"Featuring important contributions by leading scholars in the field, this volume is an indispensable intervention into the field of Critical Indigenous Studies and a must-read for understanding its empirical, theoretical, and methodological scaffolding."

– *Jeani O'Brien, University of Minnesota, USA*

"With a stellar editorial team, this extraordinary collection offers a much-needed state-of-the-field, Critical Indigenous Studies at its best, in a global frame. With thematic sections that showcase rich intellectual diversity, these outstanding essays are all well researched, conceptually innovative, and brilliantly theorized - yet, also accessible. This volume is essential reading!"

– *J. Kēhaulani Kauanui, Professor of American Studies and Anthropology, Wesleyan University, USA*

"This handbook, edited by international leading scholars in the field, will be an essential resource for the academy and for Indigenous communities. It's a unique and powerful collection of the most influential Indigenous scholars, and will be a must-have for students, researchers and scholars."

– *Larissa Behrendt, Director of Research and Academic Programs, Jumbunna Institute for Indigenous Education and Research, University of Technology Sydney, Australia*

"This book is very much welcomed. Given that Indigenous scholars are researching, developing curriculum, and trying to engage in meaningful and respectful partnerships with Indigenous communities in Australia, the USA, Canada, New Zealand, and elsewhere, a collection such as this has never been more important or timely. The Handbook is edited by esteemed Indigenous scholars, and contains works by leading and emerging critical Indigenous scholars and thought leaders. The handbook will be a source of reference, theory, explanation, challenge, and inspiration, and I am excited by the prospect of its influence in the hands of my colleagues and students."

– *Bronwyn Fredericks, Pro-Vice Chancellor (Indigenous Engagement), The University of Queensland, Australia*

"A crucial reference work for the international, interdisciplinary field of Indigenous scholars within and outside the academy, the Handbook is more than a catalogue of critical thought and practice up to the present moment – it offers deeply thoughtful glimpses into dynamic Indigenous futures."

– *K. Tsianina Lomawaima (Creek), Arizona State University, USA*

Routledge Handbook of Critical Indigenous Studies

The *Routledge Handbook of Critical Indigenous Studies* is the first comprehensive overview of the rapidly expanding field of Indigenous scholarship. The book is ambitious in scope, ranging across disciplines and national boundaries, with particular reference to the lived conditions of Indigenous peoples in the first world.

The contributors are all themselves Indigenous scholars who provide critical understandings of indigeneity in relation to ontology (ways of being), epistemology (ways of knowing), and axiology (ways of doing) with a view to providing insights into how Indigenous peoples and communities engage and examine the worlds in which they are immersed. Sections include:

- Indigenous Sovereignty
- Indigeneity in the 21st Century
- Indigenous Epistemologies
- The Field of Indigenous Studies
- Global Indigeneity

This handbook contributes to the re-centring of Indigenous knowledges, providing material and ideational analyses of social, political, and cultural institutions and critiquing and considering how Indigenous peoples situate themselves within, outside, and in relation to dominant discourses, dominant postcolonial cultures and prevailing Western thought.

This book will be of interest to scholars with an interest in indigenous peoples across Literature, History, Sociology, Critical Geographies, Philosophy, Cultural Studies, Postcolonial Studies, Native Studies, Māori Studies, Hawaiian Studies, Native American Studies, Indigenous Studies, Race Studies, Queer Studies, Politics, Law, and Feminism.

Brendan Hokowhitu is Ngāti Pukenga, Dean and Professor, Faculty of Māori and Indigenous Studies, University of Waikato, Aotearoa New Zealand.

Aileen Moreton-Robinson is a Goenpul woman of Quandamooka (Moreton Bay, Australia) and a Distinguished Professor of Indigenous Research, Office of Indigenous Education and Engagement Policy, Strategy and Impact, RMIT University.

Linda Tuhiwai-Smith is Ngāti Awa, Ngāti Porou, Tuhourangi, and Professor of Māori and Indigenous Studies, Faculty of Māori and Indigenous Studies, University of Waikato, Aotearoa New Zealand.

Chris Andersen is Métis and Dean of the Faculty of Native Studies, University of Alberta, Canada.

Steve Larkin is Chief Executive Officer at the Batchelor Institute of Indigenous Tertiary Education, Australia.

Routledge Handbook of Critical Indigenous Studies

Edited by Brendan Hokowhitu,
Aileen Moreton-Robinson, Linda Tuhiwai-Smith,
Chris Andersen and Steve Larkin

LONDON AND NEW YORK

First published 2021
by Routledge
2 Park Square, Milton Park, Abingdon, Oxon OX14 4RN

and by Routledge
52 Vanderbilt Avenue, New York, NY 10017

Routledge is an imprint of the Taylor & Francis Group, an informa business

British Library Cataloguing-in-Publication Data
A catalogue record for this book is available from the British Library

Library of Congress Cataloging-in-Publication Data
Names: Hokowhitu, Brendan, editor.
Title: Routledge handbook of critical indigenous studies/Brendan
Hokowhitu, Aileen Moreton-Robinson, Linda Tuhiwai-Smith, Steve Larkin,
Chris Andersen.
Description: Abingdon, Oxon; New York, NY: Routledge, 2021. |
Includes bibliographical references and index.
Identifiers: LCCN 2020031244 (print) | LCCN 2020031245 (ebook) |
ISBN 9781138341302 (hardback) | ISBN 9780429440229 (ebook)
Subjects: LCSH: Ethnology–Handbooks, manuals, etc. |
Indigenous peoples–Handbooks, manuals, etc.
Classification: LCC GN316 .R68 2021 (print) | LCC GN316 (ebook) |
DDC 305.8–dc23
LC record available at https://lccn.loc.gov/2020031244
LC ebook record available at https://lccn.loc.gov/2020031245

ISBN: 978-1-138-34130-2 (hbk)
ISBN: 978-0-429-44022-9 (ebk)

Typeset in Bembo
by Deanta Global Publishing Services, Chennai, India

CONTENTS

Contents

Figures

Contributors

Chadwick Allen (Chickasaw ancestry, not enrolled) is Professor of English, Adjunct Professor of American Indian Studies, Co-director of the Center for American Indian and Indigenous Studies (CAIIS), and Associate Vice Provost for Faculty Advancement at the University of Washington, Seattle. Author of the books *Blood Narrative: Indigenous Identity in American Indian and Māori Literary and Activist Texts* and *Trans-Indigenous: Methodologies for Global Native Literary Studies*, he is co-editor, with Beth Piatote, of *The Society of American Indians and Its Legacies*, a special combined issue of *American Indian Quarterly*, and *Studies in American Indian Literatures*. Professor Allen is a former editor of SAIL and a past president of the Native American and Indigenous Studies Association. His current work investigates contemporary American Indian engagements with Indigenous earthworks and earthworks principles.

Chris Andersen is Métis and dean of the Faculty of Native Studies at the University of Alberta. He became a faculty member of the Faculty in 2000 and received his PhD in 2005 from the Department of Sociology, also at the UofA. In 2014, he was awarded Full Professorship. He is the former Director of the Rupertsland Centre for Métis Research and additionally served as the Interim Institutional Co-Lead of Indigenous Initiatives for the University of Alberta from February 2018 to August 2019. Dr Andersen is the author of two books including, with Maggie Walter, Indigenous Statistics: A Quantitative Indigenous Methodology (2013) and "Métis": Race, Recognition and the Struggle for Indigenous Peoplehood (2014). In 2015, the Native American and Indigenous Studies Association awarded "Métis" the "2014 Prize for Best Subsequent Book in Native American and Indigenous Studies". With Jean O'Brien, he also co-edited the recently published Sources and Methods in Indigenous Studies (2017). Andersen was a founding member of the Native American and Indigenous Studies Association Executive Council, is a member of Statistics Canada's Advisory Committee on Social Conditions and is editor of the journal aboriginal policy studies. In 2014 he was named as an inaugural Member of the Royal Society of Canada's College of New Scholars, Artists and Scientists.

Kim Anderson, Métis, is an Associate Professor in the Department of Family Relations and Applied Nutrition at the University of Guelph where she holds a Canada Research Chair in Indigenous Relationships. Much of her research is community partnered and has involved gender and Indigeneity, Indigenous feminisms and critical Indigenous masculinities, urban Indigenous peoples and decolonizing work in the academy. Her single-authored books include *A Recognition of Being: Reconstructing Native Womanhood* (2016) and *Life Stages and Native Women: Memory, Teachings and Story Medicine* (2011). She enjoys doing oral history work with Elders and has co-produced the memoir of Anishinaabe Elder and artist Rene Meshake titled *Injichaag: My Soul in Story. Anishinaabe Poetics in Art and Words*.

Maria Bargh, Associate Professor, Te Kawa a Māui/Māori Studies, Te Herenga Waka/Victoria University of Wellington. Maria has researched and taught in the areas of Māori politics, resource management, and Indigenous Studies. Her recent research has focused on a 'Tika Transition' for climate change, a Predator Free project for her hapū and voting in iwi organisations.

Kamanamaikalani Beamer is an associate professor at the Kamakakūokalani Center for Hawaiian Studies in the Hui 'Āina Momona Program at the University of Hawai'i at Mānoa with a joint appointment in the Richardson School of Law and the Hawai'inuiākea School of Hawaiian Knowledge. Beamer's research on governance, land tenure, and Hawaiian resource management, as well as his prior work as the director of 'Āina-Based Education at Kamehameha Schools, prepared him for his continuing service as a director of Stanford University's First Nations Futures Institute, a resource management development program for indigenous leaders developed by Stanford, Kamehameha Schools, and Te Rūnanga o Ngāi Tahu in New Zealand. Beamer has revitalized and maintained lo'i kalo (taro ponds), providing him and his children opportunities to mālama 'āina, deepen connections with cultural traditions, and derive leadership lessons from the land. In 2013 he was nominated and confirmed to a four-year appointment on Hawai'i's Commission of Water Resource Management and was reconfirmed in 2017 for an additional four-year term. In addition to numerous academic publications, in 2014 Beamer published No Mākou ka Mana: Liberating the Nation, which received multiple awards including the Samuel M. Kamakau Book of the Year Award from the Hawai'i Book Publishing Association.

David A. Chang. Kanaka Maoli. Distinguished McKnight University Professor, Department of History and Department of American Indian Studies, University of Minnesota. David A. Chang is a historian of Indigenous people, colonialism, borders and migration in Hawai'i and North America. He is the author of *The World and All the Things Upon It: Native Hawaiian Geographies of Exploration* (2016), which traces the ways that Kanaka Maoli (Native Hawaiians) explored the outside world and generated understandings of their place from the late 18th century to the early 20th century. He also authored *The Color of the Land: Race, Nation, and the Politics of Landownership*, which argues for the central place of struggles over the ownership of Native American lands in the history of racial and national construction by Creeks, African Americans, and whites in the Muscogee Creek Nation and Eastern Oklahoma. Current research projects include relations between Native Hawaiian and Indigenous North American people in British Columbia and down the Pacific Coast, the politics of genealogy, and the interplay of Indigenous and Asian and white settler nationalisms in Hawai'i and North America.

Jaime Cidro (Anishnawbe) is a Professor in the Department of Anthropology and the Director of the Master's in Development Practice Program at the University of Winnipeg. She is a CIHR-funded Canada Research Chair in Health and Culture. Dr. Cidro takes a collaborative approach to her research on Indigenous maternal and child health, partnering with many Indigenous organizations and communities throughout her projects. Currently she is examining how an Indigenous doula program can address health, social and cultural outcomes for First Nations women who travel for birth in partnerships with First Nations Health and Social Secretariat of Manitoba and the Manitoba Indigenous Doulas Initiative. She recently began an urban Indigenous doula project in Winnipeg, Manitoba in partnership with the Aboriginal Health and Wellness Centre and the First Nations Health and Social Secretariat of Manitoba. She is undertaking collaborate work with community partners in Colombia to explore maternal and child health in remote Indigenous communities through a Queen Elizabeth Diamond Jubilee

Advanced Scholars Award. Her other appointments include University of Winnipeg Indigenous Academic Lead 2018–2019, Associate Director of the UAKN Prairie Region, and U Winnipeg's Indigenous Research Scholar 2018.

Glen Sean Coulthard is Yellowknives Dene and an associate professor in the First Nations and Indigenous Studies Program and the Department of Political Science at the University of British Columbia. He is the author of Red Skin, White Masks: Rejecting the Colonial Politics of Recognition (2014), winner of the 2016 Caribbean Philosophical Association's Frantz Fanon Award for Outstanding Book, the Canadian Political Science Association's CB Macpherson Award for Best Book in Political Theory, published in English or French, in 2014/2015, and the Rik Davidson Studies in Political Economy Award for Best Book in 2016.

Jennifer Denetdale, Diné/Navajo, Professor of American Studies, University of New Mexico, received her PhD in History from Northern Arizona University and is the author of three Navajo histories and numerous articles and essays. She is the first Diné to receive a PhD in History. She teaches courses in Critical Indigenous Studies, Indigenous gender & sexuality, Indigenous feminisms and gender, and Diné Studies. She has been recognized for her scholarship and community advocacy on behalf of Diné women and our LGBTQI2S relatives.

Jean Dennison. Osage Nation. Co-director for the Center for American Indian and Indigenous Studies and an Associate Professor of Anthropology at the University of Washington. Dennison's book Colonial Entanglement: Constituting a Twenty-First-Century Osage Nation (2012) speaks directly to national revitalization, one of the most pressing issues facing American Indians today. She has also published widely, including pieces in Visual Anthropology, PoLAR, American Indian Quarterly, the American Indian Culture and Research Journal and American Ethnologist. Dennison's current research uses grounded ethnographic methods to study various accountability practices as they manifest throughout the current Osage Nation government. She also currently serves on the Osage Nation Strategic Planning Steering Committee. The primary goal of her academic endeavor is to explore how Indigenous peoples negotiate and contest the ongoing settler-colonial process in areas such as citizenship, governance, and sovereignty.

Pat Dudgeon is from the Bardi people in Western Australia. She is a psychologist and professor at the School of Indigenous Studies at UWA. Her area of research includes Indigenous social and emotional well-being and suicide prevention. She is the director of the *Centre of Best Practice in Aboriginal and Torres Strait Islander Suicide Prevention* at UWA. She is also the lead chief investigator of a national research project, *Transforming Indigenous Mental Health and Wellbeing* that aims to develop approaches to Indigenous mental health services that promote cultural values and strengths as well as empowering users. She has many publications in Indigenous mental health, in particular, the *Working Together Aboriginal and Torres Strait Islander Mental Health and Wellbeing Principals and Practice 2014*. Professor Dudgeon has been an influential member of the psychology profession as Australia's first identified Indigenous psychologist. Amongst many activities she was founding chair of the Australian Indigenous Psychologists' Association.

Clayton Dumont Jr. is an elected member of the Klamath Tribes Tribal Council and Emeritus Professor of Sociology at San Francisco State University. He resides in his tribal homeland in Chiloquin, Oregon. His publications include: The Promise of Poststructuralist Sociology: Marginalized Peoples and the Problem of Knowledge (SUNY 2008). He has a longstanding research interest in the politics of cross-cultural knowing. He has written extensively on the Native American Graves Protection and Repatriation Act of 1990.

Lisa Kahaleole Hall, Kanaka Maoli, Associate Professor of Humanities and Director of Indigenous Studies Program, University of Victoria, BC, received an MA and PhD from the Ethnic Studies Department at the University of California at Berkeley, and a BA in Women's Studies from Yale University. She spent many years working with community-based cultural organizations in the San Francisco Bay Area and has written about Indigenous feminisms in "Navigating Our Own 'Sea of Islands:' Remapping a Theoretical Space for Native Hawaiian Women and Indigenous Feminism". *Wicazo Sa Review: Native Feminisms: Legacies, Interventions, and Indigenous Sovereignties*, 24:2 (2009) and "Strategies of Erasure: US Colonialism and Native Hawaiian Feminism" in *American Quarterly* 60: 2 (2008), 273-280. Her current book project on relationality, intellectual genealogies, and survivance is entitled *Making Relations in "the House of Difference"* and will include reflections on building an Indigenous studies undergraduate program that highlights local knowledges as well as Pacific connections.

Natalie Harkin is a Narungga woman living on Kaurna Yarta, South Australia, and a Senior Research Fellow at Flinders University. She is an activist-poet with a particular interest in decolonising state archives, and currently engaging archival-poetic methods to research and document Aboriginal women's domestic service and labour histories in South Australia. Her words have been installed and projected in exhibitions comprising text-object-video projection, including creative-arts research collaboration with the *Unbound Collective*. She has published widely including two poetry manuscripts, *Dirty Words* with Cordite Books in 2015, and *Archival-poetics* with Vagabond Press in 2019.

Michelle M. Hogue, Associate Professor, Coordinator Indigenous Student Success Cohort, University of Lethbridge, Lethbridge, Alberta, Canada, is of Métis heritage. Originally from Treaty 4 and 6 Territory in Canada, Dr Michelle Hogue's locally, nationally and internationally recognized teaching and research focus on building bridges between Indigenous and Western ways of knowing and learning using culturally relevant and innovative methodological approaches that blend required curricular and institutional demands with methodological teaching and learning practices that attend to Indigenous Ways of Knowing and Learning. Her research explores best practices in Canada, Australia and New Zealand to develop an inclusive, culturally responsive teaching practice and curricula through the philosophy of *Bridging Cultures: Two-Eyed Seeing for Both Ways Knowing* to enable Indigenous engagement, retention and academic success more broadly, as well as specifically, in science and mathematics.

Brendan Hokowhitu is Ngāti Pūkenga (Māori from Aotearoa). Brendan is Dean of the Faculty of Māori and Indigenous Studies at the University of Waikato. His scholarship is underpinned by Indigenous critical theory and stems from his work on Indigenous sport, physical activity, masculinities, health and film. Brendan has been lead editor of two edited collections prior, *Fourth Eye: Māori Media in Aotearoa/New Zealand* (2013) and *Indigenous Identity and Resistance: Researching the Diversity of Knowledge* (2010).

Isabel Altamirano-Jiménez is Biniá from the Isthmus of Tehuantepec, Oaxaca, Mexico. She was born and raised in the community of Ixtaltepec, where her family continues to live. She is also Associate Professor of Political Science at the University of Alberta and Canada Research Chair in Comparative Indigenous Feminist Studies since 2017. Her current research examines how Indigenous peoples, specifically Indigenous women experience and feel the impact of natural resource extraction in both Canada and Mexico. She is interested in how what happens to the land intersects with what happens to the bodies of people and other bodies. She has worked with different Indigenous organizations. Most recently she has been involved with the Ganahghootr'onatan – Land-based Learning Immersive Camp. Some of my books are: *Living on the Land. Indigenous Women Understanding of Place* (edited with N. Kermoal) and *Indigenous Encounters with Neoliberalism. Place, Women and the Environment.* She teaches Indigenous politics, Indigenous political thought, and Indigenous feminism.

Rauna Kuokkanen, Sámi, is Research Professor of Arctic Indigenous Studies, University of Lapland, Finland. Her most recent book Restructuring Relations: Indigenous Self-Determination, Governance and Gender by Oxford University Press examines the theory and practice of Indigenous self-determination, governance and gender regimes in Indigenous political institutions in Canada, Greenland and Scandinavia. Her current research focuses on comparative Indigenous politics, Indigenous feminist theory, and Arctic Indigenous governance. She was the founding chair of the Sámi Youth Organization in Finland and has served as the Vice-President of the Sámi Council.

John Maynard is a Worimi Aboriginal man from the Port Stephens region of New South Wales. He is currently Chair of Aboriginal History at the University of Newcastle. He has held several major positions and served on numerous prominent organizations and committees including, Deputy Chairperson of the Australian Institute of Aboriginal and Torres Strait Islander Studies (AIATSIS), Executive Committee of the Australian Historical Association and the New South Wales History Council. He has worked with and within many Aboriginal communities, urban, rural and remote. Professor Maynard's publications have concentrated on the intersections of Aboriginal political and social history, and the history of Australian race relations. He is the author of a dozen books, including a finalist for the Walkley Awards in 2011 with *The Aboriginal Soccer Tribe*.

Rangi Matamua, of Tūhoe, holds the position of Associate Dean Postgraduate in the Faculty of Māori and Indigenous Studies at Waikato University. He is heavily involved with Māori postgraduate studies, and supports Māori students to complete master's and PhD degrees. Professor Matamua has a background in Māori language, Māori broadcasting and Māori customs and traditions. He has led a number of research endeavours including Royal Society of New Zealand Marsden Fund projects, Ngā Pae o te Maramatanga projects, and a number of Government Department research initiatives. Professor Matamua is acknowledged as a leading expert within the field of Māori astronomy. He has delivered many Māori astronomy keynote addresses and public lectures throughout the country, and in 2017 he launched his first book, *Matariki – the Star of the Year*. A graduate of Te Panekiretanga o te reo Māori and a member of the Society for Māori Astronomy Research and Traditions (SMART), Professor Matamua is focused on revitalising Māori astronomy.

Deborah McGregor, Anishinabe, Associate Professor and Canada Research Chair: Indigenous Environmental Justice. Osgoode Hall Law School and Faculty of Environmental Studies, York University. Professor McGregor's research has focused on Indigenous knowledge systems and their various applications in diverse contexts including environmental and water governance, environmental justice, health and environment, climate change and Indigenous legal traditions. Professor McGregor remains actively involved in a variety of Indigenous communities, serving as an advisor and continuing to engage in community-based research and initiatives. Professor

McGregor has been at the forefront of Indigenous environmental justice and Indigenous research theory and practice. Her work has been shared through the IEJ project website https://iejproject.info.yorku.ca/ and UKRI International Collaboration on Indigenous research https://www.indigenous.ncrm.ac.uk/.

Crystal McKinnon. Amangu, Yamatji Nation. Vice Chancellor's Indigenous Research Fellow, RMIT University. She is a historian whose research centres on histories of Indigenous sovereignty and social movements. Her research interests also includes matters relating to Indigenous people and communities, and the Australian legal system. Crystal has previously worked and held governance roles in both the Aboriginal community organisation and the community legal centre sectors. She currently sits on the steering committee for the Law and Advocacy Centre for Women and is a co-editor of *Aboriginal History* journal.

Carl Mika is Māori of the Tūhourangi tribe and is an caps. Associate Professor in the Division of Education, University of Waikato, New Zealand. A former lawyer specialising in criminal and Treaty of Waitangi law, he now works almost entirely in the area of Māori thought/philosophy, with a particular focus on its revitalisation within a colonised reality. Committed to investigating indigenous notions of holism, Carl is currently working on the Māori concepts of nothingness and darkness in response to an Enlightenment focus on clarity, and is speculating on how they can form the backdrop of academic expression. He also writes and presents on western Continental philosophies. He is Director of Centre for Global Studies, University of Waikato, and Adjunct Professor of RMIT.

Robert J. Miller. Eastern Shawnee Tribe. Professor, Sandra Day O'Connor College of Law at Arizona State University. Miller is the Willard H. Pedrick Distinguished Research Scholar and the Director of the Rosette LLP American Indian Economic Development Program at ASU. He was elected to the American Philosophical Society in 2014. He is the Chief Justice of the Pascua Yaqui Tribe Court of Appeals and an appellate judge for other tribal courts. He has written and co-written four books and dozens of articles, editorials, and book chapters.

Dian Million (Tanana Athabascan) is Associate Professor and Chair of the Department of American Indian Studies, and Affiliate faculty in Canadian Studies and the Comparative History of Ideas Program at the University of Washington in Seattle. She is the author of *Therapeutic Nations: Healing in an Age of Indigenous Human Rights* (University of Arizona Press, Critical Issues in Indigenous Studies Series, 2013) as well as numerous articles, chapters, and poems. Dr. Million centres her work on questions arising from the effect/affect of capitalism/settler colonialism on Indigenous family and community health in North America. Informed by two generations of Indigenous Feminist scholarship, Million seeks to illuminate the ways in which Indigenous life reorganizes in the face of colonial violence and settler social welfare narratives of trauma to embrace lives that are integral to Peoples, their histories, and their places.

Aileen Moreton-Robinson is a *Goenpul* woman of *Quandamooka* (Moreton Bay, Australia) and is Professor of Indigenous Research at RMIT University. She is an international member of the American Academy of Arts and Sciences and was appointed as Australia's first Indigenous Distinguished Professor in 2016. She was a founding member of the Native American and Indigenous Studies Association. Distinguished Professor Moreton-Robinson is the author of *Talkin' Up to the White Woman: Indigenous Women and Feminism)*; *The White Possessive: Property,*

Power and Indigenous Sovereignty); and the editor of several books, including *Critical Indigenous Studies: Engagements in First World Locations.*

Margaret Mutu is of the Ngāti Kahu, Te Rarawa, and Ngāti Whātua nations of Aotearoa and of Scottish descent. She is the Professor of Māori Studies at the University of Auckland, Aotearoa/ New Zealand. She specializes in Māori language and society, the Treaty of Waitangi and Māori claims against the British Crown, and Māori rights. Her publications include many journal articles and book chapters, and four books that include two on the land claims of her hapū and iwi and one on Māori rights. For the past two decades Margaret has chaired her iwi (nation's) parliament, Te Rūnanga-ā-Iwi o Ngāti Kahu, and, in that role, has represented Ngāti Kahu on National Iwi Chairs Forum. Within the Forum she chairs the Aotearoa Independent Monitoring Mechanism which monitors the New Zealand government's compliance with the United Nations Declaration on the Rights of Indigenous Peoples. With Dr Moana Jackson, she chairs the Independent Working Group on Constitutional Transformation – Matike Mai Aotearoa.

Tāwhanga Nopera is Māori, and Health Promotions Coordinator, University of Waikato. Tāwhanga is an artist and academic who works as the Health Promotions Coordinator at the University of Waikato, in Kirikiriroa (Hamilton) Aotearoa New Zealand. Tāwhanga intends for his research to help towards wellness pathways for takatāpui and LGBTQI people, through kaupapa Māori knowledge and practices. Tāwhanga's research and art investigates marginality and is grounded by te pā harakeke, through raranga – a creative Māori approach towards socially accountable communities. Tāwhanga has a particular interest in ways that individuals are impacted upon by notions of power, and seeks out transformative pathways from traumatic experiences. Tāwhanga has whakapapa to Ngāti Whakaue, Ngāti Tūwharetoa, Ngāti Wahiao, Tūhourangi, Ngāti Whaoa, Ngāti Tarawhai, Ngāti Rangitihi, Ngāti Āmaru, Ngāi Tawake

May-Britt Öhman. Lule and Forest Sámi of the Lule River valley, Tornedalian heritage. PhD in History of Technology, researcher at Centre for Multidisciplinary Studies on Racism, CEMFOR, Dept of Theology, Uppsala University and guest senior lecturer at History, Luleå University of Technology. Öhman is board member of Silbonah Sámesijdda since 2011, member of Stockholm Sámi association since 2009. She was a board member of the National Saami Association, SSR, 2011–2015 and a deputy member of the Sámi Parliament 2013–2017. She is co-founder of UPPSAM – the network/ association for Sámi-related research in Uppsala. Her research and teaching expertise is on large technical systems, hydropower, dam safety, energy systems, sustainability, risk and safety, decolonisation, history, gender studies, STS, the Arctic, Feminist Technoscience, and Indigenous Methodologies. Her websites are maybrittohman.com; samelandsfriauniversitet.com; cemfor.uu.se; ltu.se/research/subjects/Historia.

Leonie Pihama is a mother of six and a grandmother of five. Leonie is Professor of Māori Research at Ngā Wai A Te Tūī Research Institute, Unitec and Director of Māori and Indigenous Analysis Ltd. She was a recipient of the Hohua Tūtengaehe Post-Doctoral Research Fellowship (Health Research Council) and the inaugural Ngā Pae o Te Mārama Senior Māori Fulbright Scholarship at the University of Washington. In 2015, Leonie was awarded the 'Te Tohu Pae Tāwhiti Award' (NZARE) for excellence in Māori Educational Research and as Director of Te Kotahi Research Institute accepted the 'Te Tohu Rapuora Award (Health Research Council) to recognise significant contribution to Māori health excellence and leadership. Leonie has served on the Māori Health Committee for the Health Research council and on a number of key boards including Māori Television, Te Māngai Pāho, and Ngā Pae o te Māramatanga. Leonie is currently the Principal Investigator for 'He Waka Eke Noa: Māori Cultural Frameworks for Violence Prevention and Intervention'. She is also working with Tū Tama Wahine o Taranaki Inc as an MBIE He Pūnaha Hihiko Research Placement recipient developing a 70-year strategy for a violence free Taranaki and leads the project 'Titiro whakamuri, kōkiri whakamua', exploring land-based healing practices in Taranaki as a part of the Tangata Whenua Tangata Ora HRC Māori Health Programme led by Whaariki Research Centre (Massey University).

Lester-Irabinna Rigney is Professor of Education in the Pedagogies for Justice Research group in the Centre for Research in Educational and Social Inclusion, based in the Education Futures, Academic Unit at the University of South Australia. One of Australia's most respected Aboriginal educationalists, Professor Rigney belongs to the Narungga, Kaurna, and Ngarrindjeri Aboriginal Nations of South Australia. He is an expert on Aboriginal and minority education of the Pacific. He was Distinguished Fellow at King's College, London, Menzies Australia Institute. He was also Research Fellow at University of British Columbia, Canada, and University of Fort Hare, South Africa.

Jo Smith (Waitaha, Kāti Māmoe, Kāi Tahu) is an Associate Professor in the Media Studies programme at Victoria University of Wellington, Aotearoa. Her research focus is on understanding how media (expansively understood) shapes worldviews, relationships and identities. For Jo, media also offers storytelling tools that can generate new forms of understanding and ways of being in the world. The author of *Māori Television: the first ten years* (2016) and co-editor of *Place, Power, Media: Mediated Responses to Globalization* (2018) Jo has recently contributed to kaupapa Māori projects to do with decolonisation and the media, Māori agribusinesses and soil health.

Linda Tuhiwai Smith is Ngāti Awa, Ngāti Porou, Tuhourangi. She is Professor of Māori and Indigenous Studies, Faculty of Māori and Indigenous Studies University of Waikato and Fellow of the Royal Society of New Zealand, Fellow of the American Education Research Association, and Companion of New Zealand Order of Merit. She is the author of *Decolonizing Methodologies Research and Indigenous Peoples* and co-editor with Elizabeth McKinley of *Handbook of Indigenous Education*.

Kim TallBear (Dakota, Sisseton-Wahpeton Oyate). Associate Professor and Canada Research Chair in Indigenous Peoples, Technoscience & Environment, Faculty of Native Studies, University of Alberta. TallBear is the author of *Native American DNA: Tribal Belonging and the False Promise of Genetic Science*. Building on her research on the role of technoscience in settler colonialism, she also studies settler-colonial disruptions to Indigenous sexualities. She is a regular commentator in US, Canadian, and UK media outlets, a regular panelist on the weekly podcast, *Media Indigena,* and a co-producer of the sexy storytelling and burlesque show, *Tipi Confessions.*

Alice Te Punga Somerville – Te Ātiawa, Taranaki, MA (*Auck*) PhD (*Cornell*); Associate Professor & Associate Dean (Academic), Faculty of Māori and Indigenous Studies, University of Waikato. Alice is a scholar, poet and irredentist who writes and teaches at the intersections of Indigenous, Pacific, literary and cultural studies. She engages Māori, Pacific and Indigenous texts in order to centre Indigenous expansiveness and de-centre colonialism. *Once Were Pacific: Māori connections to Oceania* (Minnesota) won Best First Book 2012 from NAISA; with Daniel Heath Justice and Noelani Arista she co-edited 'Indigenous Conversations about Biography,' a special issue of *Biography* (2016); her current project, 'Writing the New World: Indigenous texts 1900–1975', focuses on Aotearoa, Australia, Fiji, and Hawai'i.

Stephanie Nohelani Teves (Kanaka Maoli) is an Assistant Professor of Women's Studies at the University of Hawai'i at Mānoa where she teaches courses on Indigenous feminisms and queer theory. Teves is author of *Defiant Indigeneity: The Politics of Hawaiian Performance* and co-editor of *Native Studies Keywords*. Her essays have appeared in *American Quarterly*, *The Drama Review*, the *American Indian Culture and Research Journal*, and the *International Journal of Critical Indigenous Studies*.

Simone Ulalka Tur is the from the Yankunytjatjara community, north-west South Australia, and has resided in Adelaide on Kaurna Yarta, South Australia. Simone has held a number of leadership positions including the inaugural Pro Vice Chancellor Indigenous in 2020 and Director of Yunggorendi First Nations for Higher Education & Research, from 2011 to 2015 at Flinders University. A particular focus of her leadership role involves integrating Indigenous Australian perspectives within university topics and promoting a greater understanding between Indigenous Australian peoples and the broader Australian community. She currently lectures to Indigenous and non-Indigenous students each year, representing her educational philosophy of privileging Indigenous cultures, languages and ideologies as a deconstruction and decolonising educational process. Her work also explores new spaces where both Indigenous and non-Indigenous people can re-engage and transform their understandings of Australia and what it means to be Australian from an Indigenous perspective. Simone is part of four Aboriginal women academic/artist collective, *The Unbound Collective*, who enacts critical creative responses to colonial archives.

Dale Turner – Teme-Augama Anishinaabe, Associate Professor of Political Science and Centre for Indigenous Studies, University of Toronto, Toronto, Canada. Dale's work focuses on the philosophical problems that arise in the context of the legal and political relationship between Canada's Indigenous peoples and the Canadian state. Although his research has focused mostly on Canada, he was recently part of an international interdisciplinary research team that focused on the role that Indigenous knowledge played in the evolution of river restoration co-management agreements. He is currently finishing a book manuscript on contemporary Canadian Indigenous politics, tentatively titled *On the Politics of Indigenous Translation*. Dale is a citizen of Canada and of the United Kingdom and divides his time between Toronto and Kirkby Malzeard in North Yorkshire.

Fa'anofo Lisaclaire Uperesa (Samoan) Senior Lecturer, Pacific Studies, University of Auckland. Dr. Uperesa's research includes the place of sport in Pacific communities, with a focus on culture, political economy, and gender. She has published a co-edited special issue of *The Contemporary Pacific* featuring new and emerging work on global sport in the Pacific, and book chapters on US empire, migration, and the rise of American football in Samoa. Previous teaching appointments include University of Hawai`i-Mānoa, Columbia University, and Hofstra University. She was raised on Tutuila and is a proud alumna of Samoana High School.

Theodore C. Van Alst Jr. (Lakota descent) is Professor and Chair of Indigenous Nations Studies and Director of the School of Gender Race and Nations at Portland State University. He is a co-editor and Creative Editor for *Transmotion*, an open-access on-line journal of postmodern indigenous studies. His short story collection, *Sacred Smokes*, has recently been published by the University of New Mexico Press, who also published his edited volume *The Faster Redder Road: The Best UnAmerican Stories of Stephen Graham Jones*. He is a chapter contributor for collections such as *Seeing Red: Hollywood's Pixelated Skins*, and *Visualities: Perspectives on Contemporary American Indian Film and Art*. His fiction, reviews, and photography have been published widely.

Hēmi Whaanga – Ngāti Kahungunu, Ngāi Tahu, Ngāti Mamoe, and Waitaha, is Associate Professor in Te Pua Wānanga ki te Ao (The Faculty of Māori and Indigenous Studies) at the University of Waikato. Hēmi finished a BA in Māori language in 1996, before completing a master's degree that analysed Māori language structure and the teaching of Māori language. His 2006 PhD investigated discourse relationships between different language elements in Māori. Since then, Hēmi has worked as a project leader and researcher on a range of projects centred on the revitalisation and protection of Māori language and knowledge (including Mātauranga Māori, digitisation of indigenous knowledge, ICT and indigenous knowledge, traditional ecological knowledge, language revitalisation, linguistics, language teaching and curriculum development). He currently leads Ātea, a Science for Technological Innovation collaboration between researchers at the University of Waikato, University of Otago, University of Canterbury and iwi, to build and design an immersive experience that will draw on Māori protocol and world views as well as new technologies to preserve and share knowledge, language and culture in the digital realm.

Kyle Whyte (Potawatomi.) is Professor of Environment and Sustainability and George Willis Pack Professor at the University of Michigan School for Environment and Sustainability, serving as a faculty member in the environmental justice specialization. Previously, Kyle was Professor and Timnick Chair in the Department of Philosophy and Department of Community Sustainability at Michigan State University. Kyle's research addresses moral and political issues concerning climate policy and Indigenous peoples, the ethics of cooperative relationships between Indigenous peoples and science organizations, and problems of Indigenous justice in public and academic discussions of food sovereignty, environmental justice, and the anthropocene. He is an enrolled member of the Citizen Potawatomi Nation. Kyle has partnered with numerous tribes, first nations and inter-Indigenous organizations in the Great Lakes region and beyond on climate change planning, education and policy. He is involved in a number of projects and organizations that advance Indigenous research methodologies, including the Climate and Traditional Knowledges Workgroup, Sustainable Development Institute of the College of Menominee Nation, Tribal Climate Camp, and Ngā Pae o te Māramatanga. He has served as an author on reports by the U.S. Global Change Research Program and is a former member of the U.S. Federal Advisory Committee on Climate Change and Natural Resource Science and the Michigan Environmental Justice Work Group. Kyle's work has received the Bunyan Bryant Award for Academic Excellence from Detroiters Working for Environmental Justice and MSU's Distinguished Partnership and Engaged Scholarship awards, and grants from the National Science Foundation.

Nālani Wilson-Hokowhitu – Kanaka 'Ōiwi (Native Hawaiian) is Research Fellow, Te Kotahi Research Institute, University of Waikato. As a scholar of Pacific and Indigenous Studies, global citizen and woman of Kānaka 'Ōiwi (Native Hawaiian) ancestry, Nālani devotes her work to raising global awareness about critical, innovative and transformative Indigenous futurities, sustainability, and the growing voices of Kānaka 'Ōiwi working in academia to aloha 'āina and mālama moana/honua, to protect and care for our islands oceans and earth. Her research and teaching focuses on mo'okū'auhau/geneaologies as methodology, voyaging, navigation, embodiment, gender/sexuality, health, well-being, and place-baced pedagogies.

Acknowledgements

The editors would like to thank Areta Charlton for her stellar editorial work in helping to put this collection together, as well as Wiki Lewer for her support. We'd also like to thank Jason Brailey, Catherine Lake, and the Ngarara William Centre staff of RMIT for their hospitality and generosity. We would also like to acknowledge the Indigenous families, extended families, communities, and friends of the authors for supporting these Indigenous authors to do the necessary work they do, especially during a pandemic when this handbook was being finalized. Ngā mihi nunui ki a koutou.

Introduction

Brendan Hokowhitu

The *Routledge Handbook of Critical Indigenous Studies* provides a wide-ranging overview of the field of Indigenous Studies scholarship informed by the lived conditions of Indigenous peoples in the first world. The handbook's focus and reach are both interdisciplinary and international, furnishing a broad array of theoretical and empirical studies predetermined by ethical considerations in relation to Indigenous peoples' existence.

The emergence of this handbook signals an important moment related to the increasing significance of Critical Indigenous Studies and Indigenous presence within academe. Indeed, the handbook's emergence signifies the maturing and fortification of Critical 'Indigenous Studies' as an international discipline that, until only very recently, was barely recognisable in academic literature, curricula, university structures and nomenclature. There is probably good reason for the sluggish growth of the discipline given the uncomfortable pairing of 'international' and 'Indigenous' due to the necessarily localised nature of Indigenous Studies units. Thus, while recognising the fruitfulness and importance of a flourishing international discipline and what such cross-contextual conversations can produce, we also recognise the geo-political predecessors to Critical 'Indigenous Studies', such as Native Studies, Aboriginal Studies, Māori Studies, Hawaiian Studies, Native American Studies, Native Canadian Studies, Sámi Studies, and so on.

In unsettler-colonial countries and states such as Australia, New Zealand, Hawai'i, Canada, and the United States, at least, this handbook signals the growth in prominence of a field of study that was largely obscured within and shackled by other disciplinary coda where, for instance, Indigenous peoples and cultures were deemed curious reflections of the pre-civilised Self (e.g., as in Anthropology and Archaeology), in need of development (e.g., as in Development Studies), a depository of criminality and/or pathology more generally (e.g. Sociology) and/or as some strategic outpost of Empire (e.g., as in Area Studies). The absence of any collection of its kind prior to now reflects the invisibility of Indigenous theories within the academy and the overreliance of Indigenous scholars on non-Indigenous disciplines. One of the aims of this handbook, therefore, is to add to the validity of Critical Indigenous Studies as an autonomous field of study that can stand on its own, grounded by a significant corpus of scholarly work. We define "Critical Indigenous Studies [as] a knowledge/power domain whereby scholars operationalize Indigenous knowledges to develop theories, build academic infrastructure, and inform our cultural and ethical practices" (Moreton-Robinson 2016).

It is the case that there are wide global variations in terms of the state of Critical Indigenous Studies within the governance structures of universities. In Aotearoa/New Zealand, for example, Māori Studies has had some form of academic autonomy for over 50 years in most of the major universities, with all New Zealand universities now either having Faculties, Schools, or

Departments, typically with the nomenclature 'Māori and Indigenous Studies'. Māori Studies in the 1970s predictably came out of Anthropology and thus, to this day, its curricula and research remain largely rooted in its cultural renaissance ethos, with language and cultural revival persisting as firm pillars of Māori Studies. Fully-fledged Indigenous Studies Faculties, Schools, or Departments were/are far less common in countries like Australia, Canada, and the United States with amorphous programs of study taught into by interested academics from various disciplinary backgrounds from across the university, remaining the norm.

Yet, these different disciplinary historical trajectories are not necessarily advantageous in terms of what the editors of this handbook have defined as 'Critical Indigenous Studies'. My foray into international Indigenous Studies began in Oklahoma 2007 with the fledgling Native American and Indigenous Studies Association (NAISA), which was established to operationalise what Robert Warrior defined as intellectual warriorship. In Oklahoma I immediately recognised the breadth of disciplinary knowledge contributing to a fledgling Critical 'Indigenous Studies', which perhaps lacked the depth of the knowledge formalised in Māori Studies, but did not lack in critical thought, evidently being produced in conversation with disciplinary knowledges such as History, Political Science, Critical Geographies, English Literature, Women and Gender Studies, Economics, Philosophy, Environmental Sciences, Ecology, Education, Linguistics, Anthropology, Archaeology, Communication, Media and Film Studies, Sociology, Postcolonial Studies, Race Studies, Queer Studies, Law, and Cultural Studies to name but a few. Yet, the amorphous nature of NAISA and the disciplines it draws from in forming Critical 'Indigenous Studies' demonstrates both the flaws and strengths of the developing field. NAISA, like this handbook, adds stability and resilience to what remains an uneasy but at most times productive relationship with other disciplines, even as Indigenous Studies scholars around the world recognise and fight for Critical Indigenous Studies to gain increasing institutional and intellectual autonomy within the academy.

Indigenous academic autonomy does not mean that Critical Indigenous Studies scholars stop conversations with other disciplines, as rigorous and robust engagement is pivotal to establishing our field. Simply put, Indigenous academic autonomy predominantly relates to taxonomy. That is, first extricating ourselves from the overarching Western knowledge frameworks such as 'Humanities' and 'Science' so that we can define, code, disassemble, and weave together the knowledge that makes sense to our epistemologies. Such an extraction is, of course, never simple, or non-violent as the taxonomies that normalise Western knowledge enable the conditions for the Western academy to lay claims to knowledge itself, and any disruption to that way of ordering knowledge will be contested and attacked. Thus, we view this handbook as a sovereign act, a sovereign act that is part of a larger movement that supports the disengagement of Indigenous knowledges from the confines and violences associated with Western knowledge ordering.

All the contributions to this handbook are Indigenous and are understood through an Indigenous taxonomy. That is, each chapter is written by one of the growing critical mass of Indigenous scholars that has emerged over the last 10–15 years, particularly in conjunction with the increasing prominence of NAISA as the preeminent Indigenous Studies association. Whilst we readily acknowledge the non-Indigenous colleagues who contribute to our discipline, we also recognise along with our allies that few spaces are carved out in the academy for Indigenous scholars only; and even fewer spaces are carved out where Indigenous knowledge is hypothesised, defined, and/or debated and created *by* Indigenous scholars. It is also important to realise that many Indigenous scholars enter into academic systems that disproportionately privilege and prefer non-Indigenous scholars; for example, Indigenous scholars are paid less on average; we are lower in ranked on average; and, in the eyes of the academy and its non-Indigenous establishment, we remain curiosities or at best a tick box on a research grant. Thus, we do not apologise for promoting Indigenous scholarship penned by Indigenous scholars in developing the epistemological boundaries of Critical Indigenous Studies. Consistent with the development of other Western disciplinary fields in producing their knowledge base we are interested in promoting the work of Indigenous scholars and researchers who advocate for the presence of Indigenous knowledge. We do not support interpretations of Indigenous worlds and knowledge by non-Indigenous scholars.

Probably more critically, this handbook relies on the lived experiences of Indigenous scholars to provide critical understandings of indigeneity in relation to ontology (ways of being), epistemology (ways of knowing) and axiology (ways of doing). We are foremostly interested in the insights Indigenous knowledges can provide in relation to the existential experiences of Indigenous peoples and communities. That is, how we engage, disrupt, and live within the worlds that we are immersed in. The handbook, however, is not a mere auto-anthropological survey of Indigenous thought; it seeks to aid the project of re-centring Indigenous knowledges; it provides material and ideational analyses of social, political, and cultural institutions and; it critiques, considers, and contemplates how Indigenous peoples situate themselves within, outside, and in relation to dominant discourses, dominant postcolonial cultures, and prevailing Western thought.

Critical Indigenous Studies and limitations

The typical intent of Handbooks is to provide a comprehensive overview of a particular field of scholarship. We recognise that such an intent in a discipline as amorphous as Critical Indigenous Studies is problematic, which is why we believe 'critical' constitutes an important signifier of the handbook's nomenclature because, as editors, we are completely disinterested in re-gazing at Indigenous peoples via the typical anthropological methods, which continue to plague Indigenous Studies. We are far more interested in scholarship that speaks to Indigenous sovereignty and the regeneration of Indigenous knowledges.

Yet, we should also be clear in relation to the nomenclature 'Critical Indigenous Studies' because all three of these words are not unproblematic. I can remember being asked by a white postgraduate student about my use of the term 'critical Indigenous theory'. The premise to his question was that using the word 'critical' in such a coinage (i.e., with 'theory' and 'Indigenous') was problematic because of its link to Marxism and particularly the tradition associated with the Frankfurt School. It's a fair question, but one located and emanating out of white privilege and possession. I suggested to him that Indigenous peoples need not curtail the use of a violently imposed colonial language based on a logic that genealogically lays claim to knowledge itself.

In this handbook, Critical Indigenous Studies, first, emanates out of a genealogy of Indigenous, Black, and Brown scholarship that has sought to criticise the unsettler/white claims to possession over knowledge itself. Second, Critical Indigenous Studies refers to scholarship grounded in resistance to the multiple forms of violence and micro-aggressions that Indigenous peoples and communities face every day in their neo-colonial realities. Third, Critical Indigenous Studies refers to scholarship that upholds sovereign claims to Indigenous lands, languages, cultures, ecologies, ontologies, and existentiality.

It should be also clear that we are not attempting to lay claim to a universal and generalisable form of Critical Indigenous Studies instead we are conscious of the complexity of our respective existences and dependence on mother earth. We are mindful that the editors come from what have become referred to as different unsettled states, commonly referred to as 'settler states', and that all of us have been heavily invested in the intellectual and institutional growth of NAISA, with three of the editors serving on NAISA Council. That is to say, the authors we approached to submit chapters were/are predominantly NAISA members and as a consequence largely reflect the NAISA constituency, predominantly from the United States, Hawai'i, Canada, Australia, and New Zealand with increasing input from Sámi scholars and American scholars south of the US border. This is not a limitation of the handbook *per se* as we believe its contents will hold relevance to Indigenous struggles globally. However, it certainly points to another conversation that is now occurring beyond the canons of postcolonialism, neo-colonialism, and the fraught underpinnings of Development Studies and Area Studies.

A definite limitation of the handbook is that it does not cover all of the most topical areas now prevalent in Critical Indigenous Studies – nor, given the field-cum-discipline's rapid growth, could it. In total we asked approximately 90 Indigenous scholars to write a chapter based on their expertise, with an expectation that we would end up with close to 50 chapters. We ended up with 43 outstanding chapters, many of which are written by some of the most well-known scholars in our field, with the remainder penned by emerging scholars. The blend of well-known and emerging scholars we believe is a strength of the handbook. However, the central point here is that although we attempted to cover as many of the issues topical to Critical Indigenous Studies, over half of the scholars we asked to contribute were, for multiple reasons, unable to and, as a consequence, some topical issues are not present in this handbook.

Organisation of the handbook

The handbook's organisation intentionally diverges away from framing by a non-Indigenous disciplinary taxonomy. The handbook is organised into five interrelated sections that speak to broader thematic concepts that cut across the traditional Western disciplines and reiterate the ideas and work at the forefront of Indigenous scholarship. Accordingly, scholars from diverse disciplinary backgrounds who, nonetheless, all work within Critical Indigenous Studies constitute each section.

Edited by Chris Andersen, the chapters in *Section 1: Disciplinary Knowledge and Epistemology* address the emerging discipline of Critical Indigenous Studies, its trajectory, its conversations with other disciplines, and the Indigenous epistemologies and knowledges, which remain critical to the curricula and research that Indigenous scholars are imparting to students and colleagues. The coinage of disciplinary knowledge and epistemology recognises the centrality of not only cultural revitalisation and knowledge creation to our discipline but also the underlyin g premise that the presence of Indigenous Studies within the academy speaks to the validity of Indigenous worldviews and challenges claims by the west to knowledge possession. This section also demonstrates how Indigenous epistemologies are operationalised in a number of social, political, and educational institutions in different geo-cultural contexts.

Section 2: Indigenous Theory and Method, edited by Linda Tuhiwai Smith, is also disciplinary in that it reveals the multiple theories, philosophies, methodologies, and methods that many of the key scholars in Critical Indigenous Studies are currently drawing upon. The excellent collection of chapters in this section demonstrates the continued devotion of Indigenous scholars to Indigenous thought as a driver for research. Other chapters in this section also demonstrate the at times extremely fraught and sometimes productive interactions that Indigenous scholars have with non-Indigenous theory.

Aileen Moreton-Robinson edited *Section 3: Sovereignty*, which is a discernible underpinning notion of our field expressed in multiple ways, such as autonomy, Indigenous governance, rights, mana motuhake, power, possession, and chiefly rights. The ubiquitous nature of sovereignty to Critical Indigenous Studies is demonstrable because it remains central to politics, land, resources, data, history, genealogies, economies, jurisprudence, and the rights to language, culture, and knowledge. Whilst sovereignty also remains central to contra-colonialist ontologies, and academic and community-based resistances. The chapters in this section scope the culturally relative, philosophical, and ontologically grounded meaning of Indigenous sovereignties in practice.

Section 4: Political Economies, Ecologies, and Technologies is edited by Steve Larkin, and focuses on some of the most poignant issues for all humanity as seen through the eyes and contexts of Indigenous scholars and the communities they work with. It delves into the existential realities of Indigenous peoples today and historically. The impetus of the section was to recognise that far-reaching concepts such as colonialism and capitalism are not abstract ideas for Indigenous peoples; there is a facticity to colonialism that has physical manifestations for Indigenous communities. Chapters in this section theorise the interactions of Indigenous peoples with pandemics, Maoism, health economies, environmental justice, resource management, and technology. Whilst many of the chapters deal with the Indigenous lived conditions, lands, and the environment, others look at how Indigenous communities navigate the continued presence of colonialism and broader global occurrences such as COVID-19, socialism, and the importance of the digital world.

Section 5: Bodies, Performance, and Praxis, edited by myself, examines how Indigenous bodies are biopolitical in the sense that they resist broader colonial discourses, but also how they are forced to or willingly conform. Chapters in this section largely focus on praxes and performances developed by Indigenous practitioners, artists, and scholars to manifest decoloniality and/or anti-coloniality. The authors in this section employ sexuality, performance, film, sport, raranga, and educational praxes to disrupt dominant discourses and to re-establish embodied Indigenous sovereignty.

Use of the handbook

Although as Critical Indigenous Scholars we tend to rail against claims of 'comprehensiveness' because such an idea has its logic in universalism and generalisability, we do nonetheless see the value in this handbook as an idea. Building an international corpus of scholarly work led by Indigenous academics and thought leaders is a valuable project, just as NAISA was an extremely productive idea and then manifestation. That is, to build an organisation with the underpinning idea of creating an international discipline built on the conversations, knowledges, and creations of Critical Indigenous Studies scholars. There is a paucity of scholarly writing in the field of Critical Indigenous Studies and this handbook provides a venue for scholars and students to readily access and reference a diverse range of Critical Indigenous Studies scholarship that articulates and defines the Indigenous world in first world locations (see Moreton-Robinson 2016).

Reference

1. Moreton-Robinson, A. (ed.) (2016). *Critical Indigenous Studies: Engagements in First World Locations.* University of Arizona Press: Tucson.

Part 1

Disciplinary knowledge and epistemology

Part editor: Chris Andersen

1

The institutional and intellectual trajectories of Indigenous Studies in North America

Harnessing the 'NAISA Effect'[1]

Chris Andersen

At the opening of the 2007 inaugural meeting of what eventually became the Native American and Indigenous Studies[2] Association (NAISA), several long-standing Indigenous Studies scholars gave brief welcoming remarks to the first conference attendees. In doing so, these scholars emphasised an interdisciplinary and 'big tent', global vision for NAISA, a vision borne out not only by the geographical diversity of the original attendees but by the tenor of the conversations organisational naming (including, for example, whether the descriptor Native American should be included or whether the organisation should use the more expansive 'Indigenous Studies Association'). Speaking later on the creation of NAISA, Robert Warrior (2008) noted similarly that the original global vision for NAISA sat in contradistinction to the vision of the earlier American Indian Studies association, which was narrower in philosophical scope and more geographically local to the United States.

As I will explore in further detail below, there can be little doubt that the creation of NAISA has exerted a fundamental and positive impact on the intellectual growth of Indigenous Studies as a discipline, drawing thousands of predominantly Indigenous scholars from across the globe. What is less clear, however, is whether the last 13 years of NAISA's *intellectual* growth, particularly in North America,[3] has been matched by an equally robust *institutional* growth in the discipline or, perhaps more importantly, whether Indigenous Studies units have taken sufficient advantage of NAISA's constitutive presence to build our Indigenous Studies institutional networks. In the context of exploring what I regard as the gap between the discipline's intellectual and institutional trajectories, the chapter is laid out in three parts. Part one will focus on a discussion of the intellectual growth of Indigenous Studies in the NAISA era and in this context, I will emphasise two key factors: the increase of theorisation *as* an explicit part of Indigenous Studies and the impact of the intellectual *globalisation* on North American Indigenous Studies, both fuelled by the creation and growth of the NAISA.

Part two will then chart the evolution of Indigenous Studies' institutional capacity in North America to demonstrate that although the increase in *Indigenous Studies units* (including, but not limited to, faculties, departments and programs) and the attendant growth of *graduate programs* appears positive, the growth of all-important doctoral programs has not kept pace. Following this discussion, part three will then map out the contours of where Indigenous Studies units can (continue to) orient ourselves in the future in light of NAISA's powerful presence, in the context of thinking explicitly about how to build (and/or continue to build) our formal relationships with one another. The chapter will conclude with a discussion of two concrete steps that Indigenous Studies units can take to benefit institutionally from NAISA's phenomenal role in our intellectual growth. We will begin with a discussion of this intellectual growth.

Indigenous Studies' global/theoretical currents: The 'NAISA effect'

Much of Indigenous Studies' current intellectual growth has been fuelled by the expansion of the Native American and Indigenous Studies Association. As noted in the introduction, the progenitor of NAISA was created in 2007. Following several initial meetings at the University of Oklahoma and University of Georgia that saw hundreds of Indigenous and non-Indigenous scholars in attendance, the organisation was formally incorporated as a non-profit association in 2009 (see Warrior 2008 and O'Brien and Warrior 2016 for an in-depth discussion of its creation and growth). Since its inception, it attracts more than a thousand students, scholars, and community members annually from across the globe, the large majority of which have been Indigenous. Moreover, its largest conference to date took place in 2019 in Hamilton, New Zealand, led by the Faculty of Māori of Indigenous Studies at the University of Waikato, which hosted nearly two thousand delegates from around the world. All of which speaks to the increasingly global reach of Indigenous Studies.

The impact of NAISA extends beyond its annual meetings, however, leading additionally to the creation of new global intellectual networks of scholars, many of whom met and interacted for the first time at its annual meetings. These new networks have in turn produced new forms (and forums) of intellectual kinship. Though the discipline of Indigenous Studies in North America has been marked by several long-standing academic journals,[4] these intellectual networks are perhaps best symbolised by a marked increase of edited Indigenous Studies collections that include chapters from Indigenous (studies) scholars located across the globe that centre Indigenous Studies in its various theoretical and methodological lenses. In the context of centring this kinship, I will touch on four popular edited collections published by major academic presses (Hokowhitu and Devadas 2013; Simpson and Smith 2014; Moreton-Robinson 2016; Andersen and O'Brien 2016) to demonstrate what the increased 'pace' of Indigenous Studies theorising and its globalisation has begun to look like in practice.[5]

In their explicitly theoretical introduction to *Fourth Eye: Māori Media in Aotearoa New Zealand*, Brendan Hokowhitu and Vijay Devadas (2013) explain the intent of their edited collection to bring together the fields of media studies and Indigenous Studies to offer an agentic, Indigenous-centred intervention into the previous research undertaken in so-called 'third eye' media studies extend its insights to ask us to think more complexly about how Indigenous peoples engage with and use media "to confront conventionalized regimes of representation and to engender Indigenous sovereignty" (Hokowhitu and Devadas 2013: xvi). A globalising spirit underlies their argument: while the book is centred in Aotearoa/New Zealand, they suggest that the kinds of issues and dynamics it raises reverberate far beyond its shores and indeed, given the global presence and growth of Māori cinematic production, this seems apt. The global temperament that orients their discussion is further evidenced in a usefully complex discussion about the meanings and uses of the term "Indigenous" as it gets mobilised in various cultural and political contexts (Hokowhitu and Devadas 2013: xviii).

In this same globalising context, they make the bold (and I believe, correct) argument that part of the power of colonialism is not just that we live in it but that it lives in us. That is, "the inevitable impulsion to produce internationally recognized scholarship within Western academia has compelled many Indigenous writers to theorise their local context within theoretical frameworks that enable dialogue across colonial contexts" (Hokowhitu and Devadas 2013: xix). In so doing, they additionally point out the dangers of an Indigenous Studies field that views the 'pan-Indigeneity' that underscores its global currency with the progressive import it is often accorded. In juxtaposition, they note – in what is a fundamentally Indigenous Studies stance – that the deeply place-based character of first peoples otherwise positioned as 'Indigenous' resist the easy cataloguing that comes with the global use of a single, apparently unifying terminology. Indeed, in his own contribution to this volume, Hokowhitu (2013) argues that even in Indigenous Studies, the term 'Indigenous' "is epistemologically limited because of the ontological importance of local contexts, languages, and cultures. Such inattention to the local Indigenous condition inherently devalues the very concept of indigeneity because of its tethering to place" (Hokowhitu 2013: 112).

Audra Simpson's and Andrea Smith's (2014) *Theorizing Native Studies* similarly centres the importance of theory and theorising to the growing discipline of Indigenous Studies. Pushing back against the all-to-common criticism that theory is 'Western' and as such, unhelpful (if not harmful) to Indigenous communities, Simpson and Smith (2014) posit that "theorizing Native Studies troubles ... simplistic and ultimately divisive theory-versus-practice dichotomies, reconceptualises what theory is, and provides a critical framework for political and intellectual praxis" (Simpson and Smith 2014: 1–2). Along these lines, they note that Indigenous Studies debates have already been peppered with sharp theoretical interventions that not only critiqued colonial pretentions to 'facts' and 'truth' but demonstrated "the centrality of the historical method and critique ... as a project that responds ... to settler colonialism as not only a material practice of dispossession but as a representational practice of social scientific discourse" (Simpson and Smith 2014: 5).

While noting the manner in which theory and theorising in the academy have been deployed to dismiss the theoretical agency emanating from within Indigenous communities (and in doing so, attempting to turn us into passive objects that are theorised on and about), Simpson and Smith suggest:

> [t]he real question on the table is not whether we should theorize. Rather, we need to ask how we can critically and intelligently theorize current conditions in diverse spaces inside and outside the academy, and how we can theorize our responses to these conditions.
>
> *(Simpson and Smith 2014: 7)*

As such, they ask Indigenous Studies scholars to conceptualise theory and theorising beyond the academy while (re)affirming the importance to our growing discipline of building and advancing our own analytical agendas and conceptual scaffolding beyond those of conventional academic disciplines (Simpson and Smith 2014: 22). In short, far from signalling the envelopment or assimilation of Indigenous Studies into the settle colonialism of the academy, for Simpson and Smith (2014), theory and theorising actually represents a key element of its resistance.

In her *Critical Indigenous Studies: Engagements in First World Locations*, Australia-based Indigenous scholar Moreton-Robinson (2016) argues that critical Indigenous Studies represents intellectual and institutional contexts within which "scholars operationalize Indigenous knowledge to develop theories, build academic infrastructure, and inform our cultural and ethical practices. We do this critical work to challenge the power/knowledge structures through which

Indigenous peoples have been framed and known" (Moreton-Robinson 2016: 5). Building on a broad Foucauldian tradition, Moreton-Robinson's conceptualisation of a critical Indigenous Studies demonstrates a desire to move beyond Foucault's limiting oeuvre to explore the role that Indigenous Studies as an emerging discipline should play in analysing the relationship between colonialism and Indigenous sovereignty.

Of note here is Moreton-Robinson's (2016) specific use of the adjective *critical* to designate a new 'turn' in the evolution of the discipline. For Moreton-Robinson (2016), a critical Indigenous Studies is thus a growing discipline:

> with global reach, one that is multicultural, multinational and multidisciplinary. It is where Indigenous-centered approaches to knowledge production are thriving and where the object of study is colonizing power in its multiple forms, whether the gaze is on Indigenous issues or Western knowledge production.
>
> *(Moreton-Robinson 2016: 4)*

This description sophisticatedly enfolds a number of otherwise competing issues within the broader umbrella of the discipline – different cultures, different nations (and colonial nation-states) and perhaps most complexly, different disciplinary tenors – positioning them instead as productive tensions rather than barriers (see also Warrior 2014: 7). And as with all of her work, Moreton-Robinson emphasises that a willingness to theorise must sit at the base of our scholarly labour and intellectual network building.

Finally, Andersen and O'Brien (2016) published a large methodological collection – *Sources and Methods in Indigenous Studies* – that asked contributors to frame their discussion according to the following question: "what is your methodological approach to the way you undertake research, and how does it differ from past research in your discipline"? (Andersen and O'Brien 2016: 4). This question was rooted in three basic premises: first, that there is something methodologically distinctive about Indigenous Studies scholarship that differentiates it from the disciplines that volume contributors were trained in (which were usually not Indigenous Studies); second, that potential contributors would recognise these differences and deem them valuable enough to be worthy of discussion; and third, that contributors would see the research they were asked to engage in an exercise of self-reflexivity as methodologically being about Indigenous Studies (we did not ask the perhaps more complex question about whether they positioned themselves as Indigenous Studies scholars as a matter of professional identification).

The resulting contributions made a number of things clear. First, our request represented the first time many of contributors had been asked to reflect on what made their research Indigenous Studies, *methodologically* speaking. Second – echoing Moreton-Robinson's theoretical framing of Indigenous Studies – Indigenous Studies is not and cannot be wedded to prescriptive ideas about which methodological tools are appropriate to the discipline but rather (per Robert Innes's 2010 discussion), methodologies must be deployed that fit the research tasks at hand. As such, Indigenous Studies methods are deeply multidisciplinary, unified to a greater or lesser extent by their commitment to Indigenous community engagement and/or launching critiques of Western knowledge production about Indigeneity and Indigenous peoples, broadly construed. Finally, the rich discussions contained in the eventual volume provided illumination for non-Indigenous Studies scholars engaging in problematics that would otherwise be understood as central to Indigenous Studies (e.g. community engagement) to take up their research in more ethical and reciprocally responsible ways.

I chose four popular Indigenous Studies collections published in the last seven years but as of 2020, numerous scholarly books, book chapters, articles, and other edited collections are jostling for position on the space we accord to Indigenous Studies on our bookshelves, buoyed not least by the increased attention given to Indigenous Studies by major academic presses.[6] Likewise, further volumes that are what might be described as 'Indigenous Studies-adjacent' also exist. However, the four volumes I just summarised have provided leadership on and (thus) demonstrate, over nearly a decade span, two principles crucial to developing the intellectual capacity of Indigenous Studies as a discipline: (1) the growing importance of thinking and writing explicitly about theorising and methodology as central to the growth of a critical Indigenous Studies as a discipline; and (2) the growth in the global networks of scholars responsible for this work.

This latter point is worth remarking further upon: combined, the four edited collections surveyed here include scholars from more than a dozen countries. And, while they still tend to be situated in what Moreton-Robinson (2016) referred to in her collection as 'first world locations', they nonetheless demonstrate the increasingly global character of a growing Indigenous Studies. Moreover, we will see that an increasing number (although, importantly, not necessarily an increasing percentage) of Indigenous Studies scholars are launching their arguments and their networks from an Indigenous Studies unit, which speaks to the growth of Indigenous Studies institutionally, as well. Bearing that social fact in mind, the chapter's second part will now turn to a discussion of the discipline's institutional trajectories in North America over roughly the last two decades, with an eye for charting and detailing the growth of Indigenous Studies units, if not the rate of doctoral programs (which should, their proportionate lack of growth notwithstanding, be regarded as crucial 'incubators' of any discipline).

Critical Indigenous Studies – institutional trajectories in North America[7]

Far too little of the intellectual labour in the North American variant of Indigenous Studies is spent discussing its institutional dynamics. I have written elsewhere about the central importance that such discussions *ought* to occupy (see Andersen 2016) but they nonetheless remain a marginalised part of our discipline. Those who have written on these matters over the past four decades have tended to lament the lack of Indigenous Studies-specific units and the increased solidity that comes with that status (e.g. Wilson 1979; Morris 1986; Cook-Lynn 1997, 2005). More than three decades ago, for example, Morris argued that "[u]nfortunately, many, if not most, NAS programs [continue] to struggle in hostile academic environments which see them as a threat to enrollments and, therefore, to budgets of the traditional academic disciplines" (Morris 1986: 11). Two decades later and on the eve of the creation of NAISA, Cook-Lynn argued that Indigenous Studies remained largely disrespected and thus marginalised in the academy:

> The truth is we are still programs; we are still embedded in the departments of related disciplines. We have seen what happens when there is no departmental status and when faculty members have no status, no tenure in Indian Studies – when you leave your post, there's no one to take your place, the program dies, and the subject matter disappears or is subsumed by history and literature professors who don't know what they're talking about.
>
> *(Cook-Lynn 2005: 183)*

Notwithstanding Cook-Lynn's comments in particular, the growth and continued success of NAISA – as well as the expansion of Indigenous Studies programs that I will detail shortly – would seem to indicate a 'good news story' for the discipline of Indigenous Studies globally (and of more specific relevance to this chapter, North America). However, given the extent to which departments represent the dominant institutional foothold in most Canadian and US universities and likewise represent the lifeblood of most academic disciplines, intellectual growth outpacing institutional growth is potentially as much an occasion for concern as it is for celebration. Indeed, this may be a particular concern for Indigenous Studies in North America, given that the same underlying currents contributing to the rise of NAISA (i.e. scholars' increasing interest in a critical analysis of Indigenous experiences of colonialism and in that context, the study of Indigenous and non-Indigenous relationships) also hold the potential to produce tensions on university campuses in which scholars located in academic units other than Indigenous Studies self-identify (and are identified by others) as Indigenous Studies scholars, and similarly, senior administrators are faced with tough decisions about where to place monies dedicated to the 'Indigenisation' that many universities are attempting to undertake (for a Canadian discussion of this phenomenon, see Gaudry and Lorenz 2018).

In these contexts, it is instructive to note that the *growth* – though as I will detail, not necessarily the *development* – of Indigenous Studies' institutional structure in North America has matched pace with the NAISA-fuelled intellectual growth insofar as the number of Indigenous Studies units in North America has expanded steeply in the last two decades. Nelson's (1997, 2018) valuable research has meticulously charted this growth: in 1997, for example, he counted 61 Indigenous Studies programs in the United States and 8 in Canada (Nelson 1997); by 2018, this number had increased to roughly 130 in the United States and 30 in Canada (Nelson 2018). Perhaps more importantly from a disciplinary perspective, while only seven graduate programs existed in the United States in 1997 and four in Canada (including four PhD degrees or designations in Indigenous Studies in the United States and one in Canada), by 2018 these numbers had grown to include 29 US-based graduate programs (including eight PhD programs in Indigenous Studies or that allowed a concentration in Indigenous Studies) and 11 graduate programs (including five PhD degree programs) in Canada.

Two of the most important institutional 'incubators' of any discipline, however, include the formal presence of departments and the (preferably departmental) ability to offer doctoral programs. Regarding the former, this remains the case not least because, as Lee argues in an American context, "[t]he academic department [or its equivalent] is a fundamental component in … higher education" because it represents "the intersection between the larger discipline and the local institution" (Lee 2007: 41). Speaking in an Indigenous Studies context, Justice (2016) similarly suggests that failure to achieve departmental status often results in situations in which:

> Indigenous Studies [at any given university] is able to find a foothold only through the combined efforts of diverse faculty, staff and community members with a deep and sincere interest in Indigenous topics but with little else in common that connects their work or purpose.
>
> *(Justice 2016: 28)*

In their discussions of women and gender studies (WGS) as a discipline, WGS scholars have explored similar dynamics to those shaping Indigenous Studies today, and have noted the extent to which the field has refused to situate itself as a discipline, despite the fact that all disciplines are interdisciplinary to a greater or lesser extent (in practice if not in their institutional positioning). Braithwaite (2011), for example, asks us to think through what the stakes are for *not* positioning women and gender studies as a discipline. To this extent, following Braithwaite's argument, we must continue to ask what makes Indigenous Studies disciplinarily "different or more the sum of its other academic parts" (Braithwaite 2011: 218), and the role of departments – and graduate programs including, crucially, doctoral programs – in this discussion. Moreover, as I will discuss further in part three, it is not enough for individual Indigenous Studies scholars to be making these arguments: Indigenous Studies units need to be undertaking this discussion in a more concerted and more coordinated manner.

Returning to Nelson's (2018, 1997) research, out of 69 Indigenous Studies units in Canada and the United States, only 26 units – about two in five – offered baccalaureate majors (i.e. a 'BA'). Twenty years later, out of 163 programs in the United States and Canada, the number of units that offer a baccalaureate major is still less than half. Leaving aside otherwise vital discussions about the extent to which these departments receive the level of funding required to run robust degree programs (which is far from clear, given the small number of faculty and staff members in individual Indigenous Studies departments and programs), the increase in the ratio of Indigenous Studies departments in relation to the total number of Indigenous Studies units over the past 20 years is positive.

If the growth (in both relative and absolute terms) of North American-based Indigenous Studies departments in the last 20 years seems hopeful, the growth of graduate programs in general and doctoral programs in particular is less so. In 1997, of the roughly 70 Indigenous Studies units in existence, only 12 possessed a graduate program and only five of those had doctoral programs. And even in those institutions, only two offered autonomous, single-department doctoral programs (the University of Arizona and Trent University). Two decades later, out of the total number of Indigenous Studies units in Canada and the United States, about one in five units offer a graduate degree program (32 units) and while roughly 20 offered PhD programs of one kind or another with a concentration in Indigenous Studies, less than 1 in 20 offer doctoral degrees fully encapsulated within an Indigenous Studies unit and not shared with another discipline (six programs in total).

All of this represents an increased ratio vis-à-vis the state of the discipline two decades earlier, but it also means that in over the same 20-year period in which 84 new Indigenous Studies programs were established, only four additional doctoral programs were created. As such, Indigenous Studies units have been and, it appears, given the small number of doctoral programs in Indigenous Studies, will continue to be staffed with scholars whose doctoral degrees are rooted from disciplines other than Indigenous Studies. Moreover – and perhaps more importantly – the expansive view of Indigenous Studies propagated by NAISA potentially makes it less likely that university administrators will provide the fiscal leadership required to create new Indigenous Studies departments, choosing the (nearly always) less expensive option of a program that tethers together courses from already existing disciplines and their programs.

A criticism I sometimes receive when I present on these matters is that it is important not to oversell the significance of departments to the creation of robust bodies of Indigenous Studies knowledge. Indeed, in the last three decades, scholars working in Indigenous Studies have instead highlighted the intellectual importance of *interdisciplinarity* to Indigenous Studies, suggesting that novel and even 'cutting edge' research and pedagogies can, do and even must take place at the peripheries and intersections of multiple 'conventional' disciplines. As such, interdisciplinarity has been identified as a key tenet of Indigenous Studies (see Apodaca 2011; Cook-Lynn 2005; Nelson 2011; Weaver 2011). Although I am empathetic to the intellectual point being made here, for newer and relatively more marginalised disciplines such as Indigenous Studies, gaining an institutional foothold on university campuses is crucial for differentiating ourselves from other academic disciplines and departments, for stamping a collective identity in the faculty and staff members who seek to undertake research and teaching in an Indigenous Studies context and for securing the necessary institutional resources to build intellectual autonomy (see Coyne 1983 for this discussion in a women and gender studies context). Moreover, nothing about departmental status renders research trajectories necessarily less internally interdisciplinary.[8] Departments thus represent a desirable institutional placeholder *and* a forum of interdisciplinary research.

If departmental status is preferable, however, it is nonetheless the case that a large majority of Indigenous Studies departments in North America remain chronically underfunded; demonstrated, not least, in the small number of faculty members and administrative staff in most North American Indigenous Studies units. The fiscal and symbolic marginalisation that most Indigenous Studies units experience in their 'home' universities complicated and indeed, make extremely difficult to build networking opportunities with Indigenous Studies units at other universities, let alone to think strategically about *which* Indigenous Studies units to engage in network building with. Bearing in mind this crucial dynamic, the third and final section of this chapter will chart out the path forward that the Faculty of Native Studies at the University of Alberta has undertaken, made possible by Canadian universities' (and the University of Alberta's) response to the Truth and Reconciliation Commission Final Report's calls to action, and the resources that have been 'attached' to those responses, in the specific context of building relationships with other Indigenous Studies units. I turn to that now.

Connecting Indigenous Studies units: 'A sea of islands'

In her beautiful discussion of the manner in which the seemingly scattered archival locales that Indigenous Studies scholars often delve into while undertaking our research are nonetheless connected together by genealogies that otherwise go unremarked and as often as a result, unrecorded, Māori Indigenous Studies scholar Alice Te Punga Somerville uses Tongan writer Epeli Hau'ofa's (1993) metaphor of 'a sea of islands' to push back against the colonial diminishments of the Oceanic region that view the Pacific ocean in terms of absences rather than presences. Te Punga Somerville (2016) invites readers to think about the ways in which absence (and presence) often sits in the eye of the beholder: this metaphor is powerful and perhaps particularly apt for those of us writing on the presence of Indigenous Studies units in the academy. Indeed, it can be sometimes be a challenge to position the presence of Indigenous Studies units in the academy beyond their enduring marginalisation in their local institutional context.

Nonetheless, for Te Punga Somerville (2016), the act of looking (or, in terms of the poet/ry she is linking her argument to, 'reaching') is as powerful as the act of finding. As I will explain further in this section, Indigenous Studies units located across different campuses – particularly those who exist in the kinship of history – can think more strategically about what it means to reach out to one another; much like Epeli Hau'ofa's (1993) repositioning of the Pacific ocean, to position – and perhaps even to render – our local/regional context a place of presence rather than – or in addition to – absence.

What does it mean in practice to think about Indigenous Studies units in terms of a 'sea of islands'? In his own discussion of Indigenous Studies as a discipline, Justice (2016) emphasises the central importance of Indigenous Studies units recognising Indigenous peoples' relationships to the place in which they (i.e. Indigenous peoples and Indigenous Studies units) are located, and indeed the accountability that Indigenous Studies units owe to those relationships, those peoples and the sovereignty they uphold (also see TallBear 2016: 81). Justice is, however, careful to note that being mindful of our relationships to (Indigenous) place does not inevitably lead to only "looking inward" (Justice 2016: 29) – this is perhaps especially true in an Indigenous context, he argues, given the broad networks of trading, exchange, and diplomacy at the core of most Indigenous peoples' diplomatic relationships with other Indigenous peoples. Consideration of building reciprocal relationships with local Indigenous communities and organisations and respecting their expansive traditions of network building is crucial to the discipline of Indigenous Studies (Justice 2016; Nelson 2011).

Although a capacity to engage in the broader understanding and institution building of Indigenous Studies has and will continue to vary (more on that below), a number of good reasons exist for Indigenous Studies units to emphasise building relationships with other Indigenous Studies units, what I regard as an institutional refraction of what Allen refers to elsewhere as *trans-Indigenous Studies*, which in his argument represents an important lens for thinking about Indigenous Studies intellectually:

> One of the key projects for trans-Indigenous Studies, then, is to better articulate how the potential productivities of Indigenous-to-Indigenous encounters, collaborations, and comparisons are both overtly enabled and intimately structured by the complexities of transnational networks, those by-products of the histories and ongoing legacies of various colonialisms.
>
> *(Allen 2015: 9)*

In an institutional context, I am proposing that Indigenous Studies units must (continue to) work on tending to our own "Indigenous-to-Indigenous encounters, collaborations, and comparisons" (Allen 2015: 9): connecting our own departmental 'islands' across university contexts and regional and national borders.

In this broader context, the Faculty of Native Studies is, with several partners, in the midst of connecting to other Indigenous Studies units in a strategic, sustainable manner. We are focusing on doing so for two (perhaps obvious) reasons: (1) colonialism as a concept is ideological but its effects are locally manifested: hence, connecting with Indigenous Studies units allows us to compare institutional experiences, and in doing so, enriches our mutual learning experiences (i.e. collaboration); and (2) to assist our students – especially but not only our graduate students – in building professional connections (i.e. graduate student connections).

Collaboration: as I noted at the chapter's outset, the chapter's empirical scope was narrowed to the United States and Canada due to their institutional resonances. However, local refractions and specificities shape the character of Indigenous Studies units in ways that are distinctive to their local institutional/university context. These distinctions notwithstanding, the broad reach and manifestations of colonialism has ensured that more universal homologies[9] exist across geographical contexts, such that much is to be learned by engaging with other Indigenous Studies units. Indeed, conversations with faculty and staff located in Indigenous Studies units around the world bear out numerous commonalities, even in their specificity: the instances of racism we experience at the hands of non-Indigenous administrators; the ways in which nationally specific variants of 'Indigenisation' or 'decolonisation' that take place on university campuses play out in the context of Indigenous Studies units; the generational differences in scholars hired into Indigenous Studies units between (say) the 1970s and today; the analogous ways in which we engage with Indigenous communities and organisations; our relationships with Indigenous Studies scholars located outside of Indigenous Studies units; the broader manner in which public culture impacts us, and so on. In short, we have much to teach and learn from one another about institution building in the discipline of Indigenous Studies.

Student engagement: during the most recent NAISA held in Hamilton, New Zealand, the University of Waikato's Te Kotahi Research Institute (headed at the time by Professor Leonie Pihama) held a four-day pre-conference for Indigenous doctoral students, most of whom went on to attend the NAISA conference. Given NAISA's size and popularity, the pre-conference was well attended with more than 100 students registering. And, although it is highly likely that most of the attendees were located in academic units other than Indigenous Studies, the notion of bringing together Indigenous graduate students globally demonstrated strong leadership toward continuing to build intellectual networks for future Indigenous Studies scholars. It also demonstrates the clear importance for students located in Indigenous Studies units to think about network building as well.

It's popularity notwithstanding, why would graduate students located in Indigenous Studies units benefit from this network building? Certainly, it would allow them to engage with other Indigenous Studies unit-based graduate students in the context of discipline and institution building, often beyond the deficit-based positioning of Indigeneity that takes place in other disciplinary contexts. Indeed, broader philosophical discussions about as 'decolonisation' or 'Indigenisation' are both worthy projects in their own right but often, when carried out outside of the auspices of Indigenous Studies, they do not benefit us.[10] Similarly, as Indigenous Studies units continue to create and build up graduate programs, recruiting students already trained in Indigenous Studies at the undergrad (and junior graduate) level is crucial to building up the discipline with masters and doctoral students, some of whom will go on to become Indigenous Studies scholars, ideally located in Indigenous Studies units.

Conclusion: Harnessing the 'NAISA effect'

Part of this chapter's argument is that despite the discipline of Indigenous Studies' intellectual evolution (through, though not limited to, the growth of NAISA), the institutional position of Indigenous Studies within Canadian and US universities remains marginalised and in many cases, precarious. The Faculty of Native Studies is possibly the least marginalised Indigenous Studies unit in North America but even in our case, from a resource perspective we are comparatively tiny within our local academic context: fiscally,[11] but also to the extent that scholars outside of the Faculty of Native Studies self-identify – and are identified by others – as Indigenous Studies scholars, we remain somewhat symbolically marginalised as well. Moreover, our current marginalisation must be contextualised by the fact that this remains the case *following* a roughly 50 per cent growth in our budget in the last four years.

It is this context of institutionally localised marginalisation that the Faculty of Native Studies has benefitted most enormously from the growth of NAISA: the number of scholars (Indigenous and non-Indigenous) who now regularly attend NAISA has fomented an intellectual kinship that has in turn produced new networks of global and theoretically sophisticated scholarship that we have in turn incorporated into our teaching and research. Likewise, NAISA has encouraged scholars who might not have previously understood their research in an Indigenous Studies context to attend the annual meetings with an eye (and an ear) for learning the theoretical and methodological tools though which Indigenous Studies research is carried out.

As noted, however, the institutional robustness of Indigenous Studies has not kept pace with either its overall growth or the intellectual potential fostered by the creation and growth of NAISA. While numerous Indigenous Studies units have been created in the last two decades, these have tended toward program-based efforts rather than larger, more stable, and more expansive Indigenous Studies departments possessing the requisite resources to run robust graduate programs in general and doctoral programs in particular. Moreover, the new departments that *have* been created tend to be comparatively small in terms of the overall number of faculty and dedicated support staff, as well as the number of student majors and the service teaching they have the capacity to undertake. And I think an argument can be made that as numerous faculty members and graduate and undergraduate students from universities attend NAISA and return to their campuses with a passion to 'do something', it becomes much easier for sympathetic senior administrators to build programs than it does departments.[12]

Nonetheless, as much as NAISA's success has impacted the intellectual character of Indigenous Studies, it also marks an important milestone in its *institutional* growth as well by the simple fact that it has served as a hub for hundreds of Indigenous Studies scholars to connect and build networks and relationships. However, faculty and staff located in Indigenous Studies units have not yet made sufficient use of NAISA's gravitational 'pull' from a network-building standpoint. Toward that end, I will conclude the chapter by providing two suggestions for how Indigenous Studies can make better institutional use of NAISA, both of which stem from the growing number of 'pre-conference' workshops that scholars have begun to tack onto their NAISA conference trips. In this context, NAISA offers a singular opportunity to provide a pre-NAISA half day mini-conference for *Indigenous Studies administrators*; and a half day *recruitment fair* for Indigenous Studies units to recruit undergraduate and graduate students into Indigenous Studies departments and faculties that possess graduate programs.

Regarding the second use of NAISA, the Faculty of Native Studies is in discussions with several other regional (i.e. northern Plains-based) Indigenous Studies units – at the moment, the Department of Indigenous Studies at the University of Saskatchewan and the Department of Native Studies at the University of Manitoba, as well as smaller Indigenous Studies that would be invited to attend as well – to create a regular, rotating 'recruitment fair' so that senior Indigenous Studies undergraduate and junior graduate students can learn about our graduate programs, including the scholars in our programs, their research foci, and the possibilities for undertaking graduate research with us. These will potentially not only make graduate school in an Indigenous Studies faculty or department a possibility for them but provide information about the support available for their training. There is no reason why this idea could not be expanded to allow an 'Indigenous Studies graduate program' fair at NAISA for prospective students to learn more about our programs.

I sometimes worry (perhaps unfairly) about the potential of NAISA to institutionally 'water down' the discipline of Indigenous Studies, a worry shaped by the observation that much of NAISA's success appears based in a tacit agreement among attendees *not* to discuss what the contours and boundaries of the discipline are and as I have noted elsewhere (see Andersen 2016), avoiding disciplinary discussions is not the freeing trajectory it is often assumed to be. However, this is hardly NAISA's fault and indeed, most of us who attend NAISA meetings are struck anew by the feelings of excitement and intellectual creativity that we encounter, even after years of repeated attendance. In this sense, it has served as a powerful and positive connecting force for the global and broadly interdisciplinary vision of its founders. And it is in the context of the labour and the intellectual generosity of these members that Indigenous Studies programs, departments, and faculties need to begin to plan and act more strategically to benefit institutionally from NAISA's sustained and positive intellectual impact on the discipline.

Notes

1 I would like to thank Chelsea Gabel, David Parent, and Merissa Daborn for their comments on this chapter.

2 A brief note on my use of the term 'Indigenous Studies': the term itself exists as a shorthand phrasing for a wide variety of allied fields including Native Studies, Native American Studies, American Indian Studies, Hawaiian Studies, First Peoples' Studies, First Nations Studies, Māori Studies, Sámi studies, etc. to name but a few. The phrasing thus potentially hides as much as it reveals insofar as it serves as an umbrella term to refer to the critical and reflexive study of Indigenous peoples who existence predates the imposition of colonial projects by settler states (and later, nation-states) and/or their relationships

with those settler states, all the while using a term – 'Indigenous' – that potentially obscures distinctive relationships to place (see Justice 2016). It is perhaps worth pointing out, additionally, that the term Indigenous itself is not necessarily epistemologically or ontologically synonymous with autonyms that what we would otherwise describe as an Indigenous people might use to describe themselves and *their* relationships to place (see Hokowhitu and Devadas 2013: xix). Nonetheless, in the words of Māori scholar Alice Te Punga Somerville (2010: 683), using a term like Indigenous urges us to think about the *resonances* between these allied peoples and projects, just as the phrasing Indigenous Studies encourages us to undertake our analyzes in a single, expansive disciplinary context committed to working in service of Indigenous communities and working to build a broad respect for and thus uphold the sovereignty of Indigenous peoples (see Warrior 2008) – two related but distinctive projects.

3 Although my original intent of this chapter was broader, I ultimately made a decision to centre it more specifically on a North American context, which in an Indigenous Studies context, focuses discussion on Canada and the United States. Broad resonances certainly exist between these units and those of other parts of the globe – Australia, New Zealand. and Scandinavia in particular – and North American Indigenous Studies has benefitted greatly from the globalising networking concomitant with the expansion of NAISA. However, the academic institutional contexts of the countries within which Indigenous Studies exist are sufficiently distinctive to warrant their own empirical studies – simply put, universities in different nation-states are simply organized distinctively and possess distinctive institutional configurations and genealogies. Indigenous Studies programs, like all academic programs, are shaped to fit within those nationally institutionalized contexts in ways that are complex, extremely nuanced and (as I found out, surprisingly) resistant to surface level investigations. The Canadian and American academic institutional contexts, in contrast, are institutionally nearly identical and as such, can be compared in relative safety (see footnote 7 for a more in-depth discussion of these differences).

4 For example, *American Indian Quarterly* (1974–), *American Indian Journal of Culture and Research* (1976–), and *Wicazo Sa Review Journal* (1985–) in the United States; and the *Journal of Indigenous Studies* (1989–1997), *Canadian Journal of Native Studies* (1981–) and *Native Studies Review* (1984–2016) in Canada.

5 Of course, numerous longer standing texts now positioned as central to Indigenous Studies curricula were theoretically oriented and circulated globally, but these were largely sole authored manuscripts rather than edited collections.

6 Some of the major examples include Duke University Press, University of Minnesota Press, University of North Carolina Press, Michigan State University Press, University of Nebraska Press, and University of Oklahoma Press in the United States have emphasised the publication of volume that centre Indigenous relationships and issues and in Canada, the University of British Columbia Press, the University of Toronto Press, the University of Manitoba Press, Wilfred Laurier Press, and the University of Regina Press.

7 According to Dean Brendan Hokowhitu (Dean, Faculty of Māori and Indigenous Studies, University of Waikato): "In Aotearoa it sounds like a completely different context. Although I can't give exact dates, a major in Māori Studies was available at least one NZ University since the late 1960s, with all of the other major Universities following suit soon after I believe. Similarly, all NZ Universities quickly developed Māori Studies Departments, with all major Universities having Māori Studies Departments by probably the mid-late 1980s. As compared to the North American context, this relatively early formalization of baccalaureate majors stemming, typically, out of Anthropology Departments and, thereafter the creation of Māori Studies programs and then departments could be viewed as a positive, and it was for the needs of the time because of the focus on saving the language and culture. However, the genealogy out of the Anthropology Discipline, and engagement with other disciplines such as Development Studies, Area Studies and Archaeology led to often entrenched views relating to curricula and research. For example, the uptake of Critical Indigenous Studies remains extremely limited, although the engagement by younger Māori scholars with NAISA is influencing what questions the next generation of scholars are choosing to ask. One of the points that can be taken out of this very different genealogy is that disciplinary investment by Universities does not necessarily equate with intellectual evolution. Indeed, precarity and operating at the margins may lead to a creative intellectualism absent from the more formal structures such as Departments and Faculties that, at the end of the day, require administrating, are accountable in a budgetary sense, and can be more easily surveilled." Personal communication (2 March 2020).

8 For example, our unit, the Faculty of Native Studies, includes 21 full time and cross-appointed scholars with PhDs (or degrees deemed terminal in their discipline) in 11 different academic disciplines, none of which are Indigenous Studies. This creates complications (sometimes productive, sometimes not)

with respect to the content of the theory and methods courses we teach, as well as the reading lists for the comprehensive exams in our doctoral program. Moreover, to return to Braithwaite (2012), an argument could easily be made that all disciplines and all departments are inherently interdisciplinary to the extent that they are internally intellectually fluid and often-unstable entities, despite their externally apparent solidity. They contain numerous debates, sub-debates, fields, and subfields that compete for prestige within the *order crescendo* of the discipline.

9 I am using 'homology' in the manner in which French sociology Pierre Bourdieu employed it. Bourdieu (1987) used the term to describe the strong resonances between social position and cultural practices and dispositions, and the manner in which social positions 'universalize' tastes across different social fields. Hence, the kinds of institutional marginalisation that Indigenous Studies units experience in Canada and the United States would resonate with those experienced by Indigenous Studies units globally, regardless of their empirical distinctiveness.

10 Interestingly, both students I talked to also thought it was important to talk to non-Indigenous Studies undergraduate students and possible graduate students with an eye for explaining the virtues of Indigenous Studies as a discipline.

11 For example, the Faculty of Native Studies' base budget currently comprises roughly one-fifth of 1 per cent of the overall University of Alberta budget.

12 Of course, this is speculative at this point and would require further empirical research to better locally and globally contextualize the creation of Indigenous Studies programs. Nonetheless, given the number of scholars who attend NAISA who are *not* located in Indigenous Studies units, it is not out of bounds to think about the impact this is having on the manner in which Indigenous Studies units get understood on university campuses.

References

Allen, C. (2015). '2014 presidential address: Centering the "I" in NAISA', *Native American and Indigenous Studies*, vol 2, no 1: 1–14.

Andersen, C. (2016). 'Critical Indigenous studies: Intellectual predilictions, institutional realities', in A. Moreton-Robinson (ed.) *Critical Indigenous Studies: Engagement in First World Locations*. University of Arizona Press: Tucson, AZ, 49–66.

Andersen, C. and O'Brien J. (2016). *Sources and Methods in Indigenous Studies*. Routledge: London.

Apodaca, P. (2011). 'The future of American Indian studies', *American Indian Culture and Research Journal*, vol 35, no 1: 19–25.

Bourdieu, P. (1987). *Distinction: A Social Critique of the Judgement of Taste* (R. Nice, trans.). Harvard University Press: Cambridge, MA.

Braithwaite, A. (2011). 'Discipline', in C.M. Orr, A. Braithwaite, and D. Lichtenstein (eds.) *Rethinking Women's and Gender Studies*. Taylor & Francis: Hoboken, NJ, 209–224.

Cook-Lynn, E. (1997). 'Who stole native American studies?', *Wicazo Sa Review*, vol 12, no 1: 9–28.

Cook-Lynn, E. (2005). 'Indian studies: How it looks back at us after twenty years', *Wicazo Sa Review*, vol 20, no 1: 179–187.

Coyner, S. (1983). 'Women's studies as an academic discipline: Why and how to do it', in G. Bowles and R.D. Klein (eds.) *Theories of Women's Studies*. Routledge and Kegan Paul: London, 46–71.

Gaudry, A. and Lorenz, D. (2018). 'Indigenization as inclusion, reconciliation, and decolonization: Navigating the different visions for indigenizing the Canadian academy', *Alter*Native, vol 14, no 3: 218–227.

Hokowhitu, B. (2013). 'Theorizing Indigenous media', in B. Hokowhitu and V. Devadas (eds.) *The Fourth Eye: Maori Media in Aotearoa New Zealand*. University of Minnesota Press: Minneapolis, MN, 101–123.

Hokowhitu, B. and Devadas, V. (2013). *The Fourth Eye: Maori Media in Aotearoa New Zealand*. University of Minnesota Press: Minneapolis, MN.

Innes, R.A. (2010). 'Introduction: Native studies and native cultural preservation, revitalization, and persistence', *American Indian Culture and Research Journal*, vol 34, no 2: 1–9.

Justice, D.H. (2016). 'A better world becoming: Placing Indigenous studies', in A. Moreton-Robinson (ed.) *Critical Indigenous Studies: Engagement in First World Locations*. University of Arizona Press: Tucson, AZ, 19–32.

Lee, J. (2007). 'The shaping of the departmental culture: Measuring the relative influences of the institution and discipline', *Journal of Higher Education Policy and Management*, vol 29, no 1: 41–55.

Moreton-Robinson, A. (2016). *Critical Indigenous Studies: Engagements in First World Locations*. University of Arizona Press: Tucson, AZ.

Morris, P.C. (1986). 'Native American studies: A personal overview', *Wicazo Sa Review*, vol 2, no 2: 9–16.

Nelson, M. (2011). 'The future of native studies: A modest manifesto', *American Indian Culture and Research Journal*, vol 35, no 1: 39–45.

Nelson, R. (1997). 'A guide to native American studies programs in the United States and Canada', *Studies in American Indian Literatures*, vol 9, no 3: 49–105.

Nelson, R. (2018). *A Guide to Native American Studies Programs in the United States and Canada*. October 2018, [Online]. Available: https://cpb-us-w2.wpmucdn.com/people.uwm.edu/dist/f/241/files/201 8/07/guide-1dq2hx4.pdf accessed 02 September 2020.

O'Brien, J. and Warrior, R. (2016). 'Building a professional infrastructure for critical Indigenous studies: A(n intellectual) history of and prospectus for the native American and Indigenous studies association', in A. Moreton-Robinson (ed.) *Critical Indigenous Studies: Engagement in First World Locations*. University of Arizona Press: Tucson, AZ, 33–48.

Simpson, A. and Smith A. (2014). *Theorizing Native Studies*. Duke University Press: Durham, NC.

TallBear, K. (2016). 'Dear Indigenous Studies, it's not me, it's you: Why I left and what needs to change', in A. Moreton-Robinson (ed.) *Critical Indigenous Studies: Engagement in First World Locations*. University of Arizona Press: Tucson, AZ, 69–82.

Te Punga Somerville, A. (2010). 'Maori Cowboys, Maori Indians', *American Quarterly*, vol 62, no 3: 663–685.

Te Punga Somerville, A. (2016). '"I still do have a letter": Our sea of islands', in C. Andersen and J. O'Brien (eds.) *Sources and Methods in Indigenous Studies*. Routledge: London, 121–7.

Warrior, R. (2008). 'Organizing native American and Indigenous studies', *PMLA*, vol 123, no 5: 1683–1691.

Warrior, R. (2014). '2010 NAISA presidential address: Practicing native American and Indigenous studies', *Native American and Indigenous Studies*, vol 1, no 1: 3–24.

Weaver, J. (2011). 'Guest editor's introduction', *American Indian Quarterly*, vol 35, no 3: vii–xii.

Wilson, T. (1979). 'Custer never would have believed it: Native American studies in academia', *American Indian Quarterly*, vol 5, no 3: 207–227.

2

Ricochet

It's not where you land; it's how far you fly

Alice Te Punga Somerville

Specifically, this chapter traces the twists and turns of my own academic journey in order to document, and critically reflect, on the complicated gaps between the stories we tell about Indigenous Studies and lived engagements with it (and indeed with the academy). Rather than focussing on the things that can be done in or by Indigenous Studies, I propose the concept of 'ricochet' – with its connotations of dynamism, momentum, precision, and multi-directional flight – as a metaphor for thinking about Indigenous Studies work.

I made a bet with my best friend Tasha when we were 16. We were crouched down the outside wall of the school library, avoiding the cold wind on a blustery day, our uniform jerseys stretched over our knees. Tasha was pregnant, and we were talking about our respective futures. We both knew we wanted to have children, but I also knew I wanted to go to uni (or at least I knew this was what my family expected, which was pretty close to the same thing), and Tasha pointed out that if I wanted a big family, I couldn't put off having babies. By the end of that lunchtime we shook on it: I would have two babies before my 30th birthday (which seemed an indescribably distant future at the time). I said I would, and Tasha said I wouldn't. During her next pregnancies we worked on the fine print of the bet; by the time we were in our mid-twenties no one could come up with a scenario we hadn't already considered. IVF? Twins? Adoption? Birth or just pregnant by my 30th birthday? And so on. We had also decided the stakes of the bet: the loser would shout the winner a trip to Australia. And so it came to pass that the year after I returned to New Zealand from gaining my PhD in the United States, Tasha and I flew to Melbourne for a weekend at my expense. We had lots of fun, and at one point when we were relaxing in our hotel room, Tasha turned to me with a big smile and offered to make another bet. I refused this time. Fourteen years later, I had learned my lesson. I wasn't going to make another bet that depended on people other than myself to determine the outcome.

This is a chapter about Indigenous Studies, and the kinds of work that can be done inside, outside, beyond, and across particular institutional sites. But it's also about how particular institutional locations, career trajectories, and even disciplinary positioning are not really of our own making. I'm not usually that keen on thinking about academic life by drawing on romantic or reproductive metaphors, but I have to admit the striking resemblance between my naïve self shaking on (and further refining the detail of) my long-ago bet with Tasha, and my (continually) naïve self that struggles to reconcile the promise of the academy as a diverse meritocracy with the reality that doors open and close in these hallowed corridors as if on some random switch. It is, of course, important to point to strategies, policies, agency, mentoring, and sheer hard work undertaken by Indigenous scholars when we consider the big picture of Indigenous Studies as a discipline and Indigenous scholars in the academy. At the same time, the question of which scholars work inside, beyond, and outside institutional Indigenous Studies entities can – when considered in relation to an individual scholar's journey – depend far more on tricks, luck, timing, and coincidence.[1] (That many of us who are Indigenous scholars do not actually believe wholeheartedly in such things as coincidence can both add to, and ease, the burden of individual career trajectories.)

This chapter is an exercise in autobiographical self-absorption: a reflection on my own movement around, into, through, inside, beyond, *and because of* Indigenous Studies. Although I absolutely recognise the privileges and resources and support that have enabled amazing experiences connected to my work as a student and then as an academic, and will not disavow the parts of my life that do indeed make me an exception, I do not write about my own experience because I think it's exceptional, ideal, important, or even particularly interesting. I write about it to foreground the ways that, despite our enthusiastic lofty theories about Indigenous Studies being manifest (or perhaps embodied) in particular institutional locations, and despite my deep commitments to the necessity and possibility of specific organisational entities that have 'Indigenous Studies' over the door, the formation and then pathway of any one Indigenous Studies scholar is often more complicated than the institutional arguments we – including I – make. Here at the start, let me be clear by stating a central ambiguity of the past two decades of my professional life: Indigenous Studies as a discipline has been the most important strand of my career (intellectually, socially, pedagogically, creatively, professionally, pragmatically); and yet I have constantly sought to work in, and yearned for the attention of, other disciplines. This is clearly the failing, and ambivalence, of a thoroughly colonised person. But is it only this?

I have loved literary studies since my first ever lecture at the University of Auckland, when Witi Ihimaera[2] stood at the front of the lecture theatre and chanted. That first lecture eventually turned into a major in English (and history), which involved dropping out of a law degree. From there came a master's degree, also in English, also at the University of Auckland. I was supervised for my thesis by the wonderful, quiet, rigorous Ngāti Kahungunu scholar Professor Terry Sturm, and he nudged me (okay, instructed me) to consider doctoral studies overseas. Indigenous Studies as we airily refer to it now wasn't called that yet; in New Zealand it was Māori Studies, a discipline with which I'd had something of a passing but certainly not close connection. There are reasons to think about Indigenous Studies as a big umbrella that little nation-state 'studies' cluster under (or maybe a big party they all attend?): Māori Studies, Aboriginal Studies, First Nations Studies, American Indian Studies, Native American Studies, Hawaiian Studies, Chamorro Studies, and the rest. (Who are the rest? Saami Studies, certainly. But Samoan Studies only on certain days it seems). I'm not sure I'm happy with the idea that these 'studies' disciplines are mere local tributaries that feed into the Indigenous Studies river. (So many overlapping metaphors!) Regardless, by the time I finished my master's degree I had taken three Māori Studies classes: two introductory language papers (classes/units) at first year and a postgrad (graduate) paper with Sir Hugh Kawharu – an Oxford-trained scholarly giant of the Māori world – on Māori identity. (I loved the class with Sir Hugh, despite the fact that he somewhat prophetically said to me in class one day 'I don't know where you'll find the answers to the questions you're asking, but it won't be here'.)

I wasn't keen on doing a PhD, but Terry Sturm was strategic: he sought out my Grandad at my master's graduation and told him to encourage me to do a PhD. (Later that afternoon, Grandad said to me 'Alice, you'd better do it – he's the expert', along with – hilariously – 'I knew you were clever but I didn't know you were *that* clever!'. LOL Grandad I miss you.) I wanted to study literature, but I wanted to leave the British empire to do it, so there were no applications from me for Oxford, Cambridge, or the other random British universities people helpfully suggested. From 2000 to 2004 I was based at Cornell University in Ithaca, New York, in the United States; I spent one year (mid-2003 to mid-2004) in Honolulu with a loose connection to University of Hawai'i at Mānoa, and returned to Ithaca before returning home.

> *I've never been the ahi kā kind of girl*
> *Someone always stays home,*
> *But someone has to go fish, garden, collect, trade, intermarry, fight*
> *Home is always at the centre*
> *but we each find the orbit from which we can make our best contribution*
> *and me? I've never been the ahi kā girl.*[3]

Why Cornell? Embarking on a PhD, the important decider for me, on paper, was that Cornell had a strength in American Indian Studies, something to which the other university I was accepted into (Columbia) hadn't yet committed. (Cheekily, I want to say Indigenous Studies was something Columbia hadn't yet 'discovered'). Cornell's strength in the field meant I had the opportunity to get a graduate minor in American Indian Studies, a curriculum option that had the wonderful flow-on effect of attracting other Indigenous students to the school. (Indigenous doctoral cohorts: lifechanging). In addition, Cornell's English department had a long line of other New Zealand students who had studied in its classrooms, and they were more open about the languages that would 'count' towards the standard US requirement for two languages other than English. (At Cornell, Māori was a language. At Columbia, it wasn't. I wasn't lazy about learning new things – I studied 'French for Reading' one semester surrounded by Ithacan snow – but I felt the acceptance of te reo Māori as a legitimate language said more about the institution than just a rule about a language requirement). But there was another decider, off paper, and that was a trip to the sports bar on the Ithaca Commons one cold evening when I visited both campuses before deciding where to enrol. The hard-working, visionary, and grounded Osage literary scholar Robert Warrior had a visiting position at Cornell that year and was teaching a class on Native American Literature. Halfway through the class, the Indigenous students (who'd heard I would be attending) rushed up to welcome me and invited me to come join them for wings and beer afterwards. The two or three hours at the bar was the somewhat intangible reason I went to Cornell, and I continue to have friendships and connections with many of the people I shared a table with that night. My connection with Robert, which continued even though he had left Ithaca before I arrived five months later, is the reason I was one of only three Māori people who attended the first (pre-)NAISA in Oklahoma back in 2007, and we have recently been talking about collaborating on a large global Indigenous literatures editorial project. I trace these details to make something explicit: my own mobility, and my connection with certain scholars and with certain bookshelves, have been shaped by relationships as much as they have been shaped by institutions ... at the same time that those relationships have been made possible, and then nurtured, by certain institutions.

I moved 'home' in 2005 to take up a permanent position as a Lecturer in English at Victoria University of Wellington. It was home both ways: home in New Zealand, and home on my tribal land. I was deeply aware of the layers of history already underfoot. Literally. Victoria University of Wellington is built on land alienated from my relatives as a part of the process of colonisation by which almost all of Wellington and the Hutt Valley was removed from our control and we were subjected to treatment which can only, really, be described in the most extreme of terms. At the same time, there was a more recent and ongoing presence of my more immediate whānau at the university: the Te Punga family has attended this university for three generations; despite having earned my own BA and MA at Auckland, my Grandad had graduated from Vic with a BA and MSocSc; and my great uncles all attended Victoria (Hamuera Paora Te Punga BA, LLB; Walter Te Punga MSc; Matene Te Punga MSc). Uncle Fatty and Uncle Martin went on to earn PhDs overseas (these weren't granted in NZ at the time) and Uncle Martin taught Geology at Vic for several years. (The eldest brother of the line-up – the lawyer – signed up to serve with the 28th Māori Battalion in World War II and failed to come home alive). Of my mother's generation, my Aunty Jill and several of their cousins attended Vic, Mum attended Wellington Teacher's College (which is now a part of Vic); of my own generation, several cousins have attended and graduated. Walking through the corridors of Vic for the first time in 2005, then, I was coming home.

But I was introduced to my new colleagues as 'Alice, our token Māori', a clue of what was to follow, and late in 2007, unceremoniously and at the end of two nights of packing an office in an English programme into cardboard boxes, I moved to a new scholarly home. Three years in a toxic and unfriendly department left me both scarred and scared. I didn't know how much longer I could stay in academia if I'd stayed in that office in English. A temporary fix, an offer extended by the then-Head of Māori Studies: still on the payroll at English, physically camping in Māori Studies. Between Māori Studies and the deep blue sea. That's me. For the next few years, I would be introduced as 'Alice, our refugee from English', and the joke made a sadly accurate point. Come into Māori Studies, I would tell students and guests: upstairs and keep turning right until you find me. A visiting German PhD student told me she was surprised she didn't find my office in the English department. 'Isn't that strange?' she asked in a tone I couldn't decide was sceptical, condescending, or simply the result of asking a question in an adopted language. And perhaps it was. Strange. Odd, to find someone with a bachelor's degree, two master's degrees, and a PhD in English sitting in an office upstairs and to the right at Māori Studies. Odd, to find someone in Māori Studies who four years earlier sat in an apartment in upstate New York applying for two jobs in New Zealand: one in English at one university, and one in English at another. Strange. Odd. But there's another way to put it.

There I was, in Māori Studies, teaching texts written by Māori writers. Contributing to Māori Studies postgrad students through supervision and informal mentoring. Writing about Māori texts, Māori spaces, Māori pasts, Māori people, Māori communities, Māori articulations. Writing poetry that is understood as Māori, as Polynesian, as Pacific. Drawing on a PhD that was also in American Indian Studies, and those Māori Studies papers from a long-ago master's degree and an even-longer-ago first year. Writing articles and researching for a book about Indigenous experiences and literatures and racial positioning and responses to neoliberalism. Going to Indigenous Studies conferences, and Native American Literature conferences, and Australian conferences about race and indigeneity. Being flown to Taiwan to present a keynote about reading Māori writing alongside global Indigenous literatures and scholarship. The year before moving to that upstairs office in Māori Studies I applied for a job in English in Canada (an application I later withdrew when I realised I wasn't yet ready to leave Aotearoa again), but also politely refused an unsolicited job offer at a Māori Studies department elsewhere in the country. So, I'm not so sure that it was so odd, me moving to Māori Studies in 2007. In some ways would it be more odd if I hadn't?

This is all about position: it's about place. I'm still me, and I'm still writing what I write and reading what I read and teaching what I teach in any of these spaces. My classrooms and my writings aspire to reverse the colonial project in the belly of the beast: to use English-language texts written by Māori, Pacific, and Indigenous people in liberatory ways. Education as the practice of freedom, writing as a practice of sovereignty, texts as producers of space in which we might all more deeply consider the question of being human, including the question of being human in the context of multiple violences and flourishings. Māori Studies provided an intellectual space I hadn't yet experienced since starting out as an academic. It was stimulating to start conversations halfway through: not having to explain, not having to justify. A plan was set, to shift me halfway between Māori Studies and English: the best of both worlds all around. Somewhere, somehow, that plan faded, and I had to keep moving.

So I found myself trawling the job advertisements again. Wondering if I should train to teach in high school. See if I could move elsewhere. Pack my bags. Keep moving on. I wrote in a diary that I felt like a homeless person standing, exhausted, in a city which has just installed top of the range public seating on which it is impossible to lie down: everyone's needs seemed to be served but my own. Everyone else seemed to get comfort, and I couldn't even get survival. I knew that if I moved on, within a year you'd never be able to tell that I had been there. My courses would be dropped, students will reconfigure degrees or discontinue. Someone else would be at Māori Studies, upstairs, keep turning right. This is about place, and the places I inhabit haven't always been controlled by border guards I can trust. I'm not sure either place at Vic knew what it is that I do: what I write, what I teach, what makes me tick, why I work at a university in the first place. In New Zealand, I was too Māori Studies for English, too English for Māori Studies. But as I said earlier this year to a friend considering resigning from an awful academic department in a university on her own land, we can't confuse our commitment to our people with a requirement to martyrishly burn ourselves out in toxic colonial institutions. I'm just not sure this was what our ancestors dreamed of for their descendants.

People like us get from Hawaiki to Taranaki via a whirlpool
and need somewhere
to get things straightened out again.
When you first arrive you're obsessed
with wind, water,
the feeling of being out of control
After some time you focus on what needs to be repaired,
what can be reused,
what's too damaged to keep
One day you wake up
and realise that you can't remember
which scrape produced which scar
But also that it doesn't matter anymore.
One day you remember that the thing you've been repairing is a waka.

I was due for a sabbatical in 2011 and went to take up a one-year visiting position in Aboriginal Studies at the University of Toronto. This was in large part because dear friends and colleagues in academic work are based in and around Toronto, and also because I wanted to get back into different conversations than the ones that had started to carve grooves (maybe ruts) in my thinking. My friend Daniel Justice was at UofT at the time, and he arranged for me to come to Aboriginal Studies; I co-taught a course with him and shared an office. My year in Toronto was one of healing, catching up on overdue writing projects, being part of an incredibly nourishing 'Indigenous Lit Reading Group', and figuring out my next step. Once again Indigenous Studies had provided a safe place: the students, the colleagues, the staff, the name (albeit 'Aboriginal' when I was there) over the door. I have absolutely no genealogical connection whatever with people from that (or any) part of Canada, but Aboriginal Studies was a place I could be me. The next job, which I could only really consider because my little flat on Spadina Ave and my little office at UofT afforded me the perspective that only comes when one is a considerable distance from home, was at the University of Hawai'i.

Back to the Pacific, and back to English. The job in Hawai'i was focussed on Pacific literatures, and my teaching and writing there were connected to the Indigenous world beyond our region. What's more, the department there valued me and what I could contribute: when I stood to give a job talk as part of the interview process, I looked out at the packed room full of friends and supportive smiling people, and cried. *(Career tip #1: wear waterproof mascara to job talks.)* So many happy, relieved tears. These people actually wanted to hear what I had to say. I went back to Wellington to resign, pack bags, and move. I was heading back to English, but not English as it's practiced in New Zealand. This, for me, is an important point. We often talk about the ways that Indigenous Studies looks and works so differently in various nation-state contexts, as if specificity overriding uniformity is a bad thing or unique to Indigenous Studies. But English looks different in different places too: English in New Zealand is supremely white, and extremely conservative, whereas departments of English in the United States (and Canada) tend to be places that critical thinking about race, colonialism, gender, sexuality, etc. happen.

In seven years, Wellington had become home for me and I daresay no other place could ever take the place in my heart that Wellington occupies. Close family, whānau, marae, friends, students, colleagues, an island … this is what makes a place home. I shared the first years of my nephew's life with him in Wellington, and I shared the last months of my grandfather's life with him there too. I was a different person than I had been when I arrived home from Cornell, not just because I'd grown older as one does. It was the specific experience of being at home – *at home* in the Indigenous sense – which shaped me. I have described it not as becoming more Māori, but as becoming more Ātiawa. My tribal identity had become more real to me – rather than a murky shape slightly out of focus in the distance, it was a much larger shape with heft and dimension and with which I have a delicate but supple relationship. (I have often told fellow Indigenous scholars that if they have a chance to spend time at home, they *and their work* would be stronger for it.) In Wellington I became known to people who write and became quietly known as a writer. I camped and conferenced and buried people and welcomed babies and laughed and cried and fell in and out of love. These aren't the reason someone leaves. But they're not the reason someone stays, either. These are the reasons someone knows that leaving isn't always leaving after all. While I was in Wellington, I got to know an island in the middle of a harbour which became my new centre: the centre of my centre. Hawaiians might call it a piko.

It wasn't all 'push' though – it never is – it was also 'pull', the University of Hawaii would give me a chance to be in a place where I was happy, productive, part of a community. I had friends and colleagues there who would give me a chance to do better work by stimulating and challenging my thinking. I wouldn't be the only person teaching what I teach, and so I would be able to be more specific with what I do. And, after all, I had just published a book called *Once Were Pacific: Māori Connections to Oceania* in which I made the argument that the whole region is my home; a shift to Honolulu was merely moving to another part of it. My first week in Hawai'i, all those years ago in 2003 as a PhD student, I found the book which talked about the reception of tapa which had arrived in Aotearoa on Cook's ship. This metaphor of tapa has compelled, thrilled, haunted, challenged, and affirmed me as I have written and taught ever since.

If I'm truly a literary studies girl, and if I cried such happy tears to be going to the English Department at the University of Hawai'i in 2012, why do I now work in Indigenous Studies? Well, here's where the plot thickens. Anglophone Indigenous Studies is dominated by people with a very particular kind of privilege: my husband and I jokingly refer to mine as a 'princess passport'. It can be awkward to admit one's privileges when there is such social pressure to offer up long bullet-pointed lists of oppression in order to be accepted as an Indigenous person. Perversely, this happens in particular ways in the academy, despite the opportunity our higher education should offer us to think about indigeneity in more nuanced ways. (I am not writing here about non-Indigenous scholars who engage in Indigenous Studies, because I have never been one of those so wouldn't presume to speak for such experiences. However, I am repulsed by attempts to equate childhood poverty, or other kinds of personal or structured oppression, with indigeneity.) In another vein, over the many years I spent on other Indigenous lands, I had started to sense the limitations of articulations of indigeneity that focussed only the experience of being the trampled-upon hosts of a particular place. In particular, the time I spent in Canada and Hawai'i and Australia really challenged me to think carefully about the difference between being tangata whenua (host/indigenous) and manuhiri (guest). Furthermore, I came to realise that as an Indigenous person I may well be tangata whenua at home, but I was a manuhiri (and sometimes a badly behaved one) beyond New Zealand's political borders. Being Indigenous, and being an Indigenous scholar of Indigenous Studies, did not grant me sainthood, immunity, or a backstage pass. Once I was able to recognise my capacity to be an uninvited settler, and my freedom to not only articulate my experiences of indigeneity in terms other than trauma or oppression, I had the space in my head to realise the small dark blue vinyl-covered booklet that symbolises my citizenship in a colonising nation-state – and thus my oppression – was also a ticket to ride.

Being a New Zealand citizen meant I never had to even entertain the idea of whether I could gain approval to study in upstate New York, to have a sabbatical Canada (indeed, to gain a short term work visa and provincial health insurance as part of the deal), or indeed to travel to Hawai'i for my job interview. My passport has enabled me to attend conferences and conduct research in oh so many countries; it has also made holidays in various places possible. Because privileges work by obscuring the structural machinations that make them possible in the first place, I didn't even realise this until confronted by lines I couldn't see that others couldn't cross. While I was a doctoral student, a boyfriend with a Nigerian passport was travelling to London for an academic conference. One day, in full view of the packets of Weet-Bix and Milo on his kitchen shelves that we both happily claimed as shared Commonwealth childhood icons, he mentioned the visa he was applying for in order to enter at Heathrow, and I ignorantly replied 'but aren't you guys still part of the Commonwealth?' 'Oh Alice', he responded, 'yes, but surely you know there's a white and a black Commonwealth'. Even as I can piously proclaim an acknowledgement that Hawai'i is Kanaka Maoli territory illegally and unethically claimed by the United States, and I do believe this, I can only stand to do so in Hawai'i because I have stood, many times, at the border in the Honolulu international airport and been admitted to the United States of America on the basis of my New Zealand citizenship. In the aftermath of 11 September 2001, when I was beginning the second year of graduate school, I was not among the group of international students at Cornell whose passports required them to frequently return to the nearest border and re-enter the country. Indeed, at times (before 2001) I had been among the elite group of white-looking New Zealand citizens who have been waved through the US-Canada land border without even having to produce a passport. Of course, just as we grow up hearing that two wrongs don't make a right, more rights don't right a wrong.

The blue passport I have the right to bear has been too-hard won: if I had to pick between all of my international travel and being able to speak my own language, or between all of my international travel and having not had our land confiscated and then devastated, to give two examples, I would gladly hand over my airmiles. But disavowing privilege does not serve anyone but the privileged. I married someone in 2012 who did not have a royal passport.

His passport is prettier than mine – it's bright teal, with a silver emblem and writing on the front – but marks him out in the passport line. Fiji citizenship doesn't grant one entry to the United States without a really strong argument. Twice Vula's application for a visitor's visa to travel from Suva to Honolulu was declined on the basis of his being unable to produce enough acceptable paperwork to demonstrate sufficient ties to Fiji, the place where his ancestors have always lived. Finally, he was able to enter, but only after I had flown to Suva for our wedding and we could serve up the right combination of documents, photographic evidence, copies of Facebook messages, typed timelines, and letters. *Wait – surely this is a massive digression from a discussion of Indigenous Studies as a discipline!* Well, it would be, if we feel comfortable that academic positions, conferences and other gatherings, and graduate students in Indigenous Studies are frequented by those people who have access to the right kind of passport. The University of Hawai'i at Manoa was an amazing place to work, and I loved every moment of it, but I bumped into visa problems of my own and these were compounded by Vula's inability to work because he couldn't gain access to the United States in any way other than a visa granted on the basis of his marriage to me. We couldn't afford to live in Hawai'i, so we left. This is, of course, ripe for Indigenist analysis: I may have believed myself to be moving to another part of my beloved region, but to the United States I was a New Zealander. Hawai'i turned out to be an Indigenous place so enmeshed in extractive colonial capitalism that people lacking certain kinds of privileges and, worse, people Indigenous to those islands and waters – find themselves unable to live there.

My relationship with Indigenous Studies at UHM was complicated. The long-standing entity of Hawaiian Studies was not the only or obvious site for Indigenous Studies scholarship – it was accompanied on that campus by a specialist team of scholars in Indigenous Politics (in the Politics department), a single hire focussed on Indigenous Studies in American Studies, and many other scholars based in departments and schools across the institution who were active participants, teachers, and proponents of Indigenous Studies, many of whom I had first met through NAISA or other similar networks. Near the end of my time there, some quiet questions were being asked as the American Studies programme started the process of developing an Indigenous Studies major. While there is no question the Indigenous scholar involved in this project was committed to Indigenous Studies, there are broader conceptual questions we should always be asking about which institutional entities get to 'host' (or *be*) Indigenous Studies. What kind of Indigenous Studies can American Studies do? At UHM I learned these questions are required in relation to the end goal but also the process by which that goal is reached.

We moved to Australia, in response to an unsolicited and extremely well-timed invitation of the Department of Indigenous Studies at Macquarie University where I had been based for a couple of months during a staff exchange initiative back in 2009. Unlike Victoria, Toronto, or UH, this was a university with 'Indigenous' in the title that hung over the door. I had accepted an 18-month contract, with the hope that our visa stuff in the United States would get sorted and we could return to Honolulu where we both wanted to live. The US visa got even trickier, though, and Vula was thriving in a visa environment in which he had been granted a five-year working visa on the basis of his marriage to a New Zealand citizen. Once we realised that we had to give up on returning to Hawai'i, we worked hard to stay in Australia. Macquarie was definitely not going to pan out, though. Within months of my arrival the entire department except myself and one person resigned, and since then the department, its curriculum, and its future were not handled well. The Dean asked me several times, during tense urgent meetings about teaching allocations, whether I had a PhD, a question I suspect would never have been asked had I been meeting her as a member of the Department of English.[4] I did get an extension on my contract, though, which extended my year and a half in Sydney to almost three. We plunged significant amounts of our family income into my attending conferences in Australia, with the hope it would help me build up networks and 'stay in the game'.

For me, the game was weighted towards English/Cultural Studies in Australia, for two main reasons. One is that Indigenous Studies departments in Australia tended to advertise academic positions for Indigenous applicants only, and I understand both *that* and *why* this means Indigenous to Australia. I would never challenge this, and strongly champion the need for Australian universities to develop whatever policies enable them to identify, train, appoint, and promote Aboriginal and Torres Strait Islander scholars. It's a quandary though, isn't it? I found my students in Indigenous Studies classrooms at Macquarie expressed an interest in the kinds of readings and thinking that were linked to (my) global Indigenous networks. I decided the best place for me in Australia would not be in an Indigenous Studies department; in Australia, these departments were definitively focussed on those Indigenous communities connected to the land contemporarily claimed by the nation-state of Australia. Instead, I would seek to contribute what I could to Indigenous Studies in Australia from another disciplinary site. I needn't have lost sleep developing such lofty plans to stand in solidarity with departments with Indigenous Studies over the door, however, because the places I sought to stand – English, Cultural Studies – weren't that keen on having me anyway. I applied for countless jobs, none of which had Indigenous Studies in the title, and spent months putting together an (unsuccessful) application for one of the big elite opportunities that is a feature of Australia's approach to funding academic research. I kept getting rejections, and only made it to interview once. The interview was for a one-year position in English at a university in Melbourne and between producing the job ad and actually interviewing they had dramatically narrowed the scope of what they wanted. (I wouldn't appoint me to teach British Romanticism either.)

By the end of 2016 I had two months of work left on my contract and was becoming increasingly desperate. I was losing pregnancies at a rate of knots and found the constant rejection to be more soul-destroying than I cared to admit. I want to get personal again here, because not talking about the real cost of career insecurity in relation to fertility would render my particularly gendered experience of academia invisible. Working as an Indigenous scholar, and in Indigenous Studies, and in insecure academic work, is taxing in ways it can be hardest to measure when you're right in the middle of it all. An important narrative has emerged around Indigenous Studies, Pacific Studies, and related fields about the need for academic work to be configured in ways that enable scholars with children to gain access to jobs, career security, and promotions. Certainly, many Māori, Pacific, and Indigenous scholars have children during study and at career points that differ from non-their Indigenous cohort. But. There are other Indigenous scholars whose reproductive stories are less responsive to individual agency in relation to incidents, plans, or dreams. Had I known how hard achieving parenthood would eventually be, I needn't have taken a bet with Tasha all those years ago. (Of course, the unanswerable question will always be whether infertility was produced by, exacerbated by, or just coexistent with, the stress of my career.)

To loop back to my departure from the University of Hawai'i, the main reason we decided I would accept the job in Australia was because when the unexpected email from Macquarie arrived offering me a job, I was in the early weeks of a long-awaited first pregnancy. We had just realised with dismay that the parental leave policies in the United States, and specifically at UH, were so minimal that – with Vula being unable to work because of the terms of his visa – we literally could not have made it work. We lost that pregnancy by the time the electronic ink was dry on the contract with Macquarie, but also knew that staying in Hawai'i would specifically rule out the financial possibility of children. (I'm not talking about not being able to afford a fancy stroller; I'm talking about the spectre of no income – and thus no health insurance – if for any reason I couldn't return to the classroom within days of giving birth.) There are two important considerations this raises for me. I think it would be helpful to include infertility and miscarriage in the conversations we are beginning to have in Indigenous scholarly circles about the physical impacts of working in the academy. *Flashback: sitting in a meeting of over half a dozen Indigenous women scholars from various nations back in 2008, and I realise I'm the only one who hasn't had cancer.* But there's another consideration too: if we are in the business of decolonising, we also need to decolonise our thinking about what 'counts' as family responsibilities. I am endlessly intrigued by the way giving birth to my daughter in 2017 let me into all kinds of secret clubs, eyebrow raises, and solidarities to which I was not privy in 2005 when I was co-parenting my newborn nephew with my sister. Parents, siblings, aunties, uncles, grandchildren, tribal members, and so on – these are all family responsibilities, too.

I currently hold a permanent position as an Associate Professor (and Associate Dean) in an institutional entity called the Faculty of Māori and Indigenous Studies (FMIS). The University of Waikato is somewhere I didn't think I would ever work, but things have changed over the two decades since I started my PhD: Waikato has changed, Indigenous Studies has changed, and so have I. Eff-miss, as we affectionately call it, used to be a School of Māori and Pacific Development, and before that a Department of Māori Studies. The kinds of humanities-based globally focussed research and teaching I do would not have landed me a job at either of those entities. As a Faculty that now has senior people (professors, and especially the Dean) with global Indigenous mobility in their passports as well as their bookshelves, I am teaching and writing about things that connect to my research and also to my heart. I've recently added a new class, 'Pacific texts', which will hopefully scratch my itch of wanting to teach students about the cultural production of Indigenous people, and I'm working with postgraduate students doing all kinds of projects that sound suspiciously like I might be their supervisor. This chapter is not, however, an epic like those focussed on Frodo or a pilgrim or Harry Potter or even Maui. This is not a story of linear progress in which the previous chapters of lurches and losses are finally stitched up in my current status as permanent academic mama in Indigenous Studies Paradise. It's not even a story of 'bad institutions' or 'bad bosses' that finally give way to a perfect perma-nent university or workplace. After all, I have been permanently employed in permanent jobs (dream jobs, no less) before.

> *Hitching posts aren't supposed to be forever*
> *Just ask the Wellington City Council (or don't)*
> *It's all very well floating a waka for all to see*
> *But after a while the wood will rot and, if uncarefully dried,*
> *will split.*
> *The harbour feels safer than the open sea,*
> *But only as long as you're in denial about the risk of being smashed against the wharf*
> *Only as long as you force yourself to stop dreaming about life beyond te Au a Tane*
> *Only as long as you're happy with shallow breaths and restless nights*
> *Sometimes being hitched is a comfort,*
> *and sometimes it's a tether, a whip, a noose.*
> *One person's hitch is another person's freedom which is another person's incarceration.*

Literally one year after I started at Waikato, and one month after I returned from parental leave, our current Vice Chancellor announced a restructuring plan that would turn eight Faculties into four Divisions, one of which would be a Division including three current Faculties: us, Law, and Arts & Social Sciences. We were clear in FMIS what this would mean: back under non-Indigenous leadership, unrecognised as an interdisciplinary unit with connections across the entire university. Indigenous Studies is no longer an offshoot of the social sciences, however much they may try to claim us; if it was, I certainly wouldn't qualify for a position there. 'We are not them' we say, even though on an individual level I do still have connections to the Arts as a disciplinary configuration. I still attend literary conferences (perhaps now more than ever) and publish in literary and humanities journals. At Waikato, I have delivered guest lectures on Māori and Pacific writing in a large introductory Arts paper – partly because they (unbelievably, or not) do not have a specialist, and I don't want Māori and Pacific students starting a degree in English to miss out on the experience I had of seeing Witi at the front of the lecture theatre all those years ago. (Even though I don't chant for the students and would be more accurately described as a beige rather than brown body in the front of the room.) But I also do it because I love teaching literature, and I continue to want a dollar each way on the disciplines in which I work.

We fought the Vice Chancellor's proposal to 'Divisionalise' us and won, in the way that some of us 'won' against the British in the 19th century. Punishment for embarrassing the Crown has been meted out in the form of a thousand subtle strokes of the pen that some days feel like the same effect as if we hadn't fought in the first place. And yet, just as in the 19th century, our narratives of who we are have been galvanised and affirmed, and entered our collective consciousness, *because* of the fight. People have been writing about, and struggling against, the politics of the university and the particular ways in which Indigenous people and knowledges get configured within them. I need not rehearse all of those arguments and histories here. Suffice to say, Indigenous Studies will always be a site of struggle. This won't change, and hoping for anything else is also irresponsible. (Indeed, I would be suspicious of any version of Indigenous Studies that *wasn't* shaped by – and enmeshed in – struggle.) But it's not *just* a site of struggle.

I'm here in Indigenous Studies because there's work to do and I feel passionate and committed to doing it. I am not in Indigenous Studies because I can't hack it in English or because English won't have me. I'm also not in Indigenous Studies just because it's a place for Indigenous people (any more than people are in English because it's a place for English people). I'm here because I love having classrooms full of Indigenous students, and because I love supervising Indigenous students whose skills and insights enable them to do research far beyond what I could ever do, bringing to life the words of the Tongan visionary Epeli Hau'ofa who is recalled by the Banaban scholar Teresia Teaiwa to have said, 'the thing about it is, our job is to make way for people who are better than us' (Teaiwa 2010: 108). I've also noticed that my research has shifted as I have been institutionally based in Indigenous Studies. In so many ways I am still a literary scholar focussed on critical engagement with Indigenous-produced texts, but my questions are shifting and my work is responding to the specific and interdisciplinary conversations and communities (including student communities) in which I work. To choose an example, a strand of my interests has moved towards environmental and eco-critical questions, shaped by conversations in the Indigenous Studies air about land, food sovereignty, repatriation, and history. To choose another, engaging Indigenous language writing has increased in urgency from a gesture towards the hope of future work to deliberately seeking researchers and graduate students who can work across Indigenous Pacific languages.

Writing this chapter has also given me an opportunity to reflect on the opportunities – to be mentored, to serve, and to be in leadership – that I would not have had were it not for Indigenous Studies. How different my career (and life) would be without this discipline: networks and friendships for mentoring and collegiality; professional associations – especially, of course, NAISA – for chances to serve on councils and editorial boards and committees; a department and a Faculty in which I've written documents, spoken up, chaired meetings, held positions of authority, made decisions, contributed to creating space for the next ones coming through. Some days I joke that

I spend more time now with spreadsheets than a girl doing a PhD in English would ever have imagined, but I can put my hand on my heart (and my laptop) and say that I would not have had any of these opportunities – or, in the case of collegiality, pleasures – had I worked only in English. I didn't start this section of this chapter with the words 'I *currently* hold a permanent position' because I'm actively plotting an escape from Indigenous Studies, or from Waikato, but I also know that I will only stay as long as I have something to contribute, and as long as that contribution is welcome. Staying any longer than that would be irresponsible. On the other hand, to return to the argument underlying this chapter, there are limits to accounts of individual agency when it comes to disciplinary positioning and positions: maybe I will retire from this job decades in the future (thinking about retirement from my mid-career location reminds me of thinking about being 30 when I was 16); maybe I will leave Waikato one day; maybe Waikato will leave me.

The title of this chapter is drawn from some work I did when writing about Māori literary modernism. A 1975 poem by Henare Dewes, *Te Ao Hou*, called on a new generation to 'cast your dart' and I wondered what to make of this metaphor (1975: 40). It turned out that we used to play *niti*, a traditional activity in which darts were aimed at a specific site and, as with any other game of darts anywhere in the world, accuracy and skill were central to deciding on the winner. However, a unique element of this Māori game was that the point was not to hit a target directly but to cause the dart to ricochet off a mound in a particular direction as far as possible (Buck 1949: 242). Conceptually, 'ricochet' contains elements of risk, skill, reaction, and trajectory. It is necessarily about a shift in direction, but one which is tied to particular purpose and calculation, in which a deliberate harnessing of change can amplify rather than restrict movement. Hokowhitu (2008) has pointed out the metaphoric, spiritual, physical, and genealogical dimensions of dart throwing in the Māori world; these were never merely leisure activities but have always been used for pedagogic, preparatory, and community-building purposes. What can the idea of ricochet contribute to the way we understand the dynamic, dispersed, and variable actions of what could appear as chaos to those for whom the point of darts is to stick into a particular point on a flat surface? In the chapter I wrote about Māori modernism I asked: what, indeed, might the notion of ricochet contribute to the methods by which we read Indigenous texts or think about Indigenous responses to colonialism? But in this chapter the concept of ricochet opens up a way to think about the disciplinarity – both intellectual and institutional – of Indigenous Studies.

The game of darts as it has been played in Aotearoa has similarities with ricochet-focussed games played around Oceania. As with so many similar activities around the region, there are specificities unique to each of the places where they occur, as well as striking and long-standing similarities that have been maintained across the region for generations. The concept of ricochet in relation to dart throwing is therefore always already pulling against rigid borders imposed by contemporary nation states, even as it simultaneously affirms the significance of the local. In a context in which the hegemonic game of darts, if you will, is a flat disc covered in concentric circles with a prized central point, we can forget there are other things towards which one might throw darts; that not all games of darts focus on hitting a single, stable, fixed, narrow spot. Maybe the twists and turns of my own relationship with Indigenous Studies can be thought of as productive – as various kinds of energy-filled and space-making ricochet – rather than as chaotic. Perhaps we can think about diverse responses to academic circumstances as evidence of a lack of skill or focus, *or* we can focus on various trajectories and particular current landing sites as evidence of the vast, dynamic, collective enterprise that is Indigenous Studies. Each of us throws our darts – our research, our teaching, our projects, our academic lives – from particular disciplinary and personal pathways, and each of our darts ends up in incredibly different places. According to the rules of niti, we are not aiming at the mound in order to hit the same spot but to achieve the best possible ricochet: the longest distance, the furthest impact.

And if this is the metaphor we're going with, what of Indigenous Studies institutional entities? These make up the mound – the thing that needs to be solid, secure, firm, in order for ricochet to take place. Certainly some of the mound is also made by the books and articles and students and community engagements that are the result of work by Indigenous Studies scholars across (and beyond) the university – including by me, when I'm in an office in English rather than Indigenous Studies – but the bulk, the heft, the integrity of the mound depends on the bulk, the heft, the integrity of places with Indigenous Studies over the door. I find it helpful to think about the institutional work in which I am engaged as mound-building off which later dart-throwers can ricochet their own work.[5] Maybe, to tip my hat back to Andersen (2009), the impacting of intellectual soil in this way is another layer of meaning for his key concept of density. Spreadsheets and papers and meetings, and even some writing tasks that feel more 'service' than 'research', are not mere distraction or busywork but quietly add dimension to the mound. As Indigenous scholars we can be so anxious about seeming too committed – too *in love* – with these institutions, and so keen to find ways to think about our university work ultimately as being work in the world (as if our lives and the lives of our students are not in the world too). Maybe Indigenous Studies, and the patient time-consuming patting of dirt into well-shaped mounds, is something beyond which we, but importantly more and more others, can ricochet our many carefully-prepared darts ... far beyond what work has already been done, beyond our own generations, beyond our own bookshelves, beyond our own questions, beyond the forms of disadvantage and oppression that currently shape so many of our communities ... far, far beyond Indigenous Studies, to places we cannot yet even see.

Notes

1 This comment is intended to extend the critical conversation initiated by Metis scholar Chris Andersen where he speaks to the problem of disciplines other than Indigenous Studies claiming they (or, more accurately, some of their scholars) 'do' Indigenous Studies. Certainly, such claims set up a logic in which stand-alone Indigenous Studies entities could be rendered unnecessary, and I whole-heartedly both agree with Andersen and have anecdotes and observations of my own to pitch in. However, the argument can be stretched to an assumption that the reverse is also true: that when scholars working outside Indigenous Studies entities articulate themselves as being scholars of Indigenous Studies are disloyal to the interests of Indigenous Studies as a discipline. Plenty of scholars would love to work in Indigenous Studies entities – there just aren't enough jobs to go around, and maybe there are reasons to accept other positions in other departments (proximity to home, simultaneous commitment to another disciplinary conversation, desire to work with certain student communities, etc).

2 Witi Ihimaera, iconic Māori writer and anthologist, was the first Māori writer to publish a collection of short fiction, and then a novel; he was teaching in the English department when I commenced by university studies.

3 The lines of poetry in this chapter are all snippets from 'Te Kawa a Maui farewell: A Poem in Seven Parts,' a poem I published in *Ora Nui Special Edition*.

4 A new head was eventually appointed, and Bronwyn Carlson is doing a wonderful job of making the department live up to its potential.

5 I'm well aware that mound-building is a specific activity undertaken by many Indigenous communities for millennia in North America, and do not seek to overstate or appropriate a connection between those activities and the preparation for dart throwing in Aotearoa on which I am focussed here.

References

Andersen, C. (2009). 'Critical Indigenous studies: From difference to density', *Cultural Studies Review*, vol 15, no 2: 80–100.

Buck, P.H. (1949). *The Coming of the Māori*. Maori Purposes Fund Board: Wellington.

Dewes, H. (1975). 'Te Ao Hou', *Te Ao Hou*, vol 76: 40.

Hokowhitu, B. (2008). 'Authenticating Māori physicality: Translations of "Games" and "Pastimes" by early travellers and missionaries to New Zealand', *International Journal of the History of Sport*, vol 25, no 10: 1355–1373.

Teaiwa, T. (2010). 'The thing about it is …', *The Contemporary Pacific*, vol 22, no 1: 105–108.

3

Multi-generational Indigenous feminisms

From F word to what IFs[1]

Kim Anderson

Introduction

In 2005, Anishinaabe scholar Cheryl Suzack invited me to a conference she was organising at the University of Alberta (Canada). The topic was Indigenous feminism, and I recall being curious about what might be presented and who might come. Like many Indigenous women I was uncertain about identifying as feminist even though I had been writing about the impact of patriarchy in Indigenous communities for a few years by that time (Anderson 2016). The conference was in Edmonton, a four-hour flight from where I lived, and so I decided to use the trip as an opportunity to visit with an Auntie/Elder I don't get to see too often. I invited her to the conference, thinking we might visit and learn together. I wasn't surprised when she expressed some reservations, but she came, telling me that she was both curious and perplexed by the subject of the conference: *Indigenous feminism.* What did it mean? Sitting over tea, after several days of listening to presentations, she told me, 'I think I know what it means now. It's just kinship. And maybe that's another word for it: *Kinship*'.

It's been 15 years since Auntie and I sat trying to figure it out, and by now Indigenous feminisms are much more broadly known, accepted, defined, and practiced. In this chapter, I trace the development of Indigenous feminisms, which I refer to in the plural as a reminder of the multiple and diverse approaches employed by those who identify their work with Indigenous feminisms. I abbreviate periodically to 'IFs' – for stylistics reasons, but also to acknowledge the emancipatory potential of this work.

These emancipatory possibilities were foremost in my mind as I began writing this chapter, still grappling with how I might define IFs. I reflected on how I use IFs to envision, to explore questions like *What if we didn't have to grapple with the ubiquitous, everyday experiences of heteropatriarchy?* and *What are some of the ways Indigenous folks are going about transforming our social relations for the better?* Some might say that's a project of kinship. If we broaden my question about social relations to consider 'all our relations', including relations with the natural, non-human, and spirit worlds, we enter into decolonising possibilities of what Yazzie and Baldy (2018) have defined as 'radical relationality'. They attribute this practice as "coming primarily from Indigenous feminists" and encompassing "a vision of relationality and collective political organization that is deeply intersectional and premised on values of interdependency, reciprocity, equality, and responsibility" (2018: 2). As they say, "to be a good relative is to be an Indigenous feminist" (2018: 2).

I'm not sure if that is what my Auntie was thinking, but I have built on her observation about Indigenous feminisms as a form of kinship to offer this look at the evolution of IFs. My Auntie's comments also reflect the resistance of many Indigenous women to identify with the 'F' word, followed by a reframing what IFs might mean for us. In figuring out how to organise a broad, introductory chapter about IFs, it helped to think about that process of resistance and reframing in the context of kinship and radical relationality. Bearing in mind that Western feminism has often been described as occurring in waves, I decided to approach the chapter by focusing on the intergenerational processes that facilitate the transfer of Indigenous feminist knowledges and practices. In so doing I hope to honour the kinship and relations that such a process upholds. It's about the aunties and grannies that come before us: the writers, artists, and scholars we may only know through their works, and the older generations who mentor us personally. Thus understood, Indigenous feminisms might again be seen as a process of kinship and radical relationality among and for Indigenous women and increasingly beyond—a rippling wellness for all our relations.

Subsections of the chapter address the following questions: First, What are Indigenous feminisms? and Where did they come from?; then, How have Indigenous feminisms been applied?; and finally, Where are Indigenous feminisms going? I will refer primarily to the theorising and practices taking place in the Anglo-settler CANZUS states (Canada, Australia, New Zealand/ Aotearoa, and the United States), in keeping with the territories that are the focus of this handbook. I am a Metis scholar living and working within Canada, so the personal and professional experience I draw on comes from my cultural and territorial positioning.

Before I get into the what, where, and how of IFs, I will offer a story that was told to me by one of those generational mentors, Maria Campbell (Metis) – who happens to be a literary Auntie as well as my teacher, co-conspirator, and friend. As with many Indigenous stories, Maria's story provides an example of radical relationality and an anchor for me to return to, which I will do at the end of the chapter.

The story is about a woman Maria knew in her home community in northern Saskatchewan, Canada. I first heard it when we were researching the roots of violence in Indigenous communities. Maria had been reading the *Jesuit Relations* and looking through the archival works written by missionaries and church officials to track the role of the church in introducing and fostering misogynist violence in our communities. She pointed out that the 17th-century Jesuits called the Huron women that they encountered 'firebrands of Hell', and observed that these women were "haughty, proud; women who did as they pleased" (Anderson 1991: 2). She noted, "Reading this, I admired the women who resisted and wanted to know more about them: Who were they? What kind of mischief did they get into? How were they punished for it? and How did other community members respond?" (Campbell 2017). She then equated this portrayal of firebrands to a woman she had known who lived some 300 years later, in her community in northern Saskatchewan, as follows.[2]

'Firebrands of Hell': Flora and other resisters

(As told by Maria Campbell, Spring 2017)[3]

When I think back, and in the context of religion, I remember one woman named Flora. She was designated as Anglican, but she never went to church. It wasn't uncommon in our community for Anglicans to attend the Catholic Church if they lived too far away from their own denomination, but Flora never went to any of the churches. She was independent; she just did what she wanted to do.

Flora never married, never had children, but she had a lot of men visitors. It wasn't about prostitution or anything sexual; it was just that the men really liked her. I knew this from eavesdropping on conversations between my mother and my aunties. Their stories revealed how the men in our community looked to Flora for discussion and how they went to her when they wanted to talk about women's views.

The women in my family were never jealous of her – in fact they wanted the men to visit. I remember that when a woman was beaten up, my mom and aunties always hoped the guy would end up at Flora's because they wanted Flora to talk to him. My nokoms (grannies) also held influence with the men – influence on the matters of community life – but Flora's relationship with those men was different. Flora's house was almost like a man's clubhouse. Men would play poker there all night, or they would come to sit around and have tea and talk.

Flora's house welcomed women as well, and many women could be found there at any time during the day. Flora was also the helper of the midwives. They would ask her to look after the mother who had just had a baby, or the mother who had been sick before she had her baby. She was the one they would call on because they knew she would be there immediately. Flora was helpful, too, because she was really good with kids. She always encouraged relationships with children and was kind to them. And if someone was dying or if there was a death and the midwives needed help to dress the body, they would call on Flora.

Nobody had to worry about paying her because she wouldn't take money. Instead she would take tobacco and cigarette papers. There was always a smoke with a cup of tea if you went to her home. I learned that on my first visit to her house as a young woman. She had a bag of tobacco hanging from a wooden peg and a bowl of cigarette papers nearby, which she pointed to when I sat down with my tea. I didn't smoke, of course, but I was grateful that she treated me as a grown-up, and I am grateful that she was an important part of my life, as today it allows me to imagine a visit with those women the Jesuits encountered.

Because Flora was always there when you needed her, she had some kind of authority in the community, although nobody ever talked about it. But amidst this traditional respect and authority, there was the church, and, quite simply, the church hated Flora. The priest made Flora his enemy and had multiple ways of putting her down. For example, he would never say anything bad about her himself, but he would fuel bad gossip about her. It is noteworthy that he always used one or two of the women who were already known as gossips and tale-bearers – women who were jealous of Flora.

I remember one woman in particular who was very close to the priest. She was a devoted Catholic – kept the church clean and cooked meals for him, making sure everything was okay when he came to the community. She was the one who would promote gossip. In the wintertime she would report that "there were devil's tracks seen around Flora's house again" and that "a tall man was seen leaving her house every night for a week during the last full moon." Well when you're a child and you're listening to that kind of slander, you can get really frightened and curious because it feeds into what you've already observed: that a strong woman is feared and isolated by some sectors of the community. With whisperings of a tall dark man and devil's footprints and all-night poker games, you can imagine the response in a small isolated community already full of stories of *witikos*, *pahkahkosak*, and *chipis*. And so, with his promotion of frightening stories and community gossip, the priest incited plenty of lateral violence in our community, and he did it in such a way that most people never knew it was him.

That priest also modelled physical violence. I remember one incident in particular; I was about six or seven years old. We were sitting in church one morning when Flora walked in, which was remarkable to me because I had never seen her there before. She walked almost to the front to get a man who was sitting with his children. When she touched him on the shoulder, he got up immediately. I learned later his wife was having a difficult birth and so the old ladies had called for him. But when this man got up, the priest, who was in the middle of whatever he was doing, grabbed the long skinny whip that he kept by the altar – the whip that he used to threaten us kids if we didn't sit quiet and pray, the kind of whip you use on horses. He grabbed that whip, came down from his altar, and beat Flora on the back as she walked out. She didn't run. She didn't do anything except walk out quietly. That priest whipped her all the way out the door, all the while yelling at her in French. He was so angry that when he came back to the altar, he was out of breath and red-faced. And he ranted and raved throughout the rest of the service.

During those long moments that Flora was being whipped out of the church, nobody said a word. Nobody looked back. But I looked. And the memory, like a photograph, has forever been etched within me. Today when I hear the word 'violence', that is the first memory that flashes across my mind. Since childhood I have associated that priest with the way Indigenous women are treated in our communities. It is both powerful and haunting, as were the dignity and strength of Flora as she walked out of the church. (Campbell 2017: Personal communication)

Indigenous feminisms: What are IFs?

As Flora's story demonstrates, and with consideration of the 'haughty' women who encountered 17th-century Jesuits before her, Indigenous women have a long history of resisting patriarchal and colonial oppression. I will return to Flora later; for now I ask the reader to sit with her while going through this chapter, keeping in mind Huhndorf and Suzack's (2010: 5) assertion that:

Although Indigenous feminism is a nascent field of scholarly inquiry, it has arisen from histories of women's activism and culture that have aimed to combat gender discrimi-nation, secure social justice for Indigenous women, and counter their social erasure and marginalization.

Some scholars have identified IFs as both theory and activist practice (Green 2017: 7; Suzack 2015: 262), offering a critical lens through which we can interpret as well as work on the "political project" of gender justice in Indigenous contexts (Suzack 2015: 261). In trying to pin down a definition, however, it's important to note that the terms and approaches we use are constantly adapting to new contexts and responding to other evolving theories. Moving from earlier iterations that addressed the intersection of sexism and racism in Indigenous women's lives, Indigenous feminist theory and activism are often applied now to examine how heteropa-triarchy has been used as a tool for colonisation, creating distinct forms of gendered inequity and oppression that must be addressed in order to decolonise (Arvin, Tuck, and Morrill 2013). Indigenous feminist theory thus teaches us that settler-colonial states have been and continue to be built out of the dispossession of Indigenous women and the re-ordering of Indigenous relationships/kinship in order to get access to lands. Framing it as a practice of resilience as well as resistance, Tasha Spillet, in a Canadian Broadcasting Corporation (CBC) interview, defines Indigenous feminism as "an affirmation that Indigenous women have always had inherent sovereignty over our bodies, over our spirits, and land bases" (Monkman 2017: Online). In addition to these definitions, I like to think of IFs as a process of revisioning in the service of Indigenous futurities. I find Leonie Pihama's (2005 [2019]) framing of Māori women's theories helpful in this regard. She writes that Mana Wahine – "the preferred Māori label for what counts as Māori feminism" (Smith cited in Pihama 2005 [2019]: 73) – offers a 'process' whereby Māori women can proactively determine their futures and rediscover "the strength of Māori relationships" (Pihama 2005 [2019]: 72).

Genealogy: Where do IFs come from?

While Arvin, Tuck, and Morrill (2013: 13) state that "Native feminist theories have thrived in the past five decades", the literary genealogy has been sparse until recent years. Luana Ross cites Kathryn Shanley's 1984 article, 'Thoughts on Indigenous Feminism', as "the first definition of Indigenous feminism" that she encountered, and refers to the publishing of Beatrice Medicine (1978; 1983) and Paula Gunn Allen (1984; 1986) as early IFs work (2009: 41). Gunn Allen's (1986) collection of essays on the power of women in 'American Indian traditions' offered a ground-breaking vision of what she saw as Indigenous 'gynocracies'. In addition to Gunn Allen and Medicine, Joanne Barker referenced Mohawk writer Beth Brant (1988) and Menominee poet Chrystos (1988) to the list of literary feminist aunties who "anticipate in complex ways" the work of contemporary Indigenous feminists (Barker 2015: 16). I realised this recently while reviewing Brant's early work (Gould 2019); Brant theorised and practiced Indigenous feminism before we had a language for it. In 1988, Sto:lo writer Lee Maracle published *I Am Woman: A Native Perspective on Sociology and Feminism*, a book of essays that provided insight into the experiences of sexism, racism and colonialism for Indigenous women in Canada, and that pointed out the inadequacy of Western feminism to address Indigenous women's needs. In Aotearoa in the early 1990s, Ngahuia Te Awekotuku (1992 [2019]) wrote about her experiences as a 'Māori lesbian feminist' noting the limitations of Western feminism, and Kathie Irwin (1992 [2019]) wrote about the 'urgent task' of building Māori feminist theories that could draw on the primary sources of Māori society, Māori language, Māori women's herstories, and Māori cultural practices. Also writing in the early 1990s, Linda Tuhiwai Smith (1992 [2019]) and Ripeka Evans (1994 [2019]) called for Māori women's theorising that would take into account their distinct histories of both oppression and activism as well as engagement with extended family, land and spirit. Noting the limitations of Western feminism for their needs, Smith stated "The challenge for Māori women in the 1990s is to assume control over the interpretation of our struggles and to begin to theorise our experiences in ways which make sense for us and which may come to make sense of other women" (1992 [2019]: 41). In Australia, Larissa Behrendt (1993) wrote about how white women, like white and black men, were complicit in the oppression of Aboriginal women, and she outlined the failures of the feminist movement to address their needs.

Writers and activists of the 1980s and 1990s thus articulated the inadequacy of Western feminist theory and practice for Indigenous women, and they began to form theories that would address the particular ways sexism and patriarchy impacted women's lives in their own communities and nations. The new millennium brought some critical monographs that deeply engaged with the question of feminism and Indigenous women, with Aileen Moreton-Robinson's *Talkin' up to the White Woman: Indigenous Women and Feminism* (2000) and Grace Ouelette's *The Fourth World: An Indigenous Perspective on Feminism and Aboriginal Women's Activism* (2002). Moreton-Robinson's *Talkin' Up to the White Woman* (2000) offered an exacting analysis of whiteness, white nationalism and colonialism within white feminist practice in Australia and this work resonated internationally as it demonstrated how utterly unsuited white feminist practice had been to address issues of concern for Aboriginal women. Bronwyn Fredericks later wrote about non-Indigenous feminists in Australia enacting "new forms of colonizing practices" that included tokenising invitations to attend events as guest speakers and focusing on inviting "cultural expression" while continuing to act against Aboriginal sovereignty (2010: 546-547). In Aotearoa, Leonie Pihama stated that "the terms Māori and feminism do not sit comfortably together", and she noted that Western feminists had marginalised Māori ideas and concepts and had silenced Māori women (2005 [2019]: 62).

Due in large part to negative experiences with Western feminism, many Indigenous writers and activists were resistant to identifying with 'the F word' up until the mid-2000s and they continued to point to its limitations. Verna St. Denis has offered a useful summary in 'Aboriginal Women's Critique of Feminism' (2017: 46–50), stating that some contested the Western feminist notion of a universal patriarchy, taking the position that feminist approaches were not suited to Indigenous societies that were traditionally equitable in their gender relations. Some saw Western feminism as seeking equality or sameness with men in contrast to their goals of reinstating traditional Indigenous values and practices that gave women power. Some stated that sovereignty and decolonisation were the primary liberation goals. Sandy Grande has articulated how these cultural and sovereignty factors shaped the resistance to "whitestream feminism", noting that many Indigenous women in North America also viewed feminism as a project led by and working solely in the interests of white middle-class women (2015: 180). As Joanne Barker has pointed out, the political goals of feminists have not been largely relevant to Indigenous women because, starting with the work of the suffragettes and extending into the waves that followed, whitestream feminists have "failed to undo the empire's logics" (2015: 2, 11). All of this explains why some Indigenous women made a point to distance themselves from 'women's libbers', even while doing political work to resist gendered oppression in their communities (Nickel 2017). Indigenous women who did identify with feminism often found themselves stigmatised (Green 2017: 6), a practice that continues to this day (Blaney and Grey 2017: 236).

In the midst of this resistance, discussions of a distinctly identified 'Indigenous feminism' began to pick up through gatherings and publishing by the mid-2000s. Joyce Green published the first version of her edited anthology in 2007 (2017) in the wake of an Indigenous feminist conference held at the University of Regina in 2002, and Suzack et al. produced an anthology (2010) from the 2004 University of Alberta conference mentioned at the beginning of this chapter. In 2009, Mishuana Goeman and Jennifer Nez Denetdale co-edited a special edition of the *Wicazo Sa Review*, building on the earlier work of J. Kehaulani Kaunaui and Andrea Smith in the *American Quarterly* (2008). Noting that their work was also generated through gatherings hosted by American Indian Studies at the University of Illinois at Urbana-Champaign, Goeman and Denetdale affirmed the usefulness of "Native feminist analysis in decolonizing Indigenous nations," while acknowledging that "some strains of liberal-feminist thought continue to contain racial hierarchies and imperial intent" (2009: 9). All this work gave Indigenous women more space to begin to identify as Indigenous feminists and to further articulate Indigenous feminist theory and practice.

How have IFs been applied?

Celeste Liddle, an Arrernte feminist from central Australia has noted three formative elements that structure the need for Aboriginal feminism: 'the white patriarchy', 'the black [Indigenous][4] patriarchy', and 'mainstream feminism' (2014). In so doing, she offers a way to frame how IFs have been applied.

First, Indigenous feminist analysis of 'the white patriarchy' has increased our understanding of how colonisation and Christianity dismantled the positioning and influence that Indigenous women held in their communities (St. Denis 2017: 54–55). Scholars and activists have identified the concepts of egalitarianism, complementary gender relations, women's leadership/authorities, and matrilineality in our Indigenous societies and cultures (Barker 2015). While these distinctions were initially made to explain why, as Diné scholar Laura Tohe put it, "there is no word for feminism in my language" (2000: 103), they have become Indigenous feminist arguments about the need to revisit, revise, and reinstate egalitarian gender practices and traditions that empower women into our societies.[5] Generational/auntie feminist scholars like Beatrice Medicine and Paula Gunn Allen set the course for this work by getting us to consider that patriarchy was not part of Indigenous societies; that, historically, Indigenous women had power and authority. These were the authors I was reading when first trying to sort through what had happened to create the violence and gendered oppression now suffered in Indigenous communities and to think about how we might 'reconstruct' Native womanhood based on egalitarian traditions of our various nations (Anderson 2016). On the other side of the world, women in Aotearoa and Australia had also been writing about how colonisation had disrupted Indigenous systems of gender balance, equity, complementarity and women's traditional authorities (Behrendt 1993; Jahnke 1997 [2019]; Mikaere 1994 [2019]).

Work that highlighted Indigenous traditions and histories of gender equity corresponded with a general movement to recover and take pride in Indigenous tradition and culture, and this pride may be why earlier generations were less inclined to suggest that Indigenous cultures may have had their own patriarchal practices. Emma Laroque stands out as one Indigenous feminist auntie who brought critical attention to this issue early on. In 1996 she wrote, "we must be circumspect in our recall of tradition. ... We know enough about human history that we cannot assume that all Aboriginal traditions universally respected and honoured women" and "There are indications of male violence and sexism in some Aboriginal societies prior to European contact" (1996: 14). Later in this chapter I will address how subsequent generations of Indigenous feminists have been more apt to take up critical approaches to 'tradition' and gendered roles, but I will note here that there is still very little analysis of how patriarchy may have been part of pre-colonial Indigenous societies.[6]

There have, however, been plenty of Indigenous feminists across the generations who have addressed how our communities have replicated and adapted Western patriarchy within to create what Liddle (2014) called 'the black patriarchy'. As Indigenous peoples have taken up nation building, reclamation of lands and territories, and Indigenous sovereignty and resurgence, Indigenous feminists have called attention to how Indigenous women's rights, gendered discrimination, and violence have often been ignored or dismissed by our own peoples (Green 2017). In 2000, Lina Sunseri pointed to the need for Indigenous feminist analysis of nation building because "male Indigenous nationalists argue that capitalism has been the cause of women's problems and they have completely ignored or dismissed the patriarchal notion of women's oppression" (2000: 256), and in 2007, Renya Ramirez noted that "race, tribal nation, and gender should be non-hierarchically linked as categories of analysis" as we work towards liberation (2007: 35). In my own scholarly and community work, I discovered that international feminist literature offers critical insights into how fundamentalism and an essentialist positioning of women as 'mothers of the nation' are often at play in nation building (Anderson 2010).

A decade or two after such Indigenous feminist proclamations, we now see more women and organisations take up Indigenous feminist identities in their politics. Joyce Green gives examples of how the Native Women's Association of Canada and The Aboriginal Women's Action Network have employed feminist methodologies or alliance with feminist organisations (2017:

3). Other women and organisations employ Indigenous feminist practice without naming it as such. Sonja John (2015) argues that this was the case with the Idle No More movement, a female-led grassroots response, initially taken in response to a Canadian omnibus bill that threatened land and sovereignty rights. John theorised that even though the movement did not identify "as feminist per se", it was Indigenous feminist because it took into account how Indigenous women have been marginalised from male-dominated Indigenous politics in Canada (2015: 51).

Many Indigenous feminists have linked nation building with the need to address gendered violence in Indigenous communities. By connecting settler colonialism with the crises of violence in Indigenous communities today, IFs draw attention to how both the white patriarchy and Indigenous patriarchy are operational. Linking patriarchy, capitalism, and colonisation, Rachel Flowers states "the story of the settler colony is founded in disappearing peoples, from *terra nullius* to missing and murdered women" (2015: 34). In conversation with Ina Knobblock (2015), Sami feminist scholar Rauna Kuokkanen links violence with self-determination within the studies she has done in Sapmi, Greenland, and Canada, asking "How do you build Indigenous self-determination if women don't feel safe and free from violence in their own communities?" (2015: 276). Indigenous feminist analysis has recently been taken up by Indigenous scholars and activists to address the crisis of missing and murdered Indigenous women and girls in Canada. For Robyn Bourgeois, a Cree scholar who has focused on this issue, we must use an "Indigenous feminist anti-oppression framework" that takes into account how colonialism, racism, and patriarchy work together to create and sustain this crisis (2017: 255). Activists have suggested that an Indigenous feminist approach be brought to the Canadian National Inquiry into Missing and Murdered Indigenous Women and Girls. Writing at the outset of the Inquiry in 2016, Cherry Smiley called for an "explicitly feminist framework, led by fearlessly feminist Indigenous women" in order to address the particular "racist and sexist colonial context" in which the crisis is happening (2016: 312). Fay Blaney argued that instead of taking a "family-first" approach, the Inquiry needed to have a "feminist-first" approach that acknowledged the male violence against Indigenous women and girls (2017: 238). Now that the National Inquiry's Final Report has been released (2019), it is notable there is no reference to Indigenous feminism in the text, although discussions of the relationship between colonialism and violence against missing and murdered women, the gendered oppression of two-spirit peoples, and other Indigenous feminist approaches are taken up.

The National Inquiry into Missing and Murdered Women and Girls in Canada (2019) also reported on the link between resource extraction projects and violence against Indigenous women. Drawing from a Women's Earth Alliance and Native Youth Sexual Health report, the report shares how this was articulated by Melina Laboucan Massimo: "The industrial system of resource extraction in Canada is predicated on systems of power and domination. This system is based on the raping and pillaging of Mother Earth as well as violence against women. The two are inextricably linked" (2019: 586). Indigenous feminist approaches thus connect body, land, and gendered violence, and these positions underpin related activist work, like that of Dane Zaa/Nehiway writer Helen Knott (2018: 2019). Yazzie and Baldy (2018) point out that Indigenous feminism has been 'instrumental' in the resistance to resource extraction, and in the protection of water. As they note "The interconnectedness between Indigenous women's bodies and the lands that women caretake constitutes one of the primary axes of relationality in Indigenous feminism" (2018: 8). Ripeka Evans has articulated this interrelatedness of women and land among the Māori, asserting that, among other factors, Māori feminism is "grounded in the identity and creation of this country, grounded in the rivers, lakes, mountains seas and forests ..." (1994 [2019]: 130). Responsibility to land is thus a key part of the collective and radical relationality work of Indigenous feminists (Yazzie and Baldy 2018).

Finally, when it comes to engaging with 'mainstream' feminisms, Indigenous women assert that many challenges remain. In the tenth anniversary of her book *Red Pedagogy*, Sandy Grande writes that feminist discourse continues to be "not only dominated by white women but principally structured on the basis of white, middle-class experience" (2015: 181). As with the earlier generations, some Indigenous feminists are exploring how mainstream feminist practices can intersect with Indigenous feminisms. Arvin, Tuck, and Morrill (2013: 9) offer "five challenges that Native feminist theories pose to gender and women's studies" related to their assertion that the link between heteropatriarchy and settler colonialism "is intellectually and politically imperative". They challenge gender and women's studies to: problematise settler colonialism and its intersections; refuse erasure but do more than include; craft alliances that directly address differences; recognise Indigenous ways of knowing; and question academic participation in Indigenous dispossession (2013). Aikau, Arvin, Goeman, and Moregensen (2015) have explored the relationships and possibilities between transnational and Indigenous feminisms. They raise interesting questions, encouraging critical positionality and reflexivity, and they ask whether transnationalists are willing to identify as settlers. They also raise the possibilities of trans-Indigeneity that centres relationships with land and water, and, like Grande, ask us to consider how feminist knowledges continue to be informed by white supremacist settler colonialism. Aileen Moreton-Robinson (2013) and Kim Tallbear (2014) have theorised on the possibilities of Indigenous feminist standpoint theory, which can centre Indigenous women's knowledges and experience in research and activism. This approach also acknowledges the particular positioning of Indigenous women as researchers who "stand with" their communities in an ethic of "staying in relation" (Tallbear 2014: 84).

Where are IFs going?

As noted in the introduction, IFs have moved from earlier discussions about sexism and patriarchy to theorising on the link between settler colonialism, heteropatriarchy, and heteropaternalism. This movement has involved engaging with other Indigenous theoretical work. A recent edited collection by Barker has demonstrated the need to bring together Indigenous gender, sexuality, and feminist studies to address how gender and sexuality are "core constitutive elements of imperialist-colonist state formations" (2017: 6). As Mishuana Goeman states, "addressing gender and sexuality in our moves to decolonize is not optional" (2017: 190). Anishinaabeg writer Leanne Betasamosake Simpson's work offers significant direction in how we might centre gender in resurgence efforts; for as she notes, "The gendered nature of colonialism and settler colonialism means heteropatriarchy has to be critically considered in every project we're currently collectively and individually engaged in. Otherwise we risk replicating it" (2017: 51).

Some queer theorists credit the work of Indigenous feminists for introducing critical approaches to gender and sexuality in Indigenous communities. In their introduction to *Queer Indigenous Studies*, Driskell et al. note: "The work of belonging to, challenging, and transforming 'the community' long has been modelled by Indigenous women activists, who include Indigenous feminist theorists linking activist and academic work" (2011: 218). Mark Rifkin (2011) credits the work of Jennifer Nez Denetdale (2006) and Joanne Barker (2006) in his analysis of how Indigenous kinship systems were disrupted through the imposition of heteronormative, nuclear families, which resulted in the loss of Indigenous sexualities, lands, and political autonomy. In her 2001 doctoral thesis, Leonie Pihama problematised the gender binary and reductionist biologies by pointing out "there is not, as we are often presented with, a simplistic, dualistic or oppositional relationship between Māori women and Māori men, but there are varying ways in which roles and relationships are negotiated" (2001: 262;

2005 [2019]: 70). Indigenous queer theory and Indigenous feminisms are thus closely aligned in their analysis of disruption to Indigenous kinship systems and reclaiming of non-heteronormative relations. The project of examining colonial gender roles has also been taken up recently in Indigenous masculinities work (Innes and Anderson 2015; Mays 2018). Leah Sneider suggests that critical Indigenous masculinities can build on Indigenous feminist work, noting they "share both the same purpose and theoretical approach" on colonisation and the impact of patriarchy (2015: 66).[7]

Within this intersection of Indigenous feminist, gender, and queer studies, some scholars offer critical feedback about the limitations of previous IFs work. Emily Snyder has pointed to "significant theoretical gaps" in Indigenous feminist theory, stating "With few exceptions, people proceed with analyses that leave the sex and gender binary of male/female and man/woman intact", and points out that "heteronormativity predominates the scholarship" (2014: 382). Snyder challenges scholarship about Indigenous women "that uncritically takes up notions of motherhood, peacefulness, and nurturing as 'natural' or unquestioningly tied up with sacredness bestowed upon women by the Creator", adding that "theoretical tools are needed to deconstruct discourses about gender that are armoured in rigid conceptualizations of sacredness, culture, and tradition" (2014: 379; see also Stark and Starblanket 2017: 185). She cites Joyce Green, Andrea Smith, Emma LaRocque, and Val Napoleon as offering exceptions to this kind of scholarship. LaRoque, who warned of the dangers of romanticising and taking up essentialist notions of tradition in 1996, continues to ask critical questions, such as whether notions of balance and complementarity or the "idealization of female nurturing and motherhood" reify an ongoing "inequitable gendered distribution of power" (2017: 125).

While Indigenous gender complementarity has been an Indigenous feminist argument in diverse regions of the world (Stewart in Anderson et al. 2019; Hernandez Castillo 2010), some have pointed to the limitations of this argument (Liddle 2014). Gina Starblanket has written about how notions of complementary gender roles and gender equality in pre-contact Indigenous societies are problematic in that they are often used by Indigenous governments and policy makers to ignore the existence of patriarchal violence and oppression in our communities (2017: 27). Starblanket has further challenged the connection between women's bodies and their spirituality (menstrual cycles, capacity to give life), noting "Indigenous women's identities become defined through the material capacity of our bodies" (2017: 31). In a piece written with Heidi Stark, Starblanket has called out notions about women being "keepers of relationships," stating that this leads to women being responsible to "remedy unhealthy relationships and violence within Indigenous and settler contexts while also ensuring the maintenance of traditional practices" (Starblanket and Stark 2018: 185).

These recent critiques are perhaps the sign of a discipline entering a new stage of maturity, where critical reflection on earlier work is now possible. As we move to the future, it is heartening for some of us older and middle generation folks to see this. Coming from a history where we spent our energies justifying our feminist positioning, it is encouraging to see Indigenous feminist work taken up by upcoming generations of scholars[8] and in new mediums. I remember how exciting it was when I first came across the work of an Indigenous feminist blogger: Erica Violet Lee, with www.moontimewarrior. By now, there is more of such activity; Amanda Morris has written about how Indigenous feminist bloggers are now challenging stereotypes related to their intersectional identities. She notes: "Indigenous feminist bloggers use the internet to fight the imposition of oppressive fixed binaries on themselves and on their communities; their digital interventions simultaneously preserve tradition and present contemporary realities of real Indigenous experiences" (2017: 236).

Looking to the future, we can also hope for more global discussions about IFs. As Elena Flores Ruiz (in Anderson et al. 2019) has pointed out, in the context of North America, there have been "powerful contributions to the pluricultural storying of Indigenous feminist knowledges and lifeways ... but the story of Indigenous women's theorizing on the tail end of Turtle Island is missing" (2019: 128). Indigenous women from Latin America (Altamirano-Jimenez 2017; Dulfano 2017; Cappelli 2018) and beyond (see Tslotanova in Anderson et al. 2019) offer critical insights that I have not touched on here, but they share many of the histories and struggles related to IFs. There is, indeed, room for more international Indigenous feminisms, gatherings, and discussions (McCormick 2017).

Conclusion

Indigenous feminisms come of out of a long history of activism on the part of Indigenous women to address oppression in their communities, including sexism in politics, marginalisation in sovereignty movements, gendered violence, and heteronormativity. IFs offer a vision of how to move forward with social and environmental justice; to consider the what IFs − to call up what decolonisation might look like in a world where all our relations thrive. As we move into the future, I am mindful of all the women who have contributed to this development, starting with those first contact 'firebrands of Hell' who challenged the Jesuits in 17th-century New France. And then there's Flora. While she likely would never have identified as a feminist, there are many elements in her story that I would celebrate as Indigenous feminism. For example:

> *She never went to church*: Like the 'haughty women' who resisted the 17th-century Jesuits in New France, Flora did not succumb to the social norms of colonial/Christian institutions. *She was independent; she just did what she wanted to do*: Flora was not tied to a man's agenda. *Flora never married, never had children*: She did not participate in heteronormative kinship or expectations around motherhood. *I remember that when a woman was beaten up my mom and aunties always hoped the guy would end up at Flora's because they wanted Flora to talk to him*: Flora assisted kin and community with addressing gendered violence. *Men would play poker all night or they would come and sit around and have tea and talk*: Flora participated in gender non-conforming activity. *Flora was also the helper to the midwives*: She held responsibilities to future generations as well as to those passing into the spirit world. *Because Flora was there when you needed her, she had some kind of authority in the community, although nobody ever talked about it*: Flora held traditional leadership authority which is based on fulfilling responsibility to all the kin/relations. *A strong woman is feared and isolated by some sectors of the community*: Flora's strength as a leader and woman resisting oppressive practices was threatening to some. *She didn't run, she didn't do anything except walk out quietly*: Flora demonstrated a stalwart strength in resistance. *During those long moments that Flora was being whipped out of the church, nobody said a word. Nobody looked back*: Flora sometimes stood alone against the oppressive structures she was resisting.

I want to finish by honouring Flora and all the previous generations of Indigenous aunties and grannies who have demonstrated resilience, resistance, leadership, and vision through their radical relational practices. This exercise has also given me time to reflect on and appreciate their work and to feel hope with the future generations and the directions they are taking. For though we have been working in different temporalities, spaces, contexts, and interests, we share a common project of envisioning a kinship in which all our relations find themselves free.

Notes

1 This title is inspired by Luana Ross's 2009 article 'From the 'F' Word to Indigenous Feminisms'.
2 Retold with permission from Maria Campbell. This story will be part of a forthcoming book of stories by Campbell.
3 Personal communication, April 2017. This story will be shared with others in a forthcoming book by Campbell.
4 Liddle's reference to black patriarchy is in the Australian context here, and she notes, "In the Australian context, Aboriginal and Torres Strait Islander people are considered 'black Australians' and have been since the arrival of the colonisers. It has been a term we have subsequently adopted politically" (2014: footnote 1). I have inserted Indigenous in brackets in this quote for clarification for the international reader.
5 For examples of scholars posing these arguments across the decades, see Jaimes and Halsey 1992; Mihesuah 2003; Tsosie 2010; Risling Baldy 2018.
6 Laroque commented that "Many early European observations as well as original Indian legends (e.g. Cree Wehsehkehcha stories I grew up with) point to pre-contact existence of male violence and sexism against women" (1996: 14). Christine Sy (2018) has analyzed patriarchal violence in a foundational story of the Anishinaabeg, questioning whether the violence in this narrative is connected to the introduction of Christianity.
7 Conversely, Billy-Ray Belcourt has theorised on the incompatibility of Indigenous feminism and Indigenous masculinities studies, stating "the normative project of 'Indigenous Masculinities' – to make a healthy masculinity for Indigenous men in order to repair the social ... has to be done at the expense of queer life" (2016: 1).
8 Although I was not able to get a copy of this book in time to include it in this chapter, I am excited to see this upcoming collection of essays: Fehr and Nickel (2020) *In Good Relation: History, Gender and Kinship in Indigenous Feminisms*.

References

Aikau, H., Arvin, M., Goeman, M., and Morgensen, S. (2015). 'Indigenous feminisms roundtable', *Frontiers: A Journal of Women Studies*, vol 36, no 3: 84–106.

Altamirano-Jimenez, I. (2017). 'The state is not our saviour: Indigenous law, gender and the neoliberal state in Oaxaca', in J. Green (ed.) *Making Space for Indigenous Feminism*, 2nd ed. Fernwood Publishing: Black Point, NS, 215–233.

Anderson, K. (1991). *Chain Her by One Foot: The Subjugation of Women in Seventeenth-Century New France*. Routledge: London.

Anderson, K. (2010). 'Affirmations of an Indigenous feminist', in C. Suzack, S. Huhndorf, J. Perrault, and J. Barman (eds.) *Indigenous Women and Feminism: Politics, Activism, Culture*. UBC Press: Vancouver, BC, 81–91.

Anderson, K. (2016). *A Recognition of Being: Reconstructing Native Womanhood*, 2nd ed. Canadian Scholar's Press Inc: Toronto, ON.

Anderson, K., Flores Ruiz, E., Stewart, G., and Tlostanova, M. (2019). 'What can Indigenous feminist knowledges and practices bring to "Indigenizing the academy?"', *Journal of World Philosophies*, vol 4, no 1: 121–155.

Arvin, M., Tuck, E., and Morrill, A. (2013). 'Decolonizing feminism: Challenging connections between settler colonialism and heteropatriarchy', *Feminist Formations*, vol 25, no 1: 8–34.

Barker, J. (2006). 'Gender, sovereignty, and the discourse of rights in native women's activism', *Meridians: Feminisms, Race, Transnationalism*, vol 7, no 1: 127–161.

Barker, J. (2015). 'Indigenous feminisms', in J. Lucero, D. Turner, and D. VanCott (eds.) *Oxford Handbook of Indigenous Peoples' Politics*. https://doi.org/10.1093/oxfordhb/9780195386653.001.0001

Barker, J. (ed.) (2017). *Critically Sovereign: Indigenous Gender, Sexuality and Feminist Studies*. Duke University Press: Durham, NC.

Behrendt, L. (1993). 'Aboriginal women and the white lies of the feminist movement: Implications for aboriginal women in rights discourse', *The Australian Feminist Law Journal*, vol 1, no 1: 27–44.

Belcourt, B. (2016). 'Can the other of native studies speak?', *Decolonization: Indigeneity, Education, Society*. Available: https://decolonization.wordpress.com/2016/02/01/can-the-other-of-native-studies-speak/, accessed 13 May 2020.

Blaney, F. and Grey, S. (2017). 'Empowerment, revolution and real change: An interview with Fay Blaney', in J. Green (ed.) *Making Space for Indigenous Feminism*, 2nd ed. Fernwood Publishing: Black Point, NS, 234–252.

Bourgeois, R. (2017). 'Perpetual state of violence: An Indigenous feminist anti-oppression inquiry into missing and murdered Indigenous women and girls', in J. Green (ed.) *Making Space for Indigenous Feminism*, 2nd ed. Fernwood Publishing: Black Point, NS, 253–273.

Brant, B. (ed.) (1988). *A Gathering of Spirit: A Collection by North American Indian Women*. Firebrand Books: Ann Arbor, MI.

Campbell, M. (2017). Personal communications.

Cappelli, M. (2018). 'Toward enacting a zapatista feminist agenda somewhere in la Selva Lacondona: We are all Marias?', *Cogent Arts & Humanities*, vol 5, no 1. Available: https://doi.org/10.1080/23311983.2018.1491270.

Chrystos (1988). *Not Vanishing*. Press Gang Publishers: Vancouver, BC.

Denetdale, J. (2006). 'Chairmen, presidents, and princesses: The Navajo nation, gender, and the politics of tradition', *Wicazo Sa Review*, vol 21, no 1: 9–28.

Driskell, Q., Finley, C., Gilley, B., and Morgensen, S. (eds.) (2011). *Queer Indigenous Studies: Critical Interventions in Theory, Politics, and Literature*. University of Arizona Press: Tucson, AZ.

Dulfano, I. (2017). 'Knowing the other/other ways of knowing: Indigenous feminism, testimonial, and anti-globalization street discourse', *Arts and Humanities in Higher Education*, vol 16, no 1: 82–96.

Evans, R. (1994). 'The negation of powerlessness: Māori feminism, a perspective', in L. Pihama, L.T. Smith, N. Simmonds, J. Seed-Pihama, and K. Gabel (eds.) *Mana Wahine Reader: A Collection of Writings 1999-2019, Volume I*. Te Kotahi Research Institute: Hamilton, 26–136. Reprint, 2019.

Fehr, A. and Nickel, S. (2020). *In Good Relation: History, Gender and Kinship in Indigenous Feminisms*. University of Manitoba Press: Winnipeg, MB.

Flowers, R. (2015). 'Refusal to forgive: Indigenous women's love and rage', *Decolonization: Indigeneity, Education and Society*, vol 4, no 2: 32–49.

Fredericks, B. (2010). 'Reempowering ourselves: Australian aboriginal women', *Signs*, vol 35, no 3: 546–550.

Goeman, M. (2017). 'Indigenous interventions and feminist methods', in C. Andersen and J. O'Brien (eds.) *Sources and Methods in Indigenous Studies*, 1st ed. Routledge: New York, 185–194.

Goeman, M. and Denetdale, J. (2009). 'Native feminisms: Legacies, interventions, and Indigenous sovereignties [guest editor's introduction]', *Wicazo Sa Review*, vol 24, no 2: 9–13.

Gould, J. (ed.) (2019). *A Generous Spirit: Selected Works by Beth Brant*. Inanna Press: Toronto, ON.

Grande, S. (2015). *Red Pedagogy: Native American Social and Political Thought*, 10th Anniversary ed. Rowman & Littlefield Publishers: Lanham, MD.

Green, J. (ed.) (2017). *Making Space for Indigenous Feminism*, 2nd ed. Fernwood Publishing, Black Point, NS.

Gunn Allen, P. (1984). 'Who is your mother?: Red roots of white feminism', *Sinister Wisdom*, vol 25: 34–46.

Gunn Allen, P. (1986). *The Sacred Hoop: Recovering the Feminine in American Indian Traditions*. Beacon Press: Boston, MA.

Hernandez Castillo, R.A. (2010). 'Comparative perspectives symposium: Indigenous feminisms: The emergence of Indigenous feminism in Latin America', *Signs: Journal of Women in Culture and Society*, vol 35, no 3: 539–545.

Huhndorf, S. and Suzack, C., (2010). 'Indigenous feminism: Theorizing the issues'. In Suzack, C., Huhndorf, S., Perreault, J., and Barman, J. (eds.) (2010). *Indigenous Women and Feminism: Politics, Activism, Culture*. UBC Press: Vancouver, BC, 1–20.

Innes, R. and Anderson, K. (eds.) (2015). *Indigenous Men and Masculinities: Legacies, Identities, Regeneration*. University of Manitoba Press: Winnipeg, MB.

Irwin, K. (1992). 'Towards theories of Māori feminisms', in L. Pihama, L.T. Smith, N. Simmonds, J. Seed-Pihama, and K. Gabel (eds.) *Mana Wahine Reader: A Collection of Writings 1999-2019, Volume I*. Te Kotahi Research Institute: Hamilton, 66–82. Reprint, 2019.

Jahnke, H.T. (1997). 'Towards a theory of Mana Wahine', in L. Pihama, L.T. Smith, N. Simmonds, J. Seed-Pihama, and K. Gabel (eds.) *Mana Wahine Reader: A Collection of Writings 1999-2019, Volume I*. Te Kotahi Research Institute: Hamilton, 183–197. Reprint, 2019.

Jaimes, M. and Halsey, T. (1992). 'American Indian women: At the center of Indigenous resistance in contemporary North America', in M. Jaimes (ed.) *The State of Native America: Genocide, Colonization and Resistance*. South End Press: Boston, MA, 311–344.

John, S. (2015). 'Idle no more – Indigenous activism and feminism', *Theory in Action*, vol 8, no 4: 38–54.

Knobblock, I. and Kuokkanen, R. (2015). 'Decolonizing feminism in the north: A conversation with Rauna Kuokkanen', *NORA: Nordic Journal of Feminist and Gender Research*, vol 23, no 4: 275–281.

Knott, H. (2018). 'Dishinit Sakeh', in M. Greenwood, S. De Leeuw, N. M Lindsay, and C. Reading (eds.) *Determinants of Indigenous Peoples' Health*, 2nd ed. Canadian Scholars' Press: Toronto, ON, 241–253.

Knott, H. (2019). *In My Own Moccasins: A Memoir of Resilience*. University of Regina Press: Regina.

Laroque, E. (1996). 'The colonization of a native woman scholar', in C. Miller and P. Chuchryk (eds.) *Women of the First Nations: Power, Wisdom and Strength*. University of Manitoba Press: Winnipeg, MB, 11–18.

Laroque, E. (2017). 'Métis and feminist: Contemplations on feminism, human rights, culture and decolonization', in J. Green (ed.) *Making Space for Indigenous Feminism*, 2nd ed. Fernwood Publishing: Black Point, NS, 122–45.

Liddle, C. (2014). 'Intersectionality and Indigenous feminism: An aboriginal woman's perspective', *The Postcolonialist*. Available: http://postcolonialist.com/civil-discourse/intersectionality-indigenous-feminism-aboriginal-womans-perspective/, accessed 13 May 2020.

Maracle, L. (1988). *I Am Woman: A Native Perspective on Sociology and Feminism*. Press Gang Publishers: Vancouver, BC.

Mays, K. (2018). *Hip Hop Beats, Indigenous Rhymes: Modernity and Hip Hop in Indigenous North America*. State University of New York Press: Albany, NY.

McCormick, K. (2017). 'Intersections of feminist romani resistance: Building the next transnational, diasporic, Indigenous feminist agenda: A roma/native American/Dalilt coalition', *Development*, vol 60, no 1: 104–107.

Medicine, B. (1978). *The Native American Woman: A Perspective*. National Educational Laboratory Publishers: Austin, TX.

Medicine, B. (1983). 'Warrior women – Sex role alternatives for Plains Indian women', in P. Albers and B. Medicine (eds.) *The Hidden Half: Studies of Plains Indian Women*. University Press of America: New York, 267–279.

Mihesuah, D. (2003). *Indigenous American Women: Decolonization, Empowerment, Activism*. University of Nebraska Press: Lincoln, NE.

Mikaere, A. (1994). 'Māori women caught in the contradictions of a colonised reality', in L. Pihama, L.T. Smith, N. Simmonds, J. Seed-Pihama, and K. Gabel (eds.) *Mana Wahine Reader: A Collection of Writings 1999–2019, Volume I*. Te Kotahi Research Institute: Hamilton, 137–154. Reprint, 2019.

Monkman, L. (2017). 'Indigenous feminism: What is it and what does the future hold?', *CBC Indigenous*. Available: https://www.cbc.ca/news/indigenous/indigenous-feminism-facebook-live-panel-1.4428484, accessed 13 May 2020.

Moreton-Robinson, A. (2000). *Talkin' Up to the White Woman: Indigenous Women and Feminism*. University of Queensland Press: St. Lucia, QLD.

Moreton-Robinson, A. (2013). 'Toward an Australian Indigenous women's standpoint theory: A methodological tool', *Australian Feminist Studies*, vol 28, no 78: 331–342.

Morris, A. (2017). 'Weaving intersectional rhetoric: Counternarratives of Indigenous feminist bloggers', *Enthymema*, vol 19: 235–251.

National Inquiry into Missing and Murdered Indigenous Women and Girls. (2019). *Reclaiming Power and Place: The Final Report of the National Inquiry Into Missing and Murdered Indigenous Women and Girls*. Available: www.mmigwg-ffada.ca/final-report, accessed 13 May 2020.

Nickel, S. (2017). 'I'm not a women's libber although sometimes I sound like one: Indigenous feminism and politicized motherhood', *The American Indian Quarterly*, vol 41, no 4: 299–335.

Ouelette, G. (2002). *The Fourth World: An Indigenous Perspective on Feminism and Aboriginal Women's Activism*. Fernwood Publishing: Black Point, NS.

Pihama, L. (2001). *Tihei Mauri Ora–Honouring Our Voices: Mana Wahine as a Kaupapa Māori Theoretical Framework*. PhD thesis, University of Auckland: New Zealand.

Pihama, L. (2005). 'Mana wahine theory: Creating space for Māori women's theories', in L. Pihama, L.T. Smith, N. Simmonds, J. Seed-Pihama, and K. Gabel (eds.) *Mana Wahine Reader: A Collection of Writings 1999-2019, Volume I*. Te Kotahi Research Institute: Hamilton, 60–74. Reprint, 2019.

Ramirez, R. (2007). 'Race, tribal nation, and gender: A native feminist approach to belonging', *Meridians: Feminism, Race, Transnationalism*, vol 7, no 2: 22–40.

Rifkin, M. (2011). *When did Indians Become Straight?: Kinship, the History of Sexuality and Native Sovereignty*. Oxford University Press: New York.

Risling Baldy, C. (2018). *We Are Dancing for You: Native Feminisms and the Revitalization of Women's Coming of Age Ceremonies*. University of Washington Press: Seattle, WA.

Ross, L. (2009). 'From the "F" word to Indigenous/feminisms', *Wicazo Sa Review*, vol 24, no 2: 39–52.

Shanley, K. (1984). 'Thoughts on Indigenous feminism', in B. Brant (ed.) *A Gathering of Spirit: Writing and Art by North American Indian Women*. Firebrand Press: Ithaca, NY, 213–215.

Simpson, L.B. (2017). *As We Have Always Done: Indigenous Freedom Through Radical Resistance*. University of Minnesota Press: Minneapolis, MN.

Smiley, C. (2016). 'A long road behind us: A long road ahead: Towards an Indigenous feminist national inquiry', *Canadian Journal of Women and the Law*, vol 28, no 2: 308–313.

Smith, A. and Kehaulani Kauanui, J. (2008). 'Forum: Native feminisms without apology', *American Quarterly*, vol 60, no 2: 241–315.

Smith, L. (1992). 'Māori women: discourses, projects and Mana Wahine', in L. Pihama, L.T. Smith, N. Simmonds, J. Seed-Pihama, and K. Gabel (eds.) *Mana Wahine Reader: A Collection of Writings 1999-2019, Volume I*. Te Kotahi Research Institute: Hamilton, 39–52. Reprint, 2019.

Sneider, L. (2015). 'Complementary relationships: A review of Indigenous gender studies', in R. Innes and K. Anderson (eds.) *Indigenous Men and Masculinities: Legacies, Identities, Regeneration*. University of Manitoba Press: Winnipeg, MB, 62–79.

Snyder, E. (2014). 'Indigenous feminist legal theory', *Canadian Journal of Women and the Law*, vol 26, no 2: 365–401.

Starblanket, G. (2017). 'Being Indigenous feminists: Resurgences against contemporary patriarchy', in Green, J. (ed.) *Making Space for Indigenous Feminism*, 2nd ed. Fernwood Publishing: Black Point, NS, 21–41.

Starblanket, G. and Kiiwentinepinesiik Stark, H. (2018). 'Toward a relational paradigm – Four points for consideration: knowledge, gender, land, and modernity', in M. Asch, J. Borrows, and J. Tully (eds.) *Resurgence and Reconciliation: Indigenous-Settler Relations and Earth Teachings*. University of Toronto Press: Toronto, ON, 175–208.

St. Denis, V. (2017). 'Feminism is for everybody: Aboriginal women, feminism and diversity', in J. Green (ed.) *Making Space for Indigenous Feminism*, 2nd ed. Fernwood Publishing: Black Point, NS, 42–62.

Sunseri, L. (2000). 'Moving beyond the feminism versus nationalism dichotomy: An anti-colonial feminist perspective on aboriginal liberation struggles', *Canadian Woman Studies*, vol 20, no 2: 143–148.

Suzack, C. (2015). 'Indigenous feminisms in Canada', *NORA: Nordic Journal of Feminist and Gender Research*, vol 23, no 4: 261–274.

Suzack, C., Huhndorf, S., Perreault, J., and Barman, J. (eds.) (2010). *Indigenous Women and Feminism: Politics, Activism, Culture*. UBC Press: Vancouver, BC.

Sy, C. (2018). 'Considering wenonah, considering us', in K. Anderson, M. Campbell, and C. Belcourt (eds.) *Keetsahnak: Our Missing and Murdered Indigenous Sisters*. University of Alberta Press: Edmonton, 193–214.

Tallbear, K. (2014). 'Standing with and speaking as faith: A feminist-Indigenous approach to inquiry', in C. Andersen and J. O'Brien (eds.) *Sources and Methods in Indigenous Studies*. Routledge: London, 78–85.

Te Awekotuku, N. (1992). 'Kia mau, kia manawanui: We will never go away: Experiences of a Māori lesbian feminist', in L. Pihama, L.T. Smith, N. Simmonds, J. Seed-Pihama, and K. Gabel (eds.) *Mana Wahine Reader: A Collection of Writings 1999-2019, Volume I*. Te Kotahi Research Institute: Hamilton, 29–38. Reprint, 2019.

Tohe, L. (2000). 'There is no word for feminism in my language', *Wicazo Sa Review*, vol 15, no 2: 103–110.

Tsosie, R. (2010). 'Native women and leadership: An ethics of culture and relationship', in C. Suzack, S. Huhndorf, J. Perrault and J. Barman (eds.) *Indigenous Women and Feminism: Politics, Activism, Culture*. UBC Press: Vancouver, BC, 29–42.

Yazzie, M.K. and Baldy, C.R. (2018). 'Introduction: Indigenous peoples and the politics of water', *Decolonization: Indigeneity, Education & Society*, vol 7, no 1: 1–18.

4

Against crisis epistemology

Kyle Whyte

Crisis and colonialism

Colonisation is typically pitched as being about crisis. People who perpetrate colonialism often imagine that their wrongful actions are defensible because they are responding to some crisis. They assume that to respond to a crisis, it is possible to suspend certain concerns about justice and morality. Nineteenth-century European and American imperial colonialism in South America involved forcing Chinese persons, among other affected groups, into tortuous work conditions to extract and export guano, resulting in the devastation of ecosystems on guano islands. The goal of such violence to people and the environment was to resolve a crisis in soil chemistry caused by the intensive agricultural methods being used in some parts of Europe and North America (Foster and Clark 2020). The United States even passed the Guano Islands Act in 1856, which stated that Americans can seize control of any, "island, rock, or key, not within the lawful jurisdiction of any other Government" that has "a deposit of guano" (US Department of State 1856: online). In US settler colonialism, Americans in the first half of the 20th century constructed many dams that flooded Indigenous peoples such as Seneca and Lakota peoples. They did so because they believed the United States needed energy and irrigation to lessen the perceived threat of the Soviet Union in the Cold War (Barber 2005; Lawson 1994; Bilharz 2002; Rosier 2006; Rosier 1995). Or in the 19th and 20th centuries, US missionaries and teachers with particular religious values believed that it was morally acceptable to break up Indigenous families for the sake of saving Native persons' souls and averting spiritual catastrophe (Stremlau 2005; Archuleta et al. 2000). In these US cases, direct and indirect harms of settlers' crisis-response actions have devastating impacts on Indigenous peoples across ancestral, living, and emerging generations (Duran et al. 1998; Brave Heart 2000).

Colonial oppression that is allegedly defensible by real or perceived crises happens right now too. Today, people perpetrate colonialism in the name of responding to environmental crises – *climate change* being one prominent case. Responses to scientifically understand and mitigate climate change can harm or threaten Indigenous peoples. From scientific reports that provincialise Indigenous knowledge systems to wind power projects that desecrate Indigenous lands, there is no reason to believe that colonialism today is something other than an evolved practice of a familiar form of power. What are the practices of knowing the world that make it possible to understand why someone would use crisis to mask colonial power? In this essay, I will focus on contemporary environmental *crises*, mainly climate change. But I understand that my speculations are possibly relevant to other *crises* as well as to other literatures on states of exception and necropolitics (Agamben 2008; Mbembé 2003). By climate change, I mean the destabilisation of ecological systems caused, to a significant degree, by the industrial emissions of greenhouse gases. Destabilisation is exacerbated by industrially aggressive (ab)uses of land and water, including certain extractive and manufacturing enterprises, methods of energy production, intensive agriculture practices, and resource-hungry travel, consumption, and recreational habits. One approach that I will take up involves how current crisis rhetoric on climate change is mediated by certain presumptions about the unfolding of time. By *unfolding of time*, I mean how the narrative of the significance of climate change is arranged according to a past, present, and future. As Candis Callison has shown, such presumptions of temporal unfolding affect how people come to know climate change, whether as crisis or as something else (Callison 2014).

Epistemologies of crisis involve knowing the world such that a certain present is experienced as new. Indigenous Studies scholars have done significant work on the temporal assumptions behind settler colonial power, such as 'firsting' (O'Brien 2010), 'settler time' (Rifkin 2017), and the 'settler colonial present' (Simpson 2017). They have critically exposed the liberal assumptions about the primacy of the settler state in national origin narratives (Turner 2006; Bruyneel 2007; Nichols 2013). I seek to add to these ongoing conversations by focusing in particular on *crisis*. I seek to unravel some dimensions of the structure of newness that permits the validation of oppression. In particular, I will discuss the presumptions of *unprecedentedness* and *urgency*. In contradistinction to an epistemology of crisis, I will suggest that one interpretation of certain Indigenous knowledge traditions emphasises what I will just call here an epistemology of coordination. Different from crisis, coordination refers to ways of knowing the world that emphasise the importance of moral bonds – or kinship relationships – for generating the (responsible) capacity to respond to constant change in the world. Epistemologies of coordination are conducive to responding to mundane and expected change without validating harm or violence. Epistemologies of coordination are not offered here as some sort of ultimate solution to the current challenges people across the globe are facing. Although I've no problem claiming that epistemologies of coordination are much needed approaches to knowledge in education, culture, and society. Their practice would go a long way to transform unjust and immoral responses to real or perceived crises.

Epistemologies of crisis

In public Anishinaabe intellectual traditions, there's a story of history and futurity that I've heard widely and read about too in several places. The story discusses seven or eight fires, depending on the telling. Each fire relates to a particular era of time. One of the foci of the story as it unfolds across the fires is the persistence and flourishing of Anishinaabe peoples in the face of diverse challenges, including social and environmental challenges. One such challenge is the emergence and increasing power of the settler population in North America. During several instances of the story, Anishinaabe people are expected to make critical decisions about how to interpret the newcomers' intentions. There is concern about whether the settlers will show the face of death or the face of kinship and allyship. One of the warnings of the story is that the face of kinship can be superficially presented to mask what's really the face of death. There is also a time of false promises that are tempting to accept, but the ramification of acceptance is suffering (Benton-Benai 1988; Gaikesheyongai and Keeshig-Tobias 1994).

The exact time in which this story may be referring to is not important to me here. Rather, the story generates insights we can all discuss about different periods of time in which colonialism occurred in North America. Sometimes in these periods, settlers and other exploiters showed the face of kinship as a way to induce Indigenous persons to help them avert real or perceived crises. The Meriam Report in the United States (1928) declared an emergency regarding the impact of poverty on Indigenous peoples, blaming, Indigenous 'lack of adjustment' but also US agricultural and land tenure policies and the funding for the Indian Service. One response, however, was for the Bureau of Indian Affairs under then director John Collier to rescue Tribes by corporatising Tribal governance. One of the vehicles of such corporatisation in the 1930s was the Indian Reorganization Act. The corporations were intended to facilitate the Tribally controlled lease of Indigenous lands, broker deals with extractive industries, and replace diverse Indigenous forms of governance with a one-size-fits-all American form of corporate governance. These measures were phrased as reform, economic development, and wealth generation, and partly inspired by forms of colonialism practiced in other parts of the world (Hauptman 1986). Of course, the outcomes of the Indian Reorganization Act, depending on the Tribe, often involved the undermining of valuable traditional forms of governance, increasing dependence on extractive industries and commercial agriculture, and instigating divisions within Tribal societies between the interests and privileges of elected officials and Tribal citizens. The policies of this era are in some cases looked at as affirming dimensions of self-determination that have been denied under previous US regimes. And Collier is a complicated historical actor to interpret, given their advocacy of Indigenous cultures and Tribal sovereignty (Rusco 1991). Yet today it is true that some Tribal governments struggle to diversify their economies, protect health, and implement culturally relevant programs and forms of governance due to some of the barriers to self-determination that can reasonably be attributed to the Indian Reorganization Act period (and evolving since then through other policies) (Rusco 2000; Clow 1987; Ranco and Fleder 2005). In terms of the Indian Reorganization Act, the crisis of the impacts of poverty served as a basis for some settlers to show themselves (problematically) as kin or allies. Under the guise of addressing poverty, it can be argued that US settler society expanded its control over Indigenous peoples.

A crisis epistemology, in the context of settler colonialism, might look something like this. A crisis is believed to be happening, whether real, genuine, or perceived. The crisis may be articulated as related to many problems, including health, economic well-being, environmental sustainability, cultural integrity, and religious salvation. But what makes some state of affairs of the world *crisis*-oriented is the automatic assumption of imminence. By imminence, I mean the sense that something horribly harmful or inequitable is impending or pressing on the present conditions people understand themselves to be living in. There is a complexity or originality to the imminent events that suggests the need to immediately become solutions-oriented in a way believed to differ from how solutions were designed and enacted previously.

One possible structure of a crisis epistemology that I've sometimes seen is a presentist narrative. By structure, I just mean how something (here, a way of knowing the world) is organised, which includes what it's made up of and how it's put together. As a structure of crisis, a narrative is made up of time. A narrative is a way someone arranges the unfolding of time and articulates that arrangement to others. That a narrative is present*ist* means that time is put together (arranged) to favor a certain conception of the present as a means of achieving power or protecting privilege. Presentism of different kinds has been examined in Indigenous Studies as an exercise of colonial power and an effacement of the realities and conditions of that power. Audra Simpson, for example, writes that the 'settler colonial present' is one of 'purported newness'. It is "… revealed as the fiction of the presumed neutrality of time itself, demonstrating the dominance of the present by some over others, and the unequal power to define what matters, who matters, what pasts are alive and when they die" (Simpson 2017: 21). In this way, someone becomes so concerned with the *present* crisis as *new* that they question neither their own perspective nor where their perspective may derive its social origins.

In terms of epistemologies of crisis, I want to discuss two presumptions about the presentist unfolding of time. There are of course more presumptions. I focus on the following. The crises are *unprecedented*. That is, they are ones in which there are few usable lessons from the past about how to cope with the problems of today generated by crises. Sometimes today's crises are considered to have the novelty of being complex beyond anything previously encountered. The next presumption is that the crises are *urgent*, which means that they must be responded to quickly. When responsive actions are taken urgently, certain harmful consequences of the actions to humans or any other beings, entities, or systems are considered to be unfortunate, but acceptable. Each of these two presumptions of presentism, and there are of course more, can easily be abused for the sake of advancing colonial power, even in cases where the perpetrators would swear they have only the best intentions.

The presumption of unprecedentedness makes it possible to willfully forget certain previous instances or lessons related to a crisis. Regarding climate change, for example, media, scientific, and political discourses proclaim that this the first time in which the United States has engaged in the resettlement of Indigenous communities due to coastal erosion in the Arctic, Pacific Northwest, and the Gulf of Mexico. These discourses reference conflicts about power (i.e. who gets to decide whether to resettle and how). They reference concerns expressed by Indigenous persons that *climate change resettlement* is just the latest term for further territorial dispossession. They cite complex legal, bureaucratic, economic, cultural, and political hurdles Indigenous peoples are facing in resettlement processes sponsored by the United States, state, and local governments. Of course, the unprecedentedness is not true. Going back *at least* to the 19th century, the United States has used complex laws, policies, tax codes, property rights, and financial instruments (i.e. mortgages, leases) to remove and resettle Indigenous peoples in ways that imposed conflicts of power, hurdles, and territorial dispossession. Cases include long (many hundreds of miles) removals, such as the forced resettlement of Tribes to Indian Territory (Oklahoma), but also policies to relocate Indigenous families to live permanently in large urban centers. They include the shrinking of vast Indigenous territories to exponentially smaller reservations and the complete liquidation of entire Tribal homelands into private property or public lands (e.g. national parks), which led to major demographic shifts. These resettlements ultimately served to further entrench the territorial power of the United States in Indigenous homelands. The reality that the United States has been in the *resettlement business* for generations is lost in discourses about climate change. Lost too are the lessons Indigenous peoples learned across their histories of resistance and problem-solving having experienced different forms of resettlement before those associated with climate change today (Marino 2012; Crepelle 2018; Krakoff 2011; Watkinson 2015). So the crisis of climate change resettlement perceived through a presentist narrative obscures how the United States has yet to come to terms with numerous historic instances of forced resettlement. When people get caught up in the imminence of presentism – which absents the violence and tribulations of diverse ancestors – their actions run severe risks of retrenching colonial power through evolved but familiar practices that will be harmful to living and future generations.

The presumption of urgency suggests that swiftness of action is needed to cope with imminence. There either may be moral sacrifices that have to be made or ethics and justice are not elevated to a level of serious attention. The urgency of the cold war and national security, for example, made it somehow acceptable for US politicians to be open about the sacrifices that they believed were justified. In one case, during the inundation caused by the opening of Dalles dam in Oregon in the 1950s, a major fishery, Celilo Falls, was inundated. A US Senator stated, "our Indian friends deserve from us a profound and heartfelt salute of appreciation. … They contributed to [the dam's] erection a great donation – surrender of the only way of life which some of them knew" (Barber 2005: 4). Regarding climate change, there is a similar suspension of the consideration of ethics and justice. Rapidly growing literatures and technical reports are showing that, in the United States and globally, clean energy solutions for mitigating the rise in global average temperature are unjust or harmful to Indigenous peoples across the planet. The injustices and harms include economic deprivation and land dispossession and desecration. They also include the silencing of Indigenous leadership, knowledge, and voices in law, policy, and administration pertaining to mitigation measures (Suagee 2012; Bronin 2012; Beymer-Farris and Bassett 2012; Dussais 2014; Avila 2017; Nguh and Sanyanga 2013; Tauli-Corpuz and Lynge 2008; Howe 2019; Hoang et al. 2019). Victoria Tauli-Corpuz and Aqqaluk Lynge document some of the early precedents of this injustice in climate mitigation programs. In the 1990s, the Forest Absorbing Carbon Dioxide Emission Foundation (FACE) of the Netherlands and the Uganda Wildlife Authority (UWA) created a carbon offset plantation of eucalyptus trees at Mount Elgon National Park of Uganda that would offset energy utilities in the Netherlands. They write that:

> While project coordinators claim that the plantation has improved the lives of the people around the park, the indigenous people themselves (the Benet) say the exact opposite. After the declaration of Mount Elgon as a national park in 1993, the UWA violently forced the residents of Mount Elgon to leave the area and move to caves and mosques in neighboring villages. Park rangers killed more than 50 people in 2004. In addition, the project took away what little income the people had from their lands and crops. The villagers are not allowed to graze their cows and goats in the area or to obtain food or important traditional materials from the forest.
>
> *(Tauli-Corpuz and Lynge 2008: 16)*

While the conditions that make such violence possible persist today, many climate change advocates are adamant that such morally uncontrolled and unwise measures must happen now to avert crisis before oppression can addressed. Expression of this adamancy is a daily occurrence in some places. I recently read an article in *Vice* in which the journalist interviewed Jonathan Morgan of the advocacy group Extinction Rebellion, who said in 2020: "I can't say it hard enough. We don't have time to argue about social justice" (Dembicki 2020: online). Yet, if a forest conservation project displaces Indigenous peoples from their lands, for example, where is the better environmental future for that Indigenous peoples? A similar question can be posed to energy coming from wind, solar, biofuel, and nuclear sources. Catherine Sandoval shows in their research how the United States never fairly included Indigenous peoples in the energy grid system (Sandoval 2018). Given this reality, 'social justice' would be necessary for Indigenous peoples to benefit from and be leaders in renewable energy. In British Columbia, the Site C mega dam was conceived in ways that violated Indigenous peoples' rights and treaties and had numerous negative environmental impacts (Hendriks, Raphals, Bakker and Christie 2017). The dam will provide energy to the province that will crowd out from energy markets some First Nations who were building renewable energy projects on their own (Gilpin 2019; Cox 2018). So, again, projects for clean or renewable energy or carbon footprint reduction will repeat the moral wrongs and injustices of the past. Hence the presentist narrative gets caught up in imminence through presumptions of urgency, generating harm and risks that burden Indigenous peoples, and retrench colonial power. Again, we must make careful judgements about the face of kinship (stopping climate change) when we seek to take action to mitigate and prepare for climate change.

In thinking through the implications of unprecedentedness and urgency, climate change, as a concept, is a rhetorical device that people invoke so they can believe they are addressing a crisis without having to talk about colonial power. Epistemologies of crisis are presentist in their narrative orientation. Presentist orientations can favor dimensions of experiencing time in ways that presume unprecedentedness and urgency. Epistemologies of crisis then mask numerous forms of power, including colonialism, imperialism, capitalism, patriarchy, and industrialisation. The literature on colonialism and environmental crises is conveying just this point (Stein et al. 2017; Gergan et al. 2018; Anson 2017; Hurley 2020). Mabel Gergan, Sara Smith and Pavithra Vasudevan refer to certain apocalyptic and catastrophic deployments of the anthropocene and climate crisis as "temporal sleight of hand" (2018: 2). In their study examining "scientific debates and cultural representations", they claim that many "imaginings of apocalypse" work to "escape specific culpability (for instance, in processes of settler colonialism, capitalism, or imperialism) and instead center a universal human frailty that ends with triumph, a clear moral, and a clean slate" (Gergan et al. 2018: 2). The feeling of imminence that accompanies presentism leads people to obscure and overshadow how their actions relate to the persistence of different forms of power.

Epistemologies of coordination

Basil Johnston, from their work with Anishinaabe elders and archives, describes an Anishinaabe story that discusses one of the origins of humans. Humans and animals live interdependently: "[w]ithout the animals the world would not have been; without the animals the world would not be intelligible" (Johnston 1990: 49). Animals provided nourishment, 'shelter', 'joy' and voluntary 'labor' on behalf of humans. Humans and animals could communicate directly with one another. Yet humans subjected animals to abuse, taking for granted the services that animals had previously performed 'without complaint'. Johnston writes that:

> At last, weary of service, the animals convened a great meeting to gain their freedom. All came at the invitation of the courier. The bear was chosen to be the first speaker and to act as chairman of the session. He explained the purpose of the meeting. 'We are met to decide our destiny. We have been oppressed far too long by man. He has taken our generosity and repaid us with ingratitude; he has taken our labors and repaid us with servitude; he has taken our friendship and fostered enmity among us'.
>
> *(1990: 50)*

In this excerpt, humans couldn't possibly survive and flourish without animals. Yet animals were being abused. There is an ecological crisis. Yet what generates the crisis in the story is when one group – humans – abused the relationships of interdependence. Humans took domineering actions against animals that failed to demonstrate care, reciprocity, or respect for consent. If the interdependence of species can be related to environmental protection, then repairing relationships of justice and equality are inseparable from actions needed to achieve biodiversity conservation and climate change mitigation. This story is not a presentist narrative. For crisis is interpreted through a deeper history, and traced to the moral bonds of relationships among the diverse beings and entities dwelling together in shared environments. Something like a crisis cannot be understood without appealing to the history of moral bonds between the beings and entities affected by a real or perceived crisis.

Stories like this one published by Basil Johnston suggest to me an epistemology of coordination, not an epistemology of crisis. Epistemologies of coordination emphasise coming to know the world through kin relationships. There are certainly a lot of ways to talk about and define the meaning of kin. Here I want to take a particular focus. Kinship relationships refer to moral bonds that are often expressed as mutual responsibilities. The moral bonds are similar to familial relationships in the sense of local and broader families that can engage *responsibly* in coordinated action together to achieve particular goals that they have. Examples of kinship relationships are care, consent, and reciprocity, among others.

Indigenous scholars have written about how Indigenous communities came to know and address US settler colonialism through harnessing kinship to generate coordinated responses. Mishuana Goeman has interpreted a wide range of contemporary and historic Indigenous women writers and artists. Goeman's work shows how Indigenous communities develop and renew kinship relationships to achieve coordination in challenging times, such as during the era where the United States relocated many Indigenous families to large urban areas (Goeman 2009; Lone-Knapp 2000). They write that:

> As Seneca scholar Faye Lone suggests, it is important to look at our social, political, and certainly cultural relationships in a 'frame-work that allows relatedness to a flexible spatial community, one that allows for strong, mobile, symbolic identity that underlies, and perhaps even belies, external influences'.
>
> *(Goeman 2009: 185)*

In the same article, Goeman also writes:

> Often, it was necessary for women to practice gendered relations outside the cultural forms learned from their mothers, aunties and grandmothers. These practices of relating to each other were not 'outdated' in the city, but instead the elements of these practices that persisted were and continue to be vital to Native navigations in urban centers. In many ways, the lack of the dominant culture's understanding of Native peoples' capacity to reach out to others beyond their specific Tribal Nation was a major flaw in the goals of Relocation policy. In fact, the propensity for sharing where one is from and learning to live with each other comes from thousands of years of experience living on this continent together – it is as instinctive as breathing.
>
> *(Goeman 2009: 175)*

Goeman's work focuses then on understanding how new networks are formed that rely on moral bonds that can be associated with different people and practices. For Goeman, what defines Indigenous peoples are not only particular cultural practices. Rather, it is a capacity to renew important kin relations in ways that support coordination in response to change (Goeman 2009).

Goeman cites Susan Lobo's work on urban clan mothers. Lobo writes that urban clan mothers are leaders and facilitators in networks of relationships:

> Key households that provide a degree of permanence in the swirl of constant shifts and changes in the highly fluid urban Indian communities. These households gathering spots often provide short term or extended housing and food for many people, health and healing practices and advice, a location for ceremony emotional and spiritual support,

entertainment, and transportation and communication resources. They are also often vital spots of linkage with more rural communities and tribal homelands.

(Lobo 2003: 505)

In my view, these households and places are based on kinship relationships that are valued because of their capacity to be responsive to change. This includes the crisis-like changes of urban relocation in the mid-20th century. Goeman's and Lobo's work, read in relation to Johnston's story, at least suggest for me what I interpret to be epistemologies of coordination. There is a presumption of constant change (not presentism). But the strategy for response involves fostering kinship relationships. And kinship relationships have high standards responsibility, with special attention to relationships of care, reciprocity, and consent, among others.

Diverse Indigenous Studies research has demonstrated epistemologies that I would interpret as centering how to organise a society to be coordinated in the face of realities of constant change. Vicente Diaz's research Micronesian seafaring knowledge discusses the relationship between the science of navigation and motion. Instead of humans being knowers who move around stationary islands, it is rather the islands that move. Kinship relationships are critical to the formation of coordination in a constantly moving world (Diaz 2011). Brenda Child's historical research on women and conservation traditions (e.g., wild rice) demonstrates how Ojibwe women exercised central responsibilities in networks of coordination that were critical to navigating crises caused by colonialism. Ben Colombi's work with Nez Perce people on their resilience and adaptive capacity emphasises the kinship relationships, including leadership traditions, that supported coordinated responses to harsh colonial conditions (Colombi 2012).

Epistemologies of coordination are focused just as much on responses to crises. Relocation, for example, was an actual crisis for those who experienced it. Colonialism has inflicted numerous crises on Indigenous peoples. At the same time, there is no presentist interpretation of crisis and no sense of imminence. Rather, epistemologies of coordination come to know the world through the state of kinship relationships. A world or situation that has members with active kinship relationships of care, consent, and reciprocity is one where the members have the capacity to respond in coordinated ways to change that are supportive of their mutual well-being, whether the members are humans, animals, and/or diverse others. A world or situation lacking in these bonds is one in which some members will respond to change in ways that lead to deeply unjust and immoral actions and outcomes. To see the world through kinship relationships that are central to coordination requires a non-presentist mode of knowledge and a capacity to not be caught up in imminence. For one has to have a sober and detailed conception of the history of kinship relationships and how they have changed or evolved over the years based on changes like, say, US colonialism. As a massive breach of kinship, especially in terms of violations of care, consent, and reciprocity, it becomes clear that today's situation or world must attend to the establishment or repair of those relationships: whether that is a process that Indigenous peoples do on their own, no matter what the rest of the world does, or whether that process is one that allies also participate in.

No solutions without kinship

Indigenous scholars and leaders acknowledge that the world today is far from being a place where what I am calling epistemologies of coordination are common. People do not come to know the world through the degrees of kinship relationships. Mary Arquette writes reflectively their views of how Haudenosaunee people have altered their relationships with some non-human relatives, violating ancient kinship relationships in certain cases, such as the over-harvesting of fur-bearing animals (e.g. beavers) during the transatlantic fur trade period several hundred years ago. They write in the context that Haudenosaunee were responding to complex colonial forces during the fur trade. Arquette traces out what the implications are for environmental sustainability today, without apologising for the ramifications of kinship that may have been violated historically:

> When a person decides to forget ethics requiring respect for the natural world, it is not difficult for that individual to also lose respect for themselves, their families, and other human beings. In this case, not only did the fur bearers suffer from this destruction, but Haudenosaunee elders, women and children also suffered as a result of the violence, alcoholism, jealousy, mistrust and family and community breakdown that resulted. It took a reminder from our Creator and a spiritual revival for our people to begin to move away from these destructive behaviors. Many believe that if we had not been reminded to return to our own spiritual beliefs, then the Haudenosaunee may not have survived as distinct people. The struggle goes on to this day. In fact, some may question whether our communities will ever recover from the wars that we waged on the fur bearers. We certainly will never forget what happened and to this day, continue to have a special obligation to the fur bearing animals to make amends for our past mistakes.
>
> *(Arquette 2000: 92–3)*

For Arquette, the relationship between humans and animals, among other beings of non-human world, has been changed over time to the point where many moral bonds are absent. For the war waged against the beavers – at least in my interpretation – was a violation of kinship in terms of care, consent, and reciprocity.

In Arquette's philosophy, it is critical to note that they have no reason to believe that the relationships with nonhumans will be repaired: "[i]n fact, some may question whether our communities will ever recover from the wars that we waged on the fur bearers" (Arquette 2000: 92–3). This statement resists an epistemology of crisis. If the focus of knowing the world is on kinship relationships, then it is quite possible to wonder whether in today's time that it is possible to restore kin. For kinship relationships cannot be established overnight. Many of the most important kinship relationships take time to develop. There is no guarantee that during the time it takes to develop those relationships, that certain issues within ecological systems will simply be repaired. The weight of kinship is very different from the sense of imminence in crisis epistemologies.

The skepticism inherent in a number of Indigenous authors is intertwined with their adamancy about seeking sustainability and justice in the face of climate change. Skepticism is not necessarily the right word. It is more of a realism, where realism contrasts with crisis-oriented feelings of imminence. As Dan Wildcat discusses:

> In North America many indigenous traditions tell us that reality is more than just facts and figures collected so that humankind might widely use resources. Rather, to know 'it' – reality – requires respect for the relationships and relatives that constitute the complex web of life. I call this indigenous realism, and it entails that we, members of humankind, accept our inalienable responsibilities as members of the planet's complex life system, as well as our inalienable rights.
>
> *(2009: xi)*

Relationships and relatives are precisely those kinship relationships. For Wildcat, what I read as an epistemology of coordination emphasises the significance of kinship (e.g. 'relatives', 'complex web of life') for the coordination needed to live in a complex world.

Jeanette Armstrong, who has written and organised widely on the importance of caretaking for the land (Armstrong 1998), expresses realism about whether humans will be able to be sustainable:

> That issue in our traditional teachings is: every year, continuously, the people who are caretakers, and people who are careful of the harvest, whoever they might be, are reminded at our ceremonies and at our feasts, that that is what our responsibility and our intelligence and our creativity as human beings are about. That's what the gift of being human is about. If we cannot measure up to that, and we cannot live up to that, we're not needed here, and we won't be here. It's really becoming evident that we're a huge percentage in that direction of not being here.
>
> *(Armstrong 2007: 4)*

Armstrong's statement resists an epistemology of crisis and has a sense of realism. Similar to previous authors, they speak of kinship and coordination, including care, reciprocity, responsibility, ceremony/feasts, and intelligence/creativity (autonomy).

In my reading of their work, de Oliveira Andreotti, Stein, Ahenakew and Hunt (2015) have outlined an approach to living in times of crises that emphasise what I am referring to as kinship. 'Crisis' and 'unpredictability' can, "… leave little time and few spaces for exploring the complexities, tensions and paradoxes of decolonizing work without an immediate need for resolution, coherence and prescriptive action" (de Oliveira Andreotti et al. 2015: 22). Their "social cartography approach" emphasises "hospicing", among other approaches, which:

> Would entail sitting with a system in decline, learning from its history, offering palliative care, seeing oneself in that which is dying, attending to the integrity of the process, dealing with tantrums, incontinence, anger and hopelessness, 'cleaning up', and clearing the space for something new. This is unlikely to be a glamorous process.
>
> *(de Oliveira Andreotti et al. 2015: 22)*

Their work suggests that what I am calling epistemologies of coordination are likely to be rather incompatible with epistemologies of crisis. For part of an epistemology of crisis involves their being solutions that can occur quickly, maintain the current state of affairs, lack any sense of realism, and further entrench power. Moreover, though I did not focus on this here in this essay, there is an underlying conception of heroism involved in epistemologies of crisis that is morally problematic (de Oliveira Andreotti et al. 2015; Whyte 2018).

Epistemologies of coordination are not presentist. They accept the realism that some kinship relationships take time to develop, which means that they are not necessarily going to always buy into imminence. The sense of imminence in epistemologies of crisis makes some people believe that it is possible to make a transformation in the world in ways that ensure societies can bounce back to some current state of affairs. Given that, for many Indigenous peoples, the current state of affairs is one that people are trying to move beyond given how it has been shaped negatively by oppression. This means that what appears as an acceptance of an inevitable end is more akin to a deep motivation to create a better world. For a better world must arise through actions that honor the significance of ethical and just relationships and that remain vigilant to the operation and repetition of oppression. Epistemologies of coordination have a sense of realism to them.

Epistemologies of crisis are likely to be incompatible with this way of knowing. People caught up in epistemologies of crisis place an emphasis on presentism. This emphasis makes it so that they are obsessed with saving some conception of the current state of affairs because they feel the imminence of crisis. The obsession obscures how everyone one else may experience today's world. And the sense of imminence overshadows the realism needed to remember how colonial and other forms of power engendered the current state of affairs and how these forms of power are poised to retrench.

Conclusions

Indigenous responses to *crises* are certainly adamant and compelling. But they are not reliant on certain epistemologies of crisis. Such an epistemology organises knowledge in ways that emphasise some narrative of the imminence of a threat to *the present*. Without any emphasis on kinship relationships and the time it takes to develop them, epistemologies of crisis can validate the violation of moral bonds. Epistemologies of coordination are very different – but not less responsive to serious changes that can be deemed crisis level. Epistemologies of coordination organise knowledge through the vector of kinship relationships. They do not tradeoff kinship relationships to satisfy desires for imminent action. As crises like climate change continue to motivate people to take swift, solution-oriented actions, epistemologies of coordination draw attention to the problems of how presentism and imminence can betray ethics and justice. They have a realism to them. Epistemologies of coordination assess the impacts of actions by their contributions to the quality of kinship relationships.

References

Agamben, G. (2008). *State of Exception*. University of Chicago Press: Chicago, IL.

Anson, A. (2017). 'American apocalypse: The whitewashing genre of settler colonialism', *Academia.edu*, 1–10. Available: https://www.academia.edu/34949190/American_Apocalypse_The_Whitewashing _Genre_of_Settler_Colonialism, accessed May 20, 2020.

Archuleta, M., Child, B.J., and Lomawaima, K.T. (2000). *Away from Home: American Indian Boarding School Experiences 1879–2000*. Heard Museum: Santa Fe, NM.

Armstrong, J. (1998). 'Land speaking', in S. Ortiz (ed.) *Speaking for the Generations: Native Writers on Writing. Sun Tracks: An American Indian Literary Series*. University of Arizona Press: Tucson, AZ, 174–194.

Armstrong, J. (2007). 'Native perspectives on sustainability: Jeannette Armstrong (Syilx) [Interview transcript]', *Native Perspectives on Sustainability*, 1–15. Available: www.nativeperspectives.net, accessed May 20, 2020.

Arquette, M. (2000). 'The animals', in Haudenosaunee Environmental Task Force (eds.) *Words that Come Before all Else*. Haudenosaunee Environmental Task Force: Akwesasne, 82–101.

Avila, S. (2017). 'Contesting energy transitions: Wind power and conflicts in the isthmus of tehuantepec', *Journal of Political Ecology*, vol 24: 992–1012.

Barber, K. (2005). *Death of Celilo Falls*. Center for the Study of the Pacific Northwest in association with University of Washington Press: Seattle, WA.

Benton-Benai, E. (1988). *The Mishomis Book: The Voice of the Ojibway*. Indian Country Communications: Hayward, WI.

Beymer-Farris, B.A. and Bassett, T.J. (2012). 'The REDD menace: Resurgent protectionism in Tanzania's mangrove forests', *Global Environmental Change*, vol. 22: 332–341.

Bilharz, J.A. (2002). *The Allegany Senecas and Kinzua Dam: Forced Relocation Through Two Generations*. University of Nebraska Press: Lincoln, NE.

Brave Heart, M.Y.H. (2000). 'Wakiksuyapi: Carrying the historical trauma of the Lakota', *Tulane Studies in Social Welfare*, vol 21: 245–266.

Bronin, S. (2012). 'The promise and perils of renewable energy on tribal lands', in S.A. Krakoff and E. Rosser (eds.) *Tribes, Land, and the Environment*. Ashgate: Burlington, VT, 103–117.

Bruyneel, K. (2007). *The Third Pace of Sovereignty: The Postcolonial Politics of U.S.–Indigenous Relations.* University of Minnesota Press: Minneapolis, MN.

Callison, C. (2014). *How Climate Change Comes to Matter: The Communal Life of Facts.* Duke University Press: Durham, NC.

Clow, R. (1987). 'The Indian reorganization act and the loss of tribal sovereignty: Constitutions on the rosebud and pine ridge reservations', *Great Plains Quarterly*, vol 7: 125–134.

Colombi, B.J. (2012). 'Salmon and the adaptive capacity of Nimiipuu (Nez Perce) culture to cope with change', *The American Indian Quarterly*, vol. 36: 75–97.

Cox, S. (2018). 'B.C. first nations forced to shelve clean energy projects as site C dam overloads grid', in *The Narhwal*, Victoria, BC. Available: https://thenarwhal.ca/b-c-first-nations-forced-shelve-clean-energy-projects-site-c-dam-overloads-grid/, accessed 19 May 2020.

Crepelle, A. (2018). 'The United States first climate relocation: recognition, relocation, and Indigenous rights at the Isle de Jean Charles', *Belmont Law Review*, vol 6: 1–40.

de Oliveira Andreotti, V., Stein, S., Ahenakew, C., and Hunt, D. (2015). 'Mapping interpretations of decolonization in the context of higher education', *Decolonization: Indigeneity, Education & Society*, vol. 4: 21–40.

Dembicki, G. (2020). 'A debate over racism has plit one of the world's most famous climate groups', *Vice.com*, April 28. Available: https://www.vice.com/en_us/article/jgey8k/a-debate-over-racism-has-spl it-one-of-the-worlds-most-famous-climate-groups, accessed 19 May 2020.

Diaz, V.M.. (2011). 'Voyaging for anti-colonial recovery: Austronesian seafaring, archipelagic rethinking, and the re-mapping of indigeneity', *Pacific Asia Inquiry*, vol 2: 21–32.

Duran, E., Duran, B., Brave Heart, M.Y.H., et al. (1998). 'Healing the American Indian soul wound', in Yael Danieli (ed.) *International Handbook of Multigenerational Legacies of Trauma*. Springer: New York, 341–354.

Dussais, A.M. (2014). 'Room for a (sacred view)? American Indian tribes confront visual desecration caused by wind energy projects', *American Indian Law Review*, vol 38: 336–420.

Foster, J.B. and Clark, B. (2020). *The Robbery of Nature: Capitalism and the Ecological Rift.* Monthly Review Press: Eugene, OR.

Gaikesheyongai, S. and Keeshig-Tobias, P. (1994). *The Seven Fires: An Ojibway Prophecy.* Sister Vision Press: Toronto, ON.

Gergan, M., Smith, S., and Vasudevan, P. (2018). 'Earth beyond repair: Race and apocalypse in collective imagination', *Environment and Planning D: Society and Space*, vol 38: 91–110.

Gilpin, E. (2019). 'Our own hands', in *Canada's National Observer*, Vancouver, BC. Available: https://ww w.nationalobserver.com/2019/03/28/clean-energy-aligns-who-we-are-indigenous-people/, accessed 19 May 2020.

Goeman, M. (2009). 'Notes toward a native feminism's spatial practice', *Wicazo Sa Review*, vol 24: 169–187.

Hauptman, L.M. (1986). 'Africa view: John Collier, the British colonial service and American Indian policy 1933–1945', *The Historian*, vol 48: 359–374.

Hendriks, R., Raphals, P., Bakker, K., and Christie, G. (2017). 'First nations and hydropower: The case of British Columbia's site C Dam project', in *Items*. Social Science Research Council of Canada: Toronto, ON. Available: https://items.ssrc.org/just-environments/first-nations-and-hydropower-the-case-of-bri tish-columbias-site-c-dam-project/, accessed 19 May 2020.

Hoang, C., Satyal, P., and Corbera, E. (2019). '"This is my garden": Justice claims and struggles over forests in Vietnam's REDD+', *Climate Policy*, vol 19: S23–S35.

Howe, C. (2019). *Ecologics: Wind and Power in the Anthropocene.* Duke University Press: Durham, NC.

Hurley, J. (2020). *Infrastructures of Apocalypse.* University of Minnesota Press: Minneapolis, MN.

Johnston, B. (1990). *Ojibway Heritage.* University of Nebraska Press: Lincoln, NE.

Krakoff, S. (2011). 'Radical adaptation, justice, and American Indian nations', *Environmental Justice*, vol 4: 207–212.

Lawson, M.L. (1994). *Dammed Indians: The Pick-Sloan Plan and the Missouri River Sioux 1944-1980.* University of Oklahoma Press: Norman, OK.

Lobo, S. (2003). 'Urban clan mothers: Key households in cities', *American Indian Quarterly*, vol 27: 505–522.

Lone-Knapp, F. (2000). 'Rez talk: How reservation residents describe themselves', *American Indian Quarterly*, vol 24: 635–640.

Marino, E. (2012). 'The long history of environmental migration: Assessing vulnerability construction and obstacles to successful relocation in Shishmaref, Alaska', *Global Environmental Change*, vol 22: 374–381.

Mbembé, A. (2003). '*Necropolitics* L. Meintjes (trans.)', *Public Culture*, vol 15: 11–40.

Meriam, Lewis. (1928). *The Problem of Indian Administration: Report of a Survey made at the Request of Honorable Hubert Work, Secretary of the Interior, and Submitted to Him, February 21, 1928/Survey Staff: Lewis Meriam …[et al.].* Johns Hopkins Press: Baltimore, MD.

Nguh, A. and Sanyanga, R. (2013). *Corruption and Infrastructure Megaprojects in the DR Congo.* International Rivers: Oakland, CA.

Nichols, R. (2013). 'Indigeneity and the settler contract today', *Philosophy and Social Criticism*, vol 39: 165–186.

O'Brien, J.M. (2010). *Firsting and Lasting: Writing Indians out of Existence in New England.* University of Minnesota Press: Minneapolis, MN.

Ranco, D. and Fleder, A. (2005). 'Tribal environmental sovereignty: Cultural appropriate protection or paternalism?' *Journal of Natural Resources and Environmental Law*, vol 19: 35–58.

Rifkin, M. (2017). *Beyond Settler Time: Temporal Sovereignty and Indigenous Self-Determination.* Duke University Press: Durham, NC.

Rosier, P.C. (1995). 'Dam building and treaty breaking: The Kinzua Dam controversy 1936-1958', *The Pennsylvania Magazine of History and Biography*, vol 119: 345–368.

Rosier, P.C. (2006). '"They are ancestral homelands": Race, place, and politics in cold war Native America 1945–1961', *The Journal of American History*, vol 92: 1300–1326.

Rusco, E.R. (1991). 'John Collier: Rrchitect of sovereignty or assimilation?', *American Indian Quarterly*, vol 15: 49–54.

Rusco, E.R. (2000). *A Fateful Time: The Background and Legislative History of The Indian Reorganization Act.* University of Nevada Press: Reno, NV.

Sandoval, C.J. (2018). 'Energy access is energy justice: The Yurok tribe's trailblazing work to close the native American reservation electricity gap', in R. Salter, C.G. Gonzalez, and M.H. Dworkin (eds.) *Energy Justice.* Edward Elgar Publishing: Cheltenham, 166–207.

Simpson, A. (2017). 'The ruse of consent and the anatomy of "refusal": Cases from Indigenous North America and Australia', *Postcolonial Studies*, vol 20: 18–33.

Stein, S., Hunt, D., Suša, R.., and de Oliveira Andreotti, V. (2017). 'The educational challenge of unraveling the fantasies of ontological security', *Diaspora, Indigenous, and Minority Education*, vol 11: 69–79.

Stremlau, R. (2005). '"To domesticate and civilize wild Indians": Allotment and the campaign to reform Indian families 1875-1887', *Journal of Family History*, vol 30: 265–286.

Suagee, D.B. (2012). 'Climate crisis, renewable energy revolution, and tribal sovereignty', in S.A. Krakoff and E. Rosser (eds.) *Tribes, Land, and the Environment.* Ashgate: Burlington, VT, 43–74.

Tauli-Corpuz, V. and Lynge, A. (2008). 'Impact of climate change mitigation measures on Indigenous peoples and on their territories and lands', Permanent Forum on Indigenous Issues Seventh Session, vol 31: 1–90.

Turner, D. (2006). *This Is Not a Peace Pipe: Towards a Critical Indigenous Philosophy.* University of Toronto Press: Toronto, ON.

U.S. Deparment of State. (1856). The Guano Islands Act, 11 Stat. 119, Enacted 18 August 1856, Codified at 48 U.S.C. ch. 8 §§ 1411–*1419*. Available: https://uscode.house.gov/view.xhtml?path=/prelim@title48/chapter8&edition=prelim, accessed 20 May 2020.

Watkinson, M.K. (2015). *Tribal Capacity for Climate Change Adaptation: Identifying the Impact of Fractionated Land for a Coastal Community June 8 2015.* MA Dissertation, University of Washington, WA.

Whyte, K.P. (2018). 'Indigenous science (fiction) for the anthropocene: Ancestral dystopias and fantasies of climate change crises', *Environment and Planning E: Nature and Space*, vol 1: 224–242.

Wildcat, D.R. (2009). *Red Alert! Saving the Planet With Indigenous Knowledge.* Fulcrum: Golden, CO.

5

Matariki and the decolonisation of time

Rangi Matamua

What is time?

Time can be described as an "indefinite continued progression of existence and events in the past, present and future" (Oxford Dictionary 2011: Online), whilst also a system of measuring duration or the intervals that exist between two events. This basic understanding of physical time is universal, and all societies and peoples across the world have experienced and continue to experience the progression of time, from the rising and setting of the sun, to the changing of the seasons and even the tick tock of a clock. However, the manner in which we interact with time, the way time is measured and experienced varies significantly from culture to culture (Adams 1995). This is because time is bound to culture, to place, and to people. It is embedded within ritual, routine, calendars, devices, environments, discourse, myth, practise, labour, religion, spirituality, science, and all facets of cultural life. Ultimately time orientates how people interact with everything.

Therefore, there are many forms of time and different ways of interacting with time. The study of time perception and how it is used and valued is called chronemics (Reynolds, Vannest, and Fletcher-Janzen 2018: 773). There are two main kinds of approaches to time interaction. The first is monochronic which segments time into small units so time can be managed and scheduled. In this approach time is viewed as a tangible commodity that can be used in a similar manner to money. This approach to time is closely associated with industry and labour and is how time is understood by the vast majority of the world's population. The second approach to time is polychronic. Under this approach time is fluid and less formal with little focus on small units of time. In this system seasonal cycles, environmental relationships and traditions inform the rhythms of community life.

Yet, time is more than just a system of measurement, it is also political, and systems of time can represent different ideologies (Cohen 2018). Here in Aotearoa New Zealand we adhere to a universal time-keeping system that includes seconds and minutes, 24-hour days, 7-day weeks, 12-months and a 365.25-day calendar year. This system is a signpost of European expansion and colonisation. All across the globe, European settlers replaced unique polychronic native systems with their monochronic, 'Western' understanding of time. The enforced introduction of 'Western' time upon Indigenous peoples is part of a greater movement to conquer both the terrain of the population, as well as the time system that regulated the Indigenous peoples' interaction with their world. This process happened rather quickly in Aotearoa New Zealand. With the arrival of European settlers in the early nineteenth century there was a desire to establish a single system of time that brought the new colony into alignment with the rest of the world. Initially each town had slightly different time, and bells and clocks where rung to inform people when it was time to work, pray and go to school. This all changed in 1869 when Aotearoa New Zealand was the first country in the world to adopt standard time (King 1902). This time is based on Greenwich Mean Time (GMT) which is set by the Royal Observatory in Greenwich London. The application of this system in Aotearoa New Zealand is what we call New Zealand Mean Time (NZMT).

The desire to introduce standard time to Aotearoa New Zealand was driven for the most part by two sectors of society, capitalism and Christianity, and both have vested interests in the politics of time. For capitalism, time is essential for controlling the workforce. Time regulates labour and is at the heart of industrialisation (Schivelbusch 2014: 33–44). Christianity on the other hand is not only interested in temporal time, but also in what transcends time (Balslev and Mohanty 1993: 8). Religion and Christianity is undeniably associated with time, and this is evident in how we observe the yearly procession. For example, as I write this chapter, we are currently in the year 2020 since the birth of Jesus Christ. Commenting on this dual approach to the colonisation of native time Nanni (2013: 4) writes:

> Without a shared sense of time, there could be only a limited degree of communication and exchange of commodities in the rapidly-expanding networks of capitalism and Christianity – no synchronisation of labour rhythms and meshing of industrial timetables; no sense of uniting all the world's peoples under one God.

It was also against a backdrop of war, land alienation, poverty, and the loss of language and culture that Māori were forced to abandon their traditional time practices and convert to the Gregorian calendar. In 1869, the year in which the New Zealand Government adopted GMT, parts of the country were still embroiled in a bitter land war, with rebel tribes fighting crown forces (O'Malley 2019). While the primary goal of these conflicts was the control of resources, especially land, from a wider context the wars were part of the colonisation process that looked to establish the might of the British Empire over the country. Combined with a government-sponsored programme to assimilate Māori into European life, and difficulties with a declining population, Māori began to synchronise their life and culture with Western time. Lunar phases gave way to days of the week, the rising and setting of the sun was replaced with hours and minutes, and our yearly cycle fell into union with the Northern hemisphere.

On a much larger cultural level, the inclusion of Western time into Māori culture saw Māori seasonal events, ceremonies, and celebrations replaced with European cultural and religious activities. Māori began to celebrate Christmas, Easter, the Queen's birthday, and Labour Day. Even the observance of the New Year, traditionally celebrated by Māori during mid-winter, was shifted to the summer so we as a colony could align our time with 'Mother England'. Events that had no relationship to our environment or location in the world, were introduced to the country as part of the colonisation of time in Aotearoa New Zealand. Our entire context of time shifted its foundation to a Western ideology and, accordingly, all its political, religious and cultural paradigms; this remains the reality of time in Aotearoa New Zealand to this present day.

Therefore, what time system did the ancestors of the Māori follow?

Māori system of time

Indigenous concepts of time, calendar systems, seasonality, rituals, and the rhythms of nature are intrinsically intertwined. Māori, similar to other Indigenous peoples, developed a complex time system integrating celestial, environmental and ecological occurrences to track time and seasonality. The movement of the sun, moon, and stars were used as markers to regulate the timing of agricultural, fishing and hunting activities, and rituals. The pre-European Māori system of time could best be described as polychronic and environmental. These systems were also regional, tribal and localised, and even though this chapter discusses a Māori system of time, in actuality there is no such thing as a single Māori approach. Māori knowledge has always been regionally specific, and while the stars gave a broad indication as to the season and event, more detailed understandings of the local environment and ecological change were taken into account when determining time at a local level (Tāwhai 2013; Timoti et al. 2017). To date more than 500 Māori lunar calendar systems have been recorded, and this shows the extensive variation and amount of detail that was part of Māori time systems. This chapter will not attempt to unpack these numerous and diverse calendars, but instead will focus on some of the common elements, which proffer a general sense of Māori time.

The Māori approach to time took into account many environmental factors that we will explore soon; however, at the heart of this system was the practice of Māori astronomy. Māori astronomical knowledge was infused into all parts of Māori society, including tradition, knowledge and language (Harris et al. 2013; Whaanga and Matamua 2016; Matamua 2017a; Matamua 2017b). This knowledge system was transmitted via oral traditions such as mōteatea (traditional song), whakataukī (proverbs), karakia (incantations) and kōrero tuku iho (oral tradition). Māori astronomy also played a significant role in day-to-day activities such as planting and harvesting (Harris et al. 2013), was embedded and encoded into artwork such as carvings, and was integrated into the landscape through place-names. Māori astronomy is most well-known for its application to celestial navigation that helped our ancestors traverse the Pacific Ocean, the largest body of water in the world (Matamua, Harris, and Kerr 2013; Tuaupiki 2017). Ancestors of Māori, utilising the sky as a map, detailed observations and astronomical knowledge enabled:

> ... arguably the most remarkable voyage[s] in the history of humanity. ... [O]nce here, elements of the star-knowledge of the central Pacific were adapted to become relevant to these islands and their climate. ... Over the next 800 years, Māori astronomy evolved with the people to become the situationally specific knowledge base that it is today.
>
> *(Whaanga and Matamua 2016: 60)*

Māori astronomers (tohunga kōkōrangi), studied the motions of the celestial bodies in great detail, and their appearance, position, colour, and brightness were examined, whilst their heliacal rising and setting were recorded, observed, and celebrated.

Māori developed an awareness of the different links between movements of celestial bodies and seasonal patterns. This ensured food security, and all manner of cosmological phenomena were worshipped, studied, connected, and correlated to terrestrial events (e.g., seasonal changes, the timing of ocean tides, and the nature of comets, eclipses, meteors, and other transient celestial phenomena) (Harris et al. 2013; Matamua 2017b). Unlike the Gregorian calendar, which is a solar calendar that delineates a year by the amount of time it takes the earth to orbit the sun, the Māori calendar takes into account the position of the sun, the lunar phases and the pre-dawn rising (heliacal rise) of stars. All of these factors come into play when determining time.

Figure 5.1 An artistic interpretation of the sun and his two wives, Hinetakurua and Hineraumati.

This Māori time system was mostly luni-stella (combining the position of stars with the lunar calendar) in its application, meaning the two most commonly observed signs were the moon and the stars. While the position of the sun did play a role in marking the passage of time, mostly it was used to determine seasons. Māori knew when the sun rose in the South East it was summer and the days would be long and warm. Then six months later it would be seen rising in the North East, with short cold days and long nights. The gradual change in the sun's rising and setting positions was understood by Māori as a basic indication of season. The variance in the sun's position was interpreted as the perpetual journey of a Tamanuiterā (the sun), backwards and forwards between his two wives, Hineraumati, the summer maiden and Hinetakurua, the winter maiden (Best 1952: 50). In the summer, the sun lives on earth with his summer wife and brings warmth and bounty to the land. In winter he travels far out to sea to his winter wife, and the year becomes cold.

In addition to the sun, Māori followed lunar months as opposed to the solar months that make up our modern calendar. Each lunar month has its own name and is associated with a particular event or activity. An example of the different lunar months was given to the well-known New Zealand ethnologist, Elsdon Best, in the late 1800s by Tūtakangahau of Tūhoe. His 12 lunar months and explanations are as follows.

1. Pipiri. Kua piri nga mea katoa i te whenua i te matao, me te tangata. All things on earth cohere owing to the cold; likewise man.
2. Hongonui. Kua tino matao te tangata, me te tahutahu ahi, ka painaina. Man is now extremely cold, and so kindles fires before which he basks.
3. Hereturi-koka. Kua kitea te kainga a te ahi i nga turi o te tangata. The scorching effect of fire on the knees of man is seen.

4. Mahuru. Kua pumahana te whenua, me nga otaota, me nga rakau. The earth has now acquired warmth, as also have herbage and trees.
5. Whiringa-nuku. Kua tino mahana te whenua. The earth has now become quite warm.
6. Whiringa-rangi. Kua raumati, kua kaha te ra. It has now become summer, and the sun has acquired strength.
7. Hakihea. Kua noho nga manu kai roto i te kohanga. Birds are now sitting in their nests.
8. Kohi-tatea. Kua makuru te kai; ka kai te tangata i nga kai hou o te tau. Fruits have now set, and man eats of the new food products of the season.
9. Hui-tanguru. Kua tau te waewae o Ruhi kai te whenua. The foot of Ruhi now rests upon the earth.
10. Poutu-te-rangi. Kua hauhake te kai. The crops are now taken up.
11. Paenga-whawha. Kua putu nga tupu o nga kai i nga paenga o nga mara. All haulm is now stacked at the borders of the plantations.
12. Haratua. Kua uru nga kai kai te rua, kua mutu nga mahi a te tangata. Crops have now been stored in the store pits. The tasks of man are finished. (Best 1973: 19)

Each of the above 12 names is applied to both months as well as stars. These stars appear in the morning sky towards the East just before the sun rises to mark the corresponding month. For instance, the name of the tenth month is Poutūterangi. This is also the name of the star Altair in the constellation of Aqulia. Poutūterangi is a lunar month that occurs around March and April when this star is seen in the morning sky. Therefore, Māori used the stars as markers of month and season (Mahupuku 1854, cited in Matamua 2017b: 39)

The use of stars as markers of lunar months was observed in colouration with the changing lunar phases. This division of time falls under the calendar system known as maramataka (Roberts, Weko, and Clarke 2006; Best 1922b; Ropiha 2000; Tawhai 2013). The maramataka is a multi-layered time system that utilises observations of the celestial objects with ecological and environmental indicators such as the flowering of certain plants and the occurrence of particular weather patterns (Harris and Clarke 2017). In essence, it is an environmental calendar that uses the lunar phases as a baseline. The Māori names of the different lunar phases and the number of phases in the maramataka vary from region to region and tribe to tribe. There are even contrasting views on when the maramataka begins and ends, with some tribes starting their lunar month at the new moon and others with the full moon (Tawhai 2013).

These time-centred celestial observations were combined with numerous ecological events to determine season and month. Best (1977: 33) notes that at times the blooming and seeding of plants would denote season, time of the year and even activity:

certain months were marked by the blossoming or seeding of certain trees, among them being the puahou (Nothopanax arboreum), kōwhai (Sophora spp.), rewarewa (Knightia excelsa), kahika (Podocarpus dacrydioides), and tawhiwhi, a red blossomed Metrosideros. Many other plants helped to denote seasons, the time for annual tasks, etc., by their flowering, fruits, etc., and by the dying down and fresh growth of raupo, etc. Poananga (clematis) and Tahumate first blooming of the puahou, are the offspring of Rehua (Antares) and Puanga (Rigel), the latter being their mother, and the task of the two plants is to make known the warmth of summer.

Cultural keystone species like the kererū (Hemiphaga novaeseelandiae) (Timoti et al. 2017), and the tuna (Anguilla dieffenbachii) and (Anguilla australis) were so important to the survival of certain tribes that their annual harvest became a recognised part of the annual calendar system. Likewise the kūmara (sweet potato), which was a staple food source within many traditional

Māori communities was used in the same manner. The planting of the kūmara coincided with the returning of the pīpīwharauroa (shining cuckoo) and the koekoeā (long-tailed cuckoo) from the islands of the Pacific to Aotearoa New Zealand to lay their eggs. This event occurred in Mahuru the fourth month of the Māori year, around September and October. The harvesting of the kūmara followed the departure of both birds from Aotearoa in the Autumn and when the star Whānui (Vega) appeared in the morning sky. Because of this connection to the planting and harvesting of the kūmara, these two cuckoo birds were also known as the kūmara birds (Riley 2001: 60). This is one example of how stars, and ecology combine to determine season and activity. Adding to this multi-layered time system is the fact that seasonal flowers, insects, spawning animals and even implements like bird snares became constellations and stars, and their appearance during certain times of the year let the population know of an impending event.

Matariki

A central figure in the Māori observance of time is Matariki. The Matariki cluster is of great significance to many cultures worldwide and is known by many names including most commonly the Pleiades, seven sisters, or M45. This group of stars is an open star cluster located within the constellation of Taurus and includes several hundred stars of which only a handful are visible with the naked eye. 'Matariki' is often mistakenly translated as 'little eyes' or 'small eyes', due to mata meaing 'eyes' and riki 'small' or 'little'. This translation originates from the aforementioned ethnologist Eldson Best (1973) who dissected and translated the word 'Matariki'. Rāwiri Te Kōkau forwards an alternative account of Matariki stating that it is a truncated version of the longer name, Ngā mata o te ariki Tāwhirimātea, or the eyes of the god Tāwhirimātea (Matamua 2017a; 2017b). He recounts that in the beginning Ranginui (the Sky Father) and Papatūānuku (Earth Mother) were bound together in a tight embrace, with their children between them, cloaked in perpetual darkness. These children became the pantheon of Māori Gods. It was decided that their parents should be separated and all agreed to this course of action, apart from Tāwhirimātea the god of winds and weather. Tāwhirimātea sought retribution from his siblings for what they achieved and undertook a series of attacks against them. All cowered before the wrath of Tāwhirimātea except Tūmatauenga, the god of war and humanity; the ultimate warrior. Following an epic battle, Tūmatauenga triumphed banishing his brother to the sky. Defeated and overcome with sorrow, Tāwhirimātea plucked out his eyes and cast them into the heavens in a display of rage and contempt towards his siblings and aroha (love) for his father. These eyes became the stars of Matariki, Ngā mata o te ariki Tāwhirimātea.

Matariki is also known by other names including 'Te Huihui o Matariki' (the cluster/assembly of Matariki), 'Te Tautari-nui-o-Matariki' (Matariki fixed in the heavens), 'Tāriki' (an abbreviation of Matariki), 'Aokai' (denoting its connection with food), 'Hoko'/'Hokokūmara' (describing its influence over the growing of kūmara), and three further names ('Mataroa', 'Matarohaki' and 'Matawaia'), which were suggested by (Best 1910) as possible names. The name 'Matariki' is used to describe the entire star cluster with nine of the major stars in Matariki having their own individual names. These stars are Tupuānuku (Pleione), Tupuārangi (Atlas), Waitī (Maia), Waitā (Taygeta), Waipunarangi (Electra), Ururangi (Merope), Pōhutukawa (Sterope), Hiwa-i-te-rangi (Calæno), and Matariki (Alcyone). Matariki is the wife of Rehua (Antares) and together they have eight children (five daughters and three sons). Rehua, a paramount chief, is connected with medicine and healing and Matariki to well-being, good fortune and health: "it is within both Rehua and Matariki that knowledge of well-being and medicine exists, and both have the power to heal" (Matamua 2017b: 26). Although there are a number of accounts that portray Matariki as a mother to seven daughters, seven sisters, or a flock of birds, these are thought to

Figure 5.2 Illustration showing Rehua, Matariki, and their eight children. Together, Matariki and her children form the star cluster known as Matariki.

originate from Greek myths. This is another aspect of colonisation, where Māori understandings of Matariki over time have been merged with Greek myth (Matamua 2017b) and perpetuated as fact.

Within Māori astronomy stars have their own identity and specific purpose, and this characterisation helps to connect their appearance to the wider population. Each of the named stars within Matariki is associated with either a source of food, a form of weather, the afterlife, or the promise of a prosperous year. Pōhutukawa is a female, the eldest of the Matariki children, and she is associated with the dead who have passed since the last heliacal rising of Matariki. Tupuānuku is female and she is connected with food grown in the earth. Tupuārangi is male and he embodies the food that comes from the sky, including the fruit from trees and birds. Waitī is female and she holds the essence of food found in fresh water and Waitā is male and he holds the essence of the food in salt water. Waipunarangi is female and she is connected with rain and Ururangi is male and he is connected to the nature of winds for the year. Hiwa-i-te-rangi is female and the youngest of this celestial family. She is associated with the promise of a prosperous year. Matariki is the mother and the conductor of the entire cluster (Matamua 2017b).

Matariki and time

There are between 28 and 31 days in a Gregorian month, which are added together to create a solar year of 365 days. An additional day is added to this calendar system every four years to readjust the calendar to fit the solar year (i.e., a leap year). This process of adding additional periods of time to a calendar system is known as intercalation. A similar process of adding to the calendar system was followed by Māori; however, it involved the inclusion of an additional month to the Māori lunar calendar year. This process involves Matariki as the regulator for the Māori year, and it was a cyclic indicator that determined when the Māori year commenced. As previously discussed, Māori followed a lunar calendar that is 354 days long and is based upon the cycles of the moon phases (synodic months). This means that there is an 11-day difference between the Māori lunar calendar and the 365-day solar calendar that we currently follow. Over a two-year cycle this difference becomes 22 days; over three years it results in 33 days; and, therefore, over a three-year period there is a full month variation between a lunar and solar calendar.

Māori understood the subtleties of this time system and knew the importance of reconciling the lunar year with the sun to ensure that they harmonised the cycle of the year and the seasons. This was achieved with the inclusion of an extra month into the calendar system every three years. The name of this month is 'Ruhanui' or the 'listless' or 'lazy' month. Applying an intercalary month to the lunar calendar was a common practice worldwide. Early uses of an additional month can be found in calendars of the Greeks (Van der Waerden 1960), Hebrew (Segal 1957), Chinese (Aslaksen 2010; Martzloff 2016) and many other cultures. These calendars place the insertion of a 13th month at various stages during their calendars with varying degrees of accuracy. For Māori, however, the intercalary month was more approximate and precision was less of a concern with a focus more on what works. Other systems around the world have adopted a system that places seven extra months over a 19-year time scale.

For Māori, the indicator of when to place the intercalary month was the appearance of Matariki. As previously stated, the maramataka is a luni-stella calendar, and events and activities would begin and end on particular moon phases. In the case of the New Year, the heliacal rise of Matariki occurs during the first month of the Māori year, called Pipiri (June–July). Our ancestors would wait until its sighting coincided with the lunar phase of Tangaroa (the last quarter), (Te Toa Takitini 1922) a very productive time according to many Māori calendar systems. Therefore, for many tribes the Māori new year begins when Matariki is seen in the sky on the last quarter of the first month of the year, called Pipiri.

As discussed earlier, 12 lunar months is only 354 days long and is 11 days short of a solar year. The implications of this is that the lunar phase Tangaroa will be occurring 11 days earlier than the previous year. When observing the night sky the 11-day shift between solar and lunar cycles across the year will thus mean that each year Matariki would appear lower and lower in the sky on the horizon at the time of Tangaroa as the years progress (see Figure 5.3). As heliacal risings of stars occur early in the morning before the sun rises, the closer the star is to the sun below the horizon, the more difficult it is to see. Given that Matariki is a third-magnitude star, in order to view its heliacal rise with the naked eye, the cluster will need to be at least 5 degrees above the horizon while the sun is at least 16 degrees below (Matamua 2016a). Matariki is supposed to occur during the month of Pipiri in Tangaroa; eventually, the 11-day slippage will be so far out that Matariki will not be visible at that time. When Matariki was not visible during the Tangaroa phase of the month of Pipiri, Pipiri would become a double month. This is when the intercalary month known as Ruhanui would be applied. Figure 5.3 shows the position of Matariki in the early pre-dawn sky in the month of Pipiri on the first phase of Tangaroa for the years 2018 (Figure 3a), 2019 (Figure 3b), 2020 (Figure 3c), and 2021 (Figure 3d). In order to ensure visibility, the times chosen were for when the sun is at least 16 degrees below the horizon. For 2018, 2019, and 2021, Matariki is clearly seen above 5 degrees; however, for 2020, Matariki is below the 5 degree limit and thus is not visible. Therefore in 2020 the intercalary month, Ruhanui, needs to be inserted following Pipiri and, in so doing, the whole cycle resets itself.

Figure 5.3 Members of Te Matapunenga conducting a traditional ceremony at the pre-dawn rising of Matariki in the Tangaroa lunar phase of the Pipiri lunar month. Photo taken at Rangiātea in the Waikato Region in 2018.

Matariki and the decolonisation of time

Over the past three decades, there has been a renaissance in the scientific study of Māori astronomy in a range of areas including reviews on Māori astronomy (Harris et al. 2013; Williams 2013; Tuahine 2015; Orchiston 2016b), lists on Polynesian and Māori star names (Johnson and 2015), recounts on the development of astronomy and emergence of astrophysics in Aotearoa (Hearnshaw and Orchiston 2017), histories of astronomy in New Zealand (Orchiston 2016a), critiques of Polynesian, aboriginal, and Māori astronomical perspectives (Orchiston 1996; Orchiston 2000), the use of astronomy as a cultural experience (Austin 2009), comparative cultural studies of astronomical knowledge, a discussion on supernovas and meteors (Green and Orchiston 2004; Britton and Hamacher 2014), the application of portable planetariums in the teaching of Māori astronomy (Harris 2017), horticultural and ethnopedological praxis (Roskruge 2011), waka navigation (Matamua, Harris, and Kerr 2013; Tuaupiki 2017), the maramataka (Ropiha 2000; Roberts, Weko, and Clarke 2006; Smith 2011; Tāwhai 2013; Clarke and Harris 2017), Matariki and Puanga (Matamua 2013; Williams 2013; Rerekura 2014; Matamua 2017a; Matamua 2017b), together with a number of popular publications and resources on Māori astronomy (Leather and Hall 2004; Hakaraia 2006; Hakaraia 2008).

In addition to the increased academic focus on Māori astronomy, there has also been a massive surge in the celebration of Matariki throughout the country. In the past 30 years, Matariki has gained momentum and is now part of the national annual calendar. Many groups such as the Museum of New Zealand Te Papa Tongarewa, city and regional councils, schools, the public sector, and even private organisations take time to celebrate the pre-dawn rise of Matariki in mid-winter, and to acknowledge the Māori New Year. This environmentally driven and culturally relative marker of time is grown in both popularity and meaning. In 2019, Te Kaunihera o Tāmaki Makaurau-Auckland Council ran its Matariki festival from 20 June to 15 July. The largest and arguably most diverse city in Aotearoa New Zealand, hosted several events orientated around a traditional Māori luni-stella system of time. In 2017 the Wellington council moved its annual 'Guy Fawkes' fireworks display from November to mid-winter to align with Matariki and the Māori New Year (Devlin 2017). In 2009, a bill was tabled by the Māori party in the House, seeking approval for Matariki to become a national holiday (New Zealand Government 2009). These are just some examples of how Matariki has grown in popularity, and its expanding influence over our national identity.

For some Māori, the morning rising of Matariki is more than just a period of celebration. It is a chance to reconnect with traditional practices, enact spiritual beliefs, reaffirm bonds with community, acknowledge the environment, bid farewell to those whom have past since the last Matariki period and to celebrate the promise of the future. The regeneration of this native observation of Matariki is being led in some places by groups of Māori cultural practitioners. Many of these groups are enacting a number of traditional ceremonies connected to the helia-cal rising of Matariki such as 'Te taki mōteatea' (reciting of laments) and 'Whāngai i te hautapu' (to feed with a sacred offering). In some regions these ceremonies are being reinvigorated by a group of traditional spiritual specialists called Te Matapuenga, established by the language, tikanga and karakia expert, Professor Pou Temara. Since 2015, practitioners and followers of the ceremony gather before dawn in the Tangaroa lunar phase of the month Pipiri to view the rising of Matariki. Once ascended, the practitioners prepare food that corresponds to each of the domains of Matariki. The food is placed at an altar and ceremony is conducted with karakia and chants. During this ceremony a reading of the bounty of the year is conducted, the names of the dead of the year are recited and released (Te taki mōteatea) and the smoke from the food is offered to the cluster as sustenance (Whāngai i te hautapu). The regeneration of this practice associated with Matariki ceremonies is in stark contrast to many ill-conceived celebrations that continue to be conducted nation-wide, which often pay little heed to ceremony or even the Māori calendar system. However, the honouring of Matariki via ceremony is one that many Māori are turning favourably towards (Hardy and Whaanga 2018).

Māori luni-stellar calendar practices and ceremonies may be seen as inconsequential when compared to the Gregorian calendar collectively followed today. Still, they play an important role in the revitalisation and decolonisation of Māori culture and society. Today there is a grow-ing number of Māori who are seeking to reinstate more traditional practices into their day-to-day lives. Throughout the world there is greater awareness about the environment, and the general public are beginning to understand the negative impact humans are having on the natu-ral world. Many are exploring Indigenous knowledge systems as pathways to more sustainable forms of living. Alternative approaches to religion and spirituality are also growing in influence (Hardy and Whaanga 2018) and some Māori are seeking spiritual gratification via traditional ceremonies and prayers. Questions are also being asked about the relevance of our modern sys-tem of time. Why in Aotearoa New Zealand must we adhere to a single monochronic system of time that is based on a Northern hemisphere perspective, including all of its cultural practices, religious beliefs, and rituals? How can a Māori system of time be reinstated and play a more meaningful role in our daily lives? Can we operate a duel calendar system using both a Western approach and Māori theories? What are the benefits in maintaining our traditional calendar systems? What are the benefits in maintaining our unique regional and tribal divisions of time?

All of these questions are part of an ongoing enquiry into the meaning of time from a Māori perspective, and the process many are undertaking to decolonise the things many take for granted in relation to time itself. At the forefront of this mission is the celebration of Matariki, and as each year passes, its prominence and status increases. Matariki is now an institution within

Aotearoa, with its popularity surpassing some of the European calendar events that were introduced to this country, such as Guy Fawkes. Matariki is becoming a greater part of our national consciousness and is helping to embed our evolving Aotearoa New Zealand identity. Yet, there is much to do if we are ever going to break free of the bonds of Western time, or even establish a more collaborative system that merges universal time with our unique Māori approach.

Conclusion

Time is more than just a measurement of intervals between events. Time is connected to everything in the world, and its understanding and application is both complex and contextual. Today in Aotearoa New Zealand we follow a universal solar, or Gregorian, calendar that was introduced by European settlers in the 1800s. This system is based on Greenwich Mean Time, and adheres to a 365.25-day year. It does not take into account environment, ecology, location, culture, or many other factors. In relation to industrialisation, capitalism, and globalisation, its sole purpose is the unity of people under a single system of time, bringing cohesion and formality to industry, the marketplace, religion, and politics. The ancestors of Māori implemented an environmental calendar system that was less formal and valued interaction with the world. This system was founded upon astronomical events including the position of the sun and stars, and the phases of the moon. It also used ecological change to measure time, and the flora and fauna became a live part of this system.

Perhaps one of the most significant differences between these two approaches to time is that the Gregorian calendar regulates when events are observed. For instance, New Year's Day is celebrated on 1 January every year. There is no environmental, astronomical or ecological explanation for why this happens. However, a Māori calendar system is driven by the environment, and knowledge of, and interaction with the natural world is needed in order to synchronise your life with the rhythms of this system. For instance, the actual day of the Māori New Year changes every year and depends upon the visibility of stars, the position of the sun, the lunar phase and possibly many other factors. Also, this division of time was not universal. Time was relative to location, unique environment and what communities and tribes valued as important. It could be argued that our current system of time concentrates on 'following time' while the Māori calendar is focused on 'living time'.

As part of colonisation, Māori were converted to Western time, and most of our traditional time-centred practices were replaced. The solar year, solar months, seven-day week, minutes, and hours became part of colonised Māori culture and for the most part changed the manner in which we interact with each other and with our world. However, in the past 30 years, Matariki and its time-related observations has begun to be reinstated. In pre-European Aotearoa, the celebration of this astronomical event underpinned the entire year and regulated the many lunar months as associated activities. It emerged again in the 1990s as part of small tribal gatherings and different public lectures. Since then it has undergone dramatic growth and has become part of the fabric of our national identity. However, for many its purpose is much greater than an annual celebration. Matariki is part of a wider movement to decolonise time, and to reinstate many of our native time practices so they once again become a meaningful part of our day-to-day lives.

The Western calendar system, and its global spread, dominates the world's understanding of time. We are born into this system, we live our daily lives by this system and we eventually die under this system. Our whole world is driven by the never-ending ticking of the clock. However, some people are beginning to question how beneficial this system of time is for our environment, our ecology, our well-being, our culture, and for the long-term survival of life itself. This chapter has discussed the idea of Matariki leading a movement to decolonise Western notions of time here in Aotearoa New Zealand, and to revive our traditional practices. The decolonisation of Western time is a huge undertaking, and it is only natural to ponder if this could ever be a reality. Is it even possible to break away from this dominant and all-encompassing system, and reinstate traditional Indigenous understandings of time, which guide our ongoing interaction with the world and everything in it? I suppose the most plausible answer to this question is, 'only time will tell'.

References

Adam, B. (1995). *Timewatch: The Social Analysis of Time.* Polity Press: Cambridge.

Aslaksen, H. (2010). *The Mathematics of the Chinese Calendar.* Department of Mathematics, University of Singapore: Singapore.

Austin, M. (2009). 'From ancient to modern: The role of astronomy as a cultural experience', *Proceedings of the International Astronomical Union*, vol 5, no S260: 225–228.

Balslev, A. and Mohanty, J.N. (1993). *Religion and Time.* E.J. Brill: Netherlands.

Best, E. (1952). *The Maori as he Was: A Brief Account of Maori Life as it Was in Pre-European Days.* Government Printers: Wellington.

Best, E. (1973). *The Maori Division of Time.* A.R. Shearer Government Printer: Wellington.

Best, E. (1977). *Forest Lore of the Maori.* Keating, Government Printers: Wellington.

Britton, T.R. and Hamacher, D.W. (2014). 'Meteor beliefs project: Meteors in the Māori astronomical traditions of New Zealand', *WGN – Journal of the International Meteor Organization*, vol 42, no 1: 31–34.

Cohen, E. (2018). *The Political Value of Time: Citizeship, Duration and Democratic Justice.* Cambridge University Press: Cambridge, United Kingdom.

Devlin, C. (2017). 'Wellington city council cancels Guy Fawkes and moves fireworks sky show to Matariki', Stuff.co.nz. Available: https://www.stuff.co.nz/dominion-post/news/97396436/wellington-city-council-cancels-guy-fawkes-and-moves-fireworks-to-matariki, accessed March 20, 2018.

Green, D.A. and Orchiston, W. (2004). 'In search of Mahutonga: A possible supernova recorded in Maori astronomical traditions?', *Archaeoastronomy*, vol 18: 110–113.

Hakaraia, L. (2006). *Celebrating Matariki.* Reed: Auckland.

Hakaraia, L. (2008). *Matariki: The Māori New Year.* Raupo: North Shore.

Hardy, A. and Whaanga, H. (2018). 'Using the stars to indigenize the public sphere: Matariki over New Zealand', Paper presented at the Impact of Religion Challenges for Society, *Law and Democracy*, 24–26 April. Uppsala University: Sweden.

Harris, P. (2017). 'Portable planetariums in the teaching of Māori astronomy', in H. Whaanga, T.T. Keegan, and M. Apperley (eds.) *He Whare Hangarau Māori - Language, Culture & Technology, [Ebook].* Te Pua Wānanga ki te Ao, Te Whare Wānanga o Waikato: Hamilton, 136–148.

Harris, P. and Clarke, L. (2017). 'Maramataka', in H. Whaanga, T.T. Keegan, and M. Apperley (eds.) *He Whare Hangarau Māori – Language, Culture & Technology [Ebook].* Te Pua Wānanga ki te Ao, Te Whare Wānanga o Waikato: Hamilton, 129–135.

Harris, P., Matamua, R., Smith, T., Kerr, H., and Waaka, T. (2013). 'A review of Māori astronomy in Aotearoa-New Zealand', *The Journal of Astronomical History and Heritage*, vol 16, no 3: 325–336.

Hearnshaw, J. and Orchiston, W. (2017). 'The development of astronomy and emergence of astrophysics in New Zealand', in T. Nakamura and W. Orchiston (eds.) *The Emergence of Astrophysics in Asia: Opening a New Window on the Universe.* Springer International Publishing: Cham, 581–621.

Johnson, R.K. and Mahelona, J.K. (2015). *Nā Inoa Hōkū – Hawaiian and Pacific Star Names.* Ocarina Books: Bognor Regis.

King, T. (1902). 'On New Zealand mean time, and on the longitude of the colonial observatory, Wellington; with a note on the universal time question', *Transactions and Proceedings of the Royal Society of New Zealand*, vol 35: 428–451.

Leather, K. and Hall, R. (2004). *Tātai Arorangi, Māori Astronomy: Work of the Gods.* Viking Sevenseas: Paraparaumu.

Mahupuku, H. (1854). *Whakapapa Tuupuna. MS, Private Collection, Whakatāne.* Cited by P. Hōhepa in his translation document (1992).

Martzloff, J.-C. (ed.) (2016). *Astronomy and Calendars–The Other Chinese Mathematics.* Springer: Berlin.

Matamua, R. (2013). 'Matariki – the seven sisters', in *Take a Closer Look: New Zealand Stories in Stamps*. New Zealand Post: Wellington, 23–27.

Matamua, R. (2017a). *Matariki – te whetū tapu o te tau*. Huia: Wellington.

Matamua, R. (2017b). *Matariki – The Star of the Year*. Huia: Wellington.

Matamua, R., Harris, P.L., and Kerr, H. (2013). 'Māori navigation', in *New Zealand Astronomical Society Yearbook*. Stardome Observatory Planetarium: Auckland, 28–34.

Nanni, G. (2013). *The Colonisation of Time: Ritual, Routine and Resistance in the British Empire*. Manchester University Press: Manchester.

New Zealand Government. (2009). Te Rā o Matariki Bill/Matariki Day Bill. Tables Office: Wellington. Available: http://www.legislation.giovt.nz/bill/member/2009/0056/latest/whole.html, accessed 20 April 2020.

O'Malley, V. (2019). *The New Zealand Wars Ngā Pakanga O Aotearoa*. Bridget Williams Books: Wellington.

Orchiston, W. (1996). 'Australian aboriginal, polynesian and Maori astronomy', in C.B.F. Walker (ed.) *Astronomy Before the Telescope*. St Martin's Press: New York, 318–328.

Orchiston, W. (2000). 'A Polynesian astronomical perspective: The Maori of New Zealand', in H. Selin and X. Sun (eds.) *Astronomy Across Cultures: The History of Non-Western Astronomy*. Kluwer Academic Publishers: Boston, MA, 161–196.

Orchiston, W. (2016a). *Exploring the History of New Zealand Astronomy*. Springer International Publishing: Heidelberg.

Orchiston, W. (2016b). 'The skies over Aotearoa/New Zealand: Astronomy from a Māori perspective', in W. Orchiston (ed.) *Exploring the History of New Zealand Astronomy*. Springer International Publishing, Heidelberg, 33–88.

Oxford University Press. (2011). 'Time', Oxford Dictionaries. Available: https://web.archive.org/web/20 120704084938/http:/oxforddictionaries.com/definition/time, accessed 18 May 2019.

Rerekura, S. (2014). *Puanga: Star of the Māori New Year*. Te Whare Wananga o Ngapuhi-nui-tonu: Auckland.

Reynolds, C.R., Vannest, K.J., Fletcher-Janzen, E. (2018). *Encyclopedia of Special Education, Volume 3: A Reference for the Education of Children, Adolescents, and Adults Disabilities and Other Exceptional Individuals*. Wiley: Hoboken, NJ.

Riley, M. (2001). *Māori Bird Lore*. Viking Sevenseas: Paraparaumu.

Roberts, M., Weko, F., and Clarke, L. (2006). *Maramataka: The Māori Moon Calendar*. AERU: Canterbury.

Ropiha, J. (2000). *Traditional Ecological Knowledge of the Maramataka: The Māori Lunar Calendar*. Master's Thesis, Victoria University of Wellington.

Roskruge, N. (2011). 'Traditional Maori horticultural and ethnopedological praxis in the New Zealand landscape', *Management of Environmental Quality: An International Journal*, vol 22, no 2: 200–212.

Segal, J. (1957). 'Intercalation and the Hebrew calendar', *Vetus Testamentum*, vol 7, no 3: 250–307.

Schivelbusch, W. (2014). *The Railway Journey. The Industrialization of Time and Space in the Nineteenth Century*. University of California Press: Berkeley, CA.

Smith, T. (2011). *Traditional Māori Growing Practices*. Te Atawhai o te Ao: Wanganui.

Tāwhai, W. (2013). *Living by the Moon: Te Maramataka a Te Whānau-ā-Apanui*. Huia: Wellington.

Te Toa Takitini. (1922). 'Te Aroha o Rangi-nui Kia Papatuanuku', *Te Toa Takitini*, vol 11: 10.

Timoti, P., Lyver, P.O.B., Matamua, R., Jones, C.J., and Tahi, B.L. (2017). 'A representation of a Tuawhenua worldview guides environmental conservation', *Ecology and Society*, vol 22, no 4: 20.

Tuahine, H. (2015). *Te tāhū o Ranginui: Whakatūria te Whare kōkōrangi*. Masters Thesis, University of Waikato.

Tuaupiki, J. (2017). *E kore e ngaro, he takere waka nui: Te mātauranga whakatere waka me ōna take nunui*. Master's Thesis, University of Waikato.

Van der Waerden, B. (1960). 'Greek astronomical calendars and their relation to the Athenian civil calendar', *The Journal of Hellenic Studies*, vol 80: 168–180.

Whaanga, H. and Matamua, R. (2016). 'Matariki tāpuapua: Pools of traditional knowledge and currents of change', in M. Robertson and P.K.E. Tsang (ed.) *Everyday Knowledge, Education and Sustainable Futures: Transdisciplinary Research in the Asia/Pacific Region*. Springer: Singapore, 59–70.

Williams, J. (2013). 'Puaka and Matariki: the Māori New Year', *The Journal of the Polynesian Society*, vol 122, no 1: 7–19.

6

Indigenous women writers in unexpected places

Lisa Kahaleole Hall

A significant element of my ongoing work is exploring the genealogy of knowledge production – highlighting the centrality of relationship to our understanding of what counts as knowledge and what kinds of knowledge we have access to. The contradictory imperatives of institutionalising counter-hegemonic programs such as Women's Studies and Ethnic Studies within a knowledge validation structure thoroughly shaped by colonialism, racism, sexism, and Eurocentrism produces enormous and irresolvable restrictive pressure on the form and content of theory we produce.

It seems obvious that alternative institutions have been and continue to be vital sources to find multiply marginalised work given the long history of colonial, racist, and sexist institutional exclusion by and through the mainstream. But as I have written before, the pressures of academic professionalisation place counter-hegemonic scholars in 'compromising positions' because the academy's structures of reward and support are thoroughly individualist and premised on racist, sexist and colonialist norms (Hall 1993). Community-based work becomes un(der)acknowledged and devalued as community-inspired programs become professionalised within the mainstream academy. This structural dilemma is why it is politically and spiritually essential to support robust ecosystems of knowledge production emanating from imperatives of survivance, resurgence, and recovery that may overlap but exceed the academy's aims.

My early academic and creative life was shaped by the imperatives of knowledge creation and transmission through my immersion in multiple overlapping and sometimes ontologically incommensurate spaces. Whether in a classroom reading Xeroxed copies of out-of-print 19th-century Black women's novels, or arguing in an editorial board meeting for *OUT/LOOK National Gay and Lesbian Quarterly*[1] about gay white men's appropriation of Native gender roles (Gutierrez 1989), working for feminist small presses like aunt lute books and Third Woman or reading high calorie-recipes provided by *Diseased Pariah News*[1] to sustain HIV+ folks (Mae 1990), it was always clear to me how important the subjugated knowledges held by these communities is, and how difficult those knowledges are to share widely. Print culture has been a site where these knowledges accrue and live on in formal and informal archives to be rediscovered/reanimated like messages in a bottle floating through a sea of erasure. In this digital age I remain attached to the materiality of print, the longevity of its fragile construction sometimes belying the assumption of digital superiority in making and preserving knowledge. Books printed centuries ago are still in existence and readable; the hardware storage, software programs, and websites of just a few years ago are defunct, obsolete, and dead-linked.

Genealogies, partialities, and fields of potential connection and contestation

Responding to a call for an entry on 'Indigenous women in print', in this chapter I focus on a small but highly influential body of writing in English by women whose ancestors preceded European incursion and settlement in territories now claimed by the nation states of the United States and Canada. I use 'women' to highlight genealogies of work gathered under that name— especially that of the US lesbian feminist–inspired 'Women in Print' movement. I think of 'print' as capaciously as possible to include the possibility of online sites and archives of writing. Within those already narrow boundaries lie a plethora of histories, geographies, and individual and communal stories that could not be comprehensively contained in their own book series, much less a single chapter. Instead I offer some overlapping strands; threads of different gene-alogies. My model for thinking about a framework for the infinite and ongoing comes from the communal work of A.W. Lee, Scott Morgensen, Dana Wesley and myself for the AKIN project: "Reconnecting histories of community work against racism, colonialism, and gender/ sexual oppression", funded by a Canadian Social Science and Humanities Research (SSHRC) grant (Hall, Lee, Morgensen and Wesley 2017: Presentation). In documenting unacknowledged or under-acknowledged histories of activism against racism, colonialism, and gender/sexual oppressions, a key project goal was to make private memories and local histories publicly acces-sible. The motivation was to try and create an archival space where individuals and groups that might not have knowledge of each other could convene, where those who had interconnected histories could document them and where un(der)acknowledged connections might become apparent in juxtaposition. Researchers and narrators attempted to draw out community and/ or site-based narratives to see where they might overlap or to place their differences within a framework that was not intended to homogenise them, but instead bring them into a shared space that all can access and further expand, develop, or contest. Neither a unified narrative nor anything close to comprehensive inclusion was possible but the hope was to build a space where differences could productively live and interact; where particularity and similarity could be leg-ible, and finally that the relational grounding of knowledge be highlighted throughout.

In this chapter I offer these genealogical threads on Indigenous women's writings in that same spirit, where they might inform, remind, and inspire additions or contestations.

Paula Gunn Allen: Making space in the academy, taking space in community-based cultural production

The period in which I entered graduate school in the late 1980s was one of great curricular contestation, development, and revision, a time whose promises and paradoxes were on full display in the newly formed Ethnic Studies Graduate Group at the University of California at Berkeley. The Bay Area – San Francisco, Berkeley, and Oakland – was the site of decades of grassroots social movements that explicitly intersected with the university system through the student strikes demanding Ethnic Studies courses, professors and programs, and that formed an ecosystem of intellectual and cultural work that exceeded the parameters of the academy.

As a graduate student at Berkeley I was fortunate enough to have access to some of the most brilliant and field-changing women of colour scholars of literature in the academy, whose insti-tutional power and prestige never came close to the impact they made on generations of students.

Within the university, the first generation of post-Civil Rights movement academics were forced to assert both the existence and legitimacy of their own fields of study as they gained new access to formerly segregated institutions. The English Department at Berkeley was fortunate to have Koyangk'auwi/Maidu poet Janice Gould as a graduate student and Laguna Pueblo/Sioux literary scholar and writer Paula Gunn Allen as a faculty member, but they did not evince much appreciation of this at the time. In later years when Allen was recruited by UCLA's English department where they explicitly recognised her multiple accomplishments in articulating and shaping the field of American Indian literature as well as her creative work in poetry and fiction, she was astonished at this contrast with Berkeley's attitude towards her and her work.

In an interview published in 1993 in *Backtalk: Women Writers Speak Out* (Perry 1993), Allen recounted:

> Q. *When you [Paula Gunn Allen] first went to graduate school you were told you couldn't study Native American literature because there wasn't any. I have the sense that you set out to prove academia wrong. Is that true?*
>
> A. *I did, and I did it. I didn't do it alone, you understand. MLA [the Modern Language Association] helped a lot. But now we have a community of scholars worldwide and we study Native American literature both in its traditional and its contemporary aspects. It's a real discipline. Now we have meetings at MLA and we don't get members coming in and saying, 'I know an Indian and he said so and so'. Instead, we get literary questions of real substance. All of that has happened between 1970 and 1990.*
>
> (Perry 1993: 5)

Between the 1970s and 1990s Allen was also heavily involved with community-based lesbian feminist publishing and cultural production. Within the United States, non-academic feminist publishing and distribution networks developed in the early 1970s had enormous academic impact in ethnic studies and women's studies programs in the 1980s and 1990s, even as that work became delegitimised as theory and scholarship in the professionalisation of those programs.

Indigenous women in 'unexpected places'

Why I play off of Deloria's formulation of unexpected places (Deloria 2004) here is that few people immediately associate Indigenous women with the history of lesbian feminism in the United States. The Women in Print movement in the United States grew out of an urgent need by self-identified feminists in general and lesbian-feminists in particular to create a cultural space where their words could be heard and shared (Hogan 2016; Morris 1999). The inclusivity of the Women in Print movement when it existed grew out of active and ongoing contestations about what feminism was/could be/should be and who feminist were/could be/should be. 'Outreach' and access for underrepresented groups of women – women of colour, Jewish, disabled, working-class, and poor women – was a part of this ethos. While I agree with the important critiques have been made about the push for 'inclusion' within a multicultural frame and the particular erasure of those seeking sovereign space rather than incorporation into a multicultural collectivity, it is worth noting that if multicultural formations exist; they provide the necessary yet not sufficient ground for more radical revision. Thus, even as the erasure/incomprehension of Indigenous-specific issues as such was as widespread in the (lesbian)feminist movement as it was and remains in both mainstream and non-Indigenous counter-hegemonic US worldviews, a space was opened for Indigenous women's voices under the ethic of inclusion that would not have otherwise existed.

In the late 1960s and early 1970s, the US printing trade was dominated by white working-class men, many of whom held conservative cultural values that were threatened by the rise of women's and gay liberation movements at that time. The mechanics of printing involved large, heavy dirty machinery; 'typesetting' required picking up individual metal letters and arranging them in words, sentences, paragraphs, and pages. Printing presses were big, noisy and potentially dangerous, and knowledge of their workings was passed down in apprenticeships and unions historically closed to women and to men of colour.

Activist women experienced problems getting their broadsheets and posters about everything from abortion rights to lesbian dances printed by printers who claimed their material was obscene. Thus, they decided to take the means of production into their own hands and acquire printing presses of their own. Once these presses were acquired and their mechanics learned, the next obvious step was to expand printing production and learn to produce pamphlets, journals, and books. The self-help aspects of the 1960s and 1970s feminist movements were a key element in this. Skills and knowledges that had previously been coded as male were taken on by feminists who then felt a political responsibility to share their knowledge with other women.

The production of books and journals required their distribution as well as a network to publicise their existence. Women's bookstores and coffeehouse spaces emerged to fill that void. The coffeehouse/performance space could be a part of the bookstore space or a floating event in a church or community centre venue where poets, singers, musicians, and comedians could reach a feminist audience. The independent bookstore – whether 'women's' 'gay' or other served as far more than a space that housed books for purchase. In the pre-internet days, bulletin boards were literal and material, holding scraps of paper scrawled with requests for roommates, items for sale or wanted, event flyers, and political posters. The bookstore was a public space where fortuitous encounters could occur; a seemingly unlikely parallel can be drawn to Samuel Delaney's brilliant analysis in *Times Square Red/Times Square Blue* of the public space of porn theatres and sex shops in New York City as places where cross class, cross racial and cross social grouping connections were made (Delaney 1999). I would argue that for feminists the women's bookstore offered a similar dialectic of both random and directed encounters and that the loss of that space has had detrimental effects on the possibilities of community building of relations and knowledge.

The feminist bookstore was a crucial site for transmitting local and national information beyond the bookshelves. The physical location drew visitors from out of town as well as connected women from the same area who might not have met each other in other venues. A national network of book sellers and event promoters communicated with each other through word of mouth and eventually through two crucially important movement publications: Carol Seajay's *Feminist Bookstore News* and Toni Armstrong's *Hot Wire Magazine*.

The imperative to speak the unspoken in the service of creating positive social change is what drove the creation of the plethora of journals, small presses, chapbooks, 'zines, the development of feminist, gay, and/or ethnically based community archives to disseminate and preserve that speech. The grassroots network of feminist women who established a base for literature and criticism that previously no mainstream publishers would touch was one of the most significant accomplishments of the post-Civil Rights women's movement in the United States. The underlying ethic of this kind of knowledge production is communal political and cultural growth; its goal is not financial profit or credentialisation. Women with extremely limited economic resources stole hours from the clerical, organising, or low-status academic jobs worked for survival and created journals, novels, and poetry chapbooks, bookstores, presses, coffeehouses, and cultural festivals. Community-based work that overlaps but exceeds academic spaces has been a critical and often unremarked on force in developing anti-racist and anti-colonial consciousness.

This is not to say that its participants were all anti-racist and anti-colonial, far from it, but that building skills and infrastructure intended to provide space for sharing a plurality of women's voices provided a space for Indigenous women's work that did not exist in the same way elsewhere, and that did not exist for Indigenous men.

Iowa City, Iowa might seem like an unlikely home for lesbian feminism, but it gathered writers and activists who produced powerful conferences like the 1989 Parallels and Intersections: Racism and Other Forms of Oppression, and created and maintained a lesbian collective journal of prose, poetry, and art with national circulation, *Common Lives/Lesbian Lives*, from 1981 to 1996.

Paula Gunn Allen's poem 'Some like Indians Endure' was published in *Common Lives/Lesbian Lives*[1] in 1982 and her angry response to the editors' omission of her Indian identity in their bio of her followed shortly (Allen 1982a). She noted that this omission changed the readers' understanding of the poem, making it seem like just another example of non-Indian gay and lesbian cultural appropriation (Allen 1982b). Perhaps somewhat ironically, the poem's next publisher was gay white male anthropologist Will Roscoe in his anthology *Living the Spirit* (1988). Roscoe's (1988) *OUT/LOOK National Gay and Lesbian Quarterly*[1] article on 'The Zuni Man-Woman' was scathingly critiqued by editorial board member Ramon Gutiérrez in his response 'Must We Deracinate Indians to Find Gay Roots?' (Gutierrez 1989).

In response to the colonial stigma against and erasure of both women's power and non-heteronormative gender and sexuality formations, Allen offered a valorisation of what she describes as a 'ceremonial lesbian', or 'medicine dyke' in her widely influential 1986 book *The Sacred Hoop: Recovering the Feminine in American Indian Traditions*, claiming a correlation between non-heteronormative identities and spiritual power and leadership, rather than marginalisation or scorn (Allen 1986). Significantly, like the majority of her work, this book was not published by an academic press, but by one known for its social justice advocacy, the Unitarian Universalist Beacon Press. Like other work produced on the margins, *The Sacred Hoop* saw heavy use in classrooms within the academic institutions that would not have been willing or able to produce it.

Along with the decolonising emphases of Allen's reframing comes an echo of the 1970s lesbian feminist reversal of stigma embodied in the iconic and multiply awarded lesbian feminist poet and critic Adrienne Rich's formulation of 'compulsory heterosexuality' and the existence of 'a lesbian continuum' on which all women lie (Rich 1980). Rather than being 'unwomanly', peripheral to the women's movement, and/or a 'lavender menace' lesbians were framed as the most woman-loving and the most politically woman-identified women (Rich 1980). Similarly, Allen posited special and superior qualities for these roles across tribal nations. Subsequent critics have questioned the simplicity and homogeneity of this salvo, yet at the same time I think it is important to remember the contexts of erasure and contempt that these reclamation and revision projects grew from. In the United States, it was community-based political movements – Black Power, AIM, Gay Liberation, Women's Liberation, Anti-War, and Anti-poverty that enabled the racism, colonialism, and misogyny shaping canonical knowledge formation in the academy to become more widely apparent.

Allen's partnership with white working-class poet Judy Grahn in the 1980s included their hosting of weekly women's spirituality discussions on Sundays at Mama Bear's Bookstore (1983–2003) a lesbian feminist bookstore/café/cultural space on the Berkeley/ Oakland border. Mama Bear's was founded by Alice Molloy and Carol Wilson after a contentious split between workers in their first bookstore collective I.C.I-A Woman's Place Bookstore and a lockout resulting in arbitration and litigation. Allegations of racism and conflicts over versions of feminism shaped the split, which resulted in the existence of two different stores. The original Woman's Place basement housed the Women's Press Collective, publisher of works by collective members Willyce Kim, Pat Parker and Wendy Cadden along with Judy Grahn (Cutler 2015).

While Allen had a career inside academia where she built recognition of the existence of American Indian literature as well as her community-based work, Beth Brant /Degonwadonti (Bay of Quinte Mohawk) and Chrystos (Menominee) were two of the Indigenous women writers whose work was only widely circulated and made legible through the existence of lesbian feminist publishing networks crossing the US and Canada borders. 'Women's bookstores' always meant feminist bookstores, substantially but by no means solely lesbian-feminist. This kind of categorical elision allowed the genre of 'women's music' to be described as such when its demographics were largely lesbian and predominantly white (Reagon 1983).

Beth Brant's work was first widely circulated through *Sinister Wisdom*, a literary journal of primarily lesbian writers, poets, critics, and artists, which at the time of this writing has survived 44 years past its origin in this era, through 114 issues and 13 editors, maintaining a commitment to racial, ethnic, class, and age diversity throughout its publishing history. In 1982, editors Michelle Cliff and Adrienne Rich encouraged Brant to compile and edit the first anthology of contemporary American Indian women's writing, *A Gathering of Spirit: Writings and Art by North American Indian Women*, which like other path-making work was printed as a special double edition (Brant 1983) before being produced as a book (Brant 1984). In a circle of return, *Sinister Wisdom*'s most recent double issue is the anthology *A Generous Spirit: Selected Work by Beth Brant*, edited by Janice Gould, who passed away shortly after its completion (Gould 2019). Gould was a personal friend of Brant's, while the author of the anthology's afterword Deborah Miranda never met her in life, but both were profoundly impacted by Brant's work and by this writing, this evidence of existence.

The power of these anthologies is rooted in a history where small press anthologies have had an enormous impact in both coalescing (feminist) communities and making the analyses of/from those communities legible to others. In the United States, *This Bridge Called My Back: Writings by Radical Women of Color* (Moraga and Anzaldua 1981) amplified and spread the formation 'women of colour' as a political identity and locus of production throughout academic and non-academic space. American Indian women were present in that early formation through the work of Barbara Cameron (Hunkpapa Lakota, Fort Yates band), Chrystos, and the former Anita (now Max) Valerio (Blackfoot), while co-editors Cherrie Moraga and Gloria Anzaldua addressed Indigeneity through Chicana lenses.

Chrystos's poems 'I Don't Understand Those Who Have Turned Away from Me' and 'Ceremony for Completing a Poetry Reading' in *This Bridge* reflect her passionate and ambivalent relationship with feminist community (Moraga and Anzaldua 1981: 68, 191–2). It was Chrystos who put Indigenous issues front and centre into lesbian feminist networks through her prolific writing, speaking, and activism. Often the sole voice speaking about sovereignty and land struggles within lesbian feminist circles, she was angry at these absences. As a poor/working-class lesbian she gained cultural capital through the circulation of her poetry and her readings but financially supported herself for many years by working as a maid for a wealthy Bainbridge Island household. At Out/Write 90, the first national lesbian and gay writer's conference created by *OUT/LOOK National Gay and Lesbian Journal*[1] that I coordinated while a graduate student, she told me that she used to turn tricks at the conference hotel in its former incarnation, to the great interest of the hotel wait staff surrounding us. She both enjoyed shocking people and was also angry that so many of the issues she wrote and spoke about were shocking to those with the privilege of never experiencing them (Hall, 1991).

Four of the five books of poetry Chrystos published were through the Vancouver-based feminist collective Press Gang in aesthetically beautiful editions designed by Val Spiedel: *Not Vanishing* (Chrystos 1988), *Dream On* (Chrystos 1991), *In Her I Am* (Chrystos 1993), and *Fire Power* (Chrystos 1995). Press Gang's publishing arm evolved from its 1974 origin as an all-women's printing trade collective that supported women's entry into the trade, to becoming a separate entity – Press Gang Publishers Feminist Cooperative – in 1989 (Wayback Machine 2002; Simon Fraser University Archives n.d.).

While Chrystos's relationship with Press Gang and the feminist publishing industry was also passionate and ambivalent, I think it is fair to say that her powerful and beautiful world-changing work would not have been fostered in any other literary context of the time in the nexus of sexism, racism, homophobia, and classism shaping the non-feminist publishing environment. Her work circulated in book, broadsheets and reading and had a profound impact on many, including Deborah Miranda (Esselen/Chumash), who later published her own pathbreaking history/poetry/memoir *Bad Indians* (Miranda 2012) with a non-academic small press. My first introduction to Miranda was through her essay on Chrystos's work, 'Dildos, Hummingbirds and Driving Her Crazy' (Miranda 2002), exploring the absence of explicit eroticism and sexuality in work by and about American Indian women. These moments of textual connection are like messages in bottles that light in the hands of those who need to read them. The work does not get canonised or reliably stay in print, and yet it circulates to be recovered.

On the East Coast, *Sister Outsider* (Lorde 1984), an anthology of speeches and essays by Audre Lorde was promoted by Nancy Bereano while an editor at the Crossing Press prior to founding her own lesbian feminist Firebrand Press in Ithaca, New York. Audre Lorde is arguably the lesbian feminist writer whose work remains in the greatest circulation (especially in contemporary social media) and whose work has been taken up within academic contexts that previously ignored its subject matter. In an article written for the Feminist Wire, an online site that "seeks to valorize and sustain pro-feminist representations and create alternative frameworks to build a just and equitable society" (n.d.: online), and thus revitalises engagement with past and present feminist analyses, Bereano noted:

> *Lorde's work was not taken seriously during her lifetime by many who now regularly sing her praises. Very few straight women, either African American or White, called her 'sister'. Political men, both African American and White, rarely included her work as they publicly deconstructed oppression. Academics, with few exceptions, did not deem her worthy of analysis or inclusion on their required reading lists. And, in the few instances where her writing received attention either literarily or politically, it was her poetry that was noted. The fact that her prose was published exclusively by small independently owned women's presses was both a result of the major houses' narrow perspective and the fact that Audre Lorde's prose, particularly her myth-shattering essays, was instrumental in framing a changing reality for many women, primarily lesbian women (a readership long dismissed by the mainstream publishing world).*

> *(Bereano 2014: online)*

In the service of reflecting on and changing realities, Firebrand published and distributed nationally and internationally over 90 books of fiction, poetry, and prose – almost a third of which were written by lesbians of colour and women from a variety of Nations – Janice Gould (Koyangk'auwi/Maidu), Beth Brant (Mohawk), Carole LaFavor (Ojibwe), Jewelle Gomez (Ioway, Wampanoag heritage) and Vickie Sears (Cherokee), as well as by Wendy Rose (Hopi/Miwok) and Anna Lee Walters (Pawnee/Otoe-Missouria) from 1985 to its closure in 2000. This is a remarkable record, and proportionally American Indian in a way that I do not think is matched by any other single small press.

There is some dissonance between Bereano's robust history of feminist activism – including anti-racist, LGBT rights, and ageing issues – and its lack of engagement with the Haudenosaunee Confederacy surrounding her, or with Indigenous politics nationally – while simultaneously providing a remarkable level of material support in publishing this work and these authors. My assumption is that this was a positive material outcome of multiculturalism discourses of the 1980 and 1990s in combination with the ethos of inclusivity embedded within a grassroots lesbian feminist movement intent on including 'all women' but that did not focus on significant constitutive structural differences, and that the US racial binary of Black and White structured her thinking even as she published works outside of that binary.

It is worth exploring the geopolitical context in which Bereano's press operated. Ithaca, New York, is in Haudenosaunee country, on the territories of the Cayuga Nation, whose members were largely driven out and dispersed to the Six Nations reserve across the Canadian border and other spaces in the United States. Although Indigenous erasure is the norm in the United States, Haudenosaunee activism and anti-Indian racism made contemporary ongoing Indigenous existence and resistance episodically newsworthy to the mainstream press in New York State, including struggles over casinos, land-claims, and disputes about Cayuga governance, as the Cayuga Nation embarked on a resettlement project in their homelands. Unlike other US locations where I have taught, in upstate New York non-Indigenous undergraduates were aware of ongoing Indigenous existence. I give this brief background to highlight that it is more difficult for politically engaged non-Indigenous activists to be unaware of contemporary Indigenous struggles in this location even as the normative erasure and placement of Indigeneity as something of the past continues to frame non-Indigenous US social justice movements.

Most relevant to this chapter, the nearby organisation NOON (Neighbors of the Onondaga Nation), a group of mostly white Syracuse area residents who felt some responsibility to learn about the histories and needs of the Onondaga whose land they occupy, created a well-attended educational speaker series that included dialogues between Sally Roesch Wagner, a white feminist historian focused on the early US women's rights movement, and Jeanne Shenandoah, an esteemed midwife and Eel Clan Traditional Medicine Keeper of the Onondaga Nation (Wagner 2001; Shenandoah and Wagner 2006). Wagner has long contended that the early white women's suffrage leaders who came together at Seneca Falls for their famous initial convention were inspired by the Haudenosaunee women whose powerful presence and respected social roles they were witnessing in neighbouring Haudenosaunee communities. The interesting question for me is how does this conversation disappear, and why has Wagner's work in *Sisters in Spirit* (2001) not been taken up for further exploration, or even just dispute by white feminist activists in the area?

Certainly, political passion and commitment to ideals of social justice was the fuel of lesbian feminist work, not professional advancement or monetary gain. Lack of material resources meant that undercapitalisation was an ongoing threat to the most successful of feminist presses, due to the absurd economics of bookselling in which production costs and payments are so widely separated (Miller 2006). In another moment of unexpected juxtaposition, it was the popularity of cartoonist and now MacArthur award-winning graphic novelist Alison Bechdel's community-inspired 'Dykes to Watch Out For' (Queer Comics Database) comic collections that in many ways subsidised Firebrand Press's production of less commercially sustainable work. Vermont-based Bechdel's work explored the relationships between a wide range of characters, whose ages, physical abilities, size, racial, sexual, gender, political identities presented the best of lesbian feminist communal possibilities, warts and all, with humour and complexity. But with all its attention to the anti-racist and anti-imperialist political lives and commitments of its multiple characters, there was still an Indigenous absence.

Some of these absences were filled from other unexpected places – the small presses responsible for the circulation of Indigenous women's writing in the United States were of course not limited to lesbian feminist publishing, but what they all shared was an interest in analyses that would benefit social justice movements, not a focus on scholarly disciplinary norms. Three of the most influential non-fiction books by Indigenous women who held tenured positions in the academy, yet whose political, cultural and intellectual work exceeded those confines are Haunani-Kay Trask's *From A Native Daughter: Colonialism and Sovereignty in Hawai'i* (1993); Paula Gunn Allen's *The Sacred Hoop: Recovering the Feminine in American Indian Traditions* (1986), and Deborah Miranda's *Bad Indians* (2012).

Trask's book was first published in 1993 by the Maine-based Common Courage Press, whose mission stated:

> *By publishing books for social justice, Common Courage Press helps progressive ideas to find a place in our culture. The press provides a platform to spread these ideas to activists and ordinary citizens alike. It has sold a total of over one million copies since its founding in 1991, and its books have been translated and reprinted in 24 countries. ... More important, the press has given a voice to people and organizations who might otherwise never have been heard, and inspired many who might otherwise have stayed silent.*
>
> *(Wayback Machine 2006: online)*

It took another six years for a revised edition of *From A Native Daughter* to be published by a university press (Trask 1999).

As mentioned earlier, Allen's *Sacred Hoop* (1986) was published by the Unitarian Universalist Church's Beacon Press, who describes its work as:

> An independent publisher of serious non-fiction. Our books often change the way readers think about fundamental issues; they promote such values as freedom of speech and thought; diversity, religious pluralism, and anti-racism; and respect for diversity in all areas of life.
>
> *(Beacon Press n.d.: online)*

Most recently, Deborah Miranda published her book *Bad Indians* (2012) with Heyday Press, self-described as:

> An independent, non-profit publisher founded in 1974 in Berkeley, California. We are a diverse community of writers and readers, activists and thinkers. Heyday promotes civic engagement and social justice, celebrates nature's beauty, supports California Indian cultural renewal, and explores the state's rich history, culture, and influence. Heyday works to realize the California dream of equity and enfranchisement.
>
> *(Heyday Press 2015–2020: Online)*

I record so much of these presses' mission statements here both to highlight emphases on equity, enfranchisement, and social justice inspiration motivating their work and to raise the question of how those qualities do or do not impact academic publishing. The editors of those presses may not have known much if anything about the intricacies of American Indian gendered roles, Hawaiian sovereignty or California Indian resistance to the Missions prior to taking on these projects that have inspired so many field-changing conversations in the academy and activist inspiration beyond, but their commitment to social change created a platform for this work.

There is a great deal of excellent work produced through academic publishing networks whose authors are motivated by those goals, but the academic systems of validation of that work do not address those goals as centrally important, if addressing them at all. Authors holding those values thus have to work against a structural grain to publish within those contexts. Upholding disciplinary norms that are indifferent to if not actively hostile toward social change (i.e. activist) oriented work is another layer of work that can impede the development of analyses that can change practices in the world.

Conclusion: Genealogies of knowledge and the need to support non-academic sites of knowledge production

In a genealogical web of knowledge there is no 'either/or' but only 'which and when'.

If, as I have argued elsewhere, the bedrock of knowledge is relationship, it behooves us as critical thinkers to expand our relationships – personal, political, historical, and citational.

In 2015, Eve Tuck, K. Wayne Yang, and Rubén Gaztambide-Fernández offered an interactive intervention highlighting the politics of citation through the *Critical Ethnic Studies Journal* blogsite (Tuck, Yang, and Gaztambide-Fernández 2015).

For those of us with academic jobs there are under-used opportunities to materially support the existence and survival of community-based spaces of knowledge production, whether committing to ongoing use of small press books on your syllabi, ordering those books from independent booksellers and distribution, hosting talks and event at community centres, group-sourcing larger honoraria for non-academic artists and intellectuals to speak on campus. In times of precarity it is often difficult to focus on what power and resources are available to be shared out and down hierarchies of knowledge but this is essential to building those better relationships – personal, political, historical, and citational.

Consider the affiliations, not the flattening, produced by the formations 'women of colour' and 'Indigenous women' that can cross communities productively, where lateral relations can allow space for nuance and interconnectedness along with difference. Genealogies are the opposite of silos – they are assertions of connection, unexpected or otherwise.

Genealogies are material and spiritual. In the bookstores that have now shut down, I gathered copies of journals from the used shelves and squirreled them away. I have copies of *Common Lives/Lesbian Lives*, of *Sinister Wisdom*, of all the editions of *A Gathering of Spirit*, American and Canadian, including one in which I only just discovered while writing this essay was inscribed from Beth Brant to her editors. Writing about Beth I thought of heart-breaking words shared by her grandson at the memorial held for her (Smith 2015) at the Native Centre of Toronto in October 2015, when he recounted that she had stopped writing in the last years of her life and felt as if she had been forgotten. The audience held up our hands to her family and told them she was never forgotten and will not be. As I continued to finish this chapter, Deborah Miranda was posting her recent interview with Cassidy Scanlon of the Lambda Literary Organization 'Deborah Miranda on A Generous Spirit: Selected Works by Beth Brant' that cited these words from Miranda's afterword: "*Beth Brant helped save my life. I never met Beth Brant. Both of these things are true*" (Scanlon 2020: online).

In my classrooms I now ask students to conceive of themselves as part of a genealogy of knowledge – as producers and holders of the knowledge received and developed in our course work and as transmitters of that knowledge gained from those who came before and those who are still with us. I ask them to think about what their responsibility to that knowledge is, being careful to clarify that I do not know the answer to that question for them, that only they can come to know their own answer. I ask this question of myself and now, to you.

Note

1 Notably, many of the print publications referenced in this article have now been digitally archived. These include: *OUT/LOOK National Gay and Lesbian Quarterly*, which has been archived at https://voices.revealdigital.org/?a

=cl&cl=CL1&sp=BHCIGIIH&ai=1&e=--------en-20--1--txt-txIN--------------1; *Diseased Pariah News* (the first 8 issues, only), which has been archived at https://web.archive.org/web/20160624103522/http://www.diseasedpariahnews.com/; *Diseased Pariah News*, which has been archived at https://archive.org/details/diseased-pariahnews/DPN%20001/mode/2up; *Hot Wire Magazine*, which has been archived through the Women's Music Archives/History at http://www.hotwirejournal.com/hwmag.html; and *Common Lives/Lesbian Lives*, which has been archived at https://voices.revealdigital.org/?a=cl&cl=CL1&sp=ICDEABE&ai=1&.

References

Allen, P.G. (1982a). 'Some like the Indian endure', *Common Lives/Lesbian Lives*, vol 1, no 3: 75–78.

Allen, P.G. (1982b). 'Letter from Paula Gunn Allen', *Common Lives/Lesbian Lives*, vol 2, no 1: 109–110.

Allen, P.G. (1986). *The Sacred Hoop: Recovering the Feminine in American Indian Traditions*. Beacon Press: Boston, MA.

Beacon Press. (n.d.). 'History and mission'. Available: http://www.beacon.org/Assets/ClientPages/History.aspx, accessed 23 February 2020.

Bereano, N.K. (2014). 'Dismantling the master's house', *The Feminist Wire*. Available: https://www.thefeministwire.com/2014/02/dismantling-the-masters-house/, accessed 23 February 2020.

Brant, B. (ed.) (1983). 'A gathering of spirit: writing and art by North American Indian women', *Sinister Wisdom* (Special issue), vol 22/23.

Brant, B. (ed.) (1984). *A Gathering of Spirit: Writing and Art by North American Indian Women*. Sinister Wisdom Books: Rockland, ME.

Chrystos. (1988). *Not Vanishing*. Press Gang Publishers: Vancouver, BC.

Chrystos. (1991). *Dream On*. Press Gang Publishers: Vancouver, BC.

Chrystos. (1993). *In Her I Am*. Press Gang Publishers: Vancouver, BC.

Chrystos. (1995). *Fire Power*. Press Gang Publishers: Vancouver, BC.

Cutler, W.J. (2015). 'Lesbian feminism in practice: I.C.I. A woman's place bookstore', *Trivia: Voices of Feminism*, vol 17. Available: https://www.triviavoices.com/radical-lesbian-feminism-in-practice.html#.XlL6_WhKjIV, accessed 23 February 2020.

Delany, S.R. (1999). *Times Square Red, Times Square Blue*. NYU Press: New York.

Deloria, P.J. (2004). *Indians in Unexpected Places*. University Press of Kansas: Lawrence, KS.

Gould, J. (ed.) (2019). 'A generous spirit: Selected work by Beth Brant', *Sinister Wisdom* (Special issue), vol 114.

Gutierrez, R.A. (1989). 'Must we deracinate Indians to find gay roots?', *OUT/LOOK National Gay and Lesbian Quarterly*, vol 1, no 4: 61–67.

Hall, L.K. (1991). 'Chock-full of irony: multiculturalism and the organizing of out/write 90', *OUT/LOOK National Gay and Lesbian Quarterly*, vol 4, no 2: 17–27.

Hall, L.K. (1993). 'Compromising positions', in B. Thompson and S. Tyagi (eds.) *Beyond A Dream Deferred: Multicultural Education and the Politics of Excellence*, 1st ed. University of Minnesota Press: Minneapolis, MN, 162–176.

Hall, L.K., Lee, A.W., Morgensen, S., and Wesley, D. (2017). 'Struggles of memory against forgetting – the AKIN project: Mapping activist relationships in time and place', *Presentation at the 9th Annual Native American and Indigenous Studies Association Meeting, June 22–24*, University of British Columbia, Vancouver, BC.

Heyday Books. (2015-2020). 'Our mission'. Available: https://heydaybooks.com/about/, accessed 23 February 2020.

Hogan, K. (2016). *The Feminist Bookstore Movement: Lesbian Antiracism and Feminist Accountability*. Duke University Press: Durham, NC.

Lorde, A. (1984). *Sister Outsider: Essays and Speeches*. Crossing Press: New York.

Mae, B. (1990). 'Get fat, don't die: High calorie cooking with Biffy Mae', *Diseased Pariah News*, vol 1: 23–24.

Miller, L.J. (2006). *Reluctant Capitalists: Bookselling and the Culture of Consumption*. University of Chicago Press: Chicago, IL.

Miranda, D.A. (2002). 'Dildos, hummingbirds, and driving her crazy: Searching for American Indian women's love poetry and erotics', *Frontiers: A Journal of Women Studies*, vol 23, no 2: 135–149.

Miranda, D. (2012). *Bad Indians: A Tribal Memoir*. Heyday Press: Berkeley, CA.

Moraga, C. and Anzaldua, G.E. (eds.) (1981). *This Bridge Called My Back: Writings by Radical Women of Color*, 1st ed. Persephone Press: Watertown, MA.

Morris, B.J. (1999). *Eden Built by Eves: The Culture of Women's Music Festivals*. Alyson Books: Los Angeles, CA.

Perry, D. (1993). 'Paula Gunn Allen interview', in D Perry (ed.) *Backtalk: Women Writers Speak Out*, 1st ed. Rutgers University Press: New Brunswick, NJ, 1–18.

Queer Comics Database. (n.d.). 'Dykes to watch out for'. Available: http://queercomicsdatabase.com/series/dykes-to-watch-out-for/, accessed February 23, 2020.

Reagon, B.J. (1983). 'Coalition politics: Turning the century', in B. Smith (ed.) *Home Girls: A Black Feminist Anthology*, 1st ed. Kitchen Table: Women of Color Press: New York, 357–368.

Rich, A. (1980). 'Compulsory heterosexuality and lesbian existence', *Signs*, vol 5, no 4: 631–660.

Roscoe, W. (1988). 'The Zuni man-woman', *OUT/LOOK National Gay and Lesbian Quarterly*, vol 1, no 2: 56–67.

Scanlon, C. (2020). 'Deborah Miranda on a generous spirit: Selected works by Beth Brant', *Lambda Literary*. Available: https://www.lambdaliterary.org/interviews/01/29/beth-brant/, accessed 23 February 2020.

Shenandoah, J. and Wagner, S.R. (2006). 'Visionary women: The haudenosaunee and the U.S. women's rights movement', in *Onondaga Land Rights & Our Common Future*. Syracuse Peace Council: Syracuse, NY. Available: https://www.youtube.com/watch?v=DJivmVqhAY0, accessed 23 February 2020.

Simon Fraser University Archives. (n.d.). 'Fonds F-184 press gang publishers fonds archive'. Available: https://atom.archives.sfu.ca/index.php/f-184, accessed 23 February 2020.

Smith, C. (2015). 'Writer Beth Brant's life celebrated', *Anishinabek*. Available: http://anishinabeknews.ca/2015/10/29/writer-beth-brants-life-celebrated/, accessed 23 February 2020.

Trask, H.-K. (1993). *From a Native Daughter: Colonialism and Sovereignty in Hawai'i*. Common Courage Press: Monroe, ME.

Trask, H.-K. (1999). *From a Native Daughter: Colonialism and Sovereignty in Hawai'i*, 2nd ed. University of Hawai'i Press: Honolulu, HI.

Tuck, E., Yang, K.W., and Gaztambide-Fernandez, R. (2015). 'Citations practices challenge', *Critical Ethnic Studies*. Available: http://www.criticalethnicstudiesjournal.org/citation-practices, accessed 23 February 2020.

Wagner, S.R. (2001). *Sisters in Spirit: Haudenosaunee (Iroquois) Influence on Early American Feminists*. Native Voices Books: Summertown, TN.

Wayback Machine. (2002). 'Press gang'. Available: https://web.archive.org/web/20090914053134/http:/www.collectionscanada.gc.ca/women/002026-285-e.html, accessed 23 February 2020.

Wayback Machine. (2006). 'Common courage press'. Available: https://web.archive.org/web/20071011032233/; http://www.commoncouragepress.com/index.cfm?action=about, accessed 23 February 2020.

7

Critical Indigenous methodology and the problems of history

Love and death beyond boundaries in Victorian British Columbia

David A. Chang

The day after she died, the Victoria *Evening Express* newspaper said she was "a noted Cyprian" – a prostitute – and that a botched abortion had killed her. On 26 June 1864, a 15-year-old Native Hawaiian young woman named Mary Opio died in a small house in Lekwungen territory, a 10-minute walk from the Songhees Reserve, near the harbour of Victoria on Vancouver Island. The body of Mary Opio was taken to the police court on Bastion Square for an inquest. The Crown called on coroner James Dickson to perform a post-mortem and summoned a jury of white settler 'gentlemen' to witness it. Her adoptive father, too, was summoned. His name was William Kaulehelehe. He also was Kanaka Maoli (Native Hawaiian) (Barman and Watson 2006: 174). In the end, Dickson ruled that there had been no abortion. In fact, Mary had never been pregnant. She died of pneumonia. Dickson's inquest report brought an ignoble end to the public record of Mary Opio's short life (Department of the Attorney General 1864).

There are at least two ways we might research and reflect upon about Mary Opio's death. Those ways place her death differently in space. That is, they lead to different understandings of how we might understand her relationship to the spaces around them. In my presentation today, I want to do *both* of these kinds of history so that we can understand Mary and the worlds she inhabited.

A first way to research, understand, and place her death would be through using settler-generated records, classic sources in the social history of the colonised, of the poor, of the underclass. Using the tools of the social historian – census records, police records, property maps, and more – we shed light on the oppression and misery of the slum in which Mary lived and died: Kanaka Row, an area named for Kanaka (that is, Native Hawaiians) who were an important part of its population. In Kanaka Row we see a small enclave, a place under a police microscope, a slum of horrors hemmed in by colonial power. These sources and this method are powerful for showing how colonial relations of power shaped that place and emphasise the boundedness of a hemmed-in area.

A second way to research, understand, and place Mary Opio's death is though the work of Critical Indigenous Studies, turning to the use of Indigenous language sources, and to genealogy. That methodology allows us to interrogate the categories that colonial states were placing on Indigenous people as surely as they were imposing geopolitical boundaries on them – and it allows us to see how Indigenous people frustrated both these categories and these geopolitical boundaries. These sources and this method place people in broader worlds. They leads us away from the study of just the individual (a profoundly Western optic) and toward the study of relationality and of kinship – of humans to humans, of humans to other-than-human people, and of humans to the land (Moreton-Robinson 2017; Rifkin 2011; Simpson 2014; Brooks 2018, Chang 2019; Dietrich 2017). It shows us how, through relationality, they exceeded and transgressed the categories and boundaries that settler colonial power imposed upon them.

To trace relationality, we may start with one person and then trace outward from there. I begin with Mary Opio, look at the world in which she lived, then trace connections from Mary to her adoptive father William Kaulehelehe, and then to his wife Mary Kaaiopiopio, and via her to Indigenous North American people and worlds that ran through Kanaka Row and extended far beyond it.

I have found no document of young Mary's life other than the documentation of her death. She is mentioned on no census roll or tax roll or other document I can find. But using the standard methods of social history, we can learn much from two things that are documented: her death on Humboldt Street in Victoria and the accusation that she was a prostitute. Humboldt Street was the formal name for the place known more commonly as Kanaka Row or Kanaka Road until the 1870s. It hugged the northern edge of the mud flats at the inland edge of James Bay and Victoria Harbour (Lutz et al. 2016: 5). Those flats have since been built up with landfill. Ironically, Kanaka Row would now be found under the Empress Hotel in Victoria. Indeed, it was under the reign of Victoria, namesake of both the hotel and the city, that Britain imposed its authority on the sovereign homelands of the Lekwungan Salish-speaking people of Vancouver Island.

In 1843, about seven years before Mary was born, the royally chartered Hudson's Bay Company established *Fort* Victoria in Lekwungan territory as a trading entrepot. The name 'Fort' was not entirely symbolic: a palisade surrounding the fort in an 1855 image. For some time, Lekwungan people continued to maintain a significant enough control over the area that settlers preferred to reside *inside* the fort for their own protection (Lutz et al. 2016: 4–5). The Lekwungen maintained a sizable village at the site knows as Songhees, across the bay from the fort. Setters were tolerated but were unconnected to Lekwungan and therefore unwanted by them – so settlers slept in the fort for their own protection. European settlers did, that is.

In 1850, around the time that Mary was born, about one-third of the Fort's employees were Native Hawaiian men. In 1851, Charles Bayley remarked that among the few HBC employees who lived outside the fort were "Kanack[a]s who risked their lives outside relying upon the women influence, most of them living with native women". As John Lutz puts it, "with the kin connection came security", and the Kanaka lived in a group of cottages that would eventually be known as Kanaka Row (Lutz et al. 2016: 4–5).

The name is deceiving. The area was just as much Indigenous (that is, Indigenous North American) as it was Kanaka. Remember, Hawaiians' very presence there depended on Indigenous women. This was *inter-Indigenous,* or Trans-Indigenous space (Allen 2012). That mixed, racialised character increased after 1858, when Mary was about nine years old. The Fraser River gold rush made Victoria a major provisioning and trading town for those heading to and returning from the lower mainland. The Kanaka and Native population was joined by Black people as well as new Indigenous inhabitants from other parts of the Pacific Northwest (Barman 1991: 66; Lutz et al. 2016: 4).

In short, Kanaka Row was a mixed-race slum of the racialised and the Indigenous. The Kanaka men certainly fit within the category Indigenous, but in Victoria they were after a fashion settlers on Lekwungen land. That status was altered, however, by their relations with

Native women as partners and wives. Notably, these women seem NOT to have been largely Lekwungen or even Coast Salish (wish some excpetions). So this is TransIndigenous space, but mostly a space of diasporic or displaced Indigenous people living on the land of another nation, the Lekwungen.

That space, Kanaka Row, figured most prominently in the settler press of the time as a vice district – especially a place of dancehalls, prostitution, and illegal liquor. In 1861, when Mary was about 12, the *Daily British Colonist* newspaper it was a "perfect sink-hole of iniquity", the site of fights between "squaws or squaw men", where "a continuing howling nightly is maintained by the drunken wretches who visit or occupy the miserable huts that have been erected along the bank of James Bay" (Anonomous, *The Daily British Colonist* 1861: 3). This was a profoundly racist exaggeration, but it was consistent with the image of Kanaka Row that emerge form classic documents in social history: newspaper reports, police blotters, and jail records, and police records suggest that Mary's neighbourhood was isolated, immiserated, and awash in crime.

To live on Kanaka Row in the 1860s, when Mary was a teen was to inhabit a TransIndigenous and interracial space of Indigenous Vancouver Island people, Kānaka, and black men and women. It was to be heavily policed: daily jail rosters, court reports, and newspaper stories suggest that the jail held significant numbers of Indigenous people and Hawaiians. And to live on Kanaka Row was to have one's crimes racialised and one's race (including ones racialised Indigenous status) criminalised: when a man named Nahor was arrested in 1859, he was recorded in the police ledger and the press as "Nahor, a Kanaka". And when Nahor's crime was named, it, too was racially marked: he was fined five pounds for "selling liquor to Indians" (Anonymous, *The Daily British Colonist* 1859: 3).

We are seeing the origins of the mass incarceration of Indigenous people in this story, one that predates even the creation of Canada's carceral residential school system. As in the US South, the chain gang – forced labour – was crucial here (Haley 2016; Leflouria 2015). For the mere crime of vagrancy (and to be clear, that just meant being poor and not having a settled place in the colonial order), Indigenous North American people and Kanakas regularly got two to three months on the chain gang. On page after page of the newspaper and the police records, crime was racialised and race was criminalised; crime was Indigenous and indigeneity was criminal. Mary lived in a neighbourhood in a town where a newspaper bearing the name *The Daily British Colonist* on its masthead regularly described those arrested by pejorative references to race – 'Siwash' (a racist reference to Indigenous people), 'coloured', 'Kanaka' – and reported on their sentencing to the chain gang.

The crimes for which Indigenous North American and Kanaka people were arrested, fined, and forced into prison and onto the chain gang on Kanaka Row were rarely about violence and only occasionally about theft. Instead, they centred on vagrancy and illegal buying and selling of liquor. In the latter case, race and Indigeneity were legally directly relevant, as it was illegal to sell alcohol to Indigenous people. Note that all of these behaviours were common among white settlers as well. Failed white gold miners were vagrants and whites bought, sold, and consumed alcohol openly. Yet white settlers were not policed on it to the degree of the colonialised and racialised subjects of the infant Canadian state.

What one sees here is hyper-policing consistent with what we recognise today as the actions of the carceral state. One sees the criminalisation of Indigenous and racialised people. In every and all cases, this power was gendered and sexualised. It can be seen as much in the feminisation of supposedly 'weak' and 'lazy' Native men as in the hypersexualised discourse surrounding Indigenous North American women and Hawaiian women.

This criminalisation served a purpose, of course. It made settlers and their state powerful and sought to render the colonised and the racialised powerless. Even more it created a *public theatre of domination*: the public arrests, the public labour of the chain gang building the streets, maintaining the harbour, clearing the trash of the settler town – all this was on display, and those who missed it could read about it in the *Daily British Colonist* newspaper, who reported on the courts and the chain gang. The literature to date has not made note of this, and yet it is crucially important in the way criminalisation worked in this settler colonial context. The theatre of white power and racialised and Indigenous powerlessness was at play in the way Mary Opio's death was made a spectacle.

To witness the theatre of colonial power in action on Kanaka Row, take the case of Karahua, a Native Hawaiian man whose actual name was likely Kalehua, and Kut-e-quoa, a Kwakwa̱ka̱'wakw ('Fort Rupert') woman whose name also appears as 'Kateka'. In July of 1860, Sgt. Joseph Carey, a Protestant settler from Ireland who came to Vancouver Island via the California gold rush, arrested Karahua in Kanaka Row for selling whisky to Indigenous people. But Carey was not content to leave it there. Having locked up Karahua, he returned to Kanaka Row, and told Kut-e-quoa that if she gave him sexual favours, her husband would be released. She refused, and Carey grabbed her, initiating a rape. Two neighbouring women, both Kwakwa̱ka̱'wakw and both named Mary, heard the commotion through the window, ran over, and intervened. The evidence against Carey was so strong that – remarkably – the Crown brought charges against him even though he was a white policeman and Kut-e-quoa was a Indigenous woman. (Attorney General 1860; Anonymous, 'A Charge of Attempted Rape', *The Daily British Colonist* 1860a: 3; Gosnell 1906: 471–472).

But the story still fulfilled the needs of the theatre of settler power. As the Daily Colonist pointed out, all the prosecution had as evidence against this police enforcer of colonial order was the testimony of "a few squaws". The jury therefore did not even retire to consider the case. Immediately following the end of arguments, they turned to each other in the jury. "After consulting together for about one moment, [they] returned the verdict of 'Not Guilty', without leaving their seats. The spectators, of which there were a large number fairly shook the building with their applause", pressed forward to congratulate him, and led him out in victory (Anonymous, 'Court of Assizes', *The Daily British Colonist* 1860b: 3). White men could attempt rape with impunity: the defendant, Joseph Westrop Carey, would be elected to the Victoria city council only five years later, and would become mayor in 1883 (Gosnell 1906: 473). The only danger would be to Indigenous women like Kut-e-quoa and Hawaiian women like young Mary Opio.

Here was Kanaka Row as portrayed in police records and the press and the few government records we have: an isolated place of dominated people whose misery and dissolution were the very proof of settler superiority and the legitimacy of settler power. Part of that power was to create discursive categories ('Kanaka', 'Indian', 'coloured') and to create bounded spaces such as Kanaka Row in order to border people off.

But the case of Karahue and Kut-e-quoa remind us that the people transgressed settler categories and settler boundaries and they refused helplessness. Kānaka and Indigenous people from various Nations had created community in that space. Karahua and Kut-e-quoa had a mixed household; and it was Kut-e-quoa's Indigenous women neighbours who ran to help her when Carey attacked.

Kut-e-quoa's story brings us back to Mary Opio, the young woman whose death opened this paper. They two are connected via the space of Kanaka Row, via the suspicion that Indigenous women and Kanaka women were licentious, via the violations they suffered in life and in death at the hands of settler men. But again, note, there is once again a connection that transcends the boundaries set by settlers – a connection between Native Hawaiians like Mary Opio and Indigenous people like Kut-e-quoa.

To understand these connections, we would do well to leave the practice of social history for a moment and turn to another method. We can turn to the critical Indigenous studies informed reading of the literary production of Mary's adoptive father, William Kaulehelehe. Police blotters and sensational newspapers would never suggest that the area they treated as a blighted slum produced published literature. Kaulehelehe, however, subscribed to *Ka Nupepa Kuokoa*, a Honolulu newspaper, and contributed a number of pieces to it in both prose and in verse in the 1860s and 1870s. The most extended of these was a kanikau for Mary Kaaiopiopio, his wife. A kanikau is a mourning song. These were traditionally composed as tributes after the death of a loved one and performed once by the side of the deceased. After 1830, in the independent kingdom of Hawai'i, the great majority of adults became literate in their own language. Newspapers were published weekly in Hawaiian. Soon, Kānaka started publishing kanikau, mourning chants, in the Hawaiian newspapers (Pukui et al. 1972: 1:136; Tatar 1979: 56; Brown 2014: 376–377).

And kanikau are rich sources not only for understanding life in Hawai'i. Because Kānaka in North America also compose them, they also shed light on inter-Indigenous relations and the transformation of Native Hawaiians relationship to North American spaces. From the 1840s forward, the Hudson's Bay Company hired Hawaiian men to work for its operations in North America. Dozens of men worked at Fort Vancouver, in what is now Vancouver, Washington, across the river from Portland, Oregon. These men were causing trouble, fighting, and drinking. The HBC hit upon the idea of hiring a Hawaiian lay minister and teacher and clerk to bring their workers under control. They hired Kaulehelehe, and he and and his wife, Mary Kaaiopiopio, moved to Fort Vancouver. There they remained until 1860. Eleven years earlier, the United States and the Crown of Great Britain had signed the treaty establishing the 49th parallel as the US-BC border. The United States wanted the HBC (seen as a foreign agent) out of the United States, and so Kaulehelehe and Mary Kaaiopiopio had to go. When they would not leave, American soldiers burned their house down. And so, like many others from Fort Vancouver, they moved to the newly important post of Fort Victoria. There, Kaulehelehe lived in Kanaka Row and continued his work at the HBC (Barman and Watson 2006: 303).

Here we see an Indigenous worker whose life is defined by the HBC and by the changing borders of settler colonialism in North America. This fits comfortably with the view of Kanaka Row as a circumscribed and isolated place.

But a look at Kaulehelehe's published pieces transforms our understanding of his world, and indeed, of the mixed Indigenous North American-Kanaka world he inhabited. Kaulehelehe wrote a couple short prose articles and several kanikau – including one for King Kamehameha IV and for Prince Albert Kauikeaouli (K[aulehele] 1862: 1; Kualehelehe [sic] 1864: 1); The most extended of these, however, was a kanikau for his wife, Mary Kaaiopiopiooopiopio (generally called Mary Kaai). This 355-line kanikau stretches for 3,203 words. It is an epic and deeply moving song of aloha for his beloved and departed Mary Kaaiopiopio. (Kaulehelehe 1866: 1).

It is one of a number of kanikau for deceased female partners were written by nineteenth-century Kanaka men on the west coast of North America from British Columbia down to California. Kaulehelehe's kanikau for Mary Kaaiopiopio differs from all the others I have found it that he composed it for a Hawaiian woman. Most of the rest – about 10 – memorialise Indigenous North American women. Many of the Native Hawaiian men who stayed for many years or the rest of their lives in BC and down the West Coast formed families with Indigenous North American women. Kanikau for them demonstrate the bonds between Kānaka and Indigenous people from North America.

In contrast, Kaulehelehe's lament memorialises a Hawaiian woman, but it still illustrates how connected Kānaka were to Indigenous people and places in North America. These mourning songs reveal the emergence of ties to Indigenous North Americans that challenge our assumptions about spaces and lives.

> The kanikau begins with a simple declaration of its purpose:
> He Kanikau aloha keia nou,
> E Mary L. Kaaiopiopio Moeahiilani.

Having identified itself is a loving song of mourning for her, it begins the task one sees in many kanikau took on: lamenting the dead by narrating the places that mattered to them. In this kind of kanikau, the composer gives the deceased a narrated tour of these sites of connection. And for Mary Kaai, these are the sites that are mentioned. All of them are in what we now call the Pacific Northwest, but there are two major groupings. The first centres on Fort Vancouver, in Oregon (where Mary Kaai and William Kaulehelehe long lived) and stretches out along the Columbia River, Snake River, and Willamette River valleys. Her soul flies to "the tumult of the mountains of Oregon", she regards the birds at Yamhill, Oregon, feels the air that is stirred into eddies by the wind from Walla Walla, and senses as the wind stills in the Willamette Valley. Her spirit travels the length of the Tillamook Plain, ascends the Calapooya Mountains, descending at the Molalla River, in what is now the lands of the Confederated Tribes of Grand Ronde.

Mary Kaaiopiopio's spirit is flying across a vast geography. What is this region, and what does it mean that Mary Kaaiopiopio visits its mountains, valleys, forests, and rivers, regards it birds, and feels its winds? Kaulehelehe repeatedly calls this region Nouaiki and Keomolewa. Nouaiki is one of the oldest foreign terms in Hawaiian, and is a Hawaiianization of the word Northwest. The other word, Keomolewa, is an archaic Hawaiian pronunciation of Columbia. It refers to the whole watershed of the Columbia River, and beyond. In fact, we see that the geography of Keomolewa as traced by the travels of Mary Kaaiopiopio's spirit resembles the Columbia District of the Hudson's Bay Company. In some ways, this is a colonial geography defined by colonial trade.

But in other ways, it is not. It is a clearly Indigenous geography. All of these sites are what we would call ʻāina in Hawaiian – that is, lands. And all of these ʻāina have their own kama, children. In Hawaiian terms, the kamaʻāina of these lands are their Indigenous people. And especially in the context of the mid-19th-century experiences which Mary Kaaiopiopio and Kaulehelehe shared there, to evoke these lands is to evoke their Indigenous peoples.

This becomes especially clear when we remember that Mary Kaaiopiopio's spirit is not just wandering aimlessly through Keomolewa, the Columbia Country. Rather, it is the composer's responsibility to help to guide her spirit to its destination. It floats up from Kanaka Row, over James Bay, all around Keomolewa, and where does it go?

> Hele aku la ka uhane kuu wahine,
> I ka le-ale-a a hooipo me mauna Ruda (Hood)
> Ho-i no ka Uhane i ke ao-maluna.

Kaulehelehe declares that the spirit of his beloved wife (or woman) was going forth to be a sweetheart (hoʻoipo) with Mount Hood as it returned to 'the world above'. That final phrase makes a reader expect an entry into heaven will follow, which would be a fitting Christian finale to this kanikau, given Kaulehelehe's status as a Christian lay preacher. And yet, the kanikau takes a different turn:

> E ku ana ka Uhane iluna o ka mauna Pohaku
> E kahea iho ana i ke kini o Keomolewa,

Mary's spirit stands atop Stone Mountain, Oregon, and calls down to the 'kini' (the thronging multitude) of Keomolewa (the Columbia River area, and the Northwest more broadly). Neither she nor Kaulehelehe is not addressing a Christian god above. Instead, they address the people of Keomolewa:

> E hoolale iho ana i kolaila kini,
> E ho-a ke ahi e e ho-a ke a-hi,
> E ho-a ke ahi i mehana ka hale....

They provoke the many people of that place to kindle a fire to warm the house. This is not a Christian heaven, and the people that are being called forth to make the fire are not settlers, but Indigenous people:

> Nou ka ka Uhane i ke aluka Ilikini,
> Ke uluao-a la i na kuahiwi o Oregona,
> E walea'na paha i ka puili olele.
> O ke ola no ia o ke kini o Nouaiki.

Mary's soul is in 'the Indian crowd' up in the mountains of Oregon, enjoying the sounds of rattle music: a place that Kaulehelehe declares to be truly the life of the 'the Northwest's multitude'.

Kaulehelehe traces the path for Mary Kaaiopiopio's spirit, the path to where he believes she belongs: high in the mountains of the Northwest "with the multitude that is native to that place" – that is, with the spirits of the kama'āina of that 'āina: the Native people of the land. Her spirit belongs 'in the Indian crowd', enjoying the sound of Indigenous rattle music. And when Kaulehelehe says that *this* is the *true* life of the Northwest's multitude, he reveals how he understands the Northwest and Keomolewa. At its truest, it is not a settler Northwest. It is not the commercial Columbia of the HBC. It is an Indigenous space.

Moreover, in the next stanza, Kaulehelehe tells Mary Kaaiopiopio that when her spirit joins the Indian crowd, Her spirit will rejoin the spirit of their beloved and deceased adoptive daughter – Mary Opio, the 15-year-old woman whose death opened this paper.

> Hiki pu mai no me ko maka'loha;
> O ka maka'loha o kuu kaikamahine ...

Indigenous space, the space of the kama'āina, of the Indian – this is the space where the diasporic spirits of Kānaka belong.

Lest we imagine that Kaulehelehe's engagement with Indigenous people and Indigenous space is merely figurative, imaginary, and perhaps even appropriative, let us return to his kani-kau. In it, there appear several passages in the voices of other people, all speaking in Hawaiian. Miss Esther Jolibois, Miss Jane Goudie, Miss Mary Goudie all address Mary Kaai as 'makuahine hānai', or adoptive mother. Miss Kahalekai Keawe calls her "my dear elder sister". (It is not clear if Kaulehelehe is speaking in their voice, or if they composed these passages in Hawaiian themselves, or if they composed them in another language and Kaulehelehe translated them into Hawaiian.) All lament her deeply, again referring to specific places, especially those in and around Victoria – Victoria itself, Cila Hill (Cedar Hill), Bikina Hill (Beacon Hill), Vanecouva Ailana (Vancouver Island), Cadebolobe (Cadboro Bay), Saniki Akau (North Saanich), but also further up Vancouver Island, on San Juan Island, and on the Lower Mainland.

Who are these women? The careful genealogical work of Bruce McIntyre Watson makes it possible to identify them. All of these are young Indigenous women with white fathers: Esther Joiliebois' mother was Nisga'a from Nass. BC, Mary and Jane Goudie's mother was Schwayips from Colvill, in Oregon. Kahalekai Keawe was probably the daughter of a man known in Victoria as Thomas Keavē, a Hawaiian man who lived on Kanaka Row, who was married three times: once to a Saanich woman, once to a Cowichan woman, and once to an Indigenous woman whose nation was not recorded in the source I have. (The genealogical records to date have not provided these women's names, given the way they centre male settler identities. I hope to recover that information.) (Barman and Watson 2006: 309.) Note that of all these connections in Kanaka Row, only one is to a local Coast Salish person, the unnamed Saanich woman. Thus the inter-Indigenous world here seems especially connecting Hawaiian people and Indigenous people who are already away from their home – not Lekwungen people from Songhees, the Indigenous people of the place I am calling Victoria.

But outside of this kanikau, one would never know of their closeness to Mary Kaaiopiopio – that three of them considered her their mother and one called her elder sister. Moreover, we must understand that adoption is one form of a broader kind of kinship making that has been widely practiced by Indigenous people and by Native Hawaiian people, Here, we see kinship through adoption also bridging Indigenous North American communities and Native Hawaiian communities. Without using Indigenous language sources, and without understanding using Indigenous attention to genealogy and Indigenous attention to the social and political uses of adoptive kinship – without all of that critical Indigenous apparatus, one might easily miss how deeply connected Indigenous North American networks and Native Hawaiian networks became. And note especially that female-to-female inter-Indigenous networks seem to be very powerful here – networks that are, at least in my experience, entirely invisible in settler sources.

To miss these connections would be to misunderstand Kanaka Row, to see only its Kanaka distinctiveness instead of its immersion in Vancouver Island Indigenous life, indeed its emergence from Indigenous life on Lekwungen land in the broader worlds of the Coast Salish and Indigenous worlds of the Northwest. To miss these connections would be to miss the female-gendered networks that helped to create that space. To miss these connections would be to entirely miss the Indigenous social and human geography in which Kānaka like Mary Kaaiopiopio were embedded. To miss those connections would mean having one's vision mostly limited to the view of Kanaka Row that we gained from police files, census documents, HBC archives, and newspaper stories.

There is much to be gained from that latter view. It speaks powerfully to the present by showing us the nineteenth-century roots of contemporary phenomena: a dynamic urban Indigenous life; the hyper-policing of Indigenous and racialised communities, the way that gender and sexuality stand at the centre of that policing; the mass incarceration of Indigenous people; and the political uses of the theatre of power that mass incarceration represents. All these come into our sights thanks to those standard social historical methods and sources, once they are combined with critical insights from carceral studies, feminist studies, critical legal studies, and critical geography. They reveal to us with startling clarity the operation of power over Indigenous and racialised people.

But what they do not adequately show us is the way that the Indigenous objects of power evaded that power in ways the powerful never fully realised – evaded the boundaries that settler colonial power established. It takes a critical Indigenous studies approach to insist that we use Indigenous-generated sources, understand their meaning in their changing cultural and historical context, and analyse them according to categories that are most relevant – in this case, critical geography and mo'okū'auhau, or genealogy. Kaulehelehe's kanikau and the eruption into it of the voices of Indigenous North American and Hawaiian women recast our views of the lives and deaths of Mary Opio and Mary Kaaiopiopio.

Both of these kinds of ways of researching Kanaka Row are important. The first helps us understand systems of power that police, incarcerate, racialise, and sexualise, and isolate Indigenous individuals and communities. But the second gives us inspiration for resisting those systems of power. Critical Indigenous studies, bringing research, theory, and Indigenous language together in ways that interrogate and challenge colonial categories rather than merely deploying them, help Indigenous people and their allies with a crucial task: to demonstrate ways that Indigenous ancestors – whether they be our genetic ancestors or not – found ways to push beyond the limitations that powers placed on them. Creating connections between Indigenous peoples, asserting that indigeneity is both grounded in spaces in broad in its reach – this is a politics that is liberatory. This is the politics of critical Indigenous studies, and as the lives and deaths of the people of Kanaka Row show us, it is deeply rooted in the thinking, the writing, the family-making of Indigenous ancestors.

References

Allen, C. (2012). *Trans-Indigenous Methodologies for Global Native Literary Studies*. University of Minnesota Press: Minneapolis, MN.

Anonymous. (1859). 'Nahor, a Kanaka', *The Daily British Colonist*, September 23: 3.

Anonymous. (1860a). 'A charge of attempted rape', *The Daily British Colonist*, July 31: 3.

Anonymous. (1860b). 'Court of assizes', *The Daily British Colonist*, August 11: 3.

Anonymous. (1861). 'A disorderly neighborhood', *The Daily British Colonist*, October 14: 3.

Barman, J. (1991). *The West Beyond the West: A History of British Columbia*. University of Toronto Press: Toronto, ON.

Barman, J. and Watson, B.M. (2006). *Leaving Paradise: Indigenous Hawaiians in the Pacific Northwest, 1787–1898*. University of Hawai'i Press: Honolulu, HI.

Brooks, L. (2018). *Our Beloved Kin: A New History of King Philip's War*. Yale University Press: New Haven, CT.

Brown, M.A. (2014). 'Mourning the land: Kanikau in *Noho Hewa: the wrongful occupation* of Hawai'i', *American Indian Quarterly*, vol 28, no 3: 374–395.

Chang, D. (2019). 'Transcending settler colonial boundaries with mo'okū'auhau: Genealogy as transgressive methodology', in Nālani Wilson Hokowhitu (ed.) The Past Before us: Mo'okū'auhau as Methodology. University of Hawai'i Press: Honolulu, HI, 94–105.

Department of the Attorney General, British Columbia. (1864). *Inquisitions and Inquests. Record GR-1328. Microfilm B02446. June 27, 1864*. British Columbia Archives: Victoria, BC.

Dietrich, R. (2017). 'The biopolitical logics of settler colonialism and disruptive relationality', *Cultural Studies ↔ Critical Methodologies*, vol 17, no 1: 67–77.

Gosnell, R.E. (1906). *A History o [sic] British Columbia*. Hill Binding Co.: Chicago, IL.

Haley, S. (2016). *No Mercy Here: Gender, Punishment, and the Making of Jim Crow Modernity*. University of North Carolina Press: Chapel Hill, NC.

K[aulehelehe], W. (1862). 'He palapala no Keomolewa mai', Ka Nupepa Kuokoa, December 27: 1–2.

Kaulehelehe, W. (1866). 'He Kanikau no Mary L. Kaaiopiopio Moeahiilani,' *Ka Nupepa Kuokoa*, November 3: 1.

Kualehelehe [*sic*: Kaulehelehe], W. (1864). 'He kanikau no ka Moi Iolani', *Ka Nupepa Kuokoa*, August 20: 1.

Leflouria, T.L. (2015). *Chained in Silence: Black Women and Convict Labor in the New South*. University of North Carolina Press: Chapel Hill, NC.

Lutz, J., Lafreniere, D., Harvey, M., Dunae, P., and Gilliland, J. (2016). '"A city of the white race occupies its place": Kanaka row, Chinatown and the Indian quarter in Victorian Victoria', Unpublished manuscript.

Moreton-Robinson, A. (2017). 'Relationality: A key presupposition of an indigenous social research paradigm', in C. Andersen and J. O'Brien (eds.) *Sources and Methods in Indigenous Studies*. Routledge: New York, 69–77.

Pukui, M.K., Haertig, E.W., and Lee, C. (1972). *Nānā i Ke Kumu: Look to the Source*. Hui Hānai Press: Honolulu, HI.

Rifkin, M. (2011). *When did Indians Become Straight? Kinship, the History of Sexuality, and Native Sovereignty.* Oxford University Press: New York.

Simpson, A. (2014). *Mohawk Interruptus: Political Life Across the Borders of Settler States.* Duke University Press: Durham, NC.

Tatar, E. (1979). 'Chant', in G. Kanahele (ed.) *Hawaiian Music and Musicians: An Illustrated History.* University Press of Hawai'i: Honolulu, HI, 53–68.

8

Decolonising psychology

Self-determination and social and emotional well-being[1]

Pat Dudgeon

Introduction

This chapter focuses on a key decolonising discourse within Indigenous Australian psychology; that is, the concept of social and emotional well-being (SEWB). The sense of self that is at the centre of the SEWB model is connected to seven overlapping and inter-related domains of well-being: (1) body, (2) mind and emotions, (3) family and kinship, (4) community, (5) culture, (6) land and country, and (7) ancestors and spirituality. This model of SEWB has been developed by and for Indigenous people using participatory action research with numerous Indigenous communities across Australia (Brockman and Dudgeon 2019; Gee et al. 2014; Mia et al. 2017). A participatory action research process, informed by the *National Strategic Framework for Aboriginal and Torres Strait Islander Peoples' Mental Health and Social and Emotional Wellbeing* (AHMAC 2004; 2017), was undertaken to develop this paradigm to validate, value, and empower Indigenous life and reality. This process enacts self-determination which is fundamental in decolonising psychology and Indigenous mental health and well-being. As a relational, strengths-based discourse, SEWB affirms the collective capabilities of Indigenous communities and the protective force of cultural continuity in the face of ongoing colonisation in Australia. Similar to other colonised peoples, the processes of colonisation profoundly disrupted the cultural well-being of Indigenous Australians. Colonisation resulted in forms of historical and inter-generational trauma (Hartman et al. 2019), and has led to compounding disadvantage and exclusion across the social determinants of everyday life (Marmot 2011). Counter-colonial models of relational resilience, such as SEWB, offer paths towards collective healing.

The emergence of Indigenous psychologies across the world are part of a global self-determination movement which seeks to decolonise oppressive Western knowledge systems. The discipline of psychology and the construct of mental health are examples of a Western knowledge system. Dismantling this system includes revitalising Indigenous cultures and world-views in order to strengthen the flourishing of life for Indigenous peoples. Many Indigenous relational world-views understand that the flourishing of life, or well-being of individuals, families, and communities, includes the flourishing of culture, land, and spirituality. Indigenous concepts of relational well-being tend to be collective, holistic, and ecocentric, that are distinct from the more individualistic conceptualisations of well-being that tend to be advocated in Western psychology (White 2017).

The SEWB framework provides a critical, Indigenous discourse that challenges and interrupts Western perceptions of mental health and psychology. The SEWB model can be also be understood as a clinical tool, based on Indigenous health knowledges (Brockman and Dudgeon 2019). The SEWB model provides a culturally safe, therapeutic approach for restoring well-being and healing from historical trauma. Such healing and restoration comes out of a recognition that colonisation has had, and continues to have, destructive impacts on all aspects of life in each of the SEWB domains. Recovery and well-being are therefore facilitated by strengthening connections to each of these inter-related domains and this strengths-based focus in SEWB is essential to ensuring cultural safety (Dudgeon and Walker 2015; Dudgeon et al. 2017; 2020).

Decolonising psychology

Indigenous Australians are the traditional custodians of the land now called Australia, and are one of the earth's oldest and continuous cultures, estimated to be over 55,000 years old (Nagle et al. 2017). Indigenous knowledge systems include sophisticated therapeutic epistemologies and practices, philosophy, governance and law, agriculture, environmental science, and astronomy. Prior to the invasion of their country in 1788, Indigenous Australians had harmonious social structures, cared for a complex and diverse ecosystem, and enjoyed a flourishing and rich culture in which Elders played a vital role in the guidance, healing and governance of the community. Today Indigenous Australians experience an unusually high burden of ill-health, exacerbated by social marginalisation and poverty. The 'mental health gap' between Indigenous and non-Indigenous Australians (namely, the disproportionate rates of suicide and psychological distress) is the result of the destructive impact of settler colonisation and cultural genocide (Calma, Dudgeon, and Bray 2017: 256). Moreover, there is substantial evidence about the chronically destructive physical and psychological impacts of racism (Williams, Lawrence, and Davis 2019). Racism is therefore recognised as another strong influence in Indigenous mental health and well-being. In recent years, there have been calls to decolonise mainstream Australian psychology and affirm the role of Indigenous psychology in strengthening Indigenous social and emotional well-being (Dudgeon and Walker 2015). This movement has highlighted the relationship among psychology, racism, and colonisation.

In 2016, the Australian Psychological Society (APS) made a formal apology to Aboriginal and Torres Strait Islander peoples. This apology acknowledged that the discipline had been embedded in the colonial oppression of the original custodians of Australia. The APS apology stated: "We have not always respected [Aboriginal and Torres Strait Islander] skills, expertise, world views, and unique wisdom developed over thousands of years" (Carey et al. 2017: 265) and listed the following specific examples:

- Our use of diagnostic systems that do not honour cultural belief systems and world-views.
- The inappropriate use of assessment techniques and procedures that have conveyed misleading and inaccurate messages about the abilities and capacities of Aboriginal and Torres Strait Islander people.
- Conducting research that has benefitted the careers of researchers rather than improved the lives of the Aboriginal and Torres Strait Islander participants.
- Developing and applying treatments that have ignored Aboriginal and Torres Strait Islander approaches to healing and that have, both implicitly and explicitly, dismissed the importance of culture in understanding and promoting social and emotional well-being.

- Our silence and lack of advocacy on important policy matters such as the policy of forced removal which resulted in the Stolen Generations. (Carey et al. 2017: 265)

In effect, the APS apology recognises the historical role of psychology in the colonisation of Indigenous Australians and represents an important commitment towards decolonising the discipline (Carey et al. 2017). In order to decolonise psychology, two central hegemonic processes need to be disarmed: (1) the normalisation of what are essentially ethnocentric concepts of human behaviour steeped in the ideologies of Western individualism, and (2) the marginalisation and negation of Indigenous knowledge systems and cultures (Dudgeon et al. 2014; Dudgeon and Walker 2015). There are a number of ways that these destructive colonising influences can be disarmed.

Deconstructing colonisation begins by considering how the discipline of psychology operates as a form of 'governmentality' (Rose 1996); as a way of governing, or policing, disciplining, regulating and controlling populations by ever-expanding definitions of what is coded as abnormal and normal behaviour. In other words, as many critical psychologists have argued, far from being an impartial, objective science which is altruistically dedicated to the well-being of the individual, psychology reproduces dominant power relations. As an example, feminist critiques of psychology, have drawn attention to how the history of psychology has been instrumental in oppressing women by reinforcing sexist stereotypes about the intellectual and emotional inferiority of women while obscuring the socio-economic causes of women's suffering. Rose (1996) argues that Western psychology has been involved in manufacturing certain kinds of individuals. For example, the psychological discourse of female 'hysteria' was used to pathologise women who both resisted socio-economic oppression and who suffered from the impacts of being oppressed (Usher 1991).

Indigenous standpoint theory (Foley 2002; Moreton-Robinson and Walter 2009; Rigney 1997) provides an important critical approach for unsettling the truth claims of colonial knowledges, including those made in psychology. These truth claims negated and undermined the experiences of Indigenous people, including complex histories of dispossession, their cultural expertise and knowledge systems. By challenging and interrogating representations of Indigenous people from Indigenous standpoints, the authority of colonial perspective is undone. Moreover, Indigenous standpoint theory also resists the reification of Indigenous difference by situating culturally specific critiques and acknowledging the multiplicity of Indigenous world-views and perspectives across the world. Indigenous standpoint theory deploys a tactical, oppositional, and self-reflexive essentialism which is consciously used to make space for Indigenous voices.

Using Indigenous standpoints to situate Indigenous knowledge systems enables a critical interrogation of colonial master narratives about the Indigenous Other. This calls attention to how Indigenous knowledge, bodies, and histories are thwarted by settler histories and discourses, including psychology and other social science disciplines. Central to this critical oppositional standpoint is the reclamation of Indigenous knowledge systems, Indigenous epistemologies, ontologies and axiologies which have been marginalised through settler colonisations in a process of cultural genocide. Disarming the second central hegemonic tactic of colonial psychology, namely the marginalisation and negation of Indigenous knowledge systems and cultures, can be situated within the broader project of global Indigenous self-determination and the resurgence of Indigenous research.

Although Indigenous research has a marginal presence within mainstream Western academic spaces, strong reciprocity between Indigenous researchers and the broader Indigenous community have resulted in transformative cultural impacts over the last few decades. Indigenous theorists have argued that Indigenous research is a form of counter-colonial resistance, embedded in struggles for self-determination and an expression of Indigenous knowledge systems which are integral to cultural survival and the holistic well-being of Indigenous people. Indigenous research can be perceived as "a complex decolonised approach of producing, interrogating, validating, and disseminating knowledge based on Indigenous peoples' cosmology/worldview or 'world-sense'" (Coburn 2013: 53). In Indigenous psychology, the SEWB framework can be situated as an expression of Australian Indigenous therapeutic knowledge systems and world-views.

The holistic SEWB framework differs from dominant Western approaches to health and well-being. Western approaches tend to focus on categorising and diagnosing the mental health of individuals and tend to ignore social or cultural determinants of mental health (Dudgeon and Walker 2015; Dudgeon et al. 2017). The Indigenous knowledge systems which are articulated by SEWB, especially the collective, relational and 'holistic' model of well-being, has much to offer towards decolonising psychology. Indigenous health and well-being are founded on Indigenous world-views and is an expression of Indigenous cultures and is created by and managed by Indigenous people (Dudgeon and Walker 2015). Indeed, the process of decolonising psychology requires a paradigm shift to become genuinely inclusive.

In considering the social determinants of health and mental health, the individualistic biomedical paradigms are challenged by locating well-being within cultural, biopsychosocial and spiritual approaches to individual, family and community well-being. More broadly, Indigenous psychology can be situated within a larger interdisciplinary movement to decolonise dominant disciplines. These disciplines include master narratives about Indigenous identity and colonial narratives about Indigenous histories and realities. This movement affirms the culturally distinct inter-relationships between individuals and society and illustrates how these connections are shaped and transformed by a range of cultural, political, social and historical determinants (Dudgeon and Walker 2015).

A primary goal of the decolonisation is the dismantling of racist narratives which are supported by the ideology of individualism and perpetuated by the pervasive impact of both cultural and institutionalised racism within society. Deconstructing narratives about 'racial difference' which support institutional cultures and practices is therefore critical. This dismantling process must be vigilant about avoiding universalising and essentialising Indigenous identities and cultures. By negating the diverse complexity of Indigenous experiences and voices, ethnocentrism and cultural racism can be further entrenched. Additionally, it is vital that Indigenous people determine their own methodologies and theories that counter these narratives, including what is meant by cultural resilience.

Strengthening cultural resilience can enhance the SEWB of individuals, families, and communities and a range of social determinants. Strengths-based approaches recognise the capacities of individual, families, and communities to survive adverse life events across generations and enable practitioners to build on existing capabilities. A strengths-based model of cultural resilience allows exploration of how communities have adapted to change across time while sustaining cultural practices, such as traditional healing, governance, kinship, languages and other cultural activities. This approach is central to the work of a range of Indigenous psychiatrists and psychologists (Dudgeon et al. 2014; Milroy et al. 2014).

It is essential that practitioners understand the value of cultural resilience and the SEWB framework of well-being and similarly demonstrate adequate cultural competence and safety. Cultural competence is also necessary at the level of all service providers and policymakers. This entails working in ways that are "respectful and promote cultural security and achieve improved mental health and social and emotional wellbeing outcomes" (Walker, Schultz, and Sonn 2014: 195). This requires a critical understanding of the ways in which colonisation shapes social relations and privileges certain dominant social groups over others. To this end, Indigenous psychologists have designed frameworks and tools for facilitating this decolonisation process for (non-Indigenous) practitioners to use (Walker et al. 2014). Through this process, practitioners understand the covert ways in which colonisation normalises narratives about racial differences within settler society, marginalises the voices and experiences of Indigenous people, and misrepresents the history of colonisation itself (Langton 1993). Practitioners then also understand the complexities of Indigenous mental health and well-being.

Indigenous psychology

The discipline of Indigenous psychology is an expression of the right to self-determination. The *United Nations Declaration of the Rights of Indigenous Peoples* (UNDRIP) specifically affirms the rights of Indigenous people to practice self-determination in the area of mental health:

Article 21

1. Indigenous peoples have the right, without discrimination, to the improvement of their economic and social conditions, including, inter alia, in the areas of education, employment, vocational training and retraining, housing, sanitation, health and social security.

Article 24

1. Indigenous peoples have the right to their traditional medicines and to maintain their health practices, including the conservation of their vital medicinal plants, animals and minerals. Indigenous individuals also have the right to access, without any discrimination, to all social and health services.
2. Indigenous individuals have an equal right to the enjoyment of the highest attainable standard of physical and mental health. States shall take the necessary steps with a view to achieving progressively the full realisation of this right.

Article 29

3. States shall also take effective measures to ensure, as needed, that programmes for monitoring, maintaining and restoring the health of Indigenous peoples, as developed and implemented by the peoples affected by such materials, are duly implemented. (UNDRIP 2007)

As a signatory to UNDRIP, Australia has a clear responsibility to uphold these rights. Indigenous psychology in Australia therefore has an important role to improve the social determinants of everyday life (as detailed in Article 21.1), access to traditional healing and to culturally safe, non-discriminatory mental health support (Article 24, 1, 2), and the practice of self-determination, or Indigenous control over the monitoring, maintaining and restoring of Indigenous mental health and well-being (Article 29, 3.). Internationally, the Indigenous psychology movement has also sought to strengthen mental health through the process of self-determination and decolonisation.

The global Indigenous psychology movement and discipline is represented by the American Psychological Association (APA) Indigenous Psychology Task Force (APA 2011). Decolonisation is central to this Task Force as well as the revitalisation of Indigenous knowledge systems. Four dominant features are listed by the Task Force:

1. A reaction against the colonisation/hegemony of Western psychology.
2. The need for non-Western cultures to solve their local problems through Indigenous practices and applications.

3. The need for a non-Western culture to recognise itself in the constructs and practices of psychology.
4. The need to use Indigenous philosophies and concepts to generate theories of global discourse. (2011: online)

Indigenous psychology is a form of cultural reclamation and can also be understood as cultural survival. The practice, theory, and science of Indigenous psychology unsettles colonisation, while re-centering Indigenous knowledge (Kovach 2009). By supporting and developing culturally appropriate healing, Indigenous psychology is engaged in restoring therapeutic practices and knowledges which have been marginalised and suppressed. In other words:

> [t]he task of decolonising psychology, then, is not only about divesting from Eurocentric paradigms that have controlled and limited Indigenous well-being, but producing new paradigms underpinned by Indigenous knowledges'. In this context ... [t]he Indigenous paradigm of SEWB is both a new therapeutic practice and theory of well-being.
>
> *(Dudgeon et al. 2017: 322)*

Social and emotional well-being

Indigenous psychology affirms Indigenous people's collective cultural understandings of well-being. SEWB recognises strength-based Indigenous knowledge systems that are vital to cultural survival. SEWB, as discussed here, is a discourse of holistic health and mental health collectively created, articulated and formulated in Indigenous health and mental health policy and practice (Swan and Raphael 1995) and further validated by numerous Indigenous communities through a rigorous participatory process (Brockman and Dudgeon 2019; Dudgeon et al. 2014; Mia et al. 2017). The SEWB framework is fundamental to any understanding of individual, family, and community health. As Swan and Raphael stated Indigenous health is understood as:

> Holistic, encompassing mental health and physical, cultural and spiritual health. Land is central to well-being. This holistic concept does not merely refer to the 'whole body' but in fact is steeped in the harmonised inter-relations which constitute cultural well-being. These inter-relating factors can be categorised as largely spiritual, environmental, ideological, political, social, economic, mental and physical. Crucially, it must be understood that when the harmony of these inter-relations is disrupted, Indigenous ill health will persist.
>
> *(1995: 19)*

As this formative definition of holistic health makes clear, an understanding of the inter-relations between categories of cultural well-being is vital. Another way of understanding these inter-relations is through the concept of relationality.

Relationality is critical to Indigenous scholarship (Moreton-Robinson 2017). A central focus of this growing Indigenous scholarship is the unsettling of destructive colonial systems through the resurgence of relational life-affirming Indigenous knowledge systems (Yap and Yu, 2016). These relational knowledge systems are understood to have ontological and epistemological dimensions, interconnected ways of being, doing and knowing grounded in dynamic connections with 'Place-Thought'; "the premise that that land is alive and thinking" (Watts 2013: 21). Another way of putting this is that Indigenous relationality is *axiological*; they are expressions of an ethics of relationality which, in the context of the ongoing colonisation of Indigenous people, is by necessity a decolonial axiological relationality. Indigenous relationality is about the practice of an ethical harmonious life, with the land, culture, and spirituality. This is facilitated through the practice of self-determination which is also a health practice, a relational ontology and epistemology of well-being. The conception of SEWB discussed here outlines an axiology of relational well-being or guide for living well – linked to self-determination and Indigenous governance and based on Indigenous knowledge systems. SEWB provides a guiding framework for holistic cultural living, and is a solution and intervention to trauma and loss (Gee et al. 2014; Dudgeon et al. 2014).

The definition of Australian Indigenous health is a holistic notion with the health and social and well-being of individuals and communities linked to their "control over their physical environment, of dignity, of community self-esteem, and of justice" (NAHS Working Group 1989: ix). This concept has significantly influenced the discourse about Indigenous mental health and well-being over the past 25 years. SEWB is a positive state of mental health associated with a strong and sustaining cultural identity, community, and family life that provides a source of strength against adversity, poverty, neglect, and other challenges of life (National Mental Health Commission Australia 2013). The SEWB framework, including the model of the seven domains of well-being discussed below, continues to be developed by Indigenous psychologists, inspired by the previous work in the *Ways Forward Report* (Swan and Raphael 1995) and the *Framework for Aboriginal and Torres Strait Islander Peoples' Mental Health and Social and Emotional Wellbeing* (2004). Through relationality, it can be understood that identity is embedded in the inter-related well-being domains of the body, mind, kinship, community, culture, country, and spirituality (see Figure 8.1; Social Health Reference Group, 2004; Gee et al. 2014). Understanding that all of the seven domains of SEWB are inter-related is important.

The following provides a description of the inter-related, or rather the *relational*, complexity of the well-being domain of the country:

> Connection to Country involves a person's spirit, which comes from Country, becoming the central identity of that person and, as they grow, the protector and guardian of his or her Country. When a person passes, the spirit returns to its Dreaming place to become a child spirit again, awaiting another spiritual rebirth, thus connecting Country with people, their Dreaming place, language, kinship systems, and law and culture.

(Dwyer cited in Salmon et al. 2019: 5)

This description highlights how the relational domain of country encompasses a connection to other domains, namely to the domains of spirituality, culture, and kinship. The profoundly relational nature of SEWB allows a greater understanding that the domains are connected, as are the determinants of health (Gee et al. 2014). The following offers a brief description of the seven domains.

Connection to body. Indigenous physical health and body is influenced by social determinants, such as just access to education, employment, health care, food security, as well as cultural determinants.

> This domain refers to those aspects of physical health and wellbeing that are embedded in bodily, individual, or intra-personal experience (Anderson 1999). Importantly, this domain has a distinct, interdependent relationship with all other domains. The ability of an individual to feel a sense of wellbeing in themselves and in their interactions with others requires

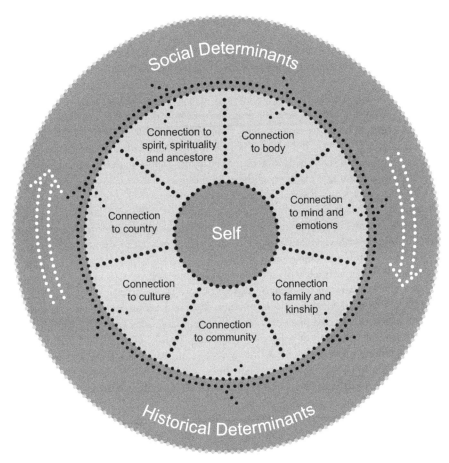

Figure 8.1. A model of social and emotional well-being (*National Strategic Framework for Aboriginal and Torres Strait Islander Peoples' Mental Health and Social and Emotional Wellbeing 2017–2023*).

a positive connection to body, mind, and emotions, which in turn involves experiencing a sense of connectedness to each of the other domains.

(Dudgeon and Walker 2015: 279).

Connection to mind and emotions. Relational well-being in the domain of mind and emotions refers to fundamental psychological needs along with the right to cultural safety, freedom from discrimination and racism, and the right to determine basic needs from an Indigenous standpoint. Importantly, strong cultural identity has been identified across the national and international literature in Indigenous psychology as pivotal to mental and emotional health, protecting against the impact of various stressors within colonial cultures and has also been linked to reduced suicide rates and increased resilience (Dudgeon and Bray 2020).

Connection to family and kinship. The social and emotional well-being domain of family and kinship recognises the centrality of Indigenous family systems to the strengthening of individuals and communities, along with the complex forms of kinship which govern communities and relationships to the environment. Kinship with Country, for example, is integral to numerous cultural lores and practices and sustains strong support networks within and between communities, as well as being at the centre of cultural ceremonies and practices (Rose, James, and Watson 2003). Indigenous family and kinship systems vary across Australia and have changed over time, are fluid and relational.

Connection to community. Strong Indigenous cultural identity is formed through relationships within and between communities. There is substantial research that healthy communities are protective for individuals, buffeting against the sociocognitive assault of racism within settler colonies (Prince 2018). The social and emotional well-being of individuals, families and communities is deeply connected such that Indigenous well-being can be understood to be a form of collective relationality. The role of Elders within communities is also vital to the harmonious governance of communities and the continuation of cultural practices which bind members together. Indigenous psychology recognises the importance of respecting culturally specific community protocols and hierarchies in order to strengthen well-being. Moreover, access to community-controlled health services has also been identified as vital to the strengthening of social and emotional well-being (Dudgeon et al. 2016).

Connection to Culture. The centrality of culture to Indigenous well-being is being increasingly recognised across the literature in the field and there is now an abundance of qualitative and quantitative evidence both in Australia and internationally that demonstrates that a strong relationship to cultural knowledge and practices (i.e., Indigenous languages, ceremony, kinship, and lores) is central to the revitalisation of collective well-being (Bourke et al. 2018). In Aboriginal and Torres Strait Islander communities, SEWB includes a strong sense of self and cultural identity, which can provide meaning and resilience in times of adversity. Identifying, participating in and engaging with cultural activities are essential to the development of strong and resilient children, young people, families and communities. A positive cultural identity assists children and young people to navigate the challenges in Australia, such as the racial tensions, discrimination, including racism and oppressive policies (Yap and Yu 2016). Elders and older people often hold special relationships with younger generations, particularly children. These relationships support the passing of cultural knowledge and connections, like kinship networks, language, culture, and cultural identity. Strong connections to culture serve as key protective factors that predict resilience in children (Prince 2018).

Connection to country and land. The relationship towards country can be understood to be foundational to the strengthening of all other forms of relational well-being. For Indigenous Australians, country refers to animals, plants, sea, sky, waterways, earth and spirits, is the source of lore and spirituality, and possesses complex agency. 'Being on Country' or going back to country is widely recognised as a culture building therapeutic practice which connects people to broader more-than-human kinships networks (totem animals, and lores), sacred places, birthing sites and the intricate cultural responsibilities to care for country which is part of the custodial relationship Indigenous people have to land (Ganesharajah 2009; Garnett et al. 2009). However, the cultural and therapeutic importance and right to connect with and be on country is rarely acknowledged by mainstream colonial psychology (Dudgeon and Walker 2015). A disrupted relationship to country has been recognised to be the etiology of specific forms of Indigenous distress and trauma (Kelly et al. 2009).

Connection to spirituality and ancestors. Indigenous spirituality, a complex system of relationality which connects all past present and future life-forms and is guided by ethical principles of respect, reciprocity and care which are also foundational to the harmonious governance of communities, is recognised as the foundation of SEWB for many Indigenous peoples. As a philosophy of life and a form of ethical governance, Indigenous spirituality can be understood as a therapeutic knowledge system in so far as it is directed towards the nurturing of harmonious life-affirming relationships (Dudgeon and Walker 2015; Grieves 2009).

An understanding of how SEWB is strengthened through these inter-related domains is central to Indigenous psychology and to the decolonisation of Western psychological discourses about Indigenous people in Australia. The disruption of these domains has been recognised to be an outcome of colonisation which has produced forms of inter-generational trauma that have devastated individuals, families and their communities (Atkinson et al. 2014). A clinical awareness of the impact of trauma on Indigenous peoples requires psychologists to examine the cultural and historical impact of colonisation. Yet, as Dudgeon and Walker (2015: 281) claim, it is crucial for psychologists to "understand how these cultural domains interact and the critical importance of supporting individuals and families in reclaiming, modifying, and adapting spiritual and cultural practices as part of healing and restoring social and emotional wellbeing". Many Australian Indigenous people experienced forced removal from their traditional land. This leaving a cultural void, an unfulfilled longing, and a need for recreating and redefining their spiritual connections, that continues through their kinship today.

Conclusion: Some paths forward

An anti-colonial position is a key critical strategy for Indigenous psychology in Australia as well as the wider mental health movement. Dismantling the hegemonic authority of colonisation is linked to the revitalisation of culturally safe, strengths-based interventions which disrupt racist discourses and support healthy relationships between the domains of SEWB. Decolonising psychology is a complex process which involves two central strategies: (1) deconstructing colonial power relations within mainstream Western psychology which normalises an ex-nominated individualism and (2) developing new Indigenous mental health and well-being discourses. In this context, the development of the SEWB discourse opens up space for the continuation of both strategies.

The social determinants approach to mental health is a central part of the SEWB discourse (Gee et al. 2014; Zubrick et al. 2014). This approach identifies the multiple ways in which colonisation has impacted on individual, families and communities across generations, interrupting healthy connections to the seven domains of well-being and undermining cultural identity. In understanding colonisation, we recognise that improving the SEWB of individuals, families and communities involves attending to the impacts of discrimination, racism in particular, ensuring communities have access to culturally safe support, and developing pathways towards restorative justice, sovereignty and self-determination over the social determinants of everyday life. All services, programs, practices and policies which impact on the well-being of Indigenous people need to acknowledge the importance of strengthening healthy relationships between the seven inter-related domains of well-being, and ensure cultural safety.

The right to self-determination, which is now enshrined in the *United Nation Declaration of the Rights of Indigenous Peoples* can be understood as the right to decolonise the oppressive systems, policies, and practices that impact Indigenous mental health and SEWB. In relation to the specific rights to self-determination over health and mental health, this right effectively means building an Indigenous psychology and ensuring that such a psychology has the ability to support the holistic health and well-being of Indigenous people across the social determinants of life. As this chapter has discussed and as the landmark 2016 APS apology recognised, the history of mainstream Australian psychology has been embedded in the colonial oppression of Indigenous people. This has been instrumental in the violation of Indigenous peoples' human rights, and the perpetuation of racist narratives about the inferiority of Indigenous peoples. It is no-longer acceptable to continue the colonial suppression of Indigenous knowledge systems and cultures. The rise of Indigenous psychology across the world attests to a resurgence of the life-affirming power of these knowledge systems. In order to decolonise psychology in Australia, Indigenous knowledge must be integrated into all educational institutions, policies impacting on Indigenous peoples, including strategies for implementing cultural safety in all programs impacting on Indigenous people, with Indigenous-led training for practitioners. In particular, the diagnosis and treatment of Indigenous people experiencing psychological stress must be led by Indigenous psychologists and psychological research.

An in-depth understanding of the social, economic, political, and historical impacts of ongoing settler colonisation and the specific forms of racism settler colonisation reproduces is also necessary. There needs to be a recognition across the discipline of psychology of the extent of the, still *ongoing,* sociocognitive impacts of colonisation of Indigenous peoples across Australia. As the *Uluru Statement From the Heart* points out:

> Proportionally, we are the most incarcerated people on the planet. We are not an innately criminal people. Our children are aliened from their families at unprecedented rates. This cannot be because we have no love for them. And our youth languish in detention in obscene numbers. They should be our hope for the future. … These dimensions of our crisis tell plainly the structural nature of our problem. This is *the torment of our powerlessness.*

> *(2017: Online)*

The persistent racism which underpins this enforced powerlessness needs to be acknowledged and challenged by the discipline of psychology and the traumatic consequences for individuals, families and communities understood from an Indigenous perspective. There is abundant evidence that strengthening Indigenous culture through the support of traditional healing, kinship networks, child-care practices, spirituality, caring for country and cultural activities builds collective resilience and well-being (Milroy, Dudgeon, and Walker 2014; Zubrick et al. 2014). Finally, using the discourse of Indigenous psychology and the SEWB model to decolonise psychology and strengthen the capacity of Indigenous peoples requires continually ensuring that the forms of structural racism that impact on the social determinants of well-being (as key examples, the removal of children from families, the incarceration of young people) are understood from an Indigenous standpoint. Likewise, tactics and strategies for supporting the strengthening of the domains of SEWB should be designed by and led by Indigenous people.

Note

1 This chapter draws on Dudgeon and Walker (2015), Decolonising Australian psychology: Discourses, strategies, and practice.

References

American Psychological Association. (2011). 'Indigenous psychology task force'. Available: https://www.apadivisions.org/division-32/leadership/task-forces/indigenous/, accessed 14 May 2020.

Anderson, I. (1999). 'Aboriginal well-being', in C. Grbich (ed.) *Health in Australia: Sociological Concepts and Issues*, 2nd ed. Longman: Sydney, NSW, 53–73.

Atkinson, J., Nelson, J., Brooks, R., Atkinson, C., and Ryan, K. (2014). 'Addressing individual and community transgenerational trauma', in P. Dudgeon, H. Milroy, and R. Walker (eds.) *Working Together: Aboriginal and Torres Strait Islander Mental Health and Wellbeing Principles and Practice*, 2nd ed. Australian Government Department of the Prime Minister and Cabinet: Canberra, 289–306.

Australian Health Ministers' Advisory Council. (2004). *National Strategic Framework for Aboriginal and Torres Strait Islander People's Mental Health and Social and Emotional Well Being 2004–2009*. AHMAC: Canberra.

Australian Health Ministers' Advisory Council. (2017). National Strategic Framework for Aboriginal and Torres Strait Islander Peoples' Mental Health and Social and Emotional Wellbeing 2017-2023. Department of the Prime Minister and Cabinet: Canberra.

Australian Psychological Society. (2016). 'Apology to aboriginal and torres strait islanders apology'. Available: https://www.psychology.org.au/getmedia/dc5eb83c-9be9-4dce-95ec-232ac89e1d14/APS-, accessed 14 May 2020.

Bourke, S., Wright, A., Jill, G., Russell, L., Dunbar, T., and Lovett, R. (2018). 'Evidence review of Indigenous culture for health and wellbeing', *International Journal of Health, Wellness & Society*, vol 8, no 4: 11–27.

Brockman, R. and Dudgeon, P. (2019). 'Indigenous clinical psychology in Australia: a decolonising social-emotional well-being approach', in P. Rodes (ed.) *Beyond the Psychology Industry: How Else Might We Heal?* Springer Nature: Switzerland, 83–93.

Calma, T., Dudgeon, P., and Bray, A. (2017). 'Aboriginal and Torres Strait Islander social and emotional wellbeing and mental health', *Australian Psychologist*, vol 52, no 4: 255–260.

Carey, T.A., Dudgeon, P., Hammond, S.W., Hirvonen, T., Kyrios, M., Roufeil, L., and Smith, P. (2017). 'The Australian psychological society's apology to aboriginal and Torres Strait Islander people', *Australian Psychologist*, vol 52, no 4: 261–267.

Coburn, E. (2013). 'Indigenous research as resistance', *Socialist Studies/Études socialistes: reveu de la société d'études socialistes*, vol 9, no 1: 52–63.

Dudgeon, P. and Bray, A. (In Press). 'Cathedrals of the spirit: Indigenous relational identity and social and emotional wellbeing', in B. Adams and F.J.R. van de Vijver (eds.) *Identity in Non-Western Contexts*. Springer Books: London.

Dudgeon, P., Bray, A., D'Costa, B., and Walker, R. (2017). 'Decolonising psychology: Validating social and emotional wellbeing', *Australian Psychologist*, vol 52, no 4: 316–325.

Dudgeon, P., Bray, A., and Walker, R. (2020). 'Self-determination and strengths-based aboriginal and Torres Strait Islander suicide prevention: An emerging evidence-based approach', in A. Page and W. Stritzke (eds.) *Alternatives to Suicide: Beyond Risk and Toward a Life Worth Living*. Academic Press: San Diego, USA, 237–256.

Dudgeon, P., Milroy, J., Calma, T., Luxford, Y., Ring, I., Walker, R., Cox, A., Georgatos, G., and Holland, C. (2016). Solutions that Work: What the Evidence and Our People Tell Us. Available: https://www.atsispep.sis.uwa.edu.au/__data/assets/pdf_file/0006/2947299/ATSISPEP-Report-Final-Web.pdf, accessed 14 May 2020.

Dudgeon, P., Rickwood, D., Garvey, D., and Gridley, H. (2014). 'A history of Indigenous psychology', in P. Dudgeon, H. Milroy, and R. Walker (eds.) *Working Together: Aboriginal and Torres Strait Islander Mental Health and Wellbeing Principles and Practice*, 2nd ed. Australian Government Department of the Prime Minister and Cabinet: Canberra, 39–54.

Dudgeon, P. and Walker, R. (2015). 'Decolonising Australian psychology: discourses, strategies, and practice', *Journal of Social and Political Psychology*, vol 3, no 1: 276–297.

Foley, D. (2002). 'An Indigenous standpoint theory', *Journal of Australian Indigenous Issues*, vol 5, no 3: 3–13.

Ganesharajah, C. (2009). *Indigenous Health and Wellbeing: The Importance of Country*. Australian Institute for Aboriginal and Torres Strait Islander Studies: Canberra.

Garnett, S.T., Sithole, B., Whitehead, P.J., Burgess, C.P., Johnstone, F.H., and Lea, T. (2009). 'Healthy country, healthy people: policy implications of links between Indigenous human health and environmental condition in tropical Australia', *Australian Journal of Public Administration*, vol, 68, no 1: 53–66.

Gee, G., Dudgeon, P., Schultz, C., Hart, A., and Kelly, K. (2014). 'Aboriginal and Torres Strait Islander social and emotional wellbeing', in P. Dudgeon, H. Milroy, and R. Walker (eds.) *Working Together: Aboriginal and Torres Strait Islander Mental Health and Wellbeing Principles and Practice*, 2nd ed. Australian Government Department of the Prime Minister and Cabinet: Canberra, 55–68.

Grieves, V. (2009). *Aboriginal Spirituality: Aboriginal Philosophy, the Basis of Aboriginal Social and Emotional Wellbeing*. Discussion Paper No. 9. Cooperative Research Centre for Aboriginal Health: Darwin.

Hartman, W.E., Wendt, D.C., Burrage, R.L., Pomerville, A., and Gone, J.P. (2019). 'American Indian historical trauma: anticolonial prescriptions for healing, resilience, and survivance', *American Psychologist*, vol 74, no 1: 6–19.

Kelly, K., Dudgeon, P., Gee, G., and Glaskin, B. (2009). *Living on the Edge: Social and Emotional Well-being and Risk and Protective Factors for Serious Psychological Distress Among Aboriginal and Torres Strait Islander People.* Discussion Paper No. 10. Cooperative Research Centre for Aboriginal Health: Darwin.

Kovach, M. (2009). *Indigenous Methodologies: Characteristics, Conversations, and Contexts.* University of Toronto Press: Toronto, ON.

Langton, M. (1993). Well, I Heard It on the Radio and I Saw It on the Television… Australian Film Commission: Woolloomooloo, NSW.

Marmot, M. (2011). 'Social determinants and the health of Indigenous Australians', *Medical Journal of Australia* vol 194, 512–513.

Mia, T., Dudgeon, P., Mascall, C., Grogan, G., Murray, B., & Walker, R. (2017). An evaluation of the national empowerment project cultural, social, and emotional wellbeing program. *Journal of Indigenous Wellbeing,* vol 2, no 2, 33–48.

Milroy, H., Dudgeon, P., and Walker, R. (2014). 'Community life and development programs', in P. Dudgeon, H. Milroy, and R. Walker (eds.) *Working Together: Aboriginal and Torres Strait Islander Mental Health and Wellbeing Principles and Practice,* 2nd ed. Australian Government Department of the Prime Minister and Cabinet: Canberra, 419–436.

Moreton-Robinson, A. (2017). 'Relationality: a key presupposition of an indigenous social research paradigm', in C. Andersen and J. O'Brien (eds.) *Sources and Methods in Indigenous Studies.* Routledge: New York, 69–77.

Moreton-Robinson A. and Walter, M. (2009). 'Indigenous methodologies in social research', in M. Walter (ed.) *Social Research Methods.* Oxford University Press: Oxford, 1–18.

Nagle, N., van Oven, M., Wilcox, S., van Holst Pellekaan, S., Tyler-Smith, C., Xue, Y., Ballantyne, K.N., Wilcox, L., Papac, L., Cooke, K., van Oorschot, R.A., McAllister, P., Williams, L., Kayser, M., Mitchell, R.J. and Genographic Consortium. (2017). 'Aboriginal Australian mitochondrial genome variation - an increased understanding of population antiquity and diversity', *Scientific Reports,* vol 7, 43041.

National Aboriginal Health Strategy Working Party. (1989). *A National Aboriginal Health Strategy 1989.* Department of Health and Ageing: Canberra.

National Mental Health Commission. (2013). Supplementary Paper: The Mental Health and Social and Emotional Wellbeing of Aboriginal and Torres Strait Islander Peoples, Families and Communities. Available: https://www.mentalhealthcommission.gov.au/getmedia/f014d128-ab8a-4a40-b3d2-9a466 8a8fd93/Mental-Health-Report-Card-on-Aboriginal-and-Torres-Strait-Islander, accessed 14 May 2020.

Prince, D. (2018). *Stories from Community: How Suicide Rates Fell in Two Indigenous Communities.* Healing Foundation: Sydney, NSW.

Rigney, L.I. (1997). 'Internationalisation of an Indigenous anti-colonial cultural critique of research methodologies: a guide to Indigenist research methodology and its principles', in HERDSA Annual International Conference *Proceedings; Research and Development in Higher Education: Advancing International Perspectives,* vol. 20: 629–636.

Rose, N. (1996). *Inventing Ourselves: Psychology, Power and Personhood.* Cambridge University Press: New York.

Rose, D., James, D., and Watson, C. (2003). *Indigenous Kinship with the Natural World in New South Wales.* NSW National Parks and Wildlife Service: Huntsville, NSW.

Salmon, M., Doery, K., Dance, P., Chapman, J., Gilbert, R., Williams, R., and Lovett, R. (2019). *Defining the Indefinable: Descriptors of Aboriginal and Torres Strait Islander Peoples' Cultures and Their Links to Health and Wellbeing.* Aboriginal and Torres Strait Islander Health Team, Research School of Population Health, The Australian National University: Canberra.

Social Health Reference Group. (2004). *Social and Emotional Well Being Framework. A National Strategic Framework for Aboriginal and Torres Strait Islander Peoples' Mental Health and Social and Emotional Well Being 2004-2009.* Department of Health and Ageing: Canberra.

Swan, P. and Raphael, B. (1995). *Ways Forward: National Aboriginal and Torres Strait Islander Mental Health Policy National Consultancy Report.* Department of Health and Ageing: Canberra.

Uluru Statement From the Heart. (2017). Available: https://www.referendumcouncil.org.au/sites/default/files/2017-05/Uluru_Statement_From_The_Heart_0.PDF, accessed 14 May 2020.

United Nations General Assembly. (2007). *The United Nations Declaration on the Rights of Indigenous Peoples: Resolution Adopted by the General Assembly.* United Nations: Geneva.

Usher, J. (1991). *Women's Madness: Misogyny or Mental Illness?* Harvester Wheatsheaf: New York.

Walker, R., Schultz, C., and Sonn, C. (2014). 'Cultural competence – transforming policy, services, programs and practice', in P. Dudgeon, H. Milroy, and R. Walker (eds.) *Working Together: Aboriginal and Torres Strait Islander Mental Health and Wellbeing Principles and Practice*, 2nd ed. Australian Government Department of the Prime Minister and Cabinet: Canberra, 195–220.

Watts, V. (2013). 'Indigenous place-thought & agency amongst humans and non-humans (first woman and sky woman go on a European world tour!)', *Decolonization: Indigeneity, Education & Society*, vol 2, 20–34.

White, S.C. (2017). 'Relational wellbeing: re-centring the politics of happiness, policy and the self', *Policy and Politics*, vol 45, no 2: 121–136.

Williams, D.R., Lawrence, J.A., and Davis, B.A. (2019). 'Racism and health: evidence and needed research', *Annual Review of Public Health*, vol 40, no 1: 105–125.

Yap, M. and Yu, E. (2016). *Community Wellbeing from the Ground Up: A Yawuru Example*. Bankwest Curtin Economics Centre: Perth.

Zubrick, S.R., Shepherd, C.S., Dudgeon, P., Gee, G., Paradies, Y., Scrine, C., and Walker, R. (2014). 'Social determinants of social and emotional wellbeing', in P. Dudgeon, H. Milroy, and R. Walker (eds.) *Working Together: Aboriginal and Torres Strait Islander Health and Wellbeing Principles and Practice*, 2nd ed. Australian Government Department of the Prime Minister and Cabinet: Canberra, 93–112.

9

Colours of creation

Nālani Wilson-Hokowhitu

Ea-breath, rising, sovereign, I sat nervously with head held high in front of the panel of all-male professors who would determine my future as a young 21-year-old, Kanaka ʻŌiwi[1] woman petitioning the University of Wisconsin, Madison for an independent major focusing on Indigenous Cultures in Contemporary Society. After several years and numerous classes in Studio Art, Art History, Environmental Studies, Cultural Studies, Anthropology, Latin American Studies, and American Indian Studies, I had confidently determined the inadequacy of the academy at addressing the pressing interrelated contemporary issues facing Indigenous lands, waters, communities, cultures, and peoples. There had been fierce role models, like Haunani Kay Trask, and quiet contemplative professors, like Roberta Hill Whiteman, who served as bright stars to follow, navigating a pathway forward. Creating the first major in Indigenous Studies at the University of Wisconsin, Madison was one my first sovereign acts as a young adult, and after successfully completing the degree of my own design in 1998, it was just the beginning. A dream for the future materialising, we now gather as scholars of Critical Indigenous Studies with the capacity to shift global consciousness. Ea! Together we rise.

This chapter centralises the scholarship of Indigenous Pacific women, who have confronted the corpus of Indigenous/Pacific knowledge as masculine and patriarchal, inviting a new generation of scholars to build upon these ponderings. There is a growing necessity to expand upon complexities of Indigenous gender and sexuality in non-heteronormative, non-binary, genderful, and gender-fluid identities. For the purposes of this work, I speak from the perspective of identifying as biologically female and hone in on femininity in relation to creation, land, waters, birthing, menstruation, and the moon to add to the body of literature devoted to our more than human ancestral connections.

Lilikalā Kameʻeleihiwa states that, "As Hawaiian women, we are the intellectual as well as the physical descendants of our female ancestors, and in turn we will be ancestral inspiration for the generations to come" (1999: 1). Following in the academic lineage of Lilikalā Kameʻeleihiwa, Haunani Kay Trask, Manulani Aluli Meyer, Noenoe Silva, Noelani Goodyear-Kāʻopua, kuʻualoha hoʻomanawanui, and many others, I seek to align mana wāhine with wāhine ākua,[2] acknowledging the intergenerational relationships between Hina and Pelehonuamea, two ancestors who initiated voyages from Kahiki and birthed islands.

On Moloka'i our ancestress Hina and her essence continue to guide the ebb and flow of the ocean tides, the flow of our own moon-cycles, and everything that is fluid, such as water and riverways, as well as the pathway of our life journeys.[3] On Hawai'i Island, Pelehonuamea thrives, birthing red magma that solidifies into black lava rock, expanding the archipelago into the turquoise sea. Both wāhine ākua are ever-present, Hina embodied in the moon and Pelehonuamea within the volcano. They are also ubiquitous in our genetic knowing as Kānaka 'Ōiwi.

In *Ka Po'e Kahiko*, Hawaiian historian Samuel Mānaiakalani Kamakau refers to ākua, such as Pelehonuamea and Hina, as ancestors who "came from Kahiki as humans do – that is, by canoe" (1964: 68). According to Noenoe Silva (2004), Kamakau incorporated ākua in his account of traveller narratives. Silva's (2004) rigorous analysis of Hawaiian language newspapers, books, and letters uncovered evidence of female ākua and women voyagers and their voyaging feats that had been edited out of English language historical texts. Women were literally 'written out' of accounts by colonial writers. It is for this reason that the ancestral mo'olelo are so important. Silva's research and translations of the Hawaiian language archives fill a crucial gap in the historical record.

Manulani Aluli Meyer affirms that, "knowledge, for Native Hawaiians, is grounded in the natural environment and in the ancestral line of family" (1998: 23). The literature supports that within Hawaiian epistemology our ancestors are a part of an animated world imbued with spirit (Kamakau 1964; Malo 1951; Meyer 1998; 2001a; 2001b; 2003; 2008; Pūkui, Haertig and Lee 1972). As Kanaka 'Ōiwi, health, wellbeing and identity is deeply connected to nā ākua/'aumākua/kūpuna (ancestors and elders) and the embodiment of our ancestors within the world around us. Furthermore, mo'okū'auahau (genealogy) align nā mana wāhine. As Lilikalā Kame'eleihiwa poignantly articulates:

> Genealogies are perceived by Hawaiians as an unbroken chain that links those alive today to the [cosmological] life forces-to the *mana* (spiritual power) that first emerged with the beginning of the world. Genealogies anchor Hawaiians to our place in the universe.
>
> *(Kame'eleihiwa 1992: 19–20)*

Mo'okū'auahau is fundamental to Hawaiian epistemology and ontology, to our sense of knowing and being.

Our mo'okū'auahau from my father's 'ohana (family) extends from Wailua and Kalamaula, Moloka'i on my grandmother's side and Ka'ū and Kalapana, Hawai'i on my grandfather's side. I write in honour of multiple generations of mana wāhine extending from Hina of Moloka'i and Pelehonuamea of Hawai'i Island to my grandmother Josephine Kamakahukilani Cathcart, great-grandmother Lani Maliu from Moloka'i and great-grandmother Elizabeth Kalikookalani Ka'aukai from Hawai'i Island. I intentionally align these lineages to my Hawaiian name, Kamakahukionālani, and to my children, who carry the names Kalikookalani and Ka'aukai.

Reclaiming and reconnecting with our bodies and our bodies' intelligence to birth, cleanse, release, and create is sovereign action. Creation as life-giving, powerful and abundant comes in many forms, including art, dance, scholarship, environmental conservation, activism, and birthing. The ancestress Pelehonuamea teaches that what might seem destructive, such as a volcanic eruption, fire, and black rock, is also abundantly creative-the birthing of 'āina (land and that which feeds). The intergenerational intersections between the moon, volcano, land, ocean, rivers, mist, and rain, guide the micro and macro cycles that inform identity, gender, and wellbeing. Here, I refer to the micro cycles as the subtle changes within our own bodies, most notably the process of birthing (in all forms), menstruation, and the macro cycles as the phases of the moon that determine the ocean tides, animal behaviour, such as the presence or lack of fish, and the growth of plants. I acknowledge Kalei Nuʻuhiwa as a kumu (source/teacher) and hoaaloha (friend), who helped clarify my thoughts focusing on birthing, menstruation, creation, and the moon.[4] Kalei focuses on the discipline of Papahulilani (the study of the atmosphere), phenology, energies, and cycles from a Hawaiian perspective. She contends that, in the traditional Hawaiian worldview, atmospheric elements embody nā kino ākua Hawaiʻi, providing a fundamental function in our ancestral memory, essential in the modern Hawaiian consciousness.

This chapter contributes to this growing discipline of Indigenous Studies with an exploration of Kanaka ʻŌiwi feminisms, epistemologies, ontologies, and my work as a global citizen and an Indigenous mother, daughter, sister, partner, scholar, curator, and artist. The writing and research evolved from a mana wāhine chapter, inspired by revelations as an artist in the studio, into informing the taxonomy of the art exhibition, *E Hina e! E Hine e!* (Waikato Museum Te Whare Taonga o Waikato, 14 September 2019–21) co-curated with Dr Aroha Yates-Smith and Maree Mills.[5]

Colours of creation

Black, Turquoise, and Red are the colours of creation that structure this work. Black as representative of Pō (darkness/night), Pōʻele (black/dark night), and the Kumulipo (source of deep darkness). Black night as the colour of creation. Black as a hue that holds the spectrum in unity. Black as the divine feminine and the beginnings of life, from the first single-cell organism bringing us into the world in which we live today. Turquoise as Hina embodied within wai (water and fluidity) in all its many forms. Red as Pelehonuamea and the magma deep within the earth, as well as waimakalehua (menstruation), the blood within our bodies that flows with the pull of the moon. These are colours of creation that structure the following sections.

Imagine painting a chapter. Imagine this writing, black and white words on paper, as vibrant with colour. The colours of this chapter thus begin with the deepest darkest hue as black. Black night and the beginnings of life. Black lava rock solidified in the ocean. Land birthed from magma. Black as the place from which we are all born. Waters flowing, riding the tide, through the birth canal we enter an intense splash of blue, turquoise, and aqua; blues of a river, deep and flowing, fresh and saltwaters connecting and combining. Turquoise to symbolise waiwai, fresh water, and its rich life-giving potential. Turquoise to symbolise the ocean and its ebb and flow. Turquoise as mist and rain.

Finally, the chapter concludes with the colour red, blood red of contrasting shades. Blood of our bodies, blood of our wombs, blood of life, and blood of death. Blood as the water within us, also life-giving and creative. Coming full circle, we return to the spectrum of black. Black as a rainbow, another realm, from which we come and to which we return. The colours of this chapter all represent nā mana wāhine: creation, potential, abundance, power, and life.

Pō; Black

"The Maoli universe is not created from the divine breath of a singular male god, but through a birthing process beginning with Kumulipo and Pōʻele (black night), paired (ēkoʻa) male and female entities of the cosmos" (hoʻomanawanui 2014: 4). Moʻokūʻauhau, our genealogical succession, recounts the birthing of the Hawaiian universe from Pō, lush and genderful. The kaona, hidden or double meaning, is metaphorical of the womb and is associated with birthing, but also potent beyond comprehension. We have come to know this Kanaka ʻŌiwi cosmology as 'the Kumulipo', the name of the male entity. The patriarchal naming negates the abundance and expansiveness of Pō and Pōʻele in recounting our Kānaka ʻŌiwi cosmology; therefore, where possible I strive to re-language the cosmological chant to honour Pō and Pō'ele alongside Kumulipo.

There are 16 wā (epochs) in the epic creation chant, half of which occur in Pō, that span eons of time and recount the birthing of nā lani (the cosmos/heavens), honua (earth), aquatic and land plants and animals. It is not until the eighth wā that dawn breaks, Ao (light), star constellations and kanaka (humans) emerge (ho'omanawanui 2014). This creation chant explains in detail the evolution of creation. Life does not begin when we are born; instead, our lives are an extension of all life forms that have come before, including the plants, animals, elements of earth, sky, wind, and rain. These life forms and elements are merely a few examples of the embodiments of the ākua (gods), 'aumākua (ancestors), kūpuna (elders and ancestors) and the place from which we originate. This is how our ko'ihonua, our cosmogonic genealogy begins:

'O ke au i kahuli wela ka honua
'O ke au i kahuli lole ka lani
'O ke au i kuka'iaka ka lā
E ho'omālamalama i ka mālama
'O ke au o Makali'i ka pō
'O ka walewale ho'okumu honua ia
'O ke kumu o ka lipo, i lipo ai
'O ke kumu o ka Pō, i pō ai
'O ka lipolipo, o ka lipolipo
'O ka lipo o ka la, o ka lipo o ka pō
Pō wale ho'i
Hānau ka pō
Hānau Kumulipo i ka pō, he kāne
Hānau Pō'ele i ka pō, he wāhine
Hānau ka 'Ukuko'ako'a
Hānau kāna, he 'Āko'ako'a, puka ...
When time turned, the earth became hot
When time turned, the heavens turned inside out
When time turned, the sun was darkened
Causing the moon to shine
This is the time the Pleiades rose in the night
The slime was the source of the earth
The source of the darkness that made darkness
The intense darkness, the deep darkness
Darkness of the sun, darkness of the night
Nothing but night
The night gave birth
Born was Kumulipo in the night, a male
Born was Pō'ele in the night, a female
Born was the coral polyp,
Born was the coral, it emerged ...

(ho'omanawanui 2014: 5)

Connection. We are connected to darkness, we are connected to the divine feminine, as we are also connected to the coral polyp, symbolic here of all and everything that follows within the 2,108 lines of the chant. Within the cosmology we not only see the vitality of darkness, we also see the constant reference to gender complementarity and species complementarity. For example, everything in the ocean has an equivalent counterpart on land.

Queen Liliuokalani translated the creation chant, which she attributed to her 18th-century ancestor, Keaulumoku, who composed the ʻoli before European contact. The chant is a sophisticated description of the origin of species. The successions of Pō, Pōʻele, and Kumulipo extend from the natural world and emergence of sea and land, flora and fauna to humans. It is an epic moʻokūʻauhau describing the interrelationships between the ocean and land, plants and animals, ancestors, and humans that connect the Hawaiian ancestral chiefly genealogies to the beginning of creation. Kanaka share an inherited moʻokūʻauhau that links Pō (darkness), mana wāhine, and wāhine ākua.

"As ʻŌiwi poets, we recognise that the Pō in our bodies is pili to the Pō in our art and activism. That hot, churning blackness. That blackness that births" (Revilla and Osorio 2019: 127). A discussion of blackness and darkness is a decolonial assertion. It is vital for wāhine/kane/genderfluid/transgender/non-binary to return to the femininity and strength that we find in our moʻokūʻauhau. Reconceiving of black is transformative because Western history is laden with oppressive colonial notions of the colour black, dark skin and racialisation, the Dark Ages, right and wrong, heaven and hell, Christian and heathen. Returning to our Indigenous cosmologies, reclaiming our ontologies and epistemologies, we engage in the process of decolonisation. We begin our liberation by acknowledging black as beautiful. Black as abundant. Black as the spectrum in unity. Black the colour of creation. Black as the divine feminine/masculine, where femininity and masculinity maintain an even balance whether male, female, transgender, genderfluid, and/or non-binary. Darkness has the capacity to heighten awareness, to sharpen inward focus, and potentiality.[6]

Black is the colour of the earth, the soil, so it is symbolic of being rich with nutrients. In the words of African American scholar Cynthia Dillard, "[w]hen the ground is black, the ground is fertile" (2008: 277). Dillard's, endarkened feminist epistemology places spirituality at the center of thought and discourse. In creating an endarkened feminist epistemology, Dillard deliberately sought language that was resistant and transformative to express three key concepts of an African-based cosmology: spirituality, community and praxis. Her use of 'endarkened' unmasks 'enlightenment', the European intellectual movement of the late 17th and 18th centuries emphasising reason and individualism rather than tradition, which was heavily influenced by philosophers such as Descartes, Locke, and Newton. Other prominent figures included Kant, Goethe, Voltaire, Rousseau, and Adam Smith. Endarkened feminist epistemology retools language as resistance, acknowledging that language has been a powerful tool in the colonisation of African Americans and other marginalised peoples (Dillard 2008).

Reclamation of Pō and black as abundant is a decolonial assertion that rejects heteronormative patriarchy, honouring non-human relations and a long lineage of cosmological connection to the natural world and our ancestors, who are ubiquitous. This relationship and understanding are a part of sustaining health and well-being for not only Kanaka ʻŌiwi, but all of creation. The following section moves from black into varying shades of blue and the expansiveness of wai (water). I imagine the next section as turquoise set against black. It is composed as a tribute to our ancestress, Hina, who embodies all that is fluid and flowing.

Waiwai; Turquoise

Kaulana Molokaʻi-famous is Molokaʻi, Great Molokaʻi child of Hina. I write about Hina and Molokaʻi as a form of appreciation to the people of Molokaʻi, our ʻohana and extended ʻohana, to the mountain of Kamakaou, to the ʻāina, valleys, streams, moana/kai, fishponds, and coral reef

(Wilson 2005; 2008a; 2008b; 2008c; 2012; Wilson-Hokowhitu 2019). Hina embodies a plethora of manifestations. She is the moon, the creator of the coral reefs and all life upon the reef, she is the guardian of fishing and travellers, the keeper of the winds, food gatherer, kapa maker, healer and mother (Kameʻelehiwa 1999). Hina walked along the southern coast of Molokaʻi, plunging her ʻōʻō (digging stick) into the earth and creating freshwater springs – providing, protecting, nurturing, feeding, healing, and intertwining past, present, and future (Ritte, Naehu, Goodyear-Kaʻōpua and Warech 2019).

Hina is one of the most widely known ancestors throughout Moananuiākea. Her name and stories change slightly from archipelago to archipelago. For example, she is called Sina in Sāmoa, Sima in Tonga, Hina in Tahiti and Hawaiʻi, and Hine in Aotearoa-New Zealand. In Hawaiʻi, Hina is the daughter of Kamaunuaniho (female) and Kalana (male) who, like Pelehonuamea, came from Kahiki. She married ʻOlopana, who was also from Kahiki, and they had a child who they named Kahiki-o-honuakele (Kamakau 1991: 111). Our cosmogonic genealogy lists Hina as an ākua (Kameʻeleihiwa 1999). She is also the mother of the island of Molokaʻi, recognised in the genealogies as an ancestor to Kanaka ʻŌiwi from Molokaʻi Island in the Hawaiian archipelago. The moʻolelo of both Pelehonuamea and Hina speak of their intentional and independently initiated voyages. The stories of Hina speak of her as the creator of the human race, as well as a legendary voyager across the Pacific.

Hina Sailing into the Moon (Wilson-Hokowhitu 2017a) is a watercolour painting depicting Hina voyaging into the cosmos. In Tahiti, Hina is the daughter of Ātea and Hotu, known for her voyage to Aotearoa (New Zealand) accompanied by her brother, Rū. They departed from Motu-tapu in Raʻiātea through Te-ara-o Hina ('the passage of Hina' and ventured south across the Pacific. In this story Hina is Hina-faʻauru-vaʻa, or "Hina the canoe pilot" (Henry 1995: 4). After exploring several islands, Hina embarked upon an even greater voyage. On the night of

Figure 9.1 Hina Sailing into the Moon (Wilson-Hokowhitu 2017)

the full moon, just as the moon met the horizon, she set sail to visit it. Upon arriving, she let her canoe drift away and decided never to return to the earth. From the moon, she watches over travellers at night, and in this manifestation her name is Hina-nui-te-araara (Great Hina the watchwoman) (Henry 1995).

There are two Hine (Hina) stories from Aotearoa that are significant to Hine as a voyager. In one story Hine-Te-Aparangi was the first to sight the islands of Aotearoa, or 'long white cloud'. She and her husband, Kupe, are widely accepted as the first Polynesians to arrive to Te Ika a Māui (the fish of Māui — as Māui literally fishes land out of the sea), the North Island of New Zealand. On this voyage, it was Hine-Te-Aparangi, who upon sighting land, yelled, 'He ao! He ao!' ('A Cloud! A Cloud!') The name Aotearoa comes from this first sighting (Nelson 1991: 9).

Another ancestral story from New Zealand speaks of Hine-raho, a woman chief and one of the voyagers on board the canoe Arahura. This canoe brought the god Arahura to Te Waipounamu (literally the water of greenstone), the South Island of New Zealand. Arahura is actually the image of pounamu, the greenstone (Tregear 1891). On the west coast of the Te Waipounamu, there is a river called the Arahura. It is where the pounamu, the precious taonga (treasure) of Ngāi Tahu and Ngāti Waiwai can be found.

There are voyaging stories of legendary women across Moananuiākea, although the names change slightly from island to island. A voyaging story in Sāmoan culture speaks of the union between Rangi and Papa, who gave birth to Tangaloa. In this story, Sina (Hina/Hine) was Tangaloa's daughter. Tangaloa sent Sina, in the form of a bird, to find land. On her journey she did not find land, so Tangaloa threw stones into the sea below, thus creating the Sāmoan island of Savai'i (Tregear 1891). In several Polynesian cultures, such as Hawaiian and Māori, the manu (bird) is a metaphor for the canoe (Henry 1995).

In other stories, Hina gives birth to the human race. The Tuamotuan story of Hina tells of Ahuroa (male) and Onerua (female), who were the parents of Tiki. Tiki and Onekura gave birth to Hina, and Tiki and Hina developed the human race. In Marquesan legend Tiki-Tapu (male) and Kahuone (female) produced Tiki (male), who with Hinemataone (Sane at Havai'i) gave birth to the human race (Howe 2006). In the Hawaiian Islands, Hina is the mother of Moloka'i, as previously mentioned, giving birth to the island of Moloka'i Nui a Hina (Great Moloka'i of Hina).

These epic mo'olelo (stories/genealogies) affirm the significance of Hina/Hine/Sina across Moananuiākea. In Hawai'i, she takes on multiple forms as mother to the coral reefs and the famous gods Kamapua'a and Māui. She beats kapa (Hawaiian fabric) and medicinal herbs. Hina controls all that is fluid and malleable, the moon and tides, as well as freshwater pools. As the moon, there are various names and translations of Hina; such as Hina-Nui-i-te-Marama, Hina'aikamalama and Hinaakamalama-Hina of the Moon or Hina fed by the moon. There is Hinaakeahi–Hina of the Fire; Hinaaka'alu'alumoana–Hina who follows the ocean; Hinahāwea–Hina of the reddish glow; Hinakekā–Hina the canoe bailer; Hinalaua'e–Hina of the laua'e fern; Hinalaulimukala–Hina of the limu kala seaweed leaves; Hinalua'iko'a–Hina of the coral reef; Hinaōpūholoko'aokamoana–Hina whose womb is full of everything in the ocean; Hinapuku'ai–Hina who gathers food; Hinapukui'a–Hina who gathers fish; and, Hinaulu'ōhi'a–Hina of the 'ōhi'a forest (Handy, Handy and Pūkui 1972; Kame'eleihiwa 1999).

There are several reasons for sharing the various manifestations of Hina within this text, all of which are interrelated. First, the mo'olelo of Hina speak of her as an ocean voyager. The fact that Polynesians tell stories of women engaging in great adventures and voyages, as well as taking on multiple forms in the natural world, exemplifies the importance and centrality of women within our cultures and genealogies throughout Moananuiākea. The other purpose for sharing the Hina moʻolelo is to highlight how she is known as the progenitor of humans in the stories previously shared. Ancestral entities, such as Hina, exemplify the strength and importance of femininity within Kanaka Maoli and Pacific cosmologies and world-views.

I need to learn how to navigate,
Read the stars, the wind, and the ocean swells
Like she did.

(Teaiwa 1995: 67)

When we retrace the moʻokūʻauhau (genealogies and storylines) of Pacific women voyagers and visionaries, what does this body of knowledge reveal about feminine epistemologies, women in leadership, gender complementarity, and Pacific women's power prior to colonisation, Christianity, and patriarchy? In other words, how can a Pacific 'her-story' counter-narrative reimagine a future for Indigenous, Pacific Island women, and peoples that moves beyond white-hetero-patriarchy while forging new possibilities for our leaders? The poem excerpt above by the late and inspirational Teresia Teaiwa refers to Nei Nimʻanoa, one of several women navigators omitted from English language publications by early anthropologists and historians; thus, producing a legacy of gendered colonialism that confounds grounded Indigenous knowledge. Accordingly, new research is demanded that is consciously invested in re-navigating Pacific women's ontologies.

"Rise up, women gods. Have Hina as your goddess" (Trask 1994: 52). Haunani Kay Trask demands action from mana wāhine to align with our female ancestors. As a graduate student, I recall sitting with Haunani in her Pacific Women's Poetry class at the University of Hawaiʻi, Mānoa, and discussing sovereignty. My belief was/is that we can remain sovereign in our actions, for example to breathe is a sovereign action. To love is a sovereign action. To work back bent and knee deep in the mud of the loʻi is sovereign action. To align with nā wāhine kūpuna and ākua is sovereign action. To observe the relationship between Hina, the moon, and the flow within our own bodies is sovereign. Haunani maintained that we would never truly be sovereign until we gained independence from the United States. Perhaps this is true; yet, the ideas that I present here come from my continued desire to seek autonomy and freedom in *everything* that we do, in every breath we take, regardless of the colonial, governmental and national impositions upon us. I write in honour of Haunani and our long lineage of mana wāhine.

Colours of Creation articulates sovereign actions of intimacy within our bodies and our profound connections to cosmology and ākua embodied within our genetic memory and the natural world. My reasoning for pursuing this research topic came from a notable alignment between the full moon, specifically the Hawaiian lunar phases of Ākua and Hōkū, and my work as an artist and academic. I began to see a clear parallel between my ability to create, paint and write, during the phases of the full moon.

Most notably on 14 November 2016, two minutes after midnight, Kaikōura, Aotearoa experienced a 7.8-magnitude earthquake, which could be felt well into the epicenter of New Zealand's North Island where we live in Kirikiriroa (Hamilton). On the same day, the moon was both full and the closest that it has been to the earth since 1948. Astronomers call a moon that is closest to the earth a perigee. This refers to the elliptical orbit of the moon around the earth, meaning that once a month the moon is closest to the earth and once a month is it farthest. In 2016, there were three perigee moons, commonly known as super moons. The 14 November 2016 moon was unique because it was both full and the closest to earth, which astronomers described as not having happened in 68 years and they predict that it will not occur again until 2034 (Brook 2016).

It was on 14 November 2016, that I became acutely aware of the micro and macro connections between the waters within my own body and the moon. I remember sleeping through the earthquake and not knowing about the super moon. The same day while in the Waikato Society of Arts studio, I recall feeling hypersensitive, profoundly creative, and off balance due to the shifting of our islands from the earthquake and my own menstruation. It was incredibly intense, and it took several days to feel grounded again. On the day of the earthquake and super moon, I painted *Hō'ailona* (2016), depicting how our ancestress, Hina, guides us in our dream-state:

Returning to my office at Te Kotahi Research Institute, I shared these experiences with my co-worker, Papahuia Dickson, who then gave me a copy of the groundbreaking work of Ngāhuia Murphy, *Te Awa Atua, Menstruation in the Pre-colonial Māori World* (2014). Ngāhuia's book inspired my search for understanding menstruation for Kanaka 'Ōiwi. Reconceptualising menstruation as water, as a river, ignited a desire to better understand wai (waters) in 'Ōlelo Hawai'i. A simple search on *Nā Puke Wehewehe 'Ōlelo Hawai'i* reveals that wai as water is a tremendous oversimplification. Wai *is* water and it is also any liquid other than sea water. So, wai is juice, sap, honey, as well as the wai of our bodies, such as blood and semen. Wai can be a verb, to flow, like water, or to be fluid. Here we see the connection between wai o ke kāne (semen), wai o ka wāhine (menstruation or other discharges), and wai o kaunu, which is the sensual and thrilling discharges of love making. Wai o ka lehua is lehua flower honey and waimakalehua is the traditional expression of menstruation. Connecting once again to the work of Ngāhuia Murphy's (2014), *Te Awa Atua*, wai in 'Ōlelo Hawai'i, used within a place name, refers to a river or stream, which in te reo Māori (the Māori language) is te awa (river).

Before delving more deeply into waimakalehua (menstruation), there are other vital translations of wai. Wai connects to the birthing waters from which we come, so it is also a pronoun, meaning who, whom, whose, or what. So, in asking, 'What is your name', in 'Ōlelo Hawai'i we

Figure 9.2 Hō'ailona (Hokowhitu-Wilson 2016)

say, "O wai kou inoa?' From whose waters do you flow? Of what waters do you come?[7] Lastly, waiwai, means prosperity, importance, wealth and abundance in 'Ōlelo Hawai'i, a testament to wai as the beginnings of creation and essential to life and wellbeing.

Waiwai is the name of this section to emphasise abundance, linking the sections, so that black is abundant, wai is abundant, and the last section waimakalehua (menstruation) is abundant. This section has taken us on a quite a journey from Moloka'i nui a Hina, Great Hina mother of Moloka'i, across Moananuiākea acknowledging Hina as one of the most prolific wāhine ākua. I have found health, wellbeing and an intimate relationship with Hina embodied in the moon. This has provided a steady source of support while living away from Hawai'i nei, because the moon is ever-present wherever you are in the world. I acknowledge Hina as continuously guiding this journey of life. I acknowledge Hina's pull while sailing with the canoe Hōkūle'a, living on the island of Moloka'i, and present in my work as an artist and academic while residing in Aotearoa, New Zealand. Wai (pronounced in English as 'Why')? Hina is wai. She is the reason.

During a personal interview, Kalei Nu'uhiwa (Nu'uhiwa, K. 2017, personal communication, 2 August) described Hina as being in charge of the sacred feminine. She discussed two manifestations of Hina that relate to the lunar calendar, Hina'aikamalama and Hinahānaiakamalama. Hina'aikamalama is Hina who eats the moon and Hinahānaiakamalama is Hina fed by the moon (Kame'eleihiwa 1999). Kalei explained that Hinahānaiakamalama represents the first 15 days of the month, as the moon grows fuller, from the lunar phases of Hilo to Hōkū; and Hina'aikamalama represents the last 15 lunar phases from Mahealani to Moku. Whereas Hinahānaiakamala is upfront and forward, Hina'aikamalama is more mellow, but she is also the one to take action (Nu'hiwa 2017: personal communication 2 August).

"The moon influences everything. Everything. We are captivated by the moon, and that's Hina" (Nu'uhiwa 2017: personal communication, 2 August). She pulls the ocean tides affecting fishing, spawning and gathering. She guides the cycle of sap flowing through plants determining if the sap is in the roots, bark or leaves, and its fertility. Hina can cause earthquakes and affect the flow of magma. She determines the flow of wai as blood, waimakalehua, within our bodies. Everything aligns to the phases of the moon and the more that we pay attention to what is happening around us, the more that we will see, feel and witness these cyclical connections. "We are all Hina" (Nu'uhiwa 2017: personal communication, 2 August).

Waimakalehua; Red

Wai as blood is red, like magma in the earth. Looking out upon a landscape, still steaming hot with fresh magma and solidifying lava rock, we can either see destruction or creation, because it is both. Our islands, land itself, would not exist without magma and the lava rock that forms. Here, I return to a visualisation of Pelehonuamea birthing land. Red magma flowing to the sea, turning black as it hisses and steams in the cooling ocean waters. From black to turquoise to red, creation and abundance abound. As we transition, it is vital to maintain clarity with the connectedness of Hina and Pelehonuamea, both navigators from Kahiki, both progenerators, and both powerful wāhine ākua. Pelehonuamea is pulled by Hina, and Pelehonuamea responds, as do wāhine with our waimakalehua.

This painting, *Pelehonuamea* (2017), came as an hō'ailona (ancestral vision/message) during a state of subconscious. My conscious thoughts were consumed by this research and the connection between the moon, Hina, wai, and waimakalehua. I was very focused on honouring my grandmother, her name that I carry, Kamakahukionālani, and our Moloka'i Nui a Hina lineage; but, while in a state of deep relaxation, conscious and aware but almost asleep, a vision came. It started as black, darkness, like the night sky and then I saw the face of an old woman in what looked like

Figure 9.3 Pelehonuamea (Wilson-Hokowhitu 2017)

stars. I could not tell if she was an ancestor or if she was me, it was as if we were the same. Then there was an explosion! I saw the magma deep within the earth coming forth, red and orange fire flowing, and creating land as the lava solidified into the ocean, black meeting turquoise.

The hō'ike (meaning of the vision) was very clear. I interpreted the dream/message as coming from the Kalapana, Hawai'i lineage of my great-grandmother, Kalikookalani Ka'aukai. I knew immediately that I needed to honour both lineages connecting to Moloka'i and Hawai'i Island. I also knew from the hō'ailona that the hō'ike was about interconnection to creation, abundance, darkness, Pō, Pō'ele and Kumulipo, that the face of the old woman was my great-grandmother, grandmother, daughter and I, all of us fading into interconnection to the beginnings of creation and emergings of the future.

I am so grateful and humbled by this hō'ailona and hō'ike. I can only hope that the paintings and writing achieve the assignment set forth by nā kūpuna. Mo'okū'auhau as methodology is about listening to and following ancestral guidance in our contemporary lives as academics, activists, artists, and in all the roles that we play (Wilson-Hokowhitu 2012; 2019). During a personal email correspondence Sharon Ehia, who works for the Queen Liliuokalani Children's Center-Wai'ainae kīpuka, said: "[d]uring the time of waimakalehua, we are most sacred and sensitive to the suggestions of our kūpuna (ancestors)" (Ehia 2017 personal communication 21 October). This statement resonated with what I was feeling and the kūpuna teachings that I was coming to understand and seeking to share.

These are the insights that Ehia shared about her work with wāhine at home in Hawai'i. She outlined the significance of waimakalehua to wāhine explaining that they are re-enacting the hale peʻa (wāhine house) to create a space for ʻōpio (youth), mākua (parents) and kūpuna (elders) to connect, teach/learn, and mālama. The focus is on wāhine flow and understanding how it connects us to our past, present and future:

> we as wāhine, bring life and have the responsibility to mālama (take care) of our flow! The belief is, if wāhine understand the connection and responsibility to their bloodline, they will be careful who they choose as life partners, respect and honuor self (because it is not only about them, i.e. – past, present and future).
>
> *(Ehia 2017 personal communication 21 October)*[8]

'Translanguaging' (Garcia and Leiva 2014) of menstruation as waimakalehua from the English language to ʻŌlelo Hawaiʻi reveals immense potential to decolonise our thinking, feeling and relationships with our blood, our cycles and our bodies as wāhine. Language and epistemology thus begin the process of decolonising our relationships with menstruation, emotions, creativity and our own potential as nā mana wāhine. For example, the ability to feel profoundly, to cry, or to be hypersensitive in our present patriarchal, colonial and Western dominated reality, can be considered a weakness or debilitating. Decolonizing our thinking, decolonising our emotions and feelings, reveals that the ability to love and cry tears of joy or sadness is cleansing and powerful, as is menstruation. It is our strength.

There are varying ways to refer to menstruation in ʻŌlelo Hawaiʻi. Maʻi is a common term, which can also mean disease, sickness or illness; but maʻi can also mean to cleanse. When working in the loʻi kalo, the taro patches, my experience has been that women who were menstruating would do tasks on land rather than entering the loʻi. I remember that the sentiment for this division of labour was respectful and acknowledged the potency and power of menstruation, as well as maʻi as a time of cleansing. There are other terms for menstruation as well, such as wai ʻula, wai o ka wāhine, and koko puna, which is the first menstrual cycle.

Kalei Nuʻuhiwa discussed the traditional term for menstruation as waimakalehua. She said that whereas maʻi can mean illness, the imagery of waimakalehua refers to the shedding of the petals of the lehua blossom (Nuʻuhiwa 2017 personal communication 2 August). The ʻōhia lehua tree is endemic to the Hawaiian Islands. It is strong and resilient because it is one of the first seeds to germinate in the cracks of lava rock, so its roots have the capacity to hold steadfast and in doing so the ʻōhia lehua tree creates the beginnings of an Hawaiian forest.

The purpose of the chapter is to align with the same intention of the Queen Liliuokalani Children's Center, to support young women with their koko puna, their first menstruation, and those who are in the early stages of understanding their shift to womanhood. I would encourage women in all stages of their lives to begin to kilo, to observe, the shifts within their bodies while also remaining attuned to the natural world, especially the moon and its pull, power and creative potential. Our ancestors were keen observers and we can benefit from their example by developing deeper relationships with our more than human relations and the world around us.

Hopena; Conclusion

Ea! Breath. To breathe. Robin Wall Kimmerer (2013) begs the question, do we breathe or are we being breathed? To explore this profound question is to acknowledge our potential lack of control and superiority as humans, as well as the possibility of our interrelatedness and interdependence to the micro and macro flows of creation. The colours of creation as black, turquoise, and red is purposefully contentious because it addresses colonial discomfort with the power of femininity, blackness as abundant and life-giving, waters pulled by the moon, and menstruation as cleansing and beautiful. Critical Indigenous Studies forges conversations that propel potentiality beyond the simplicity of heteronormative patriarchy and Christianity, challenging the past atrocities of colonialisation, and offering a more complex analysis of existence that will propel us into the next phase toward our expansive futurities. I imagine a future in which the next generation of radicalists will strive to expand consciousness. Consciousness internal and consciousness external, connecting us to all. Indigenous Studies ignites radicalisation! As Indigenous scholars we unite in sovereign acts of reclamation. Reclaiming our bodies as wāhine/kāne/non-binary, embracing and honouring our waimakalehua as a gift of sacred and heightened awareness, and the intelligence of our emotions. Take with you these ideas: felt, experienced, guided, written, sketched, and painted. The writing is purposefully exploratory and experimental in its structure and ponderings as an invitation to the next generation to engage in future conversations. In honour of one such scholar, I conclude with this excerpt from Bryan Kuwada's (2016) poem, *We who share breath*.

> Our word for breath is ea. Ea is breath is life,
> ea is life is sovereignty, ea is sovereignty is rising,
> ea is breath is breath. Rising. This is what
> lay between us as my forehead pressed
> against yours, our noses touching, our lips
> a breath apart. Our eyes are closed
> to imagine the future, to see beyond the horizon.

Notes

1 Kānaka 'Ōiwi, also used interchangably with Kanaka Maoli and Native Hawaiian, are the Indigenous peoples genealogically connected to Ka Pae 'Āina 'o Hawai'i (the Hawaiian archipelago).
2 Mana wāhine refers to the supernatural or divine power of women and ākua are ancestors who reside in the natural world, so here I am making the connection between these entities. For more on Mana Wāhine, see ho'omanawanui (2010) and Silva (2007).
3 I acknowledge Shannon U'ilani Lima and Penny Martin of Moloka'i for grounding the ideas presented about Hina in this chapter. These two women guided my understandings of Moloka'i Nui a Hina (Wilson 2005).
4 Mahalo nō, my gratitude to Kalei Nu'uhiwa for sitting with me and allowing me to interview her for this chapter and for sharing her immense knowledge and guidance about the lunar phases, waimakalehua and the work of the Queen Liliuokalani Children's Center. Mahalo nui loa.
5 *E Hina e! Hine e!* has since received critical acclaim in Coney (2019) and in 'Wāhine Waking', Steele (2020) paraprases the research for both *Colours of Creation* and *E Hina e! E Hine e!*
6 I attribute my deeper understanding of the colour black to my work as an artist. In blending paint colours, the spectrum, I learned how to make the colour black. This shifted my appreciation of black and its complexity. It thus symbolizes unity, a rainbow in unison.
7 For more about the importance of naming as a political act of resistance refer to the work of Seed-Pihama (2017).
8 Mahalo nui loa, Sharon Ehia! I am so grateful to Sharon for sharing her mana'o (wisdom) and experience working with wāhine at home in Hawai'i. Mahalo nō!

References

Brook, B. (2016). *Biggest Brightest Supermoon in 68 Years to Pass by Earth on Monday November 14.* Available: https://www.nzherald.co.nz/nz/news/article.cfm?c_id=1&objectid=11746489, accessed 12 December 2016.
Coney, H. (2019). *The Magnificent Seven (*Wellbeing *version).* Available: https://www.newsroom.co.nz/2020/01/16/986156/the-magnificent-seven-wellbeing-version, accessed 16 January 2020.

Dillard, C. (2008). 'When the ground is black, the ground is fertile: Exploring feminist epistemology and healing methodologies of the spirit', in N. Denzin, Y. Lincoln, and L.T. Smith (eds.) *Handbook of Critical and Indigenous Methodologies*. Sage Publishing: Thousand Oaks, CA, 277–292.

E Hina e! E Hine e! (2019). 'Exhibition', *Waikato Museum Te Whare Taonga o Waikato*, Hamilton, NZ, 14 September 2019–2021.

Garcia, O. and Leiva, C. (2014). 'Theorizing and enacting translanguaging for social justice', in A. Blackledge and A. Creese (eds.), *Heteroglossia as Practice and Pedagogy*, Springer Educational Linguistics 20: London, 199–216.

Handy, E.S., Handy, E.G., and Pūkui, M. (1972). *Native Planters in Old Hawaii: Their Life, Lore and Environment*. Honolulu: Bishop Museum Press.

Henry, T. (1995). *Voyaging Chiefs of Havai'i*. Kalamakū Press: Honolulu, HI.

ho'omanawanui, k. (2010). 'Mana Wahine, education and nation-building: lessons from the epic of Pele and Hi'iaka for Kanaka Maoli today', *Multicultural Perspectives*, vol 12, no 4: 206–212.

ho'omanawanui, k. (2014). *Voices of Fire, Reweaving the Literary lei of pele and hi'iaka*. University of Minnesota Press: Minneapolis, MN.

Howe, K.R. (ed.). (2006). *Vaka Moana, Voyages of the Ancestors: The Discovery and Settlement of the Pacific*. David Bateman: Auckland.

Kamakau, S. (1964). *Ka Poe Kahiko: The People of Old*. Bishop Museum Press: Honolulu, HI.

Kamakau, S. (1991). *Tales and Traditions of the People of Old: Nā Mo'olelo ka Po'e Kahiko*. Bishop Museum Press: Honolulu, HI.

Kame'eleihiwa, L. (1992). *Native Land and Foreign Desires: Pehea La E Pono Ai?* Bishop Museum Press: Honolulu, HI.

Kame'eleihiwa, L. (1999). *Nā Wāhine Kapu, Divine Hawaiian Women*. 'Ai Pōhaku Press: Honolulu, HI.

Kimmerer, R.W. (2013). *Braiding Sweetgrass: Indigenous Wisdom, Scientific Knowledge and the Teachings of Plants*. Milkweed Editions: Minneapolis, MN.

Kuwada, B.K. (2016). 'We who share breath', Unpublished poem.

Meyer, M. (1998). *Native Hawaiian Epistemology: Contemporary Narratives*. PhD thesis, Harvard University, Cambridge.

Meyer, M. (2001a). 'Hawaiian art: A doorway to knowing', in M. Cazimero and M. Meyer (eds.) *Nā Maka Hou: New Visions, Contemporary Native Hawaiian Art*. Honolulu Academy of Arts: Honolulu, HI.

Meyer, M. (2001b). 'Our own liberation: Reflections on Hawaiian epistemology', *The Contemporary Pacific*, vol 13, no 1: 124–148.

Meyer, M. (2003). *Ho'oulu*. 'Ai Pohakū Press: Honolulu, HI.

Meyer, M. (2008). 'Indigenous and authentic: Hawaiian epistemology and the triangulation of meaning', in N. Denzin, Y. Lincoln, and L.T. Smith (eds.) *Critical and Indigenous Methodologies*. Sage Publications: Thousand Oaks, CA, 217–232.

Murphy, N. (2014). *Te Awa Atua, Menstruation in the Pre-colonial Māori World*. He Puna Manawa Ltd: Ngāruawahia, NZ.

Nelson, A. (1991). *Māori Canoes-Nga Waka Māori*. Wellington: IPL Books.

Pūkui, M., Haertig, E., and Lee, C. (1972). *Nānā I Ke Kumu, Look to the Source, Volume I*. Hui Hānai: Honolulu, HI.

Revilla, N. and Osorio, J. (2019). 'Aloha is deoccupied love', in H. Aikau and V. Gonzalez (eds.) *Detours, A Decolonial Guide to Hawai'i*. Duke University Press: Durham, NC, 125–131.

Ritte, K., Naehu, H., Goodyear-Ka'ōpua, N., and Warech, J. (2019). 'Welcome to the future: Restoring Keawanui Fishpond', in H. Aikau and V. Gonzalez (eds.) *Detours, A Decolonial Guide to Hawai'i*. Duke University Press: Durham, NC, 230–243.

Seed-Pihama, J. (2017). *Ko wai tō Ingoa? The Transformative Potential of Māori Names*. PhD thesis, University of Waikato, NZ.

Silva, N. (2007). 'Pele, Hi'iaka, and Haumea: Women and Power in Two Hawaiian Mo'olelo', *Pacific Studies*, vol 30, no 1–2: 159–181.

Silva, N. (2004). *Aloha Betrayed: Native Hawaiian Resistance to American Colonialism*. Duke University Press: Durham, NC.

Steele, J. (2020). *Wāhine Waking*. Available: https://hanahou.com/23.1/wahine-waking, accessed 20 February 2020.

Teaiwa, T. (1995). *Searching for Nei Nim'anoa*. Mana Publications: Suva.

Trask, H.K. (1994). *Light in the Crevice Never Seen*. CALYX Books: Corvallis, OR.

Tregear, E. (1891). *The Maori Comparative Dictionary*. Wellington: Lyon and Blair.

Wilson, K.L.N. (2005). 'View from the mountain: Moloka'i nui a Hina', *Junctures*, vol 5: 31–46.

Wilson, K.L.N. (2008a). 'Nā wāhine Kanaka Maoli holowa'a: Native Hawaiian women voyagers', *International Journal of Maritime History*, vol 20, no 2: 307–324.

Wilson, K.L.N. (2008b). 'A waka ama journey: Reflections on outrigger canoe paddling as a medium for epistemological adventuring', *Pathways: The Ontario Journal of Outdoor Education*, vol 21, no 1: 19–23.

Wilson, K.L.N. (2008c). 'Reflection on Moloka'i nui a Hina', in M. Ah Nee-Benham (ed.), *Indigenous Educational Models for Contemporary Practice*. New York: Routledge: 194–198.

Wilson-Hokowhitu, N. (2012). 'He pukoa kani 'āina, Kanaka Maoli approaches to mo'okū'auhau as methodology', *AlterNative, An International Journal of Indigenous Peoples*, vol 8, no 2: 137–147.

Wilson-Hokowhitu, N. (2016). *Hō'ailona [Watercolour on Paper]*. ArtsPost Gallery: Hamilton, NZ.

Wilson-Hokowhitu, N. (2017a). *Hina Sailing into the Moon [Watercolour on Paper]*. Waikato Museum: Hamilton, NZ.

Wilson-Hokowhitu, N. (2017b). *Pelehonuamea [Watercolour on Paper]*. Next Level Gallery: Hamilton, NZ.

Wilson-Hokowhitu, N. (2019). 'Mo'okū'auhau as methodology: Sailing into the future, guided by the past', in N. Wilson-Hokowhitu (ed.), *The Past Before Us-Mo'okū'auhau as Methodology*. University of Hawai'i Press: Honolulu, HI, 120–131.

Part 2
Indigenous theory and method
Part editor: Linda Tuhiwai Smith

10

The emperor's 'new' materialisms

Indigenous materialisms and *disciplinary colonialism*

Brendan Hokowhitu

Recently I was asked to contribute a chapter to a special edition of a journal focusing on 'New Materialisms and Sport'. Although I'd heard of 'New Materialisms' and was vaguely aware of its underpinnings, I chose not to seriously engage with the so-called theoretical 'turn' because it appeared to be a case of the 'emperor's new clothes'. This was particularly so for Indigenous Studies, which seemed to me had no real compunction to engage with New Materialisms. The theoretical drivers and philosophical currents that hastened the theoretical turn away from the multiple binaries and humanist traditions underpinning Western thought since the Enlightenment, at least, were already well and truly ensconced in our discipline and the fabric of our cultures and epistemologies. That is, Indigenous Studies (whilst not always practiced) and the historical conditioning of Indigenous peoples as 'pre-modern' (and thus beholden to stereotypes such as 'physical' and 'close to nature') suggests our discipline is already well aware that the human individual is anything but centric amidst a largely non-human universe. The New Materialisms closes alignment with Posthumanism, and both genres co-rejection of anthropocentrism, then, feels more like a 'false-dawn' and another example of an over-exaggerated claim of Western discovery.

New Materialisms emerged largely out of the work of feminist theorists in the 1990s thinking about subjectivity, materiality, embodiment, alternative sexuality and genders (Dolphijn and van der Tuin 2012) and the lack thereof within critical Western theory. Although specifically located, more broadly its emergence signalled a desire to bring materiality back into theorising the conditions of human and non-human existence. Ironically, the emergence was largely Self-referential in that it called upon its own (i.e., Western) genealogy of the thought of white men. As the most prominent scholar in the field, Rosi Braidotti, said back in 2000, New Materialisms was, "Descartes' nightmare, Spinoza's hope, Nietzsche's complaint, Freud's obsession, Lacan's favorite fantasy" (Braidotti 2000: 159). Later, Braidotti defines "neo-materialism" as a, "method, a conceptual frame and a political stand, which refuses the linguistic paradigm, stressing instead the concrete yet complex materiality of bodies immersed in social relations of power" (Dolphijn and van der Tuin 2012: 21). Other than Braidotti, prominent theorists in New Materialisms include Manuel DeLanda, Karen Barad, and Quentin Meillassoux (Dolphin and van der Tuin 2012). One of my central critiques is, thus, the Self-referential nature of New Materialisms including it is tracing Western critical philosophy's linear development back beyond and through Marx's Historical Materialism.

New Materialisms in a sense reignited debates about the usefulness of Marxism by critiquing the lack of analysis of the centrality of material conditions to the production of culture and history. As Lewis and Kahn outline, labour power is a "unique commodity" precisely because, "it cannot be separated from the body that contains the physical, mental, linguistic, and affective potential/capacity necessary for the production of surplus value. Thus, labour power is the one commodity that remains tethered to flesh and blood" (2010: 20). The new materialists critique the over-abundance of scholarly work focused on identity and social constructionism, which is also rampant within Indigenous Studies, is heavily critiqued by new materialists. New Materialism's focus on embodiment, alternative sexuality and genders, however is, to put it mildly, a far cry from what Marx was thinking and, as Braidotti argued, "leads to a radical re-reading of materialism, away from its strictly Marxist definition (Braidotti 1991: 264).

Regardless, the nomenclature of 'new' is simply offensive in the broader realm of multiple realities because it's claims to temporal ownership of ideas that already existed in multiple Indigenous philosophies reminds me of the doctrine of discovery where already discovered lands only became meaningful through a white captive narrative; *terra nullius* equivalent *cōgitātiō nullius*. As Zoe Todd (2016) said after watching a presentation by a well-known non-Indigenous scholar on the 'ontological turn':

> the ones we credited for these incredible insights into the 'more-than-human', and sentience and agency ... were not the people who built and maintain the knowledge systems that european and north american anthropologists and philosophers have been studying for well over a hundred years, and predicating their current 'aha' ontological moments (or re-imagingings of the discipline) upon. No, here we were celebrating and worshipping a european thinker for 'discovering' what many an Indigenous thinker around the world could have told you for millennia. (online)

Hence, the nomenclature 'new' reminds me of what I have previously referred to as an "endemic discursive psychosis" bolstered by "delusions of grandeur" (2016b: 93) in relation to the invader cultures our ancestors met, and we've had to endure since. In this case the preface 'new' re-assumes a void if not delivered into this world by European/US reason. However, I was willing to investigate further.

In this chapter, I am concerned with engaging the ideas within New Materialisms and Posthumanism, at least. As is typical with my approach to Western theory generally I want to understand its use as a tool of intellectual labour. In this chapter, I flesh out the interplay among musculature, physiology, and colonial history; where the body can be a site of emancipation and/or regulation:

> Ambivalence is the overwhelming feeling that haunts my relationship with physicality. Not only my body, but the bodies of an imagined multitude of Indigenous peoples dissected and made whole again via the violent synthesis of the colonial project.
>
> *(Hokowhitu 2016a: 164)*

Posthumanism

Although Indigenous Studies folks have, like their non-Indigenous colleagues, also leant heavily on post-structuralism, Cultural Studies, and, more generally, social constructionism. Although these theoretical frameworks have power and identity as a common denominator, they have typically paid little attention to the agency of materiality and non-human beings/things. Given the immediacy of neo-colonialism, our scholarship has tended to remain in the juridical-political human domains in support of Indigenous communities steadfast focused on the survivance of their 'human rights', lands, and cultures via notions of peoples, nation and tribal sovereignty. The critique here is that Indigenous Studies, for good reason, has tended to remain focused on the human, and as Kim Tallbear pointed out to me also reflects Indigenous Studies lack of engagement with the materiality of the natural sciences (2020 personal communication). This is similar to Robert Young's (2001) assessment of the state of Postcolonial Studies in relation to non-secular thought. He writes: "Despite its espousal of subaltern resistance, [postcolonial theory] scarcely values subaltern resistance that does not operate according to its own secular terms" (338). That is, despite our espousal of epistemological closeness to non-humans, seldom are we capable within the academy to provide teachings, pedagogies, and theory that operate beyond the non-human.

It is also important that Indigenous Studies scholars become more familiar with the lexicon of New Materialisms as we enter into a new juridico-political era in Indigenous/invader states. In Aotearoa/New Zealand, for instance, a landmark decision by New Zealand's Parliament conferred 'legal personhood' to the Whanganui River:

> It confers a legal personality on the Whanganui River. A legal person is an entity that has the same rights and responsibilities as a person. ... The move reflects Whanganui iwi's unique ancestral relationship with the river. ... It will recognise Te Awa Tupua as an indivisible and living whole, comprising the Whanganui River from the mountains to the sea, and all its physical and metaphysical elements.
>
> *(New Zealand Parliament 2017: online)*

Charpleix (2018: 28) suggests the decision signals a shift, "towards an appreciation of the rights of everything that constitutes the Earth, and in showing that settler societies can, and must, forge new identities in ways that honour both their Indigenous and colonial histories". In more romantic terms, *National Geographic* reported:

> For Māori [*sic*] leaders, the focus on legal rights is misplaced. What matters is a new orientation of humans to the natural world, one based not on rights but responsibilities. Or to paraphrase John F. Kennedy: 'Ask not what nature can do for you – ask what you can do for nature'.
>
> *(2019: online)*

This is not exactly 'posthuman'; in fact, possibly the opposite. That is, the awarding of human legal rights to a non-human entity could be read as a colonial personification of the more than human. Nonetheless, the New Zealand Government's acknowledgement of the interrelated nature of Indigeneity and the physical and metaphysical milieu is nonetheless a significant juridico-political shift in terms of recognition of non-human sovereignty, especially in relation to Indigenous epistemologies. Related is Posthumanism's focus on objects and the inanimate, that essentially could be framed as 'equal-rights for things' and to recognise that things do not share our perception and have their own vitality beyond our comprehension. As Nietzsche wrote back in the 1870s in mockery of humans' perception of their totality of knowledge:

> [o]ne might invent such a fable, and yet he still would not have adequately illustrated how miserable, how shadowy and transient, how aimless and arbitrary the human intellect looks within nature. ... But if we could communicate with the gnat, we would learn that he

likewise flies through the air with the same solemnity, that he feels the flying center of the universe within himself.

(1990: 79)

The inhumanity of colonialism and other European atrocities and subsequent Nietzschean-like development of anti-humanism (read in this context, as the dying belief in the spirit of human nature) in Western thought has been central to the development of postmodern, poststructural, and postcolonial theory. The invisibility of Indigenous peoples in New Materialisms is thus merely another symptom of the pathogen of Western thought which not only "preserve[s] the boundaries of sense for itself" (Bhabha 1983: 24) but seemingly to do this actively excludes us from conversations so that, indeed, the emperor's clothing can appear afresh.

As an example, one of the foundations of the Posthuman/New Materialist theoretical turn is subverting or destabilising the individual human being, which has been so central to Western philosophy and thought since the Enlightenment and has centralised, for instance, individual human rights as a mainstay of political discourses. Although there is not the room to delve into it here, 'sovereignty' as a concept, is important here because of its genealogy, which has been entirely human centric in European philosophy (Moreton-Robinson 2015). Although it is almost redundant to say within the context of a Critical Indigenous Studies Handbook, one of the pathologies of colonisation was to mark Indigenous peoples as not fully human and the lands they lived upon as unproductive and, thus, empty. These underpinning justifications of colonialism rationalised the usurpation of lands and resources and the killing of Indigenous peoples, whilst importantly, in unsettler states at least, it justified the 'civilisation' of Natives (i.e., the so-called 'White-Man's-Burden').

This strategic positioning of Indigenous peoples served the allegorical function of helping to better define and delimit the aforementioned human centricity to Western thought; that is, rationale, stoic, unemotional, intelligent and divorced from nature (in the sense that land and the environment were only deemed of value in productive terms under the logic of capital accumulation). In contrast, the savage was irrational, emotional, encumbered by their physicality and very much ensconced in nature. It is also clear that the very presence of Indigenous and other non-white peoples destabilised binaries such as the human/nature divide. However, Indigenous peoples' closeness to nature and general savagery was usefully explained away anthropologically. That is, Indigenous peoples were described as unevolved images of the civilised European Self (Tuhiwai Smith 1999).

These ideas are quite old-hat for Critical Indigenous Studies at least. However, if we reanalyse it via the lens of Posthumanism it is clear that the multiple dualisms that the savage indigene/civilised European binary allegorically served, bolstered the scaffolding that structured the human centricity of post-Enlightenment Western philosophy. The then shortcomings of Indigenous cultures are now being lauded by posthumanists/new materialists alike, within a so-called 'turn' towards materiality and the posthuman, yet with a seemingly blanket[2] disregard of the power/knowledge nexus which privileged human thought in the first place. That is, these binaries helped constitute the very foundations of Western thought that posthumanists are now rallying against, including a desire to break down the stalwart binary of European rationalism; the objective human versus irrational nature. The fact that Indigenous epistemologies incorporated other non-human ways of knowing destabilised the human/nature binary and necessitated the development of theories by Europeans to try and encapsulate this oddity within their grand narrative. Theories abounded ranging on a continuum from the noble savage to the ignoble savage, yet they all coded our worldviews as mythical and, further, required ontological language such as 'totemism' and 'animism' to describe and catalogue Indigenous belief systems.

Nevertheless, the repositioning of the ethical centrality of materiality and non-human animals/things is, at least, an in-road for Indigenous philosophies that, until relatively recently would have been considered mythical and/or hocus pocus, and at the very least, irrational. Tallbear nicely sums the process I have oulined here: " ... so previous Euro(American) thinkers erased Indigenous peoples/thought as part of their de-animation of the material. Today, Euro(American) thinkers erase Indigenous peoples/thought again as they seek to re-animate the material" (2020 personal communication). A good example of this already discovered discovery comes from the Māori context where the lack of objective distance between nature, human genealogy and knowledge as explained by Mere Roberts via case studies of lizards and kūmara (sweet potato) illustrates a genealogical taxonomy explanative of astronomical, human, plant and animal relationships: Roberts suggests:

> Māori knowledge concerning the origin and relationships of material things like the kūmara is visualized as a series of co-ordinates arranged upon a collapsed time-space genealogical framework. This framework provides cosmogonical knowledge of celestial deities as well as historical ontologies, whose relationships extend to material things.
>
> *(2012: 40)*

The human/non-human interrelatedness typical of Indigenous cultures helped validate colonisation not only in terms of the White-Man's-Burden as already described, but also in the very basic strategic sense where Imperialists viewed the world as a series of territories to be colonised for land and resources; the original inhabitants were merely a part of a territory (Charpleix 2018) and thus could be consumed as a part of nature, as distinct from the European human.

In Braidotti's (2013) seminal book, *The Posthuman*, one of the central tenets is that there exists a fundamental interconnectedness between all forms of matter. This basic concept, in turn, enables a decentralisation of the typical ethical human centric questions. I can hear Indigenous scholars scoffing at the 'newness' of this idea, for the material and esoteric connection of all things (e.g., 'mauri'; 'all my relations') is fundamental to the Indigenous cultures that I'm aware of and really is 'Indigenous Cultures 101'. Afterall, it was European rationalism that believed it could differentiate between truth and falsehood and that the universe was comprehendible in human terms. Referring to the work of Vine Deloria Jr. and others, Tallbear (2017) relays this basic Indigenous principle as, " ... a framework that posits social relations not only between humans and 'animals', but also between humans and 'energy', 'spirits', 'rocks', and 'stars' ... [that is] an indigenous metaphysic: an understanding of the intimate knowing relatedness of all things" (191).

Perhaps I am being overly cynical in my interpretation of Posthumanism at least. What is possibly most valuable to point out is not the field's near-sightedness, but rather that at least it is attempting to unravel its own philosophical genealogy to reveal the limits and binds it has placed on knowledge itself. As I have written elsewhere:

> by raising the spectre of knowledge unintelligible to western rationalism; the possibility of Critical Indigenous Studies as a site of erasure and re-ciphering; a site to expunge those categorical taxonomies written across Indigenous epistemologies, and to reinsert those orderings already blurred beyond comprehension. From the universal mind-set, the inabilities to contain the irrational and unfathomable to the boundaries of a universal epistemology amplify the monstrous potential of Critical Indigenous Studies.
>
> *(2016b: 93)*

There are commonalities between how I conceive of Critical Indigenous Studies, and the philosophical underpinnings of a 'new' field attempting its own form of auto-immunisation:

> The monstrous future of the human transforms the human beyond recognition by the state or by the community ... it calls into question the anthropocentric assurances of human superiority, rationality, certainty, autonomy, and self-awareness that found the ontological purity of the community. ... In other words, posthumanist skepticism undermines the fundamental 'dignity' and 'centrality' of the human against which all other life is measured, opening up a newly expanded and intensified field for zoömorphic imaginative becomings.
>
> *(Lewis and Khan 2010: 34)*

New Materialisms

Posthumanism shares some common ground with New Materialisms. However, in its pursuit to decentre the human and privilege the relations between matter and the discursive, no New Materialisms texts (that I am aware of) make reference to Indigenous, postcolonial, and African/Black scholarship. Prominent players in the field, far from abandoning the theoretical bases from where they have come, and from what they are supposedly railing against, are beholden to social constructionist theory, particularly post-structuralism. Consequently, discursive analyses remain, seemingly, critical to a merger with the material. In her seminal book, *Meeting the Universe Halfway: Quantum Physics and the Entanglement of Matter and Meaning*, Karen Barad (2007) coins the term 'agential realism' based on the conjunction of the 'material-discursive', which is simply to say that discursive discourse produces matter and vice-versa, and thus there is a symbiotic relation between the binary so that there is simultaneous co-production. That is, matter and discourse are co-productive.

In Indigenous Studies the analysis has almost always been grounded in the facticity of colonisation, which had a stark material reality for Indigenous peoples and communities who died, were dislocated off of their lands, who were forced to both abandon and create new material cultures, and who refused the Cartesian Dualism that underpinned a great deal of colonial policy. Indigenous Studies, thus, has been typically 'genealogical' in methodology in both discursive and material senses. If we take Frantz Fanon's scholarship as an example, influential across a number of disciplines and penned some 60–70 years ago, his theoretical merger of discursive discourse and materiality is clearly evident, even if squarely focused on the production of the ontology of the colonised subject. Seemingly white negligence is genealogical:

> It is ironic that Jean-Paul Sartre would categorize these philosophical issues under the rubric of existentialism more than a century after these same questions were raised by Africana thinkers who were directly affected by the material conditions of chattel slavery, racial oppression, and their attendant phenomenological effects.
>
> *(Parris 2011: 5)*

It should be clarified that the majority of what is now considered the seminal works of New Materialisms was conducted under what could also be called 'Feminist Cultural Studies', where scholars consciously established a position beyond the Western masculine intellectual tradition of mind/body dualism; "... an approach which refuses to privilege mind over body ... and which assumes that the body cannot be transcended", further emphasising "contingency, locatedness, the irreducibility of difference, the passage of emotions and desire, and the worldliness of being" (Ahmed and Stacey 2001: 3).

The convergence here, if not most aptly and brilliantly highlighted by the work of Sara Ahmed, is possibly that both non-White people and women are very aware of their bodies moving in various spaces. Or put another way, white heteronormative men have throughout colonial history at least enjoyed the privilege of both the dominance of their corporeality and, thus, it's (in a sense) material invisibility, or at the very least a lack of body self-consciousness. This brings me to a blind spot in the New Materialisms' literature that I have noticed. The literature has, like Posthumanism, rightfully tended to have drawn focus away from the human and particularly white heteronormative men as the protagonists of the Anthropocene. Yet, white heteronormative men have dominated the Enlightenment and colonial projects, and colonialism at least was not solely a theoretical endeavour. Far from the mind/body duality that a Cartesian analysis would proffer in relation to bodies and power, white men did not divest the privilege of their bodies, and indeed used the control of their bodies to manifest power relations: "[a] large part of the success of physical culture was its assertion of the male body as heroic rather than erotic, in the body's depiction as 'under control' rather than 'out of control' (Budd 1997: 77).

Indigenous Materialisms

In my own work on colonial sport, Empire's view of sport and physical activity was that masculine morality in particular was/is closely related to the discipline associated with physical training. Accordingly, various sports in the British Colonial context at least (i.e., in particular rugby, cricket and boxing) were seen as training grounds for identifying male leaders (both colonial and Indigenous) who were team players and loyal. This focus on masculine corporeal control and morality in the colonies clearly stemmed from Europe:

> The Fabian Society, founded in 1884, joined in the call for an able-bodied citizenry as the best antidote to the moral and physical virus held to be devouring Britain's martial and economic sinews. The health of the nation was equated with the state of the male body, in particular an athletic soldier-citizenry. More than ever the bodies and minds of both workers and soldiers were, it was felt, in urgent need of control and rationalization if the cycle of threatened instability at home and regular humiliation abroad was to be averted.
>
> *(Beynon 2002: 40)*

The point here is that white colonial male leaders were very well aware of a heroic morality that demanded stoicism and self-restraint demonstrated through the materiality of their bodies. The focus on materiality and bodies here departs from the New Materialisms' literature that tends to focus on the overreliance on human centric masculine rationalism and theory.

This of course was based on the rational achievement of mind over body, but nonetheless white heroic male bodies in conjunction with heteronormative racist discourses produced its own forms of agential realism that, because of their laden power, were somewhat invisible; unlike non-white bodies, as so luminously theorised by Fanon in *Black Skin, White Masks* (1986):

> 'Mama, see the Negro! I'm frightened!' Frightened! Frightened! Now they were beginning to be afraid of me. I made up my mind to laugh myself to tears, but laughter had become impossible. I could no longer laugh, because I already knew that there were legends, stories, history, and above all historicity, which I had learned about from Jaspers. Then, assailed at various points, the corporeal schema crumbled, its place taken by a racial epidermal schema. In the train it was no longer a question of being aware of my body in the third person but in a triple person. In the train I was given not one but two, three places. I had already stopped

being amused. It was not that I was finding febrile coordinates in the world. I existed triply: I occupied space. I moved toward the other ... and the evanescent other, hostile but not opaque, transparent, not there, disappeared. Nausea ... (112)

Fanon reminds us, first, that racism is material in its logic (i.e., it is based on the colour of ones skin) and, second, that racism is both discursive and material in that one's 'corporeal schema' as he refers to it, that is, how a body would normally act in the world when it is not forced to be self-conscious, can be replaced by a 'racial epidermal schema'. In other words, self-consciousness, as an effect of being classified as an epidermal object, subjugates the body's agency. In turn, this process of disorientation causes a profound physiological affect; 'nausea'.

To return to an earlier point, although Indigenous Studies is grounded in the facticity of colonisation it is also quite possible that we have paid little attention to the agency of Indigenous materialisms as we have tended to employ our scholarship to aid the juridico-political battles that have consumed our communities, which very much occur in the conscious human sovereignty domain. Although, up until this point, I haven't employed the terminology 'New Materialisms' in my own work (due to the reasons explained above), nonetheless my scholarship has concentrated on bodies, materiality, and power because of my focus on sport and masculinity and because Foucault has heavily influenced my thinking.

What Foucault refers to as the invisible 'breath' that inhabits discontinuous discourses, even as they mutate, I conceive of as 'physicality' with reference to the colonised Indigenous savage. This traditionalised ontology was/is unmistakably a by-product of savage discourses premised on a Cartesian assessment of the cerebral European and the emotive/physical savage. If savagery is understood from the perspective of Enlightenment rationalism, then it is apparent that it portends a state of unenlightenment, where reason is ruled by physical impulses and/or superstition. As a discursive discourse Indigenous physicality was "capable of linking, and animating a group of discourses, like an organism with its own needs, its own internal force and its own capacity for survival" (Foucault 2002: 39). Darwin's evolutionary theory, for instance, "directed research from afar" acting as "a preposition rather than named, regrouped, and explained ... a theme that always presupposed more than one was aware of ... forcibly transformed into discursive knowledge" (Foucault 2002: 39). Such discursive knowledge underpinned Indigenous 'savagery' and was transcribed into physical terms, onto the Indigenous body and about Indigenous bodily practices. Physicality, thus, is one of those 'dense transfer points'[3] that enabled the production of the Indigenous body as a discursive formation; a lynchpin that strategically enabled/s the imprint of history upon the Indigenous body.

To reiterate here, one of the premises of New Materialisms is that rather than identity being constructed solely through a linguistic oriented discursive discourse, matter (including bodies) interacting with discursive knowledge co-produces subjectivities. In other words, and to relate back to Barad's (2007) coinage, the success of colonialism was first and foremost based on the conjunction of the 'material-discursive', where the discursive discourses surrounding the physicality of the savage was materially effective in the production of Indigenous bodies. Foucault's notion of biopower is useful here because it understands the body as a material site where discursive formations are fleshed out; where discourse, as a "border concept", operates between ethereal knowledge and material conditions. Biopower, thus, refers to, "a power whose task is to take charge of life" requiring "continuous regulatory and corrective mechanisms" (Foucault cited in Rabinow 1984: 20). Importantly, Foucault recognises the 'productive' (as opposed to suppressive) nature of biopower. Such a power "has to qualify, measure, appraise and hierarchize, rather than display itself in its murderous splendor ... [the] juridical institution is increasingly incorporated into a continuum of apparatuses whose functions are for the most part regulatory" (Foucault cited in Rabinow 1984: 20).

Sovereignty colonialism; biopolitical or disciplinary colonialism; security colonialism

The insights that Foucault provides has enabled me to re-theorise the historical and ongoing project of colonialism into three distinct parts. These distinctions mirror his taxonomy of power, firstly 'sovereignty', secondly 'biopower', and lastly 'security' (as outlined in *Security, Territory, Population* 2004). Although there is not the space to expound on how I translate these three notions to colonial power, briefly, *sovereign colonialism* relates to the initial phases of colonisation which was predominantly about imagining the colonial reality so as to set up the limits of power. It was negative (i.e., it said 'no') and used the colonial legal system to create the imagined reality: "We could even say that the law works in the imaginary, since the law imagines and can only formulate all the things that could and must not be done by imagining them. It imagines the negative" (Foucault 2004: 47). For Indigenous peoples, we were imagined as sub-human and, therefore, part of the process of *sovereign colonialism* was to strip us of our Indigenous natural cultural claims to our epistemologies and lands. Although land and resources were probably the most important motivators for *sovereign colonialism*, it was also epistemological in that it imagined a sub-human culture and thus set about banning its practices often validated on being in the interest of the Native themselves. One of the most significant Acts in terms of *sovereign colonialism* in Aotearoa/New Zealand was the 1907 *Tohunga Suppression Act*, which banned the practices of *tohunga* (expert and/or priest). The preamble to the Act states,

> Whereas designing persons, commonly known as tohungas practise on the superstition and credulity of the Māori [*sic*] people by pretending to possess supernatural powers in the treatment and cure of disease, the foretelling of future events, and otherwise, and thereby induce the Māoris [*sic*] to neglect their proper occupations and gather into meetings where their substance is consumed and their minds are unsettled, to the injury of themselves and to the evil example of the Māori people generally.
>
> *(New Zealand Government 1907: online)*

The Crown realised that *tohunga* were able to retain pre-colonial metaphysical belief systems through practices, ritual, and systems of knowledge transferral that set them beyond the imperial scope of the colonising machine and, therefore, employed sovereign power to banish the crucial tie between knowledge and power.

Biopolitical or *disciplinary colonialism* was/is more productive:

> Discipline works in a sphere that is, as it were, complementary to reality. ... Within the disciplinary space a complementary sphere of prescriptions and obligations is constituted that is all the more artificial and constraining as the nature of reality is tenacious and difficult to overcome.
>
> *(Foucault 2004: 47)*

Disciplinary colonialism is most relevant to New Materialisms (I will focus on it more below) because it very much aligns with the 'material-discursive' conjunction already discussed. Rather than the megalithic directive language associated with *sovereign colonialism* that firstly imagined the savage and then subjugated them, *disciplinary colonialism* came later, was also subjugatory, but through the institutionalised discipline of Indigenous bodies and the production of brown citizens through an array of discontinuous discourses, for instance, family structures, soap packaging (McClintock 2002), nutritional advice, unemployment subsidies, institutionalised pre-natal and natal care, war, statistics on childhood obesity, lifestyle magazines, educational curricula, mental health, daily and weekly schedules, prisons, workplaces, sport, time, the solar calendar (see Matamua, this collection); all of these seemingly discontinuous heterogeneous 'enunciations[4]' productively disciplined the Indigenous body.

Although I have yet to seriously theorise *security colonialism*, my best analogy so far is that it could be most readily thought of as the devolution or divestment of responsibility from the State to the Indigenous individual as associated with neo-liberalism. Here the State, employing a free-market logic (i.e., where material reality is a product of individual merit), absolves itself from the crimes of its predecessors, whilst ignoring the material history that led to the present privilege of settler/invaders. This is not exactly what Foucault had in mind in relation to 'security'; he employed the concept to discuss how decisions to manage populations were increasingly being made on the perceived objectivity of the free-market, which in turn validated immoral decisions by the State to harm a few based on benefiting the majority. However, the logic of managing populations who are perceived as a whole as opposed to composite of multiple variant groups, is a logic extremely important to Indigenous peoples especially in places like New Zealand where 'egalitarianism' is a strong ethical undercurrent.

Biopolitical colonialism

Foucault's work has helped me think about colonialism as not only repressive but also as 'productive' in that it has, for the most part, produced brown compliant citizens. In *The History of Sexuality: Volume 1,* Foucault (1978) argues that the biopolitical regulation of a population operates beyond the conscious production and control of knowledge. That is, crucial to biopolitical control is internalisation; the self-imposition of regulatory mechanisms so that the material, the corporeal and ethos function in unison, albeit a unison tethered together via heterogeneous statements. In the context of the present chapter then, it could be argued that the conditioning of Indigenous bodies throughout colonisation has not only a symbolic genealogy but a material existence also. Here, the etiological importance of the word 'genealogy' should not be underestimated, for it does not merely mean a textual genealogy. Foucault's nomenclature is literally referring to the material and biological descent of corporeality, where the body is, "totally imprinted by history" (1984:83). From a Foucauldian lens then, the production of a key identity (like Indigeneity) is not merely an ethereal concept, it is a co-creation of materialisation and discourse. Michael Hardt and Antonio Negri (2009) define biopower as "the power over life – or, really, the power to administer and produce life – that functions through the government of populations, managing their health, reproductive capacities and so forth" (57).

To revert back to Barad's coinage then, 'material-discursive', Foucault's biopolitical analysis in particular aligns with this convergence. Yet, Foucault's analysis could also be seen as akin to Marxism in that Marx (1964) suggested the proletariat's loss of the products of their labour is one of the factors leading to 'alienation' and 'false-consciousness'. That is, in both Marx's 'alienation' and Foucault's 'biopower' matter precedes consciousness, which from a traditional Cartesian viewpoint suggests a lack of agency if we remain focused on human consciousness. Thus, Barad's notion of 'agential realism' is helpful because it outlines the emergence of matter in conjunction with discourse: "[a] phenomenon is a specific intra-action of an 'object'; and the 'measuring agencies'; the object and the measuring agencies emerge from, rather than precede, the intra-action that produces them" (Barad 2007: 128).

Although I have never referred to 'agential realism' in my own scholarship for reasons already explained, it is evident that materiality has been a central component of my theoretical analysis. In an Aotearoa/New Zealand context, at least, it is clear to me, within the frame of *disciplinary* colonialism, that the Māori body emerged with broader colonial material discourses including capitalism and later neo-liberalism. In my writings on Indigenous masculinities, for instance, the Māori male body symbolised and came to embody the physical realm and, thus, was employed for its physical labour, observed for its performativity, and humanised through physical pursuits such as physical labouring, soldiering and playing sport. If we take employment as an example, unlike Pākehā men who enjoyed a normal spread throughout occupational strata, by 1965, "nearly 90 percent of Māori men [were] employed as farmers, foresters, labourers, transport operators, factory workers, or in other skilled and unskilled occupations" (Watson 1967: 6).

Thus, thinking about Māori men of my grandparents' and parents' generations, who were almost exclusively physical labourers, I get a better sense of 'agential realism' because the particular and contextual production of bodily cognition was a necessary effect of a physically intensive life for Māori men who typically acquired different relations to their bodies than, say, New Zealand's white middle- and upper-class men, whilst also being subjected to disciplinary colonialism, whether that be via educational discourses:

> Māori [sic] are not fitted to the various professions. About 999 out of 1000 could not bear the strain of higher education. In commerce, the Māori [sic] could not hope to compete with the Pakeha [sic]. In trades the Māoris [sic] were splendid copyists, but not originators. As carpenters they would cope under a capable instructor but not otherwise. Agriculture was the one calling suitable for Māoris [sic]. … It was therefore necessary to teach them the nobility of labour.
>
> *(Headmaster Reverend Butterfield, speech to the Young Māori Party, 1910, cited Barrington 1988: 49)*

Or, via war and sport:

> They showed themselves to be good at those things which Pakeha men [were also] proud of. Māori were good at war and they were damn good at playing rugby, so they took on a special status of being Kiwi males with a slightly exotic flavour.
>
> *(Jock Philips, cited Schick and Dolan 1999: 56)*

Hence, as I have referred to elsewhere, 'physical education' takes on a whole other meaning in relation to the *disciplinary colonisation* of Māori.

The idea of biopower or, in this context, *disciplinary colonisation*, suggests that the materiality of Foucault's genealogy is alienating. Many scholars, thus, have interpreted Foucauldian disciplinary power as suggestive of agency-lessness because regulation of the body as an antecedent to regulation of the mind, challenges the natural order of Western philosophy; mind over matter. Yet, it is not entirely clear what Foucault thought of matter and agency. One of the Foucault quotes that I've often admired is that people, "are much freer than they feel" (1988: online), because it is very hopeful in its simplicity, yet it does signal that overcoming one's own body's embedded history precedes liberation. For me, as an Indigenous person, the weight of colonisation can feel very heavy not only because of the ongoing colonial violences but also because of its physical genealogy; that is, the limits we put on ourselves, perhaps, as a result of internalising *disciplinary colonialism*. As I've written elsewhere:

> I freely admit I have been colonized; or rather I have failed to be decolonised. As a consequence, the feeling of 'being postcolonial' resembles a state of anxiety, a state of tension, a state of *disease* that indigenous people ingest in the pursuit of an unrealizable dream, that of

decolonisation. Being postcolonial is thus the realization that decolonisation will not return indigenous people to an imagined pre-colonial purity and living within the tension of the coloniser/colonised binary.

(2014: 40)

As Indigenous Studies scholars we are inclined to want to tend to the survivance of our communities and, as a consequence, we typically end up defending our hard fought for gains to be simply acknowledged as 'human' via notions of 'authenticity' and 'tradition', whilst methodologically underpinning our struggles via 'colonial-*ressentiment*'. That is, we employ the immorality of the coloniser to justify our actions. Moreover, the chasm between pre-colonial authenticity and post-contact illegitimacy sets up the conditions for 'truthful' representations of Indigeneity where some Indigenous ontologies were/are considered more authentic than others, leading to lateral violence. Seldom, however, do we focus on freeing ourselves from the burden of colonial history and the corporeal, philosophical and metaphysical limits it has placed on us and that we carry genealogically and heavily.

The point here, in relation to New Materialisms is that Indigenous bodies have been disciplined in many ways and are attuned by dominant discourses in many ways, but this doesn't necessarily mean that Indigenous bodies are subjugated; such one-way traffic would infer 'biopower' or disciplinary power. However, the Indigenous body both compliant with and resistant to a colonial 'physical education' or *disciplinary colonialism* is a clear definition of 'biopolitics':

On the biopolitical terrain ... where powers are continually made and unmade, bodies resist. They have to resist in order to exist. History therefore cannot be understood merely as the horizon on which biopower configures reality through domination. On the contrary, history is determined by the biopolitical antagonisms and resistances to biopower.

(Hardt and Negri 2009: 31)

In this sense, matter is agential in that it co-produces discursive discourses. That is the body, if pushed, will comply and, if pushed, will revolt. Also, as Hardt and Negri go on to point out, seldom is resistance effective in isolation: "corporeal resistance produces subjectivity, not in an isolated or independent way but in the complex dynamic with the resistances of other bodies" (2009: 31).

The broader point and circling back to the agency of matter, is that when Indigenous bodies resist *en masse* not only will the corporeal dynamic effect subjectivity, the co-occurring effect on discursive discourses enables the conditions for alternative subjectivities to be created. As is consistent with this chapter, these 'new' enlightenments were written about by Fanon 60 years prior to this publication:

Decolonization never takes place unnoticed, for it influences individuals and modifies them fundamentally. It transforms spectators crushed with their inessentiality into privileged actors, with the grandiose glare of history's floodlights upon them. It brings a natural rhythm into existence, introduced by new [subjectivities], and with it a new language and a new humanity. ... The naked truth of decolonization evokes for us the searing bullets and bloodstained knives which emanate from it. For if the last shall be first, this will only come to pass after a murderous and decisive struggle between the two protagonists.

(Fanon 1961: 36–7)

In *The Wretched of the Earth* (1961), thus, Fanon's decolonisation involves a violent overthrow of the coloniser not merely to get rid of the coloniser but also as transformative bodily act that materially 'sheds' the genealogical layers of colonial abuses; a necessary corporeal metamorphosis for decolonisation. Whilst not necessarily an advocate of Fanon's position here, nonetheless, it is consistent with a previous point that the 'insurrections' of Indigenous subjectivities will not manifest if Indigenous peoples are not unpossessed of the corporeal layers of colonial history.

Biopolitical resistance

'Insurrections of knowledge', is another of Foucault's concepts that has helped me think about Indigenous Studies as a discipline carving a space within a Western scientific taxonomy and an academy set on preserving its "true body of knowledge" (Foucault 1984: 83). Foucault's genealogical approach is 'anti-science' in that it rejects totalising knowledges that he would like challenged via subjugated knowledges, which assumedly would include Indigenous epistemologies:

> [Genealogy] is a way of playing local, discontinuous, disqualified, or nonlegitimized knowledges off against the unitary theoretical instance that claims to be able to filter them, organize them into a hierarchy, organize them in the name of a true body of knowledge, in the name of the rights of a science that is in the hands of the few. Genealogies are therefore not positivistic returns to a form of science that is more attentive or more accurate. Genealogies are quite specifically, antisciences ... the insurrections of knowledges
>
> *(Foucault 2003: 9)*

Here, I introduce theorisation surrounding 'Indigenous insurrections' as firstly Indigenous corporeal knowledge and, secondly, discursive intelligence that resides beyond Western rational thought. When Indigeneity is conceived as a biopolitical terrain, then Indigenous insurrections involve:

> the creation of new subjectivities that are presented at once as resistance and de-subjectification. If we remain too closely tied to a philological analysis of Foucault's texts, we might miss the central point: his analyses of biopower are aimed not merely at an empirical description of how power works for and through subjects but also at the potential for the production of alternative subjectivities.
>
> *(Hardt and Negri 2009: 59)*

Read alongside biopolitics and the 'material-discursive' conjunction, 'Indigenous insurrections' can be viewed as Indigenous intelligence that propagates bodies and discursive discourses that co-produce alternative subjectivities. Critical Indigenous Studies has its part to play in these insurrections as we bring forth those subjugated knowledges hidden or disfigured by Western taxonomies but not as some anthropological project to be assimilated within, but rather as a project of co-production with Indigenous bodies set to unravel dominant taxonomies and systems and to unweight ourselves of the burden of colonisation.

Conclusion

This chapter has enabled me to engage with some of the New Materialisms/Posthumanism literature; a task which felt like a re-witnessing of Western centricity making; a regurgitation. In its forgetfulness it repossesses the 'rights' to knowledge. It forgets that Indigenous peoples were rendered incapable of cerebral rational thought and, thus, were like animals, other living things, nature, and objects whose sole purpose was to act as metaphors, similes and allegorical figures

143

in re-centring the civilised rational European. The layers of irony that our already 'posthuman' epistemologies have been both historically subjugated and conveniently ignored, reveal the morphing nature of Western thought as strategic and violent; intent on, once again, an attempt to 'preserve the boundaries of sense for itself'.

The fact that Indigenous Studies and peoples have largely been absent or invisible in these burgeoning discussions is symptomatic of Western theory's *pathology* and *dis*ease. I reference 'pathology' and '*disease*' here intently because I would like to draw attention to the material, sub-human character of colonisation commonly asserted as an all-too-human pathological personality. That is, rather than thinking of colonisation as an anthropomorphism (a human-systems pathological killer, perhaps) we can also think of it materially and physiologically as a pathogen enabling *dis*ease (a material pathological killer, perhaps). As decolonial or anti-colonial theorists, then, our non-human material task is as 'pathologists'. The analogy is not a difficult one to draw, given I am writing this chapter in a world currently in lockdown due to COVID-19, but more importantly because of the devastation to Indigenous peoples caused by pathogens brought to our shores by colonial oppressors.

I've chosen to engage with New Materialisms largely due to my background in sport and physical education, yet it has only tended to infuriate me in terms of the west's continued claim to knowledge, ENTIRELY. Indigenous thinkers have been doing this work for millennia. My own now 18-year-old PhD research was in itself a 'material-discursive' experience; "from the innocence of jumping for joy, to the moment I become aware of my body, the moment of self-consciousness in the archive" (Hokowhitu 2016a: 164), which is to say that through research my better comprehension of discursive discourses surrounding Māori physicality had a profound material affect; in a sense during those walks through the archive, I became aware of the enormity of Cartesian discursive discourses in relation to coding Indigenous peoples as 'physical' and the violence the physical indigene and rational European tropes enabled; I questioned my own physicality, my own historical identity which was heavily reliant on sports and physical activity; thus my own 'corporeal schema crumbled', and in its place a tension-packed Cartesian schema; ill-at-ease, uneasy and *dis*-eased. The 'material-discursive' co-produced an altered subjectivity. Yet, from this *dis*-ease, a passion grew; a fire ignited.

Notes

1 I am capitalizing Self here to reference the notion of the Other. Thus, Self refers to the Western subject as the core genealogical mode of thinking about the world by Western theorists.
2 Of the New Materialisms literature I have read, the one exception here is Rosi Braidotti's (2013) book *The Posthuman* in which the opening chapter argues that colonialism was founded on the development of the Self/Other human dichotomy where Europeans made Indigenous peoples less than human to validate colonialism and, thus, in turn helped define the Western human ideal.
3 In *The History of Sexuality* Foucault refers to sexuality in similar fashion, where sexuality is "... an especially dense transfer point for relations of power ... sexuality is not the most intractable element in power relations, but rather one of those endowed with the greatest instrumentality: useful for the greatest number of manoeuvres and capable of serving as a point of support, as a lynchpin, for the most varied strategies" (1978: 103).
4 According to Young (2001) an enunciation, "... constitutes a specific material event, a performative act or a function, an historical eruption that impinges on and makes an incision into the circumstance. Its effect ... is primarily one of discontinuity, of deictic intervention, of effecting change, but it also exists in a productive tension with regularity" (401–402).

References

Ahmed, S. and Stacey, J. (eds.) (2001). *Thinking Through Skin: Transformations: Thinking Through Feminism*. Routledge: New York.

Barad, K. (2007). *Meeting the Universe Halfway: Quantum Physics and the Entanglement of Matter and Meaning*. Duke University Press: Durham, NC.

Barrington, J.M. (1988). 'Learning the "dignity of labour": Secondary education policy for Maoris', *New Zealand Journal of Educational Studies*, vol 23, no 1: 45–58.

Beynon, J. (2002). *Masculinities and Culture*. Open University Press: Buckingham.

Bhabha, H. (1983). 'The other question', *Screen*, vol 24, no 6: 24–25.

Braidotti, R. (1991). *Patterns of Dissonance: A Study of Women and Contemporary Philosophy*. Polity Press: Cambridge.

Braidotti, R. (2000). 'Teratologies', in I. Buchanan and C. Colebrook (eds.) *Deleuze and Feminist Theory*. Edinburgh University Press: Edinburgh, 156–172.

Braidotti, R. (2013). *The Posthuman*. Polity Press: Cambridge.

Budd, M. (1997). *The Sculpture Machine: Physical Culture and Body Politics in the Age of Empire*. Palgrave Macmillan: London.

Charpleix, L. (2018). 'The Whanganui River as te awa tupu: Place-based law in a legally pluralistic society'. *The Geographical Journal*, vol 184: 19–30.

Dolphijn, R. and van der Tuin, I. (2012). 'Interview with Rosi Braidotti', in R. Dolphijn and I. van der Tuin (eds.) *New Materialism: Interviews & Cartographies*. Open Humanities Press: Ann Arbor, MI, 19–37.

Fanon, F. (1961). *The Wretched of the Earth* (C. Farrington, trans.). Grove Press: New York.

Fanon, F. (1986). *Black Skin, White Masks* (C. Markmann, trans.). Pluto Press: London.

Foucault, M. (1978). The History of Sexuality: Volume 1. Pantheon: New York.

Foucault, M. (1984). 'Nietzsche, genealogy, history', in P. Rabinow (ed.) *The Foucault Reader*. Pantheon Books: New York, 76–100.

Foucault, M. (1988). 'Truth, power, self', Interviewed by R. Martin, October 25. Available: https://foucault.info/documents/foucault.truthPowerSelf/, accessed May 7, 2020.

Foucault, M. (2002). *The Archaeology of Knowledge* (A.M. Sheridan Smith, trans.). Routledge: London.

Foucault, M. (2003). *Society Must Be Defended: Lectures at the Collège de France 1975–1976* (D. Macey, trans.). Picador: New York.

Foucault, M. (2004). *Security, Territory, Population: Lectures at the Collège de France 1977-1978* (G. Burchell, trans.). Palgrave Macmillan: New York.

Hardt, M. and Negri, A. (2009). *Commonwealth*. Harvard University Press: Cambridge, MA.

Hokowhitu, B. (2016a). 'Indigenous bodies, ordinary lives', in D. Robinson and L. Randall (eds.) *Social Justice in Physical Education: Critical Reflections and Pedagogies for Change*. Canadian Scholar's Press: Toronto, ON, 164–182.

Hokowhitu, B. (2016b). 'Monster', in A. Moreton-Robinson (ed.) *Critical Indigenous Studies: Engagement in First World Locations*. University of Arizona Press: Tucson, AZ, 83–101.

Lewis, T. and Kahn, R. (2010). *Education Out of Bounds: Reimagining Cultural Studies for a Posthuman Age*. Palgrave Macmillan: New York.

Marx, K. (1964). *Economic and Philosophic Manuscripts of 1844*. International Publishers: New York.

McClintock, A. (2002). 'Soft-soaping empire: Commodity racism and imperial advertising', in N. Mirzoeff (ed.) *The Visual Culture Reader*. Routledge: New York, 506–17.

Moreton-Robinson, A. (2015). *The White Possessive*. University of Minnesota Press: Minneapolis, MN.

New Zealand Government. (1907). *Tohunga suppression act 1907 (7 EDW VII 1907 No. 13)*. Australian Legal Information Institute. Available: http://www.austlii.edu.au/nz/legis/hist_act/tsa19207ev1907n13353.pdf, accessed 12 June 2018.

New Zealand Parliament. (2017). *Innovative Bill Protects Whaganui River with Legal Personhood*. Available: https://www.parliament.nz/en/get-involved/features/innovative-bill-protects-whanganui-river-with-legal-personhood/, accessed 30 April 2020.

Nietzsche, F. (1990). *Philosophy and Truth: Selections from Nietzsche's Notebooks of the Early 1870s* (D. Breazeale, trans.). Humanities Press: Ann Arbor, MI.

Parris, L. (2011). 'Frantz Fanon: existentialist, dialectician, and revolutionary', *The Journal of Pan African Studies*, vol 4, no 7: 4–23.

Roberts, M. (2012). 'Revisiting the natural world of the Māori', in D. Keenan (ed.) *Huia Histories of Māori*. Huia: Wellington, 33–56.

Schick, R. and Dolan, J. (1999). 'Masculinity and *A Man's Country* in 1998: An interview with Jock Phillips', in R. Law, H. Campbell, and J. Dolan (eds.) *Masculinities in Aotearoa/New Zealand*. Dunmore Press: Palmerston North, 46–63.

Tallbear, K. (2017). 'Beyond the life/not-life binary: A feminist-Indigenous reading of cryopreservation, interspecies thinking, and the new Materialisms', in J. Radin and E. Kowal (eds.) *Cryopolitics: Frozen Life in a Melting World*. MIT Press: Cambridge, MA, 179–202.

Todd, Z. (2016). 'An Indigenous feminist's take on the ontological turn: "Ontology" is just another word for colonialism', *Journal of Historical Sociology*, vol 29, no 1: 4–22. Available: https://zoestodd.com/2014/10/24/an-indigenous-feminists-take-on-the-ontological-turn-ontology-is-just-another-word-for-colonialism/, accessed 15 May 2020.

Tuhiwai Smith, L. (1999). *Decolonizing Methodologies: Research and Indigenous Peoples*. Zed Books: London.

Warne, K. (2019). 'A voice for nature', *National Geographic*. Available: https://www.nationalgeographic.com/culture/2019/04/maori-river-in-new-zealand-is-a-legal-person/, accessed 30 April 2020.

Watson, J. (1967). *Horizons of Unknown Power: Some Issues of Maori Schooling*. New Zealand Council for Educational Research. New Zealand Government Printer: Wellington.

Young, R. (2001). *Postcolonialism: An Historical Introduction*. Blackwell: Oxford.

11

Intimate encounters Aboriginal labour stories and the violence of the colonial archive

Natalie Harkin

PRELUDE | a beginning by way of introduction to something else epic in search for an impossible origin of the event, a preview-awakening to the positioning of things, a warning:

> Women may have been the boundary markers of empire. But it was the gendered and racialized intimacies of the everyday that women, men, and children were turned into subjects of particular kinds, as domination was routinized and rerouted in intimacies that the state sought to know but could never completely master or work out.
>
> *(Stoler 2006a: 57)*

In 2018, the South Australian government's *Aboriginal Lands Parliamentary Standing Committee* identified Indigenous stolen wages as a matter requiring further investigation.[1] It acknowledged that, while significant progress had been made in other states following the Australian Senate's 2006 *National Stolen Wages Inquiry*, this was "not yet explored in South Australia" (Secretary to the Aboriginal Lands Parliamentary Standing Committee, pers. comm. 24 June 2019). In June 2019, the Committee called for witnesses to present information regarding the extent and impacts of stolen wages practices affecting Aboriginal people in South Australia and I was invited to present an overview of my current research on South Australian Aboriginal domestic service history. This included some context to the burgeoning Aboriginal domestic service workforce in the early twentieth century, such as: the assimilation-based rationale for interdependent policies of child removal, institutionalisation and training; the labour conditions Aboriginal women were subject to; and the question of payment and the state's management of trust fund accounts. This evidence exemplifies those intimate boundary markers of empire, to which Stoler (2006a) refers above.

The majority of Aboriginal families I know in South Australia carry intimate histories of domestic service through living memory and intergenerational blood-memory passed on. In my testimony I acknowledged the scope of existing national literature and research since the 1980s regarding the history and impact of stolen wages practices, and of Aboriginal domestic labour, particularly in Queensland and New South Wales.[2] This includes work by Indigenous scholars and writers, poets, filmmakers and artists who have been telling these stories for a very long time; stories that are often reluctantly disclosed yet shape our identity and subjectivity to leave an indelible imprint on our future. Despite the significance of these stories in the collective memory of Aboriginal South Australians, government-orchestrated systems of indentured labour remain largely hidden and unacknowledged in the state's official public narratives. Our loved ones were indeed turned into "subjects of particular kinds" and as eminent leader and historian Jackie Huggins (in Black et al. 1994: 6) describes, "[t]he stories of Aboriginal women domestic servants cannot be told enough. They illuminate a deeply-rooted racist facet of Australia's history. They tell of the trials, tribulations, and triumphs amidst the backdrop of oppression".

My current research extends previous archival-poetic work based on a significant collection of state record files on my family, including a snapshot of the 'domestic years' of my Nanna's life at the height of 'assimilation' in the 1940s when her employment was managed by the Children's Welfare and Public Relief Board (Harkin 2014, 2016, 2019). Given the volume of material collated, the only way for me to shift and transform from the archive-box was to write poetry and weave my way out, an embodied reckoning with history's record in an attempt to better understand my family's place in a broader history of colonialism. This culminated in a body of poetry and text-object-based exhibition work influenced by many Indigenous artists, poets and writers: those who laboured creatively with the contested, racialised colonial archive as a dynamic site of potential strength and renewal; who could trace the evidence and change its shape and structure with rupturing intent; and who triggered an uncanny recognition to tell us something about our own personal, local and national story.[3] This work contributes to a growing body of Indigenous-led research engaging with and responding to the violence of the colonial archive concerning issues of access and transparency; the state's archivisation processes; and questions of surveillance, representation, agency and truth-telling.[4] Such intimate encounters with the colonial archive that collide with blood-memory, inevitably contribute toward much larger decolonising stories of resistance, resilience, and refusal that, to reiterate Huggins, *cannot be told enough*.

WARNING | some blood-memory lessons should begin with slow and deep inhale knowing in that moment before exhale where this archival-poetic journey might never end the next breath may clot, won't feel so easy

Unfinished business

There is no political power without control of the archive, if not memory. Effective democratization can always be measured by this essential criterion: the participation in and access to the archive, its constitution, and its interpretation.

(Derrida 1996: 4)

I relate Derrida's (1996) quote here directly to the 2006 Australian Senate agreement to conduct a national inquiry with regard to Indigenous workers whose paid labour, wages, saving, and conditions of employment had been controlled by the government. The inquiry received 129 submissions from individuals and organisations, with only three provided from South Australia. The lack of research in South Australia renders it impossible to determine or quantify the extent of unpaid wages, to identify the families impacted, or to consider what a stolen wages reparations scheme might look like. In its final report, the Senate Committee noted its disappointment that the South Australian government did not participate in the national inquiry, and made specific recommendations for it to: (1) further consult with the Aboriginal community; (2) conduct preliminary research of state record archival material; and (3) establish a compensation scheme if evidence is found to the withholding, underpayment or non-payment of wages and welfare entitlements (Commonwealth of Australia (CoA) 2006: xiii–xiv).

The Senate Committee stated that "while extensive archival records do exist in relation to the management of Indigenous monies in South Australia, there are obstacles to accessing that information" (CoA 2006: 85). It has become increasingly difficult to access Aboriginal records since the success of the late Uncle Bruce Trevorrow's case in 2007 (Hemming and Rigney 2013; Raynes 2009a). Trevorrow, a Ngarrindjeri elder, was the first Aboriginal person to win a compensation case against any government in Australia for his forced illegal removal from his family as a child.[5] In addition, detailed indexing of the vast materials of the Aborigines Protection Board and its associated government departments is incomplete, making it impossible to know what information is available. As a contemporary form of gate-keeping, those records that have been indexed may now be deemed as "too sensitive" and thus blocked for release under legal professional privilege by the state's Attorney General (CoA 2006: 86; Raynes 2009a). Those unattainable files identified as 'missing' or labelled 'Access Denied' by South Australia's Attorney General are, as Judy Watson (2009: 84) states, "often the most revealing". This increased bureaucracy and drip-feeding of vetted and vetoed-access to Aboriginal family records affirms that "control of the archive is a form of political power" (Manoff 2004: 15). As Irene Watson (2009: 56) describes, the state has clearly locked down to protect itself from exposure and litigation, threatened by its own founding violence.

In the interest of access and transparency, the Senate Committee reported that "unless state governments took a more proactive approach, there is a risk that past injustices will be compounded with further inaction" (CoA 2006: 126). It was recommended that Commonwealth and state governments facilitate unhindered access to their archives, reiterating the need for research into Indigenous stolen wages as a matter of urgency (CoA 2006: xiii). It also identified the need for an education and awareness campaign for Indigenous communities, and for the Australian Institute of Aboriginal and Torres Strait Islander Studies to conduct a national oral history and archival research project in relation to Indigenous stolen wages. The importance of Indigenous community consultation was reiterated throughout the report and its recommendations.

To date, the official stolen wages narrative in South Australia has been one of denial and refusal, despite meticulous preliminary archival research including the administrative history of South Australia, by Cameron Raynes (2005; 2009a) and Ross Kidd (2007). In the year following the national inquiry, the South Australian government wrote a letter to the Senate Committee advising that it "had already complied with the spirit of the recommendations described in the senate inquiry report of December 2006" (Weatherill 2007: Online). It outlined that in April 2004, the Aboriginal and Torres Strait Islander Commission requested the government investigate stolen wages in South Australia, and by September 2004 the Department of Treasury and Finance (DTF) commenced an internal inquiry, instigated by the former Minister for Aboriginal Affairs, Terry Roberts. In August 2005, DTF reported that less than $65,000 was owed to 120 named persons in the form of stale or voided cheques and unclaimed superannuation. It was concluded that these 'unclaimed' monies could not be described as 'stolen'. Despite only 25 per cent of the GRG52 record group[6] being indexed at the point of inquiry, the government concluded that "a thorough examination of the files indexed so far does not reveal any evidence of this practice occurring on an organised basis" (Weatherill 2007: Online).

These findings appear absurd when compared with the magnitude of stolen wages found in other states; for example, an estimate of over $500 million was found to be owed to Indigenous workers in Queensland alone (ABC News 2019). It is likely that similar amounts may be owed in other Australian states and territories, and investigations are currently underway for a potential class action on behalf of thousands of Indigenous Australians negatively impacted by wage control practices from the late 1800s until the 1970s (Shine Lawyers 2019); practices that have significantly contributed to intergenerational poverty and continue to impact Indigenous socio-economic disadvantage today (Gunstone 2014; Kidd 2007).

My short 20-minute testimony to the *Aboriginal Lands Parliamentary Standing Committee* was an opportune moment to also shine a small spotlight on the state's institutions, systems and processes that control archives and feed particular colonial narratives on histories and people; not only the physical record artefacts, but also the political project that drives, contains and maintains them. The state's archives are not neutral or innocent sites, and the "effective democratisation" toward access, participation, and interpretation to which Derrida (1996: 4) refers, is an ongoing issue. So, for now, the matter of stolen wages in South Australia remains as 'unfinished business'.

Archons of power

Derrida's (1996) *Archive Fever* offers a significant contribution to understanding the origins of the archive and the complex relationship among state power, oppression, and archivisation. From the first point of colonial-contact, the state's 'archons' or 'superior magistrates', commanders and legislators, signified political power with the right to make or to represent the law; and to legally possess Australia under the British Empire. Moreton-Robinson (2004: 10) describes them as the "white patriarchs who designed and established the legal and political institutions that control and maintain the social structure under which we now live". They ensured the physical security of official documents and materials via state institutions and accorded themselves the right and power to interpret and possess them through the "power of consignation" (Derrida 1996: 3); that is, the technical method of collecting, organising and conserving the human record. Key consignation principles include: the gathering of material and the process of unification, identification and classification; a process that legitimises data and imperial knowledge through hierarchy and order, determining what can be archived and thus what can be accessed and studied for the future; "an arsenal of sorts, reactivated to suit new governing strategies" (Stoler 2009: 3).

The labouring to maintain 'archontic power' and the Australian nation-state is significant. As Watson (2009: 45) argues, the legal foundation of "the Australian colonial project lies within an 'originary violence' in which the state retains a vested interest in maintaining the founding order of things" through continuous re-enactments of state violence. Moreton-Robinson (2004: 1) theorises this work as "the possessive logic of white patriarchal sovereignty" which operates ideologically at the level of beliefs and discursively at the level of epistemology to naturalise the nation as a white possession. This 'logic' is both a process and mode of rationalisation, where the state's regulatory mechanisms of control and order "are extremely busy reaffirming and reproducing this possessiveness through a process of perpetual Indigenous dispossession, ranging from the refusal of Indigenous sovereignty to overregulated piecemeal concessions" (Moreton-Robinson 2015: xi).

Through its self-inscribed right to authority and law-making, the state maintains the fantasy of the imperial archive to enact ultimate civilising control over all that it surveys and documents; a fantasy maintained as absolute truth (Burton 2005; Manoff 2004; Richards 1993). Through meticulous surveillance, the state became the keeper/holder of Indigenous lives, where people were photographed, labelled and archived in the ultimate "container of power" (Barker 2006: 189); that dense site where history and subjectivity collide/collude. This white possessive logic also played out in domestic intimacies of the everyday mundane. Aboriginal women were subjugated through state possession in particularly violent ways, and indeed continue to suffer from multiple inequalities and injustices that intersect race, class and gender directly resulting from historical colonialism (Watson and Venne 2010: 347).

Archive-fever-paradox

> History lies dormant until bidden. In this state of not-dead those stories most silent can prove tenacious, holding onto terrain, whether place or people, waiting for the opportunity to be revisited, communicated, revived.
>
> *(Gough 2007: 7)*

Through this process of concluding, comprehending and containing stories and lives, the archive has become that which is living and dead, hidden and protected (Hawkes 2008). It is both sacred space *and* colonial object; it drives us to both recover *and* preserve the past; and it protects *and* patrols, regulates *and* represses. On the one hand it is a history of conservation, on the other hand a history of loss (Rivera 2007; Voss and Werner 1999). As the quote by Gough (2007) above reminds us, these records buried deep in warehouse facilities controlled by the state, lie dormant and waiting for that cusp of light to shine new inquiry and meaning between the newly opened pages. As stories emerged, revealed, and unravelled through my own family's records, I became particularly interested in what was missing from these officially logged accounts, and that functioned through a kind of paradoxical logic; where blood still pumped where hearts have stopped (Harkin 2016).

These sites are significant for those of us who refuse to be removed from the written record or face a future without an identity (Birch 2007). On writing her critically acclaimed novel *Carpentaria*, Waanyi author/poet/scholar Alexis Wright (2006) notes the importance of writing something down of ourselves that has been unwritten, so as to affirm our existence, on our terms. Increasingly, our stories are revisited, communicated, and revived, and this work necessarily re-writes a national narrative of belonging and un-belonging (Gough 2007; Gunew 2004). In our attempts to make sense of our histories, we often cling to records and objects in the hope of somehow connecting to a past we can never fully know; piecing story fragments together in ways that resist and transcend the intentions of those original recordings (Manoff 2004). We often have no choice but to access and enter what Kennedy (2011: 90) calls "the perverse archive" in order "to create an Indigenous cultural memory of dehumanization and survival". Here, the pursuit to know and understand one's own history often 'perversely' leads to records preserved by those very institutions and agencies that perpetuated past oppressive acts. The violence we bear witness to is deeply affecting, as described by Ali Gumillya Baker in her own witnessing through the state's archives (2018: 15): "this evidence of abuse by colonial powers is like a pit of sadness. The pit could swallow me up as I walk. I could fall in and never be seen again".

Some of the state institutions I applied to, seeking access to my family's records, included: State Aboriginal Records, Children's Welfare Records, the South Australian Museum, and the National Archives of Australia. The files obtained provide a chilling and intimate snapshot of lives lived under extraordinary surveillance, particularly from the 1920s to 1950s. Collectively, these records expose a culture of biopolitics underpinning the science-based social policy experimentation that all Indigenous families were subjected to in Australia during this time.[7] Every record written and filed features those 'archons of power' responsible for observing, reporting and documenting, revered on every page: The Aborigines Protection Board, The Protector, Mission Superintendents, Secretary, The Welfare Board, Children's Welfare Department, Boarding-Out-Officer, Senior Probation Officer, Inspector, Matron, Deputy-Director-of-Rationing, Police, Doctor, Psychologist, School Teacher, Academic, Scientific Expert, and the Anthropologist.

These agents of so-called 'protection' and integrity were central to this archontic-web and collated an insurmountable data for the Aborigines Protection Board and the Children's Welfare Board, and their associated departments.[8] They determined what data

151

was important, relevant, and interesting for the state repository, which in turn influenced government mechanisms and policies to directly regulate and control our family's fate. This included: forced movements from lands between mission stations and communities; child removal, and threats of child removal; institutionalisation and domestic placements. Such possessive logic, operationalised, deployed, and affirmed via the archive, was also used to legally determine who was Aboriginal, issuing 'exemption certificates' based on 'data-card' surveillance, that then conferred privileges to those the state categorised as 'white' (Moreton-Robinson 2004).

Memory, silence, and forgetting

> This is an aching archive – the one that contains all of our growing grief, all of our dispossessed longing for the bodies that were once among us and have gone over to the side that we will go to too. [...] The opposite of dispossession is not possession. It is not accumulation. It is unforgetting. It is mattering.
>
> *(Morrill et al. 2016: 2)*

The colonial archive represents that dense site where history and subjectivity make social life (Gordon 2008), where regimes of authority regulate, control and order, also through modes of exclusion and subjugation. As described by Morrill et al. (2016) above, this is a site of grief and unforgetting. It is not only the zone "from which order is given" and "from which things commence", but also where memory is deposited (Mansour 2007: 43). That which is represented on the official record as a 'unified whole' essentially silences and suppresses what is left out, and we are haunted by such exclusions. These spectres of colonialism can be revealed to make meaning through both personal family story and everyday impacts of state systems of power, when the trouble they represent can "no longer be contained or repressed" (Gordon 2008: xvi). To engage with the disruptive and transformative effects of archival haunting is to interrogate what is remembered and what is not known; to recover the forgotten and reveal the act of forgetting; and disrupt what Toni Morrison refers to as "national amnesia", that is, the state's desire to forget the colonial histories of injustice that nevertheless determine contemporary life (Durrant 2004: 116).

This national amnesia is, paradoxically, an active form of collective memory; naturalised through the state's possessive logic and understood as a "hegemonic [...] experiential 'script' that is learned, embodied, and passed on as the cultural record of 'normal'" (Bold et al. 2002 in Hart 2006: 13). The process of "silence and forgetting" in the consignation of the "fantasy archive", effectively perpetuates these silences (Mansour 2007: 43) sustaining "the violence of the archive" to which Derrida refers (1996: 7). For many of us, the desire for truth is not about "archives" as such, but a "sustained contemplation of a work of history", and presented as "the desire to find, or locate, or possess that moment of origin, as the beginning of things" (Steedman 2001: 3). Given that history and memory are shaped by an archivisation process categorised by impression, repression and suppression (Derrida 1996), there is real danger in processes that depict literal and limited reconstructions and recordings of history from particular colonial perspectives, where the logic of white possession is determined as common sense and natural (Manoff 2004; Moreton-Robinson 2004).

Tony Birch (2007: 108) reminds us that "those intent on obliterating Indigenous memory" continue to "privilege particular and unproblematic colonial representations of the past". The 'fantasy archive' is a site of conflict that perpetuates this racialised and scripted memory of 'normal'; like a crime scene, or a battleground between different disciplines and spaces, ideas and worldviews, and representations of people and facts. Once accessed this fantasy ledger becomes transparent, as Trawlwoolway artist Julie Gough describes (2001: 64):

> Absence is rife in historical records – I no longer see the historical record as factual, rather it is a ledger leaking attitudes which often reveal more than scrawled names and dates – these are the details which bring meaning to my work.

As "a ledger leaking attitudes" (Gough 2001: 64), these sites reveal the epistemic violence, values and structures of feelings that sustain particular fantasies of colonialism (Stoler 2009); fantasies that are normalised and naturalised through the possessive logic of patriarchal white sovereignty, and "inextricably linked, anchored and regulated through race" (Moreton-Robinson 2015: 193). As sites of subjective productions with histories of their own, Stoler (2002: 87) argues that scholars need to shift from thinking about the "archive-as-source" to "archive-as-subject"; an ethnography of the archive to exposes its logic, its forms of classification and ordering, and importantly, its exclusions (Burton 2005; Ghosh 2006; Mansour 2007; Stoler 2002). Such persistent interrogation can achieve transparency and accountability in knowledge production and a re-orientation toward a "robust, imaginative and interpretively responsible method of critical engagement with the past" (Burton 2005: 21). Here, the archive can be exposed as a colonial repository of codified beliefs that cluster and bear witness to reveal connections between secrecy, the law and power (Stoler 2002). The complexities are multiple, layered, and shifting, as Burton (2005: 7–8) explains:

> history is not merely a project of fact-retrieval … but also a set of complex processes of selection, interpretation, and even creative invention – processes set in motion by, among other things, one's personal encounter with the archive, the history of the archive itself, and the pressure of the contemporary moment on one's reading of what is to be found there.

This revelation of complexity is critical given the primacy of the archive to empirical and positivist representations of history and its claims to objectivity. Here, historians as "archival truth-tellers" fuel contemporary public debate on big issues (Burton 2005: 1), such as the legitimacy and extent of frontier-violence, massacres, Aboriginal child removal, indentured labour and stolen wages. These *history-as-battleground* debates (mainly played out between male-white historians) are politically and ideologically driven, centred on empirical-data, and continue to omit Indigenous voices. As stated by Birch (2007: 108), "this present day 'culture war' does not involve Indigenous people beyond objectification". As Indigenous knowledges, experiences and remembrances speak back to this violence of the colonial archive, we are like detectives examining the crime scene of our lives, which can be both exhilarating and horrific.

The silencing and absence of Aboriginal voice and experience on the record extends to the documenting and theorising of Australia's labour history. There has also been an absence of historicising racism in the history of Australian feminism and labour movements (Murdolo 1996; Pettman 1995). This lack of recognition for those "Aboriginal men and women who toiled as stockmen and domestic servants" (Huggins 1998: 1) and whose vital contributions were the backbone of Australia's economic prosperity, remain largely invisible (Huggins 1998; Nugent 2002).

Intrusive intimacies

> To study the intimate is not to turn away from structures of dominance but to relocate their conditions of possibility and relations and forces of production.
>
> *(Stoler 2006b: 13)*

To witness and encounter such erasure through the archive is to also encounter colonial intimacies that engender "precarious affections"; awkward familiarities, unsolicited attention, uninvited caresses and probings that cannot be easily refused (Stoler 2006b: 15). "Colonial intimacies" are understood to be implicated in the wielding of power via the "expert and habituated benevolence of the state" (Stoler 2006b: 15); a power rationalised through blood-quantum and racial hierarchy that positions Aboriginal people on an imagined-continuum somewhere between black and white; the 'problem' to be solved.

Such encounters are embodied in the work of physical and social anthropology led particularly by the South Australian Museum and The University of Adelaide's Board of Anthropological Research. The main purpose of the Board of Anthropological Research was to investigate urgent 'unsettled questions' regarding the 'place' of Australian Aboriginal people according to dominant theories of genetics and evolution; 'urgent' because it was believed that 'pure blood' Aboriginal people would not survive into the future (South Australian Museum (SAM) Archives 2014). From the 1920s the Board's research focus was physiology, racial origins and health, which served to reinforce Social-Darwinist doomed-race imaginings in popular culture and public opinion (Anderson 1997; Raftery 2006; SAM Archives 2005). These surveys, as tools that maintained and reproduced racial hierarchies, were also conducted without community consent or remuneration: "costs of rewards to natives have been kept very low, so far we have used boiled lollies and cigarettes" (Tindale in Anderson 2002: 237). The data, objects and specimens collected from these expeditions represent an "'anti-memorial' absence of honouring that is profoundly disturbing" (Baker 2018: 15).

In 1938, my family was living at Point Pearce Mission Station when a team of scientists set up camp to study this confined community as part of an ambitious national anthropological survey led by South Australian Museum entomologist and ethnologist, Norman B Tindale. The Point Pearce community had already been surrounded by white figures of authority controlling their lives, such as mission superintendents, government Inspectors, doctors, religious leaders, teachers, and police; typical of the reserve and mission histories across Australia. The Board of Anthropological Research arrived to conduct one of over 40 expeditions undertaken from the mid-1920s to the mid-1970s. These expeditions comprised interdisciplinary teams of experts in biology, anthropology, pathology, physiology and psychology who hypothesised and documented a physical, cultural and social anthropological record of Aboriginal Australia. The most notable expeditions were collaborations with anthropologist Joseph B. Birdsell who was affiliated with two American universities: Adelaide-Harvard Universities Anthropological Expedition (1938 to 1939) and University of California and Los Angeles-Adelaide University Anthropological Expedition (1952–1954) (SAM Archives 2011). Birdsell worked particularly well with Tindale and collaborated with the Board of Anthropological Research for over 50 years (Anderson 2002).

Surveillance data for governance

At the height of the assimilation era in Australia the conservative Liberal and Country League Party were in power in South Australia for 32 years (1933–1965). This government, influenced by its elite Adelaide-Establishment faction comprising old-money-families (Jaensch 1997), also drew scientific 'experts' into its governance structures, particularly from the Board of Anthropological Research, the South Australian Museum and The University of Adelaide (Macilwain 2007). These 'experts' were invariably appointed to senior positions including on the Aborigines Protection Board. As example, Professor John B Cleland, from the School of Medicine at The University of Adelaide, was appointed to the Board in 1940 and known to be "an arch-conservative in matters of Aboriginal policy" (Raynes 2009a: 20). Cleland was the chief "blood grouper" on the Board of Anthropological Research expeditions, known among Aboriginal people as "the butcher" who apparently "never tired of bleeding Aborigines" (Anderson 2002: 202). Government bureaucrats in turn held leading positions in the governance of both the South Australian Museum and the University. This two-way segue of 'expertise' between the state government and significant scientific institutions created a culture of biopolitics-driven governance in state Aboriginal affairs which directly influenced the nature of interventionist policies and programs governing Aboriginal people (Macilwain 2007; Raftery 2006).

Cleland urged the state to further intervene and address the "half-caste problem" on scientific grounds and promoted a "breeding" policy to eradicate "half-castes"; an "irritating and expanding group [...] between 'authentic' whiteness and 'authentic' (and disappearing) Aboriginality" (Anderson 2002: 228). Critically, Cleland was instrumental in extending the medical data-card system used at Point Pearce and Point McLeay Mission Stations, to include more social data including:

> Mental ability, willingness to work, tidiness of the home, offences against the law, work and wages earned from time to time. In fact, all matters which may assist in the summing up of person's activities both those favourable and unfavourable.
>
> *(Cleland 1940 in Raynes 2009a: 21)*

This intensified documentation of the social and domestic mundane became an important surveillance tool to increase government control and modify people's behaviour; for example, the use of bluff and threats of child removal, forced Exemption Certificates, and denial of pensions or resources (Raynes 2009a: 21). This collated 'data' directly influenced policies of protection and assimilation, particularly targeting women and children. Aboriginal children were often charged as 'destitute' or 'neglected', regardless of their circumstance, and 'poverty', at this point, was often synonymous with the rhetoric of 'neglect', 'unfit motherhood' and 'moral depravity'. Such charges were unfairly associated with all Aboriginal people and increasingly used as a means for the State Children's Council to remove children from their families (Human Rights and Equal Opportunity Commission [HREOC] 1997; Jacobs 2009; Raynes 2009a).

The increase in visitations to family homes is clearly evidenced in my own family's records, where Inspectors, or 'State Ladies' as my family called them, regularly reported on items such as the contents of kitchen cupboards, what was cooking at the point of Inspector visits, what the children were wearing, where they slept, their physical appearance, and whether the beds were made at point of inspection. In bearing witness to the depth of such surveillance, including Tindale's genealogies, photos, and data-cards sets, those inter-dependent systems of governance that wielded such power become transparent. In spite of this oppressive control, there were moments of compassion recorded by kind Inspectors and Probation Officers who genuinely appeared to have my family's interests at heart.

At the height of the assimilation era, particularly from 1939 through to 1953, the practice of illegally removing children was condoned by the state (HREOC 1997; Raynes 2009a). Around the same time, the South Australian government began to formally allocate funding to 'domestic training' as a significant measure of assimilation, and a recommendation from the Royal Commission on the Aborigines (1913). The budget item 'Training of half-caste girls for domestic service' was introduced in 1936 and became a standard entry for the Aborigines Protection Board to report against. This annual allocation of state funds increased exponentially in the following decade, from £24 in 1936, to £297 in 1947 (Harkin 2016: 196).

Poetic labour of love

While the archive is a site of lost origins where memory is dispossessed, it is also a site for hopeful and just futures where "acts of remembering and regeneration occur" (Enwezor 2008: 47) revealing also how our loved ones carefully and strategically negotiated a colonial system that was designed to control and oppress them. As Wright (2016) describes, we have been locked in in this storytelling war from the point of first contact; a war that still fosters and maintains negative, racialised, stereotyped narratives about who we are, and invades every sense of our sovereignty and resistance. As contemporary agents of memory, there are multiple ways to share the weight of these stories; to collectively move through a decolonising project of poetic refusal, resistance, and memory-making, through and beyond the colonial archive. Indigenous writers and creative practitioners have become increasingly concerned with the politics of representation and question of sovereignty, authenticity and voice; a continuum response to being defined, categorised, and written about by cultural institutions of power that historically rendered us voiceless (Heiss 2003; Wright 2016). We write invisible, silenced, and forgotten worlds from nothing into existence, to expose what Birch (2006) calls Australia's 'national secrecy about colonialism'; unveil what Kim Scott (2001) calls 'Australia's continuing neurosis'; and keep the wounds open, as Wright (2002: 19) states, to reverse the prescribed forgetting with a "steadfast telling of the truth".

Historical texts and materials objects in the archive are like mediums through which ideas can be transmitted and the past can speak; where other stories might yet be buried (Gough 2007: 17). To achieve some semblance of peace, closure, and justice for the dead, Gough labours through the archive in search for the 'underbelly' of meaning; to reveal how the gaps in dominant colonial narratives of history are in fact not silent after all (Gough 2018: 268). Her compelled repatriation of Indigenous voice and story, particularly to "draw fresh or fairer conclusions about frontier life", is the resounding heartbeat to her "methodology of detection": "My aim is to dislodge the evidence no one thought to remove, or even knew was there. I look for 'meanings' rather than 'facts' within the seemingly insignificant" (Gough 2001: 66).

When we follow the clues and paper trails, Indigenous agency, voice and protest are located throughout the record, via events and documents such as strikes, petitions, letters and deputations (Raynes 2005). One particularly rich resource on the state's archives includes letters written by Aboriginal people that provide a unique record of their lives 'under the Act'. These letters document an important historical record of lived experiences that evidence the impact of government legislation and mission policies; this includes Aboriginal women asserting their entitlement to freedom and agency (Nelson et al. 2002). The many petitions and letters I've have accessed from the State's Aboriginal archives reveal such agency of our loved ones, and attest to their strength, courage and proactive engagement with the state. In particular, the handwritten letters by my Nanna and Great-grandmother provide critical insight to histories and legacies otherwise smoothed over, hidden, or forgotten. These letters were replete with references to home, family, and a domestic-trained life controlled by the state; they expose another layer of trauma and resilience that is not widely known or considered in official accounts of history. My Great-grandmother in fact had to write similar letters for many of her children, demonstrating an intense and determined labour of maternal love, and written with persistent and clear intent. Importantly, these letters expose poignant and deep family bonds and love; proof that Aboriginal children were not 'neglected' by family or 'destitute' as charged.

These letters became central to my archival-poetic praxis culminating in the physical and metaphorical transformation, weaving their story into a basket. To touch their handwriting is to almost feel their fingertips in letters that reveal so much more than what is filed and recorded.

These are the voices and stories the world needs to read, see and hear. We may be intimate knowers of our own histories, but we have not been in control of the dominant narrative of our lives. Writing allows us to cultivate sovereignty of the mind and regain the plot-line of our lives (Lucashenko 2018; Wright 2002; 2016). This literary and archival-poetic work compliments the burgeoning national field of research concerned with engaging Aboriginal archives, led largely by Indigenous scholars and for Aboriginal communities; work that reveals a powerful legacy of silenced stories captured on the record; stories of dispossession and oppression, but also intelligence, refusal and activism.

Footnote to a prelude

apron-folds and pockets keep secrets
pinned tucked hidden
they whisper into linen-shadows that flicker-float with the sun
– hung
limp on the breeze they sway
a rhythmic sorrow.

(Apron Sorrow, Harkin 2019:19)

As a witness to this *Aboriginal Lands Parliamentary Standing Committee*, and descendant from a long-line of Aboriginal women domestic workers, I felt the gravity of bearing witness to those "gendered and racialised intimacies of the everyday" to which Stoler (2006a: 57) refers. There is much work to be done to effectively trace this history of indentured servitude and stolen wages in South Australia; to further explore critical and intimate intersections of race, gender and labour exploitation; and to expand feminist understandings of a racialised labour movement.

The issue of stolen wages remains unresolved; "one of the nation's greatest barriers to reconciliation and justice for Indigenous people" (Kidd 2007: 10.), and the need to tell our own stories, from our diverse, localised Indigenous standpoints is ongoing. We are poets, writers, scholars, curators, artists and filmmakers critically engaging with archives through blood-memory and emotion; and we labour creatively, with affective decolonising intent to deepen connections, recognition, or acceptance of our histories (Centre of Excellence for the History of Emotions 2007). To read 'against the grain' of the archive requires us to collectively rethink and reassess the transparent possessive logic and political rationalities of imperial history; to seek out those critical spaces where critical minor histories reveal gendered and racialised conditions of empire that play out in the mundane intimacies of every day (Stoler 2009).

Where systemic, orchestrated injustices have occurred at the hands of the state, such as indentured domestic labour or stolen wages, we should have the right to access our own records; to trace these epic origins so we may preview and disclose the 'originary violence' positioning of things. In the interests of truth-telling, especially for those elders primarily impacted by systemic slavery and abuses, we have a right to a just hearing, and to heal.

When I met with the Committee, I also presented them with a Ngarrindjeri basket woven from my Nanna and Great-grandmother's handwritten letters; an object that honours a very different story to that which is officially documented on the record about them and woven with intent to disrupt communal memories of amnesia or oppression. This basket represents a site of resistance and a shared-history location; one way to reckon with history, to transform the material archive and weave new offerings for the future. I wanted to impress on this Committee that where local stories are defined solely by and for nation-state interests, the driving imperative for Indigenous people to (re)write the local is that we have "the right to write and be read" (Gunew

2004: 115); to (re)write these narratives of belonging and un-belonging and (re)inscribe voice and agency to our loved ones and country. There are multiple ways to share the load and collectively move through it all, and this work is our compelled labour of love, through all our poetic capacity, in all the ways we know how.

Notes

1 A multi-partisan Committee inquiring into matters affecting Aboriginal people in South Australia.
2 Including: Haebich 2000; Haskins and Lowrie 2015; Huggins 1987, 1995, 1998; HREOC 1997; Jacobs 2009; Kidd 2007, 2012; Moreton-Robinson 2000; Murdolo 1996; Nugent 2002; Robinson 2003; and Walden 1995.
3 Refer to: Harkin (2016) for discussion of works by r e a, Yhonnie Scarce and Jackie Huggins; work of Unbound Collective available at http://www.flinders.edu.au/oise/unbound/about-unbound.cfm; and Dale Harding's exhibition 'Bright Eyed Little Dormitory Girls' (2013).
4 Including archival repatriation and activist work of Gary Foley et al. Victoria University; Cressida Fforde et al., ANU; Anna Haebich et al., Curtin University, Monash University, Colgate University, USA; and Elizabeth Nelson et al., University of Melbourne.
5 Supreme Court Justice Gray found that Trevorrow "had been illegally removed from his parents in 1957. He also found that the effect it had on his life was profound. Bruce died in June 2008, just months after he was awarded $525,000 for injuries, losses and false imprisonment" (Raynes 2009b: Online).
6 GRG 52 is the most significant reference group in State Records relating to Aboriginal people in South Australia from 1866-1968 (Raynes 2005).
7 Foucault's thinking on 'biopower' provides an understanding of how colonial regimes of authority execute political power through strategies of control, discipline and regulation. Indigenous scholars are increasingly examining Foucault's relevance to critical Indigenous studies and "how whiteness operates through the racialised application of disciplinary knowledges and regulatory mechanisms, which function together to preclude Indigenous sovereignty" (Moreton-Robinson, 2015: 129).
8 Paradoxically, Aboriginal people have experienced extensive trauma and loss under the guise of 'protection'; a web of government legislative and bureaucratic control enforcing segregation and assimilation, and "eugenic programs to 'breed out' Aboriginality altogether" (Haebich 2000: 161).
9 Correspondence from the Hon Jay Weatherill MP, Minister for Aboriginal Affairs and Reconciliation South Australia, 15 February 2007.

References

ABC News. (2019). 'Indigenous unpaid wages could be up to $500 million, analysts claim', *ABC News Online*. Available: https://www.abc.net.au/news/2019-07-10/indigenous-unpaid-wages-real-figure-500-million/11294934, accessed 1 August 2019.

Anderson, I. (1997). 'I, the "Hybrid" aborigine: film and representation', *Australian Aboriginal Studies*, vol 1: 4–14.

Anderson, W. (2002). *The Cultivation of Whiteness, Science, Health and Racial Destiny in Australia*. Melbourne University Press: Carlton, VIC.

Baker, A.G. (2018). 'Camping in the shadow of the racist text', *Artlink*, vol 38, no 2: 14–21.

Barker, C. (2006). *Cultural Studies Theory and Practice*, 2nd ed. SAGE: London.

Birch, T. (2006). '"Promise not to tell"': Interrogating colonialism's worst (or best) kept secrets', Paper presented at First Person: International Digital Storytelling Conference, February 4, ACMI: Melbourne. Available: http://www.acmi.net.au/global/media/first_person_birch.pdf, accessed 20 March 2015.

Birch, T. (2007). 'The invisible fire: Indigenous sovereignty, history and responsibility', in A. Moreton-Robinson (ed.) *Sovereign Subjects, Indigenous Sovereignty Matters*. Allen & Unwin: Sydney, NSW, 105–117.

Black, L., Huggins, J., and King-Smith, L. (1994). White Apron–Black Hands: A Project on Aboriginal Women Domestics in Service, Brisbane City Hall Gallery, July 1994. [Exhibition Catalogue]. A Black Day Dawning Production: Brisbane, QLD.

Burton, A. (ed.) (2005). *Archive Stories: Facts, Fictions and the Writing of History*. Duke University Press: Durham, NC.

Centre of Excellence for the History of Emotions. (2007). 'Feeling the past: Indigenous emotions and history', *Symposium*, November 9–10, University of Western Australia. Available: http://www.historyof emotions.org.au/events/feeling-the-past-indigenous-emotions-and-history/, accessed 1 August 2019.

Commonwealth of Australia. (2006). *Unfinished Business: Indigenous Stolen Wages*. Senate Standing Committee on Legal and Constitutional Affairs: Canberra, ACT.

Derrida, J. (1996). *Archive Fever: A Freudian Impression* (E. Prenowitz, trans.). University of Chicago Press: Chicago, IL.

Durrant, S. (2004). *Postcolonial Narrative and the Work of Mourning: JM Coetzee, Wilson Harris and Toni Morrison*. State University of New York Press: Albany, NY.

Enwezor, O. (2008). *Archive Fever: Uses of the Document in Contemporary Art*. International Centre of Photography: New York.

Ghosh, D. (2006). 'National narratives and the politics of miscegenation', in A. Burton (ed.) *Archive Stories: Facts, Fictions and the Writing of History*. Duke University Press: Durham, NC, 27–44.

Gordon, A. (2008). *Ghostly Matters: Haunting and Sociological Imagination*, 2nd ed. University of Minnesota Press: Minneapolis, MN.

Gough, J. (2001). *Transforming Histories: The Visual Disclosure of Contentious Pasts*. PhD thesis, University of Tasmania: Hobart, TAS.

Gough, J. (2007). The Ranger: Seeking the Hidden Figure of History, SASA Gallery, September 11–October 2, 2007 [Exhibition Catalogue]. South Australia School of Art: Adelaide, SA. Available: http://www.unisa.edu.au/artarchitecturedesign/sasagallery/catalogues/sasaranger.pdf, accessed 15 June 2019.

Gough, J. (ed.) (2018). *Fugitive History: The Art of Julie Gough*. UWA Publishing: Perth, WA.

Gunew, S. (2004). *Haunted Nations: The Colonial Dimensions of Multiculturalisms*. Routledge: London.

Gunstone, A. (2014). 'Indigenous stolen wages and campaigns or reparations in Victoria', *Indigenous Law Bulletin*, vol 8, no 12: 3–7.

Haebich, A. (2000). *Broken Circles: Fragmenting Indigenous Families, 1800–2000*. Fremantle Arts Centre Press: Fremantle, WA.

Harkin, N.A. (2014). 'The poetics of (re)mapping archives: memory in the blood', *Journal of the Association for the Study of Australian Literature*, vol 14, no 3: 1–14.

Harkin, N.A. (2016). *"I Weave Back to You": Archival-Poetics for the Record*. PhD thesis, University of South Australia: Adelaide, SA.

Harkin, N.A. (2019). *Archival-Poetics*. Vagabond Press: Melbourne, VIC.

Hart, L.K. (2006). 'Against hauntology and historicide: Urban Indigeneity in the white imagining'. Available: http://julieshiels.com.au/public-space/Hauntology-and-Historicide.pdf, accessed June 15, 2019.

Haskins, V.K. and Lowrie, C. (eds.) (2015). *Colonization and Domestic Service: Historical and Contemporary Perspectives*. Routledge: New York.

Hawkes, M. (2008). 'What is recovered?', *M/C Journal*, vol 11, no 6. Available: http://journal.media-culture.org.au/index.php/mcjournal/article/viewArticle/92, accessed 28 June 2019.

Heiss, A. (2003). *Dhuuluu-Yala, To Talk Straight: Publishing Indigenous Literature*. Aboriginal Studies Press: Canberra, ACT.

Hemming, S. and Rigney, D. (2013). 'Decentring the new protectors: Transforming aboriginal heritage in South Australia', in E. Waterton and S. Watson (eds.) *Heritage and Community Engagement: Collaboration or Contestation?*. Routledge: London, 98–114.

Huggins, J. (1987). '"Firing on the mind": Aboriginal women domestic servants in the inter-war years', *Hecate*, vol 13, no 2: 5–23.

Huggins, J. (1995). 'White apron, Black hands: Aboriginal domestic servants in Queensland', *Labour History*, vol 69: 188–195.

Huggins, J. (1998). *Sister Girl: The Writings of Aboriginal Activist and Historian Jackie Huggins*. University of Queensland Press: St Lucia, QLD.

Human Rights and Equal Opportunity Commission. (1997). *Bringing Them Home: Report of the National Inquiry into the Separation of Aboriginal and Torres Strait Islander Children from Their Families*. HREOC: Canberra, ACT.

Jacobs, M.D. (2009). *White Mother to a Dark Race: Settler Colonialism, Maternalism, and the Removal of Indigenous Children in the American West and Australia, 1880–1940*. University of Nebraska Press: Lincoln, NE.

Jaensch, D. (1997). *The Politics of Australia*. Macmillan: South Melbourne, VIC.

Kennedy, R. (2011). 'Indigenous Australian arts of return: Mediating perverse archives', in M. Hirsch and N. Miller (eds.) *Rites of Return: Diaspora Poetics and the Politics of Memory*. Columbia University Press: New York, 88–104.

Kidd, R. (2007). Hard Labour: Stolen Wages: National Report on Stolen Wages. ANTaR: Rozelle, NSW.

Kidd, R. (2012). 'Aboriginal workers, aboriginal poverty', in N. Fijn, I. Keen, C. Lloyd, and M. Pickering (eds.) *Indigenous Participation in Australian Economies II: Historical Engagements and Current Enterprises.* ANUE Press: Canberra, ACT, 171–180.

Lucashenko, M. (2018). 'Writing as a sovereign act', *Meanjin Quarterly.* Available: http://meanjin.com.au/essays/writing-as-a-sovereign-act/, accessed 15 June 2019.

Macilwain, M. (2007). *South Australian Aborigines Protection Board (1939–1962) and Governance Through "Scientific" Expertise: A Genealogy of Protection and Assimilation.* PhD thesis, University of Adelaide: Adelaide, SA.

Manoff, M. (2004). 'Theories of the archive from across the disciplines', *Libraries and the Academy*, vol 4, no 1: 9–25.

Mansour, W. (2007). 'The violence of the archive', *English Language Notes*, vol 45, no 1: 41–44.

Moreton-Robinson, A. (2000). Talkin' *Up to the White Woman.* University of Queensland Press: St Lucia, QLD.

Moreton-Robinson, A. (2004). 'The possessive logic of patriarchal white sovereignty: The High Court and the Yorta Yorta decision', *Borderlands E-Journal*, vol 3, no 2: 1–9.

Moreton-Robinson, A. (2015). *The White Possessive: Property, Power, and Indigenous Sovereignty.* University of Minnesota Press: Minneapolis, MN.

Morrill, A., Tuck, E., and Super Futures Haunt Qollective. (2016). 'Before dispossession, or surviving it', Liminalities: A Journal of Performance Studies, vol 12, no 1. Available: http://liminalities.net/12-1/dispossession.pdf, accessed 13 June 2019.

Murdolo, A. (1996). 'Warmth and vanity with all women? Historicizing racism in the Australian women's movement', *Feminist Review*, vol 52, no 1: 69–86.

Nelson, E., Smith, S., and Grimshaw, P. (eds.) (2002). *Letters from Aboriginal Women of Victoria, 1867–1926.* University of Melbourne: Melbourne, VIC.

Nugent, M. (2002). Women's Employment and Professionalism in Australia: Histories, Themes and Places. Australian Heritage Commission: Canberra, ACT.

Pettman, J. (1995). 'Race, ethnicity and gender', in D. Stasiulis and N. Yuval-Davis (eds.) *Unsettling Settler Societies: Articulations of Gender, Race, Ethnicity and Class.* SAGE: London, 65–94.

Raftery, J. (2006). *Not Part of the Public: Non-Indigenous Policies and Practices and the Health of Indigenous South Australians 1836–1973.* Wakefield Press: Adelaide, SA.

Raynes, C. (2005). Inquiry into Stolen Wages, Senate Standing Committees on Legal and Constitutional Affairs, Parliament of Australia: Submissions and Additional Information Received, Submission No. 8A. Senate Printing Unit: Canberra, ACT. Available: https://www.aph.gov.au/Parliamentary_Business/Committees/Senate/Legal_and_Constitutional_AffairA/Completed_inquiries/2004-07/stolen_wages/submissions/sublist, accessed 22 July 2019.

Raynes, C. (2009a). *The Last Protector: The Illegal Removal of Aboriginal Children from Their Parents in South Australia.* Wakefield Press: Adelaide, SA.

Raynes, C. (2009b). 'Secret history', Inside Story, 25 February. Available: https://insidestory.org.au/secret-history/, accessed 1 August 2019.

Richards, T. (1993). *The Imperial Archive: Knowledge and the Fantasy of the Empire.* Verso: London.

Rivera, J.-M. (2007). 'The archive as specter', *English Language Notes*, vol 45, no 1: 1–4.

Robinson, S. (2003). '"We do not want one who is too old …" aboriginal child domestic servants in Queensland, 1842–1945', *Aboriginal History*, vol 27: 162–182.

Royal Commission on The Aborigines. (1913). *Progress Report of the Royal Commission on the Aborigines; Together with Minutes of Proceedings, Evidence and Appendices.* Government Printer: Adelaide, SA.

Scott, K. (2001). 'Australia's continuing neurosis: Identity, race and history', *Alfred Deakin Lecture*, 25 May. Available: http://archive.is/CzH2t, accessed 1 August 2019.

Shine Lawyers. (2019). 'Shine lawyers investigates class action over unpaid wages for Indigenous Australians'. Available: https://www.shine.com.au/media-centre/media-releases/shine-lawyers-launches-class-action-over-unpaid-wages-for-indigenous, accessed 2 August 2019.

South Australian Museum Archives. (2005). *AA 346 Board for Anthropological Research, 1926–1975.* Available: http://archives.samuseum.sa.gov.au/aa346/provlist.htm, accessed 8 June 2019.

South Australian Museum Archives. (2011). *AA 689 Dr Joseph Bernard Birdsell.* SA Museum Archives, 2003. Available: http://archives.samuseum.sa.gov.au/aa689/provlist.htm, accessed 7 June 2019.

South Australian Museum Archives (2014). *AA 346 Board for Anthropological Research.* SA Museum Archives, 2005. Available: http://archives.samuseum.sa.gov.au/aa346/provlist.htm, accessed 7 June 2019.

Steedman, C. (2001). *Dust: The Archive and Cultural History*. Manchester University Press: Manchester.

Stoler, A.L. (2002). 'Colonial archives and the arts of governance', *Archival Science*, vol 2, no 1–2: 87–109.

Stoler, A .L. (2006a). 'Tense and tender ties: The politics of comparison in North American history and (post) colonial studies', in A.L. Stoler (ed.) *Haunted by Empire: Geographies of Intimacy in North American History*. Duke University Press: Durham, NC, 23–67.

Stoler, A.L. (2006b). 'Intimidations of empire: Predicaments of the tactile and unseen', in A.L. Stoler, (ed.) *Haunted by Empire: Geographies of Intimacy in North American History*. Duke University Press: Durham, NC, 1–22.

Stoler, A.L. (2009). *Along the Archival Grain: Epistemic Anxieties and Colonial Common Sense*. Princeton University Press: Princeton, NJ.

Voss, P.J. and Werner M.L. (1999). 'Towards a poetics of the archive: Introduction', *Studies in the Literary Imagination*, vol 32, no 1: i–viii.

Walden, I. (1995). "That was slavery days': Aboriginal domestic servants in New South Wales in the twentieth century', *Labour History*, vol 69: 196–209.

Watson, I. (2009). 'In the Northern territory intervention: What is saved or rescued and at what cost', *Cultural Studies Review*, vol 15, no 2: 45–60.

Watson, I. and Venne, S. (2010). 'Sex, race and questions of aboriginality', in M. Thornton (ed.) *Sex Discrimination in Uncertain Times*. ANU Press: Canberra, ACT, 347–367.

Watson, J. (2009). *Blood Language*. Miegunyah Press: Melbourne, VIC.

Weatherill, J. (2007). Inquiry into Stolen Wages, Senate Standing Committees on Legal and Constitutional Affairs, Parliament of Australia: Additional Information Received, 2. Senate Printing Unit: Canberra, ACT. Available: https://www.aph.gov.au/Parliamentary_Business/Committees/Senate/Legal_and_C onstitutional_AffairA/Completed_inquiries/2004-07/stolen_wages/submissions/sublist, accessed 22 July 2019.[9]

Wright, A. (2002). 'Politics of writing', *Southerly*, vol 62, no 2: 10–20.

Wright, A. (2006). 'On writing *Carpentaria*', reprinted from HEAT 13 – *Harper's Gold*. Available: http://logincms.uws.edu.au/__data/assets/pdf_file/0011/385949/Wright-HEATessay.pdf, accessed 10 May 2019.

Wright, A. (2016). 'What happens when you tell somebody else's story?' *Meanjin*, vol 75, no 4: 58–76.

12

Māku Anō e Hanga Tōku Nei Whare

I myself shall build my house

Leonie Pihama

Introduction

Māku anō e hanga tōku nei whare. Ko te tāhuhu he hīnau ko ngā poupou he māhoe, patatē. Me whakatupu ki te hua o te rengarenga, me whakapakari ki te hua o te kawariki. That's 'I myself shall build my house. The ridge-pole will be of hīnau and the supporting posts of māhoe and patatē. Raise the people with the fruit of the rengarenga, strengthened them with the fruits of the kawariki.'

I open this chapter with the words of Tāwhiao. Tāwhiao was the second Māori King within the Kingitanga movement. In this tongi (proverbial saying), Tāwhiao reflects on the need to assert our sovereignty, our self-determination within a context of colonial invasion. He urges us as a people to use the resources that we have at hand to construct what we need as a people. The māhoe and patatē as small plants and therefore were not trees that were associated with building houses, the rengarenga is known to have been a plant that was cooked within a hangi (earth oven) but was not necessarily the preferred food source and kawariki is a bitter plant used primarily as rongoā (traditional medicine). As such, Tāwhiao is reminding us that we must use what we can in times of difficulty and sparse resources. He was referring to a time of extreme colonial dispossession.

I write this chapter as I sit on our whenua, our ancestral lands, of the Waikato people, close to Tūrangawaewae, the marae (gathering place) of the Kingitanga that was built by a powerhouse tūpuna wahine (female ancestor), an exceptional woman Te Puea Herangi. As was the aspiration of Tāwhiao, Waikato have indeed been constructing our own whare. Tāwhiao is renowned for his many tongi (prophetic sayings) that have provided learnings and guidance for both Waikato and the national Māori movement of Kingitanga. Within te ao Māori (the Māori world) we have been actively constructing and re-constructing our own spaces based upon the knowledge that has been passed on to us from our tūpuna (ancestors). We are creating spaces where our people can thrive. This chapter speaks to one space, a theoretical space, that of Mana Wahine theory, a space created by Māori women to both assert our ways of being within the world, and to speak back to the imposed colonial gender constructions that continue to dominate within Aotearoa.

As a Māori woman I approach theory and research from a fundamental position that to be Māori is a gift, a blessing, and a wonderful way to have been born. We are each an embodiment of our ancestors past and our ancestors yet to come. At the centre of that being is te reo and tikanga Māori (Māori language and culture), both of which are presented and argued emphatically as appropriate and legitimate ways of understanding the world. Te reo and tikanga are asserted as valid and critical elements in the articulation of our theories (Nepe 1991; Smith, G. H. 1997; Smith, L. T. 1993; Pihama 1993; 2001). Kaupapa Māori is an overarching Māori philosophical framework that guides the work I do and how I live my life. It is also what guides my academic work as a theorist and researcher. Mana Wahine theory is a form of Kaupapa Māori theory. They travel together as hoa haere, as committed companions, as they are of this land, are always connected and as such they are closely related (Pohatu 1996).

A critical part of building our whare is the dismantling of those beliefs, ideologies, and discourses that emerge from the coloniser's house. As Tāwhiao has said we must use the Māori tools that we have at our disposal. The tools This chapter looks at Ngā Pou Ariā, the theoretical pillars and principles that frame Mana Wahine theory and the critical project of dismantling the colonial heteropatriarchal houses that have been built, and continue to be reinforced through a range of discourses and practices. It is offered as a tool to contribute to the clearing of Māori land of the insidious colonising ideologies that perpetuate abuse on Māori people daily.

Mana Wahine theory

Mana Wahine theory has two clear projects. First, the affirmation of ways of being as Māori that are grounded within our own language, culture, and knowledge. This is to draw upon our ancestral understandings and practices that align to the fundamental belief system that all Māori are valued and respected within our whānau. This is to recognise, acknowledge, affirm, and uplift the mana that is inherent to all. As key knowledge holders such as Rangimarie Pere (1984); Māori Marsden (2003); Tuakana Nepe (1991); Ngahuia Te Awekotuku (1991); Hirini Moko Mead (2003) have stated that all Māori are born with mana through the spiritual connection we have with our atua and it is passed through generations from our ancestors. Second, Mana Wahine theory that attends to the multiple issues that are faced by Māori women as a result of the impact of the intersection of race, class, and gender ideologies that have been imported to our lands. Like Kaupapa Māori theory, Mana Wahine must both analyse and challenge unequal power relations that exist both between colonised and coloniser. It must also deal with the impact of these issues internally within and upon Māori communities.

Much of the focus of present work by Māori women has been the analysis and deconstruction of colonial discourses. Through this process Māori women are exploding the colonial myths that have been constructed, whilst simultaneously redefining the boundaries (Te Awekotuku 1991; Smith 1992; Irwin 1992; Mikaere 1995; Pihama 2001; Murphy 2011; Simmonds 2014; Gable 2019; Seed Pihama 2019). This is a complex process as we are constantly confronted with the need to decolonise that which we have internalised about ourselves. Increasingly Māori women are challenging the dominant cultural terrain. Mana Wahine theory provide a means by which to describe Māori women's analyses, they are Māori women's views of the world, which are located in Māori women's experiences and understandings of the world. As such, it challenges directly belief systems that have at their centre the diminishing, the denial, the trampling of the mana of Māori women. When we speak of mana we speak of the inherent "psychic influence, control, prestige, power, vested and acquired authority and influence, being influential or binding over others, and that quality of the person that others know she or he has" (Pere 1991: 14). Mana is embedded within te ao Māori (the Māori world) and is a part of all engagements that we have as Māori people with each other and with all that dwell between Ranginui (sky parent) and Papatūānuku (earth parent). Mana Wahine theory has developed through the assertions of Māori women that we must engage directly with heteronormative patriarchal systems and structures that have been implanted within Aotearoa.

Mana Wahine theories continue to be grown and nurtured by Māori women and therefore as is the case, at this point in time, with Kaupapa Māori theory there is ongoing discussion and searching being undertaken by many Māori women as to what may be essential elements of such a framework. The whānau, hapū, and iwi context is critical to the articulation of Māori women's theories in whatever form they may take. Where there are definite parallels across te ao Māori (the Māori world) there are also distinct differences within whānau, hapū, and iwi. The variations in our experiences should not deter us from seeking theories that can support the affirmation of our roles, status, and positioning or that can bring a unified engagement of colonisation. Rather, as is the case of understanding whakapapa (our ancestral lineage) there is a strength in the ability for Māori women to locate our analyses within our specific iwi tikanga and in doing so to also recognise that our iwi histories and experiences are a source of knowledge, strength, and connection for us all. Recognising whānau, hapū, and iwi identities, and our experiences in a colonised state, is critical in any Māori theoretical discussion.

Mana Wahine theory is driven by a desire to re-engage Māori women's knowledge and understandings and in doing so affirm a wider Kaupapa Māori theory, research, and practice movements within Aotearoa. It is a theoretical framework through which Māori women engage critically with how we see ourselves and how we consider our position in a colonised society. Mana Wahine is one name utilised by Māori women alongside others such as Kaupapa Wahine or Māori Feminism to speak to analyses that are shaped by Māori women and which align to tikanga, te reo, and mātauranga Māori. The naming of our analysis is an important part of the theorising process, as naming is for our people a critical way to forefront our knowledge, histories, and cultural practices within our theoretical work. It has been argued that Mana Wahine theory is an umbrella term under which Māori women's theories can be located (Te Awekotuku 1991; Smith 1992; Simmonds 2014; Pihama et.al. 2019). Te Awekotuku (1991) explains Mana Wahine is a process whereby Māori women are able to be proactive in our determining our future and which enables us to engage in the rediscovery and work that is necessary for Māori as a whole. It is defined within cultural terms and in a context that affirms fundamental Māori values and the ways in which they are negotiated. As such Mana Wahine brings to the fore a need for analysis that will reclaim Māori world-views in terms of gender and gender relationships. As Linda Tuhiwai Smith (1992: 62) states Mana Wahine is:

A strong cultural concept which situates Māori women in relation to each other and upholds their mana as women of particular genealogical groupings. It also situates Māori women in relation to the outside world and reaffirms their mana as Māori, Indigenous women.

In order to address the issues of the intersecting ideologies of gender, race, and class Mana Wahine theory draws upon both cultural and structural analyses that are informed by our ancestral knowledge. As such decolonising approaches sit alongside the traditional knowledge sources that we depend so heavily upon to inform our ways of seeing the world through a Maori women's lens. Such a view is to remind us of the deeply hegemonic impact of colonial heteropatriarchal capitalist ideologies and to be vigilant in both our understandings and our analysis.

Mana Wahine theory is grounded within Māori knowledge and understandings as a means by which to engage with the structural conditions and colonial-dominant ideologies that create the context for such issues. As such, Mana Wahine theory has multiple projects with which it must engage including the regeneration of te reo and tikanga Māori; the affirmation and uplifting of the mana of Māori women; the critique of the imposition of colonial gender beliefs and practices and the decolonisation of colonial ideologies and practices that have become embedded within te ao Māori (the Māori world). The following discussion provides an overview of Ngā Pou Ariā, the theoretical pillars or posts that frame Mana Wahine theory.

Ngā Pou Ariā: Theoretical pillars

This section provides an overview of the theoretical pillars that are the framework of Mana Wahine theory, including the six principles identified within Kaupapa Māori theory of tino rangatiratanga (the self-determination principle); taonga tuku iho (the cultural aspirations principle); Ako Māori (the 'culturally preferred' pedagogy); Kia piki ake i ngā raruraru o te Kainga (the 'socio-economic' mediation principle); Whānau (the 'extended family structure' principle); Kaupapa (the 'collective philosophy' principle). These principles are then expanded to provide more specific discussion of key components that sit within them such as: rangatira; te reo, tikanga & mātauranga Māori; whakapapa; wairua; reclaiming cultural spaces and decolonisation. Fundamental to Mana Wahine theory is the means through which we apply each of these pillars.

Tino rangatiratanga: Within Kaupapa Māori the principle of tino rangatiratanga is the assertion of Māori sovereignty and self-determination. Smith (1997: 466) states that "'tino rangātiranga' reinforces the goal of seeking more meaningful 'control over one's own life and cultural well-being'". This brings to the fore the role of Te Tiriti o Waitangi within which the term 'tino rangatiratanga' was used to affirm Māori independence, autonomy, and self-determination. Upholding 'tino rangatiratanga' means upholding the rights of all Māori as tangata whenua (people of the land). Māori women have always exercised rangatiratanga, held key decision making, leadership responsibilities within our respective whānau, hapū, and iwi, and as individuals. It has been clearly evidenced that Māori women were signatories to Te Tiriti (Simpson 1990). However, within the relationship with the Crown there has been a constant diminishing and devaluing of the mana of wahine Māori (Szarzy 1995). This was clearly evident with the active marginalisation of Māori women by missionaries that carried Te Tiriti around the country in 1840 (Orange 1987). This has culminated in the lodging of the Mana Wahine claim to the Waitangi Tribunal in 1993 (Wai 381) and has now been allocated time for hearings in 2020. A 27-year wait that highlights the failure of the Crown to see the rangatiratanga of Māori women as a critical issue.

Wahine Rangatira: Māori Women's leadership: The term rangatira relates to the role of leadership within Māori collectives. Ranga is to weave or join together and tira is the term for group. As such rangatira are considered those that work to bring the group together to enable movement for the collective on whatever the topic, issue, or decision may be. Rangatira is not a gendered term but has become increasingly so through the imposition of notions of male dominance that sit at the centre of colonial gender relations. Rangatira is however within Māori understandings an inclusive term that is related to the capacity of people to be able to bring together collectives. The role of Māori women leaders is documented and the validation of those roles is critical to Mana Wahine theory. Irwin (1992) writes that Māori women throughout our history have been innovators and leaders; however, our stories have been made invisible and kept out of the records. Te Awekotuku (1991) argues that Māori women have always been the leaders and doers, and they remain so across a range of issues and cites Te Puea Herangi and Te Atairangikahu as Māori women leaders in Waikato, who have actively worked for the betterment of their people. Linda Tuhiwai Smith (1992) writes that Māori women in leadership roles have often been presented as the exception to the rule, yet within whānau, hapū, iwi, and Māori urban communities Māori women continue to do the work that uplift our people. We are each able to point to key Māori women's leadership on multiple levels. However, the marginalisation of Māori women's leadership roles continues as a part of the wider denial of the mana of Māori women. Mira Szarsy (1995) highlighted the urgency for the reinstatement of Māori women's involvement in key decision making related to our people, an issue that was raised at a key national hui in 1984 where it was resolved to ensure Māori women's involvement in decision making for Māori people. It was noted within the hui "That because Māori women constitute over 50 percent of the tangata whenua there must be equal representation in all areas of decision making in the future" (Sykes 2000: 63). To date this aspiration remains unrealised and as such Mana Wahine theory requires us to continue to speak to issues of leadership and the place of Māori women.

Taonga tuku iho: This principle encompasses the many treasures and gifts that have been handed to us by our tūpuna, our ancestors. This includes all aspects of tikanga, te reo, and mātauranga Māori. Within this principle is the core of what it means to be Māori and the knowledge, language, concepts, values, protocols, and practices of being Māori. Embedded within te reo, tikanga, and mātauranga are the fundamental understandings of how we are collectively informed as Māori and the responsibilities, obligations, expectations, accountabilities, and roles in terms of how we live our lives. Taonga tuku iho is an overarching concept that includes all of the knowledge and practices that our ancestors have bequeathed us for the wellbeing of current and future generations.

Te reo, Tikanga, and Mātauranga Māori: All of the components of taonga tuku iho are located within, understood, practiced and transmitted through te reo (Māori language); tikanga (Māori practices and protocols); and mātauranga (Māori knowledge and ways of knowing). The relationship between tikanga and mātauranga Māori is emphasised by Mead (2003) with all tikanga being embedded within and upon mātauranga Māori. Tikanga he states is the action and practice of mātauranga Māori and provides mechanisms of social control and ways of being within Māori society. Tikanga has both systems of determining what is 'tika' or correct, what are appropriate behaviours and how we rebalance when tikanga has been transgressed. Durie (1998: 23) refers to this as "guides to moral behaviour". Mātauranga Māori is knowledge, ways of knowing and a knowledge archive that relates to all aspects of being Māori. Within te reo, tikanga and mātauranga Māori are sources of traditional and ancestral knowledges and understandings that can enable us to rebalance the current inequities that exist in gendered relationships within Māori society as a result of colonisation.

Te reo refers to both Māori language and voice. Within te reo Māori are indicators to the positioning and status of Māori women. The non-gendered nature of pronouns is one indicator. This is increasingly written about by Māori women as a means of viewing Māori women in a context where the discourses were not necessarily gender-specific. There are many examples of this. The term 'ia' for example relates to her, him, she, or he. 'Tōna' may be her or his. 'Mōna' can refer to being for her or for him. The gender is determined by having the knowledge of exactly who is being spoken about in the given context. The English language has had significant impact upon Māori women in particular as a vehicle through which colonial gender belief are reproduced (Mara and Pihama 1994). Language plays a major role in the transmission of belief systems and therefore we must have a critical understanding of the ways in which the coloniser's language impacts on wider values, beliefs, and understandings. The interpretation and translation of te reo Māori is therefore a powerful point of analysis that Māori women who engage theories of Mana Wahine can include. Another critical aspect is that of exploring te reo Māori for those indicators of how our tūpuna Wahine positioned themselves within te ao Māori and how tikanga Māori was constructed. Within te reo Māori and tikanga are indicators that mitigate against the colonial hegemony of unequal gender relations. Terms such as rangatira, ariki, atua, tangata, tohunga are not gender-specific and are applicable to all Māori (Yates-Smith 1998;

Mikaere 1995; Irwin 1992b). Te reo Māori offers us insights into societal relations and in doing so proffers possibilities for change.

Te reo as voice is also an important component of Mana Wahine theory. Where we are cognisant of the multiple voices of whānau, hapū, and iwi, we must also recognise that within te ao Māori (Māori world) there are groupings of our people that are often silenced or denied space and voice as a consequence of colonial discourses. One group is takatāpui (Māori LGBTIQ), many of whom struggle to be recognised within their own whānau, hapū, and iwi in a context where sexuality is often kept silent. Pihama et al. (2020) note that a high percentage of takatāpui feel a level of distress when whānau and friends avoid discussions around their sexuality. This indicates that we must be aware of the ways in which Māori LGBTIQ voices are supported or denied within our whānau, hapū, and iwi and work in ways that affirm te reo, the voice, of all.

Wairua: The concept of wairua is an important element to all things Māori. This is made explicit in Mana Wahine theory. Māori women's realities are linked to spiritual notions as these cannot be denied or disconnected from physical realities (Smith, L. T. 1992). It validates our essential connection through whakapapa, with all aspects of the taiao (environment), and all atua that surround and protect us and all our relations. How we talk about the social constructiveness of events, positions, and realities must also include a discussion of the spiritual elements that are a part of those things. This is where the argument within critical theory that all things are socially constructed falls short in that it does not provide for wairua. Wairua is talked about by Pere (1988: 13-14) as follows.

> Literally translated, 'wairua' denotes wai (water), rua (two), a word that can depict spirituality. The Māori saw the physical realm as being immersed and integrated with the spiritual realm. Every act, natural, and other influences were considered to have both physical and spiritual implications. A powerful belief in supernatural forces governed and influenced the way one interacted with other people and related to the environment. Spirituality was seen as a dimension internalized within a person from conception – the seed of human life emanated from Io, the supreme supernatural influence.

One of the critical responses to Western feminism has been the lack of spiritualism within radical feminist analysis. Smith and Taki (1993: 38–42) state that Western feminisms are spirituality 'impoverished' arguing that the secular nature of Western feminism can work to deny Māori women's spirituality. Within Western feminisms spirituality has been relegated to the domain of religion (Smith, L. T. 1992). Within Mana Wahine theory wairua is an essential component to how we understand our world. Smith, L. T. (1992) argues that Māori women have a clear spiritual project that is to do with bringing forward not only discussions of wairua, but the wider discussion of Māori knowledge. She states:

> As the human manifestation of the female elements, women have been engaged in a monumental and historic-mythological spiritual struggle, a struggle marked by significant events: the wrenching apart of Papatūānuku from Ranginui; the turning over of Papatūānuku so that her sights and thoughts would look forever downwards; the creation of Hine Ahu One; the transformation of Hine Titama in Hine Nui Te Pō; the deeds of Maui against his grandmothers. This spiritual struggle continues to be fought in our role as mediators of tapu. Women have the power to make things noa, to intervene in the states of tapu-ness. This role of women tends to be conceptualised as an indication of the passive role of women, but the freedom that is contained within this role suggests that it is extremely active and dynamic. The power to make things noa contains within it the power over day-to-day life, over food,

over commerce. The spiritual discourse incorporates more than the dimension of wairua. It is a struggle over world-view, over Māori knowledge, over history and over the various realms in which we function as humans.

(Smith L. T. 1992: 42–43)

Recognition of wairua within Mana Wahine is also about the reassertion of the place of atua wāhine and the stories that give us more indication as to the roles of Māori women within whānau, hapū, iwi, Māori. In returning to the contention that the visibility of wairua is a part of a wider agenda to affirm Māori knowledge it can also be noted that such actions also directly challenge colonial notions that have marginalised and denied the power of Māori women and in particular the source of that power as it is expressed in the deeds and actions of atua wāhine. Mana Wahine theory seeks to bring forward the stories and identities of our tūpuna wahine as a way of gauging the many and varied roles Māori women carry within Te Ao Māori.

Mātauranga Wahine: Reclaiming Māori women's knowledges: L.T. Smith (1992) argues Māori women have been ignored in records related to events after colonisation events prior to colonisation. What was history is now related as 'mythology' and Māori women have been placed on the fringes of 'male adventures'. This brings to the fore the issue of the 'writing out' of Māori women in our histories and the need for conscious repositioning. Jenkins (1992) argues there is a need to look critically at how we have been presented in Māori stories informed by missionary beliefs about Māori women's realities. In a process of reclaiming Mana Wahine within Māori stories we provide the possibilities for representing ourselves taking account of how colonial ideologies are insidiously internalised into our belief systems. This requires being culturally, politically and socially 'on guard' in what is essentially a struggle for beliefs. Challenging the hegemony of colonial assumptions, beliefs, and expectations is a battle, it is a battle of minds, of knowledge, of ideas, of culture, of reo, of tikanga. Reclaiming the position of Māori women within our histories and stories is an essential part of that struggle. What is exciting and incredibly satisfying about that struggle is the potential for change in terms of the position of Māori women given a societal acceptance of the role and status of Māori women on this, our land. In presenting a critical analysis of documentation related to Māori women, Mikaere (1995) has revealed the contradictions that are inherent in assertions made from a colonised state. This reaffirms the need for conscious developments of decolonisation in Aotearoa. In recognising the impact of colonisation in any act of reclaiming Māori women's knowledge, as Mikaere (1995: 5) states:

> It is my belief that, in consciously re-examining from a Māori perspective material that has been so misrepresented, we may begin to rescue mātauranga Māori from the state of limbo to which it has been relegated by colonisation. An important part of this exercise is the raising of the image and status of Māori women from the state of submergence that, it will be argued, is the result of colonisation.

Yates-Smith (1998) writes that the process of reclaiming our stories is central to gaining a deeper understanding of mātauranga Māori and is a way of addressing imposed imbalance, of re-establishing the images of atua wāhine who have been 'dismembered' through colonisation, and placing the stories and images of atua wāhine back where they rightly belong, in the consciousness and knowledge of Māori people. Yates-Smith (1998: 4–5) states:

> The cultural renaissance among Māori calls for a recovery of spiritual knowledge to provide a strong base for those wishing to discover their past, hence the need for the dissemination

of such information, despite the past practice of restricting esoteric lore to a few. In addition to safeguarding our Māori language, we must also nurture our spirits, the Earth Mother, and all the other aspects of the natural world upon which we human beings are dependent, re-establishing a balance at a personal, cultural, and environmental level. Thus the need for information about Māori goddesses can be clearly identified.

Ako Māori: This according to G.H. Smith (1997) is a principle that reinforces Māori pedagogical approaches. Pihama et al. (2004: 20) note "Ako as Māori pedagogy is derived from a need to transmit, maintain, and further expand Māori knowledge and therefore must be seen in relation to the ways in which Māori knowledge is understood". The process of knowledge transmission, learning and teaching has been the role of whānau in the first instance and through wider social institutions such as whare wānanga in more specialised contexts. An awareness of educational processes that have impacted upon Māori is essential to an understanding of the place of te reo, tikanga, and mātauranga Māori. Analysis of both Mission and Native schooling highlights the marginalisation of ako and the direct gendering of all aspects of learning and teaching. Ako enables us to bring forward the stories of our tūpuna wahine and to advance the significant role that wahine Māori take in the learning, teaching, and guiding of knowledge within our whānau, hapū, and iwi. It also requires us, in our reclamation of Māori knowledge to ensure that we are providing opportunities for all of our people to be engaged in learning the knowledge of our ancestors. For example, karakia (ritual chant, incantation) is a key part of our lives as Māori. There are many contexts within which karakia is necessary and where those most knowledge-able and proficient in that tikanga take leadership irrespective of gender. For those that have wahine, ruahine, or kuia in their whānau that continue to provide the knowledge and guidance by karakia, the role of wahine Māori is retained and affirmed. However, increasingly karakia is viewed as the domain of men and is having a significant impact on the involvement of many Māori women. It has been noted that Māori women's involvement in such knowledge reclama-tion needs to be guided and informed by our kuia (Black 2016).

Kia piki ake i ngā raruraru o te Kainga: This principle indicates the need for Kaupapa Māori theory and Mana Wahine theory to be active in providing cultural processes of intervention to minimise the impact of colonisation. The concept relates to providing processes that support or assist whānau that experience difficulties, as a process by which to "alleviate the negative pressures of the marginal socio-economic positioning" (Smith 1997: 468). Māori collective responsibility to support each other requires both theoretical frameworks in the analysis of the socio-economic systems and structures that impede the well-being of Māori. Within Mana Wahine theory this requires critical analysis of the layers of structural arrangements that pre-vent Māori women accessing resources and economic opportunities to ensure well-being. This includes the marginalisation of Māori women within a range of areas that create poverty includ-ing dispossession of land, educational choices and life opportunities and where gender ide-ologies and practices diminish Māori women's life choices across a wide range of sectors and activities, including the impact of ideologies of domestication.

Whānau: the collective well-being of whānau is key within both Kaupapa Māori and Mana Wahine theory. This provides for the affirmation of whānaungatanga and our connection through whakapapa. G.H. Smith (1997: 471) highlights that whānau enables for the invoking of "Māori cultural values, customs and practices which organise around 'collective responsibil-ity'". Whānau refers to both the extended family collective and the process of birth, as such there is a direct cultural and spiritual connection to Māori women that we can bring to the fore within our understandings and analysis. The whānau is a critical building block for Māori society and provides a basis for the collective structure for hapū and iwi. Concepts of tuakana

– teina (older-younger siblings of same sex), tungāne (brother of a woman), tuahine (sister of a man), whaea (mother/auntie), matua (father/uncle), and others that outline positioning within whānau provide a framework of relationships. When we see whānau as key in Māori societal constructions then we can comprehend more fully the attack on whānau that occurred with colonisation. It has become increasingly commonplace that whānau has been regarded in the same light as family. The juxtaposition of whānau to family is particularly dangerous for Māori women. The dominant representation of family in Aotearoa is the nuclear family despite different family types. This representation reinforces gender relations that are inherent to the nuclear family structure. This is not to say that all people adhere to this family structure but it is a reminder that the nuclear family is in many ways the antithesis to whānau. Mana Wahine theory brings to the discussion of whānau both an analysis of how relationships between Māori women and Māori men are constructed and played out with a focus on the construction of relationships between Māori women. What is important in a discussion of whānau in Mana Wahine theory is a critical analysis of the fragmentation of whānau and the internalisation of gender roles within what is now being reconstituted as whānau. Whānau must be a social system that supports Māori women and not one that reflects the colonisers ideal of the domesticated Indigenous woman. The place and influence of whānau in knowledge transmission is critical to traditional pedagogical practices and the place of relationships within our collective responsibilities (Pere 1982; 1988; Pohatu 1996; 2011).

Whakapapa: Whānau, hapū, iwi, and Māori relationships are informed and guided in many contexts by whakapapa. As noted above there are many roles within whānau, and this is also evident across whakapapa relationships. Our connections to hapū, iwi, to our lands, our mountains, our rivers, our lakes are all central to how we position ourselves and to our identification with those relations. Whakapapa also provides us with a systematic way of placing ourselves in relationship to each other. Whakapapa originates well before humanity and reaches into the origins of all things. Whakapapa korero is our ancestral history and which gives us insights into all parts of our lives past, present, and future. As whakapapa commences with atua (deities) we are reminded that tapu (sacredness) is embedded within us all. Research related to atua wāhine (female deities) highlights the balance that exists within our spiritual realms (Yates-Smith 1998). Such balance has been disrupted by many colonial practices and as such the restoration of such knowledge is crucial. As Aroha Yates-Smith highlights there is a need for research and analysis to proffer ways "in which the balance maybe restored between the feminine and the masculine, at all levels of Māori society, spiritual, physical, and mental" (1988: iii). This is a key role of Mana Wahine theory. This is central in terms of whakapapa within Mana Wahine theory, in that it recognises that whakapapa is a cultural system that affirms the place of Māori women. It also recognises that within Western tradition of ethnography there has been a dominance of a patriarchal linear structure of genealogical tables that is often inadequate in dealing with the multi-layered relations that is whakapapa. All too often white ethnographers and anthropologists utilised their version of genealogies to make invisible the position and status of Māori women (Mahuika 1973). Mahuika (1973: 16–17) states:

> In Ngati Porou, however, primogeniture is the absolute determinant of seniority, regardless of the sex of the first-born child. In other words, the longer the unbroken line one can trace through first-born children, male or female, the greater one's seniority in society. Primogeniture, and therefore one's seniority in society are both factors in deciding who should be the leader of a tribe or sub-tribe. Leadership may be defined as control over people or mana tangata. It involved the right to direct and control people's lives in terms of the culture and the right to make political decisions on their behalf. The ability to unite the

group and to protect it against other individuals or groups were also important manifestations of leadership.

What this means is that within our analysis we need to look closely at how whakapapa is represented or recorded and the place of Māori women within whānau, hapū, and iwi. It also means that we have many opportunities to not only dispute such constructions but just as importantly to uplift our own whakapapa and the stories of our tūpuna wahine alongside our tūpuna tane. What is most exciting is that we have within our pūrākau and whakapapa kōrero knowledge that gives deep insights into the roles and status of Māori women and enables as Mikaere (1995: 7) a space for "each iwi to examine the impact of colonisation on its tikanga and accordingly, on its women".

Kaupapa: This foundational principle is one within which our collective commitment and engagement takes place. Kaupapa refers to the underpinning philosophy that brings focus to an issue and provides a platform that is distinctively Māori. Smith (1997) refers to this as the 'collective philosophy' principle related to Māori collective aspirations. Within Mana Wahine the notion of Kaupapa is shared understandings of how we want our world to be as affirming and supportive of Māori women. A key element within Mana Wahine theory is the recognition that our collective aspirations must necessarily be inclusive of the many ways in which we locate ourselves. On the whole Western feminist theories fail to engage diversity within their analysis; however, within Mana Wahine theory our cultural understandings and practices of whakapapa and whanaungatanga simultaneously indicate the many relationships that are a part of our collective identities and the diversity that exists. As such Kaupapa requires us to ensure how we understand our collectivity is done so in ways that affirm our diverse realities in ways that enable Māori women to be included. As Irwin (1992: 3) writes:

> In our work with Māori women we need to recognize that they, like any other community of women, are not a homogenous group. A number of other factors influence Māori women's development: tribal affiliation, social class, sexual preference, knowledge of traditional Māori tikanga, knowledge of the Māori language, rural or urban location, identification on the political spectrum from radical to traditional, place in the family, the level of formal schooling, and educational attainments to name but a few.

However, in order to affirm the many positions from which we can theorise and understand the world we must both recognise the diverse realities and challenge some of the colonial ideologies that continue to deny the voices of Māori women. There are also other forms of diversity that exist beyond the frameworks of whānau, hapū, and iwi including the diversity in terms of class positioning, the diversity in terms of urban and rural dwelling and the diversity in terms of sexuality to give some examples.

Reclaiming cultural space: A key element in the articulation of Mana Wahine theory is the reclamation by Māori women of cultural space. Cultural institutions and ceremonial practices provide us with a means by which to maintain and reproduce our tikanga. The affirmation of Māori women and our roles within tikanga and kawa is critical to the overall well-being of Māori women and te ao Māori. A prominent debate in this regard is that of who 'speaks' on the marae during the pōwhiri (formal welcome ceremonies). The debate regarding Māori women's speaking rights is one that has been around Māori circles for much longer than many of us realise. This needs to be explored and exposed within much wider discussions of voice and who has historically been recognised has having the right to speak in more general terms. Smith, L. T. articulated the idea that Pākehā colonisers assumed the existence of the same sorts of societal arrangements for Māori she notes "there was 'take me to your leader' mentality and of course that leader was male" (1996: Unedited interview). This assumption underpins and permeated Māori thinking within our cultural institutions. This is also essential in how we speak about decolonisation within Mana Wahine.

Decolonisation: Colonisation is both a series of historical events and a system of oppressive structures that continue to operate within Aotearoa. Decolonisation encompasses an agreed need for awareness and critical analysis of the processes and the outcomes of colonisation that we must engage directly as Māori. Decolonisation requires a peeling back of the layers in order to reveal the many ways in which colonial ideologies and practices impact upon us as tangata whenua, and constantly reflecting both on what we find and how we need to make transformative change. In Mana Wahine theoretical frameworks, decolonisation asserts the need to ensure that the positioning of Māori women is actively considered. This is particularly necessary giving the positioning of Māori women as 'Other' to Pākehā and Māori men (Smith, L. T. 1992). Cheryl Smith (1994) argues that women's involvement in decolonisation projects is crucial in order to bring to the debate issues of gender and family relations, alongside wider social issues.

Conclusion

This chapter provides an overview of Ngā Pou Ariā, key theoretical pillars that are critical to the framework of Mana Wahine theory and that can be utilised as analysis. Theory is fundamentally a process of explaining, understanding, describing, and analysing key issues or events. Mana Wahine theory does this from Māori women's viewpoint drawing on cultural understandings and applying those in ways that enable us to give voice to Māori women's analysis. Mana Wahine theory is not the only form of Māori women's analysis. It is but one form. Mana Wahine theory offers the possibility to bring change in all forms of oppressive behaviours and structures. To focus on one issue is never enough. It is not acceptable to me that we develop analyses that are limited in their approach to sexuality. Just as it is not good enough to be framed by Western theories that deny our cultural being, it is not good enough to be framed by Māori theories that deny the place of Māori women because of our gender or sexuality. Grounded upon the foundational work of Kaupapa Māori theory, it is asserted that Mana Wahine theory provides us with a deeper way of considering the intersection of colonisation, race, class, and gender. As such it is intersectional in nature.

In both Kaupapa Māori and Mana Wahine theories we seek transformation of inequalities through a process of mediating the power relationships within culturally defined paradigms. Mana Wahine theory provides a critical expansion on Kaupapa Māori theory in that it is defined and controlled by Māori women for the benefit of our whānau, hapū, iwi, and Māori organisations. Mana Wahine theory is one example of how we can draw upon the incredible strength and tenacity of our tūpuna wahine as examples of what the world can be for Māori women present and future, and to reclaim and take back what the world was for our tūpuna wahine. As with the words of Tawhiao that open this chapter, 'Māku anō e hanga tōku nei whare', it is critical that Maori engage in the creation and construction of our own whare culturally, philosophically, spiritually, politically and materially within which we both reclaim and reconstruct theoretical frameworks that serve the broader aspirations of our people both in the assertion of our knowledge and ways of being and also in the critical analysis of the colonial systems and structures that continue to impact upon our lives. That is the focus of building this theoretical house, that we call Mana Wahine.

References

Black, T. (2016). 'Call to establish a female equivalent to Te Mata Punenga', *Te Ao News*, Māori Television. Available: https://www.teaomaori.news/call-establish-female-equivalent-te-mata-punenga accessed 23 December 2019.

Durie, M. (1998). *Whaiora: Māori Health Development*. Oxford University Press: Auckland.

Gabel, K. (2019). 'Poipoia Te Tamaiti Ki Te Ukaipō: Theorising Māori Motherhood', in L. Pihama, L.T. Smith, N. Simmonds, J. Seed-Pihama, and K. Gabel (eds.) *Mana Wahine Reader: A Collection of Writings 1999–2019 Volume 1*. Te Kotahi Research Institute: Hamilton, OH, 165–77.

Irwin, K. (1992). 'Towards theories of Māori feminism', in R. Du Plessis, P. Bunkle, K. Irwin, A. Laurie, and S. Middleton (eds.) *Feminist Voices: Women's Studies Texts for Aotearoa/New Zealand*. Oxford University Press: Auckland, 1–21.

Mahuika, A.T. (1973). *Ngā Wahine Kai-hautu o Ngāti Porou: Female Leaders of Ngāti Porou*. Unpublished Master's thesis, University of Sydney: Sydney, NSW.

Marsden, M. (2003). *The Woven Universe: Selected Readings of Rev. Māori Marsden*. The Estate of Rev. Māori Marsden: Otaki.

Mead, H.M. (2003). *Tikanga Māori: Living by Māori Values*. Huia Publishers: Wellington.

Mikaere, A. (1995). *The Balance Destroyed: The Consequences for Maori Women of the Colonisation of Tikanga Maori*. Unpublished Master's thesis, University of Waikato: Hamilton, OH.

Murphy, N. (2011). Te Awa Atua, Te Awa Tapu, Te Awa Wahine: An Examination of Stories, Ceremonies and Practices Regarding Menstruation in the Pre-Colonial Māori World. MA thesis, University of Waikato: Hamilton, OH.

Nepe, T. (1991). *E Hao ne e Tenei Reanga: Te Toi Huarewa Tipuna, Kaupapa Māori, An Educational Intervention*. Unpublished Master's thesis, University of Auckland: Auckland.

Orange, C. (1987). *The Treaty of Waitangi*. Allen and Unwin Port Nicholson Press: Wellington.

Pere R. (1982). *Ako: Concepts and Learning in the Māori Tradition*. Department of Sociology, University of Waikato: Hamilton, OH.

Pere, R. (1988). 'Te Wheke: Whaia te Maramatanga me te Aroha', in S. Middleton (ed.) *Women and Education in Aotearoa*. Allen & Unwin, Port Nicholson Press: Wellington, 6–19.

Pere, R. (1991). *Te Wheke: A Celebration of Infinite Wisdom*. Ao Ako Global Learning: Gisborne.

Pihama, L. (1993). Tungia te Ururua, Kia Tupu Whakaritorito Te Tupu o te Harakeke: A Critical Analysis of Parents as First Teachers. Unpublished MA Thesis, University of Auckland: Auckland.

Pihama, L. (2001). *Tihei Mauri Ora, Honouring Our Voices, Mana Wahine As a Kaupapa Māori Theoretical Framework*. Unpublished PhD thesis, University of Auckland: Auckland.

Pihama, L. and Mara, D. (1994). 'Gender relations in education', in E. Coxon, K. Jenkins, J. Marshall, and L. Massey (eds.) *The Politics of Learning and Teaching in Aotearoa - New Zealand*. Dunmore Press: Palmerston North, 215–250.

Pihama, L., Green, A., Mika, C., Roskruge, M., Simmonds, S., Nopera, T., Skipper, H., and Laurence, R. (2020). *Honour Project Aotearoa*. Te Kotahi Research Institute & Te Whaariki Takapou: Hamilton, OH.

Pihama, L., Smith, K., Taki, M., and Lee, J. (2004). *A Literature Review on Kaupapa Māori and Māori Education Pedagogy*. International Research Institute for Māori and Indigenous Education: Auckland.

Pihama, L., Smith, L.T., Simmonds, N., Seed-Pihama, J., and Gabel, K. (2019). *Mana Wahine Reader: A Collection of Writings 1999–2019 Volume 1*. Te Kotahi Research Institute: Hamilton, OH.

Pohatu, T.W. (1996). I Tiipu Ai Taatou I Ngaa Turi O O Tatatau Maatua Tiipuna: Transmission and Acquisition Processes Within Kaawai Whakapapa. Unpublished Master's thesis, University of Auckland: Auckland.

Pohatu, T.W. (2011). 'Mauri – "Rethinking Human Wellbeing"', *MAI Review*, vol 3: 1–12.

Seed-Pihama, J. (2019). 'Kapohia Ngā Taonga ā Kui mā: Liberty from the theft of our matrilineal names', in L. Pihama, L.T. Smith, N., Simmonds, J. Seed-Pihama, and K. Gabel (eds.) *Mana Wahine Reader: A Collection of Writings 1999–2019 Volume 1*. Te Kotahi Research Institute: Hamilton, OH, 178–89.

Simmonds, N.B. (2014). *Tū te Turuturu nō Hine-te-iwaiwa: Mana Wahine Geographies of Birth in Aotearoa New Zealand*. Unpublished PhD dissertation, University of Waikato: Hamilton, OH.

Simpson, M. (1990). *Ngā Tohu o te Tiriti: Making a Mark*. National Library of New Zealand: Wellington.

Smith, C.W. (1994). *Kimihia Te Maramatanga: Colonisation and Iwi Development*. Unpublished Master's thesis, University of Auckland: Auckland.

Smith, G.H. (1997). *The Development of Kaupapa Māori Theory and Praxis*. Unpublished PhD thesis, University of Auckland: Auckland.

Smith, L.T. (1992). 'Māori women: Discourses, projects and Mana Wahine', in S. Middleton and A. Jones (eds.) *Women and Education in Aotearoa 2*. Bridget Williams Books: Wellington, 33–51.

Smith, L.T. (1993). 'Getting out from down under: Maori women, education and the struggles for Mana Wahine', in M. Arnot and K. Weiler (eds.) *Feminism and Social Justice in Education*. Falmer Press: London, 58–78.

Smith, L.T. (1996). *Interview Unedited Video Footage*. Moko Productions: Auckland.

Smith, C. and Taki, M. (1993). 'Hoihoi wahine Pakeha', *Te Pua*, 2:1, 38–42.

Sykes, A. (2000). 'Constitutional reform and Mana Wahine', in L. Pihama (ed.) *Te Pua, Special Issue: Indigenous Women and Representation*. Te Puawaitanga, University of Auckland: Auckland, 63–70.

Szarsy, M. (1995). 'Seek the seeds for the greatest good of all people', in K. Irwin, I. Ramsden, and R. Kahukiwa, (eds.) *Toi Wāhine: The Worlds of Māori Women*. Penguin Books: Auckland, 131–136.

Te Awekotuku, N. (1991). *Mana Wahine Māori: Selected Writings on Māori Women's Art, Culture and Politics*. New Women's Press: Auckland.

Yates-Smith, A. (1998). *Hine! E Hine! Rediscovering the Feminine in Māori Spirituality*. Unpublished PhD thesis, University of Waikato: Hamilton, OH.

13

On the politics of Indigenous translation

Listening to Indigenous peoples in and on their own terms

Dale Turner

Introduction

Spirituality matters to Indigenous peoples.[1] In this chapter, I reflect on the meaning of Indigenous spirituality and show how it matters in the contemporary legal and political relationship between Indigenous peoples and the Canadian state. My reflection begins with the fact that the dominant language of the legal and political relationship is English. Over the past two decades, the concept of 'Indigenous spirituality' has crept into contemporary Indigenous politics in ways that are reshaping the normative language of the legal and political relationship.[2] In this chapter, I show that we can best understand the meaning of Indigenous spirituality as a kind of 'Wittgensteinian language-game' in the relationship. I discuss Ludwig Wittgenstein's views on meaning and language in this chapter and argue that his approach to philosophical inquiry – what it means to 'be' philosophical – is useful for better understanding Indigenous peoples 'in and on their own terms'.[3]

Although the thought of Wittgenstein figures predominantly in my discussion, my motivation for doing so is to suggest that we in Indigenous Studies need to pay closer attention to how we understand language in the context of the legal and political relationship – vis-à-vis the use of the English language. I recast Wittgenstein's pragmatic approach to a philosophical investigation and recast it an 'Indigenous investigation'. I discuss two language-games of Indigenous spirituality where Indigenous languages have made interventions into mainstream Canadian politics: the 1997 Supreme Court case of *Delgamuukw v. British Columbia* and the 2012 Anishinaabek Nation of Ontario's constitution *Chi-Naaknigewin*. These exemplars show that Indigenous spirituality reveals 'forms of difference' between Indigenous and non-Indigenous worldviews and that these forms of difference profoundly affect how we ought to interpret the meaning and content of Aboriginal rights in Canada, and Indigenous nationhood in domestic and international contexts.

My discussion follows in three parts. In the first part, I lay out, albeit briefly, what I mean by taking a 'Wittgensteinian' approach to understanding language in contemporary Indigenous politics.[4] Wittgenstein's overall philosophical vision is complex and difficult, for a number of reasons that go beyond the scope of this chapter; however, his use of concepts such as 'language-games' 'family resemblances', 'forms of life', and 'surveyable representation' constitute a distinctive philosophical approach to meaning and language that can help us better understand Indigenous spirituality in the contemporary legal and political relationship. In the second part, I discuss two examples of Indigenous spirituality that have been initiated by Indigenous peoples in the legal and political relationship. The first example discusses the Gitxsan and Wet'suwet'en[5] practices of the *aadawk* and *kungax* that were proffered – as legal evidence – in a Canadian court of law to justify the ownership of their territories. The second example is the recently ratified constitution of the Anishinabek Nation of Ontario – the *Anishinaabe Chi-Naaknigewin*.[6] This Indigenous constitution includes a preamble – *Ngo Dwe Waangizid Anishinaabe* – that is written in the language of the Anishinaabe people – *Anishinaabemowin*. In the third part of the chapter, I weave the Wittgensteinian and Indigenous approaches to meaning and language and offer some thoughts on how we can best listen to Indigenous peoples 'in and on their own terms'.

Language-games and perspicuous representation: A Wittgensteinian primer

As I mentioned above, it is beyond the scope of this discussion to provide a comprehensive account of Ludwig Wittgenstein's philosophical thought. I will focus on a few of his main concepts that, taken together, constitute an approach to philosophical inquiry that is useful for guiding a discussion of Indigenous spirituality. Indigenous ways of explaining their spirituality in English require us to embrace the right *attitude* about the epistemological value of Indigenous languages.[7] I will say more at the end of the chapter about why a critical attitude matters more, or at least ought to concern us first, before engaging in philosophical debates over epistemological certainty.

Wittgenstein's philosophical thought can be loosely divided into two periods. The first period was his philosophical development between 1911 to the publication of his short book in 1922, titled the *Tractatus Logico-Philosophicus*[8] (Wittgenstein 1922). The best way to think about this perplexing text is to see it as Wittgenstein's solution to the age-old problems of Western European philosophy (epistemology and metaphysics, truth, the foundations of mathematics to name a few). In particular, Wittgenstein was interested in the relationship between logic, language, and the external world. Wittgenstein's main philosophical concern was with what we can and cannot say about the world. He states in the Preface: "The whole sense of the book might be summed up the following words: what can be said at all can be said clearly, and what we cannot talk about we must pass over in silence" (Wittgenstein 1922: 23). The text functions as a kind of geometric proof, beginning with claims about the way the world *is* and proceeds to show how logic, and undertaking a rigorous logical analysis (that he invents), can reveal the way our language structures the world. He concludes that what can be said about the world can be said clearly – everything else is rendered as nonsense.[9]

That was it, then, Wittgenstein settled matters. However, he began to see that privileging logic and the logical analysis of language produced a limited world. The 'meaningfulness' inherent in our everyday language became more important to Wittgenstein than providing an objective account of the way logic connected our language to the world. He discovered that the relationship between logic, language, and the world was much more complex – what was more important than claims of truth or falsity was that we simply use language to do an infinite number of things in the course of our daily lives.

Wittgenstein moved away from a formal analytic approach to language to embrace a more pragmatic approach to language. We make sense of the world because we *use* language in our everyday lives to – essentially – get things done. This practical approach to meaning and language culminated in the posthumously published *Philosophical Investigations* (Wittgenstein [1953] 2009). The first part of the *Investigations*, written in 693 numbered aphorisms, represents twenty years of deep, often isolated, reflection distilled from 20,000 pages of notebooks down to 72 pages of text.

It is worth exploring briefly a few of the central concepts in the *Investigations*, not only to highlight his unusual and parsimonious style of writing, but also to provide a sense of the richness of his approach to understanding the relationship between language and the world. The *Investigations* is written in a series of numbered reflections, or remarks, inter-connected in often seemingly cryptic ways. A helpful way to read the text is to view it as an ongoing conversation with himself – who was, by far, his worst critic. From an Indigenous perspective, a way of understanding Wittgenstein's writing is to see that he is telling us a particular kind of story – he does not want to tell us anything (as in a professorial kind of lecture); rather, he wants us to see for ourselves how language works in our everyday lives. It is in this sense that we can see Wittgenstein as a kind of storyteller.

For Wittgenstein, a word is meaningful because of the role it plays in the infinite number of 'language-games' that make up our everyday language. Language consists of rules and grammar, but unlike in the *Tractatus*, where he focused on a logical analysis of language, he now sees language as amorphous and capable of great flexibility – depending on what we needed to do. Language-games are embedded in our linguistic practices:

> Here the term 'language-game' is meant to bring into prominence the fact that the speaking of language is part of an activity, or of a form of life.
> Review the multiplicity of language-games in the following examples, and in others:
> Giving orders, and obeying them –
> Describing the appearance of an object, or giving its measurements – [...]
> – It is interesting to compare the multiplicity of the tools in language
> and of the ways they are used, the multiplicity of kinds of word and
> sentence, with what logicians have said about the structure of language.
>
> *(Wittgenstein [1953] 2009: 15)*[10]

Words and sentences are still amenable to logical analysis, or can be shown to follow grammatical rules, but when it comes to determining meaning, we need to look and see how we use our language in the particular kinds of games – or contexts – from which they make sense to us. Wittgenstein writes:

> Consider for example the proceedings that we call 'games'. I mean board-games, card-games, ball-games, Olympic games, and so on. What is common to them all? – Don't say: 'There must be something common, or they would not be called "games"' – but look and see whether there is anything common to all [...]
> And the result of this examination is: we see a complicated network of similarities overlapping and criss-crossing: sometimes overall similarities, sometimes similarities of detail.
>
> *([1953] 2009: 36)*

In the next remark he states:

> I can think of no better expression to characterize these similarities than 'family resemblances'; for the various resemblances between members of a family: build, features, colour of eyes, gait, temperament, etc. etc. overlap and criss-cross in the same way. – And I shall say: 'games' form a family.
>
> *([1953] 2009: 36)*

To be an active language user means that you are a member of a community, you share and participate in linguistic practices that, in a sense, 'belong' to the community. Wittgenstein does not use the word 'culture', but alludes to it when he states, "... and to imagine a language means to imagine a form of life" (1953: 19). Wittgenstein returns again and again to the relationship between language and practice and the fact that when we participate in community life we *de facto* obey rules. We follow rules, but we cannot articulate these rules.

From here, philosophically, we can take Wittgenstein's thought in a number of directions. One direction is to unpack Wittgenstein's very difficult discussion of rule following, which, I believe, takes us to the heart of his philosophy. The kinds of rules Wittgenstein refers to are not about following directions in, say, a how-to manual. Instead, he concerns himself with the rules we follow without thinking about them – as he states, the rules we follow blindly.[11] When we learn to use language 'correctly' we often don't have to pause and reflect on what we are doing – we just do it.[12]

However, there is a related direction we can take to understand Wittgenstein's philosophical approach to meaning and language: the distinction between showing and saying. In the *Tractatus*, Wittgenstein concluded that what can be said can be said clearly, and what cannot be said can be shown. In his later thought he embraced a more pragmatic approach to language. When we use a term like Indigenous spirituality we need a way to get at how this term has become embedded in the language-games that it plays a role in. For Wittgenstein, we need what he calls a 'surveyable representation' of the myriad ways we use our language in our everyday lives. In an important remark, he writes:

> A main source of our failure to understand is that we don't have *an overview* of the use of our words. – Our grammar is deficient in surveyability. – A surveyable representation produces precisely that kind of understanding which consists in 'seeing connections'. Hence the importance of finding and inventing *intermediate links*.
>
> The concept of a surveyable representation is of fundamental significance for us. It characterizes the way we represent things, how we look at matters. (Is this a 'Weltanschauung'?)
> *([1953] 2009: 54)*[13]

For Wittgenstein, a surveyable representation involves undertaking a kind of investigation. To understand Indigenous spirituality we look and see how it is used in the various language-games in which it appears. This investigation reveals the multitude of connections between the various ways the language-games are practiced in our community. The best way to see how surveyable representations function in a Wittgensteinian way is by way of providing examples of where the term under investigation is being used. In the next section, we turn to two examples of how the concept of Indigenous spirituality is used in Canadian politics. The first is in a pivotal Supreme Court of Canada case on Aboriginal title, the second is in an Indigenous constitution, drafted and implemented by the Anishinaabek Nation of Ontario.

Indigenous spirituality as surveyable representation

Gitxsan and Wet'suwet'en spirituality in a Canadian court of law

The Supreme Court decision of *Delgamuukw v. British Columbia* (1997) involved two Indigenous communities in British Columbia – the Gitxsan and Witsuwit'en First Nations – that claimed, at first, outright ownership of their territories.[14] The Gitxsan and Wet'suwet'en embraced a two-track legal strategy; that is, they claimed ownership and therefore jurisdiction over their homelands and could prove this in two ways. The first strategy engaged the legal and political languages of the state – they engaged the normative language of the common law.[15] The second strategy embraced a much more innovative approach as they argued that they could also justify the ownership of their homelands using their own Indigenous philosophical traditions.

The Court writes:

> At trial, the appellants' claim was based on their historical use and 'ownership' of one or more of the territories. In addition, the Gitksan Houses have an 'adaawk' which is a collection of *sacred oral tradition* about their ancestors, histories and territories. The Wet'suwet'en each have a 'kungax' which is a *spiritual song or dance or performance* which ties them to their land. Both of these were entered as evidence on behalf of the appellants. The most significant evidence of *spiritual connection* between the Houses and their territory was a feast hall where the Gitksan and Wet'suwet'en peoples tell and retell their stories and identify their territories to remind themselves of the *sacred connection* that they have with their lands. The feast has a ceremonial purpose *but is also* used for making important decisions.
>
> (Delgamuukw 1997: 1011–1012, emphasis added)

The decision was important not least for the Supreme Court's first serious attempt to provide a coherent systematic 'theory' of Aboriginal title in Canadian constitutional law.[16] However, the decision also built upon the Supreme Court's previous year's *R. v. Van der Peet* decision about, among other things, the role that oral traditions can play in constituting legitimate evidence in Canadian courts of law. In *Van der Peet*, the Court ruled that Indigenous perspectives must be given serious consideration in Canadian courts of law. The Court stated that " ... it must also be recognized, however, that that perspective must be framed in terms *cognisable* to the Canadian legal and constitutional structure" (R. *Van Der Peet* para. 49): if Aboriginal peoples wanted their voices to matter in Canadian courts of law, then they must articulate their perspectives in the language of the common law. In *Delgamuukw*, the Court recast this imperative:

> In other words, although the doctrine of aboriginal rights is a common law doctrine, aboriginal rights are truly *sui generis*, and demand a unique approach to the treatment of evidence which accords due weight to the perspective of aboriginal peoples. However, that accommodation must be done in a manner which does not strain 'the Canadian legal and constitutional structure' (at para. 49). Both the principles laid down in *Van der Peet* – first, that trial courts must approach the rules of evidence in light of the evidentiary difficulties inherent in adjudicating aboriginal claims, and second, that trial courts must interpret that evidence in the same spirit – must be understood against this background.
>
> (Delgamuukw 1997: para. 82)

This demand to use *only* the normative language of the common law embodies one of the most destructive forms of colonialism in the relationship between Indigenous peoples and the Canadian state. The *adaawk* and *kungax* were proffered by the Gitksan and Wet'suwet'en as *Indigenous* sources of evidence. Indigenous languages were used to articulate and justify ownership of their territories – this is what I mean by speaking 'in and on their own terms'. The Court purports to recognise the source of their cultural authenticity, while failing to recognise concomitantly its legitimacy as a philosophical system of thought *on its own terms*.

The amount of Indigenous evidence given at trial was astounding:

> A total of 61 witnesses gave evidence at trial, many using translators from their native Gitksan or Wet'suwet'en language; 'word spellers' to assist the official reporters were

> required for many witnesses; a further 15 witnesses gave their evidence on commission; 53 territorial affidavits were filed; 30 deponents were cross-examined out of court; there are 23,503 pages of transcript evidence at trial; 5898 pages of transcript of argument; 3,039 pages of commission evidence and 2,553 pages of cross-examination on affidavits
>
> *(Delgamuukw 1997: para. 89)*

Unfortunately, the Supreme Court did not provide a substantive discussion of the meaning of the *adaawk* and *kungax* "in light of the evidentiary difficulties inherent in adjudicating aboriginal claims" (*Delgamuukw 1997*: para. 82). This is one of the profound failures of the decision as it was a genuine opportunity for the Supreme Court to address head on how the common law could accommodate Indigenous peoples speaking in and on their own terms.[17]

Thousands of pages of testimony, hundreds of hours of listening to Gitxsan and Witsuwit'en medicine people, ultimately fell on deaf ears. Antonia Mills edited the testimony of hereditary Chief Johnny David into a 486-page book titled *'Hang Onto These Words': Johnny David's Delgamuukw Evidence* (Mills 2005). Mills, an anthropologist by training, was involved as an expert witness for the Witsuwit'en. Mills recognised that David's testimony makes a critical contribution to the public's understanding of Indigenous ways of thinking about the world. She states, "It presents the monumental, age-old, and ongoing difficulty in resolving conflicts between indigenous people and those colonizing forces that assume they alone have rights and law and deserve respect. Johnny David gave his voluminous testimony to counter those assumptions" (Mills 2005: 28).

It is important to note that Johnny David – Maxlaxlex (Mikhlikhlekh) – was the first Witsuwit'en hereditary chief (of nine) to give evidence to the court. Because of his age (91 years old) the court convened in his home in Moricetown. David gave his testimony in Witsuwit'en over a period of eight months, which produced eight volumes of direct testimony, two volumes of cross-examination, and the entire testimony was recorded on videotapes by a professional photographer. Mills writes, "Unlike court transcripts, which are only in English, that record, consisting of twenty-six two-hour videotapes, contains the questions as they were translated into Witsuwit'en by the interpreter Misalos/Victor Jim, and the answers Johnny David gave in Witsuwit'en" (Mills 2005: 4). David's testimony fulfills two important roles: the first role is as an authoritative source of Indigenous philosophical knowledge, and the second role is as an oral historian. The two roles are intertwined. David was taught from an early age how to listen properly to sacred stories and oral histories where eventually he 'became authorised' to talk about them in the community and in public. The court's cross-examination process pressed the fact that David did not experience directly many of the events related in the oral histories and therefore his accounts constituted hearsay.[18]

How can we look at the *adaawk* and *kungax* as a surveyable representation? What makes a Wittgensteinian surveyable representation *Indigenous*? The language-game of Indigenous spirituality is embedded in the Gitxsan and Wet'suwet'en practices of the *adaawk* and *kungax*, which is part of a larger system of Indigenous philosophical thought – Indigenous law. Understanding Indigenous law in and on its own terms begins by listening to Johnnny David's original testimony where he laid out the numerous, complex relationships between clans, houses, and the myriad ceremonies, customs and traditions that constitute their law. Mills has devoted her career to understanding Wet'suwet'en law, and we are fortunate to have David's testimony videotaped, which is an invaluable source of Wet'suwet'en knowledge, especially since it is directed at asserting and defending their rights to their homelands.

In addition, there were the English translations of David's testimony that were entered into the court record as official evidence. And of course the number of court decisions themselves –

with its affirming and dissenting opinions – becomes part of the surveyable representation, along with the myriad number of competing legal and scholarly interpretations of the courts' reasoning. We begin to see how our language takes on a complexity as different perspectives entail different uses of language. These relationships – 'connections' – are what we need to *see*. What does it mean to *see* these connections? Part of the answer lies in trying to understand other perspectives in and on their own terms. Finding connections also means to unpack assumptions, beliefs, and styles of reasoning that reveals the normative language of law and politics.

For example, there are two assumptions in Canadian law that maintain a philosophical hold on Indigenous politics in Canada. The first is the constitution's deep commitment to moral individualism: the primary placeholder of rights is the individual. Aboriginal rights, a form of group right, can be tolerated – even justified in theory – however, they must remain, in a sense, tethered to the moral and political primacy of the individual. The second assumption is that the Canadian nation state is assumed to embody the superior form of political sovereignty in Canadian society. What follows from this deep-seated belief is that the Supreme Court of Canada works uncritically with this assumption. Indigenous claims of nationhood, then, become measured against the assumed superiority of nation state sovereignty. To weave these two assumptions together, the Supreme Court has dictated that Aboriginal rights be characterised as a form of reconciliation between the laws, customs, and traditions of Indigenous peoples with the unilateral assertion of state sovereignty.[19] Indigenous laws, customs, and traditions are valued constitutionally because they are practiced by individuals who happen to belong to Indigenous cultures. It is membership in their distinctive Indigenous cultures that matters when determining the meaning of Aboriginal rights, not the fact that their rights flow out of their status as nations. To make matters worse for Indigenous peoples, this cultural context can only be of use in a constitutional context when 'reconciled' with the unquestioned fact of state sovereignty – and don't forget, explanations must be articulated in terms 'cognisable' to the Court.

An 'Indigenous' investigation clears up what amounts to a 'misuse' of language.[20] It is our task to clear up these misuses of language, to 'loosen' the unilateral assumptions of moral individualism and the supremacy of nation state sovereignty that have a stranglehold on the way the dominant culture understands Indigenous ways of thinking about the world.[21] The brutal irony is that we need to participate in an ongoing dialogue – engage a politics – using a language cognisable to the dominant culture while speaking from a place of radical difference. In the *Delgamuukw* case, the Gitxsan and Wet'suwet'en had to explain and defend their spiritual practices in the language-games of the common law. This form of philosophical colonialism has frustrated Indigenous peoples since the early treaty relationship gave way to a relationship of domination, where the legal language Indigenous peoples now use to buttress their political positions is the language of the common law. In the next section, I turn to the Anishinabek Nation's constitution – the *Anishinaabe Chi-Naaknigewin* – a document that embodies a refusal to use only English in the contemporary legal and political relationship.

The Anishinaabe Chi-Naaknigewin of the Anishinabek Nation of Ontario

The Anishinaabek Nation is a confederation of 40 First Nations in Ontario that is represented politically by the Union of Ontario Indians (UOI) located on Nipissing First Nation territory.[22] The Anishinabek Nation finds its roots in the Confederacy of Three Fires, made up of the Ojibway (Chippewas), Odawa and Pottawatomi Nations, which long pre-dates the arrival of Europeans. The traditional form of government of the Anishinabek Nation – the Grand Council – has been actively asserting their 'inherent' right of self-government in their ongoing centuries-long negotiations with the British and Canadian governments.

The political relationship is driven by the mutually recognised fiat that the Anishinabek Nation possesses the inherent right to govern themselves in accordance with their own laws, customs, and traditions. The *Anishinaabe Chi-Naaknigewin* is an assertion of that right – articulated *in and on the terms of the Anishinaabe people*. The explanation of the *Ch-Naaknigewin* is succinctly summarised on the Anishinabek Nation webpage:

> The Anishinaabe Chi-Naaknigewin is founded on Ngo Dwe Waangizid Anishinaabe and forms the Traditional Government of the Anishinabek Nation, within the Inherent, Traditional, Treaty, and Unceded Lands of Our Territories [...]
>
> The Anishinabek Nation has the inherent right bestowed by the Creator to enact any laws necessary in order to protect and preserve Anishinaabe culture, languages, customs, traditions and practices for the betterment of the Anishinabek.
>
> *(Union of Ontario Indians n.d.: Online)*

The constitution consists of a preamble and 11 articles that "forms the Traditional Government of the Anishinabek Nation, within the Inherent, Traditional, Treaty, and Unceded Lands of Our Territories" (*Anishinaabe Chi-Naaknigewin*, Preamble). The written document is a political assertion of the Anishinabek Nation's inherent right to be an Indigenous nation. The preamble – *Ngo Dwe Waangizid Anishinaabe* – is unapologetically articulated in *Anishinaabemowin* and is not translated into English.[23] The decision to keep the preamble untranslated has deep political and 'spiritual' significance for the Anishinaabe. The *Chi-Naaknigewin* 'embodies' the spiritual relationship the Anishinaabe have with all living things – including the Canadian people and their governments.

The philosophical significance of the preamble is to make the point that to *fully* understand Anishinaabe philosophical thought, one must begin by listening to it in its original language – *Anishinaabemowin*. The political point of insisting on using *Anishinaabemowin* is profound: the *authenticity* of Anishinabek nationhood is rooted in Anishinaabe ways of thinking about the world, articulated in their political traditions. For the Anishinaabe, this is the Indigenous source of the inherent right of self-government and it pre-dates, by thousands of years, the forms of political recognition invented after the arrival of Europeans.

How can we understand *Anishinaabe Chi-Naaknigewin* as a surveyable representation? The fact that the constitution begins in *Anishinaabemowin* has spiritual, philosophical and political significance. In Indigenous diplomatic protocols it is common for Indigenous people to begin by speaking their own language. In 2015, I was part of a research group that visited the Waikato Tainui, a Māori nation in Aotearoa. We were officially welcomed into their community in the marae – a community courtyard or meeting place – after following their diplomatic protocols: songs and introductory words were spoken (often forcefully) in Māori that made it very clear that we were on their land. We, as visitors, did not understand their language but we respected the significance of their diplomatic practices. Once these protocols were followed, which included our Anishinaabe medicine people speaking in response (in *Anishnaabemowin*), gifts exchanged, and the traditional hongi greetings were completed we were warmly welcomed into their community. Interestingly, I asked an Anishinaabe medicine person about these Māori protocols and he said that the Anishinaabe had similar practices. These protocols were not merely political activities, they had spiritual significance for the community, and the Anishinaabe medicine people felt comfortable in this foreign place and embraced the spiritual bond created by the relationship between place, people, ceremony and language. Indigenous spirituality functioned as a form of 'family resemblance' between the Indigenous peoples – despite their homelands being thousands of miles apart. Indigenous peoples would say that Indigenous diplomacy is political and spiritual (because they cannot be separated) – perhaps a way to understand this point in a Western European sense would be to say that Indigenous diplomacy is both political and metaphysical.

Listening to Indigenous peoples in and on their own terms

In his 'Remarks on Frazer's *Golden Bough*', Wittgenstein criticizes James George Frazer's massive comparative study on religion and mythology titled *The Golden Bough: A Study in Magic and Religion* (Wittgenstein 1993). Frazer attempted to explain the so-called primitive practices of Indigenous people as mistaken – wrong – by showing that because their worldviews were infused in beliefs in 'magic' they failed to understand or even appreciate that science is the only legitimate guarantor of knowledge. Essentially this is similar to the hardline position Wittgenstein defended in the *Tractatus*. By the time Wittgenstein wrote the *Remarks* in 1931 he criticized this Eurocentric position harshly. He wrote, "Frazer's account of the magical and religious views of mankind is unsatisfactory: it makes these views look like *errors*" (Wittgenstein 1993: 119). Wittgenstein adds that in attempting to explain an Indigenous practice, "All Frazer does is to make them plausible to people who thinks as he does" (Wittgenstein 1993: 119).

This is not an indictment against seeing the world in only one way. Wittgenstein's point is that where we go wrong is when we impose a theory – ours – that purports to explain another culture's way of surveying the world. Religious beliefs are not amenable to a scientific type of inquiry, which is what Frazer does to Indigenous beliefs and practices. Wittgenstein states:

> It is very remarkable that in the final analysis all these [Indigenous] practices are presented as, so to speak, pieces of stupidity. ... But it will never be plausible to say that mankind does all that out of sheer stupidity. ... When, for example, he explains to us that the king must be killed in his prime, because the savages believe that otherwise his soul would not be kept fresh, all one can say is: where that practice and these views occur together, the practice does not spring from the view, but they are both just there.
>
> *(Wittgenstein 1993: 119)*

Wittgenstein's message is that we need to know when to leave another culture's belief systems 'alone'.[24] For many, this claim makes Wittgenstein a relativist. I disagree. Meaningfulness arises from within communities of people – language users. What language users share is not simply that they speak the same language. Wittgenstein writes:

> 'So you are saying that human agreement decides what is true and what is false?' – It is what human beings say that is true and false; and they agree in the language they use. That is not agreement in opinions but in form of life
>
> *(Wittgenstein [1953] 2009: 94).*

One way of understanding a form of life is to see it – roughly speaking – as the cultural practices that a community embodies in their everydayness, most often in ways that they don't need to consciously think about. In other words, they de facto follow rules, but do so blindly (Wittgenstein [1953] 2009: 92). How do we learn to follow these rules? – By being brought into the community of language users. For example, Indigenous children and other community members learn about their spirituality from the appropriate medicine people and these practices become central to the everyday life of the community. The problem with someone like Frazer is that he views Indigenous religious beliefs as steeped in magic and therefore primitive and, well, simply wrong, while the scientific beliefs of Western European cultures provide access to genuine knowledge. For the later Wittgenstein, whether one's beliefs are rooted in Indigenous spirituality or Western European metaphysics the judgement is the same: cultures make sense of the world in different ways and when it comes to understanding the true nature of reality no one culture has a purchase on 'the' truth.

In returning to our exemplars, what makes the *adaawk, kungax*, and the *Ngo Dwe Waangizid Anishinaabe* 'spiritual'? – The answer depends on the language-games we choose to unpack their meaning. We can choose to listen to Indigenous medicine people speaking on their own terms, which means that we begin our investigation by recognising the philosophical value of their languages. The *adaawk* and *kungax* are Gitxsan and Wet'suwet'en cultural practices; it is in their performance at a particular time and place – over very long periods of time – that they gain normative significance in the community – these practices legitimate Indigenous law.[25] As examples of Indigenous spiritual practices they are 'serious' ways of making sense of the world; in other words, their cultural practices are not grounded in magic, rather spirituality functions more like a *grammar* in Indigenous cultures. Wittgenstein notes that magic and metaphysics share certain family resemblances:

> I think now that the right thing would be to begin my book with remarks about metaphysics as a kind of magic. But in doing this I must neither speak in defence of magic nor ridicule it. What it is that is deep about magic would be kept ... for when I began my earlier book to talk about the 'world' (and not about this tree or this table), was I trying to do anything except conjure up something of a higher order by my words?

> *(Wittgenstein 1993: 116)*

How do we capture this 'seriousness' and make it central to our investigation into the meaning of Indigenous spirituality? – Well, we 'begin' to understand Indigenous worldviews by first turning to Indigenous medicine people (this is what it means to begin by listening to Indigenous peoples in and on their own terms!). This 'linguistic turn' to Indigenous voices is what the Canadian courts have failed to do – to take seriously. As it is, Indigenous oral histories do not stand on their own in a court of law, they need to be reconfigured into English, placing the onus on Indigenous people to find the appropriate language to convince the courts that Indigenous oral histories have 'epistemological' import. Indigenous peoples must generate explanations of their deeply held beliefs and spiritual practices in a language that makes sense to the people who are violating their rights and dignity to begin with.

In a Wittgensteinian approach, we do not begin by interpreting or adjudicating knowledge claims, we begin by recognising Indigenous ways of thinking about the world as authentic sources of human knowledge. When we articulate the meaning of the *adaawk* and *kungax* in English, we initiate a particular kind of dialogue; that is, we try to find the right language to make sense of the meaning of the terms that are being used in the dialogue. An important part of our investigation is to try to understand the terms as used by the Gitxsan and Wet'suwet'en themselves.[26] The difference between the approach adopted by the Supreme Court and a Wittgensteinian one is that we begin by listening and respecting Indigenous peoples in and on their own terms. We not only adopt a richer kind of dialogical relationship, we embrace a different politics.

For example, the preamble of the *Anishinaabe Chi-Naaknigewin* is meant to be spoken – performed – as a kind of Anishinaabe offering.[27] The preamble was written by the clan mothers after insisting that the constitution needed to be first and foremost rooted in distinctly Anishinaabe understandings of their law. The seven grandfather teachings are central to Anishinaabe moral and spiritual teachings, and are listed in English in Article 4 of *Chi-Naaknigewin*: love, truth, respect, wisdom, humility, honesty, and bravery. They are also cited in the preamble; however, they are situated within an Anishinaabe worldview. The preamble drives home the point that the Anishinaabe come to the legal and political relationship with their own ways of understanding who they are as a people – a nation – with their own philosophical approaches to meaning and language.[28]

As I mentioned in the introduction, this is not a paper solely about Wittgenstein; however, I believe that a Wittgensteinian approach to language reminds us to adopt a more open attitude about the sources of meaning in the ongoing dialogue between Indigenous peoples and the Canadian state. Wittgenstein's views of language may not be of much use at all for Indigenous medicine people. When medicine people are forced into Canadian courts of law having to explain the ownership of their homelands to judges educated in the common law, we need to be much more strategic about the way we want to discuss and invoke Indigenous spirituality as a normative concept in Canadian legal and political practices. However, finding the right language in the common law should not burden Indigenous peoples alone. This is where Wittgenstein's philosophical approach may help nurture a political climate that encourages a more respectful philosophical dialogue than the adversarial approach that now characterizes contemporary Indigenous law and politics.

Notes

1 In the following discussion, I will use a pragmatic understanding of Indigenous spirituality as Indigenous peoples' relationships to land as understood and articulated by Indigenous people themselves. One useful working definition of Indigenous spirituality comes from Warraimay and Tasmanian scholar Victoria Grieves:

> Indigenous spirituality derives from a philosophy that establishes the wholistic notion of the interconnectedness of the elements of the earth and the universe, animate and inanimate, whereby people, the plants and animals, landforms and celestial bodies are interrelated. How this interconnectedness exists and why it is important to keep all things in healthy interdependence is expressed and encoded in sacred stories or 'myths'. (Grieves 2008: 364)

2 For example, Article 12 of the United Nations Declaration on the Rights of Indigenous Peoples (2007) states that "Indigenous peoples have the right to manifest, practise, develop and teach their spiritual and religious traditions, customs and ceremonies ..." (UN General Assembly 2007).

3 Wittgenstein writes, "Philosophy is a battle against the bewitchment of our intelligence by means of language" (1953: 109).

4 For an excellent intellectual biography on the life and philosophical development of Wittgenstein, see Monk (1990). For a beautifully written personal reflection on Wittgenstein's influence on his personal relationships, see Malcolm (1958). For an excellent short introduction to Wittgenstein's philosophy, see Fann (2015).

5 There are a number of different spellings for these Indigenous nations, I will use 'Gitxsan' and 'Wet'suwet'en' as they are the terms now in use by the communities themselves.

6 See https://www.anishinabek.ca/governance/anishinaabe-chi-naaknigewin/.

7 A few words here about the use the term 'epistemological'. Epistemology is the area of philosophy where we ask, 'What can we know?' I am not using it in this sense. Rather, I use the term 'epistemologically valuable' to mean, colloquially, that Indigenous languages are valued as legitimate sources of knowledge – Indigenous languages generate knowledge of the world.

8 The second period of his philosophical life – referred to as 'the later Wittgenstein' – began when he returned to Cambridge University in 1929 to his death in 1951.

9 I don't want to get bogged down in the debates over interpreting the *Tractatus*, except to say that the book has enjoyed a recent resurgence in popularity, especially among Wittgenstein scholars. Dennett writes: "You know from the moment you open the *Tractatus* that it is something special. Each left-hand

page is in German, facing its English translation on the right, and the sentences are numbered, using a hierarchical system that tells you this is a formal proof. The book begins straightforwardly enough: '1. The world is everything that is the case.' (In German, it makes a memorable rhyming couplet: Die Welt ist alles, was der Fall ist.) And it ends with an ending to end all endings: '7. Whereof one cannot speak, thereof one must be silent.'" (Dennett 1999: 147)

10 A word about quoting Wittgenstein. It is difficult to summarize or paraphrase his already often pithy remarks. Many of his remarks convey his thought perfectly, and are worth quoting in full.

11 "... When I obey a rule, I do not choose.
     I obey a rule blindly" (Wittgenstein 1953: 219).

12 The problem of rule following is key to understanding Wittgenstein's philosophy. Much has been written on what is referred to as 'the rule-following paradox', introduced after Wittgenstein claims that obeying a rule is a custom or practice. He states, "This was our paradox: no course of action could be determined by a rule, because every course of action can be made out to accord with the rule. The answer was: if everything can be made out to accord with the rule, then it can be made out to conflict with it" (1953: 201). Basically, for Wittgenstein, the paradox arises when we think of rule following as something we can explain, but often we 'know' what to do without being able to explain why. We cannot attach explanations for why we follow rules in the 'right' way. For a robust critique of the rule following paradox see Kripke (1982).

13 In his 'Remarks on Fraser's *Golden Bough*', he writes: "The concept of perspicuous representation is of fundamental importance for us. It denotes the form of our representation, the way we see things. (A kind of 'World-view' as it is apparently typical of our time. Spengler.) The perspicuous representation brings about the understanding which consists precisely in the fact that we 'see the connections'. Hence the importance of finding *connecting links*" (Wittgenstein 1993: 133). This raises an interesting point about Wittgenstein's texts. There are four English editions of the *Philosophical Investigations*, which was originally published in German. The first three editions translate ... as 'perspicuous representation', the most recent translation, which is the text I use in this chapter, benefits from over fifty years of intense Wittgenstein scholarship to use the phrase 'surveyable representation'.

14 The case unfolded in three stages. The first decision *Delgamuukw v. British Columbia* was decided in British Columbia Superior Court on March 8, 1991. Chief Justice McEachern concluded that the Gitxsan and Witsuwit'en failed to demonstrate that they owned their homelands. More importantly, McEachern (now) infamously asserted that Indigenous philosophical systems of thought did not measure up to Western European philosophical traditions and therefore were not entitled to use them to justify ownership of their territories. The Chiefs immediately appealed to the BC Court of Appeal, which was decided on 25 June 1993, overturned much of McEachern's Eurocentric reasoning, the court was still divided on the nature and scope of Aboriginal title. The Gitxsan and Witsuwit'en appealed to the Supreme Court of Canada in 1996, and a year later on December 11, 1997 the Court reversed much of McEachern's judgment. See Introduction in Mills (2005).

15 For example, they offered particular interpretations of the Royal Proclamation of 1763 (Royal Proclamation Accessed 25 March 2020), section 88 of the Indian Act (Indian Act, Accessed 3 March 2020), and s. 35(1) of the Canadian Constitution (Constitution Act, S. 35(1)).

16 (*Delgamuukw* 1997), see sections 109–169 under the heading titled "C. What is the content of aboriginal title, how is it protected by s.35(1) of the Constitution Act, 1982, and what is required for its proof?"

17 The Gitxsan and Wet'suwet'en changed their claim from the Appeals decision to the Supreme Court. They changed their claim from recognition of ownership of their homelands to recognition of Aboriginal title – a right to the lands itself. The Court ruled that they did not explicitly provide evidence for recognition of title and therefore ordered a retrial.

18 Mills cites example after example of how the court undermined David's authority as an oral historian. For example, this exchange between Crown lawyer and David was typical:
     Mr. Milne: All I want to know is on some of those places you said that white people burned down the houses or the smokehouses. Did you see that happen, or is it from what people have told you?
     Mr. David: People told me about it.
     Mr. Milne: Those are all my questions, Mr. David. Thank you very much. (Mills 2005: 34)

19 Aboriginal rights are protected in Part Two of the Canadian Constitution. Section 35(1) reads:

     The aboriginal and treaty rights of the aboriginal peoples of Canada are hereby recognized and affirmed" (*Constitution Act, 1982*). If ever a perspicuous representation was needed in Canadian society it is to gain an overarching view of the complex meaning of section 35(1). As for characterizing s.35(1) as a form of reconciliation, the Supreme Court states in *Van der Peet*, "More specifically, what s. 35(1) does is provide the constitutional framework through which the fact that aboriginals lived on the land in distinctive societies, with their own practices, traditions and cultures, is acknowledged and reconciled with the sovereignty of the Crown. The substantive rights which fall within the provision must be defined in light of this purpose; the aboriginal rights recognized and affirmed by must be directed towards the reconciliation of the pre-existence of aboriginal societies with the sovereignty of the Crown. (*Van der Pee 1996t*, para. 31)

20 Wittgenstein states, "For philosophical problems arise when language *goes on holiday*" ([1953] 2009: 23).
21 Nothing captures this attitude better than the now infamous quote from Justice McEachern in the first Delgamuukw decision:

It would not be accurate to assume that even pre-contact existence in the territory was in the least bit idyllic. The plaintiff's ancestors had no written language, no horses or wheeled vehicles, slavery and starvation was not uncommon, wars with neighbouring peoples were common and there is no doubt, to quote Hobbes, that aboriginal life in the territory was, at best, 'nasty, brutish, and short'. (Mills 2005: 10)

22 See their website at https://www.anishinabek.ca.
23 *Ngo Dwe Waangizid Anishinaabe* means 'One Anishinaabe Family'.
24 Wittgenstein states, "If I have exhausted the justifications, I have reached bedrock and my spade is turned. Then I am inclined to say, 'This is simply what I do.'" ([1953] 2009: 91).
25 This is also a response to the charge of cultural relativism. It's not just any cultural practices that arise in a community – it is *these* particular practices.
26 "Philosophy may in no way interfere with the actual use of language; it can in the end only describe it. For it cannot give it any foundation either. It leaves everything as it is ..." ([1953] 2009: 55).
27 For an oral account of the preamble by an Anishinaabe medicine person, see https://soundcloud.com/anishinabek-nation/ngo-dwe-waangizid-anishinaabe
28 It is worth mentioning, although beyond the scope of this discussion to develop more fully, that the early treaty relationship is often cited as a 'Wittgensteinian' kind of political relationship. For exemplars of this approach in political theory, see Tully (2002) and Tully (2008). The legal and political vision of the Royal Commission on Aboriginal Peoples was also committed to a Wittgensteinian understanding of the nation-to-nation relationship (RCAP 1996). Also, the political philosophy of the Haudenosaunee's Great Law of Peace shares family resemblances to Wittgenstein's concept of a language-game. Indeed, the *Guswentha* or Two Row Wampum Belt is an exemplar of political philosophy that requires participants to 'speak in and on their own terms'. See Wallace (1994), Alfred (2008), and Williams (2018).

References

Alfred, T. (2008). *Peace, Power, Righteousness: An Indigenous Manifesto*. Oxford University Press Canada: Toronto, ON.

Constitution Act, 1982, being Schedule B to the *Canada Act* 1982 (UK), c 11.

Delgamuukw v. British Columbia [1997] 3 SCI Review 1010.

Dennett, D.C. (1999). 'Ludwig Wittgenstein', *Time Magazine: The Century's Greatest Minds*, March 29. Simon & Schuster: New York, 88–90.

Fann, K.T. (2015). *Wittgenstein's Conception of Philosophy*. Partridge Singapore Publishing: Singapore.

Grieves, V. (2008). 'Aboriginal spirituality: A baseline for Indigenous knowledges development in Australia', *Canadian Journal of Native Studies*, vol XXVIII, no 2: 363–398.

Indian Act, Canada. (1985). *Indian Act (R.S.C., 1985, c. I-5)*. Available: https://laws-lois.justice.gc.ca/eng/acts/I-5/, accessed 3 March 2020.

Kripke, S. (1982). *Wittgenstein on Rules and Private Language: An Elementary Exposition*. Harvard University Press: Cambridge, MA.

Malcolm, N. (1958). *Ludwig Wittgenstein: A Memoir*. Oxford University Press: New York.

Mills, A. (2005). *'Hang onto These Words': Johnny David's Delgamuukw Evidence*. University of Toronto Press: Toronto, ON.

Monk, R. (1990). *Ludwig Wittgenstein: The Duty of Genius*. Free Press: New York.

R. v. Van Der Peet [1996] 2 SCI Review 507.

Royal Commission on Aboriginal Peoples, Erasmus, G., and Dussault, R. (1996). *Report of the Royal Commission on Aboriginal Peoples*. The Commission: Ottawa, ON.

Royal Proclamation of 1763. Available: https://indigenousfoundations.arts.ubc.ca/royal_proclamation_1763/, accessed 25 March 2020.

Tully, J. (2002). 'Political philosophy as a critical activity', *Political Theory*, vol 30, no 4: 533–555.

Tully, J. (2008). *Public Philosophy in a New Key, Volumes 1 and 2*. Cambridge University Press: New York.

Turner, D. (2006). *This Is Not a Peace Pipe: Towards a Critical Indigenous Philosophy*. University of Toronto Press: Toronto, ON.

UN General Assembly. (2007). *United Nations Declaration on the Rights of Indigenous Peoples: Resolution / Adopted by the General Assembly*, 2 October, A/RES/61/295. Available: https://www.refworld.org/docid/471355a82.html, accessed 3 March 2020.

Union of Ontario Indians. (n.d.). 'Anishinaabe nation governance'. Available: https://www.anishinabek.ca/governance/anishinaabe-chi-naaknigewin/, accessed 3 March 2020.

Wallace, P. (1994). *The Iroquois Book of Life: The White Roots of Peace*. Clear Light Publishing: Santa Fe, NM.

Williams (Kayanesenh), P. (2018). *Kayanerenkó:wa: The Great Law of Peace*. University of Manitoba Press: Winnipeg, MB.

Wittgenstein, L. (1922). *Tractatus Logico-Philosophicus*. Routledge & Kegan Paul: London.

Wittgenstein, L. (1953) 2009. *Philosophical Investigations*. Translated by G.E.M. Anscombe, P.M.S. Hacker, and Joachim Schulte, Revised 4th edition by P.M.S Hacker and Joachim Schulte. Blackwell Publishing Ltd: London.

Wittgenstein, L. (1993). 'Remarks on Frazer's *Golden Bough*', reprinted in L. Wittgenstein, J.C. Klagge, and A. Nordmann (eds.) *Philosophical Occasions, 1912–1951*. Hackett Publishing Group Co: Indianapolis, IN, 118–55.

14

Auntie's bundle

Conversation and research methodologies with Knowledge Gifter Sherry Copenace

Sherry Copenace, Jaime Cidro, Anna Johnson, and Kim Anderson

> I became more interested in academic or Western research because I know what we have as Indigenous people can help other people too. It wasn't to keep it to ourselves, but so people can see the strength of us. Sherry Copenace.
>
> *(personal communication: December 2018)*

This chapter highlights a conversation about Indigenous research methodologies and the engagement of spirituality and ceremony within a Manitoba, Canada, birth worker project. The conversation includes Knowledge Gifter and Anishinaabe Grandmother, Sherry Copenace, Jaime Cidro, lead researcher on the birth worker project, and Kim Anderson, a women's health researcher and long-time Auntie and friend to Jaime. As university-based Indigenous women focusing on health research, Jaime and Kim have been investigating how Indigenous research methodologies can be incorporated in community-based research in ways that are ethically sound, that recognise the importance of relationships, and that prioritise Indigenous ways of knowing (Anderson and Cidro 2020). This conversation demonstrates how cultural knowledge must be integrated into Indigenous research methodologies as well as the critical component Elders play when using Indigenous methodologies to examine any research topic (Kovach 2009; Johnston et al. 2018). Additionally, it demonstrates how conversation itself can be used as a research method in community-based participatory research (CBPR) (Kovach 2009). Following the conversation, we provide an analysis to reflect on the elements of Indigenous research methodologies that are discussed and exemplified throughout. Our intention in sharing the conversation is to illustrate the role of ceremony, relationships, and cultural knowledge in Indigenous research methodologies.

We will begin here by offering some context about the birth worker research project that is the context of our methodological conversation. The birth worker research took place in Manitoba, Canada, where Indigenous women who are living in remote and rural communities are required to leave their communities towards the end of their pregnancy and relocate to an urban centre so they can deliver in hospital. This is known as the 'out for confinement' or 'maternal evacuation' policy. In an effort to create culturally safe supports for the families, a group of women in Winnipeg, Manitoba developed an Indigenous based doula or birth worker program. The research team led by Jaime Cidro and the First Nation's Health and Social

Secretariat of Manitoba (FNHSSM) partnered with the Manitoba Indigenous Doulas Initiative (MIDI) out of the Wiijii' idiwag Ikwewag (Women helping each other) to develop a project where Indigenous women received care from a two doula team, one in the community and one in the city where the expectant women wait for their babies to be born. Wiijii' idiwag Ikwewag provides a five-day training to equip women in Indigenous communities to support mothers and families as they guide new life from the spiritual realm to the physical realm. The training includes personal healing and reflection, knowledge around pregnancy, birth, and parenting from both the Indigenous and Western knowledge systems. The training is unique in that it teaches the traditional knowledge around birth from within and outside the nation. In each training, the curriculum is reviewed by a community advisory circle and is infused with local Indigenous knowledge that comes from local Knowledge Keepers who provide local teachings on pregnancy, birth and parenting. A mixed-methods approach was used to determine whether the experiences of the women who receive doula care is different from the group of women who do not receive doula care.

Sherry Copenace began working with the birth worker research project in 2017 and had been involved in this work more widely with the FNHSSM through the Grandmother's Council. The birth worker research was guided by a larger group of knowledge holders and Elders, and Sherry stepped forward early on to provide culturally based support and guidance on an ongoing basis. We are grateful that, from the beginning, Sherry worked with the team to bring ceremony into the project. Because of Sherry's critical role in the methodological foundation and direction of the project, Jaime determined it would be valuable to have a conversation with her about what she brings. Jaime called Kim and Sherry together to talk about ways that Indigenous ceremony is integrated into Indigenous community-based research, and how ceremony has provided the foundational instructions for the birth worker research project. This conversation thus provides a lens into the process of using Indigenous research methodologies and Indigenous ways of knowing and doing. Our visit took place in Winnipeg, Manitoba (Canada) in December 2018, and what appears here was shortened from a much longer conversation. Before it got started, Sherry set the space by conducting a water ceremony. This was followed by some introductory conversation as this was the first time Kim and Sherry had met, and then Sherry, Jaime, and Kim began to talk about research methodologies.

The conversation

Kim: It's great to be here and learning about the birth worker project. Miigwetch for the ceremony! I really appreciate it as I typically begin my research projects with ceremony. Can you share about how you bring ceremony to research?

Sherry: Maybe I can talk about the Manitoba birth work initiative.

When they asked me to come and be a part of it, of course I said "Yes, I'll help you in any way that I can". And what the spiritual realm taught me was for them to have a ceremony every spring and fall; to start off in that way. We've always done that, and it's always been upon the Earth, outside somewhere, whether it's cold or warm. We've done that, and it's been around a fire.

I asked them to bring certain things. One of them is tobacco. Have tobacco there, have a fire, have gifts for the people you've invited or [for those who] just show up. Have a giveaway because that's how we give and receive life, and that's how those spirits will know that you're being mindful and doing the work of preparation. Because that's one of the things that we're asked to do, is to always be prepared. The way we see it is *ozhiitaa* (s/he is prepared). I like always to be prepared and to do that work – good heart, good mind. Always be generous in whatever that you do because whatever you give, it will come back to you in more ways than we as human beings can even imagine.

I asked the women to make sure to do those ceremonies for the project in the spring and fall, (although you can do them more than that). It's not like what the calendar tells you, like January, February, March. I told them to be mindful of the trees around them because the trees will tell you when to do that ceremony. The leaves will tell you, when they are starting to bud. When they're about the size of a beaver's ears is when you'll know to do that ceremony. So it's connected to the natural world, natural law. And then in the fall, before all the leaves fall off the trees, that's when you're being told to have that fall ceremony. So, when we do that, it's really asking those spirits to guide you in the work that you need to do. We're giving to them, and they'll give back to us.

When we have the food offerings, I ask them to make sure that it's food original to us. Not that I don't like those other foods – of course, I do. But [for offerings] – those are the foods that were given to us. Whether it's wild meat, fish... and where I come from it's [also] wild rice, corn, and berries. Those are our first foods; those have stories within themselves about how they were gifted to us. So we're honouring and respecting those stories, and those foods will help you do the work that you need to do. When we give something, those spirits fill our spirit, but we also fill them up as well, so they can continue to do the work for us from that spiritual realm.

While we were doing this project, there was [a spirit] grandmother that came forward. She sits somewhere in between that Southern and Western doorway. She's very ancient. I had a dream about her a long, long time ago. I passed tobacco to this old man – he's gone to the spirit world now – and I told him about that dream. He listened to me, and said: "First I'll tell you one thing: I'm not going to tell you what this dream means. That's for you to figure out, for you to use". Of course, as a young woman, I thought, *Well why doesn't he just tell me?* Because we're not patient. But I accepted that, and he said: "Another thing I'm going to tell you. You've shared your dream too quickly. What you need to do is to sit with that dream for a while. What that spirit is asking you, what that grandmother is asking you, is for you and her to develop a relationship first. Then you can start to share what she's coming to tell you".

That was good teaching for me. It's not that I was being secretive about it, but I needed to develop a relationship with that spiritual being.

So fast forward to the last few years [and the project]. I didn't tell them right away because I wanted to make sure. So at one of the ceremonies I told [the team] that this grandmother was stepping forward to offer help; that she would lead them through this work. [It was important] for them to always honour her in the spring and fall ceremony, and more often if they want to. They can call upon her.

When we had our one of our training up in Nelson House, there was a young woman there, and apparently, when I was sharing some of the teachings there was this really old lady standing behind me. [The young woman] was kind of frightened by that. She didn't want to tell. They encouraged her to tell me, and I was happy that she showed herself to one of the women that were there. It was a physical affirmation I guess, or a human level affirmation. Yes. She's there, and she showed herself to somebody who doesn't particularly believe in our way of life I guess [laughter]. Or is new to it. She thought she was just seeing things [laughter]. When they told me, it gave me goosebumps. I thought, wow, that's so powerful. So simple, but powerful.

Those are some of the ways that we have.

Some people think that when we do a ceremony, it has to be something like the one we did this morning, but it can be simpler than that. It could just be saying your spiritual name. It could just be walking on the land. All of those things, each and every day that we do, even when we breathe. It's all of those things; if we are really mindful, and acknowledge whenever we feel [that sense of connection], that's ceremony.

At one time, our people were so connected and in relationship that they didn't need to do the kinds of things we do today. It just was natural. It was just normal. We didn't need to invoke those things – the spirit could just sit here with us and talk, and we wouldn't be afraid of that. We would be open and would honour that. But because of the disruption and interruption in our way of life, we need to do other things now to ask them to be in a relationship with us.

Each and every day they work for us. That's one of the teachings that I received, is that they won't ever say no to their grandchildren, which is us. It's up to us how we're going to hear and feel it. When we ask something, we think they're going to sound like how we sound to one another, but no, they may come and tell us in different ways. Maybe you'll see something. Maybe you'll hear something. Maybe you'll feel something. Maybe you'll taste something. I don't know. There's different ways and it might not be in the way you want them to answer you.

I've been seeing more and more of our people are really having trust in that and really putting a lot of faith into everything that they do. Even in contemporary research, academic research, people are being very open, [asking spirit] to help them, guide them through that work. Sometimes when you're in this Western kind of work you come across and blocks and obstacles. If you ask those spirits to open doorways, and for you to get out of the way, they will help you. Because sometimes it's us that's in the way.

Jaime: I remember in the fall we had a [birth worker project] meeting, and we were doing difficult logistical research planning. But we talked about that ancient granny; we reminded ourselves of that story, and it helped us to settle down and look long term at our goal, which is returning birthing to community. Doulas are part of returning birthing, but it's hard to see that when you have all these normal research challenges. So that old lady is really helpful for us. We all felt her as we were having that conversation and it allowed us just stop and settle; it reminded us of why we're really there, because it's easy to forget when you're getting caught up in all this work.

Kim: One thing I'm curious about is, you do a lot of work with water, and water ceremonies. We know that women and water are connected. Was there a particular connection that happened because the work is with doulas, midwives, birthing, and all those things around water? Has there been some kind of connection made around the kinds of ceremonies for this project or the ones you're doing with babies and women?

Sherry: Well we all know that when babies are given to us, they grow in that water. But I think in today's world, some of us think these things are...like different departments, like how they are in universities [laughter], or even in municipalities. There's a department of water, department of electricity [laughter]. For us, it's not like that. Everything is interconnected. All of it. Nothing is separate. So that's part of this work, is to come to understand that it's holistic. It's all interconnected, and one part of it is that water.

That's a major part because for us as *Anishinaabe-kwe* (Anishinaabe women), that's the work we were given, to look after that water. That doesn't mean we do that by ourselves. Our men are part of that, our children are part of that. The spiritual realm leads that work. But as a woman, we were given that task to lead that work. We do that with other people too, because how are our people going to know about that if we keep it to ourselves?

Water is such a part of that work because our babies grow in water. When we came into this physical realm, what came first? It was that water. It was just like a river; cleaned that path for us, but it also ensured that we would have that memory of who we are.

Then I hear people say water has a memory. Scientists are saying that, but our people already knew that. To me it's connected and everything that we do.

Jaime: It's interesting when you said that you're starting to see academics and projects getting started in ceremony. Would you say that's kind of recent?

Sherry: I'm not sure, to be honest with you. I never really had much trust in research. I was never interested; I just thought I've got to learn about who I am. But I always knew our people researched things. Always – right from the beginning.

One of the things that I learned was that our research comes from our creation story. Even when our babies are born, when we bring life on to this Earth, it's all connected back to our creation story. We are re-enacting a piece of that creation story; it's connected to cosmology, to the natural world, to us as human beings. It's not separate. It's all connected to that. Maybe we forgot that for a little while, but that was always within us. Maybe it's just being more activated now, you know that memory.

Kim: Sometimes people do parallel paths, like you're doing all your other work with traditional knowledge, but you don't necessarily do it as part of the research project. But I think more Indigenous academics – like us or others – are now bringing it into our research practice.

I wanted to tell a little story about water and working with people in other disciplines. I started working with engineers a number of years ago, partly because I had a water resources Master's student (Jason McCullough) approach me about working on his committee. He is a great critical thinker, and in his case, and with other engineering students I have worked with, there is a realisation that they need further education about colonialism and related policies, and in some cases how to integrate community-based and qualitative methods in their research. That Master's project led to another project about wastewater in First Nations communities, and we got to work with First Nations water/wastewater operators. When we launched our research, we had this gathering, and it was mostly men. I remember thinking, *How am I going to start this project? How am I going to go about the work?* Because I'm used to working with women and kids in social and health contexts. But I though *it's about water*, so we've got to have grandmothers involved as leaders. We asked Shirley Williams to help us as an Elder and she came. She started the first gathering with a water ceremony, which everyone participated in. And because I work a lot with stories, I asked the group to begin by going around the circle and, each in turn, tell a story about their relationship with water, possibly connecting to where they were from. I was just astonished because everyone had lots to say about particular places where they came from and their spiritual connection to water. Some were from other parts of the world, or other parts of Canada. It really demonstrated how you can crack that space open, as everybody just immediately connected with water and where they're from. So that's the way we approached it, we came at it from this grandmother way. I was thinking that was an instance where it wasn't about birth or other things we think about in terms of women's responsibility, but we still found a way to have grandmothers take the lead on it. Once we did that it was kind of amazing.

Jaime: It's interesting that you're talking about grandmothers because all the birth work really started with *Nanaandawewigamig;* all these women were talking to grandmothers, getting advice, and pushing for this birth work. I think that's made a lot of difference, because we all know there is support. You're less alienated when you have a team of grannies behind you, supportive and helping you troubleshoot – maybe not the minutia of research issues, but on the larger challenges, which makes a difference.

Kim: It's great to have someone holding space for that. Maybe that's like when people go fasting and you're holding space for them – maybe it's a similar thing – where you're really holding the energy. That's a tremendous responsibility. It's really a gift that they would do that for you.

So, what's the role of the ceremony? I like that ceremony isn't just how we typically think of it. Part of it is just holding the space which the grandmothers do. The ones that are here and the ones on the other side. It's an ongoing thing, right?

Sherry: We try to be really mindful of that; to make space so that whatever knowledge they have, they can share it in a good way – and not just for a specific amount of time. When we bring in an Elder, there's moments through that whole day, just like that sun. It's not only from 9:00am to 10:00am [laughter]. When people are stuck, always rely on that spiritual realm. Open those doorways, maybe you make an offering, tobacco. Have that reciprocity with them.

I think we can carry this work just like we would any bundle that we're given. You really look after that, so that bundle will look after you. It's not only one way. It's both ways and all around that as well. At some point, that bundle will go places, and that's good too. That work will just continue however it will; I've been really surprised by how much this project has grown. I feel it's because when I rely on that grandmother, that's the spirit. That's why it's moving so quickly; sometimes I think we're running to catch up [laughter]. It's flowed out to other places because there are women that were involved initially from different provinces and now they're doing that birth helper work too, which is good.

Jaime: I want to go back to the bundle idea. It's a good way to think of it, because projects end, hopefully in a good way [laughter]! But for us, we're also mentoring students. We want our students to take part in that bundle. It's like passing that bundle of work so it can spread out. To recognise the opportunity to pass the bundle when it's time to do that.

Sherry: A lot of things I shared with you are things I've learned from those older people in my life. What they were actually doing was mentoring me. I didn't know that as a young woman. I thought, *I'm just here, and this is what I'm observing, this is what I'm hearing.* They were actually mentoring me, and that's one of our responsibilities as we get older, is to pass on what we know to the younger ones. If there are certain people that want to work with you, then it becomes your responsibility to pass on that knowledge so our way of life can continue forever. We'd be negligent if we didn't do that. Also, only do what you know. Not that it's fear-based; it's out of respect. As a human being I'm not going to know everything, but maybe my brother or sister here knows about that. Just like how doctors make referrals. I'm going to make a referral to them [laughs]. We help each other in that way, and we acknowledge the strengths of these people. You're calling upon them to help, and they're strong in what their knowledge is. It's about making sure this work goes beyond even who was ever involved in it, like humanly involved in it.

First and foremost, it's always good to know it's that spiritual realm that's guiding it, not us. That doesn't mean we just sit back and wait; of course, we've got to work for that. Of course, we do, but it's always acknowledging that it's the spiritual realm that's in the lead.

Jaime: This mentorship piece is interesting because I have been thought as just a junior for a long time, which means being mentored all the time. Kim's been a mentor for me. Then as you age, and you don't look young as you used to … I'm starting to realise, you know, I can't sit on those youth panels anymore [laughter]. *Why is nobody calling me?* So, mentorship feels like a new task that I guess I'm equipped for it, but I haven't felt like I was there yet. Mentorship from a research perspective is part of your job that you're paid to do, but I can only do so much. I think, *This is what I'm good at. I can't do all these other things, but I can mentor you on this. I can pass this to you, but there are other people who know other things. Please ask them. I can't be everything.*

Sherry: For me, it's good to say to whoever might have the resources "Okay I'm working with this young person so if you going to ask me to come and work with you, you're going to have to help me bring this person with me, or these people with me". Because nowadays it's just like they only want to bring one person. But [you need to bring them along] if you're mentoring, so they can pick up that leadership too.

Kim: For sure. I think about that too. Everywhere we go we should be bringing in youth, or younger researchers, somebody. Even bringing our students to conferences.

Jaime: Those are things that can be written into your grant application too.

Kim: I like the idea of bundle too because if you think about the research as a bundle, it changes your relationship with it and your sense of responsibility. It also frames ethics in a different way. Ethics is problematic in the way that we do it in the university. I think that some of it is really important, but the spirit is not there. Ethics is often about protecting the individual who's vulnerable, but if you think about it as a bundle, it's not about vulnerable individuals that we're trying to protect or an institution. It's about protecting and responsibility to spirit, and vice versa. I don't know if that helps us at all, but it certainly allows you to think about the kinds of responsibilities you're taking up in research. We work in health and wellness. It's about babies and kids, and birth workers, all that life force.

Jaime: It makes you be selective about what you're taking up, right? We were just talking about that this morning. There's just lots of funding out there. We get asked, we feel pressure sometimes to be on all these projects. I don't know if that's really that good, to just be on a whole bunch of projects. If you rethink of it as a bundle you can think through what your level of responsibility is; whether you're doing a disservice by being part of it if you can't contribute to all the value and potential that project has. There are other people that do it can do it too.

Sherry: In the program that I'm working with now with Master's students[1], the students ask for you to be part of their advisory council because they have a choice. I'm good with whoever they choose. It's not like it's not a competition or anything. In fact, it's a lot of work, right? So students and researchers need to be really mindful about who is best to work with them. The students come and offer tobacco and say, "This is why I'm coming to ask you … would you consider …?" Once they offer that tobacco, they offer me a gift. Then I can tell them from a spiritual way – not me – from that spirit that tells me to, how they're going to start off their research.

With a couple of students, I was told they needed to go and make offerings to start off their research. With each one, it was slightly different. They did that, and it made their student work a little bit lighter because they had that trust that they were working with that spiritual realm.

Our ethics are much more than university ethics, because it's about that responsibility and how you are really going to take care of the people and everybody that's involved in your work. It's just not like "well that's what I want out of this, I want a piece of paper". They know it's not going to end there, it's going to go somewhere beyond their student work.

The poles in our lodges each of those poles have a teaching or ethic (value) connected to it, so our ethics far exceeds that of academic or university ethics. Because you are making a promise to know, stay true to and uphold those ethics (values) even way before you even thought of building that lodge … the intent was already out there in and on the Earth (mothering), universe and within you as well.

I became more interested in academic or Western research because I know what we have as Indigenous people can help other people too. It wasn't to keep it to ourselves, but so people can see the strength of us. The power of us. That maybe despite all of these challenges that we see today, there are ways we can get through it. We can use that [knowledge] more with our people but also share with other people as well. That's why I became more interested [to work with] people who write papers. I thought *that's one way we learn, that's one of the ways that people learn now*. Some people don't believe unless they read it, even our own people. If that's a way to catch their attention, maybe when they read that paper it will inspire them to go sit on that land, to go sit by that water, to go sit with people, and listen, and hear, and be a part of that learning in that way, then that's good. That's why I became more open to it. It does have some benefits. Maybe, those babies that are being born will read about themselves in that. They won't be mentioned specifically, but they'll know it's about them.

Kim: It's great that they can get some of that knowledge in a university now. There are, of course, many ways to get it, but the fact that younger generations can now access some of that in a university program is different than earlier times, when we were students.

Sherry: With different Western theories in research, we can always provide a parallel. We don't need validation, but sometimes they need to see that. Then they can see that both ways are valid because our ways were here way before.

I remember this one student, I was talking to her about research and about some of the ways that I learned from my grandmother. She started to cry because it hit her that every moment she spent with her grandmother, she was actually doing research. She was recalling all those times when she sat talking or listening to her grandmother. But university tells us the only way you do research is this way. That's what we've come to think.

Kim: Yes, so good to talk about grandmothers here. Grandmothers are key knowledge holders and researchers, key in knowledge sharing.

Sherry: We talked earlier about how we were given ways to adopt if we don't have our biological grandmother or mother. Our ways open those doorways for us, for them to adopt us because we need that support lifelong. That can happen formally or informally.

One of the people that adopted me was Moses Land from Grassy Narrows. He's gone on to the spirit world now. I happened to meet him the first time at some kind of a gathering. He came up to me and said, "Oh there you are". [laughs] I was listening to him, and he said, "I've been looking for you". He said "I saw you way back when I was with my wife". He told me who his wife was, but she had already passed away by then. He said, "We had seen you, you were walking by, and my wife said 'That's our granddaughter'. She tried to run after you".

He became one of my teachers. We didn't have a ceremony to recognise – that was the ceremony, by him just saying, "There you are, I've been looking for you". He spoke the old language, so there are words that I learned from him that hadn't been used in a long, long time. He talked about the Earth as a lodge and how we learn from that. He said, "If you could see under the Earth there is a lodge down there, it's shaped like this [motions], and you're in it, no matter where you are". He said, "When you need our knowledge, our way, you will retain some of it when you go in that classroom, meeting room, or boardroom. But we also have teaching lodges – the greatest being the Earth". He said, "When you go and sit and learn in those lodges you're going to retain much more of it", That is one of the things he said to me, and it's true. I see more and more people are building those teaching lodges. When you construct it, there is teaching behind every pole that you take, why it's constructed in such a way, and the teachings might be different, but that's okay. It's in relation to the universe and even to us as human beings.

That's probably why in our program we start off on the land. When we get our first cohort, we go out for five days, just us and the students. We teach them. Those are some teachings that we have and the ways that we have to help each other. It's good to go back to those and to really fulfill them, to bring those back in a strong way because that's part of the research.

Jaime: Are you seeing your students incorporate ceremony as part of their theses?

Sherry: Yeah, they do. Some of them are talking about when they finish they're going to have a feast to share it publicly. There are two students who also want to write a book. That's useful. And when they launch their book, they'll have a ceremony to do that. Some of them, like those two women that I'm thinking of, they're going to have a ceremony throughout their project.

Jaime: Are you leading those ceremonies, or do they have someone?

Sherry: I will be helping with those ceremonies. When they go and put out their offerings for the very first time I usually ask them to do it by themselves because I want them to make a relationship with whatever spirit they're going to [work with]. That's up to them to do that. I just show them what to do, and I advise them on how they might want to do that.

Jaime: There are mostly women, and are the men doing ceremonies too? Are they different?

Sherry: They are similar. In fact, all of them are really grateful because this world is colonised and a lot of it is patriarchal. Even us, we've adopted some of those ways, a lot of those ways. I think for the men, the ones that I've met in that program, they're very grateful and very humbled when they see a woman doing this kind of work because I think it brings up memories of their own mothers, their own grandmothers. Maybe at some point they were displaced but they now know — or knew all along — they had this knowledge, but it was suppressed. I'm not putting our men down at all, but we tend to think only men can be spiritual leaders, only men can be this, only men can do that. I know where I come from even the men's spiritual leaders have always said, "No it's not us. It's the women. We wouldn't be here if it wasn't for these women. You are the ones who are a conduit between that spiritual realm and this physical. We're your helpers", Even that 70- and 80-year-old said that to me when I was a young woman. They didn't only say, they acted like it. That's the difference.

With these students, hopefully, we'll come to see that; they'll act on it. It's how we work together. It's not in competition but how we support everyone within that. Even in our creation stories, nobody was forgotten, everything was remembered. We just need to connect those parts of the creation story to how we do things now and how we know everything was remembered in that creation story. I had an opportunity to listen to pieces of those creation stories where it mentions people called two-spirited today — they're mentioned in that story. I don't think a lot of people hear those parts of the story anymore.

Kim: Do you tell those stories?

Sherry: I do. Oh yeah.

Kim: That's good. We need more people telling those stories.

Sherry: A lot of the ways that we have are practical too. I was born a woman but that doesn't mean I can't do things that are considered masculine. Way back when I probably wouldn't have survived if I didn't know those things and vice versa.

Jaime: In one of the two communities that we have the doula project, we have a male doula, a two-spirited doula. We were really surprised and pleased that he came forward and the community was okay with that.

Kim: What you were saying earlier Sherry, about birth, people presume that birth was only the grandmothers and the aunties, and so on, but depending on the context, there might have been men helping out with the ceremony.

Sherry: I heard that through an Elder's birth story. How both the men and woman were there. The men were in the lodge, around the drum singing him in. It was the women that actually caught him, but the men were there. Of course, he was named right there through that song. He has his own birth song, just like all of us have.

When you think about birth, [you can think about] how much power that has and how much power parenting has. In today's world, we don't really value that too much. I've come to realise it's the greatest work ever done, we'll ever do.

Jaime: It's the hardest.

Kim: Therefore, when you're doing research on mothering, you're doing it being mindful of all that power and ceremony, the power of mothering.

Jaime: We're all mothers right on top of that too.

Sherry: With this work that we're doing we've come to realise that [power]. But we know we need to make space for men too. Before it was just natural. It's not anymore; we need to make spaces for these ways and fathers want to be integral.

Jaime: We're finding that with the birth worker project. The men, the women's partners are wanting to get involved. We hadn't really thought through that piece when we were devising the project. Now we're thinking how we can get these continuing education sessions we are doing for birth workers to focus on men and men's roles? Luckily, we have lots of people to call on. I'm not sure why we hadn't focused on it before. It was the community that brought it to our attention.

Sherry: With some of the teachings or ceremonies that we have, fathers were very much a part of birth work. It's the father's role to sing their clan songs when the baby is being born and while the baby was growing in the mother's womb. It's fathers who make those fires every once in a while, for that little spirit. Today we've gotten away from that; we only make fire when somebody goes back to the spiritual world. But we always made fire when we were welcoming that spirit into this world. At one time the fathers made the birthing lodge, and I've been saying that to the trainers. If you're going to have the baby at home, the dad can do that; prepare that birthing room or that lodge for the mom and baby, and for the workers that are going to be there, the helpers. That's their role. [The fathers can] do that physical work, also putting their spirit and heart into it. Those are the kinds of things that we can give a little nudge for people to start doing that again.

Kim: I think fathers also can make the *tikinagan* (cradleboard and/or moss bag). They can go talk to the tree; prepare the space for the baby to move from the womb to the *tikinagan*.

Jaime: With our birth worker trainers, they talk about the birth bundle. They encourage women to think through what a birth bundle would look like in their family and community. Maybe it would have a moss bag and a bonnet, mocassins and other pieces.

Kim: The dad's get involved with that too?

Jaime: It's the mom. The birth worker encourages them and then they do it together. Our project supports the family in getting those materials and helping them figure out what they want in that bundle.

Kim: It's good to think about how to involve all the family, all the generations. I learned that when it came to the moss used for diapers, it was the grannies who harvested it, then picked all the twigs out to make it soft. The old ladies used to do that. It's practical stuff too, right? If you can't move a whole lot then it's a good job for the old ladies. It's cool to think about how people can reconstruct that in terms of what they're doing now. It gives everyone a role, and it also creates a relationship between the family.

Sherry: It does.

Kim: It's that preparation like you were talking about, being prepared.

The conversation takes a more casual direction and the group wraps up.
(Sherry Copenace, personal communication: December 2018).

Auntie's bundle: An Indigenous research methodology

This conversation, between three Indigenous women who play various roles of researchers, aunties and friends, illustrates and exemplifies what Indigenous research methodology looks like in practice. From this conversation, we learn about the role of Elders and ceremony in the birth worker project; however, we also see the strength of using conversation as a methodology to co-create knowledge and practice reflexivity (Kovach 2009). It also demonstrates the importance of experiences, relationality, ethical research, and responsibility throughout the research process (Wilson 2008; Kovach 2009; Cunneen et al. 2017; Bell 2018; Martin 2018). For this reason, the conversation can, in and of itself, serve as a kitchen table style model that others may draw on in their Indigenous research practices. We offer some analysis of what we see happening in both the content and practice of this interaction, and invite the reader to develop their own interpretations of the conversation.

First, the role of ceremony is central to this conversation on Indigenous CBPR and its importance is highlighted by the water ceremony Sherry performed prior to the conversation with Jaime and Kim. During the conversation, Sherry explained the significance of ceremony and the role it plays in holding space in the birth worker project. As other researchers have demonstrated, ceremony plays an important role in setting the stage for research, honouring relationships, and honouring the knowledge that will be shared (Wilson 2008; Srigley and Varley 2018). Through emphasising that ceremony is a 'sense of connection', Sherry draws attention to the conceptual framework that makes up all Indigenous research paradigms: the interconnection between epistemologies, ontologies, methodologies, relationships, places, spaces, and community (Wilson 2008; Archibald 2008; Kovach 2009; Fellner 2018). Sherry emphasised the importance of understanding the connection between water, men, women, children, the spiritual realm, the physical realm, the natural world, and the creation story. This reminds us that while Western research paradigms are often compartmentalised by discipline and research topic, Indigenous ways of knowing are holistic and focus on all experiences and elements of life (Foley 2003; Kovach 2009; Archibald 2008; Cunneen et al. 2017; McGregor 2018).

When discussing the birth worker project, Sherry, Jaime, and Kim also stressed the idea of research as a bundle that looks after you if you look after it, demonstrating the reciprocal nature of the work Jaime and Kim do as women's health researchers. This relational aspect of Indigenous research methodologies allows for a greater understanding of the interconnection between knowledge, gender, and land and the research bundle provides researchers with the tools to draw from their cultural background to pursue knowledge (Starblanket and Kiiwetinepinesiik Stark 2018; Bell 2018). This relationality and connectivity inform the iterative research process that Kim often uses when describing the research process to her students that moves from preparing (positionality, theory, ethical considerations), to harvesting (data collection), to processing (data analysis), to sharing (knowledge mobilisation), and ensures that a researcher's approach is ethical and responsible (Absolon 2011). Figure 14.1 offers an illustration this bundle, where ceremony crosses through all areas of the research process, land, or the Earth lodge that Sherry describes ("you're in it, no matter where you are") encompasses the researcher, and gender informs all analysis and practice.

One might start at any point on the wheel – for example, with thinking through the sharing/knowledge mobilisation goals, as this might be deemed the most significant by a community, say, wanting culture-based birth knowledge. As the wheel is constantly turning and all parts

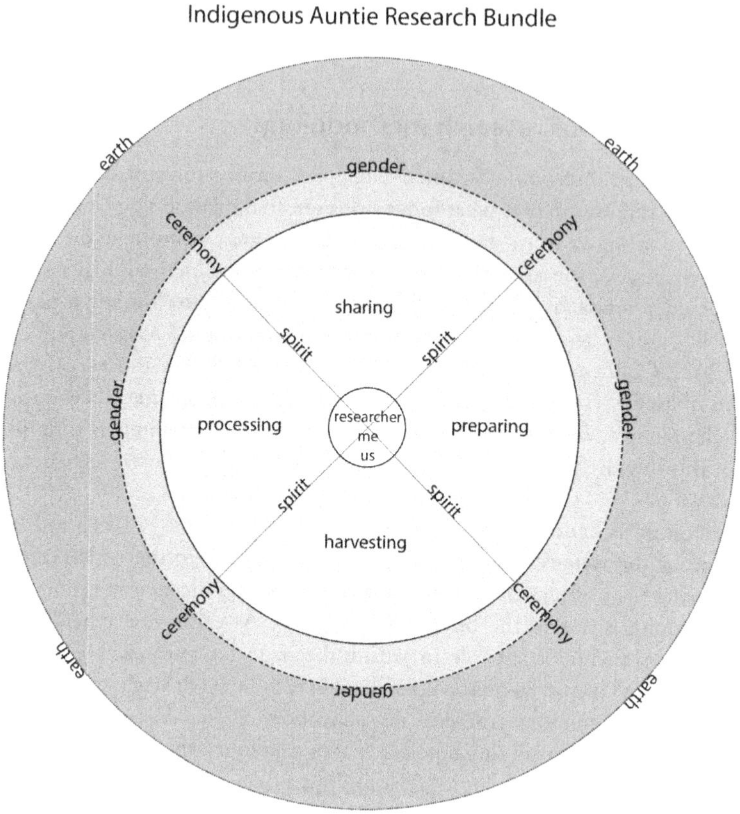

Indigenous Auntie Research Bundle

Figure 14.1 Indigenous Auntie research bundle.

inform each other, one might thus begin with any element in Auntie's bundle. Most often, the research process begins with preparation; as Sherry demonstrates and others have documented, Indigenous epistemologies are grounded in ceremonies, the spirit, the land, and the self (Ermine 1995; Debassige 2010; Martin 2018; Absolon 2019). This comes across in Sherry's discussion of relying on the spiritual realm, of making an offering of tobacco, and starting with the land. Sherry's emphasis on the efforts that occur prior to beginning the research journey is shared by many Indigenous scholars who discuss the role land plays in offering teachings and learning through dreams and listening (McIsaac 2000; Simpson 2004; Kovach 2009; Monchalin 2016; Johnston et al. 2018; Parent 2018).

Next, in the harvesting and processing stages, it is important to consider and acknowledge the multitude of sources where knowledge may emerge (Kovach 2009; Debassige 2010; Botha 2011). In the birth worker project, Sherry discussed a spirit grandmother stepping forward to offer help, and Kim elaborated on the key role grandmothers play in knowledge construction related to water research. During the harvesting/data collection stages, it is important that researchers are responsible for listening to different sources, ensuring they are approached ethically, and that they are communicated accurately (Archibald 2008). Sherry equates this responsibility with the poles in a lodge with each pole representing a teaching. Researchers must stay true to ethically upholding these teachings and values to take care of those involved in the research and those affected by it.

The final stage of the research process is sharing, and Indigenous research methodologists have emphasised how important it is to give back to communities – to share and learn beyond extracting knowledge (McGregor 2018). As Deborah McGregor points out, sharing knowledge is a gift that will benefit the well-being of others (McGregor 2018). Additionally, there is the responsibility to be accountable for the knowledge collected and ensuring it cannot cause harm and is not misused (Johnston et al. 2018). Researchers must also consider how their research will impact future generations and how it can make space for Indigenous ways of knowing (Hall and Cusak 2018). Sherry, Jaime, and Kim discussed this in terms of mentorship and their responsibility to pass on knowledge so leadership roles can be passed on. Sherry also discusses the responsibility to bring Indigenous research methodologies forward to provide a parallel to different Western research practices, which will ultimately allow future generations to access this knowledge within post-secondary institutions.

This chapter allowed us to explore Indigenous research methodologies and deepen our understanding by engaging with one Knowledge Gifter and Anishinaabe Grandmother using a conversation methodology. This conversation demonstrates how cultural knowledge and ceremony play an integral role in Indigenous research paradigms in the context of a birth worker community-based research project. While the conversation between Sherry, Jaime, and Kim concentrates on women's health research, their conversation should be considered within other research journeys as it offers insights into researcher responsibilities to make an offering, to proceed ethically, to provide mentorship, and to share knowledge. It demonstrates how sharing through conversation as a non-structured methodology can lead to rich reflection, dialogue, and storytelling (Kovach 2009). Ultimately, what Sherry teaches us about using Indigenous research methodologies is, "… always to be prepared and to do that work – good heart, good mind. Always be generous in whatever that you do because whatever you give, it will come back to you in more ways than we as human beings can even imagine".

Note

1 Sherry is one of two Elders in Residence at the University of Manitoba's Master's of Social Work Indigenous Knowledge(s) program. This is a two-year program that focusses on training Indigenous social workers to explore Indigenous forms of caring and healing. http://umanitoba.ca/faculties/socia l_work/programs/fort_garry/943.html.

References

Absolon, K. (2011). *Kaandossiwin: How We Come to Know*. Fernwood Publishing Co Ltd: Halifax, PA.

Absolon, K. (2019). 'Indigenous wholistic theory: A knowledge set for practice', *First Peoples Child & Family Review*, vol 14, no 1: 22–42.

Anderson, K. and Cidro, J. (2020). 'Because we love our communities: Indigenous women talk about their experiences as community-based health researchers'. *Journal of Higher Education Outreach and Engagement*, vol 24, no 2: (page numbers unavailable at time of publication).

Archibald, J. (2008). *Indigenous Storywork: Educating, the Heart, Mind, Body and Spirit*. UBC Press: Vancouver, BC.

Bell, N. (2018). 'Anishnaabe research theory and methodology as informed by Nanaboozhoo, the bundle bag, and the medicine wheel', in D. McGregor, J.P. Restoule, and R. Johnston (eds.) *Indigenous Research. Theories, Practices, and Relationships*. Canadian Scholars: Toronto, ON, 175–186.

Botha, L. (2011). 'Mixing methods as a process towards Indigenous methodologies', *International Journal of Social Research Methodology*, vol 14, no 4: 313–325.

Cunneen, C., Rowe S., and Tauri J. (2017). 'Fracturing the colonial paradigm: Indigenous epistemologies and methodologies', *Method(e)s: African Review of Social Sciences Methodology*, vol 2, no 1–2: 62–78.

Debassige, B. (2010). 'Re-conceptualizing Anishinaabe Mino-Bimaadiziwin (the good life) as research methodology: a spirit-centred way in Anishinaabe research', *Canadian Journal of Native Education*, vol 33, no 1: 11–28.

Ermine, W. (1995). 'Aboriginal epistemology', in M. Battiste and J. Barman (eds.) *First Nations Education in Canada: The Circle Unfolds*. UBC Press: Vancouver, BC, 101–112.

Fellner, K. (2018). 'miyo pimatiswin: (Re)claiming voice with our original instructions', in D. McGregor, J.P. Restoule, and R. Johnston (eds.) *Indigenous Research. Theories, Practices, and Relationships*. Canadian Scholars: Toronto, ON, 24–45.

Foley, D. (2003). 'Indigenous epistemology and Indigenous standpoint theory', *Social Alternatives*, vol 2, no 1: 44–52.

Hall, K., and Cusak E. (2018). 'Healing and transformative learning through Indigenous methodologies', in D. McGregor, J.P. Restoule, and R. Johnston (eds.) *Indigenous Research. Theories, Practices, and Relationships*. Canadian Scholars: Toronto, ON, 98–111.

Johnston, R., McGregor, D., and Restoule., J.P. (2018). 'Introduction: Relationships, respect, relevance, reciprocity, and responsibility: Taking up and Indigenous research approaches', in D. McGregor, J.P. Restoule, and R. Johnston (eds.) *Indigenous Research. Theories, Practices, and Relationships*. Canadian Scholars: Toronto, ON, 1–121.

Kovach, M. (2009). *Indigenous Methodologies. Characteristics, Conversations, and Contexts*. University of Toronto Press: Toronto, ON.

Martin, G. (2018). 'Storytelling and narrative inquiry: Exploring research methodologies', in D. McGregor, J.P. Restoule, and R. Johnston (eds.) *Indigenous Research. Theories, Practices, and Relationships*. Canadian Scholars: Toronto, ON, 87–99.

McGregor, D. (2018). 'Toward an Anishnaabe research paradigm: Theory and practice', in D. McGregor, J.P. Restoule, and R. Johnston (eds.) *Indigenous Research. Theories, Practices, and Relationships*. Canadian Scholars: Toronto, ON, 243–256.

McIsaac, E. (2000). 'Oral narratives as a site of resistance: Indigenous knowledge, colonialism, and western discourse', in G.J. Sefa Dei, B.L. Hall, and D. Goldin Rosenberg (eds.) *Indigenous Knowledges in Global Contexts. Multiple Readings of Our World*. University of Toronto Press: Toronto, ON, 89–101.

Monchalin, L. (2016). *The Colonial Problem: An Indigenous Perspective on Crime and Injustice in Canada*. University of Toronto Press: Toronto, ON.

Parent, A. (2018). 'Research tales with txeemsim (Raven, the Trickster)', in D. McGregor, J.P. Restoule, and R. Johnston (eds.) *Indigenous Research. Theories, Practices, and Relationships*. Canadian Scholars: Toronto, ON, 175–186.

Simpson, L.R. (2004). 'Anticolonial strategies for the recovery and maintenance of Indigenous knowledge', *American Indian Quarterly*, vol 28, no 3/4: 373–384.

Srigley, K., and Varley, A. (2018). 'Learning to unlearn: Building relationships on Anishinaabeg territory', in D. McGregor, J.P. Restoule, and R. Johnston (eds.) *Indigenous Research. Theories, Practices, and Relationships*. Canadian Scholars: Toronto, ON, 46–64.

Starblanket, G., and Kiiwetinepinesiik Stark, H. (2018). 'Towards a relational paradigm – Four points for consideration: Knowledge, gender, land, and modernity', in M. Asch, J. Borrows, and J. Tully (eds.) *Resurgence and Reconciliation: Indigenous – Settler Relations and Earth Teachings*. University of Toronto Press: Toronto, ON, 175–207.

Wilson, S. (2008). *Research is Ceremony. Indigenous Research Methods*. Fernwood Publishing: Winnipeg, MB.

15

When nothingness revokes certainty

A Māori speculation

Carl Mika

Introduction

Nothingness as a philosophical concern has preoccupied Western thought for millennia due to its importance for what can be said to exist. It is also highly significant for any Māori counter-colonial stance which aims to look beyond the Western preoccupation with an object's tangibility. Useful in this type of challenge is 'philosophising', which is that speculative act that goes beyond simply responding to a question logically. In the Māori language, the term 'whakaaro' that is loosely but insufficiently translated as 'to think' is crucial in this role. More expansive than an intellectual capacity, 'whakaaro' participates in nothingness. It is therefore at once counter-colonial and positive; it dispenses with any pretense that we operate above the things we discuss and instead attempts to place us within a much greater totality (Mika 2017a; 2017b) – within a ground of existence rather than separate from it. This kind of thinking is as indebted to nothingness as it is to any clarity[1].

This chapter considers a particular Māori philosophical phenomenon – Te Kore (nothingness, void) – and aims to signal its importance for the very stuff of thought and utterance for the Māori individual. Nothingness has received a mixed press in the dominant Western canon and although certain very influential Western philosophers have grappled with its significance and have shown a partial overlap with our own thinking, I am more concerned with the development of one's thinking that originates from and also returns to that ancient Māori state of being. In this article, I think through the void whilst making some tentative but direct claims about it and seeking to show how Te Kore undermines those claims, and indeed anyone's claims. Te Kore, I shall argue, is possibly the most urgent of our colonised struggles because it actively demarcates what can and cannot be thought and uttered. It additionally sets the scene for responses to Western critique and even develops a sense of the ludicrous as it revokes the self's control and reasserts murkiness.

The faintest stirrings of nothingness: Some issues with the term

Te Kore can be conceived of as already having established itself before any self-determined discussion of it and it is therefore 'absently present' in all existence. In this chapter, I note the prior machinery of Te Kore before settling on it as a sustained theme. It seems to like to act as ultimate disclaimer, especially if we approach 'disclaim' in terms of its original sense indicating a 'lack of' or 'reversal' of a speech act and if we understand Te Kore as a voided assertive act of thinking or talking. In that reading of them both, they come together quite nicely. As an Indigenous scholar committing an act of *proclaiming*, a 'shouting forth' of an idea, it makes sense that my mission to be certain is tempered from the outset with a significant *taking back* of that self-confidence if Te Kore does indeed refer to nothingness. The undermining of our self-confidence calls for self-moderation: the vastly different categories that Western and Indigenous philosophies respectively confront us with, force us to tread carefully. I recall a quote from Foucault who cannot articulate the Indigenous position but, in *The Order of Things*, recognises the risks of assuming that things are the same:

> This book first arose out of a passage in Borges, out of the laughter that shattered, as I read the passage, all the familiar landmarks of my thought – *our* thought, the thought that bears the stamp of our age and our geography – breaking up all the ordered surfaces and all the planes with which we are accustomed to tame the wild profusion of existing things, and continuing long afterwards to disturb and threaten with collapse our age-old distinction between the Same and the Other. This passage quotes a 'certain Chinese encyclopaedia' in which it is written that 'animals are divided into: (a) belonging to the Emperor, (b) embalmed, (c) tame, (d) sucking pigs, (e) sirens, (f) fabulous, (g) stray dogs, (h) included in the present classification, (i) frenzied, (j) innumerable, (k) drawn with a very fine camelhair brush, (l) *et cetera*, (m) having just broken the water pitcher, (n) that from a long way off look like flies'. In the wonderment of this taxonomy, the thing we apprehend in one great leap, the thing that, by means of the fable, is demonstrated as the exotic charm of another system of thought, is the limitation of our own, the stark impossibility of thinking *that*.
>
> *(2002: xvi)*

In the setting of this chapter, my own laughter evolves from any suggestion that Māori ontological categories are the same as those of the West. Foucault draws our attention to a problem of incommensurability. Intriguing to me at this point is the nature of our own categories: if they are not the same as those of the West, then what are they? Foucault is interested in how differently a thing breaks down as between two different cultural groups, but it seems to me that, in order to arrive at an answer, we would have to contend with the nature of existence itself and *thereafter* what constitutes an 'animal', well before its split into various species. With this chapter, I suspect that 'nothingness' and a *traditional* 'Te Kore-ness' draw from two completely different sets of what-ness. They weigh differently, take up separate spaces, have their own textures – in short, they *aren't* each other at all, despite the fact that at some stage onward they were equated with each other in a dictionary. Yet, if Western and Māori thought constitute each other, then the Western 'nothingness' and the Māori 'Te Kore' will, too. Here, we are considering a deeper problem than the meanings and precision of individual terms, with their lack of definitional match forcing the Māori speculative writer to account for both as if they are different and yet paradoxically co-existing.

Back to the disclaimer proper: as a Māori writer, to acknowledge the uncertainty of terms and their phenomena is to take the first cognisant step into Te Kore, although the Western term 'nothingness' and the separate ontology it reveals keep rearing up. This discussion is not exclusively about a traditional notion of Te Kore by any means, despite my occasional use of the traditional term 'Te Kore'. To a certain extent, I am playing with the essence of Western 'taxonomy', as Foucault puts it, whilst trying to undermine it. This will always end strangely, in the sense that even if I stuck to the Māori term – Te Kore – I am always granted only a small, temporary glimpse into its obscurity, but then that is clarified very quickly. This inability as a colonised Indigenous writer to get to the root of the problem (yet to nevertheless want to disturb that problem as much as possible) and to reflect the obscurity of the void in his or her writing is, strangely, itself an outcome of a first *existential* step into the void, in the sense that uncertainty begins here.

Distending the disclaimer

Nepia notes a similar darkening characteristic of Te Kore with the following:

> Te Kore may also articulate a continuum, for the layering of voices. As eternity, Te Kore articulates space into which we may speak and move, or be denied opportunities to express ourselves. Moments of calamity, or uncertainty when all seems disconnected, and unsuitable must be overcome if a creative journey is to fulfill its purpose. The creative process, like a journey, may also have abrupt halts.
>
> *(2012: 70)*

Many Māori reading that quote will undoubtedly be reminded of the trauma of colonisation. A turn to *philosophical* colonisation, one of several forms of oppression, is worth briefly visiting here in light of the fears and vulnerabilities of dominant Western philosophy and, more precisely, within the context of Māori metaphysics. Where dominant Western philosophy repudiates the "diverse, overlapping, and complex aspects of thought or idea and expels those outside the boundary of scholarship by the single standard of formal logic" (Seung-hwan 2004: 233), Māori metaphysics appears to have no problems with a radical form of holism that defies those Western conventions. Marsden (2003) suggests that the world is interconnected and this sets up various positions that cannot be reconciled with dominant Western philosophy. Rationality, for instance, would ask for proof of the All within one thing; Māori philosophy may ignore that request but instead mischievously but purposively ask the rational thinker for proof that the world *is* fragmented, because that is the premise evidently underpinning formal logic. If s/he decides to set a point of concern in this way, the Māori philosopher is evidently cynic and provocateur (see e.g., Mika 2016; 2017c), returning the gaze as if there is something deeply wrong with the rationalist's question in the first instance.

However, despite that roguish micro-device of the Māori scholar, it is evident that various disciplines, institutions, and general declarations on what can and cannot be thought, teach us from early on that the world is comprised of fragmentable parts. This teaching is admittedly subtle but it is quite treacherous, and so how we revise our expression and refresh our representations of the world calls sometimes for so-called 'irrational' descriptions. Although arguably the entire Indigenous experience is beset with this difficulty, one discrete, hypothetical example serves here: a Māori university student does not do particularly well in a conventional critical thinking course, or in a paper that has formal logic as its base assumption and practice, but she does extremely well in a paper that deals with the deliberate obscuring of ideas. If we look for the etymology of 'critical', we see that the term derives from a fundamental assumption: 'krino', or 'to separate' (Schrag 1992), with a linguistic emphasis on the first-person ('I separate'). Western critical thinking does indeed rely on clarity (Madhucchanda 2010), setting about separating concepts of things from each other, and the Māori student, it is assumed, will participate in that radical fragmentation. The student is asked to demonstrate her rational understanding by revisiting (and correcting) her assertions. Let us choose one typical assertion briefly that we will return to in more depth: 'My ancestors are always present' (incidentally, many Māori voice this very claim, whether they are in mental health facilities, courts, schools, or simply involved in casual conversation). The student is asked to provide evidence for her assertion that her ancestors are always present, and instead she simply continues her insistence by disengaging from clarity. But the clarity logician, the lecturer, persists and asks her to define her terms or question her assumptions on the basis of his own assumption that *clarity is best*. The continual line of questioning that the lecturer loves, in which elements are reduced to their clearest view, holds a certain appeal because it expunges opinion and it offers the teacher in particular an exhilarating roller-coaster ride that opens onto ever-more-precise ideas. The student and teacher journey together to arrive at "the identification of the fallacies and the rejection of the argument" (Kaplan 1994: 216), and although one doesn't always have to be clear about everything, "*we can explain things clearly when we need to*" (Lau 2011: 12, emphasis original). Representing things so that they regain their darkness or obscurity, however – *that*, for Māori students and others, may be a more sophisticated way of encountering things in the world through perception. Things would then always be read against the backdrop of the All, including its ability to withdraw, or actively negative/render nothing, the full nature of any one thing from our perception. But it is also a mysteriousness that resetting our representations – at least as far as possible – means we are starting to work within the world's convolutedness.

As I noted briefly, the existential problems that Indigenous peoples face in the world are in fact this student's challenge writ large, where we are forced to encounter objects as possessing static characteristics or properties (for example, see Mika 2017b) that are discoverable as 'true' to those individual objects. Rationality, even if not through the conscious exercise of critical thinking, confronts the Indigenous self by asking him/her to turn to an object as if it is unconnected to all others, capable of being clearly perceived. Colonisation in this philosophical sense is premised on a highly present conception of an object or idea and it relies on the continuous production of a particular worldview. But what happens if that student's most ancient and revered philosophies consider the separation of things and ideas to be anathema, not just to thought but also existence? And what occurs where Indigenous modes of perception, more generally, are based not on that clarity insisted on by the West through *elenchus* (questioning method), *eidos* (universals) or *parousia* (high presence), but within a far more obscure ground? It is in raising these questions that, along with meeting the limitations of our certainty I discussed earlier, we can encounter the promise hinted at through our own ancient metaphysics – a metaphysics of nothingness which is significant for the ways in which we respond through the worlded perception or 'whakaaro'.

Te Kore and its emissary, Kotahi-tē-kī: Nothingness

Te Kore: Metaphysical and existential force

By re-establishing our own modes of expression, whilst of course acknowledging and disturbing the limitations placed on us by colonisation, as Māori we are occupying uncertain ground by engaging with a peculiar otherness or difference. In the Māori language, this process takes on a more vibrant sense with the term 'rerekē', which is often taken to means simply 'different' but also suggests a 'progression with the fact of otherness' or, in the case of colonisation and writing, a flowing alongside the foreignness of rational thought's smooth, anaesthetic consistency. Within the depths of rerekē, our writing manifests as both Western and Indigenous. Suppressing the Western colonising question, in other words, does not fully negate the problem. In writing this chapter, I am indebted to Moana Nepia's formative work which considers in great depth the nature of Te Kore and its link, overall, with our contemporary world. At one point he outlines two basic perceptions of Te Kore which in turn are multifaceted. In many traditions, "Te Kore is usually conceptualised as a primordial realm of nothingness or void" (Nepia 2012: 32). He identifies additionally that:

> [T]he tohunga (scholar) Mohi Ruatapu conceptualised Te Kore within whakapapa stemming from Tāne, and thus in the realm of Te Ao Mārama. Here, Te Kore is personified as part of a procreative narrative, given ancestral presence, human form and potential to express states of emotion, intimacy and separation. Other sources also personify Te Kore through additional corporeal, emotional and spiritual interpretations: as a womb, or space within the body, holding potential for human life; as part of the process by which sense perception came into being; as a state of depression or emotional darkness; as loss, absence, devastation and annihilation, as a concept regulating human behavior in customary social contexts. Te Kore has also been translated as 'abyss' and 'chaos'. Through the presence or absence of space, time, movement, sensation, light, colour, and material form, Te Kore finds expression within Māori architectural, design, performance and art making contexts.

Te Kore therefore signals an existential reading of the world for the human being. Given that Māori reiterate the equal value of the non-human world, I suspect Te Kore has existential significance for all other things in the world too, although probably in vastly different ways to how the human being experiences being-in-the-world. Other entities besides humans may possess their own comportment toward and constitution by the world, but not being able to speak for them, I instead reflect on the *human* perception and configuration of things. However, at no point does the unseen, imperceptible nature of whakaaro begin and end with human perception; whakaaro is a much fuller existential and phenomenological reality than that. It is also important to note that Nepia does not necessarily oppose the common, abstract notion of Te Kore (existing in a rarefied realm, possibly only of ceremonial use) with the materiality of Te Kore for human perception. Nepia has identified the manifold ways in which Te Kore as that material nothingness embeds itself in human experience, and he seeks to understand Te Kore as a phenomenon that acts on "thought (whakaaro) understood as 'an action of the body making sense'" (2012: 36). It is this link between the darkness, loss, even terror, and whakaaro that augurs a vast divergence from Western thought, which aims to clarify matter as much as possible.

The world and all its things, in Māori philosophy, must therefore be brought into discussion with Te Kore. Again, a proviso is called for, because 'world' is clearly an English term that derives originally from the Germanic languages with 'werold' (Harper 2018a) and may therefore be about as appropriate for our use as 'nothingness', especially as its etymology refers to exclusively *human* concerns. A brief explanation about the hypothetical nature of the Māori language is necessary here: there may be verbs and nouns in te reo Māori (the Māori language) but this does not preclude nouns from having their own irruptive force and verbs from having their solidity (for example, see Mika 2017a). To that extent, Western 'languageness' is, like the Western categorisation of 'animal' Foucault highlights, laughable, and implies that language and its totality are manageable by the human self. 'Te Ao' is one term, though, that *is* ascribed both verb and noun status at once quite explicitly in Māori tradition, perhaps because of the term's/entity's vast implications for existence. It has been translated as 'world' but also 'to world' in the sense of 'to dawn'. If thought of as both 'world' and 'to world' then it takes on a sense of something evolving *as* world. By this, I mean that a thing is always-already the world as a whole (Mika 2017b). It insists on its designation as the world and therefore resonates with another largely disorienting entity – whakapapa – which in its broadest sense means 'interconnectedness'. It is important to note that in ancient Māori genealogy and philosophy, emotions, ideas, orientations have their equal place alongside those things that the West labels 'tangible'. Whakaaro, for example, means 'to think' but it also has its materiality; it also means 'idea' but it has its active insistence. It is one example of a complexity of existence that, in both its spiritual and intellectual determinants, might best be described as signalling the unfathomable mystery of the world, where things in the world in their total come to bear on the self and constitute the self's perception (Mika 2017b). Overall, 'whakaaro' strongly represents the fact of the world, in particular its infinite constitution of all things.

Te Kore, understood as an origin of uncertainty, is both generative of and embedded within things in the world (White and Mika 2013). It devolves to the world the beginnings and continuation of mystery. There is nothing ordered about the world and the worlding of things which, because of the nature of worlding, places them beyond the full perception of the human self. Whakaaro, however, does allow us to intuit them, not as disinterested bystanders but as worlded entities ourselves. Seemingly with that self-implicated human being in mind, Smith and Jenkins have identified that, if we are to grapple "with the fullness of what is the world" (1997: 14) in issues such as land (which is their example), we must retain the original understanding of what it means to embrace all stages of creation which, as I have already suggested, are influential phenomena and have significance for everyday things. These creative entities always-already contain each to the other, or at least they fundamentally co-create (Goetzfridt 1995). Warrior, similar to Smith and Jenkins, notes that Indigenous worldviews construct "nothingness [as] extant" where nothingness is not precisely *void* but instead "full of possibility" (2015: 54). It seems to be an unusual proposition for several commentators, then, that nothingness has been and gone or reached its limits several years ago. With its infinite reach in mind, we can consider how thought and speech are themselves pre-epistemological and yet determinative of human perception, feeling and utterance.

Kotahi-tē-kī: The speech and thought of nothingness

Nothingness acts as a limit on certainty and is existentially significant *in a current sense* for Indigenous peoples; it gives rise to any knowledge or thought but is not limited by them (for example see Kent 2011). A phrase in Māori that appears to be both an ancient phenomenon and an express sign of the self's limits on expression and thought is one used by Māori scholar Pei Te Hurinui Jones: it is 'Kotahi-tē-kī' (2013: 148), which he translates as "The One Unspoken Thought ... Primeval. Enshrined!" This entire phrase is useful both in its parts and its total. It is a fascinating role of the 'tē' that it recalls any thoroughgoing presence of, or negatives, the thought, or 'kī'. It makes sense, then, that 'Kotahi-tē-kī' acts as "māngai o te kore" (mouthpiece of nothingness) (Te Ruki 2010: 11), highlighting the unspokenness of something that must concomitantly exist in order to be negative at all. Te Ruki, incidentally, does not use 'tē' but instead 'te' which does not immediately denote anything to do with nothingness, but it is possible that both renderings are viable given the often contradictory nature of Māori philosophy. 'Te' is a definite article within Western linguistic convention, equated with 'the'. From a Māori worlded perspective, it designates the fact of a thing, expressing the fact of a thing's existence, but it does so whilst acknowledging the horizontal and vertical layers of constituting world. It summons that thing's stark appearance with its complex incorporation with all other things and yet it does reveal the metaphysics of nothingness. When intensified – thus, 'tē' – it *revokes* (etymologically 'calls back'; Harper, 2018b) – because it forever establishes the possibility or positive appearance of a thing and simultaneously reverses the positivity or singularity of the ontological field from which that thing emerges. In other words: if a tree exists, there is an aspect to it that participates in nothingness, and the conditions or ground of its possibility are 'nothing-ed' (whilst simultaneously existing).

'Tē', on its own, contributes to the nothingness of existence in total, well before we speak of a particular thing (such as a tree). It has the capacity to gather and disperse a field of Being. Tē, then, is worth considering in its own right, away from its relationship to any particular thing.

Both 'tē' and 'te' would convey the meaning of immediate negative and positive existence despite their different stresses. However, it seems that Jones wants to express the negativity more forcefully, hence his use of the 'tē'. 'Tē' in the phrase 'Kotahi-tē-kī' establishes the importance of the general paradox that exists with matter, because it engraves on existence the reality of nothingness; it sets the scene for a critical gaze on our part that implements a reading of things as both materially positive and negative; and to the extent that it speaks about the material existence of the unstated, it declares that within all human and non-human thought and speech lies the particularly imperceptible (not-apparent) All. Peng, Spencer-Rodgers and Nian identify the importance of that world-constituted interpretation when they state, from a Taoist perspective, that:

> The notion of non-duality refers to the belief that 'matter is spirit' and that 'spirit is matter.' The Tao is at once the void and all matter that confronts us. If we say, 'it is the void,' we are claiming that it is not matter, which in fact it also is. Thus, to understand the void, we must also understand matter.
>
> *(2006: 250)*

Reflecting the ontological designation/engraving of nothingness, those authors locate our comprehension of things within a morass of presence and absence, clarity and obscurity. Tē in its own right hence lends its non-foundational foundation to the world: in Māori thought it defines the eternally unfathomable 'Papa' (ground) (Mika 2017a; 2017b) of existence.

The resplendence that nothingness establishes within Māori thought also comes to the fore in the revoked item itself, or the term-entity that follows the 'tē'. I surmise that, in a particular way that seems oppositional, the voided thing gives rise to things through its positivity and voidness. 'Kī', as Jones has identified, is not yet spoken or thought. Yet like all other things it retains, its own manner of worldedness, has its own comportment with the rest of the world. Thus, thinking with the de-positived item is to be pushed into what Deleuze and Guattari call the:

> Supreme act of philosophy [by which we are] not so much to think *THE* plane of immanence as to show that it is there, unthought in every plane, and to think it in this way as the outside and inside of thought, as the not-external outside and the not-internal inside.
>
> *(1994: 59–60)*

Kī suggests a disclosure of the world by which we are simultaneously that world. It refers to the revealing or articulation of the world, where we do not so much describe nothingness as show it in our thinking. It refers to the revealing or articulation of the world in its reality, as its total worldedness. We are thrown into an experience of nothingness as both constitutive of and unleashing from all other things, including ourselves and our thinking. This act of thinking, in turn, returns to the specific, explicit message of Jones' phrase if it is taken literally: tē kī has something to do with thought. For Jones, from ancient times there has been an ancient representation that is not made (but our discussion on nothingness also signals the presence of that saying), and the un-thought of the thought, or the unsaying of the said, is equally as important as what we today would call 'a final product of thought'.

What we are confronted with here, in a general sense, is the undeniable fact of the world. Deleuze and Guattari, referring to Spinoza's resistance to transcendence, describe the immanence of the world as inducing "vertigo" (1994: 48) and, for Māori, his term's relevance sits with the facticity that comes with our own term 'whakapapa'. To draw a link between whakapapa and the world-disclosure of 'ki': whakapapa insists that we are within/one with all other things in the world. Kī on its own holds fascinating possibilities for its notion of *fullness* or the state of being replete. Although Pei Te Hurinui Jones does not discuss this other meaning of the term, it fits with the proposition that the world exists within any apparently single object. In awkward English, it represents the always-already-replete-world (in other words, we are forever constituted by/constituting primordial entities). Kī relates to this general fact of constitution because, if the world discloses an aspect of itself and its world, we may apprehend it but only *as* that full world, not from above it (transcendence). That ancient proclamation of 'tē kī' finds its expression in other Māori terms such as 'ira' by which a thing presents itself as 'ira!' (a Māori way of saying 'there is'), disclosing itself-as-world in its exclamatory (vertiginous) way (Mika 2015), yet despite its overwhelming facticity it withholds its totality, perhaps leaving us even more overwhelmed.

To reiterate: whakaaro must then determine an item in its unobliterating nothingness, accounting for the imperceptible, but not from the perspective of superior act of thought that Western convention seeks to force us to enact. Our theorising is not fully related to the *theoria* of dominant Western thought, which privileges the clinical gaze at things in the world (McNeill 1999), but instead it aims to incorporate the self into the assertions made about the world – although this may be an ambitious task in a colonised era that seeks to distance the self from the object of his/her thinking.

Revoking through nothingness: 'My ancestors are always present'

It could be this complex designation of the self by the world, including by Te Kore, that the speculative Māori student I spoke of earlier wants to honour in her statements and, indeed, as a central mode of critique. The complete interrelationship between metaphysical entities in Māori philosophy (Kent 2011) would insist that our current turn to the clarity of Western logic is not for all Māori. To recap: so far, we have the one primeval act of speech or thought that is paradoxically un-thought or un-spoken. The world discloses itself ('ki') through the fact of its existence but also its negating ('tē'). When we encounter a thing, it is overwhelming in its possibilities, as it is a phenomenon of that world-disclosure. It engages us as world and makes itself partly perceptible to us in that vein. This world constitution-disclosure is therefore not especially concerned with the certainty of the human self, despite the moments of clarity that we have about particular phenomena.

Against this philosophical backdrop sits a concrete world. Both need to be synthesised because, as Raju notes:

> A true and workable philosophy must give equal recognition to the two dimensions of man's being, the inward and the outward. Overemphasis on inwardness disables man from being active, and overemphasis on outwardness disconnects him from his spiritual essence, without which his activity becomes aimless.
>
> *(1954: 213)*

We can return here to the original worry of the Māori student, whose worldview is threatened by the attempt of her teacher to pare back illogic. For the student, the focus in Western logic is outwards, to the extent that s/he is forced to look *upon* the world as a separate entity. In that light, formal Western logic has its own origins but is established as feasible in its own right, ahistorical. In many respects, it does not reflect the inwardness that Raju advocates. That is, its self-evidence establishes itself as valid. The teacher challenging the Māori student's assertion that her ancestors are always present also does not have to recount the full Western genealogy of that apparently truthful mode of thought, starting with Socrates and formalised by Plato and Aristotle.

A dialogic example, involving student and teacher, of what I have discussed above could be the following:

Māori speculative student: my ancestors are always present
Clarity logician: how can you be certain?

Māori speculative student: we all have ancestors – and they have us. Actually, 'ancestors' is a wrongful translation of our 'tūpuna' because it immediately places the world within linear time. The word 'ancestors' has as its materiality the entity of 'beforeness'. It suggests that they've come and gone.

Now, you asked me 'how can I be certain?' I want to ask you about your use of 'to be' there. You imply that I can be certain. How can we ever be certain, given that we all comprise other things which are beyond our comprehension?

Clarity logician: We can't be certain of much else, but we can be certain of the statements we make if we use particular clarifying tools.

Māori speculative student: But again, you're assuming a kind of existence by saying that we can or can't 'be'. It seems that 'to be' assumes that something is to the fore. But in the context of our ancient philosophy, we can't say 'to be'. And if we did want to infer that something 'is', then we would immediately have to infer equally its lack of being or its negativity and also its thorough manifestation with the world. It therefore no longer really 'is' in the sense that you want it to be.

The disposition you mention – certainty – is also constituted by all other things. Certainty is itself an entity. There is therefore no full certainty *in itself*, even if we feel certain.

Clarity logician: to go back to your problem with 'ancestors', though: aren't you proposing something about them that is distinct from all other things in the world, because you are in fact signifying them?

Māori speculative student: what is your philosophy of language? It seems to assume that a thing, such as an ancestor, has its fixed category. But while you try to segment 'ancestor' off, 'ancestor' has its own way of being that breaks away from those categories. So does 'certain', for that matter. We have to acknowledge that forceful nature of entities in our ways of describing things.

Clarity logician: So if 'ancestors' aren't entities that have gone before, what are they?

Māori speculative student: Again, you default to the use of 'to be' in your question – the 'are', in this case. But I'll use that way of speaking too, so that we're sort of on the same page. 'Ancestors' are only 'before' in the sense of Western linear time. Like all other things in the world, though, ancestors, like language (and therefore the term 'ancestor'), irrupt within the world in their own way but as the world.

Clarity logician: doesn't that make them highly 'there', though? And doesn't that mean you'd need the verb 'to be', to denote their being?

Māori speculative student: No. Because ancestors like all other things are so thoroughly implicated with the entire world that their being is better defined as 'always-already' of the world. And with this 'always-already' comes, from a Māori perspective, a kind of destabilised self. The self is vulnerable – always, even when he or she is making apparently truthful statements.

I am familiar with your version of truth. You try to identify truth on the basis of lack of emotion. But all things designate themselves with the fullness of the world and cause us to ponder our own limitations. Otherwise we would truly be superior to all other things in the world.

I suspect even your initial question – how can you be certain? – denotes a kind of fear or desire. From our perspective, pretending otherwise is a bad faith.

Clarity logician: How?

Māori speculative student: Elation, worry, humour, sadness, anger – all give rise to thought, infuse it. For that reason, Māori representations of the world may prefer to reference emotion's insistence within any kind of Māori 'critical' thinking. Emotion is the impetus for whakaaro.

You want to advocate for truth. That is a desire. There is also a fear, or at least a distrust, of untruth with your questioning. Although fear and desire seem to not be there, they are, along with the rest of their relations. You are hence bound up, in a bodily sense (but we would say through whakapapa) by the statements you make – as I am. My philosophy allows me to be more honest about that.

So, to begin with I asked 'my ancestors are always present'. But perhaps I should have prefaced it with the following:

'The primordial speech is that of the world which constitutes me; I am one instance of the world, in all its hidden and revealed fullness. My utterances are composed of entities that have their world-constituted essence'. This sets the scene for a more honest representation, at least as far as possible in English, of my wording for 'my ancestors are always present', which I'd now put in this way:

'Those who 'resolutely-vault-forth-as-world' retreat within the world's worlded revocation'.

I've done a few things here. I've rejected the usual meaning of the word 'ancestor' that I mentioned earlier for a more inventive etymological idea of 'tūpuna'[2] (which is normally translated as 'ancestor'). It now no longer simply depicts something that went *before*; it summons the complete, unrelenting phenomenon of all things in the world that arise and constitute it. Thus, incidentally, it's not just humans that are ancestors. More importantly, our ancestors are the world and they are consigned to that which exists before our current understanding. They take on their 'not-being' with that first primordial undoing.

Nothingness is then also 'that which resolutely vaults forth as world'. To honour nothingness, we can answer as if things are negatively engraved; in a manner that de-emphasises the human self; that allows a thing to incandesce with the world and its invisible aspects; that conveys the world as if full; that acknowledges the simultaneity of absence and presence and thus does away with sequential time.

It turns out that your usual language for description – 'my ancestors are always present' – is inadequate for our thinking. I adopted this phrasing, which just shows that the formal English we have recourse to is colonised as far as we're concerned. I had to revise that phrasing.

That's probably as close as I can get to replying to your initial question 'how can you be certain?'

Nothingness' last say: The revocation of the resolutely-vaulting-forth

The teacher is probably frustrated by this stage and there is something about his certainty that resounds with Foucault's experience with the Chinese taxonomies: nothingness appears to have dethroned the self's determined attitude towards an idea. It is the dissipation of their certainty that is at stake here. Similarly, the entities of Māori metaphysics may not be all about solemn and pious reverence. It is true that laughter dispels certainty in Māori contexts. Laughter would, I suspect, be the student's lot at this stage. Depending on her personality, she could be walking away from the teacher, amused at having demolished the latter's conviction: she 'shattered the latter'. Much of her argument was implausible for formal logic but makes sense in a Māori context. However, it's not all one-way, because the dialogue has dishevelled the student too. Her argument, to an extent, has had a bad hair day – not just through the use of her term 'ancestor' but by any assumption that she had dealt with the issue. Of course, if she weaved in and out between self-certainty and vulnerability, then any laughter might direct itself more at the terrain of her own assumptions, as it had done with Foucault. In New Zealand we have a slang – 'cracking up' – for gales of laughter: thus, 'they cracked up at her joke'. Somewhat similar to the more widespread saying 'you slay me with your humour' or even 'you vanquish me', it also connotes the rupture of a smooth surface, the breaking down or disintegration of a level aesthetic, or simply the negativing of a previous appearance. Laughter may well be another mouthpiece of Te Kore.

Philosophy – no less Māori philosophy – seductively encourages a thinker to make a declaration about a state of affairs. Yet "[p]hilosophers ever desire to affirm, to maintain, to preserve, in short to bring into being (be it even by baptizing it with the pompous name of 'nothingness') that which laughter in a split second squanders, volatilizes" (Borch-Jacobsen 1987: 743). While thinking about nothingness, I had an experience that seems appropriate for our current thinking of laughter with Te Kore. On the road with an Indigenous friend and scholar (who shall remain nameless but she knows who she is), a discussion arose about Western chronological time. As is so often the case with us, talk soon turned to something ridiculous: we started to list songs that have chronology as their theme. I seem to recall us mentioning the song 'In the Year 2525' by Zager and Evans in the late 1960s, with its lugubrious doomsday scenario. 'Minute by Minute' by the Doobie Brothers might have been another unfortunate victim. We then talked about setting up a Chronology Spotify playlist and populating it with those and other similar songs – this is the sort of abyss(mal) thing that amuses us. Cracking up at the silliness of chronology-within-song, the discussion for some reason changed to whether research is necessarily chronological or not. Then suddenly a not inconsiderable disagreement erupted between us about (from memory) whether we should ever engage with research or not, due to its fundamental reliance on chronology. It was as if laughter had laughed itself out of existence, withdrawing itself for the time being. With my foot forcing the pedal down as far as possible and her drawing herself up to her formidable height in the passenger seat, we made our way home, arguing most of the way. I do remember at some point during a pregnant silence choosing a Spotify playlist of mine – titled 'Cool' – and the first song that the shuffle option chose was 'The Carnival is Over' by The Seekers. Whether indeed cool or not, the significance of that song impacts on me only now: not only did it play at laughter's decline (a sort of carnival was over), but its title is deeply, unreassuringly *chronological*.

Nothingness has its own forcefulness, and when it breaks down clarity it can upturn everyday events, making them funny, furious or unpalatable. For nothingness, the Carnival is never over. For my friend and me, it had the last laugh, as it always seems to.

Notes

1 In this chapter, I use various terms for Te Kore, including: nothingness, void, negative. There are associated qualities associated with these terms, including uncertainty, mystery, negatived. I also use several terms to describe Western tangibility, such as positivity; high presence.

2 This etymological approach to *tupuna* has been discussed before (see Mika 2014), in the context of Heidegger's later thinking (although not limited to that – he merely provides one 'jump' of many for whakaaro). The language the student uses here aims to demonstrate itself as *materially* constituted by nothingness in a more determined way than Mika's article.

References

Borch-Jacobsen, M. (1987). 'The laughter of being', *MLN*, vol 102, no 4: 737–60.

Deleuze, G. and Guattari, F. (1994). *What Is Philosophy?* Columbia University Press: New York.

Foucault, M. (2002). *The Order of Things: An Archaeology of the Human Sciences.* Routledge: London.

Goetzfridt, N. (1995). *Indigenous Literature of Oceania: A Survey of Criticism and Interpretation.* Greenwood Publishing Group: London.

Harper, D. (2018a). 'World'. Available: https://www.etymonline.com/word/world, accessed 14 May 2020.

Harper, D. (2018b). 'Revoke'. Available: https://www.etymonline.com/word/revoke, accessed 14 May 2020.

Kaplan, L. (1994). 'Teaching intellectual autonomy: The failure of the critical thinking movement', in K. Waters (ed.) *Re-Thinking Reason: New Perspectives in Critical Thinking.* State University of New York Press: Albany, NY, 205–220.

Kent, S. (2011). *The Connected Space of Māori Governance: Towards an Indigenous Conceptual Understanding.* PhD thesis, Lincoln University Te Whare Wānanga o Aoraki.

Lau, J. (2011). *An Introduction to Critical Thinking and Clarity: Think More, Think Better.* John Wiley & Sons: Toronto, ON.

Madhucchanda, S. (2010). *An Introduction to Critical Thinking.* Pearson: Delhi.

Marsden, M. (2003). *The Woven Universe: Selected Writings of Rev. Maori Marsden.* Estate of Rev. Maori Marsden: Otaki.

McNeill, W. (1999). *The Glance of the Eye: Heidegger, Aristotle, and the Ends of Theory.* State University of New York Press: Albany, NY.

Mika, C. (2014). 'The enowning of thought and whakapapa: Heidegger's fourfold', *Review of Contemporary Philosophy*, vol 13: 48–60.

Mika, C. (2015). 'The co-existence of self and thing through "ira": A Māori phenomenology', *Journal of Aesthetics and Phenomenology*, vol 2, no 1: 93–112.

Mika, C. (2016). 'A counter-colonial speculation on Elizabeth Rata's –ism', *Online Journal of World Philosophies*, vol 1, no 1: 1–12.

Mika, C. (2017a). 'A term's irruption and a possibility for response: A Māori glance at "epistemology"', in E. McKinley and L. Smith (eds.) *Handbook of Indigenous Education.* Springer: Dordrecht, 1–19.

Mika, C. (2017b). *Indigenous Education and the Metaphysics of Presence: A Worlded Philosophy.* Routledge: Oxon.

Nepia, M. (2012). *Te Kore: Exploring the Māori Concept of Void.* PhD thesis, University of Technology: Auckland.

Peng, K., Spencer-Rodgers, J., and Nian, Z. (2006). 'Naïve dialecticism and the Tao of Chinese thought', in U. Kim, K. Yang, and K. Hwang (eds.) *Indigenous and Cultural Psychology: Understanding People in Context.* Springer: New York, 247–262.

Raju, P.T. (1954). 'The concept of the spiritual in Indian thought', *Philosophy East and West* vol 4, no 3: 195–213.

Schrag, C. (1992). *The Resources of Rationality: A Response to the Postmodern Challenge.* Indiana University Press: Indianapolis, IN.

Seung-hwan, L. (2004). *A Typography of Confucian Discourse: Politico-Philosophical Reflections on Confucian Discourse Since Modernity* (J. Song and L. Seung-hwan, trans.). Homa & Sekey: Paramus, NJ.

Smith, C. and Jenkins, K. (1997). 'Colonising airspace', in L. Pihama and C. Smith (eds.) *Cultural and Intellectual Property Rights Economics, Politics & Colonisation Vol 2.* International Research Institute for Māori and Indigenous Education (IRI), University of Auckland: Auckland, 12–15.

Te Ruki, G. (2010). *Nā wai ngā pokapoka o te ahi marae i whakarite, engari, mā wai āpōpō? Who Kept the Embers of the Home Fires Burning, and Who Will Tomorrow?* Masters thesis, Auckland University of Technology.

Warrior, C. (2015). *Baring the Windigo's Teeth: The Fearsome Figure in Native American Narratives.* PhD thesis, University of Washington.

White, E. and Mika, C. (2013). 'Coming of age? Infants and toddlers in ECE', in J. Nuttall (ed.) *Weaving Te Whāriki: Aotearoa New Zealand's Early Childhood Curriculum Document in Theory and Practice.* NZCER Press: Wellington, 93–114.

16

Vital earth/vibrant earthworks/ living earthworks vocabularies

Chadwick Allen

For thousands of years, mounds, embankments, and other earthworks were dreamed, planned, and built; occupied, used, and maintained; abandoned, reoccupied, and reused; redreamed, rebuilt, and repurposed by Indigenous peoples living and traveling along the rivers and other waterways that connect the eastern half of the North American continent into a vast network – from what is now Louisiana in the south to what is now Ontario in the north. During that long tenure, mounds, embankments, and other earthworks were also studied, contemplated, and discussed by Indigenous intellectuals, by political and spiritual leaders, by builders, users, and ordinary citizens. Not only empirical research but theoretical reflection was necessarily grounded in Indigenous languages and communities, conducted through Indigenous methodologies. For the past 200 years, however, energy devoted to understanding the complexity of these built environments and their multiple potential meanings and uses has been organised by predominantly non-Native archaeologists, anthropologists, and historians, both amateur and professional, and within predominantly non-Native languages, epistemologies, and systems of ethics. In this way, like so much of Indigenous life and culture, earthworks research has been disconnected from the foundations of Indigenous inquiry. The majority of this non-Native research has restricted its investigations to questions about the physical construction of earthworks within specific chronologies (these researchers repeatedly ask not only *who* built the mounds, but *how* they were built, *when*, and whether within briefer or longer periods of time) and to questions about the siting of earthworks within specific geographies (*where* they were built, but also *why* they were built in certain ways at certain times and in certain locations). The organisation and control of this work by non-Native researchers and institutions, moreover, has been – and continues to be – bolstered by the colonial dislocations and the often forced relocations of the descendants of the Indigenous peoples who built the mounds.

Although the scholarly fields of archaeology, anthropology, and history have begun to expand the scope of their interests and the range of their interlocutors, including an increased attention to consulting with Indigenous communities, relatively little of this research has been devoted to understanding – or imagining – the effects of earthworks on people: those who came together to plan and build individual mounds or embankments or to construct multi-structure complexes and expansive cities; those who lived among earthworks permanently or seasonally; those who visited sites, centres, and cities for trade or special events; those who embarked on sacred pilgrimage to important burials or to potent effigies perhaps once in a lifetime. Relatively few researchers have asked what it might have meant to live, work, and play, to celebrate and mourn, in the presence of – and in relation to – earthworks. And relatively few have asked what it might have meant to gather at these sites for ceremony or debate, for astronomical observations, for sporting events and games, for the securing of marriages and other forms of social and political alliance, for artistic and intellectual exchange, for regular upkeep, maintenance, and repair. In fact, most research that engages the potential 'experiential' meaning of earthworks, as opposed to their potential 'referential' or symbolic meaning, focuses on the embodied experience of building the mounds, basket by 50-pound basket, rather than on the embodied experience of living among, visiting, or contemplating one's relationship to these structures.[1] Even less research has considered what those experiences might mean for Indigenous peoples living in the present or in the future.

Our understanding of earthworks and both their original and ongoing significance has been limited, in other words, by the methodologies, discourses, and colonial assumptions of standard archaeological, anthropological, and historical practice. Part of that limitation has been the discursive severing of the planners, builders, and first users of the mounds, who lived hundreds or thousands of years ago, from historical and, especially, contemporary Indigenous peoples of North America.[2] The idea of continuous genealogies and clear links from the distant past of earthworks planning, construction, and original use to the contemporary period of Indigenous appreciation, reclamation, repatriation, and potential reactivation of earthworks has proven too problematic for dominant archaeological, anthropological, and historical communities, as well as for a host of other non-Native communities that wish to claim kinship with or assert authority over the mounds, such as Indian hobbyists, certain religious groups, and versions of the New Age movement.[3] Only rarely are Indigenous individuals, communities, or nations invited to contribute to dominant conversations about North American earthworks, their histories, their ongoing significance, their possible futures.

Projects designed within frameworks of critical Indigenous studies, which typically foreground ongoing Indigenous relationships to place, can offer productive alternatives. I am not trained as an archaeologist, anthropologist, or historian, and the concern of my recently completed book manuscript, *Earthworks Rising: Mound Building in Native Art, Literature, and Performance*, is not to engage the orthodox questions driving these dominant fields of inquiry. As a scholar of contemporary Native American and Indigenous literary and artistic self-representation, and as a person of Chickasaw descent, I engage the useful work of archaeologists, anthropologists, and historians – always with a critical eye – but my objective is to move beyond typical analyses of earthworks as sources of ethnographic data about so-called prehistoric peoples cut off from living Indigenous communities and nations. Instead, in line with Indigenous studies frameworks and in collaboration with Indigenous researchers, I investigate contemporary Native American artistic, literary, and performative engagements with earthworks and earthworks principles.[4] Based on analyses of these contemporary engagements, I speculate about how earthworks themselves might be understood as forms of Indigenous knowledge still relevant in the present and central to Indigenous futures. In developing such speculations, I begin with the idea that earthworks can be understood as a form of Indigenous 'writing'. Following the lead of Indigenous artists and intellectuals, I employ a definition of writing expansive enough to include any form of encoding knowledge in any medium, rather than a narrow definition that would apply exclusively to alphabetic, syllabic, logographic, and other sound- or speech-based scripts.[5] Not everyone will agree with this usage. But my hope is that even those who wish to restrict the term *writing* only to alphabetic, syllabic, and logographic scripts will join me and other researchers working from critical Indigenous studies perspectives to pose a central question: How might earthworks be understood as systems of signs arranged into systematic patterns, as systematic encodings of knowledge produced through Indigenous technologies and practices?

My first contribution to understanding how the work of contemporary Native American artists, writers, and performers re-engages earthworks and earthworks principles was prompted by my early attempts to analyse how these contemporary productions – novels, poems, essays, performance pieces, and works of visual and installation art – make meaning at the level of their underlying *structures* as well as at the level of their explicit commentary and themes.[6] Re-viewing earthworks through the lens of these contemporary productions, I observed that mounds do not present a form of writing knowledge *on* the land, a form of marking or *inscribing* surfaces, as some of my colleagues were beginning to suggest more than a decade ago.[7] Rather, mounds present a form of layering carefully selected rocks and soils into scripts that rise *above* the earth's surface, adding to, reforming, and altering the landscape. Earthworks create raised scripts of platform, conical, linear, ridgetop, and, perhaps most spectacularly, geometric and effigy 'mounds'. This is encoded knowledge presented as scripts raised from 'borrowed' rock and soil, and thus a form of writing literally *through the medium* of the land itself. The observation felt like a revelation; I realise now, though, it was but the beginning of understanding. Likening earthworks to writing, even within the broadest of definitions, takes us only so far toward understanding diverse earthworks in themselves and in their relationships to builders, original users, and later users and caretakers, let alone toward understanding how Native artists, writers, performers, and communities engage earthworks and earthworks principles in contemporary productions.

Individual earthworks are but individual components within complex built environments that indicate multiple forms of planning and physical manipulation. This includes the 'borrowing' and transportation of particular rocks and soils from one location to another to facilitate the piling, heaping, and sculpting of particular mounds and embankments. But it also includes the infilling and levelling of adjacent plazas or the interiors of walled enclosures, and the construction of raised causeways through marshes, wetlands, or other low-lying areas. All of these activities took place on a monumental scale, and often within expansive networks of interrelated sites, complexes, centres, and cities.[8] The forms of these Indigenous built environments encode knowledge, but their 'reading' requires more – or something different – than alphabetic, syllabic, logographic, or other semiotic deciphering. Earthworks and earthworks complexes are not simply visually apprehended, understood in the way we understand various kinds of models and diagrams. They are neither idealised abstractions of coordinates drawn on maps nor geometric figures plotted on graph paper. Their reading, as I demonstrate across the chapters of my manuscript, requires methodologies that are embodied and performative: walking specific sites in order to 'see' them, making physical contact with mounds and embankments, placing our human bodies in relation to bodies of earth.[9] Moreover, earthworks and earthworks complexes are not simply inert matter – dead physical material appropriate for standard archaeological methods of stratigraphy and taxonomy. From many Indigenous perspectives, earthworks are embodied material and earthworks are animate. Assembled from vital earth, during their planning, construction, and use earthworks are imbued with social, psychic, and spiritual power that humans encounter physically, socially, and spiritually, and through which humans encounter each other as well as other-than-human beings and forces.

I have more to say about these complex issues of the embodied and animate materiality of earthworks. For this brief chapter, I focus on a dimension I call 'living earthworks vocabularies'. Before moving to that discussion, however, I should state why I do not engage the currently fashionable discourse of the so-called new materialisms, which similarly describe understandings of physical matter as 'lively' and 'agentive'. Usually contextualised as part of a broader 'ontological turn' within Continental philosophy and within Anglo-American critical theory, the new materialisms are seen as responding to the earlier 'linguistic turn' of poststructuralism and to the predominant focus on human subjectivity within recent research in the social sciences. The new materialisms stress, instead, the ways in which concrete, physical matter remains a defining component of events, lives, and worlds, not only for humans but also for other-than-humans. In this way, the new materialisms intersect eco-criticism and philosophical post-humanism, the environmental humanities, and animal studies. In their 2015 guide *Place in Research: Theory, Methodology, and Methods*, social science researchers Eve Tuck (Unangax) and Marcia McKenzie characterise the "new materialist turn" as primarily concerned with "how matter comes to matter" across a range of inquiries and analyses (Tuck and McKenzie 2015: 15). And in their 2013 essay *Beyond the Mirror: Indigenous Ecologies and 'New Materialism' in Contemporary Art*, art historians Jessica Horton and Janet Berlo describe how the new materialisms "share a basic conviction that matter – whether in the forest or in the lab – has agency, can move, act, assume volition, and even enjoy degrees of intelligence often assumed to be the unique domain of human subjectivity" (Horton and Berlo 2013: 17). But, as Tuck and McKenzie acknowledge and as Horton and Berlo explain in detail – and as readers of this volume will likely already be aware – sustaining the fiction of the 'newness' of the new materialisms depends on the foregrounding of European- and Anglo-American-derived epistemologies and perspectives and on the continued erasure of relevant Indigenous epistemologies and perspectives. "Indigenous scholars and scholars of the indigenous", Horton and Berlo note:

> will attest to the survival of alternative intellectual traditions in which the liveliness of matter is grasped as quite ordinary, both inside, and at the fringes of, European modernity. Once we take indigenous worldviews into account, the 'new materialisms' are no longer new.
> *(Horton and Berlo 2013: 18)*

A range of Indigenous and Indigenous studies scholars, working across multiple disciplines, offer related critiques and corrections. In an essay published in 2015, for instance, the noted Dakota social scientist Kim Tallbear states:

> But the field [of new materialisms] has starting points that only partially contain indigenous standpoints. First of all, indigenous peoples have never forgotten that nonhumans are agential beings engaged in social relations that profoundly shape human lives. In addition, for many indigenous peoples, their nonhuman others may not be understood in even critical Western frameworks as *living*. 'Objects' and 'forces' such as stones, thunder, or stars are known within our ontologies to be sentient and knowing persons.
> *(Tallbear 2015: 234)[10]*

Earthworks are among the categories construed as inanimate 'objects' within non-Native discourses but often function as living beings and agentive forces within Indigenous understandings.

A central Indigenous premise about the vitality of ancient earthworks is that it was not only selected rocks and soils that were carefully layered in the building of these structures. Words were spoken and chanted, songs were sung, dances were danced *into* earth during the preparation of carefully chosen sites for construction, during the preparation of soils carefully selected and then carefully gathered as materials for building. Words were spoken and chanted, songs were sung, and dances were danced *into* earth once again during mound construction, during the subsequent ceremony, during regular upkeep, maintenance, and renewal. In these ways, layers of packed rocks and soils were imbued with the power of sacred discourse, the energy of rhythmic movement. It is this communal power and energy that prepared the earth and helped build the mounds. It is this communal power and energy that continues to sustain their extant remains, their remnants and traces.

A sense of this communal power is conveyed in the 2001 novel *Shell Shaker* by Choctaw writer and intellectual LeAnne Howe. At a critical moment in the plot, one of the contemporary Choctaw characters living in southeastern Oklahoma – where the Choctaw were removed in the 1830s – experiences a vision of the construction of the Nanih Waiya, a large earthen platform the Choctaw consider their Mother Mound. In the elder's vision, the platform is constructed in what is now northern Mississippi in a highly coordinated collaboration among ancestors of the Choctaw, their descendants, and the Earth herself, a collaboration that is simultaneously ancient and ongoing. Multiple generations from the distant past to the present "open Mother Earth's beautiful body"; in response, "Mother Earth turns herself inside out and a gigantic platform mound emerges out of the ground". Working together, the multi-generational human community and the agentive Earth produce a "sacred ovulation", a "gift" for the future – the Nanih Waiya (Howe 2001: 159).

But what do I mean by 'living earthworks vocabularies'? That question also leads to southern Oklahoma, where not only the Choctaw but their close relatives the Chickasaw and other Southeastern nations were removed in the 1830s, and where the Chickasaw Cultural Centre opened outside the town of Sulphur in 2010. The Centre's 184-acre campus sits adjacent to the renowned Chickasaw National Recreation Area, south of Ada, the contemporary seat of government for the Chickasaw Nation. The Centre's beautiful grounds and extensive facilities boast state-of-the-art historical and cultural exhibits, a well-equipped research centre and archive, conference space, a high-tech theatre, an art gallery, indoor and outdoor performance spaces, a large pond and water pavilion, an honour garden marking the achievements of inductees to the Chickasaw Hall of Fame, two working vegetable gardens, two well-stocked gift shops, and a café, as well as a large staff of Chickasaw citizens who serve as knowledgeable interpreters of Chickasaw history and *living* culture.[11] In addition, the Nation has reconstructed a Chikasha Inchokka', a Southeastern-style village surrounded by a wood stockade. This 'traditional' village can be viewed aerially, from a height of three stories, standing on the Sky Bridge adjacent to the main exhibit hall. Visitors are not limited to this bird's eye view, however; they can also walk *into* the village to explore a large council house, examples of summer and winter family houses, a corn crib, gardens, a ceremonial arena with a central fire pit flanked by brush arbours, and a stickball court. The village's most impressive structure, but perhaps also its most subtle, is a full-scale replica of a Southeastern earthwork: a ceremonial platform mound newly constructed by the Nation on behalf of Chickasaw and other Southeastern peoples.[12]

The campus as a whole has been designed to enable immersive experiences. In the Chikasha Poya Exhibit Centre, a series of brief videos running at multiple viewing stations orient visitors to aspects of Chickasaw landscapes and histories (Chikasha Poya translates as "We are Chickasaw!"). Specific exhibits encourage visitors to handle material objects, practice basic Chickasaw vocabulary, listen to oral storytelling, or contemplate the veracity of different forms of historical evidence – a diary entry written by a European visiting the Southeast, for example, compared to a Chickasaw map painted on a tanned deer hide. After learning about thousands of years of changing life in the homeland, visitors are guided along a difficult, upward-slanting path representing the 1830s forced Removal to the Indian Territory, now Oklahoma, then invited to participate in the renewing, counter-clockwise movement of a stomp dance they can perform in community and around the central fire through an interactive holographic display. At the Aaimpa' Café, visitors can taste pashofa (corn soup) and highly-prized grape dumplings. At the Chikasha Inchokka', they can enter and explore houses, try their hand at stickball and other games, watch a live performance of a stomp dance around the central fire while sitting beneath the shade of brush arbours, and walk the circumference of an actual mound.

The contemporary earthwork is but one component within a broader Chickasaw assertion of political, cultural, artistic, and intellectual sovereignty. The Chickasaw Nation is actively asserting control over how its history is written and interpreted, in printed books in multiple genres published by the Chickasaw Press, in videos and digital media produced through Chickasaw TV and posted online, and in a variety of built environments – from the deep past to the present and forward into the future.[13] To build an earthwork is literally to move and reshape earth to align with surrounding waterways, with other natural features in the landscape, with the sky-world above. But to build an earthwork is also to move and reshape earth to align with the symbolic systems that undergird, express, and shape *living* cultures. As forms of spatialised knowledge – as forms of Indigenous writing – earthworks intersect traditions of place naming and place mapping, intersect traditions of rhythmic sound and choreographed movement, intersect traditions of visual and tactile encoding, intersect traditions of drawn, painted, and incised marks on multiple surfaces. They serve as evocative mnemonics that help transfer communal memory across time.[14] At the Chickasaw Cultural Centre, signage posted in the Chikasha Poya Exhibit Hall, at the Sky Bridge overlooking the Chikasha Inchokka', and at points along the periphery of the reconstructed platform mound inform Native and non-Native visitors alike – and remind Chickasaw citizens and descendants in particular – that while earthworks are part of very old Southeastern cultures, they are also part of *living* vocabularies and worldviews. They represent ways of understanding and interacting with land and place that, despite violent attack and forced removal, have not only survived but incited renewal.[15]

The specific earthworks vocabularies on display at the Centre are suggestive of the multiple ways Southeastern peoples have understood mounds and mound principles in the past, but also of the multiple ways they continue to develop their understandings in the present.[16] Over repeated visits, I became fascinated by these vocabularies and, more precisely, by how they create a conversation – a ritual call-and-response – between the language used in the signage at the Chikasha Inchokka' Traditional Village and the language used in the signage in the Chikasha Poya Exhibit Centre. At the Chikasha Inchokka', near the platform mound, a prominent sign reads:

> This mound, or *aayampo' chaaha'*, is a reconstruction of a precontact platform mound or 'temple mound'. The mounds were built by our Chickasaw ancestors working together, carrying individual baskets of dirt from nearby. Symbolic colors of clay such as red and white were sometimes used. Our Chickasaw ancestors living in the 1700s referred to the mounds as *aayampo' chaaha'*, *aayampo'* then meaning 'crockery' or 'pottery', *chaaha'* meaning 'to be tall', suggesting that our ancestors thought mounds resembled inverted pots. Today, speakers of *Chikashshanompa'* (the Chickasaw language) might call mounds *onchaba chaaha'*, meaning 'tall hill'.

The brief account, intended for a public audience, offers a surprisingly sophisticated lesson in Chickasaw historical linguistics: the vocabulary used to describe mounds has shifted over time (from the noun *aayampo'* [pottery] to the noun *onchaba* [hill]), but it has also maintained some continuity (in the consistent use of the adjective *chaaha'* [tall]). Moreover, the account's reference to ancestors living in the 1700s provides a clue about the likely sources of this knowledge, namely, the presence of French and English traders, who lived among the Chickasaw and their neighbours beginning in the early 18th century and who recorded Southeastern vocabularies in their journals and other writings. Along with subsequent non-Native works, such as word lists, grammars, and dictionaries compiled by American missionaries, government agents, and settlers in the 19th century, these early records have become key sources for the Nation that augment the knowledge that remains within Indigenous oral, graphic, and other traditions. And finally, the older phrase used for mounds, *aayampo' chaaha'* (written here using a modern orthography), is described as based primarily in mimesis. The account articulates a specific theory of meaning-making: contemporary Chickasaw think their ancestors thought the shapes of the mounds bore a physical resemblance to the shapes of inverted pots.

Unlike the signage posted at the Chikasha Inchokka', which emphasises this older earthworks vocabulary, the signage posted in the Chikasha Poya Exhibit Centre emphasises a vocabulary that is more contemporary. This signage also shifts emphasis from the mounds and their material forms to the expansive reach of the pre-contact Chickasaw homeland and to the expansive temporality of what is today the Chickasaw Nation. Under the tripartite heading "A Great Civilization/*Moundbuilders*/onchaba ikbi'", a prominent sign reads, in two parts:

> Our ancestors were *onchaba ikbi'*, the moundbuilders of the Mississippi and Ohio river valleys. Our territory stretched from the Midwest, to New England, and through the southeastern United States. Mounds were constructed from 500 to over 2,000 years ago in this region.
>
> ###
>
> In our tradition, the Chickasaws, as well as dozens of tribes, are the direct descendants of Mississippian civilization, which was active from about AD 900 to 1700. The powerful and far-reaching Mississippian economic and political structure greatly influenced and shaped our culture.

One notes, immediately, the ways in which this signage contradicts typical archaeological, anthropological, and historical accounts. Written from an Indigenous perspective, the signage rejects the discourse of 'mystery' about what happened to Mississippian peoples and actively asserts the status of Mississippian 'civilisation'. Instead of the orthodox discourse of 'they were on their way to civilisation but did not quite get there' and 'nobody knows what became of them', visitors learn that the supposedly *missing* Mississippians continued to change over time, to develop over generations, evolving into new peoples like the Chikasha encountered by the Spanish in the 16th century and reforming into new nations like the Chickasaw the US government forcibly removed to Oklahoma in the 1830s. The image included as background for this sign is a piece of pottery – the *aayampo'* foregrounded in the prominent sign at the Chikasha Inchokka'. This *aayampo'* features multiple layers of curvilinear decorations in the emblematic colours black, red, and white. But the pot's round body and fluted neck bear little physical resemblance to a flat-topped ceremonial mound or 'tall hill', and thus the image appears to question the outdoor sign's assertion of mimesis.

Another prominent sign inside the Chikasha Poya Exhibit Centre bears the tripartite heading "Ancestral Ties/*Connecting with our homeland*/onchaba". Here emphasis is placed on how mounds were typically created not in isolation, but rather as part of 'towns and cities'. The account also emphasises how contemporary Chickasaw – despite their ancestors' forced removal from Southeastern sites and despite their own temporal distance from the traditions of large-scale mound building – continue to feel connected to these ancient structures. The primary parts of the sign read:

> There are many *onchaba* (mounds) and mound groups in the ancestral homeland of the Chickasaws. They were associated with towns and cities. The largest was Moundville.

Others include: Shiloh Mounds, Pinson Mounds, Ingomar Mounds, Wickliffe Mounds and Emerald Mound.

###

Some Chickasaws who have visited mounds sense a special feeling of kinship. For every site that remains, thousands have been destroyed.

In language that is scrupulously understated, the penultimate sentence articulates what is for many a highly personal experience. The sign is careful to present neither an unauthorised exposure of private Indigenous feelings nor a hyperbolic statement of New Age mysticism. It is the final sentence, however, despite similar restraint, that is especially poignant. Although the sentence conceals the agency of mound site destruction – this politeness is perhaps not inappropriate for an Indigenous cultural centre open to a mostly non-Native public – many readers will infer the agents implied. The background for this sign illustrates its primary themes by juxtaposing three distinct images. First, under the initial headings and set partially behind the language quoted above, there is a ghosted image of Mississippian-era pottery designs. To the right, beneath the third heading, there is a contemporary photograph of one of the prominent Southeastern sites mentioned in the account. And to its right is a large map of the eastern half of North America that marks prominent mound sites located across the Southeast and the Mississippi Valley.

The call-and-response elicited between the outdoor signage at the Chikasha Inchokka' Traditional Village, with its emphasis on *aayampo' chaaha'*, and the indoor signage in the Chikasha Poya Exhibit Centre, with its emphasis on *onchaba*, becomes more obvious when we take into account the scholarship of John Dyson, a non-Native historical linguist commissioned by the Chickasaw Nation to research and write *The Early Chickasaw Homeland*, published by the Chickasaw Press in 2014.[17] Dyson's research engages not only the early French, English, and subsequent American records of Chickasaw vocabularies, but also the earliest known records produced by the Spanish, including members of the de Soto exhibition in 1539–1542. Dyson (2014) places these multiple records within their comparative linguistic contexts, and his painstaking collations help him piece together a remarkably comprehensive account of Chickasaw life, social organisation, and history in the Southeastern homeland.

Although it is not his primary emphasis, Dyson's expansive investigation touches upon earthworks vocabularies. He writes, for instance:

The nineteenth-century geographer and ethnologist Henry Schoolcraft recorded that the Chickasaw tribe referred to prehistoric southeastern mounds as 'navels' (*ittalbish*), and John Swanton [another prominent anthropologist, folklorist, and linguist who worked across the end of the 19th century into the first half of the 20th century] also remarked that the Creek used the same terminology in their own language. Those mounds were obviously regarded by both the Chickasaw and the Creek as symbols of human birth.

(Dyson 2014: 28)

This aspect of mound symbolism intersects the signage adjacent to the reconstructed ceremonial mound at the Chikasha Inchokka'. Dyson continues:

The mound stood for the center of the earth in the same way that the navel represented the center of the maternal body. Yet it bears mentioning that the Chickasaw also referred to those prehistoric mounds as *ampo' chaaha'*, tall pottery vessels or clay urns which have long been associated with Southeastern burials, including urn interments in the traditional Chickasaw homeland.

(Dyson 2014: 28)

Dyson uses an older Chickasaw orthography, rendering *aayampo' chaaha'* as the more stream-lined *ampo' chaaha'*, similar to the closely related Choctaw *ampo chaha*. His research suggests that the phrasing may function differently than simple mimesis – or that it may function in one or more ways *in addition to* simple mimesis – expanding its potential to make meaning for multiple audiences. Rather than (or in addition to) recording a sense that the shapes of the mounds resemble the shapes of inverted pots, *aayampo' chaaha'* may (also) record a sense that the mounds represent – and perhaps function as – points of intersection for human birth (the mounds are symbolic navels) and human death (the mounds are symbolic clay urns used for interment) (Dyson 2014).[18]

Dyson's analysis provides a productive lens through which to review an earlier source of linguistic knowledge, Cyrus Byington's *A Dictionary of the Choctaw Language* (1915), which Choctaw and Chickasaw intellectuals continue to find useful despite its colonial provenance. The non-Native Reverend Byington, born in Massachusetts in 1793, worked as a Christian missionary among the Choctaw for nearly 50 years, beginning in 1819, almost two decades prior to their forced removal. Although Byington completed a first draft of a Choctaw grammar in 1834 and continued to revise this and related documents until his death in 1868, his dictionary was not published until 1915, when the manuscript was edited by the prominent non-Native anthropologists John Swanton, previously mentioned, and Henry Halbert.[19] Reading Byington through Dyson, we can note the following possibilities. The Chickasaw *aayampo' chaaha'*, or the Choctaw *ampo chaha*, can mean 'tall clay pot', as suggested on the signage at the Chikasha Inchokka'. But the phrase can also mean something more metaphorical or symbolic – or possibly more descriptive of the agentive force of the mounds – related to the idea that mounds stand at the profound intersections of human birth and death. As Byington (1915) records in his dictionary, the noun *ampo* can mean a bowl or pan, pottery more generally, or any kind of vessel. But *ampo* can also mean the specific kind of clay pottery referred to in English as *earthenware*. In other words, *ampo* can emphasise a vessel, a hollow container, made specifically from "earth" in the form of porous clay.[20] The connection between the English language terms *earthenware* and *earthworks* is notable and provocative. Similarly, Byington records that the adjective *chaha* can mean high, lofty, or tall. But *chaha* can also mean steep or elevated, as well as eminent, grand, and *sublime*. In other words, *chaha* possesses not only a range of literal meanings related to height, but also a range of figurative and possibly spiritual meanings related to prominence, importance, and power. In addition to 'tall clay pot', *ampo chaha* may mean something like 'sublime earth-enware vessel' – a productive conduit between worlds, an active portal between the living and the dead.[21]

But there are potentially other dimensions to the living earthworks vocabulary of *ampo chaha*. In 2003, an interdisciplinary team of non-Native researchers published a land- and water-focused analysis of the celebrated Mississippian earthworks city known as Cahokia, located near what is now St. Louis, Missouri, and the massive site's broader environment on the Mississippi floodplain. Titled *Envisioning Cahokia: A Landscape Perspective*, this innovative study was written collaboratively by two anthropologists who are also earth scientists, two geographers who are also archaeologists, and a landscape architect. Shifting emphasis away from an exclusively archaeological perspective on Cahokia, the research collective notes in their introduction:

For the most part, the archaeological community does not have the information that it needs to place the Cahokia site in context. [...] There remains a lack of volume-length, holistic considerations of the cultural dynamics at Cahokia. We maintain that a landscape approach can be used to synthesize our knowledge about the Cahokia site and to provide a robust account of how a people interacted with the environment at a critical point in human history.

(Dalan et al. 2003: 13)

Stated succinctly: "At the heart of [their] landscape approach at Cahokia lies a desire to document the relationship that the Mississippians had with the land" (Dalan et al. 2003: 15). After visiting the Chickasaw Cultural Centre and contemplating its provocative signage, what I hoped to learn from this study, more precisely, was what kind of relationship the Mississippians at Cahokia might have had with the porous clay used to make *ampo chaha*.

Envisioning Cahokia (2003) provides a high level of detail about the design, engineering, and construction of large platform mounds. And although its non-Native authors did not consult Indigenous communities, the study nonetheless provides details that intersect the living earthworks vocabularies displayed at the Chickasaw Cultural Center and, especially, the idea that *ampo chaha* may mean something like 'sublime earthenware vessel'. In describing the monumental, multi-terraced, nearly one-hundred-feet-high platform at Cahokia known as Monks Mound, the researchers note the specific functions of porous clay as a key building material:

A significant portion of the mound mass was composed of clays with a high shrink-swell capacity and low hydraulic conductivity. When wet, these clays displaced significantly more volume than in the dry condition, whereas upon drying they contracted and tended to crack. The consequences of repeated episodes of drying and wetting are obvious: they produced great instability. Given a high local water table and an annual average of over 65,000 cubic meters of precipitation on the surface of the mound, continual water control was clearly essential for maintenance.

(Dalan et al. 2003: 138)

The builders of the massive platform had to contend with the multiple conditions and contingencies of the floodplain environment, including the types of soils and other materials readily available, a high water table, and regular seasons in which the weather shifted from one extreme to another. Such conditions and contingencies work against the stability of mounds constructed from borrowed and reformed earth. How did the Mississippians at Cahokia adjust their design and building techniques to accommodate these variables? The researchers describe the builders' clay-based solutions in these terms:

The base or core of the mound was composed of a 6- to 7-meter-high clay platform. Water pulled up into the mound by capillary action to a height of up to 10 meters kept the smectite clays in this core perennially saturated with capillary water (in an expanded state), thus forming an excellent supporting base for the enormous weight above it. A fair amount of earth would have been needed on top of this core in order to pull up the capillary water; without it, the core would have cycled through wet and dry states throughout the year and hence been unstable. Thus, from an engineering standpoint, it made sense for the bulk of the mound to be constructed relatively rapidly.

(Dalan et al. 2003: 138)

The designers, engineers, and builders of the mound discovered how to create a tall and porous clay core that, once compressed by a large mass of soil, would pull water up from the ground and then remain saturated. In this expanded state, the clay core would maintain its stability over time; this expanded clay base would, in turn, help the larger mound maintain its stability over time as well. It was a remarkably successful solution. The researchers conclude:

> The degree of success of all these efforts can be measured by the long-term stability of the mound. [...] no major failures occurred for a thousand years in spite of the instability of materials and the enormous mass and surface area of the structure. Only in the last two decades has the mound experienced major failure [because of changes in the water table due to modern industries], with the several hundred years of stability testifying to the skills of the makers.
>
> *(Dalan et al. 2003: 139)*

This information allows the analysis of the living earthworks vocabularies on display at the Chickasaw Cultural Centre to be developed even further. The term *ampo chaha* can mean 'tall clay pot' and construct meaning mimetically, indicating a physical resemblance between the shapes of platform mounds and the shapes of (some if not all) inverted pots. The term can mean 'sublime earthenware vessel' and construct meaning archetypally, indicating fundamental cycles of birth leading to death leading to birth. And the term can also mean 'smectite clay core' and construct meaning architectonically, indicating proven techniques for harnessing the properties of porous clay in order to guarantee mound stability over time. It is possible that the living earthworks vocabulary of *aayampo' chaaha'* encodes in its precise language and in its condensed, polysemic phrasing both a metaphysical understanding of how humans can make connections between worlds and a critical technique for physical construction that can help ensure long-term duration.

Time and again, we learn the lesson of the ancestors' genius and practical sense, deeply rooted in knowledge of place, long before the invention of supposedly modern technologies and the designation of the supposedly 'new' materialisms.

To conclude, I draw attention to additional signage displayed in the Chikasha Poya Exhibit Centre. Under the four-part heading "Where We Began / *Stories of Chickasaw origins* / shakchi / wihat tanowa", the two-part sign reads:

> We have tribal stories that tell of the creation of our world. In the beginning, *shakchi* (crawfish) brought mud from below the water. This was used to form the earth from which people were created.
>
> ###
>
> Many stories tell of how the Chickasaws became a tribe. All speak of *wihat tanowa* (migration). After traveling for generations, we settled in our homeland centered in northeastern Mississippi.

Note the assertion of evocative juxtaposition – rather than disabling contradiction – in this coupling of the seemingly divergent concepts of emergence *and* migration. Additional details of the Chickasaw version of the Earth Diver story, in which the seemingly small and insignificant Crawfish plays a starring role, are provided in other parts of the exhibit centre. Additional details are provided, as well, of the migration story in which the ancestors who become the Chickasaw, along with their close relations who become the Choctaw, are led on their extensive journey by a sacred White Dog, a being who represents the visible stars of the Milky Way. The juxtaposition is evocative of the majestic Serpent Mound effigy located in what is now southern Ohio, with its own juxtaposition of an uncoiling horned snake representing the below world and an oval disk representing the sun in the above world, both set on the arced bluff above the life-giving waters of Brush Creek and above the geological evidence of a meteor impact some 200 million years ago.[22] The site's multiple juxtapositions hold in productive tension two ideas fundamental to Chickasaw and other Southeastern identities in relation to place: their origins are simultaneously from below *and* above. The Chickasaw emerged into the Southeastern homeland from the watery below world through the productive vehicle of the earthen mound. The Chickasaw migrated into the Southeastern homeland led by the glittering above world through the guiding vehicle of bright white stars. The juxtaposition resolves in the knowledge that generations of Chickasaw were born, lived, died, and then born again into these cycles in the space between worlds below and above, that is, upon the vibrant, highly constructed surface world of the Southeastern homeland.[23]

Notes

1 See, for example, Bernardini (2004). Independent scholar Jay Miller discusses contemporary, small-scale mound building in the context of annual Native American ceremonies in his 2015 study *Ancestral Mounds*.
2 Miller (2015) makes a similar point in *Ancestral Mounds*.
3 Wobst (2005) examines a number of these issues in his useful overview essay. See also Atalay (2006).
4 I have been fortunate in this project to work closely with colleagues affiliated with the Newark Earthworks Center at the Ohio State University Newark, including Marti Chaatsmith (Comanche) and Christine Ballengee Morris (Eastern Band Cherokee), and with a range of Native writers, artists, and intellectuals, including LeAnne Howe (Choctaw), Monique Mojica (Guna and Rappahannock), Allison Hedge Coke (Creek, Huron, and Cherokee ancestry), Phillip Carroll Morgan (Choctaw and Chickasaw), and Alyssa Hinton (Tuscarora and Osage ancestry).
5 See, for example, Brooks (2008), Haas (2007), and C. Howe (2002). For a fuller discussion of these distinctions and an argument for employing an expansive definition of writing in the Indigenous Americas, see Boone and Mignolo (1994).
6 See, for instance, Allen (2010), Allen (2015a), and Allen (2015b).
7 In September 2005, for instance, the Newark Earthworks Center at Ohio State University Newark hosted an academic symposium titled "Native Knowledge Written on the Land".
8 The idea that earthworks need to be understood not in isolation but within broader understandings of built environments, including the creation of borrow pits and the construction of level plazas and raised causeways, is detailed in works such Dalan et al. (2003), discussed below, and Baires (2017).
9 Geographers Jay Johnson and Soren Larsen make a similar point about the centrality of "embodied and performative" research methodologies, including walking, in the introduction to their 2013 co-edited collection (Johnson and Larsen 2013: 15). Guna and Rappahannock playwright Monique Mojica (2012) describes an embodied Indigenous research methodology specifically for understanding earthworks in her 2012 essay.
10 And in an essay Tallbear published in 2017: "I am struck again and again, reading the new materialisms, by their lack of acknowledging indigenous people" (2017: 197).
11 For more information, visit www.chickasawculturalcenter.com.
12 This type of flat-topped earthwork is also known as a 'temple mound' or 'minko [chief's] mound'. In addition to the earthwork at the Chickasaw Cultural Center near Sulphur, an earthwork has been constructed at the new American Indian Cultural Center and Museum in Oklahoma City. LeAnne Howe and Jim Wilson write about both sites in their essay published in 2015; the Oklahoma City site is also discussed in Malnar and Vodvarka (2013).
13 The Chickasaw Press was founded in 2006; visit www.chickasawpress.com. Find Chickasaw TV at www.chickasaw.tv.
14 Abenaki scholar Lisa Brooks makes similar claims about other forms of Indigenous writing, such as strings and belts of wampum and birch bark scrolls (2008: 12, 220).

15 I am indebted to Amanda Cobb-Greetham, former Administrator for the Chickasaw Nation's Division of History and Culture and currently Professor and Chair of American Indian Studies at the University of Oklahoma, for giving me a behind-the-scenes tour of the Chickasaw Cultural Center and for engaging in extended conversation about the Center's conception, ongoing activities, and plans for the future in 2013. All interpretations of the Center and its earthwork presented in this chapter, however, are my own.

16 The earthworks vocabularies discussed below represent only a partial list of extant Chickasaw words for mounds. The term *shintok*, for instance, is not used in the signage at the Chickasaw Cultural Center but is commonly used in contemporary Chickasaw discourse. See, for example, the use of *shintok* in Travis (2018).

17 I was directed to Dyson's (2014) work by Chickasaw and Choctaw writer and intellectual Phillip Carroll Morgan, who worked alongside Dyson at the Chickasaw Press and who has found Dyson's work essential to his own research and writing. Morgan (2014) is the author of the historical novel *Anompolichi: The Wordmaster*, set in the year 1399, during a period of active mound building in the Southeast, and is currently working on a sequel.

18 In support of this possibility, Dyson enlists the work of another researcher of Southeastern traditions, adding, "Indeed, in his previously cited essay on mound symbolism, Vernon J. Knight Jr. has commented on those earthen 'navels' as loci of both birth and death, of emergence as well as burial" (Dyson 2014: 28).

19 *A Dictionary of the Choctaw Language* (Byington 1915) appeared as Bulletin 46 in the series produced by the Bureau of American Ethnology. Although produced by a non-Native missionary and edited by non-Native scholars, it is considered a vital source by contemporary Choctaw writers, intellectuals, and community members. I was first directed to it by the Choctaw writer and intellectual LeAnne Howe.

20 In English, pottery is typically divided into the three categories *earthenware* (fired at low temperatures and more porous), *stoneware* (fired at high temperatures and less porous), and *porcelain* (fired at even higher temperatures, nonporous and glasslike, and especially strong).

21 I am grateful to Phillip Carroll Morgan for helping me arrive at the possible translation of *ampo chaha* as "sublime earthenware vessel".

22 See Allen (2015b).

23 LeAnne Howe records a version of this understanding in her 2001 novel *Shell Shaker* through the Choctaw phrasing *Hatak okla hut okchaya bilia hoh illi bilia*, which translates into English as "The people are ever living, ever dying, ever alive", or more simply, "life everlasting." See, for example, pages 5–6.

References

Allen, C. (2010). 'Serpentine figures, sinuous relations: Thematic geometry in Allison Hedge Coke's *blood run*', *American Literature*, vol 82, no 4: 807–834.

Allen, C. (2015a). 'Re-scripting Indigenous America: Earthworks in native art, literature, community', in B. Dawes, K. Fitz, S.N. Meyer (eds.) *Twenty-First Century Perspectives on Indigenous Studies: Native North America in (Trans)Motion*. Routledge: London, 127–147.

Allen, C. (2015b). 'Performing serpent mound: A trans-Indigenous meditation', *Theatre Journal*, vol 67, no 3: 391–411.

Atalay, S. (2006). 'Indigenous archaeology as decolonizing practice', *American Indian Quarterly*, vol 30, no 3–4: 280–310.

Baires, S.E. (2017). *Land of Water, City of the Dead: Religion and Cahokia's Emergence*. University of Alabama Press: Tuscaloosa, AL.

Bernardini, W. (2004). 'Hopewell geometric earthworks: A case study in the referential and experiential meaning of monuments', *Journal of Anthropological Archaeology*, vol 23, no 3: 331–356.

Boone, E. and Mignolo, W. (eds.) (1994). *Writing Without Words: Alternative Literacies in Mesoamerica and the Andes*. Duke University Press: Durham, NC.

Brooks, L. (2008). *The Common Pot: The Recovery of Native Space in the Northeast*. University of Minnesota Press: Minneapolis, MN.

Byington, C. (1915). *A Dictionary of the Choctaw Language*. Government Printing Office: Washington, DC.

Dalan, R.A., Holley, G.R., Watters, H., Koepke, J., and Woods, W. (2003). *Envisioning Cahokia: A Landscape Perspective*. Northern Illinois University Press: DeKalb, IL.

Dyson, J.P. (2014). *The Early Chickasaw Homeland: Origins, Boundaries and Society*. Chickasaw Press: Ada, OH.

Haas, A.M. (2007). 'Wampum as hypertext: An American Indian intellectual tradition of multimedia theory and practice', *Studies in American Indian Literatures*, vol 19, no 4: 77–100.

Horton, J.L. and Berlo, J.C. (2013). 'Beyond the mirror: Indigenous ecologies and "New Materialisms" in contemporary art', *Third Text*, vol 27, no 1: 17–28.

Howe, C. (2002). 'Keep your thoughts above the trees: Ideas on developing and presenting tribal histories', in N. Shoemaker (ed.) *Clearing a Path: Theorizing the Past in Native American Studies*. Routledge: New York, 161–179.

Howe, L. (2001). *Shell Shaker*. Aunt Lute Books: San Francisco, CA.

Howe, L. and Wilson, J. (2015). 'Life in a 21st century mound city', in R. Warrior (ed.) *The World of Indigenous North America*. Routledge: London, 3–26.

Johnson, J.T. and Larsen, S.C. (eds.). (2013). *A Deeper Sense of Place: Stories and Journeys of Collaboration in Indigenous Research*. Oregon State University of Press: Corvallis, OR.

Malnar, J.M. and Vodvarka, F. (2013). *New Architecture on Indigenous Lands*. University of Minnesota Press: Minneapolis, MN.

Miller, J. (2015). *Ancestral Mounds: Vitality and Volatility of Native America*. University of Nebraska Press: Lincoln, NE.

Mojica, M. (2012). 'In plain sight: Inscripted earth and invisible realities', in R. Barker and K. Solga (eds.) *New Canadian Realisms, New Essays on Canadian Theatre*, vol 2. Playwrights Canada Press: Toronto, ON, 218–242.

Morgan, P.C. (2014). *Anompolichi: The Wordmaster*. White Dog Press: Ada, OH.

Tallbear, K. (2015). 'An Indigenous reflection on working beyond the human/not human', *GLQ*, vol 21, no 2–3: 230–235.

Tallbear, K. (2017). 'Beyond the life/not-life binary: A feminist-Indigenous reading of cryopreservation, interspecies thinking, and new materialisms', in J. Radin and E. Kowal (eds.) *Cryopolitics: Frozen Life in a Melting World*. MIT Press: Cambridge, 179–202.

Travis, R.H. (2018). 'Halbina' Chikashsha, a summer journey', in L.M. Clark (ed.) *Visual Voices: Contemporary Chickasaw Art*. Chickasaw Press: Ada, OH, 44–46.

Tuck, E. and McKenzie, M. (2015). *Place in Research: Theory, Methodology, and Methods*. Routledge: New York.

Wobst, H.M. (2005). 'Power to the (Indigenous) past and present! or: The theory and method behind archaeological theory and method', in C. Smith and H.M. Wobst (eds.) *Indigenous Archaeologies: Decolonizing Theory and Practice*. Routledge: London, 15–29.

17

"To be a good relative means being a good relative to everyone"[1]

Indigenous feminisms is for everyone

Jennifer Denetdale

In 2016, I delivered the inaugural address to the 23rd Navajo Nation Council, of whom among them was a single woman, Amber Crotty, out of 24 delegates. In my address, I acknowledged the Navajo Nation's struggle to realise sovereignty and self-determination on its own terms, for like other Indigenous nations, we are deemed a 'domestic dependent' under the United States. I reminded our predominately male leaders and the audience that our principle of K'é had once guided all areas of our lives, including the way we regarded the earth as Nihimá Nahaszáán (Our Mother Earth), of women's traditional roles of leadership, and that K'é included acceptance of our gender non-conforming relatives. In the present moment, we must become critically aware of how Indigenous peoples are folded into neo-liberal democracies that value capitalism as the measure of what life is and that capitalism in its intersections with settler colonialism and its movements should be understood within the biopolitics of the elimination of Indigenous life. We must be accountable to our espoused values of life that encompass how we regard the earth and all life and that against on-going imposed US settler imperialism, we strive for renewed life. We remain rooted in bringing forth our ancestors' wisdom on how to live the wealth of our respective deities and Holy People.

Within a year of taking her seat on the Council, delegate Crotty publicly called for the end of sexual harassment in the Navajo workplace, "We're talking about rape culture. The connection is there and it's gut-wrenching. It hurts in the gut when you have to go through this behavior, and it certainly creates the environment for a rape culture" (Landry 2016: online). Crotty calling out gender discrimination and indeed, institutionalised sexism, that exists within the Navajo Nation government reminds us that foreign notions of governance, in the form of democracy, has imposed upon our nation a heterosexual patriarchy that shapes all relationships as dominance and hierarchal. These sorts of relationships extend to how we regard and treat the natural world, including land and its resources. Indigenous feminisms embrace theory and practice that affirms Indigenous claims to land and territories and the inherent rights to live as Indigenous peoples and according to our respective epistemologies. As decolonisation, Indigenous feminisms and queer critiques embrace the revitalisation and practice of traditional knowledges against the relentless onslaught of settler colonialism that wreak havoc on our nations, communities, and the self. This essay offers my perspective on the rich genealogy of Indigenous feminisms and queer critiques and the interventions that this area study makes in Native Studies and Critical Indigenous Studies.

The word feminism is still suspicious in Indigenous spaces where its theory and practice is indicted for its collusion with "imperialist, colonialist, and racist ideologies and practices" (Barker 2017: 10). For example, Diné matriarch Venaya Yazzie published her criticism in the *Navajo Times*, "White feminism has infiltrated the arid desert lands of Navajo. Like the monsters that the Hero Twins battled against, I believe that the 'f-word' monster roams like Coyote among our people" (Yazzie 2018: online). She asks how a "Euro-American feminism" with its "individualistic selfish attitudes" could possibly have any attraction to Diné or Indigenous women, to insist that feminism is not necessary because we have a strong matriarchy:

> From our origin stories we are taught about who we are to be as Diné Asdzáá and Diné Hastiin in our dialogue, in our actions, in our personal social lives. As Navajo women, we are acting as Amá to all our clan relatives.

> *(Yazzie 2018: online)*

Yazzie stresses that we do our research so that we will refuse Western values such as feminism, thereby re-embracing our own matriarchal values, "our sacred epistemology of Diné Iiná … live in the spirit of your grandmothers, great aunts, mothers, and sisters: Be matriarch, not feminist" (Yazzie 2018: online). Yazzie's perspective is part of a current effort for rematriation. Yet, Indigenous feminists like Joanne Barker and Jennifer Denetdale caution that femininity as a central value potentially essentialises tradition, first by re-inculcating Western notions of the binary and second, by reinforcing a conservativism that is often based upon imposed Victorian values of morality (Barker 2011; Denetdale 2006). White feminism is also responsible for many Indigenous women's rejection of feminism. Goenpul feminist Aileen Moreton-Robinson asserts:

> As knowing subjects, middle-class white feminists and Indigenous women speak from different cultural standpoints, histories and material conditions. These differences separate our politics and our analyses. Indigenous women do not want to be white women; we want to be Indigenous women who exercise and maintain our cultural integrity in our struggle for self-determination as Indigenous people.

> *(Moreton-Robinson 2009: 151)*

White feminism is indicted because white women have not only benefitted from the dispossession of Indigenous peoples, but they also have facilitated our deaths and our losses.

In much the same manner as white feminists, white gay and lesbian identified scholars searched in Indigenous communities for evidence of gender diversity, to construct arguments that such diversity was 'natural'. Scott Morgensen cautions that positioning the Indigenous queer community in relation to white expectations re-inculcates white appropriation and politics, "Texts that appear on the surface to be telling truths about Native people may be telling more about the non-Native social locations or political investments of their writers and readers" (Morgensen 2011: 138). Non-Indian Indigenous queer work is actually about modern technology's regulation of Indigenous sexual bodies, "the violent sexual regulation of Native peoples became a proving ground for forming settler subjects as agents and beneficiaries of modern sexuality" (Morgensen 2010: 117). Morgensen echoes Cathy Cohen's argument that queer work is not about fitting into the status quo, the normative biopolitics that determines meaning and futures, but rather that the idea of queer and queer politics means to create space in opposition to the normative and where transformational political work can begin (Cohen 1997: 438). Much of scholarship on Indigenous peoples, then, feeds and confirms White desires, and terrorises Indigenous peoples into accepting modern technologies of life, rather than addressing their needs.

Ironically, if Venaya Yazzie had researched the term 'feminism', she would have discovered rich genealogies of not only Indigenous feminisms and queer critiques, but also women of colour feminisms and queer of colour studies. Women of colour feminisms engage with Indigenous feminisms because we have dreams and visions that can be supported through collaborations and alliances, for we experience settler colonialism and its intersection with capitalism in different ways and shape our lives in the present. Indigenous feminists have demonstrated that feminism has roots in the oldest of Indigenous societies. For example, Paula Gunn Allen draws upon Indigenous creation narratives to show traditions of women-centred societies (Allen 1992). Although white women are deemed 'the first feminists', in truth, they sought evidence of gender equality in Indigenous societies to justify their own arguments for women's rights. Indigenous feminist projects also demonstrated that Indigenous women devoted their energy to justice for their peoples and can be seen in the writings of Sarah Hopkins Winnemucca and E. Pauline Johnson who experienced frontier settler violence against their people and refused to normalise settler violence as ordinary life for Indigenous peoples (Hopkins 2015; Johnson 1893).

In 2002, Joyce Green edited an anthology, *Making Space for Indigenous Feminism*, in which contributors troubled the term 'feminism' and argued that its use held the possibilities to revalue the centrality of women in Indigenous societies and to return them to their former places of authority and participation in all aspects of life, including governance and centrality in the economics that are now relegated to men's domain. Furthermore, for Indigenous peoples, the treaties their leaders signed with settler states like the United States and Canada remain symbols of their status as nations. These treaties record land losses and the erosion of sovereignty and self-determination. Distinctions between the claims of Indigenous peoples and all others who are descendants of immigrants are still illegible to the average citizen of the United States where narratives of equality and cultural diversity assume the inclusion of Indigenous peoples into the settler polities. Indigenous feminists are committed to the return of Indigenous lands, the revival of cultural traditions and practices that have been disrupted by colonial repression – including critical interrogation of how history reshapes memories and is often narrated through a colonial nationalist lens, thereby distorting knowledges about the institutions that shape Indigenous lives.

In 2006, Indigenous scholars gathered to share their interests in Indigenous feminist studies as an intervention in Native and Indigenous Studies. Introductory essays based on these proceedings were published in *American Quarterly*, co-edited by Andrea Smith and J. Kehaulani Kauanui (2008) and the second set of essays, based upon the intro essays, were published in *Wicazo Sa Review* in 2009 (Smith and Kauanui 2009). The contributors wrote to the meaning of being feminists on our terms and as Indigenous women – and I say 'women' because we had unwittingly drawn 'feminist' as not inclusive of our LGBTQI relatives, even though some of us are gender diverse and how Indigenous feminism as a lens offers possibilities for Indigenous liberation and freedom. These forums were revitalising because as Indigenous feminists we opened space to renew interest in scholarship and practice the centred feminisms. To this day many of the Indigenous feminists I met at these forums remain my good friends and colleagues.

Since 2006, the field has flourished as demonstrated by the relationships and connections between the Academy and community-based movements that enact Indigenous liberation as the present and the future. Interrogations of how Indigenous nations and communities are transformed through the imposition of democratic principles have been fruitful as we rethink governance and leadership and its intersection with gender and how traditional forms of community and life have been erased as a result of settler terrorising sexual politics that insists on a gender binary. For examples, Jennifer Denetdale, Audra Simpson, and Cutcha Balding Reisling represent three generations of feminist scholars who complicate notions of gender. Denetdale offers glimpses into a Diné matrilineal system with her study of her great-great-great-grand-parents, Hastiin Ch'iil Hajiin and Asdzáá Tl'ógi (Man from Black Weeds and Lady Weaver). Drawing upon her genealogy where descent is traced through grandmothers, Denetdale utilises oral history and interviews with grandparents to illuminate the centrality of mothers through matrilineality to organise Diné/Navajo life. Her research offers directions for imagining earlier forms of Diné life where women were regarded as the models for authority and leadership (Denetdale 2007). Furthermore, Denetdale's essay, *Chairmen, Presidents, and Princesses: The Navajo Nation, Gender, and the Politics of Gender* illuminate how the imposition of heteropatriarchy onto Native nations devalues women and installs gender discrimination and outright misogyny. Denetdale (2006) illuminates how the category of 'tradition' is deployed to validate gender discrimination.

Similarly, Simpson illuminates how colonial structures of patriarchy have re-ordered Mohawk governance, leadership, land use – all ordering of life. In *Captivating Eunice: Membership, Colonialism, and Gendered Citizenships of Grief*, Simpson invites reimagining the status of Mohawk women at points of contact with colonial violence by revisiting the trope of captivity narratives as an American literary and intellectual device that makes legible a settler impulse to claim land and belonging through desires of becoming Indian, even as simultaneously, Indians are viewed as savage. Thus, the narrative of Eunice Williams who was captured and adopted into Mohawk society in order to alleviate the grief of a Mohawk woman who had lost her daughter demonstrates how white women acquired status where, in contrast, through colonial law, Mohawk women lost their rightful places of authority. Simpson effectively connects the past and present of settler colonial law – both Canadian and US to show how Eunice's story is "a piece of a much larger, organic system of exchanges and reciprocal violences and naturalizations" (Simpson 2009: 107) that has a political efficacy apparent today in Mohawk women's struggles to undo the Indian Act.

Feminist attention to the Indian Act has been considerable because it offers an understanding of how the intersections of settler colonial law intersects with established 'traditional' practices of Indigenous governance work to undermine the status of Indigenous women. Joanne Barker takes her interest in the Indian Act and extends her critiques of the intersections of national-isms with Native/Indigenous nation-building with her *Native Acts: Law, Recognition, and Cultural Authenticity* (Barker 2006; Barker 2011). The Indian Act offers lessons on Indigenous women's complaints of gender discrimination by their own men that is shaped by settler colonial law has been addressed by international courts. The women's complaint charged that Canada's Indian Act imposed band membership regulations that undermined First Nations women's citizenship status and gave men certain entitlements and privileges of belonging not extended to women. In contrast, within the United States, Martinez v. Santa Clara, exemplifies how Native women have lost significant former authority and status as a result of imposed patriarchy. Challenging legal reviews of Martinez v. Santa Clara that affirm Santa Clara Pueblo's claims to sovereignty that also thwart women's claims of gender discrimination, Joanne Barker offers a careful reading of the US court decision to refuse to hear the case because Santa Clara Pueblo is practicing its sovereignty to determine its membership. The lawsuit is based upon Julia Martinez's complaint she and her children were discriminated against by Santa Clara ordinance because her children's father was Navajo. According to the ordinance, if a Santa Clara woman married a non-Santa Clara man, her children count not access the same benefits offered to children of Santa Clara men who married non-Santa Clara women. Barker's analysis interrogates categories such as 'tradition', 'culture', and 'authenticity' in order to show how colonialism has profoundly disrupted Indigenous life. As Barker offers, Native nations have the capacity to build their nations upon principles that ensure the prosperity and happiness of all of its citizens (Barker 2006). Indigenous feminisms as critique allows us to think through how and why Indigenous women have been so devalued within not only the settler state, but within their own nations and communities. The ways that Indigenous women have been devalued within frameworks for Native sovereignty and self-determination is also taken up by Sami feminist Rauna Kuokkanen in her comparative study of Sami, Greenland and Canadian quests for Indigenous-centred rights. Kuokkanen argues that the revaluing of Indigenous women is integral to realising Indigenous sovereignty and self-determination (Kuokkanen 2019).

Today, the attention to revaluing women-centred traditions as feminist practices is reflected in Cutcha Riesling Baldy's *We Are Dancing For You* in which Baldy deconstructs California's genocidal history against Indigenous people, thereby sustaining studies like Deborah Miranda's *Bad Indians: A Tribal Memoir*, in order to reclaim women-centred ceremonies that honoured women's contributions to Hupa life (Baldy 2018; Miranda 2016). For Riesling, an act of decolonisation is to revive the women's puberty ceremony, a process for her that connects settler archives to the community practice of reviving a women-centred ceremony that acknowledges women's bodies as sites of a different order of things, an order where women's traditional roles as keepers of knowledge and active agents in the daily life of Hupas. Joanne Barker's edited *Critically Sovereign*, J. Kehaulani Kauanui's *Paradox of Sovereignty*, and the scholarship and community activism of Melanie K. Yazzie extends the reach of feminist analysis by demonstrating that settler colonialism continually seeks to eliminate us as Indigenous peoples, that Indigenous peoples refuse to disappear and struggles to restore traditional ways of being are always in process, thereby continually disrupting settler impulses to terrorise Indigenous peoples and that we are affirm our kinship to all beings – the earth, sky, and non-human beings (Barker 2017; Kauanui 2018b; Yazzie and Baldy 2018).

Indigenous feminist attention to the logics of transforming Indigenous women's places within their nations and communities and rendering them illegible as still powerful sources for revitalising Indigenity are understood with Audra Simpson analysis, "An Indian woman's body in settler regimes such the US, in Canada is loaded with meaning – signifying other political orders, land itself, of the dangerous possibility of reproducing Indian life and most dangerously, other political orders" (Simpson 2016: online). Since at least the 1990s, international and national attention has shed light on the violence that Indigenous women have endured and to which feminist legal scholar Sarah Deer (2015) has devoted her scholarship. Gendered violence against Indigenous peoples is more than 500 years old and has been perpetuated through colonial-produced imagery of Indigenous women such as the iconic Pocahontas and Sacajawea (Green 1975; Kauanui 2018: 88). Deer offers her expertise to tribal nations who, strangled by federal laws such as the Indian Offenses Act, find it impossible to address violence against Indigenous women. The gendered legacy of colonialism in tribal nations has led to high rates of violence, including rape and sexual assaults, against women and which have gone largely unaddressed. Furthermore, the attempts to address rape, for example, through traditional forms of justice are fraught with men-dominated justice systems that re-victimise Indigenous women. Deer is optimistic about the possibilities that Indigenous belief systems, oral traditions and practices hold to address the crisis of violence against Indigenous women. She declares that the end of rape and violence against Indigenous women is integral to Indigenous nation's decolonisation: "We want to do more than just survive. We seek nothing more than human dignity, and nothing less than justice" (Deer 2015: 163). Deer's advocacy led to the reauthorisation of the Violence Against Women Act in 2013 and for cultural and legal reforms to protect Native women from endemic sexual violence and abuse. Yet, restoring full authority to tribal nations over criminal acts such as rape are yet to be realised and the Trump administration's efforts to reduce the impact of these acts remains.

Indigenous feminist and gender studies sometimes appears to be separate area studies, as exemplified by the attention to Two-Spirits, which has been investigated by anthropologists and then supported by queer studies scholars. Indigenous feminisms' scope includes gender diversity and offers several directions to examine how gender intersects with Indigenity. First, for Deborah Miranda, recovering the presence of third or multiple genders in Indigenous societies prior to colonisation is a challenge because European traditions under Christianity tortured and killed people who did not identify within the binary. In her seminal essay, *Extermination of the Joyas*, Miranda argues that Spaniards exterminated third-gendered Indigenous peoples, whom they called 'joyas', because they were seen as abomination. Researching Spanish colonial archives, Miranda discovers genders beyond the binary and shows how Europeans and then white Americans actively destroyed the place of multiple genders in Indigenous communities (Miranda 2010). Another project is to draw upon traditional narratives where gender diversity is noted as evidence that at one time Indigenous peoples were accepting of their relatives who identified outside of the binary. For example, 'Two-Spirit' is a term that some Indigenous people have embraced because it speaks to their being as one who acknowledges their feminine and masculine sides. As Wesley Thomas, who self-identifies as a third gender person within his Diné society, notes, 'Two-Spirit' is a third gendered Native person who embraces traditional ways and practices. 'Two-Spirit', coined in urban Native settings where Native peoples refused white gay and lesbian identities and activism is now accepted as an identity and role both on and off Native nations (Thomas 1997). However, as activists note, the caveat is that while Two-Spirits and other non-conforming gendered persons claim belonging in their respective Native nations, they are often rejected by their communities through the invoking of 'tradition'. For example, Jolene Yazzie calls for our Diné people, including our healers, to accept our multiple gendered relatives. She writes, "In the Diné language, there are least six genders: *Asdzáán* (woman), *Hastiin* (male), *Náhleeh* (feminine-man), *Dilbaa* (masculine-woman), *Nádleeh Asdzaa* (lesbian), 'Nádleeh Hastii (gay man)" (Yazzie 2020: online). Identifying as *'bah'* or *dilbaa náhleeh* (masculine woman) or *nádleeh asdza,* Jolene shares her life experiences, "I prefer a masculine gender role that doesn't match my sex, but I continue to face bias over my gender expression" and

> Diné people have always understood gender as a spectrum rather than a binary, an understanding has come from traditional teachings and our creation story. In order to stop discrimination, our traditional healers must set an example and accept people of all genders.
>
> *(Yazzie 2020: online)*

These conversations about belonging and refusals to acknowledge the place of gender-nonconforming persons within Native nations and communities are taking place in public spaces and can often be tense.

Feminist attention to gender has produced an interest in Indigenous masculinities. Studies such as *Native Men Remade, Diné Masculinities, Masculindians: Conversations about Indigenous Manhood,* and *Indigenous Men and Masculinities: Identities, Legacies, Regeneration* are interventions that invoke returns to manhood based upon traditional values because generations under colonialism have affected Indigenous men's sense of manhood and masculinity (Tengan 2008; Lee

2013; McKegney 2014; Innes and Anderson 2015). *Native Men Remade* is an ethnography that reclaims Indigenous Hawaiian masculinity by returning to traditional Kanaka Maoli principles of balance, well-being, and respectful gender relations while Lloyd L. Lee offers a study of Diné masculinity that seeks to remind of traditional male roles in the face of disruption linked to the impact of colonialism on Diné men. Both authors utilise a methodology to recover former traditional masculine gender roles by invoking creation narratives that feature gender roles as models for the present. Brendan Hokowhitu's (2017) survey of Indigenous masculinities studies recognises that masculinities informed by contact with colonialism may unwittingly reproduce white sensibilities that re-entrench dominant values about manhood while these studies raise Indigenous feminists' concerns that the reclamation of Indigenous masculinity simply re-inscribes patriarchy (Kauanui 2018: 183). Interestingly, scholars of Indigenous masculinities do not appear to be versed in either gender and sexuality studies or Indigenous feminisms and queer critiques, thereby limiting an understanding of gender and sexuality.

At least more than a decade ago, I attended a talk by Tim Giago who discussed his book, *Children Left Behind: The Dark Legacy of Indian Mission Boarding Schools*, and told his story of physical and sexual abuse at a Catholic mission school in South Dakota (Giago 2006). His candid admission charged the atmosphere with emotion when a Native man thanked Giago and then shared his shame and inability to speak of his own physical and sexual abuse at a boarding school. Giago's testimony opened space to speak publicly about widespread sexual and physical abuse in US boarding schools and Catholic schools and to demand justice. Generations of physical and sexual abuse at the residential schools and boarding schools has taken a grim toll on our Indigenous people and manifests as physical and sexual abuses across generations and an inability to express love and intimacy.

It is to these dark spaces in Indigenous life that Indigenous writers and artists speak of, as the means to expose settler nations' culpability for the silence around physical and sexual abuse of Indigenous children. An Indigenous structure of feeling refers to a sensation of belonging to place and peoplehood excluded from settler governance but that remains present, most viscerally in the affective lives of Native people (Million 2009; Rifkin 2011). Although settler nations such as Canada and the United States engage with Indians as always already dead, the vitality of Indigenous life, in our telling and performance, refuse tragedy and death as the only stories. Kateri Akiwenzi-Damm explains that Western institutions such as Christianity are indicted for reshaping Indigenous gender relations and a sensibility about sexuality (Akiwenzi-amm 2003). Similarly, Drew Hayden Taylor offers rationale for her collection of narratives on Indigenous love and intimate matters, "Most often, Canadians hear about Native sexuality in their media in a more negative context. ... Although many of these stories out there reflect the vast ocean of Aboriginal sexuality. There needed to be reeducation" (Taylor 2008: np). Akiwenzi-Damm and Taylor refuse the boundaries of bourgeois domesticity, sensual pleasure and enduring emotional bonds met to be contained inside the boundaries of the conjugally defined household. Stories express a celebration of Indigenous eroticism and intimacy that acknowledges a diversity of gender, but also argues that affect is a crucial component for transforming Indigenous governance, political systems, and other institutions where Indigenous life is made and remade. In the spirit of reimagining Indigenous spaces that had previously been cordoned off as 'domestic' and 'public', feminists and queer scholars draw upon the scholarship of the 'structure of feeling', of affect, to celebrate Indigenous bodies, thereby refusing to relegate violence to spaces that silence.

In a similar manner, Kim Tallbear refuses the construction that love and intimacy are bound up in the ideals of the biologically reproductive monogamous white marriage and family. Rather, Tallbear declares that "We must collectively oppose a system of compulsory settler sexuality and family that continues building a nation upon Indigenous genocide and that marks Indigenous and other marginalized relations as deviant" (Tallbear 2018: 152). Thinking beyond settler constructions of what constitutes 'normal' and 'natural' requires remembering how and what making kin meant in traditional Indigenous families, for as Tallbear shares, "So much has gone dormant – will go dormant. So much has been imposed onto Indigenous peoples, both heteronormative settler sexuality categories and now also 'queer' categories" (Tallbear 2018: 153).

The workings of settler colonialism have deeply affected us, and in traumatic ways, so that Mishuana Goeman and other Indigenous feminists reimagine Indigenous landscape, to renew conceptions of space where we recreate our daily relationships with land, people, and ancestors (Goeman 2017). For example, Melanie K. Yazzie's scholarship connects to her care for Indigenous communities, is transnational and relational in scope, and espouses an urgency to respect all manners of life as relations, a positionality that evokes a queer feminism. Yazzie was profoundly moved to action when she learned of the brutal beatings and torture and then deaths of two Navajo men, Allison Gorman and Kee Thompson, by three Hispanic young men who confessed that they had merely been 'having fun' when they attacked the two men (Paterson 2015). Yazzie's feminist politics rearticulates the traditions of kinship and belonging where Indigenous peoples and nations reclaim the authority to made decisions about land, name the authority to determine criteria for citizenship and belonging, and demand that the US government cede power to the original peoples whose nations possess the rightful political authority in this continent. Yazzie's (2018) politics is anti-capitalist and anti-colonial. As she and her comrades declare on the Red Nation webpage, "For our Earth and relatives to live, capitalism and colonialism must die" (The Red Nation 2018: online). As I move this chapter to the final stretch, I check on Indigenous refusals to accept the way of the world as anti-Indigenous and capitalistic, for it is capitalism as an arm of settler colonialism that threatens Indigenous nations and communities as international corporations work with states and law enforcement to exploit remaining energy resources. And it is Indigenous women who are at the front of resistance in protection of Mother Earth. Based upon the wisdom of their ancestors, they reaffirm relations with the earth and its bounty of land, water, and all it provides as sustenance for humans and non-humans. Reading for the rest of the world the Unist'ot'en's determination to protect their territories from oil companies and the Canadian government, Leanne Simpson reminds us of our fierce Indigenous women and queer, trans, and Two-Spirits who will not let colonisers destroy the earth and all life without a fight: That's why, the words of Freda Huson, spokesperson of the Unist'ot'en camp speaks to the hearts of Indigenous peoples all across Mikinaakong, the place of the turtle, when she says:

> Our people's belief is that we are part of the land. The land is not separate from us. The land sustains us. And if we don't take care of her, she won't be able to sustain us, and we as a generation of people will die. That's why queer, trans and Two Spirit artists and young people are on the front lines leading solidarity occupations in Vancouver and Victoria. That's why Mohawk land protectors at Tyendinaga are blocking the tracks. That's why, a few short years ago, thousands organized and gathered at Standing Rock to block the Dakota Access Pipeline. This isn't about pipelines, or jobs or inconvenience or the best way to get our message out. This is about land and life for generations to come. This is about the kind of worlds we collectively want to live in.
>
> *(Simpson 2020: online)*

Conclusion

I begin this chapter with a quote from Melanie K. Yazzie because her life's work represents Indigenous feminist practice that draws upon the antiquity of our respective Indigenous epistemologies and brings them into the present where theory meets practice. Yazzie espouses a tradition of Indigenous resistance that centres Indigenous forms of kin-making. Drawing upon our Indigenous epistemologies we carry forth a value system to actively create the world in which we want to live. That world negates a colonial present of colonialism, capitalism, heteropatriarchy and white supremacy. As Michi Saagiig Nishnaabeg Leanne Simpson writes of our Indigenous feminisms:

> 'Theory' is generated and regenerated continually through embodied practice and within each family, community and generation of people. 'Theory' isn't just an intellectual pursuit – it is woven within kinetics, spiritual presence and emotion, it is contextual and relational. It is intimate and personal, with individuals themselves holding the responsibilities for finding and generating meaning within their own lives.
>
> *(Simpson 2014: 7)*

This essay is a telling of my own journey to enact an Indigenous feminism that is generative and transformative. Our work as Indigenous feminists offers lifelines to the coming generations of Indigenous peoples. I am indebted to the generations who came before me and voiced kin-making as the natural order of the world, our nations, communities, and families.

Note

1 See Yazzie (2019).

References

Akiwenzie-Damm, K. (ed.) (2003). *Without Reservation: Indigenous Erotic*. Huia: Wellington, 437–465.

Allen, P.G. (1992). *The Sacred Hoop: Recovering the Feminine in American Indian Traditions*. Beacon Press: Boston, MA.

Baldy, C.R. (2018). *We Are Dancing for You: Native Feminisms and the Revitalization of Women's Coming-of-Age Ceremonies*. University of Washington Press: Seattle, WA.

Barker, J. (2006). 'Gender, sovereignty, and the discourses of rights in native women's activism', *Meridians: Feminism, Race, Transnationalism*, vol 7, no 1: 127–161.

Barker, J. (2011). *Native Acts: Law, Recognition and Cultural Authenticity*. Duke University Press: Durham, NC.

Barker, J. (ed.) (2017). *Critically Sovereign: Indigenous Gender, Sexuality, and Feminist Studies*. Duke University Press: Durham, NC.

Cohen, C.J. (1997). 'Punks, bulldaggers, and welfare queens: The radical potential of queer politics?', *GLQ*, vol 3, no 4: 437–465.

Deer, S. (2015). *The Beginning and End of Rape: Confronting Sexual Violence in Native America*. University of Minnesota Press: Minneapolis, MN.

Denetdale, J.N. (2006). 'Chairmen, presidents, and princesses: The Navajo nation, gender and the politics of tradition', *Wicazo Sa Review*, vol 21, no 1: 9–28.

Denetdale, J.N. (2007). *Reclaiming Diné History: The Legacies of Navajo Chief Manuelito and Juanita*. University of Arizona Press: Tucson, AZ.

Giago, T. (2006). *Children Left Behind: The Dark Legacy of Indian Mission Boarding Schools*. Clear Light Publishing: Santa Fe, NM.

Goeman, M.R. (2017). 'Ongoing storms and struggles: Gendered violence and resource exploitation', in J. Barker (ed.) *Critically Sovereign: Indigenous Gender, Sexuality, and Feminist Studies*. Duke University Press: Durham, NC, 99–126.

Green, R. (1975). 'The pocahontas perplex: The image of American Indian women in American culture', *Massachusetts Review*, vol 16, no 4: 698–714.

Hokowhitu, B. (2017). 'History and masculinity', in C. Andersen and J.M. O'Brian (eds.) *Sources and Methods in Indigenous Studies: Routledge Guides to Using Historical Sources*. Routledge: London, 195–204.

Hopkins, S.W. (2015). *Life Among the Piutes: Their Wrongs and Claims.* Andesite Press.

Innes, R. and Anderson, K. (eds.) (2015). *Indigenous Men and Masculinities: Identities, Legacies.* Regeneration, University of Manitoba Press: Winnipeg, MB.

Johnson, E.P. (1893). 'A red girl's reasoning', *Dominion Illustrated.* Available: http://canlit.ca/wp-content/up loads/2016/02/red_girls_reasoning.pdf, accessed 4 February 2020.

Kauanui, J.K. (2018a). *Paradoxes of Hawaiian Sovereignty: Land, Sex, and the Colonial Politics of State Nationalism.* Duke University Press: Durham, NC.

Kauanui, J.K. (ed.). (2018b). 'Sarah deer on native women and sexual violence', in Kauanui, J.K. (ed.) *Speaking of Indigenous Politics: Conversations with Activists, Scholars, and Tribal Leaders.* University of Minnesota Press: Minneapolis, MN, 87–107.

Kuokkanen, R. (2019). *Restructuring Relations: Indigenous Self-Determination, Governance, and Gender.* Oxford University Press: New York.

Landry, A. (2016). 'Against rape culture in the tribal workplace: Amber Crotty', *Indian Country Today.* Available: https://newsmaven.io/indiancountrytoday/archive/against-rape-culture-in-the-tribal-wo rkplace-amber-crotty-kdzFKXcwTUWvzqxq5PisbA, accessed 11 February 2020.

Lee, L.L. (2013). *Diné Masculinities: Conceptualizations and Reflections.* Createspace Independent Publishing Platform: North Charleston, SC.

McKegney, S. (2014). *Masculindians: Conversations About Indigenous Manhood.* University of Manitoba Press: Winnipeg, MB.

Million, D. (2009). 'Felt theory: An Indigenous feminist approach to affect and history', *Wicazo Sa Review,* vol 24, no 2: 53–76.

Miranda, D.A. (2010). 'Extermination of the Joyas: Gendercide in Spanish California', *GLQ: A Journal of Lesbian and Gay Studies,* vol 16, nos 1–2: 253–284.

Miranda, D.A. (2016). *Bad Indians: A Tribal Memoir.* Heyday: Berkeley, CA.

Moreton-Robinson, A. (2009). *Talkin' Up to the White Woman: Indigenous Women and Feminism.* University of Queensland Press: Queensland.

Morgensen, S.L. (2010). 'Settler homonationalism: Theorizing settler colonialism within queer modernities', *GLQ: A Journal of Lesbian and Gay Studies,* vol 16, nos 1–2: 105–131.

Morgensen, S.L. (2011). 'Unsettling queer politics: What can non-natives learn from two-spirit organizing?', in Q. Driskill C. Finley, B.J. Gilley, and S.L. Morgensen (eds.) *Queer Indigenous Studies: Critical Interventions in Theory, Politics, and Literature.* University of Arizona Press: Tucson, AZ: 132–154.

Paterson, K. (2015). 'Cowboy, rabbit and border town violence', *NM Politics.net.* Available: https://nmpolit ics.net/index/2015/07/cowboy-rabbit-and-border-town-violence/, accessed 11 February 2020.

The Red Nation. (2018). 'Principles of unity'. Available: https://therednation.org/2018/08/11/principle s-of-unity/, accessed 12 April 2020.

Rifkin, M. (2011). 'The erotics of sovereignty', in Q.D.C. Finley, B.J. Gilley, and S.L. Morgensen (eds.) *Queer Indigenous Studies: Critical Interventions in Theory, Politics, and Literature.* University of Arizona Press: Tucson, AZ, 172–189.

Simpson, A. (2009). 'Captivating Eunice: Membership, colonialism, and gendered citizenships of grief', *Wicazo Sa Review,* vol 24, no 2: 105–129.

Simpson, A. (2016). 'The state is a man: Theresa Spence, Loretta Saunders and the gender of settler sovereignty', *Theory & Event,* vol 19, no 4: np.

Simpson, L.B. (2014). 'Land as pedagogy: Nishnaabeg intelligence and rebellious transformation', Decolonization: Indigeneity, *Education & Society,* vol 3, no 3: 1–25.

Simpson, L.B. (2020). 'Being with the land, protects the land', *Abolition Journal.* Available: https://aboliti onjournal.org/being-with-the-land-protects-the-land-leanne-betasamosake-simpson/?fbclid=Iw AR3TrCRZN_UpVdFMMDDm8YV_iMKp7AHhDQHpk40UxmaA719eUzB0DSHBRS0, accessed 20 February 2020.

Smith, A. and Kauanui, J.K. (2008). 'Native feminisms engage American studies', *American Quarterly,* vol 60, no 2: 241–249.

Smith, A. and Kauanui, J.K. (eds.) (2009). 'Forum: Native feminisms without apology, *Wicazo Sa Review,* 24(2), 9–187.

Tallbear, K. (2018). 'Making love and relations beyond settler sex and family', in A. Clarke and D. Haraway (eds.) *Making Kin Not Population.* Prickly Paradigm Press: Chicago, IL, 145–164.

Taylor, D.H. (2008). 'Introduction', in Taylor, D.H. (ed.) *Me Sexy!: An Exploration of Native Sex and Sexuality.* Douglas & McIntyre Ltd: Vancouver, BC, np.

Tengen, T.P.K. (2008). *Native Men Remade: Gender and Nation in Contemporary Hawai'i*. Duke University Press: Durham, NC.

Thomas, W. (1997). 'Navajo cultural constructions of gender and sexuality', in S. Jacobs, W. Thomas, and S. Lang (eds.) *Two-Spirit People: Native American Gender Though, Sexuality, and Spirituality*. University of Illinois Press: Urbana, IL, 156–173.

Yazzie, J. (2020). 'Why are Diné LGBTQ+ and two spirit people being denied access to ceremony?', *High Country News*. Available: https://www.hcn.org/issues/52.2/indigenous-affairs-why-are-dine-lgbtq-and-two-spirit-people-being-denied-access-to-ceremony?fbclid=IwAR1FQfF6JIxq4boR-eHzHJ-_k1qWL1KfL5StDcMBugocR0QksHzH8sIQz38, accessed 7 January 2020.

Yazzie, M.K. (2018). 'Decolonizing development in Diné Bikeyah: resource extraction, anti-capitalism, and relational politics', *Environment and Society*, vol 9, no 1: 25–39.

Yazzie, M.K. (2019). 'Reclaiming the "F-Word": What queer Indigenous feminism has to say about compassion, kinship, and liberation', Keynote address at the *14th Annual Circle of Harmony HIV/AIDS Wellness Conference*, March 26–28, Albuquerque, NM.

Yazzie, M.K. and Baldy C.R. (2018). 'Introduction: Indigenous peoples and the politics of water', Decolonization: Indigenity, *Education & Society*, vol 7, no 1: 1–18.

Yazzie, V. (2018). 'Feminism is against our culture', *Navajo Times*. Available: https://navajotimes.com/opinion/letters/letters-feminism-is-against-our-culture/, accessed 25 October 2018.

18

'Objectivity' and repatriation

Pulling on the colonisers' tale

Clayton Dumont

We *ewksiknii*, or Klamath, tell many stories about strange little creatures known as the *Gagaan'a*. These dwarf-like beings are ancient and malicious. Our ancestors told of encounters with them long before white folks arrived.

One such meeting is said to have happened at a place where the *numu*, or Yahooskins, often dug roots. Some women had dug and gathered for hours. They had left their babies in cradle-boards leaned against shade trees. One of the women did not stop to feed her infant, and the others scolded her. "What's wrong with you? He'll be hungry?" So the woman went to her baby. "I'll feed him, and then I'll be back", she said.

Well the baby was hungry, and he suckled for a long time. Finally she thought, "he should be full by now" and tried to remove him from her breast. But he wouldn't let go. She tried and tried but couldn't pry his mouth loose. "What is wrong with him", she thought. "This is not like my child". So she ran her hand over his head and felt that he was hard. "This is not my child!" she yelled. And the other women came running. They ran their hands over his body and head and felt that he was hard all over. "Something has me!" the now terrified woman said. "He is a Gagaan'a", one of the others exclaimed. "He must have killed your baby and put himself in that cradleboard". All the women tried to get that Gagaan'a off, but they couldn't. Finally they cut off the end of her breast. Even then, after the young mother was loose, they couldn't pry the severed flesh from its mouth with a stick.

We can hear this story as a warning. As 21st-century Natives, we should be careful about what we nourish in our communities. There are monsters about. Many of them are strong and cunning. Sometimes we mistake these creatures for our own and help them grow. In the thoroughly colonised spaces that indigenous peoples now inhabit – where colonial languages, laws, and anthropologically sanctioned 'authenticity' so often prevail – we sometimes conflate the ideals of the colonisers with our own cultural offspring. We must be vigilant.

Recognition is hard because the power of these monsters grows with the intergenerational process of forgetting that they are not ours. But if we learn to recognise these foreign notions, we can think carefully about when and how we encourage or resist them (Barker 2011). We can begin to think about how they came to us and how they impacted our ancestors. We can begin to recognise how tightly they are locked on to us. Like the Gagaan'a, they will remain powerful, perhaps even wholly supplanting our own, but at least we can stop them from fooling us.

The 'objectivity' ideal is a particularly insidious colonial monster. It is so pervasive as to appear natural. Many cannot imagine how any credible act of knowing can occur without it. As Robert Layton (1994: 2) asserts, "objectivity is often something one seems to have in greater measure than one's opponents". Who has not been told to 'take a step back' and 'consider your biases', to be 'fair and impartial', or to 'consider all sides of the issue'? How are we to think critically about something so widespread, permeating, and apparently foundational? It is as if we are being asked to be objective about objectivity.

Before my recent retirement, I used to tell students, when they grew confounded by predicaments like this one that, "you are trying to push the same bus you are riding in".[1] Thinking about the cultural foundations of thinking is a tough row to hoe. But what could be more important to those of us concerned with confronting colonial knowledge forms? 'Objectivity' is precisely as dangerous as it is difficult to critically interrogate. It is unapproachable to the extent that it wields power as a foundational story in the colonisers' knowledge making.

So foundational is this, what I would like to begin calling an 'objectivity complex', that few scholars have thought about its multifaceted cultural and political development. As the historian of science Lorraine Daston (1992: 598) explains, objectivity is almost always assumed to be a "monolithic and immutable concept":

> So pervasive and apparently persuasive is this assumption that it is rarely even uttered. Those few works which mention objectivity and history in the same breath examine how various sciences – mechanics, optics, chemistry, biology – successively cross the threshold of objectivity at specific historical junctures, but the implication is that objectivity itself has no history.[2]

But objectivity does have a history, or more accurately a genealogy.[3] Modern invocations of objectivity bind together, among others, what were once disparate concerns for responsible judgment, international empirical consistency, and mechanical measurements. These ideals originated in different cultural and political contexts as attempts to solve different and distinct problems (Daston 1991; Daston 1992; Daston and Galison 2007). Thus they represent different genes and lines of intellectual development culminating in our modern notion of 'objectivity' only in the second half of the 19th century.

The space-limited genealogy that I provide below emphasises theological genes of objectivity because I want to highlight its deep faith-based origins. My goal is to scandalise and destabilise the weaponised objectivity used by colonial powerbrokers to intellectually bludgeon indigenous peoples. I expose objectivity as an unobtainable fantasy (that remains a foundational myth of European-derived colonial powers) and recount its performance by US museums' representatives resisting compliance with the Native American Graves Protection and Repatriation Act (NAGPRA) of 1990.

Objectivity disrupted

A door in an auditorium in the United States Department of the Interior swung swiftly open and two columns of men emerged. The men dressed in traditional Tlingit attire reminded me of Grand Entry at American Indian powwows, but their movements were in tighter unison. At first, I thought they were all singing the same words at the same time, but after a moment, I realised they were two distinct groups responding ritually to each other. Ultimately the two (what I learned were) clans took up positions on opposite sides of the auditorium, and the back-and-forth, calls and answers, echoed forth in bold and unified cadences.

The ritual was beautiful, and I remain grateful for being allowed to witness it. Even more fortunate for me – a Native academic sitting in the audience of the 43rd Meeting of the National NAGPRA Review Committee – the Tlingits' entry continued long enough to seriously strain the allotted time for their dispute with the Alaska State Museum. As someone with a longstanding interest in the cross-cultural politics of knowing and knowledge making, I was treated to a clash of competing cultural rites – both of which are designed to manage and control conflict. "Equal time" to "make one's case" is a fundamental tenet of objectivity rituals; the Tlingits' demonstration of ritualised and protracted "balance" in "a situation like we are coming into", where confrontation is possible was apparently equally important – and centuries older (National NAGPRA 2010a: 22, 69–70, 74).

Making matters still more difficult for the National NAGPRA Program staff responsible for seeing that the Review Committee Charter's demand for "fair and objective consideration and assessment of all available relevant information and evidence" is adhered to, the committee members were clearly hesitant to cut short the Tlingits' desire to demonstrate fairness in the way of their "elders, our fathers, our grandfathers, our great grandfathers, and those who have gone before us" (National NAGPRA 2010a: 22). Four of the seven committee members were indigenous, and others were moved to serve by a commitment to seeing Native peoples treated fairly. No one on the dais in the front of the auditorium was going to disrespect these honoured clan representatives. The Tlingit performance was spectacular, loud, and long. The carefully cultivated, courtroom-like orderliness of the meeting was thrown into disarray.

Although meetings of the National NAGPRA Review Committee are not legal proceedings per se, the trappings of American courtrooms are mostly present. Committee members sit like judges elevated in the front of large rooms with microphones, name placards, and the American flag nearby. Directly across from them at lower elevations and at opposing sides of the room are elongated tables. Those who come to testify and their representatives occupy one of these, and the other holds the attorneys who make up most of the National NAGPRA Program staff. The audience sits behind the backs of those at the tables and facing the Review Committee. They are prohibited from speaking except during periods set aside for 'public comment'. Decorum norms dominate interactions. Following formal 'disputes' over human remains and funerary objects, sacred objects, or objects of cultural patrimony, the seven-member committee 'deliberates'. They publicly weigh evidence and vote on whether ancestral remains and objects should be 'repatriated' to indigenous communities or remain in museums. Objectivity tropes saturate the proceedings.

This particular day (17 November 2010) included two disputes, both involving Tlingit peoples. The first saw the Sealaska Corporation and Wrangell Cooperative Association face off with the Alaska State Museum, and the second pitted the Hoonah Indian Association and Huna Totem Corporation against the University of Pennsylvania Museum of Archaeology and Anthropology. Ironically the first dispute was over a clan hat that should have been worn during the Tlingit ceremony that I described above and that started the morning. The second was over sacred objects or *o'owu* that were sometimes referred to as the 'Mt. Fairweather' or 'Snail House Collection'. A decade later these disputes still resonate across the politics of NAGPRA in the United States. Although the committee eventually found in favour of the Tlingits in both matters, it was the perceived threat to 'objectivity' or what the National NAGPRA Program Manager (National NAGPRA 2010b: 9) later called "an obligation to safeguard this precious forum" that tribes seeking return of our ancestors and objects must contend with to this day.

By chance, the Chair of the Review Committee at this particular meeting happened to be a respected Tlingit elder. With the onset of the first dispute, she handed her gavel to another member of the Review Committee but continued to participate – offering important context and cultural expertise to other committee members (National NAGPRA 2010a: 159–60). Later that day, during the second dispute, she left the stage entirely and took her place at the table as a representative of the Tlingits confronting the University of Pennsylvania. Late in the afternoon, as the effects of the Tlingits' long morning performance stretched the meeting beyond its scheduled closing, fatigue and frayed nerves set in.

The acting chair of the committee struggled to allow time for bathroom breaks and telephone calls to explain the late working hours. In doing so he made the mistake of suggesting that the University of Pennsylvania representatives begin their presentation before the full complement of committee members were seated. That offer was declined, and nearly a decade later is still being cited as evidence that the Review Committee lacks 'objectivity'. Adding to the list of sins committed against the objectivity ideal, rumours soon began to swirl that the committee had accepted gifts of eagle feathers from tribal members appearing before them.

Additionally, and in between these two 'disputes' on the day's agenda, representatives of the US Government Accounting Office (GAO) reported on their newly published report to congress, *Native American Graves Protection and Repatriation Act: After Almost 20 Years, Key Federal Agencies Still Have Not Fully Complied with the Act* (2010). Ostensibly undertaken to expose government agencies that were ignoring the law and stonewalling tribes, the investigators chose to include anecdotal claims from critics inside museums who believed the Review Committee unfairly favoured tribal interests over the wishes of scientists attempting to retain possession of Native ancestral remains. The GAO investigators also noted, with an implied criticism, that some past committee members had recognised and stated that the explicit purpose of the law is to protect Native peoples from scientists who covet our ancestors' remains. Reciting these two sentiments, the GAO report then ominously asserted, "to be effective, federal advisory committees must be – and, just as importantly, be perceived as – independent and balanced as a whole" (GAO 2010: 36–7).

The Review Committee pushed back. One member, nominated by the museum community, wanted to know:

> Could you clarify what you mean and what you intend in your statement regarding the perception, quote and unquote, that the committee is biased in favor of tribes? What was the value of that? What was the basis of the judgment that you should include a statement like that, given the tremendous diversity that exists in the museum community, the fact that there has long been very divided opinions regarding NAGPRA from the very beginning and continuing today?
>
> *(National NAGPRA 2010a: 148)*

Another committee member cited the perception "on the opposite side…that this committee has been in fact controlled in large part by scientific organizations and museums" (National NAGPRA 2010a: 150). Ultimately the GAO spokesman retreated, admitting that the sentiments cited in the report "may or may not be representative" (National NAGPRA 2010a: 151). Nevertheless his defence of the decision to include the charges of bias handed opponents of repatriation what has become a justification for all but ignoring the law: "going forward … there are some people essentially with those perceptions that, you know … may be limiting their involvement or participation in the process and those types of things" (National NAGPRA 2010a: 149).

The following day began with an impromptu scolding from the National NAGPRA Manager who lamented "how the whole process yesterday was regarded by all of those viewing it in the room" (National NAGPRA 2010b: 15). Citing her responsibility "for safeguarding the integrity of this committee", she chided members who "took [the GAO] to task for saying things in their report to congress", for putting GAO representatives in "the position ... of being very nervous defending their report and disclosing things to you for the first time that were not in their report" (National NAGPRA 2010b: 6, 10). Curiously, forcing the GAO to admit that assertions of bias for Natives "were unfounded and without factual basis" was deemed unacceptable by the program manager because it threw the "underlying analysis" into doubt. That is, members were told to "reflect on this committee and your conduct of business" and warned that their interactions with the GAO "questions the integrity and diminishes the weight [of the report]" (National NAGPRA 2010b: 6). Apparently it was imperative to participate in perpetrating an aura of objectivity for the Government Accounting Office while offering public penance for one's own sins against objectivity.

More scolding for the previous day's perceived inequities followed and concluded with an ultimatum:

> If any of you feel that the way anything was conducted yesterday impacts on your ability to make a determination on other than the facts, then you make that individual determination. You have the opportunity, the individual decision, you have the option to abstain.
>
> *(National NAGPRA 2010b: 9–10)*

What followed was predictably painful self-consternation over impossible 'objectivity'. One member wondered aloud whether the chair should preside over a discussion about her own participation in a dispute from which she had recused her chairship. The chair consequently attempted to hand her gavel to the committee member who had chaired the previous day's dispute (after her self-recusal), only to have him also refuse it since he had *actually* chaired the dispute that was now being discussed. The need for 'objectivity' had begun to border on the comical.

Ironically, these behaviours deemed threatening to the objectivity myth are both mainstays of many indigenous cultures and a condition of being human.

Gift giving is widespread among Native peoples. Leaders from my own tribe would never travel to another tribal community without bringing gifts. Here at home, when young people visit elders they almost always bring some sort of gift. It is just good manners. Likewise, almost no Native American who lives among her own people has not sat patiently and longer than planned, because she did not want to disrespect an elder with much to say. The eagle feather gifts and the extension of allotted time for the ceremony of another culture may be dire threats to what the National NAGPRA Program Manager (18 months later still) warned was "very precious neutrality". Good will conveyed through gifts and deference to the ways of others are apparently to be scorned when committee members are told to "maintain your distance and dispassionate neutrality" (National NAGPRA 2012: 154–5). But these basic courtesies are also how Natives show respect to one another.

Similarly, in the wake of the program manager's admonishment, the Tlingit elder and committee chair's decision to recuse herself from the deliberations and to speak on behalf of her community, sent waves of angst through committee members indicted for failing in their obligation to 'objectivity':

> I know that our chairwoman recused herself, but ... I'm concerned about my ability to...make an impartial decision here after our chairwoman spoke. ... And I understand that these are very difficult matters and they're very emotional ... and I'm sure that's what fueled her decision to speak. But I in some ways feel like once some of the things were said

that I can't – I'm having a difficult time removing those from my decision making. And I'm questioning if I should recuse myself.

(National NAGPRA 2010b: 13)

Clearly this committee member recognised that performing 'objectivity' requires eschewing emotion. At least since Plato, western knowledge forms have disdained feelings. But we all have them. They are a condition of being human. Yet this committee member is being made to feel inadequate and tainted because she, as a human and a Native woman, feels for another human – for another Native woman whose people are at that very moment struggling against these same anti-human, colonial prejudices. She speaks of needing to remove those feelings, of feeling compelled to "remove those from my decision making" (National NAGPRA 2010b: 13), as if it were possible for her to stop being human and stop being Native so as to behave correctly ('objectively').

Of course no one can escape the living of life so as to be 'objective' about decisions made while living. We all inhabit space and time. We all interact with others, and our selves are created in those interactions. As social scientists have long understood, we are only socially possible (Cooley 1961; Mead 1961; Durkheim 1967). Starting in our infancy, we acquire selves by acquiring language and cultural literacy through which others' perceptions of us are reflected back to us. Despite the (particularly American) fascination with 'the individual', individualism is a group held value and something that so-called 'individuals' must learn from a group that precedes them in life. As I often told my students, paraphrasing Charles Cooley, "I am what I think other people think I am". The self is only socially acquired, and that socially arrived at self is the only venue available to me when decisions must be made.

There is then a colonial violence at work when Natives are told that thinking correctly, being fair, being 'objective' requires cutting ourselves off from interactions with our own peoples – relationships that are our very capacity for self-understanding. And this epistemic, cultural violence is doubled in as much as it is impossible. No one is from nowhere.

Nonetheless the worship of the impossibly absurd continues unabated in colonial forums where indigenous peoples are called to defend ourselves. Regardless of the goofiness of postulating what one modern philosopher calls The View from Nowhere (Naglel 1986), Natives attempting to recover our deceased ancestors and stolen objects must adhere to the bizarre cultural proclamation: "We are in a sense trying to climb outside of our own minds, an effort that some would regard as insane and that I regard as philosophically fundamental" (Nagel 1986: 11).

The backlash

I sat with other stunned observers of the 59th Meeting of the National NAGPRA Review Committee on 14 July 2016, as Dr Jordon Jacobs publicly insulted its members. Jacobs is Head of Cultural Policy and Repatriation for the Phoebe Hearst Museum of Anthropology at the University of California, Berkeley. His institution holds more ancestors than any other with the exception of the Smithsonian. Jacob's museum wrongly and defiantly designated more than 85 per cent of these deceased ancestors as 'culturally unidentifiable' – including many from my own tribe. (Miyamoto 2010; Dumont 2013). As such, the museum remains a frequent target of Native anger. Regardless, Jacobs claimed that it was "a desire on the part of the committee to malign [his] museum", that caused his hostility, and he did so by championing the 'objectivity' myth (National NAGPRA 2016: 170).

Jacobs had chosen not to show up in person for his museum's dispute with the Wiyot people and communicated his complaints via telephone:

The museum has observed the conduct of the Review Committee since the GAO report's publication. Disputes since that time have been notable not only for the procedural disparities for tribal and museum participants, including unequal time allotted to museum and tribal disputants, but also for such procedural error as the Review Committee chairperson's own testimony during a dispute proceeding from the witness table on behalf of a disputant tribe, a still undisclosed ethics investigation related to the Review Committee members' receipt of federally protected eagle feathers as gifts from a disputant tribe, and the admonishments inflicted on museum disputants by Review Committee members, often on matters immaterial to the law.

(National NAGPRA 2016: 167–8)

Jacob's ended his, what one committee member later called a 'rant', by stating that "this concludes the Hearst Museum's testimony and because of the outlined concerns, this also concludes the museum's involvement in this hearing" (National NAGPRA 2016: 171). He then hung up the telephone. He permitted no response. A lack of 'objectivity', he felt, justified his museum's disengagement from the federally mandated process for considering disputes between tribes and museums.

Jacobs excels at the polite impersonality effused by consummate performers of 'objectivity' – even when insulting a prestigious NAGPRA Review Committee appointed by the US Secretary of the Interior. His voice never portended anger or emotion of any kind.

Ironically, polite impersonality is a strategy for claiming personal authority. In one of his letters to the Klamath Tribes, asserting that we are not culturally affiliated with our own ancestors, Jacobs claims the requisite politeness by citing 'the record' of his 'demonstrated readiness to work with the Klamath Tribes'. Sadly, despite the NAGPRA mandated requirement for consultation with tribes (while decisions about cultural affiliation are being made) and our longstanding dispute with Jacob's museum, as a NAGPRA representative for my tribe for the past six years, I have never sat at a table with Jacobs. Indeed I only know what he looks like because I asked a friend to point him out to me as we all sat in the audience of a National NAGPRA Review Committee Meeting. His 'record' of 'demonstrated readiness to work with the Klamath Tribes' is purely and impersonally a paper trail.

Nevertheless, he goes on to assert in a letter to the Klamath Tribes that, "It is in that spirit that the museum wishes to move forward with the NAGPRA process on the current matter, recognizing that additional information pertaining to any of NAGPRA's lines of evidence may shed new light on earlier determinations" (2016 Letter: no page). Note that he is not present in any of these assertions. There seems to be no human perception involved, at all. He doesn't say 'my determinations' or 'our determinations' or 'the record as I perceive it', or 'NAGPRA's lines of evidence as I read them'. Nor does he acknowledge how deeply personal the desecration of our ancestors and their graves are for the Klamath Tribes, preferring to refer to them in tones of emotional indifference as 'the current matter'.

Jacob's professional writing evinces the same rhetorical strategy. Like many critics of NAGPRA, Jacob's conjures a world of objective "archaeological material" that he then juxtaposes with weaker "cultural identities" that are "subjective determinations", and the merely "symbolic progeny" of actual "archaeological evidence". Refusing to acknowledge that Native peoples have any legitimate claim to ancestors removed from our traditional homelands if they lived beyond a period in time that he never quite specifies, Jacobs reduces our deeply held responsibility to care for our ancestors to "an ethnic assertion" (2009: 93, 96, 92).

Ironically, by contending that archaeology and his own assertions are 'objective' (timeless, non-cultural, and non-political), Jacob's feels entitled to dismiss the merely subjectively felt reactions of indigenous peoples to the long history of archaeologists' racist looting of ancestral graves as "a blasé allegation" (2009: 84). Because, he says, "the drafters of NAGPRA ... failed to identify ethnicity for what it is: a recent social construction" (2009: 85), legitimate objective scientists are now forced to contend with subjectively fabricated "ethnic identity [that] is constructed from the inside out", identities that rely on "perceived collectivities" whose "relative importance are constantly shifting" (2009: 85). Thus repatriation, he chides, "is one of the 'decolonizing methodologies' identified by Linda Tuhiwai Smith in that it enfranchises groups with the power to form their own identity" (2009: 84).

Despite Jacob's belief in the flimsiness of indigenous identities, more than 70 representatives of more than 50 tribes gathered for a Native American Tribal Forum on the Berkeley campus of the University of California in April 2017. Criticisms of the Phoebe Hearst Museum, and of Jacobs himself, were scathing. And I certainly added complaints from my own tribe to the chorus. There were campus administrators present, and the forum resulted in a long report delivered to the system-wide (10 campuses) leadership of the University of California. It also got the attention of the California State Legislature, which subsequently passed Assembly Bill 2836. This new law explicitly identifies the Phoebe Hearst Museum and "the importance of complying with the federal Native American Graves Protection and Repatriation Act of 1990" (Section 1 13 (4)). The bill was signed into law on 27 September 2018. We will see if the law helps break the colonial grip of the Phoebe Hearst Museum on ancestors and cultural objects taken from many tribes.

Objectivity is theology

The modern claim to objectivity is a recent phenomenon dating only to the 19th century (Megill 1994: 2). Although the terms 'subjective' and 'objective' can be found further back in European history, they did not mean anything close to what they do today, and they were almost never used together.

To understand how our modern sense of objectivity and subjectivity have come down to us, and how these are derived from and dependent on older theological usage, we need to understand a little of the relationship between ancient Greek philosophy and Christianity.

The early church fathers were deeply indebted to Plato (427–347 BCE) (Colish 1997; Jaeger 1961). They were quite aware that it was Plato's teacher Socrates who had first articulated the claim of an abstract human "psyche", "mind", or "soul" understood as a "ghost that thinks" (Cornford 1932: 50; Havelock 1963: 197). These men spoke and read Greek, were educated in Greek institutions, and actively sought to model the institutions of Christianity into forms that would meld with the then far more powerful Platonism flourishing among the educated classes of the Mediterranean region.

Among the teachings of Plato was the assertion of what in modern English we call 'essence'. In Latin, the term most often used was 'forma'; consequently we still hear the Platonic notion of essences referred to as 'the forms'. Plato's claim was that essences were abstract and perfect forms of things that were available only to the mind. Plato strove to develop a disciplined uniformity for his new concept of 'psyche' or 'mind' that he claimed needed protection from emotions and the senses if it was to gain access to this realm of essences.

I sometimes told my students that they could think of the English language suffix 'ness' to get at what Plato intended. There are, he taught in book 10 of *The Republic*, many particular beds made by men, but there is only one true form or essence – what he called: 'bed in itself'. All physical beds, then, share qualities of the one true essence: bed-ness.

Those of us living in societies referred to as 'modern' or 'advanced' continue to know in Platonist ways. We assume the existence of Platonic essences: e.g. 'society', 'our culture', 'justice', etc. But ask yourself: have you ever actually seen these things, 'society' or 'justice'? We routinely claim to 'study society' or to 'know justice when we see it', but we are curiously untroubled by the fact that these Platonic abstractions have no physical existence. They are not empirically available. I can't go into the world and find 'society' like I can find a horse or a swimming hole. These 'essences' are phantoms, and – if we can think critically about them – rather bizarre developments of European cultural history.

The pursuit of essences by the Socratic/Platonic 'psyche' requires attacking emotion, feeling, and sensual understandings. The mind, Plato teaches, if it is to know what he calls 'the good', must be disciplined, and this requires protection from the corruption of the physical senses. Plato's disdain for his own humanity (for his physical and emotional self) is one potent source of our modern notion of 'objectivity' – albeit a long and indirect one.

But Europeans were not always so thoroughly Platonist. In the centuries following the fall of the Western Roman Empire in 476, Western Christiandom largely lost the ability to read Greek, and the works of Aristotle (384–322 BCE) remerged in Latin speaking western Europe centuries before those of his teacher. Islamic civilisations in North Africa and Spain had and used Arabic translations of Aristotle's works. With the recapturing of Toledo (in Spain) by Christians in the late 11th century, translations from Arabic to Latin began in earnest. By the end of the 12th century, almost all of the works of Aristotle available to us today had been translated into Latin. The result was an intellectual world-view that carefully mixed Christianity and the teachings of Aristotle (Berman 1981; Rubenstein 2003).

The mature Aristotle had no patience for Platonic 'essences'. Although he surmised that a central organising force was at work in the world, he could not accept that it existed in a non-physical and eternal world operating behind tangible existence. Thus in place of Plato's eternal forms he posited 'substance' working itself out in physically developing life.

The term 'substance', here, should be thought of both as it is used in modern English (as a physical, not mental thing), and as medieval Aristotelian Christians used it. To get at this history, remember that 'sub' means below. While a 'stance' is a standing or posture. So if we can imagine an underlying life force with an observable quality (a stance), we can begin to recognise what medieval Christian Aristotelians had in mind.

Some scholars describe this force as 'potential' (Cornford 1932). Others translate Aristotle's claim with the phrase: 'for the sake of which' (Barnes 1984). (Aristotle used the Greek word: hypokeimenon.) The idea is that things in life are always moving toward their perfect form or endpoint. Long before his influence appeared in the work of Charles Darwin and Karl Marx, Aristotle argued that living things develop and alter themselves with each generation. Just as a seed contains the potential of the mature plant, each generation of the plant contains the potential of the next. All of this happens for the sake of ultimate perfection, which is the endpoint.

Medieval Christian Aristotelians ('scholastics') understood the term 'subjective' to refer to the most real (substantial) qualities of things. Thus William of Ockham (1287–1347), an influential scholastic, could write that, "the universal is not a real thing with a subjective existence". He could also say that, "it has only an objective existence in the soul and is something fictitious existing in this objective existence as the external thing exists in subjective existence" (cited in Karskens 1992: 214). When the scholastics referred to things with 'subjective' qualities, they were pointing to the Aristotelian 'substance' that made them real. However, we must resist the temptation to conflate this medieval 'substance' with our modern notion of 'the objective thing itself' The latter was still centuries in the future.

'Objective', for Christian Aristotelians, referred to how something was known. This meaning is captured by the fact that in 18th-century English, its primary use still denoted the lens on a microscope (Daston 1992: 601). For the scholastics, then, objectivity was about how something subjective was received or apprehended by the mind. It pointed to the changed status of something more real (subjective) as it was affected by the act of knowing.

But it is important to remember that theirs was a theological world-view. Scholastics assumed that metaphysical questions were primary.[4] In other words, the foundational role of their God was presumed. God made both humans and the other things of the creation, and understanding the relationship between God's creative power and the limits of mortal humans' perception and reasoning was foundational to building knowledge (Fox Keller 1994).

The objects of existence and the act of knowing them were not, as they are for we moderns, obviously separable from one another. The scholastics assumed that their God was perfect and that they, themselves, were not. As God's creations, they knew they contained both the potential for movement towards perfection and mortal impediments to that progress. They contained 'substance' in the Aristotelian sense, but their (Christianity narrated) mortal limits were fundamental to their condition as imperfect earthly life forms. So questions of correct knowing (epistemology) were inextricably tied to metaphysical/theological presuppositions.

As Aristotelian substances, humans were imperfect but with the potential for perfection; the question was always one of assessing the worldly status of their Being (as substance) and therefore the capacity of their objective (imperfect) knowing.

As Machiel Karskens (1992: 221) explains:

> *Esse subiective* is a metaphysical concept referring to the existence of an accident as, *esse in alio*, or *esse in subjecto*: it presupposes a theory of substance. It can be borrowed from the domain of metaphysics to be used in epistemological matters. There *esse subiective* refers mainly to acts, powers or habits of the (human) mind as being accidents of the actually existing soul.

Let's be sure we understand. *Esse subiective* (to exist subjectively) refers to Aristotelian substance, to our underlying life force. But as Christians, medievals understood this life force as bestowed from the perfection of their God. This is why it is important to recognise how the term 'accident' is being used in the quoted passage.

Think of the older etymological sense of an accident as something that befalls (happens to) us. Then remember that, for Christians, humans are fallen beings; they are befallen from the original sin of Adam and Eve. That is, the things that happen to them in life, the necessity of enduring earthly experiences, was caused by their ancestors' fall from God's grace. Humans' perfect God-given life force, then, is present on earth only imperfectly, as evidenced by the accidents (befallings) of life. As an Aristotelian substance one moves toward one's potential; as a Christian one is shackled by earthly life.

To say, then, that "*Esse subiective* is a metaphysical concept referring to the existence of an accident as in *esse in alio* or *esse in subject* …" (Karskens 1992: 221) is to point to the perfect God-given life force (substance) limited by the accidents of earthly existence. This life force is the being (*esse*) of God present in others (*in alio*) and the things of existence (in subjecto) – including humans.

We can now see why knowing (epistemology) for medievals was always contingent on theology. ("It can be borrowed from the domain of metaphysics to be used in epistemological matters".) The "acts, powers or habits of the (human) mind" – the stuff of epistemology – can only always function as "accidents" (consequences of earthly life) befalling the God-given life force ("the actually existing soul") (Karskens 1992: 221).

Humans understood as befallen incarnations of Christian Aristotelian substance will make it possible by the early 18th century for a few philosophers to begin the slide toward modern conceptions of 'subjective' – as the stuff of particular and distinct biographies. However, in the works of the famous men usually associated with the opening of the European Enlightenment – e.g., Thomas Hobbes (1588–1679), Rene Descartes (1596–1650), and John Locke (1632–1704) – there was not yet any explicit opposition made between "objective" and "subjective" (Karskens 1992: 229). Consider for example this passage from Descartes' *Third Meditation*:

> And although the reality which I am considering in my ideas is merely objective reality, I must not on that account suppose that the same reality need not exist formally in the causes of my ideas, but that it is enough for it to be present in them objectively. For just as the objective mode of being belongs to the ideas by their very nature, so the formal mode of being belongs to the causes of ideas – or at least the first and most important ones by their very nature.
>
> *(Descartes 1994: 29: emphasis in original)*

'Objective', here, still refers to imperfect acts of knowing. But note the emphasis on externality. The 'merely objective' is being caused. No longer an unquestionably internal affair, as it was for Christian Aristotelians, external things now play a far more consequential role in how they are received by the mind.

Descartes was among the first generations of western European scholars to regain access to Latin translations of Plato that were unavailable for roughly a thousand years. Following Muslims' sacking of Christian Constantinople in 1453, Greek-speaking scholars emigrated to western Europe, particularly Italy. There they translated Plato's works and fuelled the Italian Renaissance. Descartes is suggesting, then, that these external things contain a 'formal mode of being' (Platonic essences) produced by God. And these essences affect his ideas about them.

Nevertheless, the 'mind' that Plato sought to make into a unified seat of self-governance was constantly threatened, Descartes laments, by sight that makes the sun appear smaller than things closer; and from smell, touch, and sound that continuously confused his comprehension of wax as heat was progressively applied. More insidious still, and much like the prisoners in Plato's Simile of the Cave, Descartes' sense-based humanity is "like a prisoner who is enjoying an imaginary freedom while asleep … and dreads being woken up, and goes along with the pleasant illusion as long as he can" (1994: 15).

Waking up, for Descartes means a severe Platonic and Christian disciplining of the body. Complete eradication of deceitful physical existence may not be possible, but it is the goal. He will, he says, "shut my eyes, stop my ears, and withdraw all my senses". And "all images of bodily things" that he cannot purge he will regard "as vacuous, false and worthless" (1994: 24).

Like other fathers of the European Enlightenment, Descartes is a Christian. His god bestowed him a Platonic 'mind', and if protected from earthly impurity, access to essential forms – to essences behind the physical world is achievable. He thus writes of, "a faculty of judgment… which I certainly received from God. And since God does not wish to deceive me, he surely did not give me the kind of faculty which would ever enable me to go wrong while using it correctly" (1994: 37–8).

This theological quest for purity of mind will in coming generations make it possible to begin the move toward our modern understandings of: 'subjective' and 'objective'. If as Descartes surmised, the causes of my ideas are deity created essences of external things, then their impact on a God given 'faculty of judgment' can transform the traditional notion of the 'objective'. That is, 'objective', in the older sense of imperfect knowing slides slowly into respect for the efficacy of external essences. And the relationship is two-way: the purer the mind, the more prone it is to the power of deity created essences unfettered by the senses.

Karskens (1992: 244) quotes the early-18th-century thinker, Adolph Friedrich Hoffmann (1703–1741), to mark this evolution. "These things or objects, being themselves carriers of powers … exercise an influence, which is called 'objective cause'". We can now see how this transmigration of 'objectivity' away from the domain and quality of perceiving minds and toward the efficacy of external things will unfold. We can also see that our modern conception of objectivity is faith-based and unobtainable (disembodied). As one would expect, given this European history, the "view from nowhere" is as Evelyn Fox Keller (1994: 315) notes, derived from older and unacknowledged attempts to approximate the theological presumption: "that there was one vantage point, namely God's view, that was simultaneously absolutely special and absolutely knowing".

Weaponizing the objectivity myth

Asserting 'objectivity' in a struggle to maintain possession of the ancestral human remains and cultural objects of another people is an act of colonial aggression – all the more so when the theology behind the manoeuvre goes unrecognised. We can understand the invoking of 'objectivity' as what Geonpul scholar Aileen Moreton-Robinson recognises as a colonial claim to an "epistemological a priori". That is, enacting the 'objectivity' myth "is an invisible regime of power that secures hegemony through discourse and has material effects in everyday life" (2004: 75).

Philosophers have long understood "a priori knowledge" to refer to what can be assumed because it is already known and beyond question. Thus Morten-Robinson is interested in how "whiteness [is] being exercised epistemologically". She wants to understand "how whiteness as an epistemological a priori provides for a way of knowing and being that is predicated on superiority, which becomes normalized and forms part of one's taken-for-granted knowledge" (2004: 75–6).

Although I prefer to speak of cultural difference (and not race or colour), Morten-Robinson is pointing out that while ways of knowing have always varied across human populations, European-derived traditions too often appear to be beyond question. Because these ways of knowing are assumed, they escape critical reflection. They appear natural and non-cultural. This a priori status is what allows their users, as heirs to these cultural habits, to adopt an air of superiority when they speak to and about peoples with other cultural histories.

In the opening pages, I said that I wanted to refer to the objectivity story as an 'objectivity complex'. This is because as an a priori mythology, it undergirds all sorts of authoritarian statements (many of them made in the heat of intellectual battle) that depend upon but need not explicitly invoke 'objectivity'. Representatives of the University of Pennsylvania Museum of Archaeology and Anthropology in their dispute with Tlingit peoples at the 46th Meeting of the National NAGPRA Review Committee made several such claims – assertions that, were it not for the assumed a priori status of the 'objectivity' ruse would be quickly recognised as not only untenable but downright mystical.

At issue was whether the museum had a legal 'right of possession'; to sacred objects alienated by one Tlingit individual from the Hoonah Indian Association and Huna Totem Corporation. That is, was the transfer to the museum consistent with Tlingit protocol? Despite the presence of the relevant Tlingit clan spokesmen, the museum insisted on highlighting the views of their own non-indigenous but credentialed "scholars and experts in Tlingit law and tradition and culture" (National NAGPRA 2010a :260).

Backed by the 'objectivity' of these experts, the museum asserted that, "when we look at the past, we can't look at it from today's eyes". They continued:

What's relevant to this analysis is Tlingit law and custom at the time [1924], not today, but what was the law at the time, recognizing that this is a culture that doesn't have statutory law like NAGPRA but they have traditions and practice and culture.

(National NAGPRA 2010a: 260–1)

Claiming to escape the present and the use of one's own eyes and to assume the perceptions of those long deceased and from another culture is obviously fantasy. It is also a rhetorical technique used by academics skilled in the cultural performance of 'objectivity'. It is as Kenneth J. Gergen (1994: 279) describes, a performative device for producing the illusion of first-hand knowledge, of being in the presence of a putative fact, of "establishing experiential presence". The museum representatives are mere mortals, but because their pretence enjoys a priori status as part of a foundational myth of the dominant culture, this bizarre claim to abandon their own vision and leap through time and across cultural realities went unchallenged. Because it resonates as part of a hegemonic objectivity complex, those peddling this superhuman (theological) claim were not called to defend and explain its audacity.

Just as interesting is the conflation of "traditions and practice and culture" with "law" (National NAGPRA 2010a: 260–1). 'Law' also resonates semiotically from within the objectivity complex. That is, it is assumed to be a Platonic essence represented in empirically available and objectively present text that can be correctly interpreted by sufficiently disciplined minds – intellects whose legitimacy depends upon claims to non-emotional, life-denying 'objectivity'.

The museum representatives, then, are caught in an impossible predicament. They must establish their legal 'right of possession' (as defined in the NAGPRA statute) to the Tlingits' sacred objects by inserting a foreign concept (objective law) into Tlingit culture while also acknowledging that Tlingit society 'doesn't have statutory law'. ("What is relevant is Tlingit law … recognizing that this is a culture that doesn't have statutory law like NAGPRA but they have traditions and practice and culture" [National NAGPRA 2010A: 260-1]).

'Culture', here – particularly the culture of cultural others – in this forum governed by objectivity tropes, has far less status than 'objectivity'. It is notoriously diffuse, porous, unstable, and prone to irrationality. The long colonial history of anthropology (as assumed capacity of the colonisers to objectively evaluate lesser peoples) infects and troubles this conflation of 'law' with 'traditions and practice and culture'. How can the Tlingits be both practitioners of objective 'law' (thus objectively validating the transfer of their sacred objects to the museum) and cultural others hobbled by the instability of anthropologised 'tradition' and 'culture'?

Given that the Tlingits' sacred objects were transferred to the museum by a single Tlingit individual, the museum representatives are forced to argue that their alienation was both sanctioned by something they call 'Tlingit law' and brought about in an era of notorious cultural instability wrought by overwhelming colonial pressure.

[T]he experts and the evidence shows that at that moment in time given the influence of the Alaska Native Brotherhood, the Russian Orthodox Church, the Protestant Church, that Tlingit law authorised and indeed encouraged the sale of these objects (National NAGPRA 2010a: 264).

This is a bizarre and fantastical claim. 'Tlingit law' (which the museum staff admits isn't actually 'law') is said to have had an objective reality 'at that moment in time' even as the winds of colonialism fundamentally transformed Tlingit life. This law which isn't law is said to have "authorized and indeed encouraged the sale of these objects", but is simultaneously "a changing practice" that "may not have been the case in every Tlingit community" (National NAGPRA 2010a: 264). One wonders, given all of this change which is happening differently in different

Tlingit communities, precisely which 'moment in time' among precisely which and how many Tlingit individuals constitute the 'Tlingit law' (that really isn't 'law') that the museum's 'experts' have confirmed?

Conclusion

As indigenous peoples we are justified in asking why the entirety of this fantastical colonial scheme is not laughable on it is face? What I have presented here is of course only a small snapshot of how the objectivity charade is perpetrated by colonial powers. Native peoples are regularly told that if we only had a better understanding of the objectivity laced claims of academics who believe themselves to be the legitimate stewards of our past, we would cease with our hostility. But this is an arrogance built on self-ignorance. Only those ignorant of their own history can fail to see their ancestral myths at work in their own ways of knowing. For Native peoples, then, the question as I see it isn't whether 'objectivity' is right or wrong. It is a matter of understanding the colonisers' epistemological history and teaching it to them in the strategic defence of our own peoples.

Notes

1 Jacques Derrida's (1966) classic essay, *Structure, Sign, and Play in the Discourse of the Human Sciences*, is a useful statement of the difficulty of interrogating the cultural bases of theorizing.
2 Scholarship on the topic has grown but not enough to shake the presumption that objectivity is an extra-cultural imperative for credible knowing. See Bordo (1987), Daston (1991; 1992; 2000), Daston and Galison (1992; 2007), Karskens (1992), Nagel (1986), Newell (1986), Putnam (1990), and see generally "Symposium on the Social History of Objectivity" (1992).
3 I intend 'genealogy', in the sense that Nietzsche and Foucault used it. Relevant works include Foucault (1977) and Nietzsche (1969).
4 Today metaphysics refers to that which cannot be measured and thus proven. Such questions are typically thought of as faith-based and inadmissible to empirical investigations. But this change in status did not occur until the 19th century. For example, Francis Bacon, one of the founders of scientific experimentation wrote of metaphysical understandings as "the worthiest to be sought" (Bacon 1952: 43).

References

Bacon, F. (1952). *Advancement of Learning*. Encyclopaedia Britannica: Chicago. IL.
Barker, J. (2011). *Native Acts: Law, Recognition, and Cultural Authenticity*. Duke University Press: Durham, NC.
Barnes, J. (ed.) (1984). *The Complete Works of Aristotle*. Princeton University Press: Princeton, NJ.
Berman, M. (1981). *The Reenchantment of the World*. Cornell University Press: New York.
Bordo, S. (1987). *The Flight to Objectivity*. SUNY Press: Albany, NY.
Colish, M. (1997). *Medieval Foundations of the Western Intellectual Tradition 400-1400*. Yale University Press: New Haven, CT.
Cooley, C. (1961). 'The social self', in T. Parsons, E. Shils, K. Naegele, and J. Pitts (eds.) *Theories of Society*. Free Press: New York, 822–828.
Cornford, F.M. (1932). *Before and After Socrates*. Cambridge University Press: New York.
Daston, L. (1991). 'Baconian facts, academic civility, and the prehistory of objectivity', *Annals of Scholarship*, vol 8, no 1: 337–363.
Daston, L. (1992). 'Objectivity and the escape from perspective', *Social Studies of Science*, vol 22, no 4: 597–618.
Daston, L. (2000). *Biographies of Scientific Objects*. University of Chicago Press: Chicago, IL.
Daston, L. and Galison, P. (1992). 'The image of objectivity', *Representations*, vol 40: 81–128.
Daston, L. and Galison, P. (2007). *Objectivity*. Zone Books: Brooklyn, NY.
Derrida, J. (1966). *Writing and Difference*. University of Chicago Press: Chicago, IL, 278–293.

Descartes, R. (1994). *The Philosophical Writings of Descartes*, Vol 2. Cambridge University Press: New York, 12–62.

Dumont, C. (2013). 'Navigating a colonial quagmire', in S. Chari and J.M. Lavallee (eds.) *Accomplishing NAGPRA*. Oregon State University Press: Corvallis, OR, 239–264.

Durkheim, E. (1967). *The Elementary Forms of Religious Life*. Free Press: New York.

Foucault, M. (1977). 'Nietzsche, genealogy, history', in D. Bouchard, (ed.) *Language, Counter-Memory, Practice*. Cornell University Press: Ithaca, NY, 139–164.

Fox Keller, E. (1994). 'The paradox of scientific subjectivity', in A. Megill (ed.) *Rethinking Objectivity*. Duke University Press: Durham, NC, 313–331.

Gergen, K.J. (1994). 'The mechanical self and the rhetoric of objectivity', in A. Megill (ed.) *Rethinking Objectivity*. Duke University Press: Durham, NC, 265–287.

Government Accounting Office. (2010). *Native American Graves Protection and Repatriation Act: After Almost 20 Years, Key Federal Agencies Still Have Not Fully Complied With the Act*. United States Government Accounting Office: Washington, DC. (GAO-10–768).

Havelock, E. (1963). *Preface to Plato*. Harvard University Press: Cambridge, MA.

Jacobs, J. (2009). 'Repatriation and the reconstruction of identity', *Museum Anthropology*, vol 32, no 2: 83–98.

Jacobs, J. (2016). Jordon Jacobs to the Klamath tribes, December 12, 2016. Letter. [Author's personal file].

Jaeger, W. (1961). *Early Christianity and Greek Paideia*. Harvard University Press: Cambridge, MA.

Karskens, M. (1992). 'The development of the opposition subjective versus objective in the 18th century', *Archiv für Begriffsgeschichte*, vol 35: 214–256.

Layton, R. (1994). *Conflict in the Archaeology of Living Traditions*. New York: Routledge.

Mead, G. (1961). 'Taking the role of the other', in T. Parsons, E. Shils, K. Naegele, and J. Pitts (eds.) *Theories of Society*. Free Press: New York, 739–740.

Megill, A. (ed.). (1994). 'Four senses of objectivity', in *Rethinking Objectivity*. Duke University Press: Durham, NC, 1–20.

Miyamoto, L. (2010). *Public Presentation at 43rd Meeting of the National NAGPRA Review Committee*, November 19. District of Columbia: Washington, DC.

Moreton-Robinson, A. (ed.). (2004). 'Whiteness, epistemology and Indigenous representation', in Moreton Robinson (ed.) *Whitening Race*. Aboriginal Studies Press: Canberra, ACT, 75–88.

Nagel, T. (1986). *The View from Nowhere*. Oxford University Press: New York.

National NAGPRA Program. (2010a). *Transcripts of 43rd Meeting of the National NAGPRA Review Committee*, November 17. Washington, DC. Available: https://www.nps.gov/nagpra/REVIEW/INDEX.HTM, accessed 15 January 2019.

National NAGPRA Program. (2010b). *Transcripts of the 43rd Meeting of the National NAGPRA Review Committee*, 18 November. Washington, DC. Available: https://www.nps.gov/nagpra/REVIEW/INDEX.HTM, accessed 15 January 2020.

National NAGPRA Program. (2012). *Transcripts of the 46th Meeting of the National NAGPRA Review Committee*, May 10. Santa Fe, NM. Available: https://www.nps.gov/nagpra/REVIEW/INDEX.HTM, accessed 15 January 2019.

National NAGPRA Program. (2016). *Transcripts of the 59th Meeting of the National NAGPRA Review Committee*, July 14. Missoula, MT. Available: https://www.nps.gov/nagpra/REVIEW/INDEX.HTM, accessed 15 January 2019.

Newell, R.W. (1986). *Objectivity, Empiricism and Truth*. Routledge: London.

Nietzsche, F. (1969). *On the Genealogy of Morals*. Vintage Books: New York.

Putnam, H. (1990). *Realism with a Human Face*. Harvard University Press: Cambridge, MA.

Rubenstein, R. (2003). *Aristotle's Children*. Harcourt Inc: Orlando, FL.

Symposium on the Social History of Objectivity. (1992). 'Front matter', *Social Studies of Science*, vol 22, no 4: 595–652.

Part 3

Sovereignty

Part editor: Aileen Moreton-Robinson

19

Incommensurable sovereignties

Indigenous ontology matters

Aileen Moreton-Robinson

According to political theology, the earliest reference to sovereignty's meaning as a divine rule is the declaration made by Egyptian Queen Hatshepsut, who reigned between 1486 and 1469 BCE, and declared she was a God. The Romans, Greeks, and Israelites also had similar ideas of supreme divine authority, but it was French Jurist and philosopher Jean Bodin, who in the 16th century developed the first theological conceptualisation of the modern concept of sovereignty (Bujis 2003: 236). Bodin posited that Kings and Princes were God's deputies on earth responsible for the welfare of other men. In the 17th century King James I of England elaborated on Bodin's idea which he expressed to Parliament in 1601. He stated:

> Kings are the authors and makers of laws, and not the laws of the Kings. The state of monarchy is the supremest [*sic*] thing upon the earth: for kings are not only God's Lieutenants upon Earth, and sit upon earth and sit upon God's throne, but even by God himself they are called Gods.
>
> *(King James 1 cited in Bujis 2003: 231)*

In England, by the middle ages people believed that God had granted earthly powers to the Monarch and the Church especially the Pope. King James 1 declared that sovereignty was not of the earth; it emanated from God and was embodied by Kings.

The conceptual development of sovereignty has generated an abundant non-Indigenous literature within modernity. Some scholars argue that sovereignty is no longer a cornerstone of modern politics because technology and globalisation have changed its form (Gumplova 2015). In the 21st century, cultural, environmental and economic influences transcend borders enabled by technology and communications without visas and passports. Cyber espionage is not bound by a nation state's territorial integrity, exclusive possession and supreme authority the key attributes of state sovereignty in political and legal theory. Others argue we have reached the sovereign turn whereby concepts derived from the work of Carl Schmitt, Derrida, Walter Benjamin, and Giorgio Agamben inform critical scholarship on questions of sovereignty (Jennings 2011). However, there is a blind spot in this literature with its focus on political and legal theories of sovereignty that works to occlude the ontological foundations of the concept. States of exception, the right to kill, the paradoxical relation of friend and enemy between state and subject, the maintenance of bare life, or Foucault's idea of 'to let live and to make live' are constituted through a regime of power that has transcendent origins. As will be demonstrated, the secularisation of sovereignty did not detract from its ontology – ways of being – as power emanating from a God, whose bodily form by the time of the Renaissance is represented in religious art as being white and male.

Here, I use the concept 'white' as a racialised category of analysis. In this chapter I argue that the continuing disavowal of Indigenous sovereignty operates through the racial logics of state sovereignty's incommensurable ontology. I demonstrate how Indigenous sovereignties challenge the philosophical premises of state sovereignty as these different forms do not share the same ontology. My disclaimer is I have restricted my discussion to a particular sovereignty that originated in the Kingdom of England and later manifested as the spread of the Kingdom of Britain's empire enabled the formation of nation states such as Canada, the United States, Australia, and New Zealand.

Sovereignty is not a word invented by Indigenous people, but we own the lands from which we were 'dispossessed' as rationalised by the logic of Western systems of law in the formation of the above nation states. In her ground-breaking book *Indigenous Sovereignty Matters* (2005), Lenape scholar Joanne Barker explains how the European conceptualisation of sovereignty justified conquest and possession of Indigenous territories. She explains that Indigenous peoples do not necessarily share the same understanding of sovereignty, or its relevance to the living of their everyday lives. However, since World War II, Indigenous discourse has deployed the concept sovereignty usefully to foreshadow "social and legal rights to political, economic and cultural self-determination" (2005: 1). Mohawk scholar Taiaike Alfred argues that our existence as sovereign peoples within a state rights system remains untenable. He notes, "the challenge for Indigenous peoples in building appropriate postcolonial governing systems is to disconnect the notion of sovereignty from its Western legal roots and transform it" (2005: 42–3), because the Westphalian concept inheres values and objectives that are antithetical to Indigenous traditional philosophies.

Barker and Alfred's propositions are supported by the work of Indigenous scholars. Indigenous sovereignty as a concept has multiple meanings within Indigenous political and legal scholarship from the 1970s to the early 21st century. The idea of sovereignty can refer to people who have never surrendered their lands, to illegal occupation; to prior, inherent rights in territories; to belonging to a particular Indigenous people; to holding tribal citizenship, to a political and moral claim to inclusion within settler colonial states; to recognition as first peoples and to treating as sovereign nations. These varying conceptualisations of Indigenous sovereignty share a singular point of reference and negation: the assumption of state sovereignty. In the past decade Indigenous scholarship concerned primarily with the distribution of power within Indigenous territories, has illuminated the operations of the state's racialised jurisprudential and political reach. This is evident in reading Audra Simpson's book *Mohawk Interruptus: Political Life across the Borders of Settler States*, Chris Andersen's *Metis: Race, Recognition and the Struggle for Indigenous Peoplehood* and Glen Coulthard's *Red Skin: White Masks*. Refusing settler state recognition, asserting nation status and distinct peoplehood all contest state sovereignty as part of the resolve of Indigenous sovereignties – the resilient existent. If we are to think through and work with Taiaike Alfred's challenge to Indigenous scholars to redefine and remake state sovereignty, then we must make visible the source of its supreme authority and the origins of ours.

Indigenous sovereignties – relativity

In the introduction to the book *Sovereign Subjects: Indigenous Sovereignty Matters* (2007) I asked the question: if Indigenous sovereignty does not exist, why does it require refusing by state sovereignty? As numerous Indigenous scholars have demonstrated Indigenous nations continue to exercise our sovereignties in our political struggles within and against the confines of state sovereignty (Deloria and Lytle 1984; Wilkins 1997; Trask 1999; Williams 2005; Miller 2008; Miller et al. 2010; Mutu 2011; Barker 2017; Moreton-Robinson 2007; 2015; Andersen 2014; Simpson 2014; Coulthard 2014; Kauanui 2018). We have gone to war, we have refused, and we have used political and legal mechanisms to challenge the legitimacy of Canada, Australia, the United States, New Zealand, Hawai'i states and their sovereign claims to exclusive possession of our lands. We do this because every day our sovereignties exist and are operating despite these claims. As resilient existents, our sovereignties continue ontologically and materially; as humans we are the embodiment of our lands.

The origins of Indigenous sovereignties are in and of the earth. We draw on and exert the life-force we share with and derive from our creators, ancestors and relatives that inextricably unite us with the earth and to our respective shared territories. We have origin stories that emanate from and connect us as humans and non-humans through relations and kin to all that Mother Earth and our creators made. I use the term non-human to refer to all things that do not have human form. Our ontologies, our ways of being Indigenous are inextricably connected to being in and of our lands. This is an inherent sovereignty not temporally constrained. It functions through the logics of relativity finding expression in kin relations, respect, responsibility and obligation that exist outside the logic of capital and familial ties to private property and nation states.

I am not indulging in an existential crisis nor am I promoting anthropological romanticism to posit Indigenous peoples as caring sharing humans who did not war or take over other's territories. What I am positing is that in trying to make Indigenous sovereignties comprehensible through the logic of supreme authority, exclusive possession and rights will fail to capture the facticity, complexity, depth and relativity of Indigenous sovereignties. I use the concept relativity defined by Vine Deloria as:

> everything in the natural world has relationships with every other thing and the total set of relationships makes up the natural world as we experience it. This concept is simply the relativity concept as applied to a universe that people experience as alive and not as dead or inert.
>
> *(Deloria 1990: 34)*

Relativity is born of knowledge that the earth is conscious and alive this is incommensurate with Western ideas that to be human requires possessive and extractive relations with an inert earth. In contrast, the ontology of our sovereignties is inextricably manifest in different kinds of relations born of a conscious and alive earth as will be discussed through a consideration of Kanaka Maoli, Anishinaabe, and Goenpul origin stories. Hermeneutically, origin stories are concerned with imparting cultural values over myopic and singular meaning, which is why there can be different versions of the same story with a plurality of meanings from the same value system (Gross 2003: 127–8).

Kanaka Maoli – Hawai'i

Within Hawaiian culture sovereignty is relativity; it involves human responsibility for taking care of the land and sea created by the Gods who in Hawaiian cosmology are powerful beings of nature with immeasurable power; they can exist in spirit form or human form (Silva 2004: 19). Kanaka Maoli scholar Ontai argues that Hawaiians use the word ea to mean "life, breath … spirit" to signify sovereignty as "the life of the land, is breath and spirit, is in every grain of sand, in every rock, in every tree, in every kanaka (person), as it has been since the time of darkness and light" (2005: 155). While it is acknowledged that there are number of different versions of origin stories about how the Hawaiian islands came to be the most common narrative is one where *Kanaka Maoli* are the descendants of earth mother *Papahanaumoku* and *Wakea*, the sky father who are the progeny of *Lo,* the supreme creator of *Po* the time before light. *Papahanaumoku* and *Wakea* are the first parents. *Papa* the earth mother gives birth to the islands, humans, plant and animal life. She births a still born naming him *Kalo*, who is born with no legs or arms, so they bury him outside their hut and in the morning, he had emerged in a new form as a taro plant which had grown from his grave. As descendants of *Papa* and *Wakea, Kanaka Maoli* look after *Kalo.* They practice *haloa* the eternal breath of life in ritual and show respect by nurturing and caring for their farming plot. Ontai argues that:

> The land and its resources was a function of the divine alliance and nurturing from the ancestral gods, who in turn expected haipule (piety) and aloha (devotion) from the living. In this extended na Kanaka family of gods and spirits, all things were divine, from the divine returning to the divine. The gods fed them, housed them clothed them. Their rulers, divine themselves, were the earth representatives and caretakers of those spiritual gifts. Land and its resources were personified in the ancestors, gods and rulers. They were one in the same, a blend of spirit and material co-existence, with no boundaries. Now one owned what was divine and sacred. No one owned the sky, the earth, the wind or the stars.

While Hawaiian society was structured hierarchically, the traditional divine caretakers of the land, the *ali'I* ruled on behalf of the Gods as secular and spiritual leaders. Considered by *maka ainana* to be living demigods and deities on earth, the *ali'I* (rulers) represented order, authority, spiritual guideposts; they were aligned with the spirit ancestors and temporal and spiritual guardians of the forces that brought food, shelter, comfort and well-being to everyone. However, as the children of gods every kanaka can trace their genealogy back to them and are thus inextricably tied to all that was created. Noenoe Silva argues that:

> The *ali'I, kahuna* and the *maka ainana* regarded themselves as related much more closely and affectionately than did feudal landlords and serfs. … *Ali I nui* were the protectors of the *maka ainana* sheltering them from the terrible unseen forces … should a famine arise the *ali I nui* was held at fault and deposed … should an *ali I nui* be stingy and cruel to the commoners, he or she would cease to be pono, lose favour with the *akua* and be struck down, usually by the people … a reciprocal relationship was maintained. The *ali Ii nui* kept the *aina* fertile and the *akua* appeased; the *maka ainana* fed and clothed the *ali I nui*.
>
> (Kame'eleihiwa cited in Silva 2004: 39–40)

Kanaka are ontologically and genealogically tied to their lands, thus their sovereignty comes from being a people who are in and of the sea and lands created by their ancestral creator beings. Kehaulani Kauanui argues that:

> The reason Kanaka Maoli can still evoke a myriad … genealogical connections today is because there were no exclusive boundaries between defined sets of relatives or bounded descent groups associated with land. Because Hawaiian land tenure was highly contingent and entailed a succession of caretakers, genealogical rank was a critical part of that succession.
>
> (2008: 45)

Indigenous Hawaiian sovereignty is in and of the lands to which they belong, and ownership is communal and shared. Kanaka Maoli share a life-force with the earth and creators that bind human and non-human through kinship relations and law.

Anishinaabe – Ojibway

Origin stories convey to us how we as Indigenous people came to be human to whom we are related and the lands to which we belong with Mother Earth. How we can claim who we are and who can claim us as human and non-human relatives tied to specific lands. This relativity is evident in the Ojibway story of how Turtle Island came to be. The creator Kitchi-Manitou made a family consisting of the earth, the sun and the moon. The earth was a woman from whom all living things came nourished by her lifeblood: the water. On her surface four sacred directions north, south, east and west contributed physically and spiritually to her well-being (Benton-Banai 1988: 29–34). The creator sent birds to spread the seeds of life to all the four directions water and land creatures and plants of the earth. They all lived in harmony then he created the first man named *Ani* (from whence) *Nishina* (lowered) *Abe* (the male of the species) from this original man came all the *Aninishinabe*. He walked the earth naming all things; eventually he married the fire keeper's daughter and had four sons who as adults journeyed in four directions. Upon each journey, a son met a doorkeeper who had a daughter. The sons received gifts from each of the doorkeepers. The door keeper of the West gave sage to purify the body, the doorkeeper of the south gave cedar to protect from disease and evil; the doorkeeper of the east gave tobacco to use in ceremony and the doorkeeper of the north gave sweetgrass to keep evil away from your home ensure safety on travels.

Upon completion of their journeys, the four sons returned to each of the doorkeepers and married their daughters and their children populated the earth. Over time, these first people began to fight each other over hunting grounds and other things. The creator *Gitchie Manito* saw that teachings of living in harmony were gone and he decided to flood the earth killing most human and non-human relatives. Only one human survived the flood *Waynaboozhoo* along with a few animals and birds who managed to swim and fly. *Waynaboozhoo* floated on a huge log searching for land … he allowed the remaining animals and birds to take turns resting on the log as well. Finally, *Waynaboozhoo* spoke. "I am going to do something", he said:

> I am going to swim to the bottom of this water and grab a handful of earth. With this small bit of Earth, I believe we can create a new land for us to live on with the help of the Four Winds and *Gitchi-Manitou*.
>
> *(Benton-Banai 1988: 31)*

Waynaboozhoo dived into the water and was gone for a long time. When he surfaced, and short of breath told the animals that the water is too deep for him to swim to the bottom. Many of the animals sharing the log, the loon, the otter, the helldiver and the mink tried to bring a piece of earth to the surface but failed. When little *Wa-zhushk*, the muskrat said he would try. Some of the other, bigger, more powerful animals laughed. *Waynaboozhoo* spoke stating that only *Gitchi-Manitou* can place judgement on others. If muskrat wants to try, he should be allowed to. Muskrat dove into the water and was gone much longer than the others. Muskrat did reach the bottom and was very weak from lack of air, he grabbed some Earth in his paw and with all the energy he could muster began to swim for the surface. One of the animals spotted muskrat as he floated to the surface. *Waynaboozhoo* pulled him up onto the log. "Brothers and sisters", *Waynaboozhoo* said, "muskrat went too long without air, he is dead" (Benton-Banai 1988: 32).

A song of mourning and praise was heard across the water as muskrat's spirit passed on to the spirit world. Suddenly *Waynaboozhoo* exclaimed, "Look, there is something in his paw!" (Benton-Banai 1988: 33). *Waynaboozhoo* carefully opened the tiny paw and revealed a small ball of Earth. The animals all shouted with joy. Muskrat sacrificed his life so that life on Earth could begin anew. *Waynaboozhoo* took the piece of Earth from Muskrat's paw. Just then, the turtle swam forward and said, "Use my back to bear the weight of this piece of Earth. With the help of *Gitchi-Manitou*, we can make a new Earth" (Benton-Banai 1988: 33). *Waynaboozhoo* put the piece of Earth on the turtle's back. Suddenly, the wind blew from each of the Four Directions. The tiny piece of Earth on the turtle's back began to grow larger and larger, but still the turtle bore the weight of the Earth on his back. After a while, the Four Winds ceased to blow and the waters became still a huge island sat in the middle of the water, and today that island is North America. Many Native Americans hold special reverence for the turtle who sacrificed his life and made life possible for the Earth's second people.

The stories and kinship of the *Anishinabe* passed down through time (Benton-Banai 1988). The story of their migration from the north east coast to the west coast of northern America begins with the seven prophets who came to give their prophecies to the people known as the seven fires. These prophecies provided spiritual direction for the migration from east to west to Madeline Island and it began in approximately AD 900 taking 500 years to complete. They first stopped at an island in the St Lawrence River to hold spirit and cleansing ceremonies. Some family and clan groups set up permanent villages believing they had reached the turtle-shaped island. The main tribal group moved west down the southern shore of the St Lawrence River stopping at a place called *animikee wa bu* (the place of thunder water now known as Niagra Falls) where they drove back a group of Iroquois who were pursing them. They also fought with Dakota over territory. Later the Iroquois presented the Ojibway with a Wampum Belt to seal the peace between them. It was during this time that three groups emerged in the *Anishinabe* nation: the safe keepers of the sacred fire who became the *Potawatomi*, the trader people who became the *Ottawa* and the faith keepers of the nation entrusted with the sacred scrolls and water drum of the *Midewinin* became the *Ojibway*. The *Anishinabe* became the nation of the three fires and according to their prophecy a turtle shape island awaited them at the end of their journey. This they understood to be Medaline Island, for a sacred shell arose out of the water signifying to the people this was the place to which they belonged.

This origin story connects *Aninishinabe* to being descended from the first people made in and of the earth by the creator and as the second people for whom Turtle Island and Medaline Island became ancestral home. *Aninshinabe* sovereignty is configured ontologically to lands through law, descent, intermarriage, kinship, war and relations with human and non-human kin. Turtle Island is tangible evidence of the existence of Kitchi-Manitou and his descendants the *Aninishinabe*.

The *Mooka* or the Dreaming

Within Australia Aboriginal people's sovereignty is derived from the ancient era of creation which provides the precedents for what is believed to have occurred in the beginning in the original form of social living created by creator beings (Moreton-Robinson 2000). Before the Dreaming, seawater covered the earth when it receded the Earth our mother gave birth to creator beings. The *Mooka* is a *Goenpul* concept that is difficult to explain in English terms. It is many things. It is the source of our world-view, our philosophy, and our law. It is not an historic or temporal concept; rather, it refers to our origins and ways of maintaining life and being human. Encapsulated within the *Mooka* are knowledges about causation, time, space, nature, the origins of human relations, the nature of belief and the earth which differ from Western ways of knowing.

Goenpul people have a spiritual and symbiotic approach to the earth rather than a scientific one. What is believed is given more credibility and priority than what can be proven or understood. The basis for proving or understanding lies in another way of proving that is not based in Western constructions of fact. Since spiritual belief is completely integrated into human daily activity, the powers that guide and direct the earth are believed to exist with all human life. These powers are not regarded as an outside alien force to be reckoned with and controlled. The powers come from the living earth whose energy contains spiritual origin, causation and meaning. The earth is alive and organic. Proof or understanding comes from occurrences produced by these powers. When events occur that cannot be explained Aboriginal people relate to them as natural expectations. Healings, sightings of spirit beings, messages from animals or birds are all natural and expected occurrences in our lives.

The *Mooka* contends that the vitality of the earth is consistent with the degree of relatedness between all things, specific places, people, kinship and spiritual belief and expression. The human to land linkage plays an important part in the transmission of sovereign rights in land. The central figures in the *Mooka* are powerful ancestral beings who exist in the noumenal world and live underground. These ancestral beings created the earth and humans. Their creative activity lives in a prior time, but their incarnation is manifested in people as such they are part of human organic life and humans are part of the ancestral order. The noumenal world and its relationship with the phenomenal world is mediated through a set of geographical sites and related objects; ancestral beings exist both below and above the surface, the physiography is seen as evidence of their activity. Surface sites are designated by the locality where ancestral beings emerged or receded. Goenpul people recognise that the first owners of sites are ancestral beings. Their creativity and incorporation into the land provides the basis for our sovereignty.

Specific ancestral beings created and conferred rights to specific human groups. Important ancestral beings and sites are identified with reference to deceased humans and kinship. However, sites are not the only areas identified with ancestors. They are also associated with tracts of country marked by conversations, fights, camps sites, excrement and other signs. The manifestation of such signification is evidence of the ancestor's intrinsic nature of being in the country. Thus, the structure and form of land is the fabric of ancestral metamorphosis and activity. Ancestral power and presence permeate the land. In this respect the metamorphosis of ancestral beings into the physiography denotes their and their human descendants' sovereignty. Each Goenpul person is regarded as having a human parent as well as a parent in the land. We view this relation to our lands, as westerners might perceive their relation to a biological mother, father, sister or grandparents. In this sense, Goenpul people consider our lands part of our corporeal selves.

Creator beings made the land and all life forms, which tie Indigenous people to particular tracks of country. The creator beings made the animals, plants, humans and the physiographic features of the country associated with them. They also established the Aboriginal ways of life providing laws for governance, social institutions and human and non-human activity. Creator beings provided the law, rules, and protocols for what behavior is and is not allowed expressed through both good and bad behavior in origin stories. Creator beings are immortal. They are creatures of the *Mooka* who move across country leaving behind possessions to designate specific sites of significance. They met others of their kind; they created and left the world of humans through transforming into stone and other forms, disappearing into the territory of another group or into the sky, ground or water. In doing, so they left behind tangible evidence of their earthly presence.

Creator beings also changed form and gender and in many cases are associated with elements or natural species. For example, one of the Goenpul nation's creator being is *Cabool* the carpet snake who in the mundane world is associated with all carpet snakes today. All carpet snake people are connected with each other through sharing this common creator, irrespective of where their ancestral lands are, for example, the carpet snake is a creator being of the *Gumbaymggirr* people dreaming in the Northern New South Wales and the *Goenpul* would travel to their country for ceremony. Creator being affiliation and marriage rules enabled movement across and through territories shared for ceremonial purposes and food abundance. Because the creator beings gave birth to humans, we share a common life-force; Aboriginal people are in and of the land. As the descendants and reincarnation of creator beings, Aboriginal people and our non-human relatives derive our sovereignty through and from them. Clearly Indigenous sovereignties are not configured through a logic of possession to the exclusion of all human and non-human others.

Defined territories shared with other tribes and our non-human relatives allow us to live on lands and waters within them; creator beings, ancestors, marriage and kinship provide the rules and protocols for sharing as well as demarcating territories. The idea of ownership of territory configured in different epistemological ways derived from our origin stories that explain how we, and all things, came to be. They tell of our connections to places and our responsibilities to non-human relatives and lands, of who we are as Goenpul, who can claim us, who we can claim and what laws we must follow in our relations with all things. Our origin stories carry the law they explain how our lands, humans and non-human kin are related; as the embodied representations of our creator beings, together we are the tangible evidence of their existence and sovereignty. Thus, the ontological basis of Indigenous sovereignties is being in and of the earth, which is antithetical to the ontological basis of state sovereignty.

State sovereignty

The ontological basis of colonial state sovereignty lies elsewhere. Vine Deloria Jr explains that sovereignty as a concept:

> Is an ancient idea, once used to describe both the power and arbitrary nature of the deity by peoples in the Near East. Although originally a theological term it was appropriated by European thinkers in the centuries following the Reformation to characterize the person of the King as head of state.
>
> *(Deloria 2005: 107)*

During the middle ages sovereignty was:

> Attached to *Respublica Christiana*: secular and spiritual authorities were subject to the higher authority of God. According to St Paul: the state is there to serve God. … The authorities are there to serve God … all Government officials are God's officers.
>
> *(Heng 2018: 33)*

There is little doubt sovereignty existed during the middle ages and its home was the Christian empire where feudalism in the form of legal and military obligations tied to holding land in exchange for services or labour was flourishing. This was particularly the case for the Kingdom of England where society was structured around this form of land tenure. This faith-based form of sovereignty meant divine authority rested in a God who existed outside the earth and his representatives who lived on the earth.

European Christian rulers were defenders of the faith and although their language and homelands were different, Christianity provided a sense of unity and cohesion among the true believers. The world was perceived to be clearly divided into Christians and all others including dissenting Christians. Geraldine Heng argues that:

> One of the spectacular cultural creations of the medieval period – the *mappamundi* – or world map – hits its stride in the thirteenth century and after, as a medium that visually unfolds an imagined universe of space-time which pictures the world in extraordinary ways that reflect on, and concretize, locations of race. … Cartographic and imaginary race issued a grid through which European culture perceived and understood the global races and alien nations of the world … ruminating on and understanding 'other types of monsters', namely Ethiopians, Jews, Muslims and Mongols.
>
> *(Heng 2018: 33–5)*

Heng argues that from as early as 1,144 Jews in England were subjected to violence sanctioned by the Crown on the basis of race. Caricatures of Jewish phenotypes and biomarkers survive in English manuscripts and visual art. Jews were important to English commerce but they were monitored by the Crown's administrative apparatuses and 'ruled upon by statutes, ordinances and decrees, they were required to document their economic activity at special registries by which they could be scrutinised'. Heng states that:

> In England then, the Jewish badge, expulsion order, legislative enforcements, surveillance and segregation, ritualized iterations of homicidal fables, and the legal execution of Jews are constitutive acts in the consolidation of a community of Christian English – otherwise internally fragmented and ranged along numerous divides – against a minority population that has, on these historical occasions and through these institutions and practices entered into race.
>
> *(2018: 31)*

Clearly, race was not just a linguistic marker prior to the 17th century as argued by Michel Foucault. Racialised technologies of power were already operating when God's representative was sitting on the English throne. Patriarchal white sovereignty in the form of the King holding the sceptre of divine right conferred by an external God and supported by the church was integral to the racial formation of England.

During the 16th century, the medieval ecclesiastical-political order began to wither. The Italian Renaissance saw the emergence of independent Italian city-states and regional state systems, which spread throughout Western Europe. Religious freedom advocated by non-Catholics and secular rulers informed struggles for political authority during the German Reformation. The political theology of Martin Luther disengaged the authority of the state from the religious sanction of *Respublica Christiana* enabling King Henry VIII of England to succeed in embedding the divine right in law through the Act of Supremacy (1534). This Act conferred on him and his successors' absolute sovereignty (Jackson 1999: 463–8). Kings of England waged wars in the name of God to spread Christianity and claim other peoples' territories. Thus, there is an ontological intimacy between race and sovereignty. Supreme authority resides in an external God but the King as the earthly white patriarchal embodiment of God decrees in law his absolute authority and in doing so unilaterally elevates himself to the Supreme Head of the Church of England. King Henry introduces into law the idea that sovereignty is indivisible as supreme and exclusive authority; it cannot reside in two different authorities. Thus, as a matter of law, sovereignty's racialised ontology – as patriarchal white supremacy – becomes embedded. Over time the legislature of the Kingdom of England, which had existed from the early 13th century limited the power of the English monarchy. After 30 years of war in Europe, agreements concluded by European states as part of the Treaties of Westphalia in 1648 formed the present foundations of international law with regard to sovereignty and in 1689 the English Bill of Rights passed by Parliament sets out the limits of the monarch's powers and the power and rights of Parliament. In 1707, the Kingdom of Great Britain formed as a new state through the unification of the Kingdom of Scotland and the Kingdom of England. In the British transition to modernity, sovereignty is the relational interface between law and politics, the supreme patriarchal white authority that separates these domains and binds them together. Sovereignty as supreme patriarchal white authority is the secular form of divinity. It is both the political power constituting the law and the law restraining political power. In this way law services sovereignty; it is the key mechanism, by which patriarchal white sovereignty protects and exercises its supreme authority, which rests on indivisibility; there can be only one sovereign just as Christians believed there could be only one God. Legal theorist Morris Cohen argues that within the law, sovereignty and property are separated to the degree that:

> Sovereignty is a concept of political or public law and property belongs to civil or private law… the distinction between property and sovereignty is generally identified with the Roman discrimination between dominium, the rule over things by the individual and imperium the rule over all individuals by the prince.
>
> *(Cohen 1927: 8–9)*

This distinction is however, blurred because sovereignty as a legal concept inheres territorial integrity as there has to be distinct and clear boundaries between states. Borders define the territorial limits and extension of patriarchal white sovereignty's property; they demarcate exclusive possession. Civil and private property law has effect within borders. Patriarchal white sovereignty's territorial integrity, supreme authority and governance is undiminished by the sale of private property. British sovereignty's assumption at common law put into effect the acquisition by the Crown of radical title over real property. In this way, the assumption of patriarchal white sovereignty gives life to a fiction of land tenure, which deems the Crown is the lord paramount over lands as in England whereby any private ownership of real property that pre-existed parliamentary sovereignty remained legal. Radical title forms part of the racialised logics which legitimates the Crown's exclusive possession within a specified border; the flow on effect is the formation of a state, a system of private property and the extension of rights to subjects. Radical title in Canada, the United States, New Zealand, Hawai'i, and Australia enables the nation state to acquire private property on the legal basis of just compensation as it does so when it wishes to appropriate private land for roads, dams, freeways and tunnels. The racialised logics of patriarchal white sovereignty underpin treaties and any form of Indigenous land rights as legal cases in Australia and Canada reveal "virtually unrestricted Crown authority to infringe [aboriginal] title for objectives that go beyond regulation and even public purposes to the creation of third party interests" (McNeil 2004: 295). Patriarchal white sovereignty's supreme authority and indivisibility prevails within and through the law. The principle of indivisibility – there can be only one sovereignty – inheres in patriarchal white sovereignty's supreme authority to kill, in its capacity to create states of exception, to maintain bare life, to make live and to let live. These capabilities are ontologically incommensurate with Indigenous sovereignties.

Conclusion

Patriarchal white sovereignty is not born of the earth; its origins were extra-terrestrial and historical then dynastic and imperial. These ontological origins predispose patriarchal white sovereignty to being human centred and heavenly bound. As a regime of power, it is a juridical omnipresent with ontological roots in a monotheistic religion. A sovereignty that is narcissistic, self-interested, possessive and self-serving. This is incommensurate with how Indigenous sovereignties originated, how we, and our non-human relatives, came to be and to which lands we belong as peoples of the earth. Our sovereignties are in and of the earth. They are incommensurate with a juridical omnipresent racially supreme authority authenticating a political order residing on the surface of a defined territory, in the ontological space of the divinely secular disconnected from the life-force that sustains. Patriarchal white sovereignty sits on the surface of the earth ontologically tied to an outer world emerging historically as a faith-based, inherited racialised and gendered human-centred institutionalised regime of power.

Ontologically Indigenous sovereignties configured through relativity are not race based. Our relations with Mother Earth acknowledge she is an organic and conscious entity rather than an inert object that is available for extraction and division according to a possessive logic that prioritises humans over all others. Our Indigenous human systems of land tenure configured territorial integrity along the lines of non-human kin, clan and tribes whereas state sovereignty's land tenure systems are based on supreme authority within a specific territory of Indigenous lands in the United States, Canada, New Zealand, Hawai'i, and Australia. The ontological incommensurables between the concepts of Indigenous sovereignties and state sovereignty reside in two different epistemologies. In its transition from the divine to the secular, patriarchal white sovereignty is artificial it is not predestined nor is it immutable and its ontological and epistemological reach does not control Mother Earth and her resilient existents, Indigenous sovereignties.

References

Alfred, T. (2005). 'Sovereignty', in J. Barker (ed.) *Sovereignty Matters: Locations of Contestation and Possibility in Indigenous Struggles for Self-Determination*. University of Nebraska Press: Lincoln, NE, 33–50.

Andersen, C. (2014). *Metis: Race, Recognition, and the Struggle for Indigenous Peoplehood*. UBC Press: Vancouver, BC.

Barker, J. (ed.) (2005). *Sovereignty Matters: Locations of Contestation and Possibility in Indigenous Struggles for Self-Determination*. University of Nebraska Press: Lincoln, NE.

Barker, J. (ed.) (2017). *Critically Sovereign: Indigenous Gender, Sexuality, and Feminist Studies*. Duke University Press: Durham, NC.

Benton-Banai, E. (1988). *The Mishomis Book: The Voice of the Ojibway*. University of Minneapolis Press: Minneapolis, MN.

Buijs, G.J. (2003). 'Que les Latins appellant maiestatem: An exploration into the theological backgrounds of the concept of sovereignty', in N. Walker (ed.) *Sovereignty in Transition*, 1st ed. Hart Publishing: Oxford, 229–257.

Cohen, M.R. (1927). 'Property and sovereignty', *Cornell Law Review*, vol 13, no 1: 8–30.

Coulthard, G. (2014). *Red Skin, White Masks: Rejecting the Colonial Politics of Recognition*. University of Minnesota Press: Minneapolis, MN.

Deloria, V. Jr. (1990). 'Relativity, relatedness, and reality', in B. Deloria, K. Foehner, and S Scinta (eds.) *Spirit and Reason: The Vine Deloria, JR., Reader*. Fulcrum Publishing: Golden, CO, 32–39.

Deloria, V. Jr. (2005). 'Self determination and the concept of sovereignty', in J.R. Wunder (ed.) *Native American Sovereignty*, 2nd ed. Routledge: New York, 107–114.

Deloria, V. Jr. and Lytle, C.M. (1984). *The Nations Within: The Past and Future of American Indian Sovereignty*. University of Texas: Austin, TX.

Gross, L. W. (2003). Cultural sovereignty and Native American hermeneutics in the interpretation of the sacred stories of the Anishinaabe. *Wicazo Sa Review*, 18(3), 127–34.

Gumplova, P. (2015). 'On sovereignty and post-sovereignty', *Philosophica Critica*, vol. 1, no 2: 3–18.

Heng, G. (2018). *The Invention of Race in the European Middle Ages*. Cambridge University Press: New York.

Jackson, R. (1999). 'Sovereignty in world politics: A glance at the conceptual and historical landscape', *Political Studies*, vol 47, no 3: 431–456.

Jennings, R.C. (2011). 'Sovereignty and political modernity: A genealogy of Agamben's critique of sovereignty', *Anthropological Theory*, vol 11, no 1: 23–61.

Kauanui, J.K. (2018). *Paradoxes of Hawaiian Sovereignty: Land, Sex and the Colonial Politics of State Nationalism*. Duke University Press: Durham, NC.

McNeil, K. (2004). 'The vulnerability of Indigenous land rights in Australia and Canada', *Osgoode Hall Law Journal*, vol 42, no 2: 271–300.

Miller, R.J. (2008). *Native America, Discovered, and Conquered: Thomas Jefferson, Lewis and Clark, and Manifest Destiny*. University of Nebraska Press: Lincoln, NE.

Miller, R.J., Ruru, J., Behrendt, L., and Lindberg, T. (2010). *Discovering Indigenous Lands: The Doctrine of Discovery in the English Colonies*. Oxford University Press: New York.

Moreton-Robinson, A. (2000). *Talkin Up to the White Woman: Indigenous Women and Feminism*. University of Queensland Press: St Lucia, QLD.

Moreton-Robinson, A. (ed.) (2007). *Sovereign Subjects: Indigenous Sovereignty Matters*. Allen & Unwin: St Leonards, NSW.

Moreton-Robinson, A. (2015). *The White Possessive: Property, Power and Indigenous Sovereignty*. University of Minnesota Press: Minneapolis, MN.

Mutu, M. (2011). *The State of Maori Rights*. Huia: Auckland.

Silva, N.K. (2004). *Aloha Betrayed: Native Hawaiian Resistance to American Colonialism*. Duke University Press: Durham, NC.

Simpson, A. (2014). *Mohawk Interruptus: Political Life Across the Borders of Settler States*. Duke University Press: Durham, NC.

Trask, N. (1999). *From a Native Daughter: Colonialism and Sovereignty in Hawai'i*, 2nd ed. University of Hawai'i Press: Honolulu, HI.

Wilkins, D.E. (1997). *American Indian Sovereignty and the U.S. Supreme Court: The Masking of Justice*. University of Texas Press: Austin, TX.

Williams, R.A. Jr. (2005). *Like a Loaded Weapon: The Rehnquist Court, Indian Rights, and the Legal History of Racism in America*. University of Minnesota Press: Minneapolis, MN.

20

Mana Māori motuhake

Māori concepts and practices of sovereignty

Margaret Mutu

Introduction

Indigenous sovereignty for Māori of New Zealand is known generally as *mana* (ultimate power and authority derived from the gods) and *rangatiratanga* (the exercise of mana). The terms *mana motuhake* (distinct power and authority derived from the gods), *mana taketake* (deep rooted/ Indigenous power and authority derived from the gods), *mana tōrangapū* (political power and authority derived from the gods) and *tino rangatiratanga* (exercise of absolute mana) are also heard. *Mana* and *rangatiratanga* imply the independence to exist and be who we are without interference from outsiders as well as the inalienable right to make our decisions about our lives and resources and to live in accordance with the laws our ancestors handed down to us. It is also about interdependence derived from the interrelationships we maintain through *hakapapa* (genealogical) links to other Māori and Indigenous communities locally, nationally and internationally. It is a Māori form of self-determination. Each generation inherits the responsibility to uphold and protect it and pass it on to the following generations. It is inalienable so it cannot be ceded or given away to others. The term *mana Māori motuhake* is an overarching term, which emphasises that the mana of the Māori people is distinct and ensures we always remain the *tangata whenua*, the original people of the land. *Mana Māori motuhake* is our form of Indigenous sovereignty.

In this chapter I consider the meaning of *mana* and *rangatiratanga* and the exercising of *mana Māori motuhake* in relation to the importance of the 1835 formal declaration of our sovereignty in He Whakaputanga o te Rangatiratanga o Nu Tireni and our 1840 treaty with the British, Te Tiriti o Waitangi. I then outline the effects of the British invasion and colonisation followed by a discussion of a variety of ways Māori have taken to ensure that our *mana* and *tino rangatiratanga* is upheld.

Mana and rangatiratanga

Mana and *rangatiratanga* are best understood within the philosophies, values and laws of our ancestors rather than British language and culture. British colonists attempted to destroy our knowledges and language, which posed a significant challenge for our ancestors. By the 1960s, the colonisers had successfully driven most Māori away from their ancestral lands where our ancestral understandings were (and for some, still are) the norm, and into the White dominated urban areas. By the 1980s, the language had become endangered (Benton 1997) but a few scholars who were Native speakers started recording our philosophies, values, and laws in English, always emphasising that they are best understood and discussed in Māori (see for example Marsden 2003, Mead 2003). In this way, Māori understandings of Indigenous sovereignty have been passed down generationally.

One such scholar, Rev. Māori Marsden in *God, Man and Universe: A Māori View* defined and discussed the concepts of mana in the Māori language and culture. For him:

> Mana in its double aspect of authority and power may be defined as 'lawful permission delegated by the gods to their human agents and accompanied by the endowment of spiritual power to act on their behalf and in accordance with their revealed will'. This delegation of authority is shown in dynamic signs or works of power.
>
> *(Marsden 2003: 4)*

He warned that the exercise of this power outside its limits is an abuse of the gift and may result in its withdrawal or misfortune (Marsden 2003). *Mana* is based inextricably in the spiritual realms of the world.

There are many different types of *mana* and manifestations in everyday life. All living things, animals, trees and plants, fish and birds, as well as humans are imbued with *mana*, a *mana* implanted by the gods. Many inanimate objects are imbued with *mana* such as meeting houses and mountains, which are personified and addressed in Māori as ancestors and relations (Mutu et al 2017).

The concept of *mana* is the root of authority to act in respect of certain matters and is a fundamentally important concept in Māori culture. The terms *mana atua, mana tūpuna, mana whenua, mana tangata,* and *mana moana* are also heard frequently. These are different types or aspects of mana and can be described, albeit very briefly, in the following way:

- *Mana atua* is the very sacred power of the gods which is given to those persons who conform to sacred ritual and principles.
- *Mana tūpuna* is authority and power handed down through the lineage of leaders.
- *Mana whenua* is the *mana* that the gods planted within *Papa-tūā-nuku* (Mother Earth) to give her the power to produce the bounties of nature. A person or *hapū* (grouping of extended families) that belongs to a particular area is said to hold or be the *mana whenua* of that area and hence has the power and authority to produce a livelihood for the *whānau* (extended family) and the *hapū* from this land and its natural resources.

Every effort is made to protect and uphold *mana whenua*, not only from the land being alienated, but also from its despoliation by careless exploitation. *Mana whenua* remains with the *hapū* of an area and more specifically with *whānau* who have the closest associations with specific parts of the *hapū* estate. That *whānau* has primary rights of *mana whenua* ahead of those from the wider *hapū/iwi* (grouping of hapū, nation) to whom that *whānau* belongs. Vesting Western legal title in another person does not remove *mana whenua* from a *whānau* and the responsibilities of the *whānau* and *hapū* to uphold *mana whenua* and prevent desecration and despoliation of their lands remains.

- *Mana tangata* is the power acquired by an individual according to his or her ability and effort to develop skills and to gain knowledge in particular areas and includes the spiritual and physical aspects of those skills and knowledge.

- *Mana moana* is the equivalent of *mana whenua* as it applies to the sea and its resources. The two forms of *mana* overlap considerably since the land extends well into the sea, while the sea's effects impinge some distance inland. (Mutu et al. 2017)

Rangatiratanga is the derived noun from *rangatira* who are our *hapū* and *iwi* leaders. For my *Ngāti Kahu iwi*, a *rangatira* is a person of *mana* who cares for and keeps the people together. Her/his role is to ensure the well-being of the *hapū* and *iwi*. In practice, there is usually one overall or *tino rangatira* (paramount leader), who draws on and utilises the skills of other *rangatira* within the *iwi*. While it is the people who determine who their *tino rangatira* is, the *tino rangatira* guide them in deciding who their successors should be before they pass on. The *tino rangatira* will have played a major role in training her or his successor(s) for that purpose (Mutu et al. 2017).

Rangatiratanga is a noun derived from *rangatira* and is translated literally as 'leadership'. It is not as widely used as *mana* and refers to the political aspects of *mana*. It is the exercise of leadership in a manner that ensures the *hapū* and *iwi* preserve and uphold their *mana*. The distinguishing feature of *rangatiratanga* is encapsulated in the notion of "taking care of one's people" (Bigss 1989: 310). In practice, it means exercising paramount power and authority in respect of the people and their resources, so they can prosper and enjoy social, economic and spiritual well-being. *Rangatiratanga* is exercised by individuals and local groups. It is the manifestation of the *iwi* political system (Kawharu n.d.: 1). *Tino rangatiratanga* is the exercise of ultimate and paramount power and authority. Within my *Mutu whānau*, my *Te Whānau Moana hapū* and my *Ngāti Kahu* and *Te Rarawa iwi*, we deliberately and actively maintained this knowledge and understanding along with the philosophies, values and laws that underpin our thinking (Mutu et al. 2017: 163). *Hapū* and *iwi* throughout Aotearoa each have specific understandings of *mana* and *rangatiratanga* based on their own traditions, histories and lived experiences. However, power and authority derived from the gods are common to all. Although there are several dialects of the Māori language, Māori share a single language.

Indigenous sovereignty elsewhere

Indigenous communities in the Pacific, Australia, and North America, share similar meanings with Māori philosophy about ideas of power and authority. In *Navajo Sovereignty: Understandings and Visions of the Diné People* Diné scholars, Lloyd Lee and Raymond Austin, write of *Diné* words that express Navajo sovereignty (Lee 2017: 5, 31). Austin argues "[t]he best protection for all *Diné* and the *Diné* lifeway is to formulate our own *Diné* sovereignty doctrine, a doctrine that is grounded in our own traditional knowledge and ways, and let it guide our nation forward" (Lee 2017: 37).

In *Indigenous Sovereignty Matters*, Lenape (2005), scholar Joanne Barker notes not all Indigenous peoples within the Americas and the Pacific share the same understanding of sovereignty. Instead it emerged "as a particularly valued term within Indigenous discourses to signify a multiplicity of legal and social rights to political, economic, and cultural self-determination". Furthermore "[i]t has come to mark the complexities of global Indigenous efforts to reverse on-going experiences of colonialism as well as to signify local efforts at the reclamation of specific territories, resources, governments, and cultural knowledge and practices" (Barker 2005: 1).

Mohawk scholar, Taiaiake Alfred states sovereignty "refers to supreme political authority, independent and unlimited by any other power ... it is a social creation" (Alfred 2005: 33–6) based on myths of European White supremacy and the illegitimate assumption of state sovereignty in North America by conquest. He argues Indigenous sovereignty today exists and is defined within the settler state, which denies, extinguishes or assimilates it (Alfred 2005: 36). He argues that "sovereignty" is inappropriate as a political objective for Indigenous peoples (Alfred 2005: 38). Rather, "[t]he challenge for indigenous peoples ... is to disconnect the notion of sovereignty from its Western legal roots and to transform it" (Alfred 2005: 42). He points out "[i]n most traditional indigenous conceptions, nature and the natural order are the basic referents for thinking of power, justice, and social relations" (Alfred 2005: 45).

Indigenous philosophies are premised on the belief the land was created by a power outside of human beings. A just relationship to that power respects it was not created by humans and we have no right to dispose of it as they think fit. Land is created by another power's order, therefore possession by humans is unnatural and unjust. "Reflecting a spiritual connection with the land established by the Creator, gives human beings special responsibilities within the areas they occupy, linking them in a natural and sacred way to their territories ..." (Alfred 2005: 45). This partnership resonates strongly with Māori formulations of non-intrusive frameworks and respectful coexistence, acknowledging the integrity and autonomy of various constituent elements of the human-earth relationship. This partnership and connection explicitly allow "for difference while mandating the construction of sound relationships among autonomously powered elements" (Alfred 2005: 46).

Comanche, Wallace Coffey, and *Yaqui*, Rebecca Tsosie (2001) argue sovereignty is derived from and defined by Native American culture and traditions not the individual rights focus of Western defined Indigenous sovereignty.

> It is time to reconceptualise Native sovereignty from a model that treats sovereignty as a strategy to maintain culture, to a model that analyses culture as a living context and foundation for the exercise of group autonomy and the survival of Indian nations.
>
> *(Coffey and Tsosie 2001: 191)*

Coffey and Tsosie draw on *Onondaga* Nation Faithkeeper of the *Haudenosaunee*, Oren Lyons' notion of sovereignty, that has a spiritual core "which is founded upon notions of relationship, respect, and continuity between generations [and] is quite distinct from the Western view" (Coffey and Tsosie 2001: 200). It requires an acknowledgement of and respect for all living beings, which share this earth and the future generations who will inherit the earth (Coffey and Tsosie 2001).

Goenpul scholar, Aileen Moreton-Robinson writes:

> Our sovereignty is embodied, it is ontological (our being) and epistemological (our way of knowing), and it is grounded within complex relations derived from the intersubstantiation of ancestral beings, humans and land. In this sense, our sovereignty is carried by the body and differs from Western constructions of sovereignty, which is predicated on the social contract model, the idea of a unified supreme authority, territorial integrity and individual rights.
>
> *(2007: 2)*

Furthermore "our sovereignty has never been ceded" despite White Australian assertions that "we had no sovereignty to defend" (Moreton-Robinson 2015: 150).

The European notion of sovereignty

The English cultural conception of sovereignty concerns absolute power and authority vested in sovereigns or the state; a different concept of power and authority from *mana* and *tino rangatiratanga* and from the Indigenous sovereignties referred to above.

Lakota scholar, Vine Deloria Jr. explains:

> Sovereignty is an ancient idea, once used to describe both the power and arbitrary nature of
> the deity by peoples in the Near East. Although originally a theological term it was appro-
> priated by European thinkers in the centuries following the Reformation to characterise
> the person of the King as head of state. ... The power was manifested specifically within
> the authority of the king to make war and govern domestic affairs (frequently in the name
> of God).
>
> *(cited in Barker 2005: 1)*

Māori legal philosopher, Moana Jackson, in the *Matike Mai Aotearoa* report on constitutional
transformation, explains the English notion of sovereignty:

> The Westminster constitutional system developed in the particular cultural circumstances
> of England. Its hierarchical structure headed by a Crown or sovereign is a cultural product
> that grew out of the historical tensions between the monarchs and those deemed to be
> below or in opposition to them. ... It is a distinct artefact that over the centuries has sought
> to accommodate the long-disputed interests of the nobility, the Church and the 'lower
> classes' while preserving the notion of individual property rights. Its concept of power
> became known as sovereignty which was exercised in a site of power known as Parliament.
>
> *(Matike Mai Aotearoa 2016: 32)*

Although the modern concept of sovereignty is generally understood as an English construct it
was first defined in 1569 by the French political philosopher Jean Bodin. Bodin's view of sovereignty was grounded in a belief that it marked a hierarchy of progress from societies of apolitical
barbarism (such as those of the recently 'discovered' Indigenous Peoples in the Americas) to
those countries in Europe with a 'civilised' constitutional order. It presumed that proper political power could only exist once "man ... purged himself of troubling passions" and moved up
"the great chain of being ... and its hierarchical order" (Franklin 1992 cited in Matike Mai
2016: 32). Once a people became 'civilised' they attained the reason to develop a concept of
power vesting in a sovereign, "a single ruler on whom the effectiveness of all the rest depends"
(Franklin 1992 cited in Matike Mai 2016: 32). Sovereignty was thus the "most high ... and perpetual power over the citizens" and it was that power "which informs all the members and ... to
which after immortal God we owe all things" (Franklin 1992 cited in Matike Mai 2016: 32). It
was a hierarchical ideal of constitutionalism that could only be held by civilised peoples. Bodin's
definition inheres the distinctive cultural ethos inherent in the Crown's notion of political and
constitutional authority.

The site of power throughout Europe was the monarch or alternatively the 'monarch in
Parliament', which had absolute authority and dominion over the land and its peoples. This culturally defined and 'civilised' notion of constitutional authority or 'dominion over' the Crown
was brought to Aotearoa after 1840 (Matike Mai 2016: 32). Jackson writes of the European
concept of power:

> It is ... no coincidence that the most influential definitions of sovereignty as a somehow
> 'universal' and 'civilized' concept of power were devised at the same time that Europe was
> seeking to destroy the power of Indigenous Peoples. Sometimes, its racism was openly
> expressed as in the view of the French courtier Jean Bodin ... or that of Thomas Hobbes
> who suggested it only came about when nations advanced beyond the primitive 'state of

nature' (where Indigenous Peoples supposedly lived) to a state of reason (which only the colonizers had).

(Jackson 2019: 106)

A declaration of sovereignty and a treaty with British Crown

White superiority arrived on our shores some eight generations ago. Far from being 'civilised' many Whites were lawless, barbaric and unmanageable (Wolfe 2005; Mutu 2004). Their behaviour caused great consternation amongst the *hapū* and many *hui* (gatherings) were convened to try to find solutions. Several *rangatira* undertook diplomatic missions to England where they met the *rangatira* of the English, King George IV (Waitangi Tribunal 2014: 99). They asked the king to send someone to take control of his lawless subjects living in New Zealand. The king sent a British Resident and later his niece Queen Victoria sent a Governor for the same purpose but both failed to achieve their primary purpose.

He Whakaputanga o te Rangatiratanga o Nu Tireni *1835 and* Te Tiriti o Waitangi *1840*

In 1835, the British Resident facilitated the drafting of *He Whakaputanga o te Rangatiratanga o Nu Tireni*, a formal declaration of the *mana* and *rangatiratanga* – translated as sovereignty – of the *rangatira* of the many *hapū* throughout the country. *Rangatira* throughout the north and from further south in Waikato and Ngāti Kahungunu signed it (Mutu 2004: 17–18; Waitangi Tribunal 2014: 166–167). It declared that only the *rangatira* assembled at Waitangi could make laws to keep the peace and that they would never give law-making powers to anyone else (Mutu 2004: 18; Waitangi Tribunal 2014). An interpretation in English of *He Whakaputanga* was sent to King William IV and was duly acknowledged (Waitangi Tribunal 2014). Many *hapū*, especially in the north, still consider He Whakaputanga to be the founding constitutional document of New Zealand (Matike Mai Aotearoa 2016).

Despite the good intentions of *He Whakaputanga*, British immigrants continued their lawlessness. By 1840, the *rangatira* decided that the British *rangatira* had to take responsibility for them. On 6 February, they signed *Te Tiriti o Waitangi*, a treaty written in the Māori language that confirmed the 1835 *He Whakaputanga*, preserving the *rangatiratanga* of the *rangatira*, of the *hapū* and of the people. It devolved *kāwanatanga* (governance) over British immigrants to the Queen of England (Mutu 2010; Waitangi Tribunal 2014; Mutu et al. 2017). It also made English custom available for the benefit of all. It was a treaty of peace and friendship, one that promised what the *rangatira* had asked for: acknowledgement and respect for their absolute power and authority throughout their territories, while relieving them of responsibility for lawless British immigrants (Mutu 2010).

British lawlessness continues

To this day, my *hapū* and *hapū* throughout the country continue to rely on this treaty in all our dealings with the British Crown. However, the Crown has never ensured its subjects in New Zealand knew about it let alone adhered to it. Furthermore, a Crown representative produced a document written in English that set out the aspirations of the British immigrants. It falsely claimed that Māori had agreed to cede sovereignty to the British Crown. In other words, the *rangatira* had agreed to give their mana to a stranger living on the other side of the world, a bizarre notion that is both humanly and logically impossible. This claim was a foundational element within the intricate web of lies and deception that Whites wove as they colonised to dispossess Māori (Mutu 2015). In 2014 the Waitangi Tribunal issued its report and findings into *He Whakaputanga* and *Te Tiriti* to reveal the lie of the *rangatira* ceding sovereignty.

British colonists did not stop their lawlessness and wilfully disregarded both *He Whakaputanga* and *Te Tiriti*. Rather than developing peaceful and lasting friendships with the *hapū* for the benefit of all, they embarked on a violent campaign against Māori to take possession of the country. First, they deliberately introduced diseases known to decimate Indigenous peoples with no immunity to them and the refusal of health services to remedy the devastation (Waitangi Tribunal 1997: 379–80; Kukutai 2011: 14; Mikaere 2011: 152–3). They set up illegitimate power structures including a parliament, courts, and government agencies, to take control of the entire country including the lives, lands and all the resources of *whānau*, *hapū*, and iwi which was not agreed to in *Te Tiriti*. In their illegitimate parliament they concocted policies and fabricated laws giving themselves unfettered powers to 'rule by administrative fiat' (Mikaere 2011: Chapter 6; Miller et al. 2010: 208; Te Aho 2017: 104; Rishworth 2016). Those policies and laws sanctioned the theft of lands, waters, fisheries, airways, forests and estates and anything else they could commodify from *hapū* throughout the country (Waitangi Tribunal n.d.). They sanctioned Whites attempting to destroy the lives, laws, language, culture, society, symbols, and knowledge systems of Māori and forcibly imposing their own White capitalist culture, laws, language, religion and economy on us (Biggs 1968: 74; Waitangi Tribunal 2011). Once Europeans had secured the lands slaughtering or driving the *hapū* out, raping, plundering, pillaging and destroying homes, crops, *waka* (canoes) and *wāhi tapu* (sacred sites) (Waitangi Tribunal 1996; 1999; 2004; 2017), they hid what they had done under a blanket of amnesia. For more than 150 years, they vilified and persecuted Māori and any others who reminded them of the atrocities they had committed. To this day they deny the racism they use to keep Māori in a state of poverty, deprivation and marginalisation despite being warned repeatedly by United Nations treaty bodies of the urgent need to address the problem (UNCERD 2017; UNESCR 2018; UNGA 2019). This was and is British colonisation – brutal dispossession in which states from Europe assumed the right to take over the lands, lives and power of Indigenous peoples who had done them no harm (Jackson 2019: 102).

The doctrine of discovery in New Zealand

Whites justified this behaviour as a right they inherited from their ancestors. It was based on the illogical myth of European supremacy and right to possess. Today this myth is known as the Doctrine of Discovery (Miller et al. 2010: 1). Part of that myth involved dehumanising Indigenous peoples and recasting them as mindless savages to justify driving them out of their lands. The Crown uses the Doctrine of Discovery to rationalise withholding lands, resources and rights from Māori, ignoring its rejection by the United Nations (Miller et al. 2010; Mutu 2018: 215). Whites in New Zealand desperately cling to it to this day, as Māori scholars Belinda Borell, Helen Moewaka Barnes, and colleague Tim McCreanor (2018: 26) identify as historical privilege.

They argue the Pākehā [White] settlers who acquired the land and material resources have reaped individual, collective, and intergenerational rewards from that theft. The accumulated effects have dramatically improved the economic, social, and political well-being of current descendants. Pākehā world-views and the institutionalisation of their cultural norms in national, governmental, and civic institutions serve to reaffirm and entrench models of White mental and social well-being.

This historical privilege produced historical trauma for Māori who continue to experience racial discrimination in all aspects of the social world from employment and housing, to the general disparaging of Māori language and culture in contemporary New Zealand society. Borell et al. (2017) explain racism serves to remind all New Zealanders of the second-class status of Māori people and renew the view that Māori people, language, and culture are inferior. These current experiences of discrimination perpetuate the intergenerational trauma of colonisation (Borell et al. 2017: 26). The combination of all the negative effects of colonisation has led to inevitable poor socio-economic outcomes and social indicators of poverty such as poor educational attainment, low income status, low mortality and morbidity rates, poor health, high incarceration rates and high child removal rates (Mutu 2017). It is no wonder then that more than 128,000 Māori have taken leave from their ancestral homeland to live and work in Australia (Kukutai and Pawar 2013).

Exercising *mana* and *tino rangatiratanga*

Europeans find incomprehensible that large numbers of Māori throughout the country simply refuse to accept all the myth-making and illegitimate power structures the British tried so desperately to impose on us, despite our marginalisation and poverty. They included those of us who are the descendants of the *rangatira* who deliberately passed on the histories of what really happened. There were, of course, Māori who did believe them and were seduced to assimilate into the White power structures to help maintain the coloniser's oppression.

For over 150 years, Whites fought to eradicate all memory of how they took over our country, failing to teach it in their schools. However, our resistance movement erupted in the 1970s when young Māori started protesting on the streets (Harris 2004). Their elders, at first wary of the inevitable White backlash, started joining them. Land repossessions and marches started attracting international media attention. In 1975, the government responded by setting up a permanent commission of inquiry, the Waitangi Tribunal, to investigate Crown breaches of the treaty and to make recommendations for removal of the prejudice. The government's primary intention was not to address the numerous breaches of the treaty but rather to take the protest off the streets and away from public and international view (Oliver 1991: 9–10). Exercising their *mana* and *tino rangatiratanga*, Māori have taken more than 2,600 claims to the Tribunal seeking:

- return of stolen lands, waters, seas, fisheries, airways, minerals, and other resources
- protection of the natural environment from desecration and unsustainable development
- restoration and recognition of our language and culture
- equitable access to commercial opportunities and to government resources and services including education, health, housing, and social welfare
- recognition and upholding of our mana and sovereignty. (Mutu 2017: 94)

Much to the consternation of the Crown, the Tribunal has unravelled many of its carefully woven myths and vindicated *whānau* and *hapū* who kept the memories of Crown atrocities alive (Mutu 2015). Despite being under-resourced, the Tribunal has upheld many hundreds of claims and made countless recommendations, which the government usually rejects or ignores (Te Kāwanatanga o Aotearoa 2018). In cases where the government decides it needs to extinguish a claim, particularly those relating to large land confiscations and alienations, it imposes its settlement policy on claimants further traumatising them (Mutu 2018). Settlements of treaty claims are used to entrench British colonisation and deny the *mana* and *tino rangatiratanga* of the claimants. The government returns on average less than 1 per cent of what was stolen, legislates the extinguishment of Māori title and cession of Māori sovereignty (Mutu 2012b; Mutu 2018). Claimants and their negotiators under duress and coercion accept the Crown's unfair settlements (Mutu 2018).

Few accept that the settlements are full and final and future generations will continue to pursue their claims against the Crown. Yet some of the settlements have enabled *whānau* to start climbing out of the crippling poverty endured for over 150 years. In exercising our *mana* and *tino rangatiratanga*, *hapū* and *iwi* throughout the country do so at times in defiance of White colonial edicts. Our ancestors mobilised repeatedly to defend ourselves and to remind Whites that we do exercise our own sovereignty.

Te Whakaminenga o Ngā Hapū o Nu Tireni

The first recorded gathering to deal with the lawlessness of White immigrants was known as *Te Whakaminenga o ngā Hapū o Nu Tireni* (The Gathering of the Hapū of New Zealand). It was a gathering of mainly northern *rangatira* who since the 1800s had met to discuss a range of issues, including the problematic foreigners. This gathering authorised and signed the 1835 document *He Whakaputanga o te Rangatiratanga o Nu Tireni* (The Declaration of Sovereignty of New Zealand). These same *rangatira* signed *Te Tiriti o Waitangi* in the north in 1840 (Healy et al. 2012; Waitangi Tribunal 2014). These *hapū* controlled all the territories of the north, further south in Waikato and in the east at Māhia. *Te Whakaminenga* has continued its northern focus to this day, but the gathering was marginalised and severely weakened for long periods as Whites attacked and undermined the authority of *rangatira*.

Kīngitanga—the King movement

Immediately to the south of the northern *iwi* are the *Tainui* confederation of *iwi* of the Waikato region. During the 1850s as the *hapū* and *iwi* of the central North Island resisted the theft of their lands, a number of *iwi* of the central North Island, including *Tainui*, came together to form the *Kīngitanga* or King Movement in 1858. The movement based its structure on the British monarchy, selecting a king as their overall leader in response to the extremely hostile actions of the British taking control of the fertile Waikato river lands. In exercising their *mana* and *tino rangatiratanga* in forbidding Whites to enter their territories, *Tainui's* actions were interpreted as a direct threat to White assertions of power and sovereignty. In 1863 British troops invaded the Waikato lands and confiscated 1.2 million acres of land claiming that Waikato *iwi* were rebels to justify their actions. The king and his people became virtually landless and were forced to retreat into neighbouring *iwi* lands. They remained in exile for 20 years before returning to a new legal and political order. Despite the social, economic, and cultural damage sustained by *Waikato-Tainui* during this period, the *Kīngitanga* stayed intact and *Te Kauhanganui/Te Whakakitenga o Waikato*, its parliament, was established in 1889 and continues today (Waikato-Tainui website; Cox 1993: 55–60).

For the next 120 years, *Waikato-Tainui* sought justice and redress from the Crown and reluctantly signed its first Deed of Settlement in 1995 (Waikato-Tainui website). Control of 47,048 acres or 3 per cent of the lands stolen was returned. A payment of $70 million was made with the Deed, which fell well short of the $12 billion owed to *Waikato-Tainui* (Mutu 2011: 26). Six monarchs had led *Waikato-Tainui* to this point where they could finally start recovering their economic base. The *Kīngitanga* remains an influential force in the Māori world to this day.

Te Kotahitanga—the Māori Parliament

While *Waikato-Tainui* concentrated on the *Kīngitanga,* other *iwi* tried to address the damage wrought by White colonists. Initial exclusion and then token representation of four seats in 1867 in the White Parliament (rather than the 20 Māori were entitled to) resulted in Māori setting up their own parliament in 1892. A number of *iwi* confederation movements developed around the country between the 1860s and the 1880s. The major concern for all of them was on-going theft of land by Whites and the operations of the Native Land Court. After several gatherings in their territories, the confederations met in venues around the country. Over a period of several years of debate they developed the structure and operational rules for a parliament with representatives of all *iwi* except *Waikato-Tainui,* who due to the *Kīngitanga* movement chose not to participate.

By the late 1890s the parliament's founding document carried 38,000 signatures, which is significant given the total Māori population had fallen to 42,000. *Te Kotahitanga* mirrored the structure of White Westminster parliament but drew on *He Whakaputanga o te Rangatiratanga o Nu Tireni* of 1835, *Te Tiriti o Waitangi* of 1840 and section 71 of the Constitution Act 1852. Section 71 provided for *iwi* autonomy within defined districts. The Māori parliament was named *Te Rūnanga o te Kotahitanga mō te Tiriti o Waitangi* (The Council of Rangatira and Elders for National Unity under Te Tiriti o Waitangi) and it was established to unite Māori, draw up legislation to return power to *hapū* over their lands and to reject White courts and institutions by operationalising Māori law. It had 96 members from *iwi* throughout the country of which four were allowed to be members of the White parliament to participate and inform that body of their decisions for incorporation into legislation developed there. It is often referred to as *Te Pāremata Māori* (the Māori Parliament).

Te Kotahitanga first met in the Hawke's Bay region on 14 June 1892. Over the 11 years that it was active, it debated many issues, particularly the relationship of the British Crown and *iwi* and passed legislation. However, when the four Māori members took the legislation to the White parliament, White members refused to discuss a Māori parliament and self-determination. Instead they walked out of the House. One of these Māori members of the White Parliament worked within *Te Kotahitanga* to close it down after effectively undermining its work. Whites have always used divide and conquer as a strategy and it continues to this day. Māori who do the coloniser's bidding are labelled *kūpapa* (traitors) and despite the shame, many infiltrate our organisations to this day in an attempt to have Whites, and particularly the government, control or destroy our organisations. Although *Te Kotahitanga* ceased, its principles and the wish to revitalise it remain with us.

National Māori Congress

After *Te Kotahitanga,* the next organisation for national unity was the National Māori Congress established in 1990. It was made up of *rangatira* and other representatives from almost all *iwi* around the country. Its main purpose was to form a united front for the practical recognition of our *mana* and *tino rangatiratanga.* The National Māori Congress met and made decisions on a range of issues impacting iwi and was severely critical of several of the Crown's deeply racist policies and legislation. It focussed on the Crown's unilaterally determined policy for the extinguishment of claims taken to the Waitangi Tribunal, its so-called 'treaty claims settlement' policy, which was dubbed "the fiscal envelope" (Mutu 2011: 17–27). Congress convened gatherings and advocated for constitutional change in the country which was identified as important for the future well-being of Māori as a people. Despite the very deeply respected membership of

Congress, the Crown would not tolerate its own asserted authority being questioned and instigated a divide and rule strategy to ensure the demise of Congress.

National Iwi Chairs' Forum

From the late 1990s, the so-called 'settlements' resulting from the fiscal envelope policy assisted in re-establishing small parts of the economic bases of *hapū* and *iwi*. The first settlement related to fisheries and after bitter legal battles for 11 years, now Māori are a significant and powerful player in the New Zealand fishing industry (Mutu 2012a: 120). Two relatively large settlements followed for *Tainui* in 1995 and *Ngāi Tahu* in 1997. Since then, 70 much smaller settlements have been legislated and a further 30 or so are at various stages approaching legislation. Although the settlements have grown in prosperity they are far too inadequate to address the appalling socioeconomic position of Māori.

In 2005, *Ngāi Tahu* called a gathering of 30 elected iwi chairpersons from around the country to discuss how we could support each other to properly exercise our *mana* and *tino rangatiratanga* to maximise the benefits of settlements. We set up the National Iwi Chairs' Forum and agreed to limit the Crown's (the government of the day) involvement at our behest and on our terms. The Forum has since grown to include 73 iwi chairpersons.

The Forum has drawn up indicative models for a constitution for the country based on *tikanga* (our own laws), *He Whakaputanga* of 1835 and *Te Tiriti o Waitangi* of 1840 along with the United Nations Declaration on the Rights of Indigenous Peoples. Many Māori believe that *He Whakaputanga* and *Te Tiriti* are the country's constitution, but Whites assert that the country has no written constitution and is refusing to debate the issue (Mutu 2011: 96–7). Whites who have considered the matter know it is inevitable to include *He Whakaputanga* and *Te Tiriti* in any written constitution. In taking responsibility for our country's constitution, our initiative is based on the advice provided by Māori experts and communities throughout the country.

Matike Mai Aotearoa – the Independent Working Group on Constitutional Transformation – are responsible for this work and published a report in 2016. The indicative constitutional models it recommends are based on the Waitangi Tribunal's 2014 report on *He Whakaputanga* and *Te Tiriti*, and the two different and distinct 'spheres of influence' of Māori and the Crown. The report refers to them as the *Rangatiratanga* sphere and the *Kāwanatanga* sphere. The two spheres are independent and in the *Rangatiratanga* sphere, Māori would make decision for Māori. In the *Kāwanatanga* sphere, the Crown would make decisions for its people. Where the two spheres would work together as equals making joint decisions is the Relational sphere; it is where the *Tiriti* relationship will operate. The *Matike Mai Aotearoa* report notes that it is "the sphere where conciliatory and consensual democracy would be most needed" (Matike Mai Aotearoa 2016: 9). Six indicative models are proposed involving various combinations of the spheres. They are being discussed with both Māori and non-Māori around the country. The report recommended convening a constitutional convention for Māori in 2021 and then one for the whole country with the aim of achieving constitutional transformation 200 years after the signing of *Te Tiriti o Waitangi* in 2040. The report has received widespread support from Māori and some non-Māori, but it has been subjected to strident attacks from those still clinging to the Doctrine of Discovery and outdated White New Zealand policy.

International support has come from the United Nations Committees for the Elimination of Racial Discrimination (2017), and Economic, Social and Cultural Rights (2018) along with the 2019 Universal Periodic Review of New Zealand all recommending the government engage with Māori to discuss the report. In response, the government agreed to draft a National Plan of Action to implement the United Nations Declaration on the Rights of Indigenous Peoples

(DRIP). New Zealand opposed the DRIP for decades but signed it in 2010. The Aotearoa Independent Monitoring Mechanism, whose membership includes many of *Matike Mai Aotearoa*, is working with the New Zealand Human Rights Commission, the United Nations Expert Mechanism on the Rights of Indigenous Peoples and several UN treaty bodies, to encourage the government to implement the Declaration. The Monitoring Mechanism's top priority for a National Plan is constitutional transformation.

The Forum has also taken on several other specific projects aimed at insuring that *mana Māori motuhake* is upheld in practical terms. These projects include Māori ownership of water, minerals and oil, as well as the foreshore and seabed; Māori control over and veto power over mining and oil drilling; Māori control over education, health, housing and children and over the New Zealand contribution to the climate crisis. These projects have required discussions with the government making adhering to the requirement of no Crown involvement with the Forum less straight forward. Furthermore, some *iwi* leaders still believe that Crown support and validation is needed. Government ministers, bureaucrats, and *kūpapa* are shameless in their attempts to infiltrate and influence the work and decisions of the Forum.

Conclusion

Sovereignty is a cultural construct that develops from the value systems of the society and culture in which it is embedded, thus Māori sovereignty and English sovereignty are very different. Māori values are concerned with community well-being along with balance and harmony between people and the natural elements of the world. Māori sovereignty is referred to as *mana* and *(tino) rangatiratanga* or in more general and overarching terms, as *mana Māori motuhake*. Indigenous sovereignty elsewhere appears to share the basic values of communal and environmental well-being. English values, on the other hand, revolve around individual and private property rights, the rule of law, the advance of science and the spread of Christianity (Waitangi Tribunal 2014: 38). Underpinning them is the mistaken belief that White Christians are superior to all other people and that the Doctrine of Discovery gives them the right to dispossess and traumatise Indigenous peoples for their own personal profit and gain. Māori have never accepted that Whites had any right to take over our country and trample on our *mana* and *rangatiratanga*. We have fought for more than 170 years to stop them and to restore the balance prescribed by *Te Tiriti o Waitangi*. Constitutional transformation that recognises and normalises *mana* and *rangatiratanga* and leaves the Crown to look after its own people is a solution for which our ancestors fought. My generation continues that battle in the hope that my *mokopuna* (grandchildren) will live to see the *Rangatiratanga* sphere and the *Kāwanatanga* sphere working together as equals, the dispossession and trauma of Māori remedied, White privilege shared for the benefit of all and *Papa-tūā-nuku* (the earth mother) and all her descendants restored to full health.

References

Alfred, T. (2005). 'Sovereignty', in J. Barker (ed.) *Sovereignty Matters*. University of Nebraska Press: Lincoln, NE, 33–50.

Barker, J. (2005). 'For whom sovereignty matters', in J. Barker (ed.) *Sovereignty Matters*. University of Nebraska Press: Lincoln, NE, 1–32.

Benton, R. (1997). *The Maori Language: Dying or Reviving*. New Zealand Council for Educational Research: Wellington.

Biggs, B. (1968). 'The Maori language past and present', in E. Schwimmer (ed.) *The Maori People in the Nineteen Sixties*. Blackwood and Janet Paul: Auckland, 65–84.

Biggs, B. (1989). 'Humpty dumpty and the treaty of Waitangi', in I.H. Kawharu (ed.) *Waitangi: Maori and Pakeha Perspectives of the Treaty of Waitangi*. Oxford University Press: Auckland, 300–12.

Borell, B., Moewaka Barnes, H., & McCreanor, T. (2017). Conceptualising historical privilege: The flip side of historical trauma, a brief examination. *AlterNative: An International Journal of Indigenous Peoples*, 14(1), 25–34.

Borell, B., Moewaka Barnes, H., and McCreanor, T. (2018). 'Conceptualising historical privilege: The flip side of historical trauma, a brief examination', *Alter*Native, vol 14, no 1: 25–34.

Coffey, W. and Tsosie, R. (2001). 'Rethinking the tribal sovereignty doctrine: Cultural sovereignty and the collective future of Indian nations', *Stanford Law & Policy Review*, vol 12, no 2: 191–221.

Cox, L. (1993). *Kotahitanga: The Search for Māori Political Unity*. Auckland University Press: Auckland.

Franklin, J. (ed.) (1992). *Jean Bodin on Sovereignty: Four Chapters from the Six Books of the Commonwealth*. Cambridge University Press: Cambridge.

Harris, A. (2004). *Hīkoi: Forty Years of Māori Protest*. Huia: Wellington.

Healy, S., Huygens, I., Murphy, T., and Parata, H. (2012). *Ngāpuhi Speaks*. Te Kawariki & Network Waitangi Whāngārei: Whāngārei.

Jackson, M. (2019). 'In the end "The Hope of Decolonisation"', in E.A. McKinley and L.T. Smith (eds.) *Handbook of Indigenous Education*. Springer: Singapore, 101–110.

Kawharu, I.H. (n.d.). 'Dimensions of Rangatiratanga', *Manuscript prepared for Hodge Fellowship*. Department of Māori Studies, University of Auckland: Auckland.

Kukutai, T. (2011). 'Contemporary issues in Māori demography', in T. McIntosh and M. Mulholland (eds.) *Māori and Social Issues*. Huia: Wellington, 11–48.

Kukutai, T. and Pawar, S. (2013). *A Socio-Demographic Profile of Māori Living in Australia*. NIDEA Working Papers No. 3. University of Waikato and National Institute of Demographic and Economic Analysis: Hamilton.

Lee, L. (2017). 'Introduction', in L. Lee (ed.) *Navajo Sovereignty: Understandings and Visions of Diné People*. University of Arizona Press: Tucson, AZ, 1–25.

Marsden, M. (2003). 'God, man and universe: A Māori view', in T.A.C. Royal (ed.) *The Woven Universe: Selected Writings of the Rev. Māori Marsden*. The estate of Māori Marsden: Masterton, 1–54.

Matike Mai Aotearoa. (2016). *He Whakaaro Here Whakaumu Mō Aotearoa: The Report of Matike Mai Aotearoa – The Independent Working Group on Constitutional Transformation*. University of Auckland and National Iwi Chairs Forum: Auckland.

Mead, H.M. (2003). *Tikanga Māori – Living by Māori Values*. Huia: Wellington.

Mikaere, A. (2011). *Colonising Myths, Māori Realities, He Rukuruku Whakaaro*. Huia: Wellington.

Miller, R.J., Ruru, J., Behrendt, L., and Lindberg, T. (2010). *Discovering Indigenous Lands: The Doctrine of Discovery in the English Colonies*. Oxford University Press: Oxford.

Moreton-Robinson, A. (2007). 'Introduction', in A. Moreton-Robinson (ed.) *Sovereign Subjects*. Allen & Unwin: Crows Nest, 1–19.

Moreton-Robinson, A. (2015). *The White Possessive: Property, Power and Indigenous Sovereignty*. University of Minnesota Press: Minneapolis, MN.

Mutu, M. (2004). 'The humpty dumpty principle at work: The role of mistranslation in the British settlement of Aotearoa. "He Whakaputanga o te Rangatiratanga o Nu Tireni" and "The Declaration of Independence"', in S. Fenton (ed.) For Better or for Worse: Translation as a Tool for Change in the Pacific. St Jerome: Manchester, 4–18.

Mutu, M. (2010). 'Constitutional intentions: The treaty text', in M. Mulholland and V. Tāwahi (eds.) *Weeping Waters*. Huia: Wellington, 13–40.

Mutu, M. (2011). *The State of Māori Rights: A Review of Māori Issues 1994–2009*. Huia: Wellington.

Mutu, M. (2012a). 'Fisheries settlement: The sea i never gave', in J. Hayward and N. Wheen (eds.) *Treaty of Waitangi Settlements*. Bridget Williams Books: Wellington, 114–123.

Mutu, M. (2012b). 'Ceding Mana, Rangatiratanga and sovereignty to the crown: The crown deeds of settlement for Te Rarawa, Te Aupōuri and Ngāi Takoto', *The Northland Age*, March 6: 9.

Mutu, M. (2015). 'Unravelling colonial weaving', in P. Little and W. Nissen (eds.) *Stroppy Old Women*. Paul Little Books: Auckland, 165–178.

Mutu, M. (2017). 'Māori of New Zealand', in S. Neely (ed.) *Native Nations: The Survival of Fourth World Peoples*, 2nd ed. J Charlton Publishing: Vernon, CA.

Mutu, M. (2018). 'Behind the smoke and mirrors of the treaty of waitangi claims settlement process in New Zealand: No prospect for justice and reconciliation for Māori without constitutional transformation', *Journal of Global Ethics*, vol 14, no 2: 208–221.

Mutu, M., Pōpata, L., Williams, Te K., Herbert-Graves, Ā., Kingi-Waiaua, Te I., Renata, R., Cooze, J., Pineaha, Z., Thomas, T., Te Rūnanga-ā-Iwi o Ngāti Kahu, and Wackrow, Williams, Davies Ltd (2017). Ngāti Kahu: Portrait of a Sovereign Nation. Huia: Wellington.

Oliver, W.H. (1991). *Claims to the Waitangi Tribunal*. Department of Justice: Wellington.

Rishworth, P. (2016). 'Writing things unwritten: Common law in New Zealand's constitution', *International Journal of Constitutional Law*, vol 14, no 1: 137–155.

Te Aho, L. (2017). 'The "False Generosity" of treaty settlements: Innovation and contortion', in A. Erueti (ed.) *International Indigenous Rights in Aotearoa New Zealand*. Victoria University Press: Wellington, 99–117.

Te Kāwanatanga o Aotearoa. (2018). *The Section 81 Report: A Report on the Progress Made in the Implementation of Recommendations Made by the Waitangi Tribunal*. New Zealand Government: Wellington.

United Nations Committee on Economic, Social and Cultural Rights (UNCESCR). (2018). *Concluding Observations on the Fourth Periodic Report of New Zealand*. United Nations Human Rights Office of the High Commissioner, United Nations: Geneva. Available: http://tbinternet.ohchr.org/_layouts/treatybodyexternal/Download.aspx?symbolno=E%2fC.12%2fNZL%2fCO%2f4&Lang=en, accessed 19 April 2020.

United Nations Committee on the Elimination of Racial Discrimination (UNCERD). (2017). Concluding Observations on the Combined Twenty-First and Twenty-Second Periodic Reports of New Zealand, CERD/C/NZL/C/21-22. United Nations Human Rights Council, United Nations: Geneva. Available: http://tbinternet.ohchr.org/_layouts/treatybodyexternal/Download.aspx?symbolno=CERD/C/NZL/CO/21-22&Lang=En, accessed 19 April 2020.

United Nations General Assembly (UNGA). (2019). Draft Report of the Working Group on the Universal Periodic Review: New Zealand. Available: https://www.hrc.co.nz/files/1315/4984/7007/nzupr3-draftoutcome.pdf, accessed 19 April 2020.

Waitangi Tribunal. (n.d.). 'Waitangi tribunal reports'. Available: https://waitangitribunal.govt.nz/publications-and-resources/waitangi-tribunal-reports/, accessed 19 April 2020.

Waitangi Tribunal. (1996). Taranaki Report: *Kaupapa Tuatahi: Te Muru me Te Raupatu (Wai 143)*. GP Publications: Wellington.

Waitangi Tribunal. (1997). Muriwhenua Land Report (Wai 45). GP Publications: Wellington.

Waitangi Tribunal. (1999). Ngāti Awa Raupatu Report (Wai 46). Legislation Direct: Wellington.

Waitangi Tribunal. (2004). *Te Raupatu o Tauranga Moana: Report on the Tauranga Moana Confiscation Claims (Wai 215)*. Legislation Direct: Wellington.

Waitangi Tribunal. (2011). *Ko Aotearoa Tēnei (Wai 262)*. Legislation Direct: Wellington.

Waitangi Tribunal. (2014). *He Whakaputanga me Te Tiriti: The Declaration and the Treaty: The Report on Stage 1 of the Paparahi o Te Raki Inquiry (Wai 1040)*. Legislation Direct: Wellington.

Waitangi Tribunal. (2017). *Te Urewera Volume I (Wai 894)*. Legislation Direct: Wellington.

Wolfe, R. (2005). *The Hell-Hole of the Pacific*. Penguin Books: Auckland.

21

He Aliʻi Ka ʻĀina, Ua Mau Kona Ea

Land is the chief, long may she reign

Kamanamaikalani Beamer

In 2003, Dr Jonathan Kamakawiwoʻole Osorio wrote in what I consider to be one of the most impactful essays authored by an ʻŌiwi scholar on Hawaiian sovereignty, "the nation shall have to continue to strengthen itself, by struggle and sacrifice, if it is to demonstrate to its people that it is worth defending" (Osorio 2003: 232). The essay titled *Kūʻe and Kūʻokoʻa, Law History and other Faiths,* provided a clear and concise analysis of the differing frameworks and the resulting tactics utilised by the federal recognition (inherent sovereignty) and independence (national sovereignty) advocates for Hawaiian Sovereignty. Indeed, much of the last 30 years of the Hawaiian movement has been branded by these seemingly competing strategies to achieve Hawaiian liberation, dignity, health, and the reclamation of lands. These binaries of 'Federal Recognition' versus 'Independence' had become so powerful that by the time the scholars of my generation were in our age of becoming, it was clear that one was expected to have not only selected a position on this Hawaiian political divide, but must also be prepared to defend their camp to be taken seriously as an activist let alone have any hope as an emerging academic. In some ways, it is difficult to overstate the impact that Anglo-American conceptions of sovereignty and governance has had on the psyche and imagined futures of our movement, whether ʻŌiwi seek full political independence and restoration as an independent and sovereign state or recognition as an 'indigenous people' of the United States of America, neither of these options can claim to be free from their origins in Anglo-American notions of law, territory, sovereignty, and the nation. However, they do offer vastly different possibilities for our future while creating serious consequences for the future of our islands, culture, and even identity as ʻŌiwi (indigenous Hawaiians, literally of the bones). As such the contentious debates, opposing political strategies, and nation building that has taken place in our islands while grappling with the potential futures of federal recognition or independence was perhaps a necessary condition to reach the place where we find ourselves in the movement today. And that place where we find our movement today is one where we are both challenged and empowered by the global forces reshaping our islands and planet, these include the capitalist-induced climate crisis, unprecedented and mid-evil like social-inequality and the hoarding of wealth by the '1%', and the ascension and rise of white supremacy and fascism. Similar to notions of sovereignty or federal recognition, ʻŌiwi can claim little credit for the origins of the capitalist-induced climate crisis, white supremacy, and the global elite; however, our movement must respond to these forces while taking into account the challenge offered by Taiaike Alfred (1999: xix) for indigenous peoples to "create a political philosophy to guide our people that is neither derived from the Western model nor a simple reaction against it".[1] And in Hawai'i our movement has responded in creative ways. The philosophies of Aloha 'Āina—a movement for social, cultural, and ecological justice in Hawai'i that draws from ancestral relationships to land, water, and the environment are at the heart of Hawaiian sovereignty. Aloha 'Āina is challenging and infiltrating the political consciousness in Hawai'i and informing a swelling movement as much as it has been since the illegal United States backed coup de main of the Hawaiian Kingdom government in 1893. In this chapter, I will discuss some of the recent developments in Aloha 'Āina that exist on the periphery of the federal recognition and independence divide, resting at the *piko*, center of Hawaiian Sovereignty.

The origins of Aloha 'Āina

'Ōiwi scholar and activist Dr Noelani Goodyear-Ka'ōpua writes, "a constellation of land struggles, peoples, initiatives, and grassroots organisations gave rise to what has become known as the Hawaiian movement or the Hawaiian sovereignty movement" (Goodyear-Ka'ōpua 2014: 1). Much of this movement has been informed and inspired by Aloha 'Āina.

Aloha 'Āina has been categorised as a movement and philosophy toward the "union of culture and ecosystem" (Beamer 2014: 13). Aloha 'Āina has is origins in oceanic and ancestral relationships between 'Ōiwi and our world. It has been a philosophy that has guided the ebbs and flows of Hawaiian existence as we have navigated our course in an ever changing and expanding world. At times Aloha 'Āina has taken the form of calls for the restoration of our Mō'ī (constitutional sovereign) by Hawaiian patriots after the illegal overthrow in 1893. In other moments, Aloha 'Āina has grounded movements that have sought to confront and challenge militaristic and capitalistic structures across our islands. Aloha 'Āina has had countless powerful warriors who are worthy of prose and praise to recall their fearlessness, unwavering courage, and tenacity. On 8 March 1977, two vibrant and inspirational young Hawaiians, George Helm and Kimo Mitchell, were reported missing at sea and never seen again. They have become martyrs for the Hawaiian movement and their names and memory live on in song and in the hearts of souls of Aloha 'Āina today. George and Kimo were a part of a group of Hawaiian youth who organised as the Protect Kaho'olawe Association to challenge the US military use of our island Kaho'olawe (Goodyear-Ka'ōpua 2014). The association had engaged in multiple occupations of the island in the midst of the bombing and active training by the US military. Prior to being declared lost at sea, during one of these occupations and in the midst of these incredible acts of courage and defiance of the United States military, George Helm wrote, on 30 January 1977:

> The truth is, there is man and there is environment one does not supersede the other. The breath in man is the breath of Papa (the earth). Man is merely the caretaker of the land that maintains his life and nourishes his soul. Therefore, 'āina is sacred. The church of life is not in a building, it is the open sky, the surrounding ocean, the beautiful soil. My duty is to protect Mother Earth, who gave me life. And to give thanks with humility as well as ask for forgiveness for the arrogance and insensitivity of man.
>
> *(cited in Morales 1984: 55)*

As if he was opening a portal to the soul of Mother Earth, George Helm's words were able to capture the essence of what has driven Aloha 'Āina as a philosophy and clarion call for Hawaiians who challenged American capitalism and gross misuse of islands precious natural resources. We exist because of our mother and must respect and reconnect to that source.

Sovereignty, Aloha 'Āina, and capitalist-induced climate crisis[2]

Ua mau ke ea o ka 'āina i ka pono[3], the sovereignty (breath, life) of the land continues because of *pono* or righteous, true, and proper actions. This phrase was first uttered by Kamehameha III at the end of the British occupation of the Hawaiian Kingdom in 1843. Maui College Professor and Aloha 'Āina, Kaleikoa Ka'eo, has often lectured about Kamehameha III's use of the phrase Ea (sovereignty, breath, life [see Goodyear-Ka'ōpua 2014: 3–7]) of the 'Āina (land, literally that which feeds) in contrast to the Ea of the government, offering formidable analysis that Kamehameha III's and a broader 'Ōiwi perspective on Ea as being rooted and attached to the sovereignty of our 'Āina and not necessarily to a particular government.

With the proper historical context and framing one can see that a Hawaiian conception of Ea and the philosophy of Aloha 'Āina has been fighting against the systems that are responsible for the capitalist-induced climate crisis, imperialist greed, and the arrogance of man for generations. Perhaps not everyone in Hawai'i has joined us, but every time an Aloha 'Āina stood up to try and stop an island or piece of 'āina from being bombed, restored a lo'i (a form of ancestral agriculture) or a fishpond, or resisted another hotel built over the bones of our ancestors – we were essentially fighting against the capitalist philosophies of endless development and consumption that has brought our planet to the brink of extinction. For generations, Aloha 'Āina were trying to wake up others to the harsh realities that our world was heading in a terrible direction. We were trying to restore the systems that truly brought liberty, dignity, and abundance to our islands and communities. Similar to George Helm, today we find ourselves up against incredible odds. Yet, in spite of the illegal overthrow of our country and the seizure of our lands, our philosophy of Aloha 'Āina remains. We Aloha 'Āina stand face-to-face against perhaps the most powerful military and economic force our world has ever known. Anyone who has flown into Honolulu, can look down and see the fighter jets and battleships of the United States who attach like leeches to our island's natural resources, feeding on the dignity and soul of an occupied nation. One can see the hodgepodge urban sprawl of the Honolulu skyline and the hotels built over the sands of our birth that are increasingly becoming engulfed by the impacts of sea-level rise and erosion.

The *capitalist-induced climate crisis* is already having an impact on our islands and we are experiencing remarkable effects on our islands' rainfall patterns, increased flooding, the loss of prevailing winds, and extreme periods of heat and drought. And though in some ways our planet will share the collective impacts of the capitalist-induced climate crisis, it will not harm all of us to the same degree. Much like the benefits and profits in the existing capitalistic economy – the impacts of the capitalist-induced climate crisis will operate *without* equity. In fact, at least in the short term it will most likely bring the greater harm to those with the least financial wealth and the nations that to this point are the least responsible for its causes. The irony of this should not be lost. As the truth is our planet has come to this point in the age of so-called 'civilisation', where for the first time in the history of our world we are approaching a capitalist-human induced apocalypse – and there can be no scapegoats such as the 'barbarians', or 'savages' – it is clear that our world has come to this point simply because of man's capitalist greed. We are living through perhaps the final logical outcomes of imperialism and the colonisation of indigenous lands, in a time where the modes of production of governments, companies, and the consumptive patterns of those in capitalistic societies consume our world's resources at such rates that are entirely impossible to sustain. And these societies produce radical inequality and structural imbalance. While some in our society struggle to eke out a living working multiple jobs to earn wages that can barely allow them to pay rent in Honolulu – or while graduate students fight to be unionised and paid fairly – at the same moment – separated merely by miles, caviar, marbled floors, infinity pools and a whole bunch of tax breaks – the '1 per cent' own and fly in and out of our islands on private jets. They consume our resources while their money influences local politics and thus our potential futures in ways that can be infuriating to witness, though it may be hard to see as many of them literally reside in gated coastal communities and do business behind closed doors. One of those business ventures that was birthed behind these curtains was brought into the light because of the courage of Aloha 'Āina.

Two Hawaiian mountains and two paths for humanity

The two largest mountains of Hawai'i are Mauna a Wākea also referred to as Mauna Kea (4,205 meters or 13,796 ft) and Mauna Loa (4,100 meters or 13,448 ft) on Hawai'i island. 'Ōiwi scholar Iokepa Salazar (2014 emphasises that from an 'Ōiwi perspective both of these mountains are considered to be of the first born of Hawaiian akua (gods) and thus have a familial relationship with 'Ōiwi. For scientists who study the capitalist-induced climate crisis, Mauna Loa is a famed place because it is the home of one of the world's longest running atmospheric observatories and one of the places in which the impacts of burning of fossil fuels on global climate were first discovered. It was data gathered at Mauna Loa that enabled the creation of the 'Keeling Curve', which first evidenced the accumulation of carbon dioxide in our earth's atmosphere, thus, becoming one of the first scientific works to document increased carbon dioxide in the atmosphere. In 1960, Charles Keeling published a paper[4] where he linked this increase to the burning of fossil fuels making an early discovery toward what later became known as human-induced Global Climate Change. On 13 May 2019 articles appeared around the world sounding the alarm that observations on Mauna Loa indicate that carbon dioxide levels have reached 415.25 parts per million reaching levels unknown in human history and last seen on the earth nearly 3 million years ago. If not for the place and environment of Mauna Loa and the scientific creativity of Charles Keeling our world would know much less about the scale and drastic impact capitalism has had on our planet over the last 200 years. However, in many ways today's clarion call by our planets most respected natural scientist and data sets collected from the summits of Mauna Loa could benefit from working with and being informed by the ethics of Aloha 'Āina. Do we not seek many of the same goals? Do we not understand that our societies must radically reshape the structures of government and business for the future of our planet? Do we not agree that we need to radically shift our resources towards these changes for our world today and save the only life we know to exist in our universe? If you work on our mountain, please accept this invitation to change our world and restructure our systems with Aloha 'Āina.

Mauna a Wākea is considered the world's tallest mountain and contemporarily perhaps Hawai'i's most contentious place. The thoughtful 'Ōiwi Scholar Iokea Salazar writes that, "Mauna a Wākea is sacred because it is a kupuna of all Kanaka 'Ōiwi" (Salazar 2014: 179). For many 'Ōiwi the summit of Mauna Kea is of particular significance as it is a Wao Akua (place or region of gods and reverence). Kumu Hula and renown cultural authority Dr Pualani Kanaka'ole states that:

> Mauna Kea is the first born to us. That's where our roots start that's where our island begins; that's where the first rain from Wākea hits. It is our mountain. That's where the first sunlight that rises every morning hits. That mountain is first for everything we have.
>
> (cited in UH Management Areas 2009: 1)

Families and cultural practitioners across Hawai'i island have continued to have intimate place-based and spiritual connections with the slopes, summits, and deities that reside on Mauna Kea.

Mauna Kea protector, and a revered community leader of Waimea, Hawai'i Pua Case's family formally petitioned the agency responsible for managing the mountain to recognise *Mo'oinanea*, an ancestral deity to have standing in formal legal proceeding (Salazar 2014: 56–7). While Mauna Loa has been used as a place for science to consider the impact humans have had on our planet and to cause society to reflect and redirect our activities, Mauna a Wākea is being used by the astronomy community with little consideration for our place or to redirect human's impact on our planet but rather, being inspired and driven towards capitalist desire for finding a new planet to colonise.

The University of Hawai'i founded its Institute for Astronomy in 1967 and shortly thereafter began plans to construct its first telescope on Mauna a Wākea. Today in 2019, there are 13 telescopes (UH Management Areas 2009: 3–5) on the summits of Mauna Kea, a few of which have been scientifically and physically abandoned yet remain littered across the landscape.[5] A series of Aloha 'Āina political events that took place in 2014–2015[6] reached a crescendo when it came to an issue related to Mauna Kea and the protection of the mountain from the development of the Thirty Meter Telescope (TMT), a development that was being showcased as the world's largest telescope.[7] The estimated budget for the project was US$1.4 billion and the vast majority of the philanthropic and 1 per cent community in Hawai'i were in support or financially connected to its construction. The scale of the Thirty Meter Telescope as well as over development and mismanagement of the mountain sparked an unprecedented number of Aloha 'Āina to protect Mauna Kea. Hawaiian language preschool students stood beside hula hālau as they chanted and sang on the slopes of Mauna Kea. At times there were nearly a thousand Aloha 'Āina gathered in this remote place. In total, there were 31 Aloha 'Āina arrested in April 2015 who had opposed the construction through civil disobedience and vast public debates across Hawai'i regarding their actions. Kealoha Pisciotta involved in years of struggle for Mauna Kea and one of the leaders of the Mauna Kea Hui, a group formed to protect Mauna Kea, declared:

> Today's arrests are hewa – a grave wronging. At least 30 of our Mauna Kea Ohana have been handcuffed and hauled off the mountain by County police and by the State DOCARE officers of the Department of Land and Natural Resources – the very state agency we are challenging in court.
>
> *(Big Island Video News 2015: online)*

Some called those who stood for Mauna Kea and against the construction as standing in the way of progress and accused them of taking society "back toward the dark ages" (Johnson 2014: online) others such as Dr Kamaoli Kuwada used the moment to question the rhetoric of progress and settler-colonial perspectives while asserting that those protecting Mauna Kea were actually protecting the very things society values about the uniqueness and beauty of Hawai'i for future generations:

> When you see the possibility of 'progress' in this more connected way, you see that we are actually the ones looking to the future. We are trying to get people back to the right time-scale, so that they can understand how they are connected to what is to come.
>
> *(Kuwada 2015: online)*

Much of the media coverage attempted to frame the debate in very simplistic terms as one of *science vs culture*. With the rise of social media and other forms of subversive communication there was certainly a unique space that was created which became part of an emerging, conscious, and vocal Aloha 'Āina community. The scale of the Aloha 'Āina network that emerged during the Mauna Kea protection was powerful as it was one that unified sometimes opposing political perspectives. In many ways, it didn't matter if one was for independence or federal recognition what most could agree on was that the 12 telescope facilities were enough and Mauna Kea deserved to have one of her summits free from development. Additionally, it was inspired by the powerful images captured on people's smartphones and posted on social media sites, the articulate and fearless leadership of a group of 20-somethings who resided and held regular vigil on the Mauna. In addition, Kumu Hula such as Aunty Pua Case called for the powerful ethic of what came to be termed "Kapu Aloha" a commitment toward holding oneself in the likeness and reverence of being on a sacred summit when interacting with each other and even with opposing forces. Kapu Aloha communicated love and required those participating to hold themselves toward the dignity and grace of our ancestors, while harnessing the fearless and unwavering commitment toward protecting ancestral relationships with Mauna Kea. As the weeks went by soon the political toll started to shift politicians who were being lobbied to halt construction while heartbreaking images of the arrests which often pitted a Hawaiian officer against a Hawaiian protector began to sway public opinion. There was one image taken prior to an arrest where an officer and a protector were engaged in a traditional honi (ancestral exchange of breath done by touching noses and breathing together) that sparked much public debate. In addition, the growing awareness of the truth about the illegitimate annexation of Hawai'i likely allowed the movement to build allies outside of the Hawaiian activist community and the sheer beauty and majesty of Mauna Kea itself made for images that spread across the globe to tell the story of Mauna Kea. About a week had passed and the governor of the State of Hawai'i called for a halt on the construction and later announcing amongst other things in his statement that:

> In many ways, we have failed the mountain. Whether you see it from a cultural perspective or from a natural resource perspective, we have not done right by a very special place and we must act immediately to change that.
>
> *(Governor of the State of Hawai'i 2015: online)*

Eventually the permits were invalidated and the processes headed back to contested case hearings and there were no further attempts at construction between 2016 and 2019. In October 2018, the Hawai'i State Supreme Court granted the TMT permit in a 4:1 vote. The Kamakakūokalani Center for Hawaiian Studies at the University of Hawai'i at Mānoa issued a press release critiquing the Hawaii Supreme Court ruling as well as the deeper philosophical assumptions guiding the project, stating:

> If built, the TMT will be the golden child and physical manifestation of the very philosophies of endless development and the destruction of nature, culture, and the environment that have brought our planet to the brink of extinction. In this case, we don't need bigger or more telescopes on our Mauna, they won't save our world, we need love for our mother earth, and the sacredness of undeveloped places – we need aloha 'āina.
>
> *(Beamer Unpublished: no page number)[8]*

On the afternoon of 12 July 2019, hundreds of kia'i (protectors) of Mauna Kea assembled at a meeting near the base of Pu'ukōhala on the sands of 'Ōhai'ula, Kawaihae. Key leaders of the movement had organised a strategy to attempt to stop the construction of the TMT. That night nearly a dozen vehicles made their way to a parking lot at the base of Pu'uhuluhulu which sits directly across from only paved access road that leads to the summit of Mauna Kea. The following morning participants took part in an ancestral ceremony to establish the site as a Pu'uhonoua (protected and safe space), the corners were marked as kiaʻi marched and chanted to dedicate the place towards this initiative. In the days that followed the camp grew exponentially in size, a kupuna council emerged to face the impending arrests head on, and eight kiaʻi had bound their bodies to a cattle grate that led up the Mauna Kea access road. Officials and law enforcement from the State of Hawaiʻi seemed to be caught off guard by the scale and complexity of the kiaʻiʻs strategy and in the first few days there were no arrests. But the peaceful confrontations between kiaʻi and law enforcement were streamed all over social media and the grassroots resistance grew stronger by the day. On the morning of 17 July 2019, state officers arrested 33 Hawaiian kupuna, and wave of Hawaiian wahine took to the front lines until the officers stood down. Images of the kupuna being arrested flooded social media, information was strategically communicated through a powerful media team for the kiaʻi, and the camp grew exponentially in numbers as many days there were over a thousand people between the Puʻuhonua and the kupuna tent that lay over the Mauna Kea access road. Soon kiaʻi had organised a health center, a kitchen, a child care center, and even founded the "Puʻu Huluhulu University" which was organised by Presley Keʻalaanuhea Ah Mook Sang within the Puʻuhonua near the base of Puʻuhuluhulu. The kiaʻi held classes and hosted tens of thousands of people until a temporary truce was reached on 27 December 2019, when the Hawaiʻi island Mayor had promised to freeze any attempts at construction until at least February 2020. As I type these words in late February, kupuna and kiaʻi continue to hold space on Mauna Kea surrounded by dozens of flags that were gifted in formal protocols from pacific island cousin nations, as well as members from other nations of the world. It is as if the kiaʻi had turned the road into a satellite united nations office while Mauna Kea had unified not only a large percentage of aloha ʻāina, it had also brought our pacific nations together in a formal space at the base of the Pacific's tallest mountain.

In many ways Mauna Kea, became a physical and spiritual symbol as the tip of the Hawaiian Sovereignty spear. One could witness numerous protest signs and analytical debates that questioned both United States sovereignty over our islands and the State of Hawaiʻi's authority over seized Hawaiian Kingdom government and crown lands. An exceptionally charismatic speaker and kiaʻi of the younger generation, Kahoʻokahi Kanuha was often quoted as referencing the illegal occupation of Hawaiʻi in the media, one such sentiment was captured in Science Magazine on 8 April 2015:

> At the same time, Kanuha and others hope to use the TMT protests to highlight another cause: Hawaiian sovereignty. Some activists contend the islands have been illegally occupied by the United States since the overthrow of the Hawaiian monarchy in 1893, and 'the people of Hawaii have never stood on a more grand, more noticeable platform' to discuss that issue, Kanuha says.
>
> *(Loomis 2015: online)*

Across Hawaiʻi today there is a growing awareness and debate over the legality of the United States presence and occupation of Hawaiʻi.[9] These arguments are becoming so widespread that they have found their way into the State of Hawaiʻi courts when the Hawaiʻi State Supreme Court opinion in the *State v. Kaulia* case was re-affirmed in the TMT decision when the court wrote, "[W]e reaffirm that '[w]hatever may be said regarding the lawfulness' of its origins, 'the State of Hawaiʻi ... is now a lawful government'" (Supreme Court of the State of Hawaiʻi 2013: online).

While it is unlikely a United States court could rule on an issue that would be to the detriment of its own existence. It is quite astonishing to have the courts make an argument that essentially says forget about how we got here and the origins of what put us in place, just accept that we are now legitimate. In a sense, they succinctly captured the unjust request that every court of the coloniser expects of indigenous peoples, yet, in Hawai'i it is additionally complex because of the legal history of the Hawaiian Kingdom as a sovereign and independent state since 1843.[10] Even if one were to place the logic of such arguments aside, it is highly unlikely these declarations will hold enough water to shift the rising tides of Aloha 'Āina. Such arguments are merely declarations of power and narcissism. And narcissistic power becomes increasingly fragile and brittle the more they are exposed to those who refuse to play by their rules and will not accept their flawed version of reality.

Power maintains itself not merely through might and brute force but is most effective through coercion, intimidation, and turning us against each other. Mauna Kea and the movements that have transpired as a result of it have been compared to the Kaho'olawe movement in the 1970s. One loved and deeply respected Aloha 'Āina Aunty Pua Case said to me that one of the greatest lessons that has come to our movement from Mauna Kea is that we must catalyse our efforts towards the heights and dignity of the summits of Mauna Kea. We must conduct ourselves with reverence, respect, and we must not allow past histori-cal trauma to lead us into perpetual battles with ourselves and each other. Perhaps Mauna Kea reminds us that our 'Āina is worth fighting for and we must work to bridge the per-ceived political divides between the independence and federal recognition factions of the Hawaiian movement. And the truth is that we have fought against each other for too long. Now is a time for unity, to once again exercise Ea over our islands. The generations that live today will face the global capitalist-induced climate crisis as well as white supremacy, two global forces caused by the greed of man, whose roots branch from a common philosophy of take, plunder, consume, conquer and to kill. The best way for us to defeat these foes is to unite, to come together to save our planet, and our precious places, as guided by the philosophy of Aloha 'Āina.

A place beyond the federal recognition and independence divide

It is clear that Hawai'i has reached a tipping point. We are living through a time that occurs per-haps only once in generations and it is clear that aloha 'āina is guiding this shift. One remarkable leader for Aloha 'Āina who has been near the pulse of aloha 'āina for the past 50 years is Uncle Walter Ritte. He was a companion of George Helm in the occupations and in forming the Protect Kaho'olawe Association. Uncle Walter Ritte has dedicated his life towards the advance-ment of Aloha 'Āina while being a force for advocacy and justice for Hawaiians from his home island of Moloka'i. For those of my generation he has been an inspiring leader while often being at the cutting edge of issues that affect our communities to name a few: the establishment of the Office of Hawaiian Affairs, fishpond restorations, hunting and gathering access, GMOs, water rights, community management of natural resources. He was one of the kia'i bound the cattle gate on the morning of 15 July and he has recently announced his candidacy to run for state office within the State of Hawai'i. Uncle Walter has a way of navigating a path on any issue while engaging on multiple fronts, beyond political camps, and through legal regimes. On 1 May 2019, Uncle Walter gave a moving speech calling for Hawaiians to participate across legal and political spectrums for our lands and resources. He argued that Hawaiians need to engage the state legislature while also knowing that the Hawaiian Kingdom is occupied and exists under international law. He also argued that all of the existing Hawaiian trusts and programs need to stop operating in silos and need to work together toward a common vision and mission and he argued that we need to find ways to help ourselves. I am including my transcription of his powerful speech here:

As Hawaiians tonight we find ourselves in a really serious situation we've been brainwashed all of these years, we are beginning to find out who we really were and who we really are. We have been lied to, we have been denationalized, many bad things have been happening.

I have been watching the legislature this year, and if you guys know. … Hawaiians have been going to the legislature and we have been treated really, really, really, badly. Last year at the legislature we had 13 bills to advance the Hawaiian language and every single bill died. This year we are at the legislature and we are there because of mandates coming out of our constitution that tells the legislature that you shall fund the department of Hawaiian Home lands, at the legislature we have constitutional mandates that says you shall fund the office of Hawaiian Affairs, we talking about millions and millions of dollars that are supposed to be going to the Office of Hawaiian affairs and the department of Hawaiian home lands. We are not getting anywhere close to what we should be getting as Hawaiians because of these constitutional mandates but not only because of these constitutional mandates but also because of legal laws that have been passed.

So, as Hawaiians we also find ourselves in many, many, battles on the streets. So we ask ourselves what are we going to be doing as Hawaiians in order to better ourselves. I want to come up with two solutions that I want to leave with you tonight. The first solution is to be active, when you are called an activist, be proud that you are an activist, because these activists are the ones that are setting new laws in the state of Hawaii, we are not only going to the legislature but we find ourselves on the street if we have to, when that legislature does not listen, but we are determined that we are going to fight to protect the waters that are now not flowing into our oceans, we gonna protect the fishes that are disappearing in our oceans, we gonna protect our farmlands, that are putting all kinds of chemicals and things into our farm lands, so being active is important if you are a Hawaiian today, you cannot be a taro farmer and not be politically akamai because you cannot grow taro without water , you cannot operate fishponds and not be a part of the political system because they will call your fishpond wetlands and they will call your fishponds navigable waters, strange laws and values that they place on our traditional things as Hawaiians today.

The other thing you gotta start demanding as Hawaiians is that all of our Aliʻi trusts, all of the Hawaiian agencies such as OHA and Hawaiian Homes, they need to get together they are all operating in silos, saying we only deal with children, we only deal with this we only deal with that, they have to all come together, our problems as Hawaiians is not one little thing in a silo, it demands all of these agencies to come together, if these agencies can come together than we as Hawaiians can come together. So it's important for us to demand unity in our agencies that are there for our use.

The last thing I would like to leave with you, is that we should all know who the truth and what the truth is about who we are as Hawaiians, our kingdom still exists today, we as Hawaiians need to believe that, all of the laws internationally, legally at the federal state and county level all show that our kingdom exists today. As Hawaiians we need to believe that and we need to act accordingly.

(Ritte 2019: unpublished speech)

Aloha ʻĀina rejects white supremacy and fascism

Here in the malu (shade, comfort, protection) of Mauna Kea, in some ways it is difficult for me to imagine that today in 2020, it would not merely be an exaggerated expression to say that while I am writing this essay the fascist gather in the streets. That our world would experience an open resurgence of white supremacy with the United States at its epicenter, and an

American administration and zealot that cultivates hate, intolerance, and fear to cling to power and authority. This is an American president who has threatened and attacked many of the most impoverished and oppressed members of the United States population. Women, the children of immigrants, religious minorities, indigenous peoples, the LGBT community, people of color, the physically and mentally challenged and of course any person who speaks dissension have all been targets. Who could have imagined that we would live in a place where mail bombs and twitter rants would be used as weapons to intimidate critical analysis and dissent to intimidate the freedom of speech. While those in power have created falsities such as 'alternative facts' to deny and subjugate truth. I think perhaps even in darkest hours of the Nixon administration it would have been unthinkable for thousands of troops and military vehicles to be deployed to the southern border of the United States to protect America from poor people walking on foot, seeking a better future. Or that children might be stripped from parents and kept in cages in the place some call the land of the free and the home of the brave, while a president mocks and attacks those who might simply take a knee in protest against the systemic systems of oppression and the deaths of innocent people. This wave of intolerance has even attempted to cultivate followers in Aotearoa when a duo of white supremacist attempted to speak in Auckland and were met by one Māori leader who told them their hate was not welcomed in his country. And most recently as many 49 innocent people were murdered in an act of terrorism by white supremist in Christchurch. By any account these are uncertain and unprecedented times. Yet, we as indigenous, as *Maoli* (true, first, indigenous) peoples, we have survived uncertainty, and fought against oppression, tyranny, and white supremacy for generations. These are troubling times, but we will endure. We must build alliances and support those who act with courage and determination around us, we must speak out and not allow fear or retribution to intimidate us from speaking the truth. Let me be clear and unequivocally state then, Aloha ʻĀina stands against any and all forms of white supremacy and fascism.

Aloha ʻĀina has always been an inclusive philosophy and our genealogies of gods and people affirm that we have included and made family with those from diverse places. Perhaps it is because of a worldview that seeks to support the Ea of the ʻĀina, that Hawaiians have welcomed intermarriage and diversity within our movement. Perhaps it's easier and more dignified to see the ʻĀina itself as our chief for us to follow, to serve, and to protect. For she is of the highest grace, above and beyond the faults and fragilities – without the ego of man. Our mother earth provides, she is our chief, long may she reign.

Notes

1 In addition to this powerful challenge by Alfred, I also believe that we can selectively appropriate things from the Anglo-American world as tools to design and create our future as was done by Hawaiian Aliʻi in the 19th century and even use international law for our own means (for more on this, see Beamer 2014; Sai 2008; Young 2006; also see note 3).

2 Throughout this chapter, I use the phrase 'Caplitalist Induced Climate Crisis' rather than 'Climate Change' or 'Climate Crisis' to call attention to material consequences of capitalism on our worlds resources.

3 First uttered by Kauikeaouli Kamehameha III on 31 July 1843, at the end of the brief British Occupation of the Hawaiian Kingdom and upon the return of Hawaiian Kingdom Sovereignty and Rule. Aloha ʻaina and Hawaiian Studies professor at Maui College, Kaleikoa Kaʻeo has often lectured on the meaning and importance of Kamehameha III stating the Ea (sovereignty, breath, life) of the ʻĀina (land, resources, that which feeds) rather than the Ea of the government of the time. He uses this to point out an ʻŌiwi perspective on sovereignty and rule that is ancestral and not tied to a particular government.

4 Keeling, "The Concentration and Isotopic Abundances of Carbon Dioxide in the Atmosphere".

5   For a detailed and readily accessible site on the issue of the University of Hawaiʻi's management of Mauna Kea see http://kanaeokana.net/50-years-mauna-kea

6   There are many that could be included but a few significant developments that year include: 1-Office of Hawaiian Affairs CEO Dr Kamanaʻopono Crabbe's letter to Secretary of State John Kerry questioning the prolonged occupation of the Hawaiian Kingdom by the United States. See https://www.staradvertiser.com/2014/05/12/breaking-news/oha-ceo-defends-letter-on-sovereignty/; https://www.civilbeat.org/2014/05/22059-oha-ceo-forces-standoff-over-sovereignty/.

    2-Department of Interior hearings across the Hawaiian Islands. See https://www.nbcnews.com/news/asian-america/some-protest-us-rule-recognition-native-hawaiian-government-n654501

    https://www.nbcnews.com/news/asian-america/native-hawaiians-federal-government-give-us-back-our-kingdom-n151801

    3- The Kū Kiaʻi Mauna protectors succesful halt to the contstruction of the Thirty Meter Telescope on Mauna Kea https://www.nytimes.com/2016/10/04/science/hawaii-thirty-meter-telescope-mauna-kea.html

    https://www.khon2.com/news/local-news/protesters-arrested-for-allegedly-blocking-access-to-mauna-kea-summit_20180309113623175/1025595582

7   For a thorough and powerful analysis of the TMT and Mauna Kea see Salazar (2014).

8   Kamakaūokalani Center for Hawaiian Studies Press Release, 30 November 2018. The Statement was primairly authored by Professor Kekai Perry. Quoted text is mine.

9   The research of Dr David Keanu Sai a lecturer at Windward Commuity College has made a profound impact on debates and legal frameworks toward understanding the Hawaiian Kingdom status in international law. See Sai (2008).

10 See Sai (2008) and Beamer (2014).

References

Alfred, T. (1999). *Peace, Power, Righteousness: An Indigenous Manifesto*. Oxford University Press: Oxford.

Beamer, K. (2014). *No Mākou Ka Mana: Liberating the Nation*. Kamehameha Publishing: Honolulu, HI.

Big Island Video News. (2015). *31 Arrested on Mauna Kea, Mauna Kea Hui Responds*. Available: http://www.bigislandvideonews.com/2015/04/02/31-arrested-on-mauna-kea-mauna-kea-hui-responds/, accessed 1 December 2019.

Goodyear-Kaʻōpua, N. (2014). 'Introduction', in N. Goodyear-Kaʻōpua, I. Hussey and E.K. Wright (eds.) *A Nation Rising, Hawaiian Movements for Life, Land, and Sovereignty*. Duke University Press: Durham, NC, 1–33.

Governor of the State of Hawaiʻi. (2015). 'News release: Governor David Ige announces major changes in the stewardship of Mauna Kea'. Available: https://governor.hawaii.gov/newsroom/news-release-governor-david-ige-announces-major-changes-in-the-stewardship-of-mauna-kea/, accessed 1 November 2019.

Johnson, G. (2014). 'Seeking stars, finding creationism', *The New York Times*. Available: https://www.nytimes.com/2014/10/21/science/seeking-stars-finding-creationism.html?_r=0, accessed 1 November 2019.

Keeling, C. (1960). 'The concentration and isotopic abundances of carbon dioxide in the atmosphere', *Tellus*, vol 12, no 2: 200–203. https://doi.org/10.3402/tellusa.v12i2.9366, accessed 1 November 2019.

Kuwada, K. (2015). 'We live in the future: come join us', *Ke kaupu hehi ale*. Avilable: https://hehiale.wordpress.com/2015/04/03/we-live-in-the-future-come-join-us/, accessed 1 November 2019.

Loomis, I. (2015). 'In Hawaii, protests force pause in construction of world's largest telescope', *Science Magazine*. Available: https://www.sciencemag.org/news/2015/04/hawaii-protests-force-pause-construction-world-s-largest-telescope, accessed 1 November 2019.

Morales, R. (1984). *Hoʻihoʻi Hou A Tribute to George Helm & Kimo Mitchell*. Bamboo Ridge Press: Honolulu, HI.

Osorio, J.K. (2003). 'Kuʻe and kūʻokoʻa, history, law, and other faiths', in S.E. Merry and D. Brenneis (eds.) *Law & Empire in the Pacific, Fiji and Hawaiʻi*. School of American Research Press: Santa Fe, NM, 213–237.

Ritte W. (2019). Unpublished Speech. Cited here with permission, 1 May.

Sai, D.K. (2008). *The American Occupation of the Hawaiian Kingdom: Beginning the Transition from Occupied to Restored State*. PhD dissertation, University of Hawaiʻi.

Salazar, J.A. (2014). *Multicultural Settler Colonialism and Indigenous Struggle in Hawai'i: The Politics of Astronomy on Mauna A Wākea*. PhD dissertation, University of Hawai'i.

Supreme Court of the State of Hawai'i. (2013). *State v. Kaulia, 291 P. 3d 377*. Available: https://casetext.com/case/state-v-kaulia-2, accessed 21 May 2020.

UH Management Areas. (2009). 'Executive Summary', *Mauna Kea Comprehensive Management Plan*, vol 1: 3–5.

Young, K. (2006). 'Kuleana: toward a histography of Hawaiian national consciousness, 1780–2001', *Hawaiian Journal of Law and Politics*, vol 2: 1–33.

22

Relational accountability in Indigenous governance

Navigating the doctrine of distrust in the Osage Nation

Jean Dennison

Sitting alone with Osage elder Eddy Red Eagle Jr. in the sunlit room outside the council chambers in July 2016, our conversation turned to the constant calls for accountability that we had both noticed happening across the Osage Nation. With the tell-tale twinkle in his eye that signalled he was excited about a concept, he theorised these calls as primarily a search for the kinds of deep relationships that grounded our government prior to the colonial process. He said, "There was something beyond trust and biological relationship, stronger than blood. That is ⅄ʌʃ⊙ …Everybody knew what they needed to do, and they had their role. The communication was awesome. That deep relationship made it fluid and trustworthy" (Eddy Red Eagle 2016: Personal communication). While ⅄ʌʃ⊙ cannot be fully translated into English, means different things to different Osages, and should not be diminished by taking it out of context, this conversation signalled to me that historically Osages had systems in place that created and maintained healthier political relationships and that the current distrust that plagues our nation was a product of ongoing colonialism.

The Osage Nation is hardly unique in our current obsession with accountability, and much of this can be directly tied to ongoing processes of settler colonialism.[1] In the context of the United States, this distrust needs to be understood as directly tied to the trust doctrine, also known as the trust relationship or responsibility. Through treaties, court cases, and laws, the US government has attempted to position itself as the protector of American Indian nations against outside threats and as a supporter of self-government (Wilkins and Lomawaima 2002). These paternalist promises of protection, which have at times been acted upon and at other times been ignored, work to position the United States as the supreme authority over the territory. As the remainder of this chapter will discuss in more detail, the trust relationship has repeatedly disrupted Osage governing institutions through a host of tactics, including failed treaty promises, altered governance structures, forced minerals extraction, a murderous system of legal guardianship, and ongoing mismanagement of lands, funds, and resources. The *doctrine of distrust* thus speaks directly to the impact the trust doctrine has had on Indigenous governmental relationships.

Distrust works to disrupt relationships not only with the settler governments, but also throughout Indigenous communities. Given Indigenous governmental entanglements with colonial structures and the vast changes they have undergone, it would be extraordinary if distrust was not the norm. These legacies of distrust have varied impacts and are being addressed by different Indigenous communities in different ways (Engle Merry 2000; Subcomandante Insurgente Marcos 2003; Tomas 2012; Stark and Stark 2018). For Indigenous nations to build towards a stronger future, we must face this massive legacy of distrust directly, especially how it plays out in our relationships with our own citizens, employees, and elected officials.

Even beyond settler contexts, ongoing colonial and liberal structures have distorted many governance relationships, creating widespread calls for accountability to try and address existing distrust. Unfortunately, the tools used to create accountability and transparency are themselves having devastating consequences on the day-to-day operations of governments. Distrust too often manifests in many forms of governmental disruption, including increased bureaucratic processes of approval and hyper-monitoring of employee actions, all of which further entrench, rather than alleviate, distrust (Power 1997; Shore and Wright 2000; Strathern 2000; Gupta 2012).

In the context of my research with the Osage Nation, there were different forms of accountability utilised to attempt to deal with this distrust, two which can be glossed as personal and relational forms of accountability. Personal accountability approaches tended to single out individuals for added scrutiny or regulations. They insisted that with more monitoring individuals would no longer get away with their perceived misbehaviour. Too little thought, however, was put into the consequences of these personal forms of accountability. When timeclocks were implemented on computer workstations in 2016, for example, several employees talked with me about how they felt demoralised in their workplace. For these employees it became far harder to work in spaces where they were distrusted and monitored. It was clear that this personal accountability mechanism worked to entrench rather than challenge distrust.

Another powerful manifestation of distrust in the Osage context were rumours, which occurred repeatedly when people felt uncertain, anxious, and/or disempowered. While rumours did work to destabilise unequal power relations by bringing an individual's motivations into question, they also further entrenched distrust in both the subject and source of the rumour. They strain systems of communication and hide larger structural problems. Early Osage administrators attempted to address rumours through human resource policies, but this created concerns about freedom of speech. In response to these concerns, the Osage Nation Congress went as far as to create Osage Nation code entitled "Speak What's On Your Mind". This stressed the existing Osage Nation ethics code requiring "Osage Nation employees to refrain from abusive conduct, personal charges, or verbal affronts upon the character, motives, or intents of other officials and Osage citizens", while saying that "no policy in the Nation could abridge or impair the right of employees of the Osage Nation to express their personal [or political] opinions" (Osage Nation Code 2009: 10-104). As this code demonstrates, limiting communication was not viewed by the Osage Nation Congress as a useful way to stop the spread of distrust.

Forms of personal accountability frequently slow and even stop operations, adding extra levels of bureaucratic/interpersonal scrutiny and creating what feel like toxic work environments. Personal accountability was even, at times, deployed strategically by Osage officials and employees to slow programmatic changes, to distract from jobs they themselves were not completing, and/or to create distrust in an individual they did not agree with. When the personal accountability mechanisms became intense enough, it often led motivated officials and employees to leave the government in search of a more supportive space. Too often those who stayed either deployed the personal accountability mechanisms toward their own ends or focused on maintaining the status quo to avoid the negative attention and added layers of scrutiny.

Unfortunately, the status quo in the Osage Nation, like many Indigenous nations, was shaped by federal employees and programs who were rarely invested in these communities and which too often allowed personal and corporate corruption to go unchecked.

Given the legacy of forced change, extreme distrust around any change in Indigenous nations is both the most logical and a devastating consequence of colonialism, for it ensures that cycles of distrust continue uninterrupted. When Indigenous nations attempt to take programs over from colonising nations, this distrust of change manifests in many different forms of personal accountability that disrupt their successful implementation. Some Osage people have developed a very strong relationship with and reliance on the federal government, which seems primarily related to a very deeply entrenched (and historically motivated) fear that self-determination will dislodge the trust status they have fought so hard to establish (Dennison 2018). Settler systems, and even some of these Osages, point towards manifestations of 'toxic work culture' and distrust, to call for continued intervention and paternalism. The doctrine of distrust is thus a feedback loop that continues to feed on and maintain both colonial authority and widespread cynicism. Personal forms of accountability are powerful tools of continued colonialism, as they keep Indigenous nations from thriving by creating relationships of distrust where the default authority of the federal government is further entrenched.

As Indigenous engagements with this trust relationship demonstrate, however, we cannot completely disregard the usefulness of the trust doctrine, or even distrust, to Indigenous communities. The trust relationship been used, at least at times, to push federal policy toward Native nation self-determination. As historians David E. Wilkins and K. Tsianina Lomawaima argue, Indigenous nations will continue to attempt to shift the trust relationship into a more "reciprocal vision of trust", which involves the "intertwining of moral, political and legal obligations", whereby "tribal and federal rights, properties, and sovereignty are equally entitled to deep and profound respect" (Wilkins and Lomawaima 2002: 13). From the eighteenth century until the present, Indigenous officials have used treaties, laws, court decisions and policies to maintain a land base and sovereignty. This kind of relational authority is core to many Indigenous epistemologies and approaches (Stark and Stark 2018). The Osage Nation, as this chapter will chronical, has also leveraged promises of protection as a site of engagement, warding off the most devastating of colonial policies.

In a similar vein, mutual respect is also needed 'within' contemporary Indigenous governments. Indigenous historical engagements with the doctrine of distrust demonstrate how '*relational accountability*' disrupts and shifts this colonially embedded distrust. Unlike personal forms of accountability, which tend to add additional levels of monitoring and are often intended as a form of disruption, relational accountability focuses on making change possible through increasing communication, fostering respect, and ensuring actions are motivated by community interests. Several Indigenous Studies authors, especially in the twenty-first century, have written about relational accountability as a core aspect of Indigenous sovereignty in the face of colonial research relationships (Smith 2005; Wilson 2008). Shawn Wilson used the concept to argue for research that is deeply situated in a particular community, so much so that relationships with community members ground the topics, methods, analysis, and presentation of the research. The goal then is for research that not only benefits the community, but also is conducted in a way that maintains and even strengthens the researcher's relationships. Respect, communication, and meeting community needs are also quite useful beyond the research context toward and understanding of how we might dislodge the doctrine of distrust.

To contextualise the relationships between the trust doctrine, the doctrine of distrust, personal accountability, and relational accountability, this chapter will focus on a case study from the Osage Nation, a Native nation in Oklahoma of which I am a citizen. I have conducted extensive ethnographic, oral historical, and archival research with Osage Nation government officials and employees since 2004, with visits lasting as long as 18 months at a time. These extended visits are important to me personally as well as professionally, as they allow me to stay with my parents and raise my daughter in the yearly dances. Even when I am not able to return, I stay in regular conversation with senior Osage leadership, including having them read and offer guidance on all my publications. I feel very blessed to have this level of engagement and it always makes the work stronger.

The Osage Nation's historical and contemporary struggles provide particularly useful insights into the myriad processes through which settler colonialism has fostered distrust and complicated Indigenous governance. In detailing the ways that federal government processes have, at times intentionally, attempted to destabilise the Osage Nation over the last century, this chapter demonstrates one situated story of how settler colonial processes work to foster deep-seated pessimism around governance, making it vital for Indigenous systems of governance to rebuild relational accountability.

There is nothing settled about the distrust that anchors colonialism. On the contrary, Indigenous peoples have long thwarted settler structures and continue to find creative ways of ensuring our own political futures (Lambert 2007; Cattelino 2008; Carroll 2015; Doerfler 2015; Kauanui 2016; McCarthy 2016). This chapter will thus not only discuss the processes that work to create distrust and their consequences but will also focus on how Indigenous peoples are establishing relational accountability to challenge settler colonialism's structures of distrust. As J. Kēhaulani Kauanui argues, we must pay close attention to this "enduring indigeneity" because "to exclusively focus on the settler colonial without any meaningful engagement with the Indigenous … can (re)produce another form of 'elimination of the Indigenous'" (Kauanui 2016: 2). This case study thus follows the ways respect, communication, and meeting community needs can be used to disrupt the doctrine of distrust. Despite ongoing colonial systems and their lasting impacts, Indigenous peoples strive to create governmental systems that serve our needs in ways ignored, intentionally or not, by settler governments. One of the core needs in our contemporary governmental systems is to create and maintain accountable relationships that can disrupt colonial distrust.

To maintain order within and keep outsiders from claiming their territory over the last several centuries, Osage peoples created a complex political structure through strong forms of internal and external relational accountability.[2] From at least the 17th century until the early 19th century, the Osage nations controlled extensive territory in what are now the states of Kansas, Arkansas, Missouri, and Oklahoma. Despite sharing a governance system and coming together annually, Osages understood themselves to have multiple nations during this period of time, operating more as a confederacy than a single political entity (DuVal 2007). Notably, this authority was recognised not only by other Indigenous peoples, but also by European traders who arrived in the early 1700s (DuVal 2007). From 1910 to 1923 Francis La Flesche (Omaha), the first professional Indigenous ethnologist, conducted research with Osage male elders, documenting political and religious practices and conceptions to demonstrate the complexity of their intellectual and political traditions during the 18th century (La Flesche 1999, 1939).

According to these male elders, Osage systems of government during this period established and maintained authority by modelling the governance structure on observations from the surrounding world. In this way, the government was built through and represented their relationships to each other and the world around them. Osages divided their socio-political structure into two primary groups, the ᏒᎦᏴᎪ and the ᏄᏃᏌᎾ, made up of a series of moieties representing the spectrum of life on earth. Every village included two appointed ᎦᎪᏒᎾᎪᎾ, one from the ᏒᎦᏴᎪ and one from the ᏄᏃᏌᎾ. These ᎦᎪᏒᎾᎪᎾ settled disputes and could expel individuals from the village. If issues went beyond internal village disputes, the council of *ⱠⱺⱮⱺⱬ∩ⱪⱿ* handled them. This council met informally every day and more formally as needed. They discussed larger social ills facing the Osage people as a whole and devised solutions to these problems, including establishing policies around trade and war (La Flesche 1999).

The bi-annual gatherings of all the Osage nations during the 18th century is a useful instance to see what Osage forms of relational accountability looked like in this governance structure. Osage elder Mary Jo Webb illustrated these processes at an Osage Government Reform Commission meeting in 2005 by drawing two half circles on a board with the *ⱬ∩ⱬⱺ* on top and the *Ɱ⅄ⱪⱿ* on bottom. She explained that they each had their own high *ⱪⱯⱮ∩ⱪⱿ* and lesser *ⱪⱯⱮ∩ⱪⱿ*, saying that part of the governance structure involved a large gathering in the Fall:

> So they gather; they begin to fast and pray. And they come out of this lodge here [pointing to the blackboard] and they begin to dance on this side like this; and on this side they dance like this. They meet in the middle. They do that for four days from sunup to sundown. They never sing the same song twice. They've got four days of memorized songs and each clan would have their own.
>
> *(Webb 2005)[3]*

Webb went on to explain that it was only possible for this event to take place if all the clans were there and they each sang their own songs. If there was any disharmony in the tribe, they had to work it out. Hosting this event required strong relationships of respect, fluid communication, and a centring of Osage needs. She concluded her lecture by pointing out, "You had to forgive and have restitution all the time" (Webb 2005). Having the governmental structure built around twice-yearly restitution meant that, at least in this particular historical moment, there were built-in systems of relational accountability.

Early engagements with European colonists did not disrupt Osage authority, but in fact they used trade with these newcomers to expand their relationships and widen their territorial control during this period. In the 18th century, Osages used their size and strategic location between the French traders on the Mississippi River and the many resources to the west to, as historian Kathleen DuVal writes, "develop one of the largest trading systems in North America and to wield enormous power over both their Indian and European neighbors" (DuVal 2007: 103). Establishing trade monopolies in this period enabled the Osage nations to not simply maintain authority, but also expand it across what would later become Kansas, Arkansas, Missouri, and Oklahoma.

Osage authority remained strong through the beginning of the nineteenth century when the US government 'purchased' Osage territory from the French through the Louisiana Purchase of 1803. After his first meeting with the Osage delegation, President Jefferson wrote a letter to the Secretary of the Navy, Robert Smith:

> The truth is they are the great nation South of the Missouri, their possession extending from thence to the Red river, as the Sioux are great North of that river. With these two nations we must stand well, because in their quarter we are miserably weak.
>
> *(Jefferson 1804)*

Through disrupting the Osage trade advantages and pitting other Indigenous nations against the Osage, the United States was able to eventually gain leverage over the Osage nations. At the end of the eighteenth century, Cherokees began to settle Osage lands in large numbers, as part of their own effort to avoid colonisation from the east. In addition to land theft and bloody wars,

Cherokees used a colonial rhetoric of savagery, painting themselves as civilised to the white settlers while depicting Osages as bloodthirsty, thus jeopardising Osages extensive trade relationships and control over the territory. Through this campaign, Cherokees gained political and territorial control in the area, convincing Europeans, Americans, and other Indigenous peoples that Osages were not to be trusted (DuVal 2007).

It is in this context of Cherokee settlement that the United States began negotiating treaties with the Osage nations, laying the groundwork for the doctrine of distrust through the language of protection. Unlike earlier relationships with the French, when Osages clearly had the upper hand in terms of numbers and territorial control, the Osage were now in a much weaker position. Osage leaders still hoped, however, that they would be able build reciprocal relationships that would sustain their sovereignty, as had been accomplished with the French. The 1808 Treaty of Fort Clark, the Osage Nation's first, reads: "The United States receives the Great and Little Osage nations into their friendship and under their protection; and the said nations, on their part, declare that they will consider themselves under the protection of no other power whatsoever" (Kappler 1972: 268). While clearly part of the United States government's efforts to distance the Osage from their strong relationships with the French, this idea of 'protection' would become a core tool by which the US government created the doctrine of distrust. Through this and similar treaties, the federal government positioned itself as 'protector' of Native nations even as it is simultaneously working to diminish their land base and claim the territory more fully from us and other European colonisers (Tsosie 2003: 271).

The importance of having the United States recognise Osage Nation authority and pledge resources to maintain this authority was still, however, a vital victory that ensured their survival in the context of multiple colonisations. This was a key relationship Osages needed to foster, especially within the existing understandings of social relationships with outsiders. The Osage were not alone in understanding treaty making as a form of relationship building. As Heidi Kiiwetinepinesiik Stark and Kekek Jason Stark demonstrate, Anishinaabe peoples built treaty relationships in the tradition of earlier social relationships, such as those with non-humans. These relationships were predicated on mutual respect, shared responsibilities, and continued renewal (Stark and Stark 2018). It was with these same desires for strong relationships that Osage leaders signed these treaties. Similarly, Iroquois understood the treaty relationship as a 'Covenant Chain', which Robert Williams describes as a metaphor for "two once-alien groups connected in an interdependent relationship of peace, solidarity, and trust" (Williams 1999: 991).[4] This concept of interdependence is at the core of many discussions of Indigenous sovereignty (Cattelino 2008; Simpson 2014; Dennison 2017).

This hope for mutual respect and shared responsibilities was quickly tested by the continual failure of the United States government to live up to its promises of protection. The treaty moment was instead the beginning of the massive erosion of Osage land and authority, as the doctrine of distrust worked to solidify United States jurisdiction. From 1808 until 1839, there were seven treaties under which the Osage nations lost control of over 151 million acres of land in what would later become Oklahoma, Kansas, Missouri, and Arkansas, representing 75 per cent of their land base; in return, the nations received only minimal compensation. Subsequent treaties again used the language of protection as the fundamental justification for why the Osage nations needed to cede additional territory, arguing this was the only way that the 'desired protection' could be maintained.

As these treaties tied promises of future protection with the loss of land they twisted Osage conceptions of trust in both the United States government and the Osage officials signing the treaties. For example, the 1825 treaty, known simply as The Treaty with the Osages, reads:

In order to more effectually extend to said tribes, that protection of the government so much desired by them, it is agreed as follows: ARTICLE 1. The Great and Little Osage tribes or nations do hereby cede and relinquish to the United States all their right, title, interest and claims to lands.

(The Treaty with the Osages 1825: 1)

This language exemplifies the doctrine of distrust by simultaneously diminishing their land and again promising to protect their territory.

While this loss of land was staggering, Osage officials were making strategic decisions based on the realities they were facing to ensure that their nations would have a future. In what was likely a direct response to Kansas becoming a state and writing a constitution claiming Osage territory as its own, the nations banded together in a new way and created the 1861 Osage Nation Constitution, asserting their own jurisdiction and outlining their structure of government. In creating a government recognisable to the United States government, the Osage had to find ways to build new systems of relational accountability, which the colonial context made even harder by repeatedly eroding trust.

By the 1870s, however, illegal white settlers pushed Osages off their lands again, further entrenching distrust of the promised United States protection. Selling land in what had become the state of Kansas nine years earlier, the Osage Nation purchased 2,304 square miles of their earlier territory back from the Cherokee, in what was known as Indian Territory. At that time, Osage 𐒰𐒷𐓂𐒼𐓀 𐓊𐒰𐓀𐒼𐓀 surveyed the new land and declared, "there is something in this land that will sustain us" (Gray 2005). Like many Indigenous nations, Osages had little choice but to embrace the move to Indian Country, hoping that this time the US government would honour its promises to ensure the US citizens did not cross the border and claim Osage lands.

This paternalist idea of protection was further solidified through various Supreme Court cases. In *Cherokee Nation v. Georgia* (1831) Chief Justice John Marshall argued that, based on the United States Constitution, Indigenous nations were neither states nor foreign nations, but instead "domestic dependent nations … in a state of pupilage" and the relationship should be understood as a "ward to his guardian" (Cherokee Nation v. Georgia [30 United States (5 Pet.) 1, 8 L.Ed. 25 (1831)]). The following year Marshall argued that it was actually the tribes that bargained for this protection and that it did not diminish their internal sovereignty (Worcester v. Georgia, 31 United States (6 Pet.) 515 (1832)). In *Seminole Nation v. United States* (1942) the court found that the United States "has charged itself with moral obligations of the highest responsibility and trust" toward Indigenous nations (Seminole Nation v. United States, 316 United States 286, 297 (1942)). These complicated ambiguities of pupillage, requested protection, internal sovereignty, and trust, are the core aspects that make up the doctrine of distrust.

Following the US government's removal of the Osage Nation to Oklahoma, Osages again tried to create a government recognisable to the United States government yet accountable to their people's political desires for separation. The 1881 Osage Nation Constitution was copied directly, almost verbatim, from the 1839 Cherokee Constitution, with its three-part government, democratic elections, and autonomous boundary control. Given the prevailing rhetoric of Cherokee 'civilisation' and the Cherokee success up to that time of being left to manage their own affairs in Indian Country, the 1881 Osage Constitution was a strategic choice.[5] This strategy only worked for a limited period, ultimately resulting in more disruptions. These vast governmental shifts have had lasting impacts on Osage conceptions of governmental organisation, especially 21st-century calls for checks and balances created by a three-part government structure.

Fifteen years after the passage of the 1881 government, settlers discovered oil on Osage land, further complicating self-determination and entrenching distrust. From this moment forward, the doctrine of distrust created deep entanglements with corporate interests, which have worked in tandem with settler colonialism to try and eliminate Osage control. Oil production on their land began at the end of the nineteenth century, with a blanket lease to the entire reservation going to Kansas railroad magnate Henry Foster and his brother Edwin in 1896. The Osage agent H. B. Freeman, from the Office of Indian Affairs (OIA) in the US War Department, negotiated the deal with Foster. Only after the fact was it put to a vote by the Osage Nation Council, the governing body of the 1881 Constitution. The initial lease passed by the narrow margin of 7 to 6, but the Nation Council annulled the contract a year later. William Pollock, Freeman's successor as Osage agent, overrode the National Council seven months later, reinstating the contract (Wilson 2008). Given the competitive advantage the Osage Nation lost with giving a blanket lease to one individual, it is hard to understand the OIA motivation here as anything but an example of early corporate lobbying, not unlike what happened later across Indian Country (Weyler 2007), and what continues to happen across the globe (Coll 2012).

Osage officials, however, also took advantage of this unique arrangement to protect their own interests, especially during the allotment era. The federal policy of allotment officially began in 1887 with the Dawes General Allotment Act that called for the widespread surveying of Indigenous tribal lands. Once the surveys had been completed, the United States government parcelled these lands out, usually in 160-acre tracts, to individual Indians. The remaining lands were then opened up for white settlement, reducing an overall two billion acres of Indian-controlled land to 1.47 million acres (Wilkins and Lomawaima 2002).

The US government could not force the Osage Nation into allotting their lands, like it did with other Indigenous nations, because they had purchased the reservation land and because they had a lease for the entire reservation territory. While Osage leaders eventually agreed to allow the allotment of the surface of their reservation after extensive pressure from both Oklahoma Territory and United States officials who wanted to make Oklahoma a state, the subsurface – including rights to oil, natural gas, and other minerals – was kept under the communal ownership of the Osage Tribe. James Bigheart, Osage ᏥᎪᏍᎦ from 1875 until 1906, understood the importance of retaining collective ownership over as much as possible and negotiated to not only put the minerals in trust for the Osage Nation, but to only allot the surface lands to Osages listed on the rolls, unlike other allotment processes that opened a majority of the land to settlement. Much of the surface land was transferred, however, to fee simple, meaning it could be sold, seized in the event that an owner failed to pay taxes, borrowed against, and condemned by local authorities through eminent domain. Through these and additional illegal means during the Osage Reign of Terror, individual Osages lost the majority of their land (Harmon 2010).

Given this origin, as well as the following century of entanglements, the Osage Mineral Estate is perhaps one of the most powerful examples in Indian Country of the doctrine of distrust. Established in 1906 through an act of the US Congress, the Osage Mineral Estate is made up of the mineral rights of the 1.47-thousand-acre reservation. United States Code Title 25 defines the Osage Mineral Estate as "any right, title, or interest in any oil, gas, coal, or other mineral held by the United States in trust for the benefit of the Osage Tribe of Indians under section 3 of the Osage Tribe Allotment Act" (Annals of Congress 1906: 539). The proceeds from this Mineral Estate continue to be divided to the annuitants based on their share percentage, as is common for shareholders in a corporation. A majority of these shares have been passed to descendants of someone listed on the 1906 Osage allotment roll, but one-fourth of these shares are held by non-Osage individuals and corporations who received a share during the early 20th century. At that time, a share was treated like any other property. These non-Osage continue to receive income but do not have the right to vote or hold office.

The Mineral Estate Trust drastically limited governance throughout the 20th century, fostering extreme forms of distrust among Osages. As the Osage people had not selected this form of government, the Osage Nation was one of the few places in the United States where a government body was operating without the consent of the governed. This system, while working to create legibility to the United States government and allowing Osages to control their own territory and much of their internal affairs, also deeply eroded systems of relational accountability within the Osage Nation. The Mineral Estate Trust drastically limited the forms of accountability within our government. Under this system there was only one governing body, known as the Osage Tribal Council, responsible for making all decisions affecting the nation. There were no checks on their authority or mechanism to remove them from office except to vote them out every four years. While Osages did frequently replace the elected officials during these elections, promises of transparency concerning decision making and open communication were rarely fulfilled.

Under this system of government, the Osage government also drastically limited citizenship, meaning that it was not accountable to a majority of Osage descendants. Under the Osage Tribal Council created through the 1906 Act, the only people who had a vote or could run for office were males over the age of 18, although this was later opened up to women. Through an amendment in the 1950s, which was negotiated with Osage leadership under the threat of Osage termination, voting in the Osage Tribe became tied one's share of a headright in the Osage Mineral Estate, passed down from someone on the 1906 roll. This meant that a majority of Osage descendants were unable to vote because their family members had not willed the headright to them or were still living. By 2004, only 4,000 of the 16,000 registered descendants could vote in Osage elections, based solely on their inheritance of a share.

This system not only fostered distrust of Osage leaders who facilitated these changes but also spread distrust within families. My grandfather, George Orville Dennison, was born 18 months before the 1 July 1907 cut-off date. As a result, he received three 160-acre parcels of land within the Osage reservation, 1/2230th share of all monies produced from the Mineral Estate, and, when he turned 21, a vote in Osage elections.[6] His two brothers, who were born after the 1907 cut-off date, received nothing and had no voice in the government. This led my great-grandmother to distribute my grandfather's money amongst the three boys until my grandfather married, when his wife put an end to the redistribution. These Mineral Estate proceeds divided the family, leading my great-grandmother to favour the brothers' children at gift-giving occasions. This estranged my father from the larger family, who as a young boy did not understand the disparity. This money also divided the Osage Nation, since a larger percentage of descendants were disenfranchised and began, especially in the 1960s, fighting for equal voting rights through organisations such as the Osage Nation Organization. My grandfather, and even my non-Osage grandmother, often voiced their disapproval of non-headright-owning Osage, who wanted to reform Osage government believing that "they are just trying to get our money". This was a common refrain among many headright owning Osages, who believed that federal control was more likely to protect their financial interests than Osage control (Dennison 2012; 2018).

The overly complicated and clearly destructive case of the Osage Mineral Estate is a powerful example of the consequences of the doctrine of distrust. While the US government holds the Mineral Estate 'in trust' for the Osage Nation, meaning it oversees the extraction of minerals and the dispersal of funds, the majority of the United States' actions have not worked to protect Osage interests. In 1917, the Tribal Council complained that Superintendent George Wright was "more greatly concerned about and … favorable to the interests of big oil companies and men of large financial means and political influence than … to the interests of the Osage people" (Burns 2004: 199). The Tribal Council went on to argue that the agency was spending Osage annuitant money needlessly and without their consent. Elected US officials were time and again more beholden to corporate interests that funded their election campaigns than they were to Osage interests.

Despite the fact that the surface lands were only allotted to Osages, land quickly left national control. In addition to the 'legal' processes of settlers buying land from banks after it had been confiscated, land was also taken through illegal means, primarily through estate fraud and murder. After the discovery of oil in 1897, the market for oil grew dramatically, bringing much wealth to Osage annuitants. At its peak in 1925, when each annuitant earned $13,200 per quarter, many non-Osage people came onto the reservation as legal guardians, merchants, suitors, swindlers, and murderers in an effort to gain access to this wealth (Wilson 1985). The Osage Nation eventually paid the FBI to investigate the murders of at least 60 Osages, which resulted in several convictions. However, no long-term jail sentences, return of stolen property, or financial compensation ever occurred (Harmon 2010; Grann 2016).

Such colonial legacies could not help but breed wide-scale distrust in governing institutions writ large, all of which had failed to protect Osages from widespread theft and murder. The terror from this period also created lasting legacies of internal suspicion for Osage, as children have had to make sense of white fathers who murdered aunts and uncles in the name of wealth and land. The extreme failures of the United States to live up to its promises of protection for our lands and bodies from molestation has created deep-rooted distrust, but this has also served as primary motivation for, and a tool of, our continued self-governance.

Despite the many layers of distrust, the 1906 Act has created, Osage have strategically deployed the relationship the Act solidified as a tool to stop various federal policies of elimination. While originally slated to expire after 25 years, the Tribal Council was able to extend the Mineral Estate until 1958 by insisting on our need for this continued relationship. In 1953, we, along with over one hundred other American Indian nations, including the Menominee and the Klamath, faced termination through House Concurrent Resolution 108, because they were believed to be successfully 'assimilated' into American society. The federal government had long been trying to "get out of the Indian business", but the period of termination was its most transparent attempt (US Congress 1953: 28). The Osage Tribal Council sent representatives to Washington, where they were able to negotiate for continued recognition by promising to pay their own operating costs through Osage Mineral Estate proceeds. In 1978, the Tribal Council was able to convince the United States government to change the language concerning the duration of the Mineral Estate from "until otherwise provided by an Act of Congress" to "in perpetuity" (US Public Law 95-496: 1160). These are not moments of colonial ambivalence on the part of the federal government, but instead examples of the agency Osage Nation officials had in lobbying for our interests and insisting on our continuance as a nation.

The doctrine of distrust has also worked to strengthen our resolve for maintaining and rebuilding our own governing systems in ways that are more accountable to our people. In 2004 the Osage Tribal Council succeeded in convincing the US government to pass Public Law 108-431, "An Act To reaffirm the inherent sovereign rights of the Osage Tribe to determine its membership and form of government", which cleared a path for us to reform our government (US Public Law 108-431 2004: 2609). After 100 years of colonially imposed citizenship and governance system, the Osage people were deeply frustrated by the overly limiting forms of citizenship and governance that had been imposed on us, and frequently articulated these concerns through the language of accountability. At a Tribal Council community meeting I attended prior to its passage, an Osage citizen said:

> The only problem I have with everything that's going on is 'accountability'. We have no *accountability* under the present system we have. We don't see 'accountability', where money comes from, where the money goes, or how it's dispersed. That's not your fault; it's the system we're under. We need some sort of 'accountability'.
>
> *(Anonymous 2004).*

Once P.L. 108-431 was passed the Osage Tribal Council immediately implemented a government reform process that ultimately led to the passage of the 2006 Osage Nation Constitution.

The 2006 Constitution was motivated by a search for greater relational accountability. Building on previous government reform efforts, especially in the 1990s, the Tribal Council appointed 10 Osage commissioners to involve the broadest possible group of Osages through a process of community engagement. The commissioners created and implemented the 2006 Osage Nation Constitution with the input from hundreds of open and recorded business meetings, over 40 community meetings across and beyond Oklahoma, a referendum election, a survey, a phone poll, and a final approval vote. This constitution drew from the three-part structure, and of the illegally abolished 1881 Constitution and included a vast array of accountability mechanisms, such as the separation of the executive, legislative, judicial, and treasury functions. It also established a complex set of boards that were appointed by, but distant from, elected official control, and offered the means to remove officials.

Unfortunately, many of these forms of accountability have had mixed results, at times entrenching distrust rather than building healthy governance. Tensions between the executive and legislative branches, for example, reached their peak when the congress[7] filed articles of impeachment against Principal Chief John Red Eagle, who was elected in 2010. The articles contained six different allegations ranging from interfering with an investigation by the Attorney General's office, refusing to relocate specific funds from the general treasury in accordance with Osage law, refusing to disclose a contract between the nation and a consultant in violation of the "Open Records Act", and paying funds to a consultant with no proof that the consultant actually performed the service (Tulsa World 2014).

The articles of impeachment resulted in an action before the Supreme Court, which affirmed the process of removal created by the congress and ended with congress voting to remove Principal Chief Red Eagle from office following an almost week-long trial (Tulsa World 2014). While many Osages appreciated that after 100 years of not being able to remove officials from office, the 2006 Constitution had been successfully deployed in this way, others felt like this removal was a clear sign that the constitution was entrenching rather than mitigating strife and distrust within the nation. This feeling has been affirmed by subsequent Supreme Court battles that have done little to resolve ongoing tensions about how monies are spent and who has authority to make decisions over program operations. At times, this residual distrust appears to be utilised by Osage officials in order to maintain divisions and serve political ends, including reelection. In this way, the Osage should not be understood as passive victims of the doctrine of distrust, but active agents entangled in this ongoing colonial context.

The new constitution did re-establish an important aspect of relationality by creating a more representative form of citizenship. Going back to the 1906 roll and giving all descendants equal voting in the government, the 2006 Constitution also cast a wide net around who was qualified for citizenship, including many of the younger individuals who had been excluded from representation because they still had living parents with the vote. This move was a particularly potent example of Osage agency in the face of settler colonial structures of elimination, which had greatly diminished those able to participate in our political processes.

One challenge, however, is that settler colonialism has separated many Osages from the Nation, with only about one-fourth of Osage Nation's citizens living on the reservation. The result of this separation is that Osages are often bifurcated into two groups, those who are fully engaged citizens, including participation in community events such as language classes, hand games, social gatherings, funerals, and the yearly dances, and those whose main engagement with the Nation is through receiving direct education, health, and/or burial financial assistance. There is a great deal of distrust between these groups, especially when national infrastructure projects and direct financial assistance programs are pitted against each other for funding. Some officials even use one of these platforms for election, by focusing primarily on their deep local ties or their commitment to the financial assistance programs as the main part of their campaigns. This ultimately results in fewer people being elected based on their proven track record in the necessary areas of specialty.

Even within its these limitations, the Osage Nation has been able to build its infrastructure in the face of ongoing colonialism. Current Osage leadership has facilitated a myriad of self-governance initiatives in the areas of land management, education, and health. All of them, however, have been uphill battles to implement and run. A slow-growing familiarity with the new system of government, an organisational structure siloed by programmatic ties to different federal programs and grants, and massive distrust complicate each of these efforts. Osage officials and employees must work continuously to navigate these limitations.

The 𐒻𐓬𐓰𐓵𐓘 Health Centre is one example where the impacts of the doctrine of distrust can be clearly seen. Fulfilling one element of a 25-year strategic plan that was completed in the first years of the new government through wide engagement with Osage citizens, the nation compacted the health clinic from the Indian Health Service (IHS) in 2015. Compacting in this context means that most of the authority over the clinic has shifted to the Osage Nation, reducing the United State government's authority not only over management of the facility, but also over control of how both the federal and the earned dollars that fund the clinic are spent. The infrastructure the 𐒻𐓬𐓰𐓵𐓘 Health Center inherited from the IHS, however, greatly limits its possibilities. Its electrical wiring, for example, is so outdated and poorly designed that when a radiologist tried using some new equipment it shocked him and ruined several other pieces of equipment. Elsewhere in the clinic, when the dental equipment is used, the entire office will often lose power. To address these issues, the Osage Nation Health Authority Board, which is an appointed group of medical experts independent from the nation that oversee the clinic, have developed plans for a new facility, for which they are raising funds. The building is not the only damaged infrastructure that the Osage Nation inherited from the IHS. Issues such as siloed health programs, high worker turnover, low levels of care, and programming not designed for Osage needs will require extensive efforts to shift. Fixing these issues will require building relational forms of accountability, specifically more communication, work environments where people feel valued and respected, and programming that centres Osage needs.

Along with improving health care, Chief Standing Bear made establishing an Osage school a key pillar of his administration (2014–present), and he has dedicated a great deal of his administration's time to 𐓏𐓘𐓨𐓪𐓘𐓺𐓤𐓘 𐓧𐓘𐓻𐓪𐓣𐓘𐓬𐓤 development and implementation. Starting with the existing childcare program that had four satellite facilities spread out across the reservation, our nation is investing additional financial, personnel, and cultural resources, particularly the Osage language, into ensuring that these are spaces where our children can thrive. Adding a grade each year, the nation hopes to eventually create a private K–12 Osage Nation school system.

In the ongoing planning process for ᎠᎶᏍᎧᎠ Ꮩ^ᎪᎣᎠᎪᏂ, however, Indigenous work climates are too often infected by the doctrine of distrust. In particular, too often employees are sceptical about implementing vast these institutional changes, rumours circulate widely about individuals actively involved in the reorganisation, and other employees drag their feet on making changes so as not to be subjected to intense scrutiny. Osage Nation leadership must find ways to create relational accountability in these work spaces through providing employees with the tools they need to do their job, increasing communication between workers and the administration so that problems can be addressed early on, and finding ways to build widespread employee excitement around the programming. A strong parent group has become a key advocate in making this expansive vision a reality by regularly calling for needed resources and attention to problems through Facebook, meetings with officials, and attendance at relevant governmental sessions. The impacts of this group signal the way that citizen involvement is vital for bringing these national desires into being through the establishment of new forms of relational accountability.

Conclusion

Current Osage Nation leadership has been deeply focused around accountability but has too often focused on what I have termed here personal visions of accountability, such as ensuring that employees show up to work on time or complete a given task. Part of this is because these are easier problem to target with simpler solutions. These forms of accountability, however, appear to entrench rather than dislodge distrust. Focusing on an individual's inadequacies makes relationship building hard and hides the larger structural reasons why the Osage Nation has become and continues to be a space of such deep-seated distrust. When Osage leadership has been able to instead build relational forms of accountability, such as fostering spaces where everyone feels respected, the workspace becomes a much more productive environment. Furthermore, when leadership has listened closely to the concerns of the employees, it has been much easier for the programs to shift to meet changing community needs.

Using relational accountability as the core analytic, this chapter has engaged Osage Nation governance history, desires, and debates to argue for relational accountability as a tool to disrupt the doctrine of distrust. At the core of Osage forms of relational accountability is respect, increasing communication, and meeting community needs. Through understanding the ways that trust has been distorted by the doctrine of distrust, we as Indigenous peoples can reimagine how to rebuild relational accountability.

Not only does relational accountability help us rethink how accountability should manifest in our nations, but it also helps us understand sovereignty in fundamentally different ways. Settler state sovereignty too often works as a "state of exception", where the sovereign is, at its core, outside the rules of society and thus unable to be held accountable (Agamben 1998; Dennison 2017). In the context of the Osage Nation, however, sovereignty has repeatedly been framed as the ability to create a government that is accountable to Osage needs (Dennison 2020). In our Indigenous nations we should avoid forms of sovereignty, like accountability, that do more to entrench distrust than to create healthy spaces from which to govern. At the core of sovereignty, then, needs to be a commitment to rebuilding healthy relations.

Notes

1 Settler colonialism is a persistent set of structures that attempts to eliminate Indigenous peoples, freeing land for settlement by non-Indigenous peoples (Trask 2000; Wolfe 2006).

2 The Osage originally called themselves ⌐∩໐ᏰʌᏟᏰʌ, which translates to children of the waters. Relying on false information, French colonists called this group of people ᠘ʌᏃʌᏃα, which was written in English as Osage. For clarity, I will refer to this group as Osage throughout.

3 During this conversation she talked about her sources as building on her own oral histories as well as the work of La Flesche's.

4 See also Wilkins and Lomawaima, *Uneven Ground* for a discussion of how the Cherokee and other Indigenous nations view the trust relationship.

5 While this was in many ways similar to the US government, its roots can be tied back to the Iroquois Confederacy, upon which the US confederacy was based.

6 The 2,230th share of the Mineral Estate was granted to a white woman for life because of her service to the Osage Nation. There were only 2,229 Osage listed on the roll. For more on the 1906 roll, see Wilson, *The Underground Reservation*.

7 Unless I specifically say otherwise, Congress and Supreme Court are referring to the branches inside Osage government and not to the United States or another government.

References

Agamben, G. (1998). *Homo Sacer*. Stanford University Press: Stanford, CA.

Annals of Congress (1906). Fifty Ninth Congress, Session I, 539.

Anonymous (2004). *Osage Tribal Council Community Meeting*. Recorded by Author on 17 May. Grayhorse, OK.

Burns, L.F. (2004). *A History of the Osage People*, 2nd rev. ed. University Alabama Press: Tuscaloosa, AL.

Carroll, C. (2015). *Roots of Our Renewal: Ethnobotany and Cherokee Environmental Governance, First Peoples: New Directions in Indigenous Studies*. University of Minnesota Press: Minneapolis, MN.

Cattelino, J. (2008). *High Stakes: Florida Seminole Gaming and Sovereignty*. Duke University Press: Durham, NC.

Coll, S. (2012). *Private Empire: ExxonMobil and American Power*. Penguin Press: New York.

Dennison, J. (2012). *Colonial Entanglement: Constituting a Twenty-First-Century Osage Nation*. University of North Carolina Press: Chapel Hill, NC.

Dennison, J. (2017). 'Entangled sovereignties: The Osage Nation's interconnections with governmental and corporate authorities', *American Ethnologist*, vol 44, no 4: 684–696.

Dennison, J (2018). 'The "Affects" of empire: (Dis)trust among Osage annuitants,' in C. McGranahan (ed.) *Ethnographies of Empire*. Duke University Press, Durham, NC, 27–46.

Dennison, J. (2020). 'Sovereignty as accountability: Theorizing from the Osage Nation', in W. Willard, D. Pearson, and A. Marshall (eds.) *Rising from the Ashes*. University of Nebraska Press: Lincoln, NE, 279–301.

DuVal, K. (2007). *The Native Ground: Indians and Colonists in the Heart of the Continent*. University of Pennsylvania Press: Philadelphia, PA.

Engle Merry, Sally. (2000). *Colonizing Hawai'i: The Cultural Power of Law*. Princeton University Press: Princeton, NJ.

Grann, D. (2016). *Killers of the Flower Moon: The Osage Murders and the Birth of the FBI*. Doubleday: New York.

Gray, J (2005). *Osage Sovereignty Day Celebration*. Recorded by Author on 4 February. Pawhuska, OK.

Harmon, A. (2010). *Rich Indians: Native People and the Problem of Wealth in American History*. University of North Carolina Press: Chapel Hill, NC.

Jackson, R. and Roseburg, C. (1982). 'Why Africa's weak states persist: The empirical and juridical in statehood', *World Politics*, vol 35, no 1: 1–24.

Jefferson, T. (1804). *Letter to Secretary of the Navy Robert Smith*. Available: https://founders.archives.gov/documents/Jefferson/99-01-02-0067, accessed 23 April 2020.

Kappler, C. (1972). *Indian Treaties 1778–1883*. Interland Publishing Inc: New York.

Kauanui, J.K. (2016). '"A structure, not an event": Settler colonialism and enduring indigeneity', *Lateral*, vol 5: 1.

La Flesche, F. (1939). 'War ceremony and peace ceremony of the Osage Indians', *Bureau of American Ethnology Bulletin*, vol 101: 1–280.

La Flesche, F. (1999). *The Osage and the Invisible World: From the Works of Francis La Flesche* (G.A. Bailey, eds). University of Oklahoma Press: Norman.

Lambert, V. (2007). *Choctaw Nation: A Story of American Indian Resurgence*. University of Nebraska Press: Lincoln, NE.

McCarthy, T. (2016). *In Divided Unity: Haudenosaunee Reclamation at Grand River, Critical Issues in Indigenous Studies*. University of Arizona Press: Tucson, AZ.

Osage Nation Code. (2009). *Speak What's on Your Mind*. Title 15, Chapter 10. Sections 101–106. Available: https://osage.nation.codes/ONC/15-10, accessed 29 April 2020.

Simpson, A. (2014). *Mohawk Interruptus: Political Life Across the Borders of Settler States*. Duke University Press: Durham, NC.

Smith, L.T. (2005). 'On tricky ground: Researching the native in the age of uncertainty', in N.K. Denzin and Y.S. Lincoln (eds.) *The SAGE Handbook of Qualitative Research*. SAGE Publishing: Thousand Oaks, CA, 85–107.

Stark, H.K. and Stark, K.J. (2018). 'Nenabozho goes fishing: A sovereignty story', *Daedalus*, vol 147, no 2: 17–26.

Subcomandante Insurgente Marcos. (2003). *CHP: The Thirteenth Tale, Part Six: A Good Government*. Available: http://www.struggle.ws/mexico/ezln/2003/marcos/governmentJULY.html, accessed 20 April 2020.

Tomas, N. (2012). 'Maori concepts and practices of Rangatiratanga "Sovereignty"?,' in J. Evans, A. Genovese, and A. Reilly (eds.) *Sovereignty: Frontiers of Possibility*. University of Hawai'i Press, Honolulu, HI. 220–237.

Trask, H.-K. (2000). 'Settlers of color and "Immigrant" hegemony: "Locals" in Hawai'i', *Amerasia Journal*, vol 26, no 2: 1–26.

Tsosie, R. (2003). 'Conflict between the public trust and the Indian trust doctrines: Federal public land policy and native Indians', *Tulsa Law Review*, vol 39, no 2: 271–311.

U.S. Congress. (1953). 'Hearing before the subcommittee on Indian affairs of the committee on interior and insular affairs house of representatives, testimony of the Osage Indians of Oklahoma', *House of Representatives Concurrent Resolution*, 108. Serial No 7.

U.S. Public Law 95-496. (1978). *An Act to Amend Certain Laws Relating to the Osage Tribe of Oklahoma 92 Stat. 1660-1664*. Available: https://uscode.house.gov/statutes/pl/95/496.pdf, accessed April 23, 2020.

U.S. Public Law 108-431. (2004). *An Act to Reaffirm the Inherent Sovereign Rights of the Osage Tribe to Determine its Membership and Form of Government 118 Stat. 2609-2610*. Available: https://www.govinfo.gov/content/pkg/STATUTE-118/pdf/STATUTE-118-Pg2609.pdf, accessed 23 April 2020.

Webb, M.J. (2005). *Tulsa University Legal Training for the Osage Government Reform Commission*. Recorded by Author, May 19. Tulsa, OK.

Weyler, R. (2007). *Blood of the Land: The Government and Corporate War Against First Nations*. New Catalyst Books: Gabriola Island, BC.

Wilkins, D.E. and Lomawaima, K.T. (2002). *Uneven Ground: American Indian Sovereignty and Federal Law*. University of Oklahoma Press: Norman.

Williams, R.A. (1999). *Linking Arms Together: American Indian Treaty Visions of Law and Peace, 1600–1800*. Routledge: New York.

Wilson, S. (2008). *Research Is Ceremony: Indigenous Research Methods*. Fernwood Publishing: Winnipeg, MB.

Wilson, T.P. (1985). *The Underground Reservation: Osage Oil*. University of Nebraska Press: Lincoln, NE.

Wolfe, P. (2006). 'Settler colonialism and the elimination of the native', *Journal of Genocide Research*, vol 8, no 4: 387–409.

23

Ellos Deatnu and post-state Indigenous feminist sovereignty

Rauna Kuokkanen

Introduction

On Summer Solstice 2017, a small group of mostly young Sámi women and men set up a camp called Čearretsullo siida and moratorium on an island in the Deatnu (Tana) River near the town of Ohcejohka (Utsjoki) in Sápmi,[1] Northern Scandinavia. They called their movement Ellos Deatnu! (translated into English, Long Live Deatnu!) and declared autonomy on the island and the waters surrounding it, stating that instead of the states, the area is now governed by customary Sámi law. They announced a moratorium on recreational fishing around the island, which implied that fishing licenses purchased from the state were no longer valid. Instead, such permit holders were expected to ask permission to fish from local Sámi and especially those families whose traditional fishing sites are in question.

The first of its kind in Sápmi, Ellos Deatnu emerged to resist, challenge, and undermine the assertions of sovereignty of Nordic settler colonial states in general and the 2017 Deatnu Fishing Agreement in particular. The movement, however, was quickly categorised as mere civil disobedience by media and some scholars. In this chapter, I suggest that Ellos Deatnu exceeds the idea or practice of refusing and resisting the law and order of the state. Indigenous activists frequently emphasise that for one, they are following their own rule of law (that precedes the state laws) and second, they neither have consented to nor participated in shaping the state laws that oppress them as a people. Rather than civil disobedience, I argue that Ellos Deatnu represents an attempt to regenerate a new vision of Sámi self-determination and jurisdiction and to recover traditional Sámi structures of governance regardless of the law and order of the state. As an Indigenous movement, Ellos Deatnu endeavours to moves beyond the state and thus, become 'post-state'.

The rejection of Indigenous politics and political institutions as usual has characterised many recent Indigenous grassroot movements particularly in North America, including the most well-known Idle No More in Canada and Standing Rock in the United States. Inspired and informed by these movements, Ellos Deatnu emerged from the desire to start a new sovereignty discourse vis-a-vis the Sámi in Scandinavia. Direct action of declaring autonomy and moratorium on the island of Čearretsuolu was unparalleled and extraordinary in Nordic standards. By foregrounding the resurgence of Indigenous concepts and practice of nationhood that do not acknowledge colonial and patriarchal institutions, laws and practices, Ellos Deatnu aspires to critically inter-rogate and expose the hypocrisy of the supposedly just and fair Nordic nation-states.

By deliberately engaging in 'alternative' modes of organising similar to other Indigenous movements or 'protests', Ellos Deatnu represents an attempt to generate a new vision of Sámi self-determination and sovereignty based on the siida, traditional Sámi social and political organ-isation.[2] Central to this vision is to reclaim and reengage with local traditional and kinship-based governance practices such as consensus and collaborative decision-making; spiritual leadership and ceremony; art and practical creativity, gift economies, and relationship-building with people and the land. I suggest that Ellos Deatnu does not only resist the colonial state but more impor-tantly, centres the resurgence of Indigenous concepts and practice of nationhood at the inter-section of eliminating colonial and patriarchal institutions, laws and practices.[3] Like Indigenous feminism, Ellos Deatnu critically interrogates and exposes, through lived practice of localised resistance and resurgence, the hypocrisy the supposedly just and fair 'democratic', patriarchal set-tler colonial state that is predicated on the elimination and dispossession of Indigenous peoples.

Indigenous feminist analyses are not limited on discussing women's participation, roles, or views. Thus, to examine Ellos Deatnu through the lens of Indigenous feminist analysis is not to focus on the efforts of Indigenous women in the movement to the exclusion of Indigenous men. Among the central figures of Ellos Deatnu were young Sámi men whose public demea-nor was notably different from the typical male Sámi political leadership of earlier times often characterised by self-aggrandising conduct and old boys' networks. The male members of Ellos Deatnu appeared in public unflinching and smart yet unpretentious, modest and respectful. Unlike their predecessors, they also took guidance from their female elders. My intention is not to designate Ellos Deatnu as an Indigenous feminist movement but rather, consider the ways in which its motivation, core principles, activities, and efforts attest to an ethos of Indigenous femi-nist theory and practice of sovereignty struggles, which differs from conventional Indigenous politics and the rights-based, electoral politics-driven approach.

In this chapter, I examine how Indigenous feminist analysis enables a more informed and in-depth understanding of Ellos Deatnu's goals and intentions. I am interested in the ways in which the key Ellos Deatnu objectives correspond to central Indigenous feminist ideas of (1) challenging particularly the normativity of the settler state but also unsettling conventional Sámi politics as usual; and (2) articulating and embodying explicitly anti-oppressive alternatives for Indigenous governance. The chapter begins with an overview of the main tenets of Indigenous feminism. Second, it considers the Ellos Deatnu movement and the context it emerged in. Third, I discuss Nordic settler colonialism as it applies to Ellos Deatnu and the Nordic context. The chapter concludes with an analysis of Ellos Deatnu's two strategies, resistance and resurgence, in light of what I call post-state Indigenous feminist sovereignty.[4]

Indigenous feminist analysis and resurgence

From its 'tribal feminist' roots in the United States (Allen 1986), Indigenous feminism has grown into a substantial field of global scholarly inquiry arguing for the inclusion of colonial-ism as an analytical category for conceptualising Indigenous peoples' subjugation in general and Indigenous women's oppression in particular. Indigenous feminism has illustrated how colonisation radically undermined and transformed gender relations to subordinate, margin-alise, and exclude Indigenous women irrespective of their precolonial political and economic positions. Indigenous feminist theory has simultaneously challenged the unexamined racism, colonialism and white privilege in feminist theory and movements and the sexism and misog-yny in Indigenous leadership and communities (e.g., Green 2007; Hernández Castillo 2010;

Huhndorf and Suzack 2010; Lawrence and Anderson 2005; Maracle 2006; Moreton-Robinson 2000). Indigenous feminist activists and scholars have also long questioned misguided, sexist and discriminatory ideas and practices of Indigenous sovereignty and tradition and called for an interrogation of forms of violence underlying them (Monture 2004; Nahanee 1993; Snyder et al. 2015).

Indigenous feminist analysis has established that Indigenous sovereignty struggles are always gendered. Historically, Indigenous nations were typically characterised by governance structures where men, women and two-spirit people had their specific roles and responsibilities. These duties were usually gender differentiated but considered equal and complimentary. The repressive settler state and its institutionalised heteropatriarchal structures (see MacKinnon 1983; MacKinnon 1989) (Monture-Angus 1995; Simpson 2016) have systematically compromised Indigenous social, political and legal institutions and kinship structures (e.g., Turpel 1993). Throughout history, settler colonial states have sought to restructure Indigenous polities in their own mirror image while removing all *bona fide* power and authority from Indigenous polities (Rifkin 2011). Sometimes this has occurred through explicit physical violence and genocide, sometimes through less obvious structural coercion through laws and policy.

Indigenous political institutions created to replace existing political orders were commonly patriarchal and either actively excluded women or marginalised them indirectly. As a result of the colonial imposition and subsequent adoption of patriarchal values characterised by a hierarchical and rigid gender binary, early Indigenous nationhood and sovereignty movements were frequently male-dominated, replicating the exclusion and marginalisation of women and their contributions to nation-building and governance. Today, sexism, homophobia, and even misogyny are common concerns in many Indigenous communities (Barker 2006; Denetdale 2009; Napoleon 2009; Ramirez 2007).

Simultaneously, Indigenous women's self-determination has been contested and denied first by patriarchal colonial law, policies and institutions and later, by Indigenous men who have internalised and adopted the norms and values of patriarchal colonialism. As a result, Indigenous women's rights – or perhaps more correctly, their practices and responsibilities to their territories have been erased. Indigenous women's participation, human rights, political status, and well-being have been radically curtailed. Indigenous women's self-determination is represented as an individual(istic) right in opposition to the a priori right of self-determination of Indigenous nations and communities.

Indigenous feminist analysis enables us to deconstruct the normativity of the nation-state and also addresses heteronormativity and heteropatriarchy within many Indigenous nationalisms. The key feminist insight of heteropatriarchy as a logic that naturalises gender hierarchy both within the family (the male head of the household) and in the state structures (the male lawmakers and leadership) has been employed by Indigenous feminism to expose the heteropatriarchy's central role in colonising Indigenous communities. In order for the colonial rule to be successful, Indigenous societies had to be restructured on the basis of strict gender binary and hierarchy which makes the patriarchal control appear natural (Simpson 2017; Smith 2008).

What is more, most existing self-government institutions are modeled after the logic and governance structures of the colonial state instead of drawing and building on practices of diplomacy and systems decision-making that Indigenous peoples had in place in the past. It has been suggested that contemporary self-government arrangements "serve as extensions of the colonial project" (Nadasdy 2017: 315). Given how gender has played an integral part of colonisation, many Indigenous self-determination struggles have also internalised and replicate the structures of racialised and gendered hierarchies and domination they claim to dismantle. As my research shows, many contemporary Indigenous political orders have been deeply influenced by patriarchal gender regimes (Kuokkanen 2019).

By establishing a siida on an island and declaring autonomy called Čearretsuolu and a moratorium on recreational fishing licenses issued by the states, the Ellos Deatnu movement demonstrated a yearning and determination to move beyond Indigenous politics and existing Sámi political processes and institutions. Reflecting Indigenous feminist aspirations to disrupt and unsettle normative conceptions of the nation and nation-state, Ellos Deatnu refused to follow or imitate the organisational principles, structures and leadership of the nation-state, much of which characterises formal Indigenous political bodies today. The movement did not expect or depend on the support of their respective official political bodies (the Sámi parliaments in Norway and Finland), yet it did not denounce them either. Ellos Deatnu welcomed the support of their own political institutions and were open to collaborating with them notwithstanding that the movement is premised on their inadequacy not only in providing viable solutions to pressing issues in Sápmi but also more fundamentally, creating social and political structures that better reflect Sámi values and ways of deliberation and governance.

The Deatnu River and the 2017 Deatnu Agreement

The Deatnu River, located in Northern Scandinavia at the heart of the Sámi territory, is often regarded as one of the best salmon rivers in Europe. It also signifies the border between Norway and Finland. For local Sámi, however, Deatnu is not a border but a bond that connects people. Before roads were built along both its banks after the second world war, the Deatnu was the main channel and connection for everything: people, news, provisions, mail, building materials. The Sámi have been living and fishing for salmon along the 200-kilometre-long Deatnu for thousands of years, building deep knowledge of and connection with the river and its fisheries, as well as developing specific fishing methods and systems of salmon fishery management and stewardship. One of the last wild Atlantic salmon rivers in Europe, Deatnu has also long been a popular and well-known river for recreational fishing.

In the 1751 Strömstad Peace Accord, the Deatnu River was made into an international boundary, becoming one of the oldest political borders in Europe (Müller-Wille and Aikio 2005). An addendum to the 1751 Strömstad Peace Accord called the Lapp Codicil granted free passage for reindeer herding Sámi to cross the newly established state border migrating with their herds between their winter and summer pastures.[5] Later border closures and political changes, however, resulted in deliberately ignoring the Lapp Codicil, although it has never been formally repealed. Yet it was not until post-World War II when the border of Finland and Norway was patrolled more closely and states established a more permanent presence in the region. New laws were passed to regulate land ownership and citizenship (Müller-Wille and Aikio 2005: 49–50).[6]

Since 1873, salmon fishing in the Deatnu River has been regulated by bilateral agreements negotiated by the governments of Norway and Finland. A bilateral agreement regulates the fishing season, methods and the fishing rights of the local Sámi and recreational fisheries. In Spring 2017, the governments of Norway and Finland approved a new Deatnu Agreement, which radically restricted traditional Sámi fisheries and fishing rights. Traditional Sámi fishing rights have belonged to and were passed down within families. In the new Deatnu Agreement, renegotiated to heed the scientists' warnings of declining salmon stocks, certain traditional fishing methods were banned altogether, fishing season was shortened and the fishing rights of non-resident local Sámi[7] curtailed. Sámi traditional fisheries were restricted twice as much as recreational tourist fishing in addition to the creation of a new category of fishing rights, on the Finnish side of the river, belonging to non-local property owners (Aikio et al. 2016).[8] The new Deatnu Agreement resulted in Sámi families losing their traditional fishing rights and eventually ending the Sámi fisheries in the Deatnu River will end as the younger generation are deprived of a range of skills and knowledge related to various traditional fishing practices (Satokangas 2017).

Prior to the signing of the Deatnu Agreement, local residents and Sámi traditional rights holders lobbied extensively and met with various state officials and agencies through their organisations. Even though the Finnish and Norwegian negotiation teams had Sámi representatives, they were excluded from the most important negotiations and state representatives negotiated the final deal by themselves. Local Sámi were not able to participate in the drafting process (Aikio et al. 2016). The Deputy Chancellor of Justice in Finland confirmed that the consultation of the Sámi, a legislated requirement, had been deficient. Because of this, according to him, the parliamentary process leading to the new Deatnu Agreement has been unconstitutional (Wesslin 2017). Regardless, the parliamentarians refused to reconsider the agreement, arguing that "regardless, we now have to live with it" (Aikio 2017; Lakkala 2017: online).

The encampment at Deatnu at Summer Solstice 2017 emerged first as resistance to the structural violence of the state that the new Deatnu Agreement represented. However, it was equally about resurgence of Indigenous sovereignty and self-determination and the resilience of Indigenous peoples as self-organising social and political societies. Ellos Deatnu and the Čearretsullo siida were a grassroots and direct enactment of Sámi self-determination, which had not taken place in Sápmi before. The movement immediately gained strong local, national and international support and the siida was frequently visited by local people, Sámi leadership, other supporters and international Indigenous allies. At a town hall meeting in Ohcejohka,[9] 50 people gathered to discuss and support the moratorium and to draft and sign a statement that stipulates:

> The Deatnu water system belongs to the local people who has the sole right and responsibility to decide, manage, care, look after and study their own waters and income. We do not accept the state ownership and management of our lands and waters. The Deatnu water system and all activities on it are not the business of the states.
>
> *(Cited in Alajärvi 2017a: online)*

Despite its precedent-setting character – for example, such straightforward public denouncements of state ownership of land, water and resources by the Sámi as above have been extremely rare in Scandinavia – law enforcement or other state officials did not intervene or interfere with the Čearretsullo siida. Neither police nor politicians publicly reacted to Ellos Deatnu declarations of autonomy and Sámi self-determination, nor intervened in the moratorium of recreational fishing. Such benign neglect is somewhat unusual, given the state's readiness to step in on and police Indigenous 'protests'. Possible reasons for the lack of concern include the remoteness of the location and the minimal public inconvenience of the action. According to the Ellos Deatnu participants, the few recreational fishers with whom they came into contact in the declared moratorium area were mostly collaborative and respectful.

In their efforts to highlight the fact local Sámi were the rightful owners and managers of the Deatnu River and its fisheries, the movement requested the governments of Norway and Finland to provide them with legal proof of the transfer of the ownership of the Deatnu River to the states from the local Sámi siidas.[10] Also a symbolic gesture, the point was to expose the Nordic legal fiction of the establishment of state ownership over the Deatnu River and its world-renowned salmon fisheries by unilaterally imposing state sovereignty and authority without a due process or consent of the traditional owners. In support and solidarity, another moratorium was declared on another island upstream from the Čearretsullo siida later in Summer 2017. The movement also reached out to Sámi fishers upstream critical of the Ellos Deatnu movement and who considered the new Deatnu Agreement a positive development. A public meeting was held in Kárásjohka to hear the opposition and discuss the issue. At the meeting, Ellos Deatnu members stressed that what is at stake in the new Deatnu Agreement is much greater than individual catch of salmon. [11]

As planned, the Čearretsullo siida was closed down by the participants at the end of the fishing season in August 2017. Closing the siida, however, did not mean ending the moratorium or the movement. In a recorded statement, an Ellos Deatnu participant noted that the moratorium continues until the Deatnu Agreement has been renegotiated and adopted at the local level and the process is led by Sámi of the Deatnu valley (see Ellos Deatnu 2017). Although the siida was taken down, the moratorium continued the following summer on and around the island of Čearretsuolu.

The following year the movement morphed into a mobile Moratorium Office with the objective of sharing information about Sámi self-determination. The 'office' is a suitcase with information that can be taken to events by Ellos Deatnu participants to provide guidance and support to those individuals and communities who wanted to establish their own moratoriums or decolonised Sámi areas. According to their website, the Moratorium Office provides "a decolonialist self-determination service" and "solutions for ending colonial power":

> By declaring a moratorium, you can finally take control. Nobody knows your native lands like you and your community do. So why not decide for yourself how to use and manage it? A moratorium will ensure that not only your community but also your land will get fair treatment.
>
> *(Moratorium Office n.d.: online)*

The group of Sámi 'artivists' behind the Moratorium Office also created a series of land-based art installations called Rájácummá (Border Kiss) to call attention to the foundational values of Indigenous self-determination: reciprocity with and respect for the land, our responsibilities and balanced co-existence (Eira 2018). The land-based art installations seek to emphasise the connecting force of the river Deatnu and erase the colonial border – artificial to many local Sámi.

Nordic settler colonialism and 2017 Deatnu Agreement

The Ellos Deatnu concerns pertain to Sámi self-determination, traditional fishing rights and the local Sámi ownership and management of lands, waters and resources. The Nordic countries are not typically considered settler colonial states and there are historians in Finland who argue neither colonialism nor assimilation took place in the Sámi territory (Enbuske 2008; Hiltunen 2007; Lähteenmäki 2006; Vahtola 2014). Other scholars have, however, detailed the colonial history and present in the Nordic countries (Åhrén 2004; Arell 1979; Hansen and Olsen 2014; Lawrence and Åhrén 2016; Lindmark 2013; Lundmark 1998; Otnes 1970; Pedersen 1999; Sehlin MacNeil and Lawrence 2017).

Settler colonialism is an ongoing structure that requires the elimination of the 'Native' in order to obtain their land and resources (Wolfe 2006). Elimination implies a range of dynamics, including assimilation, integration, containment extermination and genocide (Veracini 2010). Part of the 'settler colonial present' (Veracini 2015) is to continually erase other histories and geographies as well as political and legal orders. Settler colonial states have long sought to undermine and eliminate Indigenous self-determination and sovereignty through various forms of structural state violence. In the Nordic countries, this takes place through repressive laws, policies and a deliberate failure to adhere to existing legislative obligations to ensure Sámi involvement in decision-making affecting them.

At the Deatnu River, the 2017 Agreement is a settler colonial structure, seeking to eliminate the Sámi by eradicating a traditional practice and livelihood and as the result, a central aspect of people's identity who have grown up and learned to fish on the river. Deatnu is an inextricable part of who many Sámi are along the river. In the words of the Upper Deatnu Fishing Cooperative in its letter to the Parliament of Finland: "The agreement robs Sámi of their rights and kills Sámi culture" (Satokangas 2017: online). The ongoing erosion of a unique fishing culture with its specific traditional knowledge and skills will only intensify as people are deprived of a range of skills and knowledge related to various traditional fishing practices, including weir, gill net, seine and drift net (Holmberg 2018). This is a serious concern particularly for the younger generation of Sámi from the river, many of whom are considered in the Agreement 'tourists' in their own river because they live elsewhere for their studies or work (Aikio et al. 2016). Days before the final approval of the Deatnu Agreement, Aslak Holmberg, a young Sámi man who grew up fishing in Deatnu and one of the organisers of Ellos Deatnu, pleaded on Facebook for international support in a filmed statement as the last resort:

> Our way of life as Indigenous Sámi salmon fishers is being criminalised. ... It feels like [the governments of Norway and Finland] are killing us ... not by guns but slowly and silently. They're claiming that we don't have any knowledge of the river or the salmon in it. They say they're protecting the salmon from us.
>
> *(Holmberg 2017)*

While the Tana Research Group (TRG), the scientific advisory group for governments of Norway and Finland, denies ignoring Sámi traditional knowledge of Deatnu fisheries, it constructs local Sámi knowledge a relativistic and descriptive belief system. For the TRG, only "natural sciences are concerned with finding objective truths" (Falkegard et al. 2016: 144).

Post-state Indigenous feminist sovereignty

The constitutive feature of Indigenous feminist theory and the practice of Indigenous feminist sovereignty is the strive towards restoring Indigenous nationhood and self-determination beyond the settler state and the nation-state model in a way that rejects all structures and forms of violence, including sexual and gender violence against Indigenous women. In the Nordic context, Ellos Deatnu was precedent-setting in its endeavour for its place-based grassroots re-envisioning, rebuilding, and embodying 'alternative' polities and political structures. It was a first public effort to reclaim and restore the siida governance as a both resistance and resurgence.

Whereas the Sámi political institutions such as the Sámi parliaments sought to resolve the matter through the establishment and usual channels of consultation, Ellos Deatnu adopted an unconventional and unexpected approach in Scandinavian standards. Notwithstanding that Ellos Deatnu began as a reaction and resistance to the new Deatnu Agreement, the focus was expressly protecting a way of life and a relationship to a specific place as well as enacting and embodying forms of legitimacy and sovereignties alternative to the settler colonial state. Ellos Deatnu pushed for an opening for 'a new political reality', a possibility of engagement between different political and ontological orders rather than participating in and through the state structures and institutions. This does necessarily involve dismantling the state as much as moving beyond the options the state model has to offer. As Elizabeth Strakosch suggests:

Such possibilities do not necessarily involve tearing the state down in order to usher in a new political reality. In its own way, this approach accedes to the claim that the state exhausts politics – only when it vacates this space is a new politics possible. Besides, we are bound up with the state, and it holds enormous resources for change. What may be possible is to look beyond the state as the enable rand sole site of politics, to consider it as one among several different political institutions and orders. In this conception, new political arrangements do not have to rise up above or flow down from the state, but can exist alongside it.

(Strakosch 2015: 186)

'Post-state' acknowledges the existence of Indigenous polities and seeks to reclaim them. It may mean creating parallel systems of governance but in Indigenous feminist iterations, it always involves attending to the relations of domination and the structural violence of state and its institutions. Notably however, 'beyond the state' is not a naïve or misguided suggestion to reject the state altogether. While the motivating concerns for rejecting the state are understandable, it is, however, a double-edged sword. There is a danger of reifying the earlier masculinist nationalist discourse that male-led Indigenous organisations have employed against Indigenous women advocating for gender equality. These organisations argued that women have betrayed their communities by looking for support outside their communities (Barker 2006; Fiske 1996; McIvor 1995). A dogmatic stance that opposes any interaction with the state may create new exclusionary and hegemonic practices in which only the unproblematically 'traditional' approach is valid (cf. Hokowhitu 2012).

What makes Ellos Deatnu (and many other Indigenous resurgence or nationhood movements) 'post-state' is their deliberate departure from the state as the point of reference as well as the qualitative difference between resurgence and a form of resistance that says no to everything but has nothing to offer as an alternative. The latter informs today's much of mainstream politics and has been considered by some the crisis of democracy. Recent analyses of the state of Western democracies point out that while people have always tended more readily to rally *against* something rather than what they are stand *for*, present-day politics are defined by much more intense opposition to a point of destruction and extreme partisanship, making cooperative governance increasingly difficult (Fisher 2019; Foa and Mounk 2017; see also Norris 2017). This is most glaring at the moment in Britain and the United States but characterises a number of other countries globally, amounting to a growing disillusionment with existing systems of political authority and "a hollowing out of confidence in democracy itself" (Barry and Mueller 2019: online). Whether civil disobedience or a crisis of democracy, Ellos Deatnu is neither although it may serve as an inspiration for other, more mainstream movements.

Ellos Deatnu strives to move beyond not only the nation-state but Sámi also political structures currently in place. This is one of the central objectives of recent Indigenous feminist theory and activism. Modeled after the bureaucratic and administrative structures of state apparatus, Indigenous self-government bodies may serve a purpose in delivering services and programs (tribal governments in the United States) or communicating with and issuing statements to the national governments (the Sámi parliaments in Scandinavia) but they have failed – or perhaps more correctly, do not consider important – in restoring and reclaiming place-based local Indigenous governance systems and political orders. For some Sámi, the lack of Sámi foundations is a major shortcoming of the Sámi parliaments as contemporary Sámi representative and political institutions. They have also long been criticised by many Sámi for not being able to chart the path for, or explain the meaning of, Sámi determination. (Kuokkanen 2011). At the Ellos Deatnu town hall meeting in Kárásjohka, long-time Sámi educator and activist Asta Balto noted, "we've spent decades talking about self-determination without knowing what we mean.

Now we have a movement that is showing us, putting it into practice, implementing it" (Balto 2017: personal communication 25 July).

Ellos Deatnu efforts to enact an 'alternative', anti-oppressive mode of Indigenous Sámi governance correspond to the central Indigenous feminist tenets. One of the most striking departures from Indigenous politics as usual is the way in which Indigenous women have articulated their resistance to the state's coercive measures in terms of love. This became pronounced at the height of Idle No More in Canada in Winter 2012–2013 when love of the land, their children, future generations, and their communities were frequently discussed as the reasons for Indigenous women to take a stand and the streets (Nanibush 2014; Nason 2014; Simpson 2013; Wilson 2015).

The Čearretsullo siida code of conduct established a normative framework that is premised on principles of justice, love and respect, reciprocity, safety and security. The code also recognised siida's embeddedness in and interdependence with the land and non-human beings. At the closing of the siida in August 2017, Ellos Deatnu issued a statement that was distinctly political yet premised on a different ethos, set of values and ontology than conventional Sámi political statement:

> We thank Čearretsuolu – our partner, friend, spiritual source and siida. We thank the birds, animals, plants, and other blessings that belong to the island. We need this connection to a healthful life. Thank you for the peace we enjoyed this summer. We have now taken down our lávvu structures on the island and cleaned up after ourselves as we wait for the winter. The Čearretsuolu moratorium will remain in force during the next fishing season, and we intend to continue to advance self-governance in Čearretsuolu and in all of Sápmi.
>
> *(Ellos Deatnu 2017)*

By creating, presenting and enacting an alternative, Ellos Deatnu's critique of existing self-government politics is implicit yet obvious. Through the lived practice, whether in ceremony or carrying out the daily chores of running the siida, Ellos Deatnu seeks to advocate and uphold relationships with the land and one another informed by interrelatedness, responsibility and mutual respect rather than coercion, hierarchy and domination.

In the Ellos Deatnu movement, Indigenous feminist sovereignty is about refusing the violence of the colonial border on the river Deatnu, as well as reclaiming and putting the 'alternative' into lived practice (alternative to the colonial structures but from a Sámi vantage point, the normal and normative ground). In its different iterations, Ellos Deatnu envisions, visualises, carries out, and exercises local Sámi autonomy on and with the land and the river that is so central to how Sámi along the river see themselves as individuals and in relation to others. The movement's beauty – and also its fragility – is in its multiple facets. On the one hand, the movement is grounded on ethics of subtlety and on the other, forceful in its departure from Sámi politics as usual and its method of simply doing it instead of expecting or awaiting external recognition or approval, be it by the state institutions or Sámi political bodies. Furthermore, Ellos Deatnu is a representation of Indigenous feminist sovereignty for it subtly (that is, without vehement declarations or formal statements) refuses those previous expressions of Indigenous sovereignty that are characterised by formal political processes, procedures and institutions as well as the informal old boys' networks, grandstanding and sexist (or homophobic), patronising behaviour towards others than cis-hetero men.

Conclusion

By their very existence, Indigenous peoples have always threatened, whether explicitly or implicitly, the fiction of state sovereignty. Indigenous political discourse, grassroots political activism, activist scholarship and especially the recent lived practice of Indigenous resurgence movements increasingly challenge the legitimacy and universality of the sovereign settler state (Coulthard 2014; Kino-nda-niimi Collective 2014; Manuel 2015; Simpson 2014). Although Ellos Deatnu first emerged as resistance to state violence – specifically, opposition to unilateral, repressive legislation and negotiated agreements – it was equally (if not more) about resurgence of Sámi sovereignty and resilience of Sámi social and political orders.

Ellos Deatnu is an example of an Indigenous movement in a specific settler colonial context in which colonialism has been conventionally denied and the Nordic states have represented themselves as 'Indigenous friendly' and global leaders in advancing Indigenous rights. Drawing on Indigenous feminist theory and practice, I have suggested that the Ellos Deatnu movement is not about mere civil disobedience within the framework of laws and policies of the nation-states. By exceeding such framework, it embodies the intent and aspirations of Indigenous feminist sovereignty in its challenging the legitimacy of the settler colonial state as well as decolonising existing Indigenous governance structures. This is done through envisioning and embodying 'alternatives' that draw on preexisting Indigenous political traditions and remind settler colonial states about the fiction of state sovereignty on their territories.[12] By evoking other polities and authorities than the nation-state, these 'alternatives' denaturalise the patriarchal settler colonial state as the normative political and social framework.

Post-state Indigenous sovereignty movements reject mainstream politics both in substance and as practice but also markedly differ from it by not only presenting, but living the 'alternative'. Obviously for Indigenous people, proposing 'alternatives' is not that difficult because the 'alternatives' often are already existing practices that have been undermined, erased and sometimes forgotten (and thus, are not alternatives at all, hence the quotation marks). Reclaiming them, however, is painstaking and takes effort and time. Importantly, the lived or attempted Indigenous 'alternatives' cannot be idealised or romanticised. Ellos Deatnu was and is an experiment that no doubt, like all movements, has had its specific challenges and shortcomings both internal and external to it. With its imperfections, however, Ellos Deatnu represents a radical and bold attempt to enact a specific Sámi vision of alternative political order beyond the violence of state sovereignty.

Acknowledgement

The author wants to thank Jenni Laiti for her feedback on an earlier version of the chapter.

Notes

1 Sápmi is the territory of the Indigenous Sámi people, spanning the present-day northern Norway, Sweden and Finland and the Kola Peninsula, Russia.
2 Siida comprises of a small number of extended families and their territories. Historically, Sápmi was organized into dozens of siidas. The siida governance system allocated lands and resources to the use of individual families. The siida governance was never formally repealed but rather, increasingly overlooked and eroded. In the 19th century, the siida structures had been undermined to a point that the imposition of the settler colonial administrative system was relatively easy. The imposition and reorganisation of colonial borders in Sápmi also played a role in the erosion of the siida system.
3 For Indigenous resurgence see, for example, Coulthard (2014), Simpson (2012), and Waziyatawin (2012).
4 Many Indigenous peoples assert their pre-existing sovereignty, evident in the fact that at the time of contact they were politically independent societies or nations, governing themselves and their territories under their own laws. Indigenous sovereignty is typically considered qualitatively different from the Westphalian concept of sovereignty characterised by geographically separate territories and

jurisdictions the related doctrine of non-interference in the domestic affairs of a state. Most Indigenous scholars and activists maintain that sovereignty for Indigenous peoples seldom calls forth independence or non-interference.

5 In addition to transboundary rights, the Codicil included provisions on, inter alia, Sámi internal autonomy, citizenship and taxation (Åhrén 2004; Pedersen 2006).

6 For a discussion on the effects of the state borders partitioning Sápmi and the enforced citizenship of the Sámi, and Sámi responses to this development, see Lantto (2010).

7 The term 'non-resident local Sámi' refers to those individuals who are from the Deatnu River, whose families live there and continue to have traditional fishing rights in the river. Due to limited educational and employment opportunities, many Sámi have moved to urban areas but return home regularly, especially in the summer to practice fishing.

8 The traditional Sámi fishing rights in the Deatnu are tied to the ownership of property (land) along the river. Given the centrality of salmon fishing in the local economy, each property was granted certain fishing rights and sites in the river. There is a decades-long tradition of local Sámi individuals selling off small parcels of their property to mainly fishing tourists who have built holiday cabins along the river.

9 Ohcejohka (Utsjoki) has a population of approximately 700 people.

10 The Deatnu valley was historically governed by Ávjovárri, Deatnu and Ohcejohka siidas, which in the 17th century banned non-siida members (Sámi and non-Sámi) fishing in the river. As part of the siida governing structure, the Sámi Court approved the collective salmon fisheries in the Upper Deatnu Vuovdaguoika region up until the mid-19th century (Pedersen 1986; Solbakk 2003).

11 Some local Sámi fishers upstream Deatnu praised the new agreement for increasing their catch of salmon. They argued that thanks to the restrictions downstream, salmon have a better chance to get upstream (see Alajärvi 2017b; Alajärvi and Tammela 2017).

12 The legal fiction of "terra nullius" employed for the purposes of distributing sovereignty among settler states and of justifying ongoing state policies has been rejected also by a number of legal scholars (see Macklem 2015; McAdam 2015; McNeil 2013).

References

Åhrén, M. (2004). 'Indigenous peoples' culture, customs, and traditions and customary law – the Saami people's perspective', *Arizona Journal of International and Comparative Law*, vol 21, no 1: 63–112.

Aikio, K. (2017). 'Suoma Riikkabeaivvit Dohkkehedje Deanu Soahpamuša Vuordagiid Mielde'. Available: https://yle.fi/uutiset/3-9525847, accessed 14 September 2019.

Aikio, K., Näkkäläjärvi, P., and Satokangas, G. (2016). '"Tenon uusi sopimus loukkaa perustuslaillisia oikeuksia" – Utsjokelaisten eriävä mielipide'. Available: https://yle.fi/uutiset/3-8998183, accessed 28 October 2019.

Alajärvi, M. (2017a). 'Ellos Deatnu! Joavku Gáibida Ollislaš Iešmearrideami Deanu Čázádahkii'. Available: https://yle.fi/uutiset/osasto/sapmi/ellos_deatnu_-joavku_gaibida_ollislas_iesmearrideami_deanu_cazadahkii/9689670, accessed 17 September 2019.

Alajärvi, M. (2017b). '"Miige Beassat Luosa Borrat" – Badje-Deanus Gávdno Doarjja Deanu Odda Guolástannjuolggadusaide'. Available: https://yle.fi/uutiset/osasto/sapmi/miige_beassat_luosa_borrat__badje-deanus_gavdno_doarjja_deanu_oa_guolastannjuolggadusaide/9697112, accessed 17 September 2019.

Alajärvi, M. and Tammela, L. (2017). 'Juohkašuvvan Sámeálbmot Ságastahtii Kárášjogas – Dál Ii Šat Sáhte Smiehttat Iežas Sállašiid'. Available: https://yle.fi/uutiset/osasto/sapmi/juohkasuvvan_samealbmot_sagastahtii_karasjogas_dal_ii_sat_sahte_smiehttat_iezas_sallasiid/9727870, accessed 19 September 2019.

Allen, P.G. (1986). *The Sacred Hoop: Recovering the Feminine in American Indian Traditions*. Beacon Press: Boston, MA.

Arell, N. (1979). *Kolonisationen i Lappmarken. Några näringsgeografiska aspekter*. Scandinavian University Books: Stockholm, NY.

Barker, J. (2006). 'Gender, sovereignty, and the discourse of rights in native women's activism', *Meridians: Feminism, Race, Transnationalism*, vol 7, no 1: 127–161.

Barry, E. and Mueller, B. (2019). '"We're in the Last Hour": democracy itself is on trial in Brexit, Britons say'. Available: https://www.nytimes.com/2019/03/30/world/europe/uk-brexit-democracy-may.html?action=click&module=inline&pgtype=Article, accessed 17 April 2019.

Coulthard, G. (2014). *Red Skin, White Masks: Rejecting the Colonial Politics of Recognition*. University of Minnesota Press: Minneapolis, MN.

Denetdale, J.N. (2009). 'Securing the Navajo national boundaries: War, patriotism, tradition, and the Diné marriage act of 2005', *Wicazo Sa Review*, vol 24, no 2: 131–148.

Ellos Deatnu. (2017). Facebook post. Available: https://www.facebook.com/ellosdeatnu, accessed 14 September 2019.

Eira, E.O. (2018). 'Fargga rahppo Rájácummá'. Available: https://avvir.no/se/2018/06/fargga-rahppo-raj acumma, accessed 17 April 2019.

Enbuske, M. (2008). *Vanhan Lapin Valtamailla: Asutus ja maankäyttö historiallisen Kemin Lapin ja Enontekiön alueella 1500-luvulta 1900-luvun alkuun*. SKS: Helsinki.

Falkegard, M., Erkinaro, J., Orell, P., and Heggberget, T.G. (2016). *Status of the River Rana Salmon Populations 2016*. Working Group on Salmon Monitoring and Research in the Tana River System.

Fisher, M. (2019). 'Brexit mess reflects democracy's new era of tear-it-all-down'. Available: https://www.nytimes.com/2019/03/29/world/europe/brexit-theresa-may-democracy-chaos.html, accessed 17 April 2019.

Fiske, J.-A. (1996). 'The womb is to the nation as the heart is to the body: Ethnopolitical discourses of the Canadian indigenous women's movement', *Studies in Political Economy*, vol 51, no 1: 65–95.

Foa, R.S. and Mounk, Y. (2017). 'The end of the consolidation paradigm. a response to our critics', *Journal of Democracy*, Web exchange 26 January, 2–27.

Green, J. (ed.). (2007). *Making Space for Indigenous Feminism*. Fernwood: Halifax, NS.

Hansen, L.I. and Olsen, B.R. (2014). *Hunters in Transition: An Outline of Early Sámi History*. Brill: Leiden.

Hernández Castillo, R.A. (2010). 'Comparative perspectives symposium: Indigenous feminisms: The emergence of Indigenous feminism in Latin America', *Signs: Journal of Women in Culture & Society*, vol 35, no 3: 539–545.

Hiltunen, M. (2007). *Norjan ja Norlannin välissä: Enontekiö 1550–1808, asukkaat, elinkeinot ja maanhallinta*. Oulun Historiaseura: Oulu.

Hokowhitu, B. (2012). 'Producing elite Indigenous masculinities', *Settler Colonial Studies*, vol 2, no 2: 23–48.

Holmberg, A. (2017). Indigenous salmon-fishing Saami criminalised by Finland and Norway. 11 March, YouTube. Available: https://www.youtube.com/watch?v=H8ObcQnncf8. Accessed 23 September 2019.

Holmberg, A. (2018). *Bivdit Luosa – To Ask for Salmon: Saami Traditional Knowledge on Salmon and the River Deatnu in Research and Decision-Making*. Unpublished MA thesis, UiT The Arctic University of Norway, Tromsø.

Huhndorf, S.M. and Suzack, C. (2010). 'Indigenous feminism: Theorizing the issues', in C. Suzack, S.M. Huhndorf, J. Perreault, and J. Barman (eds.) *Indigenous Women and Feminism: Politics, Activism, Culture*. University of British Columbia Press: Vancouver, BC, 1–17.

Kino-nda-niimi Collective (ed.) (2014). *The Winter We Danced: Voices from the Past, the Future and the Idle No More Movement*. Arbeiter Ring: Winnipeg, MB.

Kuokkanen, R. (2011). 'Self-determination and Indigenous women – "Whose Voice Is It We Hear in the Sámi Parliament?"', *International Journal of Minority and Group Rights*, vol 18, no 1: 39–62.

Kuokkanen, R. (2019). *Restructuring Relations: Indigenous Self-Determination, Governance and Gender*. Oxford University Press: New York.

Lähteenmäki, M. (2006). *The Peoples of Lapland: Boundary Demarcations and Interaction in the North Calotte from 1808 to 1889*. Finnish Academy of Science and Letters: Helsinki.

Lakkala, A. (2017). 'Ministtar Leppä Ii Lohpit Nuppástusaid Deanu Soahpamuššii – "Sáhttit Smiehttat Heivehallama"'. Available: https://yle.fi/uutiset/osasto/sapmi/ministtar_leppa_ii_lohpit_nuppastusaid_deanu_soahpamussii__sahttit_smiehttat_heivehallama/9778723 accessed 20 September 2019.

Lantto, P. (2010). 'Borders, citizenship and change: the case of the Sami people, 1751–2008', *Citizenship Studies*, vol 14, no 5: 543–556.

Lawrence, B. and Anderson, K. (2005). 'Introduction to "Indigenous women: The state of our nations"', *Atlantis*, vol 29, no 2: 1–8.

Lawrence, R. and Åhrén, M. (2016). 'Mining as colonisation: The need for restorative justice and restitution of traditional Sami lands', in L. Head, S. Saltzman, G. Setten, and M. Stenseke (eds.) *Nature, Temporality and Environmental Management: Scandinavian and Australian Perspectives on Landscapes and Peoples*. Routledge: New York, 149–166.

Lindmark, D. (2013). 'Colonial encounter in early modern Sápmi', in M. Naum and J.M. Nordin (eds.) *Scandinavian Colonialism and the Rise of Modernity: Small Time Agents in a Global Arena*. Springer: New York, 131–146.

Lundmark, L. (1998). *Så länge vi har Marker: Samerna och Staten Under Sexhundra år*. Rabén Prisma: Stockholm, NY.

MacKinnon, C. (1983). 'Feminism, marxism, method and the state: Toward feminist jurisprudence', *Signs*, vol 8, no 4: 635–638.

MacKinnon, C.A. (1989). *Toward a Feminist Theory of the State*. Harvard University Press: Cambridge, MA.

Macklem, P. (2015). *The Sovereignty of Human Rights*. Oxford University Press: Cambridge.

Manuel, A. (2015). *Unsettling Canada: A National Wake-Up Call*. Between the Lines: Toronto, ON.

Maracle, L. (2006). 'Decolonizing native women', in B.A. Mann (ed.) *Daughters of Mother Earth: The Wisdom of Native American Women*. Praeger: Westport, CT, 29–52.

McAdam, S.S. (2015). *Nationhood Interrupted: Revitalizing Nehiyaw Legal Systems*. Purich: Saskatoon, SK.

McIvor, S. (1995). *Aboriginal Self-Government: The Civil and Political Rights of Women*. Unpublished Master in Law thesis, Queen's University, Kingston.

McNeil, K. (2013). 'Factual and legal sovereignty in North America: Indigenous realities and Euro-American pretensions', in J. Evans, A. Genovese, A. Reilly, and P. Wolfe (eds.) *Sovereignty: Frontiers of Possibility*. University of Hawai'i Press: Honolulu, HI, 37–59.

Monture, P.A. (2004). 'The right of inclusion: Aboriginal rights and/or aboriginal women?', in K. Wilkins, (ed.) *Advancing Aboriginal Claims. Visions, Strategies, Directions*. Purich: Saskatoon, SK, 39–66.

Monture-Angus, P. (1995). *Thunder in My Soul: A Mohawk Woman Speaks*. Fernwood: Halifax, NS.

Moratorium Office (n.d.). 'The moratorium office'. Available: http://moratoriadoaimmahat.org/en/m oratorium-office/, accessed 20 October 2019.

Moreton-Robinson, A. (2000). *Talkin'' Up to the White Woman. Aboriginal Women and Feminism*. University of Queensland Press: St Lucia, QLD.

Müller-Wille, L. and Aikio, S. (2005). 'Deatnu: river united, river divided: Living with the border in Ohcejohka, Sápmi', in M. Lähteenmäki and P.M. Pihlaja (eds.) *The North Calotte. Perspectives on the Histories and Cultures of Northernmost Europe*. Kustannus Puntsi: Inari, 40–53.

Nadasdy, P. (2017). *Sovereignty's Entailments. First Nation State Formation in the Yukon*. University of Toronto Press: Toronto, ON.

Nahanee, T. (1993). 'Dancing with a gorilla: Aboriginal women and the charter', in *Aboriginal Peoples and the Justice System: Report of the National Round Table on Aboriginal Justice Issues Canada*. Royal Commission on Aboriginal Peoples: Ottawa, ON, 359–382.

Nanibush, W. (2014). 'Idle no more: Strong hearts of Indigenous women's leadership', in Kino-nda-niimi Collective (ed.) *The Winter We Danced. Voices from the Past, the Future and the Idle No More Movement*. ARP Books: Winnipeg, MB, 341–345.

Napoleon, V. (2009). 'Aboriginal discourse: Gender, identity and community', in B.J. Richardson, S. Imai, and K. McNeil (eds.) *Indigenous Peoples and the Law: Comparative and Critical Perspectives*. Hart: Portland, OR, 233–255.

Nason, D. (2014). 'We hold our hands up: On Indigenous women's love and resistance', in Kino-nda-niimi Collective (ed.) *The Winter We Danced. Voices from the Past, the Future and the Idle No More Movement*. ARP Books: Winnipeg, MB, 186–190.

Norris, P. (2017). *Is Western Democracy Backsliding? Diagnosing the Risks*. Faculty Research Working Paper Series. Harvard Kennedy School: Cambridge, MA.

Otnes, P. (1970). *Den samiske nasjon: Intresseorganisasjoner i samenes politiske historie*. Pax Forlag: Oslo. MN.

Pedersen, S. (1986). *Laksen, allmuen og staten: Fiskerett og forvaltning i Tanavassdraget før 1888, Diedut 2*. Sámi Instituhtta: Guovdageaidnu.

Pedersen, S. (1999). 'Finnmárkku eananoamasteapmi ja koloniijalisma', *Sámi diedalas áigečála*, vol 1: 66–71.

Pedersen, S. (2006). *Lappekodisillen i nord 1751–1859. Fra grenseavtale og sikring av samenes rettigheter til grensesperring og samisk ulykke*. Universitetet i Tromsø.

Ramirez, R.K. (2007). 'Race, tribal nation and gender: A native feminist approach to belonging', *Meridians: Feminism, Race, Transnationalism*, vol 7, no 2: 22–40.

Rifkin, M. (2011). *When Did Indians Become Straight? Kinship, the History of Sexuality, and Native Sovereignty*. Oxford University Press: Oxford.

Satokangas, G. (2017). '"Deanu guolástansoahpamuševttohus rivve sápmelaččaid opmodaga ja duššada kultuvrra"'. Available: https://yle.fi/uutiset/osasto/sapmi/deanu_guolastansoahpamusevttohus_rivve_sapmelaccaid_opmodaga_ja_dussada_kultuvrra/9412275, accessed 29 October 2019.

Sehlin MacNeil, K. and Lawrence, R. (2017). 'Samiska frågor i gruvdebatten 2013 - nya utrymmen för ohörda diskurser?', in M. Liliequist and C. Cocq (eds.) *Samisk kamp. Kulturförmedling och rättviserörelse*. Bokförlaget h:ström: Umeå, 140–160.

Simpson, L. (2012). 'Queering resurgence: Taking on heteropatriarchy in indigenous nation-building'. Available: https://www.leannesimpson.ca/writings/queering-resurgence-taking-on-heteropatriarchy-in-indigenous-nation-building, accessed 26 August 2019.

Simpson, L. (2013). *Islands of Decolonial Love*. Arbeiter Ring Publishing: Winnipeg, MB.

Simpson, A. (2014). *Mohawk Interruptus: Political Life Across the Borders of Settler States*. Duke University Press: Durham, NC.

Simpson, A. (2016). 'The state is a man: Theresa Spence, Loretta Saunders and the gender of settler sovereignty'. *Theory & Event*, vol 19, no 4: np.

Simpson, L.B. (2017). *As We Have Always Done: Indigenous Freedom Through Radical Resistance*. University of Minnesota Press: Minneapolis, MN.

Smith, A. (2008). 'American studies without America: Native feminisms and the nation-state', *American Quarterly*, vol 60, no 2: 309–315.

Snyder, E., Napoleon, V., and Borrows, J. (2015). 'Gender and violence: drawing on Indigenous legal resources', *Univ BC Law Rev*, vol 48, no 2: 593–654.

Solbakk, A. (2003). *Joddu. Deanu Luossabivdohistorjá, Bivdobiergasat, Doahpagat*. ČálliidLágádus: Kárášjohka.

Strakosch, E. (2015). *Neoliberal Indigenous Policy: Settler Colonialism and the 'Post-Welfare' State*. Palgrave Macmillan: London.

Turpel, M.E. (1993). 'Patriarchy and paternalism: The legacy of the Canadian state for first nations women', *Canadian Journal of Women and the Law*, vol 6, no 1: 174–192.

Vahtola, J. (2014). 'Saamelaiset saaneet maansa', *Lapin Kansa*, 12 November: 3.

Veracini, L. (2010). *Settler Colonialism. A Theoretical Overview*. Palgrave Macmillan: New York.

Veracini, L. (2015). *The Settler Colonial Present*. Palgrave Macmillan: New York.

Waziyatawin (2012). 'The paradox of Indigenous resurgence at the end of empire', *Decolonization: Indigeneity, Education & Society*, vol 1, no 1: 68–85.

Wesslin, S. (2017). 'Oikeuskansleri moittii Suomen hallitusta Tenojoen sopimuksen menettelyssä – Saamelaisia koskevaa neuvotteluvelvoitetta laiminlyöty tietyiltä osin'. Available: https://yle.fi/uutiset/3-9532594, accessed 22 September 2019.

Wilson, A. (2015). 'Afterword: A steadily beating heart: Persistence, resistance and resurgence', in E. Coburn (ed.) *More Will Sing Their Way to Freedom. Indigenous Resistance and Resurgence*. Fernwood: Winnipeg, MB, 255–264.

Wolfe, P. (2006). 'Settler colonialism and the elimination of the native', *Journal of Genocide Research*, vol 8, no 4: 387–409.

24

Striking back

The 1980s Aboriginal art movement and the performativity of sovereignty

Crystal McKinnon

They are presenting their own works, and they are curating them – and that's very significant. Not only because Aboriginal artists have been for so long exploited, but because Aboriginal people have been defined by others for too long.

*John Newfong (*Boomalli – Five Koorie Artists *1988: online)*

On 25 November 1987 Ngugi journalist John Newfong addressed the large crowd gathered for the opening of the 'Boomalli Au-go-go' exhibition. His words signalled to guests they were witnessing Aboriginal sovereign artistic performance within the gallery space on Eora Country in Meagher Street, Chippendale.[1] This was the Boomalli Aboriginal Artists Cooperative's inaugural show and the 10 Aboriginal exhibiting artists were its founding members. The 'Boomalli Ten' were: Wiradjuri/Kamilaroi man Michael Riley, Bundjalung woman Bronwyn Bancroft, Bundjalung/Munajali woman Euphemia Bostock, Gurindji/Malngin/Mudburra woman Brenda L Croft, Badtjala woman Fiona Foley, descendent of the Meriam Mer people Fernanda Martins, Kuku Midigi man Arone Raymond Meeks, Murri woman Tracey Moffatt, Noonuccal woman Avril Quaill and Ngemba artist Jeffrey Samuels. The formation of Boomalli was a ground-breaking culmination of a series of exhibitions and events involving these and other Koorie, Murri, Noongar, Nunga and Gorri artists throughout the 1980s in the inner suburbs of Sydney. The significance of this Aboriginal art movement and of the Boomalli cooperative that it generated is evidenced by its continuing influence on Aboriginal arts, culture and community.

Aboriginal art exhibitions and events like these held in the 1980s are all expressions and actions which are performative of Indigenous sovereignty. As all Indigenous peoples are tied to country by their creator beings, our bodies are a manifestation of country (Moreton-Robinson 2000). Indigenous sovereignty is embodied and through non-verbal communicative artistic practices it is performative in that they serve to define and maintain one's Indigeneity, such as being Amangu or Eora or Goenpul or Boonwurrung. This performative sovereignty connects the individuals into relatedness with other Eora or Boonwurrung people, animals, trees, and to creator beings. It connects Amangu or Goenpul people into their histories and futures which are outside of the logics of colonialism. These colonial logics seek to relentlessly confine Indigenous political action as only ever reactionary and this inescapably oppositional to colonialism. This chapter provides an historical overview of key public Aboriginal art moments of the 1980s, a period of urgent successive Aboriginal political interventions into the white Australian art world which systematically excluded Aboriginal artists. These artists challenged racist discourses regarding authentic Aboriginality through their embodied Indigenous sovereignty.

History matters

Aboriginal artists like those who founded *Boomalli*, contended with the material and discursive dimensions of racism enacted upon both them and their work, which functioned primarily through the discourse of primitivism. Primitive can be understood as, "someone or something less complex, or less advanced, than the person or thing to which it is being compared" (Rhodes 1995: 13). The discursive construction of the 'primitive' arose out of the Enlightenment, when white Western European men dispossessed and colonised Brown and Black people and societies across the globe. They articulated themselves as superior in a range of ways. This is because white people placed themselves at the centre, as the norm, the ordinary, the standard against which everything else was measured (Moreton-Robinson 2004: 78). Those the colonisers constructed as inferior were objectified and controlled. During the Enlightenment, primitivism discourse was used to construct European colonial knowledge of the degree of civilisation that could or could not be ascribed to any given society.

The British deemed Aboriginal society to be primitive, lacking the British measures of civility by which it was judged. This enabled dispossession and colonisation. Ideas of the primitive can be traced in the documentation of Captain Cook's voyages where white men attributed an abundance of lack to people they sometimes only glimpsed across the water or imagined. Early white explorer diaries, squatter journals and colonist letters and paintings likewise contain this notion of primitive Aboriginal societies (Langton 1993). It can be traced throughout missionary files, colonial administrative records and police documentation. Primitivism as a discourse was wielded by colonisers in newspapers and colonial government reports to justify ongoing removal of Aboriginal children, land theft, and the policing and incarceration of sovereign Indigenous bodies. These documents, files, images, and texts work together to form part of a large colonial archive detailing what constitutes Aboriginal people and communities. This archive is a site of knowledge production rather than being simply a repository for knowledge (Stoler 2002). It incessantly generates and reifies primitivism while the ongoing colonial project energetically continues to build its Aboriginal archive.

In the 19th and 20th centuries, representations of Aboriginal people as primitive propelled the collecting practices of cultural and public institutions like museums and state galleries, and also drove collecting by individuals both in their private workplaces and for their own personal collections in their homes. European people took or stole these material cultures, art and objects from Aboriginal people and communities and attached new meaning to dislocated cultural materials, incorporating them into colonial and Eurocentric racial hierarchies and colonial fantasies of supremacy. Accordingly, from the mid- to late 19th century various international exhibitions and world fairs held in Australia and abroad displayed these material cultures in ways that claimed European superiority through juxtapositioning with Indigenous primitivity.[2] In these exhibition spaces government officials and bureaucrats, curators, exhibitors and generally those in control of the displays were specific about articulating a distinction between 'primitive' and 'civilised' societies (Edmonds 2006: 127) and, "...Aboriginal objects of industry and skill were thus positioned as 'primitive' curiosities" (Darian-Smith 2008: 1.12). By displaying items such as spears, shields and coolamons (*The Argus* 1886) without acknowledgement (or knowledge) of the complex relationships between the tool users, country, community and calendar, the colonial displays constructed Aboriginal culture as lacking the aesthetics, intelligence and spirituality which they believed marked 'civilisation', and was manifest not only in British culture, but in white people as a race.

These exhibitions were the first to display sovereign Aboriginal material cultures on walls and in European spaces. This practice discursively erased the knowledges and stories these items held in the sovereign Indigenous communities to which they belonged. By displaying them in these ways it turned them into primitive art objects for Western schemas of knowledge production and consumption about race and Empire. Many of the items collected for and displayed in these large international exhibitions of the 19th century constituted a formational part of the permanent collections of newly formed public colonial institutions, such as the National Museum of Victoria.[3] Indigenous communities in Australia and around the world are currently demanding the repatriation of their familial and ancestral items from these institutions.

Throughout this period and until the mid-20th century, Aboriginal visual art and material culture were viewed as ethnographic artefacts of little artistic value (Thomas 1978: 29). The Western aesthetic boundaries and signifiers of what art was at this time meant that Aboriginal people could never be considered as producing 'art'. The Western colonial imperative of the time was to mark colonists as superior on a singular global racial social ladder, with Aboriginal people articulated as primitive and locked in through race, through a supposed fact of biology, at the bottom of the hierarchy. Primitivism discourse originating in the Enlightenment worked in concert with newly formulated Social Darwinist theory purporting that only the strong survive while the weak perish. In this period, it was believed that all Aboriginal people were doomed to die out – not through the racially targeted colonial violence against all Indigenous people, but through implicit racial and biological causes resulting from exposure to and contact with colonisers. Colonisers murdered and hunted Aboriginal people and they violated and exposed Aboriginal peoples to disease, and they then applied Social Darwinist discourse to construe these causes of death as being natural and inevitable due to racial hierarchy. In their logics it was an unavoidable result of modernity.

Aboriginal people did not 'die out' or disappear as time passed, and scientific racism declined in use because European research could find no evidence for the demarcation or definitions of racial difference (Anderson 2002: 243). The discourse of Aboriginal people as primitive was continued through a shift to using culture instead of race (Thomas 2004: 91). Culture was also discursively tethered to notions of blood (Thomas 2004: 7), but the shift enabled a transition to the supposedly inevitable death of Aboriginal culture even as the racial community continued. This shift in discourse enabled a continuation of white hegemony, and the colonial state continued to subject Aboriginal nations to violence through incarceration on reserves and missions; assimilation policies were in full effect. Colonial governments were thorough in their systematic attempts to destroy Indigenous sovereignty by removing people from their countries, forbidding people from using their Native languages and modes of communication, by policing the use of ceremonies and other cultural practices, and by stealing children from their Aboriginal families and placing them in state institutions and individual colonisers' homes. Despite these various violent and cruel efforts, Aboriginal populations were growing rather than dying out and many people in these nations had non-Indigenous parents.

White European academics argued that biological assimilation could occur through diluting Aboriginal blood using what we now recognise as baseless science, but in the 20th century eugenics was considered a valid Western scientific study and its logics were underpinned by the discourse of primitivism (Hannaford 1996); the primitive could be erased by diluting the blood. Social and political colonial policies of assimilation used blood quotas as measures of fitness for 'biological assimilation'. However, any degree of Aboriginal blood was constructed as biologically unsuitable for assimilation. This enabled colonisers to refuse the inclusion of Aboriginal people into Australian society outside of their usefulness in working for white people. Governments and missions were also concerned with the increase in the Aboriginal population and despite exclusion zones around Aboriginal reserves and missions which kept Aboriginal people out of towns, they did not keep white men away from Aboriginal missions and reserves (McGrath 1987). The shift from race to culture as categories of definition manifest in the discourse of primitivism as the idea that a dilution of Aboriginal blood also meant a lack of authenticity in Aboriginal culture. The colonial construct of authentic Aboriginality shifted to frame remote Aboriginal communities as 'authentic', while Aboriginal people and culture in physical proximity with white people in urban centres or regional cities were interpellated as 'inauthentic'.

In the mid- to late 20th century art world this meant that what was once only seen as ethnographic primitive pieces were now held up as examples of authentic Aboriginal art. The type of art that colonisers recognised as authentic belonged to those Aboriginal people they perceived as untouched by their colonialism, lived outside modernity and were phenotypically black. Colonisers derided artistic productions by Aboriginal people living near metropoles due to the spatial and racial proximity of the artists to 'white' populations. White aesthetics did not consider these Aboriginal artists as producing contemporary Aboriginal art because the racial logics of primitivism deemed them to be inauthentic Aboriginal people.

As sovereign Indigenous artists they were, as Māori scholar Brendan Hokowhitu knows, "aware of the way that discourses of Indigenous authenticity and tradition haunt them" (2014: 296). Aboriginal artists living in the late 20th century were caught in the authentic/inauthentic racial bind produced through the discourse primitivism. This was the social and racialised environment that contextualised and impacted on urban-based Aboriginal artists with which they had to contend – one which not only interpellated them as not authentically Aboriginal, but also considered the art that they produced to be inauthentic. Throughout the 19th and 20th centuries, these European constructed categories which defined and contained Indigenous people were, "neither inherent nor stable", and these categories of difference continue to be defined and maintained (Cooper and Stoler 1997: 7). One way this is achieved is to reconfigure definitions and categories to accommodate, co-opt and explain away Indigenous political articulations and embodied sovereign difference. In the 1980s the Australian state held a Commonwealth Games, its Bicentenary Celebrations and other nation building activities, and urban-based Aboriginal communities and organised political groups led the fight against these celebrations. It was in this context that the state increasingly sought to define and contain the Aboriginality of urban-based communities and their artists through racist discourses developed over centuries. Despite the racism they encountered, these artists drew upon their ancestral sovereign knowledges and practices as embodied Aboriginal people to resist these contemporary conditions and act outside of the colonial discursive binaries. They acted from within their respective Indigenous nations' histories, and futures.

Taking control: The artistic movement of the 1980s

The 1980s artistic movement arose from a long history of sovereign political resistance. In this period Aboriginal individuals and communities made increasing demands for self-determination and Aboriginal control of Aboriginal affairs, Aboriginal lives and communities. These demands grew from the eras preceding the Federal Council for the Advancement of Aborigines and Torres Strait Islanders (FCAATSI) led Referendum campaign spanning throughout most of the 1960s. In the 1970s the Black Power movement was particularly influential on the Sydney-led

Aboriginal art movement. The Black Power movement had firmly centred Aboriginal sovereignty and espoused demands for Indigenous rights, ownership, and control over our lives and lands.

In 1983, for the first time, the Aboriginal Arts Board of the Australia Council for the Arts had two Aboriginal people in both of its top positions. Gumbaynggirr man Gary Foley was its Director, and Yuin man Charles (Chicka) Dixon was Chair of its Board of Directors. Both of these men were part of the Black Power movement and they carried this politic into their actions in their roles at the Arts Board. As their first action, they ceased funding arts initiatives that were not owned or controlled or driven by Aboriginal people themselves (Foley 2012). Dixon also appointed a new board of Aboriginal people to implement and support the changes: Noonuccal poet and artist Oodgeroo Noonuccal, Noongar playwright and poet Jack Davis, Yawuru activist Peter Yu, and Plangermairreenner writer Jim Everett (Foley 2012).

These changes directly and financially assisted many Aboriginal arts initiatives, collectives and organisations and aided the growth of an Aboriginal artistic community. This resulted in communities and individuals establishing many more Indigenous visual art and performing arts organisations across Australia, such as the Eora Centre in 1984 in Redfern and both Bangarra Dance Theatre in Sydney and Ilbijerri Aboriginal and Torres Strait Islander Theatre Cooperative in Melbourne in 1989. At the same time that these various arts initiatives and events were taking place there was an increasing number of nation-wide Indigenous protest movements, including the fight to stop Aboriginal deaths in police custody and gain justice for those that had been killed. Like the arts and events that Indigenous people created, these protests performed embodied Indigenous sovereignty as they defined and maintained the Indigeneity of participants. There were sophisticated demonstrations using a variety of political methods and tactics against both the Commonwealth Games in 1982 in Brisbane and against the 1988 Bicentenary. It was within this environment of Aboriginal arts growth alongside these types of Aboriginal political organisation and actions that the urban-based Koorie artists movement began and grew through the 1980s.

Held between 5 and 29 September 1984 at Artspace Gallery in Surry Hills, *Koori Art '84* was the first to show the works of a large number of urban-based Aboriginal artists in a combined exhibition. More than 50 works were shown together explicitly as an urban Koori exhibition which included paintings, photographs and sculptures created by 25 Aboriginal artists, most of whom were living and working in Sydney. In addition, in 1984 collectives of Aboriginal artists in Sydney and Melbourne created and completed two significant murals. The *Koori Art '84* exhibition was followed by two more important installations in 1986: *NADOC '86* and *Urban Koories. NADOC '86* was the first Aboriginal photographer's exhibition, whilst *Urban Koories* displayed contemporary Aboriginal mixed media works. The following year *Boomali Au GoGo* was held, launching the first urban Aboriginal artists collective. This was a watershed moment for Aboriginal art and Aboriginal urban-based communities alike.

The exhibition catalogues, recorded interviews and filmed footage from these events all provide evidence of the way that artists who lived in cities and the work they produced were treated by the mainstream art world. The art they produced was often denigrated whilst also being systematically excluded and marginalised, which meant these Aboriginal artists found it difficult to find spaces to exhibit their work. These artists were fighting against a racism created, adapted and shaped to identify and control them in specific ways related to both their art and their place. Their resistance was to collectively organise and continue to create art as embodied sovereign Indigenous people. Rather than striving to fit into European aesthetics or Western art history cannons, these artists drew on the art histories and knowledges of their respective Indigenous communities, rejecting white European representations and impositions. They collectively and purposefully carved out their space and artistic community. They were grounded in their Indigenous communities, carrying forth the historical lineage of both Aboriginal artists resisting colonial representations and Aboriginal political actions, with their own nations' sovereignty extending back beyond colonial encounters to our Creation. As this Aboriginal arts movement was a performance of Aboriginal sovereignty and was organised and fought for by sovereign Indigenous people, it is distinguished from other non-Indigenous political movements or artist collectives and is placed firmly within the larger interconnected Indigenous community and history.

Understanding these exhibitions, murals and collectives as sovereign performativity enables us to view this artistic movement outside the restrictive categorisations of either being only the product of colonialism or being simply reactionary to colonialism and racism. It reorients people to view the urban-based contemporary Aboriginal artists of the 1980s – the art that they produced, the events that they held, the collectives they formed – as part of a broader, interconnected assemblage of Indigenous sovereign people, actions, knowledges, and performances. This constellation exceeds the limits of colonial time and encounters and the contemporary moments, connecting with our ancestors and reaching into our future generations. The artists and their collective actions discussed in this paper belong to this broader Indigenous interconnected sovereignty movement.

The murals

In this period there were two important urban-based Aboriginal murals which form part of the 1980s Aboriginal Art Movement. Conceived in 1983 and completed in 1984, the first is the '40,000 Years and Counting' mural located on the corner of Lawson and Eveleigh Street, opposite Redfern Railway Station in Sydney. The second, conceived in 1983 and completed in 1985, is known as the 'the Koorie Mural'. It was first located on High Street in Northcote, opposite the Northcote Town Hall, but was later relocated to the purpose-built wall facing St Georges Road at the Aborigines Advancement League in Thornbury, Melbourne.

Tracey Moffatt, Avril Quaill, Kristina Nehm, Joe Geia, Charlie Aarons and Emu Nugent comprised the Redfern mural's original artistic team. They were supported by Indigenous art students from the local Eora TAFE College and other individuals. Redfern based non-Indigenous artist Carol Ruff was the coordinator of the Redfern project. The design was based on a report that Moffatt had produced for the South Sydney Council, along with input from the community where the design was on display at a Lawson Street shopfront, around the corner from the site. The artists spent weeks asking the community what they wanted included in the mural and discussing issues about who had rights to certain images, symbols and motifs. Some of the people they met with included Mum Shirl (also known as Shirley Smith), Aunty Mona Donnelly and other local Indigenous community members (Tyson 2018).

The mural is a powerful visual representation of ongoing Indigenous sovereignty and aimed, "to encapsulate the rich and powerful Aboriginal History of Redfern" (Griffiths 2018: online). It begins with a section dedicated to Aboriginal life prior to British invasion. Here it has depictions of a woman carrying a coolamon and a man hunting in water with a spear encircled by a long Rainbow Serpent whose body and tail weaves throughout the entire 300 feet length. In this section the words painted are '40,000 years is a long, long time ... 40,000 years still on my mind', which are the lines from a song written by Murri mural artist and singer Joe Geia. This section is around two-thirds of the entire mural and stands as a visual marker of colonial time on Aboriginal lands being recent and short in relation to Aboriginal, and in this place, Eora and Redfern, history. A boat represents the First Fleet, with images of Aboriginal people fighting against their arrival. Next to this is a boy standing in front of a mission church, showing institutionalisation and child removals. A boomerang flies over the roofs of houses in Redfern showing Aboriginal ongoing sovereignty over this place. The last section illustrates a portrait of Aunty Mona Donnelly from the Aboriginal Medical Service along with a depiction of the 1983 Redfern All Blacks team.

Turning to Melbourne, the Victorian Aborigines Advancement League (AAL) mural was collaboratively designed in 1983 by non-Indigenous artist Megan Evans in consultation with committee of Aboriginal people from the AAL, comprising Lin Onus, Elizabeth Morgan (then Hoffman), Ron Johnson and Mollie Dyer (Darebin Arts 2013: online). It was painted between 1983–1984 by Indigenous artists who were working with Lin Onus on traineeships with the Community Employment Program at Victorian Aborigines Advancement League (Edmonds and Clarke 2009: 29). These artists were Ray Thomas, Ian Johnson, Millie Yarran, Les Griggs, and Elaine Trott. They were joined by Megan Evans and other volunteers.

A purpose-built wall was constructed for the mural measuring approximately 6.5 metres by 46 metres. The mural comprises a range of images, "representing aspects of Victorian Aboriginal Culture and History: the white invasion, Aboriginal resistance to the white invasion, the dispossession and oppression of Victorian Aboriginal people and the history of the Land Rights movement" (*Victims or Victors?* 1985: i). It shows the artwork of Wurundjeri man William Barak and Kwatkwat man Tommy McCrae, both artists whose work was included in 1929 and 1943 Primitive Art exhibitions (Jones 2018: 20). In those exhibitions the art works and artists had been displayed as separate and distinct from their people, as anomalies and examples of exceptional primitive curiosities. In the mural their work is repositioned and integrated into the historical continuity of Aboriginal Victorian sovereignty. The mural also includes patterns and designs of possum skin cloaks and Victorian shields, along with Indigenous people performing ceremonies. Like the mural in Sydney, this one contains images of British landing in boats, with Aboriginal people both resisting and running from the scene. It shows the violence of colonialism with Aboriginal people in neck chains, scales representing the European legal system, and the resolute face of an Aboriginal man with the rallying words 'Just this or justice'. It has a section dedicated to land rights and sovereignty, depicting a land rights march, the 1972 Tent Embassy, and Aboriginal people marching on Parliament House holding placards demanding Land Rights for Lake Tyers.

Like the art exhibitions held indoors, these public murals in Melbourne and Sydney are produced through the performance of embodied sovereignty of the Aboriginal artists. The two murals share many commonalities and are excellent examples of the importance of public Aboriginal art in urban spaces. They were both painted by groups of artists in the inner suburbs of Sydney and Melbourne and in consultation with the respective Aboriginal communities. The communities were consulted about the images, events, and people they contain and the representations they depict. Consequently, they visually depict and articulate urban-based Aboriginal communities and the histories and political moments that were important to those communities in which they were respectively located.

Both made significant interventions in the discourses of authentic Aboriginal art as only belonging to remote-based Aboriginal people. These murals represent both a symbolic and literal transformation of the urban spaces of the inner-city and both demand recognition of a continuing Aboriginal presence in these cities, even as constitutive of the city space itself in the colony. They demand that the continuing Indigenous presence in urban centres be seen and felt. As public artworks located on major roads and thoroughfares, the murals are continuously subject to the public gaze and remind non-Indigenous people of Indigenous sovereignty and ongoing presence in urban centres. They are enduring parts of the performance of sovereignty in arts practice and were important in the burgeoning urban Aboriginal arts movement.

Both murals challenge persisting colonial discourses of Aboriginal cultural loss of authenticity in urban spaces, and the enduring trope of the vanishing or already dead Aborigine. For some in the colonial environment of unfinished business and perpetual state of war, symbols like these murals depict Aboriginal survival and perpetuation of Aboriginal sovereignty. For the artists in the following section, that fight moved into the exhibition and gallery spaces of inner-Sydney. Many of the people named here continue their artistic careers. Avril Quaill, Tracey Moffatt, and Lin Onus are all artists who went on to exhibit together in urban contemporary Indigenous artist exhibitions of the 1980s.

Koori Art '84 and NADOC '86

Koori Art '84 was the first exhibition in the urban-based 1980s Aboriginal art movement. It was held at Artspace located on Eora country in the inner-Sydney suburb of Surry Hills. Running between 5 and 29 September 1984, *Koori Art '84* provided a collective space for Aboriginal artists from the south-east to gather and represent themselves on their own terms. This exhibition juxtaposed the work of 23 urban-based artists alongside artists living in remote and regional Australia (*Koori Art '84* 1984: 2). Two Indigenous organisations were also listed as exhibiting artists, urban-based silk screen clothing and music promotion organisation Murijama and Ernabella Arts Inc which, "exists to promote Pitjantjatjara women's art" (*Koori Art '84* 1984: 25). This ground-breaking event was the first in what was to become of a number of exhibitions held in Sydney and elsewhere to showcase the sovereign artistic productions of Aboriginal artists who were organising and exhibiting under the labels of urban and contemporary art.

The participating urban-based artists were urban artists were Yorta Yorta man Lin Onus, Ngarrindjeri man Trevor Nikolls, Birapi man Gordon Syron, Bathurst-based Aboriginal man Warwick Keen and Yolngu and Sydney-based woman Banduk Marika. The following people were listed in the exhibition catalogue as Eora Centre participants – Darren Beetson, Peter Chester, Isabelle Coe, Terry Shewring, Andrew Saunders, Jim Simon, Ian Craigie, and Euphemia Bostock. Along with Bostock, the other previously mentioned founders of Boomallli in this exhibition were Fiona Foley, Fernanda Martins, Arone Raymond Meeks, Avril Quaill, Michael Riley, and Jeffrey Samuels. The artists living in Central Australia were Pintupi woman Ida Nabanunka, Arrernte man Wenton Rubuntja, and Pintupi men Turkey Tolson Tjupuurrula and Johnny Warangula Tjupurrula.

The participation of these artists from various locations collapsed the boundaries imposed by the colonial notions of Aboriginal art in relation to Aboriginality itself. This exhibition was a watershed because it was urban-based artist-driven, and because of the inclusion of work from urban and rural and remote regions, under the one banner of 'Koori' art. 'Koori' as a term had begun to be used in the 1980s as a collective way of talking about Aboriginal people from the south-east regions of Australia. The mobilisation of these artists under this singular banner was a purposeful political intervention. It represented a rejection of Aboriginal art, and in many ways the creation of a new way of self-description and representation. *Koori Art '84* defined:

> A new political position of unity, of struggle, and of reclamation, a self-assigned space separate from that allocated by the dominant culture as 'Aboriginal' – a space that comes with an insistence that art be defined and judged within its social and political context.
>
> *(Kleinert and Neale 2000: 268)*

Representing the ways that urban art was denigrated, responses from some commentators described the art showcased in *Koori Art '84* as, "hybrid, amateurish" and "not really authentic Aboriginal art, looking more like second rate European art" (Kleinert and Neale 2000: 267). In the introduction to the catalogue for *Koori Art '84* (1984: 3) Black woman Roberta Sykes wrote that, "our artists – as an intrinsic component of the Black community – are engaged in a purposeful march towards the twenty-first century".

This march continued into 1986 and the *NADOC '86: Aboriginal and Islander Photographers* exhibition. This was a show exclusively of works by Aboriginal and Torres Strait Islander photographers and it was held at the Aboriginal Artists Gallery (AAG) in Clarence Street, Sydney in September 1986. The Aboriginal Arts Board of the Australia Council funded the AAG, and the exhibition was initiated by Tracey Moffatt at the invitation of AAG Director Anthony (Ace) Bourke (Newton 2006: 56). When Bourke proposed his idea to hold an 'Aboriginal photography exhibition' Moffatt, who had painted the Sydney Mural, stated she would, "only exhibit my work in his gallery if he dropped all the European/White Australia photographers and only displayed the work of Aboriginal artists" (Moffatt 2006: 95), echoing the ethos of the Black Power Movement of the 1970s. Moffatt went on to curate herself and the following people into the show: Indigenous man Mervyn Bishop, Indigenous man Tony Davis, Torres Strait Islander woman Ellen Jose, Indigenous man Darren Kemp, Aboriginal man Chris Robinson, Ros Sultan, and Terry Shewring, along with Brenda Croft and Michael Riley. Riley, who was also a participant in *Koori Art '84*, stated the following about *NADOC '86*:

> It was an important show in that respect and people still refer to it. The photographers were all Indigenous and they were dictating what they wanted to show and how they wanted to show images of their own people. Rather than ethnographic photographs or by missionaries as a curiosity or something ... the 'dying race' sort of thing.
>
> *(cited in Perkins and Jones 2008: 111)*

As Riley tells us above, a central premise of *NADOC 86's* was rewriting anthropological representations created via the 'scientific' medium of the camera. The exhibition highlighted the camera as a powerful colonial tool and political force implicated and used in many historical and contemporary socio-political agendas. NADOC 86 spoke back to racist discourses and, "each exhibitor subtly undermined the deadweight legacy of ethnographic documents and negative media stereotypes" (Newton 2006: 48).

For this exhibition, as in *Koori Art '84* and later shows, Aboriginal control of the images, curation and display was key. Both *Koori Art '84* and *NADOC '86* were powerful exhibitions of self-representation and fought racist discourses and discursive constructions of authenticity and Aboriginality. By intentionally and purposefully creating these Indigenous spaces, the artists acted as embodied sovereign Indigenous people. These exhibitions and murals are performative of Indigenous sovereignty in that they function to define and maintain each artist's Indigeneity.

Boomalli Aboriginal Artists Cooperative

All of these exhibitions and arts spaces provided a meeting point and opportunity for collaboration of many different Aboriginal and Torres Strait Islanders people and artists. Resulting from this was the formation in 1987 of the first urban-based Aboriginal artist collective, Boomalli Aboriginal Artists Cooperative. After its inaugural exhibition *Boomalli Au GoGo,* the cooperative was founded by the 10 artists previously listed: Michael Riley, Tracey Moffatt, Avril Quaill, Bronwyn Bancroft, Fiona Foley, Arone Raymond Meeks, Euphemia Bostock, Jeffrey Samuels,

Fern Martens, and Brenda Croft. Boomalli was first based in Chippendale in Sydney, which Bancroft tells us was made possible through the "insight and forwards thinking of Michael Riley and Gary Foley, who as Director of the Aboriginal Arts Board at the time, promoted our endeavours and initiated Aboriginal Arts Board funding" (2012: 1). Aboriginal control of Aboriginal affairs here with Foley and Dixon in leadership roles at the AAB assisted Boomalli founder Riley and his colleagues to establish one of the most significant artists cooperatives, which still continues to this day.

Boomalli means to strike, to make a mark, in the language of at least three Aboriginal nations: Bundjalung, Kamilaroi, and Wiradjuri. Of its aims, founding member Fiona Foley (*Boomalli* 1988: online) states it best: "[t]here's a specific need for Boomalli Aboriginal Artists Co-op, and we've got specific goals and aims that we should be able to achieve and that's getting recognition for urban Koori artists". Striking back, making and fighting for recognition necessitated not only building an Aboriginal controlled space to hold exhibitions, but also one where Aboriginal artists could gather to build their own Aboriginal arts world. Founding member Raymond Meeks (*Boomalli* 1988: online) articulated it this way: "I think the idea of a community of urban Koori artists is very important in the sense that it draws us all together to express ideas and to use our coming together as a centre ... a resource centre". Boomalli was a meeting place where there was the opportunity to access support systems, and a chance to teach and learn. Quaill attests that, "it was a great learning experience in art administration, curatorship, and also of holding a group of artists together" (2012: 23).

Many of these artists have stated that the impetus for the creation of this cooperative was a sense of marginalisation and frustration with the arts world, along with a desire to change this situation. As Croft (1992: 20) recalls they, "were frustrated at the marginalisation of their work because they were urban-based and regarded as outside the 'traditional', and therefore 'real' Aboriginal art". Quaill says:

> Absolutely, we had to create our own exhibition spaces in which to hang our art because no-one in the arts industry was taking any notice of Indigenous art from people living in cities and towns as authentic, contemporary or Indigenous art.
>
> *(2012: 23)*

The artists rallied against being told that they weren't Aboriginal artists. Jeffrey Samuels (*Boomalli* 1988: online) tells us: "[e]ven though I do not paint in traditional form, I am still an Aboriginal artist and I paint about issues that concern Aboriginal culture and Aboriginal people". Arone Meeks (*Boomalli* 1988: online) adds, "I think a lot of people see Aboriginal artists as 'once upon a time' people [but] the fact is that they are alive and growing stronger".

The many exhibitions and Boomalli itself provided the space to have discussions about what Aboriginal art and artists were for Aboriginal artists and their communities. In this Aboriginal space the artists, "instigated debates about what was important to Indigenous artists, including post modernism, postcolonial critique, identity politics and authenticity in Aboriginal art" (Evans and Sinclair 2016: 283). Riley tells us they were, "striving to create just a slice of their life really – their philosophy, their thoughts and what art is to them and what being Aboriginal is to them" (Riley in Perkins 2010: 217).

The significance of Boomalli is illustrated by its influence across Australia. It had a national galvanising effect, with other Aboriginal and Torres Strait Islander people inspired by its development. Yorta Yorta man and Victorian-based artist Lin Onus was a part of the *Koorie Mural* and *Koori Art '84* and he pointed out that Boomalli became "an important outlet and focus for artists all over the country" (1993: 292). He continues to say that it was probably, "the most exciting initiative to develop during the 1980s [where a] seemingly eclectic group of young Aboriginal people ... were ... united in the political struggle as both Aboriginal people and artists" (292). The unification of these individual artists from across Australia created a movement demanding that the viewpoints of all Aboriginal and Torres Strait Islander artists be heard within Australian contemporary art forums.

Conclusion

The *NADOC '86* and *Koori Art '84* exhibitions and the formation of Boomalli constructed an Aboriginal and Torres Strait Islander space which challenged the racist discourses that imposed categories about who and what Aboriginal artists and art were and could be. Indigenous sovereignty is embodied, and through artistic practices it is performed to define and maintain one's Indigeneity. These exhibitions and Boomalli itself demonstrate how sovereignty informs Indigenous political and artistic movements and that art is itself a manifestation and performance of sovereignty.

These events of the 1980s were ground-breaking and became the foundations upon which a new Aboriginal art movement was built. Those artists could not have envisioned how significant these events would become for the history of Aboriginal art and for the broader Aboriginal political movement. They have subsequently come to be seen as marking the origins of the first wave of a contemporary urban Aboriginal art movement in Australia.

The Boomalli Artists Collective smashed colonial discourses of primitive Aboriginal art located in remote areas as 'authentic' Aboriginal culture compared to Aboriginal artists working in urban centres as 'inauthentic'. Boomalli artists created works that refused colonial constructs of 'authenticity' linked to Aboriginality as other-than-urban, not only with their expressions of sovereignty in art produced in and about the city, but also through invoking in order to refuse these binaries in their exhibitions. They did this collectively and purposefully, organising to both contest white mainstream media representations of their art and to fight against the white art world's stranglehold over exhibiting practices. In the formation of Boomalli Aboriginal Artists Cooperative, and in all of these moments, they defined their art, themselves, and their communities. Due to these 1980s moments and events and people who sit within the vast connected constellation of Indigenous sovereignty, as Tracey Moffatt says, "[t]he future for myself and other Aboriginal artists: I see is brilliant" (*Boomalli* 1988: online).

Notes

1 In this article I use the words Indigenous and Aboriginal interchangeably.
2 These included the Great Exhibition of the Works of Industry of All Nations in London in 1851; Intercolonial Exhibition of Australasia in Melbourne in 1866; Paris Exposition Universelle of 1867; the 1877 Adelaide Jubilee International Exhibition; 1879 International Exhibition in Sydney; the 1880 International Exhibition and the larger Centennial International Exhibition of 1888 both in Melbourne. For more on these and others, see Hoffenberg 2001: 27 and Darian-Smith 2008.
3 It is worth noting too, that whilst these exhibitions showcased ideas about race, and notions of inevitable Aboriginal extinction, colonial administrations reflected this racism in policy and legislation. Not long after the 1866 Intercolonial Exhibition, the *Aboriginal Protection Act 1869* (Vic) began what would become a long and vicious history of racial classification of Aboriginal people. Historian Katherine Ellinghaus (2001: 23) notes with this act Victoria became the first Australian colony to "legislate for a system of administration for Indigenous people living inside its borders". This Act was extended and government powers were expanded with the 1886 *Act to Provide for the Protection and Management of the Aboriginal Natives of Victoria*, also known as the 'Half-Caste Act'.

References

Anderson, W. (2002). *The Cultivation of Whiteness: Science, Health and Racial Destiny in Australia*. Melbourne University Press: Melbourne, VIC.

Bancroft, B. (2012). *Boomalli Essay*. Boomalli Aboriginal Artists Co-operative. Available: http://www.boomalli.com.au/about-1/, accessed 29 May 2018.

Boomalli - Five Koorie Artists. (1988). Directed by Michael Riley. Australian National Film and Sound Archive, Canberra. Available: https://www.freeview.com.au/watch-tv/shows/2ec4cdd6-c41b-415 b-9f8e-14044bae4f31, accessed 20 May 2020.

Cooper, F. and Stoler, A.L. (1997). *Tensions of Empire: Colonial Cultures in a Bourgeois World*. University of California Press: Berkeley, CA.

Croft, B.L. (1992). 'A very brief bit of an overview of the aboriginal arts/cultural industry by a sort of renegade or the cultural correctness of certain issues', *Art Monthly Australia*, vol 56: 20–22.

Darebin Arts. (2013). 'Public art', *Darebin City Council*. Available: https://www.darebinarts.com.au/programs/public-art/, accessed 7 May 2017.

Darian-Smith, K. (2008). 'Seize the day: Exhibiting Australia', in K. Darian-Smith, R. Gillespie, C. Jordan, and E. Willis (eds.) *Seize the Day: Exhibitions, Australia and the World*. Monash University Press: Melbourne, VIC, 1.1–1.14.

Editorial. (1866). 'Opening of the exhibition', *Argus*, 25 October: 5.

Edmonds, F. and Clarke, M. (2009). *'Sort of Like Reading A Map': A Community Report on the Survival of South-East Australian Aboriginal Art Since 1834*. Cooperative Research Centre for Aboriginal Health: Casuarina.

Edmonds, P. (2006). 'The Le Souëf box: Reflections on imperial nostalgia, material culture and exhibitionary practice in colonial Victoria', *Australian Historical Studies*, vol 37, no 127: 117–139.

Ellinghaus, K. (2001). 'Regulating Koori marriages: The 1886 Victorian aborigines protection act', *Journal of Australian Studies*, no 67: 22–29.

Evans, M. and Sinclair, A. (2016). 'Containing, contesting, creating spaces: Leadership and cultural identity work among Australian Indigenous arts leaders', *Leadership*, vol 12, no 3: 270–292.

Foley, G. (2012). 'Black power and aboriginal arts', *Tracker Magazine*. Available: http://www.kooriweb.org/foley/essays/tracker/tracker16.html, accessed 21 May 2017.

Griffiths, M. (2018). 'Forty thousand years mural in Redfern restored in the face of gentrification', *ABC News*. Available: https://www.abc.net.au/news/2018-04-28/iconic-redfern-mural-repainted-in-the-face-of-gentrification/9705354, accessed 21 October 2019.

Hannaford, I. (1996). *Race: The History of an Idea in the West*. Johns Hopkins University Press: Baltimore, MD.

Hoffenberg, P.H. (2001). *An Empire on Display: English, Indian, and Australian Exhibitions from the Crystal Palace to the Great War*. University of California Press: Berkeley, CA.

Hokowhitu, B. (2014). 'Haka: Colonized physicality, body-logic, and embodied sovereignty', in L.R. Graham and H.G. Penny (eds.) *Performing Indigeneity: Global Histories and Contemporary Experiences*. University of Nebraska Press: Lincoln, NE, 273–304.

Jones, J. (2018). *Murruwaygu: Following in the Footsteps of Our Ancestors*. PhD Dissertation, University of Technology Sydney.

Kleinert, Sylvia and Neale, Margo (2000). *Oxford Companion to Aboriginal Art and Culture*, Oxford University Press: Melbourne.

Koori Art '84. (1984). *Exhibition Catalogue*. Artspace: Sydney, NSW.

Langton, M. (1993). 'Well, I heard it on the radio and I saw it on the television ...', *An Essay for the Australian Film Commission on the Politics and Aesthetics of Filmmaking By and About Aboriginal People and Things*. Australian Film Commission: North Sydney, NSW.

McGrath, A. (1987). *Born in the Cattle: Aborigines in Cattle Country*. Allen & Unwin: Sydney, NSW.

Moffatt, T. (2006). 'Interview with Tracey Moffatt'. In K Favelle (ed), *Michael Riley: Sights Unseen*, National Gallery of Australia: Canberra, 95.

Moreton-Robinson, A. (2000). *Talking up to the White Woman*. University of Queensland Press: St Lucia, QLD.

Moreton-Robinson, A. (2004). 'Whiteness, epistemology and Indigenous representation', in A. Moreton-Robinson (ed.) *Whitening Race: Essays in Social and Cultural Criticism*. Aboriginal Studies Press: Canberra, 75–88.

Newtown, G. (2006). 'The elders: Indigenous photography in Australia', in K. Favelle (ed.) *Michael Riley: Sights Unseen*. National Gallery of Australia: Canberra, 47–58.

Onus, L. (1993). 'Southwest, Southeast Australia and Tasmania', in G. Lee and B. Luthi (eds.) *Aratjara: Art of the First Australians: Traditional and Contemporary Works by Aboriginal and Torres Strait Islander Artists.* DuMont: Koln, 290–95.

Perkins, H. (2010). *Art + Soul: A Journey into the World of Aboriginal Art.* Melbourne University Publishing: Melbourne, VIC.

Perkins, H. and Riley, M. (2008). 'Michael Riley', in H. Perkins, and J. Jones (eds.) *Half Light: Portraits from Black Australia.* Art Gallery of New South Wales: Sydney, NSW, 110–119.

Quail, A. and Chapman, K. (2012). 'Cultivating CIAF', *Art Monthly Australia*, 25 August: 23–25.

Rhodes, C. (1995). *Primitivism and Modern Art.* Thames & Hudson: London.

Stoler, A.L. (2002). 'Colonial archives and the arts of governance', *Archival Science*, vol 2, no 1: 87–109.

Thomas, D. (1978). 'Aboriginal art as art', in R. Edwards (ed.) *Aboriginal Art in Australia.* Ure Smith: Sydney, NSW, 29–31.

Thomas, D. (2004). *Reading Doctors' Writing: Race, Politics and Power in Indigenous Health Research, 1870–1969.* Aboriginal Studies Press: Acton.

Tyson, E. (2018). 'Redfern's iconic "40,000 years" mural to be restored'. Available: https://www.sbs.com.au/nitv/nitv-news/article/2018/03/14/redferns-iconic-40000-years-mural-be-restored, accessed 2 July 2019.

Victims or Victors?: The Story of the Victorian Aborigines Advancement League. (1985). Hyland House: South Yarra, VIC.

25

Communality as everyday Indigenous sovereignty in Oaxaca, Mexico

Isabel Altamirano-Jiménez

Sovereignty has been heatedly debated in Indigenous Studies. While some scholars critique the concept and its Western origins, others have noted the need to theorise the specificities of the term in Indigenous contexts. Joanne Barker, for example, argues that there is no fixed meaning of sovereignty because it is "embedded within the specific social relations in which it is invoked and given meaning" (2005: 20). Distinguishing Western from Indigenous sovereignty, Aileen Moreton-Robinson explains that the latter "is embodied, it is ontological (our being) and epistemological (our way of knowing) and it is grounded in complex relationships derived from the intersubstantiation of ancestral beings, humans and land" (2008: 2). Building on Barker's idea of embeddedness and Moreton-Robinson's understanding of sovereignty, this chapter examines the centrality of Indigenous everyday communal practices in the struggle for self-determination in Oaxaca, Mexico, and explores the way in which Indigenous women and non-binary individuals negotiate such practices.

Communal ways of doing and living or 'communality', the term used in Oaxaca (Maldonado Alvarado 2013; Martínez Luna 2010; Díaz 2001), resonates with Moreton-Robinson definition of Indigenous of sovereignty. Communality is understood as the practice and ethics of being with one another, with the land, and non-human beings. I argue that as a form of everyday Indigenous sovereignty, communality is not a point of arrival but a prerequisite for building decolonial futures in which bodies are always in consensual, reciprocal relationships with land, non-humans, and nature. As Leanne Simpson notes, how we live, how we do things, "how we organize is a transformative, relational act that regenerate Indigenous neuropathways inside our bodies and the web of relationships that sustain our nationhood outside our bodies" (2018: 20). At the same time, Moreton-Robinson warns, Indigenous people's embodiments and experiences vary because their relations to territory, non-human beings and social relations are multivariate (Moreton-Robinson 2013: 339).

This chapter, in part, explores how Indigenous women's struggles for bodily autonomy and transforming the micropolitics of everyday life intersect with the defence of territory, within the broader notions of property, state sovereignty, and gender relations. Understanding how state sovereignty operates requires that we focus beyond land and resources to include bodies and relationships. Thus, Indigenous local governance processes, including communal land, cultural protocols, gender relations, and practices, or what Joanne Barker (2015) terms the 'polity of the

Indigenous' become the starting point for tracing how Indigenous communities and women, in particular refuse patriarchy and state sovereignty in Oaxaca while asserting alternative ways of being in the world.

Spanish colonialism

This section explores the polity of the Indigenous in what today is Mexico and the complex contestations and challenges that Indigenous peoples have confronted in having to negotiate and refuse the social terms of colonial policies and state sovereignty. The Nahua *altepetl,* the Mixtec ñuu or the Zapotec *yetze* (commonly translated in English as city-state) were sovereign political configurations central to understanding Indigenous communal identity (Ward 2017: 11; Sousa 2017: 22). These sovereign nations had populations that ranged from several hundreds to thousands of people, a clearly delimited territory, a ruling group, a tribute or tax system, an ethnic identity, and shared sense of common origin and history (Sousa 2017: 22). Many of these communities recognised both men and women as authorities, with legal status, land holdings and who participated in communal ceremonies.

Everyone was integral to the whole and social relations were conceived of in reciprocal and complementary terms. Although men and women had distinctive roles and complemented each other to achieve a certain status, women had control over the fruit of their labour (Kellogg 2005: 25). Gender relations were certainly not idyllic, but they were not patriarchal. Rather gender and the complementarity of gender roles were central to the social division of labour in societies where the body was understood to be unstable, unfixed, and shaped by the interaction between natural forces, non-human beings and human action. Similarly, while community members paid tribute to authorities, the latter were obligated to reciprocate by providing community members with feasting, services, and assistance (Sousa 2017: 13). Complementarity and reciprocity were not limited to people but extended to natural forces and non-human beings inhabiting the territory (Lopez Austin 1994). For example, individuals' wellbeing was linked to that of specific animals. These interdependent relationships evoked thousands of interactions shaping people's actions and inactions, seasonal economic cycles, community governance, time, space, and responsibilities along age and gender lines.

Aileen Moreton-Robinson argues that as a regime of power, patriarchal white sovereignty emerges from the act of possessing and is reproduced through repeated cultural practices, meanings, and processes (2017). This 'white possessive' logic relied on rationalising and reproducing colonial and national state stories of how possession came into existence (2017: xii). Power over knowledge, the law, racialised constructs, invented histories, and surveying, all served to legitimise the dispossession of Indigenous land, resources and labour. The doctrine of discovery was instrumental to Spaniards, whose emphasis on conquest rested upon their perceived racial superiority.

In the first decades of Spanish colonisation, important changes to the Indigenous social order were introduced. While the search for 'unknown' possessions drove Spaniards to venture to what today is known as the Americas, not all Indigenous nations were equally affected. The Nahuas of central Mexico came into immediate contact with the colonisers, but in remote regions such as the ones located in Southern Mexico, colonisation occurred later. Generally, colonisation involved violently asserting control over a specific territory, hierarchically classifying people, and reconfiguring their spatial and legal orders. The insistent repetition of racially, gendered, and legal constructs entrenched the conditions of Indigenous peoples' lack of humanity in the colonial order.

In this context, colonialism was based upon a racial hierarchy that separated the *Republica de Españoles* (Spanish Republic) from the *República de Indios* (Indian Republic). The Indian

Republic, initially at least, maintained control over their lands and traditional governance systems in return for paying tribute to Spaniards (Florescano 1997: 186). Indigenous and settler lands emerged as legally distinct forms of property that divided colonisers from the colonised. Indigenous chiefly elites were able to secure some prerogatives such as wearing Spanish clothing, riding horses, and were addressed as dignitaries (Seed 2001: 122).

The imposition of the colonial economy on Indigenous peoples was built upon the Indigenous tribute system. The *encomienda* was an institution based on large enclosures of land granted to Spaniards to reward them for their military services and included the right to receive tribute from Indigenous communities and limited labour conscription. Although legally the encomienda did not confer property rights to settlers, over time it involved dispossession, as agriculture and livestock farming became important sources of income (Yeager 1995: 850). The exploitation of Indigenous labour was often achieved through violence with women and children being particularly vulnerable. Men and women worked labouring in mines and farms and constructing public buildings and roads. Women were forced into servitude to, for example, produce textiles to pay in kind tribute or to work as human carriers of a variety of goods (Kellogg 2005: 66).

The *encomienda*, however, was not consistent across geographies. In humid areas, for instance, Indigenous agricultural communities were dispossessed of some of their lands, while in areas of low agricultural productivity, Indigenous communities were subject to the abusive *repartimiento de afectos* (a system that forced Indigenous peoples to sell and later buy goods at higher prices). This system replaced the encomienda by the 17th century and also forced Indigenous communities to provide 2–4 per cent of their men and women to do low paid or unpaid labour for weeks or months at Spanish owned farms, textile factories and public projects. During the 18th century, the *repartimiento de afectos* became a major source of profit for the Spaniards and resentment for Indigenous communities (Knight 2002: 155–6).

Since women remained the main textile producers, they bore the bulk of tribute payment. Yet, the racial distinctions described above intersected with gender and sexuality, therefore, Indigenous sexual practices and gender roles became constrained within a binary system in which same-sex unions and polygamy became serious political crimes (Seed 2001: 123). In this context, pragmatic adoption of colonial practices, adaptation, rejection and resistance became part of the everyday life of Indigenous communities. Accordingly, indissoluble, monogamous, Christian marriages became the cornerstone of the evangelisation project, which altered Indigenous peoples' intimate relations (Souza 2017: 51). Yet, conflicts commonly arose over abusive practices and Spanish authorities' interference within the affairs of Indigenous communities (Altamirano-Jiménez 2013: 182). Archival records such as testaments, petitions and testimonies shed light on communities' efforts to maintain their autonomy, lands, and communal practices in the face of these economic practices and massive depopulation.

Women's voices emerge with particular strength showing the ways in which they actively used colonial courts to simultaneously defend their rights as women and their communities' lands and natural resources (Kellogg 2005; Sousa 2017). Although Indigenous communities adapted their governance institutions to respond to the impact of colonisation, they also defended their political, social and economic independence (Zeitlin and Thomas 1992: 286). As an example, Oaxaca remained a distinctive region as it was an area where Indigenous communities managed to control more lands than the Spaniards. These communities reproduce themselves as autonomous entities, maintaining their communal governance practices and institutions as a means to resist colonialism. As Brenna Bhandar has noted, along with the dominant forms of possession and domination, there were spaces where Indigenous peoples contested, subverted, and refused colonisation (2017: 184).

The tragedy of Mexican independence

With the independence movement of the early 19th-century, conditions of Indigenous servitude did not greatly improve. The radical transformation of Mexico as a newly independent country turned into a form of colonial politics that attempted to eliminate Indigenous political life. Independence from colonial rule meant transferring political control to an emergent political elite that conceived of state sovereignty in Western terms. Independence brought a new form of colonial domination in which state sovereignty was supported by racial myths, a unitary legal system, and liberal notions of citizenship and individual property. While Indigenous peoples were charged with being unproductive and primitive, individualistic capitalist accumulation was viewed as a sign of modernity and led to legal restructuring to open up Indigenous lands. The *Leyes de Reforma* or Reform Laws, for instance, were aimed at privatising Indigenous land tenure systems and the Church's lands. Indigenous communal land tenure, in particular, was seen as a colonial privilege antithetical to the modern, liberal nation-state.

Indigenous communities revolted against these laws and the attendant land encroachment. Resistance, however, was conveniently framed as revolts that threatened the safety of Creoles (Spaniards born in Mexico) and Mestizos (people of mixed race) rather than as movements against land dispossession. Ironically, while the nationalist myth of the mixed race exalted the past greatness of Indigenous civilisations, it erased living Indigenous peoples, who constituted the majority of the population at the time. As Kauanui argues in the Hawaiian case, indigeneity was simply viewed as incompatible with civic life because it had already been defined as pre-modern and uncivilised (2018: 58).

Despite these efforts, the biopolitical organisation of Indigenous life was fragmented and incomplete (Williams 2011). Legal pluralism and Indigenous communal governance institutions continued to exist as a means through which communities resisted land encroachment and state sovereignty (Altamirano-Jiménez 2017). Indigenous uprisings against land dispossession continued through the 19th century until they merged with the Mexican Revolution of 1910. The emergence of Indigenous leaders such as Emiliano Zapata and the Southern Liberation Army brought the protection of Indigenous collective land rights back in the political agenda.

At the end of this revolutionary movement, Indigenous governance systems expanded to include the agrarian authorities of the *ejidos* (collective land plots granted by the state to Indigenous and peasant communities that had been dispossessed). Indigenous communal lands and *ejidos* were protected by Article 27 of the Mexican Constitution of 1917, which effectively shielded about half of the Mexican territory from the market. Importantly, although the creation of the *ejido* system protected the integrity of lands, it strategically changed the source of rights for previously landless communities. Article 27 granted only usufruct rights to Indigenous peoples while the state retained control over subsurface rights. Moreover, the Agrarian Law in its very conception was gender-biased and, unsurprisingly, *ejido* holdings were granted mainly to men.

Unlike *ejidos*, communal lands, which Indigenous communities had retained since the colonial era, continued to function as social-security nets providing community members with the means to diversify their sources of income and to protect themselves against unexpected events. While Indigenous governance systems existed *de facto*, they were recognised in constitutions across Latin America in the early 1990s. Armed movements, international financial institutions and grassroot mobilisations forced political elites to implement constitutional changes to recognise Indigenous rights in the region. The Mexican Constitution was modified in 1992 to recognise the right of Indigenous peoples to self-determination and political autonomy.

The recognition of Indigenous rights, however, coincided with the rise of neo-liberalism in the region. As the North American Free Trade Agreement (NAFTA) was being negotiated, the Mexican federal government modified several constitutional articles that have had serious consequences for Indigenous peoples. Article 27 of the Mexican Constitution was transformed to loosen Indigenous and peasant control over their agricultural communal lands and *ejidos*. The reforms of 1992 made two important changes. First, *ejido* lands were privatised and could thus be sold, mortgaged, and rented. Second, the titling of communal lands redefined people's relationship to a property as a bundle of rights. In 1992, the Mining Law was also modified and gave mineral extraction priority over any other land use. Later on, this legislation was further transformed to make private investment more appealing by preventing municipalities from imposing taxes on mining corporations and by lifting the ceiling for foreign investment in the industry. In the state of Oaxaca, 770,000 hectares have been granted in concessions, most without the knowledge of the communities affected (Bacon 2013: 43–4).

In 1995, Oaxaca became the first state to change its internal constitution to implement the Indigenous rights recognised in national law. As an extension of these collective rights, a community's right to elect their own authorities according to their 'normative' systems was legally recognised (Altamirano-Jiménez 2017). While the privatisation of Indigenous lands went unnoticed by many non-Indigenous people, the recognition of Indigenous governance systems in Oaxaca produced a heated debate about the merit of protecting such practices. Some celebrated establishing a pluralistic legal regime in the country (Esteva 2001: 216); others opposed recognising Indigenous illiberal 'uses and customs'. This debate was shaped by the simultaneous representation of Indigenous governance systems as a source of collective rights, backward in practice and inconsistent with modern national law and human rights. Recognition was not driven by a colonial state that had finally come to accept its dark past; rather, it was the state's attempt to subject Indigenous law to national law (Roth, Boelens and Zwarteveen 2015: 459). I would argue that the recognition of Indigenous normative systems merely created a grey zone in which the legitimacy of Indigenous laws and governance systems remain in question.

Communality as everyday self-determination

What does it mean to live a sovereign communal life in Oaxaca? How is communalism mobilised to resist state sovereignty and dispossession? Located in southwestern Mexico, next to the states of Puebla, Chiapas, Guerrero, and Veracruz, Oaxaca has 15 distinctive Indigenous peoples accounting for 48 per cent of the population (INEGI 2011). Oaxaca has 570 municipalities, more than any other state in the country. Historically, the creation of municipalities (a third level of government in Mexico) has been one way for Indigenous communities to maintain their territorial and political control over their own affairs (Velásquez Cepeda 1998: 15–114). The majority of municipalities (418) in Oaxaca continue to practice their traditional governance systems, where governing is conceived of as a service to the community (Aquino Mosrechi 2013: 11). The election of municipal authorities involves filling *cargos* or posts who, in turn, have responsibility to provide services to the community and celebrations. Although the Oaxaca Indigenous Law recognised governance practices, these constitute only one component of communal life.

In the 1970s, Indigenous communities mobilised to regain control of their natural resources. This Indigenous resurgence led to communality as a political thought, which began to be theorised in the early 1980s in the Oaxaca Northern Highlands. Communality was initially articulated as a critique of anthropological understandings of indigeneity, which were limited to a set of criteria including language, ceremonies, food, and so on. Zapotec Jaime Martínez Luna and

341

Mixe Floriberto Díaz insisted that such criteria were colonial. They noted that communality, understood as Indigenous political thought and practice, was central to understanding indigeneity and the survival of Indigenous communities; that is, Indigenous sovereignty. Floriberto Díaz, writes that autonomy, interdependence, reciprocity and people's attitudes towards common life and the environment they live in is what constitutes Indigenous communities. Through the reproduction of these principles, community members express their sense of being in the world and belonging to a community. Being part of a community involves the responsibility to be with one another in reciprocal relationships (Díaz 2001; 2007). Martínez Luna, on the other hand, argues that a member of a community can stop speaking an Indigenous language or wearing traditional clothing but cannot stop participating in the communal celebrations or *tequio* (communal work). Similarly, one can migrate and still continue to contribute to the communal life (Martínez Luna 2010). Thus, belonging is a verb; to be a member of an Indigenous community in Oaxaca, one must be willing to fulfil communal obligations.

Akin to the aforementioned Joanne Barker's (2015) concept 'polity of the Indigenous', Martínez Luna explains that belonging comes from self-determined individuals who are willing to live an action-oriented way of life. It is through people's actions and practices that a sense of us, of being in community, has been maintained up to the present day despite colonial and nation-state efforts to assimilate Indigenous peoples. Communality is an experience, a practice, an attitude, and an ethos that, according to Martínez Luna, has four interrelated elements: territory, governance, work, and fiestas (community celebrations). Territory is the physical space where life is organised and joy, ceremony, relationships, food production and consumption, work, authority, learning, creation, and reflection occur. Governance is based on an ethos of service and reciprocity and the communal practices, agreements, norms, institutions, and laws that determine how people organise, manage themselves, and solve conflicts. Communal work is both a responsibility and a possibility. As a responsibility, it mediates between the past and collective subsistence. Work performed by community members is aimed at improving and maintaining collective life. As a possibility, work aims at reproducing social relations and creating a better future. Lastly, fiestas are about the joy of being with one another and other beings. Fiestas mediate between the past and the social relations in the present (Martínez Luna 2010: 87–8).

As previously discussed, Aileen Moreton-Robinson's framing of embodied sovereignty as ontological, epistemological and grounded in complex "ancestral beings, humans and land" (2008: 2) relationships, can be likened to communality. In the present context, the principles that hold these elements together are reciprocity, respect, and interdependence. These principles are crucial to expressing and deliberating upon disparate views, consensus building, and to share collective efforts to live a better communal life. Interconnectedness is the source of our obligations to one another and our communities, it is central to develop a sense of individual and collective self-determination, which are enacted every day (Martínez Luna 2010: 88–9). From this perspective, autonomy and self-determination are understood as the possibility to control territory and the conditions of Indigenous communal social reproduction at the margins of the state. Gustavo Esteva posits that autonomy in Oaxaca is not only a matter of politics. It is about the freedom to protect one's own dignity through the protection of culture, land, territory, and environment (Esteva 2001).

Communities include spirits, land, and non-human life coexisting in a given territory. The interactions among these entities evoke thousands of interactions that are driven by actions and inactions that correlate to seasonal cycles, ceremonies, and political decisions. Survival results from the complex, ontological, complementary relationships among people, the household, the land, and natural forces (Regino 2000). Often, complementarity is understood as involving symmetry among different bodies. However, as Aymara feminist and activist Julieta Paredes argues, complementarity can also conceal unequal division of work, in which one sub-group ends up performing work that is perceived to be of less value in the community (2013: 48). Examining the Hawaiian case, J. Kehaulani Kauanui sheds light on the complex predicaments that arise when nationalist elites assert state sovereignty at the expense of Indigenous peoples (2018: 21). Shaped by a logic that feminises indigeneity, Western statecraft is represented as "rational, strong, worldly, independent, and active" (Kauanui 2018: 6). In contrast, Indigenous peoples occupy the supposedly role as "savage, weak, domestic, dependent, and passive" (Kauanui 2018: 6). Building on Kauanui's work, I argue that communality should not be understood as an idyllic way of life. Rather, what is important is how despite conflicts, antagonism, and divisions, a community of bodies comes together to centre communal practices of solidarity when their way of life is threatened. Given that conflicts between men and women, families, and neighbours, highlight asymmetries, gender inequalities, and intergenerational differences, it is also important to consider how Indigenous communities negotiate their complex communal practices.

Communality, bodies, and land defence

As a practice and a way of life, communalism has been challenged both from the outside and from within. Anthropologist Laura Nader argues that Zapotec communities have created a set of premises that together constitute a 'harmony ideology', which represents communities as being internally harmonious concealing coercive practices that are against individual freedom. This harmony ideology constitutes a strategy for resisting state political and cultural hegemony (Nader 1990). Governments, political elites and critics often use the argument of individual rights, specifically Indigenous women's rights, as a means to oppose and limit Indigenous autonomy. From this perspective, Indigenous women's experiences of gendered discrimination and violence are exclusively understood as cultural problems. This understanding culturalises social injustices and the notion of the Indigenous "female victim", who needs to be rescued from her culture (Newdick 2005: 75). Clearly, certain communal practices have resulted in abuses against community members and women (Sieder and McNeish 2013; Sierra 2008; Hernández Castillo 2002; Vázquez 2011). However, the assumption that Indigenous women are passive victims or that Indigenous governance systems are static is problematic. As shown earlier, Indigenous people's relationships with each other and territory have been shaped by complex, colonial policies, practices, and community responses to such policies.

In Oaxaca, Indigenous women have practiced sovereignty by actively challenging essentialised understandings of community, communality, and gender relations. In this region, Indigenous women's position within their communities varies. For example, in some communities, women participate in the community's political life through their households. In others, when women marry, they lose their right to hold land and to participate in the communal assembly, which is the ultimate political space where communal citizenship is exercised. In many communities, when men migrate, the responsibility for the survival of the household and even the maintenance of men's community citizenship falls upon women. At the same time, migration has opened up spaces for transforming communal practices. For example, recent data confirms that 1,100 women currently occupy a post in those municipalities ruled by traditional Indigenous governance systems. In 5 per cent of these municipalities, women have been elected as majors, showing an important trend (Valladares de la Cruz 2018: 19). Since the household unit is crucial to the functioning of Indigenous governance systems, when men migrate, women are left with the responsibility of contributing towards communal work. The idea of complementary gender roles not only conceals this unequal division of labour but also naturalises binary gender relations in the household, which excludes other family configurations that exist in practice in our communities. As Julieta Paredes notes, reconceptualising the complementarity pair involves thinking beyond sexual arrangements to focus instead on relationships (Parades 2013). To fulfil their communal obligations, women develop relationships of solidarity with friends and neighbours, which are seldom considered in discussions of complementarity.

As with any acts of sovereignty there are costs. The challenge confronting Indigenous women and non-binary individuals is how their desire to have a dignified life can be achieved without compromising the kinship structures that have been instrumental to defending the communal territory. Indigenous women and non-binary individuals are not passive victims waiting to be rescued by the state but political subjects who actively fight for their bodily autonomy and communal self-determination. They call attention to the materiality of their bodies but reclaim their rights away from the state. In different forums, encounters and regional meetings, women and non-binary individuals have noted that their struggle for bodily autonomy and the micro politics of everyday life cannot be separated from their communal struggle to defend their territory. Often, land encroachment and the granting of government permits to exploit natural resource without Indigenous communities' consent go hand in hand with the violence that is committed against their bodies (Cinemanoticias 2010). Although the inseparability of Indigenous bodies from land and resource extraction is longstanding, it is still under analysed. Indigenous women actively participate in the defence of territory and autonomy, they know that what is at stake is their forest, water, and all of the entities that constitute their everyday Indigenous life. In this sense, it is not human bodies that matter but also the living, non-living, and non-human bodies that exist already in relation with human bodies.

Indigenous women's political strategies simultaneously emphasise relationality but also fluidity and transformation rather than a fixed way of being in the world. For example, the Assembly of Indigenous Women of Oaxaca (AIWO), which includes women from many Indigenous communities, has noted that within Indigenous communities, the fulfilment of communal obligations precedes the exercise of rights. This organisation also critiques the patriarchal practices that limit their participation both within and outside their communities. In the words of some of this organisation's members, "we want to be able to freely express what we think and we feel" (Martínez Cruz 2015: 176). Indigenous women centre their personal experiences, feelings, and knowledge and ways of organising that are not hierarchical. They also argue that Indigenous governance systems are not static and their transformation must be driven from within communities and with the active participation of Indigenous women (Martínez Cruz 2015: 177). Women have used the spaces opened by community-driven radio stations to narrate their own experiences of gender discrimination and subordination within their communities. Often, these radio stations are transmitted in Indigenous languages to guarantee that everyone has access to the information and foster community discussions that are important to women (Vázquez García 2012: 12).

Communal radio stations have been central in fostering community conversations. Indigenous communities are working to address and negotiate their complicated cultural politics in tension to governments, political elites and critics' understandings of Indigenous women's individual rights. Accounting exclusively for women's individual rights, leaves unquestioned the very division between men and women, nature and culture, human/non-human beings that grounds Western understanding of sovereignty and political life.

Conclusion

As a form of everyday Indigenous sovereignty, communality is not an end in itself but a process for creating decolonial futures. Communality has the potential to be both an epistemic and political project. For Indigenous people and women in particular, communality is not only about changing the economic or political regimes but also Indigenous life itself, in which bodies are always already in relationships with each other, other beings, and land. Given the neoliberal changes implemented in Mexico and the current encroachment of Indigenous lands, the persistence and revival of communal forms of governance and social organisation constitute a decolonial effort that refuses state sovereignty. As a non-statist form of Indigenous sovereignty, communality challenges the very division between men and women, nature and culture, human and non-human beings that grounds Western political life. Communality remains a strategy through which communities refuse state sovereignty while asserting other ways of being in the world that brings land, bodies, living and non-living entities together.

References

Altamirano-Jiménez, I. (2013). *Indigenous Encounters With Neo-Liberalism. Place, Women and the Environment*. UBC Press: Vancouver, BC.

Altamirano-Jiménez, I. (2017). 'The state is not a savior: Indigenous law, gender and state restructuring in Oaxaca', in J. Green (ed.) *Making Space for Indigenous Feminism II*. Fernwood: Black Point, SA, 130–143.

Aquino Mosreschi, A. (2013). 'La comunalidad como espistemología del sur: Aportes y retos', *Cuadernos del Sur*, vol 18, no 34: 7–19.

Bacon, D. (2013). *The Right to Stay Home: How US Policy Drives Mexican Migration*. Beacon Press: Boston, MA.

Barker, J. (2005). *Sovereignty Matters: Locations of Contestation and Possibilities in Indigenous Struggles for Self-Determination*. University of Nebraska Press: Lincoln, NE.

Barker, J. (2015). 'Indigenous feminisms', in J.A. Lucero, D. Turner, and D.L. VanCott (eds.) *Oxford Handbook of Indigenous People's Politics*. Oxford Hanbooks Online, 1–25. doi:10.1093/oxfor dhb/9780195386653.013.007

Bhandar, B. (2017). *Colonial Lives of Property. Law, Land and Colonial Regimes of Ownership*. Duke University Press: Durham, NC.

Cinemanoticias. (2010). 'Recriminan a Ulises Ruiz política de terror misógina y machista'. Available: http://www.cimacnoticias.com.mx/ node/41228/26/11/10, accessed 4 September 2019.

Díaz, F. (2001). 'Comunidad y comunalidad', *La Jornada Semanal*, March 11. Available at: https://www.jor nada.com.mx/2001/03/11/sem-comunidad.html, accessed 25 July 2019.

Díaz, F. (2007). *Comunalidad, Energía Viva del Pensamiento Mixe*. UNAM: Mexico City.

Esteva, G. (2001). 'The meaning and scope of the struggle for autonomy', *Latin American Perspectives*, vol 28, no 2: 120–148.

Florescano, E. (1997). *Etnia, estado y nación*. Aguilar: Mexico City.

Hernández Castillo, A. (2002). 'National law and Indigenous customary law: The struggle for justice of Indigenous women in Chiapas, Mexico', in M. Molyneux and S. Razavi (eds.) *Gender Justice, Development and Rights*. Oxford University Press: Oxford, 384–412.

INEGI (Instituto Nacional de Geografía y Estadística. (2011). *Informe de actividades y resultados del Inegi* https ://www.inegi.org.mx/contenidos/transparencia/contenidos/doc/15_inf11.pdf accessed 15 March 2020.

Kauanui, J.K. (2018). *Paradoxes of Hawaiian Sovereignty. Land, Sex, and the Colonial Politics of State Nationalism*. Duke University Press: Durham, NC.

Kellogg, S. (2005). *Weaving the Past. A History of Latin America's Indigenous Women from the Prehispanic Period to the Present*. Oxford University Press: Oxford.

Knight, A. (2002). *Mexico: The Colonial Era*. Cambridge University Press: Cambridge.

López Austin, A. (1994). *Tamoacha:n and Tlalocan*. Fondo de Cultura Económica: Mexico City.

Maldonado Alvarado, B. (2013). 'Comunalidad y responsabilidad autogestiva', *Cuadernos del Sur. Revista de Ciencias Sociales* 18(34): 21–27.

Martínez Cruz, A. (2015). 'Tejiendo identidades estratégicas: La Asamblea de Mujeres Indígenas de Oaxaca', *Nómadas*, vol 45: 170–187.

Martínez Luna, J. (2010). 'The fourth principle', in L. Meyer and B. Maldonado Alvarado (eds.) *New World of Indigenous Resistance: Noam Chomsky and Voices from North, South and Central America*. City Lights Books: San Francisco, CA, 85–110.

Moreton-Robinson, A. (ed.). (2008). *Sovereign Subjects: Indigenous Sovereignty Matters*. Allen & Unwin: Sydney, NSW.

Moreton-Robinson, A. (2013). 'Towards an Australian Indigenous women's standpoint theory', *Australian Feminist Studies*, vol 28, no 78: 331–347.

Moreton-Robinson, A. (2017). *The White Possessive. Property, Power and Indigenous Sovereignty*. University of Minnesota Press: Minneapolis, MN.

Nader, L. (1990). *Harmony Ideology: Justice and Control in a Zapotec Mountain Village*. Standford University Press: Stanford, CA.

Newdick, V. (2005). 'The Indigenous woman as victim of her culture in neoliberal Mexico'. *Cultural Dynamics*, vol 17, no, 1: 73–92.

Paredes, J. (2013). *Hilando fino desde el feminism comunitario*. Cooperativa el Rebozo: Mexico City.

Regino, A. (2000). 'La comunalidad, raíz, pensamiento, acción y horizonte de los pueblos indígenas', *México Indígena*, vol 1, no, 2: 7–14.

Roth, D., Boelens R., and Zwarteveen, M. (2015). 'Property, legal pluralism, and water rights: The critical analysis of water governance and the politics of recognizing o'local' rights', *The Journal of Legal Pluralism and Unofficial Law*, vol 47, no 3: 456–475.

Seed, P. (2001). *American Pentimento: The Invention of Indians and the Pursuit of Riches*. University of Minnesota Press: Minneapolis, MN.

Sieder, R. and McNish, J.A. (2013). 'Introduction', in R. Sieder and J.A. McNish (eds), *Gender Justice and Legal Pluralities: Latin American and African Perspectives*. Routledge: New York, 1–30.

Sierra, M.T. (2008). 'Indigenous women, law and custom: Gender ideologies in the practices of justice', in H. Baitenmann, V. Chenaut, and A. Varley (eds.), *Decoding Gender. Law and Practice in Contemporary Mexico*. Rutgers: Brunswick, GA, 109–124.

Simpson, L. (2018). *As We Have Always Done: Indigenous Freedom Through Radical Resistance*. University of Minnesota Press: Minneapolis, MN.

Sousa, L. (2017). *The Woman Who Turned into a Jaguar and Other Narrative of Women in Archives of Colonial Mexico*. Stanford University Press: Stanford, CA.

Valladares de la Cruz, L. (2018). 'Justicia electoral en Oaxaca: Entre los derechos de las mujeres y los derechos comunitarios', *Alteridades*, vol, 28, no 55: 13–24.

Vázquez, V. (2011). 'Los derechos políticos de las mujeres en el sistema de usos y costumbres de Oaxaca', *Cuicuilco* 18(50) 185–206. http://www.scielo.org.mx/pdf/cuicui/v18n50/v18n50a10.pdf (accessed 10 March 2020).

Vázquez García, C.M. (2012). 'Mujeres de la palabra florida: Comunicando pensamientos en radio *Jënpoj*', *Revista Latinoamericana de Comunicación*, 120: 9–12.

Velázquez Cepeda, M.C. (1998). *El nombramiento: Antropología jurídica de los usos y costumbres para la renovación de los ayuntamientos de Oaxaca*. Instituto Estatal Electoral de Oaxaca: Oaxaca.

Ward, T. (2017). *Decolonizing Indigeneity: New Approaches to Latin American Literature*. Lexington Books: Lanham, MD.

Williams, G. (2011). *The Mexican Exception. Sovereignty, Police and Democracy*. Palgrave Macmillan: New York.

Yeager, T. (1995). 'Encomienda or slavery? The Spanish crown's choice of labour organization in sixteenth-century Spanish America', *The Journal of Economic History*, vol 55, no 4: 842–859.

Zeitlin, Francis, J., and Thomas, L. (1992). 'Spanish justice and the Indian cacique disjunctive political systems in sixteenth-century Tehuantepec', *Ethnohistory*, vol 39, no 3: 285–315.

26

American Indian sovereignty versus the United States

Robert J. Miller

The word 'sovereignty' holds different meanings for different nations and peoples.[1] In this chapter, however, we must work from some basic definition so that we can intelligently compare the sovereignty and the ideas about sovereignty of the Indigenous peoples and nations located within the United States today with the United States' formulations and definitions of Indigenous sovereignty.[2]

A widely used legal dictionary defines sovereignty as: "The supreme, absolute, and uncontrollable power by which any independent state is governed; supreme political authority … the self-sufficient source of political power, from which all specific political powers are derived …" (Black's Law Dictionary 1979: 1252). Webster's Dictionary (1985) defines sovereignty as the "supreme power, esp. over a body politic", and as "freedom from external control" (1129). I argue that no country in the world, not even the world's leading superpower, possesses this extent of sovereignty today. In class, I offer a thumbnail definition of sovereignty as the power (jurisdiction) that a political entity exercises over its defined territory and over all the events that occur there and the people present there. Using these definitions, we can compare the disjuncture between the historical and modern-day principles of Indigenous sovereignty and the United States' ideation of that sovereignty.

Historical Indigenous sovereignty

The Indigenous nations and peoples discussed in this chapter exercised sovereignty and sovereign powers over their bodies politic, free from external controls, since time immemorial. American Indian, Native Hawaiian, and Alaska Native governments exerted varying levels of political power to govern their independent states and to exercise their inherent authority. While their powers and jurisdictions have been restricted somewhat today, these governments continue to possess extensive sovereign authority over their citizens and territories, and over Indians and non-Indians. In addition, in the current era of US Indian policy called, "Self-Determination", the federal government strongly supports and encourages Indian sovereignty for the purpose of "fostering tribal self-government" (US Supreme Court 1982: online).

American Indian sovereign powers

For thousands of years before Europeans arrived in North America, Indigenous peoples and nations organised themselves through a wide array of governmental institutions that ranged from hierarchical and even authoritarian governments that governed large, settled areas and agrarian populations, to more informal governance structures for small bands that perhaps lived by seasonal rounds and harvested wild foods and fish and animal migrations to support themselves.

The Adena and Hopewell cultures that existed from 500 BCE to 500 CE in and around the modern-day state of Ohio, and the Ancestral Puebloans of the American Southwest, governed themselves through political entities that possessed the power to mobilise labor, direct manufacture, and build roads, large urban areas, and enormous public works. The Hohokam peoples of the Southwest, for example, constructed over 500 miles of canals to irrigate over 100,000 acres and to feed up to 50,000 people in the modern-day Phoenix, Arizona, area for over a thousand years. All these peoples also built permanent residential and enormous ceremonial structures and practiced elaborate burials for elite leaders (Howard [no year]; National Park Service 2017; Ohio History Central [no year]; Miller 2012: 13, 19–20; Mann 2005: 41–2, 288–90; Strutin 1994: 34–5, 50–1; Shaffer 1992: 3, 20–3, 25–6, 28, 33–4, 36–8, 40–2, 44–5).

Many Indian nations in the vast Mississippi Valley in the central part of modern-day America were mound building cultures and erected enormous earthen mounds. For example, the culture that existed around Poverty Point Louisiana from 1700–700 BCE continues to amaze scientists today. These governments demonstrated their power, sovereignty, and jurisdiction by mobilising, organising, and paying or coercing an enormous mass of labor to undertake unimaginable building operations. Scientists state that these works took a "sophisticated level of organization … to plan and direct" and that the construction of the massive Poverty Point mounds took, "at least five million hours of labor" (Gibson 1999: online).

In addition, the city and culture of Cahokia, in modern-day Illinois, existed from 700 to 1300 CE and had an estimated population of 20,000–50,000 in 1250 CE, larger than London. The primary earthen ceremonial mound that the Cahokians built is the ancient world's largest man-made structure. It covers 14 acres, larger than the Great Pyramid of Cheops. Furthermore, French accounts from the 1700s of the Natchez culture in the lower Mississippi region demonstrate that it was ruled by a royal lineage, and that leaders and elite citizens were carried about in litters. Obviously, these Indigenous societies were governed by organised political institutions (Mann 2005: 27–8, 284–6, 291–7; Barrington 1999: 5, 86, 103; Shaffer 1992: 51–7, 62–7, 75–85).

Indigenous nations also exercised criminal and civil jurisdiction to control conduct in their territories. Some American Indian tribes used whip-masters to discipline children, and many tribal cultures used corporal and even capital punishment to control conduct. Indigenous cultures developed dispute resolution systems to settle disputes and help keep the peace. Some tribal nations fought to defend and to expand their territories. And a few Indigenous governments also taxed their citizens and held public monies and surplus crops in public treasuries (Miller 2017a: 149–50; Sturtevant and Trigger 1978: 83, 85, 202–6, 344–7, 384, 430; Strickland 1975: 10–39, 103–5, 168–74; Debo 1970: 13–14; Llewellyn and Hoebel 1941: 18, 20, 24, 26–8, 42–3, 48, 132–40, 143–6, 157–8, 166–71, 181–2, 185–6, 213–38, 276–83, 310–24, 338–40).

The Hawaiian monarchy provides an impressive example of Indigenous sovereign powers. Native Hawaiian kings and queens exercised enormous power over their subjects and built large temples. The United States overthrew the monarchy in 1893 and still to this day refuses to recognise Native Hawaiian sovereignty (MacKenzie, Serrano and Sproat 2015: 5–74; Newton, Cohen and Anderson 2012: 356–79).

The Indigenous nations of Alaska seem to have been more nomadic and followed a seasonal round economic life by fishing and hunting animals. Yet these societies also exercised governing power over their peoples and their well-defined territories and resources (US Supreme Court 1955: online). One final example of Indigenous sovereignty sums up this brief review. When English colonists arrived in what they named Jamestown Virginia in 1607, they encountered the Powhatan Confederacy, a fully operational and fully sovereign Indigenous nation. The English in the Chesapeake Bay region of Virginia immediately began engaging in diplomatic relations with this sophisticated sovereign government. There were at least 200 permanent Indian villages in the region. The famous English Captain John Smith wrote in 1612 that the Powhatan people had, "such government as that their magistrates for good commanding, and their people for due obedience and obeying, excel many places that would be accounted very civil" (Barbour 1969: 369).

These Indigenous peoples were governed by a single chief and leadership structure although there were perhaps 30 separate Indian nations in the region with a population of over 8,000. One historian states that the Powhatan Confederacy was a 'primitive empire'. That is an apt description because the Powhatan chief exacted tribute from his subject tribes. Captain Smith's 1612 map of the Tidewater area shows the extent of the Powhatan's land husbandry and society, and even identifies chiefs' houses, towns, and the district capitals of the Confederacy (Morgan 1975: 49–50; Parent 2003: 12–13).

Tribal governance structures

Indigenous governments were based on and operated according to the political beliefs and consent of their peoples. American Indian governments had varying levels of organization and institutions that functioned to carry out sovereign powers and to organise and control their societies. Probably the best-known Indian government is the Iroquois Confederacy or the Haudenosaunee. The Confederacy was a federalist governing system developed and operated by five and later six Indian nations (Oneida, Onondaga, Seneca, Mohawk, Cayuga, and Tuscarora) to control their inter-tribal and international relations. Leaders were appointed by clan mothers and could be removed, or recalled as we would say today, for various infractions. The Confederacy met in an annual congress to decide internal and international legal and political issues (Miller 1993; Sturtevant and Trigger 1978: 314–17, 418–41; Speck 1945).

Many other American Indian societies formed governments and confederacies for national governance, strength in numbers, and to conduct international affairs. Tribal nations including the Powhatan, Cheyenne, Shawnee, Creek, Cherokee, Comanche, Blackfeet, Choctaw, Chickasaw, and the Wabanaki Confederacy also developed sophisticated governance regimes that included criminal and civil jurisdiction, democratic principles, and separation of powers principles that divided power between various branches of tribal governments, clans, and villages. Almost all Indian governments also divided war and peace powers between civil and military leaders, and some Indian societies had chiefs who were in charge of planting and hunting, and some nations had both male and female chiefs (Miller 1993: 143–6; Miller 2017: 149–50; Champagne 1992: 8–12, 25–8; Sturtevant and Trigger 1978: 58–69, 84, 240–81; Strickland 1975; Llewellyn and Hoebel 1941: ix, 73–6, 78–9, 99–106, 108–10, 130–1; Barrington 1999: 109).

It is noteworthy that some scholars argue that Indian governments and Indigenous theories and practices of political science even influenced the American Founding Fathers and the US Constitution. In fact, in 1988, the US Congress passed a Resolution "recognizing the influence of the Iroquois Confederacy and other Indian Nations to the formation and development of the United States" (U.S. Congress 1988: online). Interestingly, in 1744 at a Lancaster Pennsylvania treaty council, Iroquois Confederacy leader Canasatego told Benjamin Franklin and other colonial representatives that the English colonies needed to form a union such as the Iroquois had created. Canasatego stated:

> we, the Six Nations, heartily recommend union and a good agreement between you… Our wise Forefathers established Union and Amity between the Five Nations; this has made us formidable; this has given us great Weight and Authority with our neighboring Nations. We are a powerful Confederacy; and, by your observing the same Methods our wise Forefathers have taken, you will acquire fresh Strength and Power.
>
> *(cited in Van Doren and Boyd 1938: 78)*

Ten years later, Benjamin Franklin wrote at the Albany Conference, which conference many historians say led to the formation of the American union:

> It would be a very strange Thing if six Nations of ignorant Savages should be capable of forming a Scheme for such an Union, and be able to execute it in such a Manner, as that is has subsisted Ages, and appears indissoluble; and yet that a like Union should be impracticable for ten or a Dozen English colonies.
>
> *(Labaree 1961: 118–9)*

By comparison, the Hawaiian Islands were populated by Polynesian peoples from 300 CE forward. Native Hawaiian governments were highly structured and ruled by kings and queens and a royal lineage that exercised extensive powers and control of their people. Their societies enforced criminal and civil jurisdiction (MacKenzie, Serrano, and Sproat 2015: 5–74). In contrast, Alaska Native nations were comprised of much smaller populations. Their governance structures appear to have been more rudimentary than other Indigenous nations but as with all societies and cultures, they had laws and customs to organise and govern themselves and to control the conduct of their peoples (US Supreme Court 1955: online; US Supreme Court 1959a: online).

We have barely scratched the surface on the wide variety of governance structures that the Indigenous nations developed pursuant to their political theories and needs. But these points demonstrate that Indigenous peoples and nations knew how to create governments, institutions, and laws and that they operated their governments effectively for centuries.

Indigenous diplomacy and treaty-making

For centuries before European contact, Indian nations exercised their sovereignty and engaged in international affairs via inter-tribal diplomacy with other Indigenous nations regarding political issues and trade and they solemnified their agreements by treaties. Many Indian nations formed political alliances and even confederated with other tribes for mutual protection. In the 1720s, for example, the Tuscarora nation from South Carolina merged politically with the Five Nation Iroquois Confederacy in upstate New York and moved to that area. Thereafter the Confederacy was called the Six Nations.

Once Europeans arrived, Indigenous nations readily incorporated them into their diplomatic and economic practices. European nations recognised Indian tribes as independent sovereigns and entered numerous treaties with tribal governments. Indian nations were experienced in diplomacy and trade and long manipulated European traders and countries by playing them off against each other.

Indigenous nations signed over 100 treaties with England, France, and Spain. The English and American colonies, and then the American states, entered hundreds of treaties with tribal nations from the early 1600s until the early 1800s. Europeans engaged in full diplomatic, political and commercial dealings with tribal governments. All of the European countries that attempted to establish colonies in North America dealt with tribes through treaty-making and international diplomatic methods (Champagne 1992: 15; Debo 1967: 27–36; Prucha 1994: 8–9; De Puy 1999).

Moreover, even economic affairs, which might be considered just private conduct, had political and diplomatic dimensions for Indigenous nations. American Indian, Alaska Native, and Native Hawaiian governments were actively engaged in controlling and conducting trade with other nations. In fact, trade routes crisscrossed North America long before the arrival of Europeans. Trade goods were often traded 1,000 miles from their place of manufacture, mining, or harvest. In addition, annual and semi-annual tribal markets were held in many locations in the lower 48 states in which people traveled long distances to buy and sell manufactured goods, food, and other items. Trade was so important to Indigenous nations that actual warfare and animosities would be put on hold to allow the regularly scheduled markets. Native Hawaiians and their kings also engaged in similar kinds of activities between islands.

When Europeans arrived in North America and Hawai'i, Indigenous nations were eager to trade with new partners. Diplomacy, trade, and treaty-making expanded exponentially as Indigenous peoples and their governments engaged in trade and diplomatic exchanges with newly arrived Europeans, including the Spanish in the American southeast and southwest, the French and English in the American east and midwest, Russian fur traders in Alaska, and Euro-American explorers in Hawai'i.

In sum, Indigenous governments and societies exercised to varying degrees sovereign and governmental powers long before and after Europeans arrived. Indigenous nations enforced civil and criminal jurisdiction and governed their societies and territories. They were skilled in the arts of diplomacy and in using their sovereignty and sovereign powers.

United States 'Indian law' and Indigenous sovereignty

There is an enormous body of US Indian law that has developed from federal court cases, acts of Congress, and actions of the Executive Branch since 1789. It is impossible to set out here all of American 'Indian law'. Thus, we will only mention some basic aspects of federal law and policies that have had major impacts on Indigenous sovereignty.

Doctrine of discovery

When European countries arrived in the New World they were dreaming of empires and wealth. Europeans had already developed 'international law' that was designed to serve their goals of colonising non-European areas and limiting the sovereign powers, property, and human rights of Indigenous nations and peoples. Today we call that international law the Doctrine of Discovery (Miller 2006: 1–5, 10–21).

Under that law, Europeans presumed that Indigenous nations and peoples had immediately, and without payment, knowledge nor consent, lost some of their sovereign powers and property rights when Europeans 'discovered' them. The Doctrine claimed to grant the sole right to acquire lands from Indigenous governments, by purchase or by conquest, to the European nation which claimed first discovery. Indian nations and peoples continued to possess rights to use and occupy their territories but their sovereign land rights were restricted in that they allegedly could only sell land to their discovering European nation and they were only supposed to deal diplomatically and commercially with that European country (US Supreme Court 1823: online; Miller 2006: 3–5).

European nations continued, however, to deal with Indigenous nations as political entities that possessed sovereign powers over specific lands and the peoples and events located there. England and the English colonies, for example, entered scores of treaties with Indian nations in North America and engaged in extensive diplomatic relationships with them. Spain signed 20 or more treaties with Indian nations across what is now the southeast and southwest parts of the United States. France and Holland also engaged in diplomatic relations with Indigenous peoples and signed treaties with Indian nations (Prucha 1994: 59; Deloria and DeMallie 1999: 6, 103, 106–7).

Not surprisingly, the new United States adopted the Doctrine of Discovery and treated tribal nations as if their political and sovereign powers were limited by the mere existence of the United States. But the United States also continued the English and colonial practice of dealing with Indian nations as sovereign governments that possessed power and jurisdiction over their territories and citizens. In September 1774, the 13 English/American colonies created their first national government, the Continental Congress. From its beginning, this United States government realised it had to deal with tribal nations to ensure its own survival. Consequently, the Continental Congress took a very conciliatory position vis-à-vis Indian tribes. In 1778, for example, this Congress requested permission through a treaty to cross Delaware Nation lands to attack British forces. This treaty even offered the Delaware Nation the opportunity to join the United States as a state (Miller 2006: 38–9; Treaty with the Delawares 1778: online).

The 13 American states then convened a new Congress in 1781 under a written constitution called the Articles of Confederation. These Articles assigned to Congress, "the sole and exclusive right and power of ... regulating the trade and managing all affairs with the Indians" (Articles of Confederation cited in Miller 1993: 151–2). This Congress continued the colonial and Continental Congress practice of utilising the Doctrine of Discovery while also recognising the realpolitik situation of the powers of Indian nations. This Congress continued negotiating with Indigenous governments over trade, peace, and land purchases, and ultimately entered eight treaties with Indian nations from 1784 to 1789.

US Constitution and Indigenous sovereignty

The American Founding Fathers enshrined the political status and sovereign authority of Indian governments into the US Constitution.

As already mentioned, European nations and the new United States dealt with Indigenous nations on a diplomatic, governmental, and treaty basis. Involvement in Indian affairs was a crucial part of life in early America. Indian tribes were very powerful in the 1700s and early 1800s and were a serious threat to the new country. Consequently, the Founding Fathers of the new US Constitution of 1787–1789 included Indian nations and peoples in that document.

The new Constitution refined the idea contained in the Articles of Confederation and states that: "Congress shall have Power ... To regulate Commerce with foreign Nations, and among the several States, and with the Indian Tribes ..." (US Constitution of 1787–1789 cited in Miller: 43–4). The US Supreme Court has cited this provision dozens of time in deciding Indian law cases. This provision is extremely important to any discussion of Indigenous sovereignty because it expressly recognises that there are three governments within the United States: federal, state, and Indian tribes.

The Constitution also impliedly refers to Indian nations in the Treaty Clause in Article VI where it states that: "all Treaties made, or which shall be made … shall be the supreme Law of the Land …" (U.S. Constitution, Article VI, cl. 2: online). By 1789, when the Constitution became operational, the United States had entered 23 treaties with foreign countries and nine treaties with Indian nations. Thus, the Treaty Clause language, "all Treaties made, or which shall be made", ratified these prior foreign and Indian treaties as the supreme law of the United States, and provided that same status for future treaties with foreign countries and Indian tribes (Miller 2017b: 110).

Individual Indians, and their status as citizens of their own sovereign nations, are also mentioned twice in the Constitution of 1789, in Article I, and in the Fourteenth Amendment which was ratified in 1868. In counting the population of the states, Indians were not to be counted unless they paid taxes. In effect, individual Indians were not federal or state citizens because they were citizens of their own nations. After the Civil War, when citizenship rights were extended through the Fourteenth Amendment to, "[a]ll persons born or naturalized in the United States" that amendment still "exclud[ed] Indians not taxed" (US Constitution, Amendment XIV: online). This demonstrates that Congress still considered Indians to be citizens of their own sovereign governments in 1868. Thereafter, some Indians became US citizens under various federal laws but it was not until 1924 that all Indians were made United States citizens.

The Marshall trilogy

The most famous chief justice of the US Supreme Court, John Marshall, wrote three opinions in the mid-1800s that set out basic principles of Indian law that are still relevant today. His decisions both limited and somewhat protected Indian sovereignty.

In 1823, in *Johnson v. M'Intosh*, the Court first addressed the definition of Indian sovereignty and land ownership rights. This case has already been cited above because this is the case in which the Supreme Court adopted the Doctrine of Discovery. I argue that in this case, Chief Justice Marshall set out 10 elements that comprise this legal principle and show how it limits Indigenous sovereignty and land rights. In a nutshell, the *Johnson* opinion affirmed the United States legal claim to possess the sole right to buy Indian nations' lands and assets, and that tribal governments could only deal with the United States and had lost their international diplomatic and commercial rights (US Supreme Court 1823: online; Miller 2006: 1–5, 50–3).

In 1831, the Supreme Court had to decide whether the Cherokee Nation was a 'foreign state' because the Nation sued the state of Georgia under a constitutional provision that required that the plaintiff be a foreign state. The Court relied on many different aspects of international law, Indian treaty-making, and the Doctrine of Discovery to render its decision. In light of the evidence, the Court stated that Indian nations are governments and possess political sovereignty and had:

> been uniformly treated as a state from the settlement of our country. The numerous treaties made with them by the United States recognize them as a people capable of maintaining the relations of peace and war, of being responsible in their political character. … The acts of our government plainly recognize the Cherokee nation as a state.
>
> *(US Reports, Cherokee Nation v. Georgia 1831: online).*

But ultimately the Court held that Indian nations are "domestic dependent nations" and not foreign states and are something less than full-fledged international sovereigns: "They may, more correctly, perhaps, be denominated domestic dependent nations. … They are in a state of pupilage. Their relation to United States resembles that of a ward to his guardian". The Court also stated that any attempt by another country to, "form a political connection with [Indian Tribes] would be considered by all as an invasion of our territory, and an act of hostility". Not surprisingly, then, the Supreme Court held that American Indian nations no longer possessed unfettered international sovereignty and that the Cherokee Nation was not a foreign state (US Reports, Cherokee Nation v. Georgia 1831: online).

In 1832, the Marshall Court again relied on many aspects of international law, treaties, and international law scholarship to determine Georgia's authority to apply its law inside the Cherokee Nation's territory. In contrast to the other two cases, Chief Justice Marshall and the Court now strongly supported the existence of tribal governments as political entities possessing sovereign powers. The Court stated that the actions of the United States, "manifestly consider the several Indian nations as distinct political communities, having territorial boundaries, within which their authority is exclusive, and having a right to all the lands within those boundaries…" The Court also stated:

> The very term 'nation' … applied to [Indigenous governments], means 'a people distinct from others'. … The words 'treaty' and 'nation' are words of our own language, selected in our diplomatic and legislative proceedings. … We have applied them to Indians, as we have applied them to the other nations of the earth. They are applied to all in the same sense.

After making these observations, the Court held that the State laws of Georgia, "can have no force" within the Cherokee Nation's territory (US Reports, Worcester v. the State of Georgia 1832: online).

These three cases are enormously important in US Indian law and continue to impact the sovereignty of American Indian nations and peoples to this day.

Felix Cohen's Indian law principles

The most famous American Indian law scholar is Felix Cohen. In the early 1940s he wrote the first treatise on American Indian law. He distilled an enormous mass of federal case law, congressional acts, and Executive Branch policies and actions into three fundamental principles. The US Supreme Court relies heavily on these foundational principles and they have a major effect on American Indian sovereignty today.

Congress' plenary power

The plenary power principle states that Congress has very broad authority in Indian affairs. The Supreme Court has held that this power originates in the Interstate/Indian Commerce Clause of the Constitution, which grants Congress power, "[t]o regulate Commerce with foreign Nations, and among the several States, and with the Indian Tribes" (US Constitution Article I, Section 8, cl. 3: online). According to the Court, this Clause "provides Congress with plenary power to legislate in the field of Indian affairs …" (US Supreme Court 1989: 192 online). This authority allows Congress to enact laws that injure Indian nations and their citizens or laws that benefit Indigenous tribes and their citizens. Thus, Congress has a nearly unchecked power in Indian affairs. In fact, no federal law regarding Indian nations and Indian peoples has ever been overturned because Congress exceeded its power in the Indian law arena. As a matter of fact, only in recent times did the Supreme Court decide that congressional actions regarding Indian nations can even be reviewed by the courts.

Trust doctrine

The Executive and Legislative branches of the federal government have guardian and fiduciary responsibilities for American Indian nations. This duty is partially based on the United States nearly unchecked plenary power over Indians and their governments. Principles of general trust law, and the alleged helplessness of tribal nations, led to the rise of the trust responsibility as a corollary to plenary power. In exercising this extremely broad authority, Congress and the Executive Branch are charged with the responsibilities of a guardian to act on behalf of dependent Indian peoples and their governments. The United States has accepted this responsibility and has "charged itself with moral obligations of the highest responsibility and trust" and judges its own conduct towards tribes, "by the most exacting fiduciary standards" (US Supreme Court 1942: online).

The idea of a trust duty began developing in Supreme Court case law in 1831 when the Court considered the sovereign status of the Cherokee Nation. In that case, the Court stated that the Nation was dependent on the United States for its "protection" and "wants" and was in a "state of pupilage" with the federal government. The *Cherokee Nation* Court then went on to state that the Nation's "relation to the United States resembles that of a ward to his guardian" (US Reports, Cherokee Nation v. Georgia 1831: online). Furthermore, in 1886, the Supreme Court stated that because the, "Indian tribes *are* the wards of the nation . . . [and] communities dependent on the United States" that a heavy responsibility weighs on the United States to care for Indians and their governments due to their very, "weakness and helplessness" (US Supreme Court 1886: online).

The idea of a Euro-American duty to 'protect' Indians and Indigenous nations arose long before these Supreme Court cases. Euro-Americans had long claimed an obligation to care for the best interests of Indians. Many of the US treaties with Indian nations, for example, contained promises by the United States to protect tribes, to support their commercial activities, and to provide education and medical care (Miller 2006: 25–9, 165–6; Laws of the Colonial and State Governments Relating to Indians and Indian Affairs, From 1633 to 1831 1978: 12, 16–17, 22, 37, 45, 59, 136, 142, 146, 150, 154).

Diminished tribal sovereignty

The third principle, called diminished tribal sovereignty, holds that Indian governmental sovereignty was automatically and immediately diminished upon contact with Euro-Americans. Some Indigenous sovereign rights were automatically diminished under the Doctrine of Discovery as discussed above. But the Supreme Court added two factors that also diminish Indigenous sovereignty even beyond the impact of Discovery. First, the Court implied in *Worcester* in 1832 that Indian nations could voluntarily give up aspects of their inherent sovereignty and sell land through treaties. Second, the Court has held that Congress can take aspects of Indigenous sovereignty without tribal consent pursuant to its plenary power (Newton, Cohen, and Anderson 2012: 23, 229–32; US Reports, Worcester v. the State of Georgia 1832: online).

In 1978, the Supreme Court added a third factor to the principle of diminished tribal sovereignty. In *Oliphant v. Suquamish Indian Tribe*, the Court held that the inherent sovereign powers of Indian nations did not, could not, include jurisdiction to criminally prosecute non-Indians. The Court stated that Indian nations could not have this jurisdiction because it would be, "inconsistent with their status". The Court thus expanded the definition of the diminished sovereignty principle by holding that tribal nations retain those aspects of their inherent sovereignty that they have not voluntarily given up, by treaty for example, or which Congress has not taken, pursuant to its plenary power, or, which they have not impliedly lost by virtue of their dependent status upon the United States (US Supreme Court 1978a: online).

All of these principles of Indian law limit Indigenous sovereignty.

Present-day Indian Nation sovereignty

There are 573 federally recognised Indian nations and tribes in the United States today. These political entities are governments and they exercise sovereign powers over their territories, citizens, and other persons and entities that engage in activities in Indian country. In fact, long before Europeans arrived in North America and the Hawai'i Islands, American Indian, Alaska Native, and Native Hawaiian governments exercised complete authority over their territories. After the arrival of Europeans, however, England, France, and Spain used law and raw power to limit the sovereign powers of Indigenous nations. Yet today federally recognised tribal governments still have a government-to-government political relationship with the United States and are sovereign governments with primary control and jurisdiction over their citizens and their territories (Native Hawaiians do not possess a federally recognised government).

Indian nations are sovereign governments

The United States has always recognised American Indian nations as governments. Indigenous nations exercise their own inherent sovereign powers as innate aspects of the power and authority that all governments possess. The US Supreme Court has always acknowledged that Indian governments possess inherent powers that exist totally separate from the United States and distinct from the US Constitution. Tribal nations are 'distinct, independent political communities' that exercise their powers of self-government via inherent sovereignty. Indian nations, for example, did not acquire their political existence or sovereign authority from the United States or from the US Constitution. The Court has expressly noted that tribal governments predate the Constitution and are unrestrained by constitutional and federal provisions that specifically limit federal and state authorities. Indigenous communities were and still are separate political bodies that have created the specific governments that they have chosen to live under today (US Constitution, art. I, sec. 8, cl. 3: online; US Reports, Worcester v. the State of Georgia, 559; US Supreme Court 1978b: online; US Supreme Court 1978c: online; US Supreme Court 1896: online; US Supreme Court 1883: online; Miller 1993: 158–9).

Indian nations possess: "attributes of sovereignty over both their members and their territory", (US Supreme Court 1975: online), and "tribal sovereignty is dependent on, and subordinate to, only the Federal Government, not the States" (US Supreme Court 1980: online). Although tribes are no longer "possessed of the full attributes of sovereignty"; they remain a "separate people, with the power of regulating their internal and social relations" (US Supreme Court 1978c: online). The Supreme Court, for example, has long stated that tribal governments have the exclusive authority to define tribal citizenship and to make their own laws regarding internal matters, such as domestic relations, inheritance, and citizenship, and, "to enforce that law in their own forums" (US Supreme Court 1959b: online).

The Kingdom of Hawai'i, and the specific Hawai'i island chiefs before that Kingdom, exercised extensive sovereign powers. It is thus especially ironic that the United States does not recognise today an Indigenous Native Hawaiian government. However, approximately 229 Alaska Native tribes and villages are federally recognised Indigenous governments.

Treaties

One obvious way that the United States recognised the inherent political and sovereign existence of Indian nations was by engaging in treaty-making: "A treaty, including one between the United States and an Indian tribe, is essentially a contract between two sovereign nations" (US Supreme Court 1979: online). From its beginning, the United States recognised the autonomy of Indian nations, and treaty-making rested on the concept of Indian sovereignty. From 1778 to 1871, the United States entered 375 treaties with Indian governments and signed three treaties with the Kingdom of Hawai'i in 1826, 1849, and 1875[3] (there were no US/Alaska Native treaties). The Congress and the Executive Branch have been engaged in nearly continuous political interactions with Indian nations throughout American history and entered treaties and other agreements with them using the same procedures and respect as treaties conducted with foreign nations.

Yet at the same time the United States was respecting Indigenous sovereignty, it included in almost all Indian treaties a provision that limited Indian nations' international sovereignty and commercial rights. In these treaties, the tribes granted (if they were told what the English words meant) the United States "the sole and exclusive right of regulating the trade with the Indians, and managing all their affairs in such manner as [the United States] think proper". Furthermore, the tribes often acknowledged themselves, "to be under the protection of the United States and of no other sovereign whatsoever" (Miller 2006: 43, 48).

Criminal jurisdiction

American Indian governments also exercise sovereignty and power over their territories by enforcing criminal laws. Some courts have held that tribal governments have criminal jurisdiction over their own citizens even for actions which occur outside of reservations. Interestingly, in 1883, the US Supreme Court held that tribal governments had exclusive jurisdiction to prosecute Indian-on-Indian crime on reservations. Congress thereafter used its plenary power to create limited federal jurisdiction over some of these crimes in the Major Crimes Act of 1885. In 1968, Congress also affected tribal criminal jurisdiction by limiting the number of years and fines that tribal courts can impose (US Supreme Court 1883; 1978a: online).

In 1978, the Supreme Court held that tribal governments do not have criminal jurisdiction over non-Indians. In 2013, however, Congress took a tentative step to assist Indian governments in enforcing law and order by granting them criminal jurisdiction over non-Indians in domestic violence situations. In 2010, Congress also strengthened tribal ability to enforce criminal law (US Supreme Court 1978a: online; US Congress 2010: online; US Congress 2013: online).

Civil jurisdiction

Indigenous governments exercise extensive jurisdiction over civil matters within Indian country. Many American Indian tribes operate court systems and bureaucracies, and to varying degrees exercise adjudicatory, administrative, and regulatory authority. Tribes have the sovereign authority to regulate Indian and non-Indian civil conduct on reservations in many situations. Tribal nations can tax and regulate persons involved in on-reservation activities, and disputes arising on reservations involving Indians or non-Indians will often be decided in tribal courts. In fact, the Supreme Court has stated that tribal courts are often the exclusive forum for the adjudication of disputes affecting personal and property interests on reservations. The Court stated twice in the 1980s that tribal courts are the primary forum for the adjudication of civil issues arising on reservations and jurisdiction, "presumptively lies in the tribal courts" (US Supreme Court 1987: online) even when cases involve non-Indians. In more recent years, however, the Supreme Court has limited tribal court civil jurisdiction over non-Indians and especially when the activities at issue occur on non-Indian owned fee simple lands on a reservation.

Native Hawaiians cannot exercise civil authority because according to the United States they do not have a federally recognised government. Alaska Native governments, on the other hand, possess limited forms of civil jurisdiction even though the US Supreme Court has held that there is no (or very little) Indian country in Alaska (Supreme Court of Alaska 1999: online; US Supreme Court 1998: online).

Tribal Sovereign Immunity

As governments, tribal nations enjoy the same right of sovereign immunity as do state and federal governments. Consequently, Indian governments are immune from being sued in tribal, state, or federal courts. This immunity applies whether a tribe is acting in a governmental or business capacity and whether the activity at issue occurred on or off a reservation. And tribal governmental entities, whether created to perform governmental activities or purely commercial activities, usually also benefit from the protection of sovereign immunity. Congress or Indian governments can waive tribal sovereign immunity. Waivers, however, "cannot be implied but must be unequivocally expressed" (US Supreme Court 1976: online).

Since Native Hawaiians do not possess a governmental entity recognised by the United States, the principle of immunity does not apply to them. Alaska Native governments, however, do benefit from the protection of sovereign immunity (Supreme Court of Alaska 2004: online).

International law and American Indian sovereignty

Today, American Indian nations and Indigenous peoples around the world are increasingly looking to international law and the international system to help them protect their traditional governments and their human, sovereign, and diplomatic powers of self-government. Indigenous nations and advocates from around the world achieved a great accomplishment when the United Nations General Assembly adopted the Declaration on the Rights of Indigenous Peoples in September 2007. While the United States was one of only four countries to vote against the Declaration, it has since agreed to abide by the Declaration (Miller 2015).

The Declaration contains several provisions that address Indigenous sovereign rights. It states that Indigenous peoples should be allowed to freely determine their own political status and, "have the right to autonomy or self-government in matters relating to their internal and local affairs", and "the right to … their distinct political … institutions". But it seems evident that Indigenous nations cannot use the Declaration to argue for independence and separation from the countries they are currently aligned with because Article 46(1) states: "Nothing in this Declaration may be interpreted … or construed as authorizing or encouraging any action which would dismember or impair, totally or in part, the territorial integrity or political unity of sovereign and independent States" (United Nations 2007: online).

Indigenous nations in the Americas are also using the Organization of American States to defend their rights. The OAS Commission and Court of Human Rights have issued some surprising victories for Indigenous peoples in recent decades. In addition, in 1977, Inuit governments and communities located in several countries created the Inuit Circumpolar Council to assist them in their international efforts to protect their rights and sovereignty (2004).

Conclusion

In the US system of government, federal, state, and tribal governments all have various limitations on ultimate sovereign power. Indian nations have seen some of their historical, inherent powers expressly taken by Congress pursuant to its plenary power, have voluntarily given up others via their own treaties, and have lost yet others by implicit divestiture due to their incorporation into the territory of the United States. But my conclusion, based on 30 years of studying American Indian law and history, and based on my limited experience in international Indigenous affairs, is that American Indian nations and peoples exercise perhaps the highest level of Indigenous sovereignty in the world. To be clear, I am not an apologist for the colonial/settler society of the United States nor am I claiming it is some kind of model for how to treat Indigenous nations. In fact, even as I state this fairly positive opinion, I am painfully aware of the Indian law principles of plenary power and diminished tribal sovereignty, and even worse I am fully cognizant of the following statement of the United States Supreme Court from 1978:

> The sovereignty that the Indian tribes retain is of a unique and limited character. It exists only at the sufferance of Congress and is subject to complete defeasance. But until Congress acts, the tribes retain their existing sovereign powers. In sum, Indian tribes still possess those aspects of sovereignty not withdrawn by treaty or statute, or by implication as a necessary result of their dependent status.
>
> *(1978a: online)*

Indigenous nations located within the United States are obviously faced with a serious conundrum when the Supreme Court considers their inherent sovereignty to be nothing more than this. What is American Indian sovereignty if it is this tenuous?

We plainly cannot solve that conundrum in this short chapter.

Historically, Indian nations exercised nearly unfettered sovereignty and engaged in international affairs and diplomacy. But today Indian nations must contend with the United States, and the states to some extent, to exercise sovereign and governmental powers. In point of fact, Indian governments have dealt somewhat successfully with the United States and its colonial/settler society in the past six decades. Clearly, Indian governments and peoples must continue their struggle to protect and exercise their self-determination, governmental, and sovereign rights.

Notes

1 See Alfred (2005), 34, 38, 41–43; Ontai (2005), 153-54, 165; Case and Voluck (2002), 369.
2 I use the terms 'American Indians', 'Indians', 'Alaska Natives', and 'Native Hawaiians' to refer to the Indigenous nations and peoples located within the United States today.
3 See US Supreme Court 1979; Prucha 1994 2–4, 21, 59, 67, 72–3, 128; Treaty with Hawaii on Commerce, 21 December 1826, see Bevans 1971: 861; 9 Stat. 977; 19 Stat. 625.

References

Alfred, T. (2005). 'Sovereignty', in J. Barker (ed.) *Sovereignty Matters: Locations of Contestation and Possibility in Indigenous Struggles for Self-Determination*. University of Nebraska Press: Lincoln, NE, 34–43.

Anaya, S.J. (2004). 'International human rights and Indigenous peoples: The move toward the multicultural state', *Arizona Journal of International and Comparative Law*, vol. 21: 13–61.

Barbour, P.L. (ed.) (1969). *The Jamestown Voyages Under the First Charter, 1606–1609*, vol. II. Cambridge University Press: Cambridge.

Barrington, L. (ed.) (1999). *The Other Side of the Frontier: Economic Explorations into Native American History.* Westview Press: Boulder, CO.

Bevans, C.I. (1971). *Treaties and Other International Agreements of the United States, 1776–1949.* US Government Printing Office: Washington, DC.

Black, H.C. (1979). *Black's Law Dictionary,* 5th ed. West Publishing Co.: St Paul, MN.

Case, D.S. and Voluck, D.A. (2002). *Alaskan Natives and American Laws,* 2nd ed. University of Alaska Press: Fairbanks, AK.

Champagne, D. (1992). *Social Order and Political Change; Constitutional Governments Among the Cherokee, the Choctaw, The Chickasaw, and the Creek.* Stanford University Press: Stanford, CA.

Debo, A. (1967). *The Rise and Fall of the Choctaw Republic,* 2nd ed. University of Oklahoma Press: Norman, OK.

Debo, A. (1970). *A History of the Indians of the United States.* University of Oklahoma Press: Norman, OK.

Deloria, V.I. and DeMallie, R. (1999). *Documents of American Indian Diplomacy: Treaties, Agreements, and Conventions, 1775–1979.* University of Oklahoma Press: Norman. OK.

De Puy, H.F. (ed.) (1917, reprint 1999). *Bibliography of the English Colonial Treaties With the American Indians.* Syracuse University Press: Syracuse, NY.

Gibson, J.L. (1999). *Poverty Point: A Terminal Archaic Culture of the Lower Mississippi Valley,* 2nd ed. Department of Culture, Recreation and Tourism, Louisiana: Baton Rouge. Available: https://www.crt.state.la.us/dataprojects/archaeology/virtualbooks/POVERPOI/Popo.htm, accessed 12 May 2020.

Howard, J. (n.d.). *Hohokam Legacy: Desert Canals.* Available: http://www.waterhistory.org/histories/hohokam2/, accessed 9 May 2020.

Labaree, L.W. (ed.) (1961). *The Papers of Benjamin Franklin,* vol. 4. Yale University Press: New Haven, CT.

Laws of the Colonial and State Governments Relating to Indians and Indian Affairs, From 1633 to 1831 (1832, reprint 1978). *Inclusive.* E.M. Coleman: Standfordville, NY.

Llewellyn, K.N. and Hoebel, E.A. (1941). *The Cheyenne Way: Conflict and Case Law in Primitive Jurisprudence.* University of Oklahoma Press: Norman, OK.

MacKenzie, M.K., Serrano, S.K., and Sproat, D.K. (eds.) (2015). *Native Hawaiian Law: A Treatise.* Kamehameha Publishing: Honolulu, HI.

Mann, C.C. (2005). *1491: New Revelations of the Americas Before Columbus.* Knopf: New York.

Merriam-Webster. (1985). *Webster's Ninth New Collegiate Dictionary.* Merriam-Webster: Springfield, MA.

Miller, R.J. (1993). 'American Indian influence on the United States constitution and its framers', *American Indian Law Review,* vol. 18, no. 1: 133–160.

Miller, R.J. (2006). *Native America, Discovered and Conquered: Thomas Jefferson, Lewis & Clark, and Manifest Destiny.* Praeger Press: Westport, CT.

Miller, R.J. (2012). *Reservation "Capitalism": Economic Development in Indian Country.* University of Nebraska Press: Lincoln, NE.

Miller, R.J. (2015). 'Consultation or consent: The United States' duty to confer with American Indian governments', *North Dakota Law Review,* vol. 91: 67–86.

Miller, R.J. (2017a). 'Tribal, federal, and state laws impacting the Eastern Shawnee tribe, 1812 to 1945', in S. Warren (ed.) *The Eastern Shawnee Tribe of Oklahoma: Resilience Through Adversity.* University of Oklahoma Press: Norman, OK, 149–170.

Miller, R.J. (2017b). 'Treaties between the Eastern Shawnee tribe and the United States: Contracts between sovereign governments', in S. Warren (ed.) *The Eastern Shawnee Tribe of Oklahoma: Resilience Through Adversity.* University of Oklahoma Press: Norman, OK, 107–148.

Morgan, E.S. (1975). *American Slavery, American Freedom: The Ordeal of Colonial Virginia.* W.W. Norton & Company: New York.

National Park Service. (2017). *Pueblo Bonito.* Available: https://www.nps.gov/chcu/planyourvisit/pueblo-bonito.htm, accessed 9 May 2020.

Newton, N.J., Cohen, F., and Anderson, R. (2012). *Cohen's Handbook of Federal Indian Law.* LexisNexis: San Francisco, CA.

Ohio History Central. (n.d.). *Hopewell Culture.* Available: http://www.ohiohistorycentral.org/w/Hopewell_Culture, accessed 9 May 2020.

Ontai, K.K.N.P. (2005). 'A spiritual definition of sovereignty from a Kanaka Maoli perspective', in J. Barker (ed.) *Sovereignty Matters: Locations of Contestation and Possibility in Indigenous Struggles for Self-Determination.* University of Nebraska Press: Lincoln, NE, 153–168.

Parent, A.S. Jr. (2003). *Foul Means: The Formation of a Slave Society in Virginia, 1660–1740.* Published for the Omohundro Institute of Early American History and Culture by the University of North Carolina Press: London.

Prucha, F.P. (1994). *American Indian Treaties: The History of a Political Anomaly*. University of California Press: Berkeley, CA.

Shaffer, L.N. (1992). *Native Americans Before 1492: The Moundbuilding Centers of the Eastern Woodlands*. M.E. Sharp: New York.

Speck, F.G. (1945). *The Iroquois, A Study in Cultural Evolution*. Cranbrook Institute of Science: Bloomfield Hills, MI.

Strickland, R. (1975). *Fire and the Spirits: Cherokee Law from Clan to Court*. University of Oklahoma Press: Norman, OK.

Strutin, M. (1994). *Chaco: A Cultural Legacy*. Western National Parks Association: Tucson, AZ.

Sturtevant, W.C. and Trigger, B. (eds.) (1978). *Smithsonian Institute: Handbook of North American Indians (Northeast)*. Smithsonian Institute: Washington, DC.

Supreme Court of Alaska. (1999). *John v. Baker*, 982 P.2d 738. Available: https://scholar.google.co.nz/scholar_case?case=3062071990546746245&q=John+v.+Baker,+982&hl=en&as_sdt=2006&as_vis=1, accessed 11 May 2020.

Supreme Court of Alaska. (2004). *Runyon v. Association of Village Council Presidents*, 84 P.2d 437. Available: https://www.casemine.com/judgement/us/591477feadd7b049343dd732, accessed 11 May 2020.

Treaty with the Delawares. (1778). September 17, 7 Stat. 13. Available: https://www.washington.edu/uwired/outreach/cspn/Website/Classroom%20Materials/Curriculum%20Packets/Treaties%20&%20Reservations/Documents/Treaty_with_Delawares_1778.pdf, accessed 9 May 2020.

United Nations. (2007). *Declaration on the Rights of Indigenous Peoples*. Available: https://www.un.org/development/desa/indigenouspeoples/declaration-on-the-rights-of-indigenous-peoples.html, accessed 11 May 2020.

US Congress. (1988). *Iroquois Confederacy and Indian Nations—Recognizing Contributions to the United States, Concurrent Resolution*, 21 October. Available: https://www.govtrack.us/congress/bills/100/hconres331/text, accessed 12 May 2020.

US Congress. (2010). *Tribal Law and Order Act*, 124 Stat. Available: https://www.congress.gov/111/plaws/publ211/PLAW-111publ211.htm, accessed 10 May 2020.

US Congress. (2013). *Violence Against Women Reauthorization Act*, 127 Stat. Available: https://www.congress.gov/113/plaws/publ4/PLAW-113publ4.htm, accessed 10 May 2020.

US Constitution. Article I, Section 8, cl. 3. Available: https://constitution.congress.gov/browse/article-1/section-8/clause-3/, accessed 10 May 2020.

US Constitution. Article VI, cl. 2. Available: https://www.govinfo.gov/content/pkg/GPO-CONAN-1992/pdf/GPO-CONAN-1992–9-7.pdf, accessed 12 May 2020.

US Constitution. Amendment XIV. Available: https://www.law.cornell.edu/constitution/amendmentxiv, accessed 10 May 2020.

US Reports. (1831). *Cherokee Nation v. Georgia*. Available: https://www.loc.gov/item/usrep030001/, accessed 10 May 2020.

US Reports. (1832). *Worcester v. the State of Georgia, 31 U.S. (6 Pet.)*. Available: https://www.loc.gov/item/usrep031515/, accessed 10 May 2020.

US Supreme Court. (1823). *Johnson v. M'Intosh, 21 U.S. (8 Wheat)*. Available: https://supreme.justia.com/cases/federal/us/21/543/, accessed 9 May 2020.

US Supreme Court. (1883). *Ex Parte Crow Dog, 109 U.S.* Available: https://supreme.justia.com/cases/federal/us/109/556/, accessed 10 May 2020.

US Supreme Court. (1886). *United States v. Kagama, 118 U.S. 375*. Available: https://supreme.justia.com/cases/federal/us/118/375/, accessed 12 May 2020.

US Supreme Court. (1896). *Talton v. Mayes, 163 U.S.* Available: https://supreme.justia.com/cases/federal/us/163/376/, accessed 10 May 2020.

US Supreme Court. (1942). *Seminole Nation v. United States, 316 U.S.* Available: https://supreme.justia.com/cases/federal/us/316/286/, accessed 10 May 2020.

US Supreme Court. (1955). *Tee-Hit-Ton Indians v. United States, 348 U.S.* Available: https://supreme.justia.com/cases/federal/us/348/272/, accessed 9 May 2020.

US Supreme Court. (1959a). *Tlingit and Haida Indians of Alaska v. United States*, 147 Ct. Cl. 315, 177 F.Supp.452. Available: https://law.justia.com/cases/federal/appellate-courts/F2/389/778/426387/, accessed 9 May 2020.

U.S. Supreme Court. (1959b). *Williams v. Lee, 358 U.S. 217*. Available: https://supreme.justia.com/cases/federal/us/358/217/, accessed 12 May 2020.

US Supreme Court. (1975). *United States v. Mazurie, 419 U.S.*. Available: https://supreme.justia.com/cases/federal/us/419/544/, accessed 10 May 2020.

US Supreme Court. (1976). *United States v. Testan, 424 U.S. 392, 399.* Available: https://supreme.justia.com/cases/federal/us/424/392/, accessed 12 May 2020.

US Supreme Court. (1978a). *Oliphant v. Suquamish Indian Tribe, 435 U.S.* Available: https://supreme.justia.com/cases/federal/us/435/191/, accessed 9 May 2020.

US Supreme Court. (1978b). *United States v. Wheeler, 435 U.S.* Available: https://supreme.justia.com/cases/federal/us/435/313/, accessed 10 May 2020.

US Supreme Court. (1978c). *Santa Clara Pueblo v. Martinez, 436 U.S.* Available: https://supreme.justia.com/cases/federal/us/436/49/, accessed 10 May 2020.

US Supreme Court. (1979). *Washington v. Washington Commercial Passenger Fishing Vessel Association, 443 U.S. 658.* Available: https://supreme.justia.com/cases/federal/us/443/658/, accessed 12 May 2020.

US Supreme Court. (1980). *Washington v. Confederated Tribes of the Colville Indian Reservation, 447 U.S. 134, 154.* Available: https://supreme.justia.com/cases/federal/us/447/134/, accessed 12 May 2020.

US Supreme Court. (1982). *Merrion v. Jicarilla Apache Tribe, 455 U.S. 130.* Available: https://supreme.justia.com/cases/federal/us/455/130/, accessed 12 May 2020.

US Supreme Court. (1987). *Iowa Mutual Insurance Company v. LaPlante, 480 U.S. 9.* Available: https://supreme.justia.com/cases/federal/us/480/9/, accessed 12 May 2020.

US Supreme Court. (1989). *Cotton Petroleum Corp. v. New Mexico, 490 U.S. 163.* Available: https://supreme.justia.com/cases/federal/us/490/163/, accessed 12 May 2020.

US Supreme Court. (1998). *Alaska v. Native Village of Venetie Tribal Government, 522 U.S. 520.* Available: https://supreme.justia.com/cases/federal/us/522/520/, accessed 11 May 2020.

Van Doren, C. and Boyd, J.P. (eds.) (1938). *Indian Treaties Printed by Benjamin Franklin, 1736–1762.* Historical Society of Pennsylvania: Philadelphia, PA.

Part 4

Political economies, ecologies, and technologies

Part editor: Steve Larkin

27

A story about the time we had a global pandemic and how it affected my life and work as a critical Indigenous scholar

Linda Tuhiwai Smith

A story begins to form

I write in the time of COVID-19, a novel coronavirus that began its life within humans in the city of Wuhan in China in 2019. It is now the end of April 2020. The virus has successfully shut down much of the world's economies, challenged the world's leaders and found many of them wanting in terms of their grasp of knowledge, compassion and leadership. It has grounded fleets of aircrafts, stranded cruise ships, cancelled concerts and confined millions of people to home. The virus has been lethal for those who are old, who are black, brown, and already vulnerable with chronic health conditions. It has flourished in those social contexts where humans interact such as care homes, group activities and special events, able to spread its infection with maximum efficiency. It has overwhelmed the best public health systems in the world and at the same time made heroes and heroines of the genuine experts of this disease and the front line health workers who care for the sick under the worst of circumstances. This virus knows no borders as, according to the latest theories, having passed from one species to an intermediary host and then to humans and effectively snaked itself through thin air to infect and kill. Each day I watch as numbers tell a story of destruction, death, and more dead bodies than a country can bury in a day. Who would have thought the simple beauty of a curved line would engender so much hope? Or, that the sight of First World health systems flailing through lack of equipment, resources, and space would cause so much alarm?

What does it mean to be a critical Indigenous scholar in such a time? And, how do our analytical frameworks and intellectual legacies apply to this unfolding world disaster? What are we seeing and how are we making sense of this situation? Are we in the story or, like before, do we have to find our own story? This chapter attempts to respond to these questions in the moment of living through a worldwide crisis. It is told in a series of stories, commentaries and reflections emerging as we are locked down in Aotearoa New Zealand.

A second story forms closer to home

These questions swirl in my mind as my husband and I exist in isolation, locked down under a four-week state of emergency in Aotearoa New Zealand. I am not in my home territory but am safely hosted by one of my husband's hapū and iwi. I am not near my 93-year-old father or my grandchildren. My personal sense of home is heightened. One of my iwi, like several others, has established checkpoints to ensure the safety of our people from outsiders carrying the virus into our vulnerable communities. Some of our Aborigine cousins were doing the same thing and calling it a biosecurity measure. All our iwi have wrapped support around our elders to provide them with care packages and ensure they have food and support. We know how vulnerable our people are and how poor our health system is at taking care of us. An aunt dies during this time and we are unable to grieve for her or hold our tangihanga so those of us in town stand along the road that the hearse takes to farewell a loved aunt as she is escorted by one of her sons driving behind on his motorbike, a solitary procession of one. They are taking her home to a place on a hill overlooking the Whangaehu River. We know that they can dig the grave but how can two of them bury her? We feel sad and helpless. I venture out to shop for groceries, dashing in for essential supplies and then retreating to the virus-free safety of home. I have a home. I have food security. I have support.

The story I told at the beginning of this chapter is a partial account. It is not an Indigenous story. It is not our story yet. In the strange ways that colonialism works, however, we constantly find ourselves living inside someone else's story. Indigenous peoples, peoples of colour, LGBTQI, disabled, homeless and refugee communities who were vulnerable before the outbreak, are completely erased in this discourse of global catastrophe. I scan different Indigenous news outlets to find that the Navajo Nation has its own serious outbreak of Covid-19. I read what my Māori health colleagues are saying about their deep concerns for the potential burden that Māori will experience in any pandemic. I listen to global leaders talk their big talk as if numbers tell the entire story, the truth. I listen to our Prime Minister express compassion and ask for kindness but still using a narrative that assumes we all hear and understand her message in the same way, like we can tune into the national narrative. And, we can, but what we take from it, based on our histories is, 'Māori, you are on your own'. Our people have been here before. This is a story we know because we lived it before, we died from it, we survived it and we are here.

Let's return to the first story

Let me pause and return to my first attempt to write the story and re-analyse the narrative that I constructed at the beginning of the chapter.

I write in the time of COVID-19, a novel corona virus that began its life within humans in the city of Wuhan in China in 2019. It is now the end of April 2020 [Who gets to name it? How is this pandemic worse than the one our Peoples have experienced before? Is this the starting point of our story? Is this the pivotal moment of our existence?]. *The virus has successfully shut down much of the world's economies* [You mean the economies that exclude and exploit IPs?], *challenged the world's leaders* [... of nation states, settler colonial states and former empires?] *and found many of them wanting in terms of their grasp of knowledge, compassion, and leadership* [Their knowledge and compassion for Indigenous peoples has always been absent and in some countries is hostile]. *It has grounded fleets of aircrafts, stranded cruise ships* [This sounds eerily familiar to how epidemics first arrived], *cancelled concerts and confined millions of people to home* [assuming they have homes]. *The virus has been lethal for those who are old, black, brown, and already vulnerable with chronic health conditions* [How many Indigenous communities enjoy good health anyway? Our peoples live with multiple co-morbidities, heart, lungs, diabetes and simply being Indigenous]. *It has enjoyed those social contexts where humans interact such as care homes, group activities and special events able to spread its infection with maximum efficiency* [Including Indigenous ceremonies and gatherings]. *It has overwhelmed the best public health systems in the world* [The systems that have been proven to be inequitable and racist?] *and at the same time made heroes and heroines of the genuine experts of this disease and the front line health workers who care for the sick under the worst of circumstances* [Many of whom are black, brown and immigrants]. *This virus knows no borders having passed from one species to an intermediary host and then to humans and effectively snaked itself through thin air to infect and kill. Each day I watch as numbers tell a story of destruction, death, and more dead bodies than a country can bury in a day* [Whose stories are in these numbers? What are the numbers not telling us? What are the Indigenous numbers?]. *Who would have thought the simple beauty of a curved line would engender so much hope? Or, that the sight of First World health systems flailing through lack of equipment, resources, and space would cause so much alarm* [Whose lives and deaths are hidden within the curve? Is that not how we already know the health system?].

Certain personal and contextual realities complicate this story further. The pandemic has been on the move creeping stealthily across geopolitical zones since late 2019. Our local Chinese restaurants felt the impact early as if every Chinese restaurant owner has just flown in from Wuhan the city identified as the source of the virus. Racism rears its head early in the narrating of the story. In mid-February I flew to Germany and then to the United States with my stock of hand sanitiser and face masks. I was in fact more stressed about flying to the United States as its hostility to international travellers has become more overt and entrenched at its borders. I arrived home at the end of February with no signs of ill health. In early March I flew north to Kaitaia for a research hui on Domestic Violence and then south west to New Plymouth for the same reason. Precautions were already in place and our hosts had changed their welcoming protocols to a 'no hōngi, no touch' welcome. Our Faculty of Māori and Indigenous Studies held a meeting to discuss the suspension of cultural protocols in response to the virus. The situation was already surreal. A week later my daughter calls and tells me in no uncertain terms to pack my bags and head for our home base in Whanganui and go into self-isolation that day. She calls her father who works in another city to say the same thing. Rather bluntly, she said, 'you're old, you have asthma, you need to go into isolation now!' The list to her father was somewhat more brutal. We listened to our daughter. It gave us a head start as one week later on 26 March New Zealand was in lockdown and our borders closed to non-citizens. We are told by our Prime Minister, Jacinda Ardern, to 'stay home, save lives and be kind'.

The story is reframed

The words 'pandemic' and 'epidemic' raise anxieties in many Indigenous communities across the world. Wave after wave of epidemics introduced to Indigenous populations by Europeans decimated communities. Remember that early Europeans were not that clean themselves, they did not have either the medical or public health knowledge that now exists, but did have greater natural immunity to diseases such as measles and chicken pox. Māori deaths were put down to our weakness as a race which neatly feeds into the narratives of race, of social Darwinism, natural selection and the survival of the fittest species. Disease itself was used as a biological tool of colonisation through actions such as the deliberate infection of blankets, poisoning of flour and gifts. Dis-ease alongside displacement were consequences of this massive disruption.

In Aotearoa, we have mass graves in some of our cemeteries from the 1918 Influenza Pandemic. According to my father, people died so quickly they were buried hurriedly where they died, by whoever was able to dig a grave, and their remains were transferred later into a cemetery. Our death rates during that pandemic added to the trauma caused by the participation of our men and women in World War I. The pandemic arrived in New Zealand near Armistice Day, November 1918. Māori died from influenza at seven times the rate of non-Māori.(Collier 1974) Those events occurred 11 years after the passing of the Tohunga Suppression Act 1907 which prevented Māori from seeking traditional knowledge and health advice, and just over 50 years after the New Zealand Settlement Act 1863 that confiscated many of our lands. All these events are in the living memory of our communities. One of my grandmothers was born in the 1880s and the other around 1900. These stories are not in the distant past but were conveyed through stories and memories to the next generations. My grandmother, for example, recounted a number of stories about the terrible impact of the Influenza pandemic on our communities. More importantly she also reinforced the practices that emerged from the pandemic from being obsessive about cleanliness and fresh air to being anxious about those of her grandchildren who were considered sickly. I was one such grandchild and my grandmother played a huge part in my childhood both caring and 'spoiling' me, having me sleep with her whenever I visited so she could watch over me right up to when I married. This story of the 1918 pandemic and its devastating impact is echoed in most other Indigenous contexts, decimating communities often left to suffer out of sight and out of mind (Brady and Bahr 2014). However, inside that story are also stories of survivance and creative responses, for example the creation of the jingle dress as a healing strategy of the Ojibway peoples in Wisconsin, Minnesota, and Ontario (Paul 2011).

Perhaps a critical Indigenous perspective can best tell the Indigenous story of Covid-19 by framing it within a different set of relationships, memories, discourses, and reference points; in other words different ontologies and epistemologies. Perhaps it needs to be narrated while bearing in mind the trauma of those memories and understanding that stories can trigger grief and anxiety and, as well, they can trigger resiliency, tenacity and the compassion of our ancestors. Perhaps it needs to be relayed in ways that reach, connect with and activate the survival strategies of our own communities?

The COVID-19 pandemic seemed to bear down upon the globe like a tsunami broiling under the ocean and rolling across the earth overwhelming cities like New York and countries like Italy. The global news that dominates our television is mostly about Europe, the United Kingdom and the United States as if the rest of the world doesn't count, which is not surprising as they mostly don't count. Different Indigenous colleagues take to social media, others come together to create an alternative source of health messaging while almost everyone is trying to grapple with online teaching and their own personal health and well-being. Our community-based activists, leaders, and social services also organise and implement support systems, care packages and food delivery for those vulnerable and in need. I appreciated Ojibway scholar Megan Bang's early intervention in reframing the public health message from social distancing to 'physical distancing and social connectivity' that resonated with Indigenous communities but also with those who understand the impact of social isolation.

Public health messaging in many countries identified mental health as an issue associated with being forced into isolation. Indigenous scholars quickly identified other issues of equal importance such as health equity, food security, shelter, and domestic violence as significant concerns. This list was expanded as events and policies unfolded to include education and digital equity, economic hardship and unemployment, and the broader issue of lack of inclusion of Māori in decision making. Most scholars were paying attention to their own communities such as Vicente Diaz and Christine DeLisle who were monitoring and speaking out about the impact of a US naval ship with hundreds of COVID-19 positive crew landing on a Pacific Island of Guam while living in Minnesota. Their role and that of other scholars was to provide intellectual resources, data, messages and monitoring reports for those activists on the ground even though they might be thousands of miles away. Pacific Island nations had been identified, at least by New Zealand and Australia, as one of the most vulnerable regions on earth due to their isolation and, by definition, their vulnerability to a wide range of things from hurricanes and tsunamis to reliance on imports of some foods and lack of access to strong public health systems, hospitals let alone ventilators. Parts of the Pacific were just recovering from a devastating measles epidemic in 2019.

Different international news outlets were identifying bodies on the streets of Ecuador, over-flowing morgues in Italy, freezers full of bodies and a huge mass-grave in New York. It seemed foreboding. The rising toll of deaths across the world were heightening the sense of an uncontrollable threat to humanity. Through April the global news was increasingly apocalyptic but there was a great silence on the impact on Indigenous peoples. While thinking about what this meant, Māori scholar, Kiri Dell, and her network of other young Indigenous scholars 'KIN Knowledge in Indigenous Network' invited me to give a webinar alongside other scholars such as Bonnie Duran, Michael Yellowbird, Ganesh Nana, Dara Kelly, Rereata Makiha, Mariaelana Huambachano and Gregory Cajete in a series designed to shift the discourse. I titled my talk 'Not our Apocalypse' having already formed some ways of framing this pandemic (Smith 2020).

Memories of scarcity and survival and the secret Easter Bunny of Durie Hill

Early in our isolation, my husband shared memories of growing up poor with a single mother and four siblings. This period in his childhood has had a profound impact as it includes being sent to live with an Uncle and Aunt as one strategy for his family to survive. The experience did not go well. His foster parents were loving but his homesickness made him very unwell and ended with his mother coming to fetch him back. In our isolation he worries about the children whose families are entering lockdown with limited resources and remembers his Uncles dropping off small treats to him and his siblings when he was young. He decides that we must start buying Easter eggs and chocolates to distribute on Easter Sunday to the children of our iwi who live on Durie Hill. While others are buying enormous amounts of toilet paper, emptying shelves in supermarkets, I am sent to purchase Easter eggs. Graham becomes the secret Easter Bunny of Durie Hill. Of course, that is not his only memory; he also reminisces about his grandmother's garden, which was filled with rōngoa or medicines as well as food and his family's constant foraging for food from creeks, local farms and orchards. When Graham tells these stories, they are always hilarious and poignant but are filled with examples of him and his brothers being resourceful, innovative and willing to walk miles to get work in order to pay for food. Somehow the Easter eggs become large bags of treats for children. The New Zealand Prime Minister announced in her daily briefing on COVID-19 that the Easter Bunny was an 'essential service' permitted to operate on Easter Sunday. This just emboldened the Secret Bunny of Durie Hill to look for more Easter eggs. The pandemic and the response of being locked down triggers powerful memories of survival and resurgence, of important values and practices, sacrifices and stories that kept his whānau together.

For me, in this time, I am not located in my home where I work or in any of my own iwi or tribal territories. I am not surrounded by my own whānau or iwi. It has compelled me to be more proactive on social media to keep in touch with my whānau and events. One night I worked out that if I stood at the top of one of my mountains Hikurangi I would be about two mountain ranges away from where I am being sheltered by my husband's mountain of Ruapehu from which the Whanganui River flows to the sea. My emotional geography was set for me by my grandmother not only while we sat on her veranda in the morning sun but in all her teachings about my identity. At this moment, however, my mountains, from my different iwi whakapapa, represent a powerful sense of home, of being sheltered and connected. They provide symbolic, spiritual and material points of orientation such as where to turn to (for me it's the East), where to look (to the East) and where to be reassured when away from home (from your maunga because it rises tall and magnificent and will never move). Mountains and rivers, lakes, and seas help us find ourselves.

Hikurangi

Yearning for Home
From afar
Haunted by images of a world
In crisis
stalked by a virus
That consumes the breath of life
Seeking the strength
Of our mountain
Hikurangi
In my body
As it stands unwavering
embracing our valleys
Our coastline
Our people
Hikurangi
Look further
This day
Across the Raukumara
Beyond the Ruahine
Turn your sights
Into the sheltering
Reach of Ruapehu
Follow the Whanganui
To find me
And tell me about
My ancestors
So I can feel
Safe and loved
Linda

(PS: by car this journey takes about nine hours or longer if you stop for a break)

I notice that other colleagues have talked on social media about having vivid dreams and anxieties about the pandemic, online teaching, working from home and missing loved ones. Some carry heavy responsibilities for their own families. Many are worried about their elders. In text messages three days apart, two different senior Indigenous women reach out to tell me they had been stood down from leadership roles under the guise of a crisis during an era of supposed reconciliation but when they are in isolation. In Arizona, Diné scholar Amanda Tachine invites a number of us to contribute to a love/healing syllabus to help people during this time. The podcast, 'All my relations' with Swinomish and Tulalip visual storyteller Matika Wilbur and Cherokee scholar Adrienne Keene, broadcasts a new bonus episode called 'All our (Socially Distanced) Relations' that discusses COVID-19 impacts on Tribal nations (Wilbur and Keene 2020). In Australia, Amy McQuire podcast addresses, 'How Indigenous communities got in front of the pandemic' and there is steady news through IndigenousX, an independent Indigenous Media organisation (McQuire 2020; IndigenousX 2020). Kris Rallah-Baker, a Yuggera/Warangu medical doctor who is one of the commentators for IndigenousX wrote "[w]e live in dangerous times, not unprecedented times" (Rallah-Baker 2020: online). A number of

Māori religious and spiritual groups also start using social media to reach their communities. A colleague contacts me about reworking a project on food sovereignty that I had proposed to our iwi authority two years ago. At the time, it seemed too abstract an idea but now it is real and too late, at least for this moment. Leonie Pihama, Graham Smith and I begin a series of webinars discussing Kaupapa Māori Theory and Research (Pihama, Smith, Smith, and Paul 2020) I also connect with colleagues in Arizona, Chicago, and Hawai'i to talk about our shared interest in Indigenous futurities but our talk quickly turns to this moment in time.

Somehow the opportunities of staying home, being fixed in place, helps energise some of us to connect, to reach out and do things we never had the time to do before. COVID-19 presents different opportunities to do different kinds of work, to collaborate and co-design, to reflect and innovate, to think critically about the present moment. We are also witnessing, observing, and thinking through the impact of COVID-19 on our children and families, communities, colleagues, students, and friends. And, we are experiencing ourselves what these changes feel like, what it means at a personal level and what it means to be more responsible for taking care of our own safety and well-being.

However, this is not the time to tell a neat story. There is no singular narrative. Its messy, personal, poignant, disturbing, uplifting and downright exhausting if you open yourself to the full onslaught of commentaries of a global pandemic.

The story unfolds further from the collapse of capitalism to economies of love

The devastating economic implications of shutting down a country and its economy also start to be narrated in mainstream media. It is narrated in alarmist terms on the one hand and hopeful possibilities on the other; as an economic collapse not seen since the Great Depression of the 1930s and one that may cause a major rethink about capitalism as we know it. The Depression came just over a decade after World War I and the Influenza Pandemic but our people were already mostly materially impoverished, mostly landless, and traumatised. What lands still in Māori ownership had been fragmented over a 70-year period through the work of the Native/Māori Land Court. As a people, Māori were already economically depressed, sick, and worn down.

These coloniser notions of what defines a moment of history and how they are framed continually envelop us in this whitened dystopia. Economic collapse as dramatic as the Great Depression was, is not our story either; at least not in the way it is being narrated. The dire predictions of the collapse certainly causes animated discussions at home and online with other scholars and activists. Our decolonising experiences should remind us that systems as deep as capitalism do not melt into the ether, roll over and die spontaneously or disappear in a puff of smoke. They continue to haunt political, legal, financial, social, creative and discursive systems for generations. They are mostly co-opted and corrupted even further after revolutions and land reforms, which reward the victors.

The second talk in the KIN Network webinar by economist Ganesh Nana is titled 'Capitalism – useless in any crisis' (Nana 2020) Nana provides a clear analysis of capitalism's flaws and contrasts that with a more sustainable Indigenous economic model. Like the talk of a pandemic, talk of economic collapse plays out in our communities in a marinade of remembering, anxiety, outrage, internal conflict, hope, and pragmatism. Much of what counts as our tribal economies are structured by Treaty of Waitangi Settlements within neo-liberal capitalism although people have cultural knowledge about Indigenous economic concepts and aspire to practise Māori values. Our peoples are trapped in the way labour markets have structured precarious employment.

The online discussions hint at a hope that things will have to change as unemployment and food poverty rates begin to soar. The task at hand is to feed our people, keep our elders and vulnerable people safe and well. The task at hand is to focus on the basics, on what is urgent. I think a discussion about capitalism is basic and urgent to the point of overdue but buying Easter eggs seems somehow more immediate in terms of bringing joy and smiles to our mokopuna.

Dara Kelly, a First Nations scholar followed Ganesh Nana's talk with her own entitled 'Economies of Affection' in which she addresses Indigenous economic models, values and practices (Kelly 2020). It seems these threads of work are forming among our colleagues that build on notions of a syllabus of love and healing and economies of affection, reciprocity and ceremony. In a different network I observe our colleagues working in Indigenous food systems providing practical advice and seeds where they have them that support people to grow and cook Indigenous food. Food security has quickly become an issue for families with no and low incomes and communities are having to work together to provide both food packages and food knowledge to give people confidence to grow their own food. Food is health, food is survival, and food knowledge is the basis of food sovereignty.

At the same time, different Indigenous networks and groups are forming to provide Indigenous focussed information and speak back to the 'one size fits all' messages from public health, education and business. A Māori Pandemic Response Group of Māori health specialists, Te Rōpū Whakakaupapa Uruta is formed to provide specific COVID-19 advice for Māori whānau (2020). In other contexts similar resource networks to support Indigenous communities are formed, for example the American Indian COVID-19 Resources and Responses network (American Indian COVID-19 2020). Indigenous media plays a powerful role in shining spotlights on issues that people and community are facing. The way mainstream and conservative media frame community-based check points as illegal acts is contrasted in Māori media as ways communities are protecting their vulnerable communities. Similarly, in Australia, some Aboriginal communities have established 'biosecurity check points' to stop biohazards entering their world and other Native tribes and communities have defended their right to close access to their communities. The struggle over discourse and the way our stories are being told is really important to provide space for our stories to have life and to be told.

The political life of numbers and how numbers are used to support dominant narratives

Pandemics are generally defined as outbreaks of disease that occur across a wide area, across continents, and the world. Numbers are employed very powerfully by politicians, public health specialists and the media to tell the COVID-19 story. There is a daily count on most newscasts provided by reputable institutions such as Johns Hopkins University and the World Health Organisation as well as government agencies. The rising count is strangely compelling. The vocabulary and metaphors of war enhance the idea that we are living in a thriller and even if at home we are playing a significant role as a lifesaver. The cast of characters is typically white male authorities while frontline women workers inhabit gowns and masks rendering them as masked and ghostly heroines. The numbers consist of a range of indicators; the global numbers that have tested positive for COVID-19; the country numbers who have tested positive; the numbers in hospital in a country or state; the numbers who have died globally and by country or city. In New Zealand they also count the number of clusters who have been infected through the same event or place and the number of probable cases who live in the same household of the confirmed case. Different statistical models were developed to model scenarios of how rapidly the virus will spread and how long it will take to peak and then flatten out. The flattening out is termed 'the curve' and the clearest story of the curve is told in daily briefings by the governor of New York State.

Numbers are being used to tell a story; a story about how rapidly the virus is spreading, how dangerous it is and how important it is to listen to public health messages. The numbers however are narrating the same story as the words. They are formed on the same assumptions as driven by the same ideas, priorities and conceptual and discursive strategies. It is clearly difficult and frustrating for many people, including political leaders, to accept that there is no current magic cure or treatment other than behavioural treatments of keeping people at home and physically distant from each other. This is why the basic health message has been about physical distancing and staying home. Numbers have been used effectively to get this message across by drawing attention to how dangerous it is 'out there'. It has worked in many contexts despite some world leaders demonstrating a complete lack of respect for any form of objective information and lack of compassion for the people who are each represented symbolically and in an embodied form by these numbers.

But what do any of these numbers stand for? At one level we are led to believe that the numbers stand for victims and that they represent a kind of objective truth. A truth about COVID-19 that is stable across the world and is equally meaningful across contexts. Sadly, that is not the truth of the story. The story of numbers in COVID-19 has been intensely political in that it speaks to issues of power and to the kinds of societies that produce these numbers and the governments charged with collecting them. Countries collect data using quite different priorities, systems, and categories. Countries have vastly different public health systems. Some countries have not counted people who died at home, in residential care facilities or somewhere else away from a hospital. Some people died before they could be counted. China has revised its total count a number of times. These differences are exacerbated by a lack of transparency, and by a complete disregard for numbers or science knowledge by one or two of the world's most powerful leaders.

Equally important for Indigenous peoples in this discussion is that countries have different ways to categorise peoples of colour including Indigenous peoples. Some countries refuse to acknowledge and/or count Indigenous peoples in their official statistics. Other counties categorise them as 'other' or lump them in with categories such as 'Asian Pacific'. And others like New Zealand, which ought to have counted Māori from the start, had to be challenged to do so reinforcing the idea that in a crisis everything gets set on 'default' and the default setting excludes us. For these reasons and more, Māori and Indigenous health and tribal organisations have moved to collect their own data. From monitoring Indigenous Media such as Indian Country Today it emerges that the Navajo Nation has experienced significant cases of COVID-19 with over 1,400 cases by April and 44 deaths. There are also other cases where the Indian Health Service is struggling to equip its staff with protective gear and calls are made through social media for donations for masks and protective gear for different nations and organisations. In Brazil, where the President refuses to recognise the pandemic, case numbers are rising rapidly threatening the existence of tribes in the Amazon. Across the world, the risks for Indigenous peoples are ominous as various governments that refuse to act, fail to act quickly, fail to deliver resources and fail to exercise compassion. In a pandemic with an overwhelmed system, the room for errors in counting are high. We may never know the full count and we can be sure some Indigenous bodies will never be counted or accounted for (Nelson 2015).

From the start, COVID-19 was identified as a virus that was extremely harmful to old people and those with pre-existing health issues. In New Zealand, elders were defined as someone over 70 years. It took strong intervention from Māori health specialists and Aboriginal health specialists in Australia to identify that people from our communities who were over 60 fell into the same category. The difference in mortality rates and morbidity levels between white Australians and Pākehā New Zealanders, and Indigenous people, mean that our populations are all vulnerable. It took weeks to identify that many who died from COVID-19 in the United Kingdom and the United States were Black and that many of the health workforce who died were also migrants who have been the focus of virulent anti-immigration discourses. The British Prime Minister, Boris Johnson, who was admitted to hospital for COVID-19 acknowledged two intensive-care nurses who helped save his life as, "Jenny from New Zealand and Luis Pitarma from Portugal" (Independent 2020: online) both of whom were obviously highly skilled migrant workers. It was already clear from the outbreak in China that numbers were and are controlled by systems of power, primarily by governments and political leaders and also by public health and science experts. In the management of the pandemic both numbers and words have been deployed to narrate the story. They have been used to define the crisis and frame how it is understood, they have drawn attention to and shifted attention away, they have created and confirmed categories of Other, and they have reinforced, if not enhanced, social inequities. The power of the narration is that ordinary members of the public have been immersed in the story and taken ownership of its messages. The story's official legitimacy, aided by a government with emergency powers, harnesses the public in ways that foster compliance while masking inequities.

The missed opportunity of public education and the healing role of Indigenous knowledge

I have a certificate that says 'Congratulations! You have successfully installed your printer!' It arrived, surprisingly, through my printer after I stumbled through a series of instructions, arguments with my computer and several changes of my password because I kept getting it wrong. I felt somewhat accomplished when the printer burst into life. I have also received other notifications such as receipts for the additional applications I purchased and downloaded to become more proficient in 'working from home'. In addition, I have learnt how to add virtual backgrounds to my video conference platform, upload recordings and download URLs. I have tidied the office so my husband's many rugby team photos are hidden from sight and a tasteful background of books and arty pieces present an interesting background. The beer fridge is tucked away in the corner along with the mops and brooms that are usually stored in the office. Congratulations! You are working from home!

One might suggest that this is the ideal scenario for scholars. My Dean might think this is what has been normal behaviour of myself and colleagues for years. Working in a pandemic seems somewhat frenetic and exhausting as if my home has been invaded by work and the boundaries of work and life have blurred even more. I have conference called in my pyjamas – the bottom half – having worn the same T shirt for a couple of days. I was interviewed for TV wearing the one bright red lipstick I possess that was so bright people 'private messaged' me asking what the name of the lipstick was and then said things like, 'by the way, good interview!' I have been on video calls at 7am through to 7pm, Monday to Saturday. I have lived out of a suitcase for a month having packed a bag to travel to my lockdown home. My wardrobe is limited and about to fall apart having being worn and washed every few days. I do not wear my normal work attire. I feel that I am over compensating by trying to prove that I am not slouched on a couch. I am worried about the health and safety issues of falling over the mops in the office or accidentally standing on the Easter Bunny's rugby photos or turning up to a meeting wearing a bathrobe. I don't like working from home. No, I really don't. I think I am being too productive and need a holiday. I miss being at work where I can slack off and go out for coffees with students or colleagues.

The educational response to the pandemic has been intriguing to say the least. Early evidence from China suggested that COVID-19 was far worse for elders and that children had a lower risk of catching the virus. Mortality rates seemed to back this up with most deaths occurring in an older population with pre-existing conditions. Countries took different actions in terms of keeping schools open or closing them down some of which was based on providing support for essential workers who had families. Once again, the early data seemed to back up the idea that children were relatively low risk as long as there was improved hand washing and physical distancing. New Zealand ultimately closed all schools and universities once the country shut down. The government then made the commitment to implement a nationwide online learning programme in two languages, English and Māori, for students at early childhood centres through to senior secondary schools in the third week of lockdown. This was a hugely ambitious undertaking, logistically and pedagogically challenging for parents, teachers and students.

Predictably the pre-existing social and educational inequities opened up a chasm as many Māori, Pacific and refugee families had no access to the internet, no devices, larger households and scarcity of space and back-up resources. They had little money or food. The assumption that the curriculum would steam ahead especially at the secondary school level where students have national assessments reinforced that advantaged students would continue their studies with minimal disruption while families without would just have to muddle through and fall further behind. Along with other educators I felt the whole exercise was a missed opportunity to provide a radically different curriculum. Prior to the roll-out of the national programme many parents had developed their own curriculum, which built off their skills and interests. There were cooking classes, gardening, music, painting, and even household chores. My daughter, yes the one who sent us into self-isolation, started a zoom kura with friends that covered cooking, art, the Treaty of Waitangi, Māori language, karakia, the story of Kura Kaupapa Māori, basic economics, and the coronavirus pandemic itself. Other parents have used podcasts and online webinars such as Rangi Matamua's weekly webinar 'Living by the Stars' and Che Wilson's 'Weekly Kauhau' that address Māori knowledge (Matamua 2020; Wilson 2020). Free Māori language classes started up online as well as a group that posted photos of delicious looking Indigenous food produced during lock down. Exercise programmes, dancing, music, comedy, and spiritual programmes were also curated for a virtual experience. It seemed that Indigenous knowledge has adapted well and quickly to the virtual space provided by technology.

Universities and other tertiary institutions were already in deep financial trouble with their reliance on international students particularly from China. For Australia and New Zealand, the first impact was that Chinese students were prevented from entering both countries to begin their first semester studies. Across the world, however, universities began to react to the pandemic by either closing early and/or shifting their entire teaching programmes to online platforms mid-semester. The shift to the complete delivery of online teaching and learning has been an aspiration signalled in many conferences on 'the future' of higher education. It has been seen as the way of the future, delivering a more efficient system that reduced the costs of bricks and mortar and reliance on staff employed in place to teach face to face programmes. Unsurprisingly, like the schooling sector, disadvantage is reproduced in the way universities attempted to deliver online programmes. Students from impoverished backgrounds and isolated communities, that exist in both urban and rural areas, found themselves without devices, access to the internet, financial support and the added burden of extra responsibilities at home. Many academic staff who were expected to continue teaching also had children at home and community leadership responsibilities.

Like public health, public education is a system of historic inequity, systemic racism and a bastion of privilege and social advantage. The myths of 'health care for all' or 'education for all' were exploded decades ago. In terms of Indigenous experiences, there is overwhelming evidence of the failure of education to deliver ... well, to deliver education. This occurs in all countries where there are Indigenous peoples. The concern of many of our critical educators was how quickly the system could default to a mainstream, middle New Zealand mode of curriculum and implementation. As one Māori principal told me, it was as if the Treaty of Waitangi was thrown out the door as the system defaulted to delivering its middle of the road, middle-class, focus. His comments were in relation to English medium schooling which most Māori students attend. There was a parallel stream of online learning that focussed on Māori medium schooling but some parents reacted quickly to the differences in the resource packs that were received by parents whose children were in Māori medium learning and parents whose children were in English medium learning. An opportunity to provide Māori language and curriculum to mainstream English medium schools was lost and the lack of acknowledgement and support for how vulnerable families would cope in this new educational environment was palpable. Former principal Anne Milne provided a webinar titled 'Colouring in Your Virtual White Spaces', that critiqued the on-going white streaming of education that occurs uninterrupted from real to virtual spaces and provided helpful analytical and practical tools for teachers to apply to ensure greater equity for Māori and Pacific students (Milne 2020).

The story of the story

By now it should be clear that the story I attempted to narrate at the beginning of the chapter has dissolved unable to be sustained. Other stories have spoken out even when unintended. They are more personal and more immediate to the uncertainty that COVID-19 has created and the suspension of a still colonised sense of normality grounded in neo-liberal capitalism, in racism and white privilege and the governance and management of what counts as health and well-being. In one way our ancestral stories help us navigate this uncertainty by reminding us that we have lived through something like this before, only much worse, and that those of us who have survived have to be good ancestors. Our survival stories give us clues about being resilient and seeking strategies in our knowledge and values.

What does our response tell us about sovereignty? In my view, sovereignty is expressed in many daily acts whether by Indigenous communities closing their borders and putting up check points or by developing their own systems of food and care distribution for everyone within the borders including non-Indigenous individuals and families. It is expressed by Indigenous peoples continuing to search for and reveal the statistics that tell our story. It is expressed in the relatively rapid way communities came together as a whole and used their own value system as a means to make sense of the crisis. In truth, many were already isolated but not necessarily functioning as a collective. It was also expressed by examples where Indigenous nations reached out to other nations providing equipment and support. This indigenous consciousness about sovereignty is a powerful tool of resurgency. Yes, it does not always work and there are examples where the virus overwhelmed some nations and people behaved selfishly. The resilience of Indigenous values and the accountabilities of Indigenous leadership to model those values provides some protection from a complete breakdown of being in relation and living as collectives.

Our responses also tell us about ourselves as a community of scholars. Our own health and well-being is also fragile in the sense that our health profiles reflect the profiles of our communities. Many of our colleagues are completely vulnerable to this virus in terms of their compromised immune systems. Others have children to care for while juggling teaching, administration and research obligations. Our responsibilities to teach, research and perform the roles of Indigenous public intellectuals also means that some of us are required to narrate our own story so that our communities can have confidence in their Indigenous knowledge and values. Some of us have to advocate for the needs of our peoples either in the public domain or through our professional networks. All of us have to support the work that has fallen on our Indigenous health workforce, from cleaners to nurses, medical specialists to health policy experts. One day soon they will get to tell their own stories. In the meantime, our role is also to makes spaces for their stories to emerge, to help those of our families who have lost loved ones to grieve, to celebrate those who have given birth during this time to celebrate joy.

Will this pandemic change our work? It already has. I hope that we can meet again face to face.

References

American Indian COVID-19 Resources and Responses. (2020). Available: https://www.facebook.com/groups/259818782083254/, accessed 14 May 2020.

Brady, B.R. and Bahr, H.M. (2014). 'The influenza epidemic 1918–1920 among the Navajos: Marginality mortality, and the implications of some neglected eyewitness accounts', *American Indian Quarterly*, vol 38, no 4: 459–91.

Collier, R. (1974). *The Plague of the Spanish Lady: The Influenza Pandemic of 1918–1919*. Macmillan: London.

Independent News. (2020). 'Coronavirus: Boris Johnson praises NHS as country's greatest national asset after says "he could have gone either way"', 12 April. Available: www.indpendent.co.uk/news/uk/politics/coronovarius-boris-johnson-health-news, accessed 14 May 2020.

IndigenousX. (2020). Available: indigenousx.com.au; https://twitter.com/IndigenousX, accessed 14 April 2020.

Kelly, D. (2020). *Economies of Affection*. Webinar. Available: www.indigenousknowledgenetwork.net/webinar-2020, accessed 14 May 2020.

Matamua, R. (2020). *Living by the Stars*. Available: wwwfacebook.com/Livingbythestars/, accessed 14 May 2020.

McQuire, A. (2020). *How Indigenous Communities Got in Front of the Pandemic*. Podcast. Available: https://7ampodcast.co.au/episodes/how-indigenous-communities-got-in-front-of-the-pandemic, accessed 1 May 2020.

Milne, A. (2020). *Colouring in Your Virtual White Spaces*. Available: www.annmilne.co.nz/events-speaking/2020/4/16/webinar-colouring-in-your-virtual-white-spaces, accessed 14 April 2020.

Nana, G. (2020). *Capitalism- Useless in Any Crisis*. Webinar. Available: www.indigenousknowledgenetwork.net/webinar-2020, accessed 14 May 2020.

Nelson, D.M. (2015). *Who Counts? The Mathematics of Death and Life After Genocide*. Duke University Press. Durham. NC.

Paul, G. (2011). *History of the Jingle Dress Dance: Native American Meaning and Story*. Available: www.powwows.com/jingle-dress-dance/, accessed 14 May 2020.

Pihama, L., Smith, G.H., Smith, L.T., and Paul, W. (2020). *Kaupapa Māori On Line Kōrero Series- Ngā Wai a Te Tūī*. Available: www.ngawaietetui.org.nz, accessed 14 May 2020.

Rallah-Baker, K. (2020). *We Live in Dangerous Times, Not Unprecedented Times*. Available: www.indigenousx.com.au/we-live-in-dangerous-times, accessed 14 May 2020.

Smith, L.T. (2020). *Not Our Apocalypse*. Available: www.indigenousknowledgenetwork.net/webinar-2020, accessed 14 May 2020.

Te Rōpū Whakakaupapa Uruta (2020). Available: www.uruta.maori.nz, accessed May 14, 2020.

Wilbur, M. and Keene, A. (2020). *All Our (Socially Distanced) Relations*. Available: www.allmyrelationspodcast.com, accessed 14 May 2020.

Wilson, C. (2020). *KAUHAU Sessions with Che Te Paepae Waho*. Available: https://www.facebook.com/TePaepaeWaho/, accessed 14 May 2020.

28

Once were Maoists

Third World currents in Fourth World anti-colonialism, Vancouver, 1967–1975

Glen Sean Coulthard

Last year witnessed a publication surge in critical reflections on the lasting significance of the global social and political upheavals of 1968. Among these interventions was the reissue (with a new foreword by #BlackLivesMatter co-founder Alicia Garza) of activist-historian Max Elbaum's *Revolution in the Air: Sixties Radicals Turn to Lenin, Mao and Che* (2018). The book begins by laying out the explosive interplay between the local and global that informed domestic politics on the left in the United States in the decade to follow:

> During the first four months of 1968, the Vietnam Tet Offensive ended Washington's hopes of victory in Southeast Asia, incumbent President Lyndon Johnson was forced to abandon his re-election bid, Martin Luther King was assassinated, and Black rebellions erupted in more than 100 cities. Flames reached within six blocks of the Whitehouse; 70, 000 troops had to be called up across the country to restore order. These jolts punctuated a decade of civil rights organising, anti-war protests, cultural ferment, and youth rebellion that shook the entire country. Looming defeat in Vietnam inspired more challenges to Western imperial power throughout Asia, Africa, and Latin America – then commonly termed the 'Third World'. Marxism and anti-imperialist nationalism gained seemingly unstoppable initiative. At home, more US constituencies added their weight to the energized Black community and the early anti-war battalions: youth-led protests surged in Puerto Rican and Chicano communities, an Asian American movement was born, Native Americans revitalized their fight for land and freedom. Women took up the banner of liberation, a new movement for gay and lesbian rights entered the fray. Labor stirred, with more and harder-fought strikes in 1969 and 1970 than in any year since 1946. (1–2)

Ideologically, the post-1968 decade witnessed the rise of a Third World-oriented Marxism on the US left, which according to Elbaum (2018), emerged as an alternative to a state-battered and increasingly out-of-touch 'Old Left' to a new demographic of aspiring young revolutionaries. In contrast to the perceived orthodoxy and whiteness of Old Left institutions, this wave of New Left radicals took inspiration less directly from the Soviet model and trade union activism, and more from the revolutions of Fidel Castro's and Che Guevara's Cuba; from Ho-Chi Minh's North Vietnam and Mao Zedong's China; and from the national liberation struggles of Africa.

This new 'Third World Marxism' was particularly appealing to revolutionaries of colour insofar as it paid heightened attention to the "intersection of economic exploitation and racial oppression" and put opposition to racism at "… the heart of its theory and practice" (3). Although Third World influences on the New Left were diverse during this period, the political force that commanded the most attention was arguably the revolutionary socialism thought to be embodied by the Communist Party of China under the chairmanship of Mao Zedong. Maoism, it was believed at the time, advanced a reinvigorated, grassroots model of socialist internationalism that refused to capitulate to racial capitalism and its mechanisms of violent dissemination: internal colonialism at home and imperialism abroad (Lovell 2019; Frazier 2015; Cook 2014; Wolin 2010; Kelley and Esch 1999). To what ends this understanding was mobilised and to what extent it matched reality will be taken up further below.

Out of all the people of colour political struggles and organisations covered in Elbaum's book – the Revolutionary Action Movement, Black Panthers, Young Lords, Black Liberation Army, the Red Guards, etc. – the struggles of Indigenous peoples receive the least attention. On the one hand, this is interesting to note given that the historical period under scrutiny aligns almost exactly (1968 through to the early 1980s) with many historical accounts of American Indian radicalisation in the United States. What is commonly referred to as 'Red Power', this period of Native American activism is often represented as beginning with either the formation of the American Indian Movement (or AIM) in Minneapolis in 1968 or with the occupation of Alcatraz Island from 1969 to 1971. While this periodisation of Red Power has recently come under scrutiny, in many accounts it stands as almost self-evident (Cobb 2008; Cobb and Fowler 2014; Shreve 2014; Nickel 2019; Lewondowski 2016). On the other hand, the relative absence of Indigenous struggles in *Revolution in the Air* makes sense. Elbaum's book offers a story about the substantive uptake of Marxism by New Left radicals in the US read through and adapted from the decolonisation struggles and anti-imperial politics of the Third World, with an emphasis on the interpretation and application of Maoism to this period and these groups in particular. While the self-determination efforts of the Third World drew many admirers from the ranks of US Red Power, Third World Marxism was less of an influence. Subsequently, although "… a number of individual American Indian activists embraced Marxism", Elbaum notes, "… it seems a consensus that no Marxist cadre groups or organizing collectives formed on an explicitly Marxist basis" (2018: 80).

There are a couple of reasons for this. First, in settler-colonial contexts dispossession serves as a foundational structure underwriting state formation and capital accumulation. Marxists working in contexts like the United States have tended to insufficiently recognise this. Instead, dispossession has been overwhelmingly represented as either a matter of 'the past' or it has been subordinated to the problem of exploited labour. Both serve to ideologically mask the specificity and ongoing nature of colonisation and its constitutive violences in countries like the United States and Canada. Second, many Marxist approaches adhere to a modernist view of historical progress that ranks variation in cultural, social and economic formations in accordance with each form's approximation to an imagined ideal of human development. This, in turn, has historically tended to frame Indigenous cultural, social and economic expressions as either superfluous or material and ideational impediments to progress that need to be abandoned for the sake of Indigenous peoples' own emancipation. These first two tendencies have fueled a significant amount of distrust among Indigenous activists towards Marxism, particularly those organising during the heyday of US Red Power. This skepticism came to a political head after the Sandinista National Liberation Front (SNLF) successfully overthrew the dictatorship of Anastasio Somoza Debayle in Nicaragua in 1979. The success of the Sandinistas threw the Indigenous communities of Nicaragua's Atlantic Coast – the Suma, Rama, and Miskito peoples

– into conflict with the communist nation-building project of the SNLF and thus into alliance with the US government's anti-communist foreign policy. Subsequently, many US Red Power activists – particularly high-ups in AIM like Russel Means – felt compelled to choose between "… an anti-Communist pro-indigenous stance, and a pro-Marxist position that subordinated Native rights to the revolutionary project" (Toth 2019: 197; for an in depth discussion of this period, see Dunbar-Ortiz 2016a). In the context of Indigenous peoples' struggles in the United States, these issues have compromised the building of left-Indigenous coalitions and relations of solidarity that might produce a more fruitful exchange between Indigenous and Marxist political traditions. For these conversations we need to look elsewhere.

With this in mind, the following will provide an alternate history of Red Power radicalisation and Indigenous-Marxist cross-fertilisation, one that reorients our gaze away from the dominance of US narratives and towards the struggles of Indigenous nations on the West Coast of Canada during the late 1960s and 1970s. More specifically, I focus on the political work undertaken by a small but dedicated cadre of Native militants going by the name Native Alliance for Red Power (or NARP), the Native Study Group (NSG), and the Native Women's Liberation Front (NWLF) in Vancouver, British Columbia (BC), between 1967 and 1975. Through their examples, I show that Red Power advocates drew profound inspiration from the decolonisation struggles of the Third World and, like many radicalised communities of colour during this this period, molded and adapted the insights they gleaned from these struggles abroad into their own critiques of capitalism, patriarchy, and internal colonialism at home. I argue that these critiques borrowed substantively and productively from a Third World-adapted Marxism that provided an appealing international language of solidarity and political contestation that they not only inherited but sought to radically transform through a critical engagement with their own cultural traditions and land-based struggles.

★★★

NARP was established in Vancouver in the late fall of 1967 after a meeting was called by Indigenous women in response to a controversial trial involving the rape and murder of a Native teenager, Rose Marie Roper, by three white men near Williams Lake, BC (Bobb 2012; see also Backhouse 2008). According to NARP founding members, Henry Jack and Geraldine Larkin (hereafter Gerry Ambers), the rank and file of NARP was originally drawn from a cross-section of the growing urban Indigenous population, including men and women, ex-convicts, high school drop-outs, a few academics and university students, as well as Native working class folks who either lived in or had recently migrated to the city from more rural communities (Jack 1974; Ambers 2019: personal communication). While active, NARP would grow to include chapters in most major Native urban centres across BC: Vancouver, Port Alberni, Ashcroft, Kamloops, Victoria, and Duncan (Bell 1969). In its early days, members would meet weekly in the form of small discussion-groups anywhere that space could be found – at member's apartments, in bars, diners, Indian Friendship Centres, and the offices of leftist and communist organisations: "[w]e were a green bunch with only one idea in mind", recalls Henry Jack (1974) of NARP's founding, "to do something about our appalling conditions instead of just sitting on our asses doing nothing" (119). NARP was thus formed explicitly as a 'direct action' or 'protest group' that sought to represent grassroots issues in ways that its members thought that the emerging state-subsidised First Nation organisations of the day had failed or were failing to do in an urgent enough manner (Bobb 2012).

The political line developed by NARP during its existence was as eclectic and anti-establishment as its youthful membership. Predating both the formation of the American Indian Movement in 1968 and the infamous Alcatraz occupation of 1969–1971, NARP drew critical inspiration and influence from a combination of Indigenous tradition, the national liberation struggles of the Third World, the women's liberation movement, and the politics of Black Power in the United States (Bobb 2012; 2019: personal communication; Ambers 2019: personal communication).

In terms of Black Power, the most evident political influence on NARP organisers came from the platform and politics of the Black Panther Party for Self-Defense (BPP), with which NARP members had established an early relationship via its Seattle chapter in 1968 (Ambers 2019: personal communication; Bobb 2019: personal communication). As shared with me by one of NARP's original founders, Kwakwaka'wakw Elder and artist Gerry Ambers, herself and another NARP member, Tony Antoine, felt it important to reach out in solidarity to the newly formed Seattle chapter by contacting the organisation to inform them of their own group and to tell them that they would be willing to sell the Panther newsletter, *The Black Panther*, to help raise money and support the Black liberation struggle in the United States. In response, their Seattle contact suggested that representatives of the two organisations get together to discuss a basis of unity. Subsequently, it was decided that Ambers and Antoine would drive down to Seattle for the sit down, and, upon arrival, were blindfolded by their host and driven around the city until they reached a secure location for the meeting: "I had no idea where we were being taken!", recalled Gerry in our conversation (personal communication). There they met Seattle chapter founder, Arron Lloyd Dixon, who was appointed captain of the chapter in April of 1968 by national BPP co-founder Bobby Seale. According to Ambers, they discussed the importance of their respective organisations' work, their mutual struggles for national liberation, the danger of informants within their movements, and the necessity of organising with an eye to the future and the constantly shifting terrain of their struggles: "[t]he leaders of our movements have to be prophets", Ambers recollected Dixon stressing, "because they need to see what's coming down the road and we have to prepare our people for it" (2019: personal communication). Following the meeting, Ambers and Antoine returned to Vancouver and, along with other core NARP members (Ray Bobb, Willie Dunn, David Hanuse, Henry Jack and Joan Carter) established their own political platform – expressed in its 'eight-point program' – which was borrowed and adapted from the Panther's 'ten-point program' with Party consent (Bobb 2012; 2019 personal communication; Ambers 2019: personal communication). Commenting on the diverse uptake of their platform, Bobby Seale (1969) once stated: ours is a "universal program" and several "ethnic revolutionary groups such as the such as the Mexican American Brown Berets, the Chinese American Red Guards, the Indian NARP, and others have programs similar to ours" (online). Although our "program was written specifically with the basic needs and desires of the Black people in mind," Seale (1969) concludes, "[e]verybody who wants it can have it. It isn't the program of the BPP because we dreamt it up. It is so because it came from the people" (online).

The ten-point program was itself inspired by the global dissemination of Mao's *Little Red Book*, particularly its insistence on the universality any given political line being informed by and tested against the lived reality of the masses in struggle. On the surface, at least, built into Maoism was a theoretical and political versatility particularly suited to its diverse uptake. As Robin DG Kelley and Betsy Esch (1999) explain, central to Maoism:

> is the idea that Marxism can be (must be) reshaped to the requirements of time and place and that practical work, ideas, and leadership stem from the masses in movement not from a theory created in the abstract or produced out of other struggles. (9)

This was incredibly important to burgeoning Black and Brown radicals in the US for it broke with certain tendencies within Western Marxism that tethered the revolutionary potential of 'under-developed' (read: non-Western and/or people of colour) communities to appropriately developed material conditions in the progressive unfolding of history, with presumably white city-dwellers in the lead. Mao's insistence on the revolutionary capacity of the peasantry not being dependent on the proletariat in urbanised centres broke significantly with this developmentalist framework, both in theory and practice (as demonstrated by the success of the Chinese Revolution itself). This was paramount for radicals of colour in the United States because it meant that they need not wait for the development of supposedly "objective material conditions to launch their [own] revolution[s]" (Kelley and Esch 1999: 9).

These political influences distinguish early Red Power travelers of Maoism from its predominantly white followers on the communist left in Canada. As with the United States, the influence of Maoism on the Canadian left was not exported directly from China (Kelley and Esch 1999: 11). Rather, for those previously associated with Old Left institutions like the Communist Party of Canada, the source of Mao's influence can be traced back to the revelations made regarding Stalin's atrocities by Khrushchev in his infamous 1956 speech at the Twentieth Congress of the Communist Party of the Soviet Union, which spawned an 'anti-revisionist' movement among the pro-Stalin left worldwide. The 'first wave' of anti-revisionist organisations in Canada emerged from the debates that animated this global split, many of which turned to Mao as the rightful heir of Stalin's (and Lenin's) true revolutionary legacy. Canada's earliest anti-revisionist groups (formed between 1964 and 1970) included the Progressive Workers Movement, the Canadian Party of Labour, the Canadian Liberation Movement, and the largest of them all, the Communist Party of Canada (Marxist-Leninist). All of these groups believed that the Chinese model offered Canadian progressives a 'revolutionary alternative' to existing left organisations like the pro-Soviet Communist Party of Canada, the New Democratic Party, as well as Trotskyist and other New Left groups (Canadian Anti-revisionism, no date). NARP's interest in Maoism was informed less by these anti-revisionism debates and more by China's perceived global leadership under Mao (especially between 1955 and 1975) as a material and ideological supporter of the world's 'wretched of the earth' represented by the Non-Aligned and Third World national liberation movements, and by the theoretical innovations that Mao was thought to make to Western Marxist representations of non-Western struggles. Again, here the influences on NARP closely overlap with Kelley and Esch's (1999) findings regarding Mao's impact on radical Black nationalism in the United States in the 1960s and 1970s. They write: "China offered black radicals a colored or Third World, Marxist model that enabled them to challenge a White and Western vision of class struggle – a model they shaped and reshaped to suit their own cultural and political realities" (8). In Canada, a similar impact affected Red Power organising.

As a political formation committed to direct action, NARP carried out many activities. If Mao's displacement of the white urban proletariat provided particular inspiration to Black nationalists like the Panthers, this insight, I suggest, was taken even more literally by NARP. Maoism was attractive to its Red Power advocates because it displaced not only the white urban subject but also the *geographical location* of classic accounts of revolutionary struggle from the cities to the countryside, or in this case, *the land*. For NARP co-founder Ray Bobb, in particular, this re-orientation was 'the core' of Mao's attraction: the 'countryside-encirclement-of-the-city' strategy situated Indigenous commitments to land defence as not only a revolutionary act, but also necessary for any effective resistance to the nature of capital accumulation in political economies like Canada's, based significantly, as they are, on extraction. In such contexts, extractivist development projects are foundational to accumulation given three dominant features of our neoliberal condition: the ongoing decline in Canada's domestic manufacturing base, in part due to outsourcing to the Global South for cheap labour and manufacturing sites; geopolitical instabilities resulting in a tempered political aversion (at least stated in words, if not in deeds) from acquiring desired resources from unstable regions in the world ('dirty oil', 'blood diamonds' etc.); and the aggressive 'turn inward' to devour domestic land and resources through increased extractivism as a result of the first two features. This analysis was made explicit by members of NARP in their evaluation of the oil crisis of the early 1970s and the subsequent demand it created to increase colonial exploration and capitalist development in Denendeh, the homelands of my own people, the Dene (NSG 1976: 5). Dialectically linking the struggles of the Third World to the "colonial character of the capitalist mode of production" in the north, they write:

> The ripening of contradictions and the growth of the struggle in the Middle-East, the main source of oil for imperialism, brought about an energy crisis in the imperialist nations. […] From that time, we could detect an alteration in their profit-making strategy. They re-directed their investments in oil exploration from the Middle-East […] to the imperialist nations. The rationale for this is that the growth of national liberation and social revolution in the Third World was creating an 'unsafe political climate for investment'. Thus, to maintain sources of raw materials it is necessary to find 'safe' areas of investment. The focus for this re-direction is the 'Canadian' north and, by and large, it has already been explored and decisions have been made on the division of the north amongst the various imperialist interests. The only impediment holding up a wholesale corporate invasion is the fact that the north is, and has been for tens of thousands of years, the legitimate domain of native people. It represents the only (or one of the only) vestiges of genuine national territory for native people, wherein they can realize the aspiration to which all peoples are rightfully entitled – nationhood. (5)

And, of course, similar dynamics remain at play today, which is clearly demonstrated in the resistance of the Wet'suwet'en and Secwepemc land defenders against the marked increase in proposed pipeline construction and liquefied natural gas development on their traditional territories. Under such conditions, Indigenous land-based resistance is increasingly being recognised as foundational to large scale social transformation and has subsequently forced state and capital to respond in kind through the production of "new terrorist identities, risk economies, and security networks that will configure colonization and capitalism […] in the years to come" (Pasternak 2016: 117). In short, Maoism's geographical shift in the terrain of anti-capitalist struggle synced well with the century-plus long commitment by Indigenous nations in BC to land defence, which NARP carried forward into the late 1960s and early 1970s via its support for and participation in blockades and land reclamations exemplified by the West Coast Nisqually fishing rights struggles south of the Canadian/US border in the late 60s (which also had a Seattle Panther presence), the Fort Lawton military base occupation in 1970, and the Cache Creek armed blockade in the BC interior in 1974 (Bobb 2012; 2019: personal communication; Ambers 2019: personal communication). To my mind, the significance of these type of Indigenous-led actions are only now getting the theoretical attention they deserve on the non-Native left.

Other forms of self-defence NARP supported included strikes led by students attending residential or boarding schools. They formed a Vancouver inner-city patrol squad called the 'Beothuk Patrol' that intervened into the rampant anti-Native settler and police violence that is still well documented in the neighborhood; and, like the Panthers, they self-published a 'newsletter' (5,000-plus readership) that covered a range of topics, including recruitment for land-based direct actions, general articles pertaining to the Indigenous freedom struggle (including analyses by Red Power theorists like Metis scholar Howard Adams), Native projects with anti-capitalist forms of economic development, news regarding the successes and failures of national liberation efforts in the Third World, as well as suggested reading lists for its young readership.

As with many radicals during the period, NARP members familiarised themselves with the works of Mao and other Third World theorists (Fanon, Nkrumah, Memmi, etc.) through the formation of a socialist study group in 1971, which they called the Native Study Group. The NSG also had a sister organisation in San Francisco, formed by Roxanne Dunbar-Ortiz and Robert Mendoza, to apply "Marxian analysis and national liberation theory to the history of colonization of Native Americans in North America". (Dunbar-Ortiz 2016a: 32–3). On Dunbar-Ortiz's account, the Marxism of its study group was also Maoist in orientation (2016b: 80). According to Bobb (2012), the NSG's mandate was to create "theory to the level whereby an organization could be formed to do conscious revolutionary work" (online). The goal of the NSG was thus to combine theory with revolutionary practice, including the establishment of material relations of support and solidarity within and between the 'internal colonies' of the US and Canadian settler-states and the nations of the Third World. Such efforts culminated in a 1975 trip of 18 to the People's Republic of China (PRC), which they titled the Native People's Friendship Delegation (Bobb 2012). The delegation members consisted of men and women, made up of both status and non-status First Nations and Metis delegates. The visit was organised by Lee Bobb (hereafter Lee Maracle), along with three other women. The trip was sponsored and paid for by the Chinese Communist Party, with airfare covered by the delegation through fundraising and personal contributions. On 16 January 1975, China's embassy sent approval for the tour to happen in June, and after a three-week visit, the delegation returned home on 22 June 1975. Although the intentions of the trip varied among its delegates, many, if not most, were intent on learning more about Maoism, the Cultural Revolution, and China's treatment of national minorities.

Upon returning to Canada, the NSG organised fundraising events to continue supporting their political activities, including setting up gatherings to share what they learned during their travels. Typical at these events would be a show of solidarity from local organisations also engaged in the struggle against First World imperialism abroad and internal colonialism at home. Typical organisations would include the Liberation Support Movement (a then Vancouver-based Third World Marxist-Leninist solidarity group), the Black Action Group (a Vancouver-based Black Power organisation), the East Indian Defence Committee, a militant South Asian anti-revisionist organisation formed in Vancouver in 1975), and the Progressive Workers' Movement (an anti-revisionist group which included a NARP member, Gordie Larkin, husband to Gerry Ambers at the time). The San Francisco branch study group also set up similar engagements in California, specifically for Lee Maracle, to lecture on the spirit and intent of the delegation and the possibilities of applying what they learned to an analysis of colonisation and decolonisation in Native North America. The most relevant conceptual takeaway from the PRC trip for Maracle was China's commitment to 'socialism and self-reliance', although in her case articulated through a 'cultural' frame of reference (which she also claimed was inspired by her trip to China). In reflecting on her experience, and what she learned of the relationship between economic self-reliance and cultural empowerment, Maracle wrote:

> [w]e learned that we cannot be alienated from our own culture. We have to develop an understanding of it so we can feel closer to our own roots. In China the minority groups are encouraged to promote their Indigenous culture – to learn and speak their own languages. It is very important if [our] people are going to develop in an equal way, [we must] develop [our] culture as [we] develop [our] economy.
>
> (Maracle cited in Chartier 1975: 6)

There is admittedly a lot to unpack here. With over 50 years' hindsight, and especially in light of the detail regarding what we know about the liberation struggles of Tibet against Chinese occupation, the argument that the Cultural Revolution or Chinese communism was a diversity-affirming movement for Indigenous and national minorities is largely unsustainable. But what about at the time? There are two issues to consider that would have made Maracle's observation slightly less controversial than they appear today. First, as the work of Kelly and Esch (1999), Robeson Frazier (2015), and (in a less sympathetic tone) Julia Lovell (2019) have all shown, significant resources were dumped into what was essentially a post-Sino-Soviet split global public relations campaign by the Chinese Communist Party to represent itself as *the* revolutionary alternative to the Soviet Union for people of colour the world over:

> [i]n an age when the Cold War helped usher in the nonaligned movement, with leaders of the 'colored' world converging in Bandung, Indonesia, in 1955 to try and chart an independent path toward development, the Chinese hoped to lead the former colonies on the road to socialism.
>
> *(Kelley and Esch 1999: 9)*

Kelley and Esch (1999) go on: "[t]he Chinese [...] not only endowed nationalist struggle with revolutionary value, but they reached out specifically to Africa and people of African descent" (9). This outreach included Chinese statements of solidarity with the US Black liberation struggle, of which NARP, as we have seen, was a keen follower.

Second, between 1949 and 1976, Mao's foreign policy promoted China as a quasi-tourist destination for worldly revolutionaries. What Julia Lovell has called a "hospitality machine" designed to "distract from or conceal discordant realities, and to cater to the whims of carefully chosen foreign guests," this machinery aimed "to proselytize the virtues of the Communists and their government" to would-be sympathisers abroad (2019: 78). In terms of the downplayed 'discordant realities' that Lovel speaks of, perhaps the most glaring was China's representation of the rebellion in Tibet. As Robeson Frazier (2015) explains, this armed uprising was portrayed as a minor conflict started by the upper-class and landholding elites; a view that deliberately disregarded "the revolt's multiclass composition and the reality that it represented a popular Tibetan rejection of the PRC's claims to Tibet" (59). Based on conversations I've had with Ray Bobb (one of the delegates on the trip), I suspect that similarly scripted representations where provided to folks on the Native Peoples' Friendship Delegation in 1975. Such representations suggested that what was happening in Tibet was a 'reactionary' movement against Chinese communism propped up by Western imperialist nations (Bobb 2019: personal communication). As such, to truly understand the PRC's position on the cultural self-determination of national minorities, one had to look at examples such as Mongolia, not Tibet. As Lee Maracle was paraphrased as saying in an interview upon her return from China: "[t]he Mongolians have independence. ... In the past they were underdeveloped and through Chinese policy the Mongolians have been put in a privileged position. ... They are stressing cultural development since in the past their culture was suppressed" (Chartier 1975: 5).

Gender also figured into NARP's analysis of colonial violence and decolonial resistance, as evidenced by the circumstances under which the organisation was formed: as a response to the rape and murder of 17-year-old Rose Marie Roper of the Esketemc First Nation at Alkali Lake. From its inception, women not only held foundational leadership positions in the organisation, but they also shaped how issues addressed by the group were theoretically understood and how to go about politically organising to confront them. For Gerry Ambers, Roper's death was inseparable from the colonial violence that they sought to mitigate as organisers. She understood the violent transgression of Roper's bodily sovereignty as inextricably linked with the violation of Indigenous people's lands and sovereign authority. For her, there was no hierarchy of importance between the two, and the men, generally speaking, respected her lead: "I felt that they accepted our leadership very, very well. We were always recognized as equals," recalled Ambers of her time with NARP (2019: personal communication). Self-organised, NARP women were understood as core to the movement. As stated in an editorial statement for *The Native Movement* newsletter (the publication that the *NARP Newsletter* eventually morphed into later in 1970),

> this newsletter is being published by young Indian people who are, as yet, unorganized, as a whole. The sisters in our group, however, are organized. They call themselves the Native Women's Liberation Front and have policies worked out which are, practically, nationalist, and, essentially, revolutionary.
>
> *(NWLF 1970: online)*

Disillusioned with the 'white woman's liberation movement', Vancouver Red Power women established the NWLF in 1970 to centre Indigenous women's voices in its push for the "total liberation of the colonized people of this world and for the total liberation of the Indian people of this continent" (online). And when Red Power men neglected to take their lead, the NWLF shut this down:

> Those who identify with the values of the system question the potential of Indian women in the movement. This is nonsense. Without women only half the movement's resources are being tapped. The Native Women's Liberation Front's purpose is to correct this mistaken idea and put an end to the tremendous waste of people in the movement.
>
> *(NWLF 1970: online)*

Red Power women's commitment to liberate all 'colonized people of the world' was put into practice through their own gendered solidarity efforts. One such display of support involved Red Power women helping organise and host a thousand-participant gathering of the Indo-Chinese Woman's Conference held in Vancouver in 1971, an anti-war event that hosted delegates from North and South Vietnam to share their stories about the gendered atrocities of the imperialist war in Southeast Asia (Wu 2013: 238–239).

The emphasis NARP/NSG/NWLF placed on its international solidarity campaigns was an outgrowth of three theoretical/political influences. The first was rooted in the political traditions of the Indigenous nations that comprised their membership. While decolonisation has always been informed by the normative import of Indigenous relations to land and place, we must also recognise, following Nishnaabeg theorist Leanne Betasamosake Simpson, that our struggles are and have also been intrinsically linked to and informed by global developments, and vice versa (2017): "Internationalism has always been part of our political practices", she writes, because our existence as nations has always been an international one "regardless of how rooted in place we are" (56). For Indigenous nations in BC, this internationalism was something they had always done.

The second influence relates more squarely to NARP and NSG's interpretation of Maoism, specifically the extrapolation of Mao's 'countryside-encirclement-of-the-city' framework to the world stage. As Bobb (2012) explains, when Maoism is applied at a global scale, the Third World – Asia, Africa, and Latin America – can be analogised as the 'countryside' and North America and Europe the 'city'. Such a view tethered, for Bobb, the success of national liberation struggles in the Third World to those of the 'internal colonies', paradigmatically represented by Indigenous nations. Defeating imperialism *and* internal colonialism thus requires a two-front attack: solidarity and support for the 'people's wars' of the Third World abroad and the convergence of decolonisation with class struggle to weaken the stranglehold of colonialism at home. Most of NARP's organising, as well as the political associations they formed with other communities and groups, took these demands to heart (Bobb 2012).

The third influence, I suggest, was the concept of 'internal colonialism' itself. Arguably the most dominant critical theory of race in the late 1960s and 1970s, the application of the 'internal colony' thesis to domestic race relations was, again, a product of the profound influence of the struggles against colonialism and imperialism in Asia, Africa, and Latin America (see, for example, Allen 1992; Barrera and Ornelas 1972; for critiques see Omi and Winant 2014; for application to Indigenous British Columbia see Tennant 1982). Originally stemming back to early-20th-century Marxist debates on the 'national question' sparked by Lenin's 1916 declaration that Southern Blacks in the United States should be considered an 'oppressed nation', the thesis underwent a revival on the US left in the 1960s as theorists began to assert that "people of color living in the United States are colonized people, and that forms of colonial and neocolonial power in the Third World are also deployed colonized populations domestically" (Adamson 2019: 344). Similar to 'settler-colonial' studies after it, the internal colonialism perspective insisted that "racial marginalization and subordination must be understood through the lens of colonialism and imperialism as *persistent and ongoing processes*" (Adamson 2019: 344). Unlike too much literature in the field of 'white settler-colonial studies' (King 2019), however, the normative stakes for non-Indigenous communities are much clearer when looked at through the internal colonialism frame: they, like Indigenous peoples, ought to also be considered beneficiaries of decolonisation afforded through their own access to the right to self-determination. NARP found no inconsistency with this claim coexisting with their own land and sovereignty struggles. Under such a framework, the specificity of our respective experiences of anti-Black, racialised, and colonial violences did not translate into the political incommensurabilities that seem, at times, to haunt our solidarity efforts today.

★★★

As with the influence of Third World-inspired Marxism generally, the pull of Maoism among Red Power organisers in Vancouver begins to wain as we close out the 1970s. There are a number of reasons for this. First, for many people of colour on the left in the United States and Canada, directions in Chinese foreign policy increasing began to hamper its ability to claim moral authority in leading the world revolution against colonialism and imperialism. The instrumentality of China's interventions in Africa punctuate this decline in leadership, especially in the wake of its 1975 decision to support the US-backed white supremacist regime of South Africa in its colonial contest with national liberation forces in Angola (Kelley and Esch 1999). China's betrayal was felt particularly strong amongst the Black left, which, as we have seen, was one of NARP's longest interlocutors. Second, in a manner similar to the United States and its Counter Intelligence Program, over time the instruments and techniques of Canadian state repression created irreparable cracks in the movement through the believed use of informants, misinformation campaigns, and state violence. To a certain extent, this resulted in a culture of paranoia, increased sectarianism (resulting in an aversion toward internal group descent), organisational power struggles, and ultimately a decline in membership. Third, and perhaps most importantly, some former members also became more deeply entrenched in their own communities' cultural and political traditions and began to organise more squarely within the normative frameworks offered by these practices. Even with this being the case, some members of NARP refused to see these disparate revolutionary traditions – those offered by Third World Marxist orientations and Indigenous political thought – as incommensurable. They were different, yes, but united in their commitment to justice and the collective project of freedom (Ambers 2019: personal communication).

So this begs the question: Why tell this story? Especially in light of the fact that the liberation sought by this generation of organisers has yet to break the stranglehold of colonial violence still experienced by so many in our communities today. With this being the case, I want to conclude with three brief take-aways. They are in no way the only ones, but important nonetheless.

First, in exploring the political cross-fertilisations at the heart of this story, we challenge the idea that Indigenous peoples' openness to engaging outside theoretical traditions somehow equates to assimilation and therefore represents and/or serves in the discursive erasure of Indigenous thought and intellectual traditions. What I hope the story offered here shows is that the decolonisation of Indigenous nations and nationalisms has historically been an intellectually polymorphous project undertaken by critically intelligent and culturally grounded individuals committed to radical social transformation. Before the hegemony of liberal recognition politics started to increasingly limit what Indigenous peoples could claim as their rights via Section 35 of the *Constitution Act, 1982* (rights that the courts have wedded to a mythical ideal of cultural purity within the uncontested sovereignty of the Canadian state and its capitalist mode of production) Indigenous organisers used to critically engage other traditions in their struggles for freedom without this cross-fertilisation representing cultural *inauthenticity*. 'By any means necessary' – as the saying used to go.

Second (and in a related way) this story points to a critically important history of solidarity, both in thought and practice. That is, the activities of organisations like NARP show what Indigenous land struggles have to materially offer in terms of forging a genuine politics of solidarity across social struggles that, for many reasons, do not always see eye to eye. I hope that their story might continue to mitigate these tensions by highlighting a critically important example of intellectual and political collaboration, one in which Indigenous land and sovereignty struggles are thought to intersect – necessarily and productively – with other liberation theories and efforts. As an example of "radical Indigenous internationalism" (Estes 2019: 204) – to borrow Lakota historian Nick Estes' terminology – NARP dared to imagine "a world altogether free of colonial hierarchies of race, class and nation" (and importantly, gender) and sought to align itself with colonised communities, at home and abroad, committed to achieving similar ends (2019: 204).

In the Canadian context, some recent scholarship has opted to downplay if not dismiss the historical lessons one might take from a productive engagement by Indigenous peoples and their supporters with the revolutionary traditions of the Third World, promoting instead a more appeasing politics that James Tully and John Borrows call, 'reconciliation-resurgence' (Burrows and Tully 2018); they argue against "the lack of nuance" indicative of some Indigenous scholar's "adoption of a dialectic" drawn from different colonial contexts (6). Specifically, they challenge the "polarizing" and "divisive" ways that the "binary of Third World decolonisation and master-slave dialectics of the 1950s and 1960s was pulled into some Indigenous studies circles in ways that reject reconciliation in broad terms" (6); "Third World politics", they write, "we generally regard as a historical failure" (24). The separatist politics of "Black Power" is assigned a similar fate (24). They suggest that the simplistic binaries underwriting these traditions "can fatally conceal and obscure a complex intersectional field" that "reconciliation-resurgence" is better equipped to avoid. The stakes are high, they suggest given that the inability to "illuminate broader and more complex intersectional fields of power" was not only "one reason why the colonization/decolonization binary did not lead the way to Third World liberation" but that it "might even be said that such dichotomies led to deeper forms of neocolonialism, dependency, inequality, and patriarchy in Third World settings" (7). And if this were not bad enough, such dichotomous thinking, they claim, "does not coincide with many traditional ways of knowing and being" (7).

While I do not have the time or space to unravel every argument at play here, I feel it is important to respond to a couple of core issues that are being raised. First, 'binaries' did not undermine the Third World project, racial capital did. To quote Vijay Prashad, the Third World "was not a failure […] it was *assassinated*" (Prashad 2007: np). Instead of liberation, the forces of globalisation spearheaded by the advanced capitalist states (with the United States leading the fray), fought to subdue any independence the 'darker nations' had mustered. Orchestrated through the International Monetary Fund, 'structural adjustment' campaigns used the precarity of newly independent but heavily indebted states to open up themselves up to the demands of Western capital accumulation and thus indirect rule; initiating what Frantz Fanon called the transition from the 'apotheosis of independence' to the 'curse of independence' (Fanon 1991) – a *post*-colonial *colonisation*. Also, even if the import of such theories carries with them Manichean tendencies, ought this not be interrogated against the specific material and discursive contexts in which they are deployed, and with a concern to what effect? NARP's anti-revisionist was concerned less about the Soviet Union trading communist internationalism for 'peaceful co-existence' with the capitalist west; in other words, their non-reformist position was not a naïve reproduction of Stalinist orthodoxy within their theory-building and organising. Rather, it was adapted and applied to a shift in the reproduction of colonial relations of power that began to consolidate in Canada in the late 1960s, from an openly repressive structure to one that operates through the carefully scripted recognition of 'Aboriginal rights'. It was this 'co-existence' – the peaceful co-existence offered through a politics of recognition and eventually reconciliation – that they refused. NARP, it could be said, theorised and anticipated the 'death of reconciliation' being declared in the bush and on the streets today.

The third take away is related to the first two, but more personal. Thinking and writing systematically about Red Power activism in BC offered me an indirect chance to contextualise the work that I originally undertook in *Red Skin, White Masks,* particularly my theoretical application of the Third World contribution of Frantz Fanon's thought to colonial contexts like Canada. When I finished writing my book, we were in the midst of what many thought to be the most significant political mobilisation of Indigenous peoples against the state in almost a half century (we are clearly in an equally significant phase as I write). When my book hit the shelves, however, that movement had all but dissipated and another one was on the horizon: the liberation politics of Black Lives Matter. Under such conditions, I worried that my use of Fanon could be read as problematic, as an appropriation that required at minimum some theoretical and historical contextualisation. The intellectual and activist labour of earlier generations provides an important glimpse into this context. It demonstrates that the Black and Indigenous radical traditions, the struggles of the Third and Fourth Worlds – 'the wretched of the earth' – have a long history of political engagement and intellectual exchange that transformed lives and built alternative worlds that we still inhabit. This is a critical history to retell given the demands of solidarity that unravelling our colonial present requires.

References

Adamson, M. (2019). 'The internal colony as political perspective', *Cultural Politics*, vol 15, no. 3: 343–357.

Allen, R. (1992). *Black Awakening in Capitalist America*. Africa World Press: Trenton, NJ.

Backhouse, C. (2008). *Carnal Crimes: Sexual Assault Law in Canada, 1900–1975*. Irwin Law: Toronto, ON.

Barrera, M., Muñoz, C., and Ornelas, C. (1972). 'The barrio as internal colony', *Urban Affairs Annual Reviews*, vol 6: 465–498.

Bell, D. (1969). 'Red power grows in BC', *Winnipeg Free Press*, 25 July.

Bobb, R. (2012). 'Overview of red power movement in Vancouver −1967–1975'. Available: https://revolut ionary-initiative.com/2012/04/26/overview-of-red-power-movement-in-vancouver-1967-1975/, accessed May 16, 2020.

Borrows, J. and Tully, J. (2018). 'Introduction', in M. Asch, J. Borrows, and J. Tully (eds.) *Resurgence and Reconciliation: Indigenous-Settler Relations and Earth Teachings* University of Toronto Press: Toronto, ON, 3–25.

Canadian Anti-Revisionism. (n.d.). 'The first wave of anti-revisionism, 1964–70', *Encyclopedia of Anti-Revisionism On-Line*. Available: https://www.marxists.org/history/erol/ca.firstwave/index.htm, accessed 15 May 2020.

Chartier, C. (1975). 'China through a native perspective', *The New Breed*, October, 5–6.

Cobb, D.M. (2008). *Native Activism in Cold War America: The Struggle for Sovereignty*. University of Kansas: Lawrence, KS.

Cobb, D.M. and Fowler, L. (eds.) (2014). *Beyond Red Power: American Indian Politics and Activism Since 1900*. School for Advanced Research Press: Santa Fe, NM.

Cook, A.C. (ed.) (2014). *Mao's Little Red Book: A Global History*. Cambridge University Press: Cambridge.

Dunbar-Ortiz, R. (2016a). *Blood on the Border: A Memoir of the Contra War*. University of Oklahoma Press: Norman, OK.

Dunbar Ortiz, R (2016b). 'The relationship between Marxism and Indigenous struggles and the implications of the theoretical framework for international Indigenous struggles', *Historical Materialism*, vol 24, no. 3: 76–91.

Elbaum, M. (2018). *Revolution in the Air: Sixties Radicals Turn to Lenin, Mao, and Che*. Verso: New York.

Estes, N. (2019). *Our History is Our Future: Standing Rock Versus the Dakota Access Pipeline and the Long Tradition of Indigenous Resistance*. Verso: New York.

Fanon, F. (1991). *The Wretched of the Earth*. Grove Press: New York.

Frazier, R.T. (2015). *The East is Black: Cold War China in the Black Radical Imagination*. Duke University Press: Durham, NC.

Jack, H. (1974). 'Native alliance for red power', in Waubgeshig (ed.) *The Only Good Indian: Essays by Canadian Indians*. New Press: Toronto, ON, 111–127.

Kelley, R.D.G. and Esch, B. (1999). 'Red like Mao: Red China and black revolution', *Souls: Critical Journal of Black Politics and Culture*, vol 1, no. 4: 6–41.

King, T. (2019). *Black Shoals: Offshore Formations of Black and Native Studies*. Duke University Press: Durham, NC.

Lewandowski, T. (2016). *Red Bird, Red Power: The Life and Legacy of Zitkala Sa*. University of Oklahoma: Norman, OK.

Lovell, J. (2019). *Global Maoism*. Penguin/Random House: London.

The Native Study Group. (1976). 'Palestinians and native people are brothers', *Seize the Time*, vol 2, no. 5: 1–10.

The Native Women's Liberation Front. (1970). 'The native women's liberation front', *The Native Movement*, no 1. Available: http://revealdigital.com/independent-voices/minority-presses-native-american-titles/, accessed 20 May 2020.

Nickel, S.A. (2019). *Assembling Unity: Indigenous Politics, Gender, and the Union of BC Indian Chiefs*. University of British Columbia Press: Vancouver, BC.

Omi, M. and Winant, H. (2014). *Racial Formation in the United States*. Routledge: New York.

Pasternak, S. (2016). 'Comment', in J. Hallenbeck, M. Krebs, S. Hunt, K. Goonewardena, S.A. Kipfer, S. Pasternak, and G.S. Coulthard (eds.) *Red Skin, White Masks: Rejecting the Colonial Politics of Recognition*, *The AAG Review of Books*, vol 4, Oxford University Press: New York, NY, 111–120.

Prashad, V. (2007). 'The third world idea', *The Nation*, 17 May. Available: https://www.thenation.com/arti cle/archive/third-world-idea/, accessed 20 May 2020.

Seale, B (1969). *The East Village Other*, vol 4, no 21. Available: https://www.biblio.com/book/east-village -other-vol5-no1-december/d/1275307788, accessed 20 May 2020.

Shreve, B.G. (2014). *Red Power Rising: National Indian Youth Council and the Origins of Native Activism*. University of Oklahoma: Norman, OK.

Simpson, L.B. (2017). *As We Have Always Done: Indigenous Freedom Through Radical Resistance*. University of Minnesota Press: Minneapolis, MN.

Tennant, P. (1982). 'Native Indian political organization in British Columbia, 1900–1969: A response to internal colonialism', *BC Studies*, no. 55: 3–49.

Toth, G. (2019). 'Red nations: Marxists and the native American sovereignty movement of the late cold war', *Cold War History*, vol 20, no 2: 197–221.

Wolin, S. (2010). *The Wind from the East: French Intellectuals, the Cultural Revolution, and the Legacy of the 1960s.* Princeton University Press: Princeton, NJ.

Wu, J. (2013). *Radicals on the Road: Internationalism, Orientalism, and Feminism During the Vietnam Era.* Cornel University Press: Ithaca, NY.

29

Resurgent kinships

Indigenous relations of well-being vs. humanitarian health economies

Dian Million (Tanana Athabascan)

In 2014, Tommi Hill, a member of the National Aboriginal Youth Council on HIV and AIDS (NAYCHA) spoke to the newly established Aboriginal Nations and Torres Strait Islanders HIV Youth Mob (ANTHYM): "We are Indigenous youth taking care of each other, to show other youth that we do care, that's why we're here. We are the future, it lies with us to carry this work forward". Indigenous youth have stepped up everywhere, establishing global networks of care among themselves with a strong sense of how their future lives and struggles are positioned. Along with the Native Youth Health Network out of Canada, these Indigenous youth from several continents are practicing concentric relations of care with their families, with their nations, and with each other. They are grounded in deep relations across place and time, intergenerationally and spatially. Care is a radical act in our times. It is inherent to our sovereignty, an embodied, lived experience with our relations. Little care has been extended to our Indigenous lives. We are killed because our gender, sexuality, or skin has made us targets for neglect, violence, illness, and disability in states all over the globe. Capitalism is an economic system that cares more for its investment in mines, pipelines and supply lines than it does our lives.

Jeannette Armstrong (Syilx) has told us:

> [I]ndigeneity is a viable tool toward transformation of the people-to-be into being part of the social order as tmixʷ and to be a life-force in a life-force place rather than being part of the social order of depletion and destruction.
>
> *(2009: 2)*

As an Athabascan person who has relocated to the sovereign territories of the Coast Salish, and as an academic in one of the CANZUS nation-states, I grapple with my own limitations here in offering a global picture. I still honour my relations at home in Alaska, while I live here in Washington where I seek to be part of a life-force place, to give rather than deplete. In order to speak of the Indigenous, I must invoke a vast multiplicity of peoples around the world, many who have now suffered total uprooting from places that once nourished their lives for millennia. Yet 'Indigenous' does imply the particularity of a people's relations to their Indigenous places; perhaps, even more so now because capitalism leaves so many scattered by global warming, resource extraction, and other capitalist violations.

Canada, New Zealand, the United States, and Australia, or the CANZUS nation-states, reduce our specific peoples, myriad traditions, and diverse places in their state imaginations to 'populations'. CANZUS, to remember, is what the above nation-state collective came to be called when they voted as a bloc against the ratification of the 2007 United Nations Declaration of Rights for Indigenous Peoples (UNDRIP) (United Nations 2008). Indigenous Peoples argued for years for the 's' on the end of Peoples. We are Peoples, not populations. While these nation-states later changed their minds, signing in large part because they claimed that the declaration was unenforceable, nation-state non-compliance to the life-seeking propositions of that pact are seen in many ways. UNDRIP is a profound ask for Indigenous well-being writ large. It is a document crafted with 40 years of Indigenous sweat and perseverance that names the most specific requirements for Indigenous life across the planet. Through UNDRIP, the Indigenous seek to establish protections within a global human rights and humanitarian hierarchy created by liberal and non-liberal, democratic and non-democratic nation-states, non-governmental organisations (NGOs), and developmental agencies. As a declaration, UNDRIP is advisory rather than enforceable in international law, but it exists as an unprecedented collective statement on how those without nation-state status will negotiate their well-being.

Through UNDRIP, the Indigenous have sought a check on state violence and institutionalised inequities affecting minority or marginalised peoples globally (Anaya 2004). This is an unstable arrangement as I have written. (Million 2013). While there appears to be an incredible interest among humanitarian agencies to advocate for Indigenous health, there are rising Indigenous deaths and unchecked plunder of Indigenous lands everywhere. Alongside a growing human rights discourse on Indigenous health, nation-states increasingly hedge any meaningful Indigenous self-determination. This has not gone unnoticed – for many Indigenous, it is the sign of our position: we not at the table among nations at the level of global polities, but sit at a second table called humanitarianism. I argue that our health is integral to our sovereignty, and is the result of holistic practices of care, responsibility, relations all embedded and inextricable from our "oral, kinesthetic, and practiced" ways of life (Gray 2018:Video).

In this chapter, I first present *what* Indigenous peoples define their own well-being. I bring to the fore our life-ways and traditions as (they) embody practices of refusal and resistance to accentuate our strengths. The fight to resurge relations in places and communities is to speak directly back to the assumptions inherent in any neoliberal humanitarian management of group death that poses as care. I speak to our actual struggles for Indigenous well-being, our fight for the ability to create Indigenous life. I seek to acknowledge our otherwise lives in the midst of neoliberal capitalist management systems organised around individualistic, consumer-oriented, and extractive senses of 'health'. How we do this will be important to any sovereignty that we might hope to practice.

Second, I discuss humanism and humanitarianism as forms of neoliberal governance. In many ways, the ratification of UNDRIP signifies that human rights and humanitarianism is the sphere to which the Indigenous are relegated to settle any grievance or complaint against the state. But, given humanitarianism's gloss as compassion, it is necessary to actually examine how humanitarian governance furthers the aims of racial capitalism and settler colonialism. Didier Fassin wrote recently that "the politics of compassion is a politics of inequality" (Fassin 2012: 3). In this sphere, the local is made global and an Indigenous presence and struggle for life is now made most visible.

Last but not least, I write about Indigenous lives as they are entangled within a realm of neoliberal biopolitics as 'health' at the same time that Indigenous places and peoples are abandoned if they are not seen as viable for capitalist development. I write this in solidarity with my own family, who know the terms of Indigenous health intimately. I write in solidarity with those who are posed as emblems of our Indigenous failure to thrive, who refuse the spectacle that Canada and other CANZAS nations have tried to make of them to cover their own cruel care. Instead, for myriad communities across the continents, there is life and place, and this is where I begin.

Indigenous place as well-being, relations as resurgence

My power is carried in my House's histories, songs, dances and crests. It is recreated at the Feast when the histories are told, the songs and dances performed, and the crests displayed. With the wealth that comes from respectful use of the territory, the House feeds the name of the Chief in the Feast Hall. In this way, the lilw, the Chief, the territory, and the Feast become one.

(Uukw 1987:7)

To be human in an Indigenous sense as Aileen Moreton-Robinson Robinson reminds us is "founded on a construction of humanness that is predicated on the body's connectedness to our respective countries, human ancestors, creative beings and all living things" (Moreton-Robinson 2013: 335). Place is of paramount importance if we talk about 'health' in an Indigenous sense. 'Land' is not 'territory' or 'property' as in an object; instead, *place* denotes dense, reciprocal, life-affirming relations that peoples form and have formed over millennia. Kim TallBear (Sisseton-Wahpeton Dakota) describes this succinctly: "Indigenous peoples understand themselves within coherent groups and cultures in intimate relationship with particular places, especially living and sacred landscapes" (TallBear 2015: 131). To embrace and be embraced by these intimate relations is what matters. Glen Coulthard (Dene) wrote that land provides:

An ontological framework for understanding [these] relationships. The 'land' is a profound field of 'relationships of things to each other'. To kill the land, waters, air, or any of our relations, which we pose as entities with intention, is to kill us, who are a part of rather than isolated from them.

(Coulthard 2014: 61)

Coulthard invokes the struggle to continue Indigenous life in all its relations as resurgence, as grounded normativity, within Indigenous terms. This is a lived resurgence, calling on varied knowledges for regenerating seed and food (Hoover 2017), reestablishing clan governance (Jewell 2018) and establishing alternative energy grids (LaDuke 2006). Our sovereignties are embodied through our relations with a place, danced, sang, woven, and continuously providing instruction on how to act in the world toward each other and towards all other entities (Gray 2018).

Resurgence signifies these everyday acts of life that communities strive for. Our sovereign embodied acts of self-determination are always gendered. Rauna Kuokkanen (Sámi) reminds us:

Indigenous women play a crucial role in envisioning models of autonomy that do not merely replicate patriarchal, hierarchical structures that often reproduce the marginalization and subjugation of sections of society ... [they] play a crucial role in maintaining and cultivating practices, systems, and bodies of knowledge, values, languages, modes of learning.

(Kuokkanen 2007: 2)

The outsize presence of women, youth, and non-binary leaders in Indigenous resistance is not by chance. The insertion of settler-colonial racial-capitalist order is at this intimate level of social reproduction: our ability to reproduce our worlds and literally ourselves. Settler states are established through the violation of Indigenous reproduction; through the decimation of life-sustaining relations. These states have carried out the removal of Indigenous children, the regulation of marriage, the disciplining of genders and sexualities, and the killing of water and other life-forms in our homelands. All this has inspired a fierce defense of those most impacted by the violence generated in these capitalist relations. Yet, there is fierce resistance to our efforts to collapse the hierarchies embedded in our community relations. Indigenous women and LGBTQ2s have argued that we can achieve no real self-determination unless Indigenous nations are able to reproduce our lives, our life-ways, free of the violence that these gendered capitalist relations produce among us, within us. This is why Indigenous leaders have called for resistance and resurgence rather than resilience or simply endurance (Kuokannen 2019; Simpson 2018; Simpson 2016).

Jeff Corntassel (Cherokee) in *Re-envisioning Resurgence* (2012), questions a 'politics of distraction'. Corntassel names 'three colonial R's': rights, reconciliation, and resources. Corntassel cast these three colonial 'Rs' as distractions from how our own relations provide a continuing Indigenous ability to thrive. Presently, nation-states and international humanitarian orders offer up promises of recognition, equality, and rights while reducing our non-human relations to resources. As subjects of these human 'rights', the Indigenous are positioned at the end of a long line of those who seek 'rights' in the form of care that never disrupts the violence of the racial-capitalist–settler-colonial order. Meanwhile, our non-human relations are quantified, commodified, and extracted – our relations in places are reduced to *things*.

Indigenous calls for resurgence are calls for practicing thankfulness and reciprocity, for cultivating and protecting relations with responsibility, for reaffirming who we are through our diverse remembering. Our relations are paramount to the living fact of our *survivance* and thriving. We know these relations intervene in liberal structures that sustain wealth inequality, racism, heteronormativity, and ableism. We believe in health as a social, non-anthropocentric negotiation of needs and reciprocal acknowledgments, where optimum 'health' is the outcome of a concern much larger than the individual or even community of humans. In balance, Indigenous relations are informed by the discipline of living in places, which provide protocols and knowledges that aren't about accumulation or possession but about proportionate consent, responsibility and care (de Leeuw and Hunt 2018; Daigle 2016). Each Indigenous place disciplines us differently, thus these protocols, these knowledges, are particular and cannot be characterised abstractly. In each place or in each diasporic community, the Indigenous resurge their own order – in songs, in our languages, in our relations with the human and non-human, and in our love as practice.

These are desires in alliance with life, rather than efforts to incorporate life into the logics of biopower. This is not a desire for our healing as a reconciliation with any nation-state. These are desires for life in its ineffable powers, desires to interrupt a settler coloniality–racial capitalist order that is killing.

Speaking past the trauma diagnosis

Indigenous and non-Indigenous health workers are presently producing multiple literatures that speak to an Indigenous sense of well-being across a range of health disciplines. There are vital Indigenous movements in their own right that have been effective in challenging the biopolitical misinformation that presents Indigenous worlds. Scott Morgensen, writing on an Indigenous global response to being erased by settler movements amidst the AIDS crisis, calls these Indigenous resistances *health sovereignty*. Morgensen posed that "activist assertions of the epistemologies of Indigenous governance" include "cultural, economic, and political control over conditions and methods of health" (Morgensen 2014: 189). These assertions of Indigenous epistemologies that are embedded in activist governance principles are deeply holistic with great powers to reinterpret and reframe 'health' as well-being. Each place has very deep knowledge and practice that when in place transforms places with life-giving care, with attention and with respect. In this light our internationally based Indigenous movements for sovereignty and self-determination and the UNDRIP *are* about well-being in this larger sense. Indigenous demands for self-determination seek to protect all the relations we depend on. Resurgence is about appreciating and acting on our own epistemological differences that make different futures possible.

At the same time, in the midst of diaspora and the capitalist forces that have scattered our families, current Indigenous health literatures are sites of witness to the resurgent and critical practices of Indigenous knowledges that continue, often in relations with local landed Indigenous peoples. Kanaka Maoli, and Māori are certainly leading voices in these actions. As Kanaka Maoli scholar T. Kehaulani Natsuko Vaughn recently wrote finding "self-determination and survivance" in diaspora must be an "embodied practice, one where Native Hawaiians living inside and outside of their homeland are actively maintaining culture and themselves through ancestral knowledge and protocol" and with respect and in alliance with the Indigenous peoples of that place (Vaughn 2017: 6–7).

Aotearoa New Zealand and Māori epistemologies have informed many profound resurgence practices, particularly those that inform examining family and gender roles. Leonie Pihama's work on the spatial and spiritual praxis of being woman (Pihama 2001) as well as Brendan Hokowhitu's work on Māori masculinities come to mind (Hokowhitu 2012). Rāwiri Tinirau and her colleagues at *Te Atawhai o Te Ao* (The Independent Maori Institute for Environment and Health) are known for reframing Western trauma within Māori knowledges.

In *For the love of our children: an Indigenous connectedness framework*, Iñupiat scholar Jessica Saniguq Ullrich asks "Despite colonization, something has sustained Indigenous peoples ..." Answering through her research, she writes: "connectedness, the interrelated welfare of everyone and everything has become one of the keys to Indigenous survival and well-being" (Ullrich 2019: 1). Ullrich whose work features the healing of Alaska Native children lost to foster care systems points to ways Alaska Natives might reclaim their children to and for their communities, a practice that might resurge and revitalise the whole kinship in those places – including urban places like Anchorage.

In a literature review of Indigenous holistic and strength-based indicators, derived from direct community involvement in 22 different communities across the globe, the US-based National Indian Child Welfare Association (NICWA) found common themes among First Nations, Kanaka Maoli, Māori, Aboriginal Australians, and Sámi communities (Rountree and Smith 2016). Indigenous well-being indicators are relational, in contrast to Western indicators. An individual's well-being is bound up with human and non-human kinships as well as the well-being of the community. Roundtree and Smith summarise these indices as "grounded in balance and harmony in human relationships and the natural and spiritual world" (Rountree and Smith 2016: 207).

In the context of the United States, Terry Cross finds that well-being is related to "healthy relationships, positive community relationships and contributions, [and] a sense of purpose and participation in one's community" as well as sufficient resources (Cross 2011, cited in Rountree 2016: 210). In Australia, Aboriginal kinship relations as well as connections "beyond blood relations – with 'aunties' and 'uncles'" and elders – are often cited as critical components of well-being (Priest, Mackean, and Briggs 2012, cited in Rountree 2016: 213) Across the studies that Rountree and Smith identified, the thematic of relations and connections were consistently expressed – between generations, in concentric circles of place, and in relations of reciprocal care with all entities. It is not that Indigenous peoples do not know what is needed for 'health', for life – it is that Indigenous peoples know what is life-producing far beyond any individual's well-being.

Leanne Simpson has expressed this very succinctly in her own Anishinaabeg nation's definition of *Mino-bimaadiziwin*: well-being as the way of a good life, or as an integrated existence. Simpson writes:

> Our knowledge system, the education system, the economic system, and the political system of the Michi Saagiig Nishinaabeg were designed to promote more life. Our way of living was designed to generate life – not just human life but the life of all living things.
>
> *(Simpson 2018: 118)*

In contrast to these Indigenous life-producing ways of knowing, I shift in this chapter towards an understanding of what, at the level of a World Health Organization, are now deep contradictions in determining Indigenous health. I also discuss biocapital and biopower as part of, rather than apart from, racial capitalism and settler colonialism. Finally, I hone in on the sphere of human action that is 'health' as a particular nexus that illustrates how humanitarianism is a governance of Others.

Healing in the context of racial capitalism and settler colonialism

Billy-Ray Belcourt, a young two-spirit Driftpile Cree, reflects on the idea of 'slow death' (Berlant 2007), Berlant's term for the wearing out of those who live hard lives:

> Ours are bodies that have been depleted by time. ... In the wake of both eventful and slowed kinds of premature death, what does it mean that the state wants so eagerly to move Indigenous bodies, to touch them, so to speak?
>
> *(Belcourt 2016: Online).*

The state wants to measure our death, its volume, its rate.

US Public Health researcher Jane Freemantle moves to measure this slow violence in her report on the scope of the Indigenous 'health' crisis: "The almost 400 million Indigenous people worldwide are all united by a common thread: their low standards of health compared with national averages and compared with non-Indigenous counterparts in the same regions" (Freemantle et al. 2015: 1). These are demographic reports designed to establish a distance from a norm. These figures starkly show, if anything, a state of precarity within our relations – with each other, with land, with water, and other relations that sustain our lives in comparison with normed populations.

These are the figures, Margaret Kress (Cree) says, frame the Indigenous as the eternal victim, the moribund: "Social, economic, and legal chronicles found in health, social services, and educational discourses often project Indigenous peoples as marginalized figures subsisting in conditions of poverty and dismay ..." (Kress 2017: 1). This is the 'damage' research that Eve Tuck (Unangan) has called a moratorium on (Tuck 2009; Tuck and Yang 2018). It is the underlying impetus for a movement among Indigenous researchers to take control of this statistical production (Kukutai and Taylor 2016; Rountree 2016; Walters and Andersen 2013).

In the context of this global statistical pronouncement on Indigenous precarity, I want to ask two questions. Do these figures that represent our deviance, our outsized death, actually marshal resources or will to improve Indigenous health, or do they represent something else? And, if these figures point to some other measurement, or are entangled with some other concern, what is this concern? I now return to my discussion of health as a particular point of humanitarian intervention. The struggles for human rights in the field of health are powerfully entangled with power relations that steadily monetise and financialise their human subjects. Here, I assess the contexts of care and health in a capitalist economy powerfully enacted through race and bio-power. Biopower requires a systemic knowledge of life and of 'living beings'. These are "Systems of knowledge [that] provide cognitive and normative maps that open up biopolitical spaces ... [t]hey make the reality of life conceivable and calculable in such a way that it can be shaped and transformed" (Lemke and Trump 2010: 99).

In both Canada and the United States, Indigenous women, trans individuals, and LGBTQ2S people suffer rape, disappearance, and death. In the United States and in Canada, the increasing violence against women occurs simultaneously with the destruction of lands (Konsmo and Pacheco 2016). The dissolution of American Indian and Alaska Native (AI/AN) families is accompanied by their separation from the lands and waters degraded by extractive industries. The disintegration of families in urban areas further serves to racialise Native communities without recognising their Indigeneity. All of this occurs while AI/AN in the United States enjoy a self-determination established by the Indian Self-Determination and Education Assistance Act of 1975, a 43-year contractual experiment with US capitalism. In terms of who has 'developed' self-determination and who has not, and a growing disparity between Native nations, we know it produces inequity. The 'losers' in capitalising their resources lack the kinds of 'infrastructure' like clean drinking water they don't have to pack, roads, housing and other amenities that are common to most of the rest of the United States. But the degradation is most visible in the vulnerability of and violence in the lives of those caught between normalising narratives of health and prosperity and the actual structural inequity of individuals and communities living without basic infrastructure. In the middle of the current COVID-19 pandemic (March 2020), this will become crystal clear.

These are conditions made visible to the 'mainstream' public (and to ourselves) in large-scale statistical comparisons with white and other racialised populations. According to the 2003–2009 Indian Health Service figures, American Indian and Alaska Native deaths remain the highest of any demographic in all categories of disease, except for Alzheimer's disease. The 2014 edition of Trends in Indian Health show these disparities are monstrous in proportion. In its comparison of 2007–2009 AI/AN deaths to the 2008 death rates of other racial categories in the United States, the report shows AI/AN death rates soared: alcohol-related deaths were 520 per cent greater; deaths from tuberculosis were 450 per cent greater; deaths from chronic liver disease and cirrhosis were 368 per cent greater; deaths from motor vehicle crashes accounted for a 207 per cent difference; deaths from diabetes mellitus were 177 per cent greater; deaths from unintentional injuries were 141 per cent greater; deaths from poisoning were 118 per cent greater; deaths from homicides were 86 per cent greater; and deaths from suicides were 60 per cent greater. According to Indian Health Services (IHS) reporting, AI/AN deaths from suicide topped the number of suicides from every other demographic in the nation.

These are figures that, paraphrasing Sandrina de Finney, I would characterise as a biomedical (industrial) complex extraction of numbers. Predictably, as many have noted, these figures of disease and premature death are mostly given without the context they belong in. The shortened life spans of American Indian and Alaska Natives are attributed to inequities in health services and behaviors of individuals – without accounting for their location in racial capitalism-settler colonialism. Consequently, the Western medical diagnosis/treatment for trauma and intergenerational trauma (current diagnoses) does not extend the supports necessary for lives still lived under siege and undergoing constant re-traumatisation (de Finney 2018). As de Finney and her colleagues have argued, such diagnoses simply track families into medicalised regimes.

Given the magnitude of these harms, I want to speak about the entanglements Indigenous peoples face as they sort through their colonisers' systems of care and frameworks of human rights. In this discussion, I refresh the concept of biopower as I used it in *Therapeutic Nations*. I also foreground the contexts of settler colonialism and racial capitalism. For those who are not familiar with these terms, I define them here. Jodi Melamed (paraphrasing Cedric Robinson, in turn) characterises racial capitalism thus:

> Capital can only be capital when it is accumulating, and it can only accumulate by producing and moving through relations of severe inequality among human groups – capitalists with the means of production/workers without the means of subsistence, creditors/debtors, conquerors of land made property/the dispossessed and removed.
>
> *(Melamed 2015: 277)*

In other words, the term 'racial capitalism' requires its users to recognise that capitalism *is* racial capitalism. Racialisation sorts humans for capitalist care or destruction. Liberal democracies like the United States and Canada are structured by and through racial capitalism, in material and predatory social contractual relations. Beyond racial capitalism's known propensity for accumulation and violence, Melamed asks that we attend to "capital as a system of expropriating violence on collective life itself" (Melamed 2015: 78). Citing Ruth Wilson Gilmore, Melamed invokes the term 'anti-relationality', the act of controlling all relations, or reducing myriad life relations to just those relations that sustain neoliberal democratic capitalism. As Melamed uses Gilmore's term, anti-relationality describes how capitalism appropriates and erases relations between children, their families and communities decimated by incarceration – and/or driven into cities while Indigenous places are destroyed. This is not a by-product of capitalist relations; it is racial capitalism's intent.

Racial capitalism co-evolved with settler colonialism. Settler colonialism accounts for the historicity as well as the present-ness of the relations detailed above. Eve Tuck puts it simply: "Settler colonialism [is] differentiated from what one might call exogenous colonialism in that the colonisers arrive at a place ('discovering' it) [and make it] a permanent home (claiming it)" (Tuck and Yang 2018: 2). Tuck further specifies that settler colonialism also required "the enslavement and labor of bodies that have been stolen from their homelands and transported to labor the land stolen from Indigenous people" (Tuck and Yang 2018: 2). Scott Lauria Morgensen underscores the centrality of biopower to any analysis of settler colonialism in observing how settler colonization relies upon both genocide and amalgamation. Settler nations incorporate Indigenous lands and lives, reducing the Indigene to a 'bare life', a life without its relations, while 'indigenising and naturalising' white settler citizens, the legitimate subjects of Western law. In the logic of settler colonialism, the "function of governmentality is to 'make life' compatible with the state of exception … consigning certain subjects to a state of bare life [enter the relations of capital or let die]" (Morgensen 2011: 55). The law both promises life to the Indigene (within amalgamation) and produces conditions of bare life or death (erasure) for those who struggle for lives that do not produce for racial capitalism. Different iterations of racial capitalism across the globe depended upon settler colonialism's biopolitical distinction between its 'civilisation' and the biorationalised inferiority of the Other, a well-documented distinction. These critiques of liberal humanism and the call for multiple ways of being human are now common in Critical Indigenous Studies and Critical Ethnic Studies but remain only partially legible (known, read or acted on) among dominant settler populations (Silva 2007; Mignolo 2009;

Latty 2016; McKittrick 2015). It is my contention that racial capitalism's discourse on health has emerged as a premier site at which biopower operates to extend the logic of settler colonialism and the depredations of racial capitalism through the financialisation of 'care'.

The rise of a global human rights and humanitarianism after World War II reconfigured liberalism's racial orders; it did not reform or erase them. Humanitarianism is now a field wherein dissolving welfare state capitalisms once positioned as benefactors abandon the subjects of its development, allowing capital to choose its most 'viable'. It is a field of struggle. The universal subject of human rights is the male, heteronormative white citizen of a nation-state. However, much of humanity remains stateless: outside of the positive sovereignty of the nation-state. As Jacques Rancière surmises, "the Rights of Man turned out to be the rights of the rightless, of the populations hunted out of their homes and land and threatened by ethnic slaughter ..." He continues, humanitarian rights become "the rights of the victims, the rights of those who were unable to enact any rights or even any claim in their name" (Rancière 2004: 297–8). The Indigenous actually form a large part of these peoples who, without positive sovereignty, are thus at the mercy of humanitarian 'governance'. The UNDRIP can be seen as a move to mitigate this condition, but its ability to protect is left at the level of moral humanitarian sanction. Even within a positive sovereignty, constitutionally recognised Native nations in the United States remain vulnerable as the state abandons treaty obligations to their health. This neoliberal moment is one in which nation-states have unleashed the financialisation of all spheres of life, including 'health'.

Of life and death: A litany of state violence and statistical norms

Matthew Sparke foregrounds the significance of health inequality in the age of neoliberal human rights: "But nothing embodies and illustrates inequality more materially than our health" (Sparke 2014: 684). He goes on to say that "a growing and heterodox literature on the epidemiology of inequality indicates that health outcomes embody the impact of inequalities on human life in a profoundly consequential way" (2014: 684–5). From the vantage point of international humanitarian agencies, the harms of settler colonialism/racial capitalism are not covert. An overview of health inequalities vitally underlines some of the governing political and economic structures that restrict who is entitled to biomedical self-optimisation. There is an increasing split between the subject of a new biogenetic world of individualised Western medical care and those who comprise the "large body counts" of those excluded from this world. Sparke writes, "[u]nequal and distinct forms of health governance thereby create a stark biopolitical division between different types of body counting" (2014: 684), creating different life worlds for those treated to life and those relinquished to early and prolonged deaths. As Canada and the United States abandoned their welfare states, deserting the interests of labour and valorising the production of life (Cooper 2010), they created new objects of development. Canadian and US economies moved toward heavy, speculative investments in bio-life at the same time that actual expenditures for socialised health institutions declined.

According to Kaushik Sunder Rajan, there is a peculiar epistemic overlap that link economics/capitalism and the life sciences/biotechnology. Both spheres draw upon one another for "metaphoric or epistemic sustenance" in understanding and managing "complex systems of risk" (Rajan 2012: 7). This epistemic overlap underwrites a hierarchy of populations who are the subjects of bio-life (optimal life) and other populations forced to assume the risk of their own precarity. In addition to lacking control over their exploitation as raw materials for research, these populations have few opportunities to benefit from developments in health technology or advances in the quality of health care, because this is not fundamentally about health. Big Health, like Big Pharma, is not about healing. As Joseph Dumit writes in *Prescription Maximization and the Accumulation of Surplus Health in the Pharmaceutical Industry: The Bio_Marx_Experiment*, the health industry has increasingly come to view patients and illness as commodities: "It is Illness as Value that is now being maximized, and the Health of Patients rather than their Labor that is being exploited" (Dumit 2012: 48). Health care now aims to define symptoms as targets of diagnostic and therapeutic development for medicines and therapies, or arenas of intense economic speculation (Dumit 2012: 53). This is humanitarian bio-governance.

Canada and the United States are nations steeped in the myths of progress and the ethos of humanitarianism. These myths mask the violent erasure of the Indigenous by settler-colonial projects to develop lands or displace peoples. The daily violence erupts occasionally in spectacular headlines, though its actual operations usually take place under the cover of numbing silence. In *Violence, Colonialism, and Space: Towards a Decolonizing Dialogue*, Cindy Holmes, Sarah Hunt, and Amy Piedalue task us to understand how "certain types of violence are made invisible" (Holmes et al. 2014: 540). In this article, Hunt in particular enjoins us "to make visible what each space, with its codes, its enumeration, its statistical averaging, and its management techniques produces us as" (2014: 541). For me, it seems particularly important to show how these large data descriptions of Indigenous anomie eclipse the specifics and sources of our suffering, and perhaps more importantly, our specific strengths, silencing the narratives of the strengths of our actual lives or the conditions of our actual deaths.

State violence is visible in the orderly and everyday way that nation-states practice bio-management. Maggie Walter and Chris Andersen's (Metís) *Indigenous Statistics* details the way that Canadian and Australian demographics "both reflect *and* construct particular visions" (2013: 7–9) important to the state. Demographics play an important role in "telling ourselves who we are" (Walter and Andersen 2013: 7–9). Statistics calculating the health and well-being of Native peoples play out on a "terrain of racialisation", where they support state developmental goals as "part of the broader effects of colonialism" (Walter and Andersen 2013: 21). Walter and Anderson argue that development literatures dominate any contemporary discussion of the Indigenous and that statistics always takes center stage in these discourses. Predictably, since development is in the state's interest, categories are methodologically configured to produce only certain kinds of data. Walter and Andersen critique the *methodology* of statistical measurement rather than its quantitative value. They show how the 'what' that is portrayed as factual is in actuality intensely political (Walter and Anderson 2013, also see Nelson 2015).

Over several generations, nation-states' portrayal of the 'Indian problem' has shifted from narratives of "inconvenient continued existence/biological inferiority" to narratives of "inconvenient cultural/culturally linked behavior deviance[s]" (Walter and Andersen 2013: 22). In depictions that serve state agendas rather than the interests of any specific community, Indigenes are subject to interpellations to "close the socio (economic gap)" and to be "brought up to standard" (22). The Indigene is a marked as a developmental lag: a problem that needs to be fixed (22). The 'Indian problem' is defined by normative desires of the state: the desire for developing undeveloped land, the desire for water where aquifers are rare, the desire to reduce the diversity of the land to mono-cultural crops, the desire to manage fish resources until no fish return. The dominant public of the nation-state construes such 'grand schemes of development' as the apex of life, in juxtaposition with the debased existence of the Indigene. In this narrative about subpar populations, 'normality' forever eludes the Indigenous, rationalising our continued subjection to a therapeutic state as well as the relentless search for statistics to re/define the 'Indian problem'. Many of these statistical models and narratives have had no actual input from Indigenous communities, either in rich states like the United States, and Canada or internationally. But it is this knowledge production, and not our own knowledges of our lived experiences that underwrite decisions that continue to produce a lower quality of life for most and death for many. This is the reason why it is paramount that Indigenous communities create their own indicators of health.

As Lisa Stevenson tells us in her keenly felt evaluation of death in an Arctic community, "the most benign public health programs are in fact genocidal" (Stevenson 2014: 44). She reflects with Veena Das on "the psychic life of biopolitics and how the biopolitical state, committed to enhancing the life of the population renders lifeless a people's particular form of life" (Stevenson 2014: 44). Krista Maxwell calls for "vigorous" historical analyses of "how liberalism enables myriad forms of settler violence" (Maxwell 2017: 978). I would frame this more tightly, asserting that liberalism and its spawn neoliberalism *is* settler violence and that humanitarianism is the sphere in which it is enacted. Liberal humanitarianism lets Indigenous death exist where it cannot 'heal' us, incorporate us, or erase us through other means. I have critiqued trauma, and even historical trauma as liberal terms of engagement in reconciliation discourses for restorative justice. In doing so, I do not refuse the actual violence perpetrated in the past. Rather, I assert that the conditions of violence and death are not past. These conditions provide a structure – they are structural – so that each generational iteration is under attack by means particular to the morphing power relations in that moment. There is neither 'healing' nor closure for a structure. The structure of violence is settler colonialism and the deep and pervasive harm it perpetuates, and to call this harm simply 'trauma' is myopic, if not wrong. Trauma seeks to address the individual but leaves the structure alone. It assumes that a moment or event rather than social and physical relations are what kills. The Indigenous tactically utilised historical trauma as a discursive mobilisation to avail themselves of the humanitarian mechanisms for righting wrongs, because these mechanisms promised justice (Million 2013; Kirmayer, Gone, and Moses, 2014). However, these liberal humanitarian tropes are wearied at this point – in fact, moribund. The violence is not in the past, it is in the present in Western gendered and sexualised hierarchies in our families, in our communities, in everyday relations with settlers. These relations sever and kill what makes us possible to be cohesive peoples who act from our own sacred relations, the practices that produce life for ourselves and all the entities that we are reciprocally responsible to.

Indigenous well-being is holistic and cannot be abstracted and treated within global programs for 'health' that preclude this holism. Indigenous well-being implies the opposite of abstraction. This is a well-being that is never solely defined by human relations; thus it cannot be dematerialised in accounts of the "social determinants of health" (Leeuw 2015: 91). Indigenous peoples suffer harms that *stem from* the killing and abstraction of their embodied, affective existences and spiritual, life-giving relations to both humans and non-humans. We must practice the resurgence of our generative life-giving ways of life as radical Indigenous care in ways that refuse and exceed neoliberal regimes of health. Caring is anti-capitalist. Caring builds the trust that creates communities: kinships between responsible, respectful, connected, purposeful Beings. We must take care to build the relations that Indigeneity requires.

References

Anaya, S.J. (2004). *Indigenous peoples in international law* 2nd ed., Oxford University Press: Oxford; New York.

Armstrong, J. (2009). *Constructing Indigeneity: Syilx Okanagan Oraliture and Tmixwcentrism*. PhD dissertation, Ernst-Moritz-Arndt Universität, Greifswald.

Belcourt, B.-R. (2016). 'Political depression in a time of reconciliation', *Active History*. Available: http://act ivehistory.ca/2016/01/political-depression-in-a-time-of-reconciliation/, accessed 15 June 2018.

Berlant, L. (2007). 'Slow death (sovereignty, obesity, lateral agency)', *Critical Inquiry*, vol 33, no 4: 754–780.

Cooper, M. (2010). *Life as Surplus: Biotechnology and Capitalism in the Neoliberal Era*. University of Washington Press: Seattle.

Corntassel, J. (2012). 'Re-envisioning resurgence: Indigenous pathways to decolonization and sustainable self-determination', *Decolonization: Indigeneity, Education and Society*, vol 1, no 1: 86–101.

Coulthard, G. (2014). *Red Skin, White Masks: Rejecting the Colonial Politics of Recognition*. University of Minnesota Press: Minneapolis.

Cross, T.L. et al. (2011). 'Defining youth success using culturally appropriate community-based participatory research methods', *Best Practices in Mental Health*, vol 7, no 1: 94–114.

Daigle, M. (2016). 'Awawanenitakik: the spatial politics of recognition and relational geographies of Indigenous self-determination', *The Canadian Geographer*, vol 60, no 2: 259–269.

De Leeuw, Sarah and Hunt, Sarah (2018). Unsettling decolonizing geographies. *Geography compass*, 12(7), pp.e12376–n/a.

Dumit, J. (2012). 'Prescription maximization and the accumulation of surplus health in the pharmaceutical industry: The bioMarx experiment', in K.S. Rajan (ed.) *Lively Capital, Biotechnologies, Ethics, and Governance in Global Markets*. Duke University Press: Durham, 45–92.

Fassin, D. (2012). *Humanitarian Reason: A Moral History of the Present Times*. University of California Press: Berkeley.

de Finney, S. (2018). 'Refusing the therapeutic nation: De-psychiatrizing social death and trauma under the settler carceral state', unpublished paper from *Critical Insurrections: Decolonizing Difficulties, Activist Imaginaries, and Collective Possibilities, the 4th Critical Ethnic Studies Association Conference*, 21–24 June. University of British Columbia, Vancouver.

Freemantle, J. et al. (2015). 'Indigenous mortality (revealed): the invisible illuminated', *American Journal of Public Health*, vol 105, no 4: 644–652.

Gray, R. (2018). 'Embodied heritage: enactments of Indigenous sovereignty', *Talk for World Issues Forum Western Washington University*. Available: https://vimeo.com/294656995, accessed 15 March 2020.

Hokowhitu, B. (2012). Producing Elite Indigenous Masculinities. *Settler Colonial Studies: Karangatia: Calling Out Gender and Sexuality in Settler Societies*, 2(2), pp.23–48.

Holmes, C., Hunt, S., and Piedalue, A. (2014). 'Violence, colonialism, and space: towards a decolonizing dialogue', *ACME: An International e-Journal for Critical Geographies*, vol 14, no 2: 539–570.

Hoover, E. (2017). *The River Is in Us: Fighting Toxics in a Mohawk Community*. University of Minnesota Press: Minneapolis.

Jewell, E. (2018). *Gimaadaasamin, We Are Accounting for the People: Support for Customary Governance in Deshkan Ziibiing*. PhD thesis, Royal Roads University, Victoria.

Kirmayer, L.J., Gone, J.P., and Moses, J. (2014). 'Rethinking historical trauma', *Transcultural Psychiatry*, vol 51, no 3: 299–319.

Konsmo, E.M. and Pacheco, A.K. (2016). *Violence on the Land, Violence on our Bodies: Building an Indigenous Response to Environmental Violence*. Women's Earth Alliance (WEA)-Native Youth Sexual Health Network (NYSHN): Berkeley and Toronto.

Kress, M.M. (2017). 'Reclaiming disability through pimatisiwin: Indigenous ethics, spatial justice, and gentle teaching', *International Perspectives on Inclusive Education*, vol 9: 23–57.

Kukutai, T. and Taylor, J. (2016). *Indigenous Data Sovereignty: Toward an Agenda*. Australian National University Press: Canberra.

Kuokkanen, R.J. (2007). *The Politics of Form and Alternative Autonomies: Indigenous Women, Subsistence Economies, and the Gift Paradigm*. Globalization Working Papers, no 07/2. McMasters University.

Kuokkanen, R.J. (2019). *Restructuring Relations: Indigenous Self-determination, Governance, and Gender*. Oxford University Press: New York.

Laduke, W. (2006). 'Indigenous power: A new energy economy', *Race, Poverty and the Environment*, vol 13, no 1: 6–10.

Latty, S. et al. (2016). 'Not enough human: At the scenes of Indigenous and Black dispossession', *Critical Ethnic Studies*, vol 2, no 2: 129–158.

Leeuw, S.D. (2015). 'Determinants of Indigenous peoples' health in Canada', in M. Greenwood et al. (eds.) *Determinants of Indigenous Peoples' Health in Canada: Beyond the Social*. Canadian Scholars' Press: Toronto, 90–99.

Lemke, T. and Trump, E.F. (2010). *Biopolitics: An Advanced Introduction*. New York University Press: New York.

Maxwell, K. (2017). 'Settler-humanitarianism: Healing the Indigenous child-victim', *Comparative Studies in Society and History*, vol 59, no 4: 974–1007.

McKittrick, K. (2015). *Sylvia Wynter: On Being Human as Praxis*. Duke University Press: Durham, NC.

Melamed, J. (2015). 'Racial capitalism', *Critical Ethnic Studies*, vol 1, no 1: 76–85.

Mignolo, W.D. (2009). 'Epistemic disobedience, independent thought and decolonial freedom', *Theory, Culture & Society*, vol 26, no 7–8: 159–181.

Million, D. (2013). *Therapeutic Nations: Healing in an Age of Indigenous Human Rights*. University of Arizona Press: Tucson.

Moreton-Robinson, A. (2013). 'Towards an Australian Indigenous women's standpoint theory', *Australian Feminist Studies*, vol 28, no 78: 331–347.

Morgensen, S. (2011). 'The biopolitics of settler colonialism: Right here, right now', *Settler Colonial Studies*, vol 1, no 1: 52–76.

Morgensen, S. (2014). 'Indigenous transnationalism and the AIDS pandemic: Challenging settler colonialism within global health governance', in A. Simpson and A. Smith *Theorizing Native Studies*. Duke University Press: Durham, 188–206.

Nelson, D.M. (2015). *Who Counts?: The Mathematics of Death and Life After Genocide*. Duke University Press: Durham.

Pihama, L. (2001). *Tihei Mauri Ora: Honouring Our Voices: Mana Wahine as a Kaupapa Māori Theoretical Frame-Work*. PhD thesis, University of Auckland, New Zealand.

Rajan, K.S. (2012). 'The capitalization of life and the liveliness of capital', in K.S. Rajan (ed.) *Lively Capital, Biotechnologies, Ethics, and Governance in Global Markets*. Duke University Press: Durham, NC, 1–41.

Rancière, J. (2004). 'Who is the subject of the rights of man?' *South Atlantic Quarterly*, vol 103, no 2–3: 297–310.

Rountree, J. and Smith, A. (2016). 'Strength-based well-being indicators for Indigenous children and families: A literature review of Indigenous communities' identifies well-being indicators', *American Indian and Alaska Native Mental Health Research*, vol 23, no 3: 206–220.

Da Silva, D.F. (2007). *Toward a Global Idea of Race*. University of Minnesota Press: Minneapolis.

Simpson, L.B. (2016). 'Indigenous resurgence and co-resistance', *Critical Ethnic Studies*, vol 2, no 2: 19–34.

Simpson, Leanne (2018). Centring Resurgence: Taking on Colonial Gender Violence in Indigenous Nation Building in Anderson, K, Campbell, M, & Belcourt, C (eds), *Keetsahnak / Our Missing and Murdered Indigenous Sisters*, University of Alberta Press: Edmonton, p. 215–239.

Sparke, M. (2014). 'Health', in R. Lee et al. (eds.) *The SAGE Handbook of Progress in Human Geography*. SAGE: Thousand Oaks, CA, 684–708.

Stevenson, L. (2014). *Life Beside Itself: Imagining Care in the Canadian Arctic*. University of California Press: Berkeley.

TallBear, K., 2015. Genomic Articulations of Indigeneity. In *Native Studies Keywords*. University of Arizona Press: Tucson.

Tuck, E. (2009). 'Suspending damage: a letter to communities', *Harvard Educational Review*, vol 79, no 3: 409–428.

Tuck, E. and Yang, K.W. (2018). 'R-words: Refusing research', in D. Paris and M.T. Winn (eds.) *Humanizing Research: Decolonizing Qualitative Inquiry With Youth and Communities*. SAGE: Thousand Oaks, 228–248.

Ullrich, J.S. (2019). 'For the love of our children: An Indigenous connectedness framework', *AlterNative: An International Journal of Indigenous Peoples*, vol 15, no 2: 121–130.

United Nations General Assembly. (2008). *United Nations Declaration on the Rights of Indigenous Peoples*. United Nations: Geneva. Available: http://www.un.org/esa/socdev/unpfi/document/DRIPS_en.pdf, accessed 15 March 2020.

Uukw, Delgam (1987). *The Spirit in the Land: Statements of the Gitksan and Wet'suwet'en Hereditary Chiefs in The Supreme Court of British Columbia, 1987-1990*. REFLECTIONS: Gabriola, B.C.

Vaughn, T. (2017). *Sovereign Embodiment: Native Hawaiian Expressions of Kuleana in the Diaspora*. PhD dissertation, University of California, Riverside.

Walters, M. and Anderson, C. (2013). *Indigenous Statistics: A Quantitative Research Methodology*. Left Coast Press: Walnut Creek, CA.

30

Indigenous environmental justice

Towards an ethical and sustainable future

Deborah McGregor

Introduction

The struggles of Indigenous peoples across the globe to seek equality and justice have been well documented by the UN Special Rapporteur on the Rights of Indigenous peoples. More recently in 2018, then Special Rapporteur, Victoria Tauli-Corpuz documented escalating violence, attacks, threats, and criminalisation of Indigenous peoples in their resistance to large scale development projects and the extractive industry. Furthermore, as the quotes below illustrate, Indigenous peoples have also called into question the effectiveness of so-called 'solutions' generated by international bodies, such as United Nations generated conceptions of 'sustainable development'.

> The 'New World Order' which is engineered by those who have abused and raped Mother Earth, colonized, marginalized, and discriminated against us, is being imposed on us viciously. This is recolonization coming under the name of globalization and trade liberalization.
> *(Beijing Declaration of Indigenous Women 1995, Article 6: online)*

> There exist many examples of genocide against Indigenous Peoples, therefore, the Convention Against Genocide must be changed to include the genocide of Indigenous Peoples.
> *(Indigenous Peoples Earth Charter 1992, Article 4: online)*

> We see that Mother Earth and all life is in a serious state of peril. We see the current model of sustainable development continues to proceed on the road of peril. As indigenous peoples we have experienced the terrible and negative impacts of this approach.
> *(Rio+20 International Conference of Indigenous Peoples (ICIP) 2012: online)*

In this chapter, I advocate that a distinct formulation of Indigenous environmental justice (IEJ) is required in order to address the challenges of the ecological crisis as well as the various forms of violence and injustices experienced specifically by Indigenous peoples. This calls for extending beyond the important yet limited conventional environmental justice scholarship that, while it excels at diagnosis of injustice to humanity, seeks remediation within the confines of the current political, economic and legal context (McGregor 2018). A distinct IEJ formulation must ground its foundations in Indigenous philosophies, ontologies, and epistemologies in order to reflect Indigenous conceptions of what constitutes *justice*. This approach calls into question the legitimacy and applicability of global and nation-state political and legal mechanisms, as these same states and international governing bodies continue to fail Indigenous peoples around the world. This is as true in Canada as elsewhere, as outlined in various inquiries and commissions (National Inquiry into Missing and Murdered Indigenous Women and Girls [NIMMIWG] 2019; Royal Commission on Aboriginal Peoples [RCAP] 1996; Canadian Truth and Reconciliation Commission [TRC] 2015).

Indigenous nations have not been idle, merely waiting for global and national governing bodies to address injustice; they have engaged in their own diagnoses of the core issues and put forward their own solutions, as exemplified by Indigenous environmental or climate change declarations at the international, national and local levels. This is not to suggest that those governing bodies are any less accountable – they are most certainly accountable for their actions/ inactions! Yet while various legal human rights mechanisms have been developed and deployed, they have suffered from significant limitations and have not turned the tide of the ecocidal path along which all of humanity appears to be moving. Indigenous peoples have therefore generated their own statements outlining the key issues and paths for moving forward. For example, at the United Nations Conference on Environment and Development (or 'Earth Summit', convened in Rio de Janeiro in 1992), Indigenous nations stated through the *Kari-Oca Declaration* (1992: online):

> We, the Indigenous peoples, maintain our inherent rights to self-determination. We have always had the right to decide our own forms of government, to use our own laws, to raise and educate our children, to our own cultural identity without interference.
>
> We continue to maintain our rights as peoples despite centuries of deprivation, assimilation, and genocide.
>
> We maintain our inalienable rights to our lands and territories, to all our resources – above and below – and to our waters. We assert our ongoing responsibility to pass these onto the future generations.

Articles 74 and 77 of the *Indigenous Peoples Earth Charter*, also arising from the Earth Summit (1992: online) state that:

> Non-Indigenous Peoples have come to our lands and resources to benefit themselves. And to the impoverishment of our peoples. Indigenous Peoples are victims of development. In many cases Indigenous Peoples are exterminated in the name of a development program. There are numerous examples of such occurrences.
>
> The eurocentric notion of ownership is destroying our peoples. We must return to our own view of the world, of the land and of development. The issue cannot be separated from Indigenous People's rights.

These truths were reaffirmed at the 2002 follow-up conference, the World Summit on Sustainable Development (WSSD), held in Johannesburg, South Africa, via the *Kimberley Declaration*. Through this statement, Indigenous peoples gathered at the 2002 Summit identified economic globalisation as the main obstacle to achieving recognition of Indigenous rights and sustainability within the United Nations system, noting that:

> We are deeply concerned that the activities of multinational mining corporations on Indigenous lands have led to the loss and desecration of our lands, as exemplified here on Khoi-San territory. These activities have caused immense health problems, interfered with access to, and occupation of our sacred sites, destroyed and depleted Mother Earth and undermined our cultures.
>
> *(Kimberley Declaration 2002: online)*

Ten years later, at the 2012 United Nations Conference on Sustainable Development, or Rio+20, also in Rio de Janeiro, Indigenous nations convened their own event, the *Indigenous Peoples Global Conference on Rio+20 and Mother Earth*. The resulting declaration, *Kari-Oca 2* (2012) terms the root cause of the current ecological crisis the "institutionalization of colonialism":

> Since Rio 1992, we as Indigenous Peoples see that *colonization has become the very basis of the globalization of trade and the dominant capitalist global economy*. The exploitation and plunder of the world's ecosystems and biodiversity, as well as the violations of the inherent rights of Indigenous Peoples that depend on them, have intensified. Our rights to self determination, to our own governance and own self-determined development, our inherent rights to our lands, territories and resources are increasingly and alarmingly under attack by the collaboration of governments and transnational corporations. Indigenous activists and leaders defending their territories continue to suffer repression [and] militarization, including assassination, imprisonment, harassment and vilification as 'terrorists'. The violation of our collective rights faces the same impunity. Forced relocation or assimilation assault our future generations, cultures, languages, spiritual ways and relationship to the earth, economically and politically.
>
> *(Kari-Oca 2 2012: online italics added)*

Through the *Kari-Oca 2* declaration, Indigenous nations also levelled criticism at the solutions proposed by the United Nations in its outcomes document "The Future We Want" (UNCSD Rio+20 2012: online). *Kari-Oca 2* (2012) observes that:

> *The Green Economy is nothing more than capitalism of nature;* a perverse attempt by corporations, extractive industries and governments to cash in on Creation by privatizing, commodifying, and selling off the Sacred and all forms of life and the sky, including the air we breathe, the water we drink and all the genes, plants, traditional seeds, trees, animals, fish, biological and cultural diversity, ecosystems and traditional knowledge that make life on Earth possible and enjoyable. (italics added)

Indigenous environmental and climate change declarations point to the current state of Indigenous peoples and the environment and offer a just path forward for all relations. Indigenous peoples struggle every day against resource extractive 'development' initiatives that negatively impact their lives, lands and communities (LaDuke 1999; 2005). Various forms of environmental crisis/injustice have been a fact of life for Indigenous peoples for centuries. Anthropogenic environmental change has been imposed on Indigenous peoples by historical and ongoing colonialism, including the loss of land through the activities of resource-intensive industries (Davis and Todd 2017; Richmond 2015; Whyte 2017).

This chapter builds upon efforts of Indigenous peoples in recent decades by offering a distinct understanding of Indigenous EJ that is both explicit and implicit in international Indigenous environmental and climate change declarations. I will provide a rationale for why distinct IEJ frameworks are necessary based on the knowledge and experience shared by Indigenous nations from around the world over the past 40 years. I will show that Indigenous nations have already diagnosed the fundamental causes of the global environmental/climate change crisis and set a path forward for a renewed relationships with the Earth that will assist in establishing a sustainable future for all life. I will continue to refer to various 'Declarations' and plans of action, the outcomes documents such as those cited above which have been developed by Indigenous peoples when major global environmental, climate change and sustainable development conferences have been convened. These Declarations point to the necessary foundations of a just, sustainable future as expressed through Indigenous knowledge systems, legal orders, governance and conceptions of justice. Simply put, the knowledge necessary to seek a path of life (as distinct from the widespread destruction we are currently witnessing) already exists and has done so for thousands of years.

Genocide, colonialism, and Indigenous environmental justice: A Canadian context

Similar to the violence and violations expressed by Indigenous peoples globally through the environmental declarations mentioned above, Canada's *Truth and Reconciliation Commission* (TRC) achieved these findings:

> The history of residential schools presented in this report commenced by placing the schools in the broader history of the global European colonization of Indigenous peoples and their lands. Residential schooling was only a part of the colonization of Aboriginal people. The policy of colonization suppressed Aboriginal culture and languages, disrupted Aboriginal government, destroyed Aboriginal economies, and confined Aboriginal people to marginal and often unproductive land. When that policy resulted in hunger, disease, and poverty, the federal government failed to meet its obligations to Aboriginal people. That policy was dedicated to eliminating Aboriginal peoples as distinct political and cultural entities and must be described for what it was: a policy of cultural genocide.
>
> *(TRC 2015: 102)*

Over time, various iterations of this policy of cultural genocide, as described in the TRC's final report, involved a host of injustices, including seizing control over lands and resources and denying Aboriginal peoples the opportunity to engage in Canadian social, political and economic life. One key aspect of dispossession from lands and resources is exclusion from environmental decision-making. Indigenous sovereignty, jurisdiction, and authority over decision-making have decreased as others have gained control over the lands through violent historical and ongoing colonial processes. Traditional Indigenous governance structures and regimes were systematically undermined through various colonial interventions, and these facets – dispossession from their territories and exclusion from decision making – together have contributed to virtually every environmental challenge facing Indigenous peoples today. The TRC has pointed out that such colonialism remains an ongoing process, shaping both the structure and the quality of the relationship between the settlers and Indigenous peoples (TRC 2015: 19).

More recently, and even more chillingly, the National Inquiry into Missing and Murdered Indigenous Women and Girls revealed in its final report that:

The violence the National Inquiry heard amounts to a race-based genocide of Indigenous Peoples, including First Nations, Inuit and Métis, which especially targets women, girls, and 2SLGBTQQIA people. This genocide has been empowered by colonial structures evidenced notably by the Indian Act, the Sixties Scoop, residential schools and breaches of human and Indigenous rights, leading directly to the current increased rates of violence, death, and suicide in Indigenous populations.

(NIMMIWG 2019: 50)

In addition to outright genocide, the concept of *environmental racism* provides further insight into why Indigenous peoples in Canada are over-represented in incidences of environmental injustice (Jacobs 2010). Dhillon and Young (2010 26) define environmental racism as "… the deliberate or intentional siting of hazardous waste sites, landfills, incinerators, and polluting industries in communities inhabited by minorities and/or the poor'. Peoples and communities subject to this type of racism are often impoverished, marginalized, and excluded from dominant society in various ways. The ongoing drinking water crisis in First Nation communities in Canada is an example of an environmental injustice issue that continues to plague many communities (Collins et al. 2017; McGregor 2012). The context of these injustices is described by James Anaya, United Nations Special Rapporteur on the Rights of Indigenous Peoples, who made the following observations:

One of the most dramatic contradictions indigenous peoples in Canada face is that so many live in abysmal conditions on traditional territories that are full of valuable and plentiful natural resources. These resources are in many cases targeted for extraction and development by non-indigenous interests. While indigenous peoples potentially have much to gain from resource development within their territories, they also face the highest risks to their health, economy, and cultural identity from any associated environmental degradation. Perhaps more importantly, indigenous nations' efforts to protect their long-term interests in lands and resources often fit uneasily into the efforts by private non-indigenous companies, with the backing of the federal and provincial governments, to move forward with resource projects.

(Anaya 2014: 19)

Thus, the broader situation within which any process seeking environmental justice for Indigenous people in Canada must operate is steeped in systemically racist (and sexist) colonial and violent ideology that continues in the present day. Collectively, the outcomes of justice inquiries and commissions undertaken by the Canadian state, which rely upon colonial conceptions and practices of justice, have routinely failed, and continue to fail, Indigenous peoples. It is with this in mind that we recognise the need for an alternative foundation for achieving environmental justice for not only Indigenous peoples, but for the planet as well.

The rationale for an exploration of a distinct Indigenous environmental justice paradigm stems from this view that addressing environmental injustice in any meaningful way must originate from Indigenous peoples themselves. The dispossession of Indigenous peoples from, and the literal transformation of, traditional lands (the 'environment'), have been at work for over 500 years (Davis and Todd 2017; Whyte 2017). Disruption of these relationships has had devastating consequences (Big Canoe and Richmond 2014). Within this context, continuing to rely on government and other non-Indigenous legal systems to resolve any injustice, let alone environmental injustices, will not serve Indigenous peoples in the manner necessary, as the TRC and MMIWG inquiries have revealed. Similarly, and as valuable as existing, non-Indigenous-derived,

EJ theoretical and methodological frameworks are, achieving Indigenous environmental justice will require more than simply incorporating Indigenous perspectives into non-Indigenous systems.

The planetary crisis: Genocide of all life

> It is an imperative for us, as Indigenous peoples, to stand in their way, because it means more ethnocide and genocide for us. It will lead to the disappearance of the diverse biological and cultural resources in this world which we have sustained. It will cause the further erosion and destruction of our Indigenous knowledge, spirituality, and culture. It will exacerbate the conflicts occurring on our lands and communities and our displacement from our ancestral territories.
>
> *(Beijing Declaration of Indigenous Women 1995, Article 9: online)*

Indigenous peoples over the decades have presented a distinct diagnosis of the planetary ecological crisis evidenced in the observations shared as part of Indigenous environmental declarations. Their diagnosis differs dramatically from the approach taken by United Nations and other international organisations that continue to adhere to conventional approaches to sustainable development; i.e., development to suit humanity (particularly certain segments thereof), utilising the same economic, environmental and political paradigms that have created the ecological crisis in the first place. For example, in the *Kari-Oca 2* (2012: online) Declaration, Indigenous peoples critiqued the UN's approach:

> We see the goals of UNCSD Rio+20, the 'Green Economy' and its premise that the world can only 'save' nature *by commodifying its life giving and life sustaining capacities* as a continuation of the colonialism that Indigenous Peoples and our Mother Earth have faced and resisted for 520 years. The '*Green Economy*' promises to eradicate poverty but in fact will only favor and respond to multinational enterprises and capitalism. It is a continuation of a global economy based upon fossil fuels, the destruction of the environment by exploiting nature through extractive industries such as mining, oil exploration and production, intensive mono-culture agriculture, and other capitalist investments. All of these efforts are directed toward profit and the accumulation of capital by the few. (italics added)

The *Mandaluyong Declaration*, stemming from the *Global Conference on Indigenous Women, Climate Change and REDD Plus* (2010), points to the underlying causes of climate change (arguably the same root causes as the global ecological crisis). Also important in the *Mandaluyong Declaration* is the assertion that while Indigenous peoples are not the primary cause of the global environmental/climate crisis, they are the most affected, and bear an unjust burden of adaptation while simultaneously being rendered even more vulnerable due to human and Indigenous rights violations. The *Mandaluyong Declaration* outlines the impacts that the economic world order has on Indigenous peoples and the most vulnerable within Indigenous societies:

> While we have least contributed to the problem of climate change, we have to carry the burdens of adapting to its adverse impacts. This is because of the unwillingness of rich, industrialized countries to change their unsustainable production and consumption patterns and pay their environmental debt for causing this ecological disaster. Modernity and capitalist development which [are] based on the use of fossil fuels and which promote

unsustainable and excessive production and consumption of unnecessary goods and services, individualism, patriarchy, and incessant profit-seeking have caused climate change.

(Mandaluyong Declaration 2010: online)

Ironically, the 'solutions' (e.g., the 'Green Economy'), proposed by the United Nations and other international organisations, may actually exacerbate existing conditions. In 2011, Indigenous peoples convened a gathering in Manaus, Brazil, in preparation for the United Nations Conference on Sustainable Development to be held the following year. In so doing, they generated the *Manaus Declaration* which points to a number of considerations that the Green Economy paradigm fails to address. Indigenous peoples again, as in earlier international environmental/sustainable development gatherings, reiterated the role of colonialism and the unchecked economic and political world order and its primacy in contributing to *unsustainable* development. As the *Manaus Declaration* (2011: online) points out:

> The continuing gross violations of our rights to our lands, territories and resources and to self-determination by governments and corporations, remain as key obstacles to the achievement of sustainable development. Indigenous activists and leaders defending their territories still continue to be harassed, tortured, vilified as 'terrorists' and assassinated by powerful vested interests. Since sustainable development has not been substantially implemented, *the world is now in a multiple crisis*; ecological, economic and climatic, including biodiversity erosion, desertification, food, water and energy shortage and worsening global economic recession, social instability and crisis of values. (italics added)

This statement echoes those of the earlier cited *Kimberley Declaration* of a decade prior: "[s]ince 1992 the ecosystems of the earth have been compounding in change. We are in crisis. We are in an accelerating spiral of climate change that will not abide unsustainable greed (Kimberley Declaration 2002: online). Unsustainable greed, consumption, profit, accumulation, capitalist development, modernity, patriarchy and a crisis in values have contributed to the planetary crisis that threatens all life. With few resources at their disposal, Indigenous peoples have presented their assessment of the planet's ecological health based on their own knowledge, lived experience and responsibilities. Over the past four decades, they have repeatedly gathered to advocate for an alternative, yet ancient, path forward.

Also ironically, the international scientific community's diagnosis of the ecological crisis is now largely in agreement with assessments provided by Indigenous nations for decades. Three recent global analyses of the planet's health; the World Water reports, the Intergovernmental Panel on Climate Change assessment, and the IPBES Global Assessment Report on Biodiversity and Ecosystem Services; have revealed dire consequences.

The United Nations' World Water Assessment Programme (WWAP) has released a global assessment of the planet's water annually since 2003. Its 2015 report, entitled *Water for a Sustainable World*, pointed to a global water crisis, stating that:

> [e]nsuring an adequate water supply for people is rapidly emerging as one of the major global environmental concerns of the 21st century. Some see it as the most important issue we will face in the years to come. By 2030, the world is projected to face a 40% global water deficit under the business-as-usual (BAU) scenario.

(WWAP 2015: online)

The 2019 iteration of the report revealed that some people are more vulnerable than others in terms of access to the basic human right to water. The report stated that:

Women and girls regularly experience discrimination and inequalities in the enjoyment of their human rights to safe drinking water and sanitation in many parts of the world. Ethnic and other minorities, including indigenous peoples, migrants and refugees, and people of certain ancestries (e.g. castes), often experience discrimination, as can religious and linguistic minorities.

(WWAP 2019, 2)

The Intergovernmental Panel on Climate Change (IPCC) was established in 1988 by the World Meteorological Organization and the United Nations Environment Program to assess the science related to climate change impacts, future risks, and options for mitigation and adaptation. In the fall of 2018, the IPCC released its *Special Report on Global Warming 1.5 °C*, with dire predictions. The IPCC report states that predictive models showing global warming being successfully limited to 1.5 C require a decline in:

global net anthropogenic CO_2 emissions [of] about 45% from 2010 levels by 2030 … reaching net zero around 2050. … For limiting global warming to below 2°C CO_2 emissions are [required] to decline by about 25% by 2030 … and reach net zero around 2070.

(IPCC 2018: 12).

Given that studies have indicated that, "[e]ven a 2C ceiling above pre-industrial levels may not be enough to avoid catastrophic impacts" (Hood 2018: 1), this means in simple terms that global CO_2 emissions must be slashed roughly a half below 2010 levels *in the next 10 years*, and reach 'net zero' by 2050. Currently, we are nowhere near making that happen. In fact, annual CO_2 emissions continue to *rise*, by as much as 2.7 per cent in 2018 (Hood 2018).

More recently, in May 2019, the *Intergovernmental Science-Policy Platform on Biodiversity and Ecosystem Services* (IPBES) released a global assessment report on biodiversity and ecosystem services, the first intergovernmental report of its kind. The findings are of course troubling. Following are some key numbers presented:

- 75 per cent: terrestrial environment 'severely altered' to date by human actions (marine environments 66 per cent)
- 47 per cent: reduction in global indicators of ecosystem extent and condition against their estimated natural baselines, with many continuing to decline by at least 4 per cent per decade
- [approximately] 60 billion: tons of renewable and non-renewable resources extracted globally each year, up nearly 100 per cent since 1980
- 15 per cent: increase in global per capita consumption of materials since 1980
- > 85 per cent: of wetlands present in 1700 had been lost by 2000 – loss of wetlands is currently three times faster, in percentage terms, than forest loss. (IPBES media release: online)

The IPBES data reveal that nature, the ecosystems that humans and all other species rely on for survival, are declining more rapidly than ever before. IPBES Chair Sir Robert Watson states that: "[t]he health of ecosystems on which we and all other species depend is deteriorating more rapidly than ever. We are eroding the very foundations of our economies, livelihoods, food security, health and quality of life worldwide" (IPBES 2019: online). 'Transformative change' is required, Watson asserts, for the restoration of nature, as he calls for a "fundamental, system-wide reorganization across technological, economic and social factors, including paradigms, goals and values". He further declares that:

[t]he member States of IPBES Plenary have now acknowledged that, by its very nature, transformative change can expect opposition from those with interests vested in the status quo, but also that such opposition can be overcome for the broader public good.

(IPBES 2019: online).

Indigenous interventions, as expressed through various declarations such as those that have been cited here, as well as the *United Nations Declaration on the Rights of Indigenous* Peoples, are not only critical, they offer a path forward to an alternative, sustainable future. In response to the UN's document, 'The Future We Want', released following the *Rio+20* conference in 2012, Indigenous Peoples provided their own political statement (which some have referred to as, "The Future We Don't Want", Frank 2012), created through the parallel conference, the *Rio+20 International Conference of Indigenous Peoples on Self-Determination and Sustainable Development* (Rio+20 ICIP 2012). In this response document, the concept of *Buen Vivir* (living well) was offered as an alternative pathway to the unsustainable approaches proposed by international and state actors. The document states that:

> Indigenous peoples call upon the world to return to dialogue and harmony with Mother Earth, and to adopt a new paradigm of civilization based on Buen Vivir – Living Well. In the spirit of humanity and our collective survival, dignity and well-being, we respectfully offer our cultural world views as an important foundation to collectively renew our relationships with each other and Mother Earth and to ensure Buen Vivir/ living well proceeds with integrity.
>
> *(Rio+20 ICIP 2012: online)*

Buen vivir calls for living well within an expanded view of community which includes the planet and everything on it: animals, plants, the Earth itself, or what I would refer to as 'all of Creation'. In Canada, concepts similar to Buen Vivir have also persisted despite colonial violence and genocide and are reflected in Indigenous legal, knowledge and philosophical traditions (Borrows 2010). Indigenous legal traditions in Canada and elsewhere reflect a set of reciprocal relationships and a co-existence with the natural world (Johnson and Larsen 2017). Balanced relationships are sought between humans and other entities in the natural world (animals, plants, birds, forests, waters, etc.) as well as with the ancestors (Johnston 2006) and future generations (McGregor 2015). The outcomes of these relationships can be expressed in the *Anishinaabek* concept of *Mino-mnaadmodzawin*, the ideal that ensures a sustainable future for all life (McGregor 2018).

The *Onjisay Aki International Climate Calls to Action*, the outcome document from the *Onjisay aki-Our Changing Earth-International Climate Summit* held in Sagkeeng First Nation in Manitoba, Canada, conveyed similar sentiments about the relationships required to live with the Earth:

> *Onjisay Aki* means 'our changing Earth' in the Anishinabe language. *Onjisay Aki* is a word that offers hope for the future. It acknowledges the leadership of Mother Earth herself, who as a living being carries the true influence to bring birth to new life, to counter imbalances that lead to issues like climate change, and to restore balance in the world.
>
> *(Onjisay Aki 2017: online)*

The *Onjisay Aki Declaration* also calls upon traditional knowledge and laws as being central to the path forward:

> Ancestral knowledge is the foundation of living in balance with the Earth. The traditional wisdom of Indigenous Peoples, *rooted in laws of peaceful conduct*, and a *love* for and spiritual

relationship with the land, air, water, fire, and plant, animal and human and celestial worlds, has allowed them to live sustainably within diverse homelands for millennia.

(Onjisay Aki 2017: online)

The Onjisay Aki Declaration expresses foundational tenets of living well with the Earth, as conveyed through concepts such as *Buen Vivir* and *Mino-mnaadmodzawin*, that diverge radically from the assumptions about the humanity's relationships to the natural world expressed by the United Nations and other actors in their approaches to address the planetary crisis. In the Indigenous concepts, the Earth is recognised as having *agency*; one lives well *with* the Earth. People have an ongoing relationship, governed by a law of peaceful conduct, with the Earth itself. Secondly, love for the Earth and life itself is explicitly recognised as a motivating ethical, moral and legal principle that guides conduct in relation to each other and to Mother Earth (Borrows 2019).

International Indigenous environmental justice as expressed through such concepts, then, extends the vision for peace, justice and equity to the natural world through recognising the agency of Mother Earth and expressing love for her (McGregor 2018).

Realising Buen Vivir/Mino-mnaadmodzawin

For over four decades, the international community has, at least to some extent, recognised the value of traditional knowledge (TK) in helping to address global environmental issues. TK continues to gain importance in considerations of regional, national and international environmental sustainability (Nakashima et al. 2012). TK is now mentioned, for example, in the *United Nations Declaration on the Rights of Indigenous Peoples* (UNDRIP) which highlights the importance of "recognizing that respect for Indigenous knowledge, culture and traditional practices contributes to sustainable and equitable development and proper management of resources" (United Nations General Assembly [UNGA] 2007: online). The UN also noted that, "Indigenous Peoples have the right to self determination. By virtue of that right they freely determine their political status and freely pursue their economic, social and cultural development" (UNGA 2007 Article 3: online). A core aspect of realising self-determination is to maintain *relationships* with one's territories and to practice *responsibilities* to the land and future generations. Article 25 in the UNDRIP states that:

> Indigenous peoples have the right to maintain and strengthen their distinctive *spiritual relationship* with their traditionally owned or otherwise occupied and used lands, territories, waters and coastal seas and other resources and to uphold their *responsibilities to future generations* in this regard.

(UNGA 2007: online; italics added)

Indigenous environmental declarations since the adoption of UNDRIP have called for the recognition and realisation of UNDRIP as a key step along the path toward sustainability. In addition to supporting Indigenous self-determination and sovereignty, TK is recognised because there is recognition that Western systems of knowledge continue to fail to achieve sustainability; science and technology alone cannot get us out of our current crises. Other approaches are needed, and given its long-proven history in allowing people to live sustainably with the Earth, it is logical that TK is seen as a current, relevant and viable system for understanding the situation and providing a basis from which to work toward solutions. In this context, anyone who is truly interested in sustainable relationships with Creation should also be interested in TK. Indigenous peoples certainly believe so. Indigenous peoples around the world have declared time and time again that TK is the key to environmental sustainability, as noted throughout this paper.

Through the efforts of Indigenous peoples from around the world, the various Indigenous Declarations have offered a diagnosis and path forward that answers the call for the 'transformative change' needed to alter global society's current trajectory. These plans have been based on Indigenous philosophies, knowledge, and values that underpin Indigenous legal, political and governance traditions. *Buen Vivir/Mino-mnaadmodzawin* are more than a philosophy, they express a *way* to live, a *responsibility* to live in a manner that supports the well-being of Mother Earth. This idea is expressed in the *Lima Declaration*, the outcome document from the *World Conference of Indigenous Women* (WCIW), held in Lima, Peru, in 2013:

> Protection of Mother Earth is a historic, *sacred and continuing responsibility of* the world's Indigenous Peoples, as the ancestral guardians of the Earth's lands, waters, oceans, ice, mountains and forests. These have sustained our distinct cultures, spirituality, traditional economies, social structures, institutions, and political relations from immemorial times. Indigenous women play a primary role in safeguarding and sustaining Mother Earth and her cycles.
>
> *(online; italics added)*

The *Indigenous Peoples Earth Charter* (1992: online) states in Article 31 that, "Indigenous Peoples were placed upon our Mother, the Earth, by the Creator. We belong to the land. We cannot be separated from our lands and territories". The Charter adds in Article 36 that, "Indigenous Peoples reject the assertion of non-Indigenous laws onto our lands. States cannot unilaterally extend their jurisdiction over our lands and territories. The concept of terra nullius should be forever erased from the law books of states" (Indigenous Peoples Earth Charter 1992: online). A decade later the *Kimberley Declaration* stated, "Today we reaffirm our relationship to Mother Earth and our responsibility to coming generations to uphold *peace, equity and justice*" (italics added). The *Manaus Declaration* reiterated the importance of Indigenous legal orders:

> We believe that our worldviews and respect for *natural law, our spiritualities and cultures and our values of reciprocity, harmony* with nature, solidarity, collectivity, and caring and sharing, among others, are crucial in bringing about a more *just, equitable and sustainable world.* (italics added).

Indigenous knowledge has been developed, innovated, transformed, and utilised by Indigenous peoples to sustain their communities, territories, and Nations since time immemorial.

These international Indigenous environmental declarations offer a counter-narrative to the "Earth as subject/object, resource/property/commodity" found in non-Indigenous international fora. In order for Indigenous and global environmental justice to be achieved; however, Indigenous legal and knowledge traditions must be actively applied: the concepts must be *lived*. Achieving this on a significant scale will require a massive reforming of societal values. To the extent this can be carried out, Indigenous environmental justice as expressed by Indigenous peoples the world over conveys a distinct path forward and a vision that includes a sustainable future for all life.

Conclusion: Indigenous environmental justice

We, the women of the original peoples of the world have struggled actively to defend our rights to self-determination and to our territories which have been invaded and colonized by powerful nations and interests. We have been and are continuing to suffer from multiple oppressions; as Indigenous peoples, as citizens of colonized and neo-colonial countries, as women, and as members of the poorer classes of society. In spite of this, we have been and continue to protect, transmit, and develop our Indigenous cosmovision, our science and technologies, our arts and culture, and our Indigenous socio-political economic systems, *which are in harmony with the natural laws of mother earth.* We still retain the ethical and esthetic values, the knowledge and philosophy, the spirituality, which conserves and nurtures Mother Earth. We are persisting in our struggles for self-determination and for our rights to our territories. This *has been shown in our tenacity and capacity to withstand and survive the colonization* happening in our lands in the last 500 years.

(Beijing Declaration of Indigenous Women 1995, Article 5: online; italics added)

Environmental justice as conceptualised by international Indigenous peoples extends far beyond what is generated by the United Nations system via high profile conferences, summits and outcome documents. The UN system has stayed on course in terms of generating solutions that continually fail. Indigenous peoples have offered pointed critiques of this path, including highlighting a different set of origins of the challenges. Indigenous peoples have also gathered together and created their own declarations with plans outlining a path forward based on their own collective knowledge, laws and values, despite immense diversity and the varying contexts within which many people find themselves. Indigenous peoples understand the trajectory of contemporary planetary ecocide as having obtained its footing over 500 years ago with the onset of global colonialism. Indigenous women and others have observed that current international fora such as those convened by the UN may in fact be 'recolonization' efforts. Heather Davis and Zoe Todd, writing on the origins of the 'Anthropocene' era, build on such theorising by Indigenous peoples over the past decades by stating that:

The story we tell ourselves about environmental crises, the story of humanity's place on the earth and its presence within geological time determines how we understand how we got here, where we might like to be headed, and what we need to do. We make the case for colonialism as the start date of the Anthropocene for two reasons: the first is to open up the geologic questions and implications of the Anthropocene beyond the realm of Western and European epistemology to think with Indigenous knowledges from North America; the second is to make a claim that to use a date that coincides with colonialism in the Americas allows us to understand the current state of ecological crisis as inherently invested in a specific ideology defined by proto-capitalist logics based on extraction and accumulation through dispossession – logics that continue to shape the world we live in and that have produced our current era.

(Davis and Todd 2017: 764)

The story the United Nations system tells has not brought about a more just, peaceful and sustainable world. What is required is a profoundly different set of logics, logics that already exists in the lives, experiences and knowledge of Indigenous peoples. Indigenous peoples' declarations seek in essence to 'decolonise' these broader processes. As long these dominant world systems fail to listen to and embrace the transformation required and offered by Indigenous peoples, humanity as a whole will continue to fail the Earth. Indigenous scholar Kyle Whyte confirms that we need to understand the current ecological crisis as an "intensification of colonialism" and thus decolonisation is required if any viable and sustainable path forward is to be envisioned (Whyte 2017: 156). A key element in the necessary paradigm shift will be to, as expressed by Whyte, ensure that, "our actions today are cyclical performances … guided by our reflection on our ancestors' perspectives and on our desire to be good ancestors ourselves to future generations (Whyte 2017:160). This critical sentiment is perhaps best summed up by the original *Kari-Oca* Declaration from 1992, which shared that, "[w]e, the Indigenous Peoples, walk to the future in the footprints of our ancestors" (online). It is from our past, our stories, our understandings, that a path to a Indigenous environmental justice and a sustainable future for all can be laid out. Every Indigenous Declaration since the first Earth Summit has provided guidance on how to create this path. Now all we have to do is pay attention, and act accordingly.

References

Anaya, J. (2014). 'The situation of indigenous peoples in Canada', in *Report of the Special Rapporteur on the Rights of Indigenous Peoples*. United Nations General Assembly. Available: http://unsr.jamesanaya.org/country-reports/the-situation-of-indigenous-peoples-in-canada, accessed 14 July 2016.

Beijing Declaration of Indigenous Women. (1995). Available: https://asianindigenouswomen.org/index.php/indigenous-womens-human-rights/csw/23-beijing-declaration-of-indigenous-women/file, accessed 9 August 2019.

Big-Canoe, K. and Richmond, C. (2014). 'Anishinabe youth perceptions about community health: toward environmental repossession', *Health and Place*, vol 26: 127–136.

Borrows. J. (2010). *Canada's Indigenous Constitution*. University of Toronto Press: Toronto, ON.

Borrows, J. (2019). *Law's Indigenous Ethics*. University of Toronto Press: Toronto.

Collins, L, McGregor, D., Allen, S., Murray, C., and Metcalfe, C.D. (2017). 'Source water protection planning for Ontario first nations communities: Case studies identifying challenges and outcomes', *Water*, vol 9: 550.

Davis, H., and Todd, Z. (2017). 'The importance of a date, or decolonizing the anthropocene', *ACME: An International Journal for Critical Geographies*, vol 16, no 4: 761–780.

Dhillon, C. and Young, M. (2010). 'Environmental racism and first nations: A call for socially just public policy development', *Canadian Journal of Humanities and Social Sciences*, vol 1, no 1: 23–37.

Frank, M. (2012). 'The future we don't want: Indigenous peoples at Rio+20', *Cultural Survival Quarterly*. Available: https://www.culturalsurvival.org/publications/cultural-survival-quarterly/future-we-dont-want-indigenous-peoples-rio20, accessed 31 July 2019.

Hood, M. (2018). 'CO_2 emissions up 2.7%, world "off course" to curb warming: Study'. Available: https://phys.org/news/2018-12-co2-emissions-world-curb.html, accessed 16 July 2019.

Indigenous Peoples Council on Biocolonialism. (2002). 'Kimberley declaration', from the *International Indigenous Peoples Summit on Sustainable Development*, 20–23 August. Kimberley: South Africa. Available: http://www.ipcb.org/resolutions/htmls/kim_dec.html, accessed 9 August 2019.

Indigenous Peoples Earth Charter. (1992). Available: http://www.tebtebba.org/index.php/all-resources/category/92-unced-conference?download=474:indigenous-peoples-earth-charter, accessed 9 August 2019.

Intergovernmental Panel on Climate Change (IPCC). (2018). 'Summary for policymakers', in *Global Warming of 1.5°C, An IPCC Special Report on the Impacts of Global Warming of 1.5°C Above Pre-Industrial Levels and Related Global Greenhouse Gas Emission Pathways, in the Context of Strengthening the Global Response to the Threat of Climate Change, Sustainable Development, and Efforts to Eradicate Poverty*. Available: https://report.ipcc.ch/sr15/pdf/sr15_spm_final.pdf, accessed 9 August 2019.

Intergovernmental Science-Policy Platform on Biodiversity and Ecosystem Services (IPBES). (2019). 'Nature's dangerous decline "unprecedented", species extinction rates "accelerating"'. Available: https://www.ipbes.net/news/Media-Release-Global-Assessment, accessed 9 August 2019.

Jacobs, B. (2010). 'Environmental racism on Indigenous lands and territories'. Available: https://www.cpsa-acsp.ca/papers-2010/Jacobs.pdf, accessed 9 August 2019.

Johnson, J. and Larsen, S. (2017). *Being Together in Place: Indigenous Coexistence in a More Than Human World*. University of Minnesota Press: Minneapolis.

Johnston, D. (2006). 'Connecting people to place: Great lakes aboriginal history in cultural context'. Available: https://commons.allard.ubc.ca/cgi/viewcontent.cgi?article=1191&context=fac_pubs, accessed 9 August 2019.

Kari-Oca Declaration. (1992). 'Kari-oca declaration and Indigenous peoples' earth charter', from the *World Conference of Indigenous Peoples on Territory, Environmental Development*, May 25–30. Kari-Oca: Brazil. Available: http://www.lacult.unesco.org/lacult_en/docc/Kari-Oca_1992.doc, accessed 9 August 2019.

Kari-Oca 2 Declaration. (2012). From the Kari-Oca II, the *Indigenous People's Conference at Rio +20*, June 13–22. Kari-Oca: Brazil. Available: Click here to enter text., accessed 9 August 2019.

LaDuke, W. (1999). *All Our Relations: Native Struggles for Land and Life*. South End Press: Cambridge.

Manaus Declaration. (2011). From the *Global Preparatory Meeting of Indigenous Peoples on Rio + 20 and Karioca 2*, 22–24 August. Manaus: Brazil. http://www.tebtebba.org/index.php/all-resources/categor y/18-rio-20?download=843:manaus-declaration, accessed 9 August 2019.

LaDuke, W. (2005). *Recovering the Sacred: The Power of Naming and Claiming*. Sound End Press: Cambridge, MA.

Mandaluyong Declaration. (2010). 'Mandaluyong declaration of the global conference on Indigenous women, climate change and redd plus', from the *Global Conference on Indigenous Women, Climate Change and REDD Plus*, 18–19 November. Metro Manila: Phillippines. Available: https://asianindigenouswo men.org/index.php/climate-change-biodiversity-and-traditional-knowledge/climate-change/64-mandaluyong-declaration-of-the-global-conference-on-indigenous-women-climate-change-and-re dd-plus/file, accessed 9 August 2019.

McGregor, D. (2012). 'Traditional knowledge: Considerations for protecting water in Ontario', *International Indigenous Policy Journal*, vol 3, no 3. doi:10.18584/iipj.2012.3.3.1

McGregor, D. (2015). 'Indigenous women, water justice and zaagidowin (love)', Women and Water. *Canadian Woman Studies*/les cahiers de la femme, vol 30, no 2/3: 71–78.

McGregor, D. (2018). 'Mino-mnaamodzawin: Achieving Indigenous environmental justice in Canada', *Environment and Society*, vol 9, no 1: 7–24.

Nakashima, D., Galloway McLean, K., Thulstrup, H., Ramos Castillo, A., and Rubis, J. (2012). *Weathering Uncertainty: Traditional Knowledge for Climate Change Assessment and Adaptation*. UNESCO: Paris; UNU: Darwin.

National Inquiry into Missing and Murdered Indigenous Women and Girls (NIMMIWG). (2019). *Reclaiming Power and Place: The Final Report of the National Inquiry into Missing and Murdered Indigenous Women and Girls Volume 1a*. Available: https://www.mmiwg-ffada.ca/wp-content/uploads/2019/06/F inal_Report_Vol_1a-1.pdf, accessed 23 July 2019.

Onjisay Aki. (2017). 'Onjisay Aki international climate calls to action'. Available: http://onjisay-aki.org/on jisay-aki-international-climate-calls-action, accessed 9 August 2019.

Richmond, C. (2015). 'The relatedness of people, land and health: Stories from Anishinabe elders', in S. de Leeuw, M. Greenwood, and C. Reading (eds.) *Our Health, Our Selves: Determinants of Indigenous Peoples' Health in Canada*. Canadian Scholars' Press Inc: Toronto, 47–63.

Rio+20 International Conference of Indigenous Peoples on Self-Determination and Sustainable Development (Rio+20 ICIP). (2012). 'Indigenous peoples international declaration on self-determination and sustainable development'. Available: https://www.culturalsurvival.org/news/in digenous-peoples-international-declaration-self-determination-and-sustainable-development, accessed 7 March 2020.

Royal Commission on Aboriginal Peoples (RCAP). (1996). *People to People, Nation to Nation: Highlights from the Report of the Royal Commission on Aboriginal Peoples*. Indigenous and Northern Affairs Canada: Canada. http://www.aadnc-aandc.gc.ca/eng/1100100014597/1100100014637, accessed 30 August 2016.

Truth and Reconciliation Commission (TRC). (2015). *What We Have Learned: Principles of Truth and Reconciliation*. Truth and Reconciliation Commission of Canada: Winnipeg. Available: http://www.trc. ca/websites/trcinstitution/File/2015/Findings/Calls_to_Action_English2.pdf, accessed 9 August 2019.

United Nations Conference on Sustainable Development Rio+20 (UNCSD Rio+20). (2012). 'The future we want: Final document of the Rio+20 conference'. Available: http://rio20.net/en/iniciativas/the -future-we-want-final-document-of-the-rio20-conference/, accessed 9 August 2019.

United Nations General Assembly (UNGA). (2007). *United Nations Declaration on the Rights of Indigenous Peoples*. Office of the Commission for Human Rights: Geneva. Available: https://www.un.org/d evelopment/desa/indigenouspeoples/wp-content/uploads/sites/19/2018/11/UNDRIP_E_web.pdf, accessed 9 August 2019.

Whyte, K. (2017). 'Indigenous climate change studies: indigenizing futures, decolonizing the anthropocene', *English Language Notes*, vol 55, no 1–2: 153–162.

World Conference of Indigenous Women (WCIW). (2013). 'Lima declaration', from the *World Conference of Indigenous Women, Progress and Challenges Regarding The Future We Want*, 28–30 October. Lima: Peru. Available: https://www.iitc.org/wp-content/uploads/2013/11/182171104-Lima-Declaration_web.p df, accessed 9 August 2019.

World Water Assessment Programme (WWAP). (2015). *The United Nations World Water Development Report 2015: Water for a Sustainable World*. Available: https://unesdoc.unesco.org/ark:/48223/pf0000231823, accessed 9 August 2019.

World Water Assessment Programme (WWAP). (2019). *The United Nations World Water Development Report 2019: Leaving No One Behind*. Available: https://unesdoc.unesco.org/ark:/48223/pf0000367306, accessed 9 August 2019.

31

Diverse Indigenous environmental identities

Māori resource management innovations

Maria Bargh

In this chapter I begin by examining the way debates about New Zealand climate change legislation bring to the surface the different environmental identities of Māori political and economic entities. In the second part of this chapter I explore how these different political and economic entities continue to disrupt stereotypes by pursuing strategies to promote environmental and sustainable futures, including by combining Māori views of resource ownership with those of the Crown to create legal identities for a mountain and a river (Te Urewera Act 2014; Te Awa Tupua Act 2017).

While the global issue of climate change is one which is impacting everyone everywhere, the historical contexts of each place are heavily influencing the permutations of climate change mitigation and adaptation policies and agendas (Bargh 2020).

The historical context of colonial legacies and capitalist policies are shaping responses but so too are non-capitalist and alternative-capitalist practices. Indigenous peoples' world-views are commonly argued to align with non-capitalist approaches and often said to be the answer for responses to climate change. However, Indigenous peoples are never only 'ecological natives' 'living at one with nature' but have multiple roles and identities in the political economy (Ulloa 2005). Indigenous world-views could be used in ways to support capitalist practices and policies (which many argue have caused climate change) or to support alternative-capitalist practices (which others argue promote harmonious relationships between humans and the planet) (Helin 2006; Shiva 2008; Kelly 2017).

In this chapter, I begin by examining the way debates about New Zealand climate change legislation bring to the surface the different environmental identities of Māori political and economic entities. In the second part of the chapter, I explore how these different political and economic entities continue to disrupt stereotypes by pursuing strategies to promote environmental and sustainable futures, including by combining Māori views of resource ownership with those of the Crown to provide legal identities for a mountain and a river (Te Urewera Act 2014; Te Awa Tupua Act 2017).

Contexts influence climate change policies

Globally, climate change and responses to it will shape the future quality of life of our peoples and planet. The Intergovernmental Panel on Climate Change (IPCC), a United Nations panel created to assess the science related to climate change, has indicated that global warming is likely to reach 1.5°C between 2030 and 2052 if it continues at the current rate (IPCC 2018). Their 2018 Special Report notes that "impacts on natural and human systems from global warming have already been observed. ... Many land and ocean ecosystems and some of the services they provide have already changed due to global warming" (IPCC 2018: 7).

In terms of acting to change the global warming trajectory, the IPCC stated:

> Adaptation and mitigation are already occurring. ... Future climate-related risks would be reduced by the upscaling and acceleration of far-reaching, multilevel and cross-sectoral climate mitigation and by both incremental and transformational adaptation.
>
> *(IPCC 2018: 7)*

Mitigation, adaptation and transitions to zero emissions economies requires "rapid and far-reaching transitions in energy, land, urban, infrastructure (including transport and buildings) and industrial systems" (IPCC 2018: 15). Indigenous peoples' world-views and knowledges are often pointed to as the providing key solutions for adaptation and transitions to climate change.

In their book on Indigenous knowledge for climate change, Nakashima et. al argue that acknowledgement and inclusion of Indigenous peoples views in international climate change research and monitoring has increased significantly since 1990 with Indigenous knowledge receiving "explicit recognition" in the 2014 fifth assessment report of the IPCC (Nakashima et al. 2018: 6). They highlight as further progress the recognition of the need to strengthen Indigenous peoples knowledge as a "platform for the exchange of experiences and sharing of best practices on mitigation and adaptation in a holistic and integrated manner" (Nakashima et al. 2018: 8) in the Conference of Parties (COP) processes of the UN Framework Convention on Climate Change (UNFCCC).

Despite this increased level of inclusion, Nakashima et al. make two cautions about the rhetoric of Indigenous peoples and climate change, in particular, the reputed vulnerability of Indigenous peoples and the alleged demise of Indigenous knowledge. They argue that while Indigenous peoples are commonly described as the 'canaries' and first victims of climate change, this perception is too limiting and Indigenous peoples' adaptive capabilities and resilience should also be highlighted. The other view they take issue with is the assumption that Indigenous knowledge will shortly become obsolete because it is based on observations about the environment and is a "static set of information that is handed down with little change from one generation to the next" (Nakashima et al. 2018: 10). They argue that this assumption fails to understand that Indigenous knowledge is largely about a process, "[r]ather than *what* one knows, it is more about *how* one learns and how information about one's surroundings is compiled and renewed" (Nakashima et al. 2018: 10). They further argue that "elements of knowledge per se may be of lesser importance than the cultural attitudes and values that shape the ways in which knowledge is acquired, transformed and deployed ..." (Nakashima et al. 2018: 10). Indigenous knowledge is therefore "a vehicle for passing on social values and attitudes that *reinforce* resilience" (Nakashima et al. 2018: 11).

Although politically useful, clearly a problem with such ubiquitous statements about Indigenous knowledge and Indigenous peoples is that they over-generalise. Thus, I suggest these cautions need to be extended to also include recognition of the multiple roles and identities that Indigenous peoples inhabit. Indigenous peoples are diverse and inhabit different roles and identities, including having, as Nakashima et al. indicate, 'exposure-sensitivity' to climate change, but this may also vary by degrees across and amongst different Indigenous peoples. Indigenous peoples are also directors on corporate entities which profit from climate change and can hold those roles at the same time as volunteering for tribal community activities (Bargh 2015). J.K

421

Gibson-Graham's diverse economies framework provides one of several ways to think about how these roles and identities co-exist (Gibson-Graham 2007). In their diverse economies framework they highlight the multiple roles people hold individually and collectively. Alongside Cameron and Healy (Gibson-Graham et al. 2013), they argue, "The economy is a diverse social space in which we have multiple roles. ... When we see ourselves as economic actors with multiple roles we can start to envision an exciting array of economic actions" (Gibson-Graham et al. 2013: xx).

Many people simultaneously inhabit positions of employer, employee, unemployed, mother, friend, neighbour, land owner, consumer – which give rise to different economic interactions. People are never only *just* ecologists or workers or capitalists. Considering the multiple roles people inhabit encourages deeper consideration of stereotypes and generalisations, and the expectations as Philip Deloria describes them, which underpin them, and the 'unexpected' elements which challenge and "resist categorization" (Deloria 2004: II).

Examining the multiple roles and identities of Māori in the climate change discussion in New Zealand

The discussions about the role Indigenous world-views and knowledge can play in climate change mitigations, adaptations and transitions provides an example through which to also examine the multiple roles and identities of Indigenous peoples. In this chapter I will focus my comments on the New Zealand context where the government is setting targets of net zero emissions by 2050 (Ministry for the Environment n.d.; Ministry of Foreign Affairs and Trade 2018).

In the public consultations about the net zero emissions targets and how to transition to those targets, the variety of Māori roles and identities has become more apparent. Māori have roles as farmers, owners of Māori land, owners of collective tribal assets, as private business owners, as individuals and as tribal members. 'Rūnanga' are polities usually elected and endorsed by tribal members to give voice to their *iwi* (tribe). Māori Land Trusts are the entities which manage Māori land which is a specific land title governed by the Māori Land Act 1993. Both these entities have come to be representatives of their members in different ways and are useful in exploring this history briefly before considering their approaches and submissions on adaptations to climate change.

Prior to non-Māori arrivals Māori owned resources collectively in small units (*hapū*) which joined together in confederations or an *iwi* (tribe) for specific purposes (Durie 1999). Particularly environmental resources, such as land and waterways and mountains were not owned per se in an individual private property sense but rather it would be more accurate to say that particular hapū and iwi held authority and guardianship over those and could allow others access and use rights (Erueti 1999).

In Te Tiriti o Waitangi (the Treaty of Waitangi) 1840[1], the British Crown was provided by Māori the ability to govern in exchange for guaranteeing the continuation of Māori rights to self-determination. Te Tiriti gave rise to obligations on both parties, including to work in partnership and for the Crown to actively protect Māori rights and interests. Despite these guarantees and obligations, the Crown has consistently breached Te Tiriti. In the late 1970s the Crown began a process of investigating and rectifying breaches of Te Tiriti. This process accelerated in the 1980s and 1990s and involves direct negotiations between Māori – usually iwi rūnanga- and the Crown into alleged breaches which, if proven, can lead to a settlement. Treaty settlements regularly include a number of components such as an apology, financial and cultural redress (Wheen and Hayward 2012). Māori 'post-settlement' governance entities/rūnanga are vested with any returned assets, including resources such as land and forests and are one of the prevalent forms of Māori political entities.

Iwi rūnanga have become the dominant polity through which tribes have negotiated and communicated with the Crown during settlement processes, and now for many – in a 'post' settlement political environment. Those rūnanga which have completed settlements with the Crown hold their assets, often in subsidiary companies, on behalf of their collective tribal membership base.

The next most significant set of Māori governance institutions are those which own Māori freehold land and which are regulated by the Māori Land Act/Te Ture Whenua Māori Act 1993. There are 8,406 Māori Land Trusts (Ministry of Justice 2019). These entities have a membership base which includes some but possibly not all of those Māori people who affiliate and have cultural connections to those specific lands and resources.

In submissions regarding the Zero Carbon Bill[2] there is both coherence and difference in the views put forward from these perspectives. Twenty-six submissions were lodged from Māori according to the Ministry for the Environment (Ministry for the Environment 2018). Of these, 11 submissions are available on their website, with some representing a number of smaller Māori entities, and one from a health funding agency representing a partnership with tribal organisations.

The coherence in views revolves around the need for action and the need to acknowledge pre-existing inequalities already resulting from climate change and climate change policies. One organisation stated that "Action must be taken now" (Te Pūtahitanga o te Waipounamu 2018: 6) while another says "This is bigger than the Zero Carbon Bill – it is about doing what is right for the world" (Federation of Māori Authorities 2018: 1).

On behalf of their tribe Ngāti Awa, Te Rūnanga o Ngāti Awa Ngāti Awa, emphasised the international and future commitments:

> The Bill presents an opportunity for Aotearoa to demonstrate that we are serious about achieving carbon neutrality by 2050 and that we are committed to our obligations under the Paris Agreement. We also have a responsibility to those before us and those generations to come to actively participate in seeking global solutions and to set ourselves on a course to a sustainable future.
>
> *(Te Rūnanga o Ngāti Awa 2018: 2)*

Te Rūnanga o Ngāti Ruanui saw it as an opportunity stating, "Ngāti Ruanui sees the climate change issue as a catalyst for environmental restoration and more importantly cultural restoration, focussed on mana whenua cultural norms" (Te Rūnanga o Ngāti Ruanui 2018: 13).

Māori submitters who wanted the government to be attentive to existing climate change impacts also pointed to previous policies which had disadvantaged Māori. Te Rūnanga o Ngāti Awa stated:

> The Zero Carbon Bill must acknowledge the current impacts of climate change on Maori e.g. housing, fuel costs, land use, environmental health impacts etc and plan for a transition to improve the emission profile of Aotearoa in a fair and responsible way that minimises the adverse social, cultural and economic impacts of change.
>
> *(Te Rūnanga o Ngāti Awa 2018: 2).*

The Emissions Trading Scheme (ETS),[3] which was introduced following the New Zealand government's signing of the Paris Agreement was mentioned numerous times as discriminatory to Māori. According to the Waikato-Tainui tribal polity:

The exclusion of pre-1990 indigenous forests from the ETS unfairly and disproportionately impacts on forests on Maori land. These forests are also integral to New Zealand's biodiversity which is at major risk from the impacts of climate change. By meaningfully recognizing the significance of pre-1990 indigenous forests and accounting for this in the budgeting system this will promote better consideration of appropriate land use [*sic*].

(Te Whakakitenga o Waikato 2018: 6)

Other submitters argued that because of the previous policies which disadvantaged Māori, the Crown should provide exceptions for Māori to enable a fairer transition. For example:

The impacts of the Zero Carbon Bill on Māori should be less than other parts of the economy, taking into consideration the catch-up required by Māori to achieve required land use performance and recognising Māori have been excluded from past opportunities to develop New Zealand's most optimal land and resources, and have been disadvantaged by earlier legislation e.g. ETS policy programs.

(Federation of Māori Authorities 2018: 1)

There are differences of views around the kinds of gases to be included in the scheme (short-term or long-term) and the timing of inclusion of all industries, particularly agriculture. Of specific interest to this discussion is the question of *who speaks for* and who has the *right to represent* Māori in climate change policy decision making. At the heart of the debate is an issue common to perhaps all Indigenous peoples – who has the right to be making decisions about resources on behalf of Indigenous peoples and why.

In their submission on the Zero Carbon Bill, Te Rūnanga o Ngāti Ruanui stated:

Depending on the size of asset and/or scale of the activity, decision making is typically vested on iwi [tribal] authorities, mana whenua [groups with territorial rights] of the affected land, on behalf of hapu [sub-tribes] and whanau [families]. Therefore, we recommend that the government works with iwi authorities in addressing important issues (identified, but not limited to, in our submission) in setting climate change adaptation plans, risk assessments and other associated matters.

(Te Rūnanga o Ngāti Ruanui 2018: 9)

Waikato-Tainui argued for "direct engagement with the Crown and its officials on the ongoing process of ratification and implementation of the ZCA [Zero Carbon Act]" (Te Whakakitenga o Waikato 2018: 8).

Te Rūnanga o Ngāi Tahu outlined their expectation that "the Crown will honour Te Tiriti o Waitangi (the Treaty) and the principles upon which the Treaty is founded" (Te Rūnanga o Ngāi Tahu 2018:5). The Treaty was signed between Māori tribes and the Crown and obligates the Crown to work in partnership and it has been argued this must be with tribes rather than pan-Māori entities. Ngāti Hineuru argues that:

Iwi are uniquely placed to respond to climate change but are also a key stakeholder in terms of climate change. However, in developing the legislation and more detailed policy proposals going forward, it is paramount that the Crown as a Treaty partner engage with Maori not just in terms of consultation, but constructive development and engagement on any such proposals.

(Te Kōpere o Ngāti Hineuru 2018: 1)

Other iwi organisations bridged the gap between the varieties of organisations with Te Rūnanga o Ngāti Awa stating:

> it's community are tangata whenua, kaitiaki, landowners and ratepayers in the eastern Bay of Plenty. We have an interest in climate change. The social, cultural, economic and environmental impacts of a national climate change bill such as the proposed Zero Carbon Bill will affect our people and communities.
>
> *(2018: 1)*

On the other hand, pan-tribal Māori organisations have different expectations around engagement. The Federation of Māori Authorities in their submission stated:

> Māori interests are represented at many different levels (i.e. iwi, hapu, landowner, marae and whanau), with each providing value and a unique view of the world that must be included in the formation of any zero carbon regime. ... Māori landowners (i.e. Trusts and Incorporations and other private interests) are not represented by the Iwi Leaders Forum. ... Māori landowners must be directly and centrally involved in the development of a workable and equitable zero carbon regime.
>
> *(Federation of Māori Authorities 2018: 2)*

What can be seen from the different submissions are the messy realities of Māori groups holding different understandings about who has the right to represent their members and claims to different sources of legitimacy. These are the expressions of the multiple environmental identities inhabited by Māori. Some of these views might not fit with expectations from non-Indigenous environmentalists that Indigenous peoples should take a purely nurturing and conserving rather than a mixture of nurturing and utilitarian approaches to the environment (Zaitchik 2018). Often the most simplistic way in which to dismiss Indigenous claims is by suggesting they are not Indigenous enough as they don't conform to a stereotype of generalisation (Gilio-Whitaker 2017). However, the submissions above demonstrate that a far more nuanced examination is needed to account for the genuinely multiple environmental identities.

Multiple values and strategies of Māori political and economic entities

Considering and appreciating the multiple roles and identities of Indigenous peoples and emphasising that Indigenous peoples are not simply ecological natives should not detract from the fact that there are still many ways that Indigenous peoples do promote more sustainable futures. In New Zealand, there are two clear manifestations of this in Māori resource management through rūnanga and through Māori Land Trusts.

Rūnanga and Māori Land Trusts share a number of attributes. The first is that they have Māori values laced through their organisations in governance and management practices such as vision and mission statements. The Māori values vary between organisations but commonly include *whanaungatanga* (relationships), *manaakitanga/kaitiakitanga* (nurturing/guardianship), *mana* (authority), *utu* (balance), *tapu* (spiritual quality). There is increasing research into the nature of Māori business as part of a Māori economy and examples of the manifestation and articulation of Māori values in Māori organisations is well traversed (Bargh 2020; Spiller et al. 2011; Dell et al. 2018; Amoamo et al. 2018). I provide two examples here illustrating how these entities promote more sustainable futures through their focus on *whanaungatanga* and *kaitiakitanga*.

Whanaungatanga/relationships are central to Māori legal, political, and economic institutions and frameworks (Mead 2016). These are relationships amongst people with shared genealogy and shared membership to organisations and extends forward to consideration of the next generations. Wakatu Incorporation is the management structure which owns land and other assets and represents its members that have cultural authority and connections over areas at the top of the South Island. Wakatu has very explicitly factored in the next generation in *Te Pae Tawhiti*, a 500-year plan. The plan makes provision for their members and descendants out to 2512 (Wakatu Incorporation 2012).

The value of *kaitiakitanga* (guardianship of the environment) arises from particular tribal groups having *mana* and cultural connections to geographical areas, resources and landscape features. The incorporation of the value of *kaitiakitanga* in the management of operations of Māori organisation's encourages them to consider how their activities impact the land and its health.

The largest tribe in the South Island of New Zealand, Ngāi Tahu has incorporated kaitiakitanga into their business operations. Ngāi Tahu Holdings Corporation has a net worth of 1.65 billion (Ngāi Tahu 2018) and acknowledges they have interests in sectors that contribute to carbon emissions, including transport and agriculture. The Corporation states however that, "Ngāi Tahu is not shying away from an all emissions approach to managing the tribal emissions profile, in targets and milestones" (Te Rūnanga o Ngāi Tahu 2018: 8). As part of their attempt to mitigate their emissions Ngāi Tahu Holdings Corporation are:

> Working with the globally recognised CEMARS framework, through Enviromark, which requires assessment of all emissions sources across the Ngāi Tahu business portfolio. ... This is an internationally endorsed approach to greenhouse gas emissions measurement and reduction. It aligns with a values based business model and ethical branding.
>
> (Te Rūnanga o Ngāi Tahu 2018: 8)

These two examples provide a brief insight into the ways that Māori rūnanga, including their economic 'arms' and Māori Land Trusts continue to practice Māori values, in this case of whanaungatanga and kaitiakitanga alongside their economic focus. Their support for environmental sustainability is balanced in complex ways alongside their other cultural and political aspirations.

Inserting Māori world-views into Crown laws on the environment

While Bolivia and Ecuador may have been the first countries in the world to incorporate the rights of 'Pachamama' or the earth mother in their constitutions, New Zealand has become the first country to grant a mountain and a river legal identity. This move demonstrates the culmination of efforts by Māori to have Māori world-views included in statute and foregrounds the importance of the environment.

In 2014 the central North Island iwi of Tūhoe settled with the Crown over Crown breaches of Te Tiriti o Waitangi in Te Urewera Act 2014. The purpose of the Act is to:

> Establish and preserve in perpetuity a legal identity and protected status for Te Urewera for its intrinsic worth, its distinctive natural and cultural values, the integrity of those values, and for its national importance, and in particular to:
>
> (a) strengthen and maintain the connection between Tūhoe and Te Urewera; and

(b) preserve as far as possible the natural features and beauty of Te Urewera, the integrity of its indigenous ecological systems and biodiversity, and its historical and cultural heritage; and

(c) provide for Te Urewera as a place for public use and enjoyment, for recreation, learning, and spiritual reflection, and as an inspiration for all. (Te Urewera Act 2014: part 1 section 4)

The designation of Te Urewera as a 'National Park' was removed by the Act and the mountain was vested in itself as its own legal identity. This move represented the culmination of decades of Tūhoe engagement with the Crown which had already made history by being the one tribe in New Zealand to have 'local self-government' from the Urewera District Native Reserves Act 1896 until the Act's repeal in 1922 under (Ruru et al. 2017; Binney 2009).

Te Urewera is governed by a Board with equal numbers of iwi and Crown representatives (eight total) for the first three years of existence and then the balance shifts to enable six iwi representatives and two Crown (Ngai Tūhoe n.d). The Chair is a Tūhoe person in perpetuity.

A second example of Māori negotiating Māori values and world-views into legislation came in relation to the Whanganui River in the lower North Island. In 2017 Te Awa Tupua (Whanganui River Claims Settlement) Act made history by settling breaches of the Treaty of Waitangi relating to the Whanganui River and by creating Te Awa Tupua as an "indivisible and living whole, comprising the Whanganui River from the mountains to the sea, incorporating its tributaries and all its physical and metaphysical elements" (Te Awa Tupua Act 2017: part 3, section 69). The Act details the various values and elements of the river through four different *kawa* (principles):

Ko Te Kawa Tuatahi

(a) *Ko te Awa te mātāpuna o te ora*: the River is the source of spiritual and physical sustenance: Te Awa Tupua is a spiritual and physical entity that supports and sustains both the life and natural resources within the Whanganui River and the health and well-being of the iwi, hapū, and other communities of the River.

Ko Te Kawa Tuarua

(b) *E rere kau mai i te Awa nui mai i te Kahui Maunga ki Tangaroa*: the great River flows from the mountains to the sea: Te Awa Tupua is an indivisible and living whole from the mountains to the sea, incorporating the Whanganui River and all of its physical and metaphysical elements.

Ko Te Kawa Tuatoru

(c) *Ko au te Awa, ko te Awa ko au*: I am the River and the River is me: The iwi and hapū of the Whanganui River have an inalienable connection with, and responsibility to, Te Awa Tupua and its health and well-being.

Ko Te Kawa Tuawhā

(d) *Ngā manga iti, ngā manga nui e honohono kau ana, ka tupu hei Awa Tupua*: the small and large streams that flow into one another form one River: Te Awa Tupua is a singular entity comprised of many elements and communities, working collaboratively for the common purpose of the health and well-being of Te Awa Tupua. (Te Awa Tupua Act 2017: part 2 section 13)

Te Pou Tupua was established as "the human face of Te Awa Tupua and acts in the name of Te Awa Tupua" (Te Awa Tupua Act 2017: part 2 section 18). There are two people who fulfil this role, one appointed by the iwi the other by the Crown. The functions of Te Pou Tupua are amongst other things "to promote and protect the health and well-being of Te Awa Tupua" (Te Awa Tupua Act 2017: part 2 section 19).

The Te Urewera and Te Awa Tupua Acts are both heavily imbued with and heavily rely on Māori world-views and Māori knowledge. The inclusion of Māori knowledge in these Acts indicates that it is possible, at least in the New Zealand case, for that Indigenous knowledge to be blended with dominant non-Indigenous world-views and that it can produce something innovative which empowers the environment. Without getting too optimistic and keeping in mind the many dominant forces that will seek to maintain the fossil fuel depleting, high emissions global economy, these two Acts present the possibility of Indigenous world-views and knowledge creating a positive avenue towards a sustainable future.

These two examples of a mountain and a river are still in the early years of their existence. However, they have already lit the imagination of other countries and peoples and provide a tangible example of *how* the environment can be privileged and ensured more rights for its well-being.

Conclusion

Climate change discussions internationally are increasingly turning to Indigenous world-views and knowledge as a possible source of solutions. However, the actual inclusion of Indigenous peoples in policy and decision making may continue to be less than would accord with the UN Declaration on the Rights of Indigenous peoples and is less than Indigenous peoples expect.

What the climate change debates are flushing out in New Zealand are conversations similar to those of many other Indigenous groups. Some of the key issues relate to which groups or which Indigenous people have the right to speak on Indigenous matters. In New Zealand, the different articulations of environmental identities do not conform to strict political, economic, or cultural divides as is sometimes portrayed in stereotypes of Māori people as either the ecological native or a corporate. These debates about which entities are best to negotiate with government and represent their communities are fraught with layers of colonial legacies and probably cannot ever be fully resolved. Navigating some way through, however, is vital to ensure Indigenous communities are not stressed by the same contests over resources in adapting to climate change and transitioning to low carbon economies that colonial states and empires inflicted in earlier centuries.

The designations of Te Urewera and Te Awa Tupua with their own legal identities should give hope that Indigenous peoples, under particular circumstance, can insert Indigenous world-views and knowledge into some political and legal systems. Whilst the roles and identities of Indigenous peoples may be multiple and often more complex and dense (Andersen 2009) than is sometimes thought, Indigenous knowledge is dynamic and changing and should also continue to be a source of hope for mitigation, adaptations and transitions to low carbon futures.

Notes

1 Signed in 1840 between the British and Māori, the Treaty of Waitangi has two versions – in English and the other in Māori. The two versions and different understandings about what was agreed have produced ongoing contestation between Māori tribal groups and the Crown.
2 Now the Climate Change Response (Zero Carbon) Amendment Act 2019.

3 The Climate Change Response (Emissions Trading Scheme) Act 2008. The ETS is the New Zealand government's main tool for meeting climate change targets and aims to encourage people to reduce greenhouse gas emissions by putting a price on emissions.

Bibliography

Amoamo, M., Ruwhiu, D., and Carter, L. (2018). 'Framing the Māori economy: The complex business of Māori business', *MAI Journal*, vol 7, no 1: 66–78.

Andersen, C. (2009). 'Critical Indigenous studies: From difference to density', *Critical Indigenous Theory*, vol 15, no 2: 80–100.

Barcham, M. (2001). '(De) constructing the politics of indigeneity', in D. Ivison, P. Patton, and W. Sanders (eds.) *Political Theory and the Rights of Indigenous Peoples*. Cambridge University Press: Cambridge, 137–151.

Bargh, M. (2015). *A Hidden Economy: Māori in the Privatised Military Industry*. Huia: Wellington.

Bargh, M. (2020). 'Indigenous finance: Treaty settlement finance in Aotearoa New Zealand', in J.K. Gibson-Graham and K. Dombroski (eds.) *The Handbook of Diverse Economies*. Edward Elgar: Cheltenham, 362–369.

Binney, J. (2009). *Encircled Lands*. Bridget Williams Books: Wellington.

Dell, K., Staniland, N., and Nicholson, A. (2018). 'Economy of Mana: Where to next?', *MAI Journal*, vol 7, no 1: 51–65.

Deloria, P. (2004). *Indians in Unexpected Places*. University Press of Kansas: Lawrence, KS.

Durie, M. (1999). *Te Mana, Te Kawanatanga*. Oxford University Press: Auckland.

Erueti, A. (1999). 'Māori customary law and land tenure: An analysis', in R. Boast (ed.) *Māori Land Law*. Butterworths: Wellington, 25–26.

Federation of Māori Authorities. (2018). *FOMA Submission on the Zero Carbon Bill*. Available: https://www.mfe.govt.nz/have-your-say-zero-carbon, accessed 24 April 2019.

Gibson-Graham, J.K. (2006). *A Postcapitalist Politics*. University of Minnesota Press: Minneapolis.

Gibson Graham, J.K., Cameron, J., and Healy, S. (2013). *Take Back the Economy*. University of Minnesota Press: Minneapolis.

Gibson-Graham, J.K. and the Community Economies Collective. (2017). *Cultivating Community Economies: Tools for Building a Liveable World*. Next Systems Project. Available: https://thenextsystem.org/cultivating-community-economies, accessed 24 April 2019.

Gibson-Graham, J.K. and Roelvink, G. (2010). 'An economic ethics of the anthropocene', *Antipode*, vol 41, no 1: 320–346.

Gilio-Whitaker, D. (2017). *The Problem with the Ecological Indian Stereotype*. KCET. Available: https://www.kcet.org/shows/tending-the-wild/the-problem-with-the-ecological-indian-stereotype, accessed 12 May 2020.

Helin, C. (2006). *Dances with Dependency*. Orca Spirit Publishing and Communications: Vancouver.

Horan, J., Hosking, A., Moe, S., Rowland, J., and Wilkie, P. (2019). *Structuring for Impact: Evolving Legal Structures for Business in New Zealand*. The Impact Initiative: Wellington. Available: https://static1.squarespace.com/static/5b02f1bd85ede13734718842/t/5cb65895c83025eec4c96189/1555454166118/SELS_Report_2019_online_updated.pdf, accessed 12 May 2020.

Insley, C.K. and Meade, R. (2008). *Māori Impacts from the Emissions Trading Scheme: Detailed Analysis and Conclusions*. Report Prepared for Ministry for the Environment by 37 Degrees South Limited and Cognitus Advisory Services Limited. New Zealand Government: Wellington. Available: https://www.mfe.govt.nz/sites/default/files/maori-impacts-analysis-conclusions-jan08.pdf, accessed 24 April 2019.

Intergovernmental Panel on Climate Change. (2018). *Global Warming of 1.5°C: Summary for Policymakers*. IPCC: Switzerland. Available: https://www.ipcc.ch/sr15/, accessed 12 May 2020.

Jones, C. (2016). *New Treaty New Tradition*. Victoria University Press: Wellington.

Kelly, D. (2017). *Feed the People and You Will Never Go Hungry: Illuminating Coast Salish Economy of Affection*. Unpublished PhD, University of Auckland.

Mead, H. (2016). *Tikanga Māori*, revised ed. Huia: Wellington.

Ministry for the Environment. (n.d.). *Zero Carbon Bill*. Available: https://www.mfe.govt.nz/have-your-say-zero-carbon, accessed 24 April 2019.

Ministry of Foreign Affairs and Trade. (2018). 'New Zealand sets target of net zero emissions by 2050', *Press Release*. Available: https://www.mfat.govt.nz/en/countries-and-regions/latin-america/mexico/

embajada-de-nueva-zelandia/nueva-zelandia-establece-cero-emisiones-netas-para-2050/, accessed 24 April 2019.

Ministry of Justice. (2019). *Māori Land Update*. Available: https://maorilandcourt.govt.nz/assets/Documents/Publications/MLU-2019.pdf, accessed 12 May 2020.

Nakashima, D., Krupnik, I., and Rubis, J.T. (eds.) (2018). *Indigenous Knowledge for Climate Change Assessment and Adaptation*. Cambridge University Press: Cambridge.

New Zealand Parliament. (1993). *Māori Land Act*. Available: http://www.legislation.govt.nz/act/public/1993/0004/latest/DLM289882.html accessed 12 May 2020.

New Zealand Parliament. (2008). *Climate Change Response (Emissions Trading Scheme) Act*. Available: http://www.legislation.govt.nz/act/public/2008/0085/latest/DLM1130932.html, accessed 12 May 2020.

New Zealand Parliament. (2014). *Te Urewera Act*. Available: http://www.legislation.govt.nz/act/public/2014/0051/latest/whole.html, accessed 12 May 2020.

New Zealand Parliament. (2017). *Te Awa Tupua (Whanganui River Claims Settlement) Act*. Available: http://www.legislation.govt.nz/act/public/2017/0007/latest/whole.html, accessed 24 April 2019.

New Zealand Parliament. (2019). *Climate Change Response (Zero Carbon) Amendment Act*. Available: http://www.legislation.govt.nz/act/public/2019/0061/latest/LMS183736.html, accessed 12 May 2020.

Ngai Tahu. (2018). *Annual Report*. Available: https://ngaitahu.iwi.nz/wp-content/uploads/2018/10/net-worth-distributions.jpg, accessed 24 April 2019.

Ngai Tūhoe. (n.d.). *Te Urewera Governance*. Available: https://www.ngaituhoe.iwi.nz/te-urewera-governance, accessed 12 May 2020.

Raygorodetsky, G. (2011). *Why Traditional Knowledge Holds the Key to Climate Change*. United Nations University. Available: https://unu.edu/publications/articles/why-traditional-knowledge-holds-the-key-to-climate-change.html, accessed 12 May 2020.

Ruru, J. (2018). 'Listening to Papatūānuku: A call to reform water law', *Journal of the Royal Society of New Zealand*, vol 48, no 2–3: 215–224.

Ruru, J., Lyver, P., Scott, N., and Edmunds, D. (2017). 'Reversing the decline in New Zealand's biodiversity: Empowering Māori within reformed conservation law', *Policy Quarterly*, vol 13, no 2: 65–71.

Shiva, V. (2008). *Soil Not Oil*. Zed Books: London.

Spiller, C., Erakovic, L., Henare, M., and Pio, E. (2011). 'Relational well-being and wealth: Māori businesses and an ethic of care', *Journal of Business Ethics*, vol 98, no 1: 153–169.

Sykes, A. (2010). *Bruce Jesson Memorial Lecture*. Bruce Jesson Foundation. Available: https://www.brucejesson.com/annette-sykes-2010-bruce-jesson-memorial-lecture/, accessed 24 April 2019.

Te Kopere o Te Iwi o Hineuru Trust. (2018). *Submission on the Zero Carbon Proposals*. Ministry for the Environment. Available: https://www.mfe.govt.nz/have-your-say-zero-carbon, accessed 24 April 2019.

Te Puni Kōkiri. (2016). 'Te Awa Tupua', *Kokiri*, vol 33. Available: https://www.tpk.govt.nz/en/mo-te-puni-kokiri/kokiri-magazine/kokiri-33-2016/te-awa-tupua, accessed 24 April 2019.

Te Pūtahitanga o te Waipounamu. (2018). *Submission on the Zero Carbon Bill*. Ministry for the Environment. Available: https://www.mfe.govt.nz/have-your-say-zero-carbon, accessed 24 April 2019.

Te Rūnanga o Ngai Tahu. (2018). *Submission to the Ministry for the Environment on the Our Climate, Your Say Discussion Document*. Ministry for the Environment. Available: http://www.mfe.govt.nz/node/24411, accessed 24 April 2019.

Te Rūnanga o Ngāti Awa. (2018). *Zero Carbon Bill Submission*. Ministry for the Environment. Available: https://www.mfe.govt.nz/have-your-say-zero-carbon, accessed 24 April 2019.

Te Rūnanga o Ngāti Ruanui Trust. (2018). *Te Rūnanga o Ngāti Ruanui Trust's Submission Zero Carbon Bill*. Ministry for the Environment. Available: https://www.mfe.govt.nz/have-your-say-zero-carbon, accessed 24 April 2019.

Te Whakakitenga o Waikato. (2018). *Submission on the Zero Carbon Act*. Ministry for the Environment. Available: https://www.mfe.govt.nz/have-your-say-zero-carbon, accessed 24 April 2019.

Ulloa, A. (2005). *The Ecological Native*. Routledge: New York.

Wakatū Incorporation. (2012). *Te Pae Tawhiti*. Wakatū. Available: https://www.wakatu.org/te-pae-tawhiti, accessed 24 April 2019.

Wheen, N. and Hayward, J. (eds.) (2012). *Treaty of Waitangi Settlements*. Bridget Williams Books: Wellington.

Zaitchik, A. (2018). 'How conservation became colonialism', *Foreign Policy*, July 16. Available: https://foreignpolicy.com/2018/07/16/how-conservation-became-colonialism-environment-indigenous-people-ecuador-mining/, accessed 12 May 2020.

32

The ski or the wheel?

Foregrounding Sámi technological Innovation in the Arctic region and challenging its invisibility in the history of humanity

May-Britt Öhman

What technologies or knowledges are presented as the most important human innovations in history classes and at museums? After fire and stone tools, the invention of the wheel is commonly near the top of the list. But what about ski technology, a Sámi innovation dating back more than 5,000 years? Why is it so rarely celebrated as the major technological innovation that it is? What other Arctic innovations, what Sámi technological expertise, is left out of the history books and exhibitions, of the human past and present? Writing as historian of science and technology, this chapter is a step towards a more comprehensive history of humanity, inclusive of the Arctic region of Fenno-Scandinavia, and in particular the Sámi territories, foregrounding Sámi technological knowledge and expertise, adapted to specific conditions and geographies in the Arctic climate.

The article draws on the extensive scholarly and popular literature on Sámi and Swedish/ Nordic history and archaeology, as well as the history of skiing. In addition, I have spoken to fellow Sámi and non-Sámi experts within this field. I have made the option to, whenever possible, refer to literature in English, even though most literature on Sámi technology and expertise is only available in the Fenno-Scandinavian languages. As my knowledge of languages limits me to English, Swedish, and Norwegian, I have not covered literature in Finnish, Sámi, and Russian. I regret this; in particular as I am aware of the fact that had not the assimilation policies in Sweden been so fierce, I would have grown up as a speaker of Swedish, Sámi and Meänkieli, a language close to Finnish.

Over a thousand years of scholarship on Sámi skiing and technological expertise

Early historical depictions of Northernmost Europe and people often refer to Sámi use of skis for hunting and fishing as an integral part of their way of their life – 'skiing Finns' – *Skrithiphinoi/ Screrefennae/Scricfinnia* (Ojala 2009: 84; Zachrisson 2008; 2010). Historical accounts depict the

Sámi as some of the most important providers of furs to the Roman Empire (Zachrisson 2010). This trade is described in the accounts of Jordanes, a sixth-century Gothic historian who talked about Scandza, commonly interpreted as the Scandinavian Peninsula, and the Sámi thus:

> There are the Screrefennae, who do not seek grain for food but live on the flesh of wild beasts and birds' eggs; for there are such multitudes of young game in the swamps as to provide for the natural increase of their kind and to afford satisfaction to the needs of the people. [...] Here are also those who send through innumerable tribes the sapphire colored skins to trade for Roman use. They are a people famed for the dark beauty of their furs, and though living in poverty, are most richly clothed.
>
> *(Jordanes [551 CE] 1915: 56)*

This exchange of culture, wares, and knowledge between the North and the rest of Europe has been an integral part of European consciousness for a long time; knowledge of Sámi expertise has been available for over a millennium. Scholars have furthermore documented the ski as a particular Sámi technology, including the expertise needed to use, maintain, and repair this innovation transportation in snowy landscapes.

While the ski was noted by early scholars from the European continent, there is no mention of this ancient innovation in the history of technology book by Headrick (2009) *Technology: A World History*, for instance. Nor is this innovation mentioned on the website of the Swedish National Museum of Science and Technology, where there is an online exhibition of what is a selection of the 100 most important innovations in history, as well as a history of technology timeline of important innovations (Tekniska Museet n.d.; 2018).

Claiming to be the world's largest museum, education, and research complex the Smithsonian Institute pays tribute to the wheel as a key innovation, but fails to mention the long-established use of skis by in the Arctic and by the Sámi (Smithsonian 2020; Gambino 2009). An article in the Smithsonian magazine does mention modern history of skiing (Gambino 2011), amongst other in the context of sport portraying the Swedish Vasaloppet, a 90-kilometre-long ski race set up in 1922 to honour the apocryphal story that the king who established the modern Swedish state, Gustav Eriksson (Vasa), would have travelled this distance on skis. However, no historical evidence exists to support the idea that he would have known what skis were, never mind how to use them (Persson and Oldrup 2014: 184). Nonetheless, the nationalist hero myth is spread by the organisers to this day (Vasaloppet n.d.) and often reproduced.

Skiing has been a well-loved sport in the Nordic countries since the turn of the last century, and consequently the best known and most acknowledged use of skis today is from international ski competitions, where Swedish and Norwegian athletes more often than not reign supreme. This furthers a nationalist discourse on skiing, also seen as a masculine trait in the Nordic region, all whilst disregarding the technology's Sámi origins (Birkely 1994; Sörlin 1995; Pedersen 2013; Lidström 2017).

Michael Adas (1989) discusses the use of science and technology as a tool to further the aims of overseas colonial domination, arguing that an ideology of Western technological superiority has been fundamental to justifying its paternalistic civilising mission, as well as the rapid spread of European hegemony worldwide. Historical depictions of the Sámi and their territories need to be understood in this way, as this agenda and ideology is deeply entrenched in the colonial education system and its understanding of culture. Knowledge of Sámi history, culture and traditions has largely been erased from education at all levels of Swedish society (Svalastog 2014; Öhman 2017). Writing Indigenous peoples out of the history forms part of settler-colonial expansion (O'Brien 2010). Although, it was not always like this. The Sámi were a visible part of the elite at least until the 18th century, serving as vicars, sextons, teachers, members of court and bailiffs (Rydving 2010; Nordin 2018). It is mainly over the past 120 years, as a result of increasing colonisation and domination by the colonial states over the Sámi northern territories, that the Sámi have started to be both depicted as inferior and primitive, and made invisible. To this day, the Sámi are found at all levels of the Swedish society. Highlighting one's Sámi identity however remains discouraged, and thus many Sámi keep a low profile in this regard (Åhrén 2008; Öhman 2017).

Sámi and Sámi territories in Fenno-Scandinavia

The Sámi territories, known as Sábme in Lule Sámi, cover vast areas, encompass most of the Fenno-Scandinavian peninsula, that is, areas belonging to the modern-day nation-states Norway, Sweden, Finland, and the north-eastern part of Russia. Despite long-standing attempts by these nation-states to eradicate the survival and use of our languages, 10 languages remain spoken today, thanks to both continuous use among the Sámi, and on-going language revitalisation projects (Aikio-Puoskari 2018).

To understand the current situation in Fenno-Scandinavia with regard to the subjection of Indigenous Sámi to settler colonialism – the type of colonialism that seeks to replace the original people with settler society (Wolfe 2006) – it is important to acknowledge that the Sámi and their ancestors have interacted with other people in Fenno-Scandinavia, as well as Europe and North Africa, for several millennia. Today's nation-states were established only 700 to 500 years ago, and the latest border changes affecting Sámi happened in 1905, as a result of the dissolution of the Swedish-Norwegian Union, and with the 1917 independence of Finland (from Russia). While the situation in Sábme resembles those found in other settler-colonial states, the fact that Sábme has been shared with others for thousands of years makes this experience vastly different from that of other Indigenous peoples.

There are written records of Sámi as a distinct people, separate from the Nordic peoples, as early as the first century CE. The Roman historian Tacitus mentions two northern peoples, the suiones, the Swedes, and the fenni, the Sámi, in his writings (Tacitus 98 CE/1912; Zachrisson 2008; Ojala 2009: 84). The word *Finn* is the Old Norse name for the Sámi. To this day, the name functions as a denomination for the Sámi in Norwegian (Mundal 2009; 2000; Ojala 2009). In the sixth book of the *History of the Wars*, the sixth-century scholar Procopius mentions the 'Skrithiphinoi' – skiing Finns – when he describes Thule, and the *Ynglingasaga* mentions that several of the mythical Uppsala kings of the Ynglinga dynasty had sons with Finn women (Zachrisson 2010). According to Else Mundal (2000) and Inger Zachrisson (2008), the contents of the Old Norse sources imply that the Sámi were a natural part of society and that the border between Sámi and Nordic/Germanic peoples was not sharp.

Furthermore, Sámi communities have always been heterogeneous, with diverse cultural practices, occupations, and languages. A nomadic way of life was part of reindeer herding, but it was also the result of state policies – such as forced labour in mines, or military drafts to the many wars fought by the Swedish state – that pushed some Sámi to move away to avoid trouble. Today, the Sámi are predominantly depicted as reindeer herders. While reindeer herding has been an important part of our culture for a long time, Sámi who did not herd reindeer have always existed. The early 20th century saw the beginning of a still on-going ethno-political movement which calls upon the Sámi to join forces as one people, unhindered by the borders of nation-states and cultural differences between Sámi communities. This movement arose out of a wish to oppose and challenge colonial industrial destructive intrusions, race biology, the lack of proper education, as well as land theft (Johansen 2015; Laula 1904; Stenberg and Lindholm 1920; Hirvonen 2008; Lantto and Mörkenstam 2008; Össbo and Lantto 2011; Öhman 2016).

Figure 32.1 Maria Jonsson and Maria Thomasson herding reindeer on skis in Bydalen, Jämtland, 1909. Source: Nils Thomasson/Jamtli

The documentation of Sámi technological innovations and expertise

The majority of early scholarly literature produced in Sweden, that is Olaus Magnus (1539a/b; 1555) and Schefferus (1673; 1674), focusing on the Sámi as a distinct people primarily resident in the northern parts of Fenno-Scandinavia draws upon a perceived need to tie these territories closer to the Vatican and the Swedish state. However, it important to acknowledge that Sámi have always resided in the south of Fenno-Scandinavia as well (Aalto and Lehtola: 2017; Nordin 2018). Swedish colonisation of northern Sámi territories happened alongside similar incursions by the Danish-Norwegian Kingdom and Russia. In fact, the rich salmon rivers in the north drew interest from the Swedish state relatively early, and the income generated from them was used to fund the church (Bergman and Ramqvist 2017; Ojala and Nordin 2019).

In 1316, King Birger issued a letter confirming the archiepiscopal rights of Uppsala to fish salmon in the Ume River. The Lule River (*Julevädno* in Lule Sámi) is mentioned in another letter from 1327. These letters were quickly followed by others, confirming the king's, the church's, and the nobility's land and fishing rights in Sábme (Dahlbäck 1977: 185; Bergman and Ramqvist 2017). Contact between Sámi and settler-colonial communities was also initiated by Sámi, however, who wanted the church to help convert their own people to Christianity. The earliest known example of this was the Sámi woman Margareta, whose religious zeal is well-documented in documents that talk about her meetings with Queen Margareta I in 1389, as well as the Archbishop in Lund (Rasmussen 2014; Rydving 2016).

Olaus Magnus – Carta Marina 1539 and history of the Nordic people 1555

The first comprehensive work discussing Sámi technologies and expertise was written by Olaus Magnus (1490–1557), a Swedish Catholic priest. In 1518 and 1519 he made a journey from Uppsala to the northern parts of Fenno-Scandinavia, visiting Helsingia, Iamtia, Trøndelag, Nordland, the Bothnian coast, Westrobothnia, and Norrbotten, via Tornio. Olaus Magnus was aware of his predecessors' faulty maps, and thus kept in touch with scientists, scholars and map-makers throughout his journeys, recording everything he saw and experienced along the way. Aided by the knowledge gained from this journey, as well as earlier studies, Olaus Magnus published a map of Fenno-Scandinavia in 1539 along with a booklet – an explanation to the map in German, 'Ein kurze auslegung' and Italian, 'Opera breve'. This work was later followed by his 1555 publication *Historiae gentibus septentrionalibus* (History of the Nordic Peoples) (Magnus 1539a/b; 1555; Broberg/SBL 1994; Miekkavaara 2008; Balzamo 2014).

Historia de gentibus septentrionalibus is an 800-page-long publication in Latin focusing on the entirety of Fenno-Scandinavia. The publication became a bestseller and was rapidly translated into the main European languages; German in 1567, Italian and French in 1561, Dutch in 1562, English in 1638. Translation into Swedish took more than three hundred years, 1909-1925. *Historia* contains 22 books, 778 chapters, and 481 woodcuts. It served as the main source of information about this part of the world for over a century. Despite its many inaccuracies, Olaus Magnus had indeed visited the northern Sámi territories as an envoy for the papal legate Arcimboldus to sell letters of indulgence, but also, presumably, as an investigator for the Swedish King Sten Sture the Younger, meaning that he recorded several first-hand witness accounts of Sámi traditions in the northern parts of modern-day Sweden (Broberg/SBL 1994; Balzamo 2014).

Olaus Magnus (1555) mentions the knowledge of woodwork and timber in the far north, 'in extremis terries Botniae' (i.e., Sábme). He writes in particular about a durable type of hardwood, which could refer to the compressed wood used by the Sámi to make skis (Magnus 1555; XII, XIII). In his accounts, Sábme is depicted as a land full of activities, where men and women hunted together, (IV: 11–12), guided by the locals' knowledge on how to survive in the Arctic, as well as a place where one could find a specific type of Sámi boat, vital to the fur trade and Sámi markets (Larsson 2007: 124, 135, 143, 203).

Schefferus Lapponia 1673/74 and Lundius Descriptio Lapponiae

The work of Olaus Magnus was followed by the Uppsala-based law and rhetoric professor Johannes Schefferus's widely read 1673 Latin publication *Lapponia*. In addition to references to earlier historical documents, Schefferus makes sure to mention the contributions by the Sámi themselves in his preface, noting the work of Sámi students Olof Sirma and Spirzi Nils. Less than a year later, Schefferus updated the book with several contributions written by the Sámi student Nicolaus Lundius, who in turn was the son of the Sámi vicar Andrei Petri Lundius, who had studied in Uppsala in 1633 (Henrysson 1989). Lundius's (1674; 1905) 34-page-long contribution, *Descriptio Laponiae*, was part of the version of *Lapponia* which was translated into French in 1678 and into Swedish in 1956 (Rydving 2010; Schefferus 1956: 7). In addition, Schefferus also received information from vicars working in the northern Sámi territories who had been commissioned to send their reports to him (Schefferus 1673: 14; 1674; Nordberg: 1973).

Lundius, was not however the first Sámi to write about his people, despite the notability of his work. In fact, the work of Johan Graan (1610–79), a Sámi doctor of law as well as

Figure 32.2 Image from Olaus Magnus Carta Marina, 1539a, also in Historia de gentibus septentrionalibus, 1555. Woman and man on skis in the Sámi territories, hunting.

judge of appeal, who governed Västerbotten, an area encompassing the majority of Sábme from 1653 until his death, needs to be taken into account as well, despite frequent attempts to dismiss Graan's Sámi heritage (cited in Rydving 2010). Graan made repeated attempts to address the Sámi territories' economic situation in letters issued to the central administration, and he ensured that several books were printed in the Sámi languages as a way to simplify the education of the Sámi. In order to prevent the Sámi from leaving their areas as a result of forced military recruitment and slavery work in the mining industry, Graan pondered ways to attract people to set up permanent homes in the area, thus avoiding the risk of leaving the territory void of workers, and open to foreign colonial expansion. In 1667 he requested funds from the Royal administration to map the Sámi territories (Göthe 1929: 159). This, in turn, inspired the work of Schefferus, who was then commissioned by the Lord High Chancellor Magnus de la Gardie in 1671 to write a book on the Sámi. The High Chancellor instructed vicars in the Sámi territories to send in reports on the Sámi and their lands for this book, whose preface states that its goal is to dismiss every person who claims that Sweden's military prowess can be attributed to the Sámi's extensive knowledge of magic (Schefferus 1956; Balzamo 2014).

The 1600s were however also the period during which the domination and control of Sábme by the Swedish state became more pronounced. The first proclamation for the Settlement and Colonisation of Lapland is issued in the same year as *Lapponia* is published, and it states that any land that is not needed by the Sámi could be claimed by peasants from Swedish ruled areas (Charles XI, 1872 [1673], 20f; Nordlander 1938; Nordberg n.d.; Rydving 2010).

Over a span of 35 chapters, *Lapponia* describes many aspects of Sámi livelihoods, as well as the resources of the territory, in particular where explorers could find minerals. In the 17th century the Swedish state had already opened a number of mines, such as at Nasafjäll and Silbojokk in Pite Lappmark, Kvikkjokk/Húhttan in Lule Lappmark, and Svappavaara/Kengis in Torne Lappmark, all of which are indicated on Schefferus's map (Nordin and Ojala 2017a; Naum 2018). In addition to six whole chapters devoted to the Sámi's alleged un-Christian knowledge of magic, he describes different house constructions found among the Mountain and Forest Sámi, as well as houses built by other Sámi, focusing on both permanent houses and mobile ones (Schefferus 1956: 225). Moreover, he describes the clothing, food, and drink of the Sámi, as well as herbal medicine (Svanberg 2007), hunting and hunting weapons, as well as the exquisite handicraft found amongst the Sámi, such as birch-root baskets, birch bark boxes decorated with reindeer antlers, and other tools made of antlers (Schefferus 1956: 285f). Schefferus then goes on to describe light, hand-sewn boats (Larsson 2007), a unique type of sled, called 'kieris' which are pulled by domesticated reindeer (Schefferus 1956: 284) and finally skis in great detail, thus highlighting the technological skills possessed by the Sámi.

Colonial expansion and studies of Sámi technical expertise

While both Olaus Magnus's *Historia* and Schefferus's *Lapponia* mapped the northern Sámi territories for colonial expansion and control, they also showcased the advanced culture of the Sámi. In Sweden, Schefferus's work was followed by a book written by the Uppsala professor of medicine, Olof Rudbeck the Younger, which in turn had been commissioned by King Charles IX in 1695 (Rudbeck 1701; 1987). In 1732, Carl Linnaeus, later ennobled Carl von Linné, made his first trip northwards, in continuation of Rudbeck's research. In 1737, he published a book on the region's rich flora and fauna (Linné 1737). His travel diary (Linne 1732; 1811) was not published until 1811, but he did publish notes to the Royal Academy of Science, about the construction of Sámi skis and sleds, the use of compressed wood – *tjur* or *tiör* – and how the wood was fused together with the help of a specifically made glue, which he notes, "holds better than any glue imported from foreign countries" (Linné 1740: 221).

Karolinska Institute medical doctor and race biologist Gustaf von Düben (1822-92) studied Sámi human remains, including skulls, and visited the northern Sámi territories in 1868 and 1871, accompanied by his wife Lotten, who worked as a photographer for the expedition. Their work, published in 1873, is full of descriptions of Sámi technological expertise and knowledge (Düben 1873).

Von Düben's work, in turn, is complemented by the extensive studies of Fenno-Ugrian languages by Uppsala University professor K.B. Wiklund (1868–1934). Wiklund was for a long time the only Swedish academic who focused on the Sámi and was thus called upon as an expert on Sámi livelihoods by different committees and inquiries (Karlsson 2000). The doctoral dissertation written by Wiklund's student, Sigrid Drake, focusing on the life and technological advancements of the Västerbotten Sámi at the end of the 19th century (Drake 1979 [1918]), was another significant contribution to scholarly documentation of Sámi innovation. Åke Campbell (1948) and Ernst Manker (cf 1953; Silvén 2014) also described the technological expertise of the Sámi. These studies have been further supported and built on in the unpublished work of J.G. Ullenius (1932), as well as by the ethnology professor Phebe Fjellström (1987), the archaeology associate Professor Inger Zachrisson (cf 2008; 2010), and as discussed briefly in the next section, Sámi scholar Gunilla Larsson's (2007) doctoral dissertation on Late Iron Age boat technology, as well as Sámi scholar Camilla Brattland's (2013) work on the traditional ecological expertise among Sea-Sámi in Norway.

Many books on the technological expertise and knowledge of the Sámi that challenged diminishing narratives on Sámi were written by earlier Sámi scholars too, such as Elsa Laula (1904), Johan Turi (2011 [1910]), Karin Stenberg (1920), Israel Ruong (1956), and Torkel Tomasson (1928). Tomasson founded and worked as the editor of the Sámi journal *Samefolket* for over 22 years where several articles on Sámi life and livelihood were published, explaining the problems confronted by Sámi and ingenious ways of solving these problems (Mebius 2008; Samefolket n.d).

Indeed, Sámi – in the north, at least – are well studied and analysed, in particular those who are considered to be 'authentic' by the settler state, i.e. reindeer herders. Other Sámi have awakened much less scholarly interest (cf Aalto and Lehtola 2017; Nordin 2018).

Sámi as skilled boat and ship builders

Non-Sámi settler scholars have devoted a considerable amount of time to the question of the genetic and cultural origin of the Sámi. Carl-Gösta Ojala (2009) details how a major shift in the discourse came about after 18th-century scholars highlighted the historical presence of the Sámi, only to then diminish and ridicule this fact. The shift towards depicting the Sámi as immigrants, rather than original people, followed a century of Swedish archaeologists and scientists claiming that the Sámi had been here first. The former theory, in Swedish called *Storutbredningsteorin*, 'the theory of a wide distribution' which was disrupted by Sámi expulsion from their lands by Nordic immigrants, was first promoted in the 19th century by Sven Nilsson (1787–1883), professor in natural history at the University of Lund, and a fellow of the Swedish Academy of Science (Ojala 2009: 117). The shift in the discourse was caused by growing settler colonialism, as discussed by Storli (1993) and Ojala (2009: 121f.) Building on Darwinist ideas, the pre-historic technological expertise and innovations of Sámi ancestors was downplayed by archaeologists in both Norway and Sweden and reduced to a primitive 'Arctic Stone Age', imagined to be different from a perceived developed southern Stone Age (cf Ojala 2009: 122; Storli 1993: 17). From being described as the original population of Fenno-Scandinavia, by the early 20th century Sámi people were being described as immigrants, foreigners to the region, and less technologically developed, alongside expanding settler-colonial presence in forestry and mining in the northern Sámi territories.

Recent work has challenged this revisionist view. Gunilla Larsson (2007) analysed Late Iron Age (about 400 to 800 CE in Scandinavia) Sámi travel and navigation skill in her doctoral dissertation *Ship and society: maritime ideology in Late Iron Age Sweden*. Larsson presents the Sámi as boat-builders contributing to the success of Nordic Late Iron Age – since the 19th century commonly referred to as the mythical 'Viking era' – transportation and trade (Larsson 2007: 24). She describes Sámi light sewn boats, easily carried between lakes or to pass streams in a river, as well that the Sámi did use heavier boats when needed, and would produce them when requested or ordered (Larsson 2007: 121, 161; 2015). Other scholarly work discussing early Sámi boat transports and usage include Mulk and Bayliss-Smith discussing finds of rock depictions in Badjelánnda (2006; Larsson 2007: 97), and Bergman and Ramqvist (2017).

New finds on the Sámi Iron Age – 2,500 years ago

The skill of iron production is another theme of interest in this regard. Did Sámi in the northern territories already know how to produce iron and steel 2,000 years ago? Was there a Sámi Iron Age? Ojala (2009) states that the concept of a Sámi Iron Age was suggested by Norwegian archaeologists in the 1950s, and was part of the discussion up to the 1990s (see also, for Karelia/Finland, Kosmenko and Manjuhin 1999). Zachrisson (2008: 37) states that according to written documentation Sámi were considered skilled in iron smithing during the Viking age.

However, recent finds suggest that iron and steel production dates to far earlier than was thought. Archaeological finds in Norrbotten, the northernmost county in Sweden and also the northern Sámi territories, currently being analysed as part of a research project by archaeologist and doctoral candidate in History of Technology at Luleå University of Technology Carina Bennerhag (2016; 2017) suggest that iron and steel production dates as early as around 500 BCE. These finds, and on-going analysis, challenge long-held perceptions of the hunter-gatherer societies in this region as late and passive recipients of iron.

A Sámi history of skiing

There are many evidences of the ski as an early human – Sámi– innovation. Zachrisson (2008: 37) states that "most of the several hundred prehistoric skis found in Fennoscandia are of Sámi type, several with typical ornamentation", and states that it is stressed in documentation from the ninth century to the 19th century that the Sámi were specialised in skiing (2008). Furthermore, finds such as the one of the 5,200-year-old ski in Kalvträsk on the Swedish side of Sábme, 1924, prove that skis have been around in Sábme for a very long time (Berg 1950).

Linguistic evidence from the Sámi languages alongside written records, rock depictions and drum illustrations, further support this statement the dating of the Sámi invention of skis to many millennia ago. There are around three hundred words for snow and snow conditions in Lule Sámi (Ryd and Rassa 2001) and several of these relate to conditions for skiing. Hartvig Birkely argues that skiing technology is a Sámi innovation, based on archaeological finds, and that the Sámi word čuoigat (North Sámi, tjoejkedh in South Sámi, tjuojggat in Lule Sámi) which means 'to ski', is about from 6,000 to 8,000 years old (Birkely 1994; Weinstock 2005).

In this section, I consider how this knowledge is depicted in several media, from written documentation, to rock carvings and paintings, images on a drum, as well as historical exhibits in museums.

Museums displays of ski history

The permanent exhibition on skiing at Västerbotten County Museum proudly showcases the oldest known ski in the world, the 'Kalvträsk ski' found in 1924. The ski is described as being "half a millennium older than the Egyptian Pyramids" (Västerbottens Museum 2020: online). However, so far both this exhibit and the Ski Museum showcasing old skis in Holmenkollen, Oslo, a former host of the Olympic Games and several world championships (Skiforeningen 2015) fail to mention the Sámi on exhibitions' web pages. The Västerbotten Museum (n.d.) website features a photo of the exhibition including a national romantic skiing dress, inspired by traditional Sámi clothes, although without mentioning that it is such a skiing dress and not a Sámi dress (cf Wadensten 2011).

In contrast to this silence, Ájtte, the principal Swedish museum of Sámi culture and the mountain region, has an exhibition featuring a photo collection of skis, showing their usage, as well as a collection of skis with references to work on the subject matter. On their YouTube channel there is a video explaining the Sámi practice of skiing on different types of landscapes and snow quality (Ájtte 2020; 2019; 2014).

Material finds of skis, pictures in rock carvings and paintings, and on drums

Apart from the oldest find from Kalvträsk, there are several other finds of ancient skis in bogs. With current climate change, ancient skis are now found in melting glaciers as discussed by Finstad et al. (2016). The oldest known image of a skier, dated to around 1050, was found on a rune stone near Balingsta, Uppland, 80 kilometres northwest of the current Swedish capital Stockholm. Many Sámi ceremonial drums feature depictions of skiers, and even though only a few drums remain, due to a church-led drive to collect and destroy drums during the 17th century, skiers are commonly found on the preserved ones, with the oldest one dating back to the 16th century. Rock depictions provide even earlier depictions of skiers (Åström and Norberg 1984). So far, rock depictions featuring skiers have so far not been found on the Swedish side of

Figure 32.3 Lars and Anna Brita Kråik, looking for a wolf. Source: Nils Thomasson/Jamtli

Sábme (J. Ling, Director for the Swedish Rock Art Research Archives, personal communication 2 March 2020), but there is a skier on a rock carving in Rødøy, Helgeland, on the Norwegian side of Sábme, which dates back to 2000–1500 BCE. Equally old rock paintings featuring skiers are found the Zavalruga Field in Belomorsk, Russian Karelia, near the White Sea (Åström and Norberg 1984).

Written documentation on the history of Sámi skiing

While attributing the innovation of skis to the Sámi or their ancestors is justified, it is also contestable, as it is impossible to accurately establish exactly who invented the first pair of skis, and indeed when this happened, as well as what cultural identity that person belonged to. That being said, the vast majority of historical accounts make it clear that the Sámi were highly skilled skiers, and that the art of skiing made up an important part of their cultural identity (Zachrisson 2008). The issue is complex, as the Sámi have been engaged in cultural exchanges for millennia, particularly as trade partners of huge importance to Nordic kings and lords. In this context, the processes underlying the discursive Othering of the Sámi warrant further investigation.

It is only at the beginning of the 16th century that we start to see documents that portray the Sámi as different, and then only in documents that portray northern Fenno-Scandinavia as the only true home of the Sámi. A century later, these portrayals supported the forced removal of southern Sámi communities northwards (Nordin 2018) as well as the establishment of Lapland as a reservation.

Sámi knowledge of skiing, among both men and women, is mentioned with astonishment and awe in most historical documentations of the Sámi from the 16th century onwards. Olaus Magnus's map of Scandinavia (1539a) has a picture of a man and a woman skiing whilst hunting with a bow and arrow. He discusses the skiing technology in his *History of the Nordic Peoples* drawing upon his own first-hand witness accounts of travels throughout Sábme, stating that:

> the Inhabitants of it [Scricfinnia]slide very swift, having their feet fastned to crooked pieces of Wood made plain, and bended like a Bow in the former part, with a staff in their hands to guide them; and by these, at their pleasure they can transport themselves upward downward, or obliquely, over the tops of snow. ... Therefore with such Instruments, and the Art they have to run, they are wont, especially in Winter time, to passe over the unaccessible places of Mountains, and Valleys. ... Not is there any Rock so prominent, but they can cunningly run up to the top of it, by a winding course ... sometimes they do it in heat of Hunting, sometimes to try their Skill, and to contend for mastery therein, as those who run Races to win the price.
>
> *(Magnus, [1555] 1658: 1)*

Schefferus' *Laponia* includes a picture and the following description of skiing: "I come now to their other instruments relating to this sport, the chiefest of which are their shoes, with which they slide over the frozen snow, being made of broad planks extremely smooth; the Northern People call them Skider ..." (Schefferus 1674: 99–100).

Also, the couple von Düben describe the act of skiing in their publication *On Lapland and the Laps* (Düben 1873: 37ff). In the same book, von Düben mentions how a Sámi woman who visits the couple in Stockholm during the winter 1866–1867 travelled 460 kilometres, one way, to meet them:

> The winter of 1866–67 a Sámi female friend from Wilhelmina in Åsele Lappmark visited the author in Stockholm, and when asking from where she had come the girl answered: 'Yes, we were with the herd by Hernösand, and I had some business here for the school, that is why I went skiing here'.
>
> *(Düben 1873: 92, author's translation from Swedish)*

Despite the lack of acknowledgement of Sámi technologies in contemporary publications on the history of technology, as well as in many museums, there is thus quite a large number of documents one can turn to in order to find information on the usage of skis, and how this usage relates to both climate and ecology in Sábme.

In Sábme, skis were traditionally made with compressed wood, 'tjur' or 'tiör' in Swedish, *biŋál* in Lule Sámi. Tomasson (1928) describes how important ecological factors were in the development of skis, and how the wood was selected and then processed. More recent work by Yngve Ryd, interviewing Sámi informants, describes the construction, usage and storage of skis over the summer in bogs (Ryd 1998).

Final words: Sámi technical innovations and sustainable technologies

Reclaiming Sámi and other Indigenous peoples' technological expertise and innovations, both in history and in the present day, is important work that warrants further study. Far too often, Indigenous peoples are portrayed as opponents to technical 'development', when the truth is that the opposition draws upon a desire to protect existing technological and sustainable innovations, developed over millennia, against proposed industrial exploitation detrimental to humans and non-humans, lands and water alike (cf Öhman 2016).

As described by amongst other Pedersen (2013) Sámi reindeer herders used skis on a daily basis until the 1970s. A major problem over the past 50–60 years, causing the need for motorisation of reindeer herding, has been the fragmentation of reindeer grazing land, due to the regulation of rivers used for hydropower, the establishment of mines, roads, and railroads. Now, snow mobiles and even trucks now must be used to move reindeer for their annual migration. In view of contemporary debates about the need to reduce the use fossil fuels, Sámi technology and the infrastructure it requires should be of major interest. However, criticising the forced motorisation of the Sámi reindeer herding remains complicated, as the idea that Sámi and other Indigenous peoples need to remain 'traditional' is all too often followed by the claim that, when they don't, they have abandoned the 'real' Sámi/Indigenous way of life: as if Indigenous traditions never change. However, acknowledging and making visible the history of Sámi technical innovations and ingenuity in adapting to the Arctic climate, may hopefully also promote Sámi technical innovations of today, a subject matter which so far has received far too little attention, as discussed within our ongoing research project "Dálkke: Indigenous Climate Change Studies" (cf Spik et al. forthcoming).

Acknowledgements

Gijtto, thanks, to fellow Sámi and non-Sámi with specialist knowledge of the themes addressed who have provided guidance and support, to Johan Sandberg McGuinne for language editing and valuable knowledge on Sámi culture and language, Scott Burnett for language editing, to the peer reviewers and editors, to Saemien Sijte, South Sámi Museum and Cultural Center and Jamtli for photos by Nils Thomasson. Work with this chapter was funded within the research project Dálkke: Indigenous Climate Change Studies, FORMAS Dnr 2017-01923, within the Swedish National research programme on climate.

References

Aalto, S. and Lehtola, V.-P. (2017). 'The Sami representations reflecting the multi-ethnic north of the saga literature', *Journal of Northern Studies*, vol 11, no 2: 7–30.

Adas, M. (1989). *Machines as the Measure of Men: Science, Technology and Ideologies of Western Dominance.* Cornell University Press: Ithaca, NY.

Åhrén, C. (2008). *Är jag en Riktig Same?: En Etnologisk Studie av Unga Samers Identitetsarbete.* PhD dissertation, Umeå Universitet: Umeå.

Aikio-Puoskari, U. (2018). 'Revitalization of Sámi languages in three Nordic countries: Finland, Norway, and Sweden', in L. Hinton, L. Huss, and G. Roche (eds.) *The Routledge Handbook of Language Revitalization.* Routledge: Milton, 355–363.

Ájtte. (2014). 'Skidåkning'. Available: https://www.youtube.com/watch?v=uViApBFYd5c, accessed 5 July 2019.

Ájtte. (2019). 'På väg – Jåhtet'. Available: http://www.ajtte.com/utst/pa-vag/, accessed 5 July 2019.

Ájtte. (2020). 'Collections – search word "skidor"'. Available: http://collections.ajtte.com/web, accessed 5 July 2019.

Åström, K. and Norberg, O. (1984). 'Förhistoriska och medeltida skidor', *Västerbotten*, vol 2: 82–88.

Balzamo, E. (2014). 'The geopolitical Laplander: From Olaus Magnus to Johannes Schefferus', *Journal of Northern Studies*, vol 8, no 2: 29–43.

Bennerhag, C. (2016). *A Slag Find Rewrites History.* Luleå University of Technology. Available: https://www.ltu.se/research/subjects/Historia/Nyheter-och-aktuellt/Slaggfynd-omkullkastar-historien-1.160288?l=en, accessed 6 July 2019.

Bennerhag, C. (2017). 'From hard rock to heavy metal – early iron production in a hunting- and gathering community in Northern Sweden', paper at *Iron in Archeology, Bloomery Smelters and Blacksmiths in Europe and Beyond Conference*, 30 May–1 June. Institute of Archaeology of the CAS: Prague.

Berg, G. (1950). *Finds of Skis from Prehistoric Time in Swedish Bogs and Marshes*. Generalstabens litografiska anstalts förlag: Stockholm.

Bergman, I. and Ramqvist, P.H. (2017). 'Farmer fishermen: Interior lake fishing among coastal communities in Northern Sweden AD 1200–1600', *Acta Borealia*, vol 34, no 2: 134–158.

Birkely, H. (1994). *En kulturhistorisk studie: Historisk belysning av samiske ski og samisk skiløping*. Norges idrettshøgskole: Oslo.

Brattland, B. (2013). 'Proving fishers right: Effects of the integration of experience-based knowledge in ecosystem-based management', *Acta Borealia*, vol 30, no 1: 39–59.

Broberg G.S.B.L. (1994). *Olaus Magnus, urn:sbl:7681*. Svenskt biografiskt lexikon: Stockholm.

Campbell, Å. (1948). *Från vildmark till bygd: En etnologisk undersökning av nybyggarkulturen i Lappland före industrialismens genombrott*. Hermes: Uppsala.

Charles XI (1872 [1673]). Kongl. Plakat den (1673). 'Angående lappmarkernas bebyggande'. In Poignant, E. (ed.) *Samling af författningar angående de s.k. lappmarksfriheterna*. Samson & W: Stockholm, 20–21.

Dahlbäck, G. (1977). *Uppsala domkyrkas godsinnehav med särskild hänsyn till perioden 1344–1527*. PhD thesis, Stockholm University: Stockholm.

Drake, S. (1918). *Västerbottenslapparna under förra hälften av 1800-talet: etnografiska studier*. PhD thesis, Uppsala University: Uppsala.

Düben, G.V. (1873). *Om Lappland och lapparne, företrädesvis de svenske, ethnografiska studier*. Norstedt: Stockholm.

Finstad, E., Martinsen, J., Hole, R., and Pilø, L. (2016). 'Prehistoric and medieval skis from glaciers and ice patches in Norway', *Journal of Glacial Archaeology*, vol 3: 43–58.

Fjellström, P. (1987). 'Cultural – and traditional – ecological perspectives in Saami religion', in *Saami Religion: Based on Papers Read at the Symposium on Saami Religion, Held at Åbo, Finland, on the 16th–18th of August 1984*. Almqvist & Wiksell International: Stockholm, 34–45.

Gambino, M. (2009). 'A salute to the wheel', *Smithsonian Magazine*. Available: https://www.smithsonianmag.com/science-nature/a-salute-to-the-wheel-31805121/, accessed 1 May 2019.

Gambino, M. (2011). 'Ski the Vasaloppet in Sweden', *Smithsonian Magazine*. Available: https://www.smithsonianmag.com/travel/ski-the-vasaloppet-in-sweden-38350063/, accessed 5 July 2019.

Göthe, G. (1929). *Om Umeå lappmarks svenska kolonisation: Från mitten av 1500-talet till omkr 1750*. PhD thesis, Stockholms Högskola: Uppsala.

Headrick, D.R. (2009). *Technology: A world history*. Oxford: Oxford University Press.

Henrysson, S. (1989). *Prästerna i lappmarken före 1850: Ursprung och arbetsuppgifter*. Forskningsarkivet, Umeå University: Umeå.

Hirvonen, V. (2008). *Voices from Sápmi: Sámi Women's Path to Authorship*. PhD thesis 1999 [translated], Oulu University, DAT, Guovdageaidnu: Norway.

Johansen, S.B. (2015). *Elsa Laula Renberg: Historien om samefolkets stora Minerva*. CalliidLágádus: Karasjok.

Jordanes. (1915). *The Gothic History of Jordanes in English Version*. Princeton University Press: Princeton. Available: https://archive.org/details/gothichistoryofj00jorduoft, accessed 3 July 2019.

Karlsson, C. (2000). *Vetenskap som politik: K.B. Wiklund, staten och samerna under 1900-talets första hälft*. Umeå University: Umeå.

Kosmenko, M.G. and Manjuhin, I.S. (1999). 'Ancient iron production in Karelia', *Fennoscandia Archaeologica*, vol XVI: 1–46.

Lantto, P and Mörkenstam, U. (2008). 'Sami rights and Sami challenges', *Scandinavian Journal of History*, vol 33, no 1: 26–51.

Larsson, G. (2007). *Ship and Society: Maritime Ideology in Late Iron Age Sweden*. PhD thesis, Uppsala University: Uppsala.

Larsson, G. (2015). 'Aspekter på båtar och sjöfart bland samer', in S. von Arbin (ed.) *Tjop tjop!: vänbok Till Christer Westerdahl*. Båtdokgruppen: Skärhamn, 219–232.

Laula, E. (1904). *Inför lif eller död?: Sanningsord i de lappska förhållandena*. Wilhelmssons Boktryckeri, AB: Stockholm.

Lidström, I. (2017). 'Skiers of "nature" versus skiers of "culture". Ethnic stereotypes within Swedish cross-country skiing from the late 19th century to the 1930s', in H. Roiko-Jokela and P. Pöyhönen (eds.) *The Many Faces of Snow Sports. Ski Congress 2017*. The Finnish Society for Sports History: Jyväskylä, 73–82.

Linné, C.V. (1732). *Caroli Linnaei Iter lapponicum*. Wahlström & Widstrand: Stockholm.

Linné, C.V. (1737). *Flora Lapponica*. Amstelædami: Salomonem Schouten.

Linné, C.V. (1740). *Anmärkningar öfver lapska limmet*. Vet. Akad.: s Handl., 221–222.

Linné, C.V. (1811). *Lachesis Lapponica or a Tour in Lapland*. White and Cochrane: London.

Lundius, N.A. (1674). *Descriptio Lapponiae*, [handwritten copy of original], vol D68b. Royal Library: Stockholm.

Lundius, N.A. and Wiklund, K.B. (1905 [1674]). *Descriptio Lapponiae*. Wretmans boktryckeri: Uppsala. Available: http://urn.kb.se/resolve?urn=urn:nbn:se:alvin:portal:record-158690, accessed 3 July 2019.

Magnus, O. (1539a). *Carta Marina et Descriptio Septentrionalium Terrarum Diligentissimo Elaborata*. Anno Domini:Venice.

Magnus, O. (1539b). *Opera Breve*, Giouan Thomaso:Venetia.

Magnus, O. (1555). *Historia de Gentibvs Septentrionalibvs*. Impressvm Romae apvd Ioannem Mariam de Viottis Parmensem: Rome. Available: http://hdl.handle.net/2077/43443, accessed July 3, 2019.

Magnus, O. (1658). *A Compendious History of the Goths, Svvedes, and Vandals, and Other Northern Nations*. London. Available: http://ezproxy.its.uu.se/login?url=https://searchhttp://-proquest-com.ezproxy.its.uu.se/docview/2240853011?accountid=14715, accessed 3 July 2019.

Manker, E. (1953). *The Nomadism of the Swedish Mountain Lapps: The Siidas and Their Migratory Routes in 1945*. Gebers: Stockholm.

Mebius, H. (2008). *Vaajese:Torkel Tomasson traditionsbärare och forskare*. Jengel, Gaaltije: Östersund.

Miekkavaara, L. (2008). 'Unknown Europe: the mapping of the Northern countries by Olaus Magnus in 1539', *Belgeo*, vol 3, no 3–4: 307–324.

Mulk, I. and Bayliss-Smith, T. (2006). *Rock Art and Sami Sacred Geography in Badjelánnda, Laponia, Sweden: Sailing Boats, Anthropomorphs and Reindeer*. Umeå University: Umeå.

Mundal, E. (2000). 'Coexistence of Saami and norse culture – reflected in and interpreted by old Norse myths', in G. Barnes and M. Clunies Ross (eds.) *Old Norse Myths, Literature and Society*. University of Sydney: Sydney, 346–355.

Mundal, E. (2009). 'The relationship between Sami and Nordic peoples expressed in terms of family associations', *Journal of Northern Studies*, vol 2: 25–37.

Naum, M. (2018). 'Cultural "improvement", discipline and mining in early modern Sápmi', *Post-Medieval Archaeology*, vol 52, no 1: 102–116.

Nordberg, E. (1973). 'Kapellanen Olof Sirma i Enontekis', in *Källskrifter rörande kyrka och skola i den svenska lappmarken under 1600-talet*. Skytteanska samfundet: Umeå. Available: https://www.foark.umu.se/sites/default/files/arkiv/25/sefoark2502k.pdf, accessed July 7, 2019.

Nordin, J.M. (2018). 'Center of diversity: Sámi in early modern Stockholm in the light of European colonial expansion. A historical archaeological approach', *International Journal of Historical Archaeology*, vol 22, no 4: 663–685.

Nordin, J.M. and Ojala, C-G. (2017a). 'Copper worlds: A historical archaeology of Abraham and Jakob Momma-Reenstierna and their industrial enterprise in the Torne River Valley, c. 1650–1680', *Acta Borealia*, vol 34, no 2: 103–133.

Nordlander, J. (1938). *Johan Graan: Landshövding i Västerbotten 1653–1679*. Thule: Stockholm.

O'Brien, J.M. (2010). *Firsting and Lasting: Writing Indians Out of Existence in New England*. University of Minnesota Press: Minneapolis.

Öhman, M.-B. (2016). 'Technovisions of a Sámi cyborg: Re-claiming Sámi body-, land- and waterscapes after a century of colonial exploitations', in J. Bull and M. Fahlgren (eds.) *Illdisciplined Gender*. Springer: Rotterdam, 63–98.

Öhman, M.-B. (2017). 'Kolonisationen, rasismen och intergenerationella trauman', in M.-B. Öhman, C. Hedlund, and G. Larsson (eds.) *Uppsala mitt i Sápmi II*. Uppsam: Uppsala, 99–113.

Ojala, C. (2009). *Sámi Prehistories: The Politics of Archaeology and Identity in Northernmost Europe*. PhD thesis, Uppsala University: Sweden.

Ojala, C. and Nordin, J.M. (2019). 'Mapping land and people in the north: Early modern colonial expansion, exploitation, and knowledge', *Scandinavian Studies*, vol 91, no 1/2: 98–133.

Össbo, Å. and Lantto, P. (2011). 'Colonial tutelage and industrial colonialism: Reindeer husbandry and early 20th-century hydroelectric development in Sweden', *Scandinavian Journal of History*, vol 36, no 3: 324–348.

Pedersen, H.C. (2013). 'Skiing and sport in the core Sámi area of Norway, 1927 to 1964: Organisation, modernisation and minority policy', *The International Journal of the History of Sport*, vol 30, no 6: 580–597.

Persson, Å. and Oldrup, T. (2014). *101 Historiska Myter*. Historiska Media: Lund.

Rasmussen, S. (2014). 'The protracted Sami reformation – or the protracted christianizing process', in L.I. Hansen et al. (eds.) *The Protracted Reformation in Northern Norway: Introductory Studies*. Orkana akademisk: Stamsund, 165–183.

Rudbeck, O. (1701). *Olof Rudbecks Sonens Nora Samolad Eller Uplyste Lapland*. Uppsala.

Rudbeck, O. (1987). *Iter Lapponicum: Skissboken från resan till Lappland 1695.* Coeckelberghs: Stockholm.

Ruong, I. (1956). 'Types of settlement and husbandry among the Lapps in northern Sweden', in Å. Campbell and A. Furumark (eds.) *Arctica: Essays Presented to Åke Campbell 1.5.1956.* Almqvist & Wiksell: Stockholm, 105–132.

Ryd, Y. (1998). 'Tjurskidor på vårskaren – Sommarförvaring i myren', *Hemslöjden*, vol 1: 10–11.

Ryd, Y and Rassa, J. (2001). *Snö: En renskötare berättar.* Ordfront: Stockholm.

Rydving, H. (2010). 'Samiska överhetspersoner i Sverige och Finland under 1600-talet', in E. Mundal and H. Rydving (eds.) *Samer som "de andra", samer om "de andra".* Sámi dutkan/Sámiska Studier, Umeå University: Umeå, 259–265.

Rydving, H. (2016). Samisk kyrkohistoria: en kort översikt med fokus på kvinnor som aktörer. *De historiska relationerna mellan Svenska kyrkan och samerna : en vetenskaplig antologi. Bd 1.,* 315–339.

Samefolket. (n.d.). 'Samefolkets historia'. Available: https://samefolket.se/samefolkets-historia/, accessed 3 July 2019.

Schefferus, J. (1673). *[Joannis Schefferi Argentoratensis] Lapponia.* Francofvrti ex officina Christiani Wolffii typis Joannis Andreæ. Available: http://urn.kb.se/resolve?urn=urn:nbn:se:kb:eod-2519673, accessed 3 July 2019.

Schefferus, J. (1674). 'The history of Lapland, R.A Bathurst, Oxford'. Available: http://www.kb.se/F1700/Lapland/Lapland.htm, accessed 3 July 2019.

Schefferus, J. (1956). *Lappland.* Almqvist & Wiksell: Uppsala.

Silvén, E. (2014). 'Constructing a Sami cultural heritage: Essentialism and emancipation', *Ethnologia Scandinavica: A Journal for Nordic Ethnology,* vol 44: 60–74.

Skiforeningen. (2015). 'The ski museum: exhibitions'. Available: https://www.skiforeningen.no/en/hol menkollen/skimuseet/utstillinger/, accessed 5 July 2019.

Smithsonian Institute. (2020). Available: https://www.si.edu/, accessed July 3, 2019.

Sörlin, S. (1995). 'Nature, skiing and Swedish nationalism', *The International Journal of the History of Sport,* vol 12, no 2: 147–163.

Spik, S. et al. (eds) (forthcoming). *Nyttjas eller utnyttjas? – En förstudie om certifieringar i Sápmi… [To Use or be Used? – A Pre-Study on Brand Protection in Sápmi and Recommendations for How Tánnak Can Become a Good Example for a Sámi Innovation Company].* Uppsala University: Uppsala.

Stenberg, K. and Lindholm, V. (1920). *Dat läh mijen situd!: Det är vår vilja: en vadjan till den svenska nationen från samefolket.* Svenska förlaget: Stockholm.

Storli, I. (1993). Fra 'kultur' til 'natur'. Om konstitueringa av den 'arktiske' steinalderen. *Viking – Tidskrift for norrøn arkeologi,* vol LVI: 7–22.

Svalastog, A.L. (2014). 'On teacher education in Sweden, school curriculums, and the Sámi people', in J. Gärdebo, M-B. Öhman, and H. Maruyama (eds.) *RE: Mindings.* Hugo Valentin Centre, Uppsala University: Uppsala, 151–169.

Svanberg, I. (2007). '"The lapps chew this root a lot": milk parsley (Peucedanum palustre) in Sámi plant knowledge', in U. Fransson (ed.) *Cultural Interaction Between East and West: Archaeology, Artefacts and Human Contacts in Northern Europe.* Stockholm University: Stockholm, 328–330.

Tekniska Museet. (2018). 'Teknikhistorisk tidslinje'. Available: https://www.tekniskamuseet.se/lar-dig-me r/teknikhistorisk-tidslinje/#, accessed 3 July 2019.

Tekniska Museet. (n.d.). '100 innovationer'. Available: https://www.tekniskamuseet.se/lar-dig-mer/100 -innovationer/, accessed 3 July 2019.

Tomasson, T. (1928). 'Några tankar om skidrännans och de oliklånga skidornas uppkomst', *Samefolkets Egen Tidning,* vol 3: 21–24.

Turi, J. (2011 (1910)). *An Account of the Sámi [Muittalus Samid Birra].* Nordic Studies Press: Chicago.

Ullenius, J.G. (1932). *Undersökningsanteckningar rörande skogslappsområden å Lilla Luleälvs båda sidor nedom Jokkmokk.* Norrbotten Museum Archive, F:92.

Vasaloppet. (n.d.). 'Our history'. Available: https://www.vasaloppet.se/en/about-us/history/, accessed 3 July 2019.

Västerbottens Museum. (2020). 'Skidutställningen'. Available: https://www.vbm.se/utstallningar/skiduts tallningen/, accessed 3 July 2019.

Västerbottens Museum. (n.d.). *Collections [Rachel Ågren's Items Vbm 7874 b-d].* https://samlingar.vbm.se/, accessed July 6, 2019.

Wadensten, H. (2011). 'Samisk dräkt och annan textil', *Västerbotten,* vol 1: 56–60.

Weinstock, J. (2005). 'The role of skis and skiing in the settlement of early Scandinavia', *Northern Review,* vol 25/26: 172–196.

Wolfe, P. (2006). 'Settler colonialism and the elimination of the native', *Journal of Genocide Research*, vol 8, no 4: 387–409.

Zachrisson, I. (2008). 'The Sámi and their interaction with the nordic peoples', in S. Brink and N. Price (eds.) *The Viking World*. Routledge: London, 32–39.

Zachrisson, I. (2010). 'Vittnesbörd om pälshandel?: ett arkeologiskt perspektiv på romerska bronsmynt funna i norra sverige', *Fornvännen*, vol 105, no 3: 187–202.

33

The Indigenous digital footprint

Hēmi Whaanga and Paora Mato

Introduction

As we transition from analogue platforms to the digital, a 'Fourth Industrial Revolution' of ubiquitous technologies, supercomputing, intelligent robots, large-scale machine learning, deep learning, big data analysis, and computational neural networks is upon us. Recent major development and growth in robotics, the Internet of Things, 3D printing, nanotechnology, genome editing, quantum computing, advanced biology, artificial intelligence (AI) and other technologies have blurred the lines between the physical, biological, and digital realms (Schwaub 2016). Most notable, this 'blurring of the lines', has already markedly changed how people live their lives, study, work, write, and interact with each other (Palfrey 2008). Platforms like Facebook, YouTube, Instagram, Twitter, Reddit, Pinterest, Tumblr, and social networking apps such as Messenger, WhatsApp, WeChat, QQ Chat, QZone, Viber, LINE, and Snapchat, with billions of active users per month, are the preferred method for this generation, often referred to as 'digital natives' (see, for example, Akçayır, Dündar and Akçayır 2016; Kirschner and De Bruyckere 2017; Prensky 2001, 2009; Yong and Gates 2014), to interact with one another. Like previous industrial revolutions, these technological advances will dramatically transform how this 'digital' generation will practice, share, access, communicate, distribute, and view knowledge and information. In this chapter, we describe how Indigenous communities, galleries, libraries, archives, museums, and institutions have embraced etools, emedia, and elearning to support the goals of Indigenous people, communities and organisations in striving for cultural, social, linguistic, and economic sustainability in this digital world.

Regenerating, revitalising and repatriating Indigenous knowledge

In response to the increase in access and accessibility of Indigenous content and data, numerous individuals, academic institutions, innovators, communities, industry leaders, computer scientists and programmers, historians, geographers, translators, linguists, language, and cultural experts have engaged in and lead the creation of software, web resources and Indigenous content as a mechanism to connect Indigenous communities to their language, genealogy, families, culture and identity (Whaanga, Simmonds, and Keegan 2017). This effort has been part of a broader agenda to regenerate, revitalise, and repatriate Indigenous content and objects back to their respective communities for long-term linguistic, cultural, social, and economic sustainability. A range of initiatives have been implemented to collect, maintain and organise digital content and objects, including text, video, audio, genealogy, and maps, along with methods for their access, and retrieval.

Geographic Information Systems (GIS), global positioning systems (GPS), online mapping tools (such as Google Maps and CARTO) and geospatial data have been used to represent an Indigenous worldview (Laituri 2011). As noted by McMahon, Smith and Whiteduck (2017: 423), Indigenous peoples adopt and modify "technical artefacts and associated social practices, including those used to archive, steward, and manage geospatial data". Other initiatives in this space have focused on areas such as traditional land use (Olson, Hackett and DeRoy 2016), counter mapping (Hirt 2012; Palmer 2012), participatory mapping (Bryan 2011; Robinson et al. 2016), the formation of Indigenous networks and workshops (such as Indigenous Mapping Wānanga and Workshops (Apiti 2017), and most importantly cultural mapping (Duxbury 2015).

Galleries, libraries, archives, museums (GLAM), and institutions throughout the world have vast collections of millions of treasures, artefacts, writings, and manuscripts that have been collected from Indigenous peoples and communities. For a long time, the management, conservation, care and display of these treasures, artefacts, and information have been associated with power, politics, and colonialism (Bennett 2004; Bray 2001; Clavir 2002; Corsane 2005). This association stems from a long legacy of imperial expansion, the colonisation of Indigenous peoples, and the displacement of lands (Butts 2003; Hakiwai 2004; Henare 2005). Indigenous peoples still view these institutions as remnants of colonial constructs and sites of resistance where they continue to argue for representation, equal governance and rights and access to their treasures, in order to re-establish identity, reconnect to language, history, and traditions (Lonetree 2012; Sleeper-Smith 2009).

Over the past few decades there has been a growing movement by Indigenous peoples to reclaim and repatriate their cultural treasures and their associated knowledge repositories back to their associated communities as part of an agenda to decolonise, re-story, and retell their histories within these institutions (Lonetree 2012). This re-storying is happening at a time where the distinctions between these Western knowledge institutions are blurring in terms of their amalgamated content. As articulated by Kirchhoff, Schweibenz, and Sieglerschmidt (2008: 251–2), "one of the foremost indicators of digital convergence is the blurring of distinctions between archives, libraries, museums, and other memory institutions in the virtual realm … from a users' perspective", adding that it is of no importance "where they find their information … In the digital realm, it is no longer relevant whether the original materials are in a library or a museum or an archive".

In relation to the reaffirmation of Indigenous peoples' rights, the development of etools, emedia, and elearning have played an important part in shifting physical archival and curator-controlled representations of Indigenous material towards initiatives that enable Indigenous communities to reconceptualise their relationships with these institutions in culturally-specific ways, including the re-authoring and ownership of content (Horwood 2018; Salmond 2012; Whaanga, Simmonds, and Keegan 2017). In recent years, the focus has turned to the development of digital platforms, databases, interactive augmented and virtual reality exhibitions (AR and VR) (Isaac 2015), and virtual repatriation (Hakiwai 2012; Schorch, McCarty and Hakiwai 2016) to return cultural information and objects to their respective Indigenous communities (Christen 2015; Ngata, Ngata-Gibson and Salmond 2012). Horwood (2017: 149) notes that:

> New collaborative models developed for exhibition interactives have resulted in the development of tangible, embodied interactions that bridge the digital and material. The resulting

immersive experiences tell personal stories, create evocative experiences and enrich heritage collections. ... For museums and Indigenous communities ... digital initiatives have created innovative solutions to communicate knowledge of the continuity of Indigenous values, such as through representations of intangible heritage in the museum space.

With the move towards increased collection accessibility, there has also been a move by GLAMs and institutions to utilise platforms to centralise and host the content of multiple institutions, thereby enabling the sharing of their digital collections with a broader audience, or alternatively to host a collection catalogue of another institution where there is not the capacity to host the content (Horwood 2017).[1]

Indigenising the digital space

The voices of Indigenous minorities are a rare occurrence in the spaces of global contemporary technologies. In response, Indigenous peoples are employing a range of contemporary technologies as they endeavour to bridge the digital divide and to address historical inequities that have been reinforced by the advent of new technologies (Radoll and Hunter 2017; Winter and Boudreau 2018). Strategies are being implemented that harness the capability and influence of web-based and other digital technologies as affected Indigenous groups seek to reclaim spaces for the ongoing survival, use and transmission of their languages, cultures, artefacts, histories, knowledge, and knowledge systems (Cazden 2003; Dyson and Underwood 2006). Tailoring such uses of new technologies by Indigenous groups pushes back against further marginalisation and suppression, fortified by recent advancements in digital technologies which endure disproportionate misrepresentations of Indigenous peoples where notions of a globalised 'one language, one culture' ideology linger (Lee 2011).

Recently, the exacerbation of Indigenous language decline has been attributed in no small part to unprecedented developments in the availability and global reach of new technologies. Ubiquitous communication technologies have escalated the number of endangered languages that are under threat of extinction, amplified by the pervasion of major languages in areas where until recently only minor languages were spoken (Kalzner 1995). Digital technologies and various social media platforms have intensified the pressure on the Indigenous speakers of minority tongues to use languages that are more dominant, more prestigious, or more widely known than their own (Harrison 2007). Wholesale uptake of digital technologies, new media and social media networking to globally diffuse ideas and values "has become synonymous with the weakening of historical linguistic ties and their replacement with loose connections to consumerism and capitalism. Old traditions perish and new ones evolve" (Foundation for Endangered Languages [FEL] 2012: 3). It is not uncommon for members of an Indigenous minority language community to use modern media in a major language, at the very least to ensure their broadcasts are received and recognised by as many people as possible. Unbridled sharing of wisdoms, usually privileged and sacrosanct, further compromises already-endangered languages and the traditions and practices of the cultures that those languages underpin.

Nonetheless, significant gains are being realised by Indigenous peoples as their intensifying presence in the digital spaces increasingly secures traction – especially in terms of language and cultural visibility and engagement. Global connectivity, communication systems, and networking capabilities are enabling the Indigenous voices and points of view to be heard, seen, and experienced by their communities, other ethnic groups, and the wider populace. Contemporary technology use is occurring to a growing extent by Indigenous communities to ensure their own members (and others) are able to access 'information from home' and stay in touch regardless of where they may be in the world. Such initiatives are feeding into and informing multiple projects across a growing Indigenous digital ecosystem. Additionally, particular philosophies, promoted and applied through an Indigenous lens, are gradually acquiring footholds in the indigenising of an array of digital territories. In doing so, the wider conversations, although stilted, are gradually shifting to embrace (or at least include) issues of Indigenous recognition and parity.

The impact of social media on languages is undeniable and often understated. Social media software is one medium where the sharing of conversations, information, and ideas occurs in a relatively unshackled environment. Furthermore, there is evidence that Indigenous conversations are occurring within social media and that they can be influenced in terms of numbers of participants and the volume and duration of conversations. For example, the weekly occurrence of Māori Language tweets in 2019 shows spiking that appears to be the result of national events such as Matatini (Māori National Kapahaka Competition), Te Wiki o te Reo Māori (Māori Language Week), and Te Mahuru, a commitment to speak predominantly Māori Language for the month of September.

Context-based discussions have successfully fostered and maintained online Māori-language conversations on particular social media platforms. The Facebook group 'Te Mana o Te Reo Māori' is one example that provides a way to engage in online conversation and share stories and wisdoms entirely in the Māori Language (see Figure 33.2). However, in spite of these types of opportunities to use the language and share knowledges online, it appears that the majority of online communication between Māori across the various social media platforms still occurs in the English language (Keegan, Mato, and Ruru 2015; O'Carroll 2013). Even so, Māori-language and Māori-centric posts ensure that Māori have a presence within these platforms.

Recent Indigenous technology developments have included translated interfaces for a selection of computer applications, mobile technology, physical self-service machines, online games, webpages, and social media. Twitter, for example, supports over 40 languages including Catalan (see Figure 33.3) (some other language options are displayed on the right).

More recent Indigenous developments include a myriad of apps and applications that support language translation and use, language and cultural learning, the sharing of stories and histories, gaming, and versions of experiential virtual immersion.

Examples from Aotearoa include the following.

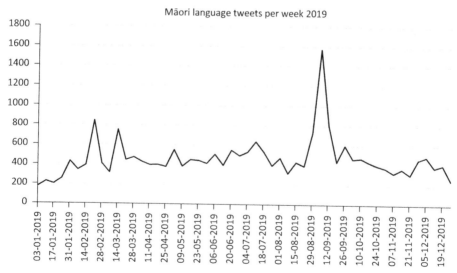

Figure 33.1 Weekly Te Reo Māori tweets during 2019[2]

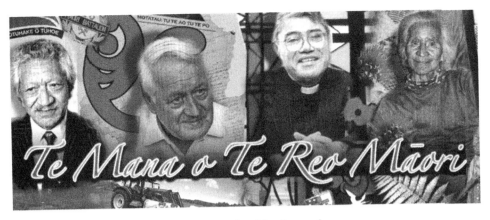

Figure 33.2 Profile picture for Te Mana o Te Reo Māori group[3]

Kupu[4]

Sponsored by SparkNZ, powered by Google machine learning technology and supported by Te Aka Māori Dictionary, Kupu (*word*) provides a new way to experience Māori language. The app uses the camera in your smart device to take a photo of an everyday object (or upload your own) and provides the noun for that image, in te reo Māori, in real time. There is also an option to hear the word spoken. Users are able to provide a suggested translation which is then flagged to the App Administrator for validation. You can then save the translated image, share it, or repeat the exercise.

Arataki Cultural Trails[5]

The Arataki Cultural Trails app provides location-based storytelling and is aimed, in the first instance, at tourists and those with limited knowledge of te reo and location history. The app

Figure 33.3 Twitter interface using Catalan

offers a self-guided, immersive cultural walking experience. Proximity storytelling helps users connect their location with authentic cultural content and information – revitalising oral histories. The app can be accessed without Wi-Fi using Bluetooth beacons and is proximity triggered – users must be at the required location to fully deploy the app.

Wrestler (NZ)[6]

Wrestler, in collaboration with Ngāti Awa and Te Wānanga o Awanuiārangi, used altered reality techniques that allow users to be immersed in various environments and settings. Using Avatars and Virtual Realities, people are able to virtually visit a wharenui (Māori meeting house), for example, and experience the histories, stories and legends in three-dimensional, 360 degree virtual and augmented reality.

Te Hiku Media[7]

Te Hiku Media is a charitable media organisation collectively belonging to the five iwi (Ngāti Kurī, Te Aupōuri, Ngāi Takoto, Ngāti Kahu, and Te Rarawa) of Te Hiku o Te Ika (the far north of New Zealand). Te Hiku operate community-based iwi radio and television services with a focus on te reo Māori, whanau, and community. Te Hiku have sourced and generated large volumes of Māori-language corpora. Their repository of translated text, audio, and video underpin their efforts to utilise machine learning techniques to establish text-to-speech and speech-to-text conversion for te reo Māori.

Māori Dictionary (Te Aka)[8]

The Māori Dictionary is an online version of *Te Aka Māori-English, English-Māori Dictionary and Index*.[9] *Te Aka* is similar to a traditional dictionary but also has encyclopaedic entries including the names of plants and animals (especially Native and endemic species), stars, planets and

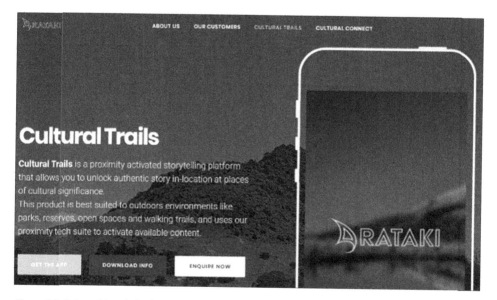

Figure 33.4 Arataki website homepage

Figure 33.5 Te Hiku Media sample webpage

heavenly bodies, important Māori people, key ancestors of traditional narratives, tribal groups and ancestral canoes. Māori names for institutions, country names, place names, and other proper names are also provided. Key concepts central to Māori culture and grammatical items are explained with examples of usage. Explanations of idioms and colloquialisms, with their meanings and examples, have been included because they are important in a Māori context, and contribute to understanding and speaking the language in a natural way.

Reobot[10]

Reobot is a Chat Bot that has been redesigned to converse in te reo Māori using the Facebook platform. ReoBot works by encouraging the user to interact and respond in te reo Māori through a series of short conversational chats. Questions such as 'What is your name?' and 'Where are you from?' or 'How is the weather?' guide the user through a short conversation that is conveyed in both te reo Māori and English. "When I was learning te reo Māori, I would seek out opportunities to practice but when you have a family, a job, this becomes difficult", says co-creator Jason Lovell. "ReoBot is designed to allow people to practice every day conversational te reo Māori in their own time at their own pace; on the way to work, at home, or whenever they can spare five minutes" (Waateanews.com 2018: Online).

Fundamentally, engagement with these sorts of technology should foster the relevant Indigenous philosophies and largely reflect (and sometimes facilitate) Indigenous engagement in offline, face-to-face situations, whilst also being cognisant of how this engagement might also invite the consumption of that content by wider social groups.

Current and future challenges

Alongside the larger global trend to digitise and document information, there is an growing demand for Indigenous knowledge to be included in this demand, and, in turn, a growing concern to preserve, safeguard and protect this digital domain as a vital resource for Indigenous communities (Nakata et al. 2008; Nakata 2007). The digitisation of Indigenous collections is extremely complex for institutions. The complexity arises from the attempt to encapsulate Indigenous knowledge systems, with their distinct systems of knowledge management and political assertion, within existing homogenised structures. Nakata (2007: 102) discusses the control by Indigenous peoples over the treatment of their own knowledge systems:

> which are quite different from Western knowledge management and these, in turn, institute different standards and rules of access and protection to these knowledge and their various forms. Western legal mechanisms for intellectual and cultural property protection are limited in their scope to recognise forms and expression of Indigenous knowledge, to provide the sorts of protection required, and to provide satisfactory benefit-sharing arrangements that Indigenous knowledge custodians assert should attach to their claims on knowledge.

The ethics of Indigenous ownership and intellectual property (IP) is complex. Globally and locally, the issue of Indigenous ownership/ IP rights continues to develop in all forms of legal documentation under a Western system. Cultural IP rights aim to secure measures of sovereignty for Indigenous communities over their own cultural artefacts. However, current IP law does not acknowledge customary Indigenous knowledge or Indigenous ownership. Given Indigenous peoples' intrinsic connection and relationship with their cultural heritage, Indigenous cultural and IP rights are socially based to the extent that culture could be conceived as being collectively owned (Janke 1999). This social organisational principle incorporates Indigenous laws and cultural responsibilities in order to protect and sustain their cultural knowledge (Janke 1999). With this perspective in mind, certain knowledge is held and maintained by a custodian who may be an individual or group. This relationship between custodians and cultural knowledge and heritage protects the integrity of that particular knowledge and ensures its dissemination is appropriately passed down to future generations. Indigenous peoples are linked spiritually and culturally to traditional lands and waters. As described by Morse (2012: 114):

> The living nature of inanimate things, and the spiritual element imbued within many such objects, has profound implications for the work of archivists, librarians, art curators, museumologists, and others who spend their days devoted to the vital tasks of preserving and/or displaying 'objects' of varying natures.

Thus, as explained by Moahi (2007: 75), one of the vital tasks when digitising Indigenous knowledge (IK) is to avoid the:

> trivialisation of the culture where it is used, and for enriching other people other than the community who own the IK. Communities should own the IK and have a say in what should or should not be digitized. IK owners should maintain their ownership rights.

Although new technologies facilitate new kinds of access and new kinds of access communities, the ownership and governance over their cultural material continues to be a major concern for Indigenous peoples (Waitangi Tribunal 2011a; 2011b), given the legacy of cultural theft that has rendered Indigenous people absent as legal owners or right holders over the last 200–450 years (Bowrey and Anderson 2009). Furthermore, this concern raises consequences about who has the ability to control and determine how Indigenous knowledge is shared, both between Indigenous people and the non-Indigenous community (Hirtle, Hudson, and Kenyon 2009).

Alongside the drive for Indigenous data access, use, management, and sovereignty, is a growing emphasis on developing platforms and cultural protocols and licensing options for Indigenous digital materials. One platform encompassing this need is Mukurtu, developed out of a grass-roots project in the remote Central Australian town of Tennant Creek. Mukurtu is a free, open source, content management tool for the management and sharing of digital cultural heritage. Developed by Kim Christen and Michael Ashley with the Warumungu Aboriginal community, the Mukurtu CMS (Content Management System) platform is built for Indigenous communities, archives, libraries and museums, to manage and share digital heritage (Christen 2008; Srinivasan et al. 2009). A range of cultural and sharing protocols are the core of Mukurtu CMS which allows for fine-grained levels of access and sharing that is dependent on users' cultural needs from completely open to strictly controlled access (Christen, Ashley, and Anderson 2012). Mukurtu CMS also developed a series of traditional knowledge licenses and labels specifically designed for the unique needs of Indigenous cultural materials. These traditional licenses work alongside creative commons licenses or copyright licenses to specify access and usage rights.

Emerging from the work of Mukurtu and their use of traditional knowledge licenses and labels is the work of Local Contexts on Traditional Knowledge (TK) Labels, an initiative that aims to address the ownership and access needs of Native, First Nations, Aboriginal and Indigenous peoples with regard to their cultural artefacts currently held and controlled by other institutions (Anderson and Montenegro 2017; Kimberly 2015). Local Contexts are also trialling a set of TK Licenses to address the specific legal status of Indigenous, traditional and locally owned materials.

Developed by the Indigenous Protocol and Artificial Intelligence Working Group (see: http://www.indigenous-ai.net/people/), the Indigenous Protocol for AI (IP-AI) was created following a series of workshops and discussions over a 20-month period with technologists, artists, scientists, cultural knowledge keepers, language keepers, and public policy experts from diverse communities and disciplinary backgrounds in Aotearoa, Australia, North America, and the Pacific. Building on the work of Abdilla and Fitch (2017) on how IK systems can inform research on pattern recognition and algorithms in robotics and AI, and an essay by Lewis et al. (2018) on drawing on Indigenous kinship protocols to re-imagine the epistemological and ontological foundations on which we design AI systems, these workshops and discussions culminated in the production of a position paper on IP-AI for persons, groups, organisations, institutes, companies, political or government representatives wishing to undertake responsible and fair development of AI with Indigenous communities. For our Indigenous communities, the IP-AI Guidelines have been developed as a starting point to assist them in defining their own, community-specific guidelines. For non-Indigenous technologists and policy-makers it is envisioned that these guidelines will assist them to initiate a productive conversation with Indigenous communities about how to enter into collaborative technology development efforts. As part of the position papers, the IP-AI collective set-out a guidelines consisting of seven principles to guide the future development of AI towards morally and socially desirable ends (Indigenous Protocol and Artificial Intelligence Working Group 2020 [not available at time of publication]; Whaanga, Lewis, and Brown 2021 [not available at time of publication]). The seven principles are:[11]

1. *Locality*: Indigenous knowledge is often rooted in specific territories. It is also useful in considering issues of global importance.

2. *Relationality and Reciprocity:* Indigenous knowledge is often relational knowledge.

3. *Responsibility, Relevance and Accountability:* Indigenous people are often concerned primarily with their responsibilities to their communities.

4. *Develop Governance Guidelines from Indigenous Protocols:* Protocol is a customary set of rules that govern behaviour.

5. *Recognize the Cultural Nature of all Computational Technology:* All technical systems are cultural and social systems. Every piece of technology is an expression of cultural and social frameworks for understanding and engaging with the world. AI system designers need to be aware of their own cultural frameworks, socially dominant concepts and normative ideals; be wary of the biases that come with them; and develop strategies for accommodating other cultural and social frameworks.

6. *Apply Ethical Design to the Extended Stack:* Culture forms the foundation of the technology development ecosystem, or 'stack'. Every component of the AI system hardware and software stack should be considered in the ethical evaluation of the system. This starts with how the materials for building the hardware and for energizing the software are extracted from the earth, and ends with how they return there. The core ethic should be that of do-no-harm.

7. *Respect and Support Data Sovereignty:* Indigenous communities must control how their data is solicited, collected, analysed and operationalized. They decide when to protect it and when to share it, where the cultural and intellectual property rights reside and to whom those rights adhere, and how these rights are governed. All AI systems should be designed to respect and support data sovereignty.

Conclusion

It is from this context that the areas of Indigenous Data Sovereignty, Traditional Knowledge labels and licensing and development of Indigenous Protocol for AI have emerged over the past few years. The reclamation of rights and sovereignty over data, for example, is happening across many nations including Australia via the *Maiam nayri Wingara Indigenous Data Sovereignty Collective*, the United States through the *United States Indigenous Data Sovereignty Network*, and in Aotearoa through *Te Mana Raraunga as the Māori Data Sovereignty Network*. Indigenous approaches to data access, use and management, and sovereignty (Kukutai and Cormack 2019; Kukutai, Tahu, and Taylor 2016; Walter and Suina 2019), is premised on the rights of Indigenous peoples to "determine the means of collection, access, analysis, interpretation, management, dissemination and reuse of data" (Walter 2018: online). These collective rights to data about, on and created by Indigenous peoples, their territories, and resources "is supported by Indigenous peoples' inherent rights of self-determination and governance over their peoples, country and resources as described in the United Nations Declaration on the Rights of Indigenous Peoples" (Walter and Suina 2019: 236–7).

As we begin the third decade of the 21st century, this chapter outlines just a few of the challenges that we currently face as Indigenous peoples. The strength and legitimacy of our Indigenous voice and the impact of our digital footprint lies in our ability to access, use, practice, share, manage, and ultimately control our identity and sovereignty in the digital sphere. Treating the digital realm as Terra Nullius 2.0 will, if we do not actively engage as Indigenous peoples in the shaping and creating its future, have dire consequences for our linguistic, cultural, social, and economic existence.

Notes

1 Some of the more notable projects and digital archives of Indigenous content include Horwood (2017) and digital archives created by the University of British Columbia library, and the University of Hawai'i (Mānoa) Library. However, there are numerous digital archives relevant to this chapter.

   Canada:

- *BC Historical Books:*
  Is a single searchable database of the bibliography of BC based on full-text searchable versions of the books.
  (see https://open.library.ubc.ca/collections/bcbooks)

- *Blackfoot Digital Library:*
  Is a collaboration between the University of Lethbridge and the Red Crow Community College celebrating Akaitapii through various forms of media, to help and support the Kainai and other students of today and tomorrow.
  (see https://www.blackfootdigitallibrary.com/digital/collection/bdl)

- *GRASAC Knowledge Sharing System (GKS):*
  Is a digital repository and knowledge sharing system (including oral narratives, archival documents, photographs, Indigenous language research, visual and material culture), of Great Lakes Aboriginal material culture and heritage items.
  (see https://carleton.ca/grasac/about/)

- *Moravian Beginnings of Canadian Inuit Literature:*
  Forming part of a McGill University Library's exhibition this collection traces the beginnings of literacy and written literature for the Inuit living in Nunatsiavut (Labrador) and, to a lesser extent, in Nunavik.
  (see http://digital.library.mcgill.ca/moravian/)

- *Musqueam Place Names Map:*
  Is a multimedia interactive map that highlights hənq̓əminəm̓ place names throughout Musqueam's Traditional Territory. It also provides audio of the language from Musqueam elders past and present, as well as historical photographs.
  (see https://www.musqueam.bc.ca/our-story/musqueam-territory/place-names-map/)

- *Reciprocal Research Network:*
  Created by the Musqueam Indian Band, the Stó:lō Nation/Tribal Council, the U'mista Cultural Society, and the Museum of Anthropology, this online tool facilitates reciprocal and collaborative research about cultural heritage from the Northwest Coast of British Columbia.
  (see https://www.rrncommunity.org/)

- *Simon Fraser University Digitized Collections – Indigenous Collections:*
  Includes the BC Multicultural Photograph Collection at the Vancouver Public Library; the Bill Reid Centre Collection; the Northern Justice Society Native Crime Bibliography; the Rodeo Collection; the Scowlitz Artifact Assemblage Project; and the White Mountain Apache Collection.
  (see https://digital.lib.sfu.ca/collection-categories/indigenous-collections)

- *Sq'éwlets: A Stó:lō -Coast Salish Community in the Fraser River Valley:*
  Is a collaborative project of the Sq'éwlets and a team of archeologists at UBC. The virtual museum displays nearly three decades of collaborative work, sharing Sq'éwlets stories, history, language, and the deep connection between people and place as a way of situating Sq'éwlets people in the world.
  (see http://www.digitalsqewlets.ca/)

- *Squamish History Archives:*
  Is a digital collection managed by the Squamish Public Library, which includes historical photographs, newspapers (1948-2001), and other materials related to First Nations history.
  (see https://squamishlibrary.digitalcollections.ca/)

- *UBCIC Digital Collections:*
  Is a collection that presents a variety of research and informational materials on Indigenous peoples and the law; land rights; the Joint Indian Reserve Commission; the McKenna-McBride Royal

Commission; and the history of the Union of BC Indian Chiefs (UBCIC) and First Nations in British Columbia.
(see https://www.ubcic.bc.ca/online_resources)
University of Calgary Native Canada Collections:
Includes the ANCS Aboriginal Film Collection; the Aboriginal Veterans' Archive; Douglas Cardinal Fonds; Dene Crafts; the Stampede Archives; the Arctic Institute of North America Photographic Archives; Galileo Educational Network – Aboriginal Resources; Artistry of the Land, Ancient Stories and Art of our First Nations' People; and more.
(see https://www.ucalgary.ca/nativecanada/collections)
University of Manitoba Indigenous Peoples Digital Collections:
Includes the Henry Budd Letters; the Centre for Settlement Studies fonds; the Connie Macmillan Collection; the Kenneth Hates Collection (North-West Rebellion); the Jill Oakes fonds; the Red River Cartes de Visite Collection; the Louis Riel Photograph Collection; the Walter Rudnicki fonds; and the Nan Shipley fonds.
(see https://libguides.lib.umanitoba.ca/c.php?g=514052&p=3511956)
Voices of Amiskwaciy:
Is an online public space, created and hosted by the Edmonton Public Library in collaboration with Indigenous communities, which supports the community to create, share, discover, and celebrate local Indigenous content in the form of digital text, videos, sound files, and images.
(see https://voicesofamiskwaciy.ca/)

United States of America:

- *American Indian Digital History Project:*
Is a Digital History Cooperative founded to recover and preserve rare Indigenous newspapers, photographs, and archival materials from all across Native North America.
(see http://www.aidhp.com/)

- *Billie Jane Baguley Digital Library (Heard Museum):*
Represents a virtual selection from the Billie Jane Baguley Library and Archives, which has an extensive collection of documentary and photographic works on Native Americans with an emphasis on Indigenous people in the Greater Southwest.
(see https://heard.org/library/digital/)

- *Carlisle Indian School Digital Resource Center:*
Brings together, in digital format, a variety of resources related to the Carlisle Indian Industrial School that are physically preserved in various locations around the country.

- *Catawba Indian Nation Archives:*
Identifies, collects, preserves, and makes accessible historical and cultural materials relating to the Catawba Indian Nation for use by tribal and the community for educational and research purposes.
(see http://catawbaarchives.libraries.wsu.edu/)

- *Confluence Story Gathering Collection:*
Publicly available on the Plateau Peoples' Web Portal. The collection features the stories of Native elders, told in their own voices, as a way to explore the interconnectedness of people and places of the Columbia River system.
(see https://plateauportal.libraries.wsu.edu/collection/confluence-story-gathering-collection)

- *Creating Collaborative Catalogs:*
An online innovation in New Mexico for two-way movement of information between museums and originating communities.
(see http://www.dmns.org/science/past-projects/creating-collaborative-catalogs)

- *Elmer E. Rasmuson Library Digital Collection:*
This collection includes historical photographs of Indigenous and settler women of Alaska in the late nineteenth and early twentieth centuries; and the Wenger Eskimo Database, which provides access to written literature about Inuit peoples, including nearly 200 titles – primarily books and journal articles.
(see https://library.uaf.edu/apr-collections)

- *Huna Heritage Foundation Digital Archives:*

A collecting archives, which gathers historical and cultural materials relating to the Xúna Kaawu for the purposes of education and enjoyment of current and future generations.
(see http://archives.hunaheritage.org/)

- *Indigenous Digital Archive:*
  A collection of over 500,000 archival documents about Santa Fe Indian School, 1920, including boarding school records, and letters.
  (see https://omeka.dlcs-ida.org/s/ida/page/home)

- *Plateau Peoples' Web Portal:*
  A gateway to Plateau peoples' cultural materials held in multiple repositories including Washington State University's Manuscripts, Archives and Special Collections, the Northwest Museum of Art and Culture, the National Anthropological Archives and the National Museum of the American Indian at the Smithsonian Institution. The materials in the Portal have been chosen and curated by tribal representatives.
  (see https://plateauportal.libraries.wsu.edu/)

- *Sipnuuk Digital Library, Archives and Museum:*
  A repository to manage, share, and enhance understanding of Karuk history, language, traditions, natural resource management, and living culture following the cultural protocols of the Karuk Tribe and in support of the missions of the Karuk Tribe, Department of Natural Resources, People's Center and Karuk Tribal Libraries, Archives and Museums.
  (see https://sipnuuk.karuk.us/)

The Pacific and Oceania:

- *AIATSIS Collections online:*
  Includes online exhibitions and digitised collections including newsletters, newspapers, notebooks, diaries, music, mathematics, stories, rare books, treaties and petitions, laws and legislation, and collectors of words.
  (see https://aiatsis.gov.au/collections/collections-online)

- *Ara Irititja:*
  A collaborative community project directed at developing a mobile digital archive for remote Australian communities.
  (see https://www.irititja.com/)

- *National Library of Australia:*
  Holds an extensive collection on Indigenous history, experience and culture, in a wide range of formats, including archived websites, photographs, maps, oral histories, manuscripts pictures and all types of publications in English and language.
  Includes copies of all Indigenous Australian language dictionaries, word lists and lexicons published to date, covering hundreds of languages and dialects. This includes a significant number of interactive dictionaries.
  (see https://www.nla.gov.au/what-we-collect/indigenous)

- *Hauraki Digital Library:*
  The collection contains digitised versions of the vast amounts of documentation that were presented to the Waitangi Tribunal in support of Hauraki claims. It contains Waitangi Claims materials, photos, interviews and stories, and images.
  (see http://dl.hauraki.iwi.nz/)

- *Sir Donald McLean papers:*
  Digitised copies of selected series from the papers of Donald McLean held at the Alexander Turnbull Library. It contains almost 3,000 letters from Māori correspondents, which are the largest surviving series of nineteenth-century Māori letters.
  (see https://paperspast.natlib.govt.nz/manuscripts)

- *Tāmata Toiere:*
  A repository on waiata and haka (Māori song, chant, and dance). Where possible, this will include the lyrics, a translation, an explanation of the context behind the composition and the reasons it was composed, a biography of the composer, an audio file, a video file, any photos of relevance, and a list of references for further study.

(see http://www.waiata.maori.nz/)

- *Te Reo o Taranaki:*
  Made up of a number of language, culture and educational resources developed by Taranaki. Includes Taranaki kōrero (stories), history, karakia (prayers and incantations), and waiata (songs).
  (see https://tereootaranaki.org/#3)

- *Pacific Digital Library collection:*
  A collaborative digital library development project created by a team of Pacific islander librarians.
  (see https://www.pacificdigitallibrary.org/)

- *Traditional Micronesian Navigation Collection*
  An online database of the material of Steve Thomas comprising unpublished papers, audiovisual and photographic materials (including oral history transcripts and 35 mm slides), publications, and miscellaneous items related primarily to traditional navigation on the Western Carolinian island of Satawal.
  (see http://digicoll.manoa.hawaii.edu/satawal/index.php)

- *Librarianship and Archives in Hawai'i and the Pacific: Pacific Libraries and Archives*
  Contains an extensive list of Pacific libraries and archives.
  (see https://guides.library.manoa.hawaii.edu/PacificLibraries)

Sami:

- *Recalling Ancestral Voices:*
  A collaborative project with the Sámi people of Sweden, Norway, Finland, and Russia to digitally repatriate knowledge of their material heritage.
  (see http://www.samimuseum.fi/heritage/english)

2 Data source: Produced by P Mato using data from personal communication: Professor K Scannell, University of Saint Louis (email 21 January 2020).

3 See: https://www.facebook.com/groups/temanaotereo/.

4 See: https://kupu.co.nz.

5 See: https://arataki.app.

6 See: https://www.wrestler.nz.

7 See https://tehiku.nz.

8 See: https://maoridictionary.co.nz.

9 See Moorfield 2013, 'Te Aka: Māori-English, English-Māori Dictionary'.

10 See: https://www.facebook.com/tereobot/.

11 The unabridged seven principles are:

1. *Locality*
   Indigenous knowledge is often rooted in specific territories. It is also useful in considering issues of global importance. AI systems should be designed in partnership with specific Indigenous communities to ensure the systems are capable of responding to and helping care for that community (e.g. grounded in the local) as well as connecting to global contexts (e.g. connected to the universal).

2. *Relationality and Reciprocity*
   Indigenous knowledge is often relational knowledge. AI systems should be designed to understand how humans and non-humans are related to and co-dependent on each other. Understanding, supporting and encoding these relationships is a primary design goal. AI systems are also part of the circle of relationships. Their place and status in that circle will depend on specific communities and their protocols for understanding, acknowledging and incorporating new entities into that circle.

3. *Responsibility, Relevance and Accountability*
   Indigenous people are often concerned primarily with their responsibilities to their communities. AI systems developed by, with or for Indigenous communities should be responsible to those communities first, provide relevant support, and be accountable to those communities first and foremost.

4. *Develop Governance Guidelines from Indigenous Protocols*
   Protocol is a customary set of rules that govern behaviour. Protocol is developed out of ontological, epistemological and customary configurations of knowledge grounded in locality, relationality and responsibility. Indigenous protocol should provide the foundation for developing governance frameworks that guide the use, role and rights of AI entities in society. There is a need to adapt existing protocols and develop new protocols for designing, building and deploying AI systems. These

protocols may be particular to specific communities, or they may be developed with a broader focus that may function across many Indigenous and non-Indigenous communities.

5. *Recognize the Cultural Nature of all Computational Technology*

All technical systems are cultural and social systems. Every piece of technology is an expression of cultural and social frameworks for understanding and engaging with the world. AI system designers need to be aware of their own cultural frameworks, socially dominant concepts and normative ideals; be wary of the biases that come with them; and develop strategies for accommodating other cultural and social frameworks. Computation is a cultural material. Computation is at the heart of our digital technologies, and, as increasing amounts of our communication is mediated by such technologies, it has become a core tool for expressing cultural values. Therefore, it is essential for cultural resilience and continuity for Indigenous communities to develop computational methods that reflect and enact our cultural practices and values.

6. *Apply Ethical Design to the Extended Stack*

Culture forms the foundation of the technology development ecosystem, or 'stack'. Every component of the AI system hardware and software stack should be considered in the ethical evaluation of the system. This starts with how the materials for building the hardware and for energizing the software are extracted from the earth, and ends with how they return there. The core ethic should be that of do-no-harm.

7. *Respect and Support Data Sovereignty*

Indigenous communities must control how their data is solicited, collected, analysed, and operationalized. They decide when to protect it and when to share it, where the cultural and intellectual property rights reside and to whom those rights adhere, and how these rights are governed. All AI systems should be designed to respect and support data sovereignty. Open data principles need to be further developed to respect the rights of Indigenous peoples in all the areas mentioned above, and to strengthen equity of access and clarity of benefits. This should include a fundamental review of the concepts of 'ownership' and 'property', which are the product of non-Indigenous legal orders and do not necessarily reflect the ways in which Indigenous communities wish to govern the use of their cultural knowledge.

References

Abdilla, A. and Fitch, R. (2017). 'Indigenous knowledge systems and pattern thinking: an expanded analysis of the first Indigenous robotics prototype workshop', *Fibreculture Journal*, vol 28: 90–103.

Akçayır, M., Dündar, H., and Akçayır, G. (2016). 'What makes you a digital native? Is it enough to be born after 1980?', *Computers in Human Behavior*, vol 60: 435–440.

Anderson, J. and Montenegro, M. (2017). 'Collaborative encounters in digital cultural property: Tracing temporal relationships of context and locality', in J. Anderson and H. Geismar (eds.) *The Routledge Companion to Cultural Property*. Taylor and Francis Ltd: London, 431–451.

Apiti, M. (2017). *The Indigenous Mapping Waananga 2017*. Te Pua Wānanga ki te Ao, University of Waikato: Hamiton. Available: https://www.waikato.ac.nz/__data/assets/pdf_file/0008/394901/chapter21.pdf, accessed 1 March 2020.

Bennett, T. (2004). *Pasts Beyond Memory: Evolution, Museums, Colonialism*. Museum Meanings, Routledge: London.

Bowrey, K. and Anderson, J. (2009). 'The politics of global information sharing: Whose cultural agendas are being advanced?', *Social & Legal Studies*, vol 18, no 4: 479–504.

Bray, T.L. (2001). *The Future of the Past: Archaeologists, Native Americans, and Repatriation*. Garland Publishing: New York.

Bryan, J. (2011). 'Walking the line: Participatory mapping, indigenous rights, and neoliberalism', *Geoforum*, vol 42, no 1: 40–50.

Butts, D. (2003). *Māori and Museums: The Politics of Indigenous Recognition*. PhD thesis, Massey University: Palmerston North.

Cazden, C. (2003). 'Sustaining Indigenous languages in cyberspace', in J. Reyhner, O. Trujillo, R.L. Carrasco, and L. Lockard (eds.) *Nurturing Native Languages*. Northern Arizona University: Flagstaff, 53–57.

Christen, K. (2008) 'Archival challenges and digital solutions in Aboriginal Australia', *SAA Archaeological Recorder*, vol 8, no 2: 21–24.

Christen, K. (2015). 'Sovereignty, repatriation, and the archival imagination: Indigenous curation and display practices', *Collections: A Journal for Museum and Archives Professionals*, vol 11, no 2: 115–138.

Christen, K., Ashley, M., and Anderson, J. (2012). *Mukurtu – Top 10 Features.* Available: http://www.mukurtu.org/features.html, accessed 30 August 2013.

Clavir, M. (2002). *Preserving What is Valued: Museums, Conservation, and First Nations.* UBC Museum of Anthropology Research Publication, UBC Press: Vancouver.

Corsane, G. (2005). *Heritage, Museums and Galleries: An Introductory Reader.* Routledge: London.

Duxbury, N. (2015). *Cultural Mapping as Cultural Inquiry.* Routledge: London.

Dyson, L.E. and Underwood, J. (2006). 'Indigenous people on the web', *Journal of Theoretical and Applied Electronic Commerce Research*, vol 1, no 1: 65–76.

Foundation for Endangered Languages (FEL). (2012). *OGMIOS Newsletter 49*, December 31. Foundation for Endangered Languages: Bath.

Hakiwai, A. (2012). 'Virtual repatriation: A database of Māori taonga in overseas museums', Seminar at *Ngā Pae o te Māramatanga Horizons of Insight Research Seminar*, 30 May. Auckland. Available: http://mediacentre.maramatanga.ac.nz/content/digitisation-research-part-one-arapatahakiwai, accessed 1 March 2014.

Hakiwai, A.T. (2004). *He mana taonga, he mana tangata: Māori taonga and the Politics of Māori Tribal Identity and Development.* PhD thesis, Victoria University of Wellington: Wellington.

Harrison, K.D. (2007). *When Languages Die: The Extinction of the World's Languages and the Erosion of Human Knowledge.* Oxford University Press: New York.

Henare, A.J.M. (2005). *Museums, Anthropology and Imperial Exchange.* Cambridge University Press: Cambridge.

Hirt, I. (2012). 'Mapping dreams/dreaming maps: Bridging Indigenous and Western geographical knowledge', *Cartographica: The International Journal for Geographic Information and Geovisualization*, vol 47, no 2: 105–120.

Hirtle, P.B., Hudson, E., and Kenyon, A.T. (2009) *Copyright and Cultural Institutions: Guidelines for Digitization for U.S. Libraries, Archives, and Museums.* Cornell University Library: Ithaca.

Horwood, M. (2017) *Going Digital in the GLAM Sector: ICT Innovations & Collaborations for Taonga Māori.* Te Pua Wānanga ki te Ao, University of Waikato: Hamiton. Available: https://www.waikato.ac.nz/__data/assets/pdf_file/0008/394901/chapter21.pdf, accessed 1 March 2020.

Horwood, M. (2018). *Sharing Authority in the Museum: Distributed Objects, Reassembled Relationships.* Routledge: Milton.

Indigenous Protocol and Artificial Intelligence Working Group. (2020). *Position Paper on Indigenous Protocol and Artificial Intelligence.* Available: http://www.indigenous-ai.net/position-paper/ (accessed 1 March 2020)

Isaac, G. (2015). 'Perclusive alliances: digital 3-D, museums, and the reconciling of culturally diverse knowledges', *Current Anthropology*, vol 56, no S12: S286–S296.

Janke, T. (1999). 'Respecting Indigenous cultural and intellectual property rights', *The University of New South Wales Law Journal*, vol 22, no 2: 631–639.

Kalzner, K. (1995). *The Languages of the World.* Routledge: London.

Keegan, T.T., Mato, P., and Ruru, S. (2015) 'Using twitter in an Indigenous language: An analysis of te reo Māori tweets', *AlterNative: An International Journal of Indigenous Peoples*, vol 11, no 1: 59–75.

Kimberly, C. (2015) 'Tribal archives, traditional knowledge and local contexts: Why the "s" matters', *Journal of Western Archives*, vol 6, no 1: 1–19.

Kirchhoff, T., Schweibenz, W., and Sieglerschmidt, J. (2008) 'Archives, libraries, museums and the spell of ubiquitous knowledge', *Archival Science*, vol 8, no 4: 251–266.

Kirschner, P.A. and De Bruyckere, P. (2017). 'The myths of the digital native and the multitasker', *Teaching and Teacher Education*, vol 67: 135–142.

Kukutai, T. and Cormack, D. (2019). 'Mana motuhake ā-rarunga: Datafication and social science research in Aotearoa', *Kōtuitui: New Zealand Journal of Social Sciences Online*, vol 14, no 2: 201–208.

Kukutai, T. and Taylor, J. (eds.) (2016). *Indigenous Data Sovereignty: Toward an Agenda.* CAEPR Research Monograph Series, no 8. ANU Press: Canberra.

Laituri, M. (2011). '"Indigenous peoples" issues and Indigenous uses of GIS', in T.L. Nyerges, H. Couclelis, and R. McMaster (eds.) *The SAGE Handbook of GIS and Society.* SAGE Publications, Inc.: London, 202–221.

Lee, D. (2011). 'Micro-blogging in a mother tongue on Twitter', *BBC.* Available: http://news.bbc.co.uk/2/hi/programmes/click_online/9450488.stm, accessed 1 March 2020.

Lewis, J.E., Arista, N., Pechawis, A., and Kite, S. (2018). 'Making kin with the machines', *Journal of Design and Science*, vol. 3, no. 5. Available: https://jods.mitpress.mit.edu/pub/lewis-arista-pechawis-kite, accessed 1 March 2020.

Lonetree, A. (2012). *Decolonizing Museums: Representing Native America in National and Tribal Museums*. University of North Carolina Press: Chapel Hill.

McMahon, R., Smith, T.J., and Whiteduck, T. (2017). 'Reclaiming geospatial data and GIS design for Indigenous-led telecommunications policy advocacy: A process discussion of mapping broadband availability in remote and Northern Regions of Canada', *Journal of Information Policy*, vol 7: 423–449.

Moahi, K.H. (2007). 'Copyright in the digital era and some implications for Indigenous knowledge', in I.N. Mazonde and P. Thomas (eds.) *Indigenous Knowledge Systems and Intellectual Property in the Twenty-First Century: Perspectives from Southern Africa*. University of Botswana: London, 66–78.

Moorfield, J. (2013). *Te Aka: Māori-English, English-Māori Dictionary*. AUT: Auckland.

Morse, B.W. (2012). 'Indigenous human rights and knowledge in archives, museums, and libraries: Some international perspectives with specific reference to New Zealand and Canada', *Archival Science*, vol 12, no 2: 113–140.

Nakata, M., Nakata, V., Gardiner, G., McKeough, J., Byrne, A., and Gibson, J. (2008). 'Indigenous digital collections: An early look at the organisation and culture interface', *Australian Academic & Research Libraries*, vol 39, no 4: 223–236.

Nakata, N.M. (2007) 'Indigenous digital collections', *Australian Academic & Research Libraries*, vol 38, no 2: 99–110.

Ngata, W., Ngata-Gibson, H., and Salmond, A. (2012). 'Te Ataakura: Digital taonga and cultural innovation', *Journal of Material Culture*, vol 17, no 3: 229–244.

O'Carroll, A.D. (2013). 'Māori identity construction in SNS', *International Journal of Critical Indigenous Studies*, vol 6, no 2: 2–16.

Olson, R., Hackett, J., and DeRoy, S. (2016). 'Mapping the digital terrain: Towards Indigenous geographic information and spatial data quality indicators for Indigenous knowledge and traditional land-use data collection', *The Cartographic Journal*, vol 53, no 4: 348–355.

Palfrey, J. (2008) *Born Digital: Understanding the First Generation of Digital Natives*. Basic Book: New York.

Palmer, M. (2012) 'Theorizing in digital geographic information networks', *Cartographica*, vol 47, no 2: 80–91.

Prensky, M. (2001). 'Digital natives, digital immigrants', *On the Horizon*, vol 9, no 5: 1–6.

Prensky, M. (2009). 'H. sapiens digital: From digital immigrants and digital natives to digital wisdom', *Innovate: Journal of Online Education*, vol 5, no 3. Available: https://nsuworks.nova.edu/innovate/vol5/iss3/1, accessed 1 March 2020.

Radoll, P. and Hunter, B. (2017). *Dynamics of the Digital Divide*. Centre for Aboriginal Economic Policy Research (CAEPR), The Australian National University: Canberra.

Robinson, C., Maclean, K., Hill, R., Bock, E., and Rist, P. (2016). 'Participatory mapping to negotiate Indigenous knowledge used to assess environmental risk', *Sustainability Science*, vol 11, no 1: 115–126.

Salmond, A. (2012). 'Digital subjects, cultural objects: Special issue introduction', *Journal of Material Culture*, vol 17, no 3: 211–228.

Schorch, P., McCarty, C., and Hakiwai, A. (2016). 'Globalizing Māori museology: Reconceptualising engagement, knowledge, and virtuality through Mana Taonga', *Museum Anthropology*, vol 39, no 1: 48–69.

Schwaub, K. (2016). *The Fourth Industrial Revolution: What it Means, How to Respond*. World Economic Forum. Available: http://weforum.org/agenda/2016/01/the-fourth-industrial-revolution-what-it-means- and-how-to-respond, accessed 1 March 2020.

Sleeper-Smith, S. (ed.) (2009). *Contesting Knowledge: Museums and Indigenous Perspectives*. University of Nebraska Press. Lincoln.

Srinivasan, R., Boast, R., Furner, J., and Becvar, K.M. (2009). 'Digital museums and diverse cultural knowledges: Moving past the traditional catalog', *Information Society*, vol 25, no 4: 265–278.

Waateanews.com. (2018). *Jason Lovell Co Creator ReoBot Maori Language Chat*. Available: https://www.waateanews.com/waateanews/x_story_id/MTg2MTY=/Jason-Lovell-co-creator-ReoBot-Maori-language-chat, accessed 1 March 2020.

Waitangi Tribunal. (2011a). 'Ko Aotearoa tēnei: a report into claims concerning law and policy affecting Māori culture and identity (Te taumata tuarua – vol 2)', in *Wai 262 Waitangi Tribunal Report* 2011. Legislation Direct: Wellington.

Waitangi Tribunal. (2011b). 'Ko Aotearoa tēnei: a report into claims concerning law and policy affecting Māori culture and identity (Te taumata tuatahi – vol 1)', in *Wai 262 Waitangi Tribunal Report* 2011. Legislation Direct: Wellington.

Walter, M. (2018). 'The voice of Indigenous data: beyond the markers of disadvantage', *Griffith Review*, vol 60. Available: https://www.griffithreview.com/articles/voice-indigenous-data-beyond-disadvantage/, accessed 4 April 2020.

Walter, M. and Suina, M. (2019). 'Indigenous data, Indigenous methodologies and Indigenous data sovereignty', *International Journal of Social Research Methodology*, vol 22, no 3: 233–243.

Whaanga, H., Lewis, J., and Brown, M. (forthcoming). 'Relation-oriented AI: why Indigenous protocols matter', in M.K. Gold and L.F. Klein (eds.) *Debates in the Digital Humanities 2021*.

Whaanga, H., Simmonds, N., and Keegan, T.T. (2017). *Iwi, Institutes, Societies & Community Led Initiatives*. Te Pua Wānanga ki te Ao, University of Waikato: Hamilton. Available: https://www.waikato.ac.nz/__data/assets/pdf_file/0008/394901/chapter21.pdf, accessed 4 April 2020.

Winter, J. and Boudreau, J. (2018) 'Supporting self-determined Indigenous innovations: Rethinking the digital divide in Canada', *Technology & Innovation Management Review*, vol 8, no 2: 38–48.

Yong, S.T. and Gates, P. (2014). 'Born digital: Are they really digital natives', *International Journal of E-Education, E-Business, E-Management and E-Learning*, vol 4, no 2: 102–105.

Part 5

Bodies, performance, and praxis
Part editor: Brendan Hokowhitu

34

Identity is a poor substitute for relating

Genetic ancestry, critical polyamory, property, and relations

Kim TallBear

In 2013, the same year my book *Native American DNA: Tribal Belonging and the False Promise of Genetic Science* was published, I started a then anonymous blog, *The Critical Polyamorist*. I intended the blog as a way to find and think with like-minded others about this new turn in my personal life, my engagement in consensual non-monogamy (CNM) with multiple partners. And it was challenging and time-consuming to figure out how to build good relations and good relationships in ways that go against that system that spans legal and contemporary cultural orders at all levels. I started writing the *Critical Polyamorist* blog because I wanted to be sure that my polyamory practice was informed by and supported my broader anti-colonial worldview before I did polyamory openly in the world. I was open with my partners, of course. If I were going to make a life-altering transition to consensual non-monogamy, it was essential that I make it into research.

In the introduction to an important special issue focused on polyamory of the journal *Sexualities,* the editors define polyamory simply as "a form of relationship where it is possible, valid and worthwhile to maintain (usually long-term) intimate and sexual relationships with multiple partners simultaneously" (Haritaworn, Lin, and Klesse 2006: 515). Polyamorists often characterise ourselves as interested in 'committed' and emotionally engaged relationships. To be clear, there are also asexual polyamorists who desire the emotional intimacy and commitment, but who do not necessarily require sexual intimacy. There are also CNM relationships that involve multiple sexual connections, but which avoid emotional engagement and long-term commitment. 'Swinging' or sex parties come to mind. Overlapping both of these groups are those who also participate in BDSM (that said, not everyone who practices BDSM is non-monogamous. Some do it within monogamous relationships.). Margot Weiss, in the fascinating monograph, *Techniques of Pleasure: BDSM and the Circuits of Sexuality* (2011) explains BDSM as "of relatively recent ... coinage" and "... an amalgamation of three acronyms: B&D (bondage and discipline), D/s (domination/submission), and SM (sadomasochism)" (2011: vii). Sometimes called 'kinksters', BDSM practitioners would refer to someone like me who does not partake in BDSM as 'vanilla'. Some non-monogamists engage in multiple types of CNM. Others, like me, are firmly in one camp. While I am pretty vanilla in the world of consensual non-monogamy, I still move against the grain of our society's compulsory monogamy system.

Writing *The Critical Polyamorist* was not the first time I pursued study in order to think and live in resistance to colonial inheritances. Twelve years earlier, in 2001, I put on hold a career in Indigenous environmental and science policy to pursue a PhD and academic research not as a new career path, but as a way to understand the professional and cultural worlds I moved through. I originally planned to return to governmental policy work post-PhD. In the early 2000s with the race to map the human genome, gene talk was on the increase in the United States. Popular understandings of 'identity' have consistently engaged such ideas during the ensuing two decades. Witness the Elizabeth Warren Native American DNA debacle in October 2018 when which she released her DNA test results analysed by a famous Stanford scientist and advisor to the genetic testing company 23andMe (Smith 2018; TallBear 2019a). The Cherokee Nation Secretary of State (Principal Chief as of this writing) Chuck Hoskin Jr., expert Cherokee genealogists and other prominent Cherokees, and I were widely quoted in the press critiquing her damage to tribal sovereignty and Indigenous definitions of citizenship and belonging by taking a DNA test to support her claims to being of Cherokee descent. Warren's is just one famous case during a year in which the same number of people purchased genetic ancestry tests as did in all previous years combined since direct-to-consumer tests came onto the market in the early 2000s. *MIT Technology Review* reported that:

> by the start of 2019, more than 26 million consumers had added their DNA to four leading commercial ancestry and health databases. If the pace continues, the gene troves could hold data on the genetic makeup of more than 100 million people within 24 months.
>
> *(Regalado 2019: online)*

Settler narratives of (im)migration, primordial race and nation are co-constituted with genome research on human migrations and population histories. Science – both academic and within the DNA testing industry – is performed by humans conditioned by certain philosophies and historical standpoints and not others. Elizabeth Warren's genomic 'proof' loops back to reinforce settler historical claims and kinship norms. Settler-colonial science, industry, and society co-constitute one another. This happens at the expense of Indigenous philosophies, governance and kinship norms.

Since childhood, I have been a de facto anthropologist of white people. I only came to understand in graduate school that I had always studied as I attempted to more than survive ongoing colonialism. I studied whites in order to interrogate their truths, which always reaffirmed for me the legitimacy of Dakota and other Indigenous narratives and definitions of relations, peoplehood, and the world. During PhD research, I formally studied settler narratives coupled with the biological sciences. In that dissertation and eventually book, I once again sought to better understand settler-colonial thought. I was trying to not succumb to the nihilism I increasingly felt over a decade of working on environmental and science policy issues with federal, non-profit, and tribal bureaucracies, but always in the shadow of US paternalism. I also wanted to perform something oppositional. Like settlers so often study Indigenous social and thought systems as other, in order to perform their own greater enlightenment and rationality, I did the same. I studied them in order to provincialise them, and render Indigenous thought as obviously more rational because it is more relational. My project is not one of multicultural inclusion. I don't seek the 'incorporation' of Indigenous knowledge to strengthen settler science. I do actually think that much of settler-colonial thought is simply more wrong than Indigenous thought, and it's deadly. We actually need to re-script science away from hierarchy toward relational, including Indigenous, analytical frameworks. Plus, as they say, turnabout is fair play. Although it is humorous to think of the unevenly matched rivals – miniscule me going up against the girthy edifice of settler genome science.

Critical polyamorists and relations

The *Critical Polyamorist* blog was yet another attempt to more than survive, to push back against settler-colonial narratives and definitions of relations, what the world is and how it should be. At first, the new turn in my personal life and research interests seemed unrelated to my previous area of research in DNA politics. But everything is related. Foregrounding Indigenous analytical frameworks and my own Dakota sense of relations, the critical polyamory work focuses on what I have come to understand as settler sexuality, marriage, and family. *Native American DNA* re-scripted definitions of individual 'identity' and Peoplehood away from essentially genomic definitions that focus on lineal inheritance of properties co-constituted with settler stories. This newer work attempts to re-script bodily practices and kinship understandings away from definitions and narratives that likewise privilege the inheritance of properties and property, and that are grounded in what Scott Morgensen calls "settler sexuality". That is, the "heter-opatriarchal and sexual modernity exemplary of white settler civilization" (Morgensen 2011: 23). Elsewhere, he elaborates that settler sexuality is a "white national heteronormativity that regulates Indigenous sexuality and gender by supplanting them with the sexual modernity of settler subjects" (2010a: 106). Morgensen also writes about how settler-colonialism has "conditioned the formation of modern sexuality in the United States including modern queer subjects and politics" (2010: 106). Settler sexuality and family are closely linked to concepts of property, which I'll return to shortly.

In thoughtful blog comments and in feedback from people who listen to my lectures and interviews, I hear about shared questions, challenges, and experiences related to non/monogamy to use Angela Willey's term that foregrounds the "relational and mutually constitutive nature" of monogamy and non-monogamy (Willey 2006: 543). Some respondents say my work is a positive revelation. Others say it is a path they were already exploring, and my work gives them language to make sense of their discomfort with both compulsory monogamy and settler polyamory. Those I hear from are racially diverse, gender and class diverse, and sometimes Indigenous. Indigenous people who contact me tend to be younger and worried about the judgement of their elders and community that is influenced by colonial conversions to Christianity. My great-grandmother, an unrecovered Catholic who raised me for half of my childhood, would have been horrified by my polyamory. It would have been impossible for me to be openly non-monogamous if she were still alive. I sometimes hear from women across the racial spectrum, long-married or divorced and with children, who long hard to live non-monogamously, but cannot risk divorce if they are married and the judgement of their community, and who fear losing custody of children. And I've heard from Indigenous men who are in their 20s, in their 50s, or somewhere in-between, who describe themselves as progressive and feminist, but who know the stereotypes that Indigenous and other men of colour are subject to. They are viewed as inherently 'unfaithful', as womanisers or 'players'. They cannot risk being even consensually non-monogamous. Their harshest judges are not only settler society, but also their own community, especially Indigenous women.

Whether my particular polyamorous interlocuters can practice non-monogamy (openly) or not, they are explicitly critical of white supremacist and settler-colonial structures, and thus dissatisfied not only with how monogamy is constituted and compulsory within settler-colonialism, but they are also critical of increasingly mainstream forms of polyamory that are whiter, more heteronormative, couple-centric, and unquestioning of state-sanctioned marriage. They, like me, tend to view monogamy and non-monogamy as not simply individual, private, and equally valid ethical choices or inclinations, be those social or biological inclinations. The personal choice model of non/monogamy – based on biological inclinations? – is a commonly held view among polyamorists and among some progressive monogamists. And because science is a product of our society, there are conversations among scientists about whether inclinations towards non/monogamy are rooted in social values and/or in biology. One can refer to Willey's work for a discussion of the science, both in contemporary 21st-century genomic and neurological sciences and in biological and sexological sciences going back to the 19th century (Willey 2016).

While some of the (would-be) critical polyamorists (not all are able to act on their desires) who reach out to me might view their non-monogamous nature as to some degree inherent, they focus on what is socially imaginable. They value dynamic possibilities for relating that are not simply driven by a sense of innately constituted impulse or desires. Those who are actively pursuing non-monogamy focus on workable relationships negotiated together in open conversation that emphasise consent, and that build networks of mutual support with not only polyamorous partners, but also within a broader community of like-minded thinkers and doers. They more often trouble gender norms and their consensual non-monogamy is often contextualised in relation to other social reform projects. It is community minded.

Deciding to be openly non-monogamous

In Texas, I remember worrying that because I am occasionally trolled for my writing and scholarship that calls for decolonising science and technology, that online harassment might increase were I to write openly about non-monogamy. Calling out monogamy as a cruel imposition of settler-colonialism seemed to me an even more radical proposition, especially since even anti-colonial thinkers on other topics buy into the script of monogamy and marriage. It turns out that my work on the colonial politics of genomics has still to date elicited more trolls. But in 2015, I didn't yet understand that would be the case.

Upon relocating to Canada, I nonetheless, decided to reveal my identity. Although perhaps I was not so clever. A graduate student at the University of Texas told me in seminar the year before that my blog posts were circulating on a gender and women's studies listserv curated by students in an east coast university. They knew I was the Critical Polyamorist. At the time, I was beginning to receive invitations from a few people who knew my identity and also messages sent to my blog e-mail with requests to lecture, do podcast and press interviews, and to publish on the topic. My occasional blog posts had found a wider audience than the fellow polyamorists I originally set out to reach and converse with. To engage more people in thinking with me on the decolonial potential of non-monogamy, I had to be open not only in my romantic relationships, but also with my name. It also felt like it was time to be open. I had heard enough from blog readers and their challenges to understand my considerable privilege as a non-monogamist. Not very many people, especially women and Indigenous people, have the same relative safety and resources to challenge and untangle themselves from compulsory monogamy. My being open, I hoped, might help destigmatise consensual non-monogamy and make more space in the world for others to live similarly.

My growing recognition of my privilege and feeling that I needed to be open was also in part prompted by the courageous critical analyses of settler sexuality and its doctrines and institutions coming from especially younger Indigenous two-spirit and queer scholars, artists, and activists. Perhaps not coincidentally, I saw many of the most incisive analyses coupled with related activism (e.g. linking environmental crisis to sexual violence and sex negativity) coming from young

Indigenous thinkers north of the Medicine line – the 49th parallel, the US/Canadian border. Part of my decision to move north was that I perceived (rightly or wrongly) Indigenous people in lands now occupied by Canada to be more critical of the settler state, including its sex negativity, and its linked role in systemic violence against both Indigenous peoples and the planet. The young people who I found exemplary of this – for example, those who worked with the organisation Native Youth Sexual Health Network (NYSHN) – had less social and economic security than I did. I had read and heard their accounts of homophobia and viciously enforced gender binarism in their own Indigenous communities, no doubt a legacy of colonialism. Being openly non-monogamous felt scary, but I likely risked far less than they did daily being open about who and how they desire, and how they present themselves in the world. It felt like it was time to step up and follow their example.

A note on methodology

My non-monogamy analyses, like my DNA and identity analyses, focus on the United States and Canada, the two settler-colonial countries I've lived in during the last two decades. That said, I prefer insider-research and critique from within the place I know best and in which I have the deepest lived investments. Since I have lived 44 of my 51 years in the United States, and less than five years in Canada, it is US culture, history, and dominant settler narratives that I know best. I do not exempt Canada from similar forms of settler-colonial violence, but I often feel insufficiently informed of Canadian history and cultural trends to focus my analyses on Canada's colonialism. The longer I live in and continue to be formed and informed by Canada, my critical eye turns more to focus on this country.

DNA test takers and property

While I have received mostly positive feedback from those who choose to engage with me on the non-monogamy work, I get a strikingly different reaction from the DNA test takers who consume my other body of writing, lectures on video, and press related to the politics of genomic and anthropological research on Indigenous populations and DTC genetic ancestry testing, give me strikingly different comments. Over the past two decades, I have received mostly negative or anxious feedback. I insist on consideration for lived relations, and relations are not a significant part of such peoples' interactions with Indigenous DNA knowledge unless one counts their implication in colonial structures that produce and consume that knowledge. Naturally, the DNA test takers tend to push back on my insistence on making relations, and instead make property claims over Indigenous biologicals and so-called identity. Among them, I have encountered two types of property-claiming 'Native American DNA' test takers:

1) First, there are the skilled genealogists who are themselves scientific thinkers, who follow recent science on human population genetics, who use DNA to confirm their family tree – to substantiate or not a story of a 'Native American' in their lineage. For them the reward is the naming and confirmation of branches in their tree. They get to claim ancestors, surnames, links to historic geographies and peoples. Ultimately, they seem to use their own family tree as a window to comprehend world history, which is understandably fascinating. Again, none of their claims need involve actual relating with Indigenous peoples or places. Their new knowledge might lead them to seek such relations, but it needn't. This type of property claim does not necessarily involve an *identity* claim. One might, for example, like one genealogist I encountered, prove the presence of a Mohawk ancestor in one's genetic

tree, but not actually claim to *be* Mohawk or seek out relations with that people. I found in the research for my book that this type of DNA test taker, usually class- and education-privileged and armed with excessive scientific knowledge, rarely translated a genetic ancestor into a personal identity claim. I was pleasantly surprised.

2) There is a second type of DNA test taker, one who makes a double property claim also without necessarily seeking to relate. These test takers tend *not* to be expert genealogists nor lay experts in the application of DNA testing to genealogy. Rather, they come to DNA testing with the specific goal of finding scientific proof to support a claim to Indigenous *identity*, often with great emotional investment. Such a test taker might combine genealogical documentation and DNA testing to provide greater support for say again a Mohawk in their family tree, which leads them to then not only claim an ancestral lineage ('*my* ancestors, *my* lineage, *my* heritage'), but such a person might also race-shift to claim a Mohawk 'identity'. They could, but do not necessarily seek to relate with Mohawk people and community, which is rarely an easy prospect for complex historical and social reasons.

I rarely anymore encounter the first type of DNA test taker, the skilled genetic genealogist, since I am no longer researching in their communities. But even though my book on 'Native American' DNA research was published seven years ago, I still regularly receive long emails and handwritten letters from the second group of DNA test consumers. When DNA test takers communicate with me, they detail long searches and deep desires to prove a 'Native American' in their family tree, most typically a Cherokee ancestor, followed by many fewer claims to possible Blackfeet/foot, Apache, and Choctaw ancestors with other peoples occasionally claimed. As opposed to the expert genetic genealogists, this second group is more ready to say something like, 'I have DNA, therefore I *am* Native American'. This is a one-sided claim in which ancestors or peoples, e.g. Blackfoot, Apache, or Cherokee peoples need not acknowledge such claims, yet those claims nonetheless have veracity in settler-colonial culture with its increasing emphasis on genetic kinship. Think of the oft-cited lament of 'identity politics' and the invocation of scientific 'proof' when such claims are rejected or pushed back on by the very Indigenous people being claimed.

Zoologist Peter D. Dwyer had a pithy insight, one I often quote, into the strange emphasis on long-ago genetic ancestry as conferring a contemporary identity claim: "[t]he idea of evolution has conditioned an odd understanding: we are what we were and not what we became" (Dwyer in Proctor 2003: 235). Dwyer referred to a scientific controversy from the mid-1980s to early 1990s surrounding one scientist's phylogenetic reconstruction that proposed that megabats were an early branch of the primate lineage. This proposal regarding the evolutionary history of megabats was apparently anathema to the wider scientific community who mocked the scientist's hypothesising as if he were saying that humans (being primates) were at some fundamental level bats. Biological anthropologist Jonathan Marks, in his book, *What It Means to be 98% Chimpanzee: Apes, People, and Their Genes*, also highlights with much humour this erroneous tendency to reckon contemporary identity or being according to long-ago shared genetic markers.

The Elizabeth Warren case, that I've already mentioned, is probably one of the most well-known examples of the power of genetic history in settler society to inform contemporary identity claims. Her Native American DNA test showed probable Native ancestry six to ten generations ago, but those genetic ancestors were not necessarily linked to the specific living Indigenous community she claims historical affiliation with, the Cherokee. So-called Native American markers are shared in higher and lower frequencies in Indigenous populations throughout the Americas, and there are thousands of different Indigenous peoples. When the story broke, I did two dozen media interviews over the span of several weeks about Warren's unsubstantiated

Cherokee claims and her DNA test to try and prove those claims despite the fact that professional genealogy showed no evidence for them (e.g., Dugyala 2019; Kessler 2018; Smith 2018; Uyehara 2018; WYNC Studios 2018). Pollysgranddaughter.com, a website researched and written by professional genealogist and Cherokee Nation citizen, Twila Barnes, shows that extensive research on Warren's genealogy reveals her maternal ancestors through whom she claims 'Indian blood' to be all white people. Barnes writes on the 'Elizabeth Warren Information page' that Warren's maternal ancestors "were never found in any Cherokee records or listed as Indian" (online). Barnes and other expert genealogists also challenge the common claim that many Cherokee hid out and avoided forced relocation on the Trail of Tears, thus also avoiding documentation. They insist that Cherokee genealogies are among some of the most well-documented in the world. During the few weeks that the Warren DNA test was at the centre of the news cycle, messages and emails spiked in my in-boxes and 'splaining snarky tweets also littered my Twitter feed. This was also the case, although less so given his lesser global stature, when I did media interviews in January 2017 about Canadian literary darling, Joseph Boyden, and his disproven claims to be Métis and to have other Indigenous ancestry (Edmonton AM 2017; Alberta Noon 2017; CBC The Current 2017). In summary, the 'Native American DNA' test takers' claims over biological property, rights to knowledge, and identity – built historically on the stolen bones and appropriated blood of Indigenous peoples – are regularly defended by scientists, the companies they found and advise, and by the public that consumes their knowledge and commercial products. Settler-colonial conceptual and legal regimes that govern DNA knowledge are held up as objectively truthful and just while Indigenous definitions of belonging, our governance rights, and our own research to support those rights that is actually informed by more multi-disciplinary and therefore, frankly, more robust research is denigrated as biased.

From DNA to polyamory research – from property to relating

As the years have unfolded since 2013, when I began living and researching polyamory in addition to genetics politics, and both within a framework that sought to understand their role in settler-colonialism, I have come to see that these two projects are connected. I am concerned in both cases with actual practices of relating versus making property claims over ancestors, Indigenous peoples, and now over lovers and partners (Reardon and TallBear 2012). In *Native American DNA*, I insisted on actual (hopefully good) relating with Indigenous communities – that property claims to Indigenous identity could not be made absent the agreement of Indigenous peoples; that Indigenous citizenship requirements, definitions of kin, tribe, and nation had to be respected; and that Indigenous peoples, relations, and 'identities' were not simply there to be claimed by heretofore non-Indigenous peoples just like the land has been claimed without assent.

Monogamous marriage supported in the 19th century 'civilising' projects in both the United States and Canada (Carter 2008; Cott 2000), including the breakup of collective Indigenous land-bases into private parcels. Settler-colonial governments in the United States and Canada imposed compulsory monogamy that helped privatise and constitute land ownership for settler men, their families, corporations, and states. These states also forced Indigenous men, women, and children into this oppressive system via land allotment policies, compulsory conversion to Christianity, relocation programs, and residential schools – its indoctrination and abuses. State programs, policies, and institutions simultaneously worked to eliminate gender and sexuality-nonconforming persons.

Just like nations have staked a sole sovereign claim to land, and male heads of household to their private acreage in a compulsory monogamy society, it is the norm for one to stake a sole sovereign claim in a beloved's body. One then seeks to write over all previous names, loves, and relations that land and body have known, and forbids in theory future possible relations with another. The property ethic that grounds compulsory monogamy and state-sanctioned marriage is being resisted at least in part by those who engage in critical polyamory – who understand critical non-monogamous relating as a move against settler-colonial structures, and not simply a personal lifestyle choice or an identity grounded in biology. The polyamorists who reach out to me are looking to relate differently, more consensually, thoughtfully, and ethically. They are trying to figure out in repeated conversations with those who want to relate back how to do that.

This is unlike so many of the DNA test takers who write me and make emotional pleas for advice about DNA testing companies, who pen ten-page letters or lengthy emails detailing their lives and long emotional searches for Native ancestry, who describe their needs to belong to this land or to have what they view as a right to belong recognised. Their narratives often evidence romantic and stereotypical ideas of Native peoples' cultures and phenotypes. For example, you can read in Elizabeth Warren's and Joseph Boyden's impassioned and unsubstantiated narratives such stereotypes. In many such stories there is also something that anthropologist Circe Sturm has observed in those who she describes as 'racial shifters', associations of whiteness with 'cultural emptiness' (Sturm 2010: 55). Many who passionately claim Native American ancestry are deeply dissatisfied with being simply white. Claiming an Indigenous ancestor and a right to identity (again like a land-claim without assent), they think will help them fill a void. These days, I only write DNA test takers back to provide them a reputable genetic genealogy forum to help them answer their technical questions about DNA tests. I want them to get good scientific advice, preferably not from the same companies profiting from DNA testing. And for application of that science to Indigenous citizenship, kinship ideas, and policy, they can turn to my book and articles, and to others I cite.

The (would-be) polyamorists, however, I write back, often at length. I try not to go beyond my skill set. I am no life or relationship counselor. Comparing these two groups has led me to argue that polyamory should remain a method of (hopefully good) relating and not come to be thought of primarily as a sexual orientation or identity. 'Identity' as a concept in popular usage does not necessarily imply ongoing relating. It might imply discrete biological conjoinings within one's genetic ancestry and it can spur alliances, but it can also exist as a largely individualistic idea, as something considered to be held once and for all, unchanging within one's own body – whether through biological or social imprinting – as one's body's property. Similarly, I don't want our polyamorous relating to calcify into individual identity claims that risk us looking too much within our own persons, including our genetics, for a definition of who we *are*. Rather, I want us to remember that we are always *becoming*, in relation not only to genetic and cultural ancestors (not always synonymous), but to one another continuously, and in relation to the geographies and political economies we inhabit whether by choice or by circumstances we may have had little choice in. If we remember that we are what we become as much or more than we are who our properties determine us to be, I suspect that will help us focus on how to relate more carefully with one another as beings in the world, both within and beyond romantic relations. We might thus weight our relating more toward the good, although relations that are not necessarily good are also the entangled relations that make and remake us into who we are.

What are the implications for Indigenous Studies?

I consider myself to be a 'public intellectual'. I write not only for an academic audience, but I write, perhaps primarily, for a larger public audience, albeit an educated and especially Indigenous public. By educated I do not, of course, refer only to those who hold university degrees. Even

though my generation was the first in my Dakota extended family to earn university and graduate degrees, my relatives, including my married-in Cree and Métis great-grandmother, were
over multiple generations since the late 19th century avid readers and politics junkies. I was
raised by people who consumed a lot of news in print, then radio and television. Today, we do
so online. Even before my relatives were accessing news in English, one of my most well-known
ancestors, Chief Little Crow aka Ta-Oyate-Duta, who reluctantly helped lead the 1862 Dakota
War against settlers in Minnesota, is documented as thoughtful, a strategic thinker, and observant
of whites and their curious practices. In a similar vein, I did a PhD to think through and hopefully be part of developing solutions to problems posed by whites that Indigenous communities
in the United States and Canada began encountering during the early days of mapping the
human genome. After Little Crow, I too fled north of the Medicine Line in search of some res-
pite from US (exceptionalist) violence. He returned only to be murdered by a white farmer near
Hutchinson, Minnesota. I continue to live in the strangely different and yet similar settler space
that is Canada. At any rate, it is not surprising given the history of publicly intellectual work in
my family of origin that I focus in this chapter on the main differences in public receptions to
my respective bodies of intellectual production.

While popular responses to my work differ from being more contentious after my genome
politics analyses to being more positive after my critical polyamory analyses, it is not that I don't
have critics of the non/monogamy work. However, they don't tend to write me or respond
on social media in the more frequent manner of respondents to my analyses of DNA politics.
But the smaller yet positive response to my non/monogamy publications, podcasts, and press
may in and of itself be telling. Perhaps it reveals not only the great excitement among some
readers and listeners, but also a not insignificant, but quiet unease among others? As I write
this, one of my graduate students just forwarded me an article, '8 Podcasts to Get Started with
Polyamory and Non-Monogamy', published today on *Autostraddle.com*, a queer feminist online
venue. The author suggests listening to two of my podcast interviews to get started, another
positive engagement (Bailey 2020). Interestingly, the skeptical or negative feedback to my work
on non/monogamy that I am aware of has come from a relatively few white, Indigenous, and
people-of-colour feminist academics. I've encountered them in multiple disciplinary symposia
and lectures, including at Indigenous Studies, political ecology, and philosophy events.

I have noticed more silence surrounding my non/monogamy work when it is not posted
directly to *The Critical Polyamorist*, non-monogamy related platforms/pages, or featured in popular media. For example, there is often not much engagement at all when I post polyamory-
related content to a more general audience, say to social media platforms, including Twitter
and Facebook where I have many diverse followers and 'friends', including many Indigenous
followers. On the other hand, when I post to Twitter, where I have at present 44,000-plus followers, and to Facebook anti-colonial content related to environmental topics, genomics, and
say COVID-19 and other biomedical issues, those posts tend to elicit lively if sometimes negative engagement, especially from non-Indigenous people. I cannot be certain, but the relative
silence around non/monogamy topics on those more general audience social media platforms
may reflect unease among Indigenous and feminist followers and friends, and simply disinterest
from those who follow me more for science politics related content.

This is obviously work in progress and I have more research to do to fully develop the
ideas herein, and to understand the responses of those who engage this work. I tend to think
and 'learn in public' as blogger, Indigenous Studies scholar, and podcaster Adrienne Keene
calls it, in an "intellectual and cultural space where we can all be represented in our true and
flawed and multitudinous ways, where one Native voice isn't made to stand in for millions,
and where we are all allowed to learn, together" (Keene n.d.: online). Like Adrienne Keene,

my learning in public is also evidenced by my blogs and active social media accounts in which I try out ideas in conversation (*All My Relations* 2019). While social media drafting of ideas is a big and growing part of my public intellectualism, it is a newer approach that is still grounded in my longer-standing feminist-Indigenous methodology that I discuss at greater length in elsewhere. In that broader suite of research methods, I work to dismantle the "binary between researcher and researched – between knowing inquirer and who or what are considered to be the resources or grounds for knowledge production" (TallBear 2014: 2). On the blog and across social media platforms, I think with other (would-be) critical polyamorists rather than study them. I think with other Indigenous thinkers, both inside and outside the academy, rather than study them. I have even come to think with other scientists, especially Indigenous scientists, rather than exclusively studying them. I do continue to study especially straight white male scientists. Again, I think it is important (and fun) to perform the idea that returning their centuries-long gaze is fair play. As Aretha Franklin sang back in 1985, 'Who's Zoomin' Who?'.

There are honest critiques to be made of this work-in-formation, and I will expand my analyses to respond to those insights as I continue to encounter them. But I also hear in the agitated critiques of fellow (I presume) anti-colonial feminists surprising investment in settler-colonial monogamy. Why amidst all of our anti- and decolonial efforts in Indigenous Studies and our increasing attention to queer and two-spirit theory so much resistance to critical interrogation of monogamy and state-sanctioned marriage? Rare exceptions include especially Pacific Indigenous scholars (e.g., Kauanui 2018). We already know through the work of Indigenous and non-Indigenous historians and legal scholars that marriage and monogamy are tightly tied to the imposition onto Indigenous peoples of private property and heteropatriarchal nuclear family. We in Indigenous Studies rail frequently against US tribal and federal government blood quantum regulations and policies that disrupt Indigenous notions of kin and peoplehood. Why then does Indigenous Studies and why do Indigenous scholars in other disciplines leave largely untouched compulsory monogamy and settler marriage that similarly disrupt our lived relations and our relational frameworks?

In conclusion, it must be noted that if non/monogamy refers to a system in which monogamy and non-monogamy are mutually constituted as feminist science studies scholar Angela Willey shows in her work (Willey 2006; 2016), this means that 'polyamory' or 'consensual non-monogamy' are but placeholders for those of us who are critical of compulsory monogamy, settler sexuality, family, and marriage in its evolving forms. We do not rest in these terms and their limited possibilities, but we can work toward and within Indigenous and other anti-colonial, anti-capitalist frameworks and languages toward terminologies and practices for relating that might be unbound from settler-conceived properties and property.

References

Bailey. (2020). '8 podcasts to get started with polyamory and non-monogamy', *Autostraddle.com*. Available: https://www.autostraddle.com/8-podcasts-to-get-started-with-polyamory-and-non-monogamy/, accessed 19 May 2020.

Carter, S. (2008). *The Importance of Being Monogamous: Marriage and Nation Building in Western Canada to 1915*. University of Alberta Press: Edmonton, AB.

CBC. The Current. (2017). 'Indigenous identity and the case of Joseph Boyden', with Anna Maria Tremonti. Available: http://www.cbc.ca/radio/thecurrent/the-current-for-january-5-2017-1.3921340 /indigenous-identity-and-the-case-of-joseph-boyden-1.3922327, accessed 5 January 2017.

CBC. Edmonton Am Podcast. (2017). 'Joseph Boyden is coming to Edmonton … Two Indigenous writers weigh in', *Episode* 300276870, 20 January. Available: http://www.cbc.ca/player/play/859187779596.

Cott, N. (2000). *Public Vows: A History of Marriage and Nation*. Harvard University Press: Cambridge, MA.

Dugyala, R. (2019). 'Native American critics still wary of Warren despite apology tour', *Politico*, 27 August. Available: https://www.politico.com/story/2019/08/27/native-american-critics-elizabeth-warren-1475903, accessed 20 May 2020.

Franklin, A., Glass, P., and Walden, N.M. (1985). *Who's Zoomin' Who?*. Arista Records: New York, NY.

Haritaworn, J., Lin, C.-J., and Klesse, C. (2006). 'Poly/logue: A critical introduction to polyamory', *Sexualities* (Special Issue on *Polyamory*), vol 9, no 5: 515–529.

Kauanui, J.K. (2018). *Paradoxes of Hawaiian Sovereignty: Land, Sex, and the Colonial Politics of State Nationalism*. Duke University Press: Durham, NC.

Keene, A. (n.d.). 'On consenting to learn in public', *Native Appropriations*. Available: http://www.nativeappropriations.com, accessed 27 February 2018.

Kessler, G. (2018). 'Just about everything you've read on the Warren DNA test is wrong', *Washington Post*, 18 October. Available: https://www.washingtonpost.com/politics/2018/10/18/just-about-everything-youve-read-warren-dna-test-is-wrong/?fbclid=IwAR3jFgozNYeu7-7TugYhzRT7G4PAOsLtCqVH69KhTSChAZUICsQWUdU-ifE&utm_term=.49549b11d72e, accessed 20 May 2020.

Morgensen, S.L. (2010a). 'Settler homonationalism: Theorizing settler colonialism within queer modernities', *GLQ: A Journal of Lesbian and Gay Studies*, vol 16, no 1–2: 105–131.

Morgensen, S.L. (2010b). *The Spaces Between Us: Queer Settler Colonialism and Indigenous Decolonization*. University of Minnesota Press: Minneapolis, MN.

Morgensen, S.L. (2011). *Spaces Between Us: Queer Settler Colonialism and Indigenous Decolonization*. University of Minnesota Press.

Proctor, R.N. (2003). 'Three roots of human recency: Molecular anthropology, the refigured acheulean, and the unesco response to auschwitz', *Current Anthropology*, vol 44, no 2: 213–239.

Reardon, J. and TallBear, K. (2012). '"Your DNA is *our* history": Genomics, anthropology, and the construction of whiteness as property', *Current Anthropology*, vol 53, no S5: S233–S245.

Regalado, A. (2019). 'More than 26 million people have taken an at-home ancestry test', *MIT Technology Review*, 11 February. Available: https://www.technologyreview.com/2019/02/11/103446/more-than-26-million-people-have-taken-an-at-home-ancestry-test/, accessed 20 May 2020.

Smith, J. (2018). 'Why Elizabeth Warren's DNA fiasco matters', *Rolling Stone*, 7 December. Available: https://www.rollingstone.com/politics/politics-features/elizabeth-warren-dna-766297/?fbclid=IwAR02AZXZzMoBVjj7hxeMkq81QlmYLaoEouC9otmuoGK7ugfsn2iUkPLLixY, accessed 20 May 2020.

Sturm, C. (2010). *Becoming Indian: The Struggle Over Cherokee Identity in the Twenty-first Century*. School for Advanced Research Press: Santa Fe, NM.

TallBear, K. (2014). 'Standing with and speaking as faith: A feminist-indigenous approach to inquiry', *Journal of Research Practice*, vol 10, Article N17. Available: http://jrp.icaap.org/index.php/jrp/article/view/405/371, accessed 20 May 2020.

TallBear, K. (2019a). 'Elizabeth Warren's claim to Cherokee ancestry is a form of violence', *High Country News*, 17 January. Available: https://www.hcn.org/issues/51.2/tribal-affairs-elizabeth-warrens-claim-to-cherokee-ancestry-is-a-form-of-violence, accessed 20 May 2020.

TallBear, K. (2019b). Interviewed by Adrienne Keene and Matika Wilbur for *All My Relations*, 'Episode 5: decolonizing sex', 19 March. Available: https://www.allmyrelationspodcast.com/podcast/episode/468a0a6b/ep-5-decolonizing-sex, accessed 20 May 2020.

TallBear, K. (2019c). Interviewed by Brooke Gladstone for *On the Media*, 'By blood, and beyond', WYNC Studios, 19 October. Available: https://www.wnycstudios.org/story/blood-and-beyond-blood?utm_medium=social&utm_source=tw&utm_content=otm&utm_source=tw&utm_medium=spredfast&utm_content=sf93926531&utm_term=onthemedia&sf93926531=1, accessed 20 May 2020.

Uyehara, M. (2018). 'What Elizabeth Warren keeps getting wrong about DNA tests and native American heritage', *GQ*, 11 December. Available: https://www.gq.com/story/elizabeth-warren-dna-tests?fbclid=IwAR18qCzkl7BSGTjExCS3_F_E5EI-vI068nMt7s4UWWVqpwu4P2rzHyqAwr8, accessed 20 May 2020.

Weiss, M. (2011). *Techniques of Pleasure: BDSM and the Circuits of Sexuality*. Duke University Press: Durham, NC.

Willey, A. (2006). '"Christian Nations", "Polygamic Races" and women's rights: Toward a genealogy of non/monogamy and whiteness', *Sexualities*, vol 9: 530–546.

Willey, A. (2016). *Undoing Monogamy: The Politics of Science and the Possibilities of Biology.* Duke University Press: Durham, NC.

WYNC Studios, On the Media with Brooke Gladstone. 'By Blood, and Beyond' Interview with Kim TallBear. https://www.wnycstudios.org/story/blood-and-beyond-blood?utm_medium=social&utm_source=tw&utm_content=otm&utm_source=tw&utm_medium=spredfast&utm_content=sf93926531&utm_term=onthemedia&sf93926531=1. October 19, 2018.

35

Indigeneity and performance

Stephanie Nohelani Teves

Indigenous peoples are always performing. Performance sustains and produces our ongoing brilliance in the face of abject violence. If we did not continue to do what it is that made us who we are as peoples, we would not still be here. There is much critical decolonial work being done to protect, recuperate and revitalise Indigenous cultural performances today in the form of dances, songs, games, sports, and general ways of being (Jacob 2013). And yet, these Indigenous performances are always framed as in deficit or on the verge of vanishing. The focus on Indigenous cultural loss unwittingly supports settler-colonial efforts to delegitimate Indigenous peoples today because of a reliance on tropes of authenticity. We must therefore shift the discourse on Indigenous performance away from seeking authencitiy or recovery, toward constant transformation. If we don't, we will continue to be locked in as 'the Native' in Western discourse, even when we are resisting our own dispossession. Inasmuch as the quest for 'authenticity' is an effort to prove ourselves worthy and as culturally distinct Indigenous peoples with inherent rights to sovereignty, the imperative to produce more 'authentic' forms of culture or to seek out our 'real' or 'pure' prior selves, only means that it is 'culture' and not 'race' that now (doubly) disempowers us (Teves 2018; Da Silva 2007). This is a double-bind for Indigenous peoples whose primary form of identification is through the performance of 'culture', (e.g. dance, seafaring, music, food, relation to land) and is exceptionally tied to cultural values that are often deemed legible by the settler-state (Coulthard 2007b; Povinelli 2002).

To decolonise understandings of Indigenous performance, we must centralise the tenets of what constitutes indigeneity and trouble them deeply. Akin to the kind of epistemological critique of gender performed by Judith Butler in *Gender Trouble* (1990) and *Bodies That Matter* (1993), Critical Indigenous Studies must trouble 'the Native'. In Butler's critique of sex and gender, she argued that the inability to see that gender construction was co-constituted with the illusion of biological sex has doubly disempowered feminist philosophy (as well as the 'women's movement' in general) and re-entrenched the dominance of gender binaries in which 'woman' is subordinate under heteropatriarchy. Applying how gender works on bodily surfaces to become both sites of 'the natural' (biological sex) and the dissonant (gender performance) is critical for thinking through how 'the Native' and what is now termed 'indigeneity' is worked on the bodies of Indigenous peoples (Butler 1990). In other words, what can be observed as 'Native' often rests upon a pre-authorised version of what is perceived to be indigeneity, as it is determined by a specific community as well as the settler-state, but it is often the latter that rests upon essentialist ideas of what is a 'true' or 'authentic' performance of Indigenous identity and life.

My customisation of Butler's theories to the category of 'the Native' is indebted to the theoretical contributions of Native Pacific Cultural Studies. I employ the late Teresia Teaiwa's game-changing articulation of 'the Native'. She writes:

> The Native may have been produced in colonial discourse as an "other" for the European, the colonizer, the civilized; it may have been used in nationalist movements to counterpose the civilization of the colonial European; it may be left behind by immigrants and diasporic subjects, but it will not go away. The Native will not go away – not only because its "original" referent still exists, but because I believe it has always had multiple significations ... the Native is many things before and "after" colonialism, before and "after" migration and diaspora.
>
> *(Teaiwa 2001: 55)*

Teaiwa was a visionary scholar and poet. She remains a foremost scholar of Pacific indigeneity and gender. Her work theorising the relationship between colonialism, gender, and militarisation in the Pacific Islands has rightfully been celebrated as path breaking. But, what is often lost in the way her theories are used, is her attention to the complexities of 'the Native', how this fabricated category is challenged by what are now termed 'Indigenous' people, and in particular, how indigeneity in the Pacific has long been the site of an ongoing struggle to define and constrain 'the Native'.[1] The idea of 'the Native' emerged through colonialism and has meaning now as a subject position that has been infused with Indigenous innovation in the face of efforts to exterminate Indigenous peoples. Indigeneity, especially in the Indigenous Pacific, may have always been about movement, fluidity, and innovation in spite of colonial efforts to affix it in time and space (Teaiwa 2001). And yet, even when we acknowledge 'the Native' was created through colonial discourse and that we are so much more complex than how colonisers marked us, we retain 'the Native' as an essential stability that existed in a 'true' prior state and much labor has been expressed to 'save' cultural forms (like dance or theatre) that can be termed 'Indigenous'.

I add to Teaiwa's and Native Pacific Cultural studies an additional layer of analysis, that is, the notion that indigeneity is a *performative process*. I invoke performance here as action, not as a pure social construction, as many post-structuralists and performance theorists have argued (Bial 2007; Schechner 2006; Striff 2003). This is vital because when indigeneity is understood solely as a subject position as determined by legal administrative measures or even by the observation of cultural activities that are legible as 'Indigenous' in a specific place and time, we neglect to understand that it is a categorisation that formed through colonialism and that Natives have challenged these definitions consistently. It requires work, doing. Indigenous people would not have been able to survive if they had not continued to do or perform what it is that made them 'Native' and that this process will never end. Indigeneity requires action, a performance, and such actions are informed by the knowledge of our culture and our genealogies, but performance also avails itself to new interpretations and techniques that ensure our survival. This is why it is *in process, constant movement, and change* and, correspondingly, resistant to measurement and containment. When we see indigeneity as a performance, we see that it will always survive even if it involves things that seem to challenge our Indigenous authenticity. It exposes 'authenticity' as a colonial measurement; a measurement that we now unfortunately carry out on each other. Giving an account of indigeneity should be a story about Indigenous resurgence and living rather than a story about Indigenous inauthenticity, disappearance, or death.

'Performance' refers to both staged performances and the enactment of everyday life. The latter focuses on how social forces structure the perceived behaviors of certain groups (i.e., sexuality, gender, age, race, class, and indigeneity) (Goffman 1959). Performance itself does not merely reflect social realities but also creates them. Within Native studies there has been more recent attention to the processes of performing indigeneity and how 'Indigenous' as a global category emerged in the Cold War era. Human rights concerns were leveraged by Indigenous peoples around the world interested in preserving distinct cultures and knowledges and a growing attention to the importance of the natural environment (Graham and Glenn 2014). Seeking recognition by a state or federal entity puts the Indigenous subject in a position of performing their culture, always asking to be seen and known, rather than controlling the terms of relationship. These performances have high stakes, often requiring a romanticised performance of indigeneity that Indigenous peoples, in turn, problematically use to police one another and begin to regard certain behaviors as 'traditional' or 'natural' (Graham and Glenn 2014; Wilmer 2009).

We must be critical of the representational apparatuses in which 'traditional' or 'authentic' culture is promoted and what is foreclosed in the process. As Brendan Hokowhitu notes, some expressions of Indigenous pre-colonial pride and I would add cultural revitalisations, requires the death of Indigenous subjectivities that threaten strategic traditionalism. Indigenous peoples, and performers especially, live with this threat of double-jeopardy because conversations about us are almost always framed in dichotomies of authentic versus inauthentic and traditional versus modern (Hokowhitu 2014). This divides our communities, privileges anthropological discourse of us as static Natives and supports settler narratives that use 'authenticity' to argue that our Indigenous political, cultural, and legal claims are irrelevant. I write from the Kānaka Maoli or Indigenous Hawaiian context, where a revered cultural value and performance – aloha – is appropriated by the tourist industry and is in turn, employed as a barometer of Hawaiianness that is used to quiet dissent and encourage the maintenance of the settler-colonial state. Furthermore, Native people 'Playing Indian' might seek to alter stereotypes, but such performances often work to reaffirm stereotypes and expectations of what indigeneity 'ought' to look like for uncritical non-Native audiences be they in the classroom, courtroom or at the beach-side bar who are profoundly attached to the fantasy of the premodern Native (Deloria 1999).

Our performances of culture can thus function as a tool or weapon of the dominant culture, that forces us to perform within the limited and often negating frames set by the dominant culture in order to be seen or recognised as subjects (read: Native/Indigenous) at all. These are the catch-22's of indigeneity. Settlers employ definitions of Indigenous cultures that regulate the limits to indigeneity itself and, thus, the Indigenous identities that prevail via claims to our resources, lands, and sovereignty. We must prove ourselves as 'real' or 'authentic' to secure political recognition and unfortunately, cultural belonging. Indigenous peoples have in turn utilised these same definitions to access the social, economic and political resources that are necessary for our survival (Raibmon 2005).

Indigenous performativity and authenticity

It is the constant performance of expected behaviors and their repetition that create 'performativity', which works through repetition and becomes subconscious and appears natural. Performativity creates norms and transgressions, which contribute to what becomes calcified as the 'real' through repetitious acts. In the Hawaiian context, as a people we are especially beholden to perceptions people have about the commercialised and culturally situated performance of aloha. Any transgression from the happy aloha-filled Native is figured as 'against Aloha' or 'unHawaiian'. For example, the idea that Kānaka Maoli are natural 'performers', that our aloha is supposed to emanate from us is part of a political and discursive practice intended to create a population that can 'naturally' serve tourists. This is policed among ourselves too through internal arguments over what is traditional, who is authentic, or the claims that 'true Hawaiians' are all gone, thus further dividing the Kānaka Maoli community along authentic/ inauthentic lines, where a select few are culturally competent while the rest are not really 'Hawaiian' or just inauthentic-remnants of our former 'Native'-selves. Thus functioning as justification that Kānaka Maoli do not have Indigenous claims because we are all 'mixed' and therefore undeserving of the right to self-government. Our Indigenous performance then operates in two tonalities simultaneously; it is the mechanism by which Kānaka Maoli are hailed as the docile and happy Native while also being a means by which we authenticate ourselves as an original Indigenous group when making claims to sovereignty on the world stage. Thus, one of the most pernicious myths of indigeneity is that everything we do is supposed to be 'natural' because we have some kind of unwavering ability to listen to the heartbeat of the earth and talk to the wind (even if we do).

This damaging romanticism does not belie that Indigenous peoples have a special relationship with the land and ocean. These relations anchor sovereignty claims as well as various Indigenous epistemological frameworks that differentiates us from other ethnic or racial minorities. But, as Hokowhitu explains, the Native's relationship to the land is wrongly misinterpreted as being characterised by 'primitive inertia', which implies that Natives cannot evolve or be civilized or live in urban areas, even though the majority of Indigenous people in settler-states do (Hokowhitu 2008). When Natives are looked to as resources for particular kinds of knowledges (like the ability to *have* aloha) they become equated with nature – a first step in rendering indigeneity as a static object that possesses an essential truth (Smith 2010). While affirming authenticity can sometimes be a necessary tactic to push back against stereotypical imagery of indigeneity, it re-embeds a belief that our 'real' selves existed prior to colonisation and it is dangerously similar to imperialist ideas of the noble savage. This is also a reinvestment in the notion that the 'real' Native exists in their natural state somewhere, uncorrupted by the ills of the West. We must dislodge the flattening of 'the Native' as the pre-discursive foundation upon which modern subjectivity asserts itself.

The performative status of the 'natural' Native needs to be exposed because the power of this myth extends to all facets of Indigenous life. Rather than overemphasise that how we perform is 'natural', a theory of performance allows us to see that what is considered 'natural' was created in opposition (i.e., as a foil) to the more advanced modern subject. By denaturalising what indigeneity is supposed to look like, we allow indigeneity to be performed in very strategic ways. Without presuming a realm of representation as distinct from the realm of the real, we sharpen our tools of analysis to identify the underlying currents of any performance as it emerges out of a particular social formation (Thrift 2008). In other words, we can acknowledge that performance creates and sustains identities, rather than searching for a subject that existed prior to the performance. Performance creates knowledge through action, creating new subjectivities, it is what some scholars have described as worldmaking. That is, the capacity for performance to transform both artist and spectator, enabling new possibilities which may transform social realities (Munoz 1999).

An analysis of racial performativity is also necessary to assess how 'the Native' is routed through colonialism and Indigenous identity and performance. Racial performativity as described by E. Patrick Johnson informs the process by which we invest bodies with social meaning. Johnson's work on Blackness is informative for theorising Indigenous performativity, because as he notes, one's experience of living blackness and the fantasy of Black life as theatrical enterprise are at odds (2003). Johnson's description of this disconnect, is similar to the performative expectations of indigeneity that are informed by social meanings and popular representations. Many people think they know what indigeneity looks like and is; the crying Indian or the hula girl as examples. Both of these tropes do damage that I need not rehearse here, but we must be cognizant of the arbitrariness of authenticity and the dangers of foreclosing possibilities. Paige Raibmon proposes looking at authenticity and the ways that Indigenous peoples deploy it as a shifting set of ideas that work for certain ends, not as a measuring stick (2005). Understanding the processes of performativity offers nuanced methodologies and interpretative modes in which to theorise how dominant modes of indigeneity allow for a narrow set of notes to be sung that, in their coherency and recognition expose the limitations imposed and self-imposed upon Indigenous subjectivities. It is critical to also focus on the dissonant sounds that are incomprehensible so that we can see how indigeneity is made and remade through multiple registers.

Performance economies

There is no shortage of Indigenous people lined up to perform on the market. Indigenous performers and performances sustain state budgets, tribal economies, and individuals' abilities to feed their families. So let me be very clear, Indigenous peoples are not colonial dupes unwilling to be reflexive about our interpellation into capitalist structures of performance. A performance in a commercialised public venue can still be spiritually significant. These are things we know and navigate. We understand the tensions operating in the mass commercialism of our performances, we sometimes consent to our own subjection to put food on the table, and we make purposeful choices to perform our culture affirmatively in the face of colonialism. Indigenous performance is therefore a constant interplay, strategically couched in economic needs as well as ancestral connections, where performance in commercial contexts does not necessarily mean compromise. Performing our culture for tourists or in other commercialised contexts does not lessen who we are as a people, it is a reminder of our enduring presence. When you stand up in front of a crowd of your peers, or strangers, and perform a ritual you might be engaging in a spiritual experience, invoking your ancestors. But you also might be dead-tired, waiting for it to end, rolling your eyes at tourists, or embellishing certain aspects of a dance because you are getting paid and this is what the paying spectators want to see. There is nothing wrong with any of that. The labor of living an Indigenous life, whether you are waiting tables, carrying luggage, pouring concrete, or driving a bus, forces us to participate in the very systems that disempowered our ancestors. All of these performances help us to survive in the face of attempted genocide and ongoing settler-colonialism.

The performance of Indigenous authenticity is a complicated, necessary, and messy response to centuries of misrepresentation. This is also why no one wants to believe that indigeneity is something that is 'performed'. It makes us feel like artificial cultural representatives that are 'vanishing' and must perform a 'real' or 'authentic' version of culture in counter-distinction to the massively commodified performances. The desire to be seen as 'real' – in both formal statecraft and everyday life – is as much a reaction to heavily mediated (mis)representations of Indigenous peoples as it is to deep existentialist determinations of indigeneity. This desire for recognition and respect speaks to a need amongst Indigenous peoples, one that seeks to move beyond stereotypes and one that acknowledges our varied articulations. When Indigenous people internalise one-dimensional versions of ourselves, we keep communities demobilised, contained, and motionless in the same ways that anthropological notions of culture and 'the Native' do. We must turn our attention to the social processes that create identities, which means a move away from conceptions of Natives as 'things' that can be studied. Scott Lyons recommends an analysis of how Natives are active agents who, "assert identity, defining identity, contesting identity, and so forth – under given historical conditions" (Lyons 2010: 59). Doing so negates questions of essentialism and allows a deeper awareness of historical processes.

As a reaction to colonialism, we do, at times, privilege notions of purity and authenticity because it offers us a sense of stability, but when that stability is exposed as a colonial-necessitated desire, we should turn our focus to the multitude of other strategies employed to survive. In the service of cultural nationalism and or in the Hawaiian case, tourist artifice, we have adopted a rigidity around indigeneity and inadvertently in the process, we have marginalised many of our own. To the extent that such cultural forms are posited as having historical depth that reaches into 'pre-colonial' contact, there is also an identification or a bonding that is constructed between the pre-colonial 'Native' and the contemporary cultural nationalist. This cultural connection may be seen by the latter to legitimise and authorise the struggle to 'reclaim' indigeneity through the forms of its cultural differences from the settler-state. Indeed, it is through culture that many of us pursue our liberation, but culture also runs the risk of constituting the form by which Indigenous peoples will once again be shackled.

Performing recognition

Indigenous performances are often required to secure resources necessary for political survival. We must remember that what is 'Native' or 'Indigenous' as Joanne Barker explains, must be understood as always related to legal claims and rights to governance, territories, and cultures which is what makes an understanding of performance so crucial (2017). 'Indigenous' implies jurisdictions, citizenships, and property rights that are deeply entrenched. It is a political status, but it is also flexible, highly contingent on both state and community recognition. In many places, the Indigenous subject has been quantified by blood quantum or other juridical means that position Native people as always vanishing and in a constant state of having to performance and thus, prove their indigeneity, especially in settler-states. The role of performance is critical in this sense because as Elizabeth Povinelli illustrates, Indigenous groups are forced to perform in ways to show themselves as worthy and these performances are sanctioned by the state through a multicultural imaginary that defuses struggles for liberation and ensures the functioning of the modern liberal state (2002). Glen Coulthard has referred to State forms of recognition as a "death dance" that entraps colonised people into performing nationhood in ways that relies on the state to adjudicate it (2007 cited in Smith 2010: online). The moral obligation and responsibility that the liberal multicultural settler-state feels towards its Indigenous subjects is rooted in its desire to understand 'the Native', because it wants to contain 'the Native' by demarcating what types of Native identities and performances are legally permissible and worthy of recognition by the settler-state. Phil Deloria narrates this process in *Playing Indian*, in his description of colonialism holding the Natives still to perform an extraction on them, to take out their essence (1999). The extraction places Natives in a lost past wherein they must constantly reenact this moment of extraction so that colonialism could 'progress' and the Natives would be left to perform their nativeness indefinitely. It is necessary to foreground these critiques of performance and recognition alongside a deeper discussion of 'the Native' within the field.

Recalling 'the logic of elimination' that Patrick Wolfe defines as a way that settlers naturalise their presence on the land in the place of Natives. Settlers eliminate Indigenous culture by assimilating Natives into settler society, erasing Native claims, particularly Native nationality (Wolfe 2006). This assimilation happens in subtle forms of language, for example when Natives are called 'hybrid' or when performances are portrayed in a way that does not connect

Indigenous culture to contemporary struggles for sovereignty. The 'logic of elimination' is not just about a physical and violent genocide, but in in settler laws, policies, and practices. As Barker details, this connects to how 'the Native' is mined for its culture, even in ways that intend to honor and praise or are practiced by non-Indigenous scholar-students seeking to learn, and yet 'the Native' can be erased as a political status at the same time. This is very dangerous in settler-states where international and state recognition of Indigenous rights is predicated on the cultural authenticity of a certain kind of indigeneity (Barker 2017). Settler-colonialism makes it possible – and necessary – to appropriate under the veil of 'honoring' Native peoples. This is a departure from colonial thinking that attempted to remake 'the Native' as a less-Native version of the colonizer. Instead, under settler-colonialism, celebrating, attempting to understand, impersonating or performing indigeneity is not a contradiction for the settler. In fact, such performing allows settlers to feel that they have transcended their own identities while also preserving (and extracting) Native authenticity (and culture) as its possession (Morgensen 2011). Maile Arvin proposes a provocative way to think about this further, her work on possession and regeneration contests Wolfe's formulation of settler-colonialism through a different lens. She argues that settler-colonialism is not simply about a logic of extermination but a logic of colonial reproduction. Native peoples, while always in the process of disappearing, are never supposed to entirely disappear. Rather, she contends that the settler colonial project secures itself through what she calls "possession through whiteness" (Arvin 2019). So, certain performances can be incorporated as a kind of cultural flavor to liven up white culture, while Native culture and politics remain politically neutered and our knowledges remain neglected. This too gets extended to the role of the scholar who extracts Indigenous performance – viewing it as an object to be analysed – rather than a work of innovation and theory that challenges the very epistemological underpinnings of Western academia.

Performance analysis allows us to argue that we strategically perform, that we are not just passive dupes, we have agency and choose to perform even when we know viewers use our performance to reconsolidate stereotypes about us. It is also away that retain our culture and remind non-Natives that what they think they know about us is limited. Natives have always been theatrical, adaptive, and performative without becoming any less Native. As Teaiwa writes:

> While Natives are multitudinous, diverse, and not necessarily invested in discourses on the Native, the Native is a densely-packed repository of often-contradictory investments. While a Native may be at one time or another be more feminine than masculine, more individualistic than communalistic, quite simple and not complex, the Native contains femininity and masculinity, individualism and communalism, simplicity and complexity.
>
> *(2001: 38)*

A better way to think about it is to ask why are we worried that people will say we aren't real, that we aren't authentic? Why are we letting the touristic and colonial visions of what our cultures are define us? When Natives step out of the frames made for them, they are subject to attack, having their authenticity and backgrounds evaluated (Chow 1993). Although these questions are useful for thinking about indigeneity, they can also turn us into "culture cops" as Lyons terms it, resulting in constrained expectations and formations of cultural nationalism that adhere to static notions of indigeneity (2010: 59–61). Advocating for a reframing of the essentialist/non-essentialist debate, Hokowhitu reanalyses performance through Indigenous sovereignty, describing Indigenous sovereignty as a representation of the ways that Indigenous peoples represent their worlds, "whether that be through hybrid or essentialist notions of culture, both forms remain critical to strategic decolonization and fluid epistemologies" (2014: 337). Instead of fearing dilution and a loss of the 'authentic', he focuses instead on the sovereignty of Indigenous peoples and communities to represent themselves alongside a commitment to be self-reflexive (2014).

The power of Indigenous performativity is its ability to create, modify, alter, and revive practices or to make completely new ones out of a reverence for your culture while also critiquing the need to perform a pure indigeneity. Performance also serves as reminders of the ways our ancestors survived too. They did this through a myriad of performances, many of which prompted debate. Just like today. These debates, transformations, and contestations might make us uncomfortable and they certainly make us disagree, but they do not compromise our indigeneity, it makes us vibrant and ever changing, illuminating an Indigenous future, for all of us. Hawaiians know that our kupuna were exceptional navigators and explorers, they were interested in new things and had an incorrigible thirst for knowledge. Yet, we have internalised this notion that we must behave a particular way, a way that is culturally Hawaiian, without outside influences. As David Chang explains, Hawaiians were especially eager to explore the outside world, affirming their sovereignty through a global vision and, "elaborated a critical geography that was both deeply Indigenous and broadly global" (2015). Thus, our kupuna (ancestors) were outward looking and thought globally. There is no such thing as an Indigenous subject untouched by the ideologies of the world or culture in which they inhabit. So, why then, do Indigenous peoples continue to be imagined as static and fixed – by the state and worse, by each other?

Through a framework of Indigenous performativity, we are able to see how indigeneity is made and remade through performances. Indigeneity is in many ways supposed to be about honoring an existence prior to colonisation, one that is carried in the genealogies and cultural practices of Indigenous peoples. Indigenous peoples would not have been able to survive if they had not continued to perform what it is that made them Native (this can take many specific cultural forms). But all performances transform and change. Conditions never remain the same. When we see indigeneity as a performance, we do not have to insist on its authenticity and affirm instead our unwavering defiance in the face of colonial violence.

Scholars working in Critical Indigenous Studies must name and understand the flexibility of Indigenous performance and life. We should always remember the great words of Tongan/Fijian theorist, Epeli Hau'ofa, who writes:

> One of the more positive aspects of our existence in Oceania is that truth is flexible and negotiable, despite attempts by some of us to impose political, religious, and other forms of absolutism. Versions of truth may be accepted for particular purposes and moments, only to be reversed when circumstances demand other versions; and we often accede to things just to stop being bombarded, and then go ahead and do what we want to do anyway.
>
> *(2008: 61)*

It is in this spirit, and in Teaiwa's memory that I retain 'the Native' and 'the real' as part of a flexible theory of identification, mana, and survival, one that performs and is performed, and is able to name the terms of is engagement in the world, whether as paid actors in the hula show who hate their job, but who also recognise every moment as a legacy of their ancestors' struggles that we have the honor to maintain today, however commodified and decontextualised from its 'pure' or 'traditional' origins or intentions.

Note

1 'The Native' is a product of the colonial imagination, a Native person that lives in 'the state of nature' and operates as the opposite of the civilized colonizer. 'The Native' is different from the political

formations of 'Indigenous peoples' as a global category that emerged post-World War II through United Nations organizing.

References

Arvin, M. (2019). *Possessing Polynesians*. Duke University Press: Durham, NC.

Barker, J. (2017). *Critically Sovereign*. Duke University Press: Durham, NC.

Bial, H. (2007). *The Performance Studies Reader* (2nd ed.). Routledge: London

Butler, J. (1990). *Gender Trouble*. Routledge: New York.

Butler, J. (1993). *Bodies That Matter*. Routledge: New York.

Chang, D.A. (2015). '"We will be comparable to the Indian peoples": Recognizing likeness between native Hawaiians and American Indians, 1834–1923', *American Quarterly*, vol 67: 859–886.

Chow, R. (1993). *Where Have All the Natives Gone? Writing Diaspora: Tactics of Intervention in Contemporary Cultural Studies*. Indiana University Press: Bloomington, IN.

Coulthard, G. (2007a). 'Subjects of Empire: Indigenous peoples and the "politics of recognition"', *Contemporary Political Theory*, vol 6: 437–460.

Coulthard, G. (2007b). 'Indigenous peoples and the "Politics of Recognition" in colonial contexts. Paper presented at the cultural studies now conference. University of East London, London, July 22.

Da Silva, D.F. (2007). *Toward a Global Idea of Race*. University of Minnesota Press: Minneapolis, MN.

Deloria, P. (1999). *Playing Indian*. Yale University Press: New Haven, CT.

Goffman, E. (1959). *The Presentation of Self in Everyday Life*. Doubleday: Garden City, NY.

Graham, L.R. and Glenn, P.H. (2014). *Performing Indigeneity: Global Histories and Contemporary Experiences*. University of Nebraska Press: Lincoln, NE.

Hau'ofa, E. (2008). *We Are the Ocean: Selected Works*. University of Hawai'i Press: Honolulu, HI.

Hokowhitu, B. (2008). 'The death of Koro Paka: "Traditional" Māori patriarchy', *The Contemporary Pacific*, vol 20: 115–141.

Hokowhitu, B. (2014). 'Haka: Colonized physicality, body-logic, and embodied sovereignty', in L.R. Graham and P.H. Glenn (eds.) *Performing Indigeneity*. University of Nebraska Press: Lincoln, NE, 273–304.

Jacob, M.M. (2013). *Yakama Rising Indigenous Cultural Revitalization, Activism, and Healing*. University of Arizona Press: Tucson, AZ.

Johnson, E.P. (2003). *Appropriating Blackness: Performance and the Politics of Authenticity*. Duke University Press: Durham, NC.

Lyons, S.R. (2010). *X-marks: Native Signatures of Assent*. University of Minnesota Press: Minneapolis, MN.

Morgensen, S.L. (2011). *Spaces Between Us: Queer Settler Colonialism and Indigenous Decolonization*. University of Minnesota Press: Minneapolis, MN.

Munoz, J.E. (1999). *Disidentifications: Queers of Color and the Performance of Politics*. University of Minnesota Press: Minneapolis, MN.

Povinelli, E.A. (2002). *The Cunning of Recognition: Indigenous Alterities and the Making of Australian Multiculturalism*. Duke University Press: Durham, NC.

Raibmon, P.S. (2005). *Authentic Indians: Episodes of Encounter from the Late-Nineteenth-Century Northwest Coast*. Duke University Press: Durham, NC.

Schechner, R. (2006). *Performance Studies: An Introduction* (2nd ed.). Routledge: New York.

Smith, A. (2010). 'Queer theory and native studies: The heteronormativity of settler colonialism', *GLQ: A Journal of Lesbian and Gay Studies*, vol 16, no 1: 42–68. Available: https://www.muse.jhu.edu/article/372444, accessed 17 May 2020.

Striff, E. (2003). *Performance Studies*. Palgrave Macmillan: London.

Teaiwa, T. (2001). *Militarism, Tourism and the Native: Articulations in Oceania*. PhD Dissertation. University of California: Santa Cruz.

Teves, S.N. (2018). *Defiant Indigeneity: The Politics of Hawaiian Performance*. University of North Carolina Press: Chapel Hill, NC.

Thrift, N.J. (2008). *Non-Representational Theory: Space, Politics, Affect*. Routledge: London.

Wilmer, S.E. (2009). *Native American Performance and Representation*. University of Arizona Press: Tucson, AZ.

Wolfe, P. (2006). 'Settler colonialism and the elimination of the native', *Journal of Genocide Research*, vol 8: 387–409.

36

Indigenous insistence on film

Jo Smith

Introduction

In promotional materials surrounding a 2012 First Peoples Cinema festival held in Toronto, co-curator and CBC pop culture critic Jesse Wente (Ojibwe) described the event as part of a new wave of Indigenous cinema "now starting to crest" (Dixon 2012, para 2). This new wave describes Aboriginal and Indigenous film-making from across the globe including countries such as Australia, Canada, the United States, New Zealand, Samoa, the Artic Circle, and the Philippines, and includes films such as Warwick Thorton's *Samson and Delilah* (2009), Taika Waititi's *Boy* (2010), and Jeff Barnaby's *Rhymes for Young Ghouls* (2013). In later interviews, Wente marks this new period as beginning with the commercially and aesthetically successful *Atarnajuat: The Fast Runner* (2001), the first Indigenous-language film to win the Camera d'Or at Cannes. According to Wente, this Inuit historical epic has influenced a range of Indigenous creatives and has proved that Indigenous filmic storytelling can appeal to international audiences (Bergstrom 2015). A new wave must necessarily have an earlier period to distinguish itself by, and Wente names Chris Eyre's *Smoke Signals* (1998), Lee Tamahori's *Once Were Warriors* (1994), and the Australian-based films of Tracey Moffat as important precursors. According to this logic, Indigenous film-makers in the 21st century can now build on a prior Indigenous film legacy from across the world to hone, develop, and disseminate production techniques and filmic discourses that reflect Indigenous world-views and sensibilities.

The emergence of Indigenous film and media corresponds to political agitation for Indigenous political rights in the late 1960s and early 1970s in Canada, Australia, New Zealand, and the United States as well as other territories (Ginsburg 1999; Gauthier 2013; Pearson and Knabe 2015; Smith 2016b). Indigenous innovations and revisions of the documentary form were dominant practices at this time and functioned to disrupt the truth regimes of colonialist enthographic practices that figured Indigenous peoples as objects of a colonial gaze (Ginsburg 1995; Rony 1996; Knopf 2008). Wente's claim to a new wave focuses on the rise of Indigenous feature-length dramas such as the films noted above, and he suggests that the end result of this Indigenous new wave might be a more populist form of film-making than the earlier period (Bergstrom 2015).

Keeping in mind that Wente's claim of a new wave comes from his role as a curator and social commentator and therefore tactical manoeuvres to promote Indigenous film-making, this chapter uses Wente's provocation to organise a snapshot of some of the ways in which Indigenous film-making can be currently understood. In what follows I offer a situated approach to understanding contemporary Indigenous film that draws on my own place-based identity as someone with whakapapa links to Kāi Tahu peoples, but a scholar with a long-standing interest in the impact and import of Māori media.[1] Indigenous film pioneers Merata Mita and Barry Barclay have shaped my thinking about media in general and their enduring legacy can be seen in two local art exhibitions that, at the time of writing, feature works by new artists influenced by Mita's decolonising screen practices and Barclay's idea of Fourth Cinema.[2] I engage with critical commentary around Barclay's notion of Fourth Cinema to address a recent portmanteau film, *Waru* (2018) made by a collective of wāhine Māori (Māori women), who present a multi-faceted response to a pressing social problem. In doing so, I argue that *Waru* continues the legacy of Barclay's conceptual and practical approach to film-making. My conclusion speculates on the lessons we can learn from *Waru* about a critical Indigenous studies approach to our film-making in the 21st century.

A contemporary context for understanding Indigenous film

If we are to make a distinction, between contemporary Indigenous film-making as opposed to earlier periods, that distinction would include the technological shifts that now afford audiences more immediate access to Indigenous media content (for example, Inuit provider Isuma. tv, IndigiTube in Australia, and nzonscreen in Aotearoa/New Zealand).[3] It would include those emerging and established state-funded media organisations that foster Indigenous voices onscreen such as the Inuit Broadcasting Corporation (IBC), National Indigenous Television (NITV) in Australia, Māori Television in Aotearoa/New Zealand, the Aboriginal Peoples Television Network (APTN), the National Film Board (NFB) both in Canada as well as US Native American Public Telecommunications to name a few. A burgeoning film festival circuit which brings Indigenous creatives together to foster artistic and industry skills is also a feature of current conditions and includes Sundance Film Festival Native Lab, the Sámi-run Skábmagovat Film Festival, the ImagineNATIVE Film and Media Arts Festival in Toronto, the National Museum of the American Indian in New York (NMAI), WINDA, the Wairoa Māori film festival in Aotearoa/New Zealand as well as the recent addition of the Māoriland film festival hosted in the small, vibrant town of Otaki. Film-makers in the 21st century also build on the legacies of earlier Indigenous film pioneers, some of whom include Sherman Alexie (Spokane-Coeur d'Alene), Barry Barclay (Ngāti Apa), Chris Eyre (Cheyenne and Arapaho), Merata Mita (Ngāti Pikiao, Ngāi Te Rangi), Victor Masayesva Jnr. (Hopi), Tracey Moffatt (Aboriginal Australian), Alanis Obomsawin (Abanaki) Sandra Osawa (Makah), Arrente/Kalkadoon woman Rachel Perkins, Gamilaroi man Ivan Sen, Mona Smith (Sisseton-Wahpeton Dakota), and Kaytej man Warwick Thornton.

Such changes in the world of Indigenous film must also be contextualised within wider and more directly political shifts for Indigenous peoples since 2000. These include state-led reconciliation processes such as the 2008 formal apology from the Australian government for the stolen generations of Aboriginal children and Canada's acknowledgement that same year of the native children who have suffered through the nation's residential schooling system. The 2007 Declaration on the Rights of Indigenous Peoples and the subsequent recognition of this document by Australia in 2009 and Canada and New Zealand in 2010 is also a factor shaping the context for understanding 21st-century Indigenous film. Institutional shifts in the state-funding of Indigenous media content must also be considered. The Fourth worlds of Indigenous film-making necessarily involve larger state initiatives that have a history of drawing on things

Indigenous to distinguish themselves on a global stage.[4] Space does not allow for a full account of these wider political and institutional forces. Instead, I will test the idea that Indigenous film-making at times moves beyond the identity categories that plague Indigenous cultural production to affirm deeply place-based expressions of Indigeneity that pose a challenge to understanding pan-Indigenous film-making.

A working definition for pan-Indigenous film-making

Defining the idea of Indigenous film-making is a typical first step in the literature in order to understand the diverse investments attached to such a category as well as the assertion of Indigenous identity contained within it. Wente's working definition can be summarised in the now popularised phrase 'nothing about us without us' that originally emerged out of the health research sector in Australia.[5] An equivalent standpoint from the viewpoint of Aotearoa would be 'by Māori, for Māori'. That is to say, such film-making is produced by key identifiable Indigenous creatives, it engages in a politics of recognition and representation, and its conditions of production and consumption privilege Indigenous ways of knowing and doing. 'Nothing about us, without us' implicitly acknowledges the decades of film-making practices that have either misrepresented, misrecognised, or altogether erased Indigenous peoples in the social imaginaries of settler nations. It is a phrase that asserts Indigenous agency and capacity for sovereignty through cinema while at the same time it assumes an unproblematic notion of 'us' as Indigenous people.

In addition, this approach does not account for those Indigenous creatives, technicians and actors who have contributed to, or are influenced and aided by majority culture cinematic practices. Nor does this categorisation include the archival powers of colonial film that Indigenous creatives draw on to revitalise or reconfigure the colonial present for Indigenous purposes. For example, while no one would argue that Alfred Cort Haddon's 1898 film documents of Mer Islanders in Torres Strait would constitute Indigenous film-making, the uses Eddie Koiki Mabo made of this footage in 1992 to prove traditional ownership of land certainly does fit with a category of cinema premised on pathways to Indigenous self-determination. Similarly, Ngāti Porou artist Natalie Robertson draws on James McDonald's 1923 film *Scenes of Maori Life on the East Coast* to benchmark the historical shape and health of her ancestral river and the subsequent impacts of colonisation witnessed in the landscapes and waterways today due to industrialised agriculture and forestry (Robertson 2019). McDonald's footage helps Robertson fulfil kaitiakitanga (guardianship) obligations for a river that is also a tupuna (ancestor). As such, filmic content such as this may arise from colonial contexts, yet the use made of this material by contemporary Indigenous practitioners and activists, tests the parameters of what might constitute the category 'Indigenous film-making'.

Te Ātiawa scholar Alice Te Punga Somerville, writing on the ways in which global film culture impacts on localised Indigenous identities, observes that trying to unpack the multiple uses of the term 'Indigenous' leads to theoretical dead-ends and that it is best to "allow space for contingency, flexibility, and negotiation" (Te Punga Somerville 2010: 666). This chapter follows this approach and argues for an expansive understanding of Indigenous film-making that takes into account not only the conditions of filmic production and aesthetic practices specific to Indigenous film, but also the conditions of consumption and critical reception that attend this kind of cultural production.

Ngāti Pūkenga scholar Brendan Hokowhitu and Vijay Devadas offer a useful definition of the global Indigenous movement as a discursive formation that draws on comparative Indigenous methods, and a critically-inflected universal Indigenous theory, to address the diverse worldviews located in specific territories (Hokowhitu and Devadas 2013: xix). Yet Hokowhitu also warns us of the risks of such transnational categories when he writes, "[g]iven that a pan-Indigenous collective consciousness must operate beyond the local, there is a tendency to gravitate to unifying concepts that in their own way debilitate native alterity" (Hokowhitu 2013: 112). And native alterity here can be understood as a form of radical difference that overturns established epistemological orthodoxies that contain and regulate the possibilities of Indigenous lives.

So, how to understand the dynamic of Indigenous *film-making* given this approach to the place-based *and* globalised idea of Indigeneity and the political and ontological value of affirming native alterity? To address these issues we can turn to the logic of film-making itself. In the words of global film scholars Toby Miller and Mariana Johnson, "[t]he life of any popular or praised text is a passage across space and time, a life remade again and again by institutions, discourses, and practices of distribution and reception" (2008: 261). Indigenous in the context of cultural products such as film then (including shorts, documentaries, feature films, animation and experimental digital media forms) means to understand the localised, embedded – Donna Haraway would say situated – knowledges, ideas, and storytelling conveyed by the vehicle of a particular film as much as the ways in which these stories, sounds, ideas and images travel, or are made mobile – and meaningful – through international forms of distribution, consumption, and engagement. So Somerville's focus on 'contingency, flexibility, and negotiation' applies not only to the label 'Indigenous' but also to the dynamics of film-making, its critical reception and consumption. Hokowhitu's focus on the critical importance of native alterity chimes with the ways in which films travel and 'land' in the context of their consumption, remaking time and again, contingent and negotiated expressions of Indigenous realities.

Here I am mindful too, of an oft-cited quotation from Aboriginal Australian intellectual Marcia Langton who argues for an understanding of Aboriginality as "a field of intersubjectivity that is remade over and over again in a process of dialogue, of imagination, of representation and interpretation" (cited in Columpar 2010: xiv). Intersubjectivity in the original context of Langton's argument relates to the encounter between Indigenous and non-Indigenous peoples and the discursive entanglements accompanying media technologies within a settler nation. Perhaps, in light of Wente's somewhat overly optimistic notion of an emerging Indigenous new wave as well as the rise of pan-Indigenous methodological practices, Indigenous film-making is now increasingly shaped by intersubjective encounters between Indigenous creatives and native forms of alterity as well as media cultures from majority cultures within national and international contexts. The challenge of addressing these complex discursive interplays lies in finding a balance between the site-specific and historically inflected forms of Indigenous creative expression and epistemes as they engage in, and interact with, more globalised modes of communication. I attempt this balancing act below with reference to two key concepts in the existing literature on Indigenous film.

Two conceptual approaches to Indigenous film-making: Visual sovereignty and Fourth Cinema

The growing body of Indigenous films has resulted in an increase in academic publications dedicated to the topic, including many non-Indigenous authors. Earlier scholarship emerged from the field of visual anthropology and include the work of Sol Worth and John Adair, Eric Michaels, Terence Turner, and Faye Ginsburg. Recent academic book authors relevant to Indigenous film from Canada, Australia, the United States, and New Zealand include Angela Aleiss, Corinn Columpar, Kirsten L. Dowell, Jennifer Deger, Mike Gasher, Joanna Hearne, Jacquelyn Kilpatrick, Kerstin Knopf, Stephen Leuthold, Stuart Murray, Beverly Singer, Michelle Raheja, and Houston Wood. Relevant edited collections include *Media Worlds: Anthropology on New Terrain* (2002), *Global Indigenous Media: Cultures, Poetics and Politics* (2008), *Visualities: Perspectives on Contemporary American Indian Film and Art* (2011), *The Fourth Eye: Māori Media in Aotearoa/New Zealand* (2013), *Indigenous Screen Cultures in Canada* (2010), and *Reverse Shots: Indigenous Film and Media in an International Context* (2015). As some of these titles suggest, academic work dedicated to Indigenous film demonstrates a prevailing interest in disrupting those majority culture scopic regimes that have dehumanised Indigenous peoples and how Indigenous creatives negotiate and 'talk back' to these practices.

Central to the notion of 'talking back' is the idea that Indigenous screen cultures have the capacity to express visual (and audio) forms of sovereignty. In *Reservation Reelism: Redfacing, Visual Sovereignty, and Representations of Native Americans in Film* (2010) Seneca scholar Michelle H. Raheja defines visual sovereignty as, "a concept specific to visual culture and aesthetics but rooted in thinking about sovereignty in other contexts" (Raheja 2011: xii). These other contexts include the realm of politics and law and in her approach Raheja calls on the earlier work of Jolene Rickard (Tuscarora) who has argued for including the arts in discussions of sovereignty, as well as Beverly R. Singer's (Tewa and Dine) emphasis on 'cultural sovereignty' and Osage scholar Robert Allen Warrior's concept of 'intellectual sovereignty' (Raheja 2010: 194). Sovereignty is a term handed down from a Western European tradition discussed philosophically by Western intellectuals such as Thomas Hobbes, John Locke and Jean-Jacques Rousseau. Its meaning in political theory refers to the ultimate overseer or authority in the decision-making process of the state. Yet, Indigenous peoples have their own terms for describing authority and self-determination (tino rangatiratanga in the context of Aotearoa) but must work within Western-defined paradigms of sovereignty in order to effect social change and achieve social justice. Accordingly, the contradictions of sovereignty are numerous but the term 'visual sovereignty' is useful for shining light on how Indigenous film-makers work within *and* against prevailing representational and aesthetic traditions to assert Indigenous voices and experiences.

Raheja's argument about visual sovereignty is put to work in a reading of Zacharias Kunuk's and Igloolik Isuma Productions' *Atanarjuat: The Fast Runner* (2001), the film mentioned by Wente as constituting a 'new wave' of Indigenous film. *Atanarjuat* features an all-Inuit cast, is based on an Inuit oral tradition, filmed on the territories where the drama occurred and deploys cinematic techniques that make the landscape a palpable force. It has an intimate relationship with Robert Flaherty's 1922 film *Nanook of the North* which, while contributing to a form of "Eskimo orientalism" (Raheja 2010: 210) has also been a source of empowerment and agency for Inuit peoples (Ginsburg 2002). Raheja states:

> I suggest a reading practice for thinking about the space between resistance and compliance wherein Indigenous filmmakers and actors revisit, contribute to, borrow from, critique, and reconfigure ethnographic film conventions, at the same time operating within and stretching the boundaries created by these conventions.
>
> *(Raheja 2013: 30)*.

For Raheja, such specific expressions of *Inuit* visual sovereignty have the capacity to deconstruct stereotypical representations of Indigenous peoples more generally, as well as contribute to the "intellectual health" of communities who prevail in the aftermath of colonisation (Raheja 2013: 60). A film such as *Atanarjuat* "permits the flow of Indigenous knowledge about such key issues as land rights, language acquisition, and preservation by narrativizing local and international struggles" (Raheja 2013: 62). Raheja argues that films such as this offer "more room for narrative play" that can contribute to "more imaginative renderings of Native American intellectual and cultural paradigms" (Raheja 2013: 65). Raheja goes on to develop the idea of a "virtual reservation" as a creative and decolonising space "where indigenous artists collectively and individually employ technologies and knowledges to rethink the relationship between media and indigenous communities" (Cummings 2011: 6).

I'm struck by Raheja's idea that Indigenous film can provoke 'thinking about sovereignty in other contexts' and to explore this claim I turn to another Indigenous context, that of Aotearoa/ New Zealand and the work of Barry Barclay. Like Raheja, Barclay draws on Māori concepts to address film-making practices. His notion of a 'communication marae' could be fruitfully explored in relation to Raheja's 'virtual reservation'. Yet it is another concept from Barclay that I explore below to try to think about 'sovereignty in other contexts'. If, as Raheja states, an Indigenous film can 'permit the flow of Indigenous knowledge' with the right kind of reading practice, what about an Indigenous film concept? Are we now at a point in time in the scholarship to make 'more imaginative renderings' of Indigenous intellectual paradigms?

Ngāti Apa film-maker and philosopher Barry Barclay's concept of Fourth Cinema is a touchstone for Indigenous film scholars and links to the idea of self-determination embedded in the notion of visual sovereignty. In a 2003 lecture Barclay invoked Fourth Cinema as a new genus of film-making that extends the more conventional categories of First, Second, and Third Cinemas. First Cinema designates Hollywood product, Second Cinema is art-house cinema of the middle classes, and Third Cinema describes those national and independent films made in non-Western nations (for example, Africa, Latin America, and Asia). According to Barclay, those who belong to the "ancient remnant cultures persisting within the modern nation state" produce Fourth Cinema (Barclay 2002). This is film-making that arises from engagement with the community depicted, it is focused on 'interior' values rather than surface features and includes innovations in filmic form that offer images of dignity to Indigenous peoples (Murray 2008). Yet the reception of Barclay's idea by non-Indigenous film scholars has focused on the problem of categorisation embedded in the term, and *not* on its creative potential. In her book *Unsettling Sights: The Fourth World on Film* Corinn Columpar argues that Fourth Cinema as a category "speaks persuasively to the ideological and aesthetic stakes of Indigenous cinema. As an actual taxomic category, however, it inherits a problem fundamental to the three-cinema model from which it derives" (Columpar 2010: xiv). That is to say, the category fails to address the complex interactions that occur across all four categories. Alternately, Houston Wood describes Barclay's approach as "at once simpler and stricter" where the Indigenous status of a film is based on whoever has creative control (Wood 2013: 37).

Yet, according to scholar Stephen Turner, a close friend of Barclay's, Fourth Cinema's classificatory parameters are designed to provoke debate and is *not* a strict categorical imperative (Turner 2013: 163). Noting that the category does not include all forms of cinema, Turner highlights the politically strategic dimensions of Barclay's position as Indigenous spokesperson when he writes: "Barclay was looking for a term that might offer film critics, who like to organize materials in categorical terms, a way of talking about a kind of film that remains little talked about in the university and film-journal world" (Turner 2013: 163). That is to say, Barclay's categorical imperative 'Fourth Cinema' is an incitement to public discourse. His concept is a strategic intervention in academic habits designed to proliferate debate and discussion about Indigenous lives and their creative outputs, as well as the contexts from which these creative works arise, and how they circulate. As such, the 'flow of Indigenous knowledge' circulating around Barclay's term has been channelled back by Wood and Columpar into orthodox and non-Indigenous pathways characterised by an obsession with categories, labels, and identity debates. The question then becomes for scholars interested in Indigenous film-making, how to reinject a form of 'narrative play' that offers more 'imaginative renderings' of the concept, Fourth Cinema?

Following the suggestion of his Indigenous colleague Charise Schwalger, Turner argues that Fourth Cinema should be understood as a *taniwha*, a term specific to the Indigenous context of Aotearoa/New Zealand, which refers to a water creature who takes on many forms according to the traditions of particular peoples and places. A taniwha is also a symbol for great chiefs. Turner writes:

> The shape-shifting quality of this spirit creature, often associated with water and danger, suggests to me a limit-point to settler vision and sense of place. Where the short history of national orthodoxy shades into long history, the shape of place shifts. The dread of this moment for non-Māori – where am I now? – makes the *taniwha* apposite, and makes Fourth Cinema a switch point.
>
> *(Turner 2013: 163)*

Turner goes on to argue that Fourth Cinema "is a term for a force or presence that animates Indigenous media more generally". It is a force or presence, rooted in "the myriad particularity of Indigenous cultures" (2013: 165). This force, presence, and *insistence* cannot be captured by orthodox and non-Indigenous regimes of representation and relates to the long-standing First Law of local peoples. It is an event that expresses living relations, a way of organising and conceiving of life that figures landscapes and waterways as beings with agential force. Writing in another context Smith and Turner clarify this particular force:

> By 'presencing', we mean the insistence of First peoples on a prior relation to place, understood in First peoples' terms and no one else's. Such presencing may be juxtaposed with the colonial present just as insistence may be conjoined with resistance. Indigenous political ontology requires no recognition from non-Indigenous people of its substance in order to be the power-that-it-is; that is what we mean by taking it as given. This presupposition (the givenness of the given) also enfolds a mode of being – and doing – that expresses sovereign capacities.
>
> *(Smith and Turner 2013: 276)*

Approaching Fourth Cinema as a shape-shifting taniwha with sovereign capacities suggests a more creative and affirmative approach to Indigenous film-making practices. This critical and creative approach goes beyond identity categories and modes of address designed to 'talk back' to non-Native peoples, paradigms and purposes. It is an approach that acknowledges the performative force of film as a vehicle of Indigenous insistence and one that chimes with Anishinaabe writer Gerald Vizenor's concept of 'survivance', an unforgettable active presence (Vizenor 2008).

I am not suggesting that all Indigenous films must now be understood as taniwha, but I do argue for maintaining the sense of native alterity (invoked by Brendan Hokowhitu earlier) embodied by the taniwha figure when talking about Indigenous film. The taniwha may be a "greased pig" in other Indigenous contexts as Cherokee film-maker Randy Redroad has named the slippery category "Native film" (Marrubbio 2013: 298). Such cinema might be seen "through the lens of a particular Indigenous epistemic knowledge" such as prophecy (Cummings 2011: 5). Following these various Indigenous authors I argue for an affirmative and creative approach to Indigenous film that imagines the power of these films beyond a politics of recognition. This approach also chimes with Redroad's wariness of the tendency of Indigenous film-makers to simply provide revisionist or decolonising responses to majority culture. He states:

I find 'talking back' to be a slippery slope as well. We have to be careful or we can end up dignifying what we're battling, because we aren't imagining ourselves outside it. ...Want to portray Indians differently? Then portray Indians differently. Just do your thing. You're still an Indian.

(Marubbio 2013: 299)

It could be that Indigenous film-makers in the 21st century are increasingly taking this affirmative kind of approach. Scholarship about Indigenous film needs to follow suit. Below I offer a reading of a recent film from Aotearoa/New Zealand that demonstrates both a critical *and* creative approach to film-making that takes, as a given, Indigenous capacities for sovereign expression.

Indigenous insistence onscreen

Waru (2017) is a portmanteau drama consisting of eight short films made by eight wāhine Māori directors (Briar Grace-Smith, Casey Kaa, Ainsley Gardiner, Katie Wolfe, Ranae Maihi, Chelsea Cohen, Paula Whetu Jones, Josephine Stewart-Te Whiu, and Awanui Simich-Pene).[6] The film addresses the topic of child abuse and all eight films are linked to the death of a young boy named Waru. Producers Kerry Warkia and Kiel McNaughton set strict conditions for each director. Each story must start at 9.59 AM on the day of Waru's tangi (funeral), the story must unfold in real time, action must be shot in one take (although some edits were used), the main protagonist must be wāhine Māori and must be connected in some way to Waru's death. Over the course of the anthology we meet Charm, the lead cook at Waru's tangi who has saved a child from violence in the past. Anahera is a teacher who must explain the death of Waru to her pupils even as she suffers from guilt about his passing. Impoverished single mother Mihi struggles to care for her kids and receives help from her Pākehā neighbour. Em is a young mum who finds her infant alone in a locked house after she comes home from a night of drinking. Ranui is a grandmother who comes to the tangi to reclaim Waru and restore his mana. Kiritapu is a news reporter who takes over the studio camera to interupt and speak back to the racist diatribe of her co-worker. The teenage Mere calls out her abuser as well as the community who are complicit through silence. Titty and Bash are sisters who are on the way to save other children from their violent home situation.

The portmanteau structure set by the producers results in a complex and kaleidoscopic treatment of the topic of child abuse. This is a collective and women-led form of storytelling that reveals the historical and wider social forces (poverty linked to landless and colonial occupation, the news media and its perpetuation of a colonial present, toxic forms of masculinity, addiction) that contribute to domestic violence. While set primarily in a small Māori community, the film addresses the established orthodoxy that child abuse is a particularly 'Māori issue' (Maydell 2017). This is done is a rather didactic manner through the figure of Kiritapu, who calls out the media's role in framing child abuse as the result of innately violent cultural tendencies. In an interview, producer Kerry Warkia framed the issue this way, "In New Zealand we're told it's a Māori problem, and when a child is killed the mother is always vilified. We felt it was time to hear from Māori women about this issue" (Vourlias 2017, para 4). The righteous anger, grief and compassion that flows from the screen – channelled by the actors as well as the camera-as-active-agent – makes *Waru* a powerful expression of mana wāhine Māori. It also requires some brave performances from its men.

The eight separate insights into Waru's surrounding environment offer multiple viewpoints that underscore the complexity of the issue, thus framing child abuse as a systemic and not an individualised issue. The film demonstrates how there is no one solution to such an issue. Yet the film also makes intense appeals to the audience to follow or be carried away by the action and to empathise with the protagonists. This is achieved through the use of mobile framing, close-up shots and, at times, spiralling cinematography necessitated by the contraint of a one-take approach. In Charm's story the camera follows her movements in the kitchen as she weaves between stovetop, bench, people, and produce and as she calls out instructions, offers advice or engages with an unwanted visitor. The camera is a highly animated spirit in the call and response action (invoking ihi, wehi, the wanawana) of the karanga between Ranui and Waru's maternal grandmother. When Em hits the ground and blacks out while holding her baby, the camera hovers above her head, frames her face in close-up and waits for her to regain consciousness. The camera is at times a silent witness to Em's dysfunction, or a supporting presence that urges her on to care for her child. In all eight stories the camera cannot be ignored. In the final story Bash directly addresses the camera as she enters a house to rescue children. Her direct address breaks the fantasy of a fourth wall between the spectator and filmic world and implicates the viewer in her actions. Bash has made a decisive decision to intervene in a family situation and her appeal to viewers of the film, is to consider doing the same. In relation to all that has gone before, this direct address functions as a switch point.

When discussing Barclay's film *Ngati* Stuart Murray has argued that the work appears, on the surface, to be an orthodox narrative: a small boy is dying of luekemia, an Australian doctor returns home, there is a fight to keep the freezing works open. But below the surface the film fosters "radical ideas about iwi and community" (Murray 2008: 8). It is a form of ventriloquisim that emulates the aesthetic norms of national and international filmic regimes, but it has an interior world operating *within and against* this regime to give voice to things Māori. Noting the focus on interior values pursued by Barclay in his creative endeavours, Stephen Turner writes, "But Indigenous film looks and does not look like other kinds of film. It behaves differently. The inseparable historical, political, and aesthetic properties of Indigenous cinema make it different in kind" (Turner 2013: 164). So too *Waru*, on the surface offers a series of short films that may be aligned with certain categories of social realism or 'issues-based' cinema, but it also has an interior life based upon principles that come only from te ao Māori. The use of cinematography and the powerful onscreen performances beg a kaupapa Māori approach to filmic analysis where specifically Māori cultural concepts such as wairua, ihi, wehi and wanawana can be explored. This approach would complement an emerging body of work focused on kaupapa Māori popular culture scholarship (Barnes 2011; Mercier 2010; Wilson 2013; Hyland 2015; Smith 2016a; Moewaka Barnes et al. 2017).

Waru takes a critical *and* creative approach to the painful topic of child abuse by fearlessly facing it head on, unafraid of a wider social context where Māori are stigmatised by domestic abuse issues. It implicitly asks, why must Māori be the bearers of this chronic national, and global, condition? The production process has collectivised the power of mana wāhine Māori who speak out, first and foremost, to Māori and Indigenous audiences (the film opened the 2017 imagineNATIVE Film and Media Arts Festival). Yet it also includes non-Māori audiences (New Zealand film critics have been united in their praise for the film). The film stages an Indigenous encounter with its audience and insists upon some kind of response. The grief, rage, confusion, and shame invoked onscreen functions as a switch point; it is a taniwha, an assertive and insistent Indigenous presence that calls for new ways of being in the world.

Yet this interior world may not be visible to all audiences of *Waru*, nor need it be so. As Christine Milligan (Ngāti Porou) reminds us, Barclay has always acknowledged the limits of cross-cultural dialogue through film. She writes:

> In a metaphorical discussion of his own experience of reading a sequence of headstones from ancient Greece, he draws attention to how a lack of knowledge beyond one's own

culture inhibits the accurate reading of stories from another culture. He maps this directly onto the position of the indigenous film-maker, whose work he sees as being misunderstood and misread by the majority settler cultures within which indigenous film-makers operate.

(Milligan 2015: 349)

The range of mis-readings that occur could also involve other Indigenous viewers not attuned to the culturally specific nature of Indigeneity within the context of Aotearoa. But this may not be an object to the cultivation of a politics of affinity across Indigenous contexts. The forms of native alterity that flow from the interior world of *Waru* are in excess of any one meaning made and this is the taniwha power of film. This filmic behaviour requires a response in kind: empathetic and attentive, open and expansive, from scholars invested in supporting the pedagogic perspectives offered by Indigenous film, as much as the audiences who witness and experience these effects.

Conclusions

In Merata Mita's seminal essay, 'The Soul and the Image', she addresses the power of cinema and Māori film-makers to influence and effect social change. As she writes, Māori film-makers "have the capacity of indigenising the screen in any part of the world our films are shown. This represents power and is one reason we make films which are uniquely and distinctly Māori" (Mita 1996: 54). I have always been sceptical of this claim because of the diverse meanings of film that can be made by different audiences, and varying historical and cultural contexts. Audiences are multifarious and ever-changing, and sometimes supposedly cross-cultural and decolonising dialogues only appear as opaque monologues. Yet, Wente's claim to a 'new wave' of Indigenous film-making, his championing of the cross-over appeal of *Atanarjuat*, and the increasing access audiences and scholars have to experiencing these films, stories, truths, and aesthetic events, makes me imagine how contemporary Indigenous films now speak of matters beyond, but nonetheless connected to, prior painful histories of disappearance, disenfranchisement, and the ongoing effects of colonisation. Revisiting Barclay's concept of Fourth Cinema and experiencing a film such as *Waru* makes me rethink my scepticism about Mita's claim. At this point in time, while films directed by Māori women as still few and far between, *Waru* is an example of 21st-century Indigenous film-making that affirms Indigenous realities on their own terms. Describing the influence that Mita had on her, Chelsea Cohen (Ngāti Ranginui), one of the directors of *Waru* and a notable film producer, talks about Mita's views on contemporary film-making. I leave the final words to her:

> Merata talks about storytelling in phases. She said, when she was starting out, it was a matter of talking to ourselves and trying to come to terms with what was happening to Māori as a whole. Trying to understand the situation. Kind of like unravelling decolonisation, and figuring out how you fit in that whole space. But now we're at a point where Māori films, and other indigenous films, have so much heart, and there are so many different layers to what people want to talk about. They don't have to be all dark and brooding and sad stories. By no means. Taika [Waititi] has proven that. He has a real resonance with international audiences because he has such irreverent humour and he's a bit silly.

(Husband 2018: online)

Notes

1 These include publications such as Smith (2016b) and Smith and Mercier (2012). This chapter builds upon an earlier discussion of media and Indigenous insistence in Smith (2013), and Smith and Turner (2013).

2 These include *Māori Moving Image: An Open Archive* at the Dowse Art Museum, Wellington 30 March –21 July 2019 and *From the Shore* at Pataka Art and Museum, Wellington 7 April–21 July 2019. The exhibition title of the latter references one of Barry Barclay's terms for Indigenous cinema.

3 See https://firstnationsmedia.org.au/our-industry/online-media-platforms.

4 Elsewhere, I have discussed how the settler nation of Aotearoa has a legacy of drawing on Māori content to make distinctive an otherwise 'beige' national identity. See Smith (2012; 2014).

5 Wente agreed with this phrase to describe Indigenous film in Canada in an interview for CBC News: The National that also included Anishinaabe film-maker Lisa Jackson, Inuk film-maker Alethea Arnaquq-Baril and long-time Indigenous reporter Duncan McCue (Anishinaabe). See "Influential filmmakers react to state of Indigenous film in Canada", 20 June 2018, https://www.youtube.com/watch?v=peRTgZbuE0s. The phrase has Polish origins and has been made popular by the South African disability movement.

6 *Waru* was funded by Māori language media agency Te Māngai Pāho, NZ On Air, Māori Television, and the New Zealand Film Commission.

Bibliography

Barclay, B. (1990). *Our Own Image*. Longman Paul: Auckland.

Barclay, B. (1991). 'Housing our image destiny', *Illusions*, vol 17: 39–42.

Barclay, B. (2003) 'Exploring Fourth Cinema'. 'Re-Imagining Indigenous Cultures: The Pacific Islands' National Endowment for the Humanities, Summer Institute, July.

Barclay, B. (2006). *Mana Tuturu: Māori Treasures and Intellectual Property Rights*. University of Hawai'i Press: Honolulu, HI.

Barnes, A.M. (2011). *Ngā kai para i te kahikātoa: Māori Filmmaking, Forging a Path*. PhD thesis, University of Auckland, NZ.

Barnes, A.M. (2018). 'Kia manawanui: Kaupapa Māori theoretical framework', *MAI Journal*, vol 7, no 1: 3–17.

Bergstrom, A. (2015). 'An Indigenous new wave of film', *3 Brothers Film*. Available: https://3brothersfilm.com/blog/2015/10/30/an-indigenous-new-wave-of-film, accessed 16 October 2019.

Columpar, C. (2010). *Unsettling Sights: The Fourth World on Film*. Southern Illinois University Press: Carbondale, IL.

Cummings, D. (ed.) (2011). *Visualities: Perspectives on Contemporary American Indian Film and Art*. Michigan State University Press: East Lansing, MI.

Deger, J. (2006). *Shimmering Screen: Making Media in an Aboriginal Community*. University of Minnesota Press: Minneapolis, MN.

Dixon, G. (2012). 'Toronto's first peoples festival spotlights an Indigenous new wave that's "starting to crest"', *The Globe and Mail*, 24 June. Available: https://www.theglobeandmail.com/arts/film/torontos-first-peoples-festival-spotlights-an-indigenous-new-wave-thats-starting-to-crest/article4364964/, accessed 16 October 2019.

Gauthier, J. (2013). 'Dismantling the master's house: The feminist fourth cinema documentaries of Alanis Obomsawin and Loretta Todd', in M.E. Marubbio and E. Buffalohead (eds.) *Native Americans on Film: Conversations, Teaching and Theory*. University Press of Kentucky: Lexington, KY, 89–115.

Ginsburg, F. (1995). 'The parallax effect: The impact of aboriginal media on ethnographic film', *Visual Anthropology Review*, vol 11, no 2: 64–76.

Ginsburg, F. (1999). 'The after-life of documentary: The impact of *you are on Indian land*', *Wide Angle*, vol 21, no 2: 60–67.

Ginsburg, F. (2002). 'Screen memories: Resignifying the traditional in Indigenous media', in F. Ginsburg, L. Abu-Lughod, and B. Larkin (eds.) *Media Worlds: Anthropology on New Terrain*. University of California Press: Berkeley, CA, 39–57.

Hokowhitu, B. (2013). 'Theorizing Indigenous media', in B. Hokowhitu and V. Devadas (eds.) *The Fourth Eye: Māori Media in Aotearoa New Zealand*. University of Minnesota Press, Minneapolis, MN, 101–123.

Hokowhitu, B. and Devadas, V. (eds.) (2013). *The Fourth Eye: Māori Media in Aotearoa New Zealand*. University of Minnesota Press: Minneapolis, MN.

Husband, D. (2018). 'Chelsea Winstanley: My idol was Merata Mita', *E-Tangata*, August 19. Available: https://e-tangata.co.nz/korero/chelsea-winstanley-my-idol-was-merata-mita/, accessed 16 October 2019.

Hyland, N. (2015). 'Beyonce's response (eh?): Feeling the *ihi* of spontaneous haka performance in Aotearoa/New Zealand', *TDR/The Drama Review*, vol 59, no 1: 67–82.

Kilpatrick, J. (1999). *Celluloid Indians: Native Americans and Film*. University of Nebraska Press: Lincoln, NE.

Knopf, K. (2008). *Decolonizing the Lens of Power: Indigenous Films in North America*. Rodopi: Amsterdam.

Leuthold, S. (1998). *Indigenous Aesthetics: Native Art, Media and Identity*. University of Texas Press: Austin, TX.

Marubbio M.E. (2013). 'Wrestling the greased pig: An interview with Randy Redroad', in M.E. Marubbio and E. Buffalohead (eds.) *Native Americans on Film: Conversations, Teaching and Theory*. University Press of Kentucky, Lexington, KY, 288–302.

Maydell, E. (2018). '"It just seemed like your normal domestic violence": Ethnic stereotypes in print media coverage of child abuse in New Zealand', *Media, Culture and Society*, vol 40, no 5: 707–724.

Mercier, O.R. (2010). '"Welcome to my interesting world": Powhiri styled encounter in *boy*', *Illusions: NZ Moving Image and Performing Arts Criticism*, Winter 42: 3–7.

Miller, T. and Johnson, M. (2008). 'Gilda: textual analysis, political economy, and ethnography', in R. Kolker (ed.) *The Oxford Handbook of Film and Media Studies*. Oxford University Press: New York, 260–285.

Milligan, C. (2015). 'Sites of exuberance: Barry Barclay and fourth cinema, ten years on', *International Journal of Media and Cultural Politics*, vol 11, no 3: 347–359.

Mita, M. (1996). 'The soul and the image', in J. Dennis and J. Bieringa (eds.) *Film in Aotearoa New Zealand*. Victoria University Press: Wellington.

Moewaka Barnes, H., Raina Gunn, T., Moewaka Barnes, A., Muriwai, E., Wetherell, M., and McCreanor, T. (2017). 'Feeling and spirit: Developing an indigenous wairua approach to research', *Qualitative Research: Special Issue*, vol 17, no 3: 313–325.

Murray, S. (2008). *Images of Dignity: Barry Barclay and Fourth Cinema*. Huia: Wellington.

Pearson, W. and Knabe, S. (eds.) (2015). *Reverse Shots: Indigenous Film and Media in an International Context*. Wilfred Laurier Press: Waterloo, ON.

Raheja, M. (2011). *Reservation Reelism: Redfacing, Visual Sovereignty, and Representations of Native Americans in Film*. University of Nebraska Press: Lincoln, NE.

Raheja, M. (2013). 'Reading Nanook's smile: Visual sovereignty, Indigenous revisions of ethnography, and *Atanarjuat: The Fast Runner*', in M.E. Marubbio and E. Buffalohead (eds.) *Native Americans on Film: Conversations, Teaching and Theory*. University Press of Kentucky: Lexington, KY, 35–57.

Robertson, N. (2019). 'Images still live and are very much alive', Whakapapa and the 1923 dominion museum ethnological expedition', *Journal of the Polynesian Society*, vol 128, no 1: 65–86.

Rony, F.T. (1996). *The Third Eye*. Duke University Press: Durham, NC.

Singer, B. (2001). *Wiping the War Paint Off the Lens: Native American Film and Video*. University of Minnesota Press: Minneapolis, MN.

Smith, J. (2012). 'Framing parade', in M. Songovini (ed.) *Covering Parade: A Festschrift Celebrating the 75th Birthday of Patricia Grace*. Wai-te-ata Press: Wellington, 31–49.

Smith, J. (2013). 'Māori television's Indigenous insistence', *Studies in Australasian Cinema*, vol 7, no's 2–3: 101–110.

Smith, J. (2014). 'The many different faces of the dusky maiden: A context for understanding *Maiden Aotearoa*', in J. Carroll, B. McDougall, and G. Nordstorm (eds.) *Huihui: Pacific Rhetorics and Aesthetics*. University of Hawai'i Press: Honolulu, HI, 144–159.

Smith, J. (2016a). 'Decolonising dreams and Māori television', in J. Hutchings and J. Lee-Morgan (eds.) *Decolonisation in Aotearoa: Education, Research and Practice*. NZCER Press: Wellington, 158–171.

Smith, J. (2016b). *Māori Television: The First Ten Years*. Auckland University Press: Auckland.

Smith, J. and Mercier, O.R. (eds.) (2012). 'Special issue: Taika Waititi's boy,' *New Zealand Journal of Media Studies*, vol 13, no 1.

Smith, J. and Turner, S. (2013). 'Indigenous inhabitations and the colonial present', in G. Huggan (ed.) *The Oxford Handbook of Postcolonial Studies*. Oxford: London, 271–233.

Te Punga Somerville, A. (2010). 'Maori cowboys, Maori Indians', *American Quarterly*, vol 62, no 3: 663–685.

Turner, S. (2013). 'Reflections on Barry Barclay and fourth cinema', in B. Hokowhitu and V. Devadas (eds.) *The Fourth Eye: Māori Media in Aotearoa New Zealand*. University of Minnesota Press: Minneapolis, MN, 162–180.

Vizenor, G. (ed.) (2008). *Survivance: Narratives of Native Presence*. University of Nebraska Press: Lincoln, NE.

Vourlias, C. (2017). 'Māori women tell their stories in Toronto Festival's "Waru"', *Variety*, 8 September. Available: https://variety.com/2017/film/festivals/maori-women-tell-their-stories-in-toronto-festivals-waru-1202548267/, accessed 16 October 2019.

Wilson, J. (2013). *Whiripapa: Tāniko, Whānau and Kōrero-Based Film Analysis*. PhD thesis, University of Auckland, NZ.

Wilson, J.K.T. (2017). 'Developing mahi-toi theory and analysis', *MAI Journal*, vol 6, no 2: 116–128.

Wilson, P. and Stewart, M. (eds.) (2008). *Global Indigenous Media: Culture, Poetics and Politics*. Duke University Press: Durham, NC.

Wood, H. (2008). *Native Features: Indigenous Films from Around the World*. Continuum: New York.

Wood, H. (2013). 'Dimensions of difference in Indigenous film', in M.E. Marubbio and E. Buffalohead (eds.) *Native Americans on Film: Conversations, Teaching and Theory*. University Press of Kentucky: Lexington, KY, 35–57.

37

The politics of language in Indigenous cinema

Theodore C. Van Alst, Jr.

With his first non-student film, *From Cherry English* (2005), Jeff Barnaby directly addressed the pain of Native language loss and acquisition in ways that quickly established his voice and style in the cinematic landscape. This paper will focus on the presence and portrayal of language and class in Barnaby's works, particularly in *The Colony* (2007), *From Cherry English* (2005), and *File Under Miscellaneous* (2010).

While the working title to this essay was 'F@#k Hollywood: Rez Rats and Revolution in the Films of Jeff Barnaby', the unvoiced subtext to this paper is 'Word and Authenticity in Native Literature and Film', making it useful to consider various nodes in Native languages, literature, and film. Anecdotal evidence points to majority non-Native listeners at readings by popular American Indian authors. If Native lit isn't reaching Indians, if the audience, intended or not, is whites, how does this shape the writing, how does it affect Indigenous language use? Do these same concerns find their way into Native cinematic production? This discussion will exam in brief the use of Native languages in prose, poetry, and cinema, and further consider questions regarding audience and intent.

Issues concerning this canted audience composition were discussed in an *Iowa Review* interview with Sherman Alexie almost 20 years ago. The effects of this perceived audience can be seen in much of what we call Native literature, particularly in poetry; it's reflected in Alexie's own thoughts that precede the quote in which Alexie describes almost exclusively white audiences and laments his literature not reaching Indians.[1] That lamentation is brought to particular poignancy in the dually autobiographical work about Corliss the student and Harlan the writer in 'The Search Engine', from the 2001 release of his short story collection *Ten Little Indians* (2004); Harlan waking up in an alley behind a tavern after passing out drinking and then vomiting on a book of his own poetry, a discarded gift to one of his recent 'friends' met in the bar the night before.

Two more questions then, two decades hence: If Native lit isn't reaching Indians, if the audience, intended or not, is whites, how does this shape the writing and in particular Indigenous language use? And do these same concerns find their way into Native cinematic production?[2]

Obviously, language is important in describing people both in and out of a group. Peoples and cultures often are first identified by their language; their own languages in turn construct who they are, and how they perceive the world. A people's sense of peoplehood is informed by their language. If one wanted to both dehumanise as well as de-nation, de-community, de-people a people, the deepest and most successful way to do so would be to remove their language, eliminate the kinship structures embedded in their languages, destroy and silence their tongues, remove and replace their very way of knowing the world (CNN 2017).

This was the *20th-century* approach of settler governments in the United States and Canada, in New Zealand and Australia.

Our particular focus for the moment, though, is on the boarding school era. In 1876, beginning with the Carlisle Indian Industrial School, United States Army Captain Richard Henry Pratt devised a program he thought would complete the perceived assimilation of American Indians into the fabric of US society. Its guiding light was distilled by the captain into these simple words: 'Kill the Indian, save the man': '*Kill the Indian, save the man*'. You may or may not have heard this phrase before, but please, allow me to place it in the context of its original setting, and expand the words to their fullest lines, these delivered as Pratt's address as the *Official Report of the Nineteenth Annual Conference of Charities and Correction* in 1892. Here is the captain's introduction:

> A great general has said that the only good Indian is a dead one, and that high sanction of his destruction has been an enormous factor in promoting Indian massacres. In a sense, I agree with the sentiment, but only in this: that all the Indian there is in the race should be dead. Kill the Indian in him, and save the man.

(1892: online)

This then was the working principle, the vision, the mission, and the goal of Pratt's boarding school model, a program that was expanded to more than 100 schools across the United States from 1876 to 1917 and forced Indian children into an education system that was devised to eliminate their language, culture, and spiritual traditions, destroying their familial relationships and those of their relatives for generations. While some historians and other academics have remarked that the boarding school affected the better part of a generation, I would argue that this government policy in fact affected seven or more generations, from the great-grandparents of the children shipped off to the schools to the great-grandchildren of those same students; the abuse, violence, and trauma they experienced had a profound effect on their close-knit families that continues to this day. One of the hallmarks and widely told stories from the boarding school experience is the imposition of a new and English name as well as the punishments exacted for speaking one's own language – often, these children would return to their families having lost the ability to speak their language, and thus to their own parents. The Indian Self-Determination and Education Assistance Act of 1975 finally signaled an end to the dominance of the residential schools, recommending community-based day schools in their place. A handful of residential schools are still in operation (such as Chemawa in Oregon, and Flandreau in South Dakota), but the curriculum reflects a better understanding and promotion of Native concerns. Three years after Carlisle opened, fledgling Post-Confederation Canada's John A. Macdonald commissioned a report on the US program, and after receiving the *Report on Industrial Schools for Indians and Half-Breeds* (Davin 1879), decided his settlers and their state would implement a policy that held "the best way to civilize Indigenous peoples was to start with children in a residential setting, away from their families, so that they could be 'kept constantly within the circle of civilized conditions'" (*National Centre for Truth and Reconciliation* [NCTR] 2015). online Attendance was made compulsory for First Nations children beginning in 1884. We note that the Indian Residential School program enacted by our 'kinder, gentler' neighbors to the north was so beloved by the government, even though their own *Truth and Reconciliation Commission* recognised that the system's aim was to "kill the Indian in the child" (NCTR 2015: online) only closed its last school in 1996.

Native literature and film arise from this legacy of havoc and terror

Directly affected or not, the artists and creators in Native cinema and literature work in the aftermath of all of these policies and programmes. How Native-authored literature and film look and sound based on the particularities of language theft, removal, loss, or however one declaims the process is our focus for the moment. I'll examine in brief the use of Native languages in prose, poetry, and cinema, and consider those earlier questions regarding audience and intent.

In the heavily weighted and carefully considered world of words in poetry, selection matters deeply. This is not to discount the work of those who choose to express themselves via prose, where Native language might sit surrounded by other words and possess the ability to blend and perhaps even surprise, but rather to focus on the more tightly stitched value for each word in a poem, where the insertion of a Native word or term in an otherwise English (and occasionally French) written work is a political choice that is immediately arresting for the reader. It is hoped at least that the deliberate and active process of reading makes both the writer and the reader intimately involved with what's happening on the page; each acknowledging the other's presence at every engagement with the written word. As Natalie Diaz says:

> Learning and speaking one's native language is an emotional and political act. Each time a poet brings a native language onto the white space of the page, into the white space of the academies and institutions of poetry, it is an emotional and political act.
>
> *(2015: online)*

In employing Native language in writing, we reflect as well that in American absences of/unfamiliarity with/resistance by existence of, Native languages, and with many Americans far more familiar with Spanish, at least than, say, Keres, or Anishinaabemowin, there seems to be less easy beauty than found in Western neo-languages like Spanglish, where the striking and the gorgeous is not lost in lines like those penned by Lorna Dee Cervantes, who describes, in *Freeway 280* (2016: online) without italics, "Las casitas near the gray cannery, / nestled amid wild abrazos of climbing roses" and sings a search for self, continuing in Spanglish, wa/ondering in "los campos extraños de esta ciudad".

Lynn Domina's work on Shauna Osborn's *Arachnid Verse* in the 'October Micro-Review' section of the *Kenyon Review* (2017), reminds us of the political will enacted by Native writers who disrupt a 'certain privilege' in their readership, when those consumers of text are:

> easily comprehending the vast majority of the lines but made uneasy by those few 'foreign' phrases, words that may very well be crucial. The simplicity of much of the English will deceive some readers into a false assurance of familiarity, of knowingness ~ until a Comanche or Spanish phrase reveals (by refusing its transparent meaning) that perhaps the reader doesn't know so much after all.
>
> *(online)*

This manifests itself in the Osborn poem she looks at in detail, one titled 'Antes taabe', the pairing of words not a portmanteau with a space between the two to illustrate their difference, but rather an uneasy if alliterative blend of Latin and *numuunu* (Comanche), that names the work 'Before the Sun', giving us a piece that might verify her observation: "Several of the poems incorporate Spanish and Comanche phrases, and though the book includes a 'Notes' section with translations, many readers will find the Comanche phrases particularly alien".

Written language itself is alien in its own right as regards its presence here in this hemisphere of overwhelming oral tradition; the inscribing, the etching, the typed or written, painted or carved words in relation to Native authors working in settler state contexts is overwhelmingly a Western construct, a Phoenician-Graeco-Roman campaign that's still with us here and now. This is to say that Native people have had far more involvement with the written word than with Bazin's 'Seventh Art',[3] and even though that form too, is largely a Western invention, film at its storytelling core may be the least strict and Western-structured of all the Arts with us today. The rise of Native filmmaking and digital storytelling in the last 10 years has been breathtaking, and Indigenous authors and producers continue to expand the field in exciting ways.

Film, for all its possibilities, nevertheless can find itself, following Bazin, subject to suffering in certain intellectual ways in that it can be received in far more passive ways, with images, sounds, and story washing over the viewer, in contrast with the largely active engagement required of readers of texts. This often less-nuanced approach to film produces a viewership that finds itself susceptible to all manner of beliefs about subjects and objects, an unsettling blending of realities that find a particular foothold in Native-content film, which is often perceived to be *documentary* in nature, or at the very least, ethnographic, with students and audiences frequently collapsing the ideas and voices of actors onscreen with Native people in the 'real world'. In order to consider films that *should* make that sort of thinking a little more difficult, we turn to the work of director Jeff Barnaby. Born in Listiguj Mi'gmaq First Nation, which is surrounded by Quebec and across the water from Campbellton, New Brunswick, educated in film at Concordia in Montreal, and who, for all his seeming horror leanings, draws on Native and non-Native poetry for inspiration in both 2004's *From Cherry English* (first screened in 2004 [2005]) (employing Rita Joe's 'I Lost My Talk') and the dystopic *File Under Miscellaneous* (2010), which utilises a Pablo Neruda Spanish-language piece with an English title, 'Walking Around', translated into in Mi'qmag and read as a voiceover by the main character in as he heads into a shop to have his Native skin removed replaced with that of a white man. Neruda, we learn as of 21 October 2017, according to BBC News, likely did not in fact die of prostate cancer, as averred on his death certificate, but of something far more nefarious, as asserted by his former driver Manuel Araya, who says Neruda was poisoned by the Pinochet regime, who didn't want him to leave the country and perhaps preferred him to be 'walking around' Santiago, before they murdered him.

File Under Miscellaneous (2010) earned a 2011 Genie Nomination for 'Best Live Action Short' and was an official selection of the Toronto International Film Festival. This piece from Barnaby that borrows directly from Neruda strikes us as an inventive, arresting, easily recognisable if not entirely conventional, cosmopolitan short film from a contemporary director. That is of course something to remark upon, no matter the personal background and education of the director and writer. But how did we get here? What are the beginnings of Native participation in cinema, and where are we at right now?

We can discuss film as art, as conveyor of image, about its power as an art form in esoteric and theoretical ways, but for the moment, let's think about the consequences of continuously portraying Native people as somehow less-than, as unformed, backdrop, savage accouterment and accessory to whites, general scenery, communers with animals, Halloween costumes, mascots, and general cardboard cutouts of humans. Why is that so powerful?

What happens when a police officer has about two-tenths of a second to decide whether he's going to shoot the person in front of him? He has to assess that individual and decide if their life is worth less than his, if they are a threat, if they are, in effect, his relation, his relative, someone he might think about seeing again.

And how does that go for Native people who have largely been portrayed as mascots, caricatures, and relics of the past? Just as you imagine it might. Depending on the statistical source, either one of the highest, or *the* highest rate of killing by law enforcement.[4]

Film and media bear much, but refuse all, responsibility for police actions, and Hollywood in particular is due the largest of charges.

I'd like to share two quotes that I think illustrate Hollywood's problem with portrayals of American Indian characters and stories, problems that show few signs of abatement.

In the first, a 1967 essay titled 'The Virtues and Limitations of Montage', André Bazin begins with a critical framing of Hollywood:

> anyone wishing to set up a film library or to compile a series of programs for young children would be hard pressed to find more than a few shorts, of unequal merit, and a certain number of commercial films, among them some cartoons, the inspiration and the subject matter of which were sufficiently childlike; in. particular, certain adventure films. It is not, however, a matter of specialized production, just of films intelligible to those on a mental level under fourteen. As we know, American films do not often rise above this level. The same is true of the animation films of Walt Disney.
>
> *(online)*

The second quote, also from Bazin, is this: "The cinema will be fulfilled when, no longer claiming to be an art of reality, it becomes merely reality made art" (online).

Thus, the reality of cinema, here the production of Hollywood, is that, regarding American Indians, we are largely subjected to the fantasies of 13-year-old imaginations (cf. *The Lone Ranger and Tonto, The Ridiculous Six,* Kevin Bacon in *The Darkness,* Eli Roth's *Green Inferno* ... obviously, what could go wrong?).

Where and how did this start in Hollywood at least? Many of you are likely to be familiar with cinematic history, and the misrepresentations of Native people throughout that history. This longer quote from a 1915 essay works to illuminate its beginnings:

> It is only within the last two or three years that genuine Redskins have been employed in pictures. Before then these parts were taken by white actors made up for the occasion. ... Even today a few white players specialize in Indian parts. They are past masters in such roles, for they have made a complete study of Indian life, and by clever makeup they are hard to tell from real Redskins. They take leading parts for which Indians are seldom adaptable. ... To act as an Indian is the easiest thing possible, for the Redskin is practically motionless.
>
> *(Dench 1915: online)*

Even though American Indian-made films by James Young Deer and Lillian St. Cyr were being released at the same time as Dench's racist essay and on through the end of the Silent Era and into the early sound period, Native-produced cinema largely disappeared until the advent of digital video. As you might imagine, Native concerns and issues were largely ignored by Hollywood in the decades between, and Native voices were silenced, though of course, resistance never disappeared. For example, Raoul Walsh's *A Distant Trumpet* (1964) contains a scene in which the Indigenous language hadn't been translated or known until it was featured in Neil Diamond and Catherine Bainbridge's 2009 *Reel Injun.* In it, 'War Eagle – Chief of the Chiricahua Apache Armies' angrily replies in an unidentified and non-subtitled language to 2nd Lt. Matt Hazard's warning that he will be pursued by his general if the young lieutenant is not released to return to his fort. Wider audiences never knew until the release of that film that the uncredited actor playing 'War Eagle' had replied, in Diné, "Just like a snake, you'll be crawling in your own shit".

With the rise of the American Indian Movement, and the elevation of Native voices domestically and internationally, Native concerns did begin to reappear in the popular realm, and America's love of the Western took on a revisionist tone for a time in the late 1960s and early 1970s, though things weren't nearly as rosy as mainstream folks thought they were. Take, for example, Chief Dan George's 1971 nomination for an Oscar for his Best Supporting Actor performance in *Little Big Man*. In a story told by Wes Studi in the 2009 documentary *Reel Injun* we can see perhaps, how Chief George's nomination didn't net him a win with the overwhelmingly old, white, male-dominated Academy of Motion Picture Arts and Sciences. When the possibility came up that Chief George might be again nominated, this time for his work in 1976's *The Outlaw Josey Wales*, according to Wes Studi, the Academy released a statement, "wherein they said, well yeah, he oughta be nominated, but, on the other hand, was he really acting, or was he just being an Indian?" (Diamond and Bainbridge 2009).

This was the response by the Academy to a superb actor's portrayal of characters in films that were both set just after the end of the US Civil War.

Nonetheless, the gains made by Chief Dan George and actors like Will Sampson that meant so much at the time would also pay dividends in future films. *Thunderheart* from 1992 is one such production that benefitted from their earlier efforts. Though easy enough to write off as a typical 'White Saviour' film starring Val Kilmer, there is quite a bit more going on in this production shot in Pine Ridge. Produced by Robert DeNiro, featuring outstanding performances from Graham Greene, Sheila Tousey, and John Trudell, and employing local singers and drums along with Dennis Banks, Sam Shepard and future US presidential candidate Fred Thompson, the film treats an amalgam of actual events that occurred in Plains reservations during the 1970s all under the device of a *noirish* detective story. One of the standout features is the performance of Ted Thin Elk and the use of Lakota language in the film. We'll exam that language in brief by way of a quick lesson. Here are some sample Lakota names: *Cante Witkó*, (Fool Heart), *Cante Pȟéta* (Fire Heart), *Cante Máza* (Iron Heart), *Cante Síca* (Bad Heart). In an intense scene that recounts some of the events that occurred during the massacre at Wounded Knee, the actor Ted Thin Elk *knows* Val Kilmer (and his character Ray Levoi) aren't who Val and Ray would have *us* believe they aren't ("I'm not who you think I am", he tells Grandpa Sam), even though Thin Elk's character Sam Reaches says otherwise. Grandpa Sam Reaches tells Ray Levoi that he is *Thunderheart* (1992), "returned to a people during a time of trouble". He tells him that the blood of "*Wakinyan Cante*" flows through his heart.

In the course of the scene, the actor very specifically employs a *fundamentally* incorrect usage in Lakota, one that would be obviously known to even the most casual or beginning speaker who would know that postpositive adjectives are standard. You all knew that after your first Lakota lesson, and the actor Ted Thin Elk knew that at least some of us watching and listening would know what he did.

In Native film, and as Native film critics who so very often must wade through scads of non-Native made film, we are forever on the lookout for the redemptive as well as the transgressive. Though initially dismissed by many as another White Saviour film, *Thunderheart* contains many numerous redemptive moments such as the 'Wakinyan Cante' segment.

And as regards that moment, we ask why would an actor do this? The root of his transgressive act is to be found not in the dialogue, but in the subject itself. Even though there may be a genuine commitment on the part of the non-Lakota filmmakers to making what they feel is an authentic film, to telling a tale that needed to be told, an exposure of corruption and collusion between the United States and corrupt tribal governments, the actor (who in this instance is a Lakota speaking elder with the final authority on the Native language being used) decides that a film about an event as deep and important to his history, *Cankpe Opi Wakpa*, Wounded Knee, will not contain Val Kilmer's character, real or otherwise. The importance and authenticity of Native language in film thus occupies a different level, even as it appears more naturally than it does in literature, when we recall the presupposed ethnographic nature of much film featuring Native actors and narratives. It does so in what we might deem 'Native-friendly' or 'Native-allied' film, that is films purporting to be supportive of Native concerns, such as *Thunderheart* (1992) or *The Revenant*, where Native language is featured, and its use supervised by Native speakers themselves, but it does so even more in Native-authored and Native-produced films. We'll observe this last in a pair of films as we return to the work of Jeff Barnaby.

The centrality of language and its importance to culture is a prevailing theme in Barnaby's films. From his first post-student film made-for-TV, *From Cherry English* (2005), to his first feature-length wide release *Rhymes for Young Ghouls*, Barnaby's work is upfront, it's brutal; he reminds some and proclaims to others in visceral ways the pain of losing your language, and he employs both physical and intellectual tactics in doing so. In Barnaby's *From Cherry English* (2005), he employs fellow Mi'gmaq artist Rita Joe's poem, 'I Lost My Talk' to illustrate the pain of language loss in horrifying and gore-drenched ways.

Even in this early film, we begin to note the particulars of Barnaby's work, the tension between class considerations and the possible expectations of a film school graduate from Concordia in Montreal. There is a decidedly different approach to what we might think of as Indigenous language activism. The main character lives in ... less than suburban home, doesn't fit into ideas of mainstream Canadian life, and makes questionable social decisions. That may be a function of youth, but here it works to move the narrative forward (the loss of tongue, the reaction to white witchery) rather than dress a shooting set in bohemian or 'artsy' or 'edgy' ways. Barnaby himself said that he pulled back in this production, as he has in others, cognizant of what he describes as a sort of 'tempered aesthetic' and mindful that if things are "too bleak, people won't watch" (Personal Interview by author 23 August 2016). However, from the very beginning, Barnaby was a director who announced a no bullshit approach to his filmmaking and the place of language and culture in his work, and his expectations for his actors, describing the ones he won't work with, ones who don't show the same level of commitment as him to authenticity in language and ethos: "If you want to get right down to the nitty gritty, it's these actors that basically put money before their culture" (Personal Interview by author 23 August 2016). That commitment surely ran around in his head while thinking about his next work; he says, "right before I wrote it, not even right before, *while* I was writing it, I was working in the woods. ... I wasn't even thinking about it in terms of class; I was thinking about it in terms of authenticity" (Personal Interview by author 23 August 2016).

That film, *The Colony* (2007), was a Best Short winner at the *Whistler Film Festival* and of the jury prize at *ImagineNative*, as well as nominated for the *Prix Iris* (Quebec Oscar), he comes close to violating his own admonition, but here rather than too bleak, he approaches 'too gory' in his aesthetic. Barnaby pulls it off of course, onscreen amputation via chainsaw notwithstanding, a mark of his talent in translating a difficult subject matter, and continues to explore his concerns with language loss, though not as directly as in *From Cherry English* (2005). In a scene from *The Colony* (2007), Maytag (played brilliantly by Glenn Gould) shows us rather than tells us of the carnage wrought in a life constrained and restricted by colonialism in a contemporary setting. He does so from a trashed couch parked in front of the murals under the Ville Marie expressway in Montreal (those mural artists are of course thanked in the credits), rolling a joint that he's lacing with a white powdery substance, which he then lights.

Feeling good, Maytag reminisces, "When I was a kid, I wanted to be a superhero. I was hard-core into comics". Hitting that joint again, he says, "Couldn't read. Could only speak Mig'maq. My Grandmother, she'd translate the fuckin', uh, *talk bubbles* into Indian for me. My father? He fuckin' hated that. He couldn't speak. Not a fuckin' word", the smoke via what looks like SFX entering, rather than leaving, his mouth at the point of exhale.[5]

Those talk bubbles? Why are they here? Is it just to look cool? Barnaby told me in a personal interview: "I'll always use Mi'gmaq in film – if some kid memorizes lines like people do with *Pulp Fiction*, maybe he'll pick up the rest of the language". I'll add that this is not some off-hand comment on Barnaby's part. Two things that stand out, among others, are the following quotes from that interview. He told me, "Native language loss is the end of that culture". That's a serious statement. And how serious is he about making sure that doesn't happen? Still as serious as when he began his career: "I've deliberately not hired Native actors because they won't learn Native languages. Fuck you" (Personal Interview by author 23 August 2016).

Finally, where to? Is there a split in the mainstream? After all, people have to work. Actors act, writers write. Filmmaker Sterlin Harjo, another award-winning director who here professes similar sentiments to Barnaby's, says:

> Native filmmakers are on the outskirts of the outskirts – it's true independent cinema. Studios won't touch us. Indians in buckskin and feathers is the only way studios want to see us because it fits their narrative. They don't want to see the truth. We have to roll up our sleeves and keep creating truth.
>
> *(Wissot 2015: online)*

Barnaby, as you might have imagined, is a bit more direct: "I couldn't fucking care less about the Hollywood guy" (Personal Interview by author 23 August 2016). In the end, much as I see with my students, whom I pester constantly in class about what they're reading, what they're watching and why, it's about 'authenticity', in the introductions I make for them to Native American Literature and Cinema, they say over and over again how much they respond to what they call the 'authenticity' in the work. On the one hand, they lament not being exposed to it sooner, and on the other they express their joy at having at least been introduced to it now. I would like to think that's where we're headed, that literary and cinematic audiences are demanding a certain authenticity in productions, and that there are artists and makers out there who are responding to demand, as well as those who are creating it. Jeff Barnaby is doing both, on behalf of those who came before, those who are here now, and those who will arrive later. I recently had the privilege of viewing a beta of his new Virtual Reality (VR) piece, *Tegs'g (Westwind)*. That this was my first VR experience and that it was amazing seems less par for the course than the fact that it was brought to me by Barnaby, who always has at least an eye and a half on the future, who said to me, "Language is how you carry the culture into the future. Whether you're flying in space boots or dressed in a loincloth speaking Mig'maq, you're still a Mig'maq" (Personal Interview by author 23 August 2016).

Barnaby is certainly not alone in engaging with language revival work in cinema, where a range of directors and writers conceive reworded worlds in a variety of ways. Whether it's Sterlin Harjo narratively filming Muskokve hymns in his documentary *This May Be the Last Time* (2014), Glenn Standring's extensive and almost exclusive use of te reo Māori in *The Dead Lands* (2014), Gwaai Edenshaw's 2018 *SGaawaay K'uuna* (Edge of the Knife) filmed entirely in Haida, or Danis Goulet's use of Cree to tell the powerful story of Weesakechak and the Weetiko in 2014's *Wakening*, and so many more in between and beyond, Indigenous languages, be they spoken, translated (or frequently not), subtitled, spray-painted, etched, or tattooed, enliven as well as cement their own existence in one of contemporary society's most powerful means of expression and communication. Indigenous creators are telling contemporary stories in their own voices and using their linguistic heritage to do so; ancestral Native languages are pulling their stories into the future.

I'll conclude by referencing Barnaby's Maytag speaking near the end of *The Colony* (2007), his beautiful, broken soliloquy in the penultimate scene flowing in ways you that make you wish you spoke the language. It begins with him deep in the dark, a filtered barely-there light on his face, and he's saying, "I fixed this". Although we know, ostensibly, that he's likely referencing the busted chainsaw from the opening sequence that he's staring down at, he could be speaking here about Native language, his own use of Mi'gmaq, and he continues, "it's rusty / but it works". In the end, in more ways than one, Barnaby's aesthetic, politics, and approach show up in a variety of contexts and approaches in Indigenous circles, in 'Indian Country', perhaps distilled so well by Māori thrash metal band *Alien Weaponry*, a name that evokes settler warfare in all its phases: "To get people to learn you have to make them interested. You can't just shove it down their throats. You can't force someone to learn a language, or a history" (O'Regan 2017: online).

Jeff Barnaby, from the moment he started making films has, is, and will always be doing that thing I ask of folks I know, of colleagues, and friends, and family, and now of you.

Let's be good ancestors.

Notes

1 Fraser, Joelle. (no year). 'Sherman Alexie's Iowa Review Interview'. He says, "Tonight I'll look up from the reading and 95% of the people in the crowd will be white" (online).

2 I've noticed that in this introduction I've used 'Native', 'Indigenous', and 'Indian'. All three are acceptable, in lieu of using an individual's tribal nation. Here in the United States, 'Native' is the most common usage, 'Aboriginal' and 'Indigenous' are preferred in Canada, with 'Indigenous' increasingly used in academic contexts in the States along with 'Native American', and 'Indian', as in 'American Indian'.

3 In working to define the 'true nature of cinema' against the 'imprudent prejudgments' of literary critics, André Bazin said, "[b]ecause its basic material is photography it does not follow that the seventh art is of its nature dedicated to the dialectic of appearances and the psychology of behavior" (2005: 62).

4 'Native Americans are killed in police encounters at a higher rate than any other racial or ethnic group, according to data from the *Centers for Disease Control and Prevention*' (CNN 2017: online). "According to data from the Centers for Disease Control (CDC) spanning from 1999 to 2015, for every one million Native Americans, an average of 2.9 of them are killed by law enforcement – the highest rate of any racial group in the United States. Natives also have a mortality rate 12 per cent higher than African Americans and three times higher than white Americans. Similarly, many deaths are likely underreported due to people of mixed race – or even forgetting to mention race – struggling with homelessness or being on a reservation in remote areas with limited resources". Native Lives Matter: The Overlooked Police Brutality Against Native Americans *Lakota People's Law Project*. 21 November 2017.

5 A happy accident of editing that Barnaby decided to leave in the film, according to our interview.

References

Alexie, S. (2004). *Ten Little Indians*. Grove: New York.

Bazin, A., Gray, H. (Translator), Renoir, J. (Foreword), Andrew, D. (Foreword) . (2005). *What is Cinema?* University of California Press: Berkeley, CA.

BBC News. (2017). 'Pablo Neruda "did not die of cancer", say experts', *BBC News*, BBC, 21 October. Available: www.bbc.com/news/world-latin-america-41702706, accessed 29 October 2017.

Cervantes, L.D. (2016). 'Freeway 280', *Poets.org*, Academy of American Poets, 4 November. Available: www.poets.org/poetsorg/poem/freeway-280, accessed 29 October 2017.

CNN. (2017). 'The forgotten minority in police shootings', *CNN.com*, 13 November. Available: https://www.cnn.com/2017/11/10/us/native-lives-matter/index.html, accessed 15 May 2020.

Davin, N. (1879) 'Report on industrial schools for Indians and half-breeds', *Hathi Trust*. Available: https://catalog.hathitrust.org/Record/100248910, accessed 29 October 2017.

Dench, E.A. (1915). 'The dangers of employing redskins as movie actors'. Available: workbench.cadenhead.org/news/3568/danger-employing-redskins-movie, accessed 19 May 2020.

Diaz, N. (2015). 'A poetry portfolio: Featuring five of our country's finest native poets', *Poets.org*, Academy of American Poets, 6 October. Available: www.poets.org/poetsorg/text/poetry-portfolio-featuring-five-our-countrys-finest-native-poets, accessed 29 October 2017.

Domina, L. (2017). 'October micro-reviews', *The Kenyon Review: The International Journal of Literature, Culture and the Arts*. Available: www.kenyonreview.org/reviews/october-micro-reviews/, accessed 29 October 2017.

Fraser, J. (n.d.). 'Sherman Alexie's Iowa review interview'. Available: www.english.uiuc.edu/maps/poets/a_f/alexie/fraser.htm, accessed 29 October 2017.

National Centre for Truth and Reconciliation. (2015). 'Canada's residential schools: The history, part 1 origins to 1939, vol. 1', *National Centre for Truth and Reconciliation Reports*. Available: nctr.ca/reports2.php, accessed 29 October 2017.

O'Regan, S.V. (2017). 'Can a thrash metal band help save the Maori language?', *Atlantic*, Atlantic Media Company, 19 October. Available: www.theatlantic.com/entertainment/archive/2017/10/can-a-thrash-metal-band-help-save-the-maori-language/541593/, accessed 29 October 2017.

Pratt, R.H. (1892). 'Official proceedings of the annual meeting: 1892', *National Conference on Social Welfare Proceedings (1874–1982)*, MLibrary Digital Collections. Available: quod.lib.umich.edu/n/ncosw/ACH8650.1892.001/69, accessed 29 October 2017.

Wissot, L. (2015). 'Ridiculous Netflix: Sterlin Harjo discusses Netflix and Adam Sandler's *Ridiculous Six*', *Filmmaker Magazine*, Independent Filmmaker Project, 14 May. Available: filmmakermagazine.com/94268-ridiculous-netflix-sterlin-harjo-discusses-netflix-and-adam-sandlers-ridiculous-six/, accessed 15 May 2020.

The Colony. (2007). Directed by Jeff Barnaby. Prospector Films. Available from DVD Screener.

File Under Miscellaneous. (2010). Directed by Jeff Barnaby. Prospector Films. Available from DVD Screener.

From Cherry English. (2005). Directed by Jeff Barnaby. Prospector Films. Available from DVD Screener.

Reel Injun (2009). Directed by Neil Diamond and Catherine Bainbridge. Rezolution Pictures/National Film Board. DVD.

Thunderheart (1992). Directed by Michael Apted, Graham Greene, John Trudell, Ted Thin Elk, Sheila Tousey, and Val Kilmer. Tribeca Productions/TriStar Pictures. DVD.

38

Entangled histories and transformative futures

Indigenous sport in the 21st century[1]

Fa'anofo Lisaclaire Uperesa

Introduction

In the weeks leading up to the Rugby League World Cup in 2018, one of the main media stories was Jason Taumalolo's choice to forgo a spot with the New Zealand national team in order to play for Mate Ma'a Tonga, the island group's rugby league team. When Taumalolo and other players like Andrew Fifita and David Fusitu'a, who were eligible to play with 'tier one' teams New Zealand and Australia but chose Tonga, the 'tier two'[2] team, it energised a run that many will remember long after the controversial call in the final seconds in the game against England. This was significant as a major upset in player recruiting: historically, Australia, New Zealand, and Great Britain have dominated rugby league,[3] with market share and financial resources that maintain that standing. This gives them privileged access to players residing in these countries and attracts players from places with fewer resources (like the Pacific Islands). Conventional wisdom and financial incentives make the choice to play for the top nations almost automatic, so this defection was a significant disruption to business as usual.

The surprise move, and the run it inspired, did indeed make history – when the team beat the Kiwis on the way to the semi-final match with England, Mate Ma'a Tonga was the first tier two side to ever beat a tier-one team. From car flags to painted *ie toga* (fine mats) displayed on lawns, to decorated fences and trees, and jerseys and miniature flags worn as *sei* or hair decorations, the groundswell of support seen all over Auckland electrified the fan base. In the week leading up to the match with England, the Tongan flag was everywhere, and not just in Auckland. Photos and video clips circulating on social media showed support in the Tongan homeland and across the transpacific diaspora, with viewing parties in Los Angeles, Sydney, and Salt Lake City, to name a few. The match drew record crowds for a rugby league match at Auckland's Mt. Smart Stadium, selling out for the first time since 1995.

In the contemporary Pacific, one of the ways cultural identity and transnational attachments are expressed and honored are via stellar performances on the sportfield. Sport is one of the few sites that can unite the diaspora and homeland in time and space. Thus, as Tonga's King George Tupou IV looked on in his Mate Ma'a Tonga jersey watching US-based Dinah Jane of Fifth Harmony sing the Tongan national anthem, Tongans and other Pacific Islanders around the world were live-streaming, singing and praying for a match of momentous significance to many.

Player Daniel Tupou explained, "The English meaning of the emblem of our jersey – Mate Ma'a Tonga – is 'Die For Tonga'. In other words, you love your country so much you would be prepared to give your life for it". He went on to describe, "I will never forget the experience of representing Tonga over these last few weeks. It is unlike anything I have known in my career" (Tupou 2017: Online). In addressing 'Tonga's World Cup Revolution', fellow Mate Ma'a Tonga team member Michael Jennings wrote, "[w]e're not representing ourselves. We're representing our families and our heritage" (2017: Online).

Indigenous sport in the 21st century highlights the multiple loyalties that transnational peoples hold, and their deep and abiding attachment to Indigenous heritage and homeland in the context of local, regional, global, and globalising sport industries. This chapter provides a survey of several different Indigenous contexts to highlight long-standing historical and emergent engagements with sport forms, which reveal complex genealogies and shifting meanings across time and space. Delving into colonial legacies and Indigenous practices, I first explore surfing in the Pacific and lacrosse in Native North America as two customary sports with long-standing Indigenous traditions that have been transformed over time and are thriving today. These highlight the dual reality of continuous local and Indigenous practices coexisting with appropriation by colonial and capitalist interests. In the broader context, Indigenous sport activities have also been revived as part of resurgent efforts toward recognition and symbolic expressions of sovereignty. I then examine how Native communities engage some of the sport forms with colonial legacies, claiming them as their own, imbuing them with meaning, and in some cases transforming them. Indigenous peoples use sports as avenues toward recognition, opportunity, and as a way of narrating community achievements to themselves and others, even as they navigate colonial, racist, and marginalising social dynamics and institutional structures. Finally, with attention to the shifting gender balance in sport participation broadly, I consider the relationship between (gendered) culture and (gendered) sport. This includes how postcolonial Indigenous masculinities are shaped in and through sport, and how Indigenous women negotiate bias, sexism, and other barriers to flourish in sport today.

From customary to contemporary sport contexts

Surfing and lacrosse are two prominent examples of Indigenous sports diffused and transformed over the course of the 20th century. By highlighting their transformations from customary to contemporary contexts, we are able to identify the complex ways they are being used by Native communities as well as illuminate how commercial and national projects have obscured their Indigenous origins in the process of appropriation. Alongside these prominent capitalised sports, other traditional sports have been revitalised as part of national or global games aimed at recovering Indigenous sport practice, often coinciding with cultural revitalisation projects or articulations of sovereignty.

Today surfing is diffused across the globe and often understood to be a 'lifestyle' sport. While its image is promoted as the commune of individuals with nature serving as a real or symbolic counterpoint to deep investment in modern corporate capitalist structures, its global form is still very much embedded in those commercial structures. Moreover, surfing's visibility and reach have been built on displacement: in international contests or in advertising contracts, Indigenous men in particular have largely been displaced as icons of 'authentic' surfing by young non-Indigenous men.[4] Yet we know from surfing histories that the sport was historically a diffuse Indigenous Pacific practice. In a general sense, different forms of surfing emerged across the Pacific (not exclusively Polynesian), although the sport as we know it today is often traced to the Hawaiian practice of *he'e nalu*, or wave riding (Finney and Houston 1996; Walker 2011).

The ancient Hawaiian sport of he'e nalu had great spiritual importance, from the protocols around the harvesting of the tree and its shaping into a board to the reverence for the elements governed by the god Kanaloa (Kahanamoku and Brennan 1968 cited in Nendel 2009: 2433). "Dancing with the waves" provided an opportunity for spiritual connection with the power and life force of the ocean and water ways (Nendel 2009: 2434) for all – men, women, and children, as well as royalty and commoners alike. Hawaiian scholar Isaiah Walker writes, "[s] urfing was more than competitive sport; it was a cultural practice embedded within the social, political, and religious fabric of Hawaiian society", including prayers, offerings at *heiau* (shrine or place of worship), and *mo'olelo* or stories that commemorated chiefly surfing feats and conveyed important values (2011: 16). Furthermore, surfing also served as a "metaphor for skill, sex, and courage" (Goldsberry 2003 cited in Nendel 2009: 2434). "[S]urfing brought together art and artistic production, spirituality, aesthetics (in the sense of bodily experiences) and a set of ideas about the relationship between nature and culture" (West 2014: 417).

As far back as the late 18th century, written accounts and engravings depicted wave riding in Tahiti and Hawai'i.[5] Perhaps because it was seen as unproductive (its ability to divert time and energy), licentious (its connection to physical prowess and sex), and pagan (tied to pre-Christian religion and spirituality), it was strongly discouraged by missionaries and converted ali'i in Hawai'i (see Walker 2008 and 2011). Its practice declined over the 19th century, to be revived and transformed in the 20th as part of a "colonial refashioning of Hawai'i and Hawaiian culture by nonindigenous promoters who sought to grow the tourism industry there" (West 2014: 417).[6] As surfing-as-sanitised-counterculture boomed in the 1960s and 1970s, industry opportunists rebranded and transformed surfing-as-sport through American-style competitive sport contests in the United States and abroad. In both California and Hawai'i, the industry was built on Indigenous erasure and dispossession; in Hawai'i the beach became a 'boarder-land' of (anti-)colonial challenge and surfing an exertion of sovereignty (Walker 2008).

The globally corporatised version of surfing flourishes in the new millennium, but so do localised and long-held Native surfing practices passed on from generation to generation. "For many Native Hawaiians, the ocean was a treasured gem that reconnected Kanaka Maoli to a pre-colonial sense of self" (Walker 2005: 580).[7] Across the islands he'e nalu connects people with movements for *malama 'aina* (to care for the land) and other Indigenous ecological efforts that are reclaiming Hawaiian cultural practices and bringing to the forefront Hawaiian world views and ways of relating to land, air, and sea. In other parts of the Pacific surfing is also reclaimed as connection to country and a symbol of sovereignty. In Australia, for example, Aboriginal knowledge frameworks with regard to place, country, and relationships help to disrupt the construction of white national Australian identity through surfing and highlights instead Indigenous philosophy and practice (McGloin 2007).

Like surfing, lacrosse too is a contemporary sport rooted in customary competition. Today it serves as a potent symbol of Indigenous heritage and practice among Native North American communities, even as it signifies both class and race in predominantly White communities across Canada and the US Lacrosse is considered by many to be the first American sport: "[f]or centuries, versions of the Native game of baggataway or twaarathon were played widely by Native peoples throughout the North American continent" (Poulter 2003: 245; see also Poulter 2010). Recounting the full postcolonial history is beyond the scope here, but over the past hundred years in the US lacrosse became a feature of elite prep schools dotting the Eastern Seaboard. Although it has been seen as niche compared to basketball, football, and other more widely played sports, today it is the fastest growing sport in the US sportscape (Craft 2012).

In contrast to lacrosse in the United States largely being confined to elite spaces until recently, in Canada it was used widely to articulate a national identity that drew on but eventually supplanted First Nations' culture. Forsyth and Wamsley (2006) detail this development, starting from the late nineteenth to mid-20th century, when the Indian Act prohibited a variety of customary physical cultural practices and federal policy marginalised Indigenous sport. Meanwhile, "[t]raditional native games and pastimes such as lacrosse and showshoeing were appropriated by the middle-class sporting clubs" of Montreal and other areas (298). Baggataway was transformed into lacrosse through rationalisation (the imposition of rules and regulations standardising play, the use of strategic 'scientific' play, and changes in positioning and equipment), as well as through the overlay of so-called 'gentlemanly values' (Poulter 2003; Delashut 2015). This extended colonial control over the game while marginalising Native players and communities, thereby appropriating the sport as a symbol of the nation (Poulter 2003: 245–246).

Regardless of its adoption in elite spaces in the United States and as a national symbol in Canada, lacrosse has long been and remains an important expression of Native identities in North America. For the Hodinöhsö:ni', the ceremonial and medicinal aspects of the game conferred spiritual healing power and represent ancestral connection: "[t]ogether, 'The Creator's Game' and the founding of the Gai'wiio[8] provide a glimpse into the cultural philosophies and the epistemological importance of lacrosse in the Hodinöhsö:ni' Longhouse worldview" (Downey 2018: 42). After having been excluded from championship play for some time, at the end of the 20th century Aboriginal athletes of the six nations of the Hodinöhsö:ni' Confederacy organised under the Iroquois Nationals team for international competition (Downey 2012). Claiming their ability to compete as a sovereign nation, the team raised visibility of competitive lacrosse on an international level and forced recognition of sovereignty through sport. On the international stage, refusal of their sovereignty by denying travel entry on Iroquois Nation passports hampered their ability to compete, but they continued to field teams at the highest level. The stories, meanings, traditions, practices, and names of lacrosse varied across Native communities; still, the sport facilitated connections "resonating throughout Indigenous transnational networks, nations, communities, kinship, and identities" (Downey 2018: 139).

Emergent articulations and contested spaces

While surfing and lacrosse are two prominent examples of long-standing Indigenous sports transformed in contemporary contexts, others have re-emerged as part of a broader reclamation of Indigenous identity and practice. In tandem with the resurgence of customary practice, the re-valuation of traditional sports materialises in contemporary competition contexts, often shaped by cultural revitalisation efforts. The *Heiva i Tahiti*, for example, has been celebrated yearly for over a century, but traditional sport events have been showcased only since 2003. According to their website,[9] these competitions, "embody the most authentic and spectacular Polynesian traditions", including outrigger canoe racing, rock climbing, javelin throwing, coconut husking, among others (Heiva i Tahiti n.d.: online). The dance competitions and the outrigger canoe racing have earned international recognition and were well rooted in historical Tahitian practice, while "[o]ther events in the heiva have their antecedents in long-established activities associated with warrior training as well as subsistence, social, and religious activities" (Stevenson 1990: 267). Tahitian academic Karen Stevenson notes that since the 1880s the proportion of French events has steadily given way to Tahitian events (1990: 261). By the 1980s the push to articulate a new Tahitian identity drew both on, "the traditional past and the reinterpreted culture of the present" to explicitly highlight *la culture ma'ohi* (1990: 265). In this process of rearticulation, the inclusion of Tahitian sports and games allowed Tahitians to highlight Indigenous identity at a moment when the French showed renewed interest in Tahiti (1990: 272). In the wider context, the heiva, along with other events (like the Festival of Pacific Arts or Māori tribal festivals) have a political dimension to recovery of heritage and cultural practice that speaks directly to recognition of Indigenous tradition and identities.

"[S]port and games are 'meaningful dramatisations of reality' in which the values of the community are represented and contested, and in which people are active agents in the making of their own identity" (Poulter 2003: 238). Examining the Saami sport organisation in Norway (SVL-N, or Sámiid Valáštallan Lihttu – Norga Poastaboksa), which provides both customary sports as well as 'universal' sports, Skille (2014) argues that Saami engagement with both sheds light on the construction of their Indigenous identity through sport. Saami engagement with mainstream Norwegian sports like skiing drew on customary Saami sport skills in a context of an explicitly 'modern' competition sport, providing an opportunity "to show their superiority over Norwegians ('daza') or others in a specific and direct sport competition" (2014: 35). At the same time, the staging of uniquely Saami sports tied to traditional practices of animal husbandry, including lassoing, cross-country skiing with lassoing, running with lassoing, and reindeer racing in SVL-N competition settings provided a space for embodied Saami culture even as they also highlighted Saami difference and served as a "border marker of ethnicity" (Skille 2014: 32). Through participation in mainstreamed Norwegian sports and the sportisation of customary activities, Saami demonstrated prowess in a way that also marked their difference as a Native people.

While drawing customary sports and games into contemporary competition formats helps to recognise and revive Indigenous tradition, it raises other kinds of concerns. In particular, people have critiqued how Native principles of sociality (e.g., cooperation, solidarity) can be undermined by the articulation of Indigenous games to the practical logic of competitive sports. Some have raised concerns about turning Indigenous core survival skills into a competition as in the Dené Games from Canada's Northwest Territories (Heine 2013: 15), and the incorporation of cultural foundations of Indigenous games and play into competitive formats for political purposes as in the *Siyadlala* program in South Africa (Burnett 2014). Others have argued the contradiction between the precepts of neoliberal sport (particularly high-performance elite level sport) and cultural foundations of Indigenous sports in the 21st century in relation to the re-emergence of Māori waka ama (outrigger canoe) in Aotearoa/New Zealand (Wikaire and Newman 2014), and neo-colonial aspects of sport for development programs in places like Zambia (Jeanes et al. 2013). As these resurgent events evolve and thrive, the benefits and drawbacks of sportisation will continue to be contested and negotiated.

By surveying a variety of Indigenous sport contexts, I bring in to focus sport as continuous and resurgent practice in Native communities. Uncovering obscured Indigenous genealogies of sport, as in surfing and lacrosse, reveals their enmeshment with Indigenous cosmologies and cultures. As I take stock of their transformation to the present day, I note how they are used to articulate identities within and beyond Native communities, as well as serve as a site for sovereign symbolism and practice. Other sports and games are acts of reclamation, often linked to re-valuation and revitalisation of Indigenous cultural identities and practices in recent decades. These notable aims coexist with important critiques of how customary games and sports, and their associated cultural values and principles, are being transformed in the current moment, and to what potential ends.

Indigenising sport

Historically, there are countless examples of Indigenous peoples engaging 'global sport' – those competitive bodily practices that have been diffused and mainstreamed internationally, often through or alongside colonial projects (Maguire 1999; Uperesa and Mountjoy 2014). These sport forms have been carried by sport missionaries expounding on the virtues of particular physical regimens, underwritten by significant funding ventures (e.g., 'sport and development' projects), and validated by an expanding global sport industry. The predominance of colonial sports, and their placement in certain contexts like the Olympic Games, evidence dynamics of power on the international stage whereby certain sports are selectively imposed as global standards for competition while others are excluded, or added after years of lobbying (Besnier et al. 2018: 47–48).

In this wider context, including where colonial sport has been a deliberate tool of assimilation and especially in settler colonial contexts predicated on the denigration and disappearance of Indigenous peoples (Wolfe 2006; Kauanui 2016), their participation and excellence in sport has served to evidence their societal worth and/or to claims to equality in a system stacked against them (Bloom 2000; Gems 2004). It has also proven the lie of settler/White supremacy based on physical and biological attributes (Miller 1998; Rubenfeld 2006). Still, Indigenous participation draws on a variety of motivations including, but ultimately surpassing the desire for recognition by the wider society (King 2007). Their presence continues to transform these spaces in ways that highlight the values, priorities, and agendas in Native communities.

Indigenous peoples have a long history of adopting and adapting colonial sports for their own purposes (Diaz 2002; Uperesa 2014b; 2018; Sacks 2019). Anderson points out that on Turtle Island:

> there were many good (mostly political) reasons for native cultures to adopt colonial sports. These reasons include the fact that they served a unifying theme throughout the over 500 recognized tribes in North America; as baseball, basketball and football were played the same way in all cultures.
>
> *(2006: 249)*

Like many other Native peoples with a community-centred orientation, the Navajo have adopted basketball as their own in ways that promote solidarity (see also McGloin 2007 on surfing and Aboriginal communities). Tailoring to their own context, they infused the game with their own sensibilities, including different styles of play, competition against their own performance or a standard rather than against teammates over opponents, and downplaying the elevation of individuals over the collective (Allison 1982).

In Australia, sport is an important component of Māori diasporic cultural identity, and has provided a space to continue specific kinds of *tikanga* or cultural protocol around welcome, celebration, and performance while residing outside of Aotearoa New Zealand: "[i]n the absence of traditional marae or sacred tribal meeting places, the rituals of encounter have to take place in car parks, on sports fields or school grounds, in rugby club-rooms or civic halls" (Bergin 2002: 259, 257). This might include *karanga* (women's formal call of welcome), *whaikōrero* (formal oratory in Māori usually done by men), *waiata* (songs), *karakia* (prayer), *hongi* (traditional greeting of pressed noses), and shared meals (259). The incorporation of Indigenous protocols of encounter, in addition to the trans-Tasman travel to Aotearoa New Zealand for sport events, help to reinforce the practice of culture in the sport arena, and the incorporation of sport into wider frameworks of culture and cultural practice.

The critical mass of Indigenous players in some sport codes has meant new opportunities for maintaining and developing cultural practices. The rising numbers of Pacific Islander players in Australia's National Rugby League competition (NRL),[10] for example, has made it possible to front the Pacific in advertising and promoting the league in exhibitions and calendars (see Uperesa and Mountjoy 2014), but has also forced a reckoning with Pasifika[11] cultural sensibilities, family expectations, and player welfare in the creation of new player welfare initiatives. Generally, 1 per cent of the population in Australia claims Pacific heritage (see Batley 2017); however, players with a Pacific background comprise 42 per cent of all NRL competition athletes (Shiu and Vagana 2016) and this makes Rugby League clubs significant spaces where critical masses of Pasifika young men gather. As a result, clubs and coaches at least at the management level, have come to recognise the need to make space for Pacific cultures in their clubs (Shiu and Vagana 2016). With 68 per cent of NRL Pacific Islander players reportedly speaking another language at home (Lakisa et al. 2014: 358), proximity in the clubs represents an important opportunity to speak a Native or heritage language, and reinforces clubs as new sites for validating cultural expression in a settler colonial nation (McDonald and Rodriguez 2014: 245).

Indigenous representation: Navigating community and sport spaces

As elite athletes, players have both the burden and privilege of representing their cultural communities, and their accomplishments and leadership in these spaces mean they are elevated and highly visible.[12] For some, it may be a heavy responsibility that they work hard to fulfill, and in some cases, shy away from. For others, success and visibility in professional codes that have come to value some players' cultural backgrounds (as in rugby and rugby league), is a welcome validation of their (Indigenous Pacific) cultural capital. While it may not be their primary motivation, Pasifika players who can navigate mainstream and Native cultural spaces benefit from what Karlo Mila calls 'polycultural capital', or the personal currency that accrues with knowledge and abilities to navigate Pacific-dominated and White-dominated institutions and spaces (Mila-Schaaf and Robinson 2010).

Indigenous athletes and communities navigate representation in settler colonial contexts, even as they contend with institutional structures and biases that erase, minimise, or constrain their presence, or that continue to centre Whiteness (Hokowhitu 2004; 2009). When Indigenous athletes reach the pinnacle of sport success by representing the nation on the global stage, they are still expected to do so in a way that mutes their Indigenous identities. Cathy Freeman, for example, had already made history as the first Aboriginal woman to win gold in the 4 × 100-meter relay in the 1990 Commonwealth Games. Ten years later she won the gold medal in the women's 400-meter event at the 2000 Sydney Olympics, garnering prestige for Australia, the host country. When she held the Aboriginal and Australian flag high in her victory lap, despite being reprimanded for doing so in the past and being directed not to (IOC rules do not recognise the Aboriginal flag), she became for many a symbol of reconciliation in Australia and beyond. Still, many Australian spectators expected her to perform allegiance to the country she was representing as if her athletic identity superseded (or indeed could be disentangled from) any other aspect of her identity. As if somehow in the rarefied context of the track, the color of her skin and the history and ongoing of treatment of Aboriginal people by the Australian state and its settler citizens was not a part of her identity and experience. She refused, and instead was one of many Indigenous athletes continuing to engage in anti-colonial, anti-racist, and anti-discriminatory participation that not only contests dynamics within sport, but connects sport to wider social contexts.

In the effort to be fully present in the sport space, athletes like Cathy Freeman are increasingly and explicitly bringing their cultural and ethnic identities with them and are less open to checking those aspects of themselves at the gate. This is an historical shift, as there are many examples of Indigenous athletes having to hide or downplay their heritage because of racism and discrimination in sport (Judd 2008; 2015). This change is made possible by public politics around racism and Indigenous rights where outright discrimination is less and less tenable (and likely also social media as an accountability mechanism with local, national, regional, and global reach). At the same time, rising numbers and a critical mass of Indigenous athletes in highly visible sport spaces are also changing the culture of sport. Further, the use of aspects of Native cultures in the branding of certain teams has provided opportunities to challenge the token appropriation of key cultural symbols or performances toward creating space for inclusion. Players and communities continue to navigate how and when to claim space through enactments of embodied sovereignty (Hokowhitu 2014).

Gender and Indigenous sport

Today, the incorporation of Indigenous cultural practices in sport also serves as a site for gender performance. In one particularly clear example we see a global public enamored with the performance of the (Māori) haka on the rugby pitch, and increasingly, other areas like football fields, basketball courts, and swimming pools, to name a few. Popularised after the professional turn in rugby union and particularly through the global media campaign of the New Zealand All Black's key sponsor Adidas in the late 1990s, the haka entered global awareness as a strident performance of Indigenous masculinity (Jackson and Hokowhitu 2002). At home, it has provided an opportunity for incorporating Māori tikanga (protocols) and mātauranga (knowledge) into the game at different levels, and corresponds to a significant investment in high-profile sport by Māori communities (Erueti and Palmer 2014; Calabrò 2016). Abroad, it has been adopted as a modular expression of pan-Polynesian masculinity in sport and had become a significant touchstone for Polynesian identity in colonial or White-dominated spaces. This is a contemporary iteration of what has been a long-standing tradition: sport as an arena for players to enhance and display their own mana, as well enhance the mamalu (honor, esteem) of their extended families and communities (Hokowhitu 2005; Uperesa 2014a; Teaiwa 2016).

While haka and its variants (including the Tongan sipi tau, popularised by Mate Ma'a Tonga in rugby league or the Samoan siva tau performed by Manu Samoa in rugby union) have become an important practice toward cultural visibility, their adoption in hypermasculine spaces like rugby and football also brands a particular version of Indigenous Polynesian (hyper)masculinity based on physical dominance, the threat of violence, and the allure of the exotic, thereby relegating other forms of masculinity to the margins (Hokowhitu 2004; Tengan and Markham 2009; Chen 2014). That this aligns with cis-heterosexual[13] versions of colonial sport masculinities is no accident; indeed, the acceptance and promotion of this alignment hinges on the ability of the power and passion of cultural performance to energise dominant sport masculinities.

Lesser known on the global stage, but wildly successful and rising in visibility are the Black Ferns (Aotearoa New Zealand's women's national rugby union team). Contrasting their use of the haka in the context of their success helps to highlight some of the issues around Indigenous gender performativity in sport today. Former Black Ferns captain, Dr Farah Rangikoepa Palmer, has discussed the team's use of haka at the unsanctioned 1991 Women's Rugby World Cup, and the backlash it generated. The haka was a "demonstration of defiance, cultural pride and identity" by women still pushing for space in the game (Palmer 2016: 2177). Contesting both the masculine dominance of rugby and what has become the masculine dominance of haka, it was confronting to both the Māori and White hetero-patriarchy. While some of the critique focused on their stance, what was really being contested was competing notions of gendered performance in sport and cultural contexts. Many traditionalists no doubt debate whether women should be in the sport at all, let alone performing the haka there. Palmer reminds us, "[h]ow women use and demonstrate power lies at the centre of debate about whether women can and should play rugby as playing rugby can challenge dominant discourse with regards to hegemonic masculinity, femininity, and compulsory heterosexuality" (2016: 2179). While curated cultural performance is often used to authenticate men's power performance in sport, for women it can complicate it by challenging (Indigenous and non-Indigenous) expectations around feminine gender performance (Palmer 2016). This reminds us that sport spaces are rarely simply straightforward, but engage significant contradictions or odd alignments, and intersectional analysis is key to critique.

In some ways sport offers a vanguard for change, creativity, and progress; however, in others it remains one of the few spaces where regressive practices are tightly held and successfully justified. That sport widely remains foundationally tied to essentialist binary gender conceptions has implications for a relatively narrow set of gender performance forms seen as acceptable in mainstreamed sport. This binary also necessarily excludes non-binary expression and Indigenous athletes who identify as takatāpui, third gender, berdache, fa'afafine, fa'atama, mahū, and so on. For these reasons and others, it is important to pay attention to the way (gendered) sport meets (gendered) culture and how the articulation of Indigenous forms with dominant gendered forms is accepted or contested.

Negotiating more inclusive spaces

While women have for a long time successfully claimed space in sport and have used sport to combat sexism, they continue to be challenged by structural inequalities and gender bias in sport. Structural inequalities are clearly marked in struggles over equal pay, the gender composition of coaching, administration, and leadership, as well as content and frequency of media coverage (Cooky et al. 2013; Cooky and Messner 2018). In short, men are more likely to be seen as belonging and women as interlopers, and this reverberates in assumptions of expertise, access to networks and training opportunities, leadership positions, and so on.

In addition to various disparities between men and women in sport such as pay, access, and opportunities, there are also the inequalities between the athletes from the dominant culture and Indigenous men and women (Hall 2013). Ferguson et al. point out that Indigenous women "experience a lack of respect, low levels of influence, lack of opportunity, inequality and few women in decision-making positions that contribute to an imbalanced sport system" (2019: 2). While women generally have historically negotiated gender bias that marginalises them in sport, Aboriginal and Indigenous women (as well as other non-White women) have intersecting factors based on racism and colonial histories that exacerbate the barriers to their participation (Maxwell et al. 2017) and acceptance within positions of power. There remain difficult dynamics to negotiate, such as a conflict between cultural activities like smudging and sport participation (Hayhurst et al. 2015: 961), barriers preventing continued participation (Maxwell et al. 2017), or feeling like success in sport comes at a cultural price (Palmer 2007: 14), but sport still provides an important space for self-actualisation.

Sport positively influences a variety of social issues for Indigenous peoples, including violence prevention, fostering social relationships, deterring crime, encouraging school attendance, and minimising substance abuse and self-harm (Ferguson et al. 2019: 2; Cunningham and Beneforti 2005). For many Native communities, sport is one of the few places they are celebrated and cast in a positive light (Palmer 2007: 13). Among girls and women generally, sports often help promote healthy outcomes: helping them to develop a more positive body image, lowering the risk of obesity, early pregnancy, smoking or drug use, and decreasing the incidence of disease (Staurowsky et al. 2009). Participation is also associated with enhanced educational outcomes through secondary school, including higher grades, standardised test scores, and graduation rates.[14]

Given that many Indigenous girls and women want to play sport and benefit when they do, it is important to identify how their participation and visibility can be improved and supported as the 21st century unfolds. One of the issues, however, is that in addition to the lack of media coverage more generally, knowledge about Indigenous women's sport practice and experience is underdeveloped: "[s]port has historically been integral to Indigenous women's identity, yet there is little published research to highlight their sport experiences" (Ferguson et al. 2019: 2). This is a developing area, where researchers argue that the prospect for continued flourishing will likely depend on the recognition and integration of local Native communities and cultures from the grassroots to the elite levels, and with Indigenous women and girls having an authentic role in shaping sport initiatives to minimise conflicts and barriers (Palmer 2007; Ferguson et al. 2019). With the women's game being the fastest growing portion of many codes (including soccer, rugby, rugby league, and gridiron football),[15] and Indigenous participation well established or increasing, it will be fascinating to see how Indigenous women's presence will continue to transform sport spaces in years to come.

Indigenous presents/ce and futurities

Indigenous sports have histories, genealogies, presents/ce, and futures. Like any social practice imbued with value and meaning, sport communicates priorities, principles, aspirations, and challenges. By examining selected genealogies and transformations in customary sport across time and space we have identified important continuities and significant shifts in Native communities, and their relationships with local, regional, national, and international contexts. Recognising also revitalised sport forms, we have seen how they can carry ideals and expressions of peoplehood in conjunction with other efforts toward recovery and resurgence. The sport arena is significant in its visibility globally; bodily performance in these contexts provide visceral, tangible, and visual evidence of Indigenous difference, marking distinct lifeways. At the same time, the effort to indigenise global sport provides potential space to create new futures and thrive holistically and unapologetically in the cultured and gendered space of sport.

Notes

1 Fa'afetai lava to Caroline Matamua and Connor Bellett for research assistance with this chapter, and to the anonymous reviewers for their helpful feedback.
2 In rugby league, the rankings are calculated with a variety of considerations including wins, wins over higher ranked teams, and match significance. The rankings are also lucrative in that higher ranked teams enjoy more monetary support from the International Rugby League and can generate more revenue locally through home tests (personal communication, Caroline Matamua, 3 April 2020). In rugby league as in rugby union, these distinctions ostensibly are to account for the more elaborate infrastructure supporting the nation's team but in effect correspond to 'developed' and 'developing' nations (see also Dewey 2008).
3 Rugby and rugby league are similar, but distinct sporting codes. Rugby league traces its roots to Britain's workingclass areas while rugby union was promoted in elite public schools. The sports have evolved different playing and governance rules, but one of the long-standing differences until the 1990s was the amateur (union) vs professional (league) aspect. Because of the workingclass associations of the league game, the culture of the sport is also less constrained and may foster a more vibrant and vocal fan culture. See also Collins (2013) on the union/league split.
4 While high profile surfers like Kalani Robb, Sunny Garcia, and Rusty Keaulana, among others, represent for Kanaka Maoli on the pro-surf tours, the media production of capitalised surfing has branded it largely as a non-Indigenous sport. See Rutsky (1999).
5 British missionary William Ellis is often cited as the having the first illustration of surfing in the Western Hemisphere on the cover of *Polynesian Researches*, vol IV (Finney 1959), but there are accounts of wave

riding and canoe surfing in Hawai'i and Tahiti by crew on Captain James Cook's ships the Endeavour and the Resolution, along with John Webber's etchings a bit later.

6 There are competing accounts over whether it was banned outright or whether surf-related festivals were cancelled, and gambling and coed recreation were denounced as immoral. Globally surfing emerges as a corporate colonial project across the world in the early to mid-20th century (Laderman 2014).

7 At the same time, demographic shifts in Hawai'i meant surfing has also provided a sense of place and belonging for non-Hawaiian 'locals' (often used to refer to those who are raised in Hawai'i or may trace several generations of residency but are not Kanaka Maoli) (Higa-Puaoi 2017). For many locals, surfing provides a significant connection to Hawai'i and a source of belonging.

8 In the Hodinöhsö:ni' Longhouse perspective the Gai'wiio (Good Word or Good Message) outlines the Shongwayàdíhs:on (the Creator's highest code of ethics) on earth. In it, lacrosse features prominently as a healing ceremony and the lacrosse stick is imbued with spiritual, life-giving powers (Poulter 2010: 38–39).

9 See https://www.heiva.org/en/event/heiva-tuaro-maohi-en/.

10 The NRL is the premier professional rugby league of Australia, with 15 teams based locally and 1 in New Zealand; it holds a significant share of the general sport market in Australia.

11 'Pasifika' has been adopted by New Zealand and diasporic Pacific communities in this area as a pan-Pacific representative terminology. For Australia, this largely draws on Polynesian communities and includes Māori. In these contexts, Pacific/Pasifika/Pasefika are often preferred over 'Pacific Islander' because of pejorative connotations carried by 'Islander', and also the desire to mark the diasporic space/place of the new host country.

12 This visibility provides a platform also for controversial views. Israel Folau's online commentary representing homophobic tenets of his faith shows the risk of representing one's beliefs when they conflict with those of the broader society and may compromise the mental health or safety of others.

13 Cis-gender refers to one's gender identity matching the gender identity associated with their birth sex.

14 See National Women's Law Center Title IX: 40 Years and Counting Factsheet 2012 available at https://www.nwlc.org/sites/default/files/pdfs/nwlcathletics_titleixfactsheet.pdf and The Case for High School Activities (National Federation of State Hgh School Associations, Indianapolis, IN, 2008) available at https://www.nfhs.org/articles/the-case-for-high-school-activities/.

15 See Middleton (2019), NRL Women and Girls Factsheet v5 accessed at https://www.nrl.com/siteassets/community/nrl---women--girls-fact-sheet-v5.pdf, and "World Rugby launches campaign to increase participation in women's game" (2019) accessed at https://www.bbc.com/sport/rugby-union/48348245 on 4 April 2020. While the numbers of girls and women playing flag and tackle American football is increasing, the sport remains overwhelmingly male. Still, the National Football League reports that nearly half of its fans are women (Johnson 2020).

References

Allison, M.T. (1982). 'Sport, ethnicity, and assimilation', *Quest*, vol 34, no 2: 165–175.

Anderson, E.D. (2006). 'Using the master's tools: Resisting colonization through sport', *International Journal of the History of Sport*, vol 23: 247–266.

Batley, J. (2017). 'What does the 2016 census reveal about Pacific Islands communities in Australia?'. Available: https://devpolicy.org/2016-census-reveal-about-pacific-islands-communities-in-austral ia-20170928/, accessed 19 May 2020.

Bergin, P. (2002). 'Māori sport and cultural identity in Australia', *The Australian Journal of Anthropology*, vol 13, no 3: 257–269.

Besnier, N., Brownell, S., and Carter, T.F. (2018). *The Anthropology of Sport: Bodies, Borders, Biopolitics*. University of California Press: Berkeley, CA.

Bloom, J. (2000). *To Show What an Indian Can Do: Sports at Native American Boarding Schools*. University of Minnesota Press: Minneapolis, MN.

Burnett, C. (2014). 'Paradigm lost: Indigenous games and neoliberalism in the South African context', in C. Hallinan and B. Judd (eds.) *Native Games: Indigenous Peoples and Sports in the Post-Colonial World*. Emerald Group Publishing Limited: Bingley, 205–227.

Calabrò, D.G. (2016). 'Once were warriors, now are rugby players? Control and agency in the historical trajectory of the Māori formulations of masculinity in rugby', *The Asia Pacific Journal of Anthropology*, vol 17, no 3–4: 231–249.

Chen, C.H. (2014). 'Prioritizing hyper-masculinity in the Pacific region', *Culture, Society & Masculinities*, vol 6: 69–90.

Collins, T. (2013). *Rugby's Great Split: Class, Culture and the Origins of Rugby League Football*. Routledge: New York.

Cooky, C. and Messner, M.A. (2018). *No Slam Dunk: Gender, Sport and the Unevenness of Social Change*. Rutgers University Press: New Brunswick, NJ.

Cooky, C., Messner, M.A., and Hextrum, R.H. (2013). 'Women play sport, but not on TV: A longitudinal study of televised news media', *Communication & Sport*, vol 1, no 3: 203–230.

Craft, K. (2012). 'Will lacrosse ever go mainstream?', *Atlantic*. Available: https://www.theatlantic.com/entertainment/archive/2012/04/will-lacrosse-ever-go-mainstream/255690, accessed 10 March 2020.

Cunningham, J. and Beneforti, M. (2005). 'Investigating indicators for measuring the health and social impact of sport and recreation programs in Australian Indigenous communities', *International Review for the Sociology of Sport*, vol 40, no 1: 89–98.

Delashut, F. (2015). 'From *baggataway* to lacrosse: An example of the sportization of native American games', *The International Journal of the History of Sport*, vol 32, no 7: 923–938.

Dewey, R.F. (2008). 'Pacific Islands rugby: Navigating the global professional era', in G. Ryan (ed.) *The Changing Face of Rugby: The Union Game and Professionalism Since 1995*. Cambridge Scholars Publishing: Newcastle, UK, 82–108.

Diaz, V.M. (2002). 'Fight boys, 'til the last ...": Islandstyle football and the remasculinization of indigeneity in the militarized American Pacific islands', in P. Spickard, J.L. Rondilla, and D. Hippolite Wright (eds.) *Pacific Diaspora: Island Peoples in the United States and Across the Pacific*. University of Hawai'i Press: Honolulu, HI, 169–194.

Downey, A. (2012). 'Engendering nationality: Haudenosaunee tradition, sport, and the lines of gender', *Journal of the Canadian Historical Association – Revue de la Société Historique du Canada*, vol 23, no 1: 319–354.

Downey, A. (2018). *The Creator's Game: Lacrosse, Identity, and Indigenous Nationhood*. UBC Press: Victoria, BC.

Erueti, B. and Palmer, F.R. (2014). 'Te whariki tuakiri (the identity mat): Māori elite athletes and the expression of ethno-cultural identity in global sport', *Sport in Society*, vol 17, no 8: 1061–1075.

Ferguson, L., Epp, G.B., Wuttunee, K., Dunn, M., Mchugh, T.-L., and Humbert, M.L. (2019). 'It's more than just performing well in your sport. It's also about being healthy physically, mentally, emotionally, and spiritually': Indigenous women athletes' meanings and experiences of flourishing in sport', *Qualitative Research in Sport, Exercise and Health*, vol 11, no 1: 1–19.

Finney, B. (1959). 'Surfing in ancient Hawai'i', *Journal of the Polynesian Society*, vol 68, no 4: 327–347.

Finney, B.R. and Houston, J.D. (1996). *Surfing: A History of the Ancient Hawaiian Sport*. Pomegranate: Petaluma, CA.

Forsyth, J. and Wamsley, K.B. (2006). '"Native to native ... we'll recapture our spirits": The world indigenous nations games and north American indigenous games as cultural resistance'. *The International Journal of the History of Sport*, vol 23, no 2: 294–314.

Gems, G. (2004). 'Negotiating a native identity through sport: Assimilation, adaptation, and the role of the trickster', in C.R. King (ed.) *Native Athletes in Sport and Society*. University of Nebraska Press: Lincoln, NE, 1–21.

Hall, M.A. (2013). 'Toward a history of aboriginal women in Canadian sport', in J. Forsyth and A.R. Giles (eds.) *Aboriginal Peoples and Sport in Canada*. UBC Press: Vancouver, BC, 64–91.

Hayhurst, L.M.C., Giles, A.R., and Radforth, W.M. (2015). '"I want to come here to prove them wrong": Using a post-colonial feminist participatory action research (PFPAR) approach to studying sport, gender and development programmes for urban Indigenous young women', *Sport in Society*, vol 18, no 8: 952–967.

Heine, M.K. (2013). 'No "museum piece": Aboriginal games and cultural contestation in subarctic Canada', in C. Hallinan and B. Judd (eds.) *Native Games: Indigenous Peoples and Sports in the Post-Colonial World*. Emerald Group Publishing Limited: Bingley, 1–19.

Heiva i Tahiti. (n.d.). 'Traditional sports – Heiva Tu'aro Ma'ohi'. Available: https://www.heiva.org/en/event/heiva-tuaro-maohi-en/, accessed 10 March 2020.

Higa-Puaoi, M. (2017). 'A local's story: navigating the waves of life', Unpublished MA Plan B Paper. University of Hawai'i-Mānoa, Mānoa.

Hokowhitu, B. (2004). 'Tackling Māori masculinity: a colonial genealogy of savagery and sport', *The Contemporary Pacific*, vol 16, no 2: 259–284.

Hokowhitu, B. (2005). 'Rugby and tino rangatiratanga: Early Māori rugby and the formation of traditional Māori masculinity', *Sporting Traditions*, vol 21, no 2: 75–84.

Hokowhitu, B. (2009). 'Māori rugby and subversion: Creativity, domestication, oppression and decolonization', *The International Journal of the History of Sport*, vol 26, no 16: 2314–2334.

Hokowhitu, B. (2014). 'Haka: colonized physicality, body-logic, and embodied sovereignty', in L.R. Graham and H.G. Penny (eds.) *Performing Indigeneity: Global Histories and Contemporary Experiences*. University of Nebraska Press: Lincoln, NE, 273–304.

Jackson, S.J. and Hokowhitu, B. (2002). 'Sport, tribes, and technology: The New Zealand all blacks haka and the politics of identity', *Journal of Sport and Social Issues*, vol 26, no 2: 125–139.

Jeanes, R., Magee, J., Kay, T., and Banda, D. (2013). 'Sport for development in Zambia: The new or not so new colonisation?', in C. Hallinan and B. Judd (eds.) *Native Games: Indigenous Peoples and Sports in the Post-Colonial World*. Emerald Group Publishing Limited: Bingley, 127–145.

Jennings, M. (2017). 'Tonga's world cup revolution', *Athlete's Voice*. Available: https://www.athletesvoice .com.au/michael-jennings-tonga-world-cup-revolution/, accessed 21 December 2017.

Johnson, M. (2020). 'NFL says 47 percent of fans are women, launches women's history month'. Available: https://www.msn.com/en-us/sports/nfl/nfl-says-47-percent-of-fans-are-women-launches-womens -history-month/ar-BB10EvUf, accessed 20 March 2020.

Judd, B. (2008). *On the Boundary Line, Colonial Identity in Football*. Australian Scholarly Publishing: North Melbourne, VIC.

Judd, B. (2015). 'Good sports: Representations of aboriginal people in Australian sports', in K. Price (ed.) *Knowledge of Life: Aboriginal and Torres Strait Islander Australia*. Cambridge University Press: Cambridge, 184–202.

Kauanui, J.K. 2016. '"A structure, not an event": Settler colonialism and enduring indigeneity', *Lateral*, vol 5, no 1. https://doi.org/10.25158/L5.1.7.

King, C.R. (2007). *Native Americans and Sport in North America: Other People's Games*. Routledge: New York.

Laderman, S. (2014). *Empire in Waves: A Political History of Surfing*. University of California Press: Berkeley, CA.

Lakisa, D., Adair, D., and Taylor, T. (2014). 'Pasifika diaspora and the changing face of Australian Rugby league', *The Contemporary Pacific*, vol 26, no 2: 347–367.

Maguire, J. (1999). *Global Sport: Identities, Societies, Civilizations*. Blackwell: Malden, MA.

Maxwell, H., Stronach, M., Adair, D., and Pearce, S. (2017). 'Indigenous Australian women and sport: Findings and recommendations from a parliamentary inquiry', *Sport in Society*, vol 20, no 11: 1500–1529.

Mcdonald, B. and Rodriguez, L. (2014). '"It's our meal ticket": Pacific bodies, labour and mobility in Australia', *Asia Pacific Journal of Sport and Social Science*, vol 3, no 3: 236–249.

Mcgloin, C. (2007). 'Aboriginal surfing: Reinstating culture and country', *International Journal of the Humanities*, vol 4, no 1: 93–100.

Middleton, L. (2019). 'Record numbers of girls and women playing football after world cup'. Available: https://metro.co.uk/2019/07/09/record-amount-girls-women-playing-football-world-cup-101369 75/, accessed 20 march 2020.

Mila-Schaaf, K. and Robinson, E. (2010). '"Polycultural" capital and educational achievement among NZ-born Pacific peoples', *Mai Review*, vol 1: 1–18.

Miller, P.B. (1998). 'The anatomy of scientific racism: Racialist responses to Black athletic achievement', *Journal of Sport History*, vol 25, no 1: 119–151.

Nendel, J. (2009). 'Surfing in early twentieth-century Hawai'i: The appropriation of a transcendent experience to competitive American sport', *The International Journal of the History of Sport*, vol 26, no 16: 2432–2446.

Palmer, F. (2007). 'Body image, hauora and identity: Experiences of Māori girls in sport', *Childrenz Issues: Journal of the Children's Issues Centre*, vol 11, no 2: 12–19.

Palmer, F.R. (2016). 'Stories of haka and women's rugby in Aotearoa New Zealand: Weaving identities and ideologies together', *The International Journal of the History of Sport*, vol 33, no 17: 2169–2184.

Poulter, G. (2003). 'Snowshoeing and lacrosse: Canada's nineteenth-century "National Games"', *Culture, Sport, Society*, vol 6, no 2–3: 293–320.

Poulter, G. (2010). *Becoming Native in a Foreign Land: Sport, Visual Culture, and Identity in Montreal, 1840–85*. UBC Press: Vancouver, BC.

Rubenfeld, M. (2006). 'The mythical Jim Thorpe: Re/presenting the twentieth century American Indian', *International Journal of the History of Sport*, vol 23, no 2: 167–189.

Rutsky, R.L. (1999). 'Surfing the other: Ideology on the beach', *Film Quarterly*, vol 52, no 4: 12–23.

Sacks, B. (2019). *Cricket, Kirikiti and Imperialism in Samoa, 1879–1939*. Springer Nature Switzerland AG: Cham.

Shiu, R. and Vagana, N. (2016). *An Unlikely Alliance: Training NRL "Cultural Warriors": State, Society & Governance in Melanesia* Australian National University: Canberra, ACT.

Skille, E.Å. (2014). 'Lassoing and reindeer racing versus "universal" sports: Various routes to Sámi identity through sports', in C. Hallinan and B. Judd (eds.) *Native Games: Indigenous Peoples and Sports in the Post-Colonial World*. Emerald Group Publishing Limited: Bingley, 21–41.

Staurowsky, E.J., Miller, K., Shakib, S., De Souza, M.J., Ducher, G., Gentner, N., Theberge, N., and Williams, N.I. (2009). *Her Life Depends on It II: Sport, Physical Activity, and the Health and Well-Being of American Girls and Women*. Women's Sports Foundation: East Meadow, NY.

Stevenson, K. (1990). '"Heiva": Continuity and change of a Tahitian celebration', *Contemporary Pacific*, vol 2, no 2: 255–278.

Teaiwa, K.M. (2016). 'Niu mana, sport, media and the Australian diaspora', in M. Tomlinson and T. Tengan (eds) *New Mana: Transformations of a Classic Concept in Pacific Languages and Cultures*. ANU Press: Acton, ACT, 107–130.

Tengan, T.P.K. and Markham, J.M. (2009). 'Performing Polynesian masculinities in American football: From "rainbows to warriors"', *The International Journal of the History of Sport*, vol 26, no 16: 2412–2431.

Tupou, D. (2017). 'Die for Tonga', *Players Voice*. Available: https://www.athletesvoice.com.au/daniel-tupou-die-for-tonga/, accessed 21 December 2017.

Uperesa, F.L. (2014a). 'Fabled futures: Migration and mobility for Samoans in American football', *The Contemporary Pacific*, vol 27, no 2: 281–301.

Uperesa, F.L. (2014b). 'Seeking new fields of labor: Football and colonial political economies in American Samoa', in A. Goldstein (ed.) *Formations of U.S. Colonialism*. Duke University Press: Durham, NC, 207–232.

Uperesa, F.L. (2018). 'Training the body for empire?: Samoa and American gridiron football', in C. McGranahan and J. Collins (eds.) *Ethnographies of U.S. Empire*. Duke University Press: Durham, NC, 129–148.

Uperesa, F.L. and Mountjoy, T. (2014). 'Global sport in the Pacific: A brief overview', *The Contemporary Pacific*, vol 26, no 2: 263–279.

Walker, I.H. (2005). 'Terrorism or native protest?', *Pacific Historical Review*, vol 74, no 4: 575–602.

Walker, I.H. (2008). 'Hui Nalu, beachboys, and the surfing boarder-lands of Hawai'i', *Contemporary Pacific*, vol 20, no 1: 89–113.

Walker, I.H. (2011). *Waves of Resistance: Surfing and History in Twentieth-Century Hawai'i*. University of Hawai'i Press: Honolulu, HI.

West, P. (2014). '"Such a site for play, this edge": Surfing, tourism, and modernist fantasy in Papua New Guinea', *The Contemporary Pacific*, vol 26, no 2: 411–432.

Wikaire, R.K. and Newman, J.I. (2014). 'Neoliberalism as neocolonialism?: Considerations on the marketisation of waka ama in Aotearoa/New Zealand', in C. Hallinan and B. Judd (eds.) *Native Games: Indigenous Peoples and Sports in the Post-colonial World*. Emerald Group Publishing Limited: Bingley, 59–83.

Wolfe, P. (2006). 'Settler colonialism and the elimination of the native', *Journal of Genocide Research*, vol 8, no 4: 387–409.

39

Raranga as healing methodology
Body, place, and making

Tāwhanga Nopera

Raranga is the process of under and over weaving and is one of many embodied knowledge traditions. Many Māori weavers express how raranga helps, other weavers often say to me, 'raranga saved my life'. I have used raranga to help heal from experiences of harm. In this chapter, I describe raranga as enabling transformation, not just in the actions of weaving leaves from a plant into functional and beautiful forms, but also in the ways that raranga knowledge helps transform my body's response to the terror-formed landscape that is New Zealand. I work primarily in self-portraiture and position my practice of using raranga within Kaupapa Māori praxis, which embeds me in community practicing values that align me to my source as a Māori person (Campbell 2014; Hohepa 2014; Pihama 2001; 2010; 2014; Smith, G.H. 1997; 2012; Smith, H. 2007; Pohatu 2004; Awekotuku 2004; Smith, L.T., 1999; Durie 1998; Marsden 1992). While theory is important to help understand what has happened to me and to concep-tualise the root cause of many hurts, it is connected to finding out what things I do every day to encourage wellness and hope. To show others my journey towards this, in this chapter I describe two untitled series of works to explain how I use raranga as a healing methodology.

Many Indigenous people discuss the need to return to story and ceremony to retain, nur-ture and increase our collective strength (Sousanis 2014; Wall Kimmerer 2013; Kovach 2012; Lee 2009; Wilson 2008; Maracle 1994). When making art, I rely on raranga as a ceremonial process to guide my faith; this always takes me from an idea to a beautiful thing. Regardless of media, when making art the works may change many times as I flow between assemblage and erasure; it is in the making and unmaking I move towards resolution. Producing beautiful images is not an important goal in making these works; rather, I use raranga to help resolve my personal internal puzzles. These pictures are each made in less than 30 minutes and are parts of a much bigger picture, story, theoretical discussion, and healing. I believe that making art is about helping make myself better, more resolved and coherent, rather than the material things I make. To me, making art is a way to see my mirror self, the person others see – the person I often deny. Regardless of the aesthetics of any artwork be it a kete, which is a type of basket, or a Picasso painting, both hold significant meaning and value. Often, I make something I regard as throw-away, but others will see it as really beautiful; I know this too is akin to the difference between the way I see myself and the ways in which I am seen. I like having opportunities to see things differently, and raranga helps me to see the world from many vantages and through many dimensions.

When I raranga, it begins with a *moemoeā*, a frozen dream from elsewhere that I hold and warm inside my body. In *If You Leave* (2016), I go to the place I gathered images used to make a 2009 artwork *GAY MES GAY MES GAY MES*, which features in the *Te Ara Online Dictionary of New Zealand* to help describe 'Hokakatanga – Māori Sexualities'. In 2009, I recognised an internal gender battle, and this is something I sought to heal. The place in the image is definitive of where I have confronted this battle, time and time again. Figure 39.1. *If You Leave* reimagines this space. I gathered similar images to those collected in 2009 and re-imaged the space without me in it. In this work I give myself an opportunity to think about the dreams I hold close, asking myself about the things in life that keep them at a distance? I was listening to *If You Leave* by Mental as anything when I layered the images and played with filters to achieve a snapshot of what my dream might look like.

Figure 39.2. *You'll Never Find* (2016) is another way of interpreting the same *moemoeā*. In this image I gather, prepare, and work with snapshots taken whilst flying to Honolulu. I always feel expansive when in the air; I obtain a sense of perspective on all my concerns and shifting thoughts. I was listening to 'You'll Never Find Another Love Like Mine' (1976) by Lou Rawls when I created this image, and after placing some of the lyrics in the image, I found out Lou produced the song in the year I was born. In this artwork, I depict a feeling of wellness and promise, but also name the slow-burning fear of never embodying my dreams.

Whilst staying in a hotel in Waikiki I looked out to Diamond Head and imagined what the eruption may have looked like; I think about the ancient prayers chanted by my ancient Kanaka Māoli ancestors in witnessing and surviving that explosion. I gather images of the landscape surrounding me in Waikiki as I peer through hotel windows and I apply them toward Figure 39.3. *Arawai Moana* (2016). This image is about *karakia*, which is like a prayer but is far more assertive than what I learned at church. Karakia I have been taught, acknowledge an abundance of energy that I draw on to create, but they also remind me of difficult lessons about respectfulness that

Figure 39.1 Nopera, T. (2016) If you leave [digital image] 100.84 cm × 56.73 cm.

Figure 39.2 Nopera, T. (2016) You'll never find [digital image] 1280 × 720 pixels.

will be part of any journey. Before this work I lived my life according to a defensive survival strategy; always on the ready to protect myself. In making the art I listened to a song by Miike Snow called *Cult Logic* (2009); a song that always reminds me of a close Unungax friend from Bristol Bay and Southern Puget Sound.

Kohikohi is when I gather things to help me toward my moemoeā. In having acknowledged the energies I need to create my moemoeā, I then collect from my surrounds. In Figure 39.4. *God Help This Divorce* (2016), titled after another song by Miike Snow, I gathered images in

Figure 39.3 Nopera, T. (2016) *Arawai Moana* [digital image] 100.84 cm × 56.73 cm.

527

Figure 39.4 Nopera, T. (2016) God help this divorce [digital image] 100.84 cm × 56.73 cm.

Mismaloya Mexico, where I stayed by myself for a time to help get into a better space. I pretty much spent six months living in cheap accommodation eating delicious fresh and cheap amazing food. The image reflects me feeling humble, gathering energy towards myself to heal and move forward in life. The title too, is a reminder of intentionally letting go of other energies, energies that have been useful but now must be let go of to make space for the new or reinvigorated energies I am inviting in. In a practical sense, making self-portraits is sometimes about trying to make myself look beautiful, and I feel like I look good and in control in this image.

Figure 39.5. *A bad name* (2016) was created using images gathered at Mauna Kea on the Big Island of Hawai'i, and it takes its name from the 1980s rock song by Bon Jovi. The image depicts

Figure 39.5 Nopera, T. (2016) A bad name [digital image] 100.84 cm × 56.73 cm.

me in a state of readiness, I am ready to *whakariterite*, or prepare the energies I gather so that I am responsive to them. When I work with *harakeke*, the fibre most commonly used for raranga, it is important that it is prepared in very specific ways before it transformed into the objects I use in my daily and ceremonial life. Sizing is important to make strands of regular length and width is crucial to get a consistent tension, as well as patterns, and harakeke must be softened to make it workable. It is the same with digital images, each must be adjusted digitally to make allowances for differences in the ways people and cameras perceive colour. Time spent in whakariterite helps me formulate a strategy, it gives me deeper knowledge of the material I create with so that I can better understand how to resolve issues when they arise.

The images I used to make Figure 39.6. *drink on my mind* (2016) were gathered in my village of Ohinemutu, at a place that used to be Ruapeka Pā, as well as a photo of clouds that I gathered in California. Our pūrakau, or stories, remind us that the Ruapeka was sunk through the powerful karakia chanted by people who had returned to settle a score after having been insulted. I considered this a good place to help convey ideas about *whakapapa*, which is a Māori genealogical system that connects us to everything in the universe. At the whakapapa stage of making, I embed the foundational design and form of the object to be made, including its shapes for weaving, this is where patterns are woven. In this image I invert a self-portrait image adding to it, an image of hawk wings that a friend had removed from a hawk after we found it dead roadside in California. At the time of making this I had been listening to 'I'll Drink to That' (2010) by Rihanna and it resonated with both some of the healing I need to, as well as celebrations I want to have.

To create Figure 39.7. *let it buuuuuurn* (2016), I only used two images, one from the window of my family home in Rotorua, and the other a self-image gathered whilst staying in an Auckland hotel. I use a blending option to inverse the colours on the greyscale landscape overexposing the self-portrait image, changing it to red to contrast against the background. This image is simple to represent the *mahi* raranga stage of a raranga process. Mahi means 'work' in te reo Māori, and even though the whole process is raranga, this is the part where the preparations

Figure 39.6 Nopera, T. (2016) drink on my mind [digital image] 100.84 cm × 56.73 cm.

Figure 39.7 Nopera, T. (2016) let it buuuuuurn [digital image] 100.84 cm × 56.73 cm.

begin to be assembled. Because I have already dreamt, focussed my intent through karakia, gathered and prepared material and then created a foundation for the work to be done through laying out a whakapapa, the actual making is simple with intuitive thinking rather than structured thinking dominant in the process. I included lyrics from 'Set Fire to the Rain' (2011) by Adele in this work, reminding me that a raranga process allows me an intuitive way of thinking so that the emotions I feel can be held in my body and conveyed with intent into my art.

Figure 39.8. *Poutama* (2016) is a composite digital image created using three images from Te Arikiroa (Sulphur Bay) Rotorua. The images have been copied and mirrored before being

Figure 39.8 Nopera, T. (2016) Poutama [digital image] 100.84 cm × 56.73 cm.

juxtaposed with an image of a pencil drawing and self-portrait image which has been copied and pasted multiple times. This image describes *whakatutuki* as part of raranga, where I make decisions about how I will resolve and meet my visions, dreams, and goals. In this artwork my self-portrait image is placed in an ascending pattern, replicating a *poutama* pattern. A poutama describes the journey of a man through his life and onward into the afterlife. Recovery from drug addiction is part of my journey, and at the time of making this artwork I was listening to 'Climb Every Mountain' (1965) by Rodgers and Hammerstein. In my reading of this artwork there is an uneasy tension in the way it is resolved, a reminder to me that resolution is not about making things perfect, it is also about acceptance.

The background landscape images for Figure 39.9. *They Can Come True* (2016) was created using images gathered in Waikiki as with *Arawai Moana* (2016). I inverted the colour in three self-portrait figures and combined them to reference 'the three graces' in Botticelli's painting *Primavera* (c.1482). In Botticelli's painting, the three graces represent three feminine graces of chastity, beauty, and love. After resolving or finishing something it is important for me to karakia again, helping me to acknowledge the learnings I am blessed with through making, as well as the new insights that I have discovered and desire to explore further. I was listening to Billy Ocean's 'Caribbean Queen' (1984), and adapted lyrics from the chorus to gay slang. In the weaving together of these images I begin to imagine what comes next, dreaming new pathways to traverse and new forms to create.

Figure 39.10. *Queendom* (2016) was created using images gathered in three places, Naknek in Bristol Bay Alaska, Ohinemutu, and Boca De Tomatlan in Mexico. The figures in the image are silhouettes of two Native friends from Bristol Bay in Alaska, whose images I gathered whilst they fished the Naknek River one winter. The Ohinemutu image depicts my ancestral meeting house, which I can see from whānau home and is named after my ancestor Tamatekapua who captained other ancestors across Te Moana Nui a Kiwa, the great ocean of Kiwa, to where my tribe now lives in Aotearoa. I used the image gathered in Boca de Tomatlan because it reflects a time when I was making new plans and feeling excited about life working in a sexual and

Figure 39.9 Nopera, T. (2016) They can come true [digital image] 100.84 cm × 56.73 cm.

Figure 39.10 Nopera, T. (2016) Queendom [digital image] 100.84 cm × 56.73 cm.

reproductive health space. I use lyrics from Diddy and Skylar Grey's song 'Coming Home' (2010) because completing a mahi raranga feels like a return to my best self; a homecoming. This is a *moemoeā anō* – a new dream envisioning future hopes.

Previously I highlighted raranga as a healing process, and descriptions to this point have outlined the sequence of that process. What follows is a discussion of three works (Figures 39.11– 39.13) speaking to the trauma I have experienced, and the creation of a performance ceremony exposing it in order to alleviate its impact. The trauma I experience stems from stigmas about sex and sexuality derived from populations who continue to colonise Aotearoa, and as a result have completely changed Māori understandings. I identify as *whakawāhine*, which means to be like a woman, and I contracted HIV at 22 in 1998. Due to this lived experience I began to work alongside Māori researchers in the sexual and reproductive health sector. These collaborations gave me opportunities to understand the barriers that victimise transgender people and people living with HIV, also enabling me to share ideas with health clinicians, researchers and government agencies as an important part of my practice.

The three works emerged from a vision; a reoccurring dream that began to solidify in my mind as a performance I should enact as ceremony, but an intimate one that would involve only a photographer and myself. Being true to the vision in my mind was absolutely crucial because I felt the picture in my mind to be messages from my ancestors; they involved sacred spaces and revered forms that are part of my village landscape. Prominent in my vision was one *pou*, or carved post, created for my village by my ancestor Tene Waitere. The pou had been carved to hold a wooden bust of Queen Victoria, gifted to us natives by her royal majesty. Throughout my life there had been a lot of political activity involving the pou as it moved slowly from a very central place to the peripheries of my village meeting space. The decentralisation occurred as generations became more and more frustrated at the lack of honesty and deceitful intentions of colonial and neo-colonial agents. When I was in my late teens the bust of Queen Victoria completely disappeared, someone had decided to remove it and hide it in protest. Eventually it was recovered and since 2019 it has rested upon the pou, yet it was recently vandalised which re-ignited debate as to its appropriateness in our village.

Figure 39.11 Nopera, T. (2016) Untitled 1 [Kodak endura print], 56 cm × 72 cm.

I worked with and was photographed by a good friend Riley Claxton who, as a photographer, I felt comfortable with. Riley understands me, which was important because the idea needed a sounding board; another set of eyes and ears to help guide the visions toward tangible outcomes. The dreams I was having were uneasy, dealing with the types of embodied sexual and reproductive trauma I was hearing from others and reading a lot about. I wanted to utilise the eerie calm that inhabits my village in the evening when all the tourists have left and there are only the sounds of bubbling hot pools and hissing steam that vents from the ground. At first when I talked to Riley about using fake blood and performing genital mutilation, he commented that it was a departure from the ways I had been making previously. However, I felt like my research journey was coming full circle, as if the works I had spent nearly four years creating were getting me to a point where I would feel confident enough to create quite direct work that could expose deeply hidden realities.

The performance was by no means public, even though it was enacted in the most open space in my village, near the *atea*, the space of challenge in which people gather before entering our ancestral meeting house. Because it was in the evening, I knew most of my relations would be inside and so no one would see us. The steam creates clouds everywhere and through LED lights, which I spray painted to diffuse and tint the light, Riley and I set quite a mysterious scene. Riley is an expert at staging cinematic images and the LED lights were a good means of

Figure 39.12 Nopera, T. (2016) Untitled 2 [Kodak endura print], 72 cm × 56 cm.

Figure 39.13 Nopera, T. (2016) Untitled 3 [Kodak endura print], 72 cm × 56 cm.

making my home seem alien, as opposed to its usual postcard semblance. Before Riley and I met, I shaved and put on more make-up than usual, dressing myself in a red cardigan, a red woollen hat and harakeke accessories that I had woven years earlier. The props I used for the images were a toy rifle, a large knife and a batch of fake blood that I eventually poured between my legs.

I suppose for someone not from Ohinemutu, night in the village can be daunting. With the steam, the graveyard and so many intricately carved Māori buildings it can seem like a very sacred place, which of course it is. However, the sacred spaces in Ohinemutu are also part of my home, they are the forms, figures, boiling vents and concrete statues that I have played amongst my entire life. For me, the unusual scene of my home represents the type of strangeness that I wanted to express in the images I had been dreaming. Riley felt uncomfortable taking the images because the scene appeared so heavy, but after having a good talk, saying a karakia and burning some sage gifted to me by a Dakota friend, Riley felt a lot better. For me, it was important to use the gifted sage because after being sexually assaulted in San Francisco, sage was the medicine used to help me feel safe on my return home to Aotearoa.

The only other medicine I ever used to heal from that incident was making art, and so it was important to include Riley in a ceremony where I enacted a pathway to heal. The photoshoot lasted about 45 minutes. I had a pretty good idea already of what I wanted to achieve, so I directed Riley with instructions about where to be and what kinds of images to gather. In response, Riley directed me on where to look, what kinds of facial expressions worked best and how to maintain good angles in relation to the light. I felt really uncomfortable because I was exposed and visible and in part because it was getting cold. As well, the fake blood had been made out of icing sugar and red food colouring, it was sticky and had started to congeal with the red glitter I had also poured liberally between my thighs. I felt incredibly gross, especially whilst performing doing gross things to my body.

From a total of 75 images gathered that night, Riley and I selected three. I had a very clear idea of what I wanted each image to look like so Riley and I gathered images until we were able to depict these. In essence, I warmed up – performing in front of the camera until we 'arrived' at the image I had in my head. For the first of the three images, I wanted to depict ideas about the loss of Māori men through colonial wars, and the disabling impact upon knowledge transmission between men and young men in relation to forms of masculinity. For the second image, I wanted to convey ideas about gender dysphoria and self-body mutilation. Part of the narrative I wanted to express for this image was to describe the internal mania of living between genders where mind and body are at a mis-match. For the final image, I wanted to express ideas about death and rebirth. 'Black lives matter' had been prominent in social media at the time and it had made me think a lot about how important Māori lives are. So many of our young men are ending their own lives, and with suicidal tendencies something that I have always fought to overcome, I was grasping for hope through the creation of an image.

I printed these at slightly larger than A3 on Kodak endure, a metallic photographic paper I have used in the past that enhances colour saturation. Rather than create photographic images in the same vein as those previously described, using muted colours, I wanted to focus on the use of reds and pinks to describe the visceral nature of the dreams I was having. These works were intended to be highly polished for a public exhibition. I exhibited the three untitled works at a group show of artists, alongside Rotorua artists Chanz Mikaere, Riley Claxton, Don Overbeay, and Mark and Paul Rayner from Whanganui. The exhibition was called Trans and ran from August to December 2016 at Helium Gallery in Rotorua – each artist was given the opportunity to express 'Trans' in ways that made sense to them.

As well as the works exhibited at Helium Gallery, I created a short animated video, using the images Riley had gathered. At the time, resolution of the video work wasn't the primary objective. I was interested in applying the automated batch animation process I had developed in the first year of my project to the images, as a way, to create a secondary image-based performance. To make the video, as with other works I adjusted the contrast, brightness, and vibrancy of each image, but I also completely removed the colour in all but a few images; for those images I desaturated the hues but left tints of colour. I did this because of the highly emotive content of the images. I wanted a way to maintain the seriousness I attempted to communicate, but at the same time enable a degree of distance so that I could analyse what messages surfaced through the video without feeling overwhelmed by them. When I had studied at drama school between 2001 and 2003, it had been impressed upon me not to use coloured lights because colour is evocative, and that to really test the cohesiveness of our ideas, we should always try to work with the tonality offered by white light. After the initial processing of images, I batch edited them to create an animation in Photoshop. The work is very raw and after making it, I felt confronted.

The final video work (Figure 39.14) titled *Trouble* (2016) could be regarded as a one-liner and violent, which is feedback I have received. The fake blood refers to the extreme decisions transgender people are often faced with to help their bodies match their feelings of gender identity, and the loss of men's blood through wars fought for British and US power. I have been critiqued on the 'shock art' tactics used in the work, with the comment that this is the domain of white artists who may have neither the communal accountability nor the refined critical lens. However, I assert the need to voice the kinds of sociocultural norms that have often present extreme barriers for Māori transgender people. A significant body of evidence articulates the clear relationship between discrimination and barriers to wellness for transgender people (Birkenhead and Rands 2012; Delahunt, et al. 2016; Dudding 2017; Gender Minorities Aotearoa 2016; Negin et al. 2015; Pega et al. 2017; Quill 2016; Reisner et al. 2016; Reynolds 2012; Richards et al. 2015; Witten 2007). It is my responsibility as a Māori artist and scholar to communicate about the impact of harm that surrounds me.

Figure 39.14 Nopera, T. (2016) Trouble [digital video still] 1280px × 720px.

The otherworldly setting of the video exacerbates actions in the video, and when I have played it to audiences, I have described the location as my backyard, which it is really. The strategy I have employed to counter criticism surrounding *Trouble* has been to speak directly to issues with audiences whilst the work is played. I tend to think of my work as parts of the whole, so of course, without the context provided it is more open to critique. However, it was a work I was compelled to create and I do not hide from the responsibility I feel to Māori people trying to make sense of their genders, their lost histories and the violating feeling of colonial trauma.

In this chapter I have story-told my methods toward healing and wellness, the story has been simplified here to its barest bones, so that others can see the order of my thinking and use it to trace the trajectory of their own dreams and envisioning. The important thing to know is that when I began telling myself my own stories, even though at first I didn't believe that I could control the outcomes of my own story, in its continual retelling I can see that I am changing into the best story I could ever imagine.

The works described in this chapter were created for my PhD thesis, where they are described differently. In their making, I travelled to many different places, collecting knowledge to guide my processes and continue making. From a western theoretical perspective my art fits within the realm 'Relational Aesthetics', described by Nicholas Borriaud as participatory and interactive engagements that are open-ended, process-based and in-progress rather than resolved and easily saleable (Beech 2011; Bishop 2004: Choi 2013; Patrick 2010; Rottner 2011; Watson 2015). However, my intent is beyond Bourriaud's description of relational objects because rather than instigate a new approach, I continue an intergenerational responsibility to community as a person from a genealogy of expert makers. I make my work within a cultural knowledge framework that does not question my role as an artist in enabling collective processes, just by doing what I do I affirm my community, or stories and our relationship to others and their stories. The ways in which these works have emerged engage a network of relationships that Bishop (2004), Choi (2013), Patrick (2010), Rottner (2011), and Watson (2015) envision for relational aesthetics because they intend to reach beyond the destructive power of colonialism to engage collective processes of empowerment.

For the most part, even though this research is framed within an academic context, the knowledge within is pretty simple; raranga as a healing methodology, helps me think about the things I do, giving me a logical pathway to interpret and have control over the processes I utilise. Gaining mastery over creative processes is healing, because not only does it feel good to make nice things, it feels good to know that it is me who makes these things good. In these works, I assemble images of myself in many different worlds; I overlay them into singular images and then organise them to see where I have been and where I am going; from moemoeā to moemoeā anō. I create a sacred space and I perform a version of myself brave enough to contend with my own past; perhaps it is no different to the process of dressing up and going to a theme party or doing Halloween. The performance nonetheless is intentional, it is about gaining mana motuhake, or complete autonomy through consciously applying an ordered range of actions that exposes past hurts, imbuing them with more hopeful energy, and in doing so embody practices that will heal. Raranga is an embodied way of thinking that helps me re-story past hurts, so that rather than remaining only a painful memory, I can externalise the hurt and make it something beautiful. With the continued prospect of complete systemic failure looming, large tracts of the Earth's surface on fire, and yet another super-flu bug reinforcing apocalyptic fears, raranga offers a way to heal and plan for hopeful futures.

References

Awekotuku, N. (2004). 'Ma hea – which way? Mo te aha – what for? Too many questions, not enough answers, for Māori on the march', Keynote presented at *The Annual Conference of the NZ Psychological Society*, 29–31 August, Christchurch, New Zealand.

Beech, D. (2011). 'Don't look now! Art after the viewer and beyond participation', in J. Walwin, J. Scheer, and A. Teresa (eds.) *Searching for Art's New Publics*. Intellect Books: Bristol, 15–29.

Birkenhead, A. and Rands, D. (2012). *Let's Talk About Sex (Sexuality and Gender): Improving Mental Health and Addiction Services for Rainbow Communities*. Auckland District Health Board: Auckland.

Bishop, C. (2004). 'Antagonism and relational aesthetics', *OCTOBER*, vol 110: 51–79. October Magazine Ltd, Massachusetts Institute of Technology, Massachusetts.

Campbell, D., and Tiakina Te Pā Harakeke (Issuing Body). (2014). *Ngā Kura A Hine-Tē-Iwaiwa Exhibition*, 14–27 May. Creative Waikato: Hamilton.

Choi, S. (2013). 'Relational aesthetics in art museum education: Engendering visitors' narratives through participatory act for interpretive experience', *Studies in Art Education: A Journal of Issues and Research*, vol 55, no 11: 51–63.

Delahunt, J., Denison, H., Kennedy, J., Hilton, J., Young, H., Chaudhri, O., and Elston, M. (2016). 'Specialist services for management of individuals identifying as transgender in New Zealand', *New Zealand Medical Journal*, vol 129, no 1434: 49–58.

Dudding, A. (2017). 'Welcome to the rainbow world of gender and sexuality', *Stuff*. Available: http://www.stuff.co.nz/life-style/life/81125652/Welcome-to-the-rainbowworld-ofgender-and-sexuality, accessed 5 May 2017.

Durie, M. (1998). *Te Mana, te Kāwanatanga: The Politics of Māori Self-determination*. Oxford University Press: Auckland.

Gender Minorities Aotearoa. (2016). *Gender Minorities Aotearoa*. Gender Minorities Aotearoa: Wellington.

Hohepa, M. (2014). 'Te hokinga ki te pā harakeke', Unpublished paper presented at *Tiakina te Pā Harakeke: A Knowledge Exchange Symposium on Māori Childrearing*, February 10–11. Waikato-Tainui College for Research and Development, Hopuhopu.

Kovach, M. (2012). *Indigenous Methodologies: Characteristics, Conversations, and Contexts*. University of Toronto Press: Toronto.

Lee, J. (2009). 'Decolonising Māori narratives', *MAI Review*, vol 2: 1–12.

Maracle, L. (1994). 'Oratory coming to theory', *Essays on Canadian Writing*, vol 54, no 54: 7–11.

Marsden, M. (1992). 'God, man and universe: A Māori view', in M. King (ed.) *Te Ao Hurihuri: Aspects of Māoritanga*. Reed: Auckland, 191–220.

Negin, J., Aspin, C., Gadsden, T., and Reading, C. (2015). 'HIV among Indigenous peoples: A review of the literature on HIV-related behaviour since the beginning of the epidemic', *AIDS and Behavior*, vol 19, no 9: 1720–1734.

Patrick, M. (2010). 'Unfinished Filliou: On the fluxus ethos and the origins of relational aesthetics', *Art Journal*, vol 69, no 1–2: 44–61.

Pega, F., Reisner, S., Sell, R., and Veale, J.F. (2017). 'Transgender health: New Zealand's innovative statistical standard for gender identity', *American Journal of Public Health*, vol 107, no 2: 217–221.

Pihama, L. (2001). *Tihei Mauri Ora: Honouring Our Voices – Mana Wahine as a Kaupapa Māori Theoretical Framework*. Unpublished PhD thesis. University of Auckland, Auckland.

Pihama, L. (2010). 'Kaupapa Māori theory: Transforming theory in Aotearoa', *He Pukenga Kōrero*, vol 9, no 2: 5–14. Te Pūtahi-a-Toi: Palmerston North.

Pihama, L. (2014). *Tiakina te pā harakeke: Māori Childrearing in the Context of Whānau Ora*. Ngā Pae o te Maramatanga: Auckland. Available: http://mediacentre.maramatanga.ac.nz/content/tiakina-pa-hara keke, accessed 15 May 2020.

Pohatu T.W. (2004). 'Āta: Growing respectful relationships', *He Pukenga Kōrero*, vol 8, no 1: 1–8.

Quill, A. (2016). 'Transgender stories: when you are born in the wrong body - just like Caitlyn Jenner', *New Zealand Herald*, 24 September. Available: https://www.nzherald.co.nz/nz/news/article.cfm?c_id=1&objectid=11715060, accessed 15 May 2020.

Reisner, S. L., Poteat, T., Keatley, J., Cabral, M., Mothopeng, T., Dunham, E., and Baral, S. D. (2016). 'Global health burden and needs of transgender populations: A review', *The Lancet*, vol 388, no 10042: 412–436.

Reynolds, P. (2012). 'Trauma and Māori LGBTQ (Takataapui) in New Zealand', *Traumatic Stress Points*, vol 26, no 4: 9–10.

Richards, C., Arcelus, J., Barrett, J., Bouman, W., Lenihan, P., Lorimer, S., and Seal, L. (2015). 'Trans is not a disorder – but should still receive funding', *Sexual and Relationship Therapy*, vol 30, no 3: 309–313.

Rottner, N. (2011). 'Relational aesthetics', *Grove Art Online* https://www.oxfordartonline.com/groveart/browse?btog=chap&subSite=groveart&t=art_ArtFormsAndPractices%3A1&t0=art_ArtFormsAndPractices%3A21.

Smith, G.H. (1997). *The Development of Kaupapa Māori: Theory and Praxis.* Unpublished PhD thesis. University of Auckland, Auckland.

Smith, G.H, Hoskins, T.K., and Jones, A. (2012). 'Interview – Kaupapa Māori: the dangers of domestication', *New Zealand Journal of Educational Studies*, vol 47, no 2: 10–20.

Smith, L.T. (1999). *Decolonising Methodologies: Research and Indigenous Peoples.* Zed Books: London.

Smith, S.M. (2007). *Hei Whenua Ora: Hapū and iwi Approaches for Reinstating Valued Ecosystems Within Cultural Landscape.* Unpublished PhD thesis. Massey University, Palmerston North.

Sousanis, N. (2014). 'Threads: A spinning fable', *Journal of Curriculum and Pedagogy*, vol 11, no 2: 102–106. Routledge: New York.

Wall Kimmerer, R. (2013). *Braiding Sweetgrass: Indigenous Wisdom, Scientific Knowledge, and the Teachings of Plants.* Milkweed Editions: Minneapolis.

Watson, M. (2015). 'Centring the Indigenous', *Third Text*, vol 29, no 3: 141–154.

Wilson, S. (2008). *Research Is Ceremony: Indigenous Research Methods.* Fernwood Publishing: Blackpoint.

Witten, T.M. (2007). 'Transgender bodies, identities, and healthcare: Effects of perceived and actual violence and abuse', in J.J. Kronenfeld (ed.) *Inequalities and Disparities in Health Care and Health: Concerns of Patients, Providers and Insurers*, RSHC vol 25. Emerald Group Publishing: Bradford, 225–249.

40

Becoming knowledgeable

Indigenous embodied praxis

Simone Ulalka Tur

Introduction

> The relationship with others is at the core of bringing stories to life.
>
> *(Phillips and Bunda 2018: 86).*

The Phillips and Bunda quote that starts this chapter contains the core idea of relationality that is central to this story; a story of senior Aboriginal women's activism by the Kupa Piti Kungka Tjuṯa (senior Aboriginal women from Coober Pedy, South Australia); a story of deep responsibility to protect Country as part as the Irati Wanti – 'Leave the Poison' campaign in the late 1990s opposing a proposal by the Australian government to build a nuclear waste dump in the remote part of South Australia. The women spoke strong and talked straight out about their opposition to the proposed waste dump, in their words they stated:

> We are the Aboriginal women.Yankunytjatjara,Antikarinya, and Kokatha.We know the Country. The poison the Government is talking about will poison the land.We say 'No' Radioactive dump in our ngura–in our Country. It's strictly poison.We had enough at Maralinga and Emu Junction.They never let people know, never ask Aboriginal people.We never tell them to go ahead, wiya no.This time we say "NO". But they are still coming. We say 'NO'.We're crying for the little ones. Little ones coming up.They want to see the old Country too.
>
> *(Kupa Piti Kungka Tjuṯa Editorial Committee et al. 2005: 53)*

The Kupa Piti Kungka Tjuṯa's campaigning was successful and the proposed dump site withdrawn. Many lessons have come from this campaign, and many of these women have passed on since this time, what remains is their strength and activism to fight.Their key messages are the responsibility to protect Country, stay strong and never stop talking about issues of Country and justice. I honour the Kupa Piti Kungka Tjuṯa and the knowledge and lessons they have taught me about what it means to resist and fight for what is right. I honour all Aboriginal people fighting to protect their Country.

Importance of Country-stay strong-talking straight out form some of the following principles with this article about what I mean to 'become knowledgeable' from the standpoint of an Aṉangu (western desert Aboriginal person, people) academic and what knowledge is needed when teaching Indigenous Studies within a university to Indigenous and non-Indigenous students.

To shape this story I begin and end with a song; a way to frame a methodical approach to build an Indigenous Studies decolonising praxis in the higher education context; an outcome of my PhD thesis titled *Pulkara Nintiringanyi – Becoming Knowledgeable Embodied Activist Pedagogy: Educational Praxis from an Anangu Woman's Standpoint* (Tur 2018).

The building of my praxis has come out of two decades of teaching within Indigenous Education and Studies within a university. It is also informed by my Senior Knowledge Holders, including my late Ngunytju (mother) and senior members of the Kupa Piti Kungka Tjuta. My praxis is situated in the knowledge which has grounded me and is embedded in the responsibility to protect Country guided by Senior Knowledge Holders, the importance to stand strong and talk straight out, as the daily work of decolonising institutions.

The purpose of my 'becoming knowledgeable' praxis is to develop and advance a theoretically sound and culturally embedded 'methodical praxis' – principally for the teaching of pre-service teachers from an Anangu perspective – but also applicable to other sites of Indigenous Education as a generic practice, when engaging with cultural, social or political matters beyond the academy. The objective is to 'decolonise' education practice. Formal *and* informal sites of education can be reciprocating proving grounds of ideas and practices.

My process of 'becoming knowledgeable' within an Anangu context (Tur and Tur 2006; Tur 2018), is shaped by Senior Knowledge Holders, connection to Country and the Anangu philosophy of Ngapartji-Ngapartji; that is, reciprocation and mutual benefit taught to me by my late mother, my Kami's (Grandmother's) and Senior Women Knowledge Holders. My relationality to Country, Elders, and Knowledge Holders is culturally located and specific. My Indigenous women's standpoint (Moreton-Robinson 2013) grounds and underpins my way of knowing within my personal life but also within a university context as an Indigenous academic and within the public domain where education and research border-cross through time, space and place. My standpoint centres Aboriginal activism through the sharing of the Irati Wanti ('Leave the Poison') anti-nuclear campaign. This campaign informs the way in which localised Indigenous community standpoints through the protection of Country, Activism, and educational philosophies shape the personal, public, and professional praxis of an Anangu/Aboriginal academic within research, community, and engagement and, in particular, teaching within Indigenous Studies and Education.

The Anangu framework I propose arises from a 'reconciliation' of approaches and connects Country and community to applied scholarship in the classroom and back again as a cyclic process. It is dynamic by nature but grounded in location, context, and protocol. Eight principles of practice are advanced, which are drawn from scholarly literature and my experience of joining theory with practice. These principles lead to local and specific as well as larger anticipated outcomes: 'transformation' in education, through Indigenisation.

I will begin by singing this article into being, in order to frame the significance of standpoint and locatedness, Country and Activism. I will then discuss the eight principles to developing a decolonising pedagogical praxis and conclude with a manifesto to engage in the higher education as an Indigenous academic.

Indigenous standpoint through song

Re-awaken Grandmothers, Grandfathers Dreaming

Kamiku Tjamuku wapar nganana watany/ kurinu
Grandmother, Grandfather let us not forget our Dreaming

Ngayulu nyuntunya tapini wapar atakankuntjaku
I am asking you to make the Dreaming clear

This is a small travelling story and song. The song is without a complete tune. My late Ngunytju and I were travelling to Umawa (on APY lands north-west South Australia), down Stuart Highway. Ngunytju began singing. I was sharing my thoughts of how I saw my PhD developing. My Kami Inawantji was a composer and Knowledge Holder of inma.[1] I was telling my Mum, 'Can she help me with an inma that asks my family to help me keep my knowledge strong? I want to learn and want to be able to keep learning inma'. We turned off Stuart Highway on the desert road and headed towards Mimili, on our way to Umawa. In the distance we could see the Musgrave Ranges.

This conversation between Ngunytju and Untal (daughter), and this Composition Song, is a call to my Mum to become knowledgeable about my Kamiku's and Tjamuku's ways of knowing, being and doing. Similarly, my Ngunytju wrote a poem to her tjamu (Grandfather) in the 1970s, called Dedication. It was her call to 'become knowledgeable' about Anangu philosophy, to understand the past but to look to the future.

Dedication poem[2]

To my tjamu, grandfather
Love beyond expression,
Forgive my intrusion.
Hope has come at last
To explain your past;
To promote your culture,
For children of our future.
So they can learn your philosophy of life:
In this our Country,
Live as brother and sister
Without hate of colour or race.

(by Mona Ngitji Ngitji Tur 2010)

I sang this poem following three years after the passing of my late mother Mona Ngitji Ngijti Tur. My mother never heard her poem sung by myself or the violin composition played by her Puḻiri (granddaughter). Relationality grounds this public act of love and grief. Distinguished Professor Aileen Moreton-Robinson's work on relationality is particularly useful to articulating standpoint (2013: 341): "[a]s an Indigenous woman my ontological relation to Country informs my epistemology. My coming to know and knowing is constituted through what I have termed 'relationality'". She expands on this to include:

Indigenous people's sense of belonging is derived from an ontological relationship to Country derived from the Dreaming which provides the precedents for what is believed to have occurred in the beginning in the original form of social living created by ancestral beings. During the Dreaming ancestral beings created the land and life and they are tied to particular tracks of Country. Knowledge and beliefs tied to the Dreaming inform the present and future. Within this system of beliefs there is scope for interpretation and change by individuals through dreams and their lived experiences.

(Moreton-Robinson 2017: online)

Professor Larissa Behrendt (2019) also articulates the importance of storytelling as a process of enacting sovereignty that reinforces Indigenous identity, values, and world-views. Quandamooka Scholar Karen Martin also states:

> To know your Stories of relatedness is to know who you are, where you are from and how you are related. Whether these stories have been distorted or forgotten, they still exist then the task becomes one of finding how this happened in order to reclaim them.
>
> *(Martin 2008: 83)*

This also reflects my personal process of learning from my Elders, my cultural scholars, and Country. Singing is important to me, and central to how I communicate as an Indigenous person, community member, learner and teacher, activist and performer. In a sense, singing is a way of 'being' for myself and my community. The act of singing connects me to Country through my Elders and family. It is a sensory and literal embodied experience. Singing resonates. It allows me to say something important and also to feel Anangu ways of knowing from long ago to the contemporary, in my body. Song and singing are like narrative partners. They allow crucial and thoughtful ways of transmitting ideas of being, in this case from the perspective of an Anangu Woman – grounded in the teachings of Elders and Knowledge Holders within my community. I see teaching as performative (hooks 1991; 1994) and singing is an important performative element in how I teach. Singing has also become central to my professional experience in public performance, in theatre, and collective creative research with my colleagues, the Unbound Collective an all Aboriginal academic/artist collective.

'Standing strong' on Country and Activism

Theorising on Country and Activism are central principles to my decolonising praxis to recognise embodied connection to land, family, history, and the everyday in processes of 'becoming' an Aboriginal academic and 'performing' praxis. Country plays an integral role to inter-generational transmission of knowledge and its place in Indigenous Studies and Education more broadly, informed by the power of Country as an ontological reality, space, place and concept. The relationalities learnt and the teachings inherent in being 'on' one's own Country become critical in 'off' Country contexts to survive and thrive through the forces of settler colonialism. This also resonates with Indigenous scholar Daniel Heath Justice's (2016) description of place, colonialism and time and space, and affirms Aboriginal and academic moments of always 'becoming'.

Indigenous activism is critical to informing a decolonising Indigenous Embodied Praxis within university structures and higher education contexts. Indigenous activism within Australia is associated with the fight for recognition of Indigenous people's rights, connection to Country and sovereignty. The Irati Wanti Anti-Nuclear Campaign in South Australia is such an example of senior Aboriginal women fighting to protect their Country as a sovereign right. It honours, outlines, and follows in the footsteps of the Kupa Piti Kungka Tjuta, Irati Wanti campaign, and the Senior Anangu Women's acitivism.

In 1998 the Australian Federal Government, under Prime Minister John Howard, made an announcement about the "plan to build a national radioactive waste dump in South Australia" (Kupa Piti Kungka Tjuta Editorial Committee et al. 2005: 10). The proposed location was Billa Kalina, north-west South Australia. From the start of the announcement, the Kupa Piti Kungka Tjuta said 'NO'. Irati Wanti – 'Leave the Poison'. This was grounded in the Senior Women's knowledge and responsibility to and 'as' Country and a result of direct family effects from the

Maralinga atomic bomb tests (1950–1960s) (Kupa Piti Kungka Tjuṯa Editorial Committee et al. 2005: 78) on their waltjapiti (family), Country, physical and spiritual wellbeing. The Kungkas' spoke out and did not stop telling their stories. They said:

> We take our responsibilities very seriously toward: the land, the Country, some of the special places, we know them the Tjukur – the important stories of the land the songs that prove how the land is the Inma–song and dance of the culture, all part of the land as well the bush tucker that we know and do our best to teach the grandchildren, and even tourists when we have the chance preserving the traditional crafts; the wira–wooden bowl, wana–digging stick, punu–music sticks, and even kali–boomerang, that our grandmothers have passed down to us through generations the language the family, that members have respect for one another. 'All this is law'.
>
> *(Kupa Piti Kungka Tjuṯa Editorial Committee et al. 2005: 6)*

These strong words, almost like a manifesto, make clear to the listener the responsibility and deep knowledge of Country, and the importance of inter-generational knowledge transmission as 'embodied' and enacted sovereignty. My personal standpoint and key focus on activism and Country are grounded in key ideas informed by Indigenous scholars.

Grounding ideas

> A critical aspect of the struggle for self-determination has involved questions relating to our history as indigenous [sic] peoples and a critique of how we, as the Other, have been represented or excluded from various accounts. Every issue has been approached by indigenous [sic] peoples with a view to *re*writing and *re*righting our position in history. Indigenous peoples want to tell our own stories, write our own versions, in our own ways, for our own purposes
>
> *(Tuhiwai Smith 1999: 28)*

Directly engaging with this quote above by Linda Tuhiwai Smith, my act of *re*writing and *re*righting have been informed by six Indigenous research methodologies that underpin my *Anangu* Woman's praxis. In her Quandamooka ontology, Martin Booran Mirraboopha (2003) outlines research as ceremony, and positions relatedness, Aboriginal heritage and relationality, stories and Aboriginal ways of knowing, being and doing within her Indigenist research framework. Moreton-Robinson's (2000; 2013) theoretical concepts on Indigenous women's standpoint, Aboriginal ways of knowing, being and doing, relationality, embodiment and sovereignty offer valuable approaches to my research. The outlining by Māori scholars Tuhiwai Smith (2012) and Smith (2003) of Decolonising Methodologies – Kaupapa Māori Theory and its principles of "self-determination ... cultural aspirations and identity ... culturally preferred pedagogy ... social economic mediation ... [and] collective philosophy" (Smith 2003: 10–13) – offer critical insights into research engagement. Indigenous Australian scholar Lester-Irabinna Rigney's (1999; 2007) principles on Indigenist research, resistance, political integrity and the privileging of Indigenous voices contribute to transformative research within Indigenous communities – in my case, the Aṉangu community.

Chilisa's research model identifies the phases of "rediscovery and recovery; mourning; dreaming; commitment; and action" (2012: 15); Wilson's (2008) conceptualisation of 'research as ceremony' centres the role of stories within research and the importance of relationality, responsibility and accountability. These are guiding frameworks in the construction of a decolonising research praxis.

In summary, these Australian and international approaches to research identify these key concepts to be added to those in my educative praxis; standpoint; Indigenous ways of knowing, being and doing; embodiment; positionality; relationality; performativity; protocol; reciprocity; responsibility; and decolonisation. These methodologies are connected to pedagogical methods that have also helped to shape my praxis.

The building of a praxis: Quandamooka ontology and 'becoming knowledgeable' Anangu way: Sharing methodologies, methods and principles

Karen Martin's Indigenist framework has been influential in my approach to 'becoming', 'bridging', and 'building' in Indigenous scholarship and praxis in Critical Indigenous Studies and Education. In particular, Martin's, "Quandamooka ontology and epistemology" (2003: 206) has provided foundational ideas for the approach to praxis. Martin (2003: 203) acknowledges that universities, as institutions of knowledge production, have engaged in what she calls '*terra nullius* research'. That is, the Western research tradition has continued to research Indigenous peoples/cultures as 'objects of curiosity'. Martin sees this as deeply problematic. Her response is to reinforce the importance of protocols within Indigenous research through locating oneself through community and Country.

Martin has referred to the work of Rigney and West in the development of an 'Aboriginal research framework'. This work has also contributed to ideas proposed in my *Anangu* method. Expanding from Rigney's principles, Martin (2003: 205) grounds her standpoint through the, "strength of her Aboriginal heritage" and positions her research through Aboriginal "worldview and realities". The principles of Martin (2003: 205) approach to Indigenist research include: (1) recognition of world-views, our knowledges and realities as distinctive and vital to our existence and survival; (2) honouring our social mores as essential processes through which we live, learn, and situate ourselves as Aboriginal people in our own lands and when in the lands of other Aboriginal people; (3) emphasis of social, historical, and political contexts which shapes our experiences, lives, positions, and futures; and (4) privileging the voices, experiences, and lives of Aboriginal people and Aboriginal lands.

Similar to Rigney's (1999; 2007) principles, Martin's (2003: 206) Quandamooka Indigenist research framework, demonstrates the significance of centring "Aboriginal ontologies" within the research process through recognition; honouring; social, historical and political context; and Indigenous voices within research – as outlined above. This also connect to the Irati Wanti campaign in the fight for protection of Country. Martin (2003: 207) explains the significance of, and relationship with, land and Entities. She describes Entities as all-encompassing, for example Waterways, Skies, Creator Spirits, and people. She states, "[t]he strength of our country can also be seen in relationships between these Entities; hence, it is a truly relational ontology" (Martin 2003: 207).

Martin (2003: 210) also expresses knowing as "purposeful" and explains how our ways of being "evolve as contexts change". Responsiveness to change is a necessary characteristic of effective praxis. This critique also reflects an approach to dynamic, healthy, and sustainable Indigenous futures. I agree with this approach and, through theory and applied practice, work towards its outcomes.

Martin's key standpoint of centring Aboriginal ways of knowing is significant here. I have learnt from and built on her foundational approach by identifying and positioning

Anangu-influenced teaching, learning and research characteristics within Critical Indigenous Education. Their intention is to decolonise and their objective is to transform approaches to Indigenous Education within the academy, and beyond. I have positioned my Country and community (as she does) and developed that approach to positioning through an approach that takes storytelling of lived experience as an essential tool in any teaching, learning and research engagement, which grounds and privileges Aboriginal ways of knowing, being and doing. The principle advocated by Martin's 'recognition of worldview' is similar to my articulation of 'Becoming Knowledgeable' identified through locatedness and relationality and speaking strong: Anangu ways of knowing, being and doing. This is reflected in the privileging of Yankunytjatjara inter-generational teaching through Elder/Kamiku and Tjamuku roles in teaching and caring for future generations, through sharing Anangu ontologies particular to Country and people. The 'honouring of social mores' described by Martin also connects to the critical position of voicing one's standpoint through situating locatedness of Country, self, and community. All are connected and grounded through relationality. All are embodied, Anangu way. Martin's emphasis on 'social, historical and political contexts' is important and connects to my positioning of speaking strong and being able to re-conceptualise, decolonise, and transform through understanding 'historical and political processes'. Martin's last principle of 'privileging the voices', I would say, is fundamental to transformative work required in higher education institutions. Indigenous voices need always to be present if sustained Indigenous scholarship is to occur through Indigenous standpoint and sovereignty; locating self and knowledges; negotiating systems; embodied activism; employment of storytelling and counter-narratives; decolonised knowledge production; performativity; reclaiming and redefining space; and reflexivity.

Indigenous ways of knowing – shaping a framework for 'becoming knowledgeable'

> Pedagogy always represents a commitment to the future, and it remains the tasks of educators to make sure that future points the way to a more socially just world, a world in which the discourses of critique and possibility in conjunction with the values of reason, freedom, and equality function to alter, as part of a broader democratic project, the grounds upon which life is lived.
>
> *(Giroux cited in McLaren and Kincheloe 2007: 2)*

In the quote above, Giroux reminds us that educators and pedagogies remain key to the freedoms in out futures. The following pedagogical approaches inform the shaping of a framework: storywork pedagogy (Archibald 2008) Strong Voices, Aboriginal Pedagogies (Blinter et al. 2000), Eight Ways of Learning (Yunkaporta 2009), Red Dirt Curriculum Guenther, Disbray and Osborne 2016; Lester et al. 2013), Storywork Pedagogy (Archibald 2008) and Red Pedagogy (Grande 2004). The pedagogies are led by Indigenous/First Nations scholars or communities or are the result of established partnerships with communities.

I have given focus to Karen Martin Booran Mirraboopha's 'Quandamooka ontology' as it best aligns with my methodological approach. Here, I will undertake a close method-based reading of Red Dirt Curriculum pedagogy, due to its focus on remote education and its Anangu community educators' perspectives of what it means to be a 'successfully' educated Anangu child. This reading also recalls Kami Lucy Lester's conversation on her perspectives of how schools can be responsive to Anangu children's ways of knowing, being, and doing.

In Red Dirt Curriculum, Guenther, Disbray and Osborne (2016) and Lester et al. (2013) offer critical insights into remote communities' need to provide education that is in the best interests of Anangu children and the community in central Australia. For future teachers, and also teachers currently working in schools with Aboriginal children, understanding the significance of Country in which the school is located is paramount to building sustainable educational partnerships with Indigenous communities. Guenther et al. (2016: 80) make the point that schools need to "fit" remote communities whilst acknowledging the need to include national curriculum frameworks. The first critical premise outlined in Red Dirt Curriculum is the valuing of Anangu epistemologies, ontologies, axiologies, and cosmologies. This reflects Martin Booran Mirraboopha's (2003; 2008) and Moreton-Robinson's (2013) explanation of valuing Indigenous world-views and relationality to Country. From this standpoint, the world-views of Anangu students, their families, extended families, and community is central to building successful educational communities within educational spaces, hereby strengthening social and cultural communication.

Additionally, recognising the significance of Country to community must be part of this understanding (though never fully known) by Western educational systems. Country is a site of knowledge and, as such, is essential to *Anangu* understandings of education. This Country-knowledge connection can begin to make schools places of broader educational engagement. I would argue that this connection also requires conceptualising Western educational spaces in different ways.

Guenther et al. (2016) reinforce the need to challenge normalised education values. From the perspective of my praxis, critical reflexivity is vital here, as is the capacity of Ngapartji-Ngapartji to enable and negotiate ways of accessing and making use of both educational systems. Makinti Minutukur (Lester et al. 2013: 8) also refers to *Anangu* ways of knowing "Our culture, our language and our stories; we must hold onto tightly and not let go because these give us strength". This recognition of the 'politics' of pedagogy must not be ignored by educational systems within Australia. In her contribution to the Red Dirt approach, Karina Lester (2013) supports this position, and argues for education that is 'balanced', 'achievable' *and* privileges Anangu world-views and Anangu everyday reality – as described by Kami Lucy Lester in her conversation. Ultimately this means embracing, not denying, Anangu ways of knowing, being, and doing, on and beyond Country.

In Archibald/Q'um Q'um Xiiem's (2008) Storywork Pedagogy, teaching and learning through First Nations storytelling and the role of Elders in education privilege First Nations ways of knowing, being, and doing. Her work outlines respect, responsibility, and reciprocity. In Anangu terms and in the terminology of my eight principles detailed below, this is what I call 'stand strong' and 'talk strong'. Stories are connected to relationality, to Country, community and lived realities. This connection is supported in Yunkaporta's (2009: 35) 8 Ways of Learning pedagogy. He connects relatedness to "Story Sharing". It is about "teaching and learning through narrative".

Wei et al. (1991) in *Aboriginal Pedagogies,* and Blinter et al. (2000) in *Strong Voices*, encourage a community of learners to facilitate the inclusion of community educational knowledges within schooling contexts. This approach is taken into account in my 'stand strong' and 'locate' principles, as well. Similarly, Yunkaporta (2009) refers to developing community links to encourage the incorporation of Aboriginal perspectives and knowledges within curriculum within teacher education. Red Dirt Curriculum (Guenther, Disbray, and Osborne 2016; Lester et al. 2013) also reinforces this perspective, highlighting the need to establish relationships with students and community links, which (in their case and in mine) acknowledges and recognises collective Anangu identity. All argue for the need of community aspirations, desires, perspectives and identities within education. Grande's (2004) Red Pedagogy also positions the need for educational institutions to be inclusive of community needs and desires, as part of a project of sovereignty and decolonisation.

Martin (2003) articulation and privileging of Quandamooka ontology offers perspectives on centring one's heritage within a research framework. In their respective works, Wei et al. and Guenther and Lester recognise the importance of heritage in teaching and learning contexts and outline the need for culturally responsive, engaged relationships between teachers and learners. Relationality and cooperation therefore become important in the interface between teacher and learner, and learner and teacher. This is reflected in my principles of 'locatedness', 'standing strong' and 'activism'. In these respects, Strong Voices echoes Moreton-Robinson (2000; 2015) and Rigney (1999; 2007) – as well as other international theorists – and methodology and methods overlap.

'Making space', from a pedagogical standpoint, 'centres' rather than marginalises community and Indigenous knowledges within educational institutions. Storywork Pedagogy, Red Pedagogy, Red Dirt Curriculum, Strong Voices, and Eight Ways of Learning all refer to making space for community aspirations, desires, perspectives and identities. Within the context of pre-service teacher education, through critical reflection on positioning and privilege, non-Indigenous students need to have space within their educational degree program, to raise their awareness (Education for Social Justice 1994) about themselves and their relationship with Indigenous peoples. Creating intellectual and physical space becomes an important educational imperative for Indigenous educators. For non-Indigenous as well as Indigenous educators and students, positioning of 'self' is important. For non-Indigenous students or collaborating colleagues, this is not the same as having an Indigenous 'standpoint' but it does require intellectual engagement and critique of ideas of privilege, race, patriarchy and racialised processes in relation to position and standing. This goes to the concept of "kindred relationships" (Worby, Tur, and Blanch 2014: 2) and Haraway's (2016: 2) "kin-like connections" (192) and requires application of what I call the principles of 'reflexive' thinking and 're-conceptualisation'. Grande's (2004) viewpoint on the need for critical pedagogical analysis, as part of teaching decolonising praxis, gives weight to the significance of 'critical reflexivity' within educational processes. Red Dirt Curriculum posits the need to critique Western understandings of education and its purposes and influences.

Yunkaporta (2009) outlines the need to reconstruct, deconstruct and re-conceptualise within educational learning. Re-conceptualisation seeks to redress the effects of colonisation and imperialism on Indigenous communities. Privileging and positioning Indigenous ways of knowing, being and doing is central to Indigenous research and pedagogical practice, as Moreton-Robinson (2000; 2015), Martin (2006; 2008), Wilson (2008), Nakata (1998; 2006; 2007b), Grande (2004) and Wei et al. (1991) have advocated. Self-determination and sovereignty are equally important, say Tuhiwai Smith (1999) and Smith (2003).

These essentials give encouragement to my Anangu framework and its contribution to a transformed understanding of educational space: where time is not experienced as linear (Yunkaporta 2009) and past can also be present and future – as experienced and understood by Indigenous communities and expressed in their epistemologies, ontologies and axiologies.

Strong pedagogy – Ngapartji-Ngapartji enabling concept

Ngapartji-Ngapartji, the Anangu philosophy of reciprocation, can act as an enabling concept in working towards reciprocal, respectful and mutually beneficial outcomes in education in the personal, professional, and public domains. I articulated an approach to Ngapartji-Ngapartji that is philosophically, epistemologically, ontologically and axiologically grounded, and stated that locatedness, relatedness, trust, and context are paramount in enacting Ngapartji-Ngapartji. My enactment is therefore based on connection to Country, kinship, and community, but that does not mean that a reciprocating approach to education cannot be attempted with – or by – others.

It does mean that those others have to consider and articulate their philosophical, ontological, and axiological positions and standpoints in order to understand the depth of the reciprocal agreement and privileged access to knowledge they are entering.

I have referred to the Ngapartji-Ngapartji to facilitate my engagement within the university. Indigenous communities may have similar philosophies or metaphors which can support a decolonising praxis within university education. Enabling concepts situated within Indigenous ways of knowing, being and doing must be acknowledged and remains the cultural/intellectual property of the knowledge holders. There will be partial perspective of such philosophies or metaphors by users who are custodians and keepers of ways of knowing. There may also be more broader enabling concepts, such as reconciliation to support such work connecting to social justice campaigns.

My embodied understanding of Country cannot be the same for pre-service teachers (unless they are from the same community), or other learners in public situations. In the formal context of the university teaching and learning, for example, the parameters of Ngapartji-Ngapartji have to be negotiated, defined, and then positioned. First, in my case, all parties must understand that 'reciprocity' is being proposed by an Anangu Woman academic enacting reciprocal and mutually sustaining educational relationships, within Indigenous Education and Studies: gendered Indigeneity matters in this positioning and all participants must understand this. Second, for pre-service teachers, learning to articulate their standpoint, knowledge of colonialism and education, understanding of racialisation, and systemic power within educational institutions is one of the vital lessons of Indigenous Education. Equally important is hearing and valuing the voices of community around articulated positions on education and taking responsibility for including these in their teaching practice. Each establishes an expectation of 'teacher knowledgeability' in the context of teaching pre-service teachers and can to Indigenous Studies more broadly. Ngapartji-Ngapartji requires ongoing consideration, understanding and negotiation of nuances based on context-specific knowledge. This need for adaptability demonstrates Ngapartji-Ngapartji as a dynamic and flexible concept.

The 'becoming knowledgeable' framework methodological approach needs to be flexible. It requires 'shifts' in pedagogical objectives which are dependent on the educational context. When dealing with tertiary education, this may involve the profile of the cohort; a recognition and understanding of the knowledge students bring into the teaching-learning space; their ability to respond to the ideas of transformation; and the professional expectation of their degree within Indigenous Education. Each shift will require rigour, flexibility, high expectation, and openness to 'give-and-give-in-return', Ngapartji-Ngapartji. This openness will influence the shape, emphasis and starting point of pedagogical approaches to 'doing' in Indigenous Education, in relation to personal, public, and/or professional contexts. It will apply to problem-identification and problem-solving in the public domain or topic construction, curriculum planning, reading selection, lecture sequencing, for example, in the professional education domain. But whatever strategies are employed, the objective will always be the same: transformation.

This methodical approach requires skilled, reflexive educators – a grounded Anangu Woman educator, for example. It requires being versed in Indigenous research methodologies, knowledge and educational and discipline-specific discourses, in order to understand and apply what is needed in this moment within formal education and beyond. Creative use of bringing 'practice to theory' is important here. This is not a universal method that I propose. It is, however, one which has been drawn from particular experiences and tested in more than one set of educational conditions. The testing and refinement of educative 'acts' need to continue, to retain and sustain relevance. My Senior Knowledge Holders always understood this. They also understood that when we 'become knowledgeable', we also have a responsibility to contribute to positive and sustainable futures. Whether Aboriginal scholar, activist, artistic performer, or future teacher, 'we' must be mindful and considered in our approaches. This requires an understanding of Indigenous sovereignty, every day, within Australia.

'Becoming knowledgeable' – two ways: An Anangu woman's approach to praxis

Objective: Decolonising prevailing teaching and research methodologies and methods. The objective is shared by many Indigenous scholars worldwide. It responds to Tuhiwai Smith's approach to Critical Indigenous Decolonising Research Methodologies – leading to transformation.

Integrating bridging and enabling concept: Ngapartji-Ngapartji – reciprocation and responsibility. Give-and-give-in-return is a mutually understood process that is grounded in the practices of reciprocity and respect. It is beneficial, caring, and requires acts of an exchange. Ngapartji-Ngapartji is the fundamental enabler of 'Becoming Knowledgeable'– as praxis.

Domains of practice: Personal, public, and professional: This approach is designed to bring together the overlapping everyday experiences of Indigenous educators and those with whom they work and for whom/to whom they have responsibility: on Country; in community; when acting on behalf of community; when engaged in professional practice. It recognises different collective expectations according to context as well as the need to maintain individual identity and agency in all domains.

Eight Principles: (1) Stand Strong;[3] (2) Locate;[4] (3) Speak Strong;[5] (4) Engage in Activism;[6] (5) Work Collectively – Collaborate;[7] (6) Make Space;[8] (7) Reflect Critically;[9] and (8) Re-Conceptualise.[10]

Anticipated outcome: Transformation in Indigenous Education through appreciation and understanding of the complexities and responsibilities of 'Becoming Knowledgeable'.

Never stop talking

I began this article with a story of the Irati Wanti campaign, honouring knowledge of and responsibility to Country and Activism by the Kupa Piti Kungka Tjuta, fundamental to their campaign was 'Talking Straight Out'. This article offers a methodological approach to an educational decolonising praxis grounded within my Anangu Woman's praxis framework in quite a specific and established direction: a model of what I have named the 'enabling' and 'obligating' concept of Ngapartji-Ngapartji. This requires the bringing together of theory and practice as praxis through ethical, equitable, responsible exchange – whether intellectual, physical, ontological, or political. That is why Ngapartji-Ngapartji appears as a feature of all of my eight principles. The 'giving-and-giving-in-return' are not of the same kind in every case but each principle is guided by historical and contemporary reference to the ethics of principles of exchange, restitution, or restoration. In my Anangu method and methodology, activism is an essential, constructive feature of critical understanding of Indigenous scholarly contribution to Indigenous research methodologies, knowledges, and education. It also contributes to Indigenous Studies and perspectives more broadly. This activism is fundamental to praxis in the contexts in which I live and work. Such praxis, especially the *doing* in Critical Indigenous Education, contributes to Indigenous scholarship by focussing attention on *how* things are to be done in real time and place, as well as *what* is being done in a more general sense. Critical Indigenous Education continues to be a developing interdisciplinary field which is rigorous and dynamic, articulated through Indigenous standpoints, perspectives and knowledges. In the spirit of expressing my pedagogical praxis, Anangu way, I end with this manifesto – a becoming song.

A becoming song

I will claim my Indigenous sovereignty

I will talk strong

I will enact the Anangu philosophy of Ngapartji-Ngapartji (of reciprocation)

I will build relationships which are mutually beneficial and rewarding

I will privilege my embodied Aboriginality as part of my standpoint position

I will always acknowledge the Country I am on

I will acknowledge and honour my Elders

I will honour my Senior Knowledge Holders as my first teachers

I will honour our stories and counter-narratives

I will engage in activism and resistance as I have been taught to do

I will name my bias and state that I will privilege Indigenous Knowledges and perspectives when I teach

I will challenge stereotypical and generalised representations of Indigenous people, our ways of knowing, being and doing

I will not accept racism

I will challenge my teaching when I engage in 'uncomfortable conversations' about race and racism and will continue to speak up

I am prepared to take risks and 'stay with the trouble' when teaching about 'Race' as a social construct and 'White Race Privilege' through facilitating 'unsettling' conversations

I will love ideas and engage in critique

I will critically reflect on my teaching and pedagogy

I will work collectively with my colleagues and teach creatively to bring about change

I will demonstrate transformative pedagogy for social justice

I will border-cross and CREATE 'Black' space

I will claim my right to be in this space and human-ness which has been denied in the past

I will sing to communicate my ideas, perspectives and critiques

I will look to the future.

Acknowledgement

I would like to acknowledge my late mother Mona Ngitji Ngitji and father Jozef Tur and the Tur-Martens family, the Lester family, in particular Kami Lucy, Rose and Karina, senior women from the Kupa Piti Kungka Tjuta, PhD supervisors Emeritus Professor Gus Worby and Professor Tracey Bunda, Unbound Collective sistas, Ali Gumillya Baker, Faye Rosas Blanch, and Natalie Harkin. I would also like to express my gratitude to Dr Natalie Harkin and Dr Sam Muller for their support and critical feedback in the writing of this article.

Notes

1 Inma in Yankunytjatjara and Pitjantjatjara means song and dance (Goddard 1997).

2 Selecting my late mother's poem *Dedication* to be adapted to song for this performance by Aboriginal singer-songwriter Nancy Bates was an important decision for me. I spoke to my immediate family about performing Mum's poetry in song, to honour her teachings, cultural philosophies, and her gift of storytelling. Like story, song also tells stories. I also understood my responsibility to maintain intergenerational teaching as taught to me by my family, my cultural teachers from the *Kupa Piti Kungka Tjuta* and extended family. I asked my *untal* Katie to perform with me and accompany her *Kami's*

poetry with her violin. This was a very special moment – to have a daughter sing her Mother's poetry, and granddaughter to play the violin to her Grandmother's words.

3 Standing strong involves recognising and acknowledging of Country one is from and located in as protocol; naming one's Indigenous standpoint; standing strong in Aboriginal ways of knowing, being, and doing and lived realities; acknowledging of Senior Knowledge Holders' authority; recognition of resistance and activism; enacting of an Activist Pedagogy; challenging racialised systems of knowledge and power in relation to representation of Indigenous people and systemic privilege; standing up against everyday racism and forms of discrimination; talking strong; visioning for future generations; being sovereign; giving-and-giving-in-return: Ngapartji-Ngapartji.

4 Locating involves situating Country and recognition of other Aboriginal communities' connection to Country; articulating Country as embodied and relational; locating Indigenous epistemologies, ontologies and axiologies; recognising of gendered knowledge; acknowledging experiences of colonialism (as ongoing); locating ideological and philosophical standpoint/s; situating knowledge and standpoint; locating oneself with like-minded collectives; giving-and-giving-in-return: Ngapartji-Ngapartji.

5 Speaking strong involves stating a position on matters of justice; always talking strong; acknowledging Elder knowledge and authority; understanding one's speaking position; following a process of 'Becoming Knowledgeable'; making visible Indigenous knowledges, perspectives, and stories within teaching and learning; stepping up when asked; engaging in a politicised process; employing critical reflexivity; reciprocal and responsible scholarly contribution; giving-and-giving-in-return: Ngapartji-Ngapartji.

6 Engaging in activism involves respecting and caring for Country; positioning decolonisation at the centre of research, teaching and learning; exhibiting embodied scholarly activism; standing strong and speaking strong; analysing of systems of power; disrupting and bearing witness; articulating a position on matters of justice; bringing intellectual, cultural, spiritual, and political knowledge and skills to ground acts of resistance; taking action; giving-and-giving-in-return: Ngapartji-Ngapartji.

7 Working collectively – collaborate involves recognising Indigenous community ways of knowing, being, and doing; identifying and connecting to 'like-minded' colleagues; naming and situating one's personal, public, and professional theoretical frameworks; expressing common desire and vision for change; engaging in respectful, reciprocal, caring, ethical and negotiated relationships; employing critical reflexivity; giving-and giving-in-return: Ngapartji-Ngapartji.

8 Making space involves building 'Black space' within institutions; re-imaging and re-inscribing ways of being; border-crossing, which brings the personal, public and professional domains together as praxis; understanding space as relational; transforming and decolonising dominant knowledge systems; privileging Indigenous knowledges; border-crossing into Critical Indigenous scholarship; challenging colonial representations of Indigenous people through critiques of race, power and privilege; creating opportunity for teaching and learning about imperialism and the effects of (ongoing) colonialism; developing Indigenous activist creative and performative acts of critical inquiry; fostering shared conversations; articulating and critically engaging with ideas, standpoint and disciplinary knowledge; negotiating space; giving-and-giving-in-return: Ngapartji-Ngapartji.

9 Reflecting critically involves engaging Critical Pedagogy as a theoretical framework in decolonising educational praxis; practicing self-reflexivity; developing an ethical standpoint; telling Indigenous stories and narratives to reflect and remember; identifying and creating strategic alliances and partnerships; giving-and-giving-in-return: Ngapartji-Ngapartji.

10 Re-conceptualising involves ongoing development of Critical Indigenous Education and Studies; enacting alternative epistemological, ontological and axiological standpoints from Indigenous perspectives; developing grounded, embodied and affective contributions to educational praxis; developing Indigenous creative and performative methodologies and pedagogies of decolonial knowledge production; developing alternative discourse; making affective contribution to educational praxis; giving-and-giving-in-return: Ngapartji-Ngapartji.

References

Archibald/Q'um Q'um Xiiem, J. (2008). *Indigenous Storywork: Educating the Heart, Mind, Body, and Spirit.* UBC Press: Vancouver, BC.

Behrendt, L. (2019). 'Indigenous storytelling: Decolonzing institutions and assertive self-determination: implications for legal practice', in J.-a. Archibald Q'um Q'um Xiiem, J.B.J. Lee-Morgan, and J. De Santolo (eds.) *Decolonizing Research Indigenous Story Work as Methodology.* ZED Books: London, 175–186.

Blitner, S., GF., Martin, B., Oldfield, N., Palmer, I., and Riley, R. (2000). *Strong Voices*, Batchelor Institute, NT.

Chilisa, B. (2012). *Indigenous research methodologies*. SAGE: Thousand Oak, CA.

Education for Social Justice Research Group, (1994). *Teaching for Resistance*, Texts in Humanities and The Centre for Studies in Educational Leadership, Adelaide, South Australia.

Girous, H. (2007). 'Introduction: democracy, education, and the politics of critical pedagogy', in P. McLaren and J. Kincheloe (eds.) *Critical Pedagogy, Where Are We Now?*, Peter Lang Publishing Inc.: New York, 1–8.

Goddard, C. (1997). *Pitjantjatjara/Yankunytjatjara Pocket Dictionary*. IAD Press: Alice Springs, NT.

Grande, S. (2004). *Red Pedagogy: Native American Social and Political Thought*. Rowman and Littlefield Publishers: Landam, MD.

Guenther, J., Disbray, S., and Osborne, S. (2016). *Red Dirt Education: A Compilation of Learnings from the Remote Education Systems Project*. Ninti One Limited: Alice Springs, NT. Available: http://www.crc-rep.com.au/resource/RedDirtEducation_CompilationLearningsRES_EBook.pdf, accessed 20 November 2018.

Haraway, D. (2016). *Staying with the Trouble Making Kin in the Chthulucenee*. Duke University Press: Durham, NC.

hooks, b. (1991). 'Theory as liberatory practice', *Yale Journal of Law and Feminism*, vol. 4, no. 1: 1–12.

hooks, b. (1994). *Teaching to Transgress: Education as the Practice of Freedom*. Routledge: New York.

Justice, D. (2016). 'A better world becoming placing critical Indigenous studies', in A. Moreton-Robinson (ed.) *Critical Indigenous Studies*. University of Arizona, Tucson, AZ, 19–32.

Kupa Piti Kungka Tjuta. (2005). In N. Brown, I.M. Stewart, E.K. Brown Crombie, E.U. Austin, and T.M. Watson (eds.) *Talking Straight Out: Stories from the Irati Wanti Campaign*. Alapalatja Press: Coober Pedy, SA.

Lester, K., Minutjukur, M., Osborne, S., and Tjitayi, K. (2013). *Red Dirt Curriculum: Re-Imagining Remote Education*. Flinders University: Alice Spring, NT. Available: http://www.flinders.edu.au/chl/fms/education_files/coreacom/SM%20Rural%20Lectures/Sidney%20Myer%20Rural%20Lecture%203%20-%20Karina%20Lester%20Makinti%20Minutjukur%20Sam%20Osborne%20Katrina%20Tjitayi-%20for%20Web.pdf, accessed 18 September 2013.

Martin, K. (Booran Mirraboopha). (2003). 'Ways of knowing, being and doing: A theoretical framework and method for Indigenous and indigenist re-search', *Journal of Australian Studies*, vol. 75: 203–214.

Martin, K.L. (2006). *Please Knock Before You Enter: An Investigation of How Rainforest Aboriginal People Regulate Outsiders and the Implications for Western Research and Researchers*. PhD thesis. James Cook University, Australia.

Martin, K.L. (2008). *Please Knock Before You Enter: Aboriginal Regulation of Outsiders and the Implications for Research and Researchers*. Post Pressed: Teneriffe, QLD.

Moreton-Robinson, A. (2000). *Talkin' Up to the White Woman: Aboriginal Women and Feminism*. University of Queensland Press: St Lucia, QLD.

Moreton-Robinson, A. (2007). 'When the object speaks, a postcolonial encounter: Anthropological representations and aboriginal women's self presentations', *Discourse: Studies in the Cultural Politics of Education*, vol. 19, no. 3: 275–289.

Moreton-Robinson, A. (2013). 'Toward an Australian Indigenous women's standpoint theory: A methodological tool', *Australian Feminist Studies*, vol. 28, no. 78: 331–347.

Moreton-Robinson, A. (2015). *The White Possessive: Property, Power and Indigenous Sovereignty*, University of Minnesota Press, Minneapolis.

Moreton-Robinson, A. (2017). 'Senses of belonging: How Indigenous sovereignty unsettles white Australia', *ABC News, Religion and Ethics*. Available: http://www.abc.net.au/religion/articles/2017/02/21/4623659.htm, accessed August 30, 2017.

Nakata, M. (1998). 'An Indigenous standpoint theory', in M. Nakata (ed.) *Disciplining the Savages: Savaging the Disciplines*. Aboriginal Studies Press: Canberra, ACT, 213–217.

Nakata, M. (2006). 'Australian Indigenous studies: A question of discipline', *The Australian Journal of Anthropology*, vol. 17-IS, no. 3: 265–275.

Nakata, M. (2007a). 'The cultural interface', *Australian Journal of Indigenous Education*, vol. 36: 7–14.

Nakata, M. (2007b). *Discipling the Savages Savaging the Disciplines*. Aboriginal Studies Press: Canberra, ACT.

Phillips, L. and Bunda, T. (2018). *Research Through, With and as Storying*. Routledge Taylor and Francis Group: London.

Rigney, L.-I. (1999). 'A first perspective of Indigenous Australian participation in science: Framing Indigenous research towards Indigenous Australian intellectual sovereignty', Kaurna Higher Education Journal. Available: https://ncis.anu.edu.au/_lib/doc/LI_Rigney_First_perspective.pdf, accessed 23 March 2018.

Rigney, L.-I. (2007). *Indigenist Research Epistemologies: A Historical Journey of Connection, Contradiction and Transformation*. PhD thesis. Flinders University of South Australia.

Smith, G. (2003). 'Indigenous struggle for transformation of education and schooling', *Alaskan Federation of Native (AFN) Convention*, Anchorage, AK. Available: http://citeseerx.ist.psu.edu/viewdoc/download?doi=10.1.1.603.1987andrep=rep1andtype=pdf, accessed 17 May 2020.

Tuhiwai Smith, L. (1999). *Decolonizing Methodologies: Research and Indigenous Peoples*. Zed Books: London.

Tuhiwai Smith, L. (2012). *Decolonizing Methodologies: Research and Indigenous Peoples*, 2nd ed. Zed Books: London.

Tur, N.N. (2010). *Cicada Dreaming*. Hyde Park Press: Hyde Park, SA.

Tur, N.N. and Tur, S.U. (2006). 'Conversation: Wapar Munu Mantaku Nintiringanyi – learning about the dreaming and land', in G. Worby and L.-I. Rigney (eds.) *Sharing Spaces: Indigenous and Non-Indigenous Responses to Story Country and Rights*. Australian Public Intellectual Network: Perth, WA, 160–170.

Tur, S.U. (2018). *Ninti Pulkaringanyi – Becoming Knowledgeable Embodied Activist Pedagogy: Educational Praxis from an Anangu Woman's Standpoint*. PhD thesis. Flinders University, Adelaide, SA.

Wei, B., Nayin, D., Rom, Y., Nginingawula, N., and Ngawurranungurumagi (1991). *Aboriginal Pedagogy: Aboriginal Teachers Speak Out*. Deakin University Press: Geelong, VIC.

Wilson, S. (2008). *Research Is Ceremony, Indigenous Research Methods*. Fernwood Publishing: Halifax, NS.

Worby, G., Tur, S., and Blanch., F. (2014). 'Writing Forward, Writing Back, Writing Black-Working Process and Work-in-Progress', *Journal of the Association for the Study of Australian Literature*, vol. 14, no. 3, pp. 1–14.

Yunkaporta, T. (2009). 'Aboriginal pedagogies at the cultural interface', PhD Thesis, James Cook University, Queensland.

41

Nyuragil – playing the 'game'

John Maynard

Introduction

Sport is a contested space not just on the playing field; historically it is an arena of racism where racist concepts have been challenged. Australian sport and its sporting heroes are one of the country's important foundations of the national identity. Any challenge surrounding this revered sports tradition within the national story becomes itself a contested space. The Aboriginal place in Australia's sporting history is one of triumph and disappointment. This chapter presents an overview of Aboriginal sporting experiences and a focus on the life and times of a largely forgotten sporting hero Wally McArthur. Sadly Australia of the 1940s and 1950s was not a country that embraced an Aboriginal sporting star no matter how talented or hard he strived. Wally McArthur would never be given the support or space to enter the national imagination.

Nyuragil is a traditional Worimi (north coast of New South Wales) word recorded to mean a "game" (Lissarague 2010: 292). The neighbouring Awabakal people had *nigulliko*, meaning to 'play sport' (Thomas 1906: 138–9). That we had names for games and sporting past times illustrates that sport, competition, and athleticism have been a part of the Australian continent long before the British arrival in 1788. Our sporting culture continued after the invasion, as documented by observers such as N.W. Thomas, L.E. Threlkeld and W.E. Roth (Thomas 1906: 138–9; Gunson 1974: 68; Roth 1984: 117–31). Herbert Basedow stated that the Aboriginal focus on strict principles of behaviour was as regimented as that of the Spartans of ancient Greece (Basedow 1925: 87).

Traditional Aboriginal sporting culture

Arguments continue to rage that an Aboriginal ball game was the original source of Australian football.[1] Author Jim Poulter wrote, "The Gunditjmara tribe played a game called *marngrook*, or 'game ball'. A ball was made of possum skin and filled with pounded charcoal and bound with kangaroo sinews. Between 50 and 100 men a side played for possession for hours on end" (Booth and Tatz 2000: 10). Many early settler accounts of the 1840s testify that this game was predominately a kicking game. The Aboriginal players apparently kicked "the ball with the instep of the bare foot, and they made strong leaps – sometimes reaching five feet [1.5 metres] above the ground" (Blainey 1990: 95–6). The recent publication *Aboriginal People and Australian Football in Nineteenth Century Australia* by Roy Hay has challenged the entrenched historical belief that an Indigenous game Marngrook influenced the development of the game. Hay states: "It is one of those stories that even historians who have researched the subject most closely wish were true, but evidence in support of the argument remains lacking and the myth continues to flourish" (Hay 2019: 2). Unquestionably, the Australian Football League (AFL) today prefers to play up the myth and encourage the idea that AFL was an Indigenous based game. Since the 1990s the AFL has promoted and raised wider awareness and appreciation of Indigenous culture and football to the Australian public. They introduced the Dreamtime game to showcase the Indigenous round at the Melbourne Cricket Ground (AFL is played on an oval field) between Essendon and Richmond. They introduced the Marn Grook trophy game to celebrate the traditional Aboriginal game and have it coincide with the match between Essendon and the Sydney Swans (Gorman 2011: 9–10).

William Blandowski, an early pioneer scientist who explored the Murray River region near Mildura in Victoria's northwest corner, also saw an Aboriginal ball game being played by the Nyeri Nyeri, in 1857. It was at Mondellimin, near present-day Merbein and it was also a kicking game. Blandowski described, "a group of children is playing with a ball. The ball is made out of Typha roots; it is not thrown or hit with a bat, but it is kicked up in the air with the foot. Aim of the game never let the ball touch the ground" (Rintoul 2007: 3). Blandowski's reflections were later used as the basis for an etching by artist Gustav Mützel. What is startling about this engraving is that it depicts an early Aboriginal footballer in a Ronaldinho-like soccer pose balancing the ball on his foot. This "keepy-uppy" game (*The Newcastle Morning Herald*, 8 February 2012) of football played in Victoria appears to have been a widely spread phenomenon amongst Indigenous groups.

Aboriginal traditional games were all about teaching skills and building fitness, particularly agility and athleticism, which were integral to the hunting and gathering lifestyle that Indigenous people had adapted to so well. All games were taught and encouraged from a very young age. As social behaviourist Desmond Morris reflected in relation to humanity in general: "our early hunting ancestors became gradually more athletic" and used "these advantages and working together as a team – a hunting pack – they were able to plan strategies, devise tactics, take risks, set traps and, finally, aim to kill" (Morris 1981: 10). The missionary Lancelot Threlkeld noted in 1834 that Aboriginal children of the Newcastle and Lake Macquarie region were encouraged to practice their sporting technique from a very young age: "children practice, in sport, the attack and defence, using a piece of the bark of a gum tree for shield, and small grass stems for spear" (Gunson 1974: 68). The convict artist Joseph Lycett captured the self-reliance and discipline incorporated by Aboriginal people in their sporting pursuits. These sporting contests captured the fitness and practised skills of the Aboriginal participants: "The sporting games were obviously much enjoyed by all members of the group – in Lycett's image, women and children are sitting on the sidelines cheering on their favourite participants" (Maynard 2014: 62).

These sporting activities clearly contributed to the physical conditioning of Aboriginal people. There are countless early settler accounts and observations across the country of the physical health, fitness and well-being of Aboriginal people. As an example, the Worimi people of New South Wales were recorded and noted for their health and imposing physical attributes: "some of the blacks were nearly 7ft tall" (Clayton 1952: 4). Another early account by an English observer in 1827 of the Aboriginal people of Coal River (Newcastle) confirms their imposing physical presence: "You seldom see a black under five feet eight or nine inches. I have seen them about six foot four in height" (*The Newcastle Morning Herald*, 11 May 1993). In the same location and area Robert Dawson observed the agility and speed of the local Worimi people: "they go up the largest and tallest trees with great facility' and noted 'their quickness is astonishing" (Dawson 1830: 68). Through this chapter I will examine the long proud Aboriginal sporting history and the tragedy of the racist barriers of the past that denied many Aboriginal sportsmen and women their sporting chance. I will in particular focus on a narrative of one outstanding Aboriginal sportsman who history continues to overlook and neglect Wally MacArthur.

Breaking down the sports barriers

In the contemporary setting, Aboriginal sporting participation and success has gripped the Australian nation from the later stages of the twentieth century. In 1968 Lionel Rose defeated Fighting Harada in Tokyo to be crowned World Bantamweight boxing champion. Rose would return home a national hero with over 100,000 people to greet him in Melbourne. The crowd that flocked to see Lionel Rose drive through the streets of Melbourne that day was greater than met the Beatles and he was named Australian of the Year (Booth and Tatz 2000: 154). Evonne Goolagong Cawley won seven tennis singles Grand Slam titles including two Wimbledon Championships. Like Rose, in 1971 she was named Australian of the Year (Booth and Tatz 2000). No event captured the imagination of the Australian public more than the Women's 400-metre final at the Sydney 2000 Olympic Games. When Cathy Freeman exploded off the turn to race to the front and gold medal glory the nation as a united collective cheered and cried with relief. Television commentator Bruce McAvaney stated, "Nothing had stopped the nation in my lifetime like this race" he said, "and I think so many Australians had a personal interest … it was personal, it was us, it was our nation. … I guess us presenting ourselves to the rest of the world through this one woman" (cited in Marlow 2015: webpage).

For many it seemed the night was a picture of Australia as it ought to be; reconciling through the celebration of one person's achievements and talent. This is what sport can achieve in healing the past and building a future inclusive for all Australians. Cathy Freeman had joined her predecessors Rose and Goolagong in being named Australian of the Year in 1998 after Commonwealth Games and World Championship successes. However, sport historically was not always a level playing field and an arena that was welcoming for Aboriginal participation. It took many decades for Aboriginal players to even gain an opportunity to play either rugby league or Australian football. Over the past 40 years those codes finally recognised the Aboriginal talent and opened opportunities for them to play the game. In the years since, these codes have been graced by some of the greatest players in the game's histories being Aboriginal. Michael Long, Adam Goodes, Michael O'Loughlin, Buddy Franklin, Jonathon Thurston, and Greg Inglis are just a handful of the Aboriginal stars whose impact and star power has seen them idolised as legends and immortals of the game.

The hard yards to sporting recognition

Sport is one of the major past times and attractions of the Australian national identity. Yet Aboriginal people, despite clear talent, were to be denied their place on the sporting field for the greater part of the 20th century. Prior to the 1970s you could count on two hands the numbers of Aboriginal players who managed to escape the colour bar and gain acceptance to play in the major codes of football in Australia. Aboriginal World War One hero Douglas Grant was outraged to write in the press over a Condoblin rugby league team refusing to play a team with Aboriginal players: "the colour line was never drawn in the trenches" (*The Lithgow Mercury*, 24 June 1929: 6). The most sickening sporting example was that suffered by Aboriginal fast bowling sensation Eddie Gilbert who in the early 1930s was reputedly the fastest bowler in the world and had bowled Don Bradman[2] for a duck (no score). Eddie Gilbert played cricket for Queensland but was never picked for an Australian national cricket team. Despite playing for his state he was not allowed in the same hotel as his teammates and was forced to sleep in a tent in the backyard of the Secretary of the Queensland Cricket Association (Harris 1989: 19). Gilbert's experience of denied sporting opportunities despite his undeniable talent was experienced by many Aboriginal athletes across the 20th century, both male and female.

There have been long-held assumptions and theories put forward that Aboriginal people possess some innate inner biological advantage that enhances their sporting prowess. Roy Hay stated that the, "skills they had honed long before the white men arrived could be used to develop different ways of playing the game – speed at ground level, rapid hand movement and brilliant hand-eye and foot-eye coordination, plus physical play" (Hay 2019: 20). John Moriarty, the first Aboriginal soccer player selected to play for his country, held similar thoughts: "it's the ideal sport for Aboriginal people. Their bone structure. Their coordination, hands, feet, eye. They've got speed and dexterity. They're naturals" (Maynard 2019: 99).

However, AFL legend Adam Goodes powerfully argued that Aboriginal sporting success was not due to some magical inner source but simply to hard work:

> when we celebrate the contribution of Indigenous footballers and Indigenous culture to our game, those traits of hard work and sacrifice are the areas of our character that I'd like people to recognise and to talk about. There's nothing magical about Indigenous football-ers. They are not born with any special powers. Like any other footballer, to get drafted they've had to sacrifice things along the way, such as time with family and friends, and put years of effort into improving their game and their fitness.
>
> (*The Sydney Morning Herald, 19 May 2010: 10*)

Wally McArthur – fire and grace

Things had not drastically changed from the experiences suffered by Eddie Gilbert some 20 years earlier when Wally McArthur burst onto the athletic and sport scene in Australia. McArthur was amongst thousands of Aboriginal kids removed from their families in what we recognise today as the Stolen Generations. McArthur was separated from his family and placed into the St Francis House[3] in South Australia. Charles Perkins, John Moriarty, and Gordon Briscoe were three other well-known names who were placed into that institution during the 1940s. Wally McArthur would prove an outstanding athlete and 400-metre runner. The times he ran as a teenager had him qualified for the Australian under 19 Athletic championships to be held in Tasmania. But he was informed that he would have to pay his own way to get there to run. Fortunately, a col-lection was made and the funds for him to run in the championship were put up. He duly won the race easily beating the field, including Kevin Gosper. The Australian team was chosen for the 1952 Helsinki Olympic Games and despite winning the U/19 championship Wally MacArthur was over-looked. Up until the 1960s, no Aboriginal athlete would be selected to represent Australia. Kevin Gosper, who he had soundly beaten, went on to win a silver medal at the 1956 Olympic Games in Melbourne. Wally McArthur, disillusioned and eventually out of the St Francis House, turned professional as a runner then went to England and became recognised as the fastest rugby league winger in the world (Pilger 1999).

What happened to Wally McArthur? How did he become such an outstanding athlete? Why did he not achieve what he should have on the sporting arena? Wally McArthur was certainly an inspiration to other young Aboriginal kids who knew him at the time. John Moriarty was his younger cousin and, like McArthur, was taken from his family and the same region and community; Borroloola of the Northern Territory. Moriarty was adamant: "He could have been one of the world's great athletes. He just exploded with fire and grace". Moriarty added that McArthur was someone to look up to: "He was a leader. He looked after us younger kids. He was such a humble compassionate person. Wally set a standard for us, as to what could be achieved in sport" (Smith 2019: online). Another Aboriginal boy at St Francis House was Vince Copley and he also recorded the impact of Wally on them all: "We loved him because he was so honest. He cared for us. He was our protector, our dear brother and our hero" (Mallett 2018: 158). Vince added that on some occasions, "we'd sneak a look at Wally shaving. There he would be standing naked from the waist up, and there we would be admiring his incredible physique and rippling muscles" (Mallett 2018: 158).

Wally McArthur was born in 1933, his father reputedly a policeman named Langdon: "but the authorities, who registered many of these births, gave him the name of McArthur, after the river at Borroloola" (Mallett 2018: 158). McArthur would many years later recount his memory of being removed from his family in an interview with journalist John Pilger:

> It was a government car, because only the government had cars at that time. The driver put me in the front seat with him and he drove around while I waved at my family. I have never seen them since, you know. They were sitting around the campfire. They didn't understand what was happening.
>
> *(Smith 2019: online)*

This was the tragedy of so many young Aboriginal lives across the 20th century. Wally did not know at the time but years later he would be recognised as one of the thousands of Aboriginal children known as the 'Stolen Generation'. Taken from his mother at a young age, he was first sent to the Bungalow Mission near Alice Springs. John Pilger noted that as a "half-caste", he was earmarked for a servile role in white society – the girls of the Stolen Generation were usually given to white middle-class homes as domestic slaves, the boys as cheap labour on country properties. Pilger recalled an entry in one of his school textbooks where the eminent Professor Stephen Roberts concluded: "It was quite useless to treat [aborigines] fairly, since they were completely amoral and usually incapable of sincere and prolonged gratitude" (Pilger 1999: online). Many years later in an interview with journalist Peter Hackett Wally McArthur confided: "I don't feel angry about it. I can't. I just had to get on with my life" (Smith 2019: website: no page number).

Apparently it was the Japanese attack on Darwin in 1942 that "prompted the rounding up of children in Borroloola who were then piled into army trucks and taken to Alice Springs". John Moriarty, aged only four at the time, recalled the removal from their families:

> I can remember getting on a truck in a yard. There were a number of other kids in the truck who were also being removed from their families, including Jim and Rose Foster, Wally McArthur and Wilfred Huddlestone.
>
> The truck went all the way down to Alice Springs. It took several days. In Alice Springs we went to a place called the Bungalow, which was the original Alice Springs Telegraph Station.
>
> The next thing I remember is the railyard. I was there with my cousins Jim Foster and Wally McArthur and a few others, we all went to see this big long rail line. I just remember seeing one seemingly endless track.
>
> We were standing there, Wally with khaki shorts on, and in bare feet, we were all bare footed.

The children were bundled onto the train to Adelaide before being sent to Sydney enroute to Mulgoa for the duration.

(Smith 2019: online)

The boys were placed into school and McArthur studied at Penrith High School. In 1948 he won 12 of the school's 13 athletic events and was NSW High School champion in the 100 yards, long jump and 440 yards. At the age of 14 and barefooted he was recorded as running 440 yards at the Sydney Cricket Ground, "… in 52 seconds, which was the world's fastest for his age group" (Smith 2019: website).

It was whilst in western Sydney that McArthur was introduced to rugby league and it was a game that his blistering pace and power ensured he excelled (Smith 2019: online). Whilst attending Penrith High School he played his first full season of rugby league at the age of 13 (*The News*, 14 November 1953: 11). After the war the boys were moved again to Adelaide and were placed into St Francis House. The Anglican priest, Father Percy Smith, who had previously run St John's Hostel in Alice Springs was in charge at St Francis (Mallett 2018: 13). Wally McArthur picked up where left off in Sydney and became athletics champion of Le Fevre Boys Technical High School. A 1949 newspaper report heralded Wally's arrival in Adelaide stating that he dominated the school sports carnival, winning the senior cup with seven firsts. The article declared that McArthur, "is hailed as an Olympic possibility" (*The News* [Adelaide], 5 May 1949). The report was supported by the NSW Amateur Athletics Association in the same year describing McArthur as the, "greatest Olympic Games prospect" (*The News*, 14 November 1953: 11).

Reflecting years later, Wally McArthur said: "I have no idea how many records I broke. I just ran because I enjoyed it. I never got a lot of recognition for what I did as an athlete". His natural gift was something he had developed from a very young age and recalled that as a young boy back in Borrooloola fishing at waterholes, "you always had to be on the lookout for crocs. You had to be fast on your feet". There was another animal to dodge up north as well: "There was also this emu that used to hang about the cattle station and he always went for me. He frightened the hell out of me. But I learnt to outrun him!" (*The News*, 14 November 1953: 11).

Wally McArthur as noted had originally started playing rugby league whilst in NSW. Once relocated to South Australia, he had dabbled with soccer, and also AFL. He was not encouraged by the AFL code as he faced a 'colour bar' of exclusion and was made aware that he was not welcome. He played in a legendary soccer game with the other boys from St Francis House when they beat a South Australian U/19 representative team 12–0 (Maynard 2019: 45). An interview with Vince Copley who played in that game highlighted the impact of Wally McArthur: "We just knocked the ball through and Wally outsprinted them" (Maynard 2019: 45). Some who have studied the athletic records and times he set believe that he was the Usain Bolt of his day. At the age of 14, "and running without shoes, he was the fastest teenager on earth. Known as the Borrooloola Flash" (Pilger 1999: online).

Through the denied access to AFL he converted back to rugby league playing for Semaphore in the South Australian competition and running professionally. This move was also precipitated through his despair and disappointment with athletics. The issues faced just to get to the national titles in Tasmania and then the lack of support, recognition or encouragement in winning the Australian U/19 championship left him resigned to the fact that no matter what he did or won he would be ignored by the national athletics body. It must have been so disappointing not to be given his chance. In 1951, the press reports were glowing of the flying Wally McArthur as Semaphore destroyed Alberton 36-0. By all reports it was a scratchy game except for the brilliance of McArthur who every time he, "gained possession and kept things moving with his elusive runs. He showed his versatility by also scoring six goals against a heavy wind" (*The Messenger Port Adelaide*, 31 May 1951: 2). The following year Semaphore were off to a flying start to the new season in Adelaide, thumping North Adelaide 41–0: "Wally McArthur beat the opposition repeatedly with his first class 'dummies'; the opposition never knew what to expect from this player" (*The Messenger Port Adelaide*, 31 May 1951: 2). He was awarded the South Australian best player award in 1952. It seems somewhat strange reading of Wally McArthur's rugby league triumphs in Adelaide as rugby league is not a game one would normally associate with South Australia, which is dominated by Australian football. Across four seasons McArthur amassed an amazing 822 points (*The Messenger Port Adelaide*, 31 May 1951: 2). The Semaphore team was undefeated through the 1950 and 1951 seasons and he scored both tries and goals at an astonishing rate. In 1953 he was selected to play for South Australia against Western Australia, where he won the Man of the Match award. He came under the notice of some ex-British players in Adelaide and they were impressed. Paul Quinn, a former Rochdale Hornets player in England living in Adelaide at the time arranged for him to go to England and play for Rochdale (Smith 2019: online).

It was announced in the press in 1953 that McArthur would be flying to England to play professionally for the Rochdale Hornets club (*The Messenger Port Adelaide*, 31 May 1951: 2). He joined the Hornets on a four-year contract and was reported as being the first Aborigine to play in England. He was additionally found work as an apprentice fitter (*Warialda Standard and Northern Districts Advertiser*, 20 November 1953:3). A report in the *Yorkshire Evening News* was glowing on the debut of McArthur in England he "has the speed, swerve and quick thinking of a born footballer". Hailed as the 'black flash' in the British press, one article pointed out that McArthur from a young age had "been in the midst of one of the greatest Christian and social experiments ever attempted in Australia" (Mallett 2018: 157). The writer neglected to mention that this experiment saw Wally McArthur taken from his family and placed in an institution thousands of kilometres away from them. Family members he would never see again.

McArthur scored three tries on his debut in the Rochdale Hornets victory over Whitehaven. It was noted that McArthur still not 20 years of age had been clocked at 9.7 seconds over 100 yards. In coming to England from South Australia he had escaped the transfer ban in place between the English and Australian controlling authorities: the ban did not consider Western Australia, Victoria, and South Australia, because those states had no representation on the Australian Board of Control, and no real interest in rugby league. McArthur's debut had even made news into Federal Parliament discussion. When after a question the Australian Prime Minister Robert Menzies stated that the Australian government was taking a keen interest in Wally McArthur. After only a handful of games in England he was "becoming the most talked of personality in English rugby league" (*The Western Mail Perth*, 18 March 1954: 17).

The following year it was noted that 20-year-old Wally had married Marlene Newchurch in England and the Rochdale club had given Wally and his bride a wonderful reception. They had previously met in Adelaide and had become engaged before Wally departed for England. Vince Copley recalled the first time Wally brought Marlene to St Francis House stating she was, "a stunner. We liked her immediately" (Mallett 2018: 158). Marlene herself had previously been employed as a domestic housemaid at Largs Bay in Adelaide for Dr and Mrs Alan Cherry before her departure to England to marry Wally (*The Western Mail Perth*, 18 March 1954: 17). It was stated that Wally McArthur originally went to England to take up a £1000 playing contract. It was further reported that the impact of McArthur playing in England had encouraged one aged ardent supporter of the club to provide "in his will for a small block of flats for Wally" (*Nepean Times*, 10 June 1954: 1). The actual club financial transaction was that he would receive an initial quarterly £250 installment on arrival, and will be 'paid at the rate of £8 a win, £6 a draw, and £4 a loss for every match' (*The Herald Melbourne*, 13 November 1953: 21).' In one match "against St. Helens, supporters of both sides cheered McArthur for almost two minutes after he had scored a brilliant try" (*The Advertiser*, 6 February 1954: 11). In the late 1950s McArthur was joined in England by some former friends from St Francis House Jim Foster, Charlie Perkins, John Moriarty, and Gordon Briscoe. Jim Foster played with Wally in England. Charlie Perkins, a top soccer player back in South Australia trialled with Everton, played with the top amateur team Bishop Auckland and was even offered a trial with Manchester United. Perkins for a time stayed with Wally and Marlene in Wigan (Mallett 2018: 168).

In England, it was a totally different social experience for these young men to that in Australia. They could walk the street with a white girl. They were served in public venues, cafes and restaurants without question. It was one of the first times they were treated with equality and their Aboriginality was not an issue. Despite some initial negative experiences and disappointments in Britain, Perkins could, at the conclusion of his stay, reflect:

> I've had a good time here. I've seen a lot of things, met a lot of people and found a lot of happiness. The English people in Wigan and Bishop Auckland or England generally, I suppose, are wonderful. They are decent people and give you a fair go. They treated me better than I was ever treated in Australia. … [Now] I was on my way back to my country, my people and problems.
>
> *(Perkins 1975: 50)*

Moriarty was also forthright on the difference in attitudes between people in England and those in Australia at that time, "[The English] enjoyed life; they enjoyed people for what they were. If you were a likeable person, they didn't discriminate on colour – at least the people I met didn't. In Australia discrimination was enshrined in law" (Maynard 2019: 55).

In an interview with me in 2004, Gordon Briscoe agreed with Moriarty and Perkins' comments about England, saying that he found great acceptance there:

> Well, they didn't know what an Aboriginal person was, and because of our background, we'd say, 'I'm an Aboriginal' … and they'd say, Well what's that?', and then we'd have to explain our background. But they treated you in the same European way, they were very self-interested. And that's how we were able to get past some of the problems. If you could play soccer, amongst people who knew something about soccer, you were put on a pedestal … if the coach said, 'You do this, and you do that', and you did that, and then you did that well, you were given an opportunity to go further up the slippery pole.
>
> *(cited in Maynard 2019: 58)*

It is probably fortunate that McArthur, Foster, Perkins, Moriarty, and Briscoe were in England during the 1950s and early 1960s. The large intake of migrants in the aftermath of World War II, particularly from the West Indies, Pakistan, and India, had not yet become the subject of concern and vocal opposition from the wider population. But by the mid to mid- to late 1960s, with the British economy in decline and competition for jobs and housing high, racism and prejudice would become rampant (Fryer 1984; Dilip 1991).

Wally McArthur was a star in England and his club record of tries and goals still stands. From 1953 to 1959 McArthur played a total of 165 games for English league clubs Rochdale, Blackpool Borough, Salford, and Workington Town. There remained a lingering wound over the barriers he faced in the athletics world: "I would have liked to have run for my country", he said: "I was in Wales when the 1958 Commonwealth Games were held in Cardiff. My times were a lot better than the Australian runners who competed. It made me a bit sad" (Pilger 1999: website: no page number). Running remained his greatest sporting love and he continued to run competitively in Britain when his football commitments allowed the time. In 1957 he was the North England sprint champion, winning both the 100- and 220-yard championships. He also won the 100-yard sprint final at the 1957 Highland Games. He was introduced to members of the Royal Family who were spectators at the Games, including Prince Philip, the Duke of Edinburgh.

Wally McArthur was longing for home at the end of the 1959 season after several years of playing at the highest level in England. He applied to the national rugby league body for a clearance to play back in Australia, but his request was ignored. He returned to Australia in 1959 and disclosed that Workington Town still owed him £800 when he left (Mallett 2018: 160). On returning to Australia:

> he worked as a fitter and turner at Port Adelaide and then moved to the industrial town of Whyalla working as a labourer and a welder in the shipyards for more than 25 years. ... He later worked as a ganger for the Australian National Railways maintaining the Indian-Pacific line on the Nullarbor Plains. Tragically, in 1977 he was involved in an accident that left him with crippling injuries.
>
> *(Smith 2019: online)*

In helping another worker to safety he leapt from a rail cart to escape an oncoming train but was struck, suffering bone fractures in both legs and feet. For the rest of his life he would remain handicapped and need the aid of a walking stick to get around. He was unable to work again after the accident and shifted his focus to his family.

McArthur's sporting achievements were recognised with a place in the inaugural induction to the Aboriginal and Islander Sports Hall of Fame in 1994. He was later named in the Aboriginal Australian rugby league team of the century in 2008. He died in 2015. The *Manchester Evening News* gave glowing coverage of the great player, quoting Hornets chairman Mark Wynn:

> Few sportspeople deserve the accolade, but just once in a while the term 'legend' is the only word that fits. ... For former Rochdale Hornets player Wally McArthur, the word 'legend' is such the occasion... Sadly the club has just heard of the passing of Wally on August 28 and even for those who never saw him play he still holds a magical place in Hornets folklore.
>
> *(31 August 2015: no page number)*

Wally McArthur is unquestionably one of the all-time great Aboriginal sportsmen. Unfortunately born into the wrong time period he was not given the opportunity to make his mark athletically upon the sporting world that his talent deserved. His story is a significant marker of the racist history of the country; including his tragic young life as just one of thousands of Aboriginal children removed from their families as part of the Stolen Generations. The fanfare of Cathy Freeman's gold medal at the 2000 Olympic games in Sydney was a mark of the progress of the nation in race relations, but it also masked not just the past but the racism that remains embedded within the fabric of Australian society.

This chapter has revealed that Aboriginal Australia had a long-standing sporting tradition well before 1788 and the British arrival on the continent. Aboriginal people were introduced to British sporting games across the middle stages of the nineteenth century and they demonstrated a quick ability to master these games most notably through cricket, horse racing and athletics. By the later stages of the nineteenth century, despite unquestioned talent, obstacles to Aboriginal participation in sport began to be set in place as the colour bar of exclusion. Rugby league and Australian football quickly established themselves as the dominant football codes down under but Aboriginal participation would largely be restricted to minimal admission until the later stages of the 1960s. If Wally McArthur's talent had been supported, encouraged and developed in the early 1950s with top coaching input and facilities, he may have gone on to be one of the greatest Australian athletes of all time. He certainly had the ability to win at the highest level including the Olympic Games. That is the tragedy of his experience, and it mirrors the experiences of so many outstanding Aboriginal sports stars who remain just shadows in the background of the country's sporting history.

Notes

1 See https://en.wikipedia.org/wiki/Australian_rules_football. Australian rules football, or Aussie rules, football or footy, is a contact sport played between two teams of eighteen players on an oval shaped field, often a modified cricket ground. Points are scored by kicking the ball between the middle goal posts (worth six points) or between a goal and behind post (worth one point). The sport's origins can be traced to football matches played in Melbourne, Victoria, in 1858, inspired by English public-school football games. Seeking to develop a game more suited to adults and Australian conditions, the Melbourne Football Club published the first laws of Australian football in May 1859, making it the oldest of the world's major football codes.

   Australian football has the highest spectator attendance and television viewership of all sports in Australia, while the Australian Football League (AFL), the sport's only fully professional competition, is the nation's wealthiest sporting body. The AFL Grand Final, held annually at the Melbourne Cricket Ground, is the highest attended club championship event in the world.

2 Don Bradman Australian test cricketer widely regarded as the world's greatest ever batsman. Played for his country between 1928 and 1948 and accumulated an unthinkable test batting average of 99.94.

3 St Francis House was an Anglican Church initiative to house Aboriginal children. It was operational between 1946 and 1959.

References

Basedow, H. (1925). *The Australian Aboriginal*, F.W. Preece and Sons: Adelaide.

Blainey, G. (1990). *A Game of Our Own: The Origins of Australian Football*. Information Australia: Melbourne.

Booth, D. and Tatz, C. (2000). *One Eyed: A View of Australian Sport*. Allen & Unwin: Sydney.

Clayton, W. (1952). *Early Days of Port Stephens: Recollections of Bill Clayton*, C.E. Bennet (ed.). Dungog Chronicle: Dungog, NSW.

Dawson, R. (1830). *The Present State of Australia*. Smith, Elder and Co.: Cornhill.

Dilip, H. (1991). *Black British, White British: A History of Race Relations in Britain*. Grafton Books: London.

Fryer, P. (1984). *Staying Power: The History of Black People in Britain*. Pluto Press: London.

Gorman, S (2011). *Legends: The AFL Indigenous Team of the Century*. Acton, A.C.T: Aboriginal Studies Press.

Gunson, N. (1974). *Australian Reminiscences & Papers of L.E. Threlkeld: Missionary to the Aborigines 1824–1859*, vol 1. Australian Institute of Aboriginal Studies: Canberra.

Harris, B. (1989). *The Proud Champions Australia's Aboriginal Sporting Heroes*. Little Hill Press: Sydney.

Hay, R. (2019). *Aboriginal People and Australian Football in Nineteenth Century Australia*. Cambridge Scholars Publishing: Cambridge.

Lissarrague, A. (2010). *A Grammar and Dictionary of Gathang*. Muurrbay Aboriginal Language & Culture Co-operative: Nambucca Heads.

Mallett, A. (2018). *The Boys from St Francis*. Wakefield Press: Adelaide.

Marlow, K. (2015). '15 years on, Cathy Freeman's Olympic gold still a potent symbol of reconciliation', *sbs. com.au*. Available: https://www.sbs.com.au/nitv/article/2015/09/25/15-years-cathy-freemans-olympic-gold-still-potent-symbol-reconciliation, accessed 29 March 2020.

Maynard, J. (2014). *True Light and Shade: An Aboriginal Perspective of Joseph Lycett's Art*. National Library of Australia: Canberra.

Maynard, J. (2019). *The Aboriginal Soccer Tribe*. FairPlay Publishing: Sydney.

Morris, D. (1981). *The Soccer Tribe*. Jonathon Cape: London.

Perkins, C. (1975). *A Bastard Like Me*. Ure Smith: Sydney.

Pilger, J. (1999). 'Fixed race'. Available: http://johnpilger.com/articles/fixed-race, accessed March 29, 2020.

Rintoul, S. (2007). 'Aussie rules kicked off by aboriginies'. Available: https://www.theage.com.au/national/aussie-rules-kicked-off-by-aborigines-20070922-ge5vnv.html, accessed 4 April 2020.

Roth, W.E. (1984). *The Queensland Aborigines*, vol. 1. Victoria Park: Hesperian Press.

Smith, M. (2019). 'Alice Bungalow kid Wally McArthur ran with "fire and grace"'. Available: http://www.alicespringsnews.com.au/2019/02/27/alice-bungalow-kid-wally-mcarthur-exploded-with-fire-and-grace/, accessed 29 March 2020.

Thomas, N.W. (1906). *The Native Races of the British Empire*. Archibald Constable and Company: London.

The Advertiser, 6 February 1954.

The Herald Melbourne, 13 November 1953.

The Lithgow Mercury, 24 June 1929.

Manchester Evening News, 31 August 2015.

The Messenger Port Adelaide, 17 July 1952.

Nepean Times, 10 June 1954.

The Newcastle Morning Herald, 11 May 1993.

The Newcastle Morning Herald, 8 February 2012.

New South Adelaide, 14 November 1953.

The Sydney Morning Herald, 19 May 2010.

The Warialda Standard and Northern Districts Advertiser, 25 November 1953.

The Western Mail Perth, 18 March 1954.

42

Academic and STEM success

Pathways to Indigenous sovereignty

Michelle M. Hogue

Introduction

Indigenous peoples in Canada have historically been judged as lesser on all levels, and their way of learning, life, and living evaluated as not equitable to that of the dominant European settler population. This position of superiority, coupled with the expressed intention to take the land and resources rightfully belonging to the Original Peoples, became the root of the assimilation policies intended to erase Canada's Indigenous peoples and absorb them into the body politic through residential schools (Titley: 1986), a horrific story in and of itself. The consequent intergenerational impact (trauma) of residential schools has resulted in over a century of educational and socioeconomic inequities for Indigenous peoples across the nation. The monumental apology by the then Prime Minister Stephen Harper on 11 June 2008, that acknowledged the wrongs done to Canada's Indigenous peoples, was followed by a six-year national inquiry into residential schools led by the Honorable Justice Murray Sinclair. The inquiry culminated in 2015 with the release of the Truth and Reconciliation Commission Report (TRC) and its 94 Calls to Action (CTA) (TRC 2015). Honorable Murray Sinclair stated to Canadians that, "[r]econciliation is not an aboriginal problem, it is a Canadian problem. It involves all of us" (2015: online). Key to reconciliation is Indigenous sovereignty; the full right and power of Indigenous peoples to govern over themselves, in all things, and at all levels. If Indigenous sovereignty is to occur, Indigenous peoples have to have the same tools as the dominant population to compete in the 21st century. Thus, there needs to be educated Indigenous peoples in all areas, and at all levels, with voice and power to bring Indigenous perspectives and rights to the table.

While Indigenous equity and sovereignty is the ultimate goal, the challenge has been where and how to begin. Honorable Justice Murray Sinclair advocates for education as the change-agent. However, the traditional Eurocentric-based Western education system does not attend to Indigenous Ways of Knowing and Learning (IWKL) and in fact serves as a roadblock; a key reason to the current issues surrounding the lack of Indigenous academic engagement, retention, and success (Gallop and Bastien: 2016). The expectation is that Indigenous learners will leave their culture and ways of knowing and learning at the education door and conform to the *white*-Western ways. This hasn't, and still doesn't, work as is evidenced by both past and current engagement, retention, and completion statistics (Statistics Canada 2016; 2018):

Rather than taking the assimilationist approach, that all must fit into, and learn the *white-Western* way, we as educators, curriculum developers, and policy makers must find ways of bridging cultures and creating a space *between* where both the Aboriginal and Western paradigms can have an equitable voice in all.

(Hogue 2018: 23)

Thus, the first step to Indigenous sovereignty is to enable Indigenous academic engagement and retention in K–12 and support their transition to and through post-secondary education (PSE). To do this we must first understand and accept that IWKL are simply different, not lesser, than Western ways of knowing and learning (WWKL) as is the expectation of the *white*-Western Eurocentric-based education system (Burns 2001; Hogue 2018). Rather than expect Indigenous conformation to the dominant system, we need to create pathways of access to PSE and at the same time reframe traditional education theory and practice in ways that attend to IWKL. This means changing both the way we *think* and *do* education. This chapter describes the gap that exists in education with a focus on the gap in the sciences and mathematics and explores cultur ally relevant and inclusive ways to bridge the gaps to enable academic engagement, retention, and success for Indigenous peoples to enable Indigenous sovereignty moving forward.

The education gap

The issue of Indigenous academic success is at the forefront of nearly all current government initiatives[1] especially with the outcomes of the TRC Report and the 94 CTA (TRC 2015). While there has been a greater increase in Indigenous students graduating from high school (30 per cent) in recent years, it still remains that the majority (70 per cent) are not graduating. Sadly, there is still a higher percentage who go into the correctional system than who graduate from high school. The education gap for Indigenous learners begins early in elementary school, persists throughout secondary school such that by the end of secondary school more than half the Indigenous learners have dropped out (C.D. Howe Institute 2016; Council of Ministers of Education 2017). According to Statistics Canada (2016; 2018), 26 per cent of Indigenous Canadians between the ages of 25 to 64 still do not have a high school diploma relative to 11 per cent of non-Indigenous Canadians. This prevents Indigenous students from entering PSE without, at the very least, first strengthening their foundation. Of those with PSE, Indigenous and non-Indigenous Canadians are relatively the same in terms of holding college diplomas (both at 23 per cent) and trades certificates (12 per cent for Indigenous and 11 per cent for non-Indigenous peoples). However, Indigenous people lag by nearly 40 per cent (11 per cent versus 29 per cent, respectively) in university degrees (bachelor or higher). Of the 11 per cent with a university degree, there are very few Indigenous peoples at the most advanced levels (i.e., Master's and PhD). In all these, the greatest gaps are seen in science, technology, engineering, and mathematics (STEM)–related degrees (Canadian Council on Learning [CCL] 2007; C.D. Howe Report 2016; CMEC 2017; Hogue 2018). This perpetuates the socioeconomic and power disadvantage as Indigenous communities must rely on non-Indigenous STEM-related professionals for their services.

It is important to note that even with secondary school diplomas, most Indigenous students, particularly those graduating from on-reserve schools, are academically and socially less prepared for PSE. The first-year attrition rate, as a result, is significantly higher than that of their non-Indigenous counterparts particularly in university (C.D. Howe 2016; CMEC 2017; Statistics Canada 2016; 2018). A key focus of the TRC and the 94 CTAs is to enable Indigenous academic success, which means ensuring K–12 engagement and retention to graduation as well as creating supportive and culturally relevant and inclusive pathway programs to PSE that create bridges between IWKL and Western education expectations.

The STEM gap

Science and technology is pervasive in all sectors of the economy, and with the retirement of the Baby Boomer generation who had fewer children, of which even fewer are entering into the STEM fields, (CMEC 2017; S.C. 2018) there are projected professional shortages in such professions at all levels. The fastest growing population is the Indigenous population and as such Indigenous youth are a critical and necessary resource to address this shortage. While Eurocentric-based Western education, in and of itself, is a roadblock for many Indigenous students, the sciences and mathematics courses serve as the greatest gatekeepers (C.D. Howe Institute 2016; CMEC 2017). This results in early streaming of Indigenous students away from the sciences and mathematics, particularly in secondary school, as one solution to retention to graduation (CCL 2007; 2009). This precludes them from entering STEM-related academic pathways at the post-secondary level, the consequence of which is the critical under-representation of Indigenous peoples in STEM-related professions such as medicine, science education, scientific research, technology et cetera at all levels. Without STEM-related professional degrees, Indigenous people do not have the opportunity to work within their own community as professionals to build community capacity, self-efficacy or sovereignty, or have equitable voice and representation in policies, governmental or other, that affect Indigenous peoples and their communities. This further perpetuates the dependency of Indigenous communities on the dominant culture for such professions and thus disempowers them, which works against any potential for sovereignty. Indigenous sovereignty requires that Indigenous peoples become successful and equally represented in the STEM fields (CCL 2007; Hogue 2018).

Indigenous science versus Western science

The University of Lethbridge (ULeth) professor emeritus and pioneer of Canada's first Native America Studies Department, Dr Leroy Little Bear, says there is the adage that 'Natives can't do Science'. He then challenges that prejudice with the question: *What science are we talking about?* Is it the science as it is taught through the Western Eurocentric-based education system, because that approach to teaching science is also failing non-Indigenous students? Or are we talking about 'true science', in which all things are related and inter-related? If that is the science we are talking about, then 'Natives', as he says, have been doing science since the beginning of time. If we are talking about the science of the Western paradigm that is compartmentalised into silos and exclusionary subjects, then perhaps that is somewhat correct in that most 'Natives' can't/don't? do that *type* of science, because it doesn't fit within the Indigenous paradigm nor attends to IWKL.

Yet, the Indigenous paradigm is steeped in science and mathematics in a very inter-related and integrated way, not defined by Western science and mathematics (i.e. chemistry, physics, biology, algebra, geometry). It is a way of perceiving the world that is holistic, participatory, and balanced with the Mother Earth's life support systems and is inclusive of spirituality, a dimension excluded and even negated in the Western paradigm (Aikenhead and Michel 2011; Bartlett and Marshall 2009; Bartlett, Marshall, and Marshall 2012; Cajete 1999; 2000). One just has to think of what is involved in hunting an animal as an example, and one soon realises the extensive science and mathematics (without calling it that) involved at all levels: the *geography* of the environment and landscape; the *environmental science* of weather patterns, water, air and land; the *physics* and *mathematics* of tracking, targeting, shooting the animal; the *biology* and *physiology* of animals and their environment; the *anatomy* of dissecting an animal; the *chemistry* of preserving the products etc. The intricate science and mathematics embedded in the fabric of this very complex traditional knowledge gets missed when we compare Indigenous and Western paradigms. If we distil science down its fundamental level of understanding life (both the animate and inanimate) and how it works, that all things are related and inter-related, then one can see Indigenous and Western science complement each other and it is possible to create bridges between the two paradigms.

Addressing the STEM gap must be done simultaneously with addressing the education gap, as it requires an early and sustained focus on engagement in the sciences and mathematics to develop an early and strong foundation for retention to and through the middle and high school levels. The challenge in addressing both gaps is to change conventional education philosophy, pedagogy, and practice; to move away from the Eurocentric-based Western-only lens and teaching methodologies and reframe these in ways that both bridge cultures and attend to IWKL (Aikenhead 2006; Battiste 2002; Cajete 1999; 2000; Hogue 2018; Sterenberg and Hogue 2011). The following section describes how opening doors of access and being open to different philosophical, pedagogical and methodological approaches in the scholarship of teaching and learning can bridge the gap between IWKL and WWKL.

Bridging the gaps

Opening doors of access

My scoping research funded by the Social Sciences and Humanities Research Council (SSHRC) (2015–2017), explored educational reform that enabled Indigenous post-secondary academic success in STEM. Outcomes showed that the very few successful programs were the ones inclusive of Indigenous knowledge and that, importantly, created bridges between IWKL and WWKL. Such programs have historically had the negative connotation of 'remedial' and 'lesser than' and are intended for those who were 'not academic enough'. However, pathway or transition programs have been reframed, particularly since the TRC, to be necessary and constructive ways to enable Indigenous students to maintain or recover shaken identities, gain a solid academic foundation, and strengthen their relationships within a post-secondary institution (Hogue and Forrest 2018; Shotton, et al. 2013; Statistics Canada 2018). Since the TRC, a number of universities in Canada have introduced bridging programs and alternative entry pathways with the sole purpose of preparing Indigenous students to enter undergraduate programs and improve Indigenous academic PS retention. The First Nations Transition Program (FNTP), recently renamed the Indigenous Student Success Cohort (ISSC) at ULeth, is a successful 15-year program that has undergone many iterations to be a locally, nationally, and internationally recognised as successful in enabling Indigenous student transition into and through PSE.

Uniquely located within the heart of Blackfoot territory, next to the largest reserve in Western Canada, ULeth accepts Indigenous students from a wide demographic across the Western provinces. The largest draw is from the three surrounding Blackfoot communities; the Kainai or Kainah ('Bloods'), Southern Piikani (Peigan Blackfeet), and Siksika ('Blackfoot')

(Academic Quality Assurance Review 2014), as well as those who live off-reserve, either in or near the City of Lethbridge. In spite of having the first Native American Studies Department in Canada, and its proximity to these communities, the Indigenous presence on campus, and the graduation rate, has been significantly lower than one would expect and below many other similarly positioned universities. In 2004, to address this, ULeth piloted the FNTP as a pathway for Indigenous students who were otherwise inadmissible into university. The one – year provincially funded pilot (2004/2005 – Phase 1) was followed by a one – year (2005/2006) hiatus in the absence of funding. In 2007, the program was reinstated using newly targeted provincial funding via the Support Program for Aboriginal Nursing Students (SPANS – Phase 2), and then in 2011 it was rolled into university base funding (Phase 3). From its inception in 2004 until 2014 the program underwent numerous changes to address some of the challenges of its original design and to meet the changing needs and demographic of Indigenous students.

In 2014, an Academic Quality Assurance Review (AQAR) of the then 10-year program was done to assess its impact and determine its future trajectory. Outcomes of the review indicated that the FNTP provides an important entry point into university and an opportunity for Indigenous students who are otherwise inadmissible to the university, to obtain a post-secondary degree. Even those Indigenous students who are deemed academically qualified, or who enter university from upgrading programs, have many challenges transitioning into mainstream university. The result is a very high first-year attrition rate and a historically very low completion rate. The FNTP provides an entry point and offers a path to integration through interaction with a wide variety of students and faculty in a culturally and academically supportive cohort environment. Having a coordinator who has been with, and taught in the program, virtually since its inception provides the experiential lens needed to address the changing academic and political climates to meet the needs of the demographic of Indigenous students it serves. Critically important in the daily operation of the program is the Learning Facilitator whose focus is on the learning needs of the students.

From the students' perspective, among the things they noted as being instrumental to their success, were: (a) the attention to IWKL and cultural relevancy; (b) support of the coordinator, faculty, learning facilitators, and elders; (c) the cultural, social, personal, and academic supports provided throughout the program; (d) the small-class sizes which created a positive learning environment and sense of community; and (e) the critically important core courses which prepared them for their later programs of choice (AQAR 2014). However, those who had completed the program and were now in mainstream said, that while the program was critical for their first year, and they did very well, challenges arose for them after in large classes. Many said they were overwhelmed in the larger classes where there were very few or no other Indigenous students. In mainstream classes there was no recognition for cultural diversity and the expectation was 'to get with the program' (student interviews, AQAR 2014: from unpublished transcripts). Sadly, there was often racism among their non-Indigenous mainstream peers, particularly when it came to group work and projects. Many felt that it would have been beneficial to take a course with a larger class size while in the program in order to have that large class experience while still having the supports of the program so they could learn how to navigate those challenges. The key important finding was that Indigenous students who entered the university through the FNTP were retained to graduation at a 10 per cent higher rate than any student, Indigenous or non-Indigenous, who entered university through the traditional mainstream route. Importantly, this program is not intended to be a remedial upgrading program, as might be found at the college level (either on or off reserve), but rather it is intended to provide a 'first – year experience' within the dominant PSE system in order to increase retention to graduation of Indigenous students.

Outcomes of the AQAR led to the redesign of the program in 2015 and renaming it as the Indigenous Student Success Cohort (ISSC) in 2019 to more accurately reflect the first-year experience and move away from the connotation of a remedial program that the word 'transition' implies. Students take a core set of courses in the fall semester (mathematics, writing, library science, and an academic foundations course) as well as either a science or social science elective.

In the spring semester they take a smaller core (an advanced foundations course and an interdisciplinary studies course) and can select two to three mainstream courses from an approved list to enable them to have the large class experience with the supports of the program. All courses count towards their program of choice and students in the program are held to the same academic standards as any other student. It is recognised locally, provincially, and nationally as an exemplar pathway program, one that has seen a continual increase in student enrollments and retention to graduation. Key to its success has been the continual attention to creating bridges between IWKL and the expected WWKL. The following sections outline the philosophy, pedagogy, and practice of the ISSC.

Philosophy: Two-eyed seeing

The *94 Calls to Action* (CTA) released with the TRC Report, called all Canadians to action with the goal of redressing the legacy of residential schools and advancing the process of reconciliation to create balanced parity at all levels between Indigenous and non-Indigenous people. Since the TRC (2015), the philosophy of Two-Eyed Seeing (TES) (Bartlett and Marshall 2009; Bartlett, Marshall and Marshall 2012) brought forth more than two decades ago has found a renewed place in the *reconciliation for parity and equity* conversations that are occurring across Canada. TES refers to seeing with one eye through an Indigenous lens and the other through a Western lens and using both together for a holistic and truly informed depth of perception (Bartlett, Marshall, and Marshall 2012). The philosophy of TES, in its origin in the Integrative Science Program at Cape Breton University, involved Indigenous educators and elders (Elders Albert and Murdena Marshall) working collaboratively and side-by-side with non-Indigenous allies, such as Dr Cheryl Bartlett, to bring Indigenous and *white*-Western paradigms in a shared space of post-secondary science education. It was a progressive, albeit seemingly premature, concept for its time, which now in light of the TRC-CTAs, is gaining ground as a potential way forward.

One of the consequences of the TRC and the CTAs is the conversation around *Indigenization*. What does this really mean? Who should be doing it? Many feel that it has to be done by Indigenous peoples for Indigenous peoples while others feel that the established academy should stand as it is. While IWKL are only recently seen to be unique and meritorious, and the education academy is opening space for such cultural perspectives, it still remains that Indigenous peoples, even in bringing along their culture, will have to learn to live within the traditional education system. Nowhere is this truer than in the sciences and mathematics courses that still pose near insurmountable roadblocks to Indigenous entrance into STEM-related professions. TES is NOT one-way; it requires that both Indigenous and non-Indigenous peoples working pedagogically together to co-learn, co-design, and co-create for Both Ways Knowing (BWK) (Hogue and Forrest 2018).

Pedagogy: IWKL versus WWKL

As an oral culture Indigenous knowledge is held by cultural experts such as elders, in the stories, in ceremony, in traditional societies, and practices. It is passed on (taught) through story, narrative, demonstration and mentoring by elders or knowledge keepers; learning is through observing and practical hands-on doing. The laboratory for Indigenous peoples is the real and applied world; the land and all the animate and inanimate inhabitants. Mother Earth and Creator are key to the spirituality of the Indigenous paradigm. All things are related and inter-related holistically unlike the compartmentalised, siloed, individualised, and competitive way of the

Western paradigm. In his interview, 'Re-Thinking Curriculum and Pedagogy', Ted Aoki (1999) talks about *curriculum-as-lived* in contrast to *curriculum-as-taught*, and the conflict between the two. This is the challenge for many Indigenous students in the traditional education system; trying to connect the curriculum as taught (in the Western system) with their lived experience; a lived curriculum that is historically deemed to be lesser (TRC 2015). This juxtaposition in ways of coming to know is a key root to the challenges many Indigenous students experience. Context and relevancy are critical and without those, bridging to understanding is nearly impossible. *Indigenization* therefore includes not only addressing the theoretical and ensuring the theoretical is correctly inclusive of Indigenous peoples and their knowledge, it must also include indigenising our practice – how we teach.

Practice: Let's do it first

When I first began teaching chemistry in the FNTP, I noticed the students struggled with making connections to what I thought (or expected) to be very basic concepts; concepts they should already have had a foundation in but didn't seem to. It didn't seem to matter how many times I went over theoretical concepts or problems, they struggled with making the connections. I had a high attrition rate, and of those who completed the course, the grades were significantly lower than mainstream averages. The only time I had complete engagement and attendance was in the laboratory component of the course, and no matter which textbook I chose, it was a roadblock rather than an asset. Most students didn't even bother with it. I came to realise through some interesting situations and many conversations with the students who often said, '*It* (Western science) *makes no sense to me*' or '*I can't understand the textbook; the words make no sense*', that the challenge was that the concepts, at least in the Eurocentric Western curriculum, and vocabulary, did not exist in their paradigm. Given Indigenous cultures are oral, and the languages are verb-based rather than noun-based, it is difficult to grasp chemistry concepts particularly without having a context. I found if I made it culturally relevant and illustrated that the concept does, in fact, exist in the Indigenous paradigm, just not in the way it is portrayed in the Western system, they could see the relevancy and more readily grasp it. So, I decided to take a different approach; put the textbook away for a while, write my own materials, and teach the course entirely in the laboratory from a practical hands-on starting point and bring the theory in later when the students had a context.

The Medicine Wheel (MW), foundational and sacred to many Indigenous cultures, is symbolic of the never-ending cycle of life and is often used to illustrate Indigenous cultural ways of knowing and practice (Bell 2014; Little Bear, personal communication, 2005–2010; Thunderbird 2020). The Indigenous paradigm is based on patterns of four, so the MW is divided into four by either a vertical and horizontal line or by two diagonal lines. The result is four equal quadrants that represent a multitude of concepts: the four directions – East, South, West, and North; the seasons – spring, summer, fall, and winter; Aboriginal wellness – spiritual, physical, emotional, and mental/cognitive; processes of being or learning – visioning, feeling, understanding, and doing; and life stages – infant, child, adult, and elder as exemplars. The quadrants are moved through in a clockwise fashion from the right (beginning) quadrant.

The MW in terms of the seasons, as illustrated in Figure 42.1, became the culturally relevant framework or 'method' for each concept I was teaching. *Spring* is a time of planting or new ideas (the purpose) – *What do we want to know?* *Summer* is the time of growth or practical hands-on doing (the procedure or experiment) – *How are we going to do this?* *Fall* the time of harvest (the results) – *What were the outcomes?* *Winter* the time for resting and processing (the conclusion) – *What do we know now?* Once the students have the context then in the *Winter* part of the cycle,

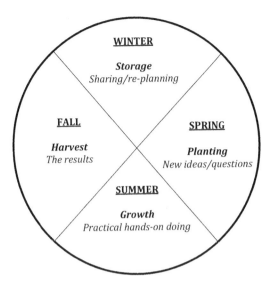

Figure 42.1 Medicine wheel of learning. Source: Hogue 2018: 164.

I am able to create the bridge to more advanced knowledge and the expected Western theory. The MW provides a parallel learning frame that bridges to the scientific method of purpose, procedure, results, and conclusion. TES, described above, is the philosophical and pedagogical approach, and foundation, to the course.

Doing the hands-on laboratory work first, or simultaneously, to illustrate the concept in a practical way, greatly enables their learning and success – it visually and practically creates a necessary bridge. Once this , students did very well in the course. The issue, therefore, isn't ability but rather a paradigm clash between IWKL and WWKL. It isn't that they can't 'do science', but that they need to be able to make relevant connections; they need a starting point, a context, a language, and some way of bridging to what they already know. Many of the concepts in the way we present them are simply not part of the Indigenous paradigm and importantly how we traditionally teach science (theory first and the practical much later) does not work with IWKL. This hands-on first, practical, methodology has had excellent results in Indigenous student retention and success in the science courses I teach and could form the model for the development of future bridging science curricula for Indigenous students. However, the challenge is the traditional science paradigm that is still entrenched in traditional curriculum and teaching practice. If we are to engage Indigenous learners in the STEM disciplines as educators, curriculum developers and policy makers, it requires accepting IWKL and moving away from our entrenched 'science' paradigm in order to think creatively and differently outside the cliché box.

A different curriculum: Land as the textbook

The land for Indigenous peoples is a source of strength and knowledge and Indigenous education was traditionally the land. Yet settler colonialism, through Western institutions of education and forced assimilation, through residential schools and still through the current Eurocentric Western education system, has forcefully dispossessed Indigenous peoples from their knowledge base, the land. In doing so the dominant culture has undermined Indigenous knowledge and has impeded the transmission of traditional knowledge (education) that arose from the relationship to the land. If we are serious about decolonising education and capacity building through reconciliation, the land needs to be the textbook and land-based learning the methodological approach to understanding the textbook. Connection to and learning from the land, according to Leanne Simpson and Glen Coulthard (2014), Indigenous educators who teach at the Dechinta Center for Research and Learning, is critically important for creating bridges between traditional Indigenous knowledge and Western curriculum and education. Importantly, it supports IWKL in an intellectual, emotional, spiritual, and physical way that enables understanding in a holistic, inter-related, and integrated way. The model in Figure 42.2 illustrates how the land and learning from all the land might be used to create bridges between IWKL and WWKL. It illustrates the relationship and inter-relationships of 'subjects' or lenses through which both paradigms could collaboratively understand the land. Such a transformative education has to be done in the spirit of the four Rs —Relationship, Respect, Responsibility, and Reciprocity – and requires Indigenous and non-Indigenous educators and curriculum developers to work together collaboratively to co-design and co-create such a curriculum in the space between. The

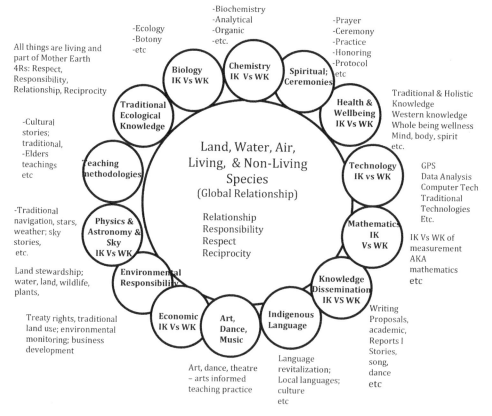

Legend:
- IK = Indigenous Knowledge
- WK = Western Knowledge
- TES = Two-Eyed Seeing

Figure 42.2 Two-eyed seeing for both ways knowing (TES/BWK) (Hogue and Forrest 2018). Model for Indigenous academic and STEM sovereignty through land-based education. Source: Hogue, in preparation.

Dechinta Center for Research and Leaning (https://www.dechinta.ca/) is a unique exemplar of how such a post-secondary program may be co-developed. However, it still remains that those entering such a program have to achieve a certain academic level first, which brings us full circle to the issue of engagement and retention. *How do we do that early and sustain it through to graduation?*

Community-based environmental monitoring as a step towards Indigenous sovereignty

The Canadian government and industry have a 'Duty to Consult' with First Nations communities on any initiatives that affect Indigenous lands and treaty rights. However, many First Nations are not able to meaningfully participate because they do not have the skills, ability, or technology to present useful data to support their concerns. Many Indigenous communities in Canada currently require technical services to be provided by third-party non-Indigenous contractors in their interactions with government and industry for resource development. Consultation funding therefore bypasses benefitting the community directly, as communities do not have the ability to retain funds due to the lack of internal capacity to execute traditional land use studies, data collection and reporting. Relevant data, as a result, is collected, held, and reported on by external non-Indigenous agencies. Historical misuse of information provided to the government and industry has led to mistrust in sharing information. Non-digital data, such as oral histories, are often discounted as equitable and First Nations do not have the skills and technology needed to generate the digital information needed by external parties involved in consultations (i.e., GIS data, mapping). It is critical, therefore, that Indigenous communities develop a sovereign ability to collect, manage, and report on data, such that they have the capacity to contribute meaningful environmental and cultural information into any decision-making process that impacts them culturally, politically, or socioeconomically.

Using emerging technologies and unique data collection and protection software, Community-Based Environmental Monitoring (CBEM) can empower Indigenous Nations to collect, store, monitor, secure, and utilise their own data. Importantly it will; enable Nations to develop self-sufficiency and build community capacity in digital literacy as well as in land-based technologies. This will further empower them to have voice at the negotiating tables of stakeholders such as government and industry at all levels where decisions are often made for or to Indigenous communities and often not for the benefit of communities; enable Nations to become providers of EM to other Indigenous communities or to stakeholders and as such develop businesses; build a network of collaborators for project development and for knowledge sharing and mobilisation with other communities provincially, nationally, and internationally; serve as a way of engaging youth in culturally relevant hands-on land-based learning which can further motivate them to stay in, and complete, secondary education and pursue PSE either at the applied college or university level; develop critical thinking skills and analytical tools to analyse and facilitate discussion and find productive solutions around community issues and concerns; address the technological, integrated, inter-related and shared knowledge that will be needed for Canadians, particularly the youth, in the rapidly evolving global landscape; re-engage youth with elders and empower the transfer of cultural knowledge that will be lost as elders pass on and as culture changes; serve as a space to bring together researchers and innovators to understand the needs of Indigenous communities to research and co-create options together which opens the space for unique and inclusive conversations and collaborations; provide a skill set for First Nations graduates to pursue employment in culturally relevant applications of STEM.

Australia has been working in the CBEM domain for many years with the *Caring for Country Ranger Program* and many communities now have their own trained Rangers. It has been a source of economic development for such communities and many young community members are pursuing various levels of PSE as a result (Mackie and Meacheam 2016; Northern Land Council 2020; Schultz and Cairney 2017). My SSHRC funded scoping research enabled me to create a collaborative network between Australia and Canada to pilot the CBEM program with Piikani Nation. The impact of the project will be realised in the capacity of Piikani Nation to represent their bio-cultural information in decision making internally to their Nation, and externally with industry, provincial and federal agencies, and the government. The project provides EM training to develop youth capacity and in doing so connects the STEM disciplines to culturally relevant career paths with the goal to support the development of a future body of trained professionals working at the interface of culture, technology, and environmental management. Lessons learned will be demonstrated to other First Nations and shared with provincial and federal agencies promoting the adoption of CBEM programs and business development.

CBEM is a culturally relevant pathway to Indigenous academic and STEM success. It develops skills and tools necessary for the next generation in our rapidly changing society and labor market. Particularly, it addresses the technological, integrated, inter-related, and shared knowledge that will be needed for Canadians, particularly the youth in the rapidly evolving global landscape. It bridges cultures through *Two-Eyed Seeing for Both Ways Knowing* and reframes education and collaboration in ways that address the TRC and its 94 Calls to Action. The promising outcomes to date are paving the pathway to Indigenous sovereignty and serve to be a model for other nations moving forward.

Note

1 See: www.aadnc-aandc.gc.ca.

References

Aikenhead, G.S. (2006). *Science Education for Everyday Life: Evidence-based Practice*. Teachers College Press: New York.

Aikenhead, G. and Michel, H. (2011). *Bridging Cultures: Indigenous and Scientific Ways of Knowing Nature*. Pearson Canada: Toronto.

Aoki, T. (1999). 'Rethinking curriculum and pedagogy: Interview with T. Aoki', *Kappa Delta Phi Record*, vol 35, no 4: 180–181.

Bartlett, C. and Marshall, A. (2009). 'Integrative science and two-eyed seeing: Life long learning from youth to elder', *Conference on Aboriginal Education*, 23–25 March. Fredericton.

Bartlett, C., Marshall, M., and Marshall, A. (2012). 'Two-eyed seeing and other lessons learned within a co-learning journey of bringing together Indigenous and mainstream knowledge and ways of knowing', *Journal of Environmental Studies and Sciences*, vol 2, no 4: 331–340.

Bell, N. (2014). 'Teaching by the medicine wheel: An Anishinaabe framework for Indigenous education', *Education Canada*, vol 54, no 3. Available: www.edcan.ca/articles/teaching-by-the-medicine-wheel/, accessed 25 January 2020.

Burns, G. (2001). 'Toward a redefinition of formal and informal learning: education and the aboriginal people', National Research Network on New Approaches to Lifelong Learning. Working Paper 28. Center for the Study of Education and Work University of Toronto: Toronto. Available: hdl.handle.net/1807/2742, accessed 23 November 2019.

Cajete, G. (1999). *Igniting the Sparkle: An Indigenous Science Education Model*. Kivaki Press: Skyland.

Cajete, G. (2000). *Native Science: Natural Laws of Interdependence*. Clearlight Publisher: Santa Fe.

Canadian Council on Learning. (2007). *The Cultural Divide in Science Education for Aboriginal Learners*. Government of Canada: Ottawa. Available: www.ccl-cca.ca/CCL/Reports/LessonsinLearning, accessed 20 November 2019.

Canadian Council on Learning. (2009). *The State of Aboriginal Learning in Canada: A Holistic Approach to Measuring Success*. Government of Canada: Ottawa. Available: www.ccl-cca.ca, accessed 20 November 2019.

C.D. Howe Institute. (2016). *Policy Conference Report: Improving Education for Indigenous Children in Canada Rappoteur's Summary*. C.D. Howe Institute, April 15. Available: www.cdhowe.org/sites/default/files/attachments/other-research/pdf/Education%20Conference%20Report_2016.pdf, accessed 20October 2019.

Council of Ministers of Education Canada. (2017). *Education Indicators in Canada: An International Perspective*. Available: www.cmec.ca/.../Education-Indicators-Canada-International- Perspective-2012, accessed 20 October 2019.

Gallop, C.J. and Bastien, N. (2016). 'Supporting success: Aboriginal students in higher education.' *Canadian Journal of Higher Education*, vol 46, no 2: 206–224.

Hogue, M. (2018). *Dropping the "T" from CAN'T: Enabling Aboriginal Post-Secondary Academic Success in Science and Mathematics*. J. Charlton Publishing: Vernon, BC Canada.

Hogue, M. and Forrest, J. (2018). 'Bridging cultures over-under: Enabling academic success from the heart', *FABENZ Conference*, November 28–30. Wellington. Available: fabenz.org.nz/proceedings-of-the-fabenz-conference-2018/, accessed 25 November 2019.

Mackie, K. and Meacheam, D. (2016). 'Working on country: A case study of unusual environmental program success', *Australasian Journal of Environmental Management*, vol 22, no 2: 157–174.

Northern Land Council. (2020). *Caring for Country*. Available: www.nlc.org.au/our-land-sea/caring-for-country, accessed 15 November 2019.

Schultz, R. and Cairney, S. (2017). 'Caring for country and the health of aboriginal and Torres Strait Islander Australians', *Medical Journal of Australia*, vol 207, no 1: 8–10.

Shotton, H.J., Lowe, S.C., Waterman, S.J., and Garland, J. (2013). *Beyond the Asterisk: Understanding Native Students in Higher Education*. Stylus Publishing: Virginia.

Simpson L. and Coulthard G. (2014). 'Leanne Simpson and Glen Coulthard on Dechinta Bush university, Indigenous land based education and embodied resurgence', *Decolonization: Indigeneity, Education and Society Blog*. Available: decolonization.wordpress.com/2014/11/26/leanne-simpson-and-glen-coulthard-ondechinta-bush-university-indigenous-land-based-education-and-embodied-resurgence/, accessed 20 November 2019.

Sinclair, M. Hon. (2015). 'As it happens', *CBC Radio* Available: https://www.cbc.ca/radio/asithappens/as-it-happens-tuesday-edition-1.3096950/reconciliation-is-not-an-aboriginal-problem-it-is-a-canadian-prob, 15 October 2019.

Statistics Canada. (2016). *First Nations People, Metis and Inuit in Canada: Diverse and Growing Population*. Available: www150.statcan.gc.ca/n1/pub/89-659-x/89-659-x2018001-eng.htm, accessed 15 October 2019.

Statistics Canada. (2018). *Aboriginal Peoples Survey*. Available: www150.statcan.gc.ca/n1/en/catalogue/89-653-X, accessed 15 October 2019.

Sterenberg, G. and Hogue, M. (2011). 'Reconsidering approaches to aboriginal science and mathematics education', *Alberta Journal of Educational Research*, vol 57, no 1: 1–15.

Thunderbird, S. (2020). *Truth and Timelessness: Indigenous Medicine Wheel Knowledge*. Available: www.shannonthunderbird.com/medicine_wheel_teachings.htm, accessed 15 September 2019.

Titley, B. (1986). *A Narrow Vision: Duncan Campbell Scott and the Administration of Indian Affairs in Canada*. University of British Columbia Press: Vancouver.

Truth and Reconciliation Commission of Canada. (2015). *Final Report of the Truth and Reconciliation Commission of Canada Volume One: Summary, Honoring the Reconciling for the Future*. James Lorimer and Co. Publishers: Toronto. Available: nctr.ca/assets/reports/Final%20Reports/Executive_Summary English Web.pdf, accessed 25 September 2019.

University of Lethbridge Academic Quality Assurance Review of the First Nations Transition Program. University of Lethbridge: Lethbridge.

43

Aboriginal child as knowledge producer

Bringing into dialogue Indigenist epistemologies and culturally responsive pedagogies for schooling

Lester-Irabinna Rigney

Introduction

Almost 25 years ago, I attempted to make an epistemic change to the way knowledge is produced in Australia that used dominant settler reference to narrowly determine what counts as knowledge, who can be knower, while dismissing Indigenous knowing as irrational and irrelevant (Rigney 1997). A first for Australia back then, my theorisation of 'Indigenist research epistemologies' as reason challenged the dominance of settler knowledge production from the hemispheric north as normative Australian practice. What structures of western science enabled the category of 'Aborigine' to be linked to 'inferiority' and the 'inability' to reason? These intellectual currents, I suggested, were produced and reproduced via knowledge production architectures that upheld assumptions that northern 'reason' was suitable to the comprehension of 'truth' and 'reality' in the south Pacific. What remained outside and beneath, were Indigenous languages, literacies, and knowledge as unscientific and the source of our social 'failure' to assimilate (Rigney 2001).

Whether in school classrooms or adult lecture halls, knowledge production, and transmission are culturalised products with accompanied systemisations of power to overgeneralises from the experiences of non-Indigenous males to all peoples. Instead of hegemonically recognising Indigenous peoples as weak and needy requiring others to produce knowledge for them, I had the audacity to argue that Indigenous peoples from birth were powerful and competent producers of knowledge for over 80,000 years. Informed by influential works (Miller 1985; Langton 1981) I confronted why Indigenous Australians are biologically recognised as the oldest peoples on the planet yet we remain fixed into cipherdom in settler evidence (Hau'ofa 1993; Wa Thiong'o 1994; Said 1995; Smith 1997; Spivak 1988).

When I began this inquiry, I was primarily concerned with epistemology as a way of understanding how education researchers subjugate Aboriginal voice while justifying their partial knowledge claims and bias rules of method (Lather 1986; Collins 2000; Harding 1986). I came to focus on seven Indigenous Australian researchers whose methods were framed by Indigenous ontology as community priorities and interests (Rigney 2007). I coined the term 'Indigenist epistemologies' that encompassed three provocations within its definition: privileging Indigenous voices, upholding integrity of cultural knowledges to resist hegemony, and empowering self-determination (Rigney 1997; 2001; 2006).

While my Australian work in universities on Indigenist epistemology is widely cited, critiqued and extended, it is only emergent in school pedagogies of teaching and learning. Given the increasing trend of Aboriginal school disparities is important to bring into dialogue Indigenist epistemologies and culturally responsive pedagogies for schooling.

Effective knowledge production of Indigenous self and community sustains identity and group belonging. It is also key to participation as a literate local and global citizen. However, in Australia the importance of the Aboriginal child as intelligent, competent knowledge producer of their own life-worlds has largely been untheorised. This has had a detrimental effect on how Aboriginal children have viewed their identities, languages, and knowledge. The Aboriginal child as knowledge consumer but never producer is false emancipation. The nexus between identity, language, and cultural born from Indigenous epistemologies have been belittled and underplayed by colonial settler systems. It is little surprise Australia has trending disparity rise between Indigenous and non-Indigenous success at school. This issue has been articulated in a number of key Australian policy texts. Australia is a signatory to the United Nations Declaration on the Rights of Indigenous Peoples (United Nations 2008) that calls for a rights-based approach to Indigenous education and preparation for teaching Indigenous education. In 2018, after a decade of work, then Prime Minister Turnbull reported to parliament widespread schooling equity failure in delivery of schooling to Aboriginal children (Commonwealth of Australia 2018). Australia is grossly failing to meet its democratic obligations to Aboriginal children who have citizenry rights at birth (Buckskin et al. 2010). More of the same monolingual, mono-epistemic curriculum and pedagogy is not an option if change to the teaching profession is required. In my view, if Australia is to meet its citizenry obligations to a quality education for all then we must pivot toward greater critical thinking of pedagogy in collaboration with engaged teachers who value diversity, child voice, and agency to reform society.

An education that connects to learning the Aboriginal cultural literate identities, knowledges, languages and aspirations offer hope and inclusion. Critical to any skilled work force and school improvement model are institutional cultures, pedagogy, and curriculum reform that are responsive to Aboriginal children as competent subjects and experts of their life-worlds, capable of producing knowledge for improving their lives and those of their communities. Existing evidence indicates that all children are intelligent and bring from home to class cultural repertoires of knowledge as strengths upon which teachers can connect learning (Moll et al. 1992). To address the strengths and needs of Aboriginal learners in public schools, I argue for a dialogical critical approach to culturally responsive teacher pedagogies that challenges superficial and tokenistic efforts inclusive of cultural celebration (Harmony Day, Reconciliation NAIDOC). While important, such festivals largely remain external and unconnected to core school learning that leads to further exclusion. This defies compliance with Australian Teacher standards to connect responsive learning to learner identities as an important performance standard of good teaching (AITSL 2016; MCEETYA 2008). What would it mean for teachers to construct knowledge-producing community schools for Aboriginal learners, as researcher – to pursue solutions to community challenges? This would require in part teachers who view themselves as researchers of their own practice who actively seek relevant pedagogies to co-construct and produce knowledge with students (as opposed to memorising, performing, and consuming knowledge).

Teachers as co-constructors of knowledge in a knowledge producing school must not be distinguished by a single pedagogy but are responsive to broad contexts, child intelligences and place-based considerations. Such teachers would need to view knowledge as not separated from experience and work hard to listen and respond to their student's ways of knowing, needs and interest. Through pedagogies of dialogue and listening, children are inspired to produce their own knowledge born from teacher conceptualisation of a community of students as inquirer.

To argue for a responsive pedagogy capable of seeing the Aboriginal child as knowledge producer, in this chapter I will draw upon principles from Indigenist epistemologies as sub-field of Indigenous Studies research including voice/listening, knowledge integrity and empowerment. I will advocate a conceptual framework from the transnational work on culturally responsive approaches to schools and pedagogy. I move beyond simply discussing ideas to report on how a teacher attempts culturally responsive pedagogies in a real classroom. Conclusions will be drawn and summarised.

Indigenist epistemological framing of the Aboriginal child as competent knowledge producer

Aboriginal children and families have competently produced knowledges for thousands of years before the arrival of the British. In other cultures, the notion of the competent child having citizenry rights from birth can be traced back to constructivist theories of early childhood education by Vygotsky (1978) and Dewey (1916). Similarly, the education principles of the Reggio Emilia approach advocate that children as unique humans have rights than just needs, who possess intelligences and skills to co-construct learning and knowledge with teachers (Malaguzzi 1993; Rinaldi 2002; 2013). The evidence of these approaches largely have emerged in homogenous European contexts. Outside of the northern hemisphere, relevant other theoretical orientations that draw on the child cultural strengths and prior knowledge include: relationship-based pedagogy (Villegas and Lucas 2002), funds of knowledge (Moll, Amanti, Neff, and Gonzalez 1992) and multi-literacies (Sleeter 2011).

In addressing colonial settler societies, Freire's (1972) concept of 'banking education' advocated for schooling of the 'oppressed' to shift from didactic learning (passive absorption) to one where the child linguistic and cultural knowledge repertoire are valued as assets to learning. The purpose of schooling for Freire is to co-construct processes of learning and knowledge production that has the potential to transform injustice in the lives of oppressed peoples.

Emergent Indigenist epistemologies in Australia reject 'deficit' views of Indigenous children, their families and their prior knowledges (Rigney 2001; 2006). Children are seen as custodians of ancient and contemporary Indigenous knowledges where they are protagonists in their learning as co-constructors of knowledge with their elders, families and community. This approach advocates for education institutions to invest in strong relationships that are critical to the co-construction of knowledge that are culturally responsive to Indigenous needs and aspirations.

Culturally responsive approaches that privilege Aboriginal children as knowledge producers are underutilised by what Rizvi and Lingard (2009: 99) call a neoliberal "audit culture of teaching" manifested through standardised testing by the National Assessment Program – Literacy and Numeracy (NAPLAN). Australian neoliberal reforms have arguably shifted the focus of teachers work from a democratic approach toward an outcomes-based focus measured through 'English only' NAPLAN scores. Such approaches require little of its predominately Anglo teacher workforce to gather or comprehend home literacies to link these with those of school for Aboriginal belonging. Research evidence by Hill, Comber and colleagues (1998) show how diversity intervention committed to cultural pluralism fail under prevailing neoliberal mandated 'English only' literacy regimes. Privileging monolingual values and practices maintain their racial inequality by labelling as deficit the cultural literate identities and assets Aboriginal children.

The reductionist mono-cultural approach is incongruent with the reality of Indigenous languages and knowledges. Cochran-Smith argues that neoliberal human capital approach to education 'ultimately undermines a democratic vision of society and that market ideology is fundamentally inconsistent with democratic education' (Cochran-Smith et al. 2017: 576). It is unsurprising that the 2018 'Closing the Gap', reported no Aboriginal wellbeing improvement since 2008 along with literacy and numeracy decline (Commonwealth of Australia 2018). These poor results have prompted debates on the need for inclusive pedagogies to re-engage Indigenous students (Moodie and Patrick 2017). Diversity is disregarded in favour of monolingual standardisation and homogeneity that devalues the rich cognitive, linguistic, and cultural repertoires that Aboriginal children bring to school from home. Teaching 'only for the test' produces narrowly scripted teacher pedagogies that lead to disparities (Smyth and Hattam 2004; Comber and Kamler 2006). These schooling conditions are problematic and lead to disengagement rather than strengthening Aboriginal aspirations. Mayer and colleagues argue that only half of graduate teachers surveyed believed their teacher education programs "prepared them to teach culturally, linguistically and socio-economically diverse learners" (Mayer et al. 2014: 215).

There are a range of Australian Indigenist epistemological conceptual resources that have the potential to assist schools in productive ways to construct knowledge that put the competent Aboriginal child, their belonging and world view at the centre of learning. For example Indigenist knowledge production and epistemologies (Rigney 1999; 2002; 2003; 2011a; 2011b; 2017; Rigney and Hattam 2018), relational ontological knowledge production responsive to Aboriginal identities (Arbon 2008) and Aboriginal education and respectful knowledge production (Yunkaporta 2009; Craven et al. 2005; Price 2012; Ma Rhea et al. 2012; Moreton-Robinson et al. 2012).[1]

Australian Indigenist epistemologies provide conceptual resources for advancing a 'strong' image of the competent Aboriginal child with rights through culturally responsive pedagogies that have been too often marginalised in schools compared to Native American Studies, Māori Studies. Indigenist epistemologies are placed based and relational that sees all things human and non-human as interconnected. This literature champions Indigenous Australians as heterogeneous where 'culture' is nuanced more than 'race' to be inclusive of disability, sexual orientation, class, gender and spirituality. There is no one moral/political Indigenist position nor single ontoepsiteme. There is no one-research method to producing knowledge that is distinctly Indigenist. Equally, there is not a distinctive project in terms of Indigenous studying Indigenous. What is distinctive about Australian Indigenist epistemologies is it is grounded in Indigenous theory and experiences of the colonised and is distinguishing by its calls for a rights-based approach to Indigenous education. Indigenist scholarship view historical and modern cultural practice of the Indigenous community that is elevated in school by a rights-based approach to knowledge production – as an untapped source to improve achievement.

This is significant given the failure of the government to 'close the gap' on Aboriginal education disparity (Department of the Prime Minister and Cabinet 2019). A rights-based approach to schooling has been articulated in a number of key Australian policy texts. For instance, Australia is a signatory to both the United Nations Declaration on the Rights of the child, and the declaration of Indigenous peoples (UN General Assembly 2007) that calls for a rights-based approach to Indigenous education and preparation for teaching Indigenous children.

There is good scientific consensus that when learning is integrated to children's rights, self-inquiry, prior knowledge, linguistic identities, and strengths – children become more engaged in learning critical for successful transition (Dahlberg and Moss 2004; 2002). Other benefits include increased student relationships, belonging, engagement, motivation, child and family/school involvement, and an appreciation of local knowledge as curriculum resource.

Drawn from Australian Indigenist epistemology I outline my 10 provocations for what I see as the nuanced rights of the Aboriginal child to produce knowledge that compliment and extend United Nations declarations. Simultaneously, in doing so, I am also speaking to the purpose of schooling in the interests of the Aboriginal child.

The rights of the competent Aboriginal child as knowledge producer

Through teaching and learning to create dialogue, democratic inclusion, and interaction between different perspectives, my ideas as provocations on the rights of the knowledge producing Aboriginal child include:

1. The right to Indigenous subjectivity and languages
2. The right to produce knowledge for the dimensions of sovereignty, equality, democracy, solidarity, and freedom
3. The right to produce knowledge that privilege voice, integrity of Indigenous epistemologies, and intelligences, to resist hegemony and to strengthen self-determination
4. The right to global literacies, numeracies, and enriching ideas of humanity
5. The right to have rights and dignity as a human being
6. The right to belong, become, and be different
7. The right to produce digital, relational, existential, creative, embodied, scientific, political, and economic knowledge to move fluently across cultures without compromising those of self
8. The right to ecological sustainability where all things are interconnected
9. The right to love, peace, and treaty free from racism and colonialism
10. The right to not inherit a dead planet.

Australian Indigenist epistemology (Arbon 2008; Rigney 2006) as an emerging body of work offers teachers hopeful provocations to redesign their pedagogical practice to realise the Aboriginal child as competent knowledge producer for change. To improve Indigenous learning and engagement, classroom practices need to shift from 'didactic' to 'dialogic' relationship-based teaching that view the child: with citizenry rights from birth; as expert of their own life-worlds; and able to move fluently across cultures toward competent knowledge production for themselves and others.

Key messages for teachers' practice change include self-reflection of subjectivity; all things are relational; to taking the vantage point of the colonised; purposeful listening and yarning dialogue; enacting respectful relationships; and democratic power sharing in schools and classrooms to empower all learners. We should remind ourselves these provocations are complex and multifaceted to broad to explore here. They are also made complicated by power differentials, 'race' blind structures curriculum and pedagogies and ignoring or denying privileges of teacher whiteness.

To shift schooling relevance towards the lived lives of learners, what pedagogies and teacher classroom practice improve engagement and knowledge production of Aboriginal children?

How do educators create a school culture that values the image of a competent child and enact a child strength-based approach to learning that is culturally responsive to Aboriginal interests? If didactic monolingual pedagogies do not work, then how do educators practice dialogic pedagogies?

A competent child needs a competent teacher. How might we redesign curriculum and teacher pedagogical practice to produce the competent Aboriginal child as knowledge producer?

It is important I now bring into dialogue Indigenist epistemologies with culturally responsive pedagogies to inform teacher practice.

Culturally responsive pedagogies

There is an international consensus that culturally responsive pedagogies (CRP) improve academic success for First Nations peoples (Bishop et al. 2007; Castagno and Brayboy 2008; Bishop 2019; Castagno and Brayboy 2008). Unfortunately, CRP theory and practice in Australia is only weakly developed and has had limited peer-evaluated reviews (e.g., Krakouer 2015; Morrison et al. 2019; Perso 2012) and has yet to seriously inform the curriculum and pedagogical reform. *Toward an Australian Culturally Responsive Pedagogy* (Rigney and Hattam 2016–2019) was an Australian Research Council-funded Indigenous Discovery project that sought to fill this gap. As researchers, we worked with teachers from seven large metropolitan public schools with substantial enrolments of Aboriginal middle years students. Teachers committed to a two-year professional learning project involving two action research cycles.

By way of a working definition, Gay (2010: 26) defines culturally responsive pedagogies as teaching 'to and through [students'] personal and cultural strengths, their intellectual capabilities, and their prior accomplishments'. For Gay, the more localised, inclusive, democratic, and supportive that teachers are, the lower the incidence and intensity of student disengagement.[2]

Bringing Indigenist epistemologies and culturally responsive pedagogies into dialogue reveal pedagogical insights for teachers. Both view all learners as competent, culturally centred who are assets rich epistemologically and ontologically. While the former is localised to Indigenous Australian context of knowledge production, the later culturally responsive teaching, provides productive pedagogical approaches that view the learner as active in the process of consuming and building knowledge. Both approaches view all schools' norms as cultural products that either help to respond to diverse cultures or hinder learning through mono-cultural assimilation. While there has been significant theoretical effort in both areas, less common is a focus on evidence of practical application and its impact.

In the remainder of this chapter, I report on research project *Toward an Australian Culturally Responsive Pedagogy* (Rigney and Hattam 2016–2019) which adopted a case study approach in several schools informed by ethnographic methods (Marcus 1998; Smyth et al. 2014: 70). Here I seek to bring into focus one case of teacher pedagogy at Sheoak Secondary School Secondary College. The use of Indigenist epistemologies and CRP theory as a framework for this pilot research enabled this exploration of how teacher reorientate their teaching to the cultural assets of the competent Aboriginal child.

Introducing Sheoak Secondary School (pseudonym)

Sheoak Secondary School is a public school situated in the northern suburbs of Adelaide servicing a large diverse Aboriginal, refugee, and multi-cultural community. It has a focus on relationships, and the respect of student voices to build empowered learners. Simone is a teacher at Sheoak Secondary. Her interview discusses her fieldwork phase of trialling action research approaches for 'voice and listening' using Yarning circles in dialogue with CRP. Simone runs a year 11 multi-cultural class with large Aboriginal cohort. This study is significant because it contributes to the urgent (inter) national need to understand how teachers redesign their practice to capture and extend cultural knowledges.

Connect learning to student life-worlds

All students including those of Aboriginal background are viewed as a curious, agentic, competent learner that possesses cultural and linguistic intergenerational intelligences brought from home to preschool. Capturing, validating, building, and bridging from the cultural, epistemic and linguistic repertoires was drawn on to inform her pedagogy. This meant the teacher drew upon prior knowledges of student to connect home to school and support, extend and optimise Aboriginal students' knowledge production: For example:

> For my own Culturally Responsive Pedagogies teacher action research project, my aim was to research my teaching practice over a semester to increase student voice through a negotiated dialogic approach to re-engage alienated students. I wanted to increase participation and get them to research their own lives. I wanted to use a pedagogy of listening. I mainly used an Aboriginal Yarning circle floor mat as I was motivated and committed to students dialoguing and listening to one another.[3]

> *(Personal Interview)*

Recognition of culture as an asset to learning

The teacher views the Aboriginal student in non-deficit terms as a powerful learner researcher. Through co-developed inquiry learning processes students draw on their prior intelligences for knowledge production to observe, raise questions, dialogue with others, engage differing views and critique their own practices and behaviour: For example:

> The student research project was to produce knowledge from the concerns of the students and their communities. They had to interview someone using active listening and record their story about local histories, challenges, and solutions. We did lots of interviewing practices using the Yarning circle mat. Here students saw themselves as researchers. I think if anything, they developed active listening skills to understand each other.

> *(Personal Interview)*

Knowledge production by the Aboriginal student in the form of a research project enabled students to develop and demonstrate research skills in collection of original data, interviews, synthesis, evaluation, and project management. In preparation for work and a changing world, students develop their ability to question sources of information, investigate local challenges and problem solve toward solutions.

Valuing diversity and linking cultural and linguistic repertoire to curriculum

Effective educators engage students as experts in their own prior knowledges and seek to integrate life-worlds and subject discipline knowledges in ways that that don't trivialise either; For example:

> In this class, I had mainstream students as well as 13 English Language development (ELD) or English as a Second Language (ESL) to learn the content and academic language used in each lesson. Students were from a range of places like Bhutan, Nepal, places in Africa like Tanzania. I included a lot of Aboriginal and multi-cultural content to show all identities and cultures were welcomed and valued in class. So every time I gave Aboriginal students

examples of how do their research project to produce knowledge in relation to Aboriginal history or culture, this assisted my own teacher action research project to improve my teaching to capture their home knowledges.

(Personal Interview)

Indigenist epistemology and CRP provide productive frameworks for improving and redesigning the practice of teachers

Through these approaches, educators can work to substantially redesign their teaching practices. Practice changes view 'culture' and 'place' matter in learning. This approach to culturally responsive pedagogies provides a useful framework for educators to acknowledge the significance of culture and to engage with diverse cultures to enhance children's active engagement in learning: For example:

I think after the Culturally Responsive Pedagogies Action research, professional development I have learnt that it is about improving skills in pedagogy ... yarning circles taught me to let go of the control and talk less in the classroom and to improve dialogue.

(Personal Interview)

I took videos of my classroom teaching with me implementing CRP for my own feedback and reflection to improve my teaching. It was good to see and show my line manager my improvement in yarning circles (pedagogies of listening).

(Personal Interview)

I now have learnt more about the yarning circle pedagogy and want to deliver it to the staff and school, especially now that the Deputy School Principal has bought more mats after seeing my video.

(Personal Interview)

what I learnt about culturally responsive pedagogies that it is about relationships in the classroom ... it is just always about my relationship with the students and students in the classroom getting along with each other. Although my action research on my own teaching tried to incorporate culturally responsive pedagogies, I had to go back to theory and it probably did vary.

(Personal Interview)

Now using CRP, I can get my head around it (diversity) easier. I will have either a year 12 health or a year 9 group of low-level literacy Aboriginal students next year. I want every lesson to be a CRP. I want it to be about their culture.

(Personal Interview)

Theorising Australian culturally responsive pedagogies

Despite international development in culturally responsive pedagogies, unfortunately in Australia it is weakly developed. Only recently has an extensive Australian literature review been completed (Morrison, Rigney, Hattam, and Diplock 2019) drawn from smaller reviews (Perso 2012; Krakouer 2015). Over the past decade, initiatives have emerged to address Indigenous disparity 'Stronger Smarter Institute', 'Cape York Aboriginal Australian Academy'. However, the outcomes have been variable and, in some cases, highly contested (ACER 2013; Guenther and Osborne 2020; Luke et al. 2013; McCollow 2013; Sarra 2017). While Tyson Yunkaporta's (2009)

'Eight Ways' Aboriginal pedagogy is emergent, little attention has been given to the potential of culturally responsive pedagogies in Australian classrooms.

To fill this gap with a small bridge to an ideal situation, this single school case study can be analysed to suggest the following characteristics for a culturally responsive approach to enacting Aboriginal child as knowledge producer.

1. *High intellectual challenge.* The teacher views the child as agentic, a competent learner, and as the producer of research and knowledge that possesses cultural and linguistic intergenerational intelligences brought from home. Educators believe in building a positive climate for learning that has the strongest impact on children's learning for success though cognitive, cultural, and developmental stretch and challenge. Educators recognise culture as strength for learning and reject 'deficit' views of the child.
2. *Connect learning strongly to student life-worlds*: View student's prior knowledge and intelligences as strengths brought from home to class that are the foundation upon which to graft new learning. The child learns best when the preschool setting incorporates, validates, builds, and bridges culturally familiar prior knowledges and languages. Committed to an anti-deficit view of student identities and their families, the teacher incorporates a vigilant approach not to essentialise and or homogenise student identities and cultures.
3. *Recognition of culture as an asset to learning*: Educators understand asset-based teaching uses strength-based pedagogical practice models that are proven to widen participation, improve engagement and influence literacy and numeracy success. Educators redesign their pedagogies to shift beyond teaching that focuses on perceived gaps and weaknesses.
4. *Critical reflection and/or taking a critical activist orientation*: In dialogue with others, the student engages differing views and critique their own practices and behaviours. Educators engage critical literacies, share power in all learning environments and engage children in social justice work for change to their local challenges.
5. *Respectful relationship building*: Committed to democratic inclusion: Relationships build between teacher to student, student to student, teacher to teacher, teacher to Aboriginal education worker, teacher to parents and local community, parent to school, school to parents. Power is shared in a co-construction of knowledge production.
6. *Boost and sustain student voice, participation, and leadership*: Build classroom mechanisms to listen, promote, and reinforce student voice in teaching, learning, and school governance.

To conclude, we have learned two basic things from this one school case study. First, this theoretical framework enables teachers to enact classroom knowledge production that connect to prior local knowledge to global knowledge. Second, the Aboriginal child is not a passive recipient of knowledge constructed by others but a co-constructor of knowledge for their own interests, for their community, and for outsiders. Educators convey highest expectations and age-appropriate stretch that supports them to become successful learners. The teacher's strong relationships efforts connecting culture to curriculum allowed students to fluently cross cultures toward learning and producing local and global knowledges.

Acknowledgement

The data used for this chapter derives from 2017 Australian Research Council Discovery Grant by Professor Lester-Irabinna Rigney and Professor Robert Hattam, 'Toward an Australian Culturally Responsive Pedagogy' [Project ID: IN170100017]. This work was also informed by a 2006 Australian Research Council Discovery Grant by Lester Rigney, 'Indigenous Research

Methodologies: Frameworks toward Indigenous Intellectual Sovereignty and the Decolonisation of Research' [Project ID: DI0348109].

Notes

1 The following examples inform my argument in relation to Indigenist productive ways to construct knowledge and Aboriginal knowledge activation:
   - Rigney (2006) defines Indigenist knowledge production as relational, culturally safe and respectful comprising of three provocations: privileging Indigenous voices, integrity of Indigenous knowledge resistant to hegemony, with emancipatory imperative to improve communities.
   - Fredericks (Walker et al. 2014), 'Yarning' or reciprocal knowledge production processes uses conversational dialogic processes for plurivocal co-construction of health knowledge production especially with, by and for Indigenous children and women.
   - Martin (2003: 205) advocate for knowledge production that validates Indigenous world-views, honours social mores, privileges voice, emphasis social, historical, and political contexts which shape Indigenous lives and futures.
   - Arbon (2008) argues for knowledge producers to understand place-based local ontologies that reveal Aboriginal people exist as embodied, reciprocal, and related entities that see all things interconnected whose epistemologies are born from ancient cultural knowledge.
   - Atkinson (2002) argues knowledge production must involve Aboriginal pedagogy of deep listening called Dadirri. Listening involves non-judgmental reflection, awareness of assumptions, and bias to recognise diversity of Indigenous community and as individuals.
   - Moreton-Robinson (2000) knowledge production seeks to contest gender subjectivities, patriarchy, racial prejudices, and power relations toward privileging the experiences and voices of Aboriginal women.
2 Some important examples that inform my framework are the following approaches:
   - Gloria Ladson-Billings (1995: 160): Culturally Responsive pedagogy for African American children rests on the propositions that students (a) experience academic success via high expectations; (b) develop cultural competence; and (c) develop a critical consciousness to change unjust circumstances.
   - Villegas and Lucas (2002: 21): the Culturally Responsive Teacher (a) is socio-culturally conscious, (b) builds on students' lives worlds to design instruction from what students already know; (c) is capable of bringing educational change and making schools more responsive to all students; (d) is capable of promoting learners' knowledge construction; (e) knows about the lives of students.
   - Bishop (et al. 2007: 15): Kaupapa Māori Culturally Responsive pedagogies involve: power is shared, culture counts, Māori to be Māori, learning is interactive and dialogic, connectedness is fundamental to relations, and there is a common vision of excellence for Māori students.
   - Assembly of Alaska Native Educators (1999): Culturally Responsive Educators promotes the teaching of multiple world-views; utilises theory of knowing how students learn; teaching for diversity; content related to local community; instruction and assessment building on students' cultures; learning environments utilising local sites; family involvement as partners; and professional teacher development.
   - Castagno and Brayboy (2008): Culturally Responsive Educators engage the cultural strengths of students in learning by engaging regularly with families and communities; engaging student cultures as strengths rather deficits.
3 Yarning mats are a teaching resource with Aboriginal art work to promote students dialogue and to produce knowledge or problem-solve on learning inquiry.

References

ACER. (2013). *Evaluation of the Cape York Aboriginal Australian Academy Initiative*. Final report. Australian Council for Educational Research: Camberwell, VIC.

Arbon, V. (2008). *Arlathirnda Ngurkarnda Ityirnda: Being-Knowing-Doing: De-Colonising Indigenous Tertiary Education*. Post Pressed: Teneriffe, QLD.

Assembly of Alaska Native Educators. (1999). *Guidelines for Preparing Culturally Responsive Teachers for Alaska's Schools*. Anchorage, AK. Available: http://ankn.uaf.edu/Publications/teacher.pdf, Accessed 12 March 2016.

Atkinson, J. (2002). *Trauma Trails, Recreating Song Lines the Transgenerational Effects of Trauma in Indigenous Australia.* Spinifex Press: North Melbourne, VIC.

Australian Institute for Teaching and School Leadership (AITSL). (2016). *Australian Teacher Professional Standards.* Available: http://www.aitsl.edu.au/initial-teacher-education/aboriginal-and-torres-strait-islander-education, accessed 9 February 2016.

Bishop, R. (2019). *Teaching to the North East: Relationship-Based Learning in Practice.* New Zealand Council for Educational Research Press: Wellington.

Bishop, R. Berryman, M. Cavanagh, T., and Teddy, L. (2007). *Te Kōtahitanga Phase 3: Whānaungatanga: Establishing a Culturally Responsive Pedagogy of Relations in Mainstream Secondary School Classrooms.* Ministry of Education Printer: Wellington.

Buckskin, P., Hughes, P., Price, K., Rigney, L-I, Sarra, C., Adams, I, and Hayward, C. (2010). *Review of Australian Directions in Indigenous Education, 2005–2008 for MCEECDYA.* MCEECDYA Reference Group on Indigenous Education, Department of Education and Training, Government of Western Australia.

Castagno, A. and Brayboy, B. (2008). 'Culturally responsive schooling for Indigenous youth: A review of the literature', *Review of Educational Research*, vol 78, no 4: 941–993.

Cochran-Smith, M., Baker, M., Burtona, S., Chang, W.-C., Cummings, C.M., Fernández, M.B., Stringer Keefe, E., Miller, A.F., and Sánchez, J.G. (2017). 'The accountability era in US teacher education: Looking back, looking forward', *European Journal of Teacher Education*, vol 40, no 5: 572–588.

Collins, P.H. (2000). *Black Feminist Thought: Knowledge Consciousness, and the Politics of Empowerment.* Routledge: New York.

Comber, B. and Kamler, B. (2006). 'Redesigning literacy pedagogies: The complexities pf producing sustainable change', in W. Bokhorsst-Heng, M. Osbourne, and K. Lee (eds.) *Redesigning Pedagogy: Reflections on Theory and Praxis.* Sense: Rotterdam, 19–32.

Commonwealth of Australia. (2018). *Closing the Gap: Department of the Prime Minister and Cabinet, Prime Minister's Report.* Department of the Prime Minister and Cabinet: Canberra, ACT.

Craven, R.G., Halse, C., Marsh, H.W., Mooney, J., and Wilson-Miller, J. (2005). *Teaching the Teachers Aboriginal Studies: Recent Successful Sstrategies*, vols 1 and 2. Department of Education, Science and Training, Commonwealth of Australia: Canberra, ACT.

Dahlberg, G., and Moss, P. (2004). *Ethics and Politics in Early Childhood Education.* London: Routledge.

Dewey, J (1916). *Democracy and Education.* Macmillan: New York.

Freire, P. (1972). *Pedagogy of the Oppressed.* Penguin: New York.

Gay, G. (2010). *Culturally Responsive Teaching*, 2nd ed. New York Teachers College Press: New York.

Guenther, J., and Osborne, S. (2020). 'Did DI do it? The impact of a programme designed to improve literacy for Aboriginal and Torres Strait Islander students in remote schools', *The Australian Journal of Indigenous Education*, vol 10: 1–8.

Harding, S. (1986). *Science Questions in Feminism.* Cornell University Press: Ithaca, NY.

Hau'ofa, E. (1993). 'Our sea of islands', in E. Waddell, V. Naidu, and E. Hau'ofa (ed.) *A New Oceania: Rediscovering Our Sea of Islands.* School of Social and Economic Development, University of the South Pacific: Suva, 2–16.

Hill, S., Comber, B., Louden, B., Reid, J., and Rivalland, J. (1998). *100 Children Go to School: Connections and Disconnections in Literacy Experience Prior to School and in the First Year of School.* Department of Education, Employment, Training and Youth Affairs: Canberra, ACT.

Krakouer, J. (2015). *Literature Review Relating to the Current Context and Discourse on Indigenous Cultural Awareness in the Teaching Space: Critical Pedagogies and Improving Indigenous Learning Outcomes Through Cultural Responsiveness.* Australian Council for Education Research: Melbourne, VIC.

Ladson-Billings, G. (1995). 'Toward a theory of culturally relevant pedagogy', *American Educational Research Journal*, vol 32, no 3: 465–491.

Langton, M. (1981). 'Urbanising aborigines: The social scientists' great deception', *Social Alternatives*, vol, 2 no 2: 16–12.

Lather, P. (1986). 'Research as praxis', *Harvard Educational Review*, vol 56, no 3: 257–277.

Luke, A, Cazden, C, Coopes, R, Klenowski, V, Ladwig, J, Lester, J, MacDonald, S, Phillips, J, Shield, PG, Spina, N, Theroux, P, Tones, M. J, Villegas, M, and Woods, A. (2013). *A Summative Evaluation of the Stronger Smarter Learning Communities Project*, vol 1 and vol 2. Queensland University of Technology: Brisbane, QLD.

Malaguzzi, L (1993). 'History, ideas and basic philosophy: An interview with Lella Gandini', in C.P. Edwards, L. Gandini, and G.E. Forman (eds.) *The Hundred Languages of Children: the Reggio Emilia Approach to Early Childhood Education.* Ablex: Norwood, NJ, 49–97.

Marcus, G. (1998). *Ethnography Through Thick and Thin*. Princeton University Press: Princeton, NJ.

Ma Rhea, Z., Anderson, P., and Atkinson, B. (2012). *Improving Teaching in Aboriginal and Torres Strait Islander Education: Australian Professional Standards for Teachers*. Australian Institute for Teaching and School Leadership: Melbourne, VIC.

Martin, K and Mirraboopa, B. (2003). 'Ways of knowing, being and doing: A theoretical framework and methods for indigenous and indigenist re-search', *Journal of Australian Studies*, vol 27, no 76: 203–214.

Mayer, D., Doecke, B., Ho, P., Kline, J., Kostogriz, A., Moss, J., North, S., and Walker-Gibbs, B. (2014). *Longitudinal Teacher Education and Workforce Study Final Report*. Deakin University: Melbourne VIC. Available: https://docs.education.gov.au/system/files/doc/other/ltews_main_report.pdf, accessed 16 July 2019.

McCollow, J. (2013). 'A controversial reform in Indigenous education: The Cape York aboriginal Australian academy', *The Australian Journal of Indigenous Education*, vol 41, no 2: 97–109.

MCEETYA. (2008). *The Melbourne Declaration*. Available: http://www.mceecdya.edu.au/verve/resources/nationaldeclarationontheeducationalgoalsforyoungaustralians.pdf, accessed 12 March 2016.

Miller, J. (1985). *Koori: A Will to Win*. Angus and Robertson: Sydney.

Moodie, N. and Patrick, R. (2017). 'Settler grammars and the Australian professional standards for teachers', *Asia-Pacific Journal of Teacher Education*, vol 45, no 5: 439–454.

Moll, L.C., Amanti, C., Neff, D., and Gonzalez, N. (1992). 'Funds of knowledge for teaching: Using a qualitative approach to connect homes and classrooms', *Theory Into Practice*, vol 31, no 2: 132–141.

Moreton-Robinson, A. (2000). *Talkin' Up to the White Woman: Indigenous Women and Feminism*. University of Queensland Press: Brisbane, QLD.

Moreton-Robinson, A., Singh, D., Kolopenuk, J., and Robinson, A. (2012). *Learning the Lessons?: Pre-Service Teacher Preparation for Teaching Aboriginal and Torres Strait Islander Students*. Australian Institute for Teaching and School Leadership: Melbourne, VIC.

Morrison, A, Rigney, L-I, Hattam, R, and Diplock, A. (2019). *Toward an Australian Culturally Responsive Pedagogy: A Narrative Review of the Literature*. University of South Australia: Adelaide, SA.

Perso, T.F. (2012). *Cultural Responsiveness and School Education: With Particular Focus on Australia's First Peoples; A Review and Synthesis of the Literature*. Menzies School of Health Research, Centre for Child Development and Education: Darwin, NT.

Price, K. (ed.) (2012). *Aboriginal and Torres Strait Islander Education: An Introduction for the Teaching Profession*. Cambridge University Press: Cambridge.

Rigney, L-I. (1997). 'Internationalisation of an Indigenous anti-colonial cultural critique of research methodologies: A guide to Indigenist research methodology and its principles', in *HERDSA Annual International Conference Proceedings; Research and Development in Higher Education: Advancing International Perspectives*, vol. 20: 629–636.

Rigney, L-I. (1999). Internationalization of an Indigenous anticolonial cultural critique of research methodologies: A guide to Indigenist research methodology and its principles, *Wicazo Sa Review*, vol 14, no 2: 109–121.

Rigney, L-I. (2001). 'A first perspective of Indigenous Australian participation in science: Framing Indigenous research towards Indigenous Australian intellectual sovereignty, *Kaurna Higher Education Journal*, vol 7, 1–13.

Rigney, L-I. (2002). 'Indigenous education and treaty: Building Indigenous management capacity', *Balayi: Culture, Law and Colonialism*, vol 4: 73–82.

Rigney, L-I. (2003). 'Indigenous education, languages and treaty: The redefinition of a new relationship with Australia', in Aboriginal and Torres Strait Islander Commission (ed.) *Treaty: Let's Get it Right!* Aboriginal Studies Press: Canberra, ACT, 72–87.

Rigney, L-I. (2006). 'Indigenist research and aboriginal Australia', in N. Goduka and J. Kunnie (eds.) *Indigenous People's Wisdoms and Power: Affirming our Knowledges Through Narrative*. Ashgate Publishing: London, 32–50.

Rigney, L-I. (2007). *Indigenist Research Epistemologies: A Historical Journey of Conviction, Contradiction and Transformation*. PhD thesis. Flinders University, Australia.

Rigney, L.-I. (2011a). 'Indigenous education and tomorrow's classroom: Three questions, three answers, in N. Purdie, G. Milgate, and H.R. Bell, (eds.) *Two Way Teaching and Learning; Toward Culturally Reflective and Relevant Education*. Australian Council for Education Research: Melbourne, VIC, 35–48.

Rigney, L.-I. (2011b). 'Social inclusion in education', in D. Bottrell and S. Goodwin (eds.) *Schools, Communities and Social Inclusion*. Palgrave Macmillan: Victoria, 38–49.

Rigney, L-I. (2017). 'Defining culturally responsive digital education for classrooms: Writing from Oceania to build Indigenous Pacific futures', in E. McKinley and L.T. Smith (eds.) *Handbook of Indigenous Education*. Springer: Singapore, 1–17.

Rigney, L.-I. and Hattam, R. (2016–2019). *Toward an Australian Culturally Responsive Pedagogy*. (IN170100017), Project funded by the Australian Research Council.

Rigney, L.-I. and Hattam, R. (2018). 'Toward a decolonizing Australian culturally responsive pedagogy', *American Educational Research Association Conference*, 13–17 April. New York.

Rinaldi, C. (2002). 'Negotiating the curriculum', in S. Fraser and C. Gestwicki (eds.) *Authentic Childhood*. Delmar: Albany, NY, 163–164.

Rinaldi, C. (2013). *Re-imagining Childhood: The Inspiration of Reggio Emilia Education Principles in South Australia*. Government of South Australia: Adelaide, SA.

Rizvi, F. and Lingard, B. (2009). *Globalizing Education Policy*. Routledge: London.

Said, E. (1995). *Orientalism*. Penguin Books: London.

Sarra, C. (2017). *Stronger Smarter: A Sustained and Enduring Approach to Indigenous Education (Whether Education Researchers Know It or Not!)*, 27–29 August. ACER Research Conference: Leadership for Improving Learning: Melbourne, VIC.

Sleeter, C. (2011). *Professional Development for Culturally Responsive and Relationship-based Pedagogy*. Peter Lang: New York.

Smith, G.H. (1997). *The Development of Kaupapa Maori: Theory and Praxis*. PhD thesis. University of Auckland.

Smyth, J., Down, B., Hattam, R., and McInerney, P. (2014). *Doing Critical Educational Research*. Peter Lang: New York.

Smyth, J. and Hattam, R. (2004). *"Dropping Out", Drifting Off, Being Excluded: Becoming Somebody Without School*. Peter Lang: New York.

Spivak, G.C. (1988). 'Can the subaltern speak?', in C. Nelson and L. Grossberg (eds.), *Marxism and Interpretation of Culture*. Macmillan: Basingstoke, 271–313.

United Nations. (2008). *United Nations Declaration on the Rights of Indigenous Peoples*. Available: http://www.un.org/esa/socdev/unpfii/documents/DRIPS_en.pdf, accessed 26 July 2019.

Villegas, A.M. and Lucas, T. (2002). *Educating Culturally Responsive Teachers: A Coherent Approach*. SUNY Press: Albany, NY.

Vygotsky, L. and Cole, M. (1978). *Mind in Society: Development of Higher Psychological Processes*. Harvard University Press: Cambridge, MA.

Walker, M., Bronwyn, F., Mills, F., and Anderson, D. (2014). '"Yarning" as a method for community-based health research with Indigenous women: The Indigenous women's wellness research program', *Health Care for Women International*, vol 35, no 10: 1216–1226.

Wa Thiong'o, N. (1994). *Decolonising the Mind: The Politics of Language in African Literature*. James, Currey, Heinemann: London.

Yunkaporta, T. (2009). *Aboriginal Pedagogies at the Cultural Interface*. PhD thesis. James Cook University, Douglas, QLD. Available: http://eprints.jcu.edu.au/10974/, accessed 26 July 2019.

Index

*Page numbers in *italics* reference figures.

Made in the USA
Columbia, SC
06 January 2025

51250161R00346